AGRICULTURE

AREA STUDIES SERIES

EDITORIAL DIRECTOR   Professor J J O'Meara
RESEARCH UNIT DIRECTOR   T F Turley
ASSISTANT DIRECTOR   S Cashman

CHIEF EDITORIAL ADVISERS

P Ford
Professor Emeritus, Southampton University
Mrs G Ford

SPECIAL EDITORIAL CONSULTANT FOR
THE UNITED STATES PAPERS

H C Allen
Commonwealth Fund Professor of American History, University College, London
Director of the London University Institute of United States Studies

RESEARCH EDITORS
Johann A Norstedt
Marilyn Evers Norstedt

This Series is published with the active co-operation of
SOUTHAMPTON UNIVERSITY

IRISH UNIVERSITY PRESS AREA STUDIES SERIES

BRITISH PARLIAMENTARY PAPERS

UNITED STATES OF AMERICA

1

Reports, correspondence
and other papers respecting
agriculture, cattle disease
and the production of
sugar and oleomargarine

1878–99

IRISH UNIVERSITY PRESS
Shannon   Ireland

PUBLISHER'S NOTE

The documents in this series are selected from the nineteenth-century British House of Commons *sessional and command papers*. All of the original papers relating to the United States of America are included with the exception of two kinds of very brief and unimportant papers. Omitted are (1) random statistical trade returns which are included in the larger and complete yearly trade figures and (2) returns relating to postal services, which are irregularly presented, of tangential USA relevance, and easily available in other sources.

The original documents have been reproduced by photo-lithography and are unabridged even to the extent of retaining the first printers' imprints. Imperfections in the original printing are sometimes unavoidably reproduced.

Many papers in this reprint are enlargements from the original octavo format.

© 1971 Irish University Press Shannon Ireland

Microfilm, microfiche and other forms of micro-publishing
© *Irish University Microforms Shannon Ireland*

ISBN 0 7165 1501 6

Printed and published by
Irish University Press Shannon Ireland
DUBLIN CORK BELFAST LONDON NEW YORK
T M MacGlinchey *Publisher* Robert Hogg *Printer*

Contents

IUP Page Number

For ease of reference IUP editors have assigned a continuous pagination which appears on the top outer margin of each page.

Cattle Disease
Correspondence respecting pleuro-pneumonia in cattle
1878–79 (111) LVIII 11

Sugar
Report on sugar production in the United States
1878–79 [C.2207] LXXIII 27

Agricultural Conditions
Royal Commission reports on the depressed condition of agriculture
1880 [C.2678] XVIII 59

Animal Diseases
Correspondence respecting animal diseases in the United States
1880 [C.2644] LVI 119

Animal Diseases
Correspondence respecting animal diseases in the United States
1880 [C.2693] LVI 241

Oleomargarine
Correspondence respecting the manufacture of oleomargarine
in the United States
1880 [C.2502] LXVII 281

Agricultural Condition
Royal Commission reports on the depressed condition of agriculture
(Reports of Mr Clay, Jun.)*
1881 [in C.2778–II] XVI 303

Animal Diseases
Correspondence respecting animal diseases in the United States
1881 [C.2787] LXXV 313

Oleomargarine
Correspondence respecting the manufacture of oleomargarine
in the United States
1881 [C.2767] LXXXIII 341

Agricultural Condition
Royal Commission reports on the depressed condition of agriculture
1882 [C.3375–VI] XV 355

Animal Diseases
Correspondence respecting animal diseases in the United States
1882 [C.3200] LII 371

Oleomargarine
Correspondence respecting the use of oleomargarine in the
manufacture of butter and cheese in New York state
1884 (275) LXXII 499

Animal Diseases
Correspondence respecting animal diseases in the United States
1884 [C.3978] LXXIV 515

*This document is extracted from a larger paper and therefore lacks an individual title page.

Continued

Contents

Continued

IUP Page Number

Sugar
Miscellaneous commercial report on the extraction of sugar from sorghum and maize
1887 [in C.4924] LXXXII 697

Sugar
Miscellaneous commercial report on the extraction of sugar from sorghum and maize
1887 [in C.4924] LXXXII 719

Sugar
Miscellaneous commercial report on the manufacture of sugar from sorghum in Kansas
1888 [C.5253–19] XCIX 731

Cattle Disease
Extracts from the Secretary of Agriculture's report on pleuro-pneumonia in cattle
1890 [C.6146] LXXIII 739

Prunes
Miscellaneous commercial report on the prune industry in California
1892 [C.6813–5] LXXX 753

Tea
Miscellaneous commercial report on tea raising in South Carolina
1894 [C.7294–2] LXXXIX 771

Agricultural Condition
Miscellaneous commercial report on the agricultural condition of the United States
1895 [C.7582–21] CIII 779

Cattle Industry
Miscellaneous commercial report on the cattle-raising industry of the United States in 1896
1897 [C.8278–2] LXXXVIII 807

Agricultural Condition
Miscellaneous commercial report on the prospects of farmers in California
1897 [C.8278–22] LXXXVIII 831

Coffee
Miscellaneous commercial report on coffee culture in the Hawaiian Islands
1897 [C.8278–24] LXXXVIII 845

Agricultural Condition
Miscellaneous commercial report on the agriculture of Maine
1899 [C.9045–8] XCVII 865

Cattle Industry
Miscellaneous commercial report on the cattle industry of the United States, 1896–98
1899 [C.9045–9] XCVII 875

CATTLE DISEASE (UNITED STATES OF AMERICA).

CORRESPONDENCE

CONNECTED WITH

THE DETECTION OF PLEURO-PNEUMONIA AMONG CATTLE

LANDED IN GREAT BRITAIN FROM THE UNITED STATES OF AMERICA.

— No. 1. —

TELEGRAM from the Marquis of *Salisbury* to Her Majesty's Minister at Washington, 30th January 1879.

PLEURO-PNEUMONIA having been detected in a cargo of cattle on board the ship "Ontario" from Portland, Her Majesty's Government are consequently considering whether it can retain the United States under the exemption of Part IV. of the 5th Schedule of the Act of 1878.

— No. 2. —

LETTER from Sir *E. Thornton* to the Marquis of *Salisbury*.

My Lord,　　　　　　　　　　　　　　Washington, 3 February 1879.

ON the receipt of your Lordship's telegram of the 30th ultimo, informing me that pleuro-pneumonia had been detected in a cargo of cattle on board the ship "Ontario" from Portland, and that Her Majesty's Government was consequently considering whether it could retain the United States under the exemption of Part IV. of the 5th Schedule of the Act of 1878, I called upon Mr. Evarts and communicated to him the contents of your telegram. He had also received one to the same effect from the United States Minister in London. He said that the information had taken him by surprise, and that he had not yet made complete inquiries upon the subject. With regard to the cases of pleuro-pneumonia, which had been discovered on board the "Ontario," he thought it very probable that the animals had contracted the disease during the voyage, and that it had been caused by bad ventilation and exposure to rough weather. He believed that there were some cases of it in different parts of the United States, but that a few always existed. They were, however, isolated cases, and there was no ground whatever for supposing that the disease was epidemic. He added that measures had now been taken for the inspection of cattle for export at the different ports of the United States, and, as it was not in the interest of the owners to ship diseased cattle, they would certainly be careful to avoid doing so. Nothing, however, could prevent isolated cases of disease contracted on board of ship; but inspection on arrival at the port of destination, and slaughter in case of need, would preclude any danger of the spreading of the disease. He expressed his opinion, that it would be hardly justifiable to stop so great a trade, and to prevent the supply of food from

reaching

reaching Great Britain on account of a few isolated cases of pleuro-pneumonia, which in this country was not considered contagious.

No. 1.

Before I saw Mr. Evarts he had sent me a short note, copy of which I have the honour to enclose, informing me that an agent of the British Government had been for some days past at New York and Alexandria, and had reported to the Canadian Government the existence of pleuro-pneumonia among cattle I had not then received his note, but he told me its contents, and asked me whether I could give him any information with regard to the agent in question; I was obliged to acknowledge that I had neither seen nor heard of him.

The next morning I addressed an official note to Mr. Evarts, transmitting him a copy of your Lordship's telegram of 30th ultimo.

Nos. 2 and 3.

I also received on that morning a private letter from the Acting Consul of Philadelphia, of which, and of its enclosure, I have the honour to enclose a copy. From this it appears that Professor D. McEachran, Veterinary Inspector of Canada, had been sent by the Government of the Dominion to inspect cattle in this country, and was doubtless the person to whom Mr. Evarts had alluded. It would appear that he ascertained that there had been many cases of the disease in Virginia, and that he discovered that it prevailed to a great and severe extent in a large cowhouse near Brooklyn, Long Island.

On the 1st instant I again called upon Mr. Evarts, and read to him the greater part of Mr. Crump's and Dr. Gadsden's letters. He still, however, expressed his opinion that these cases did not affect the general cattle of the country, and particularly those which were exported.

Mr. Evarts informed me that he had made inquiries with regard to the cargo of the "Ontario." It appeared that the bulk of the cargo were American cattle, but a few, about 22, were Canadian. He did not know amongst which of these the cases of pleuro-pneumonia had been discovered. When these cattle were about to be shipped, the collector of customs had offered to order an inspection of them, and provide them with a certificate; but their owner declined an inspection, on the ground that a certificate would not be required in England.

It is probable that should Her Majesty's Government still allow cattle to be imported from this country, a very strict supervision will be exercised over them at the ports of embarkation, and care will be taken to prevent the shipment of diseased cattle.

No. 4.

Mr. Evarts sent me a copy of a telegram which he forwarded on the 1st instant to Mr. Welsh, copy of which I have the honour to enclose.

I have made inquiries of several persons in and about Washington as to the prevalence of pleuro-pneumonia among cattle in the neighbourhood; I find that there are isolated cases of the disease here and there, but many less than in June last, when there were several deaths on account of it. The cases seem to be confined to milch cows, and more particularly to those kept in stables.

In the latter case the disease will attack a good many cows, but will not spread outside of the stable, and seems to be due to local causes.

Dr. Fairfax, a gentleman of English descent, who has lived for many years on a farm in Maryland, 9 or 10 miles from here, who is thoroughly acquainted with such matters, and whose statements can be entirely relied upon, says that the disease in this country is not the same as in England; that it is not considered to be contagious, and that it has not become epidemic, although it will spread in a stable where the animals are subjected to the same local circumstances.

I have this afternoon received a telegram from the Governor General of Canada, informing me of the Order of the Privy Council of the Dominion, prohibiting for three months, from the 1st instant, the introduction of cattle from the United States into the different provinces of the Dominion.

I have, &c.
(signed) *Edward Thornton.*

CATTLE DISEASE (UNITED STATES OF AMERICA).

Enclosure 1, in No. 2.

LETTER from Mr. *Evarts* to Sir *Edward Thornton*.

Department of State, Washington,
30 January 1879.

My dear Sir Edward,

I HAVE received information that an inspector of the British Government has been in New York and Alexandria for some days past, and has reported to the Canadian Government the existence of pleuro-pneumonia among cattle.

I presume that information to the same effect may have been communicated to you by him. I am not myself aware of the existence of the disease, but as the cattle trade between this country and Great Britain is of so great importance, and as any interruption of it is likely to have such serious results, I shall be very glad indeed to be informed of any intelligence which you may have received upon the subject, or to confer with you.

I am, &c.
(signed) *Wm. M. Evarts.*

Enclosure 2, in No. 2.

LETTER from Mr. *Crump* to Sir *Edward Thornton*.

British Consulate, Philadelphia, U.S.
(No date).

I THINK I ought to write you with reference to the latest development in the cattle disease. You may not be aware that Professor D. McEachran, Veterinary Inspector of Canada, who, I am told, was introduced to you in Canada, has been through some of the cities of the United States on a confidential mission inspecting cattle, particularly with reference to the existence of pleuro-pneumonia. He was in this city, Washington, and Virginia last week, and returned to Canada a few days ago, after making inspections on Long Island that resulted in painful developments. I am informed that he did not desire to visit any official of the Imperial Government as he was not instructed to do so; that he did not call upon you while he was in Washington, and declined a pressing invitation to confer with me while in this city. He discovered in Williamsburgh, near Brooklyn, a shocking state of things. There is a byre, a cowhouse connected with a distillery, where cows are housed to the number of 800 at a time, and fed with hot swill running along the troughs in front of the cattle connected with the distillery. The object to be attained is to increase the production of milk, which is obtained to an extraordinary extent. The cattle never get out of this place in a healthy condition, and but few alive, the pleuro-pneumonia killing them off several per day; or rather they are sold for a small sum before death, to Jew dealers, who kill and dress the meat for New York to be retailed, not to Jews, but only to the Christian consumers. A few young cattle, when first infected, are returned to the country, there, in all probability, to spread the disease. The milk and meat of these animals are dangerous to the human system. They are not allowed to be sold in Brooklyn, but can be passed through that city to New York. The temperature of the numerous cases of pleuro-pneumonia examined by Dr. McEachran was as high as 105 degrees, and in some cases 107, showing the most virulent type of the complaint. The animals get no exercise whatever, leaving their stalls, to which they are chained, for slaughter when attacked by the contagion. The filth, heat, and fetid steam of the place, it is reported, are of the most revolting character. Dr. McEachran's entrance into this place was clandestine, and upon being discovered he narrowly escaped personal violence. I have requested my informant, a veterinary surgeon of this city of ability, and the highest character in the city, Dr. Gadsden, to write me a letter. He has done so, and I beg to forward it to you.

I should also state that Dr. McEachran found much pleuro-pneumonia in Alexandria, Virginia, where two or three hundred cases terminated fatally last year. He says the complaint extends all over the State of Virginia. Dr. McEachran has returned to Canada with a determination to have steps taken for the protection of the Canadian stockyards from this infection, and the stigma that will follow the disclosure of these facts.

To-day cable news has been received in this city that a cargo of live cattle from Portland had been found afflicted with pleuro-pneumonia on arrival at Liverpool, and the animals were all killed. This news came to Eastman, of New York, the largest shipper in the country, and who is said to be carrying out the plans of Vanderbilt and the New York Central Railway. Other cable news has been received that steps are about to be taken to forbid the landing of cattle from American ports. Samuel Allerton & Co., of Chicago, the largest shippers of dead meat—and from this port—as well as others engaged in this fast becoming most important trade, are much exercised.

A certificate of inspection of a cargo of live cattle per steam ship "Lord Clive," sailed to-day from Philadelphia to Liverpool, was presented to me for authentication, but as I did not know the character of the inspector I declined to certify to it. Subsequently, however, when it was returned attested by the collector of the port, that the inspector was appointed by him to perform the duty, I certified to the official act of the collector.

The merchants here engaged in the trade are willing to adopt any plan that I may suggest to them regardless of the expense, to insure the shipment of healthy animals and meat to England.

Dr. McEachran made no discoveries in this district unfavourable to the general healthy condition of the cattle.

P.S.—Dr. McEachran had a long interview with the Commissioners of Agriculture in your city. I believe he did not visit Boston. Large numbers of live cattle are shipped from Boston in the winter, which come originally from Canada, and are on Canadian account.

Enclosure 3, in No. 2.

LETTER from Mr. *Gadsden*, M.R.C.V.S., to *George Crump*, Esq.

134, North 10th Street, Philadelphia,
28 January 1879.

KNOWING you wish all the information respecting contagious diseases of cattle, I send you a report of my examination of some with Professor D. McEachran, the Veterinary Inspector of Canada, who was sent by his Government to investigate it, and report at once.

The inspector called on me first on his way to Washington (18th instant), again on the 23rd of this month, when he reported to me he had examined several cases of contagious pleuro-pneumonia in cattle at Alexandria, Virginia.

I started with him on the 24th to New York to find out the truth of the report that a contagious disease was prevalent on Long Island. We found very many cases of contagious pleuro-pneumonia in a large byre, or cowhouse, containing about 800 cows (all in a filthy condition), at Williamsburg, near Brooklyn. This large cowhouse adjoins the distillery of Gaff, Flieschman & Co., where they are fed on hot swill and hay, to force the milk. This place is a regular pesthouse for the disease; the cows belong to a large number of milkmen, who pay a small sum (77 cents. per cow a week) for the stall and swill. It is quite impossible for me to inform you how many of these 800 cows have the disease at the present time, but I should think from what I saw that several hundred have it now, and it is only a question of time for all the others to take it. The men would not allow us to examine many of them in one part; we found very few healthy cows there. We made a *post-mortem* examination of the lungs of one of the cows that had this disease in the last stage, which leaves no doubt of its character, as all the pathological anatomy of this malady was present (one lung was very heavy and quite solid). Just before the cows die, they are killed and sent into New York market as good beef (at night).

From inquiry made by us from cattle men and veterinary surgeons at Brooklyn, we have no doubt that this disease is prevalent in many parts of Long Island, as these diseased cows from Williamsburg are often sent away alive to other parts of the island.

I have made inquiry from several veterinary surgeons in Pennsylvania, but cannot hear of any contagious diseases in cattle in the State.

Enclosure 4, in No. 2.

TELEGRAM from Mr. *Evarts* to Mr. *Welsh*, United States Minister, London.

1 February 1879.

Cattle by "Ontario," part Canadian, part Western. Inspection offered by Government was declined by shippers on their view that British regulations did not require it. There is no evidence of any disease in the cattle of this country that affects domestic or foreign trade in them. This Government would regard any proscription of our trade in live cattle as wholly unjustified by any condition of things known or suspected here. The appearance of pleuro-pneumonia in a cargo at the end of a voyage can scarcely warrant a restriction of this trade with a country free from any epidemic among cattle. Communicate to Salisbury.

— No. 3. —

LETTER from the United States Minister, London, to the Marquis of *Salisbury*.

Legation of the United States, London,
4 February 1879.

My Lord,

THE arrival of the Dominion steamer "Ontario," from Portland last week at Liverpool, with a number of cattle, a few of which were said to have had the pleuro-pneumonia, has been the occasion of much anxiety to those who have recently embarked very largely in the importation of cattle from the United States.

It has been asserted in the newspapers that these cattle were brought from
Chicago

CATTLE DISEASE (UNITED STATES OF AMERICA).

Chicago and Buffalo, in the United States, and further, that an expert, having been employed by the Canadian authorities for the purpose, had visited the United States and found in Washington and elsewhere some cattle affected by the disease.

These circumstances have caused me to make such inquiries as were essential to an understanding of the facts of the case, the results of which I beg to place before your Lordship.

From reliable parties in Liverpool, I learn that whilst a part of the cattle by the "Ontario" came from Chicago, and a part from Buffalo, at least 45 head of them came from Toronto, and were so mixed with the others that the Canadian and United States cattle could not be distinguished. It is also beyond dispute, that those which came from the United States, passed for several hundred miles over the Grand Trunk-road, through the Dominion of Canada, that all the cattle were exposed to weather of unusual severity, that they remained for a considerable time in Portland without food or water, and that they had undergone an exceptional amount of hardship and bad usage before entering upon a voyage which was made at an inclement season, and during excessively rough weather. Under these circumstances, it is strange that so few were found whose lungs were diseased. In fact, the fact that so few were found diseased is almost a conclusive proof that they were healthy when they left their several places of departure, for had they been then affected by a contagious or infectious malady, as the pleuro-pneumonia is asserted to be, would it not have been communicated to most, if not to all, of the herd.

What I have just narrated is the result of my inquiry on this side. So soon as the report reached me I telegraphed to the Department of State at Washington for the facts, both in regard to this special case and to the existence of pleuro-pneumonia amongst the cattle in the United States; Mr. Evarts replied as follows:—

"Cattle by 'Ontario,' part Canadian, part western; inspection offered by Government was declined by shippers on their view that British regulations did not require it. There is no evidence of any disease in the cattle of this country that affects domestic or foreign trade in them.

"This Government would regard any proscription of our trade in live cattle as wholly unjustified by any condition of things known or suspected here. The appearance of pleuro-pneumonia in the cargo at the end of a voyage can scarcely warrant a restriction of this trade with a country free from any epidemic among cattle."

The accounts from both sides, so far as this cargo is concerned, seem to me not to warrant the inference that the pleuro-pneumonia exists either in Canada or the United States, but if the few cattle which were diseased really had it, the hardships and exposure which they underwent are quite sufficient to account for it.

Your Lordship should not lose sight of the fact that our laws exclude the importation of all cattle from Europe into the United States on account of the fear of disease, unless under the special permission of the Secretary of State; and then only of such kinds as are needed for breeding purposes.

Since the arrival of the "Ontario" several vessels have reached here from the United States with cattle which were entirely healthy.

I trust it will prove that the alarm which has arisen from this single case has been quite unnecessary, and that nothing further will occur to check the development of a trade which promises such large employment for the tonnage of Great Britain, and an advantageous market for the abundant herds of America. I am quite sure, however, that in no event will your Lordship allow of hasty and inconsiderate action unfavourable to the interests of the United States.

It will come to the knowledge of your Lordship, from authoritative sources, that the representatives of about one-third of the entire steam tonnage of the United Kingdom, the Shipowners' Association of Liverpool, believe that the true interests of the people of Great Britain are to be promoted, not by a greater restriction in existing rules, but by their enlargement; so that the cattle coming from North America shall be subject to the same regulations which control cattle coming from Ireland, and from one port in the kingdom to another.

I have, &c.
(signed) *John Welsh.*

— No. 4. —

Letter from the United States Minister, London, to the Marquis of *Salisbury*.

Legation of United States of America,
London, 7 February 1879.

My Lord,

Since I wrote to you on the subject of the transit of cattle from America, and the alarm which the few cases of disease on the " Ontario " had occasioned, the following vessels, viz., the " Victoria," " England," " State of Alabama," " Illyrian," " Pembroke," and " Iberian," have arrived at Liverpool and discharged their several parcels of cattle without a single case of disease, all having passed, after a most critical inspection. Notwithstanding this, rumours exist in Liverpool that the Privy Council will, at an early day, put the United States on the schedule, and subject all cattle coming thence to slaughter on arrival.

This has created the greatest alarm, because of the large interests involved, and, as it is claimed, of the great injustice to which the parties will be subjected without any adequate notice.

The freedom from disease in the cattle from the United States which have hitherto been brought to England, and among recent arrivals, seem to me to forbid any action which would be so serious in its consequences, or even any interruption in the trade now existing, and I shall be glad to be authorised by you to say that the present apprehensions are unfounded.

I have, &c.
(signed) *John Welsh.*

— No. 5. —

Letter from the Clerk of the Council to the Under Secretary of State, Foreign Office.

Veterinary Department, Privy Council Office,
44, Parliament-street, Westminster, S.W.,
12 February 1879.

Sir,

I have submitted to the Lords of the Council your letter of the 8th instant, inclosing copies of two notes from the United States Minister respecting the cases of pleuro-pneumonia recently detected at Liverpool among cattle, *ex* " Ontario," from the United States, and deprecating any increase of the restrictions in the cattle trade with America.

In reply, I am directed to state, for the information of Lord Salisbury, that in consequence of the reports which have reached the Lords of the Council of the existence of pleuro-pneumonia in the United States of America, coupled with the fact that animals affected with that disease have been landed at Liverpool, their Lordships have no option under the terms of The Contagious Diseases (Animals) Act, 1878, but to revoke that portion of the Order of Council by which the United States were exempted from the provisions of that Act.

I beg to inclose a copy of the Order of Council which the Lords of the Council have considered it necessary to pass, and which comes into operation on the 4th proximo.

I am, &c.
(signed) *C. L. Peel.*

Enclosure in No. 5.

(467.)

At the Council Chamber, Whitehall, the 10th day of February 1879.

By the Lords of Her Majesty's Most Honourable Privy Council.

PRESENT:

Lord President. | Lord John Manners.

The Lords and others of Her Majesty's Most Honourable Privy Council, by virtue and in exercise of the powers in them vested under The Contagious Diseases (Animals) Act, 1878 (in this Order referred to as the Act of 1878), and of every other power enabling them in this behalf, do order, and it is hereby ordered, as follows:

1. This

CATTLE DISEASE (UNITED STATES OF AMERICA). 7

1. This Order shall take effect from and immediately after the Third day of March One thousand Eight hundred and Seventy-nine; and words in this Order have the same meaning as in the Act of 1878.
2. This Order extends to Great Britain only.
3. Article 13 of The Foreign Animals Order is hereby revoked as far as it relates to cattle brought from the United States of America, and declares that the same may be landed without being subject under the Act of 1878, or under that Order, to slaughter or to quarantine.

(signed) *C. L. Peel.*

— No. 6. —

LETTER from the British Consul General at New York to the Marquis of *Salisbury*.

British Consulate General, New York,
My Lord, 30 January 1879.

I HAVE the honour to report to your Lordship that in order to obtain the latest and most authentic information in regard to the sanitary condition of animals in this consular district, I addressed on the 24th instant a circular letter to the secretaries of the respective State Governments of New York, New Jersey, Connecticut, Delaware, and Rhode Island in this Consular District, calling attention to the statements of a professor of veterinary science, that cases of pleuro-pneumonia are not infrequent in these States, and requesting to be furnished with any information in their possession on this subject. Requesting also that my communication might be referred to the State Agricultural Department or Society, and asking that the desired information should be furnished to me as speedily as possible.

In case of the known existence of any cases, requesting further that, with regard to the nature of the disease, it might be stated whether or not it is regarded as contagious; had become epidemic; to what extent it had proved fatal; the treatment adopted for its cure; and what, if any, provision had been made for arresting its extension.

I received from the Secretary of State of the State of New York a reply, of which I enclose a copy, informing me that that Department has no knowledge relative to pleuro-pneumonia existing among animals in this State. From the Secretary of the State Agricultural Society, with whom I also communicated, I received replies, of which I enclose extracts, from which it will be seen that he questions the existence of contagious pleuro-pneumonia in this country.

No. 1.

Nos. 2 and 3.

I enclose also copies of the last annual report of the society recently adopted, in which while reference is made to the Act of the Legislature of last year respecting infectious and contagious diseases of animals (copies of which I transmitted to Her Majesty's Legation at Washington in September last), no allusion whatever is made to the existence of contagious diseases among live stock in this State.

From the State of Connecticut, however, I have received a letter from Mr. T. S. Gold, one of the "Commissioners on Diseases of Domestic Animals," of which I enclose a copy, reporting the outbreak of contagious pleuro-pneumonia in one herd of cows in the town of Watertown in that State. He adds that the disease is not epidemic, but is confined to this one herd, which is strictly quarantined. That the commissioners know of no other cases in the State, and are quite sure that none others exist.

No. 4.

In regard to the State of New Jersey, I have received from a member of the State Board of Health a letter, of which I enclose a copy, informing me that he has recently investigated the sanitary condition of live stock in that State, and finds that contagious pleuro-pneumonia has existed, and at the present time does exist, to a more or less degree. That so far as he can learn, it has never assumed the epizootic form. That at the present time it is found in isolated cases, which might be the means of superinducing an outbreak.

Nos. 5 and 6.

From the States of Delaware and Rhode Island I have, as yet, received no replies to my inquiries.

On receipt of the communication from Connecticut, and the statement therein of the supposition that the disease had been imported from New York in

August

August last, and upon a report made to me that pleuro-pneumonia among cows was supposed to lurk in some of the dairies in the suburbs of New York and Brooklyn, more especially in dairies in connection with large breweries, I addressed a letter to the respective mayors of the two cities, calling their attention to the matter, and requesting that an investigation might be made, and that I might be informed of the result.

No. 7. — I think it well to enclose a copy of a letter from the agricultural editor of the "American Agriculturist," supposed to be well informed in such matters, stating that among grazing cattle there is now no disease reported in any part of the country. That occasionally a few cases of pneumonia occur in ill-conducted dairies, but that it is not of an epizootic character, and remains in the States where it originated. He concludes by stating that there now is none of this existing, a conclusion, however, which is at variance with the positive reports from Connecticut and New Jersey.

I have to-day seen and conversed with Mr. Eastman, who is the principal shipper of fresh meat from this port, and who in the summer time has exported live stock, from hence to Great Britain. He largely supplies this market, and handles about 2,500 head of cattle every week. He assures me that in the Western States, from whence he draws his supplies, there are absolutely no diseases, certainly no contagious diseases among cattle.

In pursuance of the information which I had received, I yesterday transmitted to your Lordship the following telegram :—

"A few isolated cases of pleuro-pneumonia among horned cattle have appeared "within this consular district. Fuller report by post."

(signed) *E. M. Archibald.*

Enclosure 1, in No. 6.

LETTER from Mr. *Allen C. Beach* to *E. M. Archibald*, Esq., Her Britannic Majesty's Consul General, New York.

State of New York.
Office of the Secretary of State, Albany,
28 January 1879.

IN answer to your favour of the 24th instant, I have the honour to state that this Department has no knowledge relative to pleuro-pneumonia existing among animals in this State.

I have applied to the secretary of the State Agricultural Society, who, I thought, would be most likely to give you the information desired, and am informed that he has written you in full upon the subject.

Enclosure 2, in No. 6.

LETTER from Secretary, New York Agricultural Society, to *E. M. Archibald*, Esq., Her Britannic Majesty's Consul General, New York.

24 January 1879.

I AM in receipt of your letter of yesterday, and have much pleasure in sending a copy of the report made by the executive committee to the general meeting of the society on Wednesday last. The society's report to the Legislature has not yet been presented.

I am not in possession of any other information on the subject of the disease among cows near Washington, other than that given in the "New York Tribune;" and I very much distrust the diagnosis given in that paper, and based upon report only. It would seem that had the disease been the contagious lung plague (pleuro-pneumonia) of Europe, we should have heard of larger losses and of continued mortality.

We have never been called upon to investigate a case of pleuro-pneumonia. We have frequently had to send to investigate mysterious outbreaks of disease reported in the newspapers, but they have invariably turned out to be splenic apoplexy (anthrax). The only diseases of cattle that have ever occurred as epidemics in our cattle markets are Texan fever and the foot-and-mouth disease. The former has given no cause for alarm since 1868, except locally, and in one town and on only one farm in 1877, where it disappeared almost before we had time to be sure of its identity. The latter did not survive the first winter after its importation, and if it occurs again it will be from a new importation.

As to pleuro-pneumonia, which in one form is of course contagious (and probably the hardest of all diseases to get rid of), opinions differ as to whether it exists in this country

or

CATTLE DISEASE (UNITED STATES OF AMERICA).

or not. Professor Law, in the Paper which he read at our annual meeting in 1876 (*see* our Transactions, vol. xxxii.), probably puts the case for the affirmative as strongly as possible. On the other hand, there is the fact that we hear of no cases in recent years of disease supposed to be pleuro-pneumonia, or pronounced to be by any competent authority. The last report of it that I know of was by Professor Cressy, to the Connecticut Board of Agriculture in 1874 and, in that case the identification of the disease with the contagious pleuro-pneumonia of Europe seems to be doubtful, because the animals were purchased in the autumn, and remained sound until the spring; whereas three months is the longest period of incubation claimed for the disease by Professor Law, and two months by Gamgee (Domestic Animals in Health and Disease, vol. 1, p. 602). I am, therefore, inclined to believe the Connecticut disease to have been the sporadic pleuro-pneumonia described by Gamgee (in the work cited), rather than the contagious form. It seems hard to believe that so fatal a disease should be lurking, as some maintain that it is, among dairies of the lower class in the neighbourhood of our large Atlantic cities, without spreading and without causing such loss as to attract attention. But if such be the fact, the situation of our important cattle markets, and the way in which the movement of cattle is carried on, render it almost impossible that the disease can become epidemic.

Enclosure 3, in No. 6.

LETTER from Secretary, New York Agricultural Society, to *E. M. Archibald*, Esq., Her Britannic Majesty's Consul General, New York.

25 January 1879.

IN reply to your note of yesterday, I have to say that if it was Professor Law who wrote the article in the "Tribune" of 27th November, it accounts for the very decided tone in which the Washington disease was pronounced to be contagious pleuro-pneumonia.

As to the disease which under the name of pleuro-pneumonia has occurred, or has been reported occasionally of late years in the United States, being identical with the contagious pleuro-pneumonia of Europe, I very much doubt, for the reasons given in my letter of yesterday.

It is generally admitted, and supposed to be established, that the disease imported in Mr. Chenery's Holland cattle at Boston in 1859, and in Mr. Richardson's shorthorns in 1847, was contagious pleuro-pneumonia.

In both these cases the disease is believed to have been extirpated.

The foundation for the statement that the same disease came to this country in 1843 and in 1850, I do not know. Writing in 1860 on the subject of the disease then prevailing in Massachusetts, the late Mr. B. P. Johnson, the Secretary of this Society, used the following language:—

"At the same time it may be proper to note that, according to evidence too full and well authenticated to be rejected, pleuro-pneumonia has in several instances made its appearance in this country previous to its introduction by Mr. Chenery's importations. Cases in past years in the vicinity of several of our cities, of its attacks, and subsequent entire extirpation, have been brought to our notice in detail, &c. (Transactions, N. Y. State Ag. Soc., 1859, p. 783)."

I think it may properly be inferred from this language that, in 1859, we supposed the country to be free from pleuro-pneumonia of the contagious form, and we knew that the authorities of Massachusetts considered that in 1861, they had completely rid that State of the contagion imported in 1859. I am not in a position to assert that there has been no later importation. I can only say that I have never heard of any.

Enclosure 4, in No. 6.

LETTER from *T. S. Gold*, Esq., to *E. M. Archibald*, Esq., Her Britannic Majesty's Consul General, New York.

29 January 1879.

YOURS of the 24th instant has been referred to me by the Honorary Secretary of State, and in reply would say, that one herd of cows in Watertown is suffering at present with pleuro pneumonia. Of 19 head, four have died, one sick cow has been killed, and most of the others are affected. It is plainly contagious, and we attribute the disease to two cows brought from New York in August. It is not epidemic, but is confined to this one herd, which is strictly quarantined. We know of no other cases in this State, and we are quite sure that none exist.

One or two similar outbreaks have been controlled by slaughter and quarantine.

Dr. Noah Cressy, V.S., is treating this herd, principally relying upon alcoholic stimulants, but it is too early to speak of results.

Enclosure 5, in No. 6.

LETTER from *Henry C. Kelsey*, Esq., to *E. M. Archibald*, Esq., Her Britannic Majesty's Consul General, New York.

25 January 1879.

YOUR favour of the 24th instant is this day referred to William M. Force, Esq., Newark, New Jersey, Secretary of the State Agricultural Society, for answer.

Enclosure 6, in No. 6.

LETTER from Mr. *J. C. Corlies*, D.V.S., to *E. M. Archibald*, Esq., Her Britannic Majesty's Consul General, New York.

Newark, New Jersey, 28 January 1879.

MY esteemed friend, Mr. W. M. Force, has requested me to answer a communication conveyed to him through the State Department from yourself in reference to pleuro-pneumonia as existing in the Atlantic coast States. I have the honour to say that, as a member of the State Board of Health, it has recently been my duty to look into and investigate the sanitary condition of the live stock of our State (New Jersey), and in so doing I find that pleuro-pneumonia has and does exist to a more or less degree at the present time; and, so far as we can learn, it has never assumed the epizootic form, while on several occasions it may be said to have presented an enzootic form. But usually, and at the present time, it is found in isolated cases, which may be the means of at any time superinducing an outbreak.

It is always of a contagious character, and entails a mortality of about 50 per cent. of the affected cases, &c. &c.

The preventive measures consist of quarantining, inoculation, and, in radical cases, occision. There have been three special Acts enacted by the State Legislature for the purpose of arresting its progress on the appearance of an outbreak, the substance of which is conferring power upon township authorities to employ competent medical advice, and, if it should be found necessary, to resort to occision; and the owner to be compensated by the State.

Enclosure 7, in No. 6.

LETTER from Editor of the "American Agriculturist" to *E. M. Archibald*, Esq., Her Britannic Majesty's Consul General, New York.

21 January 1879.

YOUR inquiry about diseases of cattle has been referred to me. In reply, I beg to say that I know of no disease that is now prevalent among cattle in any part of the country. We have occasionally a few scattered cases of pneumonia occurring in ill-conducted dairies, but it is not of an epizootic character, and remains in the stables where it originated. Amongst grazing cattle there is now no disease reported in any part of the country. Our climate fortunately forbids the occurrence of those diseases which prevail in some European countries; and past experience has shown that the cases of pleuro-pneumonia which have occurred at times a few years ago were neither virulent nor difficult to deal with, and that ordinary sanitary precautions now practised are sufficient to keep it in check. Just now there is none of this existing.

— No. 7. —

TELEGRAM from Consul General *Archibald* to the Marquis of *Salisbury*.

"8 February 1879.

"THE cattle disease near Brooklyn, Long Island, is decidedly contagious; pleuro-pneumonia extensively prevalent; there is possibility of contagion affecting western cattle shipped from this port."

CATTLE DISEASE (UNITED STATES OF AMERICA).

— No. 8. —

TELEGRAM from Consul General *Archibald* to the Marquis of *Salisbury*.

"9 February 1879.

"MY telegram yesterday meant extensively prevalent in large stable near Brooklyn, in which are about 800 cows, and from whence diseased cows are said to have been sent to other parts of Long Island."

— No. 9. —

TELEGRAM from Foreign Office to Consul General *Archibald*.

"12 February, 3.50 p.m.

"REFERENCE to your telegram of 8th instant. Report by telegram name and owner of stable and address where disease is situated; also the veterinary evidence that it is contagious pleuro-pneumonia. Write full particulars by next post."

— No. 10. —

LETTER from Consul General *Archibald* to the Marquis of *Salisbury*.

My Lord,   30 January 1879.

WITH reference to my Despatch (No. 8) of the 21st instant, I have the honour to transmit herewith enclosed, for your Lordship's information, copy of a Despatch, and of its Enclosures, received by me from Sir Edward Thornton, communicating the report of an investigation made by the health officer of the district of Columbia, in regard to the real nature of the disease reported to exist among cows in the vicinity of Washington, and referred to in the Enclosure of your Lordship's Despatch, No. 1, of the 2nd instant, from which report it appears that the disease is pleuro-pneumonia.

The author of the observations in the "Tribune" newspaper, of the 27th November last, on the reported "plague" at Washington, is Dr. James Law, Professor of Veterinary Science in the Cornell University, at Ithaca, in this State, and one whose opinions are well deserving of consideration.

I have not as yet received from the President of the New York College of Veterinary Surgeons his promised report upon this subject.

Referring your Lordship for further information to my Despatch (Consular No. 10) of this date,

I have, &c.
(signed)   E. M. Archibald.

Enclosure 1, in No. 10.

LETTER from Sir *Edward Thornton* to *E. M. Archibald*, Esq., Her Britannic Majesty's Consul General, New York.

Washington, 30 January 1879.

I HAVE the honour to transmit herewith copy of a note and of its enclosures, which I have received from Mr. Evarts, from which you will perceive that it is admitted that there have been cases of pleuro-pneumonia, or lung fever, among the cows in the neighbourhood of Washington. As it would appear from the Order in Council of the 6th ultimo that the above-mentioned disease is considered to be contagious, I have addressed a further note to Mr. Evarts, inquiring as to the extent of the disease, and what steps have been taken to prevent its spreading.

Enclosure 2, in No. 10.

LETTER from Mr. *Evarts* to Sir *Edward Thornton*.

Department of State, Washington,
27 January 1879.

Sir,

I HAVE the honour to acknowledge the receipt of Mr. Drummond's note of the 16th instant, in which, on behalf of Her Majesty's Government, inquiry is made in reference to the existence among the cows, in the vicinity of Washington, of a disease similar to the rinderpest, and also as to whether any such or other form of disease has lately prevailed among the cows in or about this city.

In reply, I have to state that the matter has been referred to the Board of Commissioners of the district of Columbia, and that a reply thereto has been received from the President of that body, dated the 24th instant, accompanied by a report on the subject from the health officer of the district, copies of both of which are herewith enclosed for your information.

I have, &c.
(signed) Wm. M. Evarts.

Enclosure 3, in No. 10.

LETTER from President of the Commissioners, District of Columbia, to Honourable *W. M. Evarts*, enclosing a Report from the Medical Officer of Health.

Office of the Commissioners
of the District of Columbia, Washington,
24 January 1879.

Sir,

IN response to your request of the 22nd instant, that the Commissioners take measures to ascertain whether the rinderpest, or any other form of disease, has lately prevailed among the cows in or about the city of Washington, the Commissioners have the honour to say that they referred the matter to the health officer of the district immediately upon the receipt of your communication for investigation, and herewith submit a copy of his report on the premises.

By Order of the Board.
(signed) S. L. Phelps, President.

Enclosure 4, in No. 10.

Office of Health Officer, 24 January 1879.

RESPECTFULLY returned to the Commissioners, District of Columbia, with the following information:—

About the 17th of October 1878, a gentleman residing in the county of Washington, near this city, called at this office and requested the examination of some cattle then ill on his farm. An inspector having considerable experience with disease of cattle was sent, he made careful and thorough examination of the animals on this and adjoining farms, and reported them suffering from pleuro-pneumonia, or lung fever.

A morning paper in this city made sensational report of the matter, heading the same "Rinderpest," and from this probably sprang the reports which are said to have appeared in certain New York papers. I have been called upon several times to deny the story, and would again state that careful inspection of the dairy farms in this vicinity has failed to reveal the existence of any disease similar to the rinderpest or cattle plague.

(signed) Smith Townshend, M.D.,
Health Officer.

Official Copy.
William Tindall, Secretary.

CATTLE DISEASE (UNITED STATES OF AMERICA).

— No. 11. —

LETTER from United States Minister, London, to the Marquis of *Salisbury*.

Legation of the United States, London,
19 February 1879.

My Lord,

I HAVE the honour to acquaint you that I have just received from Mr. Evarts a circular, of which I enclose copy, and which has been addressed by the Secretary of the Treasury of the United States to collectors of customs and others.

Your Lordship will observe that by this document collectors of customs are instructed not to permit shipments of live animals from their respective ports until after an inspection of such animals with reference to their freedom from disease, and the issuance of a certificate showing that they are free from the class of maladies mentioned.

I beg to express the hope that these precautionary measures may have some influence in inducing Her Majesty's Privy Council to rescind or modify their Order in relation to this matter of the 10th instant.

I have, &c.
(signed) *John Welsh*.

Enclosure in No. 11.

COPY of a CIRCULAR in relation to Cattle Disease, issued by the Secretary of the Treasury, 1st February 1879.

CIRCULAR.

Information in regard to Cattle Disease.

Treasury Department,
Washington, District of Columbia,
1 February 1879.

BY Department's Circular of 18th December 1878, it was directed that live cattle shipped from the various ports of the United States might be examined with reference to the question whether they were free from contagious diseases, and that if found to be free from such diseases, a certificate to that effect should be given.

By that circular such inspection was not made compulsory, but the certificate was to be issued only upon the application of parties interested.

As the export trade in live cattle from the United States is of vital importance to large interests, every precaution should be taken to guard against the shipment of diseased animals abroad, and such a guarantee given as will satisfy foreign countries, especially Great Britain, that no risk will ensue from such shipments of communicating contagious or infectious diseases to the animals in foreign countries by shipments from the United States.

Collectors of customs are therefore instructed that in no case will live animals be permitted to be shipped from their respective ports until after an inspection of the animals with reference to their freedom from disease, and the issuance of a certificate showing that they are free from the class of diseases mentioned.

Notice of rejected cattle should be promptly given to this Department.

In order that this Department may be fully informed in regard to such diseases in any part of the United States, collectors of customs are requested to promptly forward to this Department any information which they may be able to obtain of the presence of contagious or infectious diseases prevailing among live animals in their vicinity.

It is probable that if the disease prevails to any considerable extent it will be noticed in the local press, and collectors are requested to send copies of any such notices to the Department for its information.

(signed) *John Sherman*,
To Collector of Customs and others. Secretary.

— No. 12. —

LETTER from the Clerk of the Council to the Under Secretary of State, Foreign Office.

Veterinary Department, Privy Council Office,
44, Parliament-street, Westminster, S.W.,
27 February 1879.

Sir,

I HAVE submitted to the Lords of the Council your letter of the 22nd instant, transmitting a Despatch, with Enclosure, from the United States Minister at this Court, on the subject of the export of cattle from the United States of America to Great Britain.

In reply, I am directed to state, for the information of Lord Salisbury, that the Lords of the Council have carefully considered the orders given by the American Government for the inspection of cattle previous to exportation. Their Lordships are, however, aware from their own experience that no system of inspection at the port, however perfect, affords complete security against the introduction of pleuro-pneumonia. So long, therefore, as that disease exists in the United States, their Lordships regret that, looking to the provisions of The Contagious Diseases Animals Act, 1878, relative to importation of foreign animals, they are unable to modify the Order of the 10th February 1879, which prohibits the introduction into Great Britain, except for slaughter, of cattle from the United States of America.

I beg to return the Despatch and Enclosure as requested.

I am, &c.
(signed) C. L. Peel.

— No. 13. —

EXTRACT from a MESSAGE from the PRESIDENT OF THE UNITED STATES, communicating, in answer to a Senate Resolution of 20th February 1878, Information in relation to the Disease prevailing among Swine and other Domestic Animals.

Executive Mansion,
27 February 1878.

To the Senate of the United States,

I TRANSMIT herewith, for the information of the Senate, the reply of the Commissioner of Agriculture to a Resolution of the Senate of the 20th instant, ",relative to the disease prevailing among swine, &c."

(signed) R. B. Hayes.

Department of Agriculture,
Washington, District of Columbia,
26 February 1878.

Sir,

IN compliance with a resolution of the Senate, adopted on the 20th instant, calling upon me for such information as may be in my possession relative to the disease prevailing among swine, commonly known as "hog cholera," with such suggestions as I may deem pertinent in this connection, I have the honour to herewith transmit a large number of letters from almost every section of the country, relating to this and the many diseases to which all other classes of domestic animals are subject. For some years past the local press, and especially the agricultural journals of the country, have been calling attention to the increase of diseases among farm stock, and the consequent heavy losses annually sustained by our farmers and stock breeders and growers.

Our wide extent of country, and its great diversity of temperature and variation of climate, the severity of frosts in some sections, and the intensity of heat in other localities, render farm stock liable to the attacks and ravages of almost every disease known in the history of domestic animals. So general and fatal have many of these maladies grown, that stock breeding and rearing has to some extent become a precarious calling, instead of the profitable business of

former

former years. This would seem to be especially true as it relates to swine. Year by year new diseases, heretofore unknown in our country, make their appearance among this class of farm animals, while older ones become permanently localised and much more fatal in their results. Farmers, as a general thing, are neglectful of their stock, and pay but little attention to sporadic cases of sickness among their flocks and herds. It is only when diseases become general, and consequently of an epidemic and contagious character, that active measures are taken for the relief of the animals afflicted. It is then generally too late, as remedies have ceased to have their usual beneficial effects, and the disease is only stayed when it has no more victims to prey upon.

— No. 14. —

Extract from Professor *James Law's* Report on Pleuro-Pneumonia, or Lung Fever.

This is a much more redoubtable affection than Texas fever, which is limited in its prevalence to our northern latitudes by the appearance of frost. Lung fever knows no limitation by winter or summer, cold or heat, rain or drought, high or low altitude. In Western Europe and America it is a purely contagious disease, dependent alone on the pre-existing virus, and never arising spontaneously. This is amply proved not only by the records of the invasion of Ireland, England, Scotland, America, Australia, the Cape of Good Hope, Norway, Sweden, and Denmark, but also by the preservation of countries (Norway, Sweden, Denmark, Schleswig-Holstein, Oldenburg, Mecklenburg, Switzerland, the Channel Islands, Massachusetts, and Connecticut) which have treated it as an exotic, and even of such localities in plague-stricken countries as breed their own stock and never import strange animals. Of the latter may be particularly mentioned the Highlands of Scotland, certain portions of the Cheviots, and parts of Normandy. This is the most insidious of all plagues, for the poison may be retained in the system for a period of one or two months, or even more, in a latent form, and the infected animal may meanwhile be carried half way round the world in apparent health, yet bearing the seeds of this dread pestilence. And this malady we harbour on our eastern seaboard, where it is gradually but almost imperceptibly invading new territory, and preparing, when opportunity offers, to descend with devastating effect on our great stock range of the west. There is abundant evidence of the existence of this affection in Eastern New York, in New Jersey, Pennsylvania, Maryland, Delaware, Virginia, and the District of Columbia (*see* Government Report on Diseases of Cattle, 1871, and many instances in current agricultural journals). Within the past year I have advised in the case of three outbreaks, one in Eastern New York, one on Staten Island, and one in New Jersey.

At present it creates little apprehension, but we are asleep over a smouldering volcano, which only wants a little more time to gather strength, when the general infection of the country will be imminent. Spreading from the port of New York, it has already gained a substantial hold upon seven different States, including the District of Columbia, and has invaded and been repeatedly expelled from two more; and it is only requisite that it should reach the sources of our stock supplies in the west to infect our railroad cars and Eastern States generally. It will create no such panic as did the Texas fever in 1868, but by its leisurely invasion of a herd, taking one victim now and another next week, or next month, and by the general infection that will be established before its true nature is suspected, it will prove far more destructive in the end than would an active invasion of Texas fever, or even rinderpest. England has lost over 10,000,000 dollars from rinderpest in the present century, but she has lost hundreds of millions from the less dreaded lung fever. To save ourselves from similar consequences, the Government should see to it, that this disease is arrested in its fatal course and thoroughly eradicated from our soil. If nothing is done the time will inevitably come when we will repeat the experience of Continental Europe, Great Britain, South Africa, and Australia, when our agriculture will be crippled, and when the extinction of the plague will be a herculean, if not an impossible, task.

CATTLE DISEASE
(UNITED STATES OF AMERICA).

CORRESPONDENCE connected with the Detection of PLEURO-PNEUMONIA among CATTLE landed in GREAT BRITAIN from the UNITED STATES OF AMERICA.

(Presented by Her Majesty's Command.)

Ordered, by The House of Commons, to be Printed,
21 *March* 1879.

111.

Under 2 *oz.*

COMMERCIAL. No. 1 (1879).

[C.—2207.] Price 4d.

REPORT

BY

MR. DRUMMOND,

SECRETARY TO HER MAJESTY'S LEGATION AT WASHINGTON,

ON

SUGAR PRODUCTION

IN THE

UNITED STATES.

Presented to both Houses of Parliament by Command of Her Majesty.
1879.

LONDON:
PRINTED BY HARRISON AND SONS.

Report by Mr. Drummond, Secretary to Her Majesty's Legation at Washington, on Sugar Production in the United States.

Sir E. Thornton to the Marquis of Salisbury.—(Received November 25.)

My Lord,   *Washington, November* 11, 1878.

I HAVE the honour to transmit herewith a letter, accompanied by a Report addressed to me by Mr. Victor Drummond, First Secretary to this Legation, relative to the cultivation and production of sugar in this country, the drawbacks allowed upon refined sugar manufactured from imported material, the amounts of these drawbacks, and the amounts exported of such refined sugar.

In conversing with the Secretary of the Treasury a few days ago respecting the drawback allowed upon sugar, he said that he disapproved of the system as adopted in the United States, and should probably comment upon it, and recommend some changes with regard to it in his next message to Congress.

I have, &c.
(Signed)   EDWD. THORNTON.

Inclosure 1.

Mr. Drummond to Sir E. Thornton.

Sir,   *Washington, November* 11, 1878.

IT may not be uninteresting to those who are engaged in the sugar trade at home and in our Colonies to have before them a short account of the present state of the sugar production of the United States, and to learn the causes why at present there is not sufficient sugar produced for domestic consumption in the union, which at first sight appears surprising, when it is known to have the advantages of climate and the very best and largest area of soil adapted for the fruitful production of the sugar cane.

This state of things may, however, shortly take a different turn, and the United States may become not only the largest sugar producers, but exporters instead of importers.

New sugars have been lately obtained which are expected to equal in quality that produced by either the sugar cane in Louisiana or the best sugar in Europe.

It has been therefore with much pleasure and interest that I have drawn up the accompanying concise Report, availing myself of information given on this matter by General Le Duc, Director of the United States' Department of Agriculture.

The new sugars which I mention above as having been lately produced are from the juice of the stalks of maize and sorghum. On account of the similarity of the juice of sorghum to that of maize the same process is applicable to both, and thus any of the varieties of sorghum may be rapidly and uniformly crystallized and sugar produced from them.

This new discovery is due to the indefatigable labour given by Mr. F. L. Stewart, of Western Pennsylvania, to the subject of the chemistry of saccharine juices for some years past.

Sugar has been made from a variety of sorghum called "Minnesota early amber," and with good results in the State of Minnesota.

General Le Duc informs me that he considers these sugars obtained as a great success.

He showed to me the extract from a newspaper in which a farmer in Maine gives an account of the results of his sugar production, who maintains that the sugar from an acre of Indian corn planting will yield him a profit equal to thirty acres of wheat.

The sugar from the corn stalks I have tested; it is very sweet and well crystallized.

With respect to the drawback duties on refined sugar exported from the United States which I have given at the end of my Report, I may mention that it is claimed by the sugar planters of Louisiana that the present Tariff does not protect the interests of the American producer of sugar in the slightest degree, but that it discriminates against the planter, and gives to the sugar refiners, who are less than fifty in number in the whole country, a monopoly of the markets. The Director of the Agricultural Department appears rather to be of this opinion, for that gentleman says: "Such protection and encouragement as the older nations of Europe have extended to their sugar interests would apply, not alone to the protection of cane sugar, but also to the manufacture of the beet sugar," &c.

I have, &c.
(Signed) VICTOR DRUMMOND.

Inclosure 2.

Report by Mr. Drummond on the Present State of Sugar Production and its Future Prospects in the United States.

GENERAL LE DUC is Commissioner or Director of the United States' Department of Agriculture, and I shall quote entirely from his Report on agriculture for the year ending 1877, when he assumed control of the Department.

The Director begins his Report by pointing out the almost unparalleled returns of the various products of the country during 1877, explaining, however, that with all these evidences of prosperous industry this is not sufficient: it is necessary that efforts should be made to produce everything which is now imported from other nations, which he believes can be accomplished from the careful cultivation of the productive soil of the country, which extends through so many different climes and offers exceptional opportunities for a nation so prosperous and self-sustaining as the United States.

Annexed is a list, which is brought to notice, of articles that are imported and that can and ought to be produced in the United States, with their value:—

Articles.		Quantity.	Value.
			Dollars.
Articles free of duty—			
Peruvian bark (Calisaya, &c.)	pounds	5,744,765	1,293,400
Bark used for tanning			184,826
Cork-bark, unmanufactured			606,169
Coffee		339,789,246	56,788,997
Eggs		4,903,771	630,393
Indigo		999,139	794,990
Madder		2,911,958	151,005
Paper materials		112,447,584	3,854,046
Tea		62,887,143	19,524,166
Total			83,827,992
Dutiable articles—			
Barley	bushels	10,285,957	7,887,886
Barley-malt	"	286,930	252,622
Rice	pounds	71,561,852	1,693,547
Hemp	tons	17,979	2,247,540
Jute and other grasses	"	60,368	2,384,881
Flax-seed	bushels	2,755,726	3,859,496
Silk			23,745,957
Straw and palm-leaf			1,856,674
Wines			4,754,110
Wool, unmanufactured		44,642,836	8,247,617
Total			56,930,340

Marginalia: General Le Duc, Commissioner of United States' Agricultural Department. Returns of agricultural products for 1877 unparalleled. Necessity of producing everything now imported from abroad. Articles imported which can be produced in the United States.

Year.	Values.	Duties.
	Dollars.	Dollars.
1874	92,614,832	34,860,278
1875	82,209,853	37,157,245
1876	75,742,466	41,898,575
Total	250,567,151	113,916,098
Annual average for three years	83,522,383	37,972,032

Fruit and Nuts.	Values.	Duties.
	Dols. c.	Dols. c.
Currants	856,425 62	209,110 61
Lemons and oranges	3,412,027 45	682,405 50
Almonds	463,106 86	240,207 89
Prunes and plums	2,333,949 00	553,660 77
Raisins	2,425,277 14	805,526 63
All other fruits and nuts	2,424,480 44	624,318 20
Total	11,915,266 51	3,115,229 60

These values amount to 236,195,981 dollars, besides the additional expense for freight and commission paid annually for imports, all of which the Director considers would be saved to the people of the United States.

General Le Duc, with particular reference to sugar, explains how strongly he has urged on all those who take an interest in sugar cultivation the necessity of the production in large quantities of this staple article of daily consumption. He says, that among the imported products of other nations which absorb the capital, retard the industry, and depress the commercial prosperity of the country, sugar holds the first importance, as the United States pay for it annually nearly 100,000,000 dollars; that with proper encouragement and support it might be produced at home. *The Director urges increase of sugar cultivation. United States pay nearly 100,000,000 dollars for sugar.*

With reference to domestic production, the Director remarks that in the State of Louisiana, from whence comes the chief source of domestic supply, the production was nearly 63 per cent. less in 1876-7 than in 1861-2; in the latter year the production amounted to 459,410 hogsheads, or 528,321,500 lbs.; in the former 169,331 hogsheads, or 190,672,570 lbs.; that it appears that a very insignificant part of the whole body of cane-bearing lands have at any time been under cultivation, and that the system of production is not calculated to produce the best results, great losses arising on account of the agricultural methods and the mechanical appliances in use, as also through unscientific handling of the bagasse there has been always a loss of at least 40 per cent., which now, however, will probably be remedied by a recently invented apparatus of Mr. Bringiers for the exhaustion of bagasse. To an improved system of labour, a division and cultivation of smaller tracts by individual owners, and a more scientific handling of the cane, the Director looks for brighter prospects. It is also to be noted that successive plantings of the same seed-cane has caused deterioration of stock which has been one of the causes of diminished crops. There are immense tracts of unoccupied and abandoned sugar-lands in Louisiana which are purchasable at low rates. In the absorption of these lands by small cultivators protection should be afforded by a good levee system, the establishment of central factories, and the construction of transportation ways; with these and the new system of ownership of small farms, growth will be given to individual independence, and draw around itself educational and refining influences, building up and strengthening new and thriving communities. *Sugar production in State of Louisiana. Mr. Bringiers' invention for exhaustion of Bagasse. Remedies for increasing production. Successive plantings of same seed a cause of diminished crops. Lands purchasable at low rates in Louisiana. What should be done to bring cultivators.*

It is reported that there are hundreds of thousands of acres of the best sugar-producing lands on the Lower Mississippi which are inundated through the broken levees. Fruitless efforts have been made by individuals, corporations, counties, and states to restrain this mighty river; it therefore, in the Director's opinion, comes to be a national duty to re-establish these levees as shall permanently secure the industries that will immediately re-occupy these lands, and which have only been abandoned on account of the overflow. It is calculated that thus the producing power of the State of Louisiana might be increased *Immense tracts of land inundated in the Lower Mississippi. Levees should be made of a permanent character. Producing-power of Louisiana might be increased 300 per cent.*

Land, 15 to 20 dollars an acre.

300 per cent. The sugar-land can be purchased for fifteen to twenty dollars an acre, having a capacity of production of 2,000 to 4,000 lbs., with a proportionate quantity of molasses.

Recommendations of sugar cultivators to assist sugar industry.

In their communications with the Director of the Agricultural Department, the sugar cultivators recommend the appointment of practical chemists to study the operation of manufacture on the ground, to analyze the soils, provide means for converting the "trash-cane" into a fertilizer, and suggest means for the re-establishment of weakened and exhausted soils; also an agricultural college and farm for determining questions bearing on the sugar industry, since experimental tests conducted by private individuals lack thoroughness on account of the expense and time required to carry them forward to complete and furnish reliable results.

Research made for soil and conditions necessary for production of sugar from beet and other vegetables rich in saccharine matter. Only one beet-sugar manufactory known to be successful.

General Le Duc is now engaged in a careful research as to soil and conditions necessary in this country to produce beets or other vegetables rich enough in saccharine matter to warrant the expenditure of capital in the machinery necessary to the successful manufacture of sugar. At present only one beet manufactory of sugar is known to be in successful operation.

Tables giving consumption of sugar in the United States.

The following Tables will be found of interest. To the imports of each year is added the amount left over from the previous year, deducting the surplus at the close. The imputation on sugar and molasses from the Pacific Coast is not given, but it is stated that in the years 1874, 32·425 tons; 1875, 22·850 tons; 1876, 30·882 tons were imported.

CONSUMPTION of Sugar in the United States.

Years.	Total Consumption.	Imported.	Domestic.
	Tons of 2,240 lbs.	Tons of 2,240 lbs.	Tons of 2,240 lbs.
1860	415,281	296,250	119,031
1861	363,819	241,420	122,399
1862	432,411	241,411	191,000
1863	284,308	231,398	52,910
1864	220,660	192,660	28,000
1865	350,809	345,809	5,000
1866	391,678	383,178	8,500
1867	400,568	378,068	22,500
1868	469,533	446,533	23,000
1869	492,899	447,899	45,000
1870	530,692	483,892	46,800
1871	633,314	553,714	79,600
1872	637,373	567,573	69,800
1873	652,025	592,725	59,300
1874	710,369	661,869	48,500
1875	685,352	621,852	63,500
1876	638,369	561,369	77,000

The importations of cane-molasses, in the same years, are shown as follows:—

Years.	Total Consumption.	Imported.	Domestic.
	Gallons.	Gallons.	Gallons.
1860	47,318,877	28,724,205	18,594,672
1861	40,191,556	20,383,556	19,808,000
1862	62,668,400	25,650,400	37,018,000
1863	37,569,088	26,569,088	11,000,000
1864	32,410,325	28,582,325	3,828,000
1865	35,185,038	34,335,038	850,000
1866	45,140,110	43,840,110	1,300,000
1867	49,776,465	46,776,465	3,000,000
1868	55,957,969	52,587,969	3,370,000
1869	54,361,092	47,961,092	6,400,000
1870	49,323,171	42,723,171	6,600,000
1871	52,065,784	41,165,784	10,900,000
1872	53,695,203	42,995,203	10,700,000
1873	51,485,526	41,985,526	9,500,000
1874	48,206,257	39,506,257	8,700,000
1875	58,608,734	46,418,734	12,190,000
1876	48,809,504	36,456,504	12,350,000

In the years named the United States produced less than 13 per cent. of the cane sugar it consumed, and little more than 21 per cent. of its molasses consumed.

The leading sources of foreign supply are:—

Countries which supply sugar.

Countries.	Quantity.	Value.
	Lbs.	Dollars.
Cuba	1,008,413,671	41,039,048
Spanish Possessions	110,445,708	3,572,400
Porto Rico	70,155,045	2,610,418
French West Indies and Guiana	49,687,265	1,751,478
Brazil	40,010,416	1,329,938
Dutch East Indies	26,187,830	1,052,953
British West Indies and Honduras	23,212,168	844,144
British Guiana	21,865,691	912,101
Sandwich Islands	20,979,374	1,051,987

Twenty-one other nations supply the remainder, which is about 3 per cent. of the whole.

The estimates of consumption per capita of the current decade for the United States, not including the Pacific States, were as follows, viz.:—

Consumption per capita in United States, except Pacific States.

In— Lbs.
1871 .. 36·80
1872 .. 35·96
1873 .. 35·71
1874 .. 37·54
1875 .. 35·39
1876 .. 32·00

With various fluctuations these figures show a steady increase in the consumption per head up to 1874, the year in which commercial stringency was inaugurated; the marked reduction in the two subsequent years results from the decrease of the purchasing-power of the people. In 1864, during the Civil War, owing to the destruction of home production, the emancipation of the slaves, and the blockade of the southern ports, the consumption per capita was only 15·37 lbs.; the close of the war in 1865 brought an advance to 24·08 lbs.

Increase of consumption up to 1874. Decrease since owing to decrease of purchasing power of the people.

Consumption during 1864 very small.

The Tables as under give an insight into the quantity of sugar and molasses produced in the State of Louisiana from 1868 to 1876. In the former year the industry began to recover from the prostrating effects of the Civil War:—

Table giving sugar production in State Louisiana, 1868 to 1876.

Year.	Pounds of Sugar Produced.			Molasses Produced.	
	Brown Sugar.	Refined.	Total.	Total Gallons.	Gallons each Hogshead of Sugar.
1868	81,506,093	13,545,132	95,051,225	6,081,907	72
1869			99,452,946	5,724,236	65
1870	147,562,588	21,346,004	168,878,592	10,281,419	71
1871	126,649,952	20,256,173	146,906,125	10,019,958	78
1872	108,501,004	16,845,489	125,346,493	8,898,640	82
1873	88,058,278	15,182,841	103,241,119	8,203,944	92
1874	110,856,363	23,648,328	134,504,691	11,516,828	98
1875	131,700,360	31,717,710	163,418,070	10,870,546	75
1876	149,904,430	40,768,140	190,672,570	12,024,108	71

I annex also the Custom-house Tables of Importation for the fiscal years 1874, 1875, and 1876, which show an annual average of imported sugar and molasses of 81,393,091 dollars. The large reduction in 1876 is attributable to the economy practised by the masses on account of the stringency of the times and an estimated falling-off in the sugar-producing countries, amounting to about 200,000 tons in the preceding year, which caused an average advance of half a cent. per lb. in the selling price. The totals below do not represent the sums that have passed into foreign hands for the foreign supply of the United States, since it is calculated that two-thirds is returned to the Treasury as duties, which for 1876 are given as amounting to 42,000,000 dollars.

Customs Tables of sugar imports, 1874, 1875, 1876.

Fiscal Year of 1874.

Articles.				Quantity.	Value.
					Dollars.
Sugar, brown	..	..	.. pounds	1,594,306,354	77,459,968
,, refined	..	..	.. ,,	39,259	3,139
Molasses	..	..	.. gallons	47,189,837	10,947,824
Melada, syrup, &c.	..	..	.. pounds	106,952,236	4,424,356
Candy, &c.	..	..	.. ,,	56,443	13,916
Total	..	..	..	..	92,849,203

Fiscal Year of 1875.

Articles.				Quantity.	Value.
Sugar, brown	..	..	.. pounds	1,695,726,353	70,015,757
,, refined	..	..	.. ,,	15,251	1,202
Molasses	..	..	.. gallons	49,112,255	11,685,224
Melada, &c.	..	..	.. pounds	101,768,386	3,313,597
Candy, &c.	..	..	.. ,,	76,816	16,737
Total	..	..	..	..	85,033,517

Fiscal Year of 1876.

Articles.				Quantity.	Value.
Sugar, brown	..	..	.. pounds	1,414,254,663	55,702,903
,, refined	..	..	.. ,,	19,931	1,685
Molasses	..	..	.. gallons	39,026,200	8,157,470
Melada, &c.	..	..	.. pounds	79,702,878	2,415,995
Candy, &c.	..	..	.. ,,	87,995	18,500
Total	..	..	..	..	66,296,553

Cotton and rice-fields not so profitable as they were.

The advantage of fostering an interest of so great financial and economic importance, which would ultimately lead to create a trade of export in sugar, is evident, particularly as it is stated that in most parts of the South the cotton and rice fields, and even some of the cotton areas, are not so profitable as formerly.

Attempts made to obtain sugar from certain vegetables with little success.
Trials with beet not been successful.

Various attempts have been made for some years to obtain good results from certain vegetables for the production of sugar, but until lately with but slight success. Beet, for instance, has received its full share of trial, but the results to produce from it sugar of good quality, and in sufficient quantity, and at a sufficiently low cost, to take the place eventually of the imported sugars produced from the tropical cane, has not been realized, notwithstanding the large sums expended to insure success, the most approved methods and apparatus of manufacture, the importation of skilled workmen, the introduction of a system of culture adapted to the proper growth of beet as understood in Europe, and the information disseminated throughout the country. Trials are, however, to be further extended to the end of this year, and further information will, it is hoped, be obtained from France and Canada, where some success has been obtained since premiums have been offered by the Government. General Le Duc laments that the same encouragement is not given by Congress.

Trials with beet to be extended to end of this year.

New discovery for production of sugar.

The "El Dorado" of sugar cultivators may, however, have been now reached. The Director of the Agricultural Department met with an agreeable surprise when he visited the State fair of Minnesota last year. He found there a sample of sugar made in that State equalizing in appearance the common brown sugar of Louisiana. This sugar he was told is made from a new variety of sorghum which, from its early ripening, quality, and fair colour of the syrup was called the "Minnesota early amber." In Rice County, 15,000 gallons of syrup were produced last year; more or less sugar has been obtained from this cane since 1875; about half the sugar has crystallized the past season to a greater or lesser extent, and it is estimated that half the crop can be made to yield sugar. For growing this variety a high clay loam of a rather loose or sandy texture is the best. Barn-yard manure should not be used, as it dilutes and injures the juice. New land is preferable to old; plant in May either in drilled rows 4 feet apart, or in hills with seven to ten seeds each, the hills 3 ft. 6 in. to 10 in. each way. Seed covered with ½ in. if earth is moist, 1 in. if dry. Rows straight, and as soon as the young plants appear the ground must be stirred close to the cane by working from each side of the row close up to the

Sugar from "Minnesota early amber" a variety of sorghum.

Conditions of soil and manner of planting.

hills with a hoe. Ground must be cultivated until the leaves shade the ground sufficiently to prevent the growth of weeds. One authority states the cane should be perfectly ripe before being cut; another produced his sugar from cane the seed of which was merely in the dough: with some of the seeds partly filled out, it did best to lie four or five days after being cut.

The amount of sugar produced from the "early amber cane" is 5 lb. to 6 lb. from a gallon of syrup weighing 13½ lbs. The yield per acre in Minnesota varies from 125 to 150 gallons of syrup. A specimen of the centrifugal-drained sugar from this cane, analyzed by the chemist of the Agricultural Department, sets at rest the quality of sugar that can be made from this species of sorghum.

Amount of sugar produced from a gallon of syrup of the "early amber cane.

Analysis of a sample.

It is as follows:—

"Sir, "*Department of Agriculture, Washington, D. C.*

"I have the honour to report that the sample of sugar from the Minnesota early amber sugar-cane, submitted for the purpose, has been analyzed and found to have the following percentage composition:—

"Cane sugar (saccharose) .. .. 88·8934
"Grape sugar (glucose) .. .. 5·6100
"Water (by drying at 110 C.) .. .. 5·8250

"The estimations of sugar were made by means of Fehling's test liquor. The principle governing the method employed is based upon the fact that glucose has the power to reduce oxide of copper, when in an alkaline solution, to the state of suboxide in such a manner that there is a fixed relation between the amount of copper oxide reduced and that of the glucose employed. Cane sugar of itself does not possess this property, but if to its solution in water about 2 per cent. by volume of strong hydrochloric or sulphuric acid be added, and the whole heated to boiling for about three hours, it will be converted into a mixture known as inverted sugar, consisting of glucose and levulose, which is possessed of the requisite power to reduce copper oxide.

"In order to prepare the solution of copper oxide for this purpose we proceed as follows: Dissolve 34·649 grains of pure crystallized sulphate of copper in about 200 cubic centim. of distilled water: make another solution of 173 grains of pure crystallized potassic sodic tartrate (Rochelle salts) in 480 cubic centim. of solution of sodic hydrate of 1·14 specific gravity; add the first solution gradually to the second and dilute the mixture to 1,000 cubic centim.

"In making the estimation in a sample of raw sugar, which contains both glucose and saccharose, we first dissolve 10 grains of the product in sufficient water for the purpose and dilute the solution to 500 cubic centim. Take a convenient quantity of the copper solution, say 10 cubic centim., heat the solution to gentle boiling, and, without interrupting the operation, carefully add a given volume of the sugar solution, say about 15 cubic centim., continue the boiling five or ten minutes longer, then allow to cool, collect the precipitate upon a filter, wash thoroughly dry, ignite in a crucible until all the paper is consumed, allow the crucible to cool, moisten the contents with strong nitric acid, and carefully ignite again. By this treatment the sub-oxide or copper will be oxidized.

"Determine the weight of the resulting cupric oxide, and from it estimate the amount of glucose corresponding to it; 100 parts of oxide of copper correspond to 45·855 parts of glucose.

"To determine the saccharose, add to 50 cubic centim. of the sugar solution to be tested about 2½ cubic centim. of strong hydrochloric or sulphuric acid, and boil the mixture about three hours, adding water as the solution evaporates. Then neutralize the free acid with sodic carbonate and add water, if necessary, to make the volume of the liquid up to 50 cubic centim., and add it to a convenient quantity of boiling copper solution as before, being careful in all cases that there shall be a slight excess of the latter.

"The subsequent treatment is precisely the same as that given above for the glucose. From the amount of copper oxide found deduct the amount corresponding to the glucose already determined, and the remainder will represent the saccharose. One hundred parts of copper oxide represent 44·864 parts of saccharose. The determination of percentages is now a simple matter of calculation, which it will be useless to describe.

"Respectfully submitted.
(Signed)   "WM. McMURTRIE, *Chemist.*

"To Hon. W. G. Le Duc,
"Commissioner of Agriculture."

Mr. Peas, of Dunreitte, Indiana, appears to have first introduced it eighteen years ago. He makes the following statement:—

Mr. Peas' account of its introduction.

"In a visit to Europe eighteen years ago, in search of seeds and plants, I bought of Vilmorin, Andrieux and Co., seedsmen in Paris, a few pounds of Chinese cane-seed, asking them for the best variety. This seed was given to a friend to plant who was an experienced grower and manufacturer of sorghum. In this lot of cane one stalk was found of a different habit from the rest, that ripened its seed before the rest of the plot was fully in bloom. Seed of this stalk was saved, and the next year planted separate to prevent admixture. This crop ripened much sooner than any other cane known to me, and the syrup was superior in colour and taste to any other produced in the neighbourhood. From its earliness and fair colour I named it "Early Amber," and under this name sent packages to customers in nearly every State and territory in the Union, especially to Minnesota and the Western and Southern States. It ripens from 90 to 100 days after the planting, yields 120 to

150 gallons of syrup per acre, and about 6 lbs. of sugar per gallon. It may be ripened in August. Means have lately been taken to separate the sugar from the syrup."

Experiments made.

Sugar has never been made in paying quantities from sorghum.

The Director of the Agricultural Department deemed extended experiments necessary, and placed in the hands of agriculturists in nearly every Congressional district of the United States a sufficient quantity of seeds for trial. Since the introduction of sorghum into the United States twenty years ago sugar has never been made in paying quantities from any of the old sorts.

In the State of Ohio, for example, the number of pounds of sorghum sugar annually produced and reported scarcely exceeded the number of acres of cane planted.

The first sugar made from sorghum.

The first sorghum sugar made in this country appears to have been by a Mr. Curtis, in Wisconsin, and it is noticeable that success was attained despite of, and most likely because of, the absence of the ordinary appliances for expressing the juice, and the substitution therefore of diffusion.

Mr. F. L. Stewart makes important discoveries.

In prosecuting further inquiries for the means of increasing the production of sugar, the Director of the Agricultural Department accidentally discovered that Mr. F. L. Stewart, a gentleman residing in West Philadelphia, had made, during the past year, some important discoveries connected with the production of sugar from maize and sorghum.

Mr. Stewart has made the subject of the chemistry of saccharine juices a speciality for some years past, and intends publishing an account of his discovery of a process by which sugar, in much larger quantities than has heretofore been supposed to exist in it, can now be made from the juice of the stalks of maize or Indian corn, taken at a period when the grain is only partially matured. His experiments seem to warrant the belief that the yield of sugar from this source may be made by a careful system of manufacture to equal, per acre of ground planted, nearly the average of sugar now produced from the sugar-cane in Louisiana, and that the American people could easily render themselves independent of foreign nations and the caprices of the foreign sugar trade, by growing and manufacturing their own sugar at comparatively small cost. Of equal importance is the statement, that on account of the similarity of the juice of sorghum to that of maize in most important particulars the same process is applicable to both; that by this means any of the prominent varieties of sorghum now known to the country may be rapidly and uniformly crystallized, and an amount of sugar be produced from any of them equal to the average product of either the sugar-cane in Louisiana or the sugar-beet in Europe. Those varieties of sorghum, which yielded heretofore only a crude table syrup, especially the old Chinese sorghum, may now be considered as the most valuable varieties. Mr. Stewart's experiments show that the regular Chinese cane of Western Pennsylvania yields 200 gallons of syrup per acre, that on good common soil 300 gallons per acre is practically attainable by the application of gypsum, phosphates, and other special manures and good cultivation; that 8 lbs. of sugar from corn and 10 lbs. from sorghum cane may be made from a gallon of dense syrup, and there is scarcely a county in the Union in which one or both of these plants cannot be successfully grown. If the above is proven, then it is demonstrable that if one acre in fifty of the area annually devoted to the growth of Indian corn in the United States be appropriated to the growth of either corn or sorghum for sugar, and properly worked up, the product would abundantly supply the present home demand.

Mr. Stewart's new process for making sugar from the juice of the stalks of maize. Yield per acre may by this process equal the average of sugar now produced from cane in Louisiana. American people will probably become independent of foreign nations for their sugar by new discovery. Similarity of juice of sorghum and maize; same process applicable to both. The old varieties of sorghum become valuable. Yield of Chinese cane.

Maize and sorghum can be grown in nearly every county of the Union. Present home demand can be supplied if the above process succeeds.

Mr. Stewart gives an interesting account of his investigations.

Mr. Stewart, at the solicitation of the Director of the Agricultural Department, has furnished him, for publication, with an account of his investigation, in the form of an article, entitled "Maize and Sorghum as Sugar Plants," which I annex herewith, as it may be of deep interest to British sugar cultivators and refiners both at home and in our Colonies.

Maize and Sorghum as Sugar Plants.

By F. L. Stewart, Murrysville, Pa.

The greatest labour they take in planting their corne. In April they begin to plant, but their chiefe plantation is in May, and so they continue till the midst of June. What they plant in April they reape in August, for May in September, for June in October. Every stalke of their corne commonly beareth two eares, some three, seldome any foure, many but one, and some none. Every eare ordinarily hath betwixt 200 and 300 graines.

The stalke, being greene, hath a sweet juice in it somewhat like a sugar cane, which is the cause that when they gather their cane greene they sucke the stalkes, for as we gather greene pease so do they their corne, being greene, which excelleth their olde.—[From the "True Travels, Adventures, and Observations of Captaine John Smith—Account of 6th Voyage, A.D. 1606, 2d Booke," London ed., A.D. 1629.]

The characteristic bread-plant of this continent is maize. Its discovered uses are so numerous, its products are so multiform, its vigour and productiveness are so wonderful in this its original home, as to give it the very foremost rank among cereals for the benefit of man. The superiority of American corn passes unchallenged in the great grain marts of the world, and we have been accustomed to consider that our knowledge of the economy and uses of the plant are well-nigh complete.

When Captain Smith landed in Virginia, nearly three centuries ago, what he saw of the plant and its uses he rehearsed to his countrymen on his return in a minute and interesting narrative of which a brief extract is given above, and from which it is evident that the Indian tribes occupying the eastern shore of America at that day were more of an agricultural people than has commonly been supposed, and the recognized uses of maize among them were widely different from those now in vogue. Its saccharine qualities were no less distinctly recognized than its value as a cereal, and the grain, both for immediate use and for preservation, was most esteemed in the immature state, when the " honey of the maize " was in its prime.

This twofold use of unrefined corn did not escape the notice of the Spanish conquerors of Mexico and Peru during the preceding century, when the plant was discovered. It is certain that in Mexico some sugar had been made from it at that period ; but the chroniclers of the conquest drew their pictures with a free hand, and it is extremely improbable that the production had attained to any importance. This appears from several circumstances, among which is the fact that maize-sugar had no prominent place, at least, in the vast enumeration of articles provided for the royal cuisine which it certainly would have held if it had ranked as a staple of the country.

The nature of this juice is such that it yields, with comparative facility, by ordinary treatment, a small proportion of its sugar, two or three per cent. We may infer, as in the case of some experiments made in this country a short time before the introduction of the Chinese cane, sugar was not obtained from it in remunerative quantity, and that is no evidence to show that sugar-making, as it existed among the Aztecs, can ever be claimed as one of the " lost arts."

Yet these statements, if not altogether mythical, have certainly some practical significance. At this time with a peculiar force, the question comes up for answer : has Indian corn, at any period of its growth, a definite value as a sugar-producing plant ?

No sufficient reply has ever been made to this question. Believing it to merit at least a thorough examination, the writer, more than two years ago, undertook some researches that have been conducted with patience and care up to the present time, and sufficient results have now been reached to furnish a decided and intelligent answer.*

But, in the course of this investigation, it was very soon discovered that maize juice, in certain important particulars, bears a strong resemblance to that of another notable plant now domesticated in this country, the value of which has been much debated, and the peculiarities of which have hitherto been very imperfectly understood—the Chinese sugar millet or sorghum.

Although the plants are strongly contrasted in some respects, it was discovered that they are so intimately related in chemical constitution as to entitle them not to be ranked together, but to separate them by a wide interval from all the known sugar plants. Natives of opposite hemispheres, they seem to have been brought together to fulfil a common destiny.

New and interesting peculiarities presented themselves in the juices of these plants, foreshadowing the necessity of improved modes of treatment, and it was at once perceived that but little practical benefit would result from an investigation, however wide its range or important its disclosures, unless a process could be devised capable of the extraction of the sugar as uniformly and certainly as, by special processes adapted to them, it is now obtained under favourable circumstances from the beet and Southern cane.

It may be confidently affirmed that not only maize in the green state, but also the Chinese and African canes, are beyond comparison superior to any other plants that can be grown in the United States for sugar production, either as to certainty of results, abundant and regular yield, ease of culture, or cheapness and facility of manufacture.

It is difficult to express in a few words the importance of this statement. It will be readily seen that the natural resources of the United States for sugar production from these plants are practically limitless, if the facts here assumed be well established. A single illustration bearing upon this point will suffice.

The area of land annually planted in Indian corn of late years in the United States averages 45,000,000 of acres, as shown by the reports to the Department of Agriculture at Washington. It is demonstrable that if the average sugar-producing capacity of either sorghum or Indian corn per acre of ground be taken at one-third less than the experiments of the past year show it to be clearly equal to, if the crop be grown and worked up with ordinary skill and care, it would require less than the one-fiftieth part, or one acre in fifty, of the acres annually devoted to the Indian-corn crop in the United States to support a growth for sugar of either sorghum or maize which would be fully adequate to supply the whole immense home demand for sugar, in value now equal annually to 100,000,000 dollars.

It can now be shown that we have the resources at perfect command, if rightfully utilized, to save to the country this vast sum which we are paying in gold every year for foreign sugars; but that in a few years hence we will be able to send to other markets a surplus of our crop, which will take equal rank with our exports of flour and corn.

To accomplish this it is not necessary that any delay should be now incurred, or that any preparation should be made involving changes in the modes of agricultural labour to which our people have become used. Nor have we to spend time in experiments new to us or to our climate and soil. To insure our success, we need not invoke the presence of any other agencies than those which the Creator has so lavishly and so opportunely laid to our hand.

The failure to recognize the value of these plants heretofore is surprising, but it is not at all unparalleled. Some of the grandest industrial monuments of the present century were not even foreshadowed during the last. It is no disparagement to us that through the swift strides our country has taken during

* Prescott extols the noble growth and saccharine qualities of the maize in these equatorial regions, and refers to the sugar made from it. Conquest of Mexico, rev. ed., 12mo, 1874, vol. i, p. 139. Carta del sic Tuazo, M. S. Oviedo, Hist. Natural de los Indias, cap. 4, ap. Barcia, tom. 1 ; Hernandez, Hist. Plant, lib. 6, caps. 44, 45, are the authorities which he cites.

the past fifty years, in some fields of material progress we have overstepped in our haste some mines of wealth which the surface concealed. The corn-plant of America, in common with many other of our indigenous productions, was not appreciated at the time of its discovery. It was recognized as an invaluable acquisition by the early colonists, and perhaps a proper estimate of its value would have been reached in the old countries if the dazzling splendour of riches brought home by the Spanish adventurers had not blinded the eyes of all Europe to all discoveries but those of gold and silver. In the enthusiasm of the time the old dream of the alchemist seemed at last to find a realization in the teeming wealth of the mines of the New World, and men were well content to accept, as the power to bring it forth, the steel of the conquistador instead of the philosopher's stone.

A full century later it was a fashionable hobby, with European writers like Abbe Reynal, to assume the essential inferiority of the productions of the New World (a mistake which the Old World has learned to correct). This whimsey imposed itself upon the sober sense of no less a naturalist than Buffon. It repressed investigation, and threw into discredit knowledge by which a later age profited by estimating at its worth, and it must be remembered that it was not until another century had rolled by that modern chemistry and the systematic "interrogation of natura" took its rise. It may be said, too, that our forefathers in this hemisphere had no immediate wants which the almost unbounded resources of the country did not supply without calling forth much technical skill, and prior to the year 1850 no crisis in the commercial history of the nation had stimulated research toward the discovery of an adequate native source of supply of sugar such as gave life to the beet-sugar industry in France.

Still, it is not a little remarkable that half the value of the plant in American agriculture has, for these three hundred years, been practically ignored. Scarcely less so is the fact that a plant so rich in sugar as sorghum cane is now shown to be should have been grown for almost a quarter of a century in this country, and in Asia from time immemorial, without any adequate realization of its value.

1. *Crystallizable Sugar.*

It is important that there should be no misapprehension as to the nature of the product now furnished by these plants.

Although chemistry recognizes a distinct class of substances to which the general term of sugar is applied, there is but one body in nature recognized in the commercial world to which the appellation of crystallized sugar can properly and honestly be applied. It is exclusively a natural product. It must pre-exist in the living plant. It cannot be counterfeited or made. In its association with other bodies in the sources from which it is obtained its presence is ofttimes only indicated by the nicest chemical tests. To break the alliance subsisting between it and the substances often in great number found along with it, and to separate the sugar without destroying it, is, in many cases, one of the most difficult problems in organic chemistry. And it becomes a new problem involving new modes of treatment every time that a crude saccharine substance is brought under examination of a different organization from others already well understood.

Sugar, as it exists in tropical sugar-cane, in the maples of our forests, in the beet, in the sorghum, and in maize, is, in its purified form, precisely the same. In saccharine value no other substance can at all compare with it; no other possesses the same crystalline form, the sweetening power, or the same chemical construction and adaptation to the uses of man as an article of food. This distinction is necessary to be made at the outset, because Indian corn has recently obtained some celebrity as a sugar plant in its capacity to furnish, from the starch of its grain, by a well-known transformation, the miserable starch sugar to which, by an amazing stretch of courtesy, the name of "corn sugar" has been applied. The misnomer should deceive no one.

I now propose to state more particularly the grounds upon which the foregoing statements of the value of maize and sorghum in this respect are based. To do this fairly, and with the conciseness which is necessary, a comparison is made in all important points between these plants respectively and the beet and the Southern cane. From this the reader will be able to decide as to their relative value for sugar production, at least in the United States. The authorities cited for the cane and beet are among the most eminent and trustworthy names associated with the sugar industry of the United States and elsewhere.

Sugar Production in Louisiana.

Although it is possible that sugar production from the tropical cane in Louisiana at certain points, and in a few other favourable localities, may be extended in the future so as to utilize to the utmost all available resources, and restore it to a condition of comparative prosperity, still it must be admitted upon all hands that we cannot in coming years reasonably look to that source to supply more than a small fraction of the sugar annually consumed in the United States.

The decline of this industry at the South during the decade preceding the late civil war was due to natural causes, affecting the growth and development of the sugar-cane itself. After years of careful experiment it was at last plainly and painfully evident that the transplantation of an exclusively tropical plant into the narrow fringe of extra-tropical territory along our gulf coast, where alone it will grow at all, was in violation of a law of the life of the plant, the ultimate result of which was disease and decay.

It was of no permanent avail that Government aid was invoked and freely given, and cuttings of new and undegenerated varieties were introduced from the most distant quarters of the globe. Nothing was left undone to foster an industry which, when it was temporarily successful, so abundantly rewarded capital and skill. Never was the ingenuity of the American mind more conspicuously displayed or more enthusiastically bestowed than in the attempt to supplement by human invention and assiduity the lack of needed qualities in the sun and air of Louisiana. Apparatus of rare workmanship and enormous cost were employed in the manufacture of the sugar, and not without reward, for in quality the sugar of New Orleans soon enjoyed a marked pre-eminence; but nothing could countervail a climatic defect by which the frost of a single night would wither the hopes of the planter for a whole season, or arrest the deterioration of his best imported canes. Contrary to a widespread belief the civil war was not the immediate cause of the prostration of this industry, although it precipitated it; and now, notwithstanding so many years have elapsed since its close, during which the stimulus of high prices has been constant, the business has not revived, and every year the disparity between the supply from this source and the demand is becoming greater. Nature has plainly set barriers to the geographical range of the plant, beyond which it cannot be grown with success. It is only within the heart of the tropics that the regions are found from which the markets of the world are now supplied, or can be expected to be with any regularity in the future.

Results of Experiments with Maize and Sorghum.

The facts adduced as to maize and sorghum have been derived from a great number of analyses and practical experiments, a detailed account of which would be inadmissible in a brief article like the present. The chemical investigations were conducted after the most approved methods now in use. For the quantitative determination of the sugars, Fehling's standard cupric solutions were generally employed. The plants tested were used when freshly cut from the ground, unless it is otherwise indicated, and they were taken at all periods of their growth, from the time when sugar began to be developed in the juice until it ceased to yield it in remunerative quantities. Many varieties of both species were tested. The action of manures upon the juice of growing plants, the influence of different soils and seasons, the effect of diverse modes of planting and culture, the comparative value under various modes of treatment of some of the most prominent varieties of corn grown for sugar alone, and for sugar as combined with the preservation in the best condition of immature grain, and the utilization of other products, have all received more or less consideration. But the most prominent attention was bestowed upon the characteristics of the juice itself, in order to secure the separation of the sugar.

In the course of this examination many preconceived opinions, both of myself and others, were shown to rest upon insufficient grounds. But it is especially gratifying to me now to say in regard to the sorghum that how muchsoever the published opinions of some eminent chemists are apparently at variance with each other, no well-established fact is discordant with what is now known. The truth, as far as ascertained, harmonizes all the facts. Notwithstanding the great diversity prevailing among different varieties of the same species in other respects, the most remarkable uniformity was found to exist in the chemical constitution of the juice at the same stage of growth of the plant.

The results of these experiments, so far as they relate to maize, were announced for the first time in the "Philadelphia Public Ledger" of the 1st December, 1876, and specimens of sugar were displayed at the Centennial Exhibition toward its close.

During the present year those results were fully confirmed, and at the same time the applicability of the process to the crystallization of the sugar of Chinese cane and the African varieties was fully established. In fact, the facility with which sorghum-juice crystallizes under this treatment is as remarkable as its obstinate refusal to do so under the other.

1. *Botanical Relationships.*

Sorghum, maize, and the tropical sugar cane are closely related. They are all simply gigantic solid pithy-stemmed grasses (not reed-like or hollow), charged at a certain period of their growth with a rich saccharine juice. There are numerous well-defined varieties of each.

The beet is remarkable as being a member of a peculiar order of plants, to which belong such alkaline seaside plants as the sampphira, saltwort, and obione. Of the same family is the common worm-seed (*Ambrina anthelmintica*). It is probable that its saccharine character has been developed largely by cultivation. Of the many varieties of beet only the white-fleshed kinds, especially that known as the Silesian, are adapted to the production of sugar.

2. *Period of Growth.*

Sorghum.—Annual, at least in temperate latitudes. The length of the period of growth differs with the variety, varying from three to five months.

Maize.—Annual, ripening its seed in from three to five months in North America.

Sugar-cane.—Perennial from the root-stalk in the tropics, flowering in from twelve to twenty months. In Louisiana it never matures its seed.

Beet.—Biennial, ripening its seed the second year from the planting, but maturing its juice during the first season in the root. The time required for this purpose is almost eight months from the time of planting.

3. *Propagation.*

Sorghum.—Propagated from seeds planted in early spring. Much labour and expense is thus saved, which Louisiana is expending in the cultivation and care of seed-cane or cuttings.

Maize.—Annually during the summer from seeds. Enjoys equal advantages with sorghum in this respect.

Sugar-cane.—Propagated always in the sugar district of our Gulf States, and ordinarily in the tropics from cuttings of the stems (joints). In Louisiana, on account of constant deterioration, it is necessary to replant from cuttings every third or fourth year, one-fourth of the whole breadth of the land devoted to sugar culture being employed constantly in the propagation of the joints from which the cane on the other three-fourths is grown.

Beet.—By seeds annually. But unlike sorghum and maize, no seed grown from the crop which produces sugar. The expense known of growing beet for seed is trifling, however, to that incurred for the sugar-cane.

4. *Ratooning or Tillering.*

Sorghum.—The crop of sorghum is capable of large increase in each season by side shoots arising from the root. It cannot be propagated from the cuttings of the stem, but when the stems are cut down they ratoon like the sugar-cane. Mr. Leonard Wray has stated that in South Africa he grew ratoons of Neazane or White Imphee six feet in height, and in two months after the first cutting sometimes fifteen stems tillered out from one root. These ripened their seed. This mode of increase is precisely analogous to the tillering of wheat when it has been cut down by the winter frost, but unlike wheat, and like the sugar-cane in some climates, it is increased, and a second crop of sorghum may be grown from the same root.

Maize.—This mode of increase is not at all a characteristic of maize.

Sugar-cane.—Ratoons regularly, as above described.

Beet.—Cannot be multiplied or propagated in any way analogous to this.

5. *Climate.*

Sorghum.—The climate of the whole territory of the United States south of Alaska, where the soil is not barren and the moisture insufficient during the summer months, is adapted in various degrees to its growth.

Maize.—A little more sensitive to cold than sorghum. All over the union where sorghum will thrive it may be grown, especially as it matures its juice within a shorter period.

Sugar-cane.—Production within the United States restricted to a very narrow belt of country bordering on the Mexican Gulf.

Beet.—May be grown for sugar in the latitude of the Middle and Northern States generally, but not at the South; but it will yield sugar remuneratively only where the summer rain-fall is equal to that of spring, and the natural peculiarities are not unfavourable.

6. *Soil.*

Sorghum.—The most suitable is a deep, rich, well-drained, and calcareous soil.

Maize.—The richest and deepest natural soils, moderately enriched. Not so sensitive to excess of moisture in the soil as sorghum.

Sugar-cane.—A deep, rich, moist loam the best. First crop off new lands yields most sugar.

Beet.—Similar requirements to the above as to depth and high fertility, but is very much more sensitive, and our best natural soils—the alluvions and prairies—have proved unfavourable to it.

7. *Manures.*

All these plants yield juices less rich in sugar and containing more impurities when supplied liberally with animal manures or those containing nitrogen in large proportion; but lime, gypsum, and the super-phosphates may be used without detriment, and sometimes with immense advantage.

8-10. *Chemical Composition.*

The Stem.

Constituents.	Sorghum.	Maize.	Sugar-cane. Avequin, Louisiana. Tahiti cane.	Sugar-cane. Avequin, Louisiana. Ribbon cane.	Sugar-cane. Dupuy. French Colonies.	Sugar-beet. Payen, France.
Sugars (12)	12·0	10·8	14·28	13·39	17·8	10·5
Woody fibre, mucilaginous, resinous, albuminous matter, and salts	22·2	19·8	9·64	9·88	10·2	6·0
Water	65·8	69·4	76·8	76·73	72·0	83·5
	100·0	100·0	100·00	100·00	100·0	100·0

The Juice.

Constituents.	Sorghum.	Maize.	Sugar-cane.		Sugar-beet (estimated).
			Avequin, Louisiana.	Erans.	Payen.
Sugars	13·5	12·0	15·78	18·2	10·66
Organic matter and salts	1·7	1·6	0·38	0·8	4·57
Water	84·8	86·4	83·84	81·0	84·77
	100·0	100·0	100·00	100·0	100·00

The intelligent reader, from the comparison as instituted above, will draw many inferences of value to which I make no reference.

Sorghum and Maize as compared with the Sugar-beet.

It is with the beet-sugar manufacture perfected, as it has been in its processes and appliances, that we must make the closest comparison; and, that it may be made with the utmost fairness, we assume as true what has been by no means proved by the experience of those who have fostered it here—that it is capable of being carried on in the United States as successfully as it is in France and Germany.

But it is well known that at the very limited point of his work, the beet-sugar er encounters the discouraging obstacle, hitherto insurmountable, of securing cheap labour for the growing of the raw material. Independent of the great expensiveness of the machinery, and the process employed, and the high degree of skill required, it is necessary that radical changes should be made in the means and methods of agricultural labour now existing, together with the great loss of time necessary to make such changes.

On the other hand, the cultivation of Indian corn and its now fully acclimatized relative, sorghum, is reduced here at present almost to a science.

It may be said that we have scarcely anything new or valuable now to learn in regard to the growth of either of them. By means of labour-saving implements and skill in the use of them, here, if anywhere, their cost is reduced to a minimum. No American who visited the Centennial Exhibition at Philadelphia and compared the maize of the valley of the Nile, of the plains of Hungary, of Portugal, Italy, or France, with the product of the valley of the Kansas or of the prairies of Iowa and Illinois, but must have felt that in all that pertains to the production of these cereals we are unrivalled by all the world.

But our very success is our peril. The over-production of corn has been almost the bane of our Western agriculture. The ease with which it is grown has a fascination to the farmer on the prairies which it is difficult to resist—so great that ofttimes to him the lack of transportation and glutted markets do not even suggest a remedy for the evil. The statistics of Washington abundantly show that in the case of this crop unrequited labour almost invariably follows in years of largely increased yield. It is just here that the new industry comes in to give immediate relief to the unremunerative labour by turning a part of the already overflowing stream into a new channel, thus utilizing our greatest waste to supply our greatest want.

It is from the uprising of such an industry as this that the highest benefits resulting from the division of labour among our people may be realized. It may be established without a jar in the routine of agricultural work, or any inroad upon established usages. The redundant population of the will flow out to meet the thus newly-created demand for labourers, and the solution of the much-vexed question may thus almost insensibly be reached.

If sorghum be grown by preference, as will often be the case, we have the advantage that it has been long enough in the country to make us familiar with all its requirements as to climate, soil, and cultivation. It is scarcely to be regretted that its full value has not heretofore been realized, for it is not probable that the attempt by our people to supplement by mechanical devices of rare ingenuity for the evaporation of the juice a defective knowledge of chemical requirements would have been made to the same extent as now. This concentration of inventive talent upon a single point, although it was not the most important one, led to the discovery of some principles in the evaporation of saccharine juice which had been overlooked. To have learned thoroughly the fact that proper evaporation, at the atmospheric pressure, of thin films of liquids containing sugar may be made to equal the results of boiling in a vacuum, is worth the past twenty years of baffled expectation. All over our land there is a large amount of capital invested in sugar-apparatus now almost idle—the result of the early interest taken in Chinese cane. Most of this, although regarded in many quarters as slight and insignificant, is just what is needed at the start in this industry; and it is widely distributed over the country and in intelligent hands. Serving a present purpose, it will lead inevitably to the rapid introduction of more perfect machinery, and to all the gains resulting from concentrated capital and skill.

These considerations, together with the fact that the crystallization of the sugar is reduced to an absolute certainty, have their value more than doubly enhanced by the circumstance that from the very outset our choice lies between maize and a still richer saccharine plant of similar requirements as to soil, climate, and general modes of treatment, but sufficiently diverse to enable us to use the one to supplant the other under a variety of circumstances, when either could not be used so well alone, both capable of having their sugar extracted by the same process, and thus giving a combination of advantages such as belong to no single sugar-plant.

There are also a large number of well-established and clearly-marked varieties of each, giving us a much wider range of subordinate qualities to adapt them to meet diverse local peculiarities of climate than are secured by any existing varieties of the beet, and the probability of still further improvement in this respect may safely be predicted.

It will be observed that the period of growth of either plant, when used for this purpose, and the time while they occupy the ground, is less by one-half than is required by the beet; and consequently the profits of a second crop, of another kind, the same season, are easily procurable from the same ground, when it is well-cared for, and are to be credited to these plants as against the beet.

The expense of preparing the ground and planting the seed is about equal for all these plants, and they have thus a great advantage over the tropical cane.

Climatic Range of Sorghum and Maize.

The climatic range of these saccharine cereals on this continent is vastly greater than that of the beet. It is also to be noted that a broad area of territory, within which it would be possible to grow the beet, toward the South, affords plants with a juice too weak to be profitable and too liable to fermentation for the establishment of factories there, a temperature of 60 degrees Fahrenheit during the working season being fatal to this pursuit with existing processes. The latitude of 45 degrees is the limit in France.

No such extreme delicacy of organization characterises maize or sorghum, and their juices are equally strong under the summer sun of either Texas or Maine.

Deficiency of moisture during our early summer—a very common occurrence—almost ruins the beet crop for sugar, and it is partly the cause of its deficient yield here. But maize can mature its juice in a season of early summer drought, being planted as late as July, in the latitude of Pittsburgh. The beet, on the contrary, requires the whole season to ripen.

Soils.

In point of adaptation to the rich, deep, natural soils of our Western prairie and the alluvions of our rivers, no plant grown either for sugar or grain, perhaps, ranks equal to Indian corn. Sorghum ranks equally as well upon them if they are not deficient in drainage, but heretofore beet-growing upon the prairies has met with but little success. Among the causes of failure the preponderance of nitric salts in the juice, derived from the soil, is assigned as the first.

Effects of Manures.

All sugar plants suffer from the effects of manures abounding in nitrogen directly applied, but the presence of certain mineral salts in constant quantity generally for each species shows that they require a soil rich in all the ordinary elements of plant growth. Normally, the azotized substances in all three of the above are not far from equal. But the presence in the beet of a great amount of mineral salts, which cannot be eliminated in process of manufacture, destroys utterly the value of the molasses for ordinary use. Indian corn, for a similar reason, does not afford as palatable a syrup as sorghum. The latter, in this respect, is capable of taking, when the syrup is purified, a front rank among plants of its class, and in the quantity of crystallized sugar which it produces it stands next to the Southern cane. It has been the aim to limit the amount of molasses (drainage) from either plant by the new process almost entirely to the glucose originally in the juice, and this has become so nearly realized in the case of sorghum as to enable us to extract $10\frac{1}{2}$ lbs. of crystallized sugar from 13 lbs. of very dense syrup readily and uniformly, a result which, in the practical manufacture of sugar, is almost unparalleled.

Cost of Production.

But it is in the vastly diminished cost of the production of well-crystallized sugar from these plants by the means now discovered, as compared with that from the beet, that the most marked disparity exists. In sugar-producing capacity the Chinese cane is in advance of Indian corn in the proportion of 12 to 14, or 6 to 7; but the greater value of the grain of corn (well dried sweet-corn being worth about 20 dollars per barrel of 300 lbs.), as compared with the grain of sorghum, fully compensates for the deficiency of sugar. The almost absolute certainty of realizing a large return from both the dried sweet-corn and sugar in our long summers is a strong argument in its favour. In this case, of course, only a large-stemmed and large-eared variety of sweet-corn should be grown. The amount of molasses (drainage) from either is small, but greater in case of maize, while that from sorghum is comparatively fine-flavoured, and free from mineral salts.

The greatly diminished cost of growing these plants, as compared with the beet, arises from the peculiar adaptation to them of our soil and climate, the use of our greatly improved agricultural implements, and substitution largely of animal instead of human labour.

But the disparity in cost becomes widest when the processes of manufacture are contrasted. Some appreciation of this will be realized when it is stated that the three items of expenditure in the beet-sugar processes are, viz., bone-black filtration, carbonation, and vacuum apparatus, in this entirely thrown out: the first two are entirely useless, and the last is unnecessary in this production. In the largest maize and sorghum sugar factories a preference may perhaps be given to vacuum finishers, but in operations of less magnitude, the comparatively simple and equally effective and rapid system of final evaporation of syrup in thin films and at a low temperature will prevail.

15

Improvement of the Soil.

Not the least of the advantages that will result from the new sugar industry in the United States will be in the improvement of the soil. Some of the rich soils of the West have borne successive crops of corn for more than twenty years, in which cases, generally, the grain was marketed, and the soil has been depleted of its most valuable mineral constituents.

Even on these soils the effects of such a system are now becoming apparent. But if sugar is grown, and the soft grain in the dried state only sent abroad, but little will be necessary to be returned to any soil already in good condition to maintain its fertility for this crop. The elements of sugar being derived from the air and water only, it abstracts from the soil nothing valuable, if the trash be carefully returned; while the ashes from the furnaces and all residual chemical products will, if properly applied, constantly supply more of the salts, &c., than immature grain takes away. But with somewhat less profit the soft corn and the seed of the sorghum may be fed on the ground, and a constant accession of the elements of fertility be thus secured to the soil. Besides, the thorough tillage which the business demands will go far to inaugurate, when it is lacking, a national system of farming, increase the value of land, and cheapen production.

The maximum crop of sugar-beets that can ordinarily be grown when an acre of ground is found to be such as to allow the rows in which they are planted to be one foot ten inches apart, and the plants one foot six inches asunder in the rows, thus producing over 21,000 beets to the acre. It is not profitable to grow beets of very large size for this purpose. They ordinarily weigh from 1 lb. to 3 lbs. each.

Yield per Acre.

It is not possible as yet to determine the maximum product of corn or cane attainable. I do not think that the best yield yet reported has reached that limit, nor perhaps can the mode of planting be indicated by which it can be secured. I recommend, however, to plant in rows three feet apart, the hills at intervals of twenty inches apart, so as to admit of cultivation across the rows once or twice in the season, by an implement drawn by horses, passed between two or three of the cross rows at once. The rows should be laid out with accuracy. The number of plants to the hill to number from two to four. The weight of the trimmed canes to the hill 2 lbs. to 8 lbs. The stems of evergreen corn in Pennsylvania will average 1 lb. each, varying from 12 oz. to 48 oz. each. Single trimmed stems of Kansas corn have equalled 6 lbs. each, but the juice of this giant growth is more impure than those of the inferior size; but an average of 3 lbs. of stem to the hill will yield 21,700 lbs. to the acre, giving 180 gallons of dense syrup, or 1,800 lbs. of crystallizable sugar, and 44 gallons of drainage molasses. If a growth of 4 lbs. to the hill is secured (an average easily obtained upon good soil with good culture), 2,400 lbs. of sugar and 55 gallons of molasses will be obtained from 225 gallons of dense syrup.

From experiments made the past summer, I conclude that an attainable limit for corn is 270 gallons of syrup per acre, 5 lbs. of stem to a hill, and 3,000 lbs. of sugar and 66 gallons of molasses upon ground which would readily yield 100 bushels of corn to the acre if grown for the grain, and which, if planted in sugar beets and tended with the usual care, would yield about the same amount of sugar. If sweet corn (evergreen) be grown for the grain and sugar combined, a reduction of one-third will have to be made in the yield of sugar in each of the above estimates respectively. The yield of sorghum in sugar will be about one-seventh greater than of corn in each of the above instances. From 100 to 350 gallons of syrup, so dense as to seem to be almost a solid mass of sugar when crystallized, can be secured ordinarily by sufficiently close and regular planting, good cultivation, and a thoroughly prepared soil. Two gallons of such syrup per square rod of ground should in all cases be aimed at as an average attainment. Of course, while the means taken to grow a crop of corn or cane vary as widely as they have done hitherto, often without any regard to system or economical management, the average production will fall far below what it ought to reach. While the maximum yield of the beet has reached in Europe about 509 lbs., the average per acre in France has dropped to 1,071 lbs. The lowest remunerative yield of sorghum (100 gallons of syrup) will produce the sam amount.

When it is considered that not a pound of sugar is wasted from the juice obtained at the mill, that the softer substance of the stalk both of corn and cane yields its juice in much larger proportion than that of the Southern sugar-cane, that the juice itself is from 10 to 50 per cent. stronger in sugar than that of beet, and the product of green fodder from maize in counties less favourable to its growth than our own has reached maxima much exceeding those upon which the above estimates are based, they will be acknowledged as fairly representing the capacities of those plants.

Corn and the Beet as Forage Plants in France.

In France, the home of the beet-sugar industry, extensive experiments have recently been made for the purpose of ascertaining the average yield of various plants for green fodder for stock, the process of ensilage, or fermentation in pits, being adopted for curing it. In the maize-growing departments of that country 26 to 35 tons of freshly-cut maize fodder per acre is estimated as the average yield. But far greater yields are announced in different quarters by higher culture. Upon a schistose sandy soil in the department of Finistère, limed and enriched with barn-yard manure and superphosphates, 44·61 tons (89,220 lbs.) in one case, and 66·91 tons (133,820 lbs.) in another, of the Caraqua, or giant maize, have already been produced there per acre.

[263]

M. Lecoreteaux,* in the "Journal Pratique d'Agriculture," summarises the comparative maximum yields of maize and sugar-beet as fodder-plants, as follows:—

	Tons.
Caraqua maize	66·96
Sugar-beets	35·68

Thus, in the gross yield for the same purpose, the maize leads the sugar-beet by almost one-half; one-third being deducted for weight of blades, immature ears, &c., will leave a weight of 44 tons or 88,000 lbs. of trimmed stems per acre, equivalent to the enormous amount of 8,800 lbs. of sugar, if juice was of the average quality.

One-half this yield is much beyond the maximum which we have assumed above for Indian corn here. It is asserted that 40 tons per acre of Chinese cane have been grown in the United States.†

The chemical composition of these plants and their juices I have made a subject of special investigation, a brief abstract of which is given in the foregoing comparative statement. The information thus gained, outside of its chief value in outlining a special mode of treatment for the extraction of sugar, possesses additional importance in its bearing upon other questions. One of these is whether a more exhaustive method of extracting the juice can profitably be employed to take the place of the ordinary cane-mills. The very great loss sustained in the expression of only the largest part of the juice of the Southern cane has led to the suggestion of a method of cutting the stem into thin slices, and exhausting the sugar by prolonged maceration and washing with hot water, and subsequent hydrostatic pressure.

The inapplicability of the latter method to the extraction of the sugar of the Chinese cane (and of maize as well) is decisively shown, if we consider the amount of soluble substances other than sugars contained in the stem, as compared with the amount of the same substances found in the juice when expressed by a sugar-mill.

A ripe stem of Chinese sorghum contains—

	Per cent.
Water	65·80
Sugar (crystallizable)	11·25
Sugar (glucose)	0·75
Gum	3·31
Pectin	0·60
Starch	7·15
Albuminoids	2·60
Cellulose	7·32
Oil	0·02
Ash: Silica, lime, potash, soda, peroxides of iron and manganese, chlorine, phosphoric acid, sulphuric acid, &c.	1·20

I have found that by washing the rasped or thinly-sliced cane repeatedly with cold water it is capable of extracting 4·5 per cent. of the albuminoids, gum, and pectin, while but 2·4 per cent. of other substances than sugar is found in the juice as it leaves the mill; but if hot-water maceration be employed to dissolve out the sugar an additional amount of pernicious substances escape with it, notably a large proportion of starch in gelatinous state, or amidin. It will also be observed that the combined weight of all the substances in the stem capable of being removed along with the sugars by acidulated or alkalized water considerably exceeds the whole of the crystallizable sugar.

On the other hand, the softer cellular structure of these plants as compared with the Southern cane facilitates very much the action of the mill, and increases the yield of juice proportionally. While from 50 to 60 per cent. only of the juice of Louisiana cane is attained ordinarily by this means, from 80 to 85 per cent. from maize and from 70 to 80 per cent. from sorghum (Chinese) may readily be obtained, as recent experiments above duly show. When light mills are used repressing may sometimes be necessary.

The following results of analyses made during the past season are of interest chiefly as showing the relative proportions of sugars in these plants at different times during the period when the extraction of sugar is profitable:—

Juice of Maize.

Varieties.	Stage of Growth.	Specific gravity.	Crystallizable sugar.	Uncrystallizable sugar.
			Per cent.	Per cent.
Pennsylvania yellow	Silk appearing; early flowering	10·44	6·98	1·92
Ditto	In early flower; roasting-ear	10·53	9·34	1·66
"Pop-corn," large	In early flower	10·44	7·25	1·65
"Stowell's evergreen"	Grain in early milk	10·60	11·34	1·56
8-rowed yellow	Ditto	10·60	11·42	1·65
Kansas yellow	Grain hardening	10·51	9·86	1·04
Ditto	Stored two weeks { Two lower joints	10·62	10·48	2·52
	{ Middle and upper joints	10·71	9·80	5·20

* Report of Department of Agriculture of United States, 1875, p. 404.
† Agricultural Report, 1857, p. 182.

Juice of Sorghum.

Varieties.	Stage of Growth.	Specific gravity.	Crystallizable sugar.	Uncrystallizable sugar.
			Per cent.	Per cent.
Chinese (regular)	Flower just expanding	10·42	6·72	2·18
Ditto	In flower a few days { Butt joints	10·60	11·30	1·60
	{ Top joints	10·53	9·75	1·25
Ditto	Seed ripening	10·58	11·52	1·18
Ditto	Seed quite ripe { Upper and middle joints	10·63	12·72	0·78
	{ Lower joints	10·55	10·57	0·93
Ditto	Mixed juice, ripe and unripe	10·60	11·34	1·56
Red imphee	Seed in early milk	10·53	9·92	0·98
Ditto	Ripe	10·60	11·92	0·98
Black imphee	Coming in flower	10·53	9·98	0·92
White imphee	Not yet in flower	10·59	10·90	1·90
Ditto	Flower just expanded	10·57	10·30	2·20
Ditto	Seed nearly ripe	10·60	10·66	2·24
Chinese imphee	{ Cut and stored (lower joints)	10·82	14·97	3·53
	{ Wisks (upper and middle joints)	10·82	16·19	2·31

Obstacles to Sugar Production from these Sources.

The two principal causes of failure in all the attempts heretofore made to produce sugar from sorghum, and which would prove almost equally formidable in the case of maize, are, first, the presence in the juice, when in the best condition, of an almost constant quantity of glucose; and, second, the uniform presence of peculiar proteine and amylaceous compounds, which distinguish these from other sugar-producing plants; consequently, the extraction of sugar from them is a problem involving entirely new conditions.

It was found that the existence of these bodies in the juice presented an almost insuperable barrier to the modes of treatment adapted to the cane of the South, and to all the processes so successful and at the same time so tedious and expensive which are employed in Europe in the extraction of sugar from the beet. By common treatment with lime, the destruction of the glucose and the speedy reduction of a large part of the sugar to the condition of levulose, the darkening of the syrup, and the incapacity of the remaining sugar to crystallize, was the inevitable result. On the contrary, if no lime was employed no defecation was possible, and the juice retained within itself the active elements of its own destruction. Thus, constantly placed between Scylla and Charybdis, the practical operator was left without resource.

It has commonly been supposed that maize contained no grape-sugar. The prevalent opinion in regard to sorghum has been that it contains it in very considerable quantity. Both these opinions are now shown to be incorrect. But that they both contain uncrystallizable sugar largely, even in larger proportion than that which is crystallizable, is proved by every analysis made of canes not taken fresh from the field. Deterioration commences within a few hours after they are cut from the ground. And to this fact almost solely are attributable all the hitherto discordant results of chemical analysis. Plants were used which, although bearing no external evidence of it, were really, as to sugars, in various stages of decomposition.

In an article like the present, which is designed merely to call public attention to this subject in its most general features, it would be useless to enter upon the minute details of the process of sugar manufacture itself which has been indicated, or to point out, except in a general way, the new and interesting relation of the chemistry of the subject to sugar manufacture, as it is at present understood. Suffice it to say, that a body has been discovered to exist possessing the remarkable quality of isolating the sugars of both kinds in solution, and protecting them as by an impenetrable shield against the action of the forces by which the other deleterious substances are either neutralized or destroyed. This is accomplished expeditiously and cheaply, and it is hoped that the information herewith communicated will be found to be sufficient to secure, during this year, the successful inauguration of this new industry in the United States.

System of Manufacture for General Use.

In the following pages I design to embody for general use the coming season the details of this system of manufacture as fully as the limits of a paper necessarily as brief as the present will admit of. Its practicability during the past year has been fully tested, and no part of it is recommended for general adoption which my own experience has not only sanctioned by repeated experiment as eminently practical, but, as in its principal new feature—the defecation of the juice—the sole discovered means by which the same ends can be attained. Its application is not limited to any special variety of either cane or corn, or by any varied conditions of climate or soil, as far as already shown. The common yellow corn yields its sugar as readily as the "sweet" corn of the gardens, and the refractory Chinese sorghum, hitherto held to be inferior to the imphees, and useless except for syrup, now seems to be unequalled by any sugar-producing plant in the world, except the Southern cane.

But it must be borne in mind that strict adherence to a well-defined system is essential to success. At the outset every available means should be resorted to to increase the productiveness and improve the quality of the saccharine plant itself. Care should be exercised in the selection of the seed, and in the choice of such varieties of corn or sorghum as will best serve the purpose of the planter. If he selects the corn, and has facilities for drying the immature grain, he will choose "Stowell's evergreen."

[263]

If he designs to feed the soft corn to stock during the working season, or after, he may take that variety or any of the large-stemmed kinds of common yellow or white corn, and either by successive plantings at intervals, or by the selection of varieties of shorter or longer period of growth, he may extend his time for the working up of corn in proper condition from the 10th August until the 1st November in the latitude of the Middle States. The "seed of Stowell's evergreen corn," grown for the two-fold purpose above-mentioned, should always be taken from the upper and best-developed ear on the stalk; the stems should be stout and well developed, and producing not fewer than two ears each.

Among the many varieties of sorghum grown in this country the Chinese, Liberian, Oomseana, white and red imphee, are perhaps the most prominent. The Chinese cane is generally the most productive. The Liberian and white imphee are objectionable on account of late ripening, but they withstand prostration by the winds much better than the former, and hence are popular in the Western country. The seed should be selected from the earliest ripened and best-developed canes.

Preparation of the Soil.

The adequate preparation of the soil, and the mode of planting and cultivation best adapted to the crop, need not be insisted upon or discussed here, but this part of the work should be of the most thorough character. The soil should be naturally rich in all the elements of plant growth. Lime, gypsum, and super-phosphates are all eligible as fertilizers; decomposed bagasse and straw, and also barnyard manure (when it is not too largely used), are all appropriate when well incorporated with the soil. Only an excess of nitrogenous manures is to be avoided. The early planting and early cultivation of cane should be insisted upon. In general, the planting of a combined crop of corn and cane will be most advisable.

Period of Harvesting.

The proper period for cutting corn, when it is a double-eared variety, is when the silk of the upper ear has become dead and the second ear is in early "roasting-ear state." The first will then have begun to harden slightly, but there is a little difference in the yield or the saccharine value from the time the first ear has its grain fully developed until the last ear has begun to harden, a period of about two weeks. "Evergreen sugar-corn" is in season for about three weeks. In the latitude of Philadelphia the grinding season will begin the first week in August.

One month later, or from the 1st to the 10th September, the Chinese sorghum will be in condition if planted the early part of April. The imphee or African canes may be worked up from the time the flower has made its appearance until the seed is ripe. The Chinese variety, from the time the glumes or external seed envelopes begin to darken in colour until perfect ripeness. On account of the slower development of the large-stemmed imphees, the Chinese cane will usually be ready first.

Curing of Green Corn.

In case of corn, the ears may be removed a week before the stems are cut without detriment. When the grain of sugar-corn is to be dried for the market, no time should be lost until it is properly cured. After being boiled for five minutes, it should be removed from the cob by cutting instruments, operated by machinery, and then dried as rapidly as possible in shallow pans, steam-heated, or on perforated plates placed on flues and constantly stirred. In from four to six hours it will be thoroughly dried if the temperature is maintained at, but not allowed to exceed, the point at which the grain remains uncoloured by the heat. If the operation is properly managed, the dried corn should be as free from colour as when cut from the cob. In the retail markets this corn bears about the same price as brown sugar. As a secondary product its manufacture would be profitable at less than half that rate. It should be packed in barrels when dry. This grain is nearly equal to green corn, fresh from the field, and in its nutritive properties and capacity to fill a place otherwise unoccupied as an article of diet, it is an important product. In its nature and uses it is very different from the ripened grain of common corn. We are thus enabled to produce at will practically two different varieties of grain from the same plant. The popular demand for dried sweet corn, both in our own country and in Europe, will always render its production a valuable adjunct to sugar manufacture from maize.

Precautions to be Observed.

I must refer here to an error into which operators are likely to fall, and which cannot be too strongly condemned. There is now the most certain evidence to show that a profound modification of the juices of these plants, setting in at the base of the stem and gradually progressing upward, begins to take place within a very few hours after they have been cut from the ground. The storing of cane for considerable periods before it is to be worked up has been a common practice heretofore, but the transformation and loss of a part and finally the whole of the crystallizable sugar is the uniform result. Therefore, it should be insisted upon, as a general rule, that both corn and cane should be worked up within twenty-four hours of their being cut in the field. In other words, the successive operations of blading, topping, cutting, removal from the field, extraction of juice, defecation, evaporation, and crystallization should directly follow each other without any loss of time. The contact of freshly expressed juice with the air is extremely injurious if prolonged for more than an hour or two. There is no point in all these successive stages of work at which it will be safe to suspend them or take rest until the defecated syrup has reached a density of about 25 degrees Baumé.

Store room, therefore, need be provided for only such an amount of canes as can be worked up in a single day. The crushing-mill should have sufficient capacity to extract with ease the juice of a considerably greater amount of corn or cane than has been apportioned regularly to one day's work.

Crushing-Mills.

The inefficiency of crushing-mills is a source of great loss. The soft texture of the stem of the cane, and especially of corn, makes this inexcusable. But the best mills may be abused by grinding at too high a rate of speed. And this is very commonly done. Good results are obtained by rollers which develop a surface of 4 or 5 yards in length per minute, so that a roll of 2 feet in diameter should only make from two to two and one-half revolutions per minute, in order to extract generally the largest amount of juice from a given weight of canes. An increase in the capacity of the mill that is required may be easily obtained by increasing the length of the rolls rather than their velocity. The fresh undried stems of corn and cane contain about 85 per cent. of their weight of saccharine juice. The ordinary crushing-mills extract but 50 to 60 per cent. of the weight of the stalk; most of the higher class of mills do not average more than 50 per cent. A perfect machine would produce 85 per cent. If in practice but 50 lbs. are obtained, 35 lbs. or more than 41 per cent. of the whole amount of juice originally contained in the stock is still retained in the bagasse. We have thus revealed the astonishing fact that about five-twelfths of the crude material is thus utterly wasted at the outset in consequence of the imperfect means ordinarily used in extracting it.

In the case of common mills of small power, a largely increased yield of juice will follow the repressing of either corn or cane. If the loss of the time incurred in this is urged as an objection, it may be replied that there is no waste of material in sugar manufacture that is justifiable, and that there is none so utterly inexcusable as that caused by the failure to extract all the juices practically separable, after a previous expenditure of time and labour in producing the crop, which is just as great when the canes are half exhausted of their juice as when they are wholly so. The difference between the product of an efficient and an inefficient mill may be almost equal to the difference between a half and a full crop.

The mill should be placed upon such an elevation that the juice as it is received from it by a pipe into the defecating tanks hereafter described, and from them into the evaporating apparatus as required. A strainer of wire gauze should be placed at the outlet of the receiving-tank at the mill to arrest any of the coarser impurities, such as fragments of cane, pith, &c., that may be floating in the juice.

Heating-Tanks.

Two heating-tanks of equal capacity, 100 gallons or more each, to be used alternately, are to be so placed as to receive the juice as it flows from the tank at the mill, and at such an elevation as to empty readily into a broad cooling-tank, which supplies the evaporator continually. The tank last named may be made entirely of 2-inch plank, closely jointed, 15 inches or more in depth, and capacity equal to that of the two heating-tanks combined. The latter may be entirely of metal (copper preferred), or they may have bottoms of sheet copper and upright wooden sides, and placed over the flue of a separate furnace in small works; or they may be heated by a steam coil or a jacket, which is preferable, in order that the ebullition of the juice may be immediately checked when the scum has perfectly formed on the surface. If they can be heated over an open fire, there should be an arrangement for throwing off the heat into another flue by means of a damper when the proper temperature has been reached. It is convenient to have these heaters large enough to contain each as much juice as is received from the mill in an hour.

Evaporating Apparatus.

The evaporator may be of any required capacity, preferably with sheet-copper bottom, and of any of the best forms now in use in sorghum manufacture, provided that its construction admits of the continual descent of a thin sheet of juice over a large heated evaporating surface, with convenient arrangements for the removal of the scum which forms immediately when the juice enters it. It is rarely the case that the form of the evaporator will admit of the syrup being reduced in it to a finishing point.

Finishing Pan.

Instead of attempting to finish in the evaporator it is much better to have a small furnace detached, over which a plain, flat copper or perfectly smooth and clean iron pan is placed; or it may be so constructed as to be heated by a steam-jacket. If heated over a flue, the most convenient finisher, perhaps, is a tilt-pan. A suitable size is 3 or 4 feet in length and breadth and 8 to 10 inches in height, the sides vertical, and the bottom perfectly smooth and flat. It should be placed upon a furnace the diameter of which externally is a little greater either way than that of the pan. From the middle of one of the sides of this furnace extends a broad beak or lip, inclined gradually upward from the bottom of the pan and projecting a foot beyond the furnace wall. From the opposite corners of the side to which the beak is attached project two short iron pins or gudgeons, forming the extremities of the axis of the pan upon which it turns. These enter sockets or staples securely embedded in the wall itself, or in the timbers directly outside of it. To a ring on the middle of the side opposite to that from which the beak projects a short chain is fastened and secured at its other extremity to the short arm of a lever pivoted to the head of an upright post, set in the ground a few inches in the rear of the pan. By bearing upon the long arm of the lever the whole contents of the pan may be instantly dumped into a cooler placed below the projecting beak. A damper should be arranged so as to throw the heat at any time into a lower flue, but particularly when the pan is tilted.

If steam is used to heat the finishing-pan, the use of the tilting apparatus may be dispensed with; but in this case the heat should be applied by means of a steam space underneath, or jacket, and not by a coil to prevent adhesion of the dense syrup to the pipes. In connection with this vessel a sharp-edged wooden scraper should be used, consisting simply of a board of hard wood, and of a length slightly less than the width of the pan, 4 or 5 inches in width, pierced with holes of $\frac{1}{2}$ inch or 1 inch in diameter, and attached by its middle to a handle of 3 or 4 feet in length, set at right angles to it. This instrument is to be moved back and forth on the whole bottom of the pan during the last two or three minutes of the concentration of the syrup.

The Cooler.

The cooler into which the finishing-pan discharges may be simply a close-jointed wooden trough, broad and flat, and capable of containing the successive batches of crystallizing sugar produced during half a day's or a day's boiling. Two of the boxes should be provided to be used alternatively.

Crystallizing Vessels.

These, as they are filled, are to be emptied into the crystallizing vessels, which may be of any convenient shape or size in which provision for drainage is secured, and which are placed in a close apartment near by, the temperature of which is kept up to about 80 degrees to 90 degrees Fahrenheit.

For experimental purposes tubs or half-barrels, with movable plugs in the bottoms, with false bottoms of slats inside and covered with coarse sacking, may be used in which to crystallize the sugar. But of a better form and scarcely more expensive are boxes 5 feet in length by 3 in breadth, the bottom formed of two planes inclined 6 inches, the intersection of which forms a groove in the middle. In this groove are twelve or fifteen holes 1 inch in diameter to permit the syrup to flow out, but temporarily closed with plugs, abruptly pointed and projecting inside 1 or 2 inches. The depth is 9 inches at the sides and 16 inches at the centre. These vessels may be made of boards 1 inch think, cemented at the joints with white lead or glycerine and litharge, and burnt out with a hot iron inside, so as to form a sloping cavity surrounding the openings for drainage. These vessels when filtered to within 3 inches of the top will hold about 75 gallons of syrup for granulation. They should be supported upon timbers above troughs connected with a cistern on a lower level, to receive the molasses as it drips from the sugar. This form of crystallizing-box originated with Dutrone la Coutusa,* one of the most eminent names connected with sugar manufacture from the Southern cane during the last century, and may still be recommended for this purpose, as combining every possible advantage in crystallizing and draining with the requisite strength. The number of these boxes that will be required will of course depend upon the amount of work to be done.

It is convenient to have the cooler mounted upon a small truck, to run from the side of the finisher into the crystallizing room where it is to be emptied.

The simple apparatus above described, together with a Baumer's syrup hydrometer and a good thermometer, which is to be immersed in a tank supplied by the heaters, is all that is indispensable for the production of a good variety of sugar from these plants by this process. Most of the machinery that is required is already in use in every State in the Union. The requirements of capital working on the large scale will necessitate the introduction ere long of that which is more expensive, but the essential features of the work on every scale of magnitude will remain the same. For it must be borne in mind that it is upon the peculiar chemical treatment of the juice that success almost entirely depends.

Process of Manufacture.

It now only remains to particularize the different steps in the system to be pursued. The whole subject of the extraction of sugar from these sources is fraught with interest at every point of view. Especially is this so in regard to the peculiarities of these juices themselves. At the first view it might seem that the art of extracting sugar from liquids so rich in it as these have proved to be ought not to be a matter of much difficulty in practice; but its apparent simplicity vanishes when it is found that the saccharine liquids constitute a distinct class by themselves, and that they contain, intimately associated with the sugar, a variety of other substances of very different chemical properties and relations. Some of them are among the most unstable of all organic bodies. Most of these substances, uncrystallizable themselves, prevent by their pressure the sugar from assuming the crystalline form, the only form in which it can be obtained pure. In order that we may make sugar, therefore, it is necessary first either to remove these extraneous substances from the saccharine solution, or by some chemical agency to change their form and characteristics, that, although present in the solution, they will present no barrier to the crystallization of the associated sugar. In this case it has been necessary to employ media operating in both these ways.

Chemical Means Employed.

But the means used for this purpose must be well chosen. They must be adequote—they must be of such kind as to use on a large scale. The defecating agents must be harmless to the health if

---

* Quoted by McCulloch, Report, p. 286. Précis sur la Canne, p. 184. Paris, 1790.

inadvertently added in excess to the juice, and must leave no hurtful compounds in any product which is afterwards to be used as an article of diet; they must be sufficient in quantity and low in price, and they must not exert any prejudicial influence upon the sugar itself.

In a problem of this kind nothing good can be accomplished at haphazard. A strict adherence to system is necessary to practical success; but it must be a system in which the means employed must be commensurate with clearly defined ends in view. Lack of information upon some of the most important points has led some persons, whom a little investigation would have taught, to adopt expensive methods of treating sorghum, borrowed from the beet and cane sugar manufacture of France and Louisiana, which in the end they have been compelled to abandon after much disappointment and loss. It is fortunate at this time that not only corn and sorghum are adapted to a single general mode of treatment, but that they do not require any considerable deviation from an established routine, provided that such due care has been observed to prevent deterioration of juice as has been already recommended.

Treatment of Juice in the Tanks.

The series of chemical changes produced in the juice follow the introduction into it at the proper time, and in graduated quantities, of two standard solutions, which for brevity I shall designate respectively as solutions A and B. Solution A consists principally of a very concentrated liquid saccharate of lime. It is of standard strength, and produces uniform results. In cases in which it cannot be procured during the coming season milk of lime may be used in its place, but with the disadvantage that the strength of the mixture is extremely variable, the lime being chiefly suspended in water instead of dissolved. In preparation of it lime of the best quality should be used, carefully slacked and washed in boiling water to remove any potash that it may contain, lime in itself being but slightly soluble in hot water. After decanting the excess of water, enough is mingled with it to form, when the coarse articles have fallen to the bottom of the vessel, a mixture with a fine sediment of the consistence of thin cream.

Taking the capacity of the heating tank to be 100 gallons each between the level of a mark made on its side six inches from the top and the level of the exit cock near its bottom, we begin by filling one of the tanks up to the mark, and then turn the flow of juice from the supply pipe into the other. One hundred gallons is a convenient measure of juice, and can be reduced to the proper density on an evaporator and finisher of moderate capacity in one hour. Heat should be applied rapidly as soon as the juice begins to enter the tank, and when it has been filled up to the mark, and the temperature of the liquid has risen to about 180 degrees, or a point just endurable by the hand immersed in it, add to it five pints of milk of lime if the juice is that of corn, or seven pints if it is that of sorghum. Stir it thoroughly, bring up the heat to a boiling point, and then shut it off and remove quickly with a large skimmer the blanket of scum formed. Allow the liquid to rest a few minutes, to permit the suspended flocculencies to subside somewhat; without waiting, however, for this to be accomplished perfectly, commence to draw off by means of a syphon or swing pipe the upper portion of the liquid into the tank below, and finally into the lower stratum down to the muddy sediment, which may then be swept out by a large pipe at the bottom into a long bag strainer. The tank is then to be refilled as before, while its companion is being exhausted. At this stage of the process the juice is strongly alkaline, and of a light wine colour. A thermometer is kept immersed in the tank supplied by the heaters, and as soon as its temperature has fallen to 150 degrees Fahrenheit, five pints of the solution B are poured into it, if it contains the contents of one of the heaters, or in that proportion.

Chemical Reactions.

The peculiar chemical reactions induced in these juices at this stage of the process may briefly be indicated as follows:—Previous to the addition of the solution to the juice, the latter had received the full benefit of the action of heat and lime, both separate and combined. Some pernicious substances are thus separated in the insoluble form, the removal of which could not so well be affected by any other means. But new compounds are formed, or are in process of formation, which would exert a still more injurious effect upon the sugars than those which they supplant. The introduction of solution B at this point arrests this action, and its effects are manifested—

1. In the preservation of sugars of both kinds from decomposition, and the production of a dark red colouring matter, which is its visible evidence, is prevented. Hence, bone black is entirely dispensed with.

2. The neutralization of the excess of lime is accomplished more perfectly than by the use of carbonic acid, and much more easily and cheaply. Hence, we drop carbonation, which is so essential in the beet-sugar processes.

3. The removal of the influence of a previously dissolved nitrogenous body in an insoluble form—that of caseine, associated with a peculiar fatty substance. These separate in curdy flocks, forming a broken, greasy pellicle. Without following out these changes further at present, it may be said that separation of these substances seems to remove the last hindrances to crystallization.*

Evaporation.

After the removal of the characteristic scum, which forms almost as soon as the juice treated as already described is admitted into the evaporator, a great change is seen to have taken place. The

---
* At the time these sheets go to press it would be premature to announce the chemical composition of the solution referred to. It need not be long delayed, but the present protection of the writer in the use of the substances so employed is the only reward that is secured him in these investigations.

juice is brilliantly transparent, and of the lightest golden colour. Except to take away the thin, curdy pellicle, which will still continue to be thrown off to some extent, no special care need be taken in the evaporation, except that it be conducted as rapidly as possible from a shallow bed of juice. After it has reached the condition of a not very dense syrup (as indicated by a boiling temperature of 225 degrees Fahrenheit), it is ready to be received into the finisher, as above described. This syrup should be of brightest golden hue, if it is from sorghum, and perfectly clear. If from maize, the colour will generally be somewhat deeper, with sometimes a faint, pinkish tinge.

In the case of sorghum, the syrup should be concentrated in a few minutes to a point at which it suddenly becomes clouded or opalescent, and scarcely flows from a ladle dipped into it and immediately held up in the air. It boils without foam except at the last, and during the last stages of concentration it should be constantly stirred with a scraper, already described.

Corn syrup should not be boiled to so great a density, but it may, without detriment, be reduced to as low a point as is indicated by a temperature, while boiling, of 236 degrees to 239 degrees Fahrenheit.

Crystallization.

The cooler should be capacious enough to contain the successive skippings of several hours' work. The type of the crystallization will be improved, and it will issue much more rapidly, if a very small quantity of well-crystallized sugar be mixed with the syrup as it cools. Therefore, when the cooler and crystallizing vessels are emptied each time to be refilled, it is advisable to allow some sugar to remain adherent to the bottom and sides, to form nuclei for the following batch, and it is as well to stir into the first batch made each season an ounce or two of well-crystallized sugar; but this need not be repeated.

The cooler when changed is to be run into the crystallizing-room and its contents dipped out into the proper vessels, as above described.

The crystallization of corn sugar will become perfected in from two to ten days. From this time forward it may be treated precisely as the sugar of Southern cane. It may be left to purge itself by natural drainage from the vessels in which it has granulated, or the molasses may be removed by inclosing the mush sugar in coarse muslin sacks and applying a hydraulic pressure, or, more expeditiously still, by means of a centrifugal machine, such as those now used in the refineries and in beet-sugar works.

The syrup of drainage is to be reboiled in the finisher, or evaporator and finisher combined, and treated at the close just as the original syrup. The first crystallization from corn should be about 6¾ lbs. from a gallon of syrup weighing 13 lbs.—total 10 lbs. About a pound and a half of uncrystallizable sugar remains in the molasses of the second crystallization, which may be fed to stock or otherwise utilized, but the mineral salts still remaining in it render it of no value as an article of human food.

Special Treatment of Sorghum in Crystallization.

Sorghum syrup should be reduced to a density that, after a lapse of from twenty-four to forty-eight hours, when kept in a warm room, it will become an almost solid mass of sugar. It requires then a special mode of treatment, the crystals being fine and held together by only a small quantity of molasses. When in this condition the mass is to be thrown into a large tub or mixing-vessel, and a small quantity (about one-tenth of its volume) of a fair, thin syrup, prepared from sorghum juice of a density of about 30 degrees Baumé, when cold, is to be poured upon it and thoroughly incorporated in it by means of a wooden stirrer.* This will bring it to the semi-fluid state, if the room in which the operation has been performed has been kept heated. The syrup dilutes the uncrystallized sugar sufficiently to render it mobile, and does not dissolve the cane-sugar. The mass may then be drained in a centrifugal, the inner drum of which is very clearly but minutely perforated and running at the highest rate of speed.

Another method which may be followed is similar to that employed in some sugar factories to extract the juice from the pulp of the beet, and also to separate the saccharine matter left in the scum.

A number of linen and coarse muslin sacks are provided, of any convenient size, but their length should be about two and a-half times their width, say twenty by fifty inches; each sack is to be about one-third filled with this sugary mixture, folded once on itself in the middle, and flattened by placing it upon a table upon a sheet-iron plate with rounded corners, a little larger on every side than the partially flattened half of the sack and its contents, the loose half being folded under. The open end of the sack may be folded twice if necessary. The plate and sack are then to be placed within a frame on the bed of a powerful screw-press, and a series of such sacks and interleaved plates laid neatly one upon another, being turned in opposite directions, and subjected to pressure, gradually applied at first, to avoid rupture of the sacks, and afterwards with sufficient power to remove all the syrup and leave the sugar nearly dry. This fine-dried sugar is then to be transferred without further drying to a heating-vessel, and about one-tenth of its weight of pure water mixed with it. Here it is to be heated very gradually, with frequent stirring, to diffuse the heat through the mass, and when it has partially remelted and it is in the liquified state, it is to be poured finally into the crystallizing boxes in a room heated to about 90 degrees Fahrenheit, where it will form a solid mass of crystals as soon as it becomes cool. The result is a very coarse-grained, beautiful sugar of a high grade. If properly prepared, it will be almost white, and the immediate yield is almost double that which may be secured in any other way without reboiling.

* An iron mixing-mill, constructed somewhat like the feed-hopper of a centrifugal sugar-drainer, with a revolving shaft in its centre, set with long projecting teeth, may be employed in regular work.

The sugar prepared from sorghum in this way has the additional advantage of not being contaminated with the secondary products usually formed by reboiling; the final crystallization is attended by no risk, is easily and cheaply done, and in quality, with due care, should rank nearly or quite equal to vacuum sugar. The very small quantity of syrup left in contact with the crystals will drain off from the crystallizers, and, being almost free from glucose, will crystallize gradually if exposed in broad trays at the temperature of the room. If the production of sugar of a softer and more open grain is desired, it can readily be accomplished by a mode of treatment almost identical with the "stirring-off" process adopted by maple-sugar producers, but with better results. As soon as the half-liquified sugary mass, produced as already mentioned, has been poured in the crystallizing-boxes, it should be stirred with a broad, oar-shaped wooden instrument, without interruption, until it is cool and the sugar has become dry.

This method of crystallization is much better adapted to sorghum than to Indian corn, and hence I recommend the mode previously given for the latter as the best.

The general principles and specific routine, as above given, should be adhered to in all cases when the extraction of sugar from these juices is the object. It will readily be seen that they are adapted to operations of very different degrees of magnitude.

There is a large class of persons in our country having lands well adapted to sugar-growing from these sources, and possessed of sufficient energy and intelligence, whose means or opportunities do not permit them to engage largely in this pursuit, but who would be glad to have it within their power to work up the cane or corn which they could grow upon their own land; and it is just this class of persons —farmers of moderate means, desirous of enhancing their own comfort, profit, and independence—by whom the initiatory steps will be taken in this pursuit. Thousands of sets of cheap apparatus, formerly used in the manufacture of crude sorghum syrup, are now scattered over the whole country in the possession of persons of this class. With but slight modification, this machinery can now be utilized in the experiment of the production of crude maize and sorghum sugars. The process is sufficiently simple as above defined to make this clearly practicable without expense.

The growth of this new branch of industry will soon give rise to large establishments in many places, supplanting, to some extent, more limited individual operations; yet it must be conceded that it is with the latter just now that this enterprise more particularly is to be identified. From the circumstance that the means are already provided for success in this stage of the work, the value of the time and money gained by putting them to an immediate practical use is almost beyond estimate.

It was only after many years of trial of mills propelled by animal power, and of inexpensive apparatus, that the sugar industry of Louisiana ever attained to any prominence, and, notwithstanding the most elaborate and expensive machinery has of late years been in use there, small planters still adhere to the simpler appliances, and with a very marked degree of success and profit. Here, also, large works will not interfere in the least with those conducted on a very moderate scale, if the latter be managed with skill and prudence. The one mill will be auxiliary to the other. In fact, the expense of transporting large quantities of canes from different parts of an extended area of country to one central manufactory is a source of great loss in many respects, and there is constant risk of deterioration by the delay which is scarcely balanced by advantages accruing from a concentration of capital and skill.

The question is asked, how can a planter work up to advantage a crop of from ten to twenty acres of cane or corn on his own land and under his own care, conducting the whole series of operations, beginning with the working of the soil and the planting of the seed, and ending with the production of a good article of crude, yellow sugar?

The importance of this question demands an answer in more explicit terms than is found in the general outline already given. In the accompanying diagram the essential features of a sugar factory to answer such a purpose are sketched. It is most convenient to have the whole work done under one roof, or within a single building. Where the location admits of it, the general arrangement here given will be found to be very advantageous. But whatever be the shape or size of the building, it is necessary that the space inside should be divided off into four separate compartments, and these should be contiguous to each other in the following order.—

(A) The mill-room; (B) the evaporating room; (D) the drying room. (See diagram.) The first two of them may be open shed, but the last two of them should be tightly closed in, and provided with the means of keeping up the temperature within them to 80 degrees Fahrenheit, whenever necessary. In addition to these there should be space for the storage of the products of the factory.

The mill (A) may be propelled by steam, water, or animal power, and, in any case, should be placed upon a strong platform of plank, supported by stout timbers. If horses are used to propel it, they work on the ground-floor below. The sweep is a straight beam, secured in a horizontal position, at a height suitable for easy draught, to a vertical wooden shaft of 10 or 12 inches in diameter, which is strongly coupled to the shaft of the driving-roll. Mills with either horizontal or vertical rolls may be used in this manner.

The convenience of this arrangement is obvious. The horses work to good advantage, and the vicinity of the mill is clear of all incumbrance, and the loss by dirt, waste, and damage to machinery, &c., is much diminished. The horizontal mills should be furnished with aprons for carrying forward the cane and removing the trash. There is room at one side, and sufficient elevation to allow the latter to be dumped over the platform outside the building, either into waggons or carts, to convey it to a barnyard for conversion into manure, or it may be utilized by burning it in the furnaces close alongside. It is convenient to have the mill-room at the base of a slight declivity or platform of rising ground, so that its floor will be on a level with the ground at the side where the cane is received to be passed through the mill.

The supply of cane or corn to the mill should be continuous. As already indicated, it should be conveyed to the mill as soon as it is cut down in the field, so that only a few hours may intervene until it is worked up. Store-room need only be provided for as much as can be passed through the mill in twenty-four hours. The mill, horses, cane, and all the machinery should be under roof, and there need be no interruption of the work.

From the tank at the mill (4) fall for the juice is secured. It is received first into the heating-tanks (6) by a pipe (pp), and thence by its downward flow successfully into the defecation tank (7), the supply tank (8), the evaporator (9), the finisher (10), and the cooler (11). Thence the cooler containing the granulating-syrup is conveyed along a tramway into the crystallizing-room adjoining, and the crystallizing-boxes (c, c, c) are filled in succession from it. Centrifugal for drying the sugar (16) (16) or the press (17) are located in the adjoining room. Brick, lime, and cemented cisterns (18) (18) (18), excavated beneath the floor of the evaporating-room, receive through pipes or troughs the syrup of drainage from the crystallizing vessels, the centrifugal, or the press. In the drying-room (D) sufficient space may be provided for the cutting from the cob by machinery, and the drying (14, 15) of the grain of sugar-corn.

The water-supply for the works should be abundant. If an engine be used to propel the crushing-mill, the boilers should be sufficiently large to supply steam for evaporating or heating purposes where furnaces are employed when animal power is used.

A few observations which have not found a place in the preceding pages will conclude this paper.

Corn stems evaporate their juices very rapidly after they are cut, and if they have not been bladed previous to being cut from the ground the evaporation, as shown by test experiments made during last summer, equalled 25 per cent. of the weight of the stem when exposed to the sun and air during a period of twenty-four hours. This was not attended by a corresponding increase in the juice, and is a source of great loss independent of that which occurs at the same time from the transformation of crystallizable into uncrystallizable sugar. This shows that the rule should be made imperative to work up the crop as it can be cut and brought in from the field. It is true that when the stripped stems of either corn or cane are kept under shelter after being cut, the evaporation is much less ($5\frac{1}{2}$ per cent. of the weight of Kansas corn and $3\frac{1}{2}$ per cent. of Chinese cane in an experiment made), and the density of the juice of both during many successive days is increased in direct proportion to the loss of water by evaporation; but it is also true that the quantity of sugar crystallizable is steadily diminished. No protection that can be given will prevent great loss if this rule be not rigidly adhered to.

It is a peculiarity of common corn, under some circumstances, that when it is allowed to stand uncut in the field after the grain has hardened it does not lose its juice as it does generally at that period, but it is as entirely destitute of sugar as is the dried stalk in mid-winter.

There is a gradual advance in the strength of the juice of corn from the time of flowering until the first ear begins to harden; and in case of stems which bear two or three ears, the juice remains in proper condition while the successive ears are hardening. Hence we have an additional reason why seed for planting should be selected from double or triple eared stems.

The variety of sweet corn known as "Stowell's evergreen" exhibits characteristics which give it marked prominence. The peculiar succulence both of the stem and grain, and the great length comparatively of the period while the ear remains in the green state, and the saccharine qualities of the juice continue unimpaired, enhance its value in this connection. At that stage of its growth when it is just "coming into roasting-ear," its juice is stronger than that of other corn, as far as tested. Generally not less than two, and often three, well-developed ears are borne upon each stalk. Although it is the latest in coming to maturity of the "sweet" varieties, it is the best "drying corn" grown, and its short, stout stalks yield as much juice as taller-stemmed sorts, and they are easier handled.

Analysis of Dried Sugar-corn.

Samples taken of the immature grain of Stowell's evergreen sugar-corn, prepared (August 1877) from it when in proper edible condition, boiling the corn in the ear for about five minutes, cutting it from the cob with a sharp knife, and drying it as rapidly as possible upon metallic plates at a regulated temperature (about 225 degrees Fahrenheit). For the purpose of comparison, I append recent analysis of the mature grain of Pennsylvania yellow corn, made by Dr. William McMurtrie, Chemist of the Department of Agriculture, and published in the Annual Report for 1873, page 178:—

	Dried Sugar-corn (Green).	Pennsylvania Yellow (Mature).
Moisture	7·12	8·87
Oil	4·20	5·17
Sugar	3·52	1·10
Gum	42·52	1·23
Starch	35·50	70·66
Albuminoids and gluten*	3·02	9·92
Cellulose	2·62	1·72
Ash	1·50	1·33
	100·00	100·00

* For convenience the azotized substances are here classed together.

It will be seen that the proportion of these substances in the dried sugar-corn is not quite equal to that contained in the ripened yellow corn, but this difference is due chiefly to the loss of gluten (diastase) occasioned by the cutting off of the germinal point of the grain of the green corn, nearly one-third of its substance, in the usual process of preparing it for drying. This circumstance, taken in connection with the fact that the cob of the green corn is exceedingly rich in saccharine matter, gum, &c., indicates the very high value of the cob with the adherent portion of the grain for stock-feeding purposes. The pith of the green corn is large, solid, and rich in sugar and gum. I regret that I am not prepared, at this time, to furnish an analysis of the cob in this condition.

The fatty matter or oil in the dried sugar-corn is about equal to that in the matured specimens of corn generally, especially in the white varieties, although it is less than in the yellow corn, with which it is here more directly compared. The saccharine matter is much greater than in the latter, and by the application of the proper chemical tests it is found to be almost entirely crystallizable. The sugar of the grain of ripened corn is generally glucose.

The most marked peculiarity of desiccated sugar-corn is the very large proportion of gummy matter which it contains (gum and dextrine) as compared with that of true starch.

Taken altogether this substance, as an article of human food, exhibits peculiarities not found in any other grain, and properly prepared it is light, rich, nutritive, and easily digested.

The proper utilization of the various secondary products arising from this industry is a subject of immense importance. This subject, in its relations to the feeding of farm stock in a systematic way, demands special attention. In these pages but one mode of utilizing the green corn is indicated; but a wide field is opened for the discovery of perhaps still more valuable modes.

In this manufacture nothing whatever should be wasted. The scums and precipitates, the washings of the sacks and of the vessels used, should be exhausted of the sugar which they contain, by reboiling and skimming, or straining and condensation to syrup for crystallization.

The rule always adopted in all well-regulated sugar-works should be enforced here. No inferior saccharine solution should ever be mixed with another of a higher grade.

The careful farmer will appreciate the importance of preserving in the best condition the top, blades, cane-seed, &c., removed in the field. The cobs from which seed-corn is cut for drying are as saccharine as the stalk, and much more nutritive. They should be fed to cattle and hogs, and cannot fail, especially in connection with other feed, to be highly valued. The bagasse, ashes of the furnaces, lime precipitates, &c., are best utilized as manures, and for this purpose they are invaluable.

Ordinary good judgment on the part of the operator, attention to details, a knowledge of the main principles involved, and a degree of practical skill easily acquired, are all that are necessary to give this new business a rapid and permanent success.

This Report will not be complete without giving the rates of drawback on refined sugar and syrup wholly manufactured from imported raw sugar, and exported from the United States. *Rates of drawback on refined sugar and syrup.*

The Treasury regulation is as follows:—

"*Rates of Drawback on Sugar and Syrup.*

"TREASURY DEPARTMENT, *September* 6, 1877.

"The following rates of drawback on refined sugar and syrup, wholly manufactured from imported raw sugar, are hereby established, to take effect on and after the 1st October, 1877:—

"On loaf, cut-loaf, crushed, granulated, and powdered refined sugar, stove dried, or dried by other equally effective process, entirely the product of foreign duty-paid sugar, $3\frac{18}{100}$ cents per pound.

"On refined white coffee sugar, undried and above No. 20, Dutch standard in colour, entirely the product of foreign duty-paid sugar, $2\frac{58}{100}$ cents per pound.

"On all grades of refined coffee sugar, No. 20, Dutch standard, and below, in colour, entirely the product of foreign duty-paid sugar, $2\frac{8}{100}$ cents per pound.

"On syrup, resulting entirely from the refining of foreign duty-paid sugar, $6\frac{1}{4}$ cents per gallon.

"The allowance on sugars will be subject to the deduction of 1 per cent., and the allowances on syrup to the deduction of 10 per cent., as prescribed by law.

"Very respectfully,
(Signed) "JOHN SHERMAN, *Secretary.*

"*Collectors and other Officers of the Customs.*"

I am also enabled to give a statement of the quantities and values of refined sugar, made from imported sugar, exported from the United States during the fiscal years ended 30th June, 1877 and 1878, with the amounts of drawback thereon. *Quantities and values of refined sugar made from imported sugar exported and*

[263]

	Exported.	1877.			1878.		
		Quantities.	Values.	Drawback.	Quantities.	Values.	Drawback.
From—	To—	Lbs.	Dols.	Dols. c.	Lbs.	Dols.	Dols. c.
New York..	Dominion of Canada	15,238,839	1,658,741	498,557 65	22,362,832	2,026,624	655,732 11
Ditto	All other countries	30,673,837	3,829,738	1,113,062 42	29,480,163	3,130,755	974,100 66
Boston	Dominion of Canada	11,828,332	1,274,603	394,336 34	12,249,515	1,156,889	384,895 79
Ditto	All other countries	5,582,706	628,415	200,978 45	6,586,151	619,600	208,163 67
Philadelphia	Dominion of Canada	..	..	..	226,986	22,417	7,145 96
Ditto	All other countries	171,790	20,890	6,122 55	838,040	91,604	28,141 20
Baltimore..	Dominion of Canada	..	..	..	..	..	..
Ditto	All other countries	105,449	12,206	3,749 62	136,886	13,831	4,023 59
San Francisco	Dominion of Canada	314,012	28,728	9,185 27	449,814	48,521	12,749 25
Ditto	All other countries	324,293	32,617	11,384 43	461,422	50,743	14,917 77
Portland, Maine	Dominion of Canada	490,641	56,885	16,582 83	1,267,111	128,223	40,213 10
Ditto	All other countries	..	..	..	..	..	..
United States	All foreign countries	64,729,899	7,542,823	2,253,959 56	74,058,920	7,289,207	2,330,083 10
United States	Dominion of Canada	27,871,824	3,018,957	918,662 09	36,556,258	3,382,674	1,100,736 21
Ditto	All other countries	36,858,075	4,523,866	1,335,297 47	37,502,662	3,906,533	1,229,346 89

Imports of sugar into the United States, 1877-78.

The imports into the United States of sugar, molasses, &c., are given in the Table below, for the fiscal years ending 30th June, 1877 and 1878:—

IMPORTS.

Sugar and Molasses.	Year ended June 30, 1878.		Year ended June 30, 1877.		1878 compared with 1877.	
	Quantities.	Values.	Quantities.	Values.	Increase.	Decrease.
	Lbs.	Dols.	Lbs.	Dols.	Dols.	Dols.
Brown sugar	1,473,480,604	89,642,368	1,584,162,924	81,187,504	..	11,545,136
Refined „	83,094	7,469	308,688	28,043	..	20,574
	Gallons.		Gallons.			
Molasses	27,490,007	6,764,119	30,188,963	7,808,257	..	1,044,138
	Lbs.		Lbs.			
Melada and syrup of sugar-cane	31,520,907	1,123,613	39,461,057	1,654,165	..	530,552
Candy and confectionery..	35,946	6,898	40,868	5,857	1,041	..

VICTOR DRUMMOND.

British Legation, Washington,
November 10, 1878.

Sugar import duties.

P.S.—The rates of duty on sugar imported into the United States are:—

Sugar—
- All not above No. 7, Dutch standard in colour .. $1\frac{3}{4}$ per lb.
- Above No. 7 and not above No. 10 .. 2 „
- Above No. 10 and not above No. 13 .. $2\frac{1}{4}$ „
- Above No. 13 and not above No. 16 .. $2\frac{3}{4}$ „
- Above No. 16 and not above No. 20 .. $3\frac{1}{4}$ „
- Above No. 20 and on all refined loaf, lump, crushed, powdered, and granulated .. 4 „

Sugar-cane—
- Other than for propagation or cultivation.. .. 10 per cent.
- If as plants .. .. 20 „

(And, in addition, an amount equal to 25 per cent. of said duties.)

Cents.
- Molasses .. $6\frac{1}{4}$ per gallon.
- „ concentrated .. $1\frac{7}{8}$ per lb.

V. D.

Addenda to Mr. Drummond's Report on Sugar Production in the United States of America.

In my letter to Sir Edward Thornton, accompanying this Report, I mention the complaint of the Louisiana sugar planters that the present Tariff does not protect their interests. With respect to this I find that the Secretary of the Treasury, in his remarks on the state of the finances, states as follows :— *[Present Tariff, and complaint by Louisiana planters. The remarks made by the Secretary of the Treasury in regard to sugar duties.]*

"The embarrassments alluded to in the last Annual Report in regard to the collection of duties on sugar have not ceased. Seizures have been made of cargoes of sugar claimed to be artificially coloured for the purpose of reducing the duties at the custom-house, and a suit involving one of these cases was tried at Baltimore, at great expense to the Government and to the importers, and was recently concluded, the verdict being that the sugars were artificially coloured after the process of manufacture was completed, but that it was not proven that the importer of the sugars had a knowledge thereof at the time of making entry. Though the claim of the Government, that the sugars had been artificially coloured for the purpose of defrauding the revenue, is maintained, it is powerless, under the Anti-Moiety Act of the 22nd June, 1874, to enforce fines, penalties, and forfeitures against persons or property unless there is proof of guilty knowledge of the fraud. *[Sugars artificially coloured. Baltimore case.]*

"It is deemed imperative that some change in the mode of collecting duties on sugar should be had, and it is preferred, as stated in the last Report, that the duty should be at one rate on all sugars up to a point which will exclude temptation, either to colour sugar for the purpose of reducing the duty, or to commit fraud by means of sampling and classification. The duties now are to a large extent dependent upon the fidelity of the sampler, one of the lowest paid officers in the public service. *[Change in collecting duties necessary. Duties dependent upon the fidelity of the sampler.]*

"In the event that duties upon sugars are made dependent to any considerable extent upon colour by the Dutch standard, it is recommended that authority be given to this Department to ascertain the true saccharine strength of imported sugars by means of the polariscope, and that the relations between the colour of sugars and their saccharine strength be definitely prescribed by Congress." *[Dutch standard. Polariscope.]*

These remarks probably have arisen from the controversy which took place at Baltimore between Mr. Perot, an importer of sugar from Demerara, and the customs authorities, who assumed that the Demerara sugars which he had manufactured were artificially coloured for fraudulent purposes. Although a verdict has been rendered adverse to Mr. Perot, it appears doubtful whether it was a rightful one. *[Verdict given in Baltimore case.]*

The Secretary of the Treasury has lately addressed a letter to the Speaker of the House of Representatives, accompanied by the draft of a Bill proposing certain alterations in the import duties on sugar. This Bill is entitled "An Act to amend existing custom laws and for other purposes," and is as follows :— *[Secretary of the Treasury proposes to Congress certain alterations in sugar import duties. Bill proposed by the Secretary of the Treasury.]*

"*Be it enacted by the Senate and House of Representatives of the United States of America in Congress assembled,* That from and after the   day of   , 1879, in lieu of the duties heretofore prescribed, the following rates of duties shall be exacted: On all sugars not above No. 13, Dutch standard in colour, and not exceeding ninety-four degrees in saccharine strength, two cents and four mills per pound : *Provided,* That any sugars not above No. 13, Dutch standard in colour, which shall test above ninety-four degrees in saccharine strength, shall pay the rate of duty chargeable on sugars above No. 13, but not above No. 16, Dutch standard in colour, and the test of saccharine strength shall be ascertained by means of the polariscope or its equivalent under such regulations as may be prescribed by the Secretary of the Treasury."

The sugar refiners and importers of sugar protest against the alleged adulteration of sugar and against the proposed Congressional action. It is said that the Southern sugar planters already enjoy a very handsome bounty, or protection, under present duties, the present rate being equal to 63 per cent. *ad valorem* on sugar. *[Protest of sugar refiners and importers. Protection afforded to Southern sugar planters.]*

The controversy as to a proposed change in the present rates of duty, and as to whether the polariscope is the most reliable means of testing sugar, claims at this moment great attention. The matter, which has been now for some days before the Committee on Ways and Means, will probably be shortly determined, as the Committee yesterday, after a careful consideration of all the facts and arguments that had been presented on the Sugar question, agreed, by a vote of six to four, to report a Bill to the House readjusting the Tariff on sugars as follows :— *[The polariscope. The Committee on Ways and Means Their Bill agreed to by six to four.]*

"On all sugars not above No. 13, Dutch standard, 2 cents 4 mil per pound; above No. 13 and not above No. 16, 2 cents ¾ mil per pound; on all above No. 16, 4 cents per pound." *[Wording of the Bill as proposed by the Committee.]*

The alleged colouring frauds being confined to sugars below No. 13, the adoption of *[This Bill prevents colouring frauds.]*

an uniform rate for lower-grade sugars leaves no incentive for colouring, and consequently obviates the necessity for any legislation to detect such reduction of the grade by artificial means.

Congress to decide. Congress will now decide what is to be done.

The Committee consider there has been no adulteration of sugars.
The Committee's decision adverse to use of the polariscope.
It is stated that the Committee on Ways and Means is unanimously of the opinion that raw sugars are not artificially darkened, as charged by the Treasury Department, and that the New York and Baltimore importers of the seized cargoes of dark Demerara sugar have not been guilty of any violation of law whatever. The Committee is also said to be unanimously of opinion in opposition to the use of the polariscope, as an absolute measure of value in assessing sugars, and will adhere to the Dutch coloured standard, modified to meet the existing necessities of the customs revenue service.

(Signed)   VICTOR DRUMMOND.

Washington, January 14, 1879.

COMMERCIAL. No. 1 (1879).

Report by Mr. Drummond, Secretary to Her Majesty's Legation at Washington, on Sugar Production in the United States.

Presented to both Houses of Parliament by Command of Her Majesty. 1879.

LONDON:
PRINTED BY HARRISON AND SONS.

AGRICULTURAL INTERESTS COMMISSION.

REPORTS

OF THE

ASSISTANT COMMISSIONERS.

Presented to both Houses of Parliament by Command of Her Majesty.
August 1880.

LONDON:
PRINTED BY GEORGE EDWARD EYRE AND WILLIAM SPOTTISWOODE,
PRINTERS TO THE QUEEN'S MOST EXCELLENT MAJESTY.
FOR HER MAJESTY'S STATIONERY OFFICE.
1880.

[C.—2678.] *Price* 8d.

Joint Report of Mr. Clare Read and Mr. Albert Pell, M.P.

Sir,

In accordance with instructions received from his Grace the Duke of Richmond and Gordon, President of the Royal Commission on Agriculture, we, as "Assistant Commissioners to inquire into the agriculture of the United States and Canada," have the honour to report that we left Liverpool on August 27th, and landed at New York on Sunday, September 7th, 1879, and left the same port on our return on December 10th. The interval of 93 days was occupied in travelling 9,400 miles on land, for the most part in the agricultural and pastural regions of the United States. Beyond a week's stay at Toronto, and another of the same duration in Manitoba, the whole of our time was spent in inquiries in the United States. Of this 20 days were devoted to the dairy districts and great towns east of the Alleghanies, and the remainder (some two months) in the western and middle States.

As regards agricultural operations, generally speaking, the harvest over this vast area was gathered in before we entered it, some of it had gone into consumption, and with grain the greater bulk was already, when we landed, the subject of active speculation; while apart from speculation in the matter of provisions, a substantial rise in prices had commenced, especially in dairy produce, and a better demand was felt for meat, owing to a revival of the iron and other industries.

A very short time for reflection satisfied us that the time of the Commission could not be turned to good account abroad during the winter months, and that the end of the year should close our work, for the time at all events, in America. That being so, any idea, if entertained, of crossing to California was dismissed from the first, as well as the hope of being able to investigate on the spot the capability of Manitoba and the north west to supersede the United States in the supply of grain to Great Britain.

Already the weather had begun to break up north of Winnipeg, frost had made itself felt and the settlers were freighting their carts and waggons with winter provisions, or fetching up their wives and families to their newly built houses and fresh broken land, to await during the long and bitter winter months the time when the whole household would throw themselves eagerly into the cultivation of the section of the land the husband had acquired and partly reclaimed during 1879. To the south of the sources of the Red River lay the wide sunny district so recently owned by the red man, but now adopted by the American citizens as the new field for enterprise among stockmen and farmers, and we naturally decided (indeed it was the only course which circumstances allowed) to spend the best part of our time on the plains and farms of the States and territories watered by the tributaries of the Missouri and Mississippi. It is here that agricultural enterprise is most vigorously developed with a display of activity and energy beyond comprehension. A restlessness and motion stir the whole body of emigrants and direct them further and further west to the occupation of new territory. They express that influence themselves by a common saying that "if hell lay in the west they would cross heaven to reach it." The truth is they are not cultivators but at present only breakers of the soil; when no virgin land is left to exhaust, and not an acre of prairie rose and weed of the plains remains to turn under the sod, the face of the succeeding race will be turned toward the east, the husbandry of the mother country will be adopted, and the earth, in answer to human diligence, will give forth her increase in richer and well earned profusion.

But it is not probable that a race so active and enterprising will confine their operations to the mere surface of the soil, when immediately below it in the Missouri basin, having Kansas City for its centre, are vast deposits of coal far exceeding in territorial expanse the great fields of Pennsylvania and Maryland.* No survey of the present, far less of the future prospects of agriculture in the United States, or consideration of the supplies she may have to spare for exportation would be otherwise than deficient and misleading, which failed to take into account the enormous population which will be called into existence by the combination, locally, of so sure a source of wealth and employment with food in abundance. Much, however, has yet to be overcome, nature even here is not invariably kind; to succeed, it will not do to rely solely on her bounty "to build," as the Americans themselves say, "large granaries and expect "the Almighty to fill them," nor to conclude that capital and toil can be dispensed with any more in the new than in the old world.

"Wonderful richness of soil, natural facilities for internal commerce afforded by rivers, and the ease with which railroads are constructed, these are the gifts of nature to the central valley, and such as will enable it, while surpassing the east in agriculture, to vie with it in commerce."*

A rough division of this great basin may be made into the pasturage and the agricultural districts, of which the former may be taken to be to the east and the latter to the west of longitude 98°. Indeed it may be said that as you leave the Mississippi and Missouri travelling westward, you enter further and further into a region of diminished rainfall, you leave trees and shrubs behind you till the foot of the Rocky Mountains are gained and the moisture they furnish is sufficient to nourish fresh vegetation.

The slight elevation above the sea and the general "plain like" character of the land are its noticeable features. The town of Cairo, 1,100 miles from the mouth of the Mississippi, is but 322 feet above the sea level. This is at the junction of the Ohio, but 975 miles higher up the latter river the elevation is very little more than doubled, being only 699 feet. We travelled up the Platte River hundreds of miles with no perceptible rise. St. Paul City is 828 feet only above the sea, but its river makes a course of 2,200 miles before reaching its mouth, while from St. Paul it is 670 miles westerly before the mouth of the Yellowstone River is reached, and then the traveller has but attained an altitude of 2,010 feet, with a rise from St. Paul of only 2 feet in the mile.

The two great ranges of hills, which form the framework of this territory are, the one, the Alleghanies, parallel with the shores of the Atlantic; the other, the Rocky Mountains following the line of the Pacific Coast. A space of 1,700 miles separates the feet of these chains at the points where they are crossed by the boundary line of the Dominion of Canada. As they trend towards the south they approach each other until the distance on the 33rd parallel is reduced to 750 miles. With the exception of an insignificant strip, through which for some 200 miles the Red River of the north flows towards lake Winnipeg, the space enclosed is drained by one mighty river. In extent it contains, exclusive of inland seas, some 800 millions of acres, and is more than 14 times the size of Great Britain. It forms the valley of the Mississippi and its tributaries. Of these, that river receives from the east the Ohio; from the north and west come the fertilising waters of the Missouri and its affluent the River Platte, while on the extreme south the River Arkansas, in its course nearly due east from the Rocky Mountains to join the Mississippi at Arkansas City, forms approximately the natural boundary in that direction of the great grain growing valley of the United States.

Grain and other crops.

Of the cereal productions the two most important in respect of human and animal food are WHEAT and MAIZE. The latter is produced in the greater abundance in the southern portion of the valley, the former in the north and north-west. There the spring variety of wheat is the principal crop for which in the States south of Minnesota and Winsconsin winter wheat is substituted where the ground is not occupied with maize.

One marked difference must in the first instance be noted with respect to the yield of these two plants. Abundance in the case of wheat is dependent on season, in that of maize on cultivation. Again, the period during which the latter may be sown and resown is a lengthy one, while the time during which it may be harvested without fear of material loss is measured by months extending into winter. The case is otherwise with wheat. However large the breadth to be sown, a few weeks in early spring or autumn should see the operation completed, and a few days only, if the best is to be done, can be allowed for harvesting. As this cereal is less dependent on cultivation than on climate

---

Note.—The dollar is worth 4s. 2d., and the cent one halfpenny. The American ton=2,000 lbs.
* Statistical Atlas of United States, p. 14.
Q 2685. Wt. 7668.

* Statistical Atlas of United States, p. 4.

and seasons, it is obviously the one selected for planting on new lands. It is *the* crop of the prairie and the newly broken lands of the Western States. Though a shy bearer, the grain commands a higher price than any other; relatively the cost of transportation in comparison with value is less, and in furnishing an annual source of speculation it fulfils with the American a function only second to that of providing human food.

While the English farmer conducts the sale of his farm produce by personal attendance at the local market, carrying with him a sample of the bulk, and is guided by the information he obtains on the spot as to the values of the day, in America the case is different. As soon as the grain is threshed, it is carted to the nearest railway depôt and deposited in the local elevator. An agent of the great grain merchants is to be found here who is always prepared to buy at "times prices;" these again are tested as far as the seller is concerned by reference to the newspaper, which, in America, owing to the universal use made of the telegraph wires, is in reality a manual of "news." Cash is paid for grain, which passes into the elevator to be graded, weighed, and cleaned, and placed through delivery notes, at the disposal of the buyer or future holders of the note.

When the facts are collected as to the cost of production and the freight of wheat, the price depends after all very much upon speculation. The facilities for speculating in wheat are more easy and tempting in America than with us, in consequence of the manner in which the wheat is there handled. Upon the wheat being delivered to any public granary store or elevator, and inspected by the officer appointed for "grading" grain, he places it in classes 1, 2, or 3, all weighing 60 lbs. per bushel. A certificate is then handed to the owner for a certain number of bushels of wheat of a certain grade, and that certificate carries with it the delivery for the wheat. The certificate may pass through several hands (each fresh buyer only depositing a small sum to guard the vendor from loss), and when the wheat is delivered, it is probable that not a single grain of the lot originally stored forms part of the delivery.

It is not only in America that articles are sometimes cheaper at the point of delivery furthest from the place of their manufacture. Occasionally a sack of Norfolk flour is cheaper at Newcastle than at Norwich, and bloaters are lower at London than at Yarmouth. But it was curious that when we quitted America, wheat was 1½d. per bushel cheaper at Liverpool than New York, and the wheat of the same quality was worth almost as much at Chicago, although 900 miles from the seaboard. It would therefore appear that the high prices which prevailed in America were due to the determination of capitalists to uphold values, rather than to the falling off of supplies or to increased demand. It is quite possible that the combination thus maintained for the purpose of enhancing prices may at another period be organised for depressing the value of grain or other produce. And, as spare capital accumulates in America, the disturbing influences of these speculative rings will probably become more general in the future than they have been in the past.

Though it may be generally said that if the cost of production exceeds the value of any article, the article will soon cease to be produced, it must be remembered that America has a yearly increasing surplus of bread-stuffs and meat, which she must sell at some price. In round numbers it may be said that nearly three-quarters of that surplus in average years finds its way to the United Kingdom. Except in seasons of general scarcity, the other countries of the world do not want, and certainly will not receive this surplus, except upon payment of heavy import duties. It may therefore follow that however low prices rule in England, the major part of the grain and meat exported from the United States will still find its way to these shores. And whenever there shall be an abundant harvest in the old world and in the new, prices may be depressed to a considerably lower level than those quoted in this report.

The cost of producing an acre of wheat, including rent and interest on capital in England is that which principally concerns the consumer. The distance intervening between him and the grower being inconsiderable, freight, insurances, and commission will not materially enhance the price, as is the case where the crop has to be transported over 3,000 or 4,000 miles.

The expenditure on the production of an acre of wheat in America can perhaps be more accurately estimated than for England, where the grain forms only one in a rotation of interdependent crops.

The prices paid for the acquisition or use of prairie land can be given, the cultivation required and money employed is also well ascertained, the agricultural operations, though the very reverse of barbarous, are simple in the extreme, and the cost of manual labour, horse, and steam power not difficult to determine. The whole may be set at a sum of 10 dollars, or two guineas per acre.* This will cover rates and cost of conveying the crop 6 miles to the local railroad, depôt, or elevator. But these factors do not determine the cost of producing a bushel of wheat, that it is obvious is governed by yield, while that again is dependent on seasons.

The yield of wheat in the United States over a long series of years appears to have just exceeded 12 bushels per acre. For the year 1879 the yield is returned at 13·1 bushels. With a yield of 12 bushels, the western farmer† could deliver from his waggon at the depôt without loss at 3s. 6d. a bushel of 60 lbs., or 28s. a quarter of 480 lbs., which is 20 lbs. short of the English weight of 5 cental.

The normal price of wheat in America on the east coast will range not with the cost of production on the farms immediately surrounding the great centres of population and industry, but with the value of land, labour, and money in the new land of the west, plus the varying cost of inland freight. As it is true that the centre of population and industrial employment in the United States is with certainty and rapidity moving westward, it is equally true that the cultivation of wheat is nomadic, and advances not in front of this movement but in the same direction, and is regarded by the farmers as more profitable, in other words, cheaper when conducted on virgin soil at a distance from the points of consumption than in the exhausted districts from which they migrate, and give place to a population for whom they have to find bread-stuff. Any estimate, therefore, of the prime cost of American wheat in England will depend materially on the cost of supply from the west.

Coming next to the consideration of freights, account has to be taken of the terms on which grain can be moved inland by "lake" and canal, or by "all rail," as well as on the ocean by sailing or by steamships. The difference between the cost of transportation from Chicago to New York by water, or by rail inland, is considerable, being on an average of five years, 1875 to 1879 inclusive, 3s. 5d. by water, lake, and canal, and 6s. 10d. by rail for the quarter of wheat weighing 480 lbs.‡ The water route is closed by ice from November to April. About 5s. 2d. is the average of the two rates.

In crossing the ocean the difference between the cost of transportation by "sails" or "steam" has been on the averages of the last five years so inconsiderable as to require no special attention. The former, however, appear by returns to have been the cheaper by about 5d. per quarter of 480 lbs.; 5s. in the one case against 4s. 7d. in the other, giving an average of 4s. 9½d.

These inland and ocean rates may be regarded as low. Those for the years preceding 1875 appear to have been higher.

In the Appendix§ will be found rates over different routes from Chicago to American ports, and from those ports to England; but though there are differences, they are not such as to interfere materially in forming a general estimate of the cost of laying down a quarter of American wheat at the British port.

In addition to the enumerated charges, those for handling and weighing have to be taken into account. These will amount in the case of grain in bulk on the other side of the water to 1s. 1d. a quarter of wheat. One gentleman stated that the quarter of wheat has been sent the 900 or 1,000 miles from Chicago to New York for 2s., while the usual winter price for that distance is 8s.

The through rates from Chicago to Liverpool are quoted by Mr. Randolph, the Secretary to the Board of Trade at Chicago, at 8s. the quarter of 480 lbs. in September 1879, while from the tables given in the Annual Report of the New York Produce Exchange for 1878, 10s. 6d. appears to have been the average for that year.

The average through rates for five years, from 1875 to 1879 inclusive, from Chicago to Liverpool are given by another informant at 10s., to which the sum of 3s. 1d. would have to be added for lake insurance, dock and town dues, and porterage at Liverpool, shortage, marine insurance, commission, and interest on money.

Liverpool charges alone, including shortage, come to 2s. 1d. per quarter.

But Chicago is not the wheat field or the spot of production. Allowance will have to be made for the carriage over some 250 to 450 miles from the farmer's station to that great emporium. The rates for these country dis-

---

* See Appendix, p. 8.
† Agricultural Report, p. 289.
‡ See App., p. 24, New York Produce Exchange Report, 1878, pp. 537-8.
§ See Appendix, p. 24, New York Produce Exchange Report, 1878, p. 330.

tances are much heavier than those we have been referring to. They are given at 6s. 8d. for 350 miles by Mr. Randolph; at 5s. for 250 miles by Mr. Dalrymple; at 6s. for 450 by Mr. Evans, of Council Bluffs; at 5s. for 450 by Mr. Underwood, of Kansas City, though in this gentleman's experience on one occasion they had been as low as 1s. 8d.

See App., pp. 4, 5, 10.

The sum of these particulars would be as follows:—

	£	s.	d.
Cost of growing a quarter of wheat (480 lbs.), in the West, including delivery to local depôt	-	1	8	0
Freight to Chicago	-	0	6	8
Thence to New York	-	0	5	2
New York to Liverpool	-	0	4	9½
*Handling in America	-	0	1	1
Liverpool charges	-	0	2	1
Total	-	2	7	9½

To bring the estimate up to English weight of five centals the quarter, one twenty-fourth or nearly 2s. would have to be added.

Besides the charges connected with the movement of grains there are commercial causes which will perpetuate great grain markets on Lake Michigan and the Mississippi. Each of the grain crops comes to maturity within a few weeks, but a year passes (not without cost) before the entire product of a season goes into consumption.†

The estimate may possibly ere long be affected by a reduction in the freights from the farms to Chicago to the extent of one-half, and special "through" contracts are said to defy any precise calculations. Allowing a deduction on this head of 3s. 9d., or about 6d. a bushel, the estimate would be brought down to 44s., or, without Liverpool charges, to 42s. the quarter.

The cultivation of wheat on unbroken prairie land is of the simplest description. If the settler's land should not be fenced he will have to trust to the law in force in certain districts for protection from the inroad of cattle, under which each owner is required to herd or tent his stock so that they should not wander among the crops of his neighbours. The improvements needed will be a house and premises adapted to the size of the occupation. The buildings will be of wood. The house, raised frequently on a basement of brick, is two-storied; the framework of pine lumber is covered with two outer skins of board and an intervening layer of paper, the inside being lath and plaster or boards, and the roof covered with wood shingles split or sawn of the size of ordinary slates. The barn (not used for the storage of grain crops, as in England,) but for winter housing of cattle, and horses, and fodder, like the house, stands frequently on a basement of stone or brick sunk partially below the surface, and divided into stalls for live stock. Above this comes the upper structure of wood, approached by an incline and entered through large doors capable of admitting a waggon load of loose fodder; on this floor frequently, in addition to the housed fodder, horned cattle and horses are also stalled. The other buildings will be yards with shedding for sheep and hogs. The whole value of these improvements, with fencing of three barbed wires on locust or tamarisk posts, 20 feet apart, costing 2 dollars 40 cents, or 9s. 9d. per 22 yards, will add 9 dols., or 37s. per acre to the cost of the land.‡

The land is broken in summer by a sulky plough constructed in part on the same principle as our old Dutch or fen plough, viz., with a wide share and rather stunt steel breast, turning a shallow furrow of the land, 14 inches in width, laid flat, and showing no crease. As in the fen plough, so here, a skeefe or revolving cutting disc takes the place of the coulter. The frame of the plough is of iron, carried on two high wheels with a pole bearing on the yoke of the oxen or collar of the horses; the driver is seated reins in hand within reach of a lever, by which the depth of the furrows may be adjusted without stopping the team. With this implement and a pair of horses at the first break, about 2½ acres are turned over in the course of the day. The men rise at 4.30, breakfast at 5.30; are on their ploughs at 6, bait their cattle in the field from 12 to 1.30, and work again till 6 or 7 o'clock. The wages paid are about 18 dollars or 75s. a month, with food, costing, 25 cents or 1s. 1d. a day from April 1 to close of the season in November. Mules, standing heat better than horses, are in many cases preferred, their pace is quite as good as that of the horse. The value of both these animals in America is dependent, on weight. Where we refer to height for description, the Americans refer to weight. A good weight for the best farm horse is 1,400 lbs.; at five years old he is then worth from 200 to 250 dollars, 40l. to 50l. A pair of mules, each weighing 1,200 lbs. to 1,300 lbs., being worth 250 to 300 dollars, 50l. to 60l., and a good ox team on the spot, 24l. to 25l. Should time allow, and the season be favourable, the land broken in the summer, after several weeks' scorching, is "back set" or ploughed back, and left in the rough condition during the bitter winter that follows. Occasionally, however, a crop of linseed or buckwheat is sown on the first ploughing, the prairie being broken early in the spring. We saw a crop of seven bushels of linseed an acre thus raised upon virgin soil, worth one dollar (4s. 2d.) a bushel, while the fee simple of the land was only from four to seven dollars an acre without improvements. In this instance on the 8th of October, the crop having been cleared off, one man unaided was working two sulky ploughs, one with three mules the other with two mules and a horse abreast, back-setting the flax stubble in furrows of a mile long, a marvellous contrast to our three-horse team at length, requiring two men with two lads to get the same number of ploughs over the ground. Occasionally, the prairie broken in the first week of June is sown with "navy" beans, which are pulled in the middle of September and command 5s. 2d. per bushel, the yield being from three to five bushels. The first furrow turned may cover up seed "corn" dropped in by the ploughman from his seat, which will produce from 15 to 20 bushels of shelled "corn."

App., p. 9.

App., p. 10.

These, however, are "catch" crops, and, perhaps, quite exceptional, which, to ensure success, should only be attempted by those who have the command of extra horse power and spare hands.

The hire of a horse for farm work struck us as reasonable, being only 50 cents or 2s. 1d. a day; and teams may be hired at from 2 to 2¼ dollars, 8s. 4d. to 9s. 6d., a day for the man, two horses, and implement. These "hack" teams will plough 2¼ acres a day, or harrow once over 14 acres a day. With three horses in the "sulky," three acres of ploughing may be completed, and 6s. an acre is the price at which contracts are made for ploughing cultivated land in the autumn. These prices are of course considerably below those ruling in England, and it seemed to be an evidence of the straitened condition of the smaller farmers to undertake this work on such apparently low, if not unremunerative, terms. In the spring the backset furrows are harrowed down, the seeder, drawn by two horses, attended by one man, distributes 1¾ bushels of seed per acre over 10 acres in the day, and one, or better still, two harrowings at 15 acres a day complete the operation. All is then left during the summer months for the undisturbed growth of grain and weeds together. During the past year the prairie rose, when the root has not been scorched or frozen to death, may here and there struggle above the surface, and some of the coarse grasses make greater pretension to recover their hold of the land. Blight, drought, and injurious insects may blast the hopes of the farmer, but, if he be spared these, in July or August another busy time comes round and the most modern example of labour-saving machinery is brought into requisition. The self-binding automatic harvester, drawn by four horses or mules, and under the charge of a single man, cuts, gathers, and binds with wire about 15 acres a day. An expert on horseback accompanies every two machines where many are at work together, and in case of any stoppage from breakage, or gearing out of order, at once gallops up and repairs the damage and sets the machine agoing. A great saving is effected by this machine over the ordinary reaper, in the clean and complete gathering of the crop, leaving hardly any scattered grain on the land; whereas, when the binding has to be done by hand, two bushels per acre at least is frequently left and lost. The sheaves are gathered into ricks of about 100 bushels placed at easy distances for stacking and in convenient groups for threshing.

App., p. 9.

App., p. 9.

App., p. 5

On some large farms moveable granaries are in use, measuring 16 × 16 and 10 feet high, into which the grain is deposited direct from the machine.

App., p. 9.

In other cases it is carried direct in bags to the elevator, where it is cleaned and graded No. 1, 2, or 3, according to quality, ready for the buyer.

Damage and destruction to wheat crops arise from drought and high wind at seed-time; drought or sunstroke in July, when the berry should fill; and noxious insects. Weeds, though mischievous, do not appear to give the trouble they cause in England, the climate being dryer and less favourable to the growth of the root-creeping grasses so difficult to destroy with us; still the "morning glory," or convolvulus major, the wild buckwheat, cockle and sunflower, or resin weed, impede and weaken the crop during its growth, while pigeon grass (setaria setosa) in many cases takes entire possession of the land after harvest, and in potato grounds before the crop is raised. Though the American farmer pays little attention to the presence of this weed among his grain,

App., p 9.

---

* Avoided on through rates.
† Transportation Committee Report, p. 27.
‡ App., p.

it is highly detrimental to the growth of potatoes and root crops, and most difficult to subdue. Dry as was the season of 1879, weeds and grasses on newly broken land in the west had so far obtained mastery as to form the bulk of many a sheaf, which the men rejecting at the threshing machine used for firing the engine. It is not at all an unusual practice to make steam with straw, inferior sheaves, flax straw, and coarse prairie hay, the furnace door being then fitted with a funnel mouthed tube, down which this vegetable fuel is thrust with a long fork.

App., p. 10. As to the growth of wheat in settled districts, though in many instances crop after crop has been taken for years without rest or restoration, the practice is admitted by the growers to be destructive to the land and impossible, except in the case of low rich river bottoms, to be maintained with impunity. The intermission of occasional crops of maize or of clover by way of change, restores the productive powers of the land sufficiently to improve the yield of wheat. If the land is cleaned and fairly cultivated between the rows of maize, wheat follows without ploughing the land. Occasionally the wheat is sown while the tall uncut maize is still standing, in which case the sower is on horseback, the horse's ears being covered with a cloth, and the seed wheat is distributed over the tops of the standing corn. After the maize is cut, an iron railway rail 28 feet long, with a small "shoe" at each end, is drawn by two horses across the rows to break down the stalks, which are afterwards collected and burnt. Sometimes, but this is in the middle and older settled States, the maize being reaped and shocked the land is ploughed between the rows and wheat sown before the maize crop is removed. Sometimes the wheat is sown on the unploughed maize stubbles. These operations are of course only carried out in the districts where "fall" or winter wheat is grown.

Manure seems never to be applied. It is an encumbrance; and buildings, when the land is not exhausted, which become surrounded with a deep accumulation of farm manure, are pulled down and removed to a clear spot. In the west straw, as a rule, is burnt where threshed in the fields, and there can be no better proof of the accumulation of fertile elements in the virgin soil than is afforded by the succeeding crop on the spots where these fires have taken place, covering from 10 to 20 poles of land. In England rank vegetation would spring up in these patches, due to the restoration to the soil of an unusual amount of fertilising inorganic matter; but the prairie is so surcharged with these elements that the addition makes no perceptible difference in the crop whatever.

The fall wheat is subject to attack from the Hessian fly, (Cecydomia destructor) shortly after it comes above ground, and several fields we saw seemed to be completely destroyed. This tiny fly* appears late in August and deposits its eggs, rarely more than three, in the creases of the leaf; in from four to ten days the maggot is hatched out, and works down the leaf within its sheath to the base, at that time only just above the root. There for three or four weeks the insect absorbs the juices of the plants, which grow feebler and feebler till they assume a yellow hue and die off, leaving too thin a stock to be worth saving for harvest. A second brood are ready to deposit eggs in April and early in May, which they do as before on spring wheat or barley if sufficiently advanced, or on the winter wheat above the first or second joints. The grub works down to the base of the sheath as before, and causes the stalk to fall by the weight of the head.

The best known and most dreaded insect is, however, the hopper, or locust, or Rocky Mountain Locust, Caloptenus spretus. The ravages made by these insects are truly terrible, and have been the subject of a valuable report of the United States Entomological Commissioners for the year 1877.† The injury committed by them in the States and territories west of the Mississippi during 1873, 1874, 1875, and 1876, were so great as to assume national importance, and resulted in a conference of the governors of these States held at Omaha in October 1876.

Out of this sprung, in pursuance of an Act of Congress, the United States Entomological Commission, with an appropriation of 18,000 dollars (3,600*l*.) for the expenses of three skilled entomologists.

The commission divide the districts they infest into three regions—the permanent or native breeding ground, where the species is always found; the sub-permanent, which they frequently invade and remain in for a period of years; and the temporary, which is only periodically invaded, and from which they generally disappear within a year.

The permanent region includes, Montana, Wyoming, and part of Colorado.

The sub-permanent—Dakota, parts of Nebraska and Colorado.

The temporary region lies east of the former, and the including line of the three regions takes in the east side of Lake Winnipeg, passes through St. Paul in Minnesota in a direction due south to the point where the Colorado River enters the Gulf of Mexico, then extending in a north-west direction it reaches Santa Fe in New Mexico, and turning westward it embraces Utah, Nevada, Idaho, and sweeping round the eastern slopes of the Rocky Mountains in Manitoba, it follows the southern limits of the forest land in latitude 53° till it reaches Lake Winnipeg; the greater part of Manitoba, in the Dominion of Canada, falling within the permanent and sub-permanent regions.

The list of locust years in Texas is rather formidable.* In 1858 they hatched by millions, and did great damage. So complete and general was the destruction that farmers had to plant again. In 1873 immense swarms suddenly appeared. For five days the multitudes kept travelling along the course of the Rio Grande. "The damage done was immense." In 1876 swarms reached Texas from the north and north-west about the middle of September, eating up succulent vegetables, the orange and cotton trees suffering particularly.† At Austin, the cars were so much obstructed on the Texas Central Railroad as to necessitate occasional halts in order to clear the track. The area of this invasion was 200 miles in width by 360 in length, or 72,000 square miles. In 1877 the approximate damage done to gardens in Texas was estimated at 790,000 dollars, or 158,000*l*.

In Missouri in 1875, by the end of the month of May, the non-timbered portions of the middle western counties were as bare as in winter; one might travel for days by buggy and find everything eaten off, and relief committees were formed.‡

In Kansas in 1866 they are described as almost darkening the sun in their flight, and in Brown County, for a width of 12 miles, trees were stripped of their leaves, and corn fields literally stripped to the stalk. They "cleaned out Topeka" of vegetables, grass, and clover, and left the ground as if burnt with fire. In 1874 these pests swept over the State, and the corn crop was ruined by them. The suffering was great. 1,842 families were reduced to destitution, and relief committees were resorted to for aid. In 1875 they ravaged the regions along the Kansas Pacific Railroad, leaving bare fields, desolated towns, and general ruin behind them.§

In Nebraska in 1874, the entire State from a point 30 miles west of the Missouri was more or less devastated, the western portion entirely so. Another invasion occurred in 1876, nearly as calamitous as that of 1874.‖

Iowa appears not to have suffered so severely, though even there they are reported to have eaten holes in waggon covers and tarpaulins, and to have turned their attention to the neck and throat of a soldier sleeping out on the prairie; and in 1875 they occasioned considerable loss in Council Bluffs and two other counties.¶

The splendid State of Minnesota has been scourged by them. We may pass by the Indian traditions of the locusts taking possession of this State for 17 years, and of the devastation caused in the valley of the Red River in 1857, when the infant Colony did not save their seed, and come down to 1874 and 1876, in which years great addition was made to the area of devastation.**

In 1877, the young hatched in over 42 counties, and never in any year in the State were so many bushels of grain destroyed, though it is stated in the same time never was so large a wheat crop raised.

In Dakota a great swarm made a descent on the prairies in 1870, and 1874 was a year of marked devastation. They came down thick like a snowstorm, and descending upon the last day of July, eat everything green through nearly all the southern counties of Dakota. In 1875 a swarm came from the Minnesota infested region along the line of the St. Paul and Sioux City Railroad in a continuous cloud, probably 1,000 miles long from east to west, and 500 miles from north to south. Partial destruction that year extended down the valley of the Big Sioux River; 1876 was a bad year for Dakota.††

In Montana, Idaho, and Wyoming, as might be expected from their proximity to the Rocky Mountains, their presence is almost uninterrupted, and the mischief resulting from it very serious.‡‡

In Wyoming in 1842 they swept every blade off; the buffalo disappeared, and the Indians moved off rapidly to

---

* The Hessian fly, a lecture by P. A. Cook, 1878, p. 8.
† Report p. 7.

* Report, p. 57.	¶ Report, pp. 78-9.
† „ p. 61.	** „ pp. 80-1.
‡ „ p. 68.	†† „ pp. 89-90.
§ „ p. 71.	‡‡ „ pp. 92-7.
‖ „ pp. 75-6.	

REPORTS OF ASSISTANT COMMISSIONERS.

avoid starvation, and thence down to the present time they have infested the territory in swarms.

In 1874 and 1875 great and destructive swarms infested Colorado and along the Main Arkansas; for four years previous to 1876 the ranch men were eaten out of house and home. This was repeated in 1876.*

In Utah, New Mexico, and Arizona, in Nevada, and in Oregon and Washington territory, the locusts are reported to have, at different times, been masters of the situation; though the locusts are said not now to thrive, in some parts of Nevada, notably in Lincoln County, since 1870, when a large swarm having deposited the eggs in a sandy "Mesa," the heat in the shade being 116° and in the ground 160°, the eggs melted like lead, and that class of hopper taking warning has not appeared since.†

A foot of snow does not appear to cause the young locust any inconvenience.

Before leaving this subject it should be added that British North America is not exempt in the west from these pests, and that there is abundant evidence of their mischievous presence, especially in the years 1872, 1874, 1875, 1876. Millions have been drowned in Lake Winnipeg, causing a horrible stench.

Many estimates of the price at which wheat can be grown in America are based on calculations made upon large tracts of land that are cultivated by the aid of the best machinery and the most perfect and economical management. However well these estimates may look on paper, experience has proved that these gigantic farms do not as a rule succeed. Other prices are based upon the figures furnished with great exactness by very small farmers. But in these estimates there is too often a very small value placed upon the labour of the farmer and his family.

Few English farmers have any idea of the hard and constant work which falls to the lot of even well to do farmers in America. Save in the harvest, certainly no agricultural labourer in England expends anything like the same time and strength in his day's work; therefore it is essential to guard against putting the value of the farmer's own labour at too low a figure, and to make due allowance for the drawback which must occur upon the most skilfully managed and best arranged big farms. The calculations are here made in the endeavour to strike an average of the cost of the production of wheat between the very large and the very small farms of America, and in estimating the cost of the latter to give a fair and reasonable value to the labour of the farmer and his family.

The readiness with which the tillers of the soil take to machinery in America would surprise some of the farmers in the old country. The skill and ease with which they are worked say something for the manufacturer, but still more for the intelligence of the farmer. In America the presence of labour-saving machinery upon even a small farm, is an absolute necessity. There is the further inducement to obtain implements of all kinds by buying them on long loans, and by paying for them by instalments, which sometimes tempts a farmer to buy more machinery than he can afford. The machines used upon the farms are well constructed and exceedingly light and handy. The land is level, the soil light, the climate dry, and the crops by no means bulky. Under these favourable conditions machines that would soon come to grief in England, work well for many seasons in America. But having got a good machine, and skilfully used it, it appears beyond the power of an American farmer to take the slightest care of it. Not only the common implements of the farm, but such costly and delicate machines as drills, mowers, self-binding reapers and thrashing machines, stand abroad all the year round. A few poles and a ton or two of that straw which is lying about in masses ready to be burnt, might protect all the spare machinery on a farm. But nothing of the sort is attempted, or at least it is so rarely done as only to prove the exception to a very general rule of wanton negligence. When, therefore, one hears of the perishable nature of the American implements, it would appear that the chief fault rests with the farmer rather than the maker. We should say that good machinery and improved implements are much more common on American than English farms. The tools are certainly lighter, better shaped, and better made. It may be true that a "good workman never finds fault with his tools," but it is truer still that a Yankee labourer is too sensible ever to work with a bad one.

Whenever the natural fertility of the virgin soil is exhausted, or indeed seriously impaired, and recuperative crops have to be introduced to repair the damage, then no doubt the expenses of growing wheat in these western prairies and the great river basins of America will be increased. That this exhaustion must come one day with continuous wheat growing followed by burning the straw is quite certain. But it cannot come immediately. The accumulated vegetable deposits of centuries and the untold number of grass crops that burn or rot upon the prairies, are not to be exhausted in a few years.

When wheat shows signs of flagging, the simple alternative of a crop of Indian corn seems sufficient to restore its fertility. And in northern latitudes where maize cannot be grown, one year's clover ploughed in suffices for another round of wheat crops. But the impoverished condition of some of the eastern states, and the necessity of manuring and rotating the crops in others, plainly indicate that the fertility of the virgin soil, however great, is not inexhaustible.

Next in importance to the wheat crop, if indeed it does not claim first rank, comes CORN, better known under the term "maize, or Indian corn."

Slowly, but surely, it is thrusting the cultivation of the noble grain northwards, and while wheat may be said to be now cultivated to the best advantage in the valleys of the Missouri, Mississippi, and Ohio with their affluents north of latitude 35°, corn will be found as a main crop from the Gulf of Mexico to the shores of the great lakes, and extending from Texas and Kansas in the west to New Jersey, Carolina, and Florida, in the east.* Good and wholesome alike for men and beast, whether as green cobs on the table or as sweet chopped fodder in the manger, or later on in the year as ground to flour for cakes and bread, or given in profusion, unshelled or shelled, to cattle and hogs, this prolific plant promises food in abundance for millions yet unborn.

Unlike wheat, the period for sowing maize, with a good prospect of a crop, is unusually long, and that during which it may be left standing, or in shocks before gathering, is still longer. While with wheat the yield depends so materially on the character of the season, in the case of corn reliance has to be placed not so much on weather as on cultivation; if that be thorough and continuous, success is sure to follow.

If the ground be prairie ground it will be broken in the summer, back-set in the autumn, and in the following spring be harrowed down and marked out for setting. The seed, about a gallon an acre, is deposited by seed dropping dibs in rows, so that the plants stand 4 feet apart every way.

The cost of growing an acre in Iowa is given at about 5 dollars 50 cents, and the cost per bushel, taking the yield at 40 bushels, at 13·825 cents. Another estimate gives the cost at 5 dollars 20 cents; this is in Missouri, also on prairie land. [App. p. 34.] [App. p. 34.]

One man with a pair of horses will sow and cultivate 40 acres of maize on prairie land, or 20 acres on woodland, in Missouri. Near Indianapolis, in Indiana, a man will cultivate 30 acres of corn. The average yield there is laid at 30 bushels, and the average price at 40 cents per bushel. Sixty bushels is now considered a very good crop, 80 bushels used to be thought so, but continuous cropping has diminished production. Within the last 10 years corn has sold at 20 cents and at 50 cents per bushel in Columbia, Missouri. Corn is "cultivated" five times till the tassel is out. It is then left standing till autumn, and the cobs are gathered by hand into waggons, or the crop is cut and shocked and the cobs afterwards plucked. When carted it is thrown into cribs, covered chambers of wood with slatted sides through which the air freely passes. The corn that has to be shelled for grinding or marketing is passed through a small machine worked by hand or other power, which strips the grain from the core. Corn saved for seed is selected and hung up to dry on rails or beams in barns and covered buildings; as the germinating power is damaged by the ordinary method of saving the corn. While the marketable weight required for wheat is 60 lbs., that for corn is 70 lbs. for unshelled and 56 lbs. for shelled corn. [App. p. 15.] [App. p. 17.] [App. p. 17.] [App. p. 15.] [App. p. 17.]

Maize as a rotation crop answers the same end as root crops in England. The land is rested, cleaned, and enriched by its introduction. There is no crop in which so little hazard is incurred as in this. With wheat the uncertainty is great; out of 18 crops in Ohio six only were full crops, some were utterly destroyed by drought; but during the same period corn never failed, and the average yield was 35 bushels. The variations of price have been as marked as with other commodities, ranging within the last 10 years from 15 cents and 20 cents a bushel up to 50 cents, the average for the United States being 42 cents from 1871 to 1878. The yield, of course, varies with the [App. p. 14.] [App. p. 10.] [Agricultural Report, 1878, p. 290.]

---

* Report, pp. 100-1-2 et seq.
† „ p. 109.
„ p. 113.

* Census Map xxxvi and xxxvia.

quality of the land from 20 bushels up to 60 bushels an acre, the average from 1863 to 1878 being 26¾ bushels. In the river bottoms 60 bushels is exceeded. While the profit which the farmer derives in England by the growth of roots is an indirect one, and is estimated by taking into consideration the value of the manure which is left from their consumption by sheep or cattle, in America the profit is a direct one. Corn bought at 25 cents a bushel brings back 30 cents when given to hogs, if the latter sell even at as low a price as 3 cents a lb. live weight.

The annual growth of corn has of late years enormously increased; in 1868 there were nearly 35,000,000 acres planted, and in 1878, 51,500,000, but the money value per acre has been steadily declining. This increased abundance and cheapness has made it the object of a considerable and growing export trade, so much so that probably over 6 per cent. of the crop finds its way abroad.

The centre line of cultivation of this cereal is not moving westward as rapidly as that of wheat. While the movement of the latter was, in 28 years, eight degrees westward, that of the former has been only four; possibly it will be still slower in the future, as the heaviest portion of the Illinois crop is still west of the centre line (longitude 89°), while Illinois produces one-fifth of the whole crop.

It is fair to assume that over a large portion of the middle and eastern States a preference for the cultivation of corn over that of wheat has been established. While large quantities are consumed in these States in the production of beef and pork, this grain is universally in requisition for human food, coming to table at all meals and in all forms, and a very considerable quantity is manufactured for export in the form of spirits.

We saw and heard but little of the cultivation of BARLEY; the few samples which we had an opportunity of examining on the farms of the United States were almost universally of a poor character, the grain being lean, irregular, and parched. The exception to this was met with on the irrigated land at the foot of the Rocky Mountains, where the sample was plump, apparently mellow, and of a good colour. The growth of this grain does not appear to be increasing; the acres grown in 1874 being 1,580,626 against only 1,790,400 in 1878. Of this quantity, over one-third is cultivated in California. The soil and climate of this State, though we did not visit it, appear to be suitable to the production of barley, and it is well known that the exports have commanded this season (1879–80) very high prices, (56s. to 60s. a quarter,) in England. The Californian established weight is 50 lbs. per bushel against 48 lbs. in New York and most other States.

It is, however, remarkable that the Canadian barley finds its way into the United States in the face of a duty of 15 cents or 7½d. per bushel, and goes into consumption there in considerable quantities in the form of malt. The natural weight of the Canadian barley is lower than that of the Californian by several pounds per bushel.

The growth of OATS appears to be steadily increasing; in 1874 the average was nearly eleven millions, in 1878 it exceeded thirteen millions. The established weight is 32 lbs. per bushel throughout most of the States. These established weights—13 stone 10 lbs. for barley, and 9 stone 2 lbs. for oats per sack,—are an evidence of the inferior quality of the grain.

The acreage devoted to the growth of POTATOES does not materially increase; it was a million and one third in 1874, and in 1878 it had only reached a million and three-quarters. The State of New York furnishes one-fifth of the total area. The quality, except in the South-western States, was universally good. The average yield is not very large, being estimated at about 88 bushels per acre, 60 lbs. to the bushel. The lifting of the roots had for the most part been completed on the farms we visited in the United States, and the land was occupied by an abundant growth of pigeon grass and other rank weeds, but in Manitoba, on the farms near the Assiniboine, we saw splendid specimens in the ground, the yield on one farm being stated by the owner to have never fallen below 300 bushels, and to have reached 400 bushels in 1879. These crops had not even been moulded up.

The production of FRUIT is a marked feature of American farming in all the settled districts, and almost every known variety of fruit is produced for the market. More than five million peach trees blossom every spring on the lands between the Delaware and Chesapeake Bays and the inter-ocean region of the north-west. In the middle States and New England hundreds of families get an income from the gathering and sale of the wild strawberry, raspberry, blueberry, huckleberry, blackberry, and cranberry. These small fruits are mostly consumed at home. In the Genessee Valley peaches were carted about in waggon loads, and orchards of pear and peach intermixed were universal. So eagerly are they cultivated here that the graveyards are covered with these plantations, and on one farm in Manitoba we found melons of three sorts, cucumbers, "citrons" for preserving, filberts, French beans, raspberries, strawberries, and grapes for preserving, with sunflowers over 11 feet high, and the seed disc 13 inches across, the seeds being used for food for poultry. The apple crop is the most important, more than two millions of acres are devoted to it, and within the last eight years the increase of production has been in a greater ratio than ever. Next in importance is the peach crop, plentiful enough to bring this fruit within reach of all classes. In New Jersey, Delaware, and Maryland are many orchards counting 10,000, 20,000, and 30,000 trees.

An important business had its beginning some 20 years ago in Baltimore in preserving fruits for market. Though there are now other establishments in Michigan, Delaware, and Illinois, the old town still maintains its supremacy, the factories there, when the fruit seasons is over, employing their plant in canning oysters. The preservation is effected by packing the prepared fruit in hermetically-sealed cans. Vegetables are treated in the same manner, and the shipments of both are rapidly on the increase. In addition to this method, the primitive one of drying in the sun is extensively practised in the middle and southern States, where at many homesteads you may see rows of boards tilted up to the sun and covered with slices of fruit. In New England the apples are pared, quartered, and strung for hanging out in the sun or in some airy covered building. Blueberries and blackberries are spread out on paper, and they are also canned in large quantities, the pickers camping out with their families on the berry plains, and being paid 3 cents to 4 cents a quart for gathering. Gradually these simple processes have been improved on, first by drying under glass, next by the use of stove heat, until finally at Baltimore and other cities, depôts were established for the reception of large quantities of fruit, furnished with machinery and appliances, and with capacity for an immense amount of work. The fruit under the modern method enters first into a moderately warm and moist atmosphere, and thus its moisture is extracted slowly and the vegetable juices not disturbed; passing on to drier and hotter chambers the evaporation is more rapid, and the fruit undergoes at the same time a chemical change by the conversion of the acids and starch into grape sugar, of which proof is given by the fact that half the quantity of sugar is needed for a pie made of this fruit to that used with fresh apples.

HOPS are grown principally in New York, Vermont, Maine, and the adjoining North-eastern States; but those of Wisconsin, California, and Oregon have greatly increased of late years. Canada seems also likely to largely contribute to the growth of hops. It would appear that the area under cultivation in America has been considerably reduced this year by reason of the low prices which prevailed in 1878 and the first half of 1879. The prices then were as low as 10 cents per lb., now they range from 30 to 40 cents. The receipts of home-grown hops in New York last autumn enormously exceeded those of the like period in 1878, and the exports from September to December were 38,000 bales (of 200 lbs.), against 7,000 bales in those months of 1878. Yet, notwithstanding this great increase of exports, Bavarian hops were freely imported into New York in the autumn of 1879.

All the hops were harvested before we arrived in America; we had, therefore, no opportunity of seeing how they were cultivated, nor indeed had we the advantage of hearing from many practical farmers their estimate of the cost at which hops can be produced in America. We were, however, informed, upon what appeared reliable evidence, that when the wholesale price falls below 12 cents per lb., however good the crop may be, the production at such a price must entail considerable loss upon the grower.

Cattle and Meat.

Anyone who has seen the splendid American oxen which are imported into this country, and the massive quarters of prime beef which find their way across the Atlantic, might be somewhat surprised and disappointed at the comparatively few really well bred cattle that are to be found in the United States. There are no doubt in Kentucky and the surrounding States thousands of beautiful robust pure bred shorthorns. But in the eastern States the cattle are mostly ordinary dairy stock, descended from the common breeds of the early settlers, with only here and there a herd of really good cattle. In the south and west the Texan and other similar breeds predominate, the originals being no doubt imported from Spain. It is only the primest bullocks that are exported dead or alive to Great Britain. The market here will not answer for any

REPORTS OF ASSISTANT COMMISSIONERS.

but the best beef, as the expenses of transit are almost as heavy upon an inferior as upon a really good beast.

As regards these and pure bred shorthorns there will be found in the appendix a paper delivered to us by Mr. John Clay, Jun., our fellow commissioner, "on the shorthorn interest and its influence on the American beef trade."

It can be hardly necessary to describe the different ways of breeding, rearing, and grazing cattle in the older States. The modes may vary with the different localities and climates; but they all exist under more or less similar conditions in the old country. In the north and east the cattle have all to be housed for many months in the winter. This necessarily much enhances the cost of keeping stock, and the farmers of those localities feel keenly the competition of the south-west and middle States. Where cattle have to be under cover in the winter it is usual for them to be stabled on the basement floor, or perhaps these stalls may be partially underground and another lot of stock kept over them. The upper portion of the building is invariably devoted to the storage of hay. The hay barn is the great feature of the American homestead, and as thatching any kind of ricks is seldom attempted, it is necessary to have a lofty and spacious building in which to safely secure the stock of winter provender. A small beam, high up in the roof, extends the whole length of the barn, upon which runs a pulley, with an unloading fork attached, and by this means the hay is easily removed from the waggons and traverses to the furthest part of the barn. The hay which is made from artificial grasses is mostly composed of Timothy grass, and looks coarse and stalky, but is eaten with great relish by horses, and is considered more valuable than clover hay. A great extent of hay is saved from the prairies and rough meadows. This is probably cut and secured in small stacks or large cocks during the summer and early autumn, and carted to the homestead in the winter months. The hay is not allowed to heat in the rick or in the barns as in England. All grasses, any British farmer would say, are allowed to become over-ripe before they are cut, thus depriving the hay of much of its value. But the climate appears much more certain for securing the crop in good order than we generally have it in England, and therefore mouldy hay, save that spoiled for the want of thatch, is seldom met with. Few roots are grown even in the eastern States; the great bulk of winter food is hay. Indian corn is given to all feeding and occasionally milking animals. Sometimes it is used in a green but more generally in a ripened state, and in a few instances, meal from other grain is also used for winter grazing. Bran, which is worth on the spot about 40s. a ton, is a favourite feeding stuff, but we came across only one instance in which either linseed or cotton cakes were given to cattle. In Canada a large number of worked oxen are fed for the English market, and though somewhat coarse and ugly, turn out capital beef. In the distilleries throughout America the refuse slop is largely employed in the manufacture of beef, and in some towns dairy cows are also fed upon it.

In many of the middle States, even where the winters are really severe, thousands of cattle are never under cover. When grazed in the winter they are fed in rough inclosures or corrals, without any shed, shelter, or bedding. Sometimes a bit of woodland is railed off and the cattle allowed to roam over the sheltered portion of it. They always have access to water, but have seldom much hay. Their food is mainly Indian corn. Sometimes this corn is given in the stalk, the leaves and tender portion of the stem affording excellent fodder. More often, however, for grazing cattle the maize is given in the cob, or ear, and as they become fat the corn may be shelled, and sometimes it is given at the last in the shape of meal. Wherever cattle are grazed upon unground corn, a considerable amount passes through the animal whole, and much that falls from the cribs would be wasted if a goodly number of pigs were not grazed with the bullocks. Two pigs to one bullock is the general proportion kept for winter grazing, and the pig not only serves the part of a scavenger, but also contributes very materially to the profits of the farmer.

Of the enormous crops of maize raised in the middle States of America the quantity exported has never exceeded 7 per cent. The rest must be consumed within the Union; a large portion of it close to the spot where it grew.

By converting his maize into beef and pork, the American farmer expects to receive double the value he could command for this corn. The manure from the stock so fed is esteemed of no value, and is generally regarded as a nuisance. This way of regarding it is altogether different from that of the English farmer, who, when he uses grain or other artificial food for his grazing animals, has invariably to look for a large portion of his return in the improved value of the manure thus produced.

Q 2685.

No great amount of cattle are raised in the maize zone of the States. They come mostly from the west, and are grazed by the farmers who grow the maize. A class of monied men give the grower so much per bushel for his Indian corn, and furnish him with stock to eat it, or they provide the cattle and pay 6 cents per lb. for the increased live weight of the cattle. Others buy the maize from their poorer neighbours, delivered at their own homesteads, and they feed large numbers of cattle and pigs. A well bred three year old steer is supposed to weigh about 1,100 lbs., and in six months will eat a ton of hay and about 90 bushels of maize, or half a bushel (28 lbs.) per day, and is expected to gain from 250 to 350 lbs. live weight. The greatest rate of increase would, at six cents per lb., give the grazier 20 dollars for his 90 bushels of maize, and the profit in the pigs would certainly pay well for the hay, the attendance, the interest on the money, and the risk of losses, the latter apparently being very small.

In addition to these winter-grazed cattle there are many others which are fattened upon the rich grass lands of Kentucky, Illinois, Ohio, Missouri, and neighbouring States, but almost all the best are supplied with Indian corn, especially in the autumn, when the grass has begun to fail or lose its quality.

It is chiefly from the corn States that the primest oxen find their way to England. These cattle are highly graded and some pure bred short-horns, but the great mass of the bullocks from the west, however well they are grazed, are not good enough to export alive, but are killed at Chicago, St. Louis, or Kansas City. The number of oxen and other cattle on January 1st, 1879, is estimated by the Agricultural Department at 21½ millions, of sheep at 38 millions, of swine at 34½ millions. The figures differ, however, widely from those of the tables of the 9th census (1870), where the cattle are returned at 28 millions, sheep at 28½ millions, and swine at 25 millions.

Agricultural Report, 1878, p. 274.

The enormous increase of cattle of late years has been upon the plains of Texas and the far west. Texas has been known as a great cattle State for years, but outside this, what was described in our old school maps as "The Great American Desert," is now stocked with tens of thousands of cattle. A vast number of the best bred young steers are driven northward every year, probably to be kept as grazing stores on the ranches of Colorado and Wyoming, and to be eventually grazed on some of the middle States. Large droves of heifers are also sent away to found herds upon the eastern slopes of the Rocky Mountains. Texas seems essentially a breeding district, and cattle that will not come to any great size if kept in that State invariably grow considerably when taken to other localities. The great heat, the occasional droughts and scarcity of water, entailing perhaps a daily ramble of some 30 to 40 miles, may be the reasons why highly graded cattle do not flourish so well in Texas.

These vast plains appear to the stranger in the autumn fearfully scorched and sterile. There is not a sprig of anything green to be seen for miles. The short stunted herbage is quite brown, and looks burnt to a cinder. But this apparently worthless grass is in reality *self-made hay*. It grows rapidly in the spring, and is *cured* by the sun before it ripens. Should a drought be followed by heavy rains in July, and the grass shoot up again, this latter growth is generally killed by the frost before it is dried by the sun, and is comparatively worthless. There are severe snow storms, called "*blizzards*," sometimes quite early in the autumn, which last for a day or two, and then lovely open weather may prevail until Christmas. Great falls of snow are rare. When they happen cattle suffer severely, but more generally the snow quickly drifts into the hollows and the stock can get at the grass without much trouble.

Cattle of both sexes and all ages herd together. The cows drop their calves at any period of the year, and about 25 cows are allotted to each bull. The dexterity with which the cow boys single out a wild calf and lasso it riding at full speed on their slim ponies is really wonderful. Each stockowner has his own brand, which is registered at the State office, and any infringement upon it is severely punished. The first lot of meaty cattle, are generally sent away early in the summer, the last drafts ending early in November. Some of these droves have to walk from 200 to 500 miles to a railway station, and are then *shipped* east, being mostly consigned to salesmen at the first great cattle market, and sold by commission.

It is very interesting to mark how the cattle in these great ranges are *bunched* up for the night. Towards sun down the distant stock which have been grazing over the plain are gradually driven by the cow boys into the centre, and when they are congregated into a sufficiently small space, the boys on their ponies continue to ride quickly round and round the cattle, halloing and cracking their long whips. The boldest calf does not venture to escape from this magic circle, but first one and then another of the older cattle lie down, and in a comparatively short time the whole herd is on the ground. The boys then camp close by and roll themselves up in their blankets for the night, and no movement takes place in the herd until the morning.

There are some States, like Utah, where the cattle receive a little hay in the winter, but in the great plains of Wyoming, Colorado, Nebraska, Kansas, &c., the cattle range over the whole country without even a single herdsman to look after them from November to April. In the spring the stockowners of the district have a great "*round up.*" The whole country is scoured, and now and then some stray oxen are found more than 100 miles from the rest of the herd. All being branded, except the calves which have been born during the winter months, the stray cattle are claimed by the representatives of the different owners, and are driven to their proper ranges for the summer months. They graze over an enormous territory, the distance being only limited by the absence of water. Cattle must be watered night and morning, and however far they may wander for their food, they must return twice in the 24 hours to the river banks.

The stockmen of the plains have mostly secured the lands bordering upon all the rivers and streams of the district. Each stockman probably owns no more than 160 acres of land, or perhaps he has acquired his right to another quarter section by pre-emption. Without means of watering stock the rest of the land is of little or no value. In some districts wells have been sunk and pumps, driven by wind, furnish a supply of water. But very many thousand acres of land are now grazed by the owners of the river side plots without paying any rent or acknowledgement whatever. The land still belongs to the Federal Government, save in Texas, where the State owns all the unsold land. These vast ranges are offered at a price which no one seems inclined to give. It is contended that the land without the water is not worth more than 12 cents per acre, whereas the price asked by the Federal Government is $1\frac{1}{4}$ dollars. There is plenty of room not only for all the cattle and sheep that have now a free range over these plains, but also for any number of new settlers who like to stock them, provided they can secure a supply of water. When the country is fully settled up then some question of ownership may arise. But that event will not happen just yet, and at present the stockman is entirely master of the position, and with actually no expense save that of herding his cattle during eight months of the year, and paying a trifle towards the local taxation of the district, there is no wonder that he makes an enormous return upon the capital he invests. It is generally acknowledged that the average profit of the stockowner has been for years fully 33 per cent. No doubt this is by far the most remunerative branch of American farming, but to secure the greatest return a large amount of money must be employed. For instance, it is computed that the owner of 10,000 cattle with 150 horses ought to have 7,000 or 8,000 dollars more in cash to work the range profitably. Small herds do not answer like large ones. It is almost as cheap and easy to manage 5,000 cattle as it is to attend to 1,000. A herd of 5,000 must have 100 horses for the cow boys or cattle men, while 10,000 would only require 150. The horses are worth from 25 to 40 dollars, and are chiefly bred in Texas. The expenses of keeping a fair sized herd of cattle for 12 months do not exceed $1\frac{1}{2}$ dollars per head, and in some instances they are as low as one dollar. Within 100 square miles of Cheyenne in Wyoming territory, are herds ranging from 1,000 to 35,000 head of cattle. Their average value is now stated to be 20 dollars per head. In this territory the losses among cattle from all causes are only put down at $2\frac{1}{2}$ per cent. per annum. In Texas and other districts the losses are estimated from 5 to 10 per cent. A herd of 10,000 cattle should annually produce from 1,500 to 2,000 head of fat stock, of these 20 per cent. will be cows, the rest $3\frac{1}{2}$ and 4 year old steers, with a value of 25 to 30 dollars. The cost of raising such a bullock including losses and all expenses could not be more than 10 dollars. The cost of "*shipping*" cattle by rail from Cheyenne to Chicago is $7\frac{1}{2}$ dollars, including freight, feeding, attendance, and commission. Arrived at Chicago they are generally sold in the market at so much per 100 lb. live weight. A few may be disposed of as stores, but most of them are killed in the great slaughter-houses of that city. Some are sent another 900 miles to New York and are there killed, but a few of the very primest do not end their long and toilsome journey until they are landed in Great Britain.

Pretty much the same mode of management is pursued in Texas and New Mexico. The cattle, however, are inferior. They are evidently descended from the old Spanish stock, and until lately have not been much improved. But now most of the herds in Texas are being crossed with short-horn and Hereford bulls, which are imported from the middle States in great numbers. One large firm of Kentucky breeders sends yearly as many as 400 short-horn bull-calves into these plains. The improvement that will take place in these cattle in a few years must be considerable. The only doubt is whether highly bred stock can endure the hardships and privations to which the old breeds have for ages been subjected, and to which they seem to have become accustomed. A more careful and expensive mode of handling these cattle will of course considerably enhance the cost of production and tend to lower the profit now made upon the money invested in rearing these animals.

It is wonderful how many hundred miles these semi-wild cattle of America travel. The young stock from Texas frequently journey to Colorado, or those from Washington, Montana, and Utah to Wyoming and Nebraska. They go by easy stages from one stream to another, and sometimes increase in weight during their long journey. Great losses now and then occur from a scarcity of water, and occasionally whole herds die from eating poisonous weeds in the spring.

The Texan fever among cattle appears a very mysterious disease. Certain it is that adult cattle imported into Texas invariably take it and die. Calves under six months' old on the other hand as a rule escape the disorder and become acclimatized. It is stated on the highest veterinary authority that the disease actually exists in a latent form among apparently the healthiest cattle of the State, and that post-mortem examinations have proved this. Be that as it may, it is only rarely that the cattle of Texas develop this fever, either in that State or in their migrations from it. But at certain times of the year, when droves of Texans are going northward, other cattle that cross their trail are smitten with it and die by thousands. It seems questionable whether the disease thus developed in the stock of other States is of a *contagious* nature. Those cattle which have escaped the infection when crossing the path of the Texan cattle do not seem to contract the fever from their dying fellows. As may be imagined such a fatal disease has strict regulations made against it by the neighbouring States, and Texan cattle are prohibited from being driven through their territories during the hot seasons of the year. But there is much difficulty in enforcing such salutary regulations in those wild districts, and great losses are experienced by their fraudulent evasion. There does not seem much probability of the dreadful disease being imported into this country, nor is it probable that it will at any time spread extensively into the middle States of America.

There can be no doubt, notwithstanding the excellent and improved provisions for the transit of live stock both by land and by sea, that a considerable amount of suffering to the cattle and loss to the consumer still result from the transit of live animals. The United States Government have doubtless reduced that suffering to a minimum by the sensible and humane arrangements which are made for feeding, watering, and resting cattle on their long railway journeys. But under the most favourable conditions the passage across the Atlantic must be more or less painful and injurious to stock. In calm weather it is stated that after a day's sail cattle become accustomed to their sea voyage, and actually improve in condition. Granted that cattle frequently cross the Atlantic without any serious loss of meat, there are too many instances of the injury many cattle receive on the passage, to say nothing of the actual loss of portions of the live cargo.

The admirable manner in which the transit of fresh meat is managed in America and on board the steamships now ensures with almost perfect certainty its arrival in prime condition on these shores. All this seems to point to a greater development of the dead meat trade, and until some more stringent methods are enforced for the eradication of pleuro-pneumonia in the United States, the unrestricted imports of live cattle into the interior of these islands cannot for the present be resumed with any safety. The American Government seem now quite alive to the necessity of stamping out pleuro-pneumonia and other contagious diseases. The fact that these disorders only exist in the Eastern States, and principally among the dairy stock of the great cities, proves pretty clearly that they are imported and are not of American origin. Nowhere in the middle or Western States do we find any traces of pleuro-pneumonia, foot and mouth, and such like contagious diseases.

Whenever America can show a clean bill of cattle health, and live imports are again introduced, a considerable trade in store stock will probably be developed. The cost of transit of great numbers of store cattle need not be so heavy as it is now. More of such stock could go in the railroad trucks and in the ship's holds than is now allotted to fat animals. And the animals themselves would not be so cumbrous and helpless, and would be more likely to withstand the evil effects of the long sea passage than the great unwieldy fat bullocks which suffer so much on the sea. The greatly improved graded cattle of the west, and the purer short-horns of the middle States, would make most valuable store stock for winter or summer grazing, and if the cost of transit could be reduced to the same per-centage on their value which is now charged for fat animals, the trade in store stock might prove profitable to the American breeder and beneficial to the English grazier. In the meantime it may be worth while to consider if some reasonable quarantine should not be allowed for the purpose of bringing over some of the high class short-horns which are now to be bought so reasonably in America. The best and purest blood of the most celebrated English herds have been long used in the central States. The constitution, flesh, and hardiness of these Anglo-American short-horns is so wonderfully developed and strengthened by the unpampered and natural conditions under which they are reared, that a few cargoes of their best pedigree stock would certainly greatly improve the common run of short-horns in these islands.

The common practice is to sell all live stock by live weight. Not only are public weighbridges common everywhere, but almost every large farm, and, indeed, many a small one, has its weighbridge. This is useful, not only for selling stock but for ascertaining the weight of all farm produce with much greater exactness than is common in England. The scale would assuredly not only dispel all doubt about the progress made by grazing animals, and test the accuracy of estimates made of the weight of cattle, but would also help to correct those wild guesses that are often made of the weight of roots and such like produce upon farms. The American weighbridge seems a cheaper and simpler machine than those in general use in this country, but if the same demand existed for them here as in America, no doubt their manufacture would speedily improve. Greatly as the custom of selling all fat stock by live weight is to be commended, it still leaves the quality of the meat and the condition of the animal to be taken into consideration in estimating its value. But in buying lean animals the criterion of weight must exercise much less influence in deciding the price, and when the plan of selling by weight is extended to horses and mules, it strikes an Englishman that a really good custom is being carried rather too far. An owner who is selling a horse, before dilating upon his pace and beauty, generally informs you of his exact weight; and many hundreds of mules are purchased without being seen by the buyer, upon being assured that they are of a certain height with an average weight of so many lbs. One would imagine that the age, shape, temper, and pace of a mule were of more consequence than his weight, which must depend very much upon the condition he is in.

Butchers in England when asked why they charge such high prices for prime joints, often state as a reason the great and increasing difficulty they experience in selling the ordinary portions of the bullock. If great differences prevail in England between the price of the best and coarsest joints, a still greater difference exists in the United States. During the recently depressed times the labouring classes in America did eat the coarse joints of beef, but with the returning activity of national prosperity there again appears a greater run than ever upon the primest meat. In New York the very best joints of a carcase of beef command 18 cents to 22 cents per lb., but the forequarters are hardly saleable at 4 cents to 6 cents. Quantities of excellent common meat are therefore always a drug and sometimes are well-nigh wasted. A further loss is also made in cooking, and in the manner in which meat is served. It is said that there is more food wasted in England in a month than would feed the French nation for a day. But such a remark would apply with tenfold force to the United States. It is, of all countries, the country of domestic waste, and with such a rude abundance of all the necessaries of life, it is neither felt nor indeed hardly noticed. Were it not for this extravagance a much larger surplus of American meat would find its way to the old world.

The method of handling cattle in the market and abattoirs differs in more points than one from that pursued in England. Of course, to begin with, the supply is on a larger scale, and the American makes commensurate preparations in the large stockyards of Chicago, Kansas City, and St. Louis. The freight cars running into the heart of these establishments discharge their loads at once into yards and sheds, where the animals are fed on prairie hay and watered; the proceedings are conducted with rapidity, though without hurry or noise. The men avoid coming into personal contact, except on horseback, with the Texan and similar western cattle, which, with their long pointed horns and wild nature, are awkward customers. Gangways of planks for stockmen and salesmen pass over the heads of these animals in the yards, and wide alleys intersect them, down which the beasts are moved from yard to yard, and ultimately to the slaughterhouse. No dogs are about, no pointed sticks or goads, the officers of the Society for the Prevention of Cruelty to Animals are never absent, and their notices meet the eye in every direction. We never saw an animal ill used, though it is alleged that much cruelty and torture is practised at country depôts and during the railway journeys. Business is expedited by the universal resort to the scales for value. The quality is estimated by the eye and acquaintance with the character of the breed rather than by the touch. Commission agents and salesmen are employed as negotiators between the stockowner and the purchaser, whether for killing or feeding, and the packers and canning companies employ agents who buy, kill, and deliver the beef they require. In Chicago stockyards one man buys one-third of the whole supply of beef cattle, and in 1878 killed in the abattoirs 335,000 oxen. He prefers for his purpose Colorado cattle, and termed shorthorn and "grades" "fool's meat." As soon as a yard of western cattle have been bought at so many cents a pound live weight, they are driven to the scales, a long enclosed platform holding some 40 beasts; there they are weighed off in a very few minutes, and a ticket is furnished by the officer of the market of the total weight. They are then driven by men on horseback along the alleys or roads, swing gates closing behind them and opening on either side to make a passage in the direction of the yard to the slaughterhouse. On arriving here they are enclosed to await their turn. When that comes a gate at the further end is opened and a mounted drover hurries out some 20 or 25 up an inclined plane into a narrow passage, upon which the doors of the killing pens open. As soon as the passage is filled, the slaughterman and his companion, who move about overhead on a narrow gangway, open one of these doors, and by aid of poles, if needed, direct one, sometimes two beasts into a pen; the door is immediately closed and another opened; this goes on till in a few minutes the passage is emptied and the pens have each then one or two occupants. The slaughterman then, taking a long dagger-pointed iron rod, commencing with the first pen, thrusts or "jobs" the point into the spine immediately behind the horns; the animal thus "pithed" sinks at once paralysed, and is said to be insensible to further pain. With incredible rapidity this angel of death hurries overhead from pen to pen and completes his task without blunder or noise in the space of two or three minutes. Before he has reached the further pen a sliding door opening into the abattoir has been raised, a chain has been attached to the horns of the first ox, this running round a pulley on the floor and worked by steam or horse-power has drawn the animal out on to the platform, a few blows on the head have been given from a heavy hammer, the veins of the throat have been opened, and the process of flaying has commenced. The passage is again filled, the sliding door is dropped, the passage door opened, and another victim has entered to continue the murderous succession. At Chicago the hides are taken off, not with a knife as in England, but by blows from the back of a heavy cleaver. Stripped in this way they are not damaged by cuts or slashes, and make therefore a somewhat better price. During skinning the carcase is raised aloft till the head is clear of the ground, this is taken off, the viscera are removed, the carcase is split down into two sides and, suspended from rollers running on an overhead rail, is pushed back into the shed, where with some hundred others it hangs a time for cooling, large wooden fans above swinging to and fro continually to drive away the animal gases and sweeten the meat. In course of time the sides pass on into the chill rooms, where the temperature is brought down by means of ice stored overhead, or by freezing mixtures forced through coils of pipes. After cooling it is quartered and sent by freight car or waggon to the canning houses or packers in the city. The best portions, however, of really good western cattle and of the graded oxen are stripped off and packed as fresh meat in boxes surrounded with ice. These, the "tender loin" and "back strips," are despatched east for the supply of hotels and restaurants. Though their journey may be a long one they take no harm in the low temperature provided by the ice, and they ultimately find a market at from 8*d.* to 10*d.* a pound. Some of the meat is despatched in quarters suspended in freight cars constructed for the purpose and cooled by a supply of ice broken small and filling a long trough down the centre of the roof. The supply is renewed if exhausted

Q 2685.

on the road, and the cargo reaches its destination in perfect condition.

All the coarser portions and all the commoner cattle, however, in Chicago stockyards find their way to the packers and canners. Some is salted and packed in tierces or barrels, while vast quantities are boiled, stripped from the bone, slightly salted, and packed tightly in air-tight tins for the canned beef of commerce, a useful supplement to the ordinary diet of the English labourer, and the food of the American miner, who litters the mineral districts of the Rocky Mountains, as the ranch men do the plains, with the empty tins. Ready cooked, free from bone and other waste, palatable and nutritious, this preserved meat has recommendations which promise to make it an article of general importance in this kingdom. The present price at which this meat as supplied in contracts in London is about 6d. per pound. The carcasses of cattle injured in transit, the diseased, and the poverty-stricken, all going by the generic term of "scallawags," are thrust promiscuously into the steam chests and ultimately reduced to a dry powder. This forms a considerable article of commerce in the southern States for the growth of cotton. The demand for it is daily increasing, as it is found that its forcing power is such as to ensure the full development of the pod before the early frosts put an end to production.

As with grain so with cattle, the prime cost of American cattle on the foot at Liverpool depends materially on ruling rates of freight by rail and ship. With these at 6l. an ox from Chicago to Liverpool in 1879, money was lost; whereas in 1878, before freights went up, money was made. Freights for western cattle have gone up considerably, from 120 dollars a car carrying 21 beasts, with a rebate of 70 dollars (or 50 dollars net), to 110 dollars a car net, a rise of over 100 per cent., this is from Dallas in Texas to St. Louis. This rise adds 12s. 6d. to the cost of the ox.

From Fort Dodge in Texas to Kansas City the freight in 1879 is 8s. 4d. per ox, to move him up to Chicago will cost 12s. 6d. more, with some 5s. additional for food, water, and yardage on the road. Freight from Chicago to New York would be over 16s. a head, food, water, and attention on the journey would cost 6s. more, and then comes the cost and risk of the sea voyage, which cannot be taken at a lower figure than for freight 5l., and for food on board ship with attendance and insurance 30s. a head. Dock charges, charges for landing, lairage, and dues upon which we are not instructed to report add to the cost before the animal enters the slaughter-house at the English port.

A general statement was made by the producers of meat and acknowledged by the exporters, that very considerable profits were made by sending live and dead meat to England in 1878. The same authorities also agreed that great losses were incurred by the exporters in the summer and autumn of 1879 in consequence of the fall in prices, which began in July and continued until the end of last year. Loud complaints were made by the shippers of the inadequate arrangements provided for the slaughter of live animals upon their arrival at Liverpool, after the order preventing the movement of American cattle inland. But since then adequate accommodation has been provided, and no complaint reached us of lack of convenience or want of room at London or any other port to which live animals are consigned. The general impression among importers undoubtedly is that no sufficient reason exists for imposing on the American cattle "slaughter at the ports of debarkation" in this country; but none of them pretended to deny the prevalence of pleuro-pneumonia among the dairy cows of the New England cities. After balancing the various opinions of the meat exporters, it appears that really prime beef can be delivered in England and sold at a fair profit at 6½d. per pound; that 7d. gave a margin for a most lucrative trade, but that 6d. per pound was hardly sufficient to pay the risks and outgoings, and would leave little or no profit to the exporter.

The exporters complain most bitterly of the manner in which their meat is "handled" in England. The moment that it leaves the chilled room of the ship no further care is taken of it. The quarters of beef are placed in barges or carts, as the case may be, piled one on the top of another, and delivered to the railway, where they are placed in common trucks and transmitted in a like careless manner to London or other great towns. Arrived at their destination there are no cool stores to which they can be consigned, consequently all the meat must be sold, however over-stocked and depreciated the market may be. And the treatment the meat has received in its transit from the port is such, that in hot weather, if it is not already injured, it must be immediately consumed. Several exporters said that if they could ensure their dead meat the same treatment here that it received in America, they could afford to take reduced prices and yet make more profit.

There appears to be little or no loss of dead meat in America. The refrigerating cars which are re-iced at certain intervals during long railway journeys, deliver not only meat, but dairy produce, and poultry in New York from Chicago and other western centres, invariably in prime condition. Every small butcher has his chilled chamber to which he consigns all his unsold meat, and it is nothing uncommon toward the close of an over-stocked poultry market, for notice to be sent round that ample accommodation in some chilled store can be had until the next market day upon very reasonable terms. Now that it is said that "compressed air is equal to ice," there seems no reason why the American should possess this exclusive privilege of preserving all his perishable commodities.

Dairy Produce.

The extraordinary depression of *Dairy Produce* which became general in 1878, and continued with increased severity until the autumn of last year, has undoubtedly reduced the number of cows kept in America for milking purposes. Cheese in the month of September 1879 nearly doubled in value, and the American farmer who is ever ready to change the operations of his farm to suit the fluctuations of the market, will soon restore the numbers of his dairy stock. But this cannot be accomplished even in the States all at once, and it is therefore likely that the better prices which now prevail in America will continue without serious reduction for some little time. Not only had the value of cheese and butter fallen to a ruinously low ebb, but the price of fresh milk near large cities had sunk so considerably that some farms which had for years been furnishing those supplies, were being devoted to more mixed husbandry. But as a general rule we did not find the retail price of milk in the American cities to be much below that commonly paid in England. On the other hand, the quantity of milk consumed everywhere in America greatly exceeds that which is commonly used in this country, and the quality is generally better.

Until the last few years the chief part of the butter and cheese made within the Union was manufactured in the Eastern States. The State of New York was regarded as the great seat of dairy farming. But now the west, 1,000 miles away, supplies New York and other eastern cities with enormous quantities of both cheese and butter. Five or six years ago large numbers of Danes settled in Iowa and started dairy farming. For a time there was a difficulty in sending the fresh products of these western States in good order to the east; but now by the aid of refrigerating railroad cars and cool stores, both at the stations where the goods are collected and also where they arrive at the point of consumption, not only butter and cheese, but eggs and such like perishable farm products can be transported safely and stored for some time without injury. The New York dairy farmers complain bitterly of the preferential railroad rates charged in favour of the western producers. After making due allowances for all the advantages which may be justly accorded to through traffic for long distances, it does appear that the railroads unfairly handicap those farmers who live a few hundred miles from the eastern cities. It was stated that at one time the same rate and even less was charged for carrying farm produce 1,000 miles, as was demanded for half that distance.

Much cannot be said in praise of the general quality of American butter. Great strides have been made of late to improve its manufacture, and since the establishment of creameries a much more scientific management of the dairy has become general. For some time past a battle has been raging between shallow and deep milk pans. The prevalent idea that a moderately even temperature was necessary for securing the largest amount of the best cream has been seriously challenged, and it is attempted to demonstrate that a consistent low temperate, but little above freezing, secures the most rapid and effectual development of cream. The shallow pans have been discarded, and deep circular tins, 19 inches by 8, immersed in running water supplemented with ice, are now used in some of the best dairies. At this low temperature it is asserted that more cream rises in 12 hours than by the old plan in 36. It is contended not only that there is a great saving of trouble, and that space is economised, but that the skim milk, especially in hot weather, is ever so much better. The "Cooley" system of placing the milk tins actually under water (covering the tins with a loose lid which excludes the water like a diving bell) is being adopted in some dairies. It certainly has the advantage of compactness, as the milk of a large number of cows may be stowed away in a good sized chest which can stand anywhere. But serious objections have been raised to this plan. It is stated by many that the cream thus raised is somewhat tainted, and that a continuous exposure to the air during its formation is necessary to expel the animal gases from the cream. The upholders of the system deny this, while their opponents further allege that the butter made from cream so produced will not keep so long as that where the cream has been exposed to the beneficial influence of pure air. There are those who reply, that even if a few natural impurities are retained, the greater danger of exposing milk to a vitiated atmosphere is avoided.

It is pleasing to notice the willingness, it may be even called ready eagerness, with which the American farmers welcome all things new. Any novelty, however revolutionary to existing plans and ideas, is sure to find admirers and may expect a fair trial. The rapidity with which these new systems of dairy management have spread, would astonish many English farmers, who, especially in dairy districts, are proverbially slow to change. But there seemed in America a reaction already setting in once more in favour of shallow pans. At the New York dairy fair held last December there was a model of an improved dairy upon the old principle of flat tins which found many admirers especially among the farmers' wives. But there appears to be a general consensus of opinion in favour of a cool temperature for the milk, even in winter. Here again the abundance of cheap ice is all in favour of the American producers. A dairy partially under ground, supplied with running water, finds most favour in the States. Where these advantages are not obtainable, a better system of ventilating the dairy might do something to improve the general quality of the butter. The other features of dairy management seemed fairly good.

Cheese factories seem more common than creameries, and their success until the remarkable fall in the price of cheese 18 months ago has been very general. While the great bulk of American butter is no doubt poor, the chief part of the cheese is now decidedly good. None of it is really first-class cheese, and it is all exported or consumed when it is very fresh. Some efforts are now being made to introduce the manufacture of different kinds of European cheeses into the States, but they can hardly be said to have been yet adopted to any great extent. The bulk of American cheese is of one uniform make, of a like quality, colour, and shape. Very little cheese is eaten in America. The amount made is 300,000,000 lbs.,* and of that quantity fully 40 per cent. is exported, while the amount of butter made is estimated at 1,000,000,000 lbs., and only a little over 2 per cent. is sent abroad. The home consumption of butter is therefore considerable, and the absence of any great export demand may result from its general inferior quality. It is startling to find the prices paid for really good butter by rich people in the great cities. While the common run of butter in the market may be bought for 10d. per lb., 2s. per lb. is sometimes charged for a supply all the year round, and as much as a dollar per lb. is paid in a few instances. In all the dairies where these fancy prices are obtained the butter is made from fresh cream, and the greatest care is observed in feeding the cows with the best varieties of food, the cows preferred being mostly those of the Channel Island breeds.

A paper on the dairy interests of Canada, from the pen of Mr. John Clay, junior, our fellow Commissioner, will be found in the Appendix.

Horses.

The American cart horse is a much lighter animal than the English. A farm horse in America is used for every purpose. He must plough and cart the corn, but there is not much manure for him to haul. Carts, save those of the Red River, which are put together without an ounce of iron, are seldom used, four wheels being invariably applied to all agricultural carriages. The state of the roads does not allow the passage of any heavy loads, and the carriages, although strongly made, are all lightly constructed. The farm horse (or rather horses, for a single horse is seldom seen in harness) has to take the farmer to the town on market day, and the family to church on Sunday. We saw but little or no soil that could not be ploughed with two horses. There is therefore no necessity for the great weight and strength of the cart horse as in England. The general price of good common farm horses would vary from 20l. to 30l., and really prime young animals from 40l. to 50l. each. If the price of the animal and the smaller number necessary are taken into consideration, it will not require half the capital to provide the horse stock on a tillage farm in America that is now needed in England. The number kept is probably more than might be considered necessary for the cultivation of such easily tilled land, but then it must be remembered that the busy season is short, that the hard work comes all at once, and that during the winter the horses may be kept in comparative idleness at very little cost, or they may be employed in earning some money in the towns, or in cartage for the improvement, rather than the usual routine work of the farm. The introduction of the Clydesdale and Shire horses from Great Britain has tended of late to produce a stronger and more valuable class of cart horse, but the horses from France and Normandy appear to find more favour with the Americans.

The farm horses in the middle and southern States have a hard time of it. They are seldom housed, fed mostly on grass, and live and die in the open. In the north the horses receive more care, are stabled during a large portion of the year, and are fed on maize, oats, and hay.

Mules are largely used as draught animals. They are common on many farms, and are said to be harder, stronger, and longer lived than horses. There certainly are some very grand animals in the States, especially those seen at the St. Louis' fairs. These mules stand 16 hands high, weigh upwards of 1,200 lbs., and cost about 30l. a head when four years old. Great attention must have been paid to breeding mules in America, or they could not have produced so many good and really noble animals.

A still lighter stamp of cart horse than those already described is bred in Texas and some of the southern States. They are weedy, worthless looking animals, and yet seem capable of much endurance, and to be useful upon a farm. Great number of ponies are bred in the Indian territory, in Montana, and some western States. They are by no means well shaped or handsome, but are reputed as fleet, sturdy, useful little animals, and are chiefly used in herding cattle in the great plains of the west. Oxen are not only used in ploughing, but in some districts are the chief draught animals. They are more easily fed and cared for on long journeys than horses. A good yoke of oxen being worth from 20l. to 30l., they come cheaper than horses, and now that there is a demand for stalled oxen for export, they make more money when they are too old for beasts of burden than they did some years ago.

Although hardly within the domain of agriculture, no notice of the live stock of America would be complete without a passing notice of its extraordinary trotting horses. The amount of space an American trotter passes over in a minute is really wonderful, and the speed seems yearly on the increase. But the style of going is hardly what would be termed trotting in England. It is more of a run than a trot, and there is little high action among these fast horses. The general pace for a riding horse is what is called a "running walk," or what goes in England by the name of a "jog trot." It is really astonishing how fast horses thus trained get over the ground.

The American horse must be a sure-footed animal, as a broken knee is seldom seen. He is also a docile, patient and hardy creature. It is no uncommon sight at market or at a school to see rows of horses "hitched" up to a rail, and standing for hours in the rain or sunshine. They are certainly well trained in many respects. The whip is seldom needed and more rarely used, as the reins are employed instead. All horses going at a great speed appear to draw the light vehicles to which they are harnessed more by the reins than by the traces. When the reins drop the horse stops, which is somewhat puzzling to a foreign driver. As railroads run along the chief roads and main streets of towns, horses are so accustomed to trains, that they seem no more inclined to shy at an engine than at another horse.

Sheep and Wool.

The sheep stock of America will require only a brief notice. The fact that their numbers do not greatly exceed the cattle in the States will prove that sheep farming does not exist to any very great extent. Vast flocks of sheep in the south-west are kept solely for their wool. Not only is the quantity and quality of the mutton of these sheep inferior, but the cost of transit of such a small animal is so great as to almost eat up the value of the carcase. There seems to have been great vicissitude among the sheep farmers all through America. Sometimes there has been a spirited and even wild demand for sheep, and every farmer seemed inclined to keep a few; at another and no very distant period, sheep were unsaleable, and some in the west were killed simply for their skins. Sheep appear to have been very dear some seven or eight years ago, and latterly could be bought for half the price which then prevailed. The recent jump in the value of wool, and the increased demand for mutton, have brought about another revival, and sheep farming is now rapidly extending.

Like the cattle of America, its sheep farming may be divided into two distinct classes; that of the cultivated

---

* Report of Department of Agriculture 1877, p. 343.

lands of the old States, and the great flocks of the far west.

The sheep in the old States are fed and managed during the summer mainly as in our midland counties. They have more hay than roots in the winter, and have to be then housed for many months. This is especially the case in Canada. So the cost of sheep rearing is considerable, and the value of folding sheep on arable land does not appear to be much known; at any rate we saw no sheep fed within hurdles during our visit. There are a few flocks of the improved English breeds to be found all over the old settlements, and at the agricultural shows some really well bred sheep, especially among the longwools are sure to be exhibited. But the more general run of sheep kept by the small farmer is of that rough and ordinary kind which is very difficult to classify or describe.

In the vast plains of the west the sheep are mostly of the Mexican type, crossed in many instances with the Merino to improve the character of the wool, which it does in a marked degree. Compared with the cattle on these ranges, sheep require much more care and attention. They must have constant shepherding, be frequently watered, be herded or folded at night, and in the winter must be fed with hay and protected from snow drifts. The worst disease to which the sheep are subjected is the scab; that tiresome skin disorder seems very common, and is only cured by frequent dressings of tobacco water. Rot seems unknown, nor did we hear any complaint of the fly. In some districts a serious drawback to the cleanliness of the wool, and even of the comfort of the sheep, was the enormous quantities of the seeds of weeds with which the wool was covered. These seeds not only changed the colour and appearance of the wool, but also were so numerous as to materially injure its quality. In the plains small wolves and cayotes prey upon the sheep, but their ravages appeared trifling compared with the devastation caused by dogs in the eastern States. As the State fully compensates the owner for all stated losses in this respect, it seems unlikely that the depredations of these horrible dogs will rapidly decrease.

There does not appear much reason to suppose that America will for some years to come export wool to any extent. At the present time a considerable amount is being imported from England and her colonies, and if the manufacture of woollen goods in the States continues to progress, there is not much chance of their supply of home grown wool meeting the increased demand. The duty on foreign unwashed wool is 12 cents per lb., and 10 to 11 per cent. ad valorem in addition; on scoured wool the duty is three times this amount. The farmers of Ohio have recently petitioned "that these duties may be maintained as a proper "protection to the growers of American wool," and this opinion seems general among the sheep farmers of the United States. The price of half bred Merino wool such as is grown in California has been during the summer as low as 20 cents per lb., in December it had advanced to 40 cents. Common coarse American wool was sold in June last at and under 10 cents per lb., at the close of the year prices ranged in the eastern cities from 23 to 30 cents. Cape wool in December was sold at 30 cents, and Australian at 42 cents per lb. It will therefore be seen that wool, like cheese and other produce of American soil, took a tremendous upward bound in the fall of 1879, and it was this advance in prices, and the consequent demand for wool in America, which caused the revival of the wool trade in this country.

Hogs and Bacon.

The PIG in America has a happy time of it. He roams everywhere at pleasure; he is monarch of all he surveys. His freedom may be purchased at the expense of shelter, for covered pens or sties are exceedingly rare, but the pig seems a much more hardy animal in the new world than in the old. He is seldom housed, except when the winters are exceptionally severe; he is fed in open sties, without any shed or shelter beyond what he can find for himself. The American hog has plenty of Indian corn from the time he can eat until he steps into those frightful slaughter pens at Chicago or St. Louis. He makes the most of his advantages, and comes at a comparatively early age to a considerable weight. The average live weight of a pig killed in winter is stated to be 280 lbs., in summer it is 240 lbs. Twenty per cent. reduction from the live weight is supposed to give the average weight of the dead carcase. Nowhere can such grand herds of swine be seen as in the maize states of the Union. Save in the Indian territory, you may see a 1,000 pigs without finding a really bad one, and there can be no doubt that the swine stock of America is generally superior to that of England. The Berkshire is the most common breed; they come to early maturity, and have a large amount of lean meat in proportion to the fat. The other most popular breed is the Poland China. These pigs fatten very readily and come to an enormous weight, but the pork is not equal in quality to that of the improved Berkshires.

The rapidity with which hogs are slaughtered and dressed in the great curing houses of America is well known. All that need be said here is that the pig is seized by the hind leg, hauled aloft, stuck, bled to death, scalded, scraped, disemboweled, beheaded, halved, and run into the chilled chamber in 10 to 15 minutes. One establishment alone at Chicago disposed of 1,000,000 hogs last year. The most is made of the offals, and the pork is salted, pickled, dried, or otherwise disposed of. Notwithstanding that beef is so plentiful and cheap, there is an enormous consumption of pork in America, and in the south it may be considered to form the principal meat diet of the labouring classes. An unreasonable prejudice still exists in many parts of England against American pork. No doubt from its being fed almost exclusively upon maize the meat is somewhat hard, and may at times be over-salted, but the great mass of the pork sent to the United Kingdom is without doubt sound and wholesome meat of very fair quality.

The pig in America is not without some drawbacks. He is exposed to various diseases, the most fatal being the hog cholera, or what is now termed in England swine fever. No cure is known for it, and no substantial reason has yet been assigned for its origin. It is highly contagious, and occasionally clears off all the pigs of the district. Its ravages in some regions are so extensive that farmers are compelled to give up keeping pigs for a time.

The great danger which must result to our home stock from importing live pigs from any country where this fatal disease is so prevalent, confirms the necessity of making the recent orders prohibiting such importations, for a time at least, permanent. The infinitesimal proportion of live pigs to the pork we receive from the other side of the Atlantic renders the prohibition of no consequence whatever to the consumers of this country. Of all domestic animals the pig appears the most costly and most difficult to transport alive by sea or by land; whereas his flesh seems capable of being sent in one form or another to any distance at a very cheap rate.

The pork and bacon on issuing from the chill room presents a totally different appearance to that it had 30 hours previously; then moist, warm, flabby, and dull coloured, now it is dry, cool, firm, and bright, stiff enough to be carried in sides on the shoulders or backs of porters to the solid block, presided over by two adepts wielding huge long bladed cleavers. With a few rapid unerring blows the feet are first removed, the next blow goes right through the side behind the elbow, the last (a great exertion) takes off the hind leg behind the loins, the ham being subsequently trimmed by knives; each portion is flung into its proper receptacle for removal.

Then comes the curing, pickling, and packing of the boxed meats or sides and shoulder pieces. For curing the salt has to come from Liverpool, and the process lasts about 3 weeks; finally the sides and shoulders, after being washed, cleansed, and dried, are forced by mechanical pressure into square wooden cases, nailed down, and are then fit for export.

The hams undergo separate treatment, being placed in pickle for some 10 weeks till they are thoroughly saturated with the salt, saltpetre, and sugar, of which it is composed. After this they are removed to the smoking chamber and suspended much as herrings are at Yarmouth in the smoke of burning sawdust. They are next brushed and sewn up in calico covers before labelling. Nothing remains but to force some two score or so into the wooden cases in which they are exported. The best parts of the viscera and scraps of trimmings are minced up for sausages of different kinds and to suit different markets, while the "leaf" is converted in steam heated chests into prime lard, and the coarse fat trimmings, brain, eyes, and other similar offal is rendered down into a lower quality, or yields lard oil now so much used in lubricating machinery.

Poultry.

Not much can be said in praise of the poultry of the United States, with the exception of the turkeys which are generally good, and are raised without much difficulty. They do not, however, appear to reach the great weight of our English birds, being of a slighter form, approaching that of the wild stock. In Kentucky we saw the best specimens gathered together in flocks of many hundreds by speculators. As evening comes on, these birds congregate in some selected and fenced woody nook, watered by a little stream; here they are plentifully fed, after which they take to the boughs of the trees, roosting by preference in lofty places. A large bare tree loaded with these creatures presents an astonishing spectacle in the clear American atmosphere, which retains much of its characteristic brightness even after sundown.

The fowls are exceptionally badly bred. If it may be said of the Texan cattle that they are all "legs and horns," the American fowl may be described as all "legs and elbows," and when plucked presents with his bright yellow skin a most uninviting appearance. They are, too, restless and sprawling, and if food were not abundant and cheap, would for the table be unremunerative. They are, however, in request for a change from the perpetual repetition of tender loin and fillet of beef, and the prices paid are somewhat high. In Detroit market ducks were over 1s. each, fowls 10d., and turkeys 6½d. a pound. At Lexington, Kentucky, when the loin of beef was from 5d. to 6¼d. a pound, turkeys ready for cooking were 5d. a pound, geese, good birds, 4d. a pound, and fowls 7½d. each. On the farms of the short-horn breeders, we saw some really good birds, pure-bred Dorkings, with whom the climate and food appeared to agree, as well as with the grand herd of Durhams, and studs of race and trotting horses. The American farmer, however, has been shrewd enough to discover that eggs pay better than birds, and he has turned attention to their production and preparation in large quantities for distant markets. The price paid by collectors seemed good. In Minnesota, on the spot where fowls sold at 6s. 3d. a dozen, eggs made 5d. a dozen; while at Lexington, with fowls at 7½d. each, eggs made as much as a penny each, and never lower than 4d. a dozen. They are packed in millboard partitions, an egg in each square cell, 36 in each layer resting on cardboard sheets, one above the other, and the whole contained in a handy sized packing case. The counting is thus made easy and few eggs are broken. Another way is to pack 70 dozen in a wooden barrel in oats. These are treated as fresh meat, chilled and kept for months in chilled chambers; collected at about 3d. a dozen in the middle States, and thus preserved, they are sold in New York at from 11d. to 1s. a dozen when eggs are scarce; the oats making the cost price again to the packer. They come over 1,500 miles, and one dealer was known in 1878 to have cleared 3,000l. by sales on a rise of prices. The abolition of slavery has affected the value of eggs, the free blacks now keeping round their little houses a good stock of hens, but even now prices are sometimes remarkably high. In January 1874, eggs sold at 20d. a dozen in New York, though before the month was out they fell to 6d.

Railroads, and Transport.

An important question naturally asked is this: as the distant lands of the west come into cultivation will not the cost of transit be so increased as to raise the price of their products at the seaboard? Judging from the past, distance appears to have comparatively little influence upon the cost of transit. Where there is a sharp competition between rival railroads, and especially where water carriage can join that competition, goods are carried for 1,000 miles as cheaply as 100 where no such competition exists. The extraordinary manner in which railroads have multiplied in the States, and the vigour with which they are now being pushed, not only in the newly developed regions, but in the older States, would point to a cheaper rather than a higher rate for inland transit. The introduction of steel rails must greatly reduce the expense of maintaining the permanent way of a railroad, and, during the recent depressed times, the cost of making new lines and renewing old ones, has been comparatively small. It may be as well, however, to bear in mind the paramount necessity of railroads in the States. Except in the limestone districts of the older settlements, and where the roads are mostly kept in repair by tolls, there are not only no good roads, but there are no tracks that we should dignify by the name of a highway in England. The water carriage, where it can be reached, is abundant and cheap; but the country now being developed is mostly destitute of great navigable rivers, and where they do exist some are blocked with ice for months in the winter, and the waters of others fall very low in the autumn. Another fact worthy of record is that a well managed railroad appears to possess so many advantages as to be enabled to run a whole fleet of steamers off good navigable rivers, a notable instance being the extraordinary decrease of boats upon the Mississippi at St. Paul.

The whole question of transportation over routes to the seaboard has for years occupied the attention of the national government. In December 1872 the senate, by resolution, authorised the appointment of a committee to consider that part of the President's message which related to this question. Their inquiry embraced, among other subjects, combinations between different lines, consolidation of lines, issuing of stock not representing money paid for construction, commonly known as "watering" stock, competition between different lines and water lines, and the relative cost of various methods of transportation.*

Besides freight charges, terminal or incidental charges incurred at various ports go to make up the entire cost of transportation. These are commissions, elevator charges, insurance, weighing, and inspection, beyond which is the marine insurance. When wheat is sold at intermediate points, or held in store, an additional charge is incurred. The committee found, in 1872, the average cost of moving No. 2 spring wheat from Chicago to New York, for freight alone, to be 15s. 3d., and, including transfer and insurances, to be 17s. 6d. per quarter, and of "corn" 14s. 9d.† The cost of transporting wheat from points west of Chicago then averaged 5s. 8d. per quarter, and for "corn" just under 5s. 4d.‡ This appears to coincide with present charges as given to us by the growers and at the Chicago produce exchange, and to be 20 per cent. higher than for the same distance between Chicago and New York. But, as the committee observe, it must be remembered that there are other commercial facts which determine the profitable shipment of grain from the interior,§ and that the extent of these shipments depend mainly on the amount of return freights, and as regards exportation upon the available supply of tonnage for foreign ports. In 1872, over 1,000,000 bushels of wheat were held at Montreal in consequence of lack of tonnage, followed by over caution of traders in 1873, through which Montreal received 1,000,000 bushels less than there was power to export. Since 1872, however, the cost of handling grain at New York and other ports has been materially reduced by the construction of elevators owned by the railroad companies, as well as by floating elevators in dock, and while grain in bulk was heretofore unloaded by hand at a cost of 4 to 5 cents per bushel,‖ the establishment of the elevators and better terminal facilities has reduced the charge for receiving, weighing, wharfage, delivery to vessels, and storage for 10 days, to 1¾ cents, or 7d. per quarter of 480 lbs. The two elevators we visited at New York of the New York Central Railroad are each capable of holding 1,500,000 bushels, mostly brought by rail and delivered into boats for transfer to ships in port.

The transport of bulky goods, such as grain, always has been less costly by canals and lake in America than by rail, but the average cost of transport by canal, something under 1 cent per 2,000 lbs. per mile,¶ is greater than it would be with larger canal facilities, without which the canal is taxed to its utmost capacity in the latter part of the season, leading to increased canal rates. The enlargement, however, of the canal, and the use of steam as a motive power, may again give the canal a marked advantage over the railroad. Quite recently a discovery has been made in the use of the steam propeller, of very simple application but of great value in rendering the power more efficacious. It consists in simply pushing instead of tugging the fleet of barges moved by the "propeller." In the face, however, of the fact that the railroad has run the steamboats off the Mississippi at St. Paul, has decimated the fleet at St. Louis, and has absorbed nearly all the traffic of the Thames above London, and of our canals, it is difficult to find reasons for not anticipating similar general effects in the United States. The railroads will always possess certain advantages which will secure them a preference, notably that grain in bad condition sustains less injury when moved in that way than by ship, and the fact that it is frequently required to be at the port to meet contracts for shipping at an earlier date than that at which the canal could deliver. While the river competition may be active and dangerous to the competing railroad in good weather, and when the river is up, with low water or ice gorges, the tables are turned.**

Whatever effect water competition may have had in reducing rates, they have been deranged and depressed in a more marked degree by competition among the railway companies themselves. The consequences of this competition were simply suicidal, and goods were transported during its active continuance at wholly unremunerative rates. In the exercise of common prudence and for self preservation, the eastern trunk lines and western roads entered into articles of organisation adopted by their representatives at a meeting held at Chicago, in December 1878.†† The joint executive committee was then established, with Mr. Albert Fink elected as permanent chairman. Members of each of the trunk lines act upon this committee for their own lines and as delegates for other western companies, and it was ordained that the committee "should

---

* Report of Committee, p. 10.
†   "   "   pp. 21–30.
‡   "   "   p. 26.
§   "   "   p. 23.
‖   "   "   p. 27.
¶   "   "   p. 61.
**   "   "   p 37
†† App. p. .

"alone have the power to make, change, and enforce all through passenger and freight rates and rules in both directions, from, to, or beyond their respective termini and common points upon all of the said competitive traffic common to any two or more of the trunk lines." The Presidents affirmed the principle of "pools," and decided to perfect such "pools," and adopt rules for the maintenance of rates as the committee might deem just. The "pool," however, does not appear, at all events in its early days, to have been maintained, and a loss was sustained on the Chicago east-bound traffic, owing to this failure, amounting to 1,840,494 dollars, between December 19th 1878, the day on which it was agreed to pool the Chicago business, and May 1st, 1879. In September 1879 the joint executive committee again met, and the chairman remarked that the good effects of the "pool" were noticeable in the better maintenance of rates, and that an agreement as to minimum rates, which took effect on August 1st, had been strictly carried out. And from information given to us by Mr. Albert Fink, in New York, in December 1879, it would seem that the "pooled" companies had really succeeded in establishing higher rates through the agency of co-operation. If this be so, and the "pool" is kept in perfect good faith, this concerted action must inevitably tend, with an increase in the cost of transportation, to raise rates and enhance the value of western grain at the seaboard. We have, however, some reason to believe that special contracts are still made over "pool" lines for large quantities and favoured customers.

App. p. 28.

App. p. 28.

The Labourer.

The farm labourer can hardly be said to exist as a distinct class in the United States, unless it be among the coloured people in the middle and southern States. These appear to be settled, domesticated, and contented to stick to one industry. In many respects agriculture suits them. They are fond of animals, and the attachment appears to be reciprocated. At a large sale of shorthorns in Kansas City, a negro in charge of a bull expressed to us a hope that he might not be separated from him by the purchaser, and that to wherever the fortunes of the auction took the bull he might be allowed to migrate. But with the whites employed in the cultivation of arable land the case is wholly different. In the large farms of the west the bothy system is carried out, and buildings are put up in which the summer men mess and sleep. In winter they are off to the towns and cities, and it is seldom the same faces are seen two years running on the farm. Mounted overseers or foremen are also engaged for the season at better pay, and these men, long-witted and keen-eyed, leave very little on trust to the ordinary hand. It should be remarked that, though wages may appear high, the hours of labour from spring to autumn are long, and winter is a period of almost complete cessation from work for man and beast on the American farm. The horses and mules then lay on flesh against the lengthening days when the soil will be released from the grip of winter, and the men either take to drinking or school, or, possibly, go "lumbering." All seem well dressed and well fed, and very ready with the implements under their care or direction. There is no need for the exercise of muscular strength and endurance for which our labourers were once so famous. Machinery does all the hard work. Ricks are small, the hay lofts are filled to their further end by machinery, the ploughs and cultivators are fitted with seats, and reapers with metal arms cut, gather, bind, and deliver the wheat, oats, and barley. As much cannot be said of labour on the smaller farms; there the owner, to all the mental cares of ownership, adds the physical stress of manual labour of the severest description. No other class of men toil so unceasingly, enduring the life of savages for a while in order to conquer the backwood or civilize the prairie. The man, sedate and serious, is attempting almost single handed to perform the work of two, if not more, English labourers. It is true he is not cultivating, but only cropping the soil, and, as far as he is able, leaves to machinery and animal power some of the drudgery that falls to the lot of the European field hand. His children are "full of health, turbulence, and energy," and their school education is carried on beyond the period which closes it with us; but the wife, though "ready to meet the ills of life without fearing and without braving them,"* betrays in her appearance the terrible trial through which the family are passing, and she, at all events, seems conscious of the fact that her lot is not lightened by the independence which is held to accompany the possession of the soil by the cultivator.

A point of interest in the future production of wheat is the supply of farm labour. We failed to see that scarcity of farm hands that we anticipated. In the very busy season of the year good labourers may be scarce, but, as a general rule, when the men are wanted they are to be found. The very few labourers that are required upon a great wheat growing farm in America during the dead winter months is surprising. In one instance we were told that only two men were kept upon 5,000 acres. There was actually no live stock upon that farm save the horses and mules, and these fed in the roughest manner. When the longer days and harder work of the American labourer, together with his being employed only when he is wanted, are taken into account, the annual cost of labour per acre is much less than the amount paid in England. The supply of labourers in the future must depend mainly upon the quantity and quality of the emigrants. There will be sure to be numbers of intending and expecting farmers who will for a time be forced to work for others before they can farm for themselves. And there will be thousands commencing farming on their own account who will be desirous then, as now, to earn good wages for themselves and horses during the busy months of the agricultural year, although their own land would probably pay much better in the end if that labour was bestowed upon it. The serious depression which so long existed among the commercial, mining, and manufacturing industries of America, no doubt tended to draw the labourer from the town to the field. Previously, the high wages and constant employment of the artisan, together with the comparative comforts of town life, made the labourer rather prefer the great cities of the east to the prairies of the west. A continuance of the recent burst of prosperity in all branches of trade in the States may again tempt men from agricultural pursuits back to the towns. Should the tide of emigration cease to flow from Europe, or the general movement of the American population towards the west be checked, agricultural labourers may be scarce, and the husbandman find himself without hands in his busiest seasons. But at present a failure of a fair supply of farm labour does not seem imminent. The prospect, for some time to come, points rather to higher wages than to a really short supply of farm hands. In domestic servants, however, there is not only a scarcity, but in farm-houses a perfect dearth of female helps. In many towns good house servants are hardly to be found, and those that are employed are mostly recent arrivals from Ireland or the Continent. The highly finished education which the poorest girls in America receive seems to make them contract a dislike to domestic service. In the south the coloured population are the chief domestics, but in the far west no indoor servant is to be had, and all the household labour falls with crushing severity upon the farmer's wife, or upon his children, as soon as they are able to do any work.

Board of Agriculture.

The American farmer has the advantage of a Government Department of Agriculture. It is quite possible that such an institution may be a curse rather than a blessing, but in a new country a Government Department, well administered, as it is now at Washington, cannot fail to be of essential service to agriculture. Not only is there this department of the Federal Government specially directed to the interest of the farmer, but every State we visited has its own Department of Agriculture, which being in direct communication with that at Washington, renders the service of the central office more useful and complete. It is wonderful that a Government Department with such slender means at its disposal can do so much good, and it is only by cordial co-operation with the different Boards of Agriculture in the various States that so much is accomplished. The central authority prepares the agricultural statistics, and publishes interim reports of the prospects of the crops throughout the United States. The statistics not only contain the acreage of the crops but an estimate of their probable yield, and this, to be of any appreciable value, can only be furnished by the different localities. In return for these valuable services rendered by the Boards of Agriculture in the different States, the Department at Washington furnishes them with all the agricultural information it can collect from foreign sources, and also supplies them and the different agricultural colleges and experimental farms that are associated with them, all the new variety of grain and seeds that are likely to be useful in their localities.

It would appear to be the laudable ambition of the great American nation "to feed the world and clothe themselves." With the great variety of soil and climate which the United States possesses, it is more than likely that they could successfully cultivate, sufficient for their own wants, almost every crop and plant which is grown throughout the world. A great effort has recently been made by the energetic head of the Department of Agriculture to promote and encourage the production of sugar. The experiment so far appears highly successful. Already a considerable

---

* De Tocqueville's Democracy in America.

amount of excellent sugar is produced in many different parts of the States. Among the varieties of sugar cane which are most successful is the Minnesota early "Amber Sorghum." This cane, has a marvellous strength and rapidity of growth, and its juice is remarkably rich in saccharine matter.

Throughout the United States and Canada the means of a young farmer for securing a good agricultural education, both scientific and practical, abound everywhere. At Guelph, in Ontario, there is a college, like our Cirencester, in which a farmer's son can obtain almost at a nominal cost an insight into the most perfect routine of farm and stock management (in both of which he is expected to assist), with the advantages of the best scientific knowledge, illustrated not only in the laboratory but in the field. The different counties into which the States are divided have invariably some such excellent institution for imparting a sound and enlightened agricultural education.

Canada.

Upon the arrival of the "City of Montreal" at New York, we were waited upon by the Hon. Robert Read, Senator, with an invitation from the Canadian Government to visit Ottawa, and make a prolonged tour in the Dominion. We were compelled to decline the greater part of this kind invitation, but Mr. R. Read courteously assisted us in our investigations in New York, and remained our guide and companion till we left Toronto.

Many of the general agricultural remarks that have been made apply equally to Canada and the United States. It will be only possible now to say a few special words upon the farming of the Dominion of Canada. We had not time to visit Lower Canada, nor did we see very much of Ontario. The arable farming around Toronto is decidedly in advance of anything we saw in the United States. The cultivation strongly resembled that of England, and for cleanliness and produce would compare favourably with some of its well farmed districts. The soil is deep and fertile. The country has almost all been reclaimed from the primeval forest, and the labour that has converted that woody region into miles of smiling corn fields, must have been no easy task. But in the great north-west, the country so recently opened to the over-populated countries of the old world, there is no forest to subdue, or scrub to uproot. The whole is one vast plain, more or less fertile, which can be converted into a grain field by the simple operation of two shallow ploughings. The soil around Portage le Prairie is a rich black loam, light of tillage, yet sufficiently retentive to withstand severe drought. In many places there appeared little or no variation to the depth of 3 feet. In some spots the land is swampy and low, but a few main dykes would dry many hundred acres, and with a soil so friable, no drainage for surface water could possibly be required. This vast region, called by some "the future wheat granary of the new world," had not in September last the advantages of any railway. In this respect Canada seems greatly in arrear of the United States. While in the latter country railroads, made sometimes with English capital, are run through a country almost unpopulated in order to develop it, in the Dominion no railroad is made until it has a population on or beyond it that may be expected to pay the working expenses of the new line. It may be that the original shareholders of the pioneer railroads of the States are often sacrificed and their line is sold for a small sum to some wealthy company. But if Canada is to be developed with a rapidity approaching that of the United States, the Dominion Parliament must spread its railway system somewhat more quickly. A far seeing policy must anticipate eventual profits from opening a now inaccessible though rich region, rather than expect immediate payment from the traffic along the new lines of railroad that must soon be made.

Much has been said against the long and severe winters of Manitoba. No doubt the cold is intense, and that for well nigh five months in the year all field work is suspended. But it is a crisp dry cold that is not so unpleasant, and with the first sharp frost and fall of snow the roads that were before impassable become excellent highways for the cartage of timber and of grain. No doubt the grasshoppers did in the years 1875 and 1876 destroy the few cereal crops of the early settlers. But should they again invade the territory, it is confidently expected that with the increased acreage planted with grain, their ravages must be distributed over a much larger area, and will not be so severely felt. It is also argued that no Indian corn can be produced in that northern latitude, and therefore it will never be a region of cattle and of sheep. Certainly stock must be housed during the winter months, and provender of some kind must be grown to feed them during that long and dreary season. But there is no reason why abundant crops of natural hay and artificial grasses, such as Timothy, rye grass, clover, and Hungarian millet should not be grown in great abundance, and the deep and friable soil seems well adapted for the cultivation of mangolds and other roots.

No man should emigrate to the far west who is not prepared to work hard and live hard. He may successfully transplant an English family into this region of "rude abundance," but he cannot expect to take with him the comforts of an English home. For years all new settlers, but especially the females, must expect to rough it. The old, the sickly, and the faint-hearted should never emigrate however poor and sad their lot may be in the old country. But to the young, the vigorous, and the courageous, who cannot get a comfortable living in England, Manitoba offers a home that will soon provide all the necessaries of life, and in a few years of steady and well directed toil, will probably ensure a competency, and possibly a moderate fortune. It may be a very good country for a farm labourer to settle in, but it appears especially adapted as a field for the practical hardworking stalwart young farmer who has a few hundred pounds in his pocket, and who would know how to spend it to the best advantage.

In the Appendix will be found the Government regulations, recently issued, respecting the disposal of public lands for the purposes of the Canadian Pacific Railway. The Order in Council of November 1877 is now cancelled, and settlers who had taken up land under the order are to be dealt with, and their claims adjusted under the new provisions, which certainly are more encouraging to settlement than the old ones. We have also added in the Appendix a short account of the land system of the different provinces of the Dominion.

To those who could not endure the rough life of the west, there are many farms of 100 or 200 acres to be bought in Ontario and Lower Canada at from 50 to 100 dollars an acre. These farms may be near a good town or railway and are well fenced, and upon which decent farm houses and suitable buildings have been erected. There are also in these localities sundry such farms to let at from three dollars to five dollars an acre; or they can be hired by the tenant paying the rent in kind by a fixed portion of the produce, while occasionally the farm is worked in shares, the landlord finding all or a portion of the live stock of the farm. This may be an easy means for a farmer without capital to work his way up, but it seldom leads to any permanent friendly relations between landlord and tenant.

Our regret at not being able to describe more fully the agriculture of Canada is considerably modified by the fact that in the autumn of last year 14 tenant farmers' delegates from Scotland and the north of England visited the Dominion, and have since written a series of most useful and exhaustive reports. These reports have been freely circulated by the Department of Agriculture of the Canadian Government, and their contents are widely known. But there was one great feature of Canadian farming, viz., its dairy produce, which seemed to us to require some special notice, and we have therefore to call attention to the separate report of Mr. John Clay, Junior, upon this subject, which will be found in the Appendix.

Land Laws.

The title to land in the first instance comes by patent from the National Government (of which a form is given in the Appendix), and is therefore extremely simple, but, as in England, in the course of time titles become encumbered with charges and trusts. The power of entailing we found legally recognised in most States, limited, as in England, to a life in being and 21 years beyond. Though this is the fact, the exercise of the right thus given by law seemed distasteful to those with whom we discussed the matter, and the love of equality so inconsistent with an accumulation of real property in one individual made its recognition revolting. We were told that large properties are "pecked at," but they nevertheless exist. Large landed properties are held by absentee holders holding on for the rise in value. And a much larger amount of farm lands is cultivated by rent paying tenants than is generally supposed. In the Appendix we have given forms relating to land transfer and occupation, which do not, however, seem to call for special remark. They are of rather an old fashioned type with indorsements which would be used here if the land were in a register county. There are two forms of mortgage, one in the shape of a trust for sale. Two forms of lease, in which the clause for re-entry is a stringent one. Several deeds of conveyance, in which the word "warrant" seems to be used as implying covenants for title, possibly by force of some American statute with which we are not acquainted.

On the whole it cannot be said we have anything to learn from these forms, and it would rather seem (as perhaps is to be expected) that they are behind the standard of the better class of English conveyancing.

One of the forms of lease (that printed in Sioux City) has been furnished to us by Messrs. Close, Benson, & Co., of the City of London, whose letter enclosing the lease we have inserted in the appendix, as it relates to the practice of letting out land to tenants in Iowa.

A reference to our notes in the Appendix will show that the existence of landlords and the practice of letting farm lands, either on shares or for a money rent, is to be met with everywhere.

See American Almanack, 1878, p. 69.

Under the homestead and exemption laws the legislature intends to secure to every head of a family or householder the possession of a permanent home, and the policy of protecting the home of a debtor from forced sale prevails in the legislation of most States. This has been greatly perverted by loose judicial construction so as to include nearly all the property of a debtor in the exemption from liability for his debts, but finally in nearly all the States the exempted property is limited either to enumerated articles or to chattels of a defined value.

Experience soon showed the necessity of prohibiting the alienation of the homestead, unless the wife joined in the deed, and in several States the courts have held that a widow takes a homestead in addition to her dower.

By the national law, also, it is provided that no land acquired under its enactments shall be liable for any debt of the settler contracted prior to the issuing of the patent for his homestead.

The legislature of Manitoba, in the Dominion of Canada, by enactment in 1872 protected the debtor's land to the extent of 160 acres and a limited amount of live stock and chattels from seizure.

Conclusion.

It would be impossible for us to close this Report without acknowledging with gratitude the kindly reception and hearty welcome which we received everywhere in America. Private individuals and public officials were alike ready to offer us every facility for prosecuting our inquiry and affording us valuable information. When questions were asked that would here be considered impertinent or inquisitive, they were answered with a frankness and readiness that pleased and astonished us. We were forced to make curt speeches, to decline many invitations, and dispense with sundry receptions which we hope were not considered uncourteous, but we found it impossible to make rapid progress when our plans were publicly known. We might apparently have commanded the services of every State official from the Governor downwards, but we found our movements less hampered, and our information more reliable and independent when we pursued our inquiries alone. Among the many kind attentions we received we must not forget to mention the ready assistance given us by the various railways. Foremost among those intelligent officials was our good friend Mr. J. H. Drake, of St. Paul. Our visit to Minnesota and to Manitoba was made singularly easy and pleasant by his accompanying us, and placing a "wild train" at our disposal, to run wherever we liked over the different lines of railway. But wherever we went we found the same generous hospitality, the same readiness to impart useful information, and the same uniform courtesy and warmth of welcome.

Private individuals too vied with each other in rendering us assistance, and our thanks are especially due to Mr. McTavish, of the Hudson's Bay Company, who drove us all over the region of Prairie Le Portage, and to Mr. Hespeller, the immigration agent, who piloted us through the extensive settlements of the Russian Memnonites.

Nor must we forget to add our thanks to the Governor-General of Canada for his hospitality and kind attention. His Excellency assisted us in every possible way, and we regret our inability to avail ourselves more fully of the facilities he so kindly placed at our disposal. Even in the far west of Manitoba, the civilities we received were, if possible, of a still more warm and hearty character. It is quite true that the Lieutenant-Governor seemed to take little or no interest in our mission, but the Prime Minister of the Province and the other members of his Government not only showed us every attention, and gave us every information, but the Hon. Mr. Norquay and the St. George's Society entertained us at magnificent banquets.

We have avoided as far as possible volunteering any speculative opinions of our own on subjects to which our attention was directed. In fact, the haste with which we were compelled to pass over the scenes of our inquiry left us no leisure for critical conclusions after devoting the requisite time to the collection of facts. The view we took of the agricultural affairs in the United States was of necessity a broad and general one, and only in some special matters were we able to go into particulars. Much that the instructions with which we were furnished required at our hands remains, we regret to say, unsatisfied, and were it not for the excellent provision made by the American railroad system for getting a night's rest while travelling, much more must have been omitted. We came to the conclusion, however, that after all America is no paradise, that in the contest for agricultural supremacy, while fresh unexhausted soil, a level surface, and the absence of stones are highly favourable for the profitable use of modern machinery, and the manufacture of grain by a scourging course of cropping, still drawbacks exist which tell in favour of the old country. They may be stated in a few words. Severe winters, putting a stop to agricultural employment, dangerous droughts, injurious insects, and in the prairie land (in the absence of lakes) a short supply of good water.

With regard to cattle, for the present the American stockman in the West is possessed of singular advantages; land for nothing, and abundance of it. In the East good markets for dairy and other produce, and in the middle States excellent pastures of blue grass (*poa pratensis*). The growth of this plant too is extending far beyond its old home of Kentucky, and is now being established to the west of the Missouri. Its success in this district opens fresh prospects to the grazier, who will in time bring the improved turf under the hoof of thoroughbred stock, or at least of highly graded cattle.

The western country, however, is poorly watered for the better class of stock, which suffer if left short of this supply, and the struggle for water rights for native cattle, which suffer less from drought, threatens ere long to become a serious difficulty; the allotment of land and the termination of free range will tend to make cattle raising more costly, though on the other hand, the increased consumption of the population as it advances towards the western plains will enhance prices. We have referred to the important part the railroad fills in developing agricultural wealth in the United States. No effort is spared on the part of the people to thrust this right arm of civilization as far as it can be made to reach; with them it is not population first, and the railroad to follow, but the latter first as a means to the former. With an intelligence, quick to design, and a spirit eager and daring, to carry out these enterprises, it is difficult to account for a dulness of apprehension which tolerates the continuance of a tariff so hurtful to foreign trade and domestic economy as, in some measure, to render the position of the English agriculturalist more advantageous than that of the American.

We are, &c.
(Signed) CLARE SEWELL READ,
　　　　　ALBERT PELL.
To W. A. Peel, Esq.,
　Secretary, Royal Commission
　　on Agriculture.
July 1880.

APPENDIX.

NOTE BOOK of Mr. CLARE READ and Mr. ALBERT PELL, M.P.

Landed at New York on Sunday, September 7th, 1879.

With MR. EDWARD HINCHEN, President, New York Produce Exchange, Sept. 8, 1879.

heat and ur. The recent exports of wheat have taken the form of ' rain in preference to flour, owing to the brand of flour having become debased and untrustworthy. A committee of the Produce Exchange (New York) are now endeavouring to establish a guaranteed brand.

an. Bran is now compressed into packages 34 inches by 16 and 16 inches deep. The price in the New York warehouse is 18 dollars a ton of 2,000 lbs., and is so sold by Messrs. A. T. Roberts & Co., corn merchants, 3, State Street, New York. The freight to Liverpool would come to about 25*s*. a ton.

eat to diterra- an. Jesse Hoyt & Co., New York, say that during the month of August 1879, a new demand began in their trade, and they sold one parcel of 100,000 bushels of spring wheat to go to Italy, also 100,000 bushels to go to Sicily.

At the produce market we saw samples of wheat, flour, and barley, and the leading men on 'Change. One large exporter said, "Should you have better harvests in Eng- " land, and reduce the price of your farm produce still more, " we shall continue to send it to you. America will pro- " duce much more than she can consume, and we must " send it to you, as your's is the only reliable market we " have for our surplus."

s. Eggs come to market wholesale in New York in barrels containing 70 dozen, priced at 15 cents per dozen. They have been preserved for several months in refrigerators, and are delivered from Toledo in Ohio. One dealer cleared 3,000*l*. by a rise in prices in 1878. He bought at 6 cents a dozen and sold at from 22 cents to 25 cents. Between June and October they are packed in oats, which in New York are worth the cost price to the packer in the west. The farmer is said to make more by eggs than by any other produce. They come over 1,500 miles from Omaha on the Missouri. The supply, after the abolition of slavery, became more abundant, as the free blacks in the south are poultry keepers. In 1874 eggs sold in New York in January at 40 cents the dozen, before the month was out they fell to 12 cents to 15 cents. The home consumption in New York has materially increased.

s. ery.

With MR. BAXTER.

er. The finest butter in New York now comes over 1,000 miles from Iowa, though originally New York was the principal butter and cheese producing district. The present prices (Sept. 9th) for the very best is 20 cents; it is salted, and travels packed in 50 lbs. and 100 lbs. tubs in refrigerators by railway and ocean steamer. The best qualities are produced in factories and creameries. The improvement in manufacture is due to the settlement of a colony of Danes in Iowa, and their butter brings the highest prices. The Iowa brand came in about five years ago.

butter. The price of creamery butter in June was 16 cents per lb. Now the same butter, having been stored in a chilled warehouse, is worth 20 cents, and is quite as good. Factory butter was selling in July and August as low as 7 cents to 8 cents, and is now worth 12 cents to 14 cents. Good butter ends in June and begins in September, if cool; for fresh butter the cows are then fed on Indian corn.

e. Good cheese is now 5 cents to 6 cents per lb.; the best may be bought at this. The price has dropped from 9 cents to 10 cents in 1878 to 5 cents to 6 cents in 1879 for household cheese. Cheese manufactured for the foreign trade at present prices makes a return of only ¾ cent per quart. There is, however, a better consumption than formerly at the table.

by We were informed at the New York Produce Exchange that during the summer wheat was charged by rail in New York State 10 cents per 100 lbs. for 500 miles, and only 8 cents from Chicago, 900 miles, for the same weight.

Sept. 9th.

Mr. F. H. Ralph, 28, Broadway, introduced us to Mr. T. C. Eastman, who took us over his vast premises, constructed for the preservation of fresh meat for exportation to England. The cattle and sheep are killed and placed for 24 hours in chill rooms, and cooled there for that time principally with cold air passed down over ice, and returned to the top where the ice is; then for 24 hours more intense cold is produced by circulating through pipes ice that has been dissolved by salt. The first process reduces the temperature to 40° and the last to 34°. The meat is then quartered, packed in clothes, taken 3½ miles in vans, specially constructed and covered with two tarpaulins, to the ship, where it is placed in a chill room, similarly cooled to that on Mr. Eastman's premises. Some 300 cattle can be killed in a day. Sheep undergo the same process, but are packed whole. The average age of the cattle killed is four years.

Beef. The present price of small cattle beef is 8½ cents per lb., bigger and better bullocks 8¾ cents, averaging 750 lbs. dead. The cattle are kept in large pens, and supplied with hay, Indian corn, and water; they are weighed alive, and 100 lbs. live weight is considered to produce 56 lbs. of beef when the bullock is good, but not more than 50 lbs. where the Texan cattle are killed. We saw several most excellent cattle in the pens, and also a drove of thin coarse-looking bullocks from Texas.

Blood. The slaughter knives are from Sheffield, the saws are American. The blood is dried, ground, and bagged up in parcels of about 175 lbs. It contains about 17 per cent. of ammonia, and goes south at from 32 dollars to 42 dollars per 2,000 lbs. (a ton).

Tankage. The slaughter-house offal ("tankage"), including the heads of oxen and sheep, is "rendered" down in steam-tight vessels; the grease is taken off, and the residuum dried and ground to powder. This contains 6 per cent. of ammonia with phosphates, and is sold in lots of 100 tons at 26 dollars per 2,000 lbs. The stench and foul air resulting from this process is drawn into a special apparatus and burnt. The best fat is rendered down separately, and goes to the manufacture of "butterine."

Butterine.

Mr. Eastman says dead meat cannot be shipped in summer with a profit against live meat, when the beast goes over to Liverpool or London for 3*l*. When he began the business of transporting the live ox, he paid as high as 7*l*. a head for the passage. Ships carrying grain, load the grain below, and require light freight for the spar deck and steerage; cattle answer the purpose very well. As to success in the trade, Mr. Eastman lost from 10 dollars to 25 dollars a head in August 1879 by live shipments. And in the same year as much as 10 dollars to 15 dollars per carcase on dead meat, owing to the drop in prices in England. The price of the best joints of beef in New York are now (Sept. 9, 1879), 25 cents per lb. The rate of shipment now, from Boston to Liverpool and from New York to Liverpool is 2 dollars per head, to which insurance at sea averaging 4½ per cent. would have to be added. The weighing is done by sworn weighers on bridges holding 50 beasts driven on at one end of the platform and out at the other. The scales (Fairbank's) weigh from 10 lbs. up to 100,000lbs. and turn with a feather.

Weighing.

Meat. On board the "City of Montreal" we had some excellent beef which had been carried from America to England; a portion of the meat came back to America again perfectly fresh and good.

At Manhattan Beach, New York, the best joints of beef and mutton cost 18 cents to 22 cents per lb., or 16 cents if any inferior meat is taken. In the iced larder of the monster hotel meat is kept at this season of the year three weeks before it is used, and is not considered ready for cooking until it has been there some time.

Elevator. We visited the elevators of the New York Central Railway. There are two of these monster *stores* for grain, each capable of holding 1,500,000 bushels. The grain is mostly brought by rail and drawn up into vast granaries, and then delivered into boats, which take it to the various ships at New York, &c.

With MR. X. A. WILLARD, Little Falls, Herkemer Co., New York State, Sept. 10, 1879.

Value of land. This country was settled up about 1770. In 1780 Mr. Willard's grandfather gave 10*s*. an acre for the ground in its old forest state. In 1800 land had risen to the value of 25 dollars to 30 dollars an acre, being then cultivated with grain.

Dairying began as a speculation in 1800, though the progress was at first slow. It spread from this to adjoining townships, and thence to other counties in the State. In 1840 land ran up to 40 dollars an acre, dairying being then well established. The price rose in 1860 to 100 dollars an acre for the best farms, and by 1875 the price had reached 150 dollars and 200 dollars, while as much as 250 dollars

AGRICULTURAL INTERESTS COMMISSION:

an acre was paid in "greenbacks" for some extra good farms near railways. By September 1879 land had lost half its value, estimated in gold. A farm near Little Falls of 100 acres was this autumn (1879) disposed of under a forced sale to a farmer at 104 dollars an acre. Within the last ten years the seller had been offered 250 dollars in greenbacks. The drop is due to depression in business. House property has gone down as well, though not to the same extent.

Landlords. Foreclosures of mortgage are now much more frequent than formerly. A landlord class has sprung up, Mr. Harris Burrell of Little Falls, a cheesefactor, owns some 3,000 or 4,000 acres of land which he lets in farms of 150 and 200 acres, usually from year to year, but occasionally on lease.

Rent. The system pursued is to let "on shares." The landlord finds land and cows and poultry, half the swine, and pays three-fifths of the taxes. The tenant finds labour, implements, all the horses or draught animals, and pays two-fifths of the taxes. The landlord receives three-fifths of the butter and cheese and one-half of the rest of the farm produce including eggs, with the exception of the hay; but any hay left over at the end of the term of tenancy becomes the landlord's,

Hay. who pays 2 dollars a ton for making. Should the hay run short the landlord has to supply the deficiency, the tenant contributing 2 dollars a ton. The average price of hay in the neighbourhood is 10 dollars a ton. One-third of the land in Herkemer county is let to tenants.

Tenants. Mr. Jas. J. Cooke, of Little Falls, lets land and prefers yearly tenants, that he may get rid of a bad one. His tenants pay all road rates and bear two-fifths of the loss of stock by death.

Landlord and tenant. Under another system the tenants find one-half the dairy stock and take one-half the produce, including calves. A demand for small hirings has arisen, and the artisans of Little Falls offer to take land within walking distance (two miles) of the town in lots of about an acre at 20 dollars an acre, the landlord ploughing the acre, worth to do, about 2 dollars. Fifteen acres were thus let last year. The factory people grow potatoes and some maize. The usual price of potatoes is from 30 cents to 60 cents, 1s. 3d. to 2s. 6d., per bushel of 60 lbs. The industries at Little Falls are textile manufactories, and there are machine shops for producing mowers. There is abundance of manageable water power on the Mohawk River. There had been an inclination on the part of capitalists to buy land with the view of letting it, but this has passed away. In some cases the artisans have bought small lots of land and given as much as 200 dollars and 300 dollars an acre, 40l. to 60l. Though for six years there has been a general "shrinkage" of business and in values, the dairyman felt nothing of it till 1879.

Values. Cows have come down from 90 dollars in greenbacks to 35 dollars and 40 dollars in gold. Horses again from 350 dollars a pair, 70l., in 1877 to 275 dollars or 55l. a pair in 1879.

Wages. Wages have dropped over 25 per cent. In 1877 farm hands were worth 16 dollars a month and board, and in 1879 they had dropped to 12 dollars to 13 dollars a month with board. The soil on Mr. Willard's farm is "Utica slate," stands drought and wet equally well, and is admirably adapted for grass. The surface is broken into long gentle swells rising into higher ridges or terraces commanding charming views of a fairly timbered cultivated country, with excellent houses and farm premises at distances of a mile to 3 miles apart.

Cows. The cows are of a mixed breed, the size of Ayrshire and of that character, with some Dutch blood about them. One farmer (Mr. Skinner) had three Dutch bulls. His calves are sold, making as much as 8 dollars each, 33s. 4d. He had 76 cows; they are milked under the barn on the basement story. One milker to 12 cows, which it is stated he completes in the hour.

Milk. The milk is set in deep tins placed in a tank, supplied through a pipe from a spring with cold water. In winter the stove pipe is carried through the same tank to raise the temperature.

EATONVILLE FACTORY, Herkemer County, New York State. Mr. SMITH, Manager.

Cheese factory. Cheesemaking commenced this year, 1879, on March 22nd, and will close in December; 575 cows from 18 farms supply the milk, which is delivered at the factory at 8.30 a.m. and at 8 p.m., some travelling 2 miles from the farm. The milk from each farm is tested against trickery, but no allowance is made for quality. The night's milk is chilled. The milk after being weighed is warmed up to 84°. The rennet is then added and the milk stands for an hour. The curd is then broken for from 60 to 75 minutes. After the curd is broken it is put into the sink; the whey goes back to the farm. The curd remains in the press for 15 hours; it is broken by hand except when sour, and then the mill is used. In the spring and fall the farmers skim the night meal and mix with the morning's meal before delivery. The fresh made cheese is put in a room with a temperature of 70°, remains there from 30 to 60 days, and is then sold off for consumption. The weight of the cheese is about 56 lbs. An account of milk delivered is entered to each man, upon which his share in the bulk is computed. *Cheese.* Cheese sells in Little Falls by reputation. It is sold in Monday's market in the town, delivered on Tuesday, and exported. *Prices.* Prices have been in 1879 as low as 5 cents in September; they were 7½ cents in May; the average price in 1878 was 8¼ cents. *Labour.* The hours of labour are not short, commencing at 4.30 a.m. and ending at 10 p.m. About 16,000 to 17,000 lbs. of milk are worked daily, producing about a pound of cheese fit for sale from 10 lbs. of milk. In the month of October a pound of cheese has been got from 8½ lbs. of milk. A gallon of milk is taken to weigh 8 lbs. 9 oz.

Sept. 11, 1879.

Utica show and State fair. At the State fair at Utica met Governor Seymour, the President, and the other officials, and were treated with great politeness. *Cattle.* Some good short-horns, mainly shown by Mr. Campbell and Mr. Haight, and a few nice Devons and Herefords, and a large show of Dutch cattle which have been recently imported to improve the milking stock of the district were exhibited. There were Southdowns, Cotswold, and Lincoln sheep fairly represented, but the exhibits of Leicester and Shropshire downs were moderate. The pigs were very grand, all breeds being in great force, the Berkshire the most numerous. There were also some big red pigs that are not seen in England. The great feature of the show was the natural condition in which the cattle were shown. Hardly a short-horn was in more than fair store order, the society excluding breeding animals that are too fat; and the sheep were all untrimmed. The show of cart horses was small, but the entries of trotting horses were numerous, and there were many carriage and other horses, most of which moved well, but had no amount of high action in them. The exhibition of fruits was remarkable, flowers poor, implements good, and mechanical contrivances numerous and clever. *Potatoes.* There was a special class for cheese and another for potatoes, the varieties of which seemed without end. It was altogether a most successful and instructive exhibition. A Lincoln ram had clipped 16 lbs. and the wool was sold for 43 cents per lb. Southdown wool was worth 35 cents, and mixed wools as low as 30 cents per lb., and inferior long wools only 27 cents.

Tillage. In Genessee Valley the land is ploughed (Sept. 12), drilled, harrowed, rolled, and dressed up with as much care as in England. Stones are gathered off into piles or built into walls. At Middleport is a large graveyard. It is just ploughed up as if for wheat sowing; some of the grave stones have been moved and reared against others to make way for the plough, while at the same time a man was busily digging a grave.

Orchards, hop, and peach gardens were all around, and a 3 by 6 feet drill was working with a pair of horses and one attendant only, driving from behind. Telegraph wires lined the roads as in England, and graveyards and orchards were in one.

A most successful breeder of Cotswold sheep and pigs in the State of New York is Mr. Joseph Harris, of Moreton Farm, Rochester, and some idea of the extent of his herd of black Essex or Fisher Hobb's pigs may be gathered from the fact that last autumn it contained 100 breeding sows.

Between Rochester and Suspension Bridge maize and lentils were being gathered. Potatoes were in plenty in *Colorado bug.* spite of serious traces of the Colorado bug. The drilled wheat was coming up, and will be reaped in the middle of July. There were many fields enclosed with stone walls *Clover* and cropped with clover for seed. It is cut with the reaper. Brank or buckwheat was also grown. Hardly an acre of ground was uncultivated, not even the graveyards. There are a few quickset hedges. The soil is of the same character as that around Syston in Leicestershire.

BOW PARK, BRANTFORD, TORONTO, Sept. 13.

We travelled with Mr. A. Smith of the Ontario Veterinary College to Brantford. The land changes from weak sand to a good loam; the fields become larger, and there are some dead fallows sown with wheat and water furrowed in *straight* lines. A few patches of healthy growing swedes appear, and the maize was standing in shocks. The ricks are thatched or covered with boards, and there is no pest except the potatoe bug.

Bricks tiles. There is a pipe tile yard close to Toronto, where 2-inch pipes 13 inches long are sold at 32s. per 1,000. Good white bricks, capital ware, at 30s. per 1,000. *Wages* Labour is a dollar a day without food.

Besides a general view of the farms along the line, we had a still better one of the larger occupations as we drove between Brantford and Paris, where Senator Christy has a farm of 500 acres, and there were several of 200 or 300 acres. The soil was mostly light and almost gravelly. The

APPENDIX TO JOINT REPORT.

land was well tilled, and there were several fields of swedes, and a lot of capital Indian corn. There were more sheep than we had seen anywhere, and which were for the most part well-bred Cotswolds. The winter wheat was being drilled, and most of it seems just planted.

The Bow Park farm contains about 900 acres, 750 of which are under the plough, the rest rough meadow, wood, and roads. It is all more or less light land, and is kept in famous condition. No wheat is grown, the grain being rye and oats. The chief feature in the cultivation of this farm was the enormous crops of Indian corn. That which we saw was being cut with a hook, laid in bunches, and tied up after lying on the ground, and put in round shocks, and fastened at the top with a band of rye straw for 8s. an acre. These shocks remain out until they are required for the cattle, when they are chaffed and steamed and mixed with meal for the stock all through the winter.

The amount of stock on this farm was truly wonderful; 400 pedigree shorthorns, 100 sheep, 100 pigs, and 34 horses. Green rye is fed off in the spring or cut for the stalls, and is followed by rape, which is also fed off.

There was some very late Indian corn which had followed some other crop. The mangolds and swedes were not so clean or so good a plant as some we saw elsewhere, nor did the rye and oats from the stubble appear to have been at all equal to the maize. The cattle were mostly in boxes, boarded at the bottom; some were in open yards, the sheds being furnished with folding doors, which confined the cattle in winter. The buildings are all of wood covered with shingle, and appear in good repair and very well arranged, but the whole have since been burnt down. Winter wheat seems the chief grain of the district, though none is this year grown at Bow Park. Several acres of hops are grown around Brantford. The chief extra food at Bow Park was Indian meal and bran; the latter to be bought at the mills of Brantford at 40s. per ton, which seems to be about the value of a ton of hay. An average of 300 bushels of Indian corn are bought per month for the stock on the Bow Park farm.

Sept. 15th, with Mr. Rennie, seedsman, of Toronto, to Messrs. Gooderham and Worts' distillery, on the outskirts of the town. Room is provided for 3,000 oxen to feed on the premises. They are put in by "runners" as lean, to remain eight months, from Oct. 15th to June 15th, the distillery finding sheds, lofts, or barns, mangers, and wash. The runners provide hay, and pay a rent of 15 dollars a beast for the wash. The daily consumption is 22 lbs. of hay and from 28 to 30 gallons of wash. The hay is bought of farmers, who deliver it in at from 16 to 18 dollars per 2,000 lbs. The oxen coming from Canada West, and costing 3½ to 3¾ cents per lb. live weight, ought to put on 200 lbs. while feeding. The English market is now the best; before there was a sale in England the price was 13 dollars for rent. It then rose to 15 dollars, and there is now a talk of raising it to 17 dollars. Mr. Lumber feeds 1,000 beasts here now out of the lot of 2,600. From 10 to 15 pigs are allowed to each 100 head of cattle to clean up waste; no charge is made for the pigs. The manure is all swilled away down troughs to the adjacent waste land, and is regarded as an incumbrance and nuisance.

A drive of over 15 miles with Mr. Rennie took us to his brother's farm at Milliken, Scarboro'. Near Toronto is a range of low-lying marsh close to the lake, from which rises some rocky ground, that is chiefly covered with trees and rough feed. At the top of the hill is a large expanse of table land, of nice quality and well farmed. It appears that farms would average about 100 acres, all divided by rails of some sort, the snake fence giving way to straight rails, some fastened by wire to the cedar posts. There were several newly built farmhouses, and other signs of prosperity, but there were also indications of great thrift and hard work. Very few roots, but plenty of second crops of clover, and that mostly for seed. Hardly any sheep, and no great amount of stock kept but for the dairy, the produce of which is made into fresh butter. Mr. Simpson Rennie's farm contains 100 acres of capital land, a dark sandy loam of great depth. All has been underdrained that requires it at a depth of 2½ feet, with 2-inch pipes and 3-inch for mains. The land here does not generally require draining except in the low spots where the water settles. Swedes good and clean, but backward; all the land singularly free from weeds; in fact, as clean as a garden. The corn crops of wheat, barley, and oats all looked good, and the clover (saved for seed) was excellent. A new orchard of some 8 acres was planted some three years ago, and looked flourishing. Mr. Rennie grows monster specimens of mangolds, carrots, and gourds. Visited a newly built farmhouse in the neighbourhood which cost 500l. The country, on our return, was more unlevel, and not so well cultivated until we struck upon Young Street, a straight road over 600 miles long, which brought us back to Toronto

Mr. Simpson Rennie values his 100 acres of land at 120 dollars an acre. Nice little house and homestead, all capital land, well fenced and cultivated. It is farmed on the six years' course, three being in grass. *Value of land.*

TORONTO EXHIBITION, Sept. 16.

At the Industrial Exhibition at Toronto the chief feature of interest to the English farmer was the collection of grain. There were some really grand samples of wheat, and one remarkably fine parcel of barley. There were sundry stands of implements and machinery, including two great contrivances for uprooting trees and smashing rocks. *Rearing stock.*

Mr. J. Watt, Salem, township of Nichol, Wellington county, breeds steers for stores. They are calved from January to March. Two are hung on to a cow for the summer; they are castrated at three weeks old, weaned and brought under cover in September or October. They are then tied up, and put on an allowance of 3 lbs. or 4 lbs. of ground peas (worth now ½d. a pound), with ¼ bushel of swedes and hay. They have the run of the "bush" and pasture during the second and third year, with the same sort of feed in the winter as before. They are sold off in June when over two years; 12l. is considered a remunerative price, but they have dropped lately to 10l. and 11l. *Toronto show.*

The hire of a farm hand is 100 dollars for seven months, from April to October. For harvest the pay is 1 dollar 25 cents a day and food. Work begins at 6 a.m., and closes with the light at 8 p.m. No spirits or beer is drank, but oatmeal and water take their place in the field. *Labour and Wages, and food.*

Two fat steers were exhibited at Toronto, one three years and eight months, the other four years old. Their live weight is 2,300 lbs. and 2,250 lbs.; 60 per cent. of this will be their dead weight, that is 1,380 lbs. or 172 stone, and 169 stone, or 1,350 lbs. In Canada, however, the "dead" weight or "dressed" weight includes the hide and tallow as well as beef. Another pair weighed 4,200 lbs.; they were three years and two months old, and worth 7 cents to ship. Another pair, one a six year old worked ox, weighed 2,950 lbs., the other, three-and-a-half years, 2,300 lbs.; these were valued at about 5½ cents per lb. live weight. *Exhibits of cattle.*

There was a fair English cart stallion for whose use the charge made was 48s., no foal, no pay. One of the judges, a butcher, says that the best joints of beef and mutton are now worth at Toronto 12½ cents, or 6¼d. per lb. Hides are worth 4½ cents per lb. Old beasts are becoming scarcer, so are sheep. The artisan eats the same cuts as his master. Cattle are killed for the best joints, the coarser ones being given away at 3 cents per lb. The show of long-woolled sheep, Leicesters and Lincolns, was excellent. The wool was rather open, due, probably, to the climate. *Stallion. Price of meal. Hides. Coarse meat. Toronto show.*

The Toronto Agricultural Show was a wonderful exhibition of stock for any country. The short-horns were the most numerous and the most meritorious class. Among the chief winners were the entries from the Bow Park herd. There were some good Herefords and a great many Ayrshires, and a few Galloways and other breeds. In sheep the long wools were the most numerous; the short and medium woolled sheep were fairly represented. The pigs here, as everywhere else in America, were the great features of the show, and could not well be surpassed at any exhibition in the old country. Among the horses the imported Clydesdale were the best, and some of them stepped as well as Norfolk cobs. Perhaps the most useful class in the show was the yearling short-horn bulls, a splendid array of well bred young animals, many of which could be had for about 20l. each.

ONTARIO AGRICULTURAL COLLEGE.—Sept. 17.

At the Experimental Farm of the Ontario Agricultural College, Oxford Down and Cotswold sheep succeed best, and are most in demand in the neighbourhood. Of two bull calves of the same age the Hereford is worth 150 dollars, the Durham only 60 dollars. The Hereford being in demand just now as an improver of western cattle, foraging better than the Durham and being considered somewhat hardier. A pair of cart horses were sold to-day on the farm for 75l., one four years the other three years old. *Guelph experimental farm. Sheep. Hereford and Durham. Horses, value of.*

The Agricultural College is a sort of Cirencester, save that instead of paying large fees the pupils are boarded, lodged, and instructed, and paid for their labour on the farm. The farm consists of 380 acres under the plough, and is worked by 10 horses. The stock on the farm was excellent, especially the Herefords, and the land well managed. The Indian corn was capital, and there were several sorts of mangold and swedes and green turnip, but all the roots looked backward though healthy. The sheep were good, and an Oxford down ram was really a prime animal.

Around Guelph the rates upon farms of 200 acres of good enclosed land would amount to about 11l. This does not include road rate, which is usually worked out by the farmer; six days on a farm of this size for one man with his two horses and waggon. *Rates.*

AGRICULTURAL INTERESTS COMMISSION:

Guelph show.

At the Agricultural Exhibition at Guelph the short-horn was again the most numerous class, and was very creditable for a local show. The long-woolled sheep were also commendable, and the trotting horses went at a great pace and fetched long prices.

The soil between Toronto and Guelph is various; some parts rocky and very poor; others light loam and nicely farmed, and many miles were almost covered with wood.

Detroit market prices, meat.

At *Detroit*, Sept. 19, the dead weight of cattle runs from 375 lbs. to 450 lbs., killed at two years old, and 4 cents or 2*d.* per lb. is the value of the dressed meat. The fore quarters 3 cents, the hind 5½ cents, the heart 10 cents. The sheep at under two years old come out about 40 lbs. the carcase, worth 6 cents or 3*d.* per lb. The fore quarters 5 cents, the hind 7 cents to 8 cents, or 4*d.* per lb. Lamb, the best, 30 lbs. to 35 lbs. the carcase, is valued at 8 cents or 4*d.*, and veal, 75 lbs. to 150 lbs. the calf, dead, at 5 cents. the lb. Every butcher is provided with his ice-chamber in the market houses, from 300 to 500 lbs. a day costing 10 cents or 5*d.* per 100 lbs.

Chilled stores.

Butter. Poultry.

The best butter costs 20 cents, or 10*d.* per lb., though it has been down to 15 cents, or 7½*d.* per lb. Ducks were selling at 25 cents, or 1*s.* 0½*d.* each; fowls at 20 cents, or 10*d.*, and turkeys were worth 6½*d.*, English, per lb.

The land west of Detroit is generally light and in places hilly, mostly nicely farmed, but towards Chicago, near Lake Michigan, it is low, swampy, and poor.

CHICAGO, Sept. 22.

Chicago. Oxen.

In the park, near the Chicago stockyards, were 12 beasts, the property of Mr. Walker and Mr. Sharman, one, now five years old, weighed a year ago 3,500 lbs. at the Exhibition here. There were "triplets," four years old, weighing 6,600 lbs. or 2,200 lbs each, live weight. We visited the Union stockyards, Chicago, with the largest buyer, "who does not want popularity." He bought in the year 1878 335,000 head of cattle, one-third of the whole supply to Chicago. His choice is Colorado oxen; they are worth 3¼ cents. in the slaughter-house. To clear 1*s.* a head is sufficient profit to the buyer, and he gave 33 dollars a head for the Colorados we saw killed, 6*l.* 17*s.* 6*d.* in English money. The Texan but not the Colorado supply is getting younger. The Hereford within the last two years is becoming *the* bull; his stock "rustles" or forages better on the plains. This buyer thinks they are killing more female Texans than before. It costs at Colorado 1 dollar a year to rear a beast from a calf. Snow storms are very destructive there, killing with starvation as many as 200, 300, or 400 at a time. Bunches and droves of cattle are bought in the stockyards by weight, which is tested on Fairbank's scales, weighing, as we saw, over 40 bullocks at one time. These were half-bred Colorados, and 42 of them weighed 41,200 lbs.; they would turn out about 56 per cent. of dressed meat. A lot of half-bred Scotch and Colorados were bought to-day at 26½ dollars each, 5*l.* 8*s.* 8*d.* The cross did not seem an advantageous one, it gave no improvement in quality. The quality of the native Colorado beast, fed as he is on the natural herbage, is excellent. It costs over 6*l.* to move a beast from Chicago to Liverpool, and a dealer told us the State ox has been shipped at a loss this year to Liverpool or Glasgow, freights having gone up; but that a profit was made on the transaction in 1878.

Triplets.

Colorado rearing.

Colorado beef.

Freights.

Loss in the English trade.

CHICAGO PRODUCE EXCHANGE, Sept. 22.

Raising wheat, cost of at Chicago.

Mr. Randolph, the secretary to the Chicago Board of Trade, gives the following as the cost of producing a bushel of wheat in the west. The bushel weighs 60 lbs.

	dols.	cents.
Preparing the ground and seeding, per acre	1	65
Seed, 2 bushels	1	50
Harvesting and stacking	2	50
Threshing and cleaning	1	40
Delivery to railway in country	0	50
Rent, say land at 20 dollars, and interest of money 6 per cent.	1	20
Total	8	75

Freight and other charges.

The estimated yield being 12 bushels, gives per bushel 73 cents or 3*s.* 8½*d.*

	c.	s.	d.
The freight for 350 miles to Chicago, per bushel	20	0	10
Chicago charges	2½		
Insurance on transit	1¼	1	1⅞
Freight to Liverpool	24		
Average Liverpool charge, including shortage		0	3⅛
Total per bushel		2	3

Value of wheat.

Which, added to 3*s.* 0½*d.* the cost of the grain on the spot, gives 5*s.* 3½*d.* per bushel or 42*s.* 4*d.* per quarter as the value of American wheat delivered in Liverpool.

Spring wheat No. 2 is worth about 2*s.* a quarter less than English grown wheat of an average quality, but three-quarters of the crop is winter wheat, the value of which at Liverpool is 1*s.* per cental (or 100 lbs.) higher than for spring No. 2; to-day (Sept. 22) the Liverpool quotation per cental for spring No. 2 is 8*s.* 9*d.* to 9*s.* 7*d.*, and for American winter wheat 10*s.*

American spring wheat No. 2 is selling to-day "off coast" (Cork) at from 46*s.* 6*d.* to 47*s.* per 480 lbs.

Yield of grain.

The average yield of wheat in the United States from 1870 to 1877 is returned at 12 bushels per acre; maize, 26 7/10; oats, 27 9/10; rye, 14 9/10; barley, 21¼.

Freights Liverpool

It is said that with better return loads wheat might be carried from New York to Liverpool for 6*d.* a bushel (this does not include Liverpool charges), and that wheat could be shipped from Chicago to New York by waterway at 10 cents per bushel, 4 cents on the lake and 6 cents on the canal.

British weights being 5 centals (500 lbs.) to the quarter against 480 lbs. United States, an addition should be made equal to over 4 per cent. on the estimated value or cost of the latter to bring it within terms understood in England when the British quarter is quoted.

Mr. J. Wentworth's farm.

On Sept. 23 had a drive of 8 or 10 miles through a black flat country to the Hon. John Wentworth's Summit farm, about 9 miles from Chicago. On the road the land seemed wet and stiff, and the grass of poor quality.

The fields on Mr. Wentworth's farm were very large, one of pasture being over 300 acres; the arable field contained upwards of 600 acres. The barn was a famous building well stocked with hay, and there were over 300 tons of hay upon the farm, half of which was in well-made stacks.

The corn too was almost all in stacks, or rather big cocks, but neither hay nor corn was thatched, nor have we seen a yard of thatch since we arrived in the United States.

There was a grand short-horn Duke of Airdrie's bull with wondrous hide, flesh, and substance. The cows were not so good, and the Southdowns were not of first-rate quality or size. But the white Suffolk pigs were indeed beauties, not a bad one in a lot of 100 or more. They were feeding as usual upon Indian corn, and had a long trough filled with common salt.

There was a good orchard of several acres in extent. The arable land did not appear to be particularly well farmed or exceptionally clean, although three men with a waggon and pair were pulling up burdocks from the sides of the road.

The pr[airie]

The first part of the journey from Chicago to St. Paul on Sept. 24, is through a region of "lumber," and it is not until Eau Claire is passed that there is much farming. Some 20 or 30 miles from St. Paul the rolling prairie begins, and the land, a deep sandy loam, seems well tilled, but the straw is burnt on the land in great heaps, and there are no cattle or sheep kept save a few cows. This is the best country we have yet seen for corn growing. The soil is easily ploughed, a two-furrow plough, with a man riding and driving two or three horses, being often used in this locality.

Sept. 25, 1879.

Milling flour.

At Minneapolis the great mills are driven by the waters of the Mississippi, which are diverted by a tunnel above the rapids. The rapids are protected by a wall and apron, the latter entirely spoiling the effects of the falls.

Patent flour.

At Minneapolis we learn that at Niagara mills they say they make out of 260 lbs. of wheat, spring No. 2, 196 lbs. of flour, of which 58 per cent. is patent or Hungarian flour. It is said that at New York it takes 270 lbs. of fall and spring wheat to produce 196 lbs. of flour, of which 49 per cent. is patent flour. Mr. Robinson Greenwood, miller, Blackburn, England, says he is certain this is got out of 266 lbs. The classes of wheat produced by milling are: 1st, patent or Hungarian; 2nd, baker's straights or snowdrops; 3rd, fine sharps, middlings, pollard, bran, and red-dog flour, the commonest flour. In the great per-centage of flour achieved by the Americans, viz., 196 lbs. out of 260 lbs. of wheat, the flour rolled and ground out of the thirds or middlings is included.

Classes of flour and grist.

Value, ferent flour.

Messrs. Hubert, Schute & Co., Minneapolis, say the State Millers' Association buy for all Minneapolis. A bushel of wheat 60 lbs., No. 2 spring, is worth now 92 cents, equal to 30*s.* 8*d.* per 480 lbs. The offals are worth 5 dollars per ton of 2,000; 4¾ bushels of wheat, equal to 285 lbs., gives 196 lbs. flour, 79 lbs. offal, and 10 lbs. waste. Of the flour 40 per cent. is patent, worth 7 dollars per barrel of 196 lbs.; 50 per cent. is baker's flour or snowdrop, worth 5 dollars per barrel, and 10 per cent. is low grade ("red-dog") worth 2 dollars per barrel.

APPENDIX TO JOINT REPORT.

Flour in bags.
Flour is now exported in bags, as they stow better on board ship than barrels, and there is great saving in expense. The bran, worth 5 dollars a ton of 2,000 lbs., is not shipped to England, it goes mainly to eastern States. 200 lbs. of bran is now pressed into a bag, without any wire to bind it, but we could not see any of the compressed bran, as shown us at New York. The freight of bran to Liverpool would be about 8 dollars per ton, so it could be sold at 3*l*. a ton, but it is poor thin bran, nothing but the outer skin of the wheat.

Bran.

ST. PAUL, MINNEAPOLIS, Sept. 25.

Value of land.
Spring and fall wheat.
Farms above St. Paul, between the city and Minneapolis, are worth 200 dollars an acre. Ninety miles south of St. Paul fall wheat ceases and spring wheat begins, the growth of which extends northwards; 100 miles from St. Paul prairie hay is supplied to the farmers at 5*s*. a ton of 2,000 lbs. for their sheep, which require nothing more but water during the winter. The agricultural engine fires are fed with hay.

Hay.

DALRYMPLE'S FARMS, DAKOTA, Sept. 26.

Drought.
In 1879 10 days' rain at the end of June saved the crop, without rain there would have been only 4 bushels an acre. "They called prayers all round wherever there was Christian "faith." Mr. Dalrymple put away 7,000 bushels of wheat for seed. Job hands travel the country with their horses and waggons, camping out on the prairie; they take ploughing and breaking up by piece-work. Wife, children, and poultry travel with them. The nomadic habits of these people are illustrated by a saying, that when the teams are "hitched to," preparatory to shifting the camp, the hens at once lie down on their backs to have their legs tied. Mr. Dalrymple's crops of 1879 are believed to have turned out about 15 3/10 bushels per acre. No ricks are thatched about here. In Mr. Dalrymple's case no stacks even are made, nor is the wheat sometimes shocked. It is picked up and carried to the engine direct from the ground. This is a hazardous practice, and on the whole said to be uneconomical. Pairs of oxen are used to plough in this district.

Job hands and hackney work.

Mules.

Harvest practice.

We had the advantage of meeting Mr. Dalrymple, and he showed us over a large portion of his gigantic farm. With a readiness that is characteristic of the American nation he imparted to us all the information we sought, and answered numerous questions with great courtesy and frankness. His is the biggest grain farm we have heard of even in America, the whole being managed in a singularly admirable manner.

The following is a verbatim report of this interesting conversation, which took place in the train as we journeyed from Fargo to Dalrymple station :—

Dalrymple.
Q. What did your farm cost?—A. The farm consists of 75,000 acres, of which I own half interest; it cost from 40 cents to 500 dollars per acre four years ago. The taxes for school, road, and county purposes amount to 10 cents per acre=364*l*. 11*s*. 8*d*. per annum on the farm. There is no governmental tax. I am general manager, and the system of farming is this: We divide the land into divisions of 5,000 acres with a superintendent over each, who has a division foreman and a gang foreman under him. The superintendent sub-divides his 5,000 acres in divisions of 2,500 acres. The finances are conducted on a regular system of vouchers. All of the supplies are in one store, and are taken out upon a requisition as in the army. The division foreman gives the order. All cash is paid on time checks, and we pay as often as a man wants his money. We are cultivating now 20,000 acres and add 5,000 acres each year.

Q. When do you sow your crops?—A. We commence in April to sow wheat and oats; we only raise oats and barley enough for our own use. It takes about three weeks to put in the crops. For wheat we sow 1 bushel and 20 quarts to the acre, and raise the Scotch Fife variety, which is used in making the new patented-process flour. Our land produces what has been graded as No. 1 hard. The yield runs from 20 to 24 bushels per acre on an average. The wheat is all sown with machines, and it takes 400 head of horses and mules to put in the crop. One seed sower sows 200 acres, and one harrow goes over 100 acres.

Q. How do you prepare new land?—A. We break new land after the crop is in. We commence cutting about August 1st, and use 115 automatic self-binding harvesters (100 W. A. Wood's and 15 M'Cormick's) which bind with wire. The crop is usually cut in 12 days. To thresh we use 21 threshers, and each machine threshes 1,000 bushels per day. It takes a gang of 25 men and 20 horses for each thresher to haul wheat to the machine (for we do not stack) and then to the cars. We thresh and ship 50 cars each day, with an average of 400 bushels per car. An expert on horseback attends to two harvesters when they are at work.

Q. What does your freight cost?—A. We pay freight to market, it costs 15 cents to Duluth, 250 miles, there the elevator's charges for storage, cleaning, and shipping are 1½ cents per bushel. It costs on an average from 10 to 12 cents for freight from Duluth to New York, or 4*s*. per quarter of 480 lbs.

Q. Where do you get your seed?—A. We take the seed from our new land, and generally aim to sell at the conclusion of harvest. The first yield of wheat from new land is usually the best. Our wheat averages a weight of 59 lbs. to the bushel.

Q. What are the class of emigrants to this part of America?—A. Mostly Norwegians, Scandinavians, and Germans.

Q. Are you well supplied with labour?—A. Yes.

Q. Does the new population supply the old?—A. Yes; the new comers get their farms into condition in two or three years, so they help their neighbours.

Q. How do you care for your cattle in this State?—A. We have the herd law; each man takes care of his own stock. He either fences the cattle in or provides a keeper for them.

Q. What is the cost of labour?—A. In the spring months we pay on an average 18 dollars per month and board. During the cutting of the grain 2 dollars 25 cents per day and board. In the threshing season 2·00 dollars per day and board. For fall work, till the ground freezes up, we pay 25 dollars a month and board.

Q. Do you keep men in the winter?—A. Only one man for each forty (40) head of horses, and pay him 30 dollars per month in winter.

Q. Have you been troubled with chinchbugs or grasshoppers?—A. The first year they injured the crop 2 to 3 bushels per acre, but they have not troubled us since, and it seems a historical fact that they make short stays in country cultivated or being rapidly cultivated.

Q. When do you commence breaking new ground?—A. We commence in the middle of May and finish the last of June. We usually plough 3 inches to 4 inches deep. The 1st of July we backset the same ground. The average distance of one man's daily ploughing is 18 miles or about 2½ acres. After we backset, we then harrow and leave the ground till next spring; every four years we sow Timothy and clover to recuperate the land and plough the clover under.

Q. What is the cost of raising wheat?—A. About 11 dollars per acre the first crop, and 8 dollars for the subsequent crops. On an average of 20 bushels to the acre a Yankee can make a fair living. The interest on the capital is about 72 cents per acre, on a basis that the land is worth 12 dollars per acre; the taxes are 10 cents, which would make a total of 82 cents.

Q. Could a man grow wheat at a profit and sell it in New York for a dollar the bushel?—A. Yes, a good living.

Q. What is the cost to open a farm?—A. To put buildings, beams, machinery, and "house" goods on a ploughed wheat farm would cost about 9 dollars per acre, which, added to 3 dollars, the original cost, comes to 12 dollars.

Q. Can you sell wheat in New York for 75 cents per bushel and not lose anything?—A. Yes.

At this point Mr. Drake asked Mr. Dalrymple if it was true, as reported, that he could raise wheat and deliver it at his station for 35 cents per bushel, and Mr. Dalrymple admitted that was pretty near the correct figure. Mr. Drake thereupon made this statement:

Cost of raising wheat in farm, 35 cents
Freight to New York, 28 cents.
Selling commission at 1½ per cent.
Marine insurance at 2 per cent.
Ocean freight, 18 cents.
For contingencies, 12 cents.
And you have the wheat sold off the coast at Cork for 96 cents per bushel.

French stallions.
Mr. N. Whitman, Fargo, bought a Norman stallion for 2,500 dollars; this year he has had 70 mares at 30 dollars each.

Gang plough.
Mr. Whitman, junr., farms 300 acres, of which 170 are broken up. He goes out with his gang-plough and ploughs land for his neighbours. He can do five to six acres a day, and charges from 1½ to 1¾ dollars an acre.

Sulky plough and child.
Mr. Hadwin, near Castleton, has a son 12 years old who began to plough last winter, and now drives a sulky plough with a team of horses, and ploughs 3 acres a day.

Landlord.
Mr. Hadwin Wheatland, County Bruce, Canada, has let his farm in Canada for four years at 20*s*. an acre, with convenants as to sale of straw and hay, and cropping, as in England.

Mr. Hadwin came west three years ago, and bought, near Mr. Dalrymple's farm, 6,000 acres at 3½ to 5 dollars an acre. He broke up 1,000 acres and grew wheat upon it in

AGRICULTURAL INTERESTS COMMISSION:

1878. The yield was 25 bushels per acre; he had 1,300 acres with wheat in 1879, which averaged 20 bushels an acre, and he has now 2,100 acres ready to sow with wheat in 1880.

Mr. Hadwin also bought 640 acres near Fargo at 25 dollars in 1877, and is now offered 50 dollars for it; it is now broken up, but not otherwise improved.

Value of meat, Fargo. At Fargo, Dakota, butchers' beef is worth, 7¾ cents the lb. for the carcase; mutton, 7 cents per lb., by the carcase; pork, 6 dollars to 7 dollars per 100 lbs.; milk, 5 cents per quart, 8d. per gallon English; hams, 10½ cents to 12½ cents per lb.; shoulder pieces 6½ cents to 7 cents per lb.; American bacon, 10 cents per lb.; salt mess pork, 200 lbs. for 12½ dollars, or 52s., or 3¼d. per lb. This has advanced rapidly in value during the last 10 days, so has cheese, partly in sympathy with wheat. *Value of worked oxen.* A pair of large Hereford working oxen are worth at Fargo to-day 20l. *Valley of Red River.* The country along the upper valley of the Mississippi and Red River of the north appears to be either rising or drying up. The water level of lakes within 40 miles of St. Paul has sunk 6 feet in 25 years, and men are living who knew hunters who once canoed over portions of the Red River Valley. This valley is about 350 miles long and from 70 to 100 in width.

Sept. 27.

Warren's Town. *Warren's Town*, between St. Paul and Pembina, consists of one saloon or restaurant and one two-roomed cottage. *Settler.* The owner had built the latter for 12l. or 15l., and had bought a "town lot" of land adjoining, 140 feet by 40 feet, of 40 dollars, 8l. 6s. 8d. Her husband was in Prince Edward's Island waiting to sell his land there. The unmarried daughter had bought 160 acres 3 miles away for 20 dollars, the cost of the deeds. This is State land. *Acquisition of land.* If she plants 10 acres of trees 2 feet apart, and cultivates them for five years, she can acquire another 160 acres for nothing. *Crops.* The daughter said wheat yields 40 bushels per acre here this year, and that the potatoes are grand. In addition to the saloon and cottage there are two elevators, a striking indication of cultivation in the surrounding district. *Character of land Red River Valley.* Below Warren's Town, however, patches of low willow appear in the prairie, with sluys (sloughs) and wet splashes. As we go north the willow predominates, and some scrubby aspen rises out of the willow. *Floods.* There is abundant suggestion of flooded land, and it is admitted that in 1873 the waters were out, but not for long. Ricks are drawn together to the homesteads. A shed is seen covered with *thatch*, lumber being far away at Minneapolis. The railway is very incomplete in construction, and we travel very slowly, but faster than a prairie "schooner," with white cotton tilt, going south, drawn by three mules, with two children, following step by step in the wheel track made on the dusty grass.

Canadian half breeds. The district along the Red River and the Assemboine is mostly occupied by half-breed French Canadians. These men do not take readily to farming, and only cultivate a few acres, and use the rest as a run for cattle and cutting prairie hay. They have mostly a narrow river frontage, which extends back into the prairie for 2 miles or more, being a singularly narrow and unmanageable bit of land.

FORT GARRY OR WINNIPEG, Sept. 28.

Manitoba hoppers. Mr. Wm. Hespeler, Dominion Immigration Agent, Winnipeg, says:—Hoppers come in the autumn and deposit their eggs. No winter kills these, and after hatching next spring and summer, if in numbers, destruction begins. This continues for four or six weeks until the wings develop, when they take flight and go south. The wheat about Portage-la-Prairie is kept in ricks during winter to be sold in the following spring and summer. *Wheat.* Wheat is now 55 cents per bushel for exportation and 65 cents for consumption. The cattle are all wanted for use, for milk, and for breeding for new settlers. *Oxen for draught.* The ploughing is done by oxen. They are the best beasts for "breaking" the new soil by the first settlers, as they keep themselves on the native grasses, and fatten on the native hay. Stall-fed oxen are brought into Winnipeg in the winter from 50 miles distant. *Value of stock.* A pair of really good working oxen is worth 120 dollars to 150 dollars, 24l. to 30l.; cows 25 dollars to 35 dollars, 5l. to 7l. each; *Horses.* horses 250 dollars to 300 dollars, 50l. to 60l. a pair. These are general purpose horses, weighing 1,000 lbs.

Winnipeg to Portage-la-Prairie. Stiff land around Winnepeg, some very wet, but can be easily drained. Not much good farming, and only a small portion of the land under the plough. Nearer to Portage-la-Prairie, a lot of well-farmed land growing good crops of spring wheat and barley. Harvest not ended, nor the cutting and carrying prairie hay. Almost all oxen in the carts good strong cattle; a few sheep, and only middling pigs. 30 to 35 bushels an acre of wheat said to be grown generally this year. Not much autumn ploughing done; most of the land expected to be ploughed before the frost, if not must wait until the spring. Wheat sown in the middle of April, and barley and oats sometimes not sown until June.

MANITOBA, Sept. 29.

Cartage. Hudson's Bay Company pay 1 cent per 100 lbs. per mile for cartage. The carts carry 1,000 lbs., and are constructed without any iron. The draught animals are frequently oxen, in very rude raw leather harness, and the teamsters are "half-breeds" (French and Indian). *Oats.* At Poplar Point, on the Assemboine River, between Winnipeg and Portage-la-Prairie, the oats were some uncut and some in shock. *Wheat.* Wheat has yielded this year 40 bushels per acre; it was sown in the end of April. Mr. Sissons, of Portage-la-Prairie, *Hungarian grass.* grows Hungarian grass. It is a gross feeder, taking much manure. It is sown early in June, and cut in the beginning of September; 3 acres produced him 11 waggon loads. It is a smothering crop. *Average of grain crops.* Mr. Sissons' average of wheat is 35 bushels of 60 lbs. per acre; barley, 35 bushels of 48 lbs.; oats, 65 bushels of 34 lbs. Mr. Sissons cultivates 85 acres out of a lot of 320 acres. *Horses, value of.* He has a pair of mares weighing 1,200 lbs. each, worth 70l. the pair. They plough 4 acres easy in a day with a double-furrow gang plough. The pay of the school-mistress here is 320 dollars, 66l. 13s.

PORTAGE-LA-PRAIRIE, MANITOBA, Sept. 30.

Mackenzie farm. Mr. Kenneth Mackenzie, of Rat Creek, owns 2,400 acres of land, and farms about 400 acres, letting off half of the 400 acres. Some low damp ground will be kept for hay, the rest may be broken up for grain, all but 400 acres of timber land. He says if he had but houses he could let every inch in shares. In "taking in" land the practice is to plough and backset before the fall, harrow down, and sow in the spring; afterwards one ploughing suffices for a crop. *Crops.* He has taken nine grain crops in succession, the first wheat crop being the best and heaviest. *Letting land.* The arrangements with a farm tenant are these: Mr. Mackenzie finds land and half the seed, and pays taxes. Tenant cultivates with his own horses and cattle, and takes one third of the crop of wheat, the crop may be 30 bushels, of which the tenant would have 10 bushels and the landlord 20 bushels. *Taxes.* Mr. Mackenzie pays 20l. a year on the 2,400 acres, and all of this is for school rate, and he thinks the average of all taxes would come to 6 cents per acre of tillage land. *Poor law.* There are no poor laws, and Mr. Mackenzie hopes there never will be any; if they are enacted it will be in the great cities first. *Value of land.* If Mr. Mackenzie could get 20 dollars an acre for the 2,400 acres, he would sell up and go away. He gave one dollar for the land he bought, and he also bought *Soldiers warrants.* soldiers' warrants (carrying 160 acres) at from 45 dollars to 150 dollars. Almost all the produce has been consumed or gone west. *Hoppers locusts.* The hoppers have been troublesome; they hatch at the end of April or beginning of May and remain till about June 30th, when they are winged and take flight. They once cleared off a field of 90 acres of wheat, leaving nothing behind them. If they come again, Mr. Mackenzie would sow no wheat or barley but oats or peas. He grows 4-rowed barley to give to horses. *Birds.* Besides hoppers, blackbirds do mischief to the oats, this was particularly the case in 1871. Below is a statement of Mr. Mackenzie's crops:

Crops and yield.

	Wheat.	Barley.	Oats.
	Bushels.	Bushels.	Bushels.
1871	28	28	50
1872	32	35	55
1873	32	35	55
1874	22	Locusts.	Locusts left no crop.
1875	Locusts.	Not sown.	40 Injured by locusts.
1876	41	45	80
1877	36	45	80
1878	35	43	80

1879 will probably give as good a yield all round as any year.

Potatoes Mr. Mackenzie never had less than 300 bushels to the acre of potatoes; this year (1879) will give, it is thought, 400 bushels, and the plants have not been moulded up. *Ploughi[ng]* An Indian with a pair of horses was at plough, the furrow turned measured 14 inches, and he gets over above two acres a day. The depth was slight for the second crop of wheat. *Shack lo[st]* There was quite four bushels to the acre of "shack" lost on the ground.

Labour. Labour costs 15 dollars a month and board, and in harvest 1¼ dollar or 5s. 3d. a day and board. Three men and the master keep the farm going with a little help in hay time, and six extra hands are required in harvest.

APPENDIX TO JOINT REPORT. 7

Oats without skins.
The oats were in stock having been sown as late as June. Some of them were Bohemian or "hulless," having no skins; they are shy yielders giving about 35 bushels to the acre.

Durham bull calf.
A good Durham thorough-bred bull calf sells for 100 dollars, 20l., the price used to be 150 dollars or 30l.

At Mr. Yeoman's farm the fields are not opened for the reaping machine, but the wheat in the first round is sacrificed to the passage of the implement. The sunflower here grows over 11 feet high, the seed disk is 13 inches across.

Fruits and field garden produce.
Melons of several sorts grew well in the open air. The sorts were the water, nutmeg, pineapple, and Canteloupe. There were also cucumbers, citron gourds for preserving, Spanish rhadish as large as swedes for pickling, French beans, wurtzels, wild filberts, raspberries, strawberries, and grapes, all good for preserving. The wild hops were particularly fine and fragrant, and Mr. Yeoman's brother, a chemist, says of them, "they are stronger for medical pur-

Hops.
"poses than any cultivated hops he had met with."

Barley.
Mr. Sissons, Maple Farm, Portage-la-Prairie, Manitoba, sowed a field of barley in 1873 on June 1st, and harvested it in nine weeks. It grew 50 bushels per acre. He has 100 acres under plough in 1879. Wheat 50 acres, barley 5 acres,

Crops.
oats 31 acres, Hungarian grass 4 acres, potatoes 10 acres, together 100 acres. He works four horses, and being in

Labour.
years, employs one man and his son, pays 15 dollars a month for the year round and his board for the man. He requires one man all the harvest and another for stacking; wages are then one dollar a day for a short time. School tax, 31

Taxes, school and road.
dollars on 480 acres. Assessment based on the capital value and not on the annual value of the land has been one dollar an acre on unimproved land and four dollars on improved land. Road tax on this farm is four days' team

Statute work on road.
work; a man, waggon, and team will count for three dollars. It will take three horses to cultivate 100 acres of land here.

Land good,
Land around Portage-la-Prairie almost all the same character, a deep tender rich loam, light of tillage and yet strong enough to resist drought. All sown in the spring, and all the land, if possible, ploughed first in the "fall."

but not developed.
Small quantity of barley and large extent of oats which yield as much as 100 bushels per acre. A great portion of the land here is held by speculators and companies, and there is quite a rush of farmers' sons to the west to acquire land under the homestead law and the right of preemption to the further quantity of 160 acres. The result is that instead of all the land being developed in this neighbourhood, three fourths will remain as prairie until the far west is settled.

Living rude.
The singular mixture of dirt and discomfort in the dress of the farmers and the house and surroundings, was enough to astonish any one who was assured of the good and affluent position of the owners.

Division of land.
The land is divided into townships of one mile square containing 36 sections. A road two chains (44 yards) wide surrounds the townships, the sections are separated by roads 33 yards wide. The Government in making a railway appropriates every alternate section adjoining the line.

October 1, 1879.

Land inferior.
Our return from Portage-la-Prairie was through the worst portion of the land, as much of it was low and wet, yet capable of being much improved with a little judicious arterial drainage. The land itself although in some places thin did not appear at all heavy, and had all the qualities of a fine alluvial deposit in the wettest spots.

October 2.

Mr. Norquay.
Went with Mr. Norquay, prime minister of Manitoba, a drive through the old Selkirk settlement, crossing the Red River by a ferry, and driving through woodland and scrub to Bird Hill. Below the hill a long stretch of prairie extended to the south, but it did not appear of the dryest and best quality. The hill formed a singular exception to the general character of the land, being composed of fine shingle or gravel, which, scooped out by a steam shovel, was being removed for ballasting the new railway.

Annuity to Indians, effect of.
Mr. Norquay tells us that there the grant of an annuity of five dollars to the Indians (full breed) had demoralised and pauperised them. Accepting it disfranchised the recipient. The best men surrendered the grant and obtained the franchise; while these improved the others retrograded. At Bird Hill Mr. McKintosh has resided for 20 years. The average price he has obtained for salt

Butter.
butter is 25 cents and for fresh 20 cents; the one, of course, being disposed of in winter the other in summer when the supply is abundant. The worth of a newly dropped calf here is three to four dollars; a reared

Value of calf.
calf four months old in the fall fetches 10 dollars or 42s.; a down calving heifer is priced at 30 dollars to 40 dollars (six to eight guineas). Butchers buy the steers at

Meat.
nine cents per lb. of dressed meat and sink the offal; 14 cows make over 130 lbs. of butter and rear their calves;

Crops.
the crop of wheat is 20 bushels, of oats 50 bushels.

One farmer, beyond Bird Hill, has sold 180 acres for

Value of land.
2,200 dollars; if 400 dollars are allowed for buildings and fencing, that would give 10 dollars an acre as the value of the land.

October 3, 1879.

Mennonites.
Mr. Hespeler, the emigration agent of Winnipeg, kindly drove us to the Russian Memnonite settlement. These Russian settlers have not selected the best spot in the Dominion, it is low and swampy. In consequence of the wet spring and summer this year the yield of wheat has varied from 8 to 12 bushels per acre, and all the corn crops, by the poor weak stubble, show a small yield.

Their buildings.
These poor people have built capital houses and barns, infinitely superior to the other settlers. The houses and sheds are all covered with thatch; some appearing to be all roof, thatched down to the ground. Cattle seem numerous and fairly good, but there are only a few sheep and horses, the work being mainly done by oxen. The settlers have taken up 120,000 acres, but only a very small portion of this is tilled. They seem to burn some of the straw, and devote a portion of it to mending the roads; they are an industrious, quiet, and frugal people; they

Their church.
are building churches, and over one is a loft for the storage of grain, against years of scarcity. There seems some reason for this precaution, as they experienced two attacks of locusts in the first years of their settlement, which did not begin before 1874. All the land to Niverville station is more or less wet, but there are some few patches of high prairie which are ploughed. It seems

Land grants.
questionable how the new land grants to railroads will work, and with a charge of 6 dollars an acre for a five-mile belt next the line, it is not likely soon to be all sold and settled.

Elevator.
Mr. Hespelers' elevator by the railway side at Niverville holds 35,000 bushels. It cost 800l. complete with the

Charges.
proper machinery. Mr. Hespeler charges 5 cents per bushel or 1s. 8d. per quarter of 400 pounds for buying, storing to May 1st, and delivery from elevators into cars. He buys for a firm in Ontario who pays this charge. There is a Glasgow house who mill at Galt, and sell their flour direct in England. This elevator is a circular one, and was put up by four carpenters complete in eight weeks, striking their own circles. Mr. Hespeler expects to receive 600

Wheat.
dollars this season for its use. He says that wheat grown in this neighbourhood is stronger, takes more water than that grown on stale land, and the wheat grown on old

Loans and interest.
land in Ontario is of less value. Mr. Hespeler advances money at 10 per cent on the Minnesota grain crop.

MINNESOTA, Oct. 6.

Game laws.
The game laws in Minnesota are severe, but refer more perhaps to a close time for breeding than to the offence of trespass. There is a close time for woodcocks, prairie chickens, grouse, quail, and partridge and pheasants, also for elk and buck, and for river and lake fish. Breach of these laws are accompanied by loss of guns and dogs, and all hunting or fishing gear found with the offender. The valley of the

Hay.
Minnesota was dotted with large hay cocks awaiting frost for removal.

For 10 miles above St. Paul the land is valued at 25 dollars to 35 dollars, six to seven guineas the acre. The hay crop

Value of hay.
which is mowed by hand comes to from 2 to 2½ tons (of 2,000 lbs.) an acre, and is worth, when delivered in St. Paul, 25 dollars or five guineas a ton. Much of it goes to the lumber region. Summer fed cattle go south to

Cattle.
Ontario for winter feeding on corn, and thence to Chicago for killing. Eggs in the Minnesota valley are 10 cents a

Eggs.
doz., they are packed in square millboard partitions in layers of three dozen, separated by a square sheet or tray of millboard; the collectors send them east.

ST. PETERS, 80 miles south of St. Paul, Oct. 6th.

A farm. Yield.
A farm in the vicinity of St. Peters which we visited is worth 35 dollars to 50 dollars an acre, yielding per acre 15 bushel of wheat, 40 to 50 bushel of corn, 60 bushel of oats

Rent-shares.
Labour.
Money rent.
Taxes.
School rate.
Assessment.
Value of land.
Milling.

(of 9 stones a sack). Land is let here on shares. The landlord finds all land, half the seed, and half the threshing, and takes half the grain. Labour is paid a dollar a day. In the case of a farm of 50 acres, 15 acres arable and 35 acres pasture, the arable let at 3 dollars or 12s. 6d. an acre, and the pasture at one dollar an acre. The taxes amount to from 18 dollars to 20 dollars on the lot, or about 1s. 7d. per acre. The school rate presses heavily. The assessment is an annual one, bringing improvements into charge. Fifty-eight acres of cultivated land with a house sold three years ago for 3,000 dollars.

At Mankato a splendid flouring mill is just started, with modern improvements of the best description. The processes in the manufacture of flour are the same as those carried out at Minneapolis. The Mankato Milling Company manufacture, under the superintendence of Mr. Wm. Pearson, the choicest family and baker's flour. That gentleman has been good enough to give us the following particulars, as well as to promise further information, which reached us at Council Bluffs.

MANKATO, MINNESOTA, October 6, 1879.

A bushel of wheat in the United States weighs 60 lbs. A ton is 2,000 lbs. About 4¾ bushels of No. 2 spring wheat will make a barrel of flour of 196 lbs., 4¾ bushels will weigh therefore 285 lbs. In manufacture this 285 lbs. is accounted for as below :—

	lbs.
Dirt and waste	12
Evaporation, about 3%	8
A. Bran, about 9 lb. per bushel	43 } =87
B. Finished middlings } 4lb. to 5lb. per bushel, say	24
C. Shorts	
D. Patent flour, 35% of barrel of 196 lbs., say	69
E. Straight or bakers' flour, 58% of barrel of 196 lbs., say	113 } =198
F. Red-dog, 7% of barrel of 196 lbs., say	14
Unaccounted for	2
Total	285

Processes in milling :—
  a. The wheat is cleaned.
  b. Warmed or sweated by passing through steam-heated cylinders.
  c. Rolled or crushed.
  d. Silked or wired to take out *germs* which are added to the "*finished*" middlings or offal.
  e. Ground. The bran A. is then stripped off, passed through porcelain rollers to free it from flour, which goes into baker's flour E.
  f. The flour is bolted and a separation effected between the flour E. and the "middlings."
  g. The middlings are next dusted for flour, which is also added to E.
  h. The middlings are next graded on silks of different numbers (fine and coarse) so as to enable the use of different silks in the "purifiers" (10 in number). The purifiers give off *finished* middlings and *cleaned* middlings.
  i. The *cleaned* middlings are rolled in porcelain rollers or re-ground and re-silked, the products are patent flour D. and red-dog F.
  j. The finished middlings (offals) are graded into finished middlings B. and shorts C.

The mild climate and weather affect milling; these are more favourable in the west than in the east of United States.

dollars
Bran A. is worth, on the spot, 5 per ton (of 2,000 lbs.)
Finished middlings B.   „   12   „   „
Shorts C.   „   7   „   „

Some millers re-grind the bran from the rollers, and take out a lower grade of flour.

N.B.—Absolute *rigidity* in fixing is sought for in erecting machinery for patent flour. The mills here are bedded on the *solid rock*, and power distributed almost entirely by *belts*, thus avoiding the jar of cogged wheels.

The number of times middlings and cleaned middlings are passed through purifiers varies in different mills, and depends also on considerations of value of the different products B. C. D. and E.

Some "germs" still remain in the flour after process "d." These are got out in process "i." Flour D. and E. are supposed to be entirely freed from "germs."

MANKATO, MINNESOTA, October 13, 1879.
DEAR SIR,
Your favour was duly received, but owing to press of business our Mr. Pearson was unable to give me the desired information until this morning.

1. Price of No. 2 spring wheat 92 dols. per bushel here.
2. Price of patent flour in New York 7 50 dols. to 8 50 dols.
3. Price of straight „ „ 6 0 dols. to 6 50 dols.
4. Price of red-dog „ „ 4 50 dols. to 5 50 dols.

Of the 24 lbs. of offal you speak of 8 lbs. are finished middlings and 16 lbs. shorts.

Trusting this will reach you in due time,
  We remain,
  Very truly yours,
  MANKATO MILL Co.
Albert Pell, Esq.,
  Council Bluffs.

In Mr. Hubbard's oil cake mill at Mankato, a bushel of linseed, weighing 56 lbs., makes 40 lbs. of cake, 15 oil and 1 lb. loss. The price of oil cake at the mill is 4 guineas per ton, and of linseed 4s. per bushel; the crop varies from 8 to 20 bushels.

General Baker of Mankato thinks the cost of producing a bushel of wheat is from 40 cents to 45 cents, plus the value of the land. This is from the soil to the granary on the farm. The cost is diminishing; competition for water carriage will reduce the present rate, which is 36 cents, or 1s. 6d., or 12s. a quarter of 400 lbs. from Mankato to New York. The value of wheat, spring No. 2, at Mankato being 85 cents per bushel, the value of the quarter on the spot would be 28s. 4d.

The Federal Government improved the waterways.

The State Governments have power to control railway rates in the case of exhorbitant charges, either for goods or passengers. "Charters" for building railways are granted by the Government of the different States through which the railways pass; but in the territories a license has to be obtained from the Federal Government.

The average yield of wheat this year at Mankato is 12 bushels.

Eggs at Mankato 3 cents to 10 cents per dozen. Hotel joints of beef and mutton 6 cents to 7 cents. Fowls, 6s. 3d. a dozen. Milk, 4 cents or 2d. per quart.

MR. HUBBARD'S statement of the cost of producing wheat is this :—

	Dols.	Cents.
Ploughing an acre once	1	25
Seed, 1¾ bushel, at 1 dol.	1	75
Sowing with seeder, at 10 cents a day, with two horses and man at 2½ dols., per acre	0	25
Harrowing 7½ acres twice over, one man and two horses at 2½ dols., per acre	0	34
(A third harrowing would pay)	0	0
To run a combined automaton harvester will, for horses and men, 4 dols. and 10 cents a day, cost per acre	0	40
For the use of the machine, per acre	1	
For wear	0	38
Shocking, highly paid and skilled labour at 3 dols. a day, per acre	0	35
Stacking, unskilled and low-priced labour, 1½ dols. a day, per acre	0	60
Threshing (machine and three men), 5 cents per bushel, do. potatoes, mowing machine carting grain to granary, 5 cents per bushel, will yield 15 bushels per acre, costs the two per acre	1	50
Rent of land of a quality to produce 15 bushels per acre continuously worth 20 dols. an acre at 8 per cent. on the value, per acre	1	60
Taxes, per acre	0	15
Herding or keeping up fences, per acre	0	15
Carting to station	0	45
Total cost per acre	10	17

Cost of production of wheat.
Freights.
Price of wheat on the spot.
Railway building.
Yield of wheat.
Prices of food.
Cost of producing an acre of wheat in Minnesota.

With a yield of 15 bushels per acre, the cost per bushel would thus be 68 cents, or 22*s.* 8*d.* a quarter of 480 lbs. Mr. Barden of Bingham, Lake Minnesota, estimates the cost of producing an acre of wheat at 10 dols. without herding.

Beer duty. Mr. William Bierbauer, of the Brewery, Mankato, Minnesota, informed us that the beer tax was 1 dollar per barrel of 31 gallons, and that he brews $2\frac{1}{3}$ bushels of malt to the barrel. He also pays a brewer's license, which is, for 500 barrels and over, 100 dollars, if less, 50 dollars. No tax is paid until the beer is sold and leaves the premises; and then the stamp is placed over the spigot. The excise officers come occasionally and visit the brewery, but never interfere with any process, or take any notice of the malt; any farmer may malt if he pleases, and feed his cattle with malt, and any person may brew without paying any tax if he does not sell the beer he produces.

Minnesota, Oct. 7.

Locusts. Farms. Crops. A branch of the St. Paul and Sioux City railway crosses the Wattenwan River. Ours is the first passenger car that has run over it. Within the last five years locusts have twice destroyed the crops. The farmhouses are built of brick; straw is used as it used to be in our fens for shedding and shelter. Cattle are seen, and good Toulouse geese. **Corn and wheat.** Maize and mixed cropping appear, also patches of the Chinese amber cane; there is no "fall" wheat. We cross the Blue Earth River at Vernon; the homesteads remind one of the fens; some land is dunged! Much of the ploughing for winter is completed, and there is a greater breadth of "corn" than of wheat. The fences are of three "barbed" wires on locust posts 20 feet apart, costing $2\frac{40}{100}$ dollars per chains of 22 yards. The homesteads are sheltered with screens of cultivated trees, chiefly the Turin poplar. **Value of land.** The land is rolling prairie, worth from 7 dollars to 8 dollars an acre to take in. There are very few "sluys," but plenty of lakes.

Wheat yield. At Mountain Lake the yield this year is only 5 bushels an acre, the best was 29 bushels two years ago all over one farm; there is more wheat planted just now than ever.

Mr. Barden's farm. Mr. R. Barden, of Barden Barden, Bingham Lake, Minnesota, owns and occupies a stock and grain farm of 2,140 acres or $3\frac{1}{2}$ sections of land, of which 1,400 acres are in cultivation carrying 500 head of horned stock and horses. There have been two years of drought, and the yield has proved 20 bushels, 12 bushels, and 12 bushels, giving an average of 15 bushels an acre on the three years. **Labour.** The staff of men consists of from 8 to 10 men engaged for eight months, and five regular hands kept through the winter. The pay for the men for the eight months is from 16 dollars to 17 dollars a month and board, and 12 dollars a month and board for the five winter hands; wages are a little higher than formerly. **Hackney work, ploughing.** During a month's sowing five to eight teams are hired at 2 dollars to $2\frac{1}{4}$ dollars a day, or 9*s.*, to include a pair of horses with implements and one man. They will plough $2\frac{1}{4}$ acres a day or harrow 14 acres once over. Mr. Barden gave this autumn $1\frac{1}{2}$ dollars an acre at the busy season for ploughing; this was done with a "sulky" plough and pair, and they move $2\frac{1}{4}$ acres a day, while three horses will clear 3 acres.

Drilling. Yield. The sower or seed distributor puts in from 10 acres to 12 acres a day. Mr. Barden says, no man ever raised 40 bushels of spring wheat in the acre, 30 bushels is an enormous crop, and 18 bushels is a *good* average. **Rotation of crops.** He intends to manure all his land and to cultivate in rotation, the course intended being clover (sown with the wheat), wheat, corn, wheat, clover, wheat, corn, &c. The clover will be grazed.

Prairie keep. Mr. Barden pays only 1 cent per acre for excellent prairie keep, hiring 640 acres of railway sectional land at this rate. He is at liberty to mow and remove the hay.

Fencing. Any unallotted land may be grazed by *any one*, but all cattle must be *herded* in Minnesota. There are consequently no corn lands inclosed; in other States where there are no herd laws, corn growers must fence in their lands.

Prairie, near Windom, Minnesota, Oct. 8.

Messrs. Thompson and Kendall's farm. On Messrs. Thompson (of St. Paul) & Kendall's farm, near Windom, flax is sown on the first break of the prairie land. **Flax and linseed on first break.** It is ploughed once in the spring, and the seed is sown broadcast and harrowed in. **Value of land.** The land is worth from 4 dollars to 7 dollars, and the crop of linseed this year has proved 7 bushels, worth about 4*s.* 2*d.*, or one dollar a bushel. **Buckwheat.** Buckwheat is also sown in the same way, but was spoilt this year by frost. This grain is used largely for cakes as soon as winter sets in. It is to be found on every breakfast table. **Competent ploughman.** One man, without any assistance, was working two sulky ploughs, each with a team of three horses, turning over the flax stubble. The furrows were about a mile long. Starting one plough in the furrow, he mounted the others, and followed it up closely with his team, dismounting at the end to turn the leading plough on the headland into the return furrow.

Moveable granaries. There are moveable granaries on this farm 16 ft. by 16 ft. by 10 ft. high. They go on runners, and cost 50 dollars or 10 guineas each.

Tenant farmers. Mr. Kendall lets off 152 acres of land. He furnishes the land ready ploughed and the seed, and takes half the crop, delivered into his moveable granary. The tenant leaves the land ploughed at the end of the term of five years, and is bound to plant half the land in wheat. The house, buildings, granaries, and stables, worth 400 dollars or 82*l.*, go with the land. **Yield of wheat and oats.** The yield this year was 1,165 bushels by measurement of wheat off 111 acres, about $10\frac{1}{2}$ bushels to the acre, and 41 acres of oats gave by measurement $3,136\frac{1}{2}$ bushels, or over 76 bushels an acre. The St. Paul harvester and self-cord binder now ties the sheaves with string instead of wire.

Blight. Noxious insects. Blight comes in July; hoppers from July to September. The "chinch bug" damaged the wheat in 1878 seriously in Houston county, Minnesota.

Breaking up. Of the 23,000 acres of which this farm consists, commencing in May 1876, 6,000 acres have been already broken up. The first crops were gathered in 1877.

A farm of Mr. Moore. Mr. Moore, of Springfield, near Windom, Minnesota, was two years in the United States Navy, and obtained a grant of 160 acres by occupation. Of this he has in wheat 30 acres, in oats 30 acres, in corn 10 acres, in oats 20 acres, and in barley 30 acres. He occasionally sows Timothy grass and clover. **Yield.** His best crop of wheat was in 1877, when he had 32 bushels, and his worst in 1879, when he had but 5 bushels an acre. He considers 15 bushels a fair average. **Weight of wheat.** He sows spring, and has never tried "fall" wheat. The natural weight of his wheat is 56 lbs. to 57 lbs. the bushel; a quarter would thus fall short about 50 lbs. of the weight of an English quarter. There is no appearance yet of deteriorations of the soil. A cross of oats or corn cleans the land, and he means to try rotation. **Locusts.** Locusts were worst in 1875.

Maize cultivation. Corn is sown from April 10th to April 20th, with "planters," a sort of dibble delivering the seed into the ground, wheat is ploughed in the spring, and repeatedly harrowed. A man will set with a planter 5 acres in the day, the seeds being 4 ft. by 3 ft. apart, and the quantity sown half a peck. The land is then harrowed again, and corn harrowed. When the corn is up it is harrowed again. This destroys infant weeds. It is then "cultivated" in both directions two or three times with a pair of horses, which "overtakes" 6 acres to 7 acres daily. **Gathering.** A man picks about an acre, giving 50 bushels of cobs, in a day. For fodder, maize is not sown till June. If the maize stubble is really clean, wheat is sown on it without any ploughing. Mr. Moore's out crop runs from 32 bushels to 60 bushels, average 45 bushels. The barley will average 30 bushels, though he has grown 35 bushels. His stock consisted of—

2 in foal mares, worth	200	dollars.
1 yearling	50	„
3 cows	60	„
12 young stock	76	„
1 plough	16	„
1 set of harrows	6	„
1 broad caster	75	„
1 cultivator	8	„
1 heavy waggon	80	„
1 light do.	35	„
1 reaper and mower combined	210	„

Mr. Moore works all the land himself, with the help of two men in hay and harvest time. He purposes foddering his straw and manuring his land. The implements were left out in the weather, not even a few forksful of straw being spread over the more costly implements.

Winds. High winds in the spring are said to blow the soil and seed corn to the devil. **Hauling.** Hauling by horse teams for 40 miles is done at 15 cents per ton per mile.

Weeds. The weeds are "morning glory" (*convolvulus major*), bird weed, wild buckwheat, cockle, pigeon grass, sunflower, or rosin weed, trundle weed, tickle weed, fathen. The cottonwood tree grows to a large size, and rapidly planted like oziers in slips.

Sheep. Sheep are wintered in yards on hay and bran at 4 dollars a ton.

Messrs. Horace Thompson and E. T. Warner of St. Paul work a large farm near Luverne, Minnesota. On Oct. 10th there were 46 ploughs going and 70 men at work. There were 96 horses and mules for draught and 150 pigs for stock; of cattle and sheep there were none. The prairie is broken in June, and sown with corn dropped by the ploughman from his seat, the yield now is 15 bushels to 20 bushels of shelled corn the acre. The land after the corn is off is backset and sown with wheat in the following spring. A second crop of wheat follows, and then comes clover for four years, which in 1880 will be fed off with hogs (swine).

Messrs. Thompson and Warner's farm.
Breaking Maize.
Clover and hops.
Dung.

Dung is an encumbrance and nuisance, and Mr. Thompson would give 50 dollars to have it cleared away.

Navy beans.

Navy beans are also sown in the first week of June on the first break of the land in the same fashion as the maize. They are pulled about the middle of September, yielding 3 to 5 bushels, worth 1¼ dollars per bushel of 60 lbs.

Ploughs.

The ploughs, all single furrow, each drawn by three mules turning 3 acres a day, are "Casaday's," of South Bend, Indiana, costing 65 dollars, or nearly 13 guineas.

Labour.

The men rise at 4.30, breakfast at 5.30, turn their teams out at 6, work till 12, when they bait in the field, resting till 1.30, and then resume work till dark, about 6 or 7 p.m. The wages are 18 dollars a month and food (costing 25 cents a day, fried pork, potatoes, tea or coffee, and milk) from April 1st to Nov. 15th, or the close of the season.

Mules.

Mules are preferred to horses, especially during hot weather; they are bought in Missouri, costing on an average 150 dollars or 31*l.*, and weighing 1,000 lbs. to 1,300 lbs. Their feed is a mixture, consisting of two-thirds oats and one-third corn. They are turned out into yards in the winter. An active horse 5 years old, weighing 1,400 lbs., is worth from 200 dollars to 250 dollars (40*l.* to 50*l.*). A pair of mules each weighing 1,200 lbs. to 1,300 lbs. is worth 250 dollars to 300 dollars (50*l.* to 60*l.*). A good ox team 120 dollars to 125 dollars (24*l.* to 25*l.*). The hire of a working horse for farm purposes is 50 cents or 2*s.* 1*d.* a day. The reaper used is the "St. Paul corn-binding reaper" which costs 320 dollars or 66*l.* 13*s.* delivered at the railway depôt. If the land is clean and has been well cultivated wheat is sown after corn without ploughing. An iron rail 28 feet long with a shoe at each end is drawn by two horses across the rows of corn stalks; this breaks them down, after which they are horse-raked together and burnt.

Horses.
Ox teams.
Hire of horse.
Wheat after corn.

Mr. Thompson's wheat ranged this year in yield from 3 bushels to 15 bushels an acre, and his corn about 40 bushels.

Yield in middle States.

Mr. J. H. Drake, of St. Paul, says that the eight middle States have not averaged more than from 8 bushels to 12 bushels of wheat per acre in the last 15 years on land worth from 40 dollars to 100 dollars per acre. In the west, the sunstroke of three hot days in July in 1878, and the drought of the spring of 1879, injured the yield of wheat. In 1877 there was snow, and the middle States grew 20 bushels to 30 bushels. 1878 was another good year, and 1879 the best of all; therefore there will be a very large acreage of winter wheat in 1880.

Drought.

Sheep.

At Worthington fair, Oct. 11th, we hear that in Nobles county, Minnesota, in 1877 there were about 2,000 sheep clipped; in 1879 about 8,000, these were fine Merinos and Cotswolds. Manufacturers recommend this cross for combing wools for producing the finest goods. Wool in 1877 was 25 cents to 30 cents the lb.; in 1878 the same, and in 1879 the same, but firmer. The tups are put to in the middle of December for the lambs to fall in the middle of May. The ewe clips 4 lbs., and the hogget not much more. Shearing time is July 1st. The wether sheep kept till four years old will weigh from 100 lbs. to 150 lbs., worth 2½ cents to 3 cents per lb. live weight. The sheep are gathered into yards for the winter in the first week of October and turned out at the end of April, getting nothing but hay during the time they are up.

ve stock.

Twenty miles north of Sioux City, Minnesota, hogs are penned and cattle are in yards. Horses and cattle are also seen in herds or droves feeding in the "corn" fields.

Wheat.

Since 1876 a larger area of wheat has been sown in the middle States, and the yield has improved up to 45 bushels an acre. The yield of wheat during the same period has dropped in the west.

Freights.

Railway freights are ultimately (if excessive) subject to the control of the States Government. This has been decided on an appeal to the Supreme (Federal) Court. Railway rates have varied but little during seven years, and it does not seem probable that they will vary. They rise as winter closes the navigation, and run down when warmer weather permits it to open. In the summer of 1879, Mr. J. C. Evans of Council Bluffs says, grain was carried for 10 cents per 100 lbs. from Chicago to New York, over a distance little less than 1,000 miles, the usual winter rate being 35 cents to 45 cents.

From Council Bluffs to Chicago, about 500 miles, the rate for transport of grain, which passes as 4th class, is 25 cents per 100 lbs. of corn and 30 cents per 100 lbs. of wheat.

Flour goes at the same rate as grain, 100 barrels to the car, the barrel weighing 200 lbs. gross. A sack of flour is 100 lbs. gross, that is to say, half a barrel.

Mr. J. F. Evans of Council Bluffs is "sorely afflicted" with tenants. They convert his fences into house fuel, destroy his house and buildings, and do not half farm his land. The rent he takes is a fixed one of 20 bushels of corn delivered into the landlord's cribs in the city within about 2 miles of the farm. Eighteen miles away his farms are rented at 13 bushels of corn in the cribs on the farm. Mr. Evans lets off 300 acres of land on these terms. The average price of corn for 10 years at Council Bluffs has been 40 cents per bushel. A bushel of shelled corn is 56 lbs., of unshelled 76 lbs.

Tenants.
Rent.
Value of maize.

We passed over the land of a gentleman who has been the owner of 300 acres or 400 acres for 25 years, during which period he has neither let or cultivated the estate. His residence is 2,000 miles away (at Vicksburg), and he patiently waits for the inevitable rise in the value to avail himself of its "natural increment" before selling. He acquired his estate of Government at 1¼ dollars an acre, and has paid taxes since he entered into possession. He is a banker.

Absentee landlord.

The farm of Mr. Orr of Hunden Dale, Council Bluffs, consists of 480 acres, 280 acres of which are cultivated and 200 acres are open. He feeds about 110 oxen in winter on corn and hay, beginning with cobs and finishing off with shelled corn. His stores are younger than they used to be. His fat cattle last year (1878) were sold at 5¼ cents (live weight) per lb. to go to Liverpool. They would weight about 1,460 lbs. at New York, and would lose about 70 lbs. a beast on the journey between Council Bluffs and that port. Their worth on the spot, weighing about 120 stone dead weight (of 8 lb. per stone), would have been somewhere near 16*l.* a beast.

Farms, Mr. Orr's.
Feeding oxen.
Age of oxen.
Weight.
Value.

The stock now in Mr. Orr's yard average three years old, and weigh about 1,200 lbs. lean; they are well bred graziers' beasts. They will put on from 225 lbs. to 250 lbs. of flesh in the winter, eating corn which has of late years been selling at 15 cents per bushel of 50 lbs., and costs from 12½ cents to 15 cents to raise. The value of the corn is doubled when converted into meat. Wheat does worse as a staple crop than in former years; it is giving place to corn. The growth of permanent seeds succeeds on this farm. The plant sown with the wheat in April looked thick and well established; while some sown in September with the rye was coming up strongly. The Kentucky blue grass forms the main growth in some of the pasture land.

Value of corn to feed
Corn and wheat.
Seeds.
Kentucky blue grass.

The railway cars coming into the depôt at Council Bluffs carry 20 to 22 large oxen. The Oregon cattle are of a larger size than those from Colorado, and answer to our large Irish cattle. They are worth in Council Bluffs 7*l.* a head, having travelled over 2,000 miles to this spot, 1,500 miles of the distance on foot, starting south in April. Great losses are incurred on the journey from poisonous weeds. One drover lost 1,400 from this cause in 24 hours, another 700.

Oregon cattle at Council Bluffs.

The railroad freight is 85 dollars a car to carry 20 to 22 oxen from Cheyenne to Council Bluffs. This puts nearly 17*s.* ahead on the value of the animal. They have been sold at Cheyenne for 28 dollars or 5*l.* 15*s.*, and bought in Oregon at from 20 dollars to 25 dollars, or four to five guineas. They are turned out once on the trip from Cheyenne for food and water. The food allowed is 50 lbs. at one cent per lb., or 2*s.* 1*d.* per bullock; 50 lbs. more is allowed at Council Bluffs, when 25 cents is charged in addition for lairage.* Twenty-five cars containing 500 oxen were unloaded in half-an-hour. Two men will bring a train of 400 or 500 cattle by rail. The stamp of cattle in Oregon has not changed for better or worse, but the old cattle are getting scarcer, and the price is rising from competition. A bunch of 100 of these oxen weighing about 1,170 lbs. each were sold at 3½ cents live weight, coming to 7*l.* 12*s.* each at Council Bluffs.

Oregon cattle.
Value.
Railway trip.
Aged cattle scarcer.

AT CHEYENNE, Oct. 15.

Leaving intense heat and the moquitos behind us on the Missouri, by slow degrees we reached an altitude of 6,000 feet, and before reaching Cheyenne met a storm of thunder, wind, and snow, violent beyond measure, which delayed

Snow storms.

---
* See p. 14.

APPENDIX TO JOINT REPORT.

Lost cattle.

the train and made movement out of doors painful and laborious. The hotel at the railway depôt is crowded with ranch men and their people, all weather bound. It is now freezing hard and the snow is drifting over the plains. 500 oxen coming down to the depôt for shipment have stampeded, drifting, heaven knows where, before the storm. They will be hard to recover. After facing the storm with Mr. Evans for half a mile to see a freight train of cattle loaded, we return to the hotel smothered in snow.

Cattle, the Texan's drive.

Mr. Sturgis remembers the first "drive" of Texan cattle, it was in 1867, and amounted to 750,000 head. It was as many the next year, but has dwindled down since that time to the present amount of 200,000.

The drive is distributed in this way. The young steers for feeding to Colorado, Wyoming, Nebraska, Missouri, Iowa, and Illinois. The heifers are placed in Colorado, Wyoming, Nebraska, and Kansas. The meaty beasts are shipped for Denison or Texas, or for Chicago or St. Louis for "canning," or killed for butchers' use in the local markets. Some Texans are killed and "canned" at Galveston, some are driven into Louisiana and so go on to New Orleans for consumption.

Cheyenne prairies.

The district in which Cheyenne is situated was formerly described as the Great American Desert. Its sparse covering of scorched grasses justifies that description. Cattle, however, get fat on the native keep. The grass springs up in the early part of the summer, and dries up brown in August before it has seeded. The saccharine matter is thus preserved which would be otherwise lost if touched by the frost while green. These grasses would be in danger of destruction if sheep were introduced. The heart of the grasses would be eaten out in spring, there would be no renewal from seed, and permanent mischief would ensue. The most luxuriant places would be turned into plain gravel beds, where the grasses will not grow again unless irrigated. The value of wool, equal to 6s. a sheep, is, however, tempting, and sheep breeding is increasing in Texas, though no mutton is exported, the object being Merino wool.

Grasses.

Sheep injurious to grass.

Sheep in Texas.

Texan cattle decrease.

The number of cattle in North and East Texas has noticeably *decreased*, giving place to corn and cotton. The total export of Texans may be as large as ever though the "drive" has diminished. During the last five years prices of every class of cattle have shrunk from 25 to 33 per cent. at Chicago. In 1875 matured Texans at Chicago made 4 cents per lb. on the live weight, in 1879 they make but 2¾ cents per lb. This drop in value has extended as well to "graded" Americans, those which fetched in 1875 4½ cents to 5 cents are now selling at 3½ cents per lb. Last year, 1878, the United States shipped 76,000 live oxen to England, but this is equal to 6 per cent only of the number handled at Chicago.

Drop in value.

The following is a rough estimate of the different herds of cattle around Cheyenne kindly furnished by Mr. Wm. Evans, who has a herd of 7,000 head of cattle :—

Herds round Cheyenne.

	Head of cattle.
Iliff Estate	35,000
The Swan Brothers	25,000
Judge Carey	21,000
Creighton	20,000
Sturgiss and Co.	20,000
N. R. Davies and Co. (8,000 old and 12,000 new this year)	20,000
C. Wright	14,000
Irwin	8,000
Kelline	8,000
Kelly	10,000
Platt and Farris	10,000
Durban Brothers	3,000
Dater Brothers	3,000
Whitcomb and Co.	12,000
Frewen Brothers	6,000
Sparks	4,000
Vantessel	4,000
Col. Babbitt	4,000
Converse	4,000
Brasison	4,000
Nagle	4,000
Philips	3,000
Reel	3,000
Arnold	2,500

Smaller owners from 1,000 to 300.

All these in the Wyoming territory, 100 miles square around Cheyenne.

Flocks.

The following is a list of the principal flocks in this locality :—

	Sheep.
Hay and Thomas	8,000
Post	20,000
Warren	10,000
Chadwick	10,000
Hubbard	15,000

and sundry others from 400 to 1,000 sheep.

Value of the cattle would average 20 dollars per head and sheep 2 dollars.

Cost of shipping cattle from Cheyenne to Chicago is 7½ dollars, which includes freight, feed, attendance, and commission.

Value of stock on ranches.

Value of cows (on the ranch, dry and fat) 17 dollars to 22 dollars; steers from 25 dollars to 35 dollars at 3½ years old. Cost of raising a bullock, including all expenses and losses, 10 dollars. About 20 per cent. of fat cattle sold would be cows; a herd of 10,000 head should produce yearly 1,500 to 2,000 fat stock. One bull is kept to 25 cows.

Winter grazing.

The want of capital among American agriculturists is keenly felt, but in no operation of farming is it so manifest as in winter grazing cattle. But the capitalist comes to the rescue, and frequently furnishes the store stock, and pays the farmer 6 cents per lb. for the increased live weight of the bullock. Suppose the average live weight of the store animal to be 1,100 lbs., by six months' good feeding, which is considered to be half a bushel of maize per day (28 lbs.), the ox would consume 90 bushels, and should in that time, if the best bred bullocks are grazed under favourable circumstances, produce as much as 350 lbs. increased live weight, or about 2 lbs. per day. The grazier would therefore receive for the increased value of the bullock (350 lbs. at 6 cents) 21 dollars. But he might also make 350 lbs. of pork by keeping two pigs to each bullock; this at 3 cents per lb. is 10½ dollars; that added to the 21 dollars for the beef would give him 31½ dollars for his 90 bushels of maize, or 35 cents per bushel, which would be about twice the market value of the corn.

Two hogs to one bullock

Profit to capitalist.

The account of the capitalist who furnished the store cattle would stand thus: Supposing he could sell the fat ox at 5 cents per lb., his 1,450 lbs. of live meat would be 70 dollars. The cost of the store bullock and the 21 dollars paid to the grazier would be 56 dollars 75 cents, and thus leave him a profit of 13 dollars 25 cents upon each bullock. This great difference in the value per lb. of store and fat animals is explained thus: A good meaty steer weighing 1,100 lbs. would, if killed, only yield, at 50 per cent. of his live weight, 550 lbs. of dressed meat, but the same bullock when really fat and weighing 1,450 lbs. alive, would furnish, at 60 per cent., 876 lbs. of beef; so that the increased live weight of 350 lbs. would actually produce 326 lbs. of dressed meat.

Profit to farmer grazing his own stock.

If the corn grower bought the bullocks himself, interest on the cost for six months at 10 per cent. would be 1 dollar 77 cents; deduct that from 13 dollars 25 cents and that leaves 11 dollars 48 cents as his profit as capitalist. This added to 31½ dollars for the increase of beef and pork, gives the gross profit at 42 dollars 98 cents, and that would be 47 7/10 cents per bushel for his corn. This calculation does not include the cost of the hay, which will be quite *one ton* for six months each bullock, and is worth at the farm about 3 dollars; nor the attendance, nor loss from death or disease, nor the capital invested in the pigs, nor the loss in bargaining with sharp dealers. However, there can be no doubt that the farmer makes twice the value of his corn when it leaves his farm in the shape of meat. (Would that the English grazier could always do half as well.) The manure is not considered of any benefit whatever, and the yards or "corrals" are of the roughest and rudest description, with hardly any sheds or shelter.

Corrals.

Losses.

The loss of cattle from all causes on these prairies is put down at the most at 2½ per cent. per annum. Mr. Davies does not consider a smaller herd of cattle than 5,000 pays. That would require 100 horses; 10,000 only 150 horses. These horses are worth from 25 to 40 dollars; and are chiefly brought from Texas.

Homestead on ranches.

The homestead of the ranches is built on land owned by the stock farmer, and, perhaps, the real estate does not exceed 160 acres; these homesteads and preemptions are invariably on the side of the valleys, which slope down to the streams and rivers, and almost all the water frontage is now legally appropriated. There are vast plains between the watered valleys, 10 to 20 miles wide, belonging to Government; upon these plains the cattle live, and the cattle owners pay no rent to anyone. It is calculated that the worth of these plains (without *water*, which is already owned by some of the stock-men,) is not more than 12 cents per acre, whereas the Government price is 1¼ dollars. Mr. Davies considers that each head of cattle would require 25 acres if the land was inclosed. Mr. Evans calculates that the owners of 10,000 cattle and 150 horses would require 7,000 to 8,000 dollars more in cash to work a ranch profitably.

Expenses cattle and sheep.

The expenses upon a sheep on these ranches for the year, including hay, shepherding, loss, &c., would be 50 cents; upon a bullock from 1 to 1½ dollars.

Profit o ranches

The acknowledged profits upon capital invested in cattle are from 25 to 33 per cent.; even the latter figure is probably below the mark.

CHEYENNE, Oct. 17.

Snow and frost.

Pike's Peak, 170 miles away, visible with the naked eye. The ground hard with frost and the wind very cold. The dry snow is blown into drifts in the hollows, but we start with two teams with Mr. Davies for his ranch, some 10 miles south of the railroad. A few small horses seen on the horizon, and the bold little prairie dog in all directions. We reached Mr. Davies' ranch in time to go with his horses to a herd of 500, the last lot for Chicago market this year. They are of all ages and differ in condition. They are held together by two cow boys on horseback; some are lying down, some are standing with heads downward and noses poked out, as is the manner of western cattle ready for a stampede if the snow and tempest bursts on them again. Mr. Davies' pair of fine grey horses do not like to face the weather, and we make our passage in tacks, avoiding the gullies and drifts. We return to dinner at his hospitable house in front of the corral and the old log hut where he first settled. A brook is close at hand from which the vegetable garden is irrigated, and under a verandah at the door lies a magnificent staghound which had taken the first prize at the Crystal Palace in England.

Prairie dogs.
Last lot for Chicago.

Mr. Davies' ranch.

Wild and dreary as the scene is outside, we find the house filled with evidences of refinement and modern comforts. We had venison steaks and Californian canned grapes at dinner and some excellent champagne, acceptable after living so long on milk and water. Before we left, a gentleman, storm clothed and with his field glass at his side, came in. He was in quest of his sheep, some thousands, which had escaped from the herdsmen during the storm, while the men who were in summer clothing had to desert in order to save their lives. He had seen a few of them, one dead, with a wolf by its side watching for another straggler. As we return we cross the recent trail of a large part of the flock, but we have no means of communicating with the owner. The only green thing on the prairie is the cactus in untouched bunches, and the brown short herbage does not half hide up the gravelly soil; the loftiest plant is a thistle 18 inches high, and a small yucca growing in tufts among the dead grass. Sheep gnaw the heart out of the grass; there will be a row some day about the "keep" between their owners and the cattle men, and between both and the Government on the land and free range question. The back lands with no water will be valueless when the water fronts are appropriated.

Lost sheep.

Coming troubles.

Mr. Davies starts to-morrow to meet, 100 miles, it may be 200 miles away, 12,000 oxen he has bought in Oregon. They have been months on the road towards his ranch. If there is grass where he falls in with them, he will leave them on that spot for the winter (which seems commencing) and fetch them on in the spring; "free range" with a vengeance.

Free range.

From Governor Hoyt's statement, the territory of Wyoming imports store stock from Oregon, Idaho, Montana, and even Nebraska, for wintering and feeding.

Store stock for Wyoming.

As the country fills up, the ranch men may come in conflict with the Government, who will then probably allot them land within limits. The value of a ranch at present depends materially on its water rights. The growth of vegetables and hay is dependent on irrigation, which is being carried out to some extent. Mr. Moreton Frewin, of Big Horn, Powder River, Wyoming, has bought his hay this year at 8 and 10 dollars a ton (of 2,000 lbs.) of a grower who has irrigated about 200 acres, and cuts about 4 tons to the acre. He has himself taken a crop of as much as 50 tons off 9 acres of damp land. In the valley of the Popo-Agie, Central Wyoming, there is said to be high cultivation, with water as complete as near Edinburgh. One farm of 160 acres there is half in grain (wheat, oats, and barley), and half in cultivated grasses (clover, Timothy, and red-top). The clover is "Alfalva," our Lucern. The sample at Governor Hoyt's in blossom measured 2 feet in height. It does not require re-sowing, being either a perennial or renewed by self-sowing. These farmers have a good market in the neighbouring Indian reservations.

Ranches.
Water right.

Hay.

Irrigation.

Alfalva.

A flock of 8,000 sheep in the Cheyenne district of the Rocky Mountains require about 80 tons of hay for the winter. A sheep is worth 2 dollars 50 cents on the ranch, the value of the wools at 25 cents per lb., unwashed, being 1 dollar 50 cents. The average loss among a well-managed flock should not exceed 3 per cent., but good sheds are required as a protection against drifting snow, which smothered as many as 1,200 in one day belonging to Mr. F. E. Warren. Scab is prevalent, but is cured by a tobacco dip, the tobacco costs 2 cents per lb., and the sheep are dipped three times for 10 cents a head, "no cure no pay;" this is an effectual specific. Wolves and cayotes are destructive among the flocks.

Sheep.
Wool.
Losses.
Snow.
Scab.
Wolves.

Mr. F. E. Warren, of Cheyenne, sheep master, in partnership with Mr. W. B. Miner, gives the following information. Merino wool shrinks in cleaning and scouring, on an average, 60 to 65 per cent. Washing will take out 10 per cent. The Mexican stock are hairy and coarse, with fleeces of 2 lbs. to 2½ lbs. Crossed with the merino gives a fleece of 6 lbs. to 8 lbs. of good quality, not quite combing, but equal to Cheviots; 9 out of 10 of the cross will go to the higher priced quality, and the 10th fleece may be coarse. Medium wool loses less than the finest by washing, and much less by scouring. Sheep have been introduced within the last eight years, and are on the increase. Cattle came in two years earlier. The freight of wool from Cheyenne to Boston is $2\frac{7}{10}$ cents per lb. Mr. Warren owns 18,000 sheep. The average weight of wool unwashed on a 13,000 lot of all ages in 1879 was just under 6 lbs. the fleece, and brought 22 cents per lb. at Cheyenne. This is a choice flock for shearing, a large proportion being pure merinos or high grades of $\frac{15}{16}$ths merino. Wolves are troublesome in winter, and are scared by lanthorns suspended at the lairs. About 10 tons of hay is the winter supply needed for 1,000 sheep. Flocks are made up of 2,000 to 2,500 head, and are managed by one man with his dogs. A good well-covered ranch will do a sheep to 2 acres; on an indifferent ranch, twice the space would be requisite, while on a very poor one 6 acres is allowed. A thousand pounds in the pocket of a working man will start him nicely with sheep; the yield from which is an annual one. Cattle have hitherto paid better than sheep, but the latter with care and attention are now producing a better return. Taking all the capital into account which has been sunk in purchase of land and improvements and in cash for stock, in 1879 the sheep-master here got by the wool 23 per cent. return; out of which expenses have to come. The increase in lambs, however, meets these outgoings, and leave them 25 per cent. clear profit. The worth of a running lot of sheep, mixed merinos, Mexicans, and bucks of all ages would be 2 dollars a head, and the clip would be worth 1 dollar. All the wethers, shearlings and older sheep were sold this year at 2¼ dollars; 1,000 were resold at 2 dollars 65 cents, to go for mutton to the Black Hills; they would weigh 110 lbs. or 115 lbs., 50 per cent. of which would be dressed meat.

Sheep. Mr. Warren. Wool.

Wolves.
Sheep, winter feed.
Flocks.
Ground required.
Capital.

Profit on sheep.

Value of flock.

Weight of fat sheep.

Scab is a very bad disease, taking three dips to get rid of. Losses equal to 3, 5, and 10 or 12 per cent. during the winter, and the expenditure of capital in the corral and on hay and care-taking will bring the value of the sheep up to 3 dollars on clip day. The interest of money on loan for short periods to sheep and cattle-owners ranges from 14 to 18 per cent. on personal security under a note of hand.

Losses.

Loans and interest.

Cattle-owners' brands, registered at the county seat, are mortgaged at 12 per cent.

Oct. 18, 1879.

Colorado farming for grain is almost all accomplished by irrigation. Cattle are kept on the plains, and do well through the winter. Mr. R. C. Bloomfield, of Denver, has a small herd of 3,000, 30 miles from Deer Trail. Bought his stock some five years ago from New Mexico, and uses pure Durham bulls from Illinois. Thinks the land of S.E. Colorado all stocked, and would give only 10 acres to each head of stock if enclosed, which indicates that the land is better than in Wyoming. Estimates losses at 6 to 8 per cent. Cattle in long and severe winters get weak and perish in snow drifts; still profits are from 30 to 40 per cent. Sends his fat cattle now to Leadville; they walk there, and it pays better than shipping to Chicago or Kansas City. Graded cattle do well, but pure herds suffer from climate. Short-horns do best, but Herefords are now coming much into favour. Cattle that are kept as in Wyoming and left out all the winter have the first "round up" in April, and the stockowner may find some of his cattle 200 miles away from his ranch. The grass in Colorado is "cured" in August, as in Wyoming; if grass grows much in July, and early frost comes before it is cured by the sun, great damage is done, as the grass is killed not cured. The discovery of the virtues of this self-made hay was in making the railroad through Wyoming, when some draught oxen had to be left there during the winter. These were found quite fat and healthy in the spring, whereas the owners expected to find them dead.

Colorado.

Ranch.

Col. Archer's farm, 16 miles from Denver, is irrigated by a ditch that diverts the water from a stream at the foot of the Rocky Mountains. If water has to be *bought* by a tenant it costs 1 dollar an acre. The Colonel thinks his wheat was 30 bushels and his barley 60 bushels per acre. He also fancies he has 200 tons of hay from meadows, only a few of which are irrigated, and that it will be worth 20 dollars a ton in Leadville. The Colonel has a tenant who pays for rent half the wheat crop, the Colonel finding the

Denver.

Col. Archer irrigation.

APPENDIX TO JOINT REPORT.

seed and ploughing the ground. All the cereal crops in this part of Colorado are grown only by irrigation.

Oct. 21, 1879.

From Denver to Kansas City. First there is the endless prairie with its herds of cattle and sheep, and all along for at least 200 miles this sort of country prevails. The Herefords have been used for crossing, and the cattle are very good useful animals. The country seems short of water, and now and then the cattle are supplied by windmill pumps. Land afterwards changes to partial cultivation. Indian corn is mostly grown, but there is a great deal of "fall" wheat, 6 to 8 inches high now. It is sown after corn ; some with the corn roots left on the field, some with the shocks of corn on the land, and in a few instances the wheat is sown among the standing corn and "cultivated" in. As we go east there are more live fences, a few of the American thorn, but mostly of the Osage orange, and a larger extent of ploughed land. There are also lots of weeds and much poor tillage as we approach Kansas City.

KANSAS CITY, Oct. 22.

At the offices of Messrs. Irwin, Allen, and Co., Live Stock Exchange Buildings, Kansas City, met with Mr. Rust, corresponding clerk to Messrs. Irwin, Allen, and Co., who says the cattle-raising States and territories of the United States comprise Texas, New Mexico, Colorado, Wyoming, Montana, Nebraska, Dakota, Kansas, and the Indian territory. These States and territories are the great pastures of America. Oregon is more of a farming country. The cattle from all districts south of the Platte River come on to Kansas City market. There they are sorted up into lots :—

I. The very best are shipped east to St. Louis and Chicago.

II. The next best butchers take for local consumption.

III. The medium good lots find buyers in the packing and canning houses at Kansas City.

IV. The next quality pass to feed off rough keep in the winter and go over to summer grazing.

V. Others are put on full corn feed at once.

VI. The "tankers," or "culls," or "scallawags" are digested in boilers, and their bones go for phosphates to the farmers in the east.

Of late years Texans have been "all horns and tails," but crossed with a good Durham or Hereford bull the produce is a good medium beast. The Texan draft is now about 300,000, but few of them reach Kansas City fat. Their ages are from five years down to six months. It takes four or five months to get them up to Wyoming. They can live in a very dry country, and will range back 25 miles for water, which they require but once a day. The further north young Texans are taken the larger they come compared with their fellows left in Texas. New Mexican stock are dun and black, much like the Texans, but few good bulls go to New Mexico. The Colorado bullock is far ahead of them. There is a native Colorado breed descendants of the early importations from the east which make good beef, rough fed one winter and corn fed the next, coming up to 1,500 lbs. or 1,600 lbs.

Kansas are an excellent breed of graded cattle, fattening at from three to five years of age, and weighing 1,200 lbs. to 1,600 lbs. Some stock is put on the Indian reserves by outsiders.

October 22, 1879.

At Kansas City, Colorado, steers selling for feeding at 2 dollars 60 cents per 100 lbs. live weight, worth three times that in England. Better cattle sell from 2 dollars 75 cents to 2 dollars 85 cents, and weigh 1,100 lbs.

Pigs sell from 3 dollars 10 cents to 3 dollars 20 cents per 100 lbs.

The Hamiltons and other Kentucky breeders had a sale of pedigree stock by Colonel Judy and Colonel Muir. First cow, six years old, made 155 dollars and her April bull calf 70 dollars, her two year old heifer 150 dollars. Another cow and six weeks' calf made 110 dollars, a third 125 dollars, and her June calf 55 dollars. One yearling bull made 130 dollars and another 100 dollars.

Mr. Hamilton has two short-horn fat bullocks ; one four years old weighed 2,600 lbs., and the other, three years old, 2,350 lbs. They would weigh dead 66 lbs. to the 100 lbs. live weight, or two-thirds dead. These two fine oxen were exhibited by the breeders to show to what a size good short-horn steers could be grown at an early age.

Mr. Armour killed this year, November 1878 to November 1879, 325,000 hogs ; price is now 3 dollars 15 cents to 3 dollars 20 cents. All the pork and bacon go to the south and west, and only the lard to England. There has recently been such a demand in the south for pork, that Mr. Armour bought two million lbs. of sides this year to supply to his customers. A winter pig weighs 280 lbs. live weight and 240 lbs. in summer. Formerly 25,000 cattle were killed, now only 3,000, packed in brine in barrels and sent east. Texan cattle used for packing now worth 2½ cents per lb. live weight ; if really fat, the same bullocks would be worth from 3½ cents to 4 cents per lb. Freight for salt meat to New York, 1,500 miles, was in the summer 18 cents to 22 cents per 100 lbs. ; now it is 66 cents. Farmers cannot live and sell hogs at 2 dollars 60 cents live weight, as they did last year. Lard is still low, and sells for 6 dollars 15 cents per 100 lbs.

Mr. Armour sold a farm in New York State seven years ago, 73 acres, for 16,000 dollars (220 dollars per acre), buyer has asked him to take it back at 8,000 dollars lately.

East Kansas, East Nebraska, and all Missouri and Iowa are the corn-feeding districts of the United States, taking the stock of the western and southern States for this purpose.

Mr. Francis Livingstone Underwood, of Kansas City, says that since 1874 large farmers (500 acre men) have been unsuccessful ; they have had to borrow and been compelled to part with their farms at a great sacrifice. This remark applies to Illinois, Iowa, Southern Minnesota, Northern Missouri, and East Kansas. The crop of wheat ought to be changed in two years even on good land. Some land, however, in Iowa has grown "corn" in the Mississippi bottoms for 40 successive years, when the land was first settled. In Kansas there have been five good crops of wheat, in the State of Illinois, North Missouri, and South Kansas three good crops of "fall" wheat, and in Indiana one good crop, that of this year exceeding 30 bushels an acre.

Mr. Underwood farms 1,900 acres in Iowa, growing "corn."

Interest on money lent in Iowa is now 7 per cent., in Kansas 9 per cent.

Mr. Underwood advances only 40 per cent. of the value of the naked land without improvements. There was a time in 1879 when a bushel of wheat could be moved to Chicago, 500 miles, for 5 cents, the charge being now 15 cents. It is thought this will be the ruling rate for some time. It will take 12,500 dollars a mile to build and equip a prairie railroad, and 40,000 dollars to 60,000 dollars a mile have been raised on them. The Union Pacific road pays interest on 120,000 dollars a mile. It might be built for 12,500 dollars on the flat.

The best farmers are getting their crops into rotation, growing clover for feeding off with swine, keeping it down in seed and grass two or three years before ploughing. Mr. Underwood's estimate of growing wheat per acre is :—

	Dols.	Cents.
Ploughing	1	0
Seed	1	25
Sowing	0	25
Harrowing twice (a third harrowing would do good)	0	50
Cutting with four horses	0	40
Wire for tying	0	45
Use of machine	0	75
Shocking	0	25
Stacking	0	50
Thrashing	1	20
Rent	1	60
Taxes	0	20
Herding or fencing	0	13
Delivery 12 miles	0	60
Total	9	10

October 23, 1879.

From Kansas City, with Mr. Vineyard, to Mr. Coppick's farm, and then to Mr. Seth Ward's, where we saw a fine herd of short-horns, and one of the best and purest Oxford bulls now in America. Mr. Ward's farm is mostly in Timothy grass and clover, and extends over 600 acres. The whole district seems nice undulating land, and there is a considerable extent of permanent grass, the Kentucky blue grass being the most prominent. The Indian corn was being gathered from the shocks, the straw being used for fodder. Every available acre of land was sown with "fall" wheat. The whole country well enclosed, mostly with live fences of the wild or Osage orange. All the farmers were in the city attending the cattle sales, which last three days.

October 24, 1879.

To Mr. Duncan's farm, near Maple Spring Station, by a narrow gauge railway. The farm contains 400 acres, 100 rough pasture, 50 under plough, (wheat 30, maize 20,) and 250 in clover and Timothy grass, 50 acres being cut for hay, 12 cut twice. The live stock consisted of 6 cows, a Durham bull, heifers and calves, 430 sheep, and 60 pigs, and some that will weigh 200 lbs. at Christmas, and are worth 3¼ cents per lb. now. Mr. Duncan sometimes feeds steers in the winter with corn and hay, has then to buy corn, some recently bought delivered at 25 cents per bushel. Butcher takes the ram lambs at 2½ dollars, if fat; ewe lambs and merino bucks kept for stock; four horses for work; two intelligent active boys, sons of Mr. Duncan, 19 and 17, do most of the work on the farm, the latter still going to school in the winter. A black man is hired for three or four months at 15 dollars a month and his dinner, odd hands hired when necessary at 1 dollar a day, some 75 cents, even in summer. Seven cents per head is paid for shearing sheep.

Labour.

Rams turned in to ewes in August and September and taken out in October, that no lambs may fall in March, as that is a cold wet month; the rams are put to again in November. The ewes lamb in an open shed or under a hay stack in a clover field, and are not housed in the winter. Good merino ewes will clip 4 to 6 lbs., and a first-class ram 20 to 25 lbs., this wool is singularly greasy. If sheep are fed under cover there is a greater amount of grease. Clover leys remain down three years if a good plant. Autumn wheat sown at one ploughing after old clover and on maize stubble. "Hoppers" came in 1876 and killed clover, wheat, and corn, but corn was replanted, and that sown late in June was a good crop.

Sheep.

Clover.

Hoppers.

Great uncertainty is a feature of the wheat crops in Ohio, where in 18 years there have been only six full crops. In 1878 all looked well, when three hot days spoilt the crops; some were never cut, and the average in Ohio was only 10 bushels. Corn in 18 years has never failed, having averaged 35 bushels; one man and a pair of horses can manage 35 acres of corn; complete cultivation ensures a crop; seasons having less influence on it than on wheat.

Poor crops of wheat.

Drought.

Corn.

In Texas, Oct. 25th. At Dallas it is allowed that Texan fever, like yellow fever, departs when frost sets in; nor does it prevail among Texan or other acclimatised cattle in Texas; nor do the Texan cattle in the drift north suffer from its attacks, but cattle, say in Colorado, and adjacent districts, coming on the trail of the Texans in their passage out of Texas in the autumn, take the disease and die in great numbers. To move Texan cattle with safety they should start when the grass starts, and accompany the advent of spring as it opens towards the north. If this is done no ill-consequences ensue. A frontier line of quarantine is established against the drive along the Canadian River. The symptoms of this malady are loss of appetite, the dung dry, weakness, inability to move, and at the time of death bleeding at the nostrils. Professor Gamgee says that post-mortem examination of Texan cattle in their own country, and in good health, in every case disclose traces of the disorder. At Dallas it is believed that the necessary expenses attending sheep farming leave no profit. On the western ranches in Texas nothing has to be paid for the land, though it is considered a "good idea" to obtain legal possession of the watered land, which may be bought at from 50 cents to 1 dollar an acre. Money is to be borrowed for short periods on cattle (not longer than for three months) at 18 per cent.

Texan fever.

Quarantine.

Sheep.

Five dollars a car is the cost of feed and water at each stop on the railroad.* Watering and feeding cattle is required by the *national* law all through the United States. The law is not enforced, possibly on account of difficulties in relation to the executive, but, nevertheless, it is generally obeyed. The numbers moved over the line here increased this year as compared with last, but not on a comparison with previous years. The return freights from east to west are much higher. Freight east of St. Louis and Chicago for a car have gone up 100 per cent. Col. Noble, the general manager of an important western line, says it costs 20,000 dollars per mile to build and equip a prairie line. If iron rails will last three years steel will hold good for 14, the difference in cost being 8 dollars; the duty on steel rails is now 28 dollars a ton, and they may be bought at 23 dollars before the duty is imposed.

Watering and feeding cattle on railroad.

Numbers moved.

Freights risen.

Cost of railroad.

Iron and steel rails.

The best wood for light work, in carriage building, and for similar purposes, is Bois d'Arc. It is the timber of the Osage orange, and is particularly valuable for machinery, as it shrinks but slightly.

Wood for machinery.

The land grant to a soldier of the Texan Republic was 4,000 acres, and is termed a "head right." There are men now living who have been subjects under five different forms of Government in Texas: i. Mexican; ii. Monarchy (Maximillian); iii. Texan Republic; iv. Southern Confederacy; v. United States.

Land grant.

Mr. A. B. Legard, Frajillo Post Office, Oldhams, County Texas, has 11,500 sheep now, and 14,000 in the summer,

Sheep in Texas.

* See p. 10.

having sold the balance in the fall to a neighbouring sheep farmer who keeps only a dry flock, mainly for wool. Mr. Legard sold his wool, delivered at the station, about 200 miles off, at 22 cents a lb., now worth 24 cents or 25 cents. Sends wool to station and brings back maize for his merino bucks, the carriage being moderate, as there is freight both ways. Government pays 1 cent per lb. per 100 miles for land transport. In 1872 ewe and lamb worth 4 dollars and 75 cents, in 1879 only 2 dollars and 50 cents. In spring of 1872 wool worth 40 cents per lb., in 1879 18 cents. Sheep have been "unsaleable as a rock," they are now "talking" about them again.

Howard Oil Company, Dallas, Texas. Cotton seed costs 10 cents a bushel, weighs 33⅓ lbs. or 3 bushels to 100 lbs. Seed brushed, and cotton wadding made from the small particles brushed off, further dressed, and then all ground or crushed twice and the meal dressed out; the husks shaken and blown out in two operations. Meal then heated and pressed into cake, oil going to refiners and sent to Italy, and comes back as salad oil. Husks used for fuel or sold for bedding; ashes are sold for making soap. The cake was of a beautiful quality, it is sent to Galveston for shipment to England.

Cotton cake

With Mr. William Hunter, Fort Worth, Texas, Oct. 27th. Cattle in stock pens, three years old, rough meaty steers, sold for 13¾ dollars here; expenses to Chicago 5¼ dollars each; they will bring 1 dollar profit if sold as Mr. Hunter expected at 20 dollars; two years old steers, poor and rough, 11 dollars, and yearlings 6 dollars. The two-year olds, if well done, would be worth 17 dollars next year, and not cost above 1 dollar " handling." A prime lot of three-year old steers weighed 1,000 lbs. at Chicago, worth now 2¾ cents per lb., two years ago were worth nearly 4 cents. No increase of cattle at Forth Worth or in the district. Loans on cattle 15 to 18 per cent. in three months' bills renewable. Stockmen do well, and make at least 33⅓ per cent. on the capital they invest.

Cattle at Fort Worth

Malaria commonly attacks new comers into the south-western States. The best treatment seems to consist in abstinence from meat and adopting a vegetable diet; but with respect to following this advice the cost of vegetables has to be considered. Cabbages at Fort Worth, 40 miles west of Dallas, cost wholesale in the market 9 cents each, 4½d., and are poor specimens at that price; they are brought 750 miles by rail from the east (St. Louis), and even here their journey is not ended; some are packed to go by waggon 400 miles further west, when having travelled over 1,100 miles, their price will be increased to 25 cents, or 1s. 0½d.

Malaria.

Cabbages.

Four miles west of Dallas Mr. Carruth owns about 5,000 acres of land, of which about 2.500 acres are cultivated and rented out. The landlord builds small houses, costing 110 dollars to 150 dollars each, and lets them with 60 or 70 acres on the terms of one-third of the grain and a quarter of the cotton ginned and baled ready for sale, and delivered at the nearest railway station. Colonel Noble lets in the same way, and the money value of his rent this year will come to 7½ dollars per acre; but this is an exceptionally good season, the average being about 5 dollars.

Land.

Tenants.

Rent.

The landlord insists on a certain acreage of cotton being planted. The cost of cultivating cotton before picking is about the same as maize. Winter or fall wheat is cut in May; 24 bushels is considered a good yield, and though in some seasons it runs up to 40 bushels, in others there is nothing.

Cotton.

Wheat.

Oct. 28.

It appears that Texas fever attacks old cattle that are imported into the State, but that usually a six months' calf becomes acclimatized and escapes. Mr. James Read, of Fort Worth, bought 12 Hereford bulls and lost eight of them. He had previously used Durhams, but likes the Herefords for crossing with the Texas cattle. Mr. Read has a farm of over 400 acres enclosed near Fort Worth, and a ranch 170 miles off. The farm next Fort Worth much cut up by drought. Wheat and maize a failure, and winter oats only 32 bushels an acre. Saw a few well graded Durham cattle near the Sulphur Springs; also from a distance saw Captain Thompson's farm, which is well enclosed. There is some good land between Dallas and Fort Worth, especially near the former town, but it is all badly farmed. Cotton is a fair crop, but maize is more or less a failure.

Mr. James Read's fa

A Mr. Harris has lately bought 25,000 acres in Texas, but has only 4,000 sheep at present upon it. Had just sold 10,000 lbs. of his fall clip at 25 cents per lb. His sheep and lambs clip nearly 2½ lbs. of wool in the fall, and 4½ lbs. in the spring. If clipped only once, sheep will hardly yield 5 lbs., so the fall clip is nearly all profit. Half-bred Merinos are kept entirely for wool; the freight of the sheep by rail eats up the value of the

Mr. Harris sheep.

Wool.

mutton, so little is made of that. Mr. Harris says that wool pays to grow at 18 cents per lb., and all above that is profit. Last winter was very severe, and half the sheep were lost by some farmers; but Mr. Harris, who looks well after his flock, did not lose 8 per cent.

'reights.

There has been no rise in freight west of Chicago for the past three years, costing now from Fort Worth to New York 230 dollars a car; but cattle generally change hands once or twice on the road. Cattle to St. Louis cost from Fort Worth 120 dollars (for $21\frac{1}{2}$ cattle) per truck, which with feed makes $5\frac{1}{2}$ dollars a head expenses. (Cattle must be fed and watered every 28 hours.) Cattle fares have gone up 100 per cent. east of Chicago. Cattle were taken at 120 dollars with 70 dollars *drawback;* now 110 dollars a car without any *drawback*.

October 29, 1879.

allas to . Louis.

From Dallas to Sherman the land is fairly good. It is mostly prairie, cultivated in cotton and maize. From Sherman to Texar-kana there is much more woodland, especially as we neared the boundary of Texas, which for miles was all forest. The same sort of farming prevailed, and some of the land appeared very good. There was a nice farm of 4,000 acres of prairie land to be sold; it was owned by a Frenchman, and would probably be bought for 5 dollars an acre. Climate appears very hot, and this year the drought is excessive. From Texar-kana to St. Louis it is mostly woodland. As we near the Mississippi, and pass into the mineral region of Arkansas, there is more land cultivated, but the crops are not by any means great.

Nov. 1, 1879.

Louis ck-yard.

To the St. Louis stock-yards (east), and saw the cattle, sheep, and pigs there. Only one pen of really nice cattle, high graded Durhams, and they sold at $4\frac{1}{4}$ cents per lb. to feed in the district. There were several lots of Colorado and Texas cattle, and sundry collections of cows and odd stock. The sheep varied considerably; the Mexicans were very poor, they weigh about 85 lbs. alive, and are sold for 2 cents a lb.; a lot of half-bred Merinos, nice sheep, sold from 3 to 4 cents, and would weigh from 100 to 125 lbs. Some extra good black faced sheep, that would weigh 160 lbs., sold at $4\frac{1}{2}$ cents.

lorado l Texan ttle.

At Mr. Whittaker's pork packing house they killed this day 2,700 hogs. They send the pork salted to the south, and the lard east.

Louis k-yards. eford ls and rham. ue of . re cattle. Gillett's k.

At St. Louis stock-yards Messrs. Hunter, Evans, and Co. state that the Hereford bull is becoming very fashionable; they prove to be hardier than Durhams. The value of the choicest beef beasts to-day, Nov. 1, is $4\frac{3}{4}$ cents live weight ("on the foot"), the net weight will be 60 per cent. of dressed beef out of animals weighing on foot 1,650 lbs. "Running" cattle are selling now at $2\frac{2}{3}$ cents to $2\frac{3}{4}$ cents. Mr. Gillett has a lot of cattle now in hand weighing over 2,000 lbs.

s.

Hogs are selling to-day at $3\frac{1}{2}$ cents to $3\frac{7}{10}$ cents, with dropping prices.

ng bulls he t. ng bulls t. Louis k-yard.

In the stock-yards we saw (belonging to Mr. Wm. Lovering) 26 young bulls, from 6 to 20 months of age. These had been gathered at Detroit to ship for breeders in New Mexico; they are from half to seven-eighths, and even full blood, and all of nice quality; their value on the stones to-day, at St. Louis, would be 4*l.* 16*s.* round.

ning.

The St. Louis Beef Canning Company "operate" at the national stock-yards St. Louis, and are represented in England by Messrs. Miller and Halls of London, and H. H. and [S. Budgell and Co. of Liverpool. This Company are now killing 500 beasts daily of an average weight of 850 lbs. They manufacture into 14, 10, 6, 4, 2, and 1 lb. tins. They also send out as fresh meat in ice "rolled ribs," "tender loin," "back strip," and "navel bit" or plate. These pieces are shipped as far as Pittsburgh, 700 miles, New York, 1,100 miles, Buffalo 650 miles. The meat having been chilled on the premises is packed in galvanized iron drums; these again are placed in a box surrounded, if the time of year requires it, with ice. On a long journey the boxes are re-iced. Hotel keepers are thus supplied direct from the stock-yards, and there is, as well, a local trade in St. Louis.

h beef ints.

hams.

Beef hams are also cut and cured here; they are smoked, and for the most part find a market in the south.

ch nd.

The trade in America is increasing rapidly for this class of meat. A trade in France has also sprung up within a year which appears likely to develop into considerable proportions; the company have an agent in Paris, and are doing a smart trade there. The rise in the value of tin had added 1*d.* to the cost of the large cans. On the whole, three years' experience in the trade goes to show that the price of the St. Louis meat has not varied, but the quality is improving. The existing price of good Texan cattle on foot, fit for canning, is $2\frac{5}{8}$ cents per lb., equal to nearly 1*s.* 6*d.* a stone English live weight (14 lbs.). The company's premises cover about 3 acres, and cost, including machinery, fixtures, and rolling stock, about 200,000 dollars or 41,000*l.* They were erected and put to use within the space of 90 days this year. About 1,200 hands are employed, the men earning from 1 dollar to $2\frac{1}{2}$ dollars a day, the girls from $3\frac{1}{2}$ dollars to 7 dollars a week, those engaged on piece-work earning the most. The men making cans and topping them by task earn from 15 dollars to 18 dollars a week, *i.e.*, over 3 guineas. The belief is held that two-thirds of the money is spent in play and drink.

in tin. . ity. e of

Cost of plant. Work and wages. Improvidence.

Nov. 3, 1879.

Renting land.

To Florissant, west of St. Louis, on a sandy loam deep and light; better adapted for corn than wheat, which delights in a stiffer soil. Quantities of land rented, mostly one year's tenancy, but others from 8 to 10 years; general rent 5 dollars an acre, landlord paying outgoings. If rented in shares, one-third of produce. All wheat planted in the fall, and, as elsewhere, an unusually large acreage sown this year. The French settlers make bad farmers; will give their manure to the Dutch, who will drive it a mile.

Farm at Florissont. Crops. Teams. Labour and wages. Manure. Cows. Milk. Team work. Value of wheat and maize. Straw manure.

From St. Louis the Jesuit Novitiate College and farm at Florissant is easily reached by railroad. The farm consists of 300 acres arable and grass; of this 65 acres are in wheat, the yield of which averages 22 bushels; 75 acres in corn, with average yield of 60 bushels; 18 acres in oats; 55 acres in Timothy grass; and 87 acres in permanent pasture; five teams of horses and mules, 10 in all, are worked, worth about 13 guineas each animal; 12 ploughs are in stock, of the value of 36*s.* each. Five men are employed at a pay of 168 dollars, or 35*l.* a year, and board and washing, and two boys at half the cost of the men. In hay time two extra hands are engaged at 4*s.* 2*d.* a day and food. In harvest time the same assistance is required, and three additional hands for binding after the machine. The manure is put mostly on the grass land. Hay at St. Louis sells at 11 dollars or 46*s.* a ton of 2,000 lbs. A few sheep are killed for the establishment at weights of about 70 lbs. Twenty-five milking cows are kept for milk and butter, and a yield of 3 gallons daily from a cow would be considered really good. Calves are sold for veal at from four to ten weeks old, averaging 90 lbs. of veal, and 9 dollars each, or 37*s.* 6*d.* A team here will plough $1\frac{1}{2}$ acres in nine hours, and will drill from 8 to 10 acres, according to the character of the ground. The mower cuts from 6 to 8 acres. The best day's work among wheat with the reaper was 15 acres, and 12 acres would be considered satisfactory. Wheat, when selling at a dollar or 33*s.* 4*d.* per quarter of 480 lbs., will pay for production; so will maize at 40 cents, and the Florissant people say it ought not to be lower. The straw is stacked with angles, affording shelter to the cattle as they pull at it, eat, and tread it under foot. The product is called manure, and is here carted on to the land.

November 5.

Manure farm at Columbia. Cropping. Live stock. Values of stock. Butter. Channel Island cows. Quality of stock.

The farm of Mr. E. C. Moore, Ingleside, Columbia, Missouri, consists of 450 acres, all cultivated. In 1879 there was no wheat (but 50 acres are now sown); of corn there were 27 acres, barley none, as it is never grown; oats, 25 acres; seed clover and Timothy mown, 150 acres; permanent grass 250 acres. The live stock carried on it are, cattle 50, sheep 65 (40 ewes and 25 lambs), hogs 80, mules 6, horses, mares, and foals 15. As to values, a thorough-bred bull calf seven months old is valued at 50*l.*; five barren cows, and one barren heifer, high grades, are worth 3 cents per lb. on foot, weighing about 1,200 lbs., coming to 36 dollars or 7 guineas each. "Elegant" butter is quoted at 24 cents or 1*s.* a lb. Good Southdown breeding ewes average in value 7 dollars or 29*s.* each. Mr. Moore himself gave for three Shropshire ewes and a ram, thorough breds, from England, at St. Louis fair, 230 dollars; taking the tup at 100 dollars or 20 guineas, the ewes would come to 9*l.* a head. There is a pure herd of Channel Island dairy cattle owned by Col. Guitar (some of them, about 12 cows and 2 bulls, just imported) within 2 miles of the town. It is remarkable that *all* the stock seen round Columbia are above the average of English stock in quality.

The University farm. Value of corn, and eaten by hogs. Price and yield of corn. Hogs.

At the University Farm, Columbia, Mr. Maddex, the manager, finds that corn bought at 25 cents will bring back 30 cents in hogs, selling at 3 cents a lb. live weight; 5 bushels of corn puts 50 lbs. live weight upon hogs. Within the last 10 years corn has sold at 20 cents and 50 cents per bushel; 40 bushels is an average crop. One man will plough, sow, and cultivate 40 acres of prairie land in maize or 20 acres of woodland. A 250 lb. live hog will net 200 lbs. of dressed meat. The manager had one lot which lost only $10\frac{1}{2}$ per cent. in killing.

Prairie land.

The prairie here, before it was broken up, was considered valueless, being then a wet pan; but, on breaking, this permanently dries up.

November 6.

Mr. Bradford's farm. At Mr. Geo. A. Bradford's farm, near Columbia, are some fine "high grade" steers running about one head to 5 acres of fair grass land; they are three years old, worth about 43 dollars, say 9*l*. They will eat, in the winter, corn worth 5*l*., but this will find food as well for two hogs following the cattle, which, if they sell at 3 cents per lb. live weight, will return one-third of the value of the corn, leaving 3*l*. 6*s*. net to be charged on the ox. A bullock during six summer months, including May and October, can be joisted out at 1 dollar a month. **Swine disease.** Cholera is very destructive now among swine. It kills "like rats a fighting," and pork becomes a dead loss. **Value of land.** One hundred and sixty acres of Mr. Bradford's land cost 4,000 dollars or about 5*l*. an acre; money having been lent on it at 10 per cent. the mortgage was foreclosed.

Springfield. Within the last five years the value of land in the neighbourhood of Springfield, Illinois, has fallen 25 per cent., but it is now rising again. Col. Jones, president of State National Bank, bought a farm of 480 acres, 2½ miles from Springfield, at 50 dollars an acre; four years ago it cost 65 dollars, and the owner spent 7,000 or 8,000 dollars in building and improvements. **Cattle at distillery.** Col. Jones has 1,260 cattle feeding at the distillery; 300 are bulls, which cost 2¼ cents per lb., and weighed 1,400 lbs.; the rest are steers, which cost 3¼ cents, and weighed 1,100 lbs. Steers will gain 200 lbs. by June, and bulls 400 lbs., and if the steers sell at 4 cents and the bulls at 3 cents a lb. live weight they will pay. They cost 3 cents a day for the *wash*, and eat 16 lbs. of hay, which costs 4 dollars a ton. They come in October and go out in May and June.

Illinois farm. Mr. Shin's. The farm of Mr. Jas. Shin, near Springfield, consists of 300 acres, bought recently for 85 dollars an acre; had previously been sold for 110 dollars, and before that for 130 dollars an acre. It is devoted to dairying, and is worked for cheese. **Dairy cheese.** The yield ought to be 1½ lb. of cheese daily from each cow for 10 months; 10 lbs. of milk should give 1 lb. of cheese. **Manufacture of cheese.** Making begins April 1st and closes December 1st. The evening's milk is put into the vat and cooled with ice down to 50° or with water to 60°. The morning's meal is added, and the whole brought up by steam to 85°. The rennet (Bavarian) is then added, and the milk stands from 25 to 35 minutes. It is then sliced, and when the curd has settled the temperature is brought up to 95°. All is left alone till the acid is up, ascertained by smelling, then the whey is drawn off, for calves and pigs. The whey is next drained off by manipulation, and the salt added in the proportion of 3 lbs. to the 100 lbs. of cheese. The curd is finally crumbled and pressed for 24 hours.

Weight, and value of cheese. The cheeses weigh from 35 to 45 lbs., and will sell in five to six weeks time at 12 to 13 cents per lb. The maker can just live, if he makes no bad debts, at 8 cents, or 4*d*. per lb., and will make money at 10 cents, or 5*d*. per lb.

Sowing wheat on horseback. There is a good deal of enterprise among wheat growers here, and corn land is sown with wheat before the stalks are removed. As they are 9 feet high the sower is mounted on horseback and sows overhead, the horses ears being protected by a cloth.

Chicago, Nov. 10, 1879.

Chicago fat stock show. At Chicago cattle show, November 10, the judges were practical butchers. Mr. J. G. Gillett of Hart City, Illinois, shows 64 head, two years and three years old. They are well bred thick-fleshed heavy cattle. The beasts never having been tied up or haltered are rather "rumbustical-looking." Mr. Gillett says that next year he intends to "subdue them before they come into Chicago. They have never been under cover. **Chicago stock show, Mr. Gillett's.** Among his exhibits are a pair of twin red steers, born September 10, 1876; the two weigh 4,250 lbs., and have never been under shelter. A roan steer calved August 1876 weighs now 2,470 lbs.; another, born March 1877, weighs 2,140 lbs.; and a red, calved April 1876, reaches 2,170 lbs. Twelve, two years old, weigh 1,580 lbs. each born from May to July. Nineteen yearlings, born in the same months in 1878, weigh 1,300 lbs. each, one a March calf, weighs 1,420 lbs. or 101 stone of 14 lbs. live weight. Mr. Gillett breeds and raises 500 calves this season; the greatest profit is made by selling two year olds. He began breeding in 1844, and kept one bull for 19 years. The produce from him in one year was 48 calves, of which 47 were bull calves. He prefers red as a colour for the bulls.

Messrs. Brown's Durhams. Messrs. J. N. Brown and Sons, Berlin, Illinois, exhibit a red thorough-bred steer, 26 months old, which weighs 1,700 lbs.; a red and white 18 months 1,370 lbs.; and a red steer, 16 months old, 1,360 lbs. Six steers sold at 20 months old to Mr. Bonallack of Montreal weighed 1,435 lbs. each, of which 72 per cent. came out dressed meat. The best inferior beasts would "dress out" 60 per cent. The thorough-breds at this show do not quite reach the weights of the best graded cattle.

Mr. E. S. Cunningham, Winchester, Kentucky, and Mr. J. H. Graves, Chilerburg, Kentucky, exhibit, jointly, a pure, bred roan steer, born March 16th, 1876, which weighs 2,060 lbs, and a red steer "graded," born February 1877, weighing 1,665 lbs.

Herefords at Chicago. Among the *Herefords*, Mr. F. L. Miller of Beecher, Illinois, shows a cow, born March 1874, weighing 1,850 lbs.; a grey brindled steer, born March 1876, weighing 1,850 lbs.; a red, graded calf, born July 28th, 1878, weighing 1,160 lbs. This animal is to be killed, and the dressed meat weighed and recorded. A red thorough-bred Hereford, born June 1878, weighs 1,180 lbs.; a rough-haired red, born December 1877, weighs 1,400 lbs.; another red thorough-bred, born January 1876, weighs 2,000 lbs., and a red half-bred just turned four years weighs 2,180 lbs.

Mr. A. S. Moore's Durhams. Mr. Amos Seth Moore exhibited three remarkable animals. A red-graded steer, born April 1877, weighing 1,845 lbs.; a roan-graded steer, born April 1877, weighing 1,780 lbs.; a red-graded steer, born April 1877, weighing 1,850 lbs. A graded steer of Mr. Moore's gained 125 lbs. a month running on grass and corn, and then kept up for six months.

Durhams. Mr. Hunt Mr. J. W. Hunt, Ashton, Illinois, exhibited three fine animals; a red steer $\frac{15}{16}$ graded short-horn, born December 12, 1876, weighing 1,810 lbs.; another, born at the same time, weighing 1,610 lbs.; another red steer $\frac{7}{8}$ graded, born April 1876, weighing 2,100 lbs.

The State Board of Agriculture prepare a report, showing the age and weights of all exhibits, in order that stockmen may judge at what period of life the greatest amount of flesh is put on, and the most profitable time for killing.

Huge cattle Eight monsters were exhibited by Mr. Sherman all named, as follows:—

"Nelson Morris," a light roan, weighs 2,840 lbs. or 203 stone, long weight;

"General Logan," red, said to have Devon blood in him, 2,478 lbs.;

"Bob Ingersoll," red, 2,090 lbs.;

"Colonel Judy," roan, 2,500 lbs.;

"J. B. Turner," light red, 2,820 lbs., or over 200 stone long weight, English;

"Hosier Boy," roan, 2,552 lbs.;

"General Morton," roan, 2,836 lbs., again over 202 stone long weight;

"John Sherman," roan, 2,309 lbs.

Sheep. The sheep exhibited are Cotswolds, Leicesters, Shropshires, Southdowns, and grades and crosses with Merinos. The farmers seem to hold the opinion that sheep will be more "run on" now. **Short wool** Short wool has risen 8 cents in value in the pound this year.

Pigs. The pigs were all good, but the "Poland Chinas" eclipsed the Berkshires.

Butter prices. Creamery butter is at the present time making 36 cents, or 1*s*. 6*d*. per lb. It was down to 14 cents, 7*d*., in July. Butter is exhibited.

Illinois Condensing Co., Elgin, Illinois, Nov. 11.

Condensed milk. Borden's condensed milk is manufactured at Elgin. The company work 3,000 gallons of milk daily. The low price has caused farmers to resort to mixed farming instead of cow keeping. The company's price for milk now is 10 cents, or 5*d*. a gallon; in summer it was 6 cents, or 3*d*. It will probably rise to 12 cents, or 6*d*. this winter. One gallon of milk weighing 9⅝ lbs.* at 60° gives 3 lbs. of condensed milk; 75 per cent. of water is expelled from the heated milk, and 10 per cent. is left in; the remaining 15 per cent. of the milk is solid matter. Sugar is added and the product is canned. Most of the work is done by women and girls, even among the tin work.

Elgin Creamery.

At this creamery milk for cream is "set" in deep tins 19 inches by 8 inches diameter. These hold four gallons, and are placed in a tank supplied with running water and ice for 24 hours while the cream rises. **Proportion of cream and butter to milk** Three pounds of butter is considered an excessive yield from 100 lbs. of milk or 11½ gallons; the quantity varies from 1 lb. up to 3 lbs. **Price of milk.** The price of milk is 1 dollar 25 cents per 100 lbs. or 11½ gallons, about 11 cents, or 5½*d*. a gallon: this from November 1st to December 1st. **Milk.** In winter it will be 12 cents, or 6*d*. the gallon. For two summers it has been down to 4 cents, or 2*d*. a gallon. These are losing prices to farmers; to pay them, milk should command 7 or 8 cents per gallon. A continuance of low prices induces farmers to abandon cow keeping. **Cheese.** "Skim cheese has been *unsaleable* this year, and we have thrown it to the hogs; we did so in June and July 1879." This is the statement of the manager of a factory taking the milk of 400 cows. **Price.** Their skim milk cheese, sold at 10 to 15 days old, is making now 9 cents or 4½*d*. per lb.

---

* A gallon of milk weighs 9¼ lbs.

APPENDIX TO JOINT REPORT.

INDIANAPOLIS, Nov. 12.

Weather charts. A weather chart is suspended in the room of the Board of Trade in Indianapolis. It is large and on canvas, with contour lines, and the points of observations, called stations, named in red. Moveable discs about the size of a farthing are daily attached near the stations, *red* for fine, *blue* for cloudy, *half blue, half white,* for cloud and rain, *white* for rain, *black and white stripes* for snow. Adjustable cardboard arrows on the map next each station indicate the direction of the wind, and slips of manuscript appended show the records of barometer and thermometer and the rainfall in inches.

Mr. Oliver Johnson's cropping. The farm of Mr. Oliver Johnson, Walnut Grove, 3 miles from Indianapolis, consists of 160 acres; 40 acres wheat, 40 maize, 20 oats and seeds, 60 wood and grazing land. The stock are 6 horses, 30 horned cattle, and 30 sheep. *Manuring.* The land is manured regularly, the dung being put on the seeds, and on wheat after wheat, and this practice, Mr. Johnson says, will have to be followed if the fertility of the land is to be maintained. *Yield and price.* The average crop of wheat is 13 to 15 bushels, and the average price 1 dollar, or 33s. 4d. a quarter of 480 lbs.; of corn, 30 bushels, at an average price of 40 cents or 1s. 8d., or 13s. 4d. the quarter of 448 lbs. *Maize.* A man and a pair of horses will prepare the land, and sow and cultivate 20 acres of corn (maize). It is well to "cultivate" this crop five times, till the tassel is out. The yield depends on cultivation more than on season.

Labour and wages. The wheat is cut in the last week of June or the first week of July. Two regular hands cost 18 dollars a month, with bed and board. The price of an extra man in busy times is 1 dollar to 1 dollar 50 cents a day, with bed and board. For three winter months, only one hand is required. *School v. drink.* The men then out of place may, and do in some cases, even when 40 years old, attend school. Others spend their time and money in drinking. *Value of farm.* The value of this farm with improvement, house buildings and fencing, at the present time is 200 dollars an acre, 41l. 10s. From as low as 10 bushels an acre of wheat has been raised up to 42 bushels, and of corn from 20 bushels up to 80 bushels.

Freights and pool. Mr. Gallup, president of the Board of Trade, Indianapolis, says that within the last eight years freights to the seaboard (say to Boston) have been 80 cents the 100 lbs., they then dropped as low as 22 cents; this was followed by combination and the establishment of "the pool" among railway companies; and freights stand now at 42 cents per 100 lbs., equivalent to a rise of 6d. per bushel or 4s. a quarter in the carriage of the grain to the seaport, which now stands at 8s. 5d. per quarter of 480 lbs.

C. Dawson's farm. Mr. Chas. Dawson owns near Indianapolis 163 acres of fair land. In 1879, 100 acres of this was in corn, the remaining 63 acres in wood. *Hog cholera.* Hog cholera has alarmed him, it has become so frequent. It is usual to follow a rotation in cropping—a simple one, wheat and corn. There are 25 acres sown with winter wheat this fall, and the truth is admitted that in this neighbourhood, to cultivate with success, farmers must begin to use fertilisers, and the sons of the present agriculturists will have to adopt the English plan. *Manuring and soiling crops.* The fertiliser here is clover; the best farmers keep one-third of their land down in this plant for the scythe or feeding off, or to turn under the furrow for autumn-sown wheat. *Maize yield.* Sixty bushels is now accepted as a good crop of corn, against the higher average of 80 bushels, which was achieved in years gone by, and it is universally admitted *Effect of continuous cropping.* that the yield of land has diminished after being subjected to continuous cropping. Rates are 1 dollar an acre on land valued at 100 dollars, to which must be added 1 per cent. on personalty, equal to 25 cents per acre, making a total of over 6s. an acre.

Luther Johnson's cropping. Mr. Luther Johnson's farm at Maidwell Grove consists of 205 acres; of this 40 acres are in wood, with some grazing ground under the trees; 62 acres have been wheat, 55 acres corn, and the balance in seeds for mowing and pasture. *Stock.* The stock are 6 horses and mules, 10 horned cattle, 75 to 150 sheep, 40 hogs; the last-named animals *Hog cholera.* being objects of suspicion and alarm. The cholera breaks out without any warning or without the introduction of any fresh stock. The animals are alive and hearty in the morning and dead at night. *Manure.* Manure is put on the clover leys in the autumn for wheat, and again is supplied in the spring to land intended for corn. *Seeds kept down.* Seeds are kept down two, three, and four years. When Mr. Johnson was a boy blue *grass* was scarce, now it is very general in pastures.

Labourer's wages. A man and a pair of horses will grow and "cultivate" 25 acres of corn five times. Mr. Johnson employs two regular hands by the month, and one extra during three months, but Mr. Johnson's boy of 16 helps. Four extra men are wanted in harvest, at 1 dollar 50 cents a day, and bed and board; this is only for six or eight days. The pay

Q 2685.

of the regular hands is 13 dollars a month, with bed and board. In the month of November a hand may be secured for 75 cents and dinner. *Hours of labour.* The labourers breakfast before sunrise, work from sunrise till 12, then lie by for one hour to work again till supper at 5, which is eaten "as fast as may be," and the day's toil is not concluded till the sun sets. *Sunrise and sunset.* On the longest day the sun rises at 4.32 and sets at 7.32. On the shortest day the sun rises at 7.22 and sets at 4.44. On April 1st it rises at 5.44 and sets at 6.24, and on October 1st it rises at 5.56 and sets at 5.43, giving *Hours of daylight.* during the year more hours of daylight for work than in England, with shorter days in summer and longer in winter.

Rent of land. Agricultural land is let at 6 dollars an acre, the owner paying the taxes. If the rent is paid in kind, the terms are these: the landlord finds all the land and pays all the taxes; he also does the repairs. For rent he takes half the grain threshed and delivered to granaries on the farm, and the corn in the ear to the farm cribs. The tenant pays another rent here by the month for the grass, which is not, as is sometimes the case, thrown into the bargain. *Taxes.* Taxes on the farm are 1 dollar 85 cents per acre, to which that on personalty adds 15 cents more, making on the whole 2 dollars, or 8s. 4d. per acre. There have been a great number of foreclosures of mortgages during the *Foreclosures.* past three years, owing to the bad times. In 1879, 46¼ *Yield of wheat.* bushels per acre of wheat were grown on 35 acres, after clover for two years pastured with sheep; 32 acres in 1879 grew 35 bushels per acre after corn and after wheat. *Yield of corn and wheat.* Corn will average in 1879 about 60 bushels per acre; though the average yield has been dropping during the past six years, and so has the yield of wheat. If that of 1879 is taken out of account, it will not rise above 18 bushels an acre on this farm, while that for the county during the same period does not exceed 13 bushels for wheat and 50 bushels for corn. *Cost of production less.* The cost, however, of raising and harvesting a crop of wheat now, compared with that of 20 years ago, is probably less.

Wool value. River washed wool was worth 75 to 80 cents in 1874; in the spring of 1879 it could be bought for 20 cents the lb., and now it has risen (November 1879) to 30 cents; 10 cents more, or 40 cents the lb., would satisfy the grower.

Abortion. At Greencastle, Indiana, abortion among cows is said to be warded off by giving a pint of hemp every other day from the time of serving to the period at which the cow last slipped calf, but a great short-horn breeder placed no reliance on this prescription.

Mr. Lockridge's bull. At Mr. Lockridge's farm is a roan bull, five years old, thorough-bred, with a splendid coat and grand rump and round; the charge for his use is 10 dollars or 2 guineas. Mr. Lockridge's herds were examined, beautiful short-horns, and in capital condition. Mr. Lockridge runs a big bullock to 5 acres this year, they are sold, and he has bought in 2 and 3 year old steers for next year's grass. They cost 3¼ cents per lb. and weighed 1,300 lbs., having grass only during the winter, save in coarse weather, when they may have hay or corn stalks. The arable land is let to tenants who give half the wheat (the *Tenants.* landlord finding seed and paying for threshing his half crop) and one-third of the corn and oats. The soil in the neighbourhood of Indianapolis and Green Castle is a limestone and deep loam along the river bottoms.

Dr. Stevenson, of Green Castle, lets his arable land and takes in cattle to graze for 1 dollar a month.

Mr. Lockridge's stock. Mr. Lockridge's thorough-bred Durhams are big thick-fleshed and are more adapted for the production of heavy feeding steers. At another of Mr. Lockridge's farms were *Large fat cattle.* seven majestic 4¾ years old graded steers. It was stated that when quartered the meat would be too large to hang between decks, and was therefore unfit on this account for exportation. They seemed, as well, to be too big and heavy for the English market, weighing as they did 2,300 lbs. They were expected to bring 6 cents a lb. at Christmas. The owner had already sold 40 away from this lot at 5¼ cents per lb., averaging 1,940 lbs. each.

Maize. The Hon. O. P. Davis of Newport, Vermillion County, Indiana, grows from 1,000 to 1,200 acres of "corn" yearly; he finds the seed and gives from 12½ cents to 15 cents per bushel for the cultivation. The land is ploughed 5 inches deep, harrowed marked, dropt, cultivated four times, harvested, and delivered into cribs at that price. Mr. Collett of Eugene, Indiana, also pays 12½ cents. for growing corn. On really good deep land corn has been grown for 50 years and averaged 60 bushels an acre.

Tenants. Professor John Collett, Indianapolis, has had from 25 to 40 tenants upon the family estate, and has let the land for 3 dollars an acre for wheat, corn, grass, and pasture: all landlord's outgoings amount to 25 cents an acre, which he pays, and also finds timber, &c. for repairs, tenants doing the labour. Mr. Isaac Porter, of Eugene, Indiana, has land worth 60 dollars an acre, which he lets for wheat growing. It has grown wheat continually for 10 years, and he receives one half the produce, which has averaged 9 dollars an acre.

Mr. J. W. Davidson, of Mahomet, Illinois, lets 250 acres; 50 acres of wheat average 30 bushels, landlord finds seed and receives half crop; 150 acres of corn yield 60 bushels and landlord receives two-fifths of the crop; 50 acres oats yield 50 bushels, landlord finds seed and receives one-half for rent. He grazes the grass land himself, allowing the tenant 20 acres of pasture for his cows; 20 acres of meadow land are cut for hay, and the crop divided between landlord and tenant. Rates and taxes always paid by owner.

Kentucky.

Mr. Alexander's herd of Woodburn.

At Mr. A. J. Alexander's farm at Woodburn, Kentucky (Nov. 17th), Mr. Lucas Broadhead has the charge of the grand herd of Bates' blood. There are 50 head of beef cattle, 60 head of Durhams, 40 of Jerseys, and grades. Of blood horses, 40 yearling thorough-breds are sold from the mares at 300 to 400 dollars each, 60 guineas to 83*l.*

Fencing.

The enclosures are made with black walnut sawn rails 1½ inches thick by 6 inches wide, fastened to split locust posts; these will last 30 years, and the rails 15.

Our fellow commissioner, Mr. John Clay, junr., well known in the short-horn world, who accompanied us through Kentucky, undertakes to give notes and statement relating to this and other short-horn herds.

Hospital.

At Lexington is the Hospital of St. Joseph, a private establishment in the charge of Roman Catholics. It is under the direction of commissioners or trustees. The city authorities make a payment of 150 dollars annually, raised from 100 dollars, for the privilege of sending in temporary paupers. Private patients are admitted on payment of about 5 or 6 dollars, 21*s.* or 25*s.*, for lodging and attendance, but the patient pays beyond this for the doctor and medicine. Other patients come in with "permits" (letters of recommendation), and are supported out of the charitable fund of the hospital, except with medicine, which is found by the city.

The number of patients is increasing. The doctors make a present of their services except in the case of the paying patients. If a free patient is found to have means of paying he would be dismissed, but such a case has not occurred.

Orphan asylum.

The Orphan Asylum at Lexington is under the management of 24 ladies. For funds they have 5,000 dollars left by a gentleman at the cholera time in 1833. Since then other legacies have come in. The capital is put out to interest, and is not drawn upon; when the interest is insufficient to meet expenses, the matron says "we go out a-begging." The city occasionally gives something, perhaps 500 dollars, over 100*l.* The "county" orphans are taken by arrangement with the county, on a contribution of 700 dollars yearly. Seven county orphans are generally in the establishment. Every county keeps its own orphans and paupers. Parents contribute nothing,

Half and double orphans.

even if able. As to "half" orphans, when the parent has succeeded in obtaining admission for the child, "he or she is satisfied," and refuses to help, though undoubtedly help ought to be given. The original rule at the founding was to receive none but "double" orphans, but this has been broken; now it has been revived, and is being acted upon; the evil consequences of sheltering "half" orphans are apparent. Mothers marry and have other children, or they decamp, in both cases leaving their children in the orphanage. There is no crowding here now. Arrangements are made to take 36 cases. The children are kept till fit to go out in the world, the boys being bound out to masters at 15, and the girls to trade or domestic service at about 16. Boys and girls are sent to school till they leave, and children under 20 months are not admitted. A right is exercised over the boys till they are 21, and the girls till they are 18, and the parents cannot take them away after binding, but this is not attempted in the case of double orphans.

At Lexington, Kentucky, Nov. 17, 1879.

Mr. Warfield, of Lexington, has some good short-horns, Booth's and Bates' combined; Southdown sheep and Berkshire pigs; his farm is all blue grass, and is well watered with ponds artificially made.

Value of live butchers' meat.

Good bullocks, "on foot," 1,800 lbs. were shipped to the number of 100 last week from here to Liverpool market at 4¼ cents per lb. The leg of mutton here makes 8 to 9 cents per lb., 4*d.* to 4½*d.* The Porterhouse steak of beef 12½ to 15 cents, 6¼*d.* to 7½*d.*; the loin of beef, 10 to

Poultry.

12½ cents, 5*d.* to 6¼*d.* A dressed turkey ready for cooking 80 cents, 5*d.* per lb; this year's fowls, 15 cents or 7½*d.* each; geese, 8 cents or 4*d.* per lb. "dressed" or trussed;

Butter, eggs and cheese. Vegetables.

butter, from 15 to 30 cents; cheese, from 10 to 15 cents; eggs, 8 to 25 cents for 12; good cabbages, now 2½ cents, in spring 5 cents each; turnips, 10 cents per bushel for the

Hay and corn.

table or stock; hay, 17 dollars, 3*l.* 10*s.* 10*d.*, per ton of 2,000 lbs.; corn, 35 cents or 1*s.* 3½*d.* per bushel delivered, or 10*s.* 4*d.* per quarter of 448 lbs.

Mr. Hamilton's estate in Missouri.

Mr. Geo. Hamilton, of Flat Creek, Mount Sterling, Kentucky, owns 2,000 acres of prairie land on limestone in Carse county, Missouri, 30 miles south of Kansas City. This estate was bought in 1854 at 1 dollar 25 cents per acre of the

Conversion from prairie to blue grass.

Government, and in 1856 under soldiers' warrants at 90 cents per acre. It remained unproductive till 1867, when it had risen in value to 10 dollars an acre. The land was broken in 1868, and put down in wheat, to be sown out in blue

Blue grass in Missouri prairie.

grass, the seed of which was taken from Kentucky. This took four or five years to complete, and now the blue grass has got complete possession of the land, which grazes 400 head of stock cattle, bred on the spot, and lying on the land without any shelter all the year round. The establishment of this grass diminishes the use of winter food by at least

Blue grass versus prairie fee[d].

one half. The very same land with prairie herbage could not be grazed for more than five months without the assistance of artificial food.

Land need[ed] to fat an o[x].

Two acres of the very best cleared pasture land in Kentucky will make off one ox in the year, raising the weight from 1,350 lbs. up to 1,750 lbs. If timbered groves are measured in, 4 acres would be required. The best cleared "blue grass" pasture round Mount Sterling commands 75 to 90 dollars for purchase, or 15*l.* 12*s.* to 18*l.* 15*s.*

Bad times.

The worst times were in 1877. A young steer worth 20 dollars in 1877 was worth 30 dollars in 1874, and is now again worth as much as in 1874. Real estate and fancy bred stock went all to pieces in 1877. Blue grass improves

Yield of grain.

with age. The average yield of wheat is 20 bushels, of corn 45 bushels.

Ranches and stock.

Mr. Hamilton, says Mr. Driscol, of Ansty, Texas, is a large ranch man in Texas and in Wyoming. Mr. Hamilton supplies him with bulls, "thorough-bred" at 125 dollars, or 26*l.* each, delivered at Kansas when 6 months old. Mr.

Cost of ke[ep].

Driscol tells him it costs a dollar a head a year to keep cattle on his ranches. A branded calf on Mr. Driscol's

Value of stock.

ranch is worth 5 dollars, or 21*s.* To freight cattle from the

Freights.

Pan Handle costs 2 dollars a head from Fort Dodge to Kansas City, and 3 dollars thence to Chicago, and there is in addition the cost of driving 50 miles.

Messrs. Hamilton[s'] farm.

Messrs. Geo. and James C. Hamilton of Flat Creek, Kentucky, have a farm in extent 3,500 acres, of which 250 acres are in arable cultivation, 150 acres corn, 30 acres wheat, 70 acres oats and rye. The average yield of wheat is 20 bushels, corn 50 bushels. Out of the 3,500 acres, 100 acres are forest and not depastured, 500 acres are in groves, (timber with grass under), leaving about 2,650 acres of good cleared blue grass pasture. In June 1879 this farm carried 420 head of thorough-bred short-horns, young and old, 200 head of beef cattle, 100 sheep, 50 horses, 20 mules, 21 jennets, 2 jacks, 100 sheep and 20 hogs. No cattle are

Sale of thorough-bred sto[ck].

housed; there is indeed but one "barn" on the estate. Ninety bulls have been sold off to one man in the Pan Handle. Messrs. Hamilton have other farms besides the large one in Missouri, and they sell annually over 400 head of pure-bred short-horns in three sales, two at Kansas City in May and October, and one at the stock farm in Clarke County.

Wages in Kentucky.

The average wages of farm hands in Kentucky are for a white man 15 to 18 dollars per calendar month, with house and an acre of garden, worth 1 dollar a week, the use of a cow worth 1½ dollars a month, and firewood, to be got in his own time with the master's team free. The coloured man comes on the same terms, but with only 8 to 10 dollars a month in money.

Mr. Van Meter's farm.

Mr. Van Meter's farm is at Sycamore, Winchester, Kentucky. About 50 bulls (of Rose of Sharon strain) sold off annually to Virginia, Tennessee, Ohio, and the West;

Bulls for ranch.

about 50 females are annually sold as well. Four bulls are needed to 100 cows out on the ranch; these are herded separately when they first arrive, and last about two years.

Mr. Van Meter's farm consists of 1,100 or 1,200 acres of land; 180 acres in Indian corn, the rest all in grass. He

Joisting cattle.

has 300 short-horns, and 80 head of other cattle taken in to graze at 1½ dollars a month; 30 or 40 sheep, 30 horses and mules, and 60 pigs. Corn averages 50 bushels per acre. Negro labour is 50 cents a day, best blacks 10 or 12

Cattle management.

dollars a month, with house and garden. Mr. Van Meter says "the less corn that is given to stock, the more money "is made by grazing. The best way is to have three "farms; one in Indian territory for breeding cattle, one in "Kansas for rearing and growing the young stock, and "one in Kentucky for grazing the cattle on good grass."

Texan c[attle] restricti[on].

By the Middle States' law, Texan cattle are not allowed to leave the Chicago stockyard alive between the beginning of April and the beginning of November, except in cars

* This will be found in page 21 of this Appendix.

on trains for passage to other markets for slaughter. Kansas "dead line" law is in force to prevent Texan cattle moving through protected countries now settled up, leaving free passage to the Texans through the unsettled countries. Stock sent into Texas take the Texan disease.

exan fever.

Old bulls invariably die of it, and of the young bulls 30 per cent. die. A larger proportion die if imported in May than if imported in December, but of the latter even 30 per cent. are lost. The Texan disease cannot be transmitted in districts north or west of Texas.

·. Renick's rm.

Mr. Abraham Renick, Sharon, Clarke County, Kentucky, farms an estate of nearly 2,000 acres. Mr. Renick has a grand herd of short-horns, all of the Rose of Sharon blood, there are 64 females and five bulls. He recently exchanged 40 females and one short-horn bull for 543 acres of this prime grass land. Mr. Renick had just sold 39 one and two years prime Southdown wether sheep, weighing about 150 lbs. each, at $4\frac{1}{2}$ cents per lb. live weight, and has bought 38 two year old short-horn steers of excellent quality, weighing 1,344 lbs. each, at 4 cents per lb. These will be sold fat next summer off the grass, being kept on the pastures and foddered with hay during the winter.

·crease of ·ight of

Mr. Abraham Renick this year grazed 47 three year old beasts from early in April to the end of October, when they averaged 1,780*l.* lbs., and had put on over 440 lbs. during the season without any corn. These were sold at $4\frac{1}{2}$ cents to go east.

·tle.

Mr. Burford Tracey, of Winchester, had 75 splendid short-horn oxen, weighing upon an average 1,800 lbs. For these he was offered $4\frac{3}{4}$ cents per lb. live weight, he asked 5 cents. Mr. Tracey considers that a well-bred bullock ought to put on from 400 to 500 lbs. in 12 months.

ue of ·d.

In Kentucky, good grass land had been worth 100 dollars an acre; it had fallen to 60, but had now recovered so as to sell at 70 dollars an acre. If the land was well farmed, and had a good house and buildings, it might fetch 75 dollars; mortgages are effected at 6 per cent. Near Lexington land lets at 4 to 5 dollars an acre, landlord paying rates and doing the repairs; tenants do not stop long.

·t of ·l. ·is to ·veland.

The land between Winchester (where we left the rail for Mr. Van Meter's farm), and Cincinnati, was all on the limestone formation. The first part of the district to Paris was chiefly pastoral, with good blue grass pastures, but beyond it became more arable. From Cincinnati to Cleveland all through Ohio was a nice farming country, mostly devoted to the growth of wheat and maize; some good cattle and only a few sheep. From Cleveland to Hudson was hilly and the farms small; some corn and wheat and hay but not much blue grass. From Cleveland along the shores of Lake Erie to Buffalo the land was flat and in places wet. It seemed fairly farmed but not to produce great crops. From Albany to Boston, 24th, the country is very hilly in parts, so barren that the land appears worth nothing. It cannot be called a farming country at all except in the valleys. Where they are of any breadth there, the land appears very fertile, and in the valley of Connecticut tobacco of a superior quality is grown. For miles there is not an acre of land under the plough.

Cleveland to Hudson, Nov. 22, 1879.

·se ·ry at ·son.

Messrs. Straight and Son, of Hudson, conduct the business of cheese making in 13 factories, from April 1st to December 1st, taking the milk of 5,000 cows. The warehouse is at Hudson. Making new-milk cheese commences in the first week of April, and is suspended about September 14th; then for the rest of the season skim milk cheese and butter are manufactured. The cows run dry during the winter, or perhaps a small quantity of butter is made

of

by the farmers. The average price of milk has been 1 dollar per 100 lbs. or $8\frac{1}{2}$ gallons, something under 6*d.* a gallon. In 1878 the average price was 80 cents. In 1879 it has ranged from 60 to 65 cents, and from April to September about 50 cents, though the closing price just now is 1 dollar 30 cents. With an average price of less than 80 cents farmers throw the business up and take to mixed farming. On September 15th the price in these factories rose from 50 to 60 cents; on September 20th from 60 to 70 cents; on October 1st from 70 cents to 1 dollar; on October 25th from 1 dollar to 1 dollar 20 cents, and on November 5th from 1 dollar 20 cents to 1 dollar 30 cents, the price rising and falling with the market price for cheese. Though the natural weight of a gallon of milk is a little over $8\frac{1}{2}$ lbs. at the factory it is taken at 10 lbs., as 10 lbs. makes one pound of cured cheese. The farmers bring the milk as far as three miles, and deliver it night and morning (on Sundays as on other days) at 8 a.m. and 8 p.m. Payment for milk is made once a month;

·e.

80 cents for 100 lbs. is about as low a price as the farmer can produce it at. In the spring cheeses are sold sometimes as young as 20 days, at other times 90 days, but this is about as long as they will bear keeping; after that they "get dead." In 1879 some of the make at these factories, owing to yellow fever in the south, and low prices, had to be almost given away; several car loads had to be sacrificed, but since September 1st the price of cheese has more than doubled, having risen from $5\frac{1}{4}$ cents to 12 cents at the factory.

Prices.

Messrs. Straight and Son make annually 50,000 cheeses of 30 lbs. each, and 300,000 lbs. of butter. A small amount of cream is taken off the milk during *all* the summer, and made into butter, which is offered for sale from time to time as made, the surplus being kept for sale in the autumn.

Milk is skimmed.

The cheese warehouse, several stories high, is built with air-spaced walls and double windows, kept closed.

Cheese warehouse.

Air by means of a blast is drawn in through a 12-inch glazed pipe, 200 yards in length, open at the far end and laid at a depth of 13 feet under ground. The blast is driven by steam. When the temperature of the external air is 80° to 90°, by passing it through the underground-pipe it is reduced to 61° or 64°. The blast is kept going for 10 hours out of the 24.

Cool air.

As ice is also used in cooling the milk, provision has to be made for a supply of 2,000 tons per annum. This costs about 1·25 dollars a ton of 2,000 lbs. to harvest and pack, exclusive of the value of the ice houses. The ice has to be hauled one or two miles by hired teams from the pond to the ice house at the factory. The ice houses are constructed of wood, double walled, placed on the level ground, and banked up. Six inches of sawdust is spread on the ground, over the drain, and the same thickness is interposed between the inner wall and the ice, finally the ice is covered over at top with 18 inches of sawdust and good ventilation is provided overhead. The blocks of ice are cut 22 inches square, and from 6 inches to 14 inches thick.

Ice houses.

The price of butter in 1879 has ranged from 17 to 38 cents per lb. for general supply. In this country and in the west the price has been 8 cents lower. Grazing and dairying are the uses to which the neighbouring land is put. In 1878, dairy butter went in the winter at 18 cents per lb.; in the fall of 1879 it makes 22 cents. To make a lb. of butter would take from 20 lbs. to 30 lbs. of milk, $2\frac{1}{3}$ to $3\frac{1}{2}$ gallons; this seems a high return.

Milk for 1 lb. of butter.

A farmer who kept from 35 to 70 cows has reduced his herd in consequence of want of help for milking. This farmer says 400 acres will keep 60 cows summer and winter; of this 75 acres are timber land, and 40 acres ploughed for wheat and corn. With wheat at 4*s.* 2*d.* a bushel, and the land producing 20 bushels an acre, a man is said to get his living.

Mixed farming versus dairying.

This farmer rents out his cows from April 1st to December 1st at 14 dollars. The hirer finds all keep on his own land. He has let out all his cows, and has taken to mixed farming with sheep and young stock.

Letting out cows.

In 1878 he had six sheep killed by dogs, and all the lambs were born dead from the mothers being worried. The State made him compensation. 100,000 sheep are said to have been killed or worried by dogs in this State (Ohio) in 1878.

Dogs and sheep.

The value of a good down calving cow is now 35 dollars, or 7 guineas, two years ago the same cow was worth 55 dollars; they will probably recover their old value.

Value of cow.

Land round here is now worth 50 dollars, or 10 guineas an acre. The clay land is good for "wheat" and grass, the sandy is best for maize. More roots (wurtzels) are grown than formerly; they are stored in cellars, and eaten in the spring. They weigh as high as 13 and 15 lbs. each, and yield 490 bushels to the acre. Labour is 1 dollar a day now and board (worth 33 cents), altogether 5*s.* 6*d.*, and this is one-fourth more than it was at the same period in 1878. People are said to get more disinclined to work, to loaf about and get into the Penitentiary, and that education is responsible for this shirking of manual labour.

Value of land.

A good hand will milk 16 cows in an hour and a half. Milk is now selling for 1 dollar 50 cents per 100 lbs. delivered at the local station, about $6\frac{1}{4}$*d.* a gallon.

Milking.

At Boston, Merchants' Exchange, Nov. 25. J. B. Brigham and Co., 38, Central Street, Boston, Massachusetts, state that the rates of grain from Chicago are 45 cents, or 1*s.* $10\frac{1}{2}$*d.* per 100 lbs., subject to a rebate of 5 cents for exportation; this is equal to 8*s.* per quarter of 480 lbs. On "through bills" (as from Chicago to Liverpool) a little concession is made.

River rates to Boston.

Mr. Joseph E. Woods, Foreign Agent, Boston, states that the ocean rates are 6*d.* per 60 lbs. of any grain (they were $2\frac{1}{2}$*d.* to 3*d.* in July); 5 per cent. must be added for primage, this would be about 4*s.* 2*d.* per quarter of 480 lbs. to cross the ocean.

Ocean rates.

The lowest ocean rate was two years ago, when it was down to 1*d.* per 60 lbs., or 8*d.* per quarter of 480 lbs.

Lowest.

The highest was in February 1878, when it stood at $9\frac{1}{2}$*d.*, or 6*s.* 4*d.* per quarter: within the last five years it is said to have been 8*s.* a quarter.

Highest.

Shipowners say 7*d.* a bushel, or 4*s.* 8*d.* per quarter, is a fairly paying rate. The elevator charges for storing and insuring for 20 days, and putting on board come to $1\frac{1}{4}$*d.* per bushel, or 10*d.* per quarter. The insurance is $\frac{5}{8}$ of 1 per cent. on

Elevator charges.

value, less a discount of 20 per cent. For flour in sacks the freight is 22s. 6d. per English ton, and for barrels 2s. 6d. a barrel, 200 lbs.

Cattle freight from Boston to England. Sheep. Hogs.
Ocean freights for live oxen are now offered at 4l. per head to Liverpool or London. They have been as high as 7l. 10s. and as low as 45s. The insurance is about the same as for grain. Sheep are generally paid for by space, coming to about 8s. each, to Liverpool or London. Hogs have been quoted as sheep, but very few are shipped. Molasses are put on board as medicine for cattle at sea.

Provisions;
The freights for boxed meats and lard and provisions, per English ton, is 25s. to Liverpool and 30s. to London; for cheese and butter not carried in a refrigerator, 35s. to Liverpool and to London 40s., but this is rather lower than usual.

in refrigerators.
In refrigerators the rate would be from 65s. to 70s. a ton to Liverpool.

Boston rates are low.
As a rule, shipping can be done on cheaper terms from Boston than from other American ports.

Chicago to Boston.
Rates for boxed meats and provisions from Chicago to Boston for export are 45 cents per 100 lbs., including putting on board.

Butter price.
The choicest butter in pounds, stamped and packed in boxes for hotels, is now 35 to 40 cents, 1s. 5½d. to 1s. 8d., per lb. Creamery butter in tubs is from 1s. 7d. to 1s. 8d. Inferior, made from pastures of prairie "wire" grass, is 21 cents or 10½d. Butter is too dear to ship to England at the present figures.

Butter. Cheese prices.
The best full milk cheese is 13 cents or 6½ per lb. wholesale for the table; retailing adds a cent a lb., making it 7d. Skim and half-skim cheese is from 3d. to 5d. a lb. wholesale.

Martin Fuller, Philadelphia.
Martin Fuller & Co., W. P. stockyards, Thirtieth and Market Streets, Philadelphia, have exported live cattle for two years from Philadelphia to Liverpool, London, Bristol, and Cardiff.

Dead meat prices.
The lowest price of dressed dead meat is 5d., the highest 7d. They have lost money this year by exporting meat to England.

Hides.
"Hidesmen" or tanners bought Martin Fuller's hides at Liverpool, and brought them back in the face of the duties. They ship from the docks, carting the meat from the stockyards. They filled last night the chilled room of one ship, which sailed at 8 this morning; a few quarters returned will be kept until the next steamer starts. A cargo of meat in boxes has been delivered in 16 days from Chicago to Liverpool viâ Philadelphia and Pennsylvania Railroad and "American" line of steamers.

Martin Fuller & Co. slaughter oxen in the stockyards. The whole arrangements are the most perfect we met with.

Fertilisers.
They manufacture a "manure fertiliser" at 2½ cents per unit of ammonia, which sells at 32 dollars a ton, 2,000 lbs.

Bones and Hides.
The raw bones are worth 1¼ cents per lb. Hides at Philadelphia are 20s. each.

Chilling meat.
In preparing the dead meat for travelling, the chilling chamber in summer is brought down to 36° or 38°, and 48 hours are allowed to complete the process of expelling the animal heat and gases. The firm work off from 700 to 800 head of cattle daily.

Paying prices. Ice. Hay. Amount of business.
Beef, they say, should make 6d. a lb. in England to be remunerative, pork 5d., mutton 6d. Ice costs, in the summer of 1879, 10s. 5d. per 2,000 lbs. at the stockyards, and 12s. 6d. on board ship. Hay in the stockyard is 8s. 4d. per 100 lbs. This firm exports weekly 300 beef carcases, 200 live oxen, and 200 hogs. They begin shipping alive in April, and continue till October. Insurance comes too high for winter transportation.

Hogs.
The general character of oxen and sheep is improving; that of swine was always good. Hogs sink 20 per cent. in dressing out of live weights, and selected meat is worth 6½ cents.

Mutton.
Western sheep are worth at Philadelphia 4 to 5 cents live weight per lb.

Skins.
Skins are now worth 1 dollar 75 cents each. Best Southdown sheep are worth 5½ cents live weight.

Stockyard charges.
Stockyard charges are for weighing and yardage 1s. 8d. per ox, and 10 lbs. of hay for feed at 2 dollars per 100 lbs. or a penny a lb., 10d. The charge for sheep is 2½d. and for swine 2⅓d.

Society for protection of cruelty to animals.
Officers of the Society for the Prevention of Cruelty to Animals are constantly in attendance, and offenders are punished.

Better demand.
During the manufacturing depression in Philadelphia for the past five or six years, the consumption of meat in the city dropped in a marked degree; it is now recovering itself, and it is admitted that more cattle than ever will be consumed at home. A good trade is also expected in England by reason of the short supply of winter food in this country.

BALTIMORE, November 28.

Poor land
Came from Philadelphia in the morning, passing through a somewhat poor country, that was said to be "deserted," but which shows signs of good farming. This portion of Maryland is intersected by broad rivers, and some parts of it appear wet and require draining. We saw several fields that had been dressed with farm yard manure or compost, and for the first time in America we discovered some artificial manure being sown by hand on a wheat field. At Philadelphia Mr. Garnett, of the Baltimore and Ohio Railway, promised us a return of past and present freights, and had a steam tug placed at our disposal to view the harbour.

Floating elevator.
We examined the elevators of the company, and saw how the floating elevators discharged and removed corn from a barge into a steam vessel. The harbour was full of ships and everything seemed busy and flourishing.

Freights.
Called on Mr. Sydney Wright (Peter Wright and Sons), who said that freights were singularly low for the season of the year, all ships having come over, many laden with iron, and others tempted by the belief that good freights could be secured for transporting grain to London, Liverpool, and the Continent.

The land between Baltimore and Washington is all poor; a gravelly subsoil with hardly any top soil, a considerable portion of it is in wood. There are a few nice patches of land in the valley, but they are by no means extensive.

VIRGINIA, December 2.

Virginia farms.
To Charlottesville with Mr. Barber, President of the Midland and Great Southern Railway. After crossing the Potomac into Virginia the soil is a stiff yellowish clay, in some places almost white, like pipe-clay. In a short distance the ground changed to red clay, which comes quite to the surface, yet it is said to be very fertile and good holding land. A little nice land around Gordonsville, and the country by Charlottesville was really pretty. Inspected a large farm and saw some good bred short-horns and a number of excellent Normandy horses, a Clydesdale stallion, and a thorough-bred from Mr. Alexander of Kentucky.

Horses.
Grass is not by any means thick upon the ground, and farmers complain of drought which has been so intense that the autumn sown wheat is not yet up.

Government offices.
The time at Washington was mainly occupied in obtaining information from the various Government offices. We were especially interested and instructed at the Department of Agriculture, of which General Le Duc is the head. We had an interview with General Sherman and we attended a sitting of Congress, where besides seeing several gentlemen we had previously met in the provinces, we received some useful facts and fresh ideas from the representatives of other States we had not the advantage of visiting.

The President.
One of us (the other being too ill) paid his respects to President Hayes, who appeared greatly interested in our mission. In all our inquiries we were cordially assisted and kindly directed by the British Minister, Sir Ed. Thorton, and the indefatigable Secretary of the Legation, Mr. Victor Drummond, and we cannot sufficiently express our grateful acknowledgments for the kindness and attention they showed us.

Produce Exchange New York.
At the produce market at New York we again made many inquiries and extracted much useful information. The President of the Exchange, and indeed every official consulted, was most obliging and attentive. Nothing seemed to trouble them, and all the questions we put were answered with courteous readiness.

Railway "pool."
One morning was spent with Mr. Albert Fink, who as Chairman of the Joint Executive Committee of all the great railways, speaks with commanding authority upon all questions of inland freights. We also visited the premises, warehouses, and docks of some large shippers and merchants, and saw the great depôt for emigrants and the capital arrangements made for their comfort on landing, and the ready means adopted for obtaining them suitable employment. At New York we had the advantage of the friendly assistance of the British Consul General, Mr. Archibald, who was ever ready to give us the benefit of his great experience.

Notes by Mr. John Clay, Junr., on the Shorthorns of America and the Dairy Farming of Canada.

The Shorthorn Interest, and its Influence upon the American Beef Trade.

The producing and rearing of pure bred cattle has an immense influence upon the agriculture of America. Notwithstanding the mighty efforts made by single individuals to improve and expand live stock farming, it may safely be said that as a nation those people who live in America did not seriously turn their attention to the production of meat till about three years ago. No doubt countless herds thronged the prairies in a semi-wild state, and there were cattle kings in Texas and other Western States possessing thousands of animals, but they were, and still are, a poor class not fitted to fetch a fourth-rate price on the home market, and at this moment, so far as England is concerned, she has only to compete with a small but rapidly increasing quantity of good animals. Two great classes of cattle thronged and are increasing upon the prairies; the Texans and the common scrub cattle, called by Illinois feeders *stockers*. The former are descended from the old importations made by the Spaniards, and resemble, somewhat, the Spanish cattle of to-day, while the stockers are, without a doubt, descendants of the cattle brought over by those early settlers from England, who sought a home amid the more northern parts of the continent. Throughout the eastern States a class of cattle, mixtures of every breed imaginable, is kept principally for dairying purposes, while occasionally a herd of good grade cattle may be found. It is not my province to inquire why most, venture to say nine-tenths of American cattle are of the poorest description, be it my mission to point out how rapidly these may be improved. Nothing can equal the rapidity with which the Americans, once having seized upon an idea, carry it into effect. As far back as 1784 shorthorns, or what were called improved shorthorns in those days, were brought across the Atlantic. In 1817 another importation was made, and a serious effort made to improve the native cattle. Then in 1834 followed, perhaps, the first practical foundation of a steady improvement. The cattle imported in those years have been most prolific, and some of the families have been with little change carried on and improved by descendants of the importers. In 1853 another notable importation took place, some of the finest shorthorns in England being carried across the Atlantic. In so great a degree was this the case that within the last few years Englishmen have had to bring back at enormous prices some of the descendants of these high bred animals. Ever since that latter date a steady influx of well bred animals has flowed in from the mother country, modified or expanded very much by the state of commerce or trade. There are now many thousands of pedigreed cattle in the American Continent, and every State in the Union, as well as every province in Canada, is well represented. More especially is this the case in Kentucky, Illinois, Iowa, and Ontario. It was very desirable to find out the exact number of shorthorn females, so that an approximation of the annual product and increase of good cattle, might be arrived at, but after communicating with the best authorities upon the subject, I cannot get any satisfactory information on this point.

As a rule the American farmers are not born stock farmers, and they do not take to it readily, but it is being forced upon them for various reasons. First, it pays better than corn farming; secondly, it is accomplished with much less labour, an important fact in a new country; thirdly, they must resort to it, in the older States at any rate, to recuperate a soil worn out with continual corn growing and straw burning. Having got thus far they find that to produce and fatten the class of animals they possess will not pay, and they will need to improve their stock before going further. The prime agent in this great work has been, and will be, the shorthorn. The unparalleled demand for young bulls for six months past shows the rapidity with which stock owners are trying to improve their herds. Towards the close of 1879 there was scarcely a bull in the market. No doubt good times had much to do with this demand, but it is an evidence how much attention is being paid to improvement.

In an extended tour I met with many valuable herds of shorthorns, a proper account of which it would be impossible to give. I take up a few herds which represent on a large scale the shorthorn interest. As I said above every State and province contributes its quota, yet Kentucky pre-eminently is the home of the American shorthorn. Everyone has heard of the famous blue grass which abounds there, and on which cattle subsist the whole year round without artificial food or shelter. Strange as it may seem, the very highest bred cattle in Kentucky and the Western States have never been under any other roof than that which nature gave them. Such treatment produces hardiness and healthiness.

One of the most historic farms in America is that owned by Mr. A. J. Alexander, Woodburn, Kentucky. It is devoted to the raising of fine stock, horses, cattle, and sheep. Although the cattle upon this place are mostly kept outside, it is one of the few places in this state where boxes are provided. There is accommodation for over 100 cattle, and previous to a displenishing sale this summer fully that number were on hand. During summer the cows are continually outside, but in winter time they are housed at night. The bulls are kept in roomy boxes, and part of every day they are turned into a paddock, where they receive healthy exercise. From this place many of the finest shorthorns in the world have gone forth, and the Dukes of Airdrie are household words in every breeder's herd that has any pretensions to owning good cattle. The principal families at this place are the Airdrie Duchesses, Barringtons, Filberts, Vellams, Filigrees, Mazurkas, Miss Wileys, &c.

Perhaps the largest owners of pedigreed shorthorns in the world have their head-quarters in Kentucky. Those are the Hamiltons, a company of gentlemen who own about 700 head. They have various places of business both in Kentucky and the west. At Flat Creek near Mount Sterling, Kentucky, the residence of Mr. George Hamilton, about 250 cows and heifers are kept. The farm is entirely a grazing one, and is perhaps one of the most suitable places for stock raising that can well be imagined. Studded with magnificent trees and gently rolling, the natural shelters are all that can be desired. Beautiful streams intersect the place, and on every side are evidences of that limestone formation which helps to grow and will ever give the lead to the shorthorns of Kentucky over the other parts of America. The families at this place are Barringtons, Kirklevingtons, Places, Ruby Duchesses, Rose of Sharons, Miss Wileys, Gems, Illustriouses, Young Mary's, Josephines and Phyllises. Mr. Van Meter, of Sycamore and Stockplace, is also a member of this firm, and has about an equal number of cattle upon his beautiful grazings; Rose of Sharons, Young Mary's, Phyllises and Josephines are the principal families kept. Each of those herds is headed by a Duke bull. At the former, Grand Duke of Geneva does good service, while, at the latter, 20th Duke of Airdrie is a valuable sire. Many of the animals are sold privately, but the firm hold two annual sales at Kansas City, Missourie, where they get the full benefit of the western demand. Bull calves from their commoner cows range in the auction ring from 100 to 150 dollars each, while the better classes sell from that price up to a 1,000 dollars. Annually this firm sell about 500 cattle bred by themselves and bought from other breeders. Nearly the whole of those cattle go west to improve the herds upon the plains.

The remarkable uniformity of those cattle is marvellous, showing the skill with which they have been bred. The great characteristic is family likeness, and the persistence with which those gentlemen have stuck to systematic breeding is worthy of the highest commendation. To accomplish those ends Kentucky and the whole continent of America, owe a great deal to Mr. Abram Renick the father of transatlantic shorthorn breeders, and perhaps the first breeder of his day. Mr. Renick sticks to one tribe, the Rose of Sharons, of which he owns 65 females. They are all descended from a cow bought from the *immortal* Thomas Bates.

The immense value of the shorthorn is nowhere better demonstrated than in Kentucky. After travelling through the other states it is a pleasure to reach a country where really good cattle are kept. Cattle that would grace the finest pastures in Great Britain. The splendid herds of young bullocks showed an immense wealth among the farmers, and the labour of years in improving those cattle will result undoubtedly in a great financial success, and a lasting benefit to the country, because we have always observed that a country which abounds in flocks and herds supports a well-to-do race of people.

Canada also boasts of many fine cattle, and at the Industrial Exhibition held at Toronto, in September, I saw many noble specimens of shorthorn. No other class of cattle seemed to compete with them. There was individuality and evidence of rapid maturity about them that gave pre-eminence to this class of cattle. The Canada West Farm Stock Association carried away the lion's share of the honours, and in a visit made to Bow Park, where this company keep their herd, the magnificence of the stock at home was only second to that in the show ring. This association own over 300 females. The system is to house all cattle during both summer and winter, and turn them out daily for exercise. They are all fed on soiled food, the principal fodder being green Indian corn stalks. This part of America is singularly well adapted for this system. To show forth that such is the case, some seasons as much as 40 tons per acre of Indian corn fodder is raised. Both in a green state, and also when cured for winter, it is most excellent food.

In this herd, the following families are largely represented, viz. :—Oxfords, Barringtons, Kirklevingtons, Wild Eyes, Places, Duchess Nancy, Waterloos, Darlingtons, Acombs, Rose of Sharons, Roan Duchess, Craggs, and many other Bates families, along with a small but choice herd of Booth cattle. Canada annually produces a large number of first class young bulls, many of which find their way to the States. But as a rule the cattle of Canada have not benefited to such a degree as might have been expected from the number of really serviceable animals that have been bred. It must, however, be borne in mind that Ontario and other provinces of Canada are not adapted to cattle breeding as the grazing is very poor. Its success, so far as cattle are concerned, will be in feeding them, drawing its future supplies from the western states, and fatting for the English market. It will reciprocate in this line the feeling of friendship in sending west a lot of young bulls every season suited to improve the cattle on the plains.

It is unfortunately impossible to get accurate statistics of the number of shorthorns on the continent of America. It may be stated, however, that herds are met in every direction, and that at one sale alone this autumn 300 head were sold in four days. It seemed to me that the shorthorn is destined to play a most important part in the agriculture of America. It seems to be the cosmopolitan of the various breeds of cattle. It thrives all over, and wherever cattle are known, there will it be found. Its rapid maturing powers will give it the preference over all other breeds.

While the cattle trade of America is expanding with wonderful rapidity, it seems to develop into certain courses which as the years roll on will be more distinctly defined. The Mississippi seems to be the line of demarcation dividing the breeding from the feeding States. There will of course be a certain amount of breeding in every part of the Continent, but the real home of the young cattle will be west of the great river which drains the centre of North America. They must inevitably come to the rich and generous soils of Illinois, Indiana, Ontario, &c., to be ripened for the butcher. On the boundless prairies they will develop bone and muscle, while on the richer feeding grounds of those other states, they will gain flesh and fat very rapidly. With such opportunities, and by systematic grading with purer breeds, the raising of good cattle will develop enormously. It is almost impossible to approximate the rate of increase, so large is the importation of thoroughbred bulls in the west. Every bull that crosses the Mississippi adds enormously directly, and still more so indirectly, to the beef producing powers of the plains. Fifteen years ago the cattle of Ireland were a poor and miserable class. One sees to-day the improvement that has taken place among them, but the energy of the Americans, and the generosity of their soil and climate will work the same amount of improvement in half the time. It is not so much an increase in quantity as in quality that we shall need to meet. The actual number of cattle that can be sent to the English market is a mere drop in the bucket in comparison with the numbers that the farmers of the American Continent possess. With systematic breeding, it is safe to say that, in 10 years from this time, the Americans will have 10 times as many cattle suited for our home markets in comparison with the present. I do not mean that the competition will increase 10 times ; for it must be understood that it is likely that, with properous times, the price of good beef and mutton will rise materially in the States and Canada. At present a first rate article rules very high, and is exceedingly scarce. With the price of everything rising in value, it is almost certain that beef and mutton must also be affected. With an increased demand at home, and a certainty of ocean freights increasing considerably, there is little fear of meat being brought across the Atlantic at the prices ruling during the last two years. One fact, however, is certain whatever may be the surplus of butcher's meat on the other side of the Atlantic, to England it must come just as surely as the overflow of American granaries crosses the ocean to feed the millions in our manufacturing cities.

The Dairy Interest of Canada.

This report refers, so far as figures and facts are concerned, to the province of Ontario, but it will be a fair representation, so far as I have been able to gather information, of the dairy interest as pursued in Canada and the Eastern States of the Union.

In the province of Ontario, dairying has been very extensively and profitably pursued for 12 or 15 years back. For many years the Canadian farmers had only one source of income, that derived from grain. Without a certain amount of live stock, grain culture is undoubtedly the most unprofitable of all farming operations. At first the returns from virgin soil are large and easily obtained, but year by year they diminish till at last the land is almost barren. For a long period of years farms that had been carved out of the backwoods rewarded munificently those hardy pioneers who sought a home amid the forests of the west. But in Ontario and the Eastern States, those days are past and a new system of culture has been forced upon the husbandman. Many districts were specially suited to dairying, and accordingly, as if by magic, cheese factories sprung up all over the country. In certain localities they have paid very well. All the evidence that I have taken tends to show that at 10 cents or 5d. per lb. for cheese of the finest quality, the business will be a very profitable one. On the basis of allowing 10 lbs. of milk to one of cheese, we get the result that the production of milk at $\frac{1}{2}d$. per lb. is a very paying business. The great disadvantage is the fluctuating propensities of the trade. During the seasons of 1878 and 1879 cheese was a perfect drug, being quoted as low as 2$\frac{1}{2}d$. to 3d. per lb. and then scarcely saleable. This was a ruinous business, but during last autumn it suddenly recovered, and we find this spring it is quoted at 7d. per lb.

It is therefore very difficult to calculate the profit and loss on a dairy farm, and more especially as it is well nigh impossible to find one solely devoted to this branch of husbandry. The practice almost universal is to find a mixed style of farming, a system of agriculture set on a pivot, so that the farmer can turn round to another branch of the business without much loss. In travelling through the dairy districts you will often come across a farm of this description. The extent we shall suppose 150 acres, cropped thus :—

	Acres.
Wheat	17
Oats	21
Pease	3
Roots	15
Hay	30
Grazing	40
Bush hand	24
	150

The live stock will consist of 12 cows and 20 to 24 young cattle, half of which will be sold annually, and the cows when they are old will be fattened and sent to the butcher at prices which will almost replace heifers, that is to say if the farmer does not rear or place in his byre some of his own breeding. The sales of cattle will average $400 or $500 (80$l$. to 100$l$.) per annum. The cows bring up a calf each, and then, calculating cheese on the basis of 10 cts. per lb., each cow will earn $30 (6$l$.) per head by sending the surplus milk to the factory. Following as near as possible notes sent for my guidance, here is a balance sheet of this farm. It is a practical balance taken down from the lips of a Canadian farmer, and while not very minute it is actual experience, and will show pretty nearly the profit of the year.

Utilisation of Breeding Herds for Dairy Purposes.

Dollars.
1. Rent of dairy land, say 150 acres at $4 per acre   -   -   -   -   600·00
   [The nature of the land is a sandy loam, dry and well adapted for nearly any crop.]

		Dollars.
2.	Live stock, kept 12 cows, 24 young cattle, probably 20 sheep, and 4 horses -	—
3.	Prime cost of cows whether bred or reared on the farm or purchased; include under this heading all stock on the farm along with implements, &c. ? Value $2,000. Interest at 7 per cent. - - -	140·00
4.	Yield of milk, butter, and cheese?—As stated above 12 cows earn $30 cts. each after bringing up calf. House will be supplied with above free of charge -	
5.	Utilisation of whey, butter, milk, &c., including rearing and feeding of calves, pigs, &c. ?—No cash return. House will reap any benefit.	
6.	Cost of food not grown on the farm?—Nothing.	
7.	Cost of labour on the farm?—Farmer and son both able-bodied men, say over and above free home, $250 each -	500·00
	Extra labour, in hay and harvest	50·00
	Wear and tear of four horses $400 at $10 per cent. - - -	40·00
	Wear and tear on implements $500 at $10 per cent. - - -	50·00
8.	Commission on sales and cost of delivery?—Nothing for commission. Delivery of milk calculated at half a cent for each pound of cheese. No charge against farm.	
9.	Cost of heifers, whether bred or purchased, to replace old or unprofitable cows?—No charge against farm.	
10.	Cost of artificial manures?—Nothing. Cost of seed?—Grass seeds, turnip seeds, &c. - - - -	80·00
		1460·00

Yield of Dairy Produce to Farmer.

1.	Gross sum received for dairy products	360·00
2.	Gross sum received for fat calves, pigs or other means of utilising refuse. Nothing in cash.	
3.	Gross sum received for young cattle and cast cows - - -	500·00
4.	Sales of other produce of the farm:	
	Grain - - - -	600·00
	Sheep, wool, &c., with occasionally a young horse - - -	100·00
		1560·00

The actual profit is very small. But over and above the cash receipts, the farmer procures the larger part of his living from the farm. In such a generous climate as Canada much more benefit is derived from the poultry yard, garden, &c. than at home. Then we allow the farmer and his son 50l. each for their labour. If the property is entirely free of debt, a total income of about $1,000 per annum (200l.) will be derived, but then that is the result of labour and interest upon capital combined along with a generous supply of produce from the farm. No cash is paid out, or at least very little. The farm is almost self-supporting. It is a case of no outlay, a life of continual saving. A man in such a position with no horrible mortgage hanging over his head is truly independent.

For further illustration I shall take a farm of 100 acres entirely devoted to dairy purposes, although it would be nearly impossible to find one of such a description. Most of the farms of this size when in a dairying district support 15 cows and just as many young cattle as there is fodder to spare. Such a farm entirely devoted to dairying would be cropped thus:—

	Acres.
Wheat - - - -	20
Oats - - - -	10
Pease - - - -	5
Roots - - - -	5
Indian corn for fodder -	10
Hay - - - -	10
Grazing - - - -	20
Bush - - - -	20
	100

To work the above two horses would be enough, but probably a third would be kept for driving milk, use of family, and various other purposes. The farmer, with the assistance of a boy, would do all the manual labour, and at milking time the family, if any, would assist, but this operation would also be overtaken by the farmer and his assistant.

Cost of Dairy Produce to Farmer.

		Dollars.
1.	Rent of dairy land - - -	400·00
2.	Number of cows kept per 100 acres, 25 cows - - - -	—
3.	Prime cost of cows whether bred or reared on the farm or purchased, say 25 cows at $40 each = $1,000 at 7 per cent. -	70·00
4.	Yield of milk, butter, cheese?—Cows well fed will yield 28 lbs. milk per day for an average of 230 days, equivalent to 600 lbs. cheese per annum	—
5.	Utilisation of whey, butter milk, &c., including rearing and feeding of calves, pigs, &c. ?—No cash return; house will reap a little benefit	—
6.	Cost of food not grown on farm?—This will depend much upon season and farmer's style of feeding, say -	100·00
7.	Cost of labour in the dairy, including attendance and manufacture of dairy products?—None; all milk taken to factory - - - -	—
8.	Commission on sales and cost of delivery, if any?—None in either case -	—
9.	Cost of heifers, whether bred or purchased to replace old or unprofitable cows, say six cows drafted at a loss of $10 each, and allow on death = $40·00 -	100·00
10.	Cost of artificial manure - -	20·00
	Cost of labour - - -	450·00
	Wear and tear of three horses = $300 at 10 per cent. - -	30·00
	Wear and tear on implements = $400 at 10 per cent. - -	40·00
	Extra labour - - -	50·00
	Seed - - - -	50·00
	Service of cows - - -	25·00
		1335·00

Yield of Dairy Produce to Farmer.

1.	Gross sum received for the dairy products?—To cover all accidents of season, &c., it is safe to calculate 25 cows give 500 lb. cheese each at 10 cents	1,250·00
2.	Gross sum received for fat calves, pigs, and other means of utilising refuse?—In this case calves will be sold shortly after birth, say, for lot -	30·00
3.	Gross sum received for cast cows?—This item allowed for on other side -	—
4.	Sales of other produce - -	—
	Grain - - - -	300·00
		1580·00

This balance sheet would represent a gain of over $200·00 to the farmer over and above his labour and interest for his capital, as well as a large portion of his living from the farm. As we have said before it is almost impossible to strike a farm balance sheet, as none of the farmers keep books. To come, however, to actual facts, we quote the experience of one of the shrewdest farmers we have met with in the dairy districts. He possessed a farm of 200 acres, 150 acres cultivated and 50 acres bush. Twenty-nine cows were kept upon the place along with a variety of other stock. The receipts for the milk from those cows delivered at a factory a short distance from his house were from $1,350 to $1,567, as near as can be calculated, $50 or 10l. per cow for the year. His actual income after supplying house and doing a little manual labour himself was on an average $1,000 per year. Allowing $600 as rental of his land, for we count nothing upon the bush land, it being a fair investment to allow it to stand, his actual profit is $400 over and above the produce used from it.

On a farm clear of debt and fully stocked there is no danger but what a practical agriculturist can make a good living, and also save money on a dairy farm. There are times of prosperity and days of depression, but on the whole it is a profitable and paying business, and it is a system of culture well suited to Canada and many portions of the eastern States, and when properly understood it will be an immense source of income to a certain number of American farmers. When the farmers who are engaged in this business find out the value of soiling crops, not only will the production of milk be far greater, but the land will recover from the outrageous treatment which it has received in years gone bye. The remark is often made that the virgin soils of America are practically unexhaustible. It is utter nonsense. No land can keep up its fertility if everything is taken away and no return is made. It is only a question of time, longer in coming in some districts than in others, when every inch of soil will need some assistance in the way of manure. Nowhere is this more clearly seen than in the Province of Ontario, on whose fertile soil after the primeval forest had been cleared away immense crops were produced, whereas to-day scarce a piece of cultivated land throughout the whole Province but shows the want of more careful and kinder treatment. For those reasons, and influenced by the immense competition in the grain trade from the western prairies, dairy farming and all branches of agriculture in which live stock is the principal feature are sure to be favourite pursuits in the older Provinces and States. The competition from those parts is sure to increase in our home markets, not only in quantity but also in quality. The old style of wheat after wheat is past. Another day has dawned upon the American farmers. Every year sees new improvements, and from what I have seen no class of farmers are more perceptive than those who live by dairy farming.

Manufacture of Dairy Products at Factories.

Nothing can be more complete than the system of manufacturing farm produce pursued at the various cheese and butter factories of America. The idea of co-operation is thoroughly worked out in all details, and it is one of the few cases in agriculture where it has succeeded. In certain districts every now and again you come across a large wood building with a hog pen near it, and as a general thing close at hand will be a stream of clear water. To the experienced eye this is a cheese factory. Enter it and you will find everything scrupulously clean and nice. Large vats stand side by side so placed that the milk which is weighed on an outside platform runs into them. Close at hand are the presses, while attached to the main building is a boiler and engine house. This drives all the machinery and heats the milk while in the vats. Far the larger part of the building is used as a store and drying house. It is not my province to go into the various ways of making cheese, for there are many different systems. Suffice it to say that year by year the quality is being improved and made more suitable for the English market. It cannot well fail to be otherwise, for hundreds of intelligent men are devoting their whole life and energy to making this valuable product. In attending this spring the Dairymen's Association of Western Ontario no one could help being struck with the intelligent appearance of the 500 or 600 persons who congregated to discuss the various points connected with their business. No outside discussions or irrelevant questions were allowed. There was, however, a free interchange of ideas, and subjects were sifted in the most complete manner. The whole question centred in milk, how best to produce it, and the most advantageous ways to convert the raw material and place it before the consumer as a manufactured article. Such meetings, devoid of all political animus, are of the greatest service to agriculture, and the example of our dairying friends is worthy of being followed in other branches of agriculture.

Twelve years ago the factory system, so far as cheese is concerned, was in its infancy. But the seed had been sown; factory after factory rose up as if by magic. The rise and progress of this trade may be gleaned from the following facts taken from among countless others :—

" Below we give a correct report of the operations of the
" past season, and also a statement of the business done
" during the 12 years of its management. During the
" season of 1879 there was received at the factory the
" quantity of 995,290 lbs. of milk, which made 1,580
" cheese, weighing 97,768 lbs., and brought the sum of
" $7,213·30. Substracting expenses, $991·43, there was
" left a dividend of $6,221·87. Quantity of milk required
" to make one lb. of cheese 10⅙ lbs."

CONDENSED STATEMENTS for the past TWELVE YEARS of the Factory.

Year.	No. of Cheese.	Lbs. of Cheese.	Lbs. of Milk.	Total Receipts.
				$
1868	647	38,844	307,243	1,669.96
1869	1,195	71,743	682,054	8,260.74
1870	1,691	101,446	988,828	11,686.45
1871	1,639	98,324	970,230	9,637.20
1872	1,590	95,344	942,403	10,841.50
1873	1,521	91,253	906,521	10,194.74
1874	1,554	112,848	1,122,754	13,720.19
1875	2,057	123,474	1,228,304	13,239.83
1876	2,307	138,416	1,385,000	13,268.22
1877	2,691	161,485	1,625,444	18,040.74
1878	3,444	213,981	2,143,482	17,785.26
1879	1,580	97,768	995,290	7,213.30
	21,916	1,344,926	13,360,523	135,558.13

Average quantity of milk per lb. of cheese, 9.93.
Average price per lb., a fraction over 10 cents. ,,

The above is a fair index of what can be done in cheese-making. The average price of 10 cts. per lbs. is a profitable one, and at such a price dairy farmers universally admit that they can make money. It will be noticed that in ten years the production increased five times, but it was carried more on account of commercial depression than anything else, to a greater extent than what the demand warranted. In 1879 an extraordinary change takes place, showing the marvellous rapidity with which agriculturists in America can change into a different course. The product suddenly falls to half the previous year's amount. Here again we have an extreme. With so little production and the trade improving all over the world we find the price of cheese double itself in six months.

But to give an idea of the inside financial work of a factory we produce a balance-sheet of one of those establishments for 1879.

APPENDIX TO JOINT REPORT.

STATEMENT of the CHEESE MANUFACTURING COMPANY for the year 1879.

Total of milk received at factory - 1,635,454 lbs.
Average lbs. of milk to the lb. of cheese - 10$\frac{45}{100}$

Amount of cheese made at factory - 156,475½ lbs.
Cheese sold for, $11,516$\frac{38}{100}$. Average price per lb. 7$\frac{36}{100}$ cents.

Dr.	
To balance cash in bank from 1878	586·70
„ cash in bank, cheques issued not paid	96·36
„ cash from cheese sales	11,036·56
„ interest on deposits	44·66
„ cash for whey	182·00
„ cheese sold patrons and others	479·82
„ cash from patrons for overmake	17·61
„ cash from ex-treasurer to treasurer	6·14
„ difference	·01
	12,449·86

Cr.	
By paid making account	1,095·75
„ „ patrons	8,723·81
„ „ teaming	1,086·71
„ „ do. in 1878	22·93
„ „ auditing	8·00
„ „ account	4·20
„ „ repairs on factory	329·73
„ „ interest on note	18·00
„ „ scale boards	21·95
„ „ boxes	307·29
„ „ printing	7·60
„ „ insurance	15·41
„ „ transmitting	17·80
„ „ sundry accounts	7·62
„ „ rent and rails	23·00
„ „ postage	1·75
„ „ expenses, travelling, &c.	16·03
„ „ shipping and weighing	13·05
„ „ taxes	12·90
„ „ salary to M. S.	51·00
„ „ salary to treasurer	15·00
„ due for cheese	15·12
„ cash in treasurer's hands	·37
„ cash in bank	634·84
	12,449·86

STATEMENT.

Building and plant cost.	
Borrowed money	300·00
	300·00

$3,500·00.	
Cash in bank	634·84
Do. in treasurer's hands	·37
Due for cheese	15·12
Stones on hand—value	20·00
	670·33

The expenses, as will be seen from the above statements, are much heavier in the one factory than the other; perhaps the result of situation, such as distance from farm to factory and from factory to railway facilities. In many cases the patrons do all the teaming. In the latter case it is charged against the factory. Both factories appear to have got about the same amount per lb. for their cheese—about 7$\frac{1}{3}$ cents per lb.—but owing to the expenses in working and otherwise the actual gain to patrons in one case was 6$\frac{1}{3}$ cents and in the other 5$\frac{60}{100}$ cents per lb., a very material difference. At those prices dairying, so far as the farmer is concerned, is a ruinous business, but with cheese now selling at 14 cents per lb., giving the farmer about 12 cents for his milk, his receipts are doubled.

The more we know of the cheese factories which are freely dispersed all over the Eastern States and Canada, the more we admire the system. In a country where labour of a certain class (it is skilled labour that is needed in this department of agriculture) is scarce and dear, cheese making could not be carried on profitably as in Great Britain. Few men can command the capital to start and carry on a farm of dimensions large enough to produce milk to keep even a factory on a small scale in running order. But with the above system it is a very easy matter. Under its beneficial influence several districts in America are destined to rise into considerable importance as agricultural centres. The land instead of being impoverished will gain ground in fertility, the people will grow richer, while food will be produced at a cheaper rate for the million.

Export of Dairy Produce, Cheese, &c.

Under this heading I do not think it necessary to go into detail. We have spoken to a great many exporters upon the subject, and their evidence, so far as cheese is concerned, simply amounts to the fact that on an average a charge of 2 cents per lb. will cover all expenses of exportation from America to Liverpool or London. This covers conveyance to seaboard, cost, freight, and insurance to Great Britain and commission upon sales there.

Concluding Remarks.

It is, of course, difficult to predict the future of the dairy business in America, and we are speaking now of the whole Continent. For a period to come, more attention will be paid to butter making. For our purpose, however, cheese and butter may be classed as one. The same raw material produces both, and at different times, as the price of the product varies, more attention will be paid to the one than to the other.

I am of opinion that in this line of agricultural produce we shall need to face an ever increasing competition. I do not say that prices will fall much, but the change from certain classes of farming into this is so rapid that in almost any year the production increases so much that the market can be flooded and the prices forced down to a ruinous point, while undoubtedly the cost of production will be lessened. The manufacture, pure and simple, of milk into butter and cheese cannot be much reduced; always excepting the gradual and steady improvement of quality, and the grading up of low class goods into a better article. But there is an immense step towards producing the raw material at a lower rate. Granted that milk at 10 cents per gallon is a very profitable business, and that it pays if the farmer can get 8 cents per gallon in an ordinary season, the time is not far distant when, with land at the same rate as at present, the American farmer can produce milk at 2 cents per gallon less than he has been doing. This will be accomplished by an improved husbandry. There are no rich and fertile pastures in the dairying districts of America as in Great Britain, nor from the climatic influences will there ever be such, but the land is suitable in every way to a splendid system of soiling. The open nature of the land influenced by a powerful sun is eminently suited to produce those crops so essential to the pursuit of dairying. When 30 to 40 tons of green fodder (Indian corn) can be raised per acre, and that food very succulent and full of saccharine matter, milk can be produced for a great portion of the year at a very cheap rate. The difficulty in America as at home is to educate the farmer to adopt new plans, but in time, as the country grows older and the development of science in agriculture is extended, new systems will replace the old. Nor is it only in summer that the American farmer has an advantage over the British dairy farmer. In winter the price of all classes of food is comparatively low, as for instance, where we reside, bran, the principal winter food of dairy cows, can be bought at 40s. per ton of 2,000 lbs., just about half of its price at home.

Q 2685.

Up to this time American farmers have not profited from those advantages to the extent they might have done. They have neither improved their herds nor fed them as liberally as they should have done, but the course on events will force them into it. To compete with the new lands upon the prairie now feeling for the first time the influence of the ploughshare, the culture of cereals must lessen every year in the East. Not only to protect themselves, but also to recuperate the energies of the land which they have abused so recklessly, the farmers in the Eastern States and Canada will be forced to enter upon a mixed husbandry, of which stock farming will be the principal part. They will be compelled to follow a more generous, and what is sure to follow, a more economical style of farming.

Average Price of Dairy Products compared with Flour and Pork in New York City during the Month of January each Year, from 1825 to 1879, arranged in Decades.

First Decade—1825 *to* 1835.

——	Cheese.	Butter.	Flour.	Mess Pork.
	Lb. c.	Lb. c.	Bbl. $	Bbl. $
1825 - -	7¼	15	5·13	13·37
1826 - -	8	15¼	4·80	11·75
1827 - -	7¼	17½	5·14	11·87½
1828 - -	6⅛	15⅓	5·58	14·12½
1829 - -	6¼	13¾	6·45	12·25
1830 - -	6¾	13½	4·98½	11·50
1831 - -	6	14¾	5·71	13·87
1832 - -	6	15⅓	5·76⅓	13·50
1833 - -	6	15½	5·56⅓	13·25
1834 - -	6¾	14	4·98	14·50

Second Decade—1835 *to* 1845.

——	Cheese.	Butter.	Flour.	Mess Pork.
	Lb. c.	Lb. c.	Bbl. $	Bbl. $
1835 - -	7¼	17½	5·86½	13·75
1836 - -	8¾	19⅓	7·49⅓	18·25
1837 - -	9⅓	19	9·14	23·50
1838 - -	8	20	7·96	21·50
1839 - -	9	19	7·30	23·25
1840 - -	6¾	17½	5·29½	14·25
1841 - -	5¾	11⅓	5·58½	13·25
1842 - -	7	11¼	5·57	9·62½
1843 - -	5¼	8⅓	4·85½	8·87½
1844 - -	4⅔	10¼	4·67	10·12½

Third Decade—1845 *to* 1855.

——	Cheese.	Butter.	Flour.	Mess Pork.
	Lb. c.	Lb. c.	Bbl. $	Bbl. $
1845 - -	6⅔	13½	4·93½	9·31½
1846 - -	7	13	5·06	13·56
1847 - -	6¾	16	6·68½	10·25
1848 - -	6¾	16	5·96	11·00
1849 - -	6	15	5·51	14·18
1850 - -	6¼	15⅓	5·55	11·81
1851 - -	5¾	14¼	4·52	12·18
1852 - -	6¾	18¾	5·00	14·68
1853 - -	8½	18	5·78	19·62
1854 - -	9½	19½	8·89½	13·43

Fourth Decade—1855 *to* 1865.

——	Cheese.	Butter.	Flour.	Mess Pork.
	Lb. c.	Lb. c.	Bbl. $	Bbl. $
1855 - -	9½	22¼	8·76	12·62
1856 - -	8½	22½	6·42	17·37
1857 - -	9½	22¼	5·78½	19·67
1858 - -	6¼	18½	4·29½	15·75
1859 - -	8½	19	4·11	17·57
1860 - -	11	16	4·30	16·18
1861 - -	10	14	5·35	16·12
1862 - -	7	15	5·50	12·25
1863 - -	12	22	6·05	14·43
1864 - -	15½	24	7·00	19·87

Fifth Decade—1865 *to* 1875.

——	Cheese.	Butter.	Flour.	Mess Pork.
	Lb. c.	Lb. c.	Bbl. $	Bbl. $
1865 - -	20	45	10·00	35·25
1866 - -	18½	30	8·75	29·12
1867 - -	17½	30	11·00	19·12
1868 - -	15	45	9·55	21·00
1869 - -	19½	40	6·60	28·00
1870 - -	17½	30	4·85	29·75
1871 - -	16¼	20	6·25	19·75
1872 - -	13½	15	6·40	14·50
1873 - -	14¼	16	6·25	13·25
1874 - -	14¾	27	6·00	16·50

Sixth Decade—1875 *to* 1879.

——	Cheese.	Butter.	Flour.	Mess Pork.
	Lb. c.	Lb. c.	Bbl. $	Bbl. $
1875 - -	15¾	29	4·50	20·50
1876 - -	13¼	26	4·35	20·75
1877 - -	14¼	28	5·50	17·50
1878 - -	12¾	27¾	....	....
1879 - -	8	20	5·00	8·25

To give some idea of the relative trade in butter and cheese, and the extraordinary fluctuations in quantities, take, for instance, the exports from the port of New York of the two articles for 18 years from January to January.

——	Butter.	Cheese.
	Lbs.	Lbs.
1861 - - -	23,159,391	40,141,225
1862 - - -	30,603,235	39,200,439
1863 - - -	23,060,999	40,731,168
1864 - - -	14,174,861	49,755,842
1865 - - -	9,718,079	41,668,213
1866 - - -	1,985,432	38,379,069
1867 - - -	4,479,456	53,429,518
1868 - - -	987,362	41,233,806
1869 - - -	1,168,447	56,413,581
1870 - - -	1,399,354	61,710,435
1871 - - -	7,500,347	70,245,881
1872 - - -	4,814,497	67,109,248
1873 - - -	3,586,103	88,860,349
1874 - - -	4,641,896	94,102,050
1875 - - -	4,226,976	92,000,960
1876 - - -	10,590,823	94,432,805
1877 - - -	19,652,176	107,594,189
1878 - - -	23,590,608	134,007,282

ORGANISATION of the JOINT EXECUTIVE COMMITTEE, as adopted December 18 and 19, 1878, with ADDITIONS and AMENDMENTS to June 18, 1878.

Office of Chairman, Joint Executive Committee, 346, Broadway, New York.

At a meeting of the representatives of the Eastern Trunk Lines and Western Roads, held at Chicago, December 18 and 19, 1878, the following Articles of Organisation of the Joint Executive Committee were adopted:—

1. That this committee be known as the joint executive committee.

2. It has been organized by the election of Albert Fink as permanent chairman, and   as permanent secretary.

3. The general office of the committee shall be located at New York, and the chairman and secretary be authorised to incur such expense as is necessary to fulfil its purpose.

4. It shall take cognizance of all through competitive freight and passenger traffic in both directions.

5. Its object shall be the maintenance of agreed rates, and the abatement of expense on all such traffic by all initial and connecting lines.

6. It shall convene at the call of the chairman or any three (3) of its members, on a notice of 48 hours, when necessary; otherwise, such additional time shall be given as may be practicable.

7. The point of meeting shall always be in New York, when no other point is specified in the call.

8. The object or objects of every special meeting shall be stated in each and every call therefor.

9. Regular meetings shall be held in New York, the third Tuesday of each month, unless the chairman advises the members in the prior week that no business will be ready for presentation thereat.

10. The committee, or a majority of the committee, or their representatives, shall constitute a quorum for the transaction of business.

11. If at any time two-thirds of the members of the committee, or their alternates or representatives authorised to act, are present, the chairman shall act and vote for the members absent or those present who are not authorised to act.

12. In case any question brought before this committee fails to receive its unanimous action, such question shall be referred to the chairman, who shall decide the case upon its merits, and whose decision shall have the same force and effect as the unanimous vote of the committee.

13. Any two or more of the members of the committee, or their alternates or representatives, may meet and act with the chairman upon questions local to them.

14. All negotiations between the committee and companies not represented by it shall be carried on solely through the chairman.

15. All companies are to make all complaints as to direct or indirect violations or evasions of rates, promptly, by wire and mail, to the chairman of the committee, accompanied, in all cases, with as much proof as may be obtainable.

16. All companies, parties thereto, agree not to take any steps to meet alleged abatements or evasions of rates by other lines until the committee has acted thereon and announced its conclusions.

17. The committee is authorized and empowered to specify and enforce against all companies such rules and regulations for its purpose as it may from time to time adopt, and the committee or the chairman acting therefor may call for all persons and papers it may desire.

18. The western members of the joint executive committee shall represent and act for all western companies which the western executive committee has heretofore represented or acted for.

19. The chairman of the joint executive committee shall ascertain promptly, and report as early as practicable, what other companies, eastern or western, do or do not agree to be bound by its proceedings; and what member, alternate or representative, upon the joint committee shall represent their several interests.

20. In the event of any company withdrawing its member upon the committee, or the authority it has given any other member, alternate or representative, to act therefor, it shall give not less than 30 days' notice to the chairman; but this agreement shall nevertheless continue in force among the remaining parties hereto.

At a meeting of the joint executive committee, April 23 and 24, the following additional articles were adopted at the recommendation of the president of the trunk lines:—

21. That each of the trunk line presidents name a member or members who shall act upon the joint executive committee, not only for his own trunk line company, but to represent with full and equal power each and every other company directly or indirectly controlled by the presidents of the trunk lines.

22. That the presidents farther authorise their so appointed representatives upon this joint executive committee to act for such other western railroad companies as may see fit to delegate such authority to them, and that all western companies be solicited by the presidents to delegate such authority to the trunk line appointees upon such executive committee, or place other permanent representatives for each of their interests upon said joint executive committee.

23. When all the members are named by the trunk lines and their connexions, the joint executive committee shall then alone have the power to make, change, and enforce all through passenger and freight rates and rules in both directions, from, to or beyond their respective termini and common points upon all of said competitive traffic common to any two or more of the trunk lines, and prescribe such other rules, regulations and orders, and exercise such power over all officers, soliciting, contracting, and other agents, as may be necessary for the maintenance and enforcement of agreed rates, classifications, rules, and penalties.

24. In the event that any connecting line fails or refuses to delegate authority to any of the other members upon such joint executive committee, or to appoint an independent representative thereon, that the presidents farther authorise the trunk line executive committee, in connexion with the joint executive committee, to take such action as to such companies as, in the judgment of the executive committees, may be deemed proper.

25. That the presidents affirm the principle of pools, in both directions, upon all through freight and passenger traffic common to any two or more of the trunk lines, and direct their representatives on the joint executive committee to call the full joint executive committee together, at an early date, to perfect such pools, and adopt such rules and regulations for the maintenance of rates, and their enforcement, as the said joint executive committee may deem just.

26. In view of the differences then likely to arise in said joint executive committee, we farther urge, as an essential to any permanently successful results, the distinct adoption of the principle of arbitration; and in order to carry it into effect, we farther recommend that a permanent board of arbitration be appointed by the said called meeting of the joint executive committee, which board shall continue in permanent session at New York.

27. That any differences, of whatever nature, arising in said joint executive committee, in the formation of such pools, or in any matter, act, or thing relating thereto, or to the maintenance of rates in the absence of pools, upon which the joint executive committee is not unanimous, shall be promptly referred to the said board of arbitration; and the decision of said board of arbitration, or that of a majority of its members, shall be final and binding upon all parties, until changed by unanimous agreement of the joint executive committee, or by the said Board of arbitration.

In accordance with Articles 26 and 27, the following gentlemen were elected as arbitrators:—

CHARLES FRANCIS ADAMS, Jr.,
DAVID A. WELLS,
JOHN A. WRIGHT.

These gentlemen have agreed to serve for one year, commencing June 1, 1879.

The following resolution, determining how the salary of the arbitrators is to be paid, was adopted at the meeting of April 23:—

28. That the salaries to be paid the members of the board of arbitration be paid by the several roads represented on the joint executive committee *pro rata* on the gross earnings from the competitive business, to be ascertained and proportioned by the chairman of the committee.

At the meeting of the joint executive committee, held in New York, June 12 and 13, the following resolutions were adopted:—

29. That all parties desiring to submit any question for arbitration, are requested to notify the chairman of the executive committee, stating the nature of the case to be decided and the time at which they wish the case heard, and that the chairman of the joint executive committee notify the chairman of the board of arbitration, and arrange for the time of hearing the case.

30. That the chairman of this committee be, and he is hereby requested to notify the managing or executive officers of all western railroads, not already represented in the joint executive committee, of the establishment and organisation of said committee, and of the selection of the board of arbitration, and request all such companies, who desire to become parties to and co-operate in the said arrangement, to appoint a member to represent them.

31. That the trunk line executive committee, representing the trunk lines, as well as all such other connecting railroad companies who may authorise the members of this committee to act for them, constitute a standing committee for the purpose of carrying out the resolutions of the joint executive committee, and to take such other action as may be thought necessary for the maintenance of rates, and the enforcing of all agreements made between the companies represented on the joint executive committee; and further,

32. That the standing committee may obtain the votes in writing or by telegram upon any subject that may be necessary to be acted upon promptly (avoiding thereby as much as possible the necessity of calling together the full joint executive committee), and such votes shall be counted, and shall have the same force as if given in full meeting of the members of

the joint executive committee; a notice of the result of the vote to be given by the chairman to all the members of the committee.

At a meeting of the board of arbitration, held on June 18, the following rules were adopted:

33. The parties concerned in the matter to be referred to arbitration shall in all cases put in writing a statement of facts, supported by such arguments and statistics as they may see fit to present, and shall transmit the same to the chairman of the joint executive committee.

34. On receipt of the foregoing statement, the chairman of the joint executive committee shall specify in writing the exact question or questions which are to be passed upon by the board, and transmit the same to it at once, together with all the statements submitted, or other information in his possession relating to the matter in dispute.

35. The board of arbitration shall, as soon as may be, after such papers are received by it, meet for the consideration of the case, and shall either decide the same or make such order in regard to procuring further information or having oral hearings as may seem necessary.

36. The final decision of the board when arrived at, shall forthwith be transmitted by it to the parties interested and to the chairman of the joint executive committee.

I certify that the above is a correct copy of the articles of organisation of the joint executive committee, as adopted on December 18 and 19, 1878, and of the amendments adopted up to June 18, 1879.

ALBERT FINK, Chairman,
Joint Executive Committee.

LIST of ROADS represented on the JOINT EXECUTIVE COMMITTEE, June 18, 1879.

Atlantic and Great Western.
Baltimore and Ohio.
Canada, Southern.
Central, Vermont.
Chicago and Alton.
Cleveland, Columbus, Cincinnati, and Indianapolis.
Grand Trunk.
Great Western.
Indianapolis and St. Louis.
Lake Shore and Michigan Southern.
Marietta and Cincinnati.
Michigan Central.
New York Central.
New York, Lake Erie and Western.
Ohio and Mississippi.
Pennsylvania Railroad.
Pennsylvania Company.
St. Louis, Vandalia, Terre Haute, and Indianapolis.
Toledo, Peoria, and Warsaw.
Wabash.

TARIFF RATES 1879, CHICAGO to NEW YORK, as furnished by MR. ALBERT FINK, 346, Broadway, New York, December 1879.

		4th Class Provisions.	Grain per 100 lb.
		Cents.	Cents.
During a severe fight.	May to June	—	10 to 12
	June 9, rates (1879)	20	15
	June 23	25	20
Higher rates made possible by large business.	August 4, good summer rate.	30	25
	August 25	35	30
	October 13	40	35
	November 10	45	40

The above rates were established and maintained since June 9 owing to the improvements made in the co-operation of the roads.

The rates prior to August 4 were too low, and were forced on the roads by former competition, which in May and June 1879 reduced the rates beyond precedents.

If the railroad company succeed in maintaining fair and reasonable rates which they desire to establish, it is fair to assume, taking the present cost of railroad operation, that they would make no lower rate on grain during the season of navigation from Chicago to New York (1,000 miles) then 20 cents per 100 lbs., say from May to August; 25 to 30 cents from August to September; 35 cents in October, 40 cents during the winter months, say November, December, and January, and 35 to 30 cents from February to May (lower rates during those months in anticipation of opening of navigation).

At present prices of railroad operation, 15 cents per 100 may be considered the very lowest, but 20 cents nearer the average of all roads, and the tendency is towards an increase in cost of transportation.

Cattle rates are at present 55 cents per 100 lbs.; never exceeds 60 cents per 100. During temporary fights they have gone down to 25 cents, and in some instances 1 dollar per car load has been charged, Chicago to New York. Hogs are shipped at 10 cents over 4th class rates.

The rates are generally better maintained than the rates on grain and provision.

Tariff from Kansas City to Chicago, about 500 miles:—

Wheat, May 6, 1878 to September 12, 1879, varies from 25 to 28 cents per 100; mostly 25 cents.

Corn, barley, and oats, same period, from 20 to 23 cents; mostly 20 cents.

Fourth class, 25 to 31 cents; mostly 25 cents.
Provision same as wheat.

TARIFF RATES FROM CHICAGO.

Date.	4th Class.	Grain.	Box Meats.
	Cents.	Cents.	Cents.
July 2, 1877	35	30	35
Sept. 4, ,,	35	35	35
Oct. 17, ,,	40	40	40
,, 22, ,,	40	40	45
Feb. 9, 1878	30	30	35
March 11, 1878	30	30	30
April 1, ,,	30	25	30
May 17, ,,	25	20	20
July 3, ,,	18	16	18
August 1, ,,	25	20	20
,, 5, ,,	30	25	30
,, 19, ,,	30	30	30
Sept. 2, ,,	35	30	35
,, 2, ,,	35	30	—
Nov. 25, ,,	40	35	—
Feb. 20, 1879	35	30	—
March 4, ,,	30	25	—
,, 17, ,,	20	20	—

CURRENT RATES FROM CHICAGO.

		Cents.
February 2, 1878	-	27½
,, 15, ,,	-	25
,, 20, ,,	-	22½
,, 22, ,,	-	20
April 1, ,,	-	25
,, 25, ,,	-	22½
,, 27, ,,	-	20
May 9, ,,	-	18 & 18½
,, 17, ,,	-	20
,, 28, ,,	-	18
July 1, ,,	-	15 & 16
August 1, ,,	-	Tariff.

Date.	4th Class.	Grain.
	Cents.	Cents.
August 5, 1878	25	20
,, 15, ,,	30	25
Sept. 2, ,,	35	30
Nov. 25, ,,	40	35
Dec. 10, ,,	35	30
,, 12, ,,	30	25
,, 17, ,,	25	25
Feb. 26, 1879	20	20
March 11, ,,	18	18
,, 17, ,,	15	15

(Circular No. 17.) Furnished by MR. ALBERT FINK.

Loss on "CHICAGO EAST-BOUND TRAFFIC," owing to failure to maintain TARIFF RATES.

Office of Chairman, Joint Executive Committee,
New York, May 27th, 1879.

The following is an estimate of the losses sustained on the Chicago east bound traffic during the period from December 19th, 1878 (the day on which it was agreed to pool the Chicago business), to the 1st of May 1879 (4 13/31 months).

This estimate is based upon the difference in the agreed rates and the rates as actually charged (approximately), and is submitted in order to show the great folly of the present and past method of conducting the competitive traffic of railroads, as well as to again demonstrate the necessity of future co-operation in maintaining reasonable and permanent rates of transportation.

APPENDIX TO JOINT REPORT.

Month.	Tons Forwarded.	Agreed Rates in Cents, per 100 lbs.			Actual Rates in Cents, per 100 lbs.			Average Reduction in Rates.	Loss of Revenue.
		4th Class Provision.	Grain.	Average.	4th Class Provision.	Grain.	Average.		
1878.									Dollars.
December, 13 days	82,532	40	35	37	35	30	32	5	82,532
1879.									
January	196,759	40	35	37	30	25	27	10	393,518
February	200,130	35	30	32	20	20	20	12	480,312
March	259,031	30	25	27	18	18	18	9	466,256
April	298,484	25	20	22	15	15	15	7	417,876
Total	1,036,936	—	—	—	—	—	—	—	1,840,494

See notes regarding rules after April 1879.

This loss of revenue, 1,840,494 dollars, distributed over the five terminal roads, and their eastern connections according to the actual tonnage carried by each road, is as follows, viz. :—

	Per Cent.	Dollars.
Michigan Central and connections	29·9 =	550,308
Lake Shore " "	24·8 =	456,442
Pennsylvania " "	41·2 =	758,284
Baltimore and Ohio " "	4·1 =	75,460
Total loss	=	1,840,494

The following table shows the gross and net earnings derived from the Chicago business for $4\frac{13}{31}$ months, the estimate being based upon the supposition that all the business went to New York. This simplifies the calculation and gives results sufficiently correct for present purposes, $95\frac{1}{4}$ per cent. of the Chicago business having actually gone to Boston, New England, New York, Philadelphia, and Baltimore. It is also assumed that fourth-class business is 40 per cent. of the total grain and fourth-class business.

The cost of transportation on east-bound business (including the return of the cars) is estimated at 12 cents per 100 lbs. from Chicago to New York, and 3 cents terminal charge, a total cost of 3·00 dollars per ton. This may be considered the lowest possible cost at this time, being only 0·35 cent per ton per mile; the average cost on the Lake Shore and Michigan Central roads during last year was 0·474 cent per ton per mile, equal to the rate of 22·8 cents per 100 lbs. from Chicago to New York.

Gross and Net Earnings from Chicago Business for $4\frac{13}{31}$ Months.

					Dollars.
December, 13 days	82,532 tons, at average rate of 32 cents per 100 lbs. actually charged	=	528,205
January	196,759 " " " 27 " " "	=	1,062,499
February	200,130 " " " 20 " " "	=	800,520
March	259,031 " " " 18 " " "	=	932,512
April	298,484 " " " 15 " " "	=	895,452
	1,036,936 " " " $20\frac{1}{3}$ " " "	=	4,219,188
Cost of transporting	1,036,936 " " " 3·00 per ton		3,110,808
	Net earnings		1,108,380
The losses sustained on account of reduction in rates have been			1,840,494
If rates had been maintained, the total net revenue would have been			2,948,874

There were carried east during the $4\frac{13}{31}$ months 1,036,936 tons, the actual net revenue (estimating the cost of transportation at the lowest possible figure, much lower than the freight can really be carried) was per ton $\frac{1,108,380}{1,036,936} = 1·07$ dollars, and the net revenue that could have been obtained, if the low and reasonable tariff, as shown in the first table, had been maintained would have been $\frac{2,948,874}{1,036,936} = 2·84$ dollars, showing that the railroad companies would have made the same net profit, if, instead of carrying the tonnage at the rates they did, they would have carried only $\frac{1·07}{2·84} = 37\frac{2}{3}$ per cent. of the tonnage at the tariff rates.

The following statement shows how much tonnage the terminal roads could lose, if rates were maintained, before there would be any reduction in the net revenue which they actually derived from the business under the low rates, viz. :—

	Per Cent.	Per Cent.
Michigan Central	from 29·9	to 11·4
Lake Shore	" 24·8	" 9·3
Pennsylvania	" 41·2	" 15·5
Baltimore and Ohio	" 4·1	" 1·5

It follows that by maintaining tariff rates any per-centage of tonnage which a road may receive above the low per-centages shown in this statement will cause an increase in the net revenue over and above the net revenue derived from the larger tonnage under the low rates which have prevailed during the last $4\frac{13}{31}$ months.

In conclusion, attention is called to the following facts :—

That on roads on which the cost of transportation is greater than 15 cents per 100 lbs. from Chicago to New York, and this is the case on most roads, a still greater reduction in tonnage could be made, if rates were maintained, before any loss of net revenue was incurred.

On roads on which the cost of transportation is at the rate of $20\frac{1}{3}$ cents per 100-lbs. from Chicago to New York, or 0·42 cents per ton per mile, no net revenue is made, and such road could give up the whole business without losing money.

The above estimate of losses incurred, viz. 1,840,494 dollars, shows only the loss incurred for $4\frac{13}{31}$ months, and from the Chicago business alone.

To estimate the loss for the year and for the whole east bound traffic, it is safe to assume that for the whole year from Chicago alone it will be twice as much as for the $4\frac{13}{31}$ months, and that the Chicago business is about one-fourth of the whole east-bound competitive business ; so that the losses per year to the railroads east of the Mississippi river and north of the Ohio to the seaboard are about $8 \times 1,840,494 = 14,724,000$ dollars.

This does not include the losses from local business, the revenue from which is affected by the low through rates. The fact that these low through rates give rise to unjustly discriminating local rates, and that the bitter feeling of the people against railroad corporations results mainly from this unjust discrimination, should also be considered, and induce railroad managers to maintain by co-operation reasonable and equitable rates of transportation.

The loss of 1,840,494 dollars for $4\frac{13}{31}$ months was no doubt due to the fact that the agreement to apportion the Chicago business between the terminal lines in December last was not carried out.

The difference in the division of traffic which led to the disagreement was 4 per cent. of the Chicago business. The net revenue derived from these 4 per cent. since the 19th of December 1878 to April 30th, 1879, at the low cost of transportation, as estimated above, was (on 41,477 tons, at 1·07 dollars) = 44,489,000 dollars.

This being the amount in dispute, the whole revenue of the railroads east of the Mississippi river and north of the Ohio river, has had to sustain a loss at the rate of 15,000,000 dollars per year. Since May 1st, up to which date the above estimates are made, still further reduction in the rates on the east-bound traffic, including live stock and also passenger traffic, have been made which will greatly increase the losses.

These facts show the great necessity of carrying out in good faith the plan of co-operation under the organisation of the joint executive committee which has lately been adopted, and according to which all differences between competing railroad companies are to be settled by arbitration.

Had the question of the division of the Chicago traffic been submitted to arbitration and settled, the enormous losses as estimated above could no doubt have been avoided.

ALBERT FINK,
Chairman.

ALL RAIL FREIGHTS, CHICAGO to NEW YORK, furnished by ED. M. ARCHIBALD, Esq., C.B., BRITISH CONSULATE GENERAL, NEW YORK, Dec. 1879.

"All rail" freight tariffs eastward from Chicago on grain per 100 lbs. These are the published tariff rates from time to time during each year from 1874 to 1879 inclusive. Large quantities of freight have been transported by rail at rates much below the published tariffs.

Grain.	Highest per 100 lbs.	Lowest per 100 lbs.
	Cents.	Cents.
1875	45	30
1876	45	20
1877	40	30
1878	40	20
1879	40	20

The average for the five years being 6s. 10d. per quarter of 480 lbs.

In March 1879 there was a break in the rail rates, when grain was taken from Chicago to New York at from 15 cents to 18 cents per 100 lbs. On the 19th of March the rates on grain were as low as 15 cents per bushel to New York, 13 cents to Philadelphia, and 12 cents to Baltimore. Again, on the 8th May there was a break on the rail rates to 15 cents on grain from Chicago to New York, 13 cents to Philadelphia, and 12 cents to Baltimore, and during May the competition reduced the rates exceptionally to 10 cents to New York, and lesser rates to Philadelphia and Baltimore.

All Rail Rates, Chicago to New York. Ed. M. Archibald, Esq., C.B.

	Flour per barrel.		Pork, Beef, Lard, per 100 lbs.		Boxed Meats, per 100 lbs.		Bulk Meat, per 100 lbs.	
	Highest.	Lowest.	Highest.	Lowest.	Highest.	Lowest.	Highest.	Lowest.
	Cents.	Cents.	Cents.	Cents.	Cents.	Cents.	Cents.	Cents.
1875	90	70	85	70	—	—	55	45
1876	90	40	70	65	—	—	55	20
1877	80	60	40	30	45	35	50	40
1878	80	32	40	16	45	18	50	23
1879*	80	40	50	30	45	25	50	30

NOTE.—Exceptional rates were made far below the foregoing during March and May 1879.

LAKE and CANAL TRANSPORTATION. (All water route.)

AVERAGE FREIGHTS, CHICAGO to NEW YORK, 1875 to 1879.

(Distance, Chicago to Buffalo, 900 miles. Buffalo to New York, 500 miles. Total, 1,400 miles.

	Wheat (per Bushel 60 lbs.)			Corn (per Bushel 56 lbs.)		
	c.	m.	fr.	c.	m.	fr.
1875	11	4	3	10	3	1
1876	9	5	8	8	6	6
1877	11	2	4	9	8	3
1878	9	1	5	8	3	1
1879	†10	0	0	9	0	0

The average for the five years will be for wheat per quarter of 480 lbs., 3s. 5d., for corn per quarter of 448 lbs., 3s. 1d.

* Cents, mills, fractions.

† This is the best estimate that can be given of the present year's freights, no statistics having as yet been published.

TARIFF of CHARGES for HANDLING and STORAGE of GRAIN at the Port of NEW YORK. ED. M. ARCHIBALD, Esq., C.B.

1878–9.

Storage.

Storage, including weighing, on all sound grain for first 10 days or part thereof, ½ cent per bushel, and for each succeeding 10 days or part thereof, ¼ cent per bushel.

Handling and Weighing.

	Per bushel.
Weighing	½ cent.
Elevating from canal boats	½ "
Screening and blowing	½ "
Turning grain	1–5 "

	Per bushel.
Transferring grain in store, including weighing	¾ cent.
Transferring, including screening and blowing	1 "
Bagging grain, including holding, loading, and tying bags	1 "
Bagging, with specific weight	1½ "

Total for grain in bulk about 1s. 5d. per quarter.

Vessel Charges.

	Per 1,000 Bhs. Dollars.
Delivering on board single-deck ocean vessels, including trimming	7·00
Delivering on board double-deck ocean vessels, and trimming	8·00
Delivering on board ocean vessels in bags	6·25
Delivering on board coastwise vessels, including trimming	2·50

OCEAN FREIGHTS, NEW YORK to LIVERPOOL and LONDON. December 1879.

Live Cattle.	Dressed Meat.	Sheep.	Pigs.
Per head.	Per ton of 40 cubic feet.	Per head.	Per head.
4l. to 5l.	20s.	5s. to 6s.	7s. to 8d.

The *average* freight during the seven months ended 31 July 1879 has been as follows:—

Cattle, 3l. 10s. per head; sheep, 5s. 6d. pigs, 10s.

Ocean Freights. New York to Liverpool and London.—1875 to 1879. Ed. M. Archibald, Esq., C.B.

RATES of OCEAN FREIGHT, BALTIMORE to LIVERPOOL.

Peter Wright & Sons,
44, Second Street, Baltimore.

—	Average.	Oilcake, per 2,240 lbs.		Grain, per Bushel.		Flour, per Barrel.	
		Highest	Lowest.	Highest	Lowest.	Highest	Lowest.
	d.			Cents.	Cents.	*s. d.*	*s. d.*
1875 -	10	—	—	13	7	3 9	2 6
1876 -	10	30*s.*	25*s.*	14	6	3 6	2 9
1877 -	$7\frac{1}{2}$	—	—	11	4	3 6	2 9
1878 -	$8\frac{1}{2}$	—	—	11	6	3 6	2 6
1879 -	$6\frac{1}{2}$	—	—	$9\frac{1}{4}$	4	—	—

Average of five years, 5*s.* 7*d.* per quarter of 480.

CHARGES.—INTERNATIONAL NAVIGATION COMPANY'S GIRARD POINT GRAIN ELEVATORS, PHILADELPHIA, 1878.

Per bushel.

Receiving, weighing, and storing from cars, including first 10 days' storage, and delivery to vessel - - - - - - $1\frac{1}{4}$ cents.

Per bushel.

Receiving, weighing, and storing from vessels, and including first 10 days' storage - - - 2 cents.
Delivering same to vessels - - - $\frac{1}{4}$,,
Every succeeding 10 days' storage - - - $\frac{3}{8}$,,
*Blowing, on delivery or in store - - - $\frac{1}{4}$,,
Weighing and transferring in store - - $1\frac{1}{4}$,,

Weighing and delivering in bags, including sewing or tying, with specific weight in each bag, one cent per bushel additional.

Weighing and delivering in bags, including sewing or tying, without specific weight in each bag, five-eighths of one cent per bushel.

Wharfage will be charged on sailing vessels at the company's docks, 2·00 dollars per day.

PETER WRIGHT & SONS, General Agents,
C. B. Rowley, 307, Walnut Street,
Manager (Room 23). Philadelphia.

Dec. 1879. Present freight to London and Liverpool, of cattle 4*l.*; grain, 4*d.*; flour in barrels, 2*s.*; bags, 1*l.* 1*s.* 3*d.* per 2,240 lbs.; salt meats in boxes and barrels, 1*l.* 5*s.* per ton of 2,240 lbs.; canned provisions, no quotations; cheese and butter, 1*l.* 15*s.*

Highest and lowest freight this year $9\frac{1}{4}$*d.* and 4*d.*

* Grain will only be screened and blown when practicable.

EXPORTS from PHILADELPHIA, furnished by JOEL COOK, Esq., PHILADELPHIA.

—		1874.	1875.	1876.	1877.	1878.	1879 to June 30.
Corn - - - -	Bush.	2,203,588	4,601,586	16,790,691	10,271,423	19,868,713	10,125,476
Wheat - - - -	,,	3,289,532	3,302,054	2,989,704	2,546,857	8,854,301	6,146,256
Rye - - - -	,,	104,616	179,872	431,223	188,613	112,567	—
Flour - - - -	barrels	186,663	161,291	217,943	132,437	212,812	36,013
Salt meats - - -	lbs.	23,037,458	36,501,997	77,457,010	65,942,522	96,904,135	40,279,257
Fresh meats - - -	,,	—	—	—	6,790,870	6,063,430	7,203,910
Butter and cheese - - -	,,	2,444,775	2,604,208	2,492,410	3,037,437	3,835,305	1,520,131
Lard - - - -	,,	8,245,342	14,056,634	14,336,924	8,190,580	18,058,998	6,458,372
Cotton - - - -	,,	14,298,118	13,551,977	18,615,475	10,681,119	14,538,168	4,782,263
Cattle - - - -	head	—	—	—	1,346	4,156	3,109
Sheep - - - -	,,	—	—	—	—	3,759	1,855
Hogs - - - -	,,	—	—	—	—	2,393	1,056
Petroleum, refined - -	galls.	70,810,711	55,112,341	55,107,836	41,280,536	67,249,735	23,188,178
,, crude - - -	,,	1,614,116	6,497,845	7,512,635	5,220,501	5,244,184	1,352,694

PHILADELPHIA to LIVERPOOL.

Highest and Lowest Freight Quotations, 1874 to 1879.

—	Grain, per 60 lbs.	Flour, per Barrel.	Oilcake, per Ton.	Tallow, per Ton.	Provisions, per Ton.	Beef, per Tierce.	Pork, per Barrel.	Cotton, per pound.	Tobacco, per Hds.	Cheese, per Ton.	Cattle.
	d. *d.*	*s. d.* *s. d.*	*s. d.* *s. d.*	*s. d.* *s. d.*	*s. d.* *s. d.*	*s. d.* *s. d.*	*s. d.* *s. d.*		*s. d.* *s. d.*	*s. d.* *s. d.*	
1874 - -	$12\frac{3}{4}$ and 4	4 0 & 2 0	40 0 & 17 6	50 0 & 20 0	60 0 & 20 0	9 6 & 4 0	7 6 & 3 0	$\frac{1}{2}$ and $\frac{1}{8}$	55 0 & 20 0	60 0 & 20 0	60*s.* to 120*s.* per head.
1875 - -	$11\frac{1}{2}$,, 5	4 0 ,, 2 0	45 0 ,, 20 0	50 0 ,, 25 0	55 0 ,, 27 6	9 0 ,, 5 0	7 0 ,, 2 6	$\frac{1}{2}$,, $\frac{3}{16}$	52 6 ,, 25 0	55 0 ,, 25 0	
1876 - -	10 ,, 6	4 0 ,, 2 0	35 0 ,, 20 0	50 0 ,, 20 0	50 0 ,, 20 0	9 0 ,, 2 6	6 6 ,, 1 9	$\frac{7}{16}$,, $\frac{7}{32}$	50 0 ,, 21 6	60 0 ,, 25 0	
1877 - -	$11\frac{1}{2}$,, 4	4 0 ,, 2 0	32 6 ,, 10 0	50 0 ,, 12 6	55 0 ,, 15 0	8 0 ,, 3 0	6 0 ,, 2 0	$\frac{3}{8}$,, $\frac{7}{32}$	47 6 ,, 22 6	70 0 ,, 20 0	
1878 - -	10 ,, $5\frac{1}{2}$	4 0 ,, 2 6	32 6 ,, 20 0	40 0 ,, 20 0	45 0 ,, 20 0	8 0 ,, 4 0	6 0 ,, 3 0	$\frac{11}{32}$,, $\frac{7}{32}$	50 0 ,, 27 6	52 6 ,, 30 0	
1879 - -	$8\frac{1}{2}$,, 4	4 0 ,, 1 9	25 0 ,, 15 0	42 6 ,, 20 0	55 0 ,, 25 0	9 0 ,, 4 0	7 0 ,, 2 $10\frac{1}{2}$	$\frac{1}{2}$,, $\frac{3}{16}$	45 0 ,, 25 0	70 0 ,, 25 0	

RATES OF INSURANCE, furnished by JOEL COOK, Esq., PHILADELPHIA.

Sailing Vessels.

	Summer.	Winter.
Grain - -	1 per cent.	$2\frac{1}{2}$ per cent.
Oil - -	$\frac{7}{8}$,,	$1\frac{1}{4}$,,

Steamers.

	Regular Liners.	Outsiders.
Grain -	$\frac{3}{8}$ to $\frac{1}{2}$ per cent.	$\frac{3}{4}$ to $1\frac{1}{2}$ per cent.
Provisions, &c. -	$\frac{3}{8}$,, $\frac{1}{2}$,,	$\frac{3}{4}$,, $1\frac{1}{2}$,,

Purchasing and shipping commission, $1\frac{1}{2}$ to 2 per cent.

INMAN STEAMSHIP COMPANY, LIMITED, LIVERPOOL, furnished by DAVID MACIVER, Esq., M.P.

Average rates of freight per 100 lbs. on grain carried by this company's steamers during the years 1875 to 1879, inclusive.

A.—Rates from Chicago to New York.

—	No. of Shipments.	Highest Rate.	Lowest Rate.	Average Rate.
		Cents.	Cents.	Cents.
1875	None.	—	—	—
1876	1	40	40	40
1877	2	$28\frac{1}{2}$	$28\frac{1}{2}$	$28\frac{1}{2}$
1878	4	40	$30\frac{1}{2}$	33·87
1879	15	$25\frac{1}{2}$	$\frac{4}{5}$	15·30

These rates include cost of transportation to New York, and putting alongside steamer. Average, 6 dollars per 480 lbs.

B.—Rates from Chicago to Liverpool.

—	No. of Shipments.	Highest Rate.	Lowest Rate.	Average Rate.
		Cents.	Cents.	Cents.
1875	None.	—	—	—
1876	1	70	70	70
1877	2	$65\frac{1}{4}$	$65\frac{1}{4}$	$65\frac{1}{4}$
1878	4	68	$63\frac{1}{2}$	65·60
1879	15	53·42	28·83	38·00

These rates include all charges for transportation, transhipment at New York, and discharging from vessel in Liverpool. Average, 11*s.* 11*d.* per 480 lbs.

C.—Rates from New York to Liverpool.

—	Highest Rate.	Lowest Rate.	Average Rate.
	d.		*d.*
1875	$16\frac{11}{24}$ and 5°/ₒ prim.	$8\frac{3}{4}$*d.*, and 5 °/ₒ	$13\frac{1}{3}$ and 5°/ₒ prim.
1876	$14\frac{4}{1}$,,	$8\frac{1}{8}$,,	$12\frac{3}{4}$,,
1877	$17\frac{17}{24}$,,	$7\frac{1}{2}$,,	$11\frac{1}{6}$,,
1878	$16\frac{1}{4}$,,	$9\frac{19}{24}$,,	$12\frac{2}{3}$,,
1879	$13\frac{1}{3}$,,	$7\frac{2}{3}$,,	$10\frac{1}{2}$,,

The above rates include putting on board in New York, transportation, and discharging from ship in Liverpool.

Quay porterage $\frac{5}{9}$ of a penny per 100 lbs.

Shortage averages 1 per cent.

Importers' profits, insurance, interest or commissions not included in above figures.

34, Lancaster Gate, W.,
10th March 1880.

DEAR MR. PELL,

I GOT my friend, young Inman, to look up his books and see what his company had been getting for bringing wheat from Chicago to Liverpool during the last five years.

Three shillings a cental looks as if it were quite an outside figure *as regards the mere cost of transportation.* This, I think, entirely bears out my estimate, which was that 5*s.* a cental more than represents the total cost of putting wheat from Chicago into the hands of the consumer in England. It looks to me as if the 5*s.* a cental really meant a handsome profit to every body all round. I do not see where 2*s.* a cental or anything approaching to it could, plus cost of conveyance, go away in expenses, and therefore it is distinctly my opinion that 5*s.* a cental is beyond the mark and leaves a *large* margin for profits.

My people were trying to get you some more information from other sources, but I do not know what they will be able to do now, as we are all busy about the election.

Yours, &c.,
DAVID MACIVER.

(Furnished by David MacIver, Esq., M.P.)

AVERAGE RATES on GRAIN from NEW YORK to LIVERPOOL during five years ending 31st December 1879. Grain free on board at New York.

—	1875.		1876.		1877.		1878.		1879.	
	Steam.	Sail.	Steam.	Sail.	Steam.	Sail.	Steam.	Sail.	Steam.	Sail.
	d.	*d.*	*d.*	*d.*	*d.*	*d.*	*d.*	*d.*	*d.*	*d.*
Freight, and 5 per cent. primage	14·84	13·20	14·05	13·33	12·06	11·55	13·24	12·37	10·85	10·32
Insurance on 10*s.*, estimated value of 100 lbs. grain, at 7*s.* 6*d.* per cent. for steam, and 20 per cent. sail.	·45	1·20	·45	1·20	·45	1·20	·45	1·20	·45	1·20
Dock and town dues, 1*s.* 8*d.* per ton = per 100 lbs.	·89	·89	·89	·89	·89	·89	·89	·89	·89	·89
Master porterage, 1*s.* $4\frac{1}{2}$*d.* per ton = per 100 lbs.	·74	·74	·74	·74	·74	·74	·74	·74	·74	·74
Per cental of 100 lbs. - -	16·92	16·03	16·13	16·16	14·14	14·38	15·32	15·20	12·93	13·15

NOTE.—Average cost of freight (steam and rail) for five years - - 5*s.* 6*d.* per quarter.
Add other charges as above, about - - - $2\frac{1}{2}$*d.* per bushel = 1*s.* 6*d.* ,,

Total - - 7*s.* 0*d.*

Liverpool, 1st March 1880.

STATEMENT of AVERAGE RATES of FREIGHT, CHARGES, &c. on 100 lbs. Grain worked out in pence and decimals, furnished by WM. RATHBONE, Esq., of LIVERPOOL.

—	1875.		1876.		1877.		1878.		1879.	
	Steam.	Sail.	Steam.	Sail.	Steam.	Sail.	Steam.	Sail.	Steam.	Sail.
	d.	*d.*	*d.*	*d.*	*d.*	*d.*	*d.*	*d.*	*d.*	*d.*
Average rate freight, including 5 per cent primage, New York to Liverpool.	—	—	13·87	12·98	12·14	11·40	13·23	12·44	10·76	10·13
Average rate freight, including 5 per cent. primage, Chicago to New York.	—	—	Rails. 14·37	—	Rails. 16·78	—	Rails. 12·90	Lake. 4·41	Rails. 13·09	Lake. 6·47
Through rate, Chicago to Liverpool.	27·50	—	25·50	—	25·41	—	23·88	—	22·55	= avge 25 = 10*s.* per quarter.
Lake insurance to be added on to lake freight, $\frac{1}{4}$ per cent. and 10 per cent.	—	—	—	—	—	—	—	0·27	—	0·27
Dock town dues, Liverpool, say at 1*s.* 8*d.* per ton.	·89	·89	·89	·89	·89	·89	·89	·89	·89	·89

AGRICULTURAL INTERESTS COMMISSION:

Statement of Average Rates, &c.—cont.

	1875.		1876.		1877.		1878.		1879.	
	Steam.	Sail.	Steam.	Sail.	Steam.	Sail.	Steam.	Sail.	Steam.	Sail.
	d.	d.	d.	d.	d.	d.	d.	d.	d.	d.
Porterage and other charges, say at 2s. per ton.	1·07	1·07	1·07	1·07	1·07	1·07	1·07	1·07	1·07	1·07
Shortage, 1 per cent., say on 10s.	1·20	1·20	1·20	1·20	1·20	1·20	1·20	1·20	1·20	1·20
Marine insurance on 10s., at 7s. 6d. per cent. for steam, and 2l. 10s., 2l. 7s. 6d., 2l., 2l. 5s., 2l. 5s. for sail.	·45	3·00	·45	2·85	·45	2·40	·45	2·70	·45	2·70
Commission, 2½ per cent., interest, &c., 1 per cent.	4·20	4·20	4·20	4·20	4·20	4·20	4·20	4·20	4·20	4·20
Average rate freight, &c., Chicago to Liverpool, per steamer.	35·31	—	33·31	—	33·29	—	31·69	—	30·36	13·1
New York to Liverpool, by steamer.	—	—	21·68	—	19·95	—	21·04	—	18·57	—
New York to Liverpool, by sail.	—	—	—	23·19	—	21·16	—	22·50	—	20·19

Note.—Average 13s. 1¾d. per quarter of 480 lbs., Chicago to Liverpool, by rail and steamer, including all charges.

Cost of Growing an Acre of Maize, near Le-Mars, Iowa, and of delivery at a Railway Station, estimated by Close Brothers & Co., 38, Cornhill, and Lemars.

	Cents.
Rent 8 per cent. on 12 dollars, value per acre (improved) 5 miles from a railway	·96
Ploughing, average price by contract, 1877-78-79	·90
Harrowing „ „ „	·20
Marking „ „ „	·10
Seed „ „ „	·06
Planting „ „ „	·35
Cultivating, three times, contract price	·90
Husking and cribbing, price by contract, with yield of over 40 bushels	·75
Hauling to station, 5 miles, 40 bushels, one team hired for 2 dollars 50 cents could make two journeys	1·25
	5·47

Lowest price at Le-Mars, 1879, 16 to 18 cents per bushel.
Highest price at Le-Mars, 1879, 28 to 30 „ „
Cost per bushel, as above, 13·825 cents per bushel.

N.B.—All these prices being contract prices, include a return of 8 per cent. on the capital invested in land, implements, and teams.

Cost of producing an Acre of India Corn.

	Dollars.
Interests on cost of land 8 per cent., at 20 dollars per acre	1·60
Ploughing	1·
Harrowing over	·25
Marking	·15
Seed	·10
Planting	·30
Cultivating three times	1·00
Husking and hibbing	·75
Delivery at station	·05
	5·20

F. L. Underwood, Esq.,
Merchants National Bank,
Kansas City.

Dear Sir, Minneapolis, Minn., September 26, 1879.

In response to the inquiries you made of me, I beg to state that the kind of wheat milled in this city is all spring wheat, mostly known as hard wheat. The value of same to-day is, for No. 1, 98 cents, and No. 2, 93 cents per bushel of 60 pounds. Four and three-fourths bushels of No. 1 spring wheat will make a bushel of flour of 196 lbs. In the manufacture of flour there is a waste of about 12 lbs. per bushel, leaving as bran and shorts about 77 lbs. per bushel. The flour made from the wheat will range about as follows, viz.:—

Thirty-eight per cent. of our Superlative, and about 5 per cent. of a grade called Imperial, worth respectively to day at the mill 7·25 dollars and 6·75 dollars per bushel. 45 per cent. of bakers' flour called Snowdrop worth at mill to-day 5 dollars per bushel, and 12 per cent. of low grade, worth about 3 dollars per bushel at mill. The price of offal to-day is but 5 dollars per ton, a very low figure, as it is sometimes worth more than double that sum. I believe that I have answered all of your questions above, but shall be glad to give you any further information in my power.

Hon. A. Pell, M.P., Very truly yours,
care of British Consul New York. C. C. Washburn.

47, Exchange Place,
Dear Sir, New York, October 27, 1879.

According to promise I send you an account of the grindings at Pillsbury's and Washburns' mills, you will see they make a great profit on what they do. I think you may take Pillsbury's as more correct of the two, as one man buys wheat for both mills, and from what I could make out 98 cents per bushel was the price of wheat on that day and not 92 cents as stated by Washburn. I send you a sample of the wheat they were grinding. They grind much higher than we do and regrind their bran; they also use a purifier to every pair of millstones, and pay very great attention to dressing their stones. I do not see they do anything that we English millers need be afraid of, or that we cannot do, but they beat us in one thing at present, i.e., they get a very good price for their flour. With kind regards to Mr. Read and yourself, and hoping you may have a pleasant passage home.

I am, &c.
A. Pell, Esq., M.P. Robinson Greenwood.

N.B.—Shall be glad to hear what your friends think of the grinding.

Wheat Grinding at Pillsbury and Washburn Mills, Minneapolis, furnished by Mr. Robinson Greenwood, of Blackburn, England.

Pillsburys.

	Currency. Dols.	Sterling. £ s. d.	£ s. d.
196 lbs. flour at	5·55	1 3 1½	
94 „ offal	·24	0 1 0	
	5·79	1 4 1½	1 4 1½
300 lbs. wheat at 98 cents per bushel =	4·90		1 0 5
			0 3 8½

This shows a profit for grinding and expenses of 3s. 8½d. per barrel of 196 lbs.

Washburns.

	Currency. Dols.	Sterling. £ s. d.	£ s. d.
196 lbs. flour at	5·55	1 3 1½	
79 „ offal	·20	0 0 10	
	5·75	1 3 11½	1 3 11½
285 lbs. wheat at 92 cents per bushel =	4·17		0 18 2½
			0 5 9

This shows a profit of 5s. 9d. for grinding and expenses per barrel of 196 lbs.

Robinson Greenwood.

APPENDIX TO JOINT REPORT.

Flour is reckoned as under—

			Dols.	£	s.	d.
40 per cent.	patent at 7 dols.	=	2·80	-	0 11	8
50 „	bakers at 5 „	=	2·50	-	0 10	5
10 „	red dog at 2½ „	=	·25		0 1	0½
			5.55		1 3	1½

(FORM OF PATENT.)

The United States of America.

To all to whom these presents shall come, greeting,

Homestead certificate }
Application

Whereas there has been deposited in the General Land Office of the United States a certificate of the register of the Land Office at   , whereby it appears that pursuant to the Act of Congress, approved 20th May 1862, " To " secure Homesteads to actual Settlers on the Public Domain," and the Acts supplemental thereto, the claim of
has been established and duly consummated in conformity to law for the   according to the official plot of the survey of the said land, returned to the General Land Office by the surveyor general.

Now know ye, that there is therefore granted by the United States and the said   the tract of land above described, to have and to hold the said tract of land, with the appurtenances thereof, unto the said
and   heirs and assigns for ever.

In testimony whereof, I,   , President of the United States of America, have caused these letters to be made patent, and the seal of the General Land Office to be hereunto affixed.

Given under my hand at the city of Washington the
day of   in the year of our Lord one thousand eight hundred and   , and of the Independence of the United States the
By the President   .
By   Secretary.
Recorder of the General Land Office.

Recorded Vol.   , page

MORTGAGE DEED.

THIS INDENTURE made and entered into the   day of
in the year of our Lord one thousand eight hundred and   between   of the county of   and State of   , the part of the first part, and   of the county of   and State of   , the part of the second part,

Witnesseth, That the said part of the first part, for and in consideration of the sum of   in hand paid, by the said part of the second part, the receipt of which is hereby acknowledged, do hereby grant, bargain, and sell unto the said part of the second part,   heirs and assigns   certain tract of land, situate, lying and being in the county of Sangamon and State of Illinois, known, designated, and described as follows, to wit :

And for the consideration aforesaid, the   part of the first part hereby waive and release , confirm and transfer and for ever relinquish to the said part of the second part all right, interest, or title   may now have or may hereafter acquire in and to the real estate herein-before described, by virtue of the laws of the State of Illinois, approved February 11th, A.D. 1851, entitled " An Act to exempt homesteads from sale on execution," and all laws amendatory thereof.

To have and to hold the aforesaid tract or parcel of land, free from all homestead exemption rights, together with all the appurtenances thereto belonging or in anywise appertaining, to the only proper use and benefit of   the said part of the second part   heirs and assigns for ever. And the said part of the first part, for   heirs, executors, and administrators, do   covenant with the said part of the second part, that   lawfully seized, that said land is free from all encumbrance, that   ha full right to convey, and will for ever warrant and defend the said tract of land from the claim of   the said part of the first part   heirs and assigns and against the claim or claims of any other person whomsoever. Nevertheless, the above indenture of mortgage is upon this express and only condition : That whereas,

In witness whereof, the said part of the first part ha hereunto set   hand and seal the day and year first above written.

In the presence of }
          (L.S.)

Q 2685.

State of Illinois, Sangamon county, SS. Before me, the undersigned   within and for the county aforesaid came   who   personally known to me as the real person by whom and in whose name the above conveyance was executed, and by whom and in whose name the same is proposed to be acknowledged, and who then acknowledged   signature thereto to be   free and voluntary act and deed, for the purpose of waving and releasing all right, title, and interest in and to said land by virtue of the homestead exemption laws of said State, and for all other purposes therein expressed; and the said   being by me first examined separate and apart from   said husband and the contents of said conveyance being first made known to   acknowledged that, freely and voluntary without any compulsion or coercion from   said husband executed the same, and for ever released and waived all right interest, and title to said real estate, by virtue of the homestead exemption laws of said State, relinquished all
right to the claim of dower in and to the lands and tenements in said conveyance, described and sold, transferred and conveyed all title in fee simple or right by inheritance, in and to the real estate aforesaid, and that   do not wish to retract.

Given under my hand and   seal, this
day of   in the year of our Lord one thousand eight hundred and

(L.S.)

QUIT-CLAIM DEED

THIS INDENTURE, made the   day of
in the year of our Lord one thousand eight hundred and
Between,   party of the first part, and
party of the second part,

Witnesseth, That the said party of the first part, for and in consideration of   dollars in hand paid by the said party of the second part, the receipt whereof is hereby acknowledged, and the said party of the second part, for ever released and discharged therefrom, ha   remised, released, sold, conveyed, and quit-claimed, and by these presents do   remise, release, sell, convey, and quit-claim, unto the said party of the second part,   heirs and assigns for ever, all the right, title, interest, claim, and demand which the said party of the first part ha   in and to the following described lot   , piece or parcel of land to wit:

To have and to hold the same, together with all and singular the appurtenances and privileges thereunto belonging, or in anywise thereunto appertaining ; and all the estate, right, title, interest, and claim whatever of the said party of the first part, either in law or equity, to the only proper use, benefit, and behoof of the said party of the second part,   heirs and assigns for ever

And the said   party of the first part, hereby expressly waive , release   and relinquish   unto the said party of the second part,   heirs, executors, administrators, and assigns, all right, title, claim, interest, and benefit whatever, in and to the above described premises, and each and every part thereof, which is given by or results from all laws of this State pertaining to the exemption of homesteads.

In witness whereof, the said party of the first part hereunto set   hand   and seal   the day and year above written.

Signed, sealed, and delivered in presence of }

(L.S.)

State of Illinois,   county, SS.   I   in and for said county, and the State aforesaid, do hereby certify, that   personally known to me as the same person whose name   subscribed to the foregoing instrument of writing, appeared before me this day, in person, and acknowledged that   he   signed, sealed, and delivered the said instrument of writing as   free and voluntary act, for the uses and purposes therein set forth.

And the said   wife of the said
having been by me examined separate and apart, and out of the hearing of her husband   and the contents and meaning of the said instrument of writing having been by me fully made known and explained to her   and she also by me being fully informed of her rights under the homestead laws of this State, acknowledged that she had freely and voluntarily executed the same, and relinquished her dower to the lands and tenements therein mentioned, and also all her rights and advantages under and by virtue of all laws of this

State relating to the exemption of homesteads, without the compulsion of her said husband, and that she does not wish to retract the same.

Given under my hand and   seal, this   day of   A.D. 18

(L.S.)

Quit-Claim Deed.

KNOW ALL MEN BY THESE PRESENTS:
That   of   county and State of   in consideration of the sum of   dollars, in hand paid by   of   county, State of   do hereby quit-claim unto the said   all our right, title, and interest in and to the following described premises, situated in the county of   and State of Iowa, to wit:

And the said   hereby relinquish   right of dower in and to the above described premises.

Signed the   day of   18
In presence of   }

(L.S.)

State of   county, SS.
On this   day of   A.D. 18   , before me, a   within and for said county personally came   personally to me known to be the identical person   whose name   affixed to the above instrument as grantor   and severally acknowledged the execution of the same to be   voluntary act and deed for the purposes therein expressed.

In testimony whereof, I have hereunto subscribed my name and affixed my official seal at   on the date last above written.

Trust Deed.—Statutory Form.

THIS INDENTURE witnesseth, that the grantor   , of the   in the county of   and State of   for and in consideration of the sum of   dollars, in hand paid, convey   and warrant to   of the   county of   and State of   the following described real estate, to wit:

situated in the county of   , in the State of   , hereby releasing and waiving all rights under and by virtue of the homestead exemption laws of the State of   in trust, nevertheless, for the following purposes:

Whereas, the said   grantor   , herein justly indebted upon   promissory note   , bearing even date herewith, payable to the order of

Now, if default be made in the payment of the said promissory note   , or of any part thereof, or the interest thereon, or any part thereof, at the time, and in the manner above specified for the payment thereof, or in case of waste, or non-payment of taxes or assessments on said premises, or of a breach of any of the covenants, or agreements herein contained, then in such case, the whole of said principal sum and interest, secured by the said   promissory note   , shall thereupon, at the option of the legal holder or holders thereof, become immediately due and payable; and, on the application of the legal holder of said promissory note   , or either of them, it shall be lawful for the said grantee, his heirs, assigns, or successor in trust, after giving thirty days' previous notice of such sale, by publication, once in each week for four successive weeks, in any newspaper at that time published in the city of   , in said   county, to sell and dispose of said premises, or any part thereof, and all right, title, benefit, and equity of redemption of the said grantor   , heirs and assigns therein, at public vendue, at any door of any building used as a court house, in said city of   , to the highest bidder for cash, at the time and place mentioned in such notice, or may postpone or adjourn the said sale from time to time, at discretion, and may sell said premises in mass, or in separate parcels; and upon making such sale or sales, shall execute and deliver to the purchaser or purchasers at such sale, good and sufficient deed or deeds for the conveyance in fee of the premises sold; and out of the proceeds of such sale, after first paying all expenses of advertising, selling, and conveying, as aforesaid, and   dollars attorney's fees, and all moneys advanced for insurance, taxes, assessments, and other liens, then to pay the principal of said note   , whether due and payable by the terms there of or not, and interest thereon at the rate of ten per cent. per annum, up to the time of sale, rendering the overplus, if any, to the said grantor   , legal representatives or assigns, on reasonable request, and it shall not be the duty of the purchaser to see to the application of the purchase money; which sale or sales so made shall be a perpetual bar, both in law and equity, against said grantor   , heirs and assigns, and all other persons claiming said premises by, through, or under said grantor

When the said note   and all expenses accruing under this trust deed shall be fully paid, the said grantee or his successor or legal representatives, shall re-convey all of said premises remaining unsold to the said grantor   , or his   heirs or assigns, upon receiving his reasonable charges therefor. In case of the death, resignation, removal from said   county, or other inability to act, of said grantee   then   of said   , is hereby appointed and made successor in trust herein, with like power and authority, as is hereby vested in said grantee. It is agreed that said grantor   , shall pay all costs and attorney's fees, incurred or paid by said grantee, or the holder or holders of said note   in any suit in which either of them may be plaintiff or defendant, by reason of being a party to this trust deed, or a holder of said note   , and that the same shall be a lien on said premises, and may be taken out of the proceeds of any sale of said premises.

Witness the hand   and seal   of the said grantor   , this   day of   A.D. 187

(L.S.)

State of   county of   , SS. I,   in and for said county, in the State aforesaid, do hereby certify, that   personally known to me to be the same person   whose name   subscribed to the foregoing instrument, appeared before me this day in person, and acknowledged that   he   signed, sealed, and delivered the said instrument as   free and voluntary act, for the uses and purposes therein set forth, including the release and waiver of the right of homestead.

Given under my hand and   seal, this   day of   A.D. 187

(L.S.)

Release Deed.

KNOW ALL MEN BY THESE PRESENTS, That   of the county of   and State of   for and in consideration of one dollar, and for other good and valuable considerations, the receipt whereof is hereby confessed, do hereby remise, convey, release, and quit-claim, unto   of the county of   and State of   all the right, title, interest, claim, or demand whatsoever may have acquired in, through, or by a certain deed, bearing date the   day of   A.D. 187   , and recorded in the recorder's office of   county, in the State of   in book   of   page   to the premises therein described, as follows, to wit

together with all the appurtenances and privileges thereunto belonging or appertaining.

Witness   hand   and seal   , this   day of   A.D. 187   .

(L.S.)

State of   , county   SS. I,   in and for the said county, in the State aforesaid, do hereby certify, that   personally known to me to be the same person   whose name   subscribed to the foregoing instrument, appeared before me this day in person, and acknowledged that   he   signed, sealed, and delivered the said instrument as   free and voluntary act, for the uses and purposes therein set forth.

Given under my hand and   seal, this   day of   A.D. 18

(L.S.)

Quit Claim Deed.—Statutory Form.

THIS INDENTURE witnesseth, that the grantor   of the   in the county of   and State of   , for the consideration of   convey and quit claim   to   of the   , county of   and State of   , all interest in the following described real estate, to wit:

situated in the county of   , in the State of   hereby releasing and waiving all rights under and by virtue of the homestead exemption laws of this State.

Dated this   day of   A.D. 187

(L.S.)

State of   county of   , SS. I   in and for said county, in the State aforesaid, do hereby certify that   personally known to me to be the same person whose name   subscribed to the foregoing instrument, appeared before me this day in person, and acknowledged that he   signed, sealed, and delivered the said instrument as free and voluntary act, for the uses and purposes therein set forth, including the release and waiver of the right of homestead.

Given under my hand and   seal, this   day of   , A.D. 18 .

(L.S.)

MORTGAGE.

THIS INDENTURE, made this   day of   in the year of our Lord one thousand eight hundred and seventy   , between   of the   in the county of   and State of   party of the first part, and   of the   in the county of   and State of   party of the second part.

Whereas, the said party of the first part is justly indebted to the said party of the second part in the sum of   dollars secured to be paid by   certain

Now, therefore, this indenture witnesseth, that the said party of the first part, for the better securing the payment of the money aforesaid, with interest thereon according to the tenor and effect of the said   above mentioned, and also in consideration of the further sum of one dollar to   in hand paid by the said party of the second part, at the delivery of these presents, the receipt whereof is hereby acknowledged, ha   granted, bargained, sold, remised, released, conveyed, aliened, and confirmed, and by these presents do   grant, bargain, sell, remise, release, convey, alien, and confirm, unto the said party of the second part, and to   heirs and assigns for ever, all the following described lot , piece , or parcel   of land, situate in the county of   and State of   and known and described as follows, to wit :

To have and to hold the same, together with all and singular the tenements, hereditaments, privileges, and appurtenances thereunto belonging, or in anywise appertaining ; and also all the estate, interest, and claim whatsoever, in law as well as in equity, which the said party of the first part ha   in and to the premises hereby conveyed, unto the said party of the second part,   heirs and assigns, and to their only proper use, benefit, and behoof, for ever ;

Provided always, and these presents are upon this express condition, that if the said party of the first part,   heirs, executors, or administrators, shall well and truly pay, or cause to be paid, to the said party of the second part,   heirs, executors, administrators, or assigns, the aforesaid sum of money, with interest thereon, at the time and in the manner specified in the above-mentioned   according to the true intent and meaning thereof, then and in that case these presents, and everything herein expressed, shall be absolutely null and void.

But it is further provided and agreed, that if default be made in the payment of the said   or of any part thereof, or the interest thereon, or any part thereof, at the time and in the manner and at the place above limited and specified for the payment thereof, or in case of waste or non-payment of taxes or assessments, or neglect to procure or renew insurance, as herein after provided, or in case of the breach of any of the covenants or agreements herein contained, then, and in such case, the whole of said principal and interest, secured by the said   in this mortgage mentioned, shall thereupon, at the option of the said party of the second part,   heirs, executors, administrators, attorneys, or assigns, become immediately due and payable ; anything herein or in said   contained to the contrary notwithstanding. And this mortgage may be immediately foreclosed to pay the same by said party of the second part,   heirs, executors, administrators, or assigns ; or the said party of the second part,   heirs, executors, administrators, attorneys, or assigns, after publishing a notice in any newspaper at that time published in the   in the State of Illinois, for   weeks before the day of such sale, may sell the said premises, and all right and equity of redemption of the said party of the first part,   heirs, executors, administrators, or assigns therein, at public auction, at the   in the   in the State of Illinois, or on said premises, or any part thereof, as may be specified in the notice of such sale, to the highest bidder for cash, at the time mentioned in such notice, or may postpone or adjourn said sale from time to time at discretion, with or without re-advertising, and may sell said premises *en masse*, or in separate parcels.

And the said party of the first part hereby specially covenant and agree to and with the said party of the second part to waive, and hereby waives,   right of equity of redemption, and further agree that   will neither assert or claim any such right on a sale of the above-described premises by virtue of this mortgage. And upon the making of such sale or sales, the said party of the first part do   hereby authorise, empower, and direct the said party of the second part, his executors, administrators, attorneys, or assigns, in his or their own name, to make, execute, and deliver to the purchaser or purchasers thereof, a deed or deeds for the premises so sold, and covenant and agree that all the recitals of such deed or deeds setting forth the fact of due notice, advertisement, and sale, and any and all such other facts and statements as may be proper to evidence the legality of such sale or sales, or conveyance or conveyances, and that the same have been duly made in all respects so as to meet the requirements herein contained, or arising in law, and necessary to convey a good title, shall be taken and considered as *primâ facie* evidence of all such facts and matters set forth in such recitals ; and out of the proceeds of such sale, or money arising therefrom, the said party of the second part,   executors, administrators, attorneys, or assigns, first to pay all costs and expenses incurred in advertising, selling, and conveying said premises, including the reasonable fees and commissions of said party of the second part, and all other expenses, including all moneys advanced for taxes, and other liens or assessments, with interest thereon at ten per cent. per annum, together with the sum of   dollars for attorney's fees, then to pay the principal of said   whether due and payable by the terms thereof or not, and interest thereon up to the time of such sale, and to render the overplus, if any, to said party of the first part   legal representatives or assigns, on reasonable request, and in case of the foreclosure of this mortgage by proceedings in court, or in case of any suit or proceeding at law or in equity, wherein said party of the second part,   executors, administrators, or assigns, shall be a party plaintiff or defendant by reason of   being a party to this mortgage, he or they shall be allowed and paid their reasonable costs, charges, attorney's and solicitor's fees, in such suit or proceeding by said party of the first part, and the same shall be a further charge and lien upon said premises under this mortgage to be paid out of the proceeds of sale thereof, if not otherwise paid by said party of the first part.

And in consideration of the money paid as aforesaid to the said party of the first part, and in order to create a first lien and incumbrance on said premises under this mortgage, for the purposes aforesaid, and to carry out the foregoing specific application of the proceeds of any sale that may be made by virtue hereof, the said party of the first part do   hereby release and waive all right under, and benefit of, the exemption and homestead laws of the State of Illinois, in and to the lands and premises aforesaid, and the proceeds of sale thereof, and agree to surrender up possession thereof to the purchaser or purchasers at such sale, peaceably on demand.

And the said   for   and   heirs, executors, and administrators, covenant and agree to and with the said party of the second part   , executors, administrators, and assigns, that at the time of the ensealing and delivery of these presents   well seized of said premises in fee simple, and ha   good right, full power and lawful authority to grant, bargain, and sell the same in manner and form as aforesaid ; that the same are free and clear of all liens and incumbrances whatsoever ; and that   will for ever warrant and defend the same against all lawful claims ; that the said party of the first part will in due season pay all taxes and assessments on said premises, and exhibit once a year, on demand, receipts of the proper persons, to said party of the second part, or   assigns, showing payment thereof, until the indebtedness aforesaid shall be fully paid ; and will keep all buildings that may at any time be on said premises, during the continuance of said indebtedness, insured in such company or companies as the said party of the second part or   assigns may from time to time direct, for such sum or sums as such company or companies will insure for, not to exceed the amount of said indebtedness, except at the option of said party of the first part, and will assign, with proper consent of the insurers, the policy or policies of insurance to said party of the second part or   assigns, as further security for the indebtedness aforesaid. And in case of the refusal or neglect of said party of the first part, or either of them, thus to insure, or assign the policies of insurance, or to pay taxes, said party of the second part, or his executors, administrators, or assigns, or either of them, may procure such insurance, or pay such taxes, and all moneys thus paid, with interest thereon at ten per cent. per annum, shall become so much additional indebtedness, secured by this mortgage, and to be paid out of the proceeds of sale of the lands and premises aforesaid, if not otherwise paid by said party of the first part.

And it is stipulated and agreed, that in case of default in any of said payments of principal or interest, according to the tenor and effect of said   aforesaid, or either of them, or any part thereof, or of a breach of any of the covenants or agreements herein by the party of the first part,   executors, administrators, or assigns, then, and in that case, the whole of said principal sum hereby secured, and the interest thereon to the time of sale, may at once, at the option of the said party of the second part, executors, administrators, attorneys, or assigns, become due and payable, and the said premises be sold in the manner and with the same effect as if the said indebtedness had matured.

In witness whereof, the said party of the first part hereunto set   hand and seal the day and year first above written.

Signed, sealed, and delivered, in the presence of
                                                                    (L.S.)

State of   , county of   SS. I, in and for the said county, in the State aforesaid, do hereby certify that   personally known to me to be the same person whose name   subscribed to the foregoing instrument, appeared before me this day in person, and acknowledged that he signed, sealed, and delivered the said instrument as   free and voluntary act, for the uses and purposes therein set forth, including the release and waiver of the right of homestead.

Given under my hand and   seal, this   day of   A.D. 187 .
                                                                    (L.S.)

Warranty Deed.—Statutory Form.

This Indenture witnesseth, that the grantor, of the   in the county of   and State of   for and in consideration of the sum of   dollars, in hand paid, convey , and warrant , to   of the   county of   and State of   the following described real estate, to wit:

situated in the county of   in the State of   hereby releasing and waiving all rights under and by virtue of the homestead exemption laws of this State.

Dated this   day of   A.D. 187 .
                                                                    (L.S.)

State of   county of   , SS. I, in and for said county, in the State aforesaid, do hereby certify, that   personally known to me to be the same person whose name   subscribed to the foregoing instrument, appeared before me this day in person, and acknowledged that he signed, sealed, and delivered the said instrument as   free and voluntary act, for the uses and purposes therein set forth, including the release and waiver of the right of homestead.

Given under my hand and   seal, this day of   187 .
                                                                    (L.S.)

Warranty Deed.

Know all Men by these Presents, that   of   county and State of   , in consideration of the sum of   dollars, in hand paid by   of   county, and State of   do hereby sell and convey unto the said   the following described premises situated in the county of   and State of   to wit:

And   do hereby covenant with the said   that   hold said premises by good and perfect title; that   have good right and lawful authority to sell and convey the same; that they are free and clear of all liens and incumbrances whatsoever; and   covenant to warrant and defend the said premises against the lawful claims of all persons whomsoever; and the said   hereby relinquishes   right of dower in and to the above described premises.

Signed the   day of   A.D. 187 .
In presence of

State of   county, SS.
On the   day of   A.D. 187 , before me a   within and for said county personally came   personally to me known to be the identical person   whose name   affixed to the above instrument as grantor and severally acknowledged the execution of the same to be   voluntary act and deed for the purposes therein expressed.

In testimony whereof, I have hereunto subscribed my name and affixed my official seal at   on the date last above written.

                                            38, Cornhill, London, E.C.,
Dear Sir,   1st July 1880.

In dealing with our property in America, we find that it is equally to our advantage to let the larger part of our arable land in small holdings; generally 160 acres.

There are always a number of men with small capital, 300*l.* and upwards, who are willing to become our tenants in Iowa.

I enclose a blank form of one of our leases. From it you will see that we have some very stringent clauses, but at the same time we know that we are dealing with men of small capital, and therefore take the greater part of our rents in "kind" instead of "money," and in case of damaged crops through grasshoppers or other causes (clause 19) we are very lenient.

The lease provides for a payment of a cash rent, and where it is so paid, it is usually 2 dollars or 8*s.* 4*d.* an acre. But when paid in "kind" the custom of country is that—

(*a.*) If the landlord finds the seed, retakes half of the crop.
(*b.*) If the tenant finds the seed, the landlord takes one-third of the crop.

We are sending out several English farmers with small capital, not less than 300*l.*, to take some of our farms, and have no hesitation in saying that it is a good opening for such men if they think of emigrating, for they go at once to a ready made farm with a good house on it, and with land ready for cultivation; and thus before they invest their own money in fixtures or land, are able to get a knowledge of the country and of values.

                                            I am, &c.
Albert Pell, Esq., M.P.   Close, Benson, & Co.

Lease.

This Indenture, made this   day of   , A.D. 18 , between   party of the first part, and   party of the second part, witnesseth, that the said party of the first part doth hereby lease to the said party of the second part the following described property, to wit:

To have and to hold the same to the said party of the second part from the   day of   18 , to the   day of   18 . And the said party of the second part, in consideration of the aforesaid leasing, hereby agrees to   to the said party of the first part as rent for the same   as follows, to wit:

part of all the wheat, oats, barley, flax, and rye, also   part of all the corn, and   part of all the   raised or grown upon said premises; all of the aforesaid to be delivered in good marketable condition at the place, in the manner, and at the time hereafter recited: and the said party of the second part further covenants and agrees as a part of said rental to accept, abide by, and perform, at his own exclusive cost and charge, in each and every particular, all of the covenants herein-after recited, by him to be kept and performed, to wit:

I.—During the pendency of this lease the party of the second part shall keep, at his expense, in good repair all buildings, sheds, fencing, wells, and all improvements now on or hereafter put on the same during the term.

II.—He shall never assign this lease, nor sublet any portion of said premises, without the written consent of the party of the first part.

III.—He shall farm and till all of said premises in a good and farmlike manner, and plant or seed all of the tillable land to crops consisting of each or all of either wheat, oats, barley, flax, rye, corn, or   crops as said party of the second part may desire, and to give his personal labour and attention to the farming of said land.

IV.—He shall furnish good and sufficient seed, labourers, teams, farm machinery, &c., to put in, seed or plant, and take care of and secure said crops.

V.—He shall clean and fan all grain used for seed, in such a manner as will free it from all foul seeds that will injure the growing crops or the land; and plant or seed each particular crop at the proper time or season.

VI.—He shall thoroughly drag or drill in all small grain when sown, and thoroughly work or cultivate the corn not less than   times during the season, and cut all foul weeds out of the growing crop.

VII.—He shall protect all crops from stock running at large from time of planting until fully harvested and stored, and also at all times protect both crops and premises from all trespassers of whatsoever kind that may do damage.

VIII.—He shall allow the said party of the first part, his agent, or anyone appointed or directed by him, to enter upon said premises and examine the manner in which it is cultivated and cared for, at any time he may see fit to do so, or authorize any one to do so.

IX.—He shall stack the wheat, oats, barley, flax, rye, and all small grain promptly, and in a good and farmlike manner cover the top of each stack with hay or slough grass in such a manner that it will shed rain; he shall tie the covering on, and in case of damage of any kind whatsoever shall repair said damage promptly and carefully; and he shall plough a good and sufficient fire-guard around all said stacks, the house, barn, sheds, &c., before the   day of   of each year.

X.—He shall thresh all small grain before the   day of   each year during this lease, and shall give to the party of the first part personally   days notice (prior to each time of threshing) of said threshing; all of said threshing to be done at one time or period unless said party of the first part agrees to and allows the contrary in writing; and, providing always, no small grain shall be threshed until it shall have gone through the sweat.

XI.—He shall husk and deliver in any crib or pile at any place that the party of the first part may elect within two miles of said premises all the rent or other corn to be delivered or belonging to the said party of the first part as rent or otherwise, on or before the   day of   of each year, and shall haul and deliver into any granary which said party of the first part may designate, at any place not more than two miles from said premises, all the small grain to be delivered or belonging to the party of the first part as rent or otherwise, directly from the machine as threshed. The landlord's share of the corn to be first husked, and the party of the second part agreeing to protect the landlord's share of all crops from weather and stock, and to deliver the same in good marketable condition.

XII.—He shall fall plough   acres of said premises on or before the   day of   during each year of this lease. He shall plough the same at least   inches deep all in a thorough and farmlike manner, and shall not skip nor cut, and cover, and in case he fails to do said ploughing the same may be done by the party of the first part at the exclusive cost and charge of the party of the second part.

XIII.—He shall not sell, mortgage, nor remove from said premises any of the crops raised thereon during this lease without the written consent of the party of the first part, unless all past due rents and rents coming due for that current year are fully paid, and all fall ploughing shall be done as hereinbefore recited.

XIV.—He shall harvest, gather, and properly care for all crops when matured as soon as it is proper to do so, or in default thereof, the party of the first part, at his election, may cause said crops to be harvested, gathered, and properly cared for at the exclusive cost and charge of the party of the second part.

XV.—He shall not commit nor allow any waste in the cutting or destruction of timber or otherwise, without the written consent of the party of the first part.

XVI.—He shall scatter all manure made on said premises, upon said premises, upon the places where it is most needed.

XVII.—He shall give diligence and care to protect and nourish any natural or artificial timber that may be now or hereafter upon said premises.

XVIII. He shall satisfy and pay at the proper time all taxes, excepting State and county taxes, which may be levied upon said premises during the time of this lease, and in consideration of such payment of said taxes the party of the first part hereby agrees to release said party of the second part from the payment of rental upon   acres of said premises at the rate of   dollars per acre.

XIX.—In case the crops on said premises are destroyed in whole or in part by grasshoppers, said party of the second part shall be relieved from the payment of so much of the cash rent of said premises as shall be in proportion to the amount of the crop destroyed; it being well understood that this condition shall not take effect unless in case of actual damage by grasshoppers, and then only in case the crops raised on said premises shall fall below the following amounts per acre in average, viz.: wheat   bushels; oats   bushels; barley   bushels; rye   bushels; flax   bushels; corn   bushels   per acre. The amount of damage to said crop to be ascertained as follows, unless mutually agreed upon, viz.: by three referees, the party of the first part to select one, the party of the second part to select a second, and the two thus selected to select the third.

XX.—He shall permit the party of the first part or his agent at any time to enter upon and take possession of all or any part of said premises in order to fall plough the same.

And it is further covenanted and agreed by the party of the second part, that at the expiration of this lease he will deliver to the party of the first part peaceable possession of the said premises in good condition and repair, the usual wear and accidents by fire and unavoidable force alone excepted; and in case the said party of the second part shall make default in any of the conditions or covenants of this lease to be by him kept or performed, either in the payment of the rent or the delivery of the share of the grain or other products of the said farm to be delivered as such rent, at the time or in the manner provided for herein, or in keeping the said premises in repair, as herein provided, or in farming or cultivating the said farm in the manner and at the times above provided, or in the payment of taxes as provided, the said party of the first part may, and hereby reserves the right, at his election, at any time during the continuance of this lease to enter in and upon the said premises, and all or any portion thereof, with his servants and employés, teams and implements, that may be necessary and proper, to make all repairs, plant or put in and cultivate any crops that should be planted or put in, or harvest, gather, or thresh any crops; to do any ploughing, or any other act, thing, work, or labour, that should be done or attended to by the party of the second part under the terms of this lease, and out of the crops, or the share of the crops belonging to, or to belong to the party of the second part, to keep and retain so much thereof as shall be necessary to pay for all such work and labour, and any damage that may accrue to the party of the first part by reason of any default of the party of the second part to properly perform the conditions and covenants aforesaid:

Or if any default shall be made in the payment of the rent above reserved, or any part thereof, or any of the covenants or agreements herein contained to be kept by the party of the second part, as aforesaid, it shall be lawful for the party of the first part, or   legal representatives, to declare this lease terminated at once and into and upon the said premises or any part thereof, either with or without process of law, to re-enter and re-possess the same at the election of the party of the first part, and to distrain from any rent that may be due thereon, upon any property belonging to the party of the second part. And in order to enforce a forfeiture for non-payment of rent, it shall not be necessary to make a demand on the same day the rent shall become due, but a failure to pay the same at the place aforesaid, or a demand and refusal to pay on the same day, or at any time or any subsequent day shall be sufficient, and after such default shall be made, the party of the second part and all persons in possession under   shall be deemed guilty of a forcible detainer of the said premises under the statute.

And it is further covenanted and agreed, between the parties aforesaid that no alteration of this lease shall be made except in writing, and endorsed hereon.

The covenants herein shall extend to and be binding upon heirs, executors, administrators, and legal representatives of the parties to this lease.

Witness the hands and seals of the parties aforesaid, the day and year first above written.

Signed, sealed, and delivered in presence of
           (L.S.)
                                                   (L.S.)

LEASE.

THIS INDENTURE, made this   day of A.D. 1870, between   party of the first part, and   party of the second part,

Witnesseth, that the party of the first part, in consideration of the covenants of the party of the second part, herein-after set forth, do   , by these presents, lease to the party of the second part the following described property, to wit:

in the   county of   and State of

To have and to hold the same to the party of the second part, from the   day of   187 , to the   day of   187 . And the party of the second part, in consideration of the leasing the premises as above set forth, covenants and agrees with the party of the first part to pay the party of the first part at   as rent for the same, the sum of   dollars, payable as follows, to wit:

And the party of the second part covenants with the party of the first part, that at the expiration of the term of this lease he will yield up the premises to the party of the first part, without further notice, in as good condition as when the same were entered upon by the party of the second part, loss by fire or inevitable accident and ordinary wear excepted.

It is further agreed by the party of the second part, that neither he nor   legal representatives will underlet said premises or any part thereof, or assign this lease without the written assent of the party of the first part first had thereto.

And it is further expressly agreed, between the parties hereto, that if default shall be made in the payment of the rent above reserved, or any part thereof, or any of the covenants or agreements herein contained to be kept by the party of the second part, it shall be lawful for the party of the first part or legal representatives, into and upon said premises or any part hereof, either with or without process of law, to re-enter and re-possess the same at the election of the party of the first part, and to distrain for any rent that may be due thereon upon any property belonging to the party of the second part. And in order to enforce a forfeiture for non-payment of rent, it shall not be necessary to make a demand on the same day the rent shall become due, but a failure to pay the same at the place aforesaid or a demand and a refusal to pay on the same day, or at any time on any subsequent day shall be sufficient; and after such default shall be made, the party of the second part and all persons in possession under   shall be deemed guilty of a forcible detainer of said premises under the statute.

And it is further covenanted and agreed, between the parties aforesaid,

The covenants herein shall extend to and be binding upon the heirs, executors, and administrators of the parties to this lease.

Witness the hands and seals of the parties aforesaid, the day and year first above written.

(L.S.)

REGULATIONS respecting the Disposal of certain Public Lands for the purposes of the Canadian Pacific Railway.

DEPARTMENT OF THE INTERIOR.

Ottawa, Oct. 14th, 1879.

Public notice is hereby given that the following provisions, which shall be held to apply to the lands in the province of Manitoba, and in the territories to the west and north-west thereof, are substituted for the regulation, dated the 9th July last, governing the mode of disposing of the public lands situate within 110 (one hundred and ten) miles on each side of the line of the Canadian Pacific Railway, which said regulations are hereby superseded:—

1. Until further and final survey of the said railway has been made west of the Red River, and for the purposes of these provisions the line of the said railway shall be assumed to be on the fourth base westerly to the intersection of the said base by the line between ranges 21 and 22 west of the first principal meridian, and thence in a direct line to the confluence of the Shell River with the River Assiniboine.

2. The country lying on each side of the line of railway shall be respectively divided into belts, as follows:—

(1.) A belt of 5 miles on either side of the railway, and immediately adjoining the same, to be called belt A;

(2.) A belt of 15 miles on either side of the railway adjoining belt A, to be called belt B;

(3.) A belt of 20 miles on either side of the railway, adjoining belt B, to be called belt C;

(4.) A belt of 20 miles on either side of the railway, adjoining belt C, to be called belt D; and

(5.) A belt of 50 miles on either side of the railway, adjoining belt D, to be called belt E.

3. The even-numbered sections in each township throughout the several belts above described shall be open for entry as homesteads and pre-emptions of 160 acres each respectively.

4. The odd-numbered sections in each of such townships shall not be open to homestead or pre-emption, but shall be specially reserved and designated as railway lands.

5. The railway lands within the several belts shall be sold at the following rates, viz.: In belt A, $5 (five dollars) per acre; in belt B, $4 (four dollars) per acre; in belt C, $3 (three dollars) per acre; in belt D, $2 (two dollars) per acre; in belt E, $1 (one dollar) per acre; and the terms of sale of such lands shall be as follows, viz.: one-tenth in cash at the time of purchase; the balance in nine equal annual instalments, with interest at the rate of 6 per cent. per annum on the balance of purchase-money from time to time remaining unpaid, to be paid with each instalment.

6. The pre-emption lands within the several belts shall be sold for the prices and on the terms respectively as follows:—In the belts A, B, and C, at $2.50 (two dollars and 50 cents) per acre; in belt D, at $2 (two dollars) per acre; and in E, at $1 (one dollar) per acre. The terms of payment to be four-tenths of the purchase money, together with interest on the latter at the rate of 6 per cent. per annum, to be paid at the end of three years from the date of entry, the remainder to be paid in six equal instalments annually from and after the said date, with interest at the rate above-mentioned on such portions of the purchase money as may remain unpaid, to be paid with each instalment.

7. All payments for railway lands, and also for pre-emption lands, within the several belts, shall be in cash, and not in scrip or military and police bounty warrants.

8. All moneys received in payment of pre-emption lands shall inure to and form part of the fund for railway purposes, in a similar manner to the moneys received in payment of railway lands.

9. These provisions shall be retroactive so far as relates to any and all entries of homestead and pre-emption lands, or sales of railway lands obtained or made under the regulations of the 9th of July, hereby superseded; any payments made in excess of the rate hereby fixed shall be credited on account of sales of such lands.

10. The Order in Council of the 9th November 1877, relating to the settlement of the lands in Manitoba which had been previously withdrawn for railway purposes, having been cancelled, all claims of persons who settled in good faith on lands under the said Order in Council shall be dealt with under these provisions, as to price of pre-emptions, according to the belt in which such lands may be situate. Where a person may have taken up two quarter sections under the said Order in Council, he may retain the quarter section upon which he has settled, as a homestead, and the other quarter section as a pre-emption, under these provisions, irrespective of whether such homestead or pre-emption may be found to be upon an even-numbered section or otherwise. Any moneys paid by such person on account of the lands entered by him under the said Order in Council, will be credited to him on account of his pre-emption purchase, under these provisions. A person who may have taken up one quarter section under the Order in Council mentioned will be allowed to retain the same as a homestead, and be permitted to enter a second quarter section as a pre-emption, the money paid on account of the land previously entered to be credited to him on account of such pre-emption.

11. All entries of lands shall be subject to the following provisions respecting the right of way of the Canadian Pacific Railway or of any Government colonization railway connected therewith, viz.:

a. In the case of the railway crossing land entered as a homestead, the right of way thereon, and also any land which may be required for station purposes, shall be free to the Government.

b. Where the railway crosses pre-emptions or railway lands, entered subsequent to the date hereof, the Government may take possession of such portion thereof as may be required for right of way or for station grounds or ballast pits, and the owner shall only be entitled to claim payment for the land so taken, at the same rate per acre as he may have paid the Government for the same.

c. In case, on the final location of the railway through lands unsurveyed, or surveyed but not entered for at the time, a person is found in occupation of land which it may be desirable in the public interest to retain, the Government reserves the right to take possession of such land, paying the squatter the value of any improvements he may have made thereon.

12. Claims to public lands arising from settlement, after the date hereof, in territory unsurveyed at the time of such settlement, and which may be embraced within the limits affected by the above policy, or by the extension thereof in the future over additional territory, will be ultimately dealt with in accordance with the terms prescribed above for the lands in the particular belt in which such settlement may be found to be situated, subject to the operation of sub-section *c.* of section 11 of these provisions.

13. All entries after the date hereof of unoccupied lands in the Saskatchewan agency, will be considered as provisional until the railway line through that part of the territories has been located, after which the same will be finally disposed of in accordance with these provisions, as the same may apply to the particular belt in which such lands may be found to be situated, subject, as above, to the operation of sub-section *c.* of section 11 of these provisions.

14. With a view to encouraging settlement by cheapening the cost of building material, the Government reserves the right to grant licenses, renewable yearly under section 52 of the "Dominion Lands Act, 1879," to cut merchantable timber on any lands situated within the several belts above described, and any settlement upon, or sale of lands within, the territory covered by such licenses, shall, for the time being, be subject to the operation of such licenses.

15. The above provisions it will, of course, be understood will not affect sections 11 and 29, which are public school lands, or sections 8 and 26, Hudson's Bay Company's lands.

Any further information necessary may be obtained on application at the Dominion Lands Office, Ottawa, or from the agent of Dominion Lands, Winnipeg, or from any of the local agents in Manitoba or the Territories.

By order of the Minister of the Interior,

J. S. DENNIS,
Deputy of the Minister of the Interior.

LINDSAY RUSSELL,
Surveyor-General.

The following is a short SUMMARY of the LAND SYSTEM of the different PROVINCES of the DOMINION of CANADA :—

In Manitoba and the north-west free grants of 160 acres are given to any head of a family, male or female, or to any person over 18 years of age, on condition of three years' settlement from time of entry. For the necessary documents for the registration and taking up a free grant the fee is 10 dollars, payable when the title is issued. A person entering for a homestead may also enter the adjoining quarter section (160 acres), if vacant, as a pre-emption right, and enter into immediate possession thereof, and on fulfilling the conditions of his homestead may obtain a patent for his pre-emption right on payment for the same at the rate of 1 dollar per acre, if outside the railroad belts, but if within such belts, at the price set forth in the regulations, the maximum price being 2 dollars 50 cents per acre.

Free grants of land are also made for the culture of forest trees outside the ralway belts, in addition to the homestead, but settlers cannot take up the pre-emption land as well as the grant for the culture of trees.

The Legislature of Manitoba in 1872 passed a Homestead Exemption Law, which in addition to exempting from seizure for debt the debtor's goods, as follows: furniture, tools, farm implements in use, one cow, two oxen, one horse, four sheep, two pigs, and 30 days' provender for the same, also enacts that his land to the extent of 160 acres shall be free from seizure, as also the house, stables, barns, and fences on the same, in the case of all writs issued by any court in the province.

Free grants of from 100 to 200 acres are also made in the provinces of Ontario and Quebec on residential conditions, and they also have homestead exemption laws, but not quite so liberal as that of Manitoba. Lands can also be purchased in these provinces at reasonable rates.

There is also land available for settlement in Nova Scotia, New Brunswick, and British Columbia on very reasonable terms.

LONDON:
Printed by GEORGE E. EYRE and WILLIAM SPOTTISWOODE,
Printers to the Queen's most Excellent Majesty.
For Her Majesty's Stationery Office.

CATTLE DISEASE (UNITED STATES OF AMERICA).

FURTHER CORRESPONDENCE

RELATING TO

DISEASES OF ANIMALS

IN THE

UNITED STATES OF AMERICA.

Presented to both Houses of Parliament by Command of Her Majesty.

LONDON:
PRINTED BY GEORGE EDWARD EYRE AND WILLIAM SPOTTISWOODE,
PRINTERS TO THE QUEEN'S MOST EXCELLENT MAJESTY.
FOR HER MAJESTY'S STATIONERY OFFICE.

1880.

[C.—2644.] *Price* 1s. 9d.

CATTLE DISEASE (UNITED STATES OF AMERICA).

FURTHER CORRESPONDENCE

RELATING TO

DISEASES OF ANIMALS IN THE UNITED STATES OF AMERICA.

No. 1.

LETTER from the BRITISH CONSUL at BALTIMORE to the MARQUIS OF SALISBURY.

(No. 12.)

My Lord Marquis, Baltimore, March 1, 1879.

With reference to my Despatch No. 9 of the 7th ultimo, as to Cattle Plague, I have the honour to report that, with the exception of a few cases at Alexandria, Virginia, I have heard of none in my district.

The cases of pleuro-pneumonia at Alexandria appear to have been entirely confined to cows in dairy-farms, and I have the honour to enclose a paragraph from one of the Baltimore papers describing the symptoms of this disease and alluding to the cases at Alexandria.

I have, &c.

The Most Honourable (Signed) DENIS DONOHOE.
    The Marquis of Salisbury, K.G.
      &c.   &c.   &c.

Enclosure in No. 1.

Baltimore "American" of 24th February 1879.

Diseased Cattle.—Cases of Pleuro-Pneumonia at Alexandria, Symptoms of the Disease. Blissville Stables. Hog Cholera.

Washington, February 23.—Dr. Gadsden, veterinary surgeon of Philadelphia, called upon Dr. Bushman, veterinary surgeon of the army, to-day, and requested the doctor to show him some cattle with contagious pleuro-pneumonia at Alexandria, Va., whither Dr. Bushman had previously taken Dr. McEachran, the agent of the Canadian Government Drs. Gadsden and Bushman accordingly went first to the stable where Dr. McEachran had previously purchased a cow for post-mortem examination. At this stable they found only one cow, three belonging to the same person having died within a few months past. The cow was suffering from contagious pleuro-pneumonia in a a chronic form. She had a peculiar cough, palled membranes, and her temperature was 103°. Dr. Bushman says the cow has lost considerable flesh since he saw her on the 22nd of January. Drs. Gadsden and Bushman found three other cows on the common, one of them having the disease in the first stage. The spasmodic action of the nostrils was well marked. When she lay down she was seized with a fit of coughing and laboured breathing.

As a matter of public as well as private interest, Dr. Gadsden furnishes the following symptoms of pleuro-pneumonia of the contagious type which, he thinks, will enable persons connected with cattle raising readily to recognise the symptoms. If the disease arises from cohabitation a cough is first noticed about the ninth day, but the disease would not perhaps be noticed by the owners of the stock before the end of a month. The first sign after the cough is a shivering fit. The coat looks dull and starving; there is an occasional cough of a dry harsh character when the animal is moved briskly. The animal looks full in the early morning, thus differing from healthy animals. The quantity of milk diminishes. There is a loss of appetite and an altered gait, the animal

Q 2337.   Wt. 6284.

standing with its elbows turned outward from the ribs. The neck and head are extended and the nostrils somewhat convulsively expanded at each inspiration, and quickness of breathing of the animal is disturbed with an audible grunt; the expression of the countenance indicates uneasiness and absolute pain. The eyes are prominent and fixed. There is much thirst and ropy saliva from the mouth, the muzzle hot and dry; the back is slightly arched, with protuding head and extended fore limbs, with the hinder ones drawn under with knuckling of the hind fetlocks. When lying down the animal rests on its briskets, or lies on the affected side, leaving the ribs on the healthy side of the chest as much freedom of motion as possible. As the disease advances the pulse quickens, but becomes more feeble. The beating of the heart, which is at first subdued, becomes marked and palpitating. The membrane of the eyes, mouth, and vagina are usually pallid; the tongue is foul, covered with fur, and the exhaled breath has a nauseous and even a fetid odour. Grunting, grinding of the teeth, diminished secretions, weakness and emaciation increase with the progress of the malady. When the animal becomes weak it lies down more frequently. It sometimes shows symptoms of jaundice, tympanitis from gases accumulating in the paunch. The gait is now so staggering that the animal appears to suffer from partial paralysis of the hind quarters. The breathing is more frequent and laboured, the animal gasps for breath, the spasmodic action of the nostrils is very marked, the grunt is very audible, and there is peculiar puckering of the angles of the mouth. The acute stage of this disorder varies from seven to twenty-one days. Convalescence extends over a period of one, two, or three months, during the greater part of which the animal is often capable of infecting healthy cattle.

Dr. Gadsden says, that on the discovery of the disease the sick animal should be immediately separated from the healthy ones to prevent contagion, as he considers treatment useless.

Information continues to be received at the Department of Agriculture relative to hog cholera. This demonstrates the fact that the disease is not only infectious but contagious, and it is also shown that other animals taking the disease from them can transmit back to the previous source. This has been made apparent by Dr. Law, of Cornell University. The only way yet suggested for the prevention of the spread of the disease is to stamp it out by killing the animal. It is estimated that swine of the value of $20,000,000 or $30,000,000 perish every year. The former appropriation to enable the Department to investigate the subject was $10,000, and a similar amount will be appropriated this year for the same purpose.

New York, February 22—Twenty cows in the Blissville, L. J., stables were ordered to be killed to-day, they having been condemned by General Patrick and Professor Law. Sixty others were taken to other slaughter-houses in Williamsburgh. The value of the slaughtered animals is about $290, which the State will allow owners.

No. 2.

LETTER from SIR E. THORNTON to the MARQUIS OF SALISBURY.

(No. 19, Consular.)

My Lord,   Washington, March 3, 1879.

With reference to my Despatch No. 18 of this series, and of the 23rd ultimo, I have the honour to enclose copies of a letter addressed by the Secretary of the Treasury to the President of the Senate, showing the value of the cattle exported from the United States, during the year ended June 30th 1878. He mentions the steps which he had taken, owing to the appearance of pleuro-pneumonia, to prevent the export of infected cattle, and he asks for authority to restrict or prohibit the export of diseased cattle, and to appoint experts to inspect cattle intended for export. He at the same time submits a bill, in which it is proposed that the Secretary of the Treasury should be authorised to adopt measures to prevent the export of diseased cattle, to appoint inspectors at different ports, and to refuse a clearance to vessels taking diseased cattle on board.

It was probably on account of this letter that the Senate adopted the amendment referred to in my Despatch above mentioned to the Bill relative to the transportation of animals, by which it was proposed that the Secretary of the Treasury should appoint inspectors at certain ports.

I have, &c.

The Marquis of Salisbury, K.G.   (Signed)   E. THORNTON.
&c. &c. &c.

Enclosure in No. 2.

LETTER from the SECRETARY of the TREASURY, in relation to the EXPORTATION of LIVE ANIMALS to FOREIGN COUNTRIES, and recommending LEGISLATION providing for an INSPECTION of the same before Shipment.

February 22, 1879.—Referred to the Committee on Agriculture and ordered to be printed.

Treasury Department, Office of the Secretary,
Washington, D. C., February 21, 1879.

SIR,

The exportation of live animals has already become an important interest, and is rapidly increasing. From statements by the Bureau of Statistics (paper marked A.), which I have the honour to inclose, it appears that the value of the exports of live animals during the fiscal year ended June 30, 1878, was nearly eight times the value of such exports during the fiscal year ended June 30, 1868.

The value of horned cattle exported from the United States during the fiscal year ended June 30, 1878, was $3,896,818; but during the first five months of the current fiscal year the value of such exports was $4,414,000, or $517,182 in excess of the value of the same during the entire preceding year. During the fiscal year ended June 30, 1878, nearly 62 per cent. of the cattle exported were shipped to Great Britain, $17\frac{1}{2}$ per cent. to Cuba, and 11 per cent. to British Possessions in North America.

On the 18th of December, 1878, a Despatch was received by this department, through the Department of State, from Liverpool, to the effect that unless cattle shipped from the United States should have the Government health-certificate when embarked, they would probably be slaughtered on landing. On the same day I issued to collectors of customs by telegraph a circular authorising them to cause an inspection to be made of all neat cattle proposed to be shipped to Great Britain, and to issue a certificate that such cattle as shall be shipped are free from all disease. A copy of such circular (marked B.) is transmitted herewith.

On the 1st of February 1879, I issued a second circular, a copy of which is inclosed (marked C.), making imperative such inspection, and prohibiting the shipment of cattle without such inspection and a certificate showing that the cattle shipped are free from disease, and requiring collectors of customs to promptly forward to this department any information which they may be able to obtain of the presence of contagious or infectious diseases prevailing among live animals in their vicinity.

In consequence of a shipment of diseased cattle from the United States to Liverpool, which were found to be infected with the pleuro-pneumonia, the British Government has deemed it necessary to make very stringent regulations for preventing the introduction of diseased animals into their ports. The powers of this department have been exhausted, if not transcended, by the orders contained in the two circulars already issued, I deem it proper, therefore, to recommend that the Secretary of the Treasury be authorised by suitable legislation to prohibit or restrict, in such manner as he may think proper, the exportation of live animals from the United States to foreign countries, whenever it shall appear to his satisfaction that any contagious or infectious diseases exist among such animals in the United States, and that he have authority to appoint such skilled persons as may be necessary to inspect animals for exportation, and to examine into questions connected with the diseases of animals, under such regulations as he may prescribe.

After a conference with the Secretary of State, who heartily concurs in supporting the proposed measure, I submit a draft of a Bill containing such provisions. The powers conferred thereby upon the Secretary of the Treasury are very liberal, but not more so than the authority conferred upon him by section 2,493 of the revised statutes, relating to the importation of neat cattle. By that section the importation of neat cattle from any foreign country into the United States is prohibited, with the proviso, in substance, that the operation of the section shall be suspended or modified at the discretion of the Secretary of the Treasury, under such regulations as he shall deem proper.

Very respectfully,
(Signed)   JOHN SHERMAN,
Secretary.

Hon. William A. Wheeler,
Vice-President, United States Senate.

Be it enacted by the Senate and House of Representatives in Congress assembled, that the Secretary of the Treasury be and he is hereby authorised to take such steps and adopt such measures, not inconsistent with the provisions of this Act, as he may deem necessary to prevent the exportation from any port in the United States, to any port in a foreign country, of live cattle affected with pleuro-pneumonia or any infectious disease.

2. The Secretary of the Treasury is, in pursuance of the authority granted by the first section of this Act, authorised to appoint one or more skilled persons as inspectors at the port of New York, and any other port in the United States from which he may have information that live cattle are being shipped, whose duty it shall be to examine carefully all live cattle offered for shipment at such port; and if, upon such examination, it shall be found that any cattle so about to be exported are infected with any infectious disease, that fact shall be reported without delay to the collector of the port, whose duty it shall be, under such regulations as may be prescribed by the Secretary of the Treasury, to refuse a clearance to any vessel which shall take on board such cattle for exportation. The exporter of such cattle as shall be found free of any such infectious or contagious disease, and not in any infected herd, shall be entitled to a certificate from the collector to that effect.

3. The Secretary of the Treasury shall have authority to prescribe all needful rules and regulations for carrying the provisions of this Act into effect, and all expenses attending the execution of the same shall be paid out of the appropriations for collecting the revenues from customs: Provided, however, that the Secretary of the Treasury may prescribe, by regulation, such reasonable fees for inspection as he may deem just and equitable, to be paid by the owners of cattle exported under the provisions of this Act.

A.

EXPORTS of LIVE ANIMALS during the last ELEVEN YEARS.

Year ended June 30.	Value.
1868	$ 733,395
1869	917,046
1870	1,045,039
1871	1,019,604
1872	1,773,716
1873	2,033,447
1874	3,310,388
1875	2,672,505
1876	2,436,287
1877	3,325,287
1878	5,844,653

NOTE.—The value of the exports of live animals during the fiscal year ended June 30, 1878, was nearly eight times the value of such exports during the fiscal year ended June 30, 1868.

EXPORTS of LIVE ANIMALS during the fiscal YEAR ended JUNE 30, 1878.

Order.	Animals.	Number.	Value.
			$
1	Horned cattle	80,040	3,896,818
2	Horses	4,104	798,723
3	Mules	3,860	501,513
4	Sheep	183,995	333,499
5	Hogs	29,284	267,259
6	All other, and fowls	—	46,841
	Total	301,283	$5,844,653

The value of horned cattle exported from the United States during the fiscal year ended June 30, 1878, was $3,896,818; but during the first *five months* of the current fiscal year, the value of such exports was $4,414,000, or $517,182 in excess of the value of the same during the entire preceding year.

EXPORTS of HORNED CATTLE to the various FOREIGN COUNTRIES during the FISCAL YEAR ended JUNE 30, 1878.

Order.	Countries.	Value.	Per cent.
		$	
1	United Kingdom	2,408,843	61·81
2	Cuba	683,563	17·54
3	Provinces of Quebec, Ontario, &c.	442,092	11·35
4	British West Indies and British Honduras	119,734	3·07
5	Germany	87,648	2·25
6	Belgium	67,850	1·74
7	France	35,700	·92
8	All other countries	51,388	1·32
	Total	$3,896,818	100·00

Nearly 62 per cent. of the cattle exported were shipped to Great Britain, 17½ per cent. to Cuba, and 11 per cent. to British Possessions in North America.

EXPORTS of CATTLE to GREAT BRITAIN from 1874 to 1878, inclusive.

Year ending June 30—	Number.	Value.
		$
1874	123	113,800
1875	110	73,000
1876	244	31,220
1877	5,091	546,829
1878	24,982	2,408,843

B.
[Circular.]
EXPORTATION of CATTLE to GREAT BRITAIN.

Treasury Department,
To COLLECTORS OF CUSTOMS AND OTHERS,　　　Washington, D. C., December 18, 1878.

THE following Despatch has been received by cable, through the Department of State, from Liverpool:

"Unless cattle shipped from United States have Government health-certificate when embarked, slaughter probably compulsory on landing, paralyzing trade. Can you cable Welsh assurance appointment veterinary officers at seaports?"

You are authorised to cause an inspection to be made of all neat cattle proposed to be shipped from your port to Great Britain, and to issue your certificate that such cattle as shall be shipped are free from all disease, and that there is no known disease in cattle at your port, or in its neighbourhood.

In States in which there are officers authorised by law to examine into the diseases of cattle, the collector may avail himself of their services, as the basis of his action, at the expense of the shippers.

Very respectfully,
(Signed)　　H. F. FRENCH,
Assistant Secretary.

C.
[Circular.]
INFORMATION in regard to CATTLE DISEASE.

Treasury Department,
To COLLECTORS OF CUSTOMS AND OTHERS,　　　Washington, D. C., Feb. 1, 1879.

BY department's circular of December 18, 1878, it was directed that live cattle shipped from the various ports of the United States might be examined with reference to the question whether they were free from contagious diseases, and that, if found to be free from such diseases, a certificate to that effect should be given.

By that circular such inspection was not made compulsory, but the certificate was to be issued only upon the application of parties interested.

As the export trade in live cattle from the United States is of vital importance to large interests, every precaution should be taken to guard against the shipment of diseased animals abroad, and such a guarantee given as will satisfy foreign countries, especially Great Britain, that no risk will ensue from such shipments of communicating contagious or infectious diseases to the animals in foreign countries by shipments from the United States.

Collectors of Customs are, therefore, instructed that in no case will live animals be permitted to be shipped from their respective ports until after an inspection of the animals with reference to their freedom from disease, and the issuance of a certificate showing that they are free from the class of diseases mentioned.

Notice of rejected cattle should be promptly given to this department.

In order that this department may be fully informed in regard to such diseases in any part of the United States, collectors of customs are requested to promptly forward to this department any information which they may be able to obtain of the presence of contagious or infectious diseases prevailing among live animals in their vicinity.

It is probable that if the disease prevails to any considerable extent it will be noticed in the local press, and collectors are requested to send copies of any such notices to this department for its information.

(Signed)   JOHN SHEARMAN,
Secretary.

No. 3.

LETTER from the BRITISH CONSUL-GENERAL at NEW YORK to the MARQUIS OF SALISBURY.

(No. 21, Consular.)   British Consulate General, New York,
March 4, 1879.

MY LORD,

I HAVE the honour to report to your Lordship that pleuro-pneumonia among horned cattle still exists on Long Island, and is reported also to exist on Staten Island, and two or three other localities in the neighbouring counties.

Vigorous measures towards extirpating the disease are being enforced, in compliance with the law, and under the instructions of the Governor of this State.

A few isolated cases are said to exist in New Jersey, but the States of Connecticut, Rhode Island, and Delaware, are reported to be free from it.

I have, &c.

The Most Honorable   (Signed)   E. M. ARCHIBALD.
     The Marquis of Salisbury, K.G.
         &c.   &c.   &c.

No. 4.

LETTER from FOREIGN OFFICE to the CLERK OF THE COUNCIL.

SIR,   Foreign Office, March 6, 1879.

WITH reference to your letter of the 27th ultimo, I am directed by the Marquis of Salisbury to transmit to you, to be laid before the Lords of Her Majesty's Privy Council, a further note from the United States Minister in this country, praying for a reconsideration of the action recently taken by their Lordships in regard to the importation of live cattle into this country from America. I am to request that Mr. Welsh's note may be returned with your reply.

I am, &c.

The Clerk of the Council,   (Signed)   T. V. LISTER.
   &c.   &c.   &c.
     Veterinary Department.

Enclosure in No. 4.

LETTER from the UNITED STATES MINISTER, LONDON, to the MARQUIS OF SALISBURY.

Legation of the United States,
London, February 28, 1879.

MY LORD,

PARDON me for again addressing your Lordship on the subject of the live cattle trade which promised to be of so much importance to England and the United States, and which, unless the late action of the Privy Council shall be modified, will be brought to an end on the 3rd proximo.

The authorities of several of the States most interested in the matter, as well as the Federal Government, have taken such prompt and vigorous measures for the extirpation of disease should it be suspected to exist, and have required so rigid an examination by experts, before shipment, that the danger of pleuro-pneumonia, or indeed any other serious ailment, has been reduced to a minimum.

I cannot but hope, therefore, that Her Majesty's Government will see fit not to depart from the policy hitherto pursued and which has resulted so favourably.

Until the arrival of the steamship "Ontario," although up to 31st of October 1878, more than 96,000 cattle from North America had been landed alive, and no cases of disease had occurred, and since her arrival 25 steamers from the United States have reached Liverpool with 3,237 head, all of which have passed inspection and 421 head now landing by the "City of Bristol," from Philadelphia await inspection. The circumstances connected with the "Ontario" shipment, which I have heretofore explained to your Lordship, were such as to make it more than doubtful whether the disease among her cattle originated in the United States, and what I have now stated will satisfy you, I trust, that it is unwise to alter, on account of it, the policy of Her Majesty's Government towards the United States.

I have, &c.
(Signed) JOHN WELSH.

The Most Honorable
 The Marquis of Salisbury,
  &c. &c. &c.

No. 5.

LETTER from the DEPUTY CLERK OF THE COUNCIL to the UNDER SECRETARY OF STATE, FOREIGN OFFICE.

SIR, March 8, 1879.

I HAVE submitted to the Lords of Council your letter of the 6th instant, transmitting a further note from the United States minister in this country praying for a reconsideration of the action recently taken by their Lordships in regard to the importation of live cattle into this country from America.

In reply, I am directed to state, for the information of Lord Salisbury, that their Lordships regret that it is not possible, in view of the provisions of the Contagious Diseases (Animals) Act, 1878, and of the existence of disease in America, to modify the provisions of the Order in Council of the 10th of February last relating to cattle brought from the United States.

I beg to return, herewith, Mr. Welsh's note as requested.

I am, &c.
(Signed) E. HARRISON.

The Under Secretary of State,
 &c. &c. &c.
  Foreign Office.

No. 6.

LETTER from the BRITISH CONSUL-GENERAL at NEW YORK to the MARQUIS OF SALISBURY.

(No. 22, Consular.) British Consulate General,
MY LORD, New York, March 8, 1879.

I HAVE the honour to transmit, herewith enclosed, for such information as they may furnish, extracts from the New York Herald newspaper of the 6th and 8th instant containing letters from the correspondents of that paper at St. Louis and Chicago, in which it is stated that Texan cattle, detained at Chicago on their way eastward, became diseased with pleuro-pneumonia, owing, as it is represented, to unhealthy stabling and feeding at the last-mentioned city. Together with the copies of the letters in question, I enclose editorial notices which appear to maintain the correctness of the reports of the correspondents. Until, however, these statements shall have been confirmed by reports of official inspectors or veterinary surgeons, it would be unsafe to accept them as conclusive.

Q 2337.

It will be seen on reference to the extract from the " Herald " of the 6th instant that certain cattle and sheep imported from Jersey, by the way of Southampton by the steamer " Lepanto " have been quarantined at this port in accordance with the recent Order of the Treasury Department, on the ground that they have been imported from an infected country.

I have, &c.

The Most Noble (Signed) E. M. ARCHIBALD.
   The Marquis of Salisbury, K.G.
     &c. &c. &c.

Enclosures in No. 6.

" New York Herald," March 6, 1879.

CATTLE DISEASE in the WEST.

An important contribution to the history of that part of the trade in live cattle which has resulted in excluding our dealers from British markets will be found in the letter we publish to-day from our correspondent at St. Louis. It has been a mystery to the general public how pleuro-pneumonia, which did not exist as an epidemic in the great cattle raising districts, and was unknown in the herds sent forward from their native plains for exportation, though it was known to exist in swill-feeding stables from which animals were not exported, yet appeared to such an extent in shipments of American cattle on their arrival at British ports, as to force the English government to make a rule against our cattle. The mystery is now cleared up by the discoveries of " Herald " correspondents in Western cities; and once more we have an illustration of the old truth that the ruin of trade is due to dishonest and unscrupulous traders. At Chicago from 8,000 to 12,000 cattle are fed every winter in stalls, to be sent eastward in the spring as fattened stall-fed cattle. How they are fed and how they are kept is a story the record of which is a vivid repetition of the descriptions that have been written of the Blissville stables. But the whole procedure is given in the St. Louis letter we print to-day. It appears that upon the arrival at the stock yards there of a large consignment of Texan cattle the animals in good condition are sold readily and shipped eastward for butchery here or exportation, and that they are sound and healthy. But in every consignment there will be poor specimens—not diseased, perhaps, but half starved, lean and feeble. These, of course, sell at a low rate and are bought by feeders, who put them into swill stables, fatten them up, and then by collusion put them into the sales of fresh cattle from the Plains. Doubtless in those swill stables pleuro-pneumonia exists permanently as in the swill stables here, and the animals remaining long enough to be contaminated are thus sent out as Texas cattle, yet with a disease caught in the swill stables.

" New York Herald," March 6th, 1879.

DISEASED CATTLE.—PROFESSIONAL SLOP FEEDERS in the WEST.—FATTENING CATTLE for EAST.—KEPT in FILTHY PENS and FED on DISTILLERY REFUSE.—The EAST ST. LOUIS SUPPLY.

St. Louis, March 2, 1879.

It has been known for some time that slop-fed and diseased cattle were shipped from this point to the Eastern markets and there disposed of as good conditioned Texas stock. This evil has been steadily growing until it has assumed so startling a magnitude that only prompt and strong measures will enable the authorities to put a stop to it. Your correspondent visited the stock yards at East St. Louis with the view of ascertaining, if possible, the extent of this evil, and the number of cattle that had been held over at this point to fatten for the Eastern market, but, owing to the shrewdness of buyers, the feeding of slops is not carried on in the yards, the owners having found from experience that it materially affects their sales; consequently a new class has sprung up, called professional feeders, who, to carry on their work more successfully and elude detection, ship the cattle off to out of the way places, re-ship them to the stock yards after putting them through the fattening process and send them East in mixed lots with through shipments, thus preventing even a fair estimate of the number of slop-fed stock that is in this way thrown on the Eastern markets. Beer slops and what is called " chop " feeding was carried on to a large extent right in the stock yards until owners found that it damaged their sales.

How it is done.

As soon as a lot of Texan cattle are brought into the yards the best appearing and most saleable are quickly disposed of and shipped off within twenty-four or forty-eight hours, but the healthy cattle that the East receives in this way have a terrible offset in what follows. After the yard is pretty well cleared, then comes the professional feeder and buys up all the poor and diseased cattle and the odds and ends of unsaleable stock, getting great bargains, as the owners are glad to get them off their hands at any price.

Where it is done.

At an expense of much time and labor your correspondent at last ferreted out the location of these feeding quarters and discovered that the business is carried on to a large extent at Greenville, Worden, Vincennes, and even up as far as Peoria. Wishing to satisfy himself as to the condition of the cattle, and the extent to which it was carried on, he took an early train yesterday and visited the sheds of one A. H. McNeil, located at Greenville, Bond county, some 40 miles north of St. Louis. The condition and surroundings of the cattle there found was enough to breed disease, even if they were fed on wholesome hay and corn. In three long, narrow sheds there was an average of 150 head of cattle, crowded into narrow stalls, with no space to move about in, breathing the same air over and over again, as no means for ventilation were provided, and filth reigned supreme. Long troughs ran the full length of the sheds, and present almost as filthy an appearance as the floors and sides of the wall, slimy, steaming, and actually rotting; these troughs are filled twice a day with beer slops and chop feed, which the cattle learn after a time to devour ravenously, as no corn or hay is given them during the whole fattening process, which generally lasts from two to three months.

Fresh arrivals.

While your correspondent was looking through the sheds a small herd arrived that were easily recognized as Texas cattle. They were thin and poor, and appeared weak, either from starvation or disease, and unable to carry without tottering the weight of their enormous horns. They were separated and driven into a vacant shed, and each assigned a stall, after which the feeding process commenced. A quantity of beer slops and bran mixed was emptied into the common trough from barrels. Although they had not undoubtedly been fed for 48 hours, and, from insufficient food while in transit, preserved a half-starved appearance, they merely sniffed at the vile mixture and utterly refused to touch it, some of them lying down as soon as they were driven into the stalls, to be quickly prodded up with the long poles in the hands of the men who had them in charge. They are penned up in this way several days before they will touch food at all, but as soon as they do commence to feed on it it is surprising how rapidly they fatten up and the healthy appearance they present. They are kept in these close sheds where no pure air can reach them for two and three months, kept in a filthy and disease-breeding condition and fed on nothing but distillery refuse and beer slops, until they present a healthy and fat appearance, when they are re-shipped to East St. Louis, and there sold from the stock yards as fresh and healthy Texan cattle, mixed up with *bonâ fide* shipments from Texas and Colorado.

Undoubtedly diseased.

In this way there are daily shoved on the Eastern market from eight hundred to a thousand head of cattle that are undoubtedly diseased, so intermixed with good condition stock that it is impossible to separate them after they reach the East. This is very easy to do at this end, there being no veterinary surgeon at the yards, and no effort is made before shipping to separate and examine even what are known to be mixed lots, and, as a consequence, it is safe to say that all are more or less diseased by the time they reach New York.

This nefarious proceeding is not confined to up-country buyers, but is also practised by the original owners. They come here daily with a miserable looking lot of cattle with the intention of holding them over in the East St. Louis yards for the purpose of slop fattening, but when they find that buyers are becoming too sharp to be imposed on in this manner, they assign them to the out of town feeders, and make some amicable arrangement whereby it will be covered up when the cattle are returned to the yards that they have been still fed.

The daily Supply.

There are to-day in the stock yards about 800 head of stock that from all appearance are half starved, and in all probability would not outlive a journey to New York in their present condition, but in a day or so they will be bought up and shipped off to some unwholesome feeding pen, and in a couple of months will be returned in a fattened condition, but with disease in every pore from the close quarters, filthy surroundings, and utter lack of care while under treatment by this economical plan; the actual cost not exceeding $3 per head, and fully 300 pounds are added to their weight. There were shipped yesterday 970 head, a large percentage of which were undoubtedly re-handled here, and have been penned up for weeks and fed on distillery refuse. This thing is going on every day, but as a matter of course is kept very quiet, and all operations are so underhanded that it is impossible to get at reliable figures as to the actual shipments, or the number of re-handled cattle that are shipped in the midst of through lots.

More Cattle at Blissville to be killed.—English stock quarantined.

When General Patrick returned to the office of the Board of Health in Brooklyn yesterday, after his conference with the Custom House officials of this city in reference to the cattle supposed to be diseased on the steamer "Lepanto," he was waited upon by Dr. McLean, sanitary inspector, who presented his report in relation to infected stables and diseased cattle within the city limits of Brooklyn. According to some of these reports it appears that during the past two days three cows were led from the Blissville stables and killed at the slaughter-house of Moses May, on Johnson Avenue. During the same period 17 cows, found to be infected with pleuro-pneumonia at the stables, were knocked on the head and thrown on the offal boat for removal to Barren Island. Only 148 cows now remain at the Blissville stables, and before the lapse of many days, all, whether sick or healthy, will have been slaughtered. Dr. McLean spurns the idea that the stables will thereafter be set apart for steers only. He says it is much more likely that the place will be filled with hogs, which will secure ample consumption for the swill. General Patrick said that he had been unable from the pressure of business to devote as much attention to the examination and slaughter of the Blissville cattle as was expected in the beginning of his labours, otherwise not one of the animals would now be living. He sends couriers every day to the stables in order to be kept informed as to the manner in which the quarantine is maintained. This insures constant vigilance on the part of the sheriff and his deputies.

Dr. McLean is preparing a statement in relation to the prevalence of pleuro-pneumonia among the cows in the Blissville stables, and he will reply therein to the opinions expressed by the veterinary surgeons who contended that there was not a case worthy of serious attention. His challenge, published in the "Herald" some days ago, has not yet been accepted. Its acceptance, he says, must come through the columns of the "Herald," the medium through which it was issued. "The high standard," said he, " hitherto maintained in the veterinary profession demands that this question be subjected " to a decisive test. I cannot conceive how there can be any backing out where profes- " sional reputations are at stake." The result of the controversy is eagerly awaited in professional circles both in this State and New Jersey, and Dr. McLean speaks with a determination on the subject that shows he is thoroughly in earnest.

Professor Law was absent from the office of the Brooklyn Board of Health during the day pursuing his investigations into the interior of Queen's county. Roslyn was the first objective point, and Mineola will have its turn next. The Quarantine Commissioners have entered on a week of increased activity. The extension of their field of operations through several counties involves heavy labors and responsibilities. The office is visited daily by dozens of owners of cows asking for permits, so they may not fall into the meshes of the law. After the application has been made a thorough inspection of the stable and cattle by one of the sanitary inspectors must be held before a permit is granted, and quarantine regulations where such may be necessary, laid down. It is worthy of notice that since the extensive slaughter of Blissville cattle the depots of the Erie and Midland Railroads in Jersey City are nightly crowded with milk wagons from the eastern and middle sections of Brooklyn. The increased demand for milk from Orange, Rockland, and Sullivan counties in this State, and Bergen, Passaic, Sussex, and Morris counties in New Jersey, has caused a stir amongst the farmers in those sections.

Feeding with Swill.

Mr. Rouse, Chairman of the Legislative Committee on the Cattle Disease in New Jersey, contends that the swill is not injurious or unhealthy of itself. If it be given to the animals while fresh and when not too hot it does not produce any deleterious effects. In this opinion he is supported by promnent veterinary surgeons, one of whom observed that frequently swill is sent away a considerable distance from the city to farms and allowed to stand till it acidulates, when it becomes very injurious as food. If to this be added want of proper ventilation the cause of the cattle disease can be easily understood.

A resolution has been passed by the King's and Queen's Counties Dairymen's Association favoring the efforts of its members to stamp out pleuro-pneumonia among the cows of the two counties above named.

Cattle Dealers discharged.

Jacob Hecht and Abraham Stern, the two cattle dealers who were arrested on the 8th ult. charged with bringing diseased cattle within the city limits, thus violating a sanitary code, were arraigned in the Court of Special Sessions yesterday for trial. Dr. Comfort of the Board of Health, was put upon the stand, and stated that the cows were sickly and affected with a cough. They were consigned to A. Stern. The Veterinary Surgeon of the Board of Health testified that he examined the cows and found seven of them in the last stages of pleuro-pneumonia and the remaining four diseased. Mr. Judson, proprietor of the Gramercy Park Hotel, said that he sold a herd of 11 cows to A. Stern from his farm in Watertown, Conn., but whether they were the same cows referred to in the complaint he could not say as he had not seen them in six months. He disposed of the cows because he could not sell the milk, and they were a great expense to him. After the examination of several witnesses and a spirited discussion between the counsel, both the prisoners were discharged on the ground that the evidence given was insufficient to convict them.

English-blooded Stock quarantined.

The live stock on board of the steamer "Lepanto," from Hull, England, was landed yesterday morning, being confined for about 20 days. As stated in yesterday's "Herald," a telegram was sent to Secretary Sherman requesting his permission to quarantine the imported cattle on the steamship company's dock, at Jersey City, for one week, so as to determine whether any disease might develop itself.

Yesterday morning an answer came from the Treasury Department, granting authority to the Collector to give permission to land the stock, but to quarantine the same in some place where it would not come in contact with other cattle. Another conference was held, at which General Patrick was present, when it was decided to impound the 24 cows, 6 bulls, and 2 rams, for the space of two weeks in the stables No. 6, 8, and 10, Seventh Avenue. If in that time no signs of pleuro-pneumonia appear, permission will be given to take them to Pennsylvania.

"New York Herald," March 8th, 1879.

WESTERN CATTLE SHEDS.—A VISIT to the "STILL-FEEDING" YARDS of CHICAGO.—THOUSANDS of CATTLE FATTENING.—SCENES of FILTH and REPULSIVENESS.—THE "STRINGS."—NO DISEASE VISIBLE.—HISTORY of an ALLEGED CASE of PLEURO-PNEUMONIA.

Chicago, March 4, 1879.

THE feeding of beef cattle on distillery slops in Chicago and at other points in Illinois is an industry of no mean proportions. There are, in all probability, but comparatively few who appreciate the magnitude of this business, or who, when they sit down to a juicy roast or steak, pause to think how the animal from which it was taken may have acquired its fat tissues. "Still slop" to the average reader is associated with swill milk and numberless foul diseases and decaying tails and suppurating hoofs and other horrible conditions not cheerful to contemplate. This may be true in some localities where the feeding of milch cows has been carried on, no sanitary regulations enforced, and the animals permitted to roll in filth; but it must be conceded that in this section of the West at least, where fattening is conducted for the world's market, there is a different condition of things observable and vitally essential. There are from eight to 12 thousand head of beef cattle fed at the distilleries of Chicago every winter, and these form important integers in the live stock markets of the East and England, to which points they are shipped every spring. The business is carried on so quietly, as far as the general public not interested in the condition of the live-stock market is concerned, that it knows but comparatively little regarding the process of preparing their beef cattle for the block.

"Still-feeding" in Chicago.

The method employed in feeding the cattle which are detained at the various distilleries in and about Chicago is the same, in a general way, as that in vogue elsewhere; but it is extremely doubtful whether a better showing on the whole, as to the condition of the animals and of the varied details of care essential to carrying on the business can be presented in any other city of the Union where this industry is followed. To be sure, it is found here, as no doubt is also manifested by examination of feeding establishments elsewhere, that there are differing degrees of cleanliness and effective shelter in the surroundings of the beasts which have been selected for the long confinement and fattening process, but, taking all things into consideration, the Chicago still-fed cattle will, beyond question, average up a full maximum per centage of first-class condition. The "Herald" representative to whom was assigned the duty of penetrating to the heart of these foul and slimy resorts for cattle, where all is filth, no matter how assiduous may be the endeavours of the workmen to keep them clean; where unsavory steam arising from moist and manure-covered beasts and long and broad channels of turgid excrement, made "puddingy"—if the term may be used—by continuous streams of urine, fills the very limited space between floor and roof, and fairly nauseates the stomach on first inhaling it; where springy boards lying on pools of filth throw sprays of fetid accumulations on every passer by, and where wild and vicious steers and unruly bulls spitefully flirt their saturated tails into the face of the unsuspecting stranger who gazes for the first time upon a scene of this kind—the "Herald" representative, who has just passed through this ordeal, finds much that is of interest in the feeding-houses in Chicago. A cattle-feeding shed is by no means an inviting place in any sense of the word. It is a region of concentrated, pungent, and penetrating nastiness at best, an offence to delicate olfactories; yet, when we contemplate what it might be and what the Chicago sheds are, we must admit that the latter are, comparatively, as a tidy parlor to the habitation of a slovenly housekeeper, where uncleanness prevails and order is not known. A general description of the manner of feeding cattle here will cover the details of each separate establishment, for they are all conducted on the same general plan. It is unnecessary to enter here into any analysis of the characteristics of still slops, or to describe the method in vogue of producing the same. It is the refuse, as all must know, of the grain, yeast, and all such other ingredients as are employed in the manufacture of alcohol, high wines, or whiskey. When the mash has passed through the last stage of manufacture—that of distillation—it is, by means of large pumps, forced into flumes having a sharp grade, and by them run into vats located a short distance from the distillery buildings. These vats hold the slop which is intended for feeding to the cattle housed upon the premises. There are also other vats in the neighbourhood for the reception of slop sold to private individuals living in the neighbourhood and who use it as feed for their small bunches of cows and beef cattle.

The Feed Vats and Trough.

The number of cattle fed on the distillery premises is pretty accurately proportioned to the capacity of the distillery to supply slop per diem, so that there is but a comparatively small amount of slop which goes to outside parties by sale in wagon loads. The vats containing the slops for feeding to the cattle are so built that there is a swift and even flow given to the soft feed when it is sent on its journey to the animals in the sheds. The several vats are supplied with main flumes, which empty the slops into a general distributer usually run through the centre of the roof and furnished with lateral box pipes to shoot it into the feeding trough below at regular intervals throughout the various "strings," so called, of cattle waiting for their meal. In one or two establishments the supply was conducted to the feeding troughs by means of box conduits ranged along the outside of each row of sheds, and thence run into the feeding troughs from one end of the building only. The first-mentioned plan would seem to be preferable, as it supplies the feed more evenly and simultaneously along the entire feeding trough, and prevents cattle impeding its flow while others are impatiently awaiting their meal. The feeding troughs are about 14 inches wide and 6 inches deep, running from one side of the building to the other, and, when the slop is let in, are filled perhaps two-thirds full. At a distance of about 3 feet apart, and leading from the floor beneath the feeding trough to the roof, are placed stanchions, and to these the beasts are fastened by means of a short chain, a little more than a foot in length, caught into a large ring that encircles the stanchion and has free play up and down. This chain is fastened to another encircling the neck, and which is provided with a thick leather pad at the point where it rests upon the top of the neck so as to prevent chafing or soreness. As a general thing the cattle are fastened to the right, but in many instances it is found necessary to fasten them right and left on account of their vicious natures.

Jammed together.

So closely together are the cattle ranged that occasionally they interfere with one another, there being no partitions or stalls, and it is not infrequently the case that serious damage results from animals getting under the feet of their neighbours. Indeed, at several of the feeding establishments visited here instances of this kind were noticed. The buildings in which the cattle are contained are, as a rule, so constructed as to width as to permit of the ranging of about 40 head in each "string" or row. They are nothing more than sheds, and, as a general thing, are so flimsily constructed that their interiors are about as much exposed to the weather as are the outer portions. In only two of the establishments visited here were the roofs perfect or the sides of the sheds so securely battened as to "expel the wintry flaw." The shed might be likened as to form to a row of salt vat covert or inverted letters V moved close together and boarded up at either end, as for instance $\wedge\wedge\wedge$. In most of the establishments the lower edges of the roofs, which are supposed to be joined, are six inches to a foot apart. These spaces are closed up by pitching in hay, and the result is that in the majority of instances there are immense gaps through which the frosty air and pelting snow drifts in upon the haunches of the animals. Two of the feeding-houses of Chicago are admirably constructed, the space from the ground to the apex of the roof being nearly double the customary height, the buildings weather proof, and glass ventilators provided in the centre for the double purpose of fresh air and light. When it is borne in mind that the cattle, from being long housed, having no exercise for fully six months, and constantly surrounded by the steam from the hot feed, grow extremely tender of flesh and sensitive to the slightest alterations of temperature, as much so as would a human being kept continually in a warm room and deprived of exercise, the necessity of protecting them from sudden drafts of chilled air or other exposure liable to induce colds or have a tendency to check the development of fat tissues will be seen. The cattle are located in these sheds so that their haunches reach that point where the lower edges of the roofs meet, and the space in each compartment is large enough to admit two "strings" standing with buttocks towards each other, and with a space of perhaps three feet intervening. In this intermediate space the floor is sunk about one foot below the floor on which the animals stand, and serves as a conduit for excrement and urine, which, falling upon the main floor, is carried to the rear by its own gravity mainly, the floor quietly sloping, and finds its way to the common receptacle. The sheds are cleansed three times daily. This is done partly by flushing with warm water, this process being facilitated by the employment of rubber scrapers, the attendants passing between the animals and drawing the manure back into the channel between the "strings." It is then forced to the exterior of the building by means of a board, to which is attached a long handle, and the interior of the shed is thus for the time being, left comparatively free from filth. This same process is repeated from the outside, the manure having found its way from each feeding section along the row of sheds into a flume extending the entire length, and is finally elevated by means of a steam pump into immense reservoirs, from whence it is finally emptied through flumes into conveyances, boats or others, and eventually finds its way into the lake before this city.

Hay Feed.

The cattle in these sheds can never be hungry, for they are fed almost continually and given all they want at each meal. At 6 o'clock a.m. they are given slops, and also at 10 a.m. and 3 and 6 p.m. Twice daily they are fed hay, and at these meals they are furnished with salt. There is no time in the day that they do not have feed before them, and if they do not fatten upon the rations provided it cannot be attributed to any lack of attention in this direction on the part of the attendants.

Beastly Disgust.

As is, perhaps, perfectly natural, all the animals brought in do not take kindly to the soft feed, and utterly refuse to partake of the steaming mess. But in case they are not indisposed by reason of sickness they eventually decide to partake of the new article of diet, and finally appear to relish it as though it was the most natural article of food in the world. They can get no other.

"*No Sickness.*"

The cattle feeders, distillers, employés about the feeding sheds, and others entirely disinterested in the business, when questioned as to the prevalence of any sickness among the beasts, were unanimous and positive in their statements that nothing of the kind ever existed. To be sure it was true that now and then, when the animals were brought in, there might be one or two, or mayhap half a dozen, in a drove of one thousand or fifteen hundred, which would exhibit some signs of indisposition, but they would be nothing serious. Perhaps an animal would be worn out with travel and would refuse to eat. Out he must come and go to the stock yards, to be sold and killed for city consumption. Perhaps an animal, unused to the new feed, would get his feet into the hot mess and they became tender. Out he came also, for it would be useless to keep him in the herd, where he could not stand, and liable to be tramped on by his neighbours. Whenever anything of this kind was discovered, and it always occurs when the animals are first housed, the feeble ones are immediately taken from the remainder of the herd, and disposed of to slaughterers.

Fat and Healthy-looking.

The testimony of all was that there was no complaint among the cattle and never had been. This statement is most assuredly borne out by the present condition of the cattle in the Chicago feeding sheds. There could scarcely be a finer lot of animals gathered together, if their outward appearance is to be taken as a criterion of their inner condition. They are all clear-eyed, plump, active, and full of that spirit of general buoyancy that can only come of good health. In a tour covering the past three days, and in which time all the distilleries in Chicago were visited, at least such as engage in cattle feeding, and often looking over about seven thousand head of steers and bulls, the " Herald " representative did not find in a single instance an animal that gave the slightest symptoms of ill-health or debility. All alike were in prime condition, and gave every evidence of perfect health. One seldom looks upon more attractive beef animals—buttocks full, level on top and rounding beautifully in their downward curves; sides fat and heavy; shoulders strong; necks lying in folds; nostrils free of all diseased exudations; eyes sharp and dry and unsunken. Add to these evidences of good condition appetites unimpaired, and one cannot but concede that the still-fed beasts in the Chicago distillery sheds are as prime in every essential as it is possible for such animals to be. It may be said that the persons feeding these cattle—the distillery proprietors and the owners of the cattle—are, of course, interested in setting forth the condition of the animals in the best possible light, and this, of course, may be so; but when one takes the trouble to look at the animals individually, passing through every alley in each of the feeding sheds, as the " Herald " representative did, and thus has before him every opportunity to discover any evidence of disease, and finds that they are just as represented, he must state the facts as they exist, and add his testimony in favor of their general healthfulness.

Few Texan Cattle.

There are comparatively few Texans fed at the Chicago distilleries. Examination shows that the great proportion of animals are natives, varied by occasional bunches of Coloradans and Cherokees. These Colorado steers are graded as Texans, and are considered by feeders as of a superior quality in that their frames, being large, will take on proportionately more fat during the feeding season, and are therefore more profitable.

The " Still-feed " Season.

The feeding season in Chicago begins about the 1st of October. From that time until about the middle of May the cattle are kept on the slops. If the market warrants their being taken out any time between the latter part of March and the 15th of May they may be disposed of, but as a general thing they remain until about the last date indicated. The price paid for feeding, provided the cattle are owned by outside parties, is 9 cents a head per day. This amount is paid to the distillers for the slops and shed-room. The cattle owners furnish men to look after the animals and feed them, and also supply their own hay. In several instances in this city the distillers are the owners of the beef cattle. Generally where the distillers feed their own cattle they also feed milch cows for other parties on contract.

The Chicago Establishments.

There are in Chicago five large distilleries where cattle are fed on slops. These are the West Side Alcohol Works, the Phœnix Distillery, No. 2; Shufeldt's Distillery, the Garden City Distillery, and the Riverdale or Black Hawk Distillery. The West Side Alcohol Works are located at the intersection of Kinzie Street and Western Avenue. This Company are feeding about 400. The animals were driven in about the 1st of October, and are now in prime condition. They are mostly native steers. The animals are fed four times daily on slops and hay twice, and are as clean as cattle can be when surrounded, as these are, by natural filth. In the opinion of the feeders the animals will take on from 300 to 400 pounds during the term of confinement. The feeding sheds cannot be considered first class. The rule here is to cut out promptly any animal that may exhibit any signs of weakness or disease, and send it to the slaughter-house. But no disease of any serious nature has manifested itself. No Spanish fever has ever been discovered.

The Phœnix Distillery, superintended by Mr. George T. Burroughs, is located beyond the northern limits of the city, on a branch of the Chicago river. Here about 1,800 cattle are fed. All are in prime condition. The gain in weight is estimated at about 400 pounds. The cattle are owned by the distilling company. About 300 are Texans, the remainder Cherokees, Coloradans, and natives. The sanitary regulations are excellent. Care is taken to cut out all cattle that may develope disease; but thus far the sheds have been free of all complaints. There have been no fevers and no symptoms of lung affections. The feeding-houses are kept pretty clean; yet it must be stated that they are not in as good condition—or were not on the occasion of the visit of the "Herald" representative—as the necessities of the case would demand. The buildings are poor, and the cattle in many cases subjected to continuous draughts of cold air, which are liable to engender lung difficulties. The animals will probably be shipped early in May. They are intended for domestic and foreign markets. They will be shipped first to the Albany (N.Y.) yards. Feeding here is conducted on the same plan as described elsewhere in this letter.

The Garden City Distillery is located in the southern portion of the city, on West Twenty-second Street, near Halstead Street. It is a large establishment, and has accommodations for fully 1,200 cattle. At present there are 1,000 feeding, mostly natives, with some Coloradans and Cherokees—few thorough Texans. There has been and is no sickness in the entire lot. The regulations require that any diseased cattle shall be promptly taken from the sheds and sent off the premises. Even if the cattle do not take to the slops and persist in not eating they are cut out. Mr. Powell, of the Garden City Company, estimates that the cattle will take on about 250 pounds each during the feeding season. The present lot came into the sheds about the latter part of November, and will probably remain until the 15th of May. They will be shipped to Albany, and many of them will, no doubt, find a market abroad. These cattle are owned by a Milwaukee party who has made a specialty of fattening beef for the English trade. The feeding-sheds here are in fair condition, and were found to be in a commendable state of cleanliness.

The Shuteldt Distillery is on the north side of the city, near Chicago Avenue, on Larrabee Street. There are about 1,600 head feeding. The sheds are spacious, well-ventilated, and warm. The floors are kept remarkably clean, and the animals are in excellent condition. The same system of feeding is followed as in the other establishments, and the sanitary regulations are extremely rigorous. No disease has been discovered. The animals are healthy and vigorous.

The Riverdale, or Black Hawk, Distillery is about 20 miles from Chicago on the Illinois Central Railroad, at a point known as Dalton. Here there are about 1,500 head of cattle feeding. There is no sickness among them, and the condition of the sheds is good in every respect. The regulations regarding sick animals are stringent, and the cattle are kept as clean as is possible. The testimony as to gain in flesh and other points concerning feeding and care is the same as was elicited at the other establishments.

Outside Stables.

Additional to the foregoing may be mentioned the feeding of cattle now being carried on at several other points in the State—namely, Springfield, Pekin, Peoria, and Sterling. From all reports received from those localities the animals are in excellent condition.

A Summary.

The slop-fed cattle in Illinois may be briefly summarised as follows:—

Chicago.	No. of Head.	Texans.
Alcohol Wells	400	—
Phœnix Distillery	1,800	300
Shufeldt's	1,600	50
Garden City Distillery	1,200	100
Riverdale	1,500	—
Pekin	2,000	—
Sterling	2,000	—
Springfield	2,000	—
Peoria	3,500	—
Scattering at Pekin and Peoria	2,000	—
Totals	18,000	450

Pleuro-Pneumonia.

In connexion with the foregoing it may be apropos to mention here a few facts in relation to the excitement that has prevailed the past week at the Union Stock Yards, Chicago, and among live stock dealers generally in the West regarding the reports which have gone out as to the discovery of a case of pleuro-pneumonia. It is very unfortunate that such a rumor should have gained credence even for a moment, for the injury it is calculated to do is very great. The whole thing was more the result of hasty judgment and nervous excitement on the part of those to whom has been intrusted the inspection of live stock at this point, than any desire to strike a blow at the cattle interests of the West, for it must be conceded that the gentlemen in whose hands this matter rests are commendably jealous of the good of this section of the country. That the report has gone abroad that a case of contagious pleuro-pneumonia was discovered here there can be no doubt, and it is due to the Western live stock interests that it should be corrected. It appears that on the 22nd of February a heifer was found at the stock yards which, as the government inspector reports, "exhibiting signs of pleuro-pneumonia." The animal was as once killed, and steps taken to examine it. Before this was done the inspector unwisely, and when labouring under great mental excitement, sought out the collector of this port and informed him that a veritable case of pleuro-pneumonia had been discovered, and assistance of experts was asked in order to make a thorough examination. At the same time an assistant of the government inspector informed the editor of the "National Live Stock Journal," in this city, that they had found a case of contagious pleuro-pneumonia. Coming from a source deemed authoritative this statement was repeated, and the announcement at once went out that the dreaded cattle disease had in fact made its appearance at the West. This was prior to the careful investigation of the lungs and pleura of the slaughtered heifer. A day or two later, when the authorities had looked into the matter with greater care, the diseased parts of the animal were found to not show any enlargement, mottled condition, or disease of the pleura. In contagious pleuro-pneumonia these conditions are always present. The hepatization of the lungs showed only that the beast had been afflicted with a sequel of some lung disease, probably common pneumonia, which is not in the slightest degree dangerous or contagious. These statements as to the condition of this animal are made by accomplished veterinarians and must be accepted as true. Meantime, however, the other report had gone out, and it will probably be some time before the effect of the false announcement can be neutralised. The government inspector has, of course, striven to shake off from himself all responsibility for the first rumor, but it would appear that his excited condition and haste to make known the fact that an animal had been found with pneumonia symptoms had the effect to falsify the true condition of things. It was nothing more than common or sporadic pleuro-pneumonia not contagious.

IMPORTATION OF CATTLE.—ASSISTANT SECRETARY FRENCH on the QUESTION of PROHIBITING the LANDING of CATTLE imported from GREAT BRITAIN.—PLEURO-PNEUMONIA and its existence in ENGLAND considered.—Continuance of the PROHIBITION advised.

Washington, March 7, 1879.

The following report from Mr. H. F. French, Assistant Secretary of the Treasury, upon the subject of the recent Treasury orders prohibiting the landing of cattle from England, was read at the Cabinet Council to-day, and upon consideration of the facts stated the Treasury order of February 26, 1879, will remain in force:—

To the Secretary:—

The question presented is whether the order of this Department of February 26, 1879, prohibiting the landing of cattle imported from Great Britain until otherwise ordered should be rescinded or modified. Said order was issued upon information that the disease known as pleuro-pneumonia, which in England is often called the cattle-plague, had appeared in Hull and other parts of England. Hull is a port on the north-eastern coast of England between which and New York a regular line of steamers plies, touching at Southampton, where cattle from the Channel Islands are taken on board and brought to the United States.

Origin of the Disease.

The pleuro-pneumonia, as it was familiarly known in Massachusetts nearly 20 years ago, was introduced from Holland by the importation of Holstein cattle by Mr. Cheney, of Belmont. I assisted in the investigation of the disease at that time, and I judge from the facts recently made known that the disease now prevalent to some extent in this country and Great Britain is of the same type. It is a contagious disease, and is supposed to be communicated not only by actual contact of sound cattle with those diseased, but through infected fodder, or bedding, or buildings. A marked feature of the disease is that it often incubates or lies dormant from 30 to 50 days, and even more, after its seeds are sown, and during this period of incubation, whether longer or shorter, not even a skilled veterinary surgeon can detect its presence. Cattle may therefore be purchased in England, shipped to this country, sold at auction and dispersed over our principal stock-breeding States without the possibility of detecting the disease by any inspection of the animals.

Measures of Prevention.

The States no doubt have full power by quarantine or other regulations to protect themselves against the spread of this disease; some of them, as Massachusetts and New York, have adopted measures for this purpose. The necessary measures for the inspection of this disease, as adopted in those States and in England, are:—The isolation of all suspected herds and the slaughter and burial of all animals found to be infected, and usually of all that have been exposed to the infection. These measures, with provision for proper compensation to the owners of the cattle thus slaughtered, are now enforced in England and in the States already named, and probably in many others. Several States into which cattle are imported, it is understood, have no such regulations. Of these I understand Maryland to be one, and Baltimore is a port both of importation and exportation of live cattle.

If Congress possesses the power to prevent the introduction of the cattle disease by enforcing the inspection and quarantine or the destruction of suspected animals, it has thus far failed to exercise such power. The only provision on this subject to be found in the laws of the United States is contained in sections 2,493, 2,494, and 2,495 of the Revised Statutes.

Section 2,493 Revised Statutes provides that:—

The importation of neat cattle and the hides of neat cattle from any foreign country into the United States is prohibited, provided that the operation of this section shall be suspended as to any foreign country or countries, or any parts of such country or countries whenever the Secretary of the Treasury shall officially determine, and give public notice thereof, that such importation will not tend to the introduction or spread of contagious or infectious diseases among the cattle of the United States; and the Secretary of the Treasury is hereby authorised and empowered, and it shall be his duty to make all necessary orders and regulations to carry this law into effect, &c.

By section 2,494 of the Revised Statutes, the President has the power to suspend the operation of the above section whenever, in his judgment, the importation of neat cattle and their hides may be made without danger of introduction and spread of the contagious diseases, &c.

I think it is clear that section 2,493 of the Revised Statutes confers upon the Secretary of the Treasury no authority whatever to quarantine or isolate, or to slaughter imported cattle. The only power conferred upon him is to suspend the operation of the section whenever he shall officially determine " that such importation will not tend to the introduction or spread of contagious or infectious diseases," and to make the necessary orders and regulations to carry this law (*i.e.*, the law to prevent the importation of neat cattle, &c.) into effect, and to suspend the same as provided. The only power that the President has under section 2,494 of the Revised Statutes is to suspend the prohibitory law whenever in his judgment the importation may proceed without danger of the introduction of disease. The only question, therefore, to be considered at present is whether the Secretary of the Treasury or the President can determine that the statute prohibiting the importation of neat cattle, &c., can be suspended without danger of the introduction of the cattle disease.

The Disease in England.

By a letter from J. D. Harrison, Secretary of the New York Agricultural Society, dated February 12, 1879, addressed to the Secretary of the Treasury, attention was called to the fact that cattle of the Jersey island are at this time brought to the United States frequently, and in considerable numbers, by steamers sailing from the port of Hull, and at least one shipment was about to arrive, and the Secretary was urged to take proper precautions against the importation of diseased or infected cattle. Mr. Harrison is a worthy representative of one of the oldest and most efficient agricultural societies in this country and a society specially interested in the importation and improvement of neat cattle. At about the same time statements had been officially made in the papers and otherwise tending to show that pleuro-pneumonia had broken out at various places in England. We had information also that the steamer " Lepanto " was about to arrive in New York from England, bring a herd of Jersey cattle from Southampton to be sold at auction in New York. In the meantime, as will presently be more fully shown, the pleuro-pneumonia had appeared in various parts of the United States, especially near New York city. The Dominion of Canada, on February 6, 1879, had published an Order of Council prohibiting the importation or introduction into the dominion of cattle from the United States for a period of three months from that date. We had learned also that two herds of cattle, one being from the United States and one from Canada, shipped from Portland, Me., by the " Ontario," had been found to be deceased with pleuro-pneumonia on their arrival, and a part or all of them condemned to be slaughtered.

Prohibitory Order issued.

No other power to deal with the disease existing by law the order of February 26, prohibiting importation from England, was issued. This order has given the department power to co-operate with the authorities of the State of New York in preventing the sale and dispersion through the country of the cattle imported by the steamer "Lepanto," which arrived at New York about March 1st. The importers readily complied with the conditions, satisfactorily to the collector of customs at New York, and to the authorities of the State of New York, and the herd, consisting of about 40 animals, is now quarantined in New York for 60 days.

A letter from Mr. Packard our Consul at Liverpool, to Hon. F. W. Seward, Assistant Secretary of State, dated February 10th, 1879 states that the London " Times " of of February 7th, published a report that pleuro-pneumonia had broken out among the cows of William Robinson, a dairyman at the north end of Liverpool. Upon inquiry of Mr. Robinson it appears that on November 27th, January 3rd, and February 4th, he had sold a cow to a butcher, and these three cows had all been found to be diseased, and that on February 7th all of his remaining cows, six in number, were slaughtered by order of the Privy Council. He says all the animals were English, and that he never brought an American cow or saw one offered for sale. Upon inquiry Superintendent Walsh, of the Bootle police, said the pleuro-pneumonia had appeared about six months ago at the dairy of Mr. Wilson, near Crosby, who kept 21 cows. Six were found diseased and all were slaughteted. On the farm of Mrs. Haines, near Bootle, about the same time, three cows had the disease and were slaughtered and buried. Pleuro-pneumonia appeared on October 28th at the dairy of Rowland Allen, near Liverpool, and of 15 cows 11 were diseased, and all were slaughtered. On October 17th, at the dairy of Mr. Lambert, one cow was attacked and 11 were slaughtered. None of these cows were American.

The article referred to, from the London " Times," is annexed to Consul Packer's letter. From this it appears that of 197 cattle landed at Liverpool by the " Ontario," from Portland, all have been slaughtered and 13 of the number only found infected.

A second letter from Mr. Harrison, secretary of the New York Agricultural Society, dated January 26, 1879, fully sets forth the danger of the trade in cattle between Hull and New York, and urges the department to take measures to prevent the introduction of the pleuro-pneumonia through that channel. He says:—

The port of Hull is, at latest mail advices, infected with lung-plague, contagious pleuro-pneumonia, of cattle. This port having a constant trade with Holland—the very home, during the present century, of lung-plague—has for a long time been one of the most dangerous of all ports as regards the receiving and disseminating of this worst of all diseases of cattle.

A letter from Dr. James Low, of the Brooklyn Board of Health, addressed to General Curtis, dated February 28th, 1879, strongly urges one of two courses—either the absolute prohibition of the importation of cattle from Europe, or the placing of newly arrived animals in quarantine for at least two months, and then an examination weekly by a veterinary expert and the burning or disinfecting of all the bedding, fodder, and other moveable objects connected with animals imported from foreign countries.

Under this state of facts the Secretary will consider whether it is safe to suspend the order of February 26th, preventing the importation, in view of the fact that this order is the only means provided by law by which any officer of the Government is authorised to interfere in any way with the importation of cattle.

Export of Live Animals.

From the Bureau of Statistics we learn that the exports of live animals have increased from $733,395 in 1868 to $5,844,653 in 1878, being an increase of about eightfold: that the exports of horned cattle during the first five months of the current fiscal year amounted to $4,414,000—$517,182 in excess of the value of the same during the entire preceding year. Of the cattle exported in 1878, about 62 per cent. went to Great Britain. The following table exhibits the number and value of the cattle entered for consumption from 1873 to 1878:—

STATEMENT showing NUMBER and VALUE of CATTLE ENTERED for CONSUMPTION from 1873 to 1878.

	Number of Cattle.	Value.
		Dolls. Cts.
Year ending June 30, 1873	34,998	826,764 51
,, ,, 1874	45,715	884,961 29
,, ,, 1875	45,310	748,151 71
,, ,, 1876	30,068	458,264 82
,, ,, 1877	31,893	314,094 37
,, ,, 1878	41,933	475,526 42
Totals	229,917	$3,707,763 12

Customs Division, March 6, 1879.

H. B. JAMES,
Chief of Customs Division.

Purposes of Importation and Exportation.

In considering this subject it is necessary to bear in mind the different purposes for which cattle are exported and imported. Our exportation of neat cattle to England is chiefly for immediate slaughter for beef, although some cattle, no doubt, are sold to be sent into the country to be fattened, and some, perhaps for dairy use. The great bulk of our cattle received at English ports are intended for immediate slaughter. Where abattoirs are provided, as is already done at several of the ports, an Order of the Council that the cattle shall be immediately slaughtered on arrival brings no great loss upon the owner, while it effectually prevents the spread of any disease from that source through the kingdom. On the other hand, the cattle imported from Great Britain are almost entirely of valuable breeds of short horn or Channel Island cattle, intended for breeding purposes and not slaughter, and, being purchased of breeders in all parts of the country, are liable to carry contagion over our whole land. An order to slaughter them upon arrival would be equivalent to an order of non-importation. While we may properly suspend the importation of cattle from England until the danger of contagion has passed, England has no similar reason for prohibiting importation into that Kingdom, but may wisely and properly maintain stringent regulations for inspection, and require slaughter of the animals at the ports of arrival as a precautionary measure.

The Disease in the United States.

I am not yet satisfied as to the extent of the prevalence of the cattle disease in the United States. We are taking measures to gain information daily upon the subject One thing, however, we may regard as certain, that England has reason to believe that the pleuro-pneumonia prevails to a considerable extent in this country. A letter from the Minister of Agriculture of Canada, dated February 24th, 1879, addressed to Mr. Le Duc, Commissioner of Agriculture, states that the cattle taken to England by the "Ontario" were purchased in Ohio and other parts of the West, and were taken immediately from cattle yards in Buffalo, and that "the imperial authorities have in-"dubitably satisfied themselves that the disease conveyed by the cattle of the "Ontario" "was pleuro-pneumonia of the most malignant type."

Further, that Professor McEachran, of Montreal, who was specially commissioned by this department, did find pleuro-pneumonia in the State of New York, in the district of Columbia, in Virginia, in New Jersey, and other places.

I should be glad to have it demonstrated that the disease does not exist in the Western States, or in Maine, Vermont, or New Hampshire in the Eastern.

I do not place full confidence in the above statement of the Canadian Minister, but it will undoubtedly be accepted in England as true. The exportation of neat cattle from this country has already almost entirely ceased. In reply to telegrams addressed to the ports of Portland, Boston, New York, and Baltimore I received answers yesterday that no exportations were contemplated at either port, so far as known, except a shipment contemplated on the 10th instant, per "Sumatra," for London. The only course by which the exportations can be resumed is the adoption on our part of energetic measures to stamp out the disease wherever it may appear.

I think the order adopted by this department prohibiting importations for the present will be everywhere regarded as a step in the right direction, and cannot be regarded by England as unfriendly to our commerce with that nation.

I send herewith a memorandum by H. B. James, of the Customs Division, showing various orders and restrictions heretofore placed upon the importation of live animals.

Very respectfully,
H. F. FRENCH,
Assistant Secretary.

AMERICAN CATTLE for FOREIGN MARKETS.

The first examination of cattle for shipment abroad since the 14th of February last was made at the yards at Sixtieth Street yesterday afternoon, and the animals will be shipped this morning. A "Herald" reporter learned upon inquiry at the office of the Collector of the Port that it is General Meritt's intention to appoint a special officer for the inspection of cattle intended for transportation abroad, but so far no authority for such appointment has been received from the Treasury Department. At present the inspections are made under the directions of the Surveyor's office. General Graham, the Surveyor of the Port, said to the reporter that the examinations were made by a veterinary surgeon under the supervision of a Custom House inspector, and he added that the inspector's who are chosen for this duty are those most familiar with disease in cattle. For further information he referred the reporter to the barge office, where Colonel Kibbe was found. Colonel Kibbe stated that the veterinary surgeon is employed by and at the expense of the exporter, but that the inspector must be satisfied of his character and capacity. The examinations are very thorough. Every animal is examined as thoroughly as if it was a question of bargain and sale, and as most of the inspectors detailed for this duty are butchers, and so in a manner experts in regard to diseases in cattle, there is little or no danger of infected animals being shipped. The eyes and nostrils are especially scrutinised. Applications for permits to ship cattle are made at the surveyor's office, and the permits are not granted until a thorough examination in every case demonstrates that the animal is free from disease.

GENERAL PATRICK preparing to change his BASE of OPERATIONS.—JERSEY CITY receiving ATTENTION.

While the sanitary squad in Brooklyn was busied yesterday in the examination of stables in the Northern and Eastern districts, General Patrick was occupied in his headquarters at the office of the Board of Health in receiving reports from several quarters in Queen's County. Among those who called were gentlemen interested in cattle traffic from Glen Cove, Mineola, Roslyn, and Jamaica, desiring to obtain more definite information in regard to the removal of cattle to New York. In every instance General Patrick informed the applicants that no cattle could be removed without a permit from the State authorities, assuring the owners at the same time that they would be subjected to as little inconvenience as possible. He stated explicitly that the officers appointed by the Quarantine Commissioners would proceed with the utmost expedition if their efforts were seconded by the proprietors of stables. To use the general's words, " I wish heartily that this business were ended in this section of the State, so that we " might turn our attention to other quarters. This matter is so important that we " cannot afford to spend too much time in one place." The general declined to state what new instructions he received from the Executive, but the movements in his office yesterday indicated that he is about to direct his efforts in other directions. The quarantine staff refused to impart any information on the subject, but an officer of the Brooklyn Board of Health told a "Herald" reporter that as soon as the cattle at the Blissville stables could be disposed of, the services of Sheriff Rushmore would be required in another portion of Queen's County. The sheriff seemed to have anticipated the order as several of his deputies were notified that their services at Blissville would be dispensed with at the end of next week. General Patrick will remain, however, at his present headquarters in Brooklyn, and direct the quarantine operations in the counties to which his jurisdiction is extended. Continual complaints arrive from Staten Island, Westchester, Suffolk, Rockland, and Orange Counties, but the work is of such magnitude that it will be necessarily slow. The general frankly stated that when the quarantine at Blissville was established he did not anticipate the immense work to be encountered by the quarantine staff. He has made a proposition to the proprietors of the stables at Blissville in regard to the establishment of a large cattle yard in that vicinity, after the cattle now in the stables have been slaughtered, and the subject will be fully discussed on Monday evening. It has been definitely settled that the new quarantine yard shall not be located within the municipal limits of Brooklyn.

Instructions have been issued that the cattle boat "Midland" shall land all the animals brought from the Jersey shore hereafter at the foot of Broadway in Brooklyn. The New Jersey Stock Yard Company has been notified that if the boat from their yards at the Long Dock transgress the rule laid down in regard to the landing at Broadway the officers of the boat will be arrested, and the boat seized by the State authorities. Although this may be regarded as an extreme measure, it has been recommended by the wholesale butchers and cattle dealers of Williamsburg, who refuse to allow the cattle consigned to them to mingle with those coming from the Long Dock.

The New Jersey Raid.

The members of the examining committee of the Jersey City Board of Health, comprising Health Inspector Cronin, and Drs. Lochner and Knauper, and Professor Chambon, continued their investigations in regard to the condition of the stables in the Greenville section of Jersey City yesterday. They found many stables in a filthy condition, and several cattle were suffering from pleuro-pneumonia. Professor Chambon and Inspector Cronin have been selected by the Legislative Committee on the Cattle Disease as examiners of stables in Hudson County, pending the passage of the Cattle Diseases Bill in the lower house.

SWILL-FED CATTLE FROM THE WEST.

Another contribution to the history of the progress of Western cattle from the plains to the seacoast is given in the letter from Chicago which we print to-day. It will be noted that it repeats with some ampler details the story given in the letter on the same subject from St. Louis which we printed on Thursday. In the account given of some particular features of the cattle trade in these two great cities, the public interested in knowing the truth on this subject—and an exact knowledge of the truth is the first step toward the discovery of a remedy—will see clearly established that connexion between swill stables where pleuro-pneumonia certainly exists, and the great cattle-breeding plains where the animals are certainly healthy. Our veterinary surgeons and our cattle breeders and sellers have denied the existence of this malady in marketable cattle as strenuously as the English officers have declared its existence, and these denials were made precisely because our surgeons and dealers were unable to comprehend that there could be any possible connexion between the healthy cattle from the plains and the cattle stewed for months on a fattening process in the foul hot air of a swill-feeding pen. How puny specimens of the healthy cattle are sold cheaply on the way, fattened in these pens, and sold again as healthy cattle from the plains we have now shown, and we leave it to those most interested to find a remedy.

No. 7.

LETTER from FOREIGN OFFICE to the CLERK OF THE COUNCIL.

Sir,　　　　　　　　　　　　　　　　　　　Foreign Office, March 26, 1879.

I AM directed by the Marquis of Salisbury to transmit to you the accompanying copy of a note from the United States Minister at this Court, stating that landing of cattle from England has been prohibited in ports of the United States owing to the alleged existence of pleuro-pneumonia in the vicinity of Hull, and requesting investigation as to the existence of the disease, and I am to request that in laying this latter before the Lords of Her Majesty's Privy Council, you will move their Lordships to cause Lord Salisbury to be informed what answer should be returned to Mr. Welsh's note.

I am, &c.

The Clerk of the Council,　　　　　(Signed)　　JULIAN PAUNCEFOTE.
&c.　　&c.　　&c.
Veterinary Department.

Enclosure in No. 7.

LETTER from the UNITED STATES MINISTER, LONDON, to the MARQUIS OF SALISBURY.

My Lord,　　　　　　Legation of the United States, London, March 19, 1879.

I HAVE the honour to acquaint you that the Secretary of the Treasury of the United States, having received authentic information that the disease known as pleuro-pneumonia has recently been found to exist among cattle in the vicinity of Hull in this kingdom, he has, under the provisions of section 2,493 of the United States Revised Statutes instructed the collectors of customs at the principal ports not to permit the landing of neat cattle from England until otherwise ordered.

I have been requested by Mr. Evarts to inform your Lordship of this temporary prohibition.

Meanwhile, the Secretary of the Treasury desires that investigation should be made through the Diplomatic and Consular Officers of the United States in England, in regard to the extent to which the disease exists here, and such other facts upon the subject as may be useful to his department in deciding what course hereafter to pursue.

I beg leave, therefore, to ask your Lordship to assist me in obtaining this information either from Her Majesty's Privy Council, or such other branch of the Government as may have official cognizance of this matter.

I have, &c.

The Marquis of Salisbury,　　　　　(Signed)　　John Welsh.
&c.　　&c.　　&c.

No. 8.

LETTER from CLERK OF THE COUNCIL to THE UNDER SECRETARY OF STATE, FOREIGN OFFICE.

　　　　　　　　　　　　　Veterinary Department, Privy Council Office,
Sir,　　　　　　　　Princes Street, Westminster, S.W., April 1, 1879.

I BEG to acknowledge the receipt of your letter of the 26th ultimo, transmitting copy of a note from the United States Minister at this Court, stating that landing of cattle from England has been prohibited in parts of the United States owing to the alleged existence of pleuro-pneumonia in the vicinity of Hull, and requesting investigation as to the existence of the disease.

I am directed by the Secretary of State in reply to transmit, for the information of Lord Salisbury, a memorandum showing the counties in Great Britain in which pleuro-pneumonia has been reported to exist during the first twelve weeks of 1879.

I am, &c.

The Under Secretary of State,　　　　　(Signed)　　C. L. PEEL.
&c.　　&c.　　&c.
　　Foreign Office.

Enclosure in No. 8.

Memorandum.

Pleuro-Pneumonia has been reported ito exist in the following 51 counties of Great Britain, during the first 12 weeks of 1879.

Berks.	Lincoln (Kesteven).	Worcester.	Edinburgh.
Cambridge.	Lincoln (Lindsey).	York, East Riding.	Fife.
Chester.	Middlesex.	York, North Riding.	Forfar.
Cumberland.	Norfolk.	York, West Riding.	Kincardine.
Derby.	Northampton.	Isle of Ely.	Kinross.
Durham.	Northumberland.	The Metropolis.	Lanark.
Essex.	Notts.	Carnarvon.	Linlithgow.
Herts.	Rutland.	Flint.	Peebles.
Huntingdon.	Stafford.	Merioneth.	Perth.
Kent.	Suffolk.	Aberdeen.	Renfrew.
Lancaster.	Surrey.	Banff.	Stirling.
Leicester.	Sussex.	Berwick.	Wigtown.
Lincoln (Holland).	Warwick.	Clackmannan.	

316 fresh outbreaks have been reported, and 942 cattle have been attacked, 914 have been killed, and 24 have died.

(Approximate).

Veterinary Department, Privy Council Office,
March 31, 1879.

(Signed) G. T. Brown.

No. 9.

(No. 32, Consular.)

LETTER from SIR E. THORNTON to the MARQUIS OF SALISBURY.

My Lord, Washington, April 15, 1879.

I have the honour to transmit herewith despatches, as marked in the margin, which have reached this Legation under flying seal from Her Majesty's Consulates at New York and Philadelphia, reporting the existence of pleuro-pneumonia among cattle in the States of New York, New Jersey, and Pennsylvania, and detailing the measures adopted by the Governments of those States to eradicate the same.

Mr. Crump states that the disease which has broken out among the dairy cattle in Pennsylvania, although not to an alarming extent, is pronounced by competent veterinary surgeons to belong to the contagious type of a malignant character.

I have, &c.

The Marquis of Salisbury, K.G.
&c. &c. &c.

(Signed) EDWARD THORNTON.

Enclosure 1 in No. 9.

No. 25.

LETTER from the British Consul-General at New York, to the Marquis of Salisbury.

My Lord, British Consulate General, New York,
April 8, 1879.

I have the honour to report to your Lordship that pleuro-pneumonia among horned cattle still prevails in this State, and in some parts of the State of New Jersey. The State Authorities are, however, making all available efforts to extirpate the disease, and inspectors have been appointed with full power to adopt and enforce such measures as may be necessary for its suppression.

I have the honour to transmit, for your Lordship's information, copies of a letter, which has recently been published in the "New York Herald," from Professor Law, of the Cornell University, on the subject of contagious pleuro-pneumonia among cattle and in regard to the measures which he recommended for exterminating the plague.

I have, &c.

The Most Noble
The Marquis of Salisbury, K.G.
&c. &c. &c.

(Signed) E. M. Archibald.

26

Enclosure 2 in No. 9.

"New York Herald," March 13, 1879.

Professor Law on Pleuro-Pneumonia.—Origin and Extent of the Disease.—Expense of Slaughtering and Quarantine.

To the Editor of the "Herald":—

As legislation is now pending in the various states infected with the contagious pleuro-pneumonia of cattle, and as there is some danger that legislators who have not for themselves studied the nature of the malady, may be betrayed into sanctioning enactments that will leave the States in question helpless to exterminate the plague, and a continued source of danger and expense to the neighbouring States, I beg that you will allow me space for a few remarks on the subject. These I shall confine to vital points in connexion with the nature of the disease, and the only effectual means of exterminating it.

That the malady is contagious, is shown every day in the course of our work. Wherever we find it existing in a herd, we obtain a history of a recent purchase or of some other form of exposure by which the herd has been infected. To give illustrations would be to record the whole history of our course in stamping it out so far. But this is not enough. The disease is not only contagious, but in this country it is only propagated by contagion. Throughout the immemorial ages of this the oldest of continents, the herds of buffaloes roaming over its plains never contracted this affection. Yet buffaloes are susceptible to the disease as well as our domesticated cattle; and if the buffaloes on the unfenced plains had once developed the malady, it would have remained as a permanent plague, as it has throughout all historic periods in the open steppes of Eastern Europe and Asia, and since 1859 in the wide stock ranges of Australia. During the long period that has elapsed since the colonisation of America, the cattle have been subjected to all the conditions of life that have beset them since 1843, but until that period, when an infected Dutch cow was imported into Brooklyn, the malady was unknown. Since that date it has never at any time been absent from Brooklyn and Long Island. On the contrary, Massachusetts, which imported this animal plague in 1850, set herself vigorously to the work of exterminating it. In the next five years she killed and paid for over one thousand cattle, but in so doing she killed the contagion, and since 1865 has not known this disease.

Never developed in the Western States.

Cattle have lived in innumerable herds in the Western States, subjected to all possible privations and to the greatest trials in the way of travel, crowding, filth, and starvation, but on no occasion has this lung-plague been developed, and to-day I believe the cattle of these States are as sound as are the buffaloes on the plains. In Europe this plague always extends on the occasion of any great war, and devastates the countries through which the armies pass, but only because the commissariat parks are supplied from infected districts. During the late American war, our commissariat herds were subjected to equal privations, with the additional drawback of the absence of the smooth paved roads of the Old World, but the plague never broke out in these herds or ravaged the states where the armies were operating. The explanation is that the cattle supplies were drawn from uninfected regions, and in the absence of the specific imported disease-germ no abuse in America was capable of producing it.

Swill in the West.

The swill-milk stables of the West are as much crowded, as filthy and as ill-ventilated as those of New York and New Jersey. But the swill stables of the West never produce this disease, while those of the seaboard, into which the germ has been introduced, are ravaged to a ruinous extent. If more proof is wanted of the purely contagious nature of the malady, it is to be found in the entire absence of the plague from the Highlands of Scotland, the Channel Islands, Brittany, much of Normandy, Spain, Portugal, Norway, and Sweden. These places breed their own stock, and rarely or never import strange cattle; therefore this poison, exotic to their soil, has never gained a foothold. Norway and Sweden have, indeed, imported the plague, but speedily expelled it by the only effectual method of exterminating the poison. The same is true of a number of other European nations, as well as of Massachussets and Connecticut.

The remark is as true to-day of Western Europe and America, as it was a century ago, when made by the immortal Haller of his own native Switzerland, that the disease never appears but as the result of the introduction into a country or district of an animal from an infected place.

Danger of Half Measures.

This being the case, any temporizing with the poison is in the highest degree injudicious and harmful. In some of our States, laws are enacted against thistles, and you may travel from side to side of such States without once beholding this emblem of agricultural shiftlessness. This success has been attained by attacking the weed in the early stages of its growth, and by preventing any specimen from reaching fructification and diffusing its myriads of seeds. So with with the "bovine lung fever." Incomparably less appreciable and less tangible than the thistle down, the seeds of this disease are being constantly exhaled from the lungs of the sick animal, and the infected air is wafted onward, loaded with a freight of death to every susceptible animal. We may quarantine the sick, but we cannot quarantine the air. We may purify the air, it is true, by an incessant disengagement of disinfectant vapours. But the cost would exceed the value of the sick animal, even if it recovered. We may shut out men and beasts from the infected premises, though even this would be found to be practically impossible when attempted on a large scale, but we cannot absolutely prevent wild animals like pigeons, rats, and mice from eluding our vigilance. We can disinfect the drains and manure heaps, but we can never be sure that every particle of poison has been decomposed, and that if removed or washed away, such products will not infect other animals. When the sick are preserved for any purpose, the poison is being constantly given off in all the products and accumulated in the air in the buildings and in the excretions to such an extent that no watchfulness can at all times guard against its escape. To quarantine the sick is therefore to maintain prolific manufactories of the poison which we wish to destroy, and to open the way for its wide diffusion.

Expense of Quarantine.

But another unanswerable objection to quarantine is its expense. The perfect isolation of sick animals from visitors, human and brute, can only be secured by a patrol to be kept up day and night. Any such course would soon incur an expense greater than the value of the animals sought to be preserved. At the Blissville stable a quarantine of seventeen days cost, in sheriffs and deputies alone, a sum of over $900. At another stable, containing only twelve cows, the sheriff's expenses for fourteen days amounted to $300. If we add to these the expenses of professional examination of the animals, of the treatment of the sick, which is a necessary corollary of the quarantine, of the constant disinfection of the air and excretions, and the repeated disinfection of the buildings, it will at once appear that this method is the most ruinously expensive, as it is the most dangerous and inefficient that can possibly be adopted.

Ineffectual Treatment.

What has been stated of quarantine is a sufficient answer to the demand for the treatment of the sick. Ruinous in its expense, and still more ruinous in its reproduction and propagation of the poison, it should be prohibited under the heaviest penalties in all countries where the extermination of the disease has been determined on. Germany, Holland, Belgium, France, and England have been treating the victims of this plague for nearly half a century, but the result has only been the increase of disease and death. Our own infected States have been treating it for a third of a century, and to-day it exists over a wider area than ever before. Contrast this with the results in Massachusetts and Connecticut, where the disease has been repeatedly crushed out at small expense, and there can be no doubt as to which is the wisest course. As all the plagues are alike in the propagation of the poison in the bodies of the sick, I may be allowed to adduce the experience of two adjacent counties in Scotland when invaded by the rinderpest. Aberdeen raised a fund of £2,000, and, though she suffered several successive invasions, she speedily crushed out the poison wherever it appeared by slaughtering the sick beasts and disinfecting the premises. The result was that little more than half the fund was wanted to reimburse the owners for their losses, and the splendid herds of the country were preserved. Forfar, on the other hand, set herself to cure the plague, with the result of a universal infection, the loss of many thousands of cattle, and the ruin of hundreds of farmers. Finally the malady was crushed out in the entire island by the method adopted by Aberdeen and other well-advised counties at the outset.

Inoculation incompatible with Extermination.

Inoculation is condemned by all those considerations that would forbid quarantine and treatment. Whatever good there is in inoculation depends on the reproduction of the poison in the system of the inoculated animal, so as to render it unsusceptible to a second attack. The inoculated animal is therefore infected, and, like a beast infected in the ordinary way, is a prolific source of the poison and a means of its diffusion. Inoculation has been largely practised in Europe, but no country which has resorted to it extensively has ever succeeded in rooting out the pestilence. Cattle have been inoculated by the tens of thousands in Belgium and Holland, and of all Europe these are the countries most extensively infected. France, Prussia, Italy, Austria, and England have each practised it on a large scale, and each remains a home of the plague. Australia has followed the practice, and is now and must continue an infected country. Our own infected States have inoculated, and the disease has survived and spread it spite of it, and even by its aid. Whatever country has definitely exterminated the plague (Norway, Sweden, Denmark, Holstein, Mecklenberg, Switzerland, Massachusetts and Connecticut) that country has prohibited inoculation and all other methods that prevail on the principle of preserving the sick, and has relied on the slaughter of the infected and the thorough disinfection of their surroundings. So will it be with us. If any State adopts or allows any of these temporizing measures, that State will only repeat the experience of the past, alike in the Old World and New, will perpetuate the disease in the country, will entail great losses on its citizens, will keep up the need for constant watchfulness and great expense by the adjoining States for their own protection, and will indefinitely postpone the resumption of the foreign live-stock trade, which a few months ago promised to be one the most valuable branches of our international commerce. In the present crisis nothing can excuse delay or inefficient legislation or work. To be successful, all the infected States must act harmoniously, and if any one comes short of a statute and administration at least as thorough as that of New York, on that State will rest the odium of proctracting what cannot but be considered otherwise than as a great national calamity.

Brooklyn, March 10, 1879. JAMES LAW.

Enclosure 3 in No. 9.

(No. 11, Consular.)

LETTER from the ACTING BRITISH CONSUL at PHILADELPHIA to the MARQUIS OF SALISBURY.

MY LORD, British Consulate, Philadelphia, April 12, 1879.

I have the honour to report to your Lordship that there have been several cases of pleuro-pneumonia among cattle in the city and county of Philadelphia during the past few weeks, while in the interior of the State of Pennsylvania the disease has broken out among dairy cattle although not to an alarming extent. This disease is pronounced by competent veterinary surgeons to belong to the contagious type of a malignant character. The State Government are about adopting stringent measures to stamp the disease out, which, it is believed, will be effectually done in a short time.

In the Western States of this Consular District, I have not been able to learn that contagious pleuro-pneumonia exists among any of the cattle herds. Should the disease in the Eastern States, however, not be effectually eradicated, it is but a question of time as to the contagion reaching the West, and there spreading amongst the vast herds whence the cattle for shipments to Europe are drawn.

I have, &c.

The Right Hon. the Marquis of Salisbury K.G., (Signed) GEORGE CRUMP.
&c. &c. &c.

No. 10.

LETTER from FOREIGN OFFICE to the CLERK OF THE COUNCIL.

SIR Foreign Office, April 24, 1879.

I AM directed by the Marquis of Salisbury to transmit to you the accompanying note from the United States Minister at this Court, relating to the restrictions at present existing on the cattle trade between the United States and this country, and I am to request that, in laying the same before the Lords of Her Majesty's Privy Council, you will move their Lordships to cause Lord Salisbury to be informed what answer should be returned to Mr. Welsh's Note, the return of which with your reply is requested.

I am, &c.

The Clerk of the Council, (Signed) W. LISTER.
  Veterinary Department.

Enclosure in No. 10.

LETTER from the UNITED STATES MINISTER, LONDON, to the MARQUIS OF SALISBURY.

MY LORD, Legation of the United States, London, April 18, 1879.

THE subject of cattle disease has very properly of late attracted much attention in the United States, and has received the most serious consideration. It has been determined that pleuro-pneumonia, in its contagious form, if it has existed at all, of which there is reasonable doubt, has been limited to certain localities, outside of the line of the cattle trade, and the dread of its consequences has caused in all parts of the Union the exercise of the utmost possible precaution against its spreading, and the use of every possible means for its extinction, so that there is no longer any reasonable ground for apprehension concerning it.

As this particular branch of trade, the live-cattle trade, between the two countries is not less important to Great Britain than it is to the United States, I will place before you a statement which will aid in its intelligent consideration.

The rigid conditions of the order of Her Majesty's Privy Council of the 10th February last must bring to an end the live-cattle trade between the United States and Great Britain. Such a result will of necessity in the first place compel the great cattle herders of the West to seek other markets, other outlets not yet discovered, for the products of this industry, which if found, as they doubtless will be, even though turning out to be less profitable, they may be slow to abandon for a resumption of British markets, presenting so much uncertainty and risk from the possibility of restrictive regulations, which may at any time be renewed without a moment's notice, and when cargoes of great value may be in transit on the ocean. Again, the main lines of railroad from the Missouri river to New York, Philadelphia, and Boston, are seriously affected by any unnecessary interruption in this important traffic, and the interest of the Transatlantic steamers, chiefly British bottoms, in which the cattle are transported directly to England is one that cannot well be lost sight of in any calm consideration of the subject. The pertinence of these observations is at once apparent from a glance at the rapid growth of the cattle export trade of the United States, and the magnitude which it has already attained. In 1871 the export of cattle on the hoof to all countries amounted in value to only $403,491, while for the year 1878 the same export to all countries reached in value to $3,896,818; and of this export in 1878, the proportion to Great Britain was in value $2,408,843, while in fresh beef or slaughtered cattle, the export of which from the United States may be said to have begun in 1874, the value of that article exported to Great Britain in that year was almost nominal, being only $12,661. The export of the same article in 1878 puts up a total to all countries of $5,009,856, the proportion to Great Britain being $4,966,152! With the almost limitless capacity for cattle-raising now available in the vast regions of otherwise unoccupied pasture land west of the Mississippi River, and north of the 37th degree of north latitude, the increase of the business in the immediate future cannot well be estimated, nor can its economic interests to the working classes of Great Britain have wholly escaped the attention of Her Majesty's Government.

It will not have escaped your Lordship's attention that subsequent to the arrival of the "Ontario" many steamers have arrived in England from the United States with cargoes of cattle on the hoof which were found, upon the most rigid examination by the officers of Her Majesty's Privy Council, to be entirely free from contagious pleuro-pneumonia, and even landed in a perfectly healthy condition, although transported through the United States and to the seaboard, and thence across the ocean during the severe winter months; nor will your Lordship have forgotten the doubt expressed by me in my letter to you of the 14th February whether the disease on the "Ontario" was in reality of a contagious character or exceeded in severity what the severity of the voyage ought naturally to have produced. The circumstance of exemption from disease in the cattle which arrived previously to, and also subsequently to, the arrival of the "Ontario," of itself goes far to show that the disease, now creating so much anxiety not unmixed with alarm in Great Britain (pleuro-pneumonia) so far as it may have been found to exist at all in the United States, is spiradic in its character, and is not found in any part of the country to have assumed the form of a cattle-plague or epidemic. Indeed, as in the case of the "Ontario," the rare and exceptional cases of that disease that have developed during the past winter amongst the cattle of the United States may be traced immediately to the exposure and the want of care and irregularity in supplying them food and water while in transit. The season has been unusually severe, and remarkable for heavy snowfalls all over the Northern, Middle, and Western States, and extending as far south as the States of Mississippi and Alabama; and the consequent delay of heavy freight trains on the great East and West lines of railroad over which cattle are shipped rendered this partial neglect in a great measure unavoidable. In like manner, the reports which found their way into the newspapers of Washington and also of New York during the autumn of 1878 in regard to the then alleged prevalence of a disease similar to the rinderpest amongst the cows in the district of Columbia and portions of the States of Maryland and Virginia, and which formed the subject of a note 16th January last, from Sir Edward Thorton to the Honourable Mr. Bates, were found upon careful inquiry by experts, at the instance and under the direction of the Secretary of the Treasury, to be almost if not wholly destitute of foundation. While occasionally there might be found at that time, as there may be found at any time, a diseased cow on a plantation in the region referred to, no such disease as the rinderpest, or any kindred malady, was found to exist among either milch cows or those being fed for the market. None is known to exist now, although careful scrutiny is still being exercised. The report itself, when traced to its original source, was discovered to have emanated from a superserviceable and interested individual, who sells milk in Washington, &c., and possesses some small dairy farms in Virginia, in the neighbourhood of Washington, who from motives that are too obvious desired to impress milk consumers with the belief that that all milch cows in the locality referred to, outside of his own domain, were infected with rinderpest, or some other mortal disease, which rendered the use of their milk deleterious to the public health. There is no doubt that a great deal of misapprehension is prevailing in the public mind of Great Britain, and that to some extent it is shared by the officers charged by Her Majesty's Privy Council with the delicate but arduous duties of the inspection of American cattle on their arrival in British ports. In the hope of at least in part removing the misapprehension, I may add a few facts, without even a seeming reflection on any one here, for while they are perfectly familiar to the Government and people of the United States, they cannot reasonably be expected to be equally well known in England.

In the first place it may be stated with the nearest possible approach to correctness that amongst the live cattle shipped from the United States to Great Britain few or none are raised for or prepared for market east of the Mississippi River. The cattle raised and fed in the States of the Ohio Valley and in the North-western States bordering on the great lakes, find a ready home market in the cities and towns in the immediate neighbourhood of their feeding, and in the New England States, where cattle feeding cannot be properly pursued, and are found it is believed insufficient for the home demand. The cities of Cincinnati, St. Louis, Chicago, Milwaukee, Detrois, Cleveland, and others of only less importance, furnish more than a sufficient market for all the cattle fed in the States referred to, and it is a well-known fact that the State of New York, vast and fertile as it is in area, does not find it profitable to raise beef in sufficient quantities for the supply of the people of that State. So, with equal accuracy it may be alleged that the cattle destined for foreign markets, including the market of Great Britain, which is sure to be not only the principal of these, but greater in its demand than all other countries together, are fed and prepared for exportation in the States and territories of the republic, north of the 36th degree of north latitude and west of the Mississippi River, embracing the States of Kanzas, Nebraska, and Colorado, and the territories of Wyoming, Montana, and Southern Dakota, the prairies and river valleys of which are noted as furnishing the richest and most healthy pasture lands of the world. It is under these exceptionally favorable circumstances that the American cattle trade has so suddenly reached its present and most marvellous proportions, and yet the enterprise may be said to be but in the infancy of its development, for the vast plains of Northern Dakota (through which the Northern Pacific railroad is projected and partly constructed) reaching west to the Red River Valley, as yet untouched, are known to offer even greater inducements to the herdsmen than the lands already occupied. It would seem needless to argue that cattle fed under such conditions, with unbounded range of pasture, pure air, and running water from the streams fed by the mountain snows, must as a rule be healthy and much less liable to contagious disease than those prepared for market in close pastures or stall fed. Moreover, the facilities for introducing and enforcing sanitary measures are greatly increased. If a disease makes its appearance in a herd, the herd can be at once assorted and separated by such a distance as will tend to prevent its spread, the infected cattle can be at once slaughtered, as they would be, for no one knows better than the herdsmen that such present sacrifice is most likely to secure him ultimately against more serious pecuniary loss.

A few words also are necessary to bring fully to your attention the precautionary measures which have already been adopted in the different sections of the Union, under the authority of the Federal and the different State Governments, and in some instances under city municipal regulations. Leavenworth, Kansas, and Omaha, Nebraska, are the two great entrepôts at which the cattle for exportation are first received by the great railroad transportation lines; those shipped at Leavenworth coming from Kansas and Colorado, and at Omaha from Nebraska, Wyoming, Montana, and Southern Dukota.

At each of these two shipping points, Leavenworth and Omaha, there has been established an inspection provided for under the laws of Kansas and Nebraska, and no cattle infected with pleuro-pneumonia or other disease are permitted to be forwarded thence to Chicago, while at the latter city, under the regulations of its board of health and the municipal authorities, these cattle again undergo an inspection before being shipped for the port of embarkation at the seaboard. With the arrangements made for inspection at New York, Philidelphia, and other Atlantic ports by the Secretary of the Treasury you are already familiar. With such precautionary measures, enforced with a reasonable degree of faithfulness and energy, as I have no doubt they are (for it is not the interest of the exporter to send to market even a doubtful article), it is quite improbable that any cattle can leave the ports of the United States that are not free from contagious or other disease. The question is one of great interest to the citizens and Government of the United States, and it is believed to be one of equal interest to Her Majesty's subjects in Great Britain.

In closing this statement I will further say to you, my Lord, that I have made it so full because of the earnest desire of the President of the United States that Her Majesty's Government may see the importance and propriety of revoking the order of the 10th February last, subjecting live cattle from the United States to immediate slaughter at the port of arrival, thus removing the present serious interruption to this great element of commerce between the United States and Great Britain, and in which the people of both countries feel so deep an interest.

With sentiments of the highest consideration,

I remain, &c.
(Signed) JOHN WELSH.

The Most Honourable
   The Marquis of Salisbury,
     &c. &c. &c.

No. 11.

LETTER from the CLERK OF THE COUNCIL to the UNDER SECRETARY OF STATE, FOREIGN OFFICE.

Veterinary Department, Privy Council Office,
Sir,   44, Parliament Street, Westminster, S.W., April 30, 1879.

I HAVE submitted to the Lords of Council your letter of the 24th instant, enclosing note from United States Minister at this Court, relating to the restrictions at present existing on the cattle trade between the United States and this country.

In reply I am directed to state for the information of Lord Salisbury that the Lords of the Council are of opinion that a reply to the note should be to the following effect:

Since the date of the landing of the cattle from the "Ontario," among which contagious pleuro-pneumonia was detected by the inspectors of the Privy Council, the disease has been discovered to exist in several other cargoes of cattle from the United States which have been landed at the ports of London and Liverpool.

The existence of contagious pleuro-pneumonia among cattle in the United States is clearly established by the documentary evidence published in a Parliamentary paper on March 21st 1879.

Under the above circumstances and having regard to the fact to which I referred in my letter of 27th February last that no system of inspection, however perfect, affords complete security against the introduction of pleuro-pneumonia, their lordships regret that they are unable to modify the Order of Council of February 10th relating to the landing of cattle from the United States.

I am, &c.
(Signed) C. L. PEEL.

The Under-Secretary of State,
   Foreign Office.

No. 12.

LETTER from the BRITISH CONSUL-GENERAL at NEW YORK, to the MARQUIS OF SALISBURY.

No. 29.

My Lord,   British Consulate General, New York, May 1st, 1879.

I HAVE the honour to report to your Lordship that although pleuro-pneumonia among cattle is still prevalent in this State, the prompt and stringent measures adopted by the State authorities have effected a marked improvement compared with the state of things a few weeks since, and more especially on Long Island, where, according to Professor Law, the disease has been almost extirpated.

The Legislature of the State of New Jersey has passed an Act similar to that of the State of New York; and in that State, as well as in Connecticut, every effort is being made to stamp out the disease.

I have, &c.
(Signed)   E. M. ARCHIBALD.

Her Majesty's Principal Secretary of State
    for Foreign Affairs, London.

No. 13.

LETTER from the CLERK OF THE COUNCIL to the UNDER SECRETARY OF STATE, FOREIGN OFFICE.

Veterinary Department, Privy Council Office,
Sir,   44, Parliament Street, Westminster, S.W., May 7, 1874.

I AM directed by the President of Council to state that typhoid fever of swine has been detected within the last few days in cargoes of swine from the United States of America landed at the ports of Hull and Liverpool, and to request that you will have the goodness to move Lord Salisbury to direct that this may be communicated to the American Minister, with an intimation that their Lordships will have to consider whether it may not be necessary to deal with swine from the United States, in the same manner as with cattle from that country under order of February 10, 1879.

I am, &c.
(Signed)   C. L. PEEL.

The Under Secretary of State,
   &c.   &c.   &c.
    Foreign Office.

Enclosure in No. 13.

(467.)

At the Council Chamber, Whitehall, the 10th day of February, 1879.

By the Lords of Her Majesty's Most Honourable Privy Council.

PRESENT:

LORD PRESIDENT; LORD JOHN MANNERS.

THE Lords and others of Her Majesty's most Honourable Privy Council, by virtue and in exercise of the powers in them vested under the Contagious Diseases (Animals) Act, 1878, (in this Order referred to as the Act of 1878,) and of every other power enabling them in this behalf, do order, and it is hereby ordered as follows:

1. This order shall take effect from and immediately after the third day of March, one thousand eight hundred and seventy-nine; and words in this order have the same meaning as in the Act of 1878.

2. This order extends to Great Britain only.

3. Article 13 of the Foreign Animals Order is hereby revoked as far as it relates to cattle brought from the United States of America, and declares that the same may be landed without being subject under the Act of 1878 or under that Order to slaughter or to quarantine.

C. L. PEEL.

No. 14.

LETTER from the BRITISH CONSUL-GENERAL at NEW YORK to the MARQUIS OF SALISBURY.

No. 33.

My Lord,   British Consulate General, New York, June 2, 1879.

I HAVE the honour to report to your Lordship in regard to the sanitary condition of horned cattle in this Consular District, that the same state of affairs mentioned in my last report still continues. The authorities of the different States are still energetically endeavouring, either by isolating or slaughtering the diseased animals, to stamp out the plague.

The attention of the New York State Commissioner is now more especially directed to some cases of the disease which have appeared among cattle located at East Hampton, Long Island, and its vicinity. A number of cattle there affected with pleuro-pneumonia have been ordered to be slaughtered, and the remainder have been quarantined.

I have, &c.
(Signed) E. M. ARCHIBALD.

Her Majesty's Principal Secretary of State
for Foreign Affairs.

No. 15.

LETTER from the ACTING BRITISH CONSUL at PHILADELPHIA to the MARQUIS OF SALISBURY.

(No. 13, Consular.)

My Lord, British Consulate, Philadelphia, June 3, 1879.

I HAVE the honour to report to your Lordship that casual cases of pleuro-pneumonia among cattle in the State of Pennsylvania have continued to occur during the months of April and May, several cases having been reported since my Despatch of April 12th, No. 11.

The Legislature of Pennsylvania has just passed an Act giving the Governor of the State authority to suppress the disease in any of the counties of the State. For this purpose he has power to issue his proclamation announcing the existence of pleuro-pneumonia or other contagious or infectious disease in any particular county or counties, and to order all persons to seclude afflicted animals in their possession as well as to take such precautions against the spreading of the contagion as the nature of the circumstances may render necessary or expedient, to order premises or farms where the disease exists, or has existed, to be put in quarantine and to prescribe such regulations as may be necessary to prevent its spread; to employ medical and veterinary practitioners and such other assistance as he may deem necessary; to prescribe regulations for the destruction of afflicted animals and for the proper disposition of their hides and carcases and of all objects which might convey infection or contagion. No animal is to be destroyed unless previously examined by a competent medical or veterinary practitioner in the employment of the Governor, who also has power to prescribe regulations for the disinfection of all premises, buildings, and railway cars, and of all objects from which infection may arise or be conveyed. The Act provides for the payment of all expenses incurred in carrying out its provisions. Animals coming into Pennsylvania from a neighbouring State that have been examined and passed by the legal examiner of such State, or that have been quarantined and discharged are not subject to the provisions of the Act.

Active steps are about to be taken under this law, and it is confidently hoped that the disease known as pleuro-pneumonia will be effectually eradicated from the State of Pennsylvania in a short time.

I have received no returns showing the existence of any contagious disease among cattle in the other six States of this consular district.

I have, &c.
The Right Hon. the Marquis of Salisbury, K.G., (Signed) GEORGE CRUMP.
&c. &c. &c.

No. 16.

LETTER from the ACTING BRITISH CONSUL at PHILADELPHIA to the MARQUIS OF SALISBURY.

(No. 16, Consular.)

My Lord, British Consulate, Philadelphia, July 8, 1879.

I HAVE the honour to report to your Lordship that during the month of June there were a few cases of pleuro-pneumonia among cattle in the State of Pennsylvania.

In the Western States of this consular district, however, no cases appear to have occurred so far as it has been in my power to ascertain.

The cattle shipped from this port to the United Kingdom are exclusively from the Western States. They remain in the city but a few hours and have been found on arrival to be free from disease.

I have, &c.

The Right Honourable
   The Marquis of Salisbury, K.G.,
    &c. &c. &c.

(Signed) GEORGE CRUMP.

No. 17.

LETTER from the ACTING BRITISH CONSUL-GENERAL at NEW YORK to the MARQUIS OF SALISBURY.

No. 41.

My Lord, British Consulate General, New York, August 12, 1879.

I have the honour to report to your Lordship that during the past month fresh cases of pleuro-pneumonia among cattle have been reported in the State of New Jersey in this consular district, more particularly in the countries of Bergen, Essex, and Hudson, which countries have been quarantined by the State Inspector in order to prevent the spreading of the disease. The Inspector in his report to me on the subject, states that pleuro-pneumonia exists also in other parts of the State, but that the largest number of cases occur in the above-mentioned countries. He further observes that so soon as sickness is reported among the herds a veterinary surgeon is despatched to the spot to inspect to animals and separate the sick from the well, and quarantine the place, the herds being re-inspected from time to time.

In regard to the state of New York, I have nothing to add to the reports heretofore made by Mr. Consul-General Archibald.

I have, &c.

Her Majesty's Principal
Secretary of State for Foreign Affairs.

(Signed) J. PIERREPONT EDWARDS,
Acting Consul-General.

No. 18.

LETTER from the ACTING BRITISH CONSUL at PHILADELPHIA to the MARQUIS OF SALISBURY.

(No. 18, Consular.)

My Lord, British Consulate, Philadelphia, August 12, 1879.

I have the honour to report to your Lordship that the disease pleuro-pneumonia among cattle has been decreased in Pickering Valley, near Phœnixville, county of Chester, Pennsylvania, within the past month, and that the Governor of the State has ordered four head to be killed and others, together with three farms, placed under quarantine.

On the farm of Mr. Richard L. Jones, at Darby, near Philadelphia, nine head have died within a few weeks, making twenty head in all lost by Mr. Jones this year. Some of the above-mentioned nine head were killed by order of the Governor, and paid for by the Commonwealth.

I beg to enclose your Lordship three printed copies of a circular issued by the Secretary of the Board of Agriculture of Pennsylvania, by command of the Governor. The circular is addressed to the owners of cattle, their agents, servants and employés, common carriers by land or by water, veterinary surgeons, and all others interested; it requests these persons to promptly report all cases, or supposed cases, of disease among neat cattle of a contagious or infectious nature, and states that the laws of 1866 and 1879 are to be fully enforced. The powers granted the Executive under these laws are clearly stated in a letter from Governor Hoyt to the Secretary of the Board of Agriculture, dated May 1st, 1879, copies of which I beg herewith to enclose.

The prompt killing of the diseased animals seems to check the progress of the disease in any herd in which it has broken out, and in such instances it is not long before the herd can be safely released from quarantine. In no case has the infection spread from the herd after it was placed under quarantine by the authorities, and it is believed that a strict quarantine and the prompt destruction of all diseased animals before the disease becomes contagious, will effectually prevent any further spread of the malady.

I have, &c.

The Right Honourable
The Marquis of Salisbury, K.G.
&c. &c. &c.

(Signed) GEORGE CRUMP.

Enclosure 1 in No. 18.

CIRCULAR issued by the PENNSYLVANIA BOARD OF AGRICULTURE.

Important to Dealers in Cattle.—It having been ascertained that an infectious and contagious disease of neat cattle, known as pleuro-pneumonia, exists in certain counties of this State, Mr. Thomas J. Edge, secretary of the Pennsylvania Board of Agriculture, on May 1st., was appointed by Governor Hoyt as his assistant for the purpose of carrying out the provisions of the Acts of 1866 and 1879, for the prevention of the spread of this disease.

The following circular has been issued by Mr. Edge:

OFFICE OF PENNA. BOARD OF AGRICULTURE, HARRISBURG, August 8, 1879.—To all owners of cattle, their agents, servants, or employés; to all common carriers by land or water; to all veterinary surgeons, and to all others whom it may concern:—His Excellency Governor Hoyt, having decided to co-operate with the Executive Officers of the States of Massachusetts, Connecticut, New York, and New Jersey, in a united effort to eradicate the disease known as pleuro-pneumonia from the herds of this State, it becomes my duty, under the foregoing commission, to request that you will promptly report to me all the cases of disease among neat cattle by you suspected to be contagious or infectious. Without your co-operation and assistance, this attempt can only result in partial success; with it, the result can scarcely be doubtful, and the work thus far accomplished gives us assurance of good results.

His Excellency is anxious that all owners of cattle and others interested should be fully impressed with the belief that this Commission, as well as the laws of 1866 and 1879 for the prevention of the spread of the disease, are in their interest, as well as that of the State. It is also the wish of his Excellency that, while the provisions of these laws are fully enforced and made most effective, and their purposes promptly and fully accomplished, it shall, at the same time, be so managed as to cause the least possible inconvenience and injury to all concerned, and with a minimum of expenditure to the State.

I would particularly call your attention to the language used by his Excellency in relation to the line of action to be pursued when interested parties have concealed the existence of the disease in their herds. This provision is very important, not only to the stock owner, but also to the State, for while the concealment of the existence of the disease will result in pecuniary loss to the owner of the stock, it, at the same time, greatly increases the danger of infection, and the subsequent expense of the State. With your active co-operation in this respect we may hope for the prompt suppression of a disease which, while it has already caused a great loss to our stock owners, will, should it become established in our Western States, inflict an incalculable and lasting injury to the stock-raising interests of the whole nation. So far as known, all infected herds in this State have been quarantined and all diseased animals promptly isolated or killed. In the future, as in the past, it will be our duty to cause as little injury and inconvenience to the owners of stock as is consistent with our duties to the State, and to carry out, to the full letter, the directions of his Excellency relative to the valuation of all stock condemned and killed.

All reports of supposed infection should be made direct to the office, and all interested are requested to accompany the report with a correct and full account of the location of the herd and symptoms, in order that all unnecessary expense to the State may be avoided. No special line of action has yet been marked out for application to cattle in motion from one portion of the State to another, or to those in transit to other States, but it will be the duty of those in charge to cause the least possible inconvenience consistent with the best interests of the State.

Hoping that the subject may receive that attention from you which its national importance warrants.

I am, &c.

Secretary, Pennsylvania Board of Agriculture.

(Signed) THOMAS J. EDGE.

Enclosure 2 in No. 18.

COMMONWEALTH OF PENNSYLVANIA, EXECUTIVE CHAMBER HARRISBURG, May 1, 1879.

To Thomas J. Edge, Secretary Pennsylvania Board of Agriculture—

SIR, it having been ascertained that an infectious and contagious disease of neat cattle known as pleuro-pneumonia has been brought into and exists in certain counties of this State, I hereby appoint you as my assistant to carry out the provisions of the Acts of 1866 and 1879 for the prevention of the spread of this disease. As such assistant you are hereby authorised:

To prohibit the movement of cattle within the infected districts, except on license from yourself after skilled veterinary examination under your direction.

To order all owners of cattle, their agents, employés or servants, and all veterinary surgeons to report forthwith to you all cases of disease by them suspected to be contagious, and when such notification is received you are directed to have the case examined and to cause such animals as are found to be infected with said disease to be quarantined, as also all cattle which have been exposed to the infection or contagion of said disease, or are located in an infected district, but you may in your discretion permit such animals to be slaughtered on the premises and the carcasses to be disposed of as meat, if, upon examination, they shall be found fit for such use.

You may prohibit and prevent all persons not employed in the care of cattle therein kept from entering any infected premises. You may likewise prevent all persons so employed in the care of animals from going into stables, yards, or premises where cattle are kept other than those in which they are employed. You may cause all clothing of persons engaged in the care, slaughtering, or rendering of diseased or exposed animals, or in any employment which brings them in contact with such diseased animals, to be disinfected before they leave the premises where such animals are kept. You may prevent the manure, forage, and litter upon infected premises from being removed therefrom, and you may cause such disposition to be made thereof as will, in your judgment, best prevent the spread of the disease. You may cause the buildings, yards, and premises in which the disease exists or has existed to be thoroughly disinfected.

Your are further directed, whenever the slaughter of diseased animals is found necessary, to certify the value of the animal or animals so slaughtered, at the time of slaughter, taking into account their condition and circumstances, and to deliver to their owner or owners, when requested, a duplicate of such certificate. Whenever any owner of such cattle, or his agent or servant, has wilfully or knowingly withheld or allowed to be withheld notice of the existence of said disease upon his premises or among his cattle, you will not make such certificate.

You are also directed to take such measures as you may deem necessary to disinfect all cars, vehicles, or movable articles by which contagion is likely to be transmitted. You will also take such measures as shall insure the registry of cattle introduced into any premises on which said disease has existed, and to keep such cattle under supervision for a period of three months after the removal of the diseased animal and the subsequent disinfection of said premises.

You are further authorised and empowered to incur such expenses in carrying out the provisions of the foregoing orders as may in your judgment appear necessary, and to see to it that all bills for such expenses be transmitted to this department only through yourself, after you have examined and approved the same in writing.

(Signed)   HENRY M. HOYT,
Governor.

Attest:

J. R. MCAFEE, Deputy Secretary of the Commonwealth.

No. 19.

LETTER from the BRITISH CONSUL-GENERAL at NEW YORK to the MARQUIS OF SALISBURY.

No. 43.

British Consulate General, New York,
September 1st, 1879.

MY LORD,

I HAVE the honour to report to your Lordship that there has been no material change in the sanitary condition of cattle in this consular district since the transmission of Mr. Acting Consul-General Edwards' Despatch, No. 41, of the 12th ultimo.

I have, &c.

Her Majesty's Principal Secretary of State   (Signed)   E. M. ARCHIBALD.
for Foreign Affairs, London.

No. 20.

LETTER from the BRITISH CONSUL-GENERAL, at NEW YORK, to the MARQUIS OF SALISBURY.

(No. 46, Consular.)
My Lord,
British Consulate General, New York,
October 1st, 1879.

I HAVE the honour to report to your Lordship, in regard to the sanitary condition of cattle in this consular district, that, while certain localities still remain affected with pleuro-pneumonia, there is reason to believe that owing to the vigorous and persistent measures of the authorities the number of cattle suffering from the disease is declining in this city and its environs; the disease has certainly decreased.

At a meeting on the 16th instant of the American Veterinary Association in this city, it was stated by one of the cattle inspectors that, up to the 1st instant the number of infected stables discovered in this city was 67, out of a total number of 1,100 stables; and the number of infected cattle, 470. The Commissioner for New Jersey, in giving the results of his experience in that State, reported he had examined 15,000 animals since last spring, quarantined 112 herds containing 874 animals, and registered 325 cases of actual pleuro-pneumonia.

Dr. Taylor, of the Bureau of Contagious Diseases, describing the manner in which the disease spreads from the city stables, makes the following observations:—

"Each stable gets fresh cows from the stock-yards, buying on credit, with the privilege of returning a cow if she is not satisfactory. Sometimes a cow is kept in a stable two or three days, exposed to the disease there, and then returned to the stock-yard, to be sent to New Jersey or some other State where the disease appears in her, and she infects a whole herd. As the proprietor of the stock-yard has forgotten his transaction with the city stable keeper, the disease is not traced to its source, but is set down as spontaneously generated. By oversights like this the disease is carried to all parts of the surrounding country from the city stables, when raging here, and the epidemic breaks out at many points almost simultaneously, giving rise to the notion that it originates in meteorological disturbances."

At the meeting above mentioned a proposition was made to secure the foundation of a National Bureau of Veterinary Inspection, and a committee was appointed to take action in the matter.

The New York Central Railway Company have, at the suggestion of the State Inspector, built stables on their land, in this city, in order to keep city cattle from coming in contact with cattle coming from the West. In these stables the cattle forwarded over the railroad are quarantined and can easily be inspected before they are sold.

I have, &c.
Her Majesty's Principal Secretary of State
for Foreign Affairs.
(Signed) E. M. ARCHIBALD.

No. 21.

LETTER from FOREIGN OFFICE to the CLERK OF THE COUNCIL.

Sir,
Foreign Office, October 4, 1879.

I AM directed by the Marquis of Salisbury to transmit to you for any remarks which the Lords of Her Majesty's Privy Council may have to offer thereupon, a Despatch from the Acting British Consul at Philadelphia, containing a report on contagious diseases among cattle in the month of August last.

The enclosure in Mr. Crump's Despatch, the return of which is requested, has been sent to the Board of Trade as bearing upon a question of quarantine upon human beings and merchandise.

I am, &c.
The Clerk to the Council,
Veterinary Department.
(Signed) JULIAN PAUNCEFOTE.

Enclosure in No. 21.

LETTER from the ACTING BRITISH CONSUL at PHILADELPHIA to the MARQUIS OF SALISBURY.

(No. 19, Consular.)

My Lord, British Consulate, Philadelphia, September 8, 1879.

I HAVE the honour to report to your Lordship that during the month of August but few cases of pleuro-pneumonia have occurred in the State of Pennsylvania, and that the State Authorities continue to exercise diligence in the endeavour to suppress the disease. Some opposition, however, is experienced on the part of a limited number of veterinary practitioners, stock raisers, and shippers, who contend, first that pleuro-pneumonia is not prevalent in the State, and, secondly, that if there are any cases of the disease, the disease itself is not contagious.

No reports come from the Western States of this consular district that the disease prevails either in Ohio, Illinois, Indiana, Michigan, Iowa, or Wisconsin, although it is not improbable that among the immense herds of cattle mustered at the Chicago stock-yards some of the cattle are attacked, but as they are forwarded to the Eastern markets for immediate consumption or foreign shipment, care being taken that none but healthy cattle are placed on ship-board, but little is thought of it, and there is no desire on the part of dealers too have the inspections too sweeping.

An interesting legal decision has been rendered by the Supreme Court of the State of Illinois as to the right of a State to protect itself from contagious diseases. It declares that all State laws interfering with the free interchange of commerce between the different States are contrary to the constitution of the United States, and shows that any legislation for the purpose of suppressing contagious diseases among cattle, to be effective must emanate from the Congress of the United States. Under this decision it would appear to be very difficult, if not impossible, for any State to enact laws touching upon the transportation of diseased cattle, sheep, swine, or other farm animals without infringing upon the rights or attempting to control the property of citizens of other States. So far as such laws affect only the people and property of their own State they may be effective, but when they affect the commerce between different States, they come in contact with the constitution of the United States, and are, therefore, invalid. I beg to enclose your lordship the only printed copy of this decision I have been able to obtain.

In connection with this report I beg to add a word with regard to the increasing trade in cattle with England, the receipts of cattle at the stock-yards in Chicago and the prices prevailing compared with those of last year. The shipments to Europe are largely on the increase. During the eleven months ending May 31st, 1879, there were shipped from the United States 118,423 head, selling for 1,470,000*l.* compared with 64,824 head during the same period in 1878, which sold for only 580,000*l.*, showing an increase of 90 per cent. and a larger price per head. The receipts of cattle, hogs, and sheep at the Chicago stock-yards since January 1st, 1879, compared with the same in 1878 are as follows:—

1879.

—	Cattle.	Hogs.	Sheep.
January	86,547	996,389	30,669
February	94,636	463,799	40,280
March	80,290	364,512	38,041
April	96,247	326,464	33,799
May	103,393	537,785	18,556
June	92,932	537,611	22,035
July	122,998	277,724	17,646
August (27th)	86,666	224,570	17,575
	763,711	3,728,854	218,601

1878.

—	Cattle.	Hogs.	Sheep.
January	78,835	879,317	36,530
February	82,536	579,161	29,192
March	79,958	342,462	30,902
April	92,479	371,969	23,636
May	97,148	438,608	20,321
June	81,376	547,727	17,109
July	96,369	325,239	18,019
August	84,188	303,572	21,875
	692,889	3,788,055	197,584

The prices for cattle ranged as follows:—

—	1879.	1878.
Extra graded steers	$5.00 to $5.25	$5.00 to $5.50
Choice steers	4.75 „ 4.95	4.60 „ 4.85
Good steers	4.50 „ 4.70	4.30 „ 4.50
Fair steers	4.20 „ 4.40	3.75 „ 4.15
Common steers	3.50 „ 4.00	3.00 „ 3.50
Corn-fed Texans	2.80 „ 3.60	3.20 „ 3.70
Thorough Texans	2.60 „ 3.10	2.75 „ 3.15
Native butcher cows	2.25 „ 3.75	2.50 „ 3.75
Veal calves	3.00 „ 4.50	3.50 „ 5.00
Milch cows, per head	15.00 „ 35.00	20.00 „ 40.00

The cost of raising cattle in the distant West is very small. In the territory of Montana it is only 60 cents per head. A three year old beef steer, including payment of taxes, which will sell on the ground for $30 per head, costs but $2 for feed and care. The losses in raising are estimated at 2 per cent., while the profits vary from 25 to 40 per cent. per annum. In 1873 there were but 86·944 head of cattle in the territory, and in 1878 there were 250,000 head, and 22,000 head having been exported.

I have, &c.
(Signed) GEORGE CRUMP.

The Right Honourable
   The Marquis of Salisbury, K.G.
    &c. &c. &c.

No. 22.

LETTER from the CLERK OF THE COUNCIL to the UNDER SECRETARY OF STATE, FOREIGN OFFICE.

Veterinary Department, Privy Council Office,
44, Parliament Street, Westminster, S.W.
October 6, 1879.

SIR,

I AM directed by the Lords of the Council to request that you will have the goodness to move Lord Salisbury that representation may be made to the Government of the United States of America, that it has been reported to their lordships that foot-and-mouth disease has been detected by the Inspectors of the Privy Council among the following cargoes of sheep landed in the port of Liverpool from Boston, namely, July 3rd, ship "Bulgarian"; September 19th, ship "Bulgarian"; September 24th, ship "Pembroke"; September 26th, ship "Palestine"; and October 4th, ship "Brazilian."

That, having regard to the provisions of the Contagious Diseases (Animals) Act, 1878, with respect to the importation of foreign animals, their Lordships regret that, should any further consignments of diseased sheep arrive from the United States, they will consider themselves compelled to issue an Order of Council treating sheep in the same manner as cattle and swine are now treated from that country, that is to say, that they shall be landed only at a foreign animals wharf for slaughter.

I am, &c.
(Signed) C. L. PEEL.

The Under Secretary of State,
  &c. &c. &c.
   Foreign Office.

No. 23.

LETTER from the CLERK OF THE COUNCIL to the UNDER SECRETARY OF STATE, FOREIGN OFFICE.

SIR, October 10, 1879.

I HAVE submitted to the Lords of Council your letter of the 4th instant, transmitting, for any remarks their Lordships may have to offer thereupon, a Despatch from the Acting British Consul at Philadelphia, containing a report on contagious diseases among cattle in the month of August last.

In reply, I am directed by their Lordships to observe, for the information of Lord Salisbury, that so long as the various States are unable to make laws against the introduction of disease, and so long as no general law exists on the subject, it is impossible for the Privy Council here to be satisfied, as required by The Contagious Diseases (Animals) Act, 1878, "that the laws thereof relating to the importation and "exportation of animals, and to the prevention of the introduction or spreading of " disease," . . . . . " are such as to afford reasonable security against the importation " therefrom of diseased animals." Had the state of things represented by the legal decision referred to by Mr. Crump been understood to exist in 1878, the United States of America would not have been included in Part IV. of The Foreign Animals Order, the Privy Council having then been informed that every State had power to make its own regulations.

I beg to return, herewith, Mr. Crump's Despatch, and am directed to request that the Lords of Council may be favoured with a copy of the legal decision therein referred to.

I am, &c.
(Signed) C. L. PEEL.

The Under Secretary of State,
&c. &c. &c.
Foreign Office.

No. 24.

LETTER from the BRITISH CONSUL-GENERAL at NEW YORK to the MARQUIS OF SALISBURY.

(No. 48.) British Consulate General, New York,
My Lord, October 9, 1879.

I HAVE the honour to transmit, herewith enclosed, for your Lordship's information, copies of a publication in the "New York Times" of this morning reporting a serious outbreak of pleuro-pneumonia among cows in Putnam county in this State.

The origin of this outbreak is doubtful, some persons attributing it to a herd of cattle which had been brought from Buffalo by way of Albany some months since. The farmers and others interested are alive to the importance of extirpating the disease, and are taking vigorous measures for that purpose under the superintendence of General Patric, the State Commissioner. It is to be feared, however, that the disease will yet make its appearance in other quarters through the spreading of the infection from Putnam County.

In the State of New Jersey also a fresh outbreak of pleuro-pneumonia is reported to have taken place, and, according to a recent statement in the newspaper, is "making " frightful ravages among cattle in the neighbourhood of Forked River in that State, " nearly every herd in the place being lessened by the malady."

In this city, through the energetic means adopted and measures enforced by General Patric, it is reported in the newspapers that the disease has almost disappeared.

I have, &c.
(Signed) E. M. ARCHIBALD.

Her Majesty's Principal Secretary of State for Foreign Affairs,
Foreign Office.

Enclosure in No. 24.

"New York Times," October 9, 1879.

THE PLAGUE AMONG CATTLE.—THREE TOWNS QUARANTINED IN PUTNAM COUNTY.

THIRTY-THREE DEATHS REPORTED.—MASS-MEETING AT BREWSTER TO CONSIDER THE SITUATION. —A GLOOMY OUTLOOK FOR THE FARMERS.—THE DISORDER UNDOUBTEDLY CONTAGIOUS.

Putnam County has been in a state of ferment for the last three weeks, in consequence of the advent of the dreaded cattle plague—contagious pleuro-pneumonia. The farmers at first declined to call the disease that had begun to decimate their herds by that terrible name, and insisted it must be something else; but three weeks ago Prof. Law, of Cornell University, Veterinary Assistant to State Commissioner Patrick, appeared on the scene, and, after a thorough investigation, both on the living and the dead subject, pronounced the disease to be contagious pleuro-pneumonia beyond peradventure. The doleful tidings aroused the whole community to action, for the wealth of Putnam County (politically a part of New York State, and geologically, topographically, and socially a part of Connecticut) lies in its grazing and dairy interest, and to strike at that is to menace the well-being of every town in the county. There are facts which give this outbreak a very special importance to the people of New York City, particularly as the milk of cows infected with the disease has been pronounced a perilous article of diet by competent scientific authorities. Although the New York market derives less milk from Putnam County than from several others, Orange among them, this tract is nevertheless, one of the large sources of supply; directly shipping large quantities in the fresh state, in the first instance, and being, in the second instance, the main source from which the condensing establishment belonging to the Borden Condensed Milk Company derives it stock. The factory is situated at Brewster's Station, a thriving place of about 1,500 inhabitants, and has proved a leading source of revenue to the farmers in the immediate vicinity.

The current news of the outbreak must first be briefly recounted, and then it will be in order to inquire into the causation, and describe the symptoms of the disease. After Prof. Law had made due examination about three weeks ago, and suggested certain necessary precautions, a week ago last Saturday Dr. Hopkins, one of the cattle inspectors in this city, under the control of Gen. Patrick, was sent to Putnam County, with a view to co-operate with the local authorities in stamping out the plague. Gen. Patrick issued an order last week quarantining three of the towns in which the infection had appeared, to wit: Philipstown, Kent, and Patterson. There are some cases in the town of Carmel, and a few, it is stated, in the town of Southeast, but in the latter so far the infected herds only have been quarantined. There were some difficulties in the way of instituting a wholesale slaughter of the infected animals, the principal one being that the appropriation placed at Gen. Patrick's disposal by the Legislature last winter has been exhausted by the campaign in this city and on Long Island, and there was no money in the treasury from which to indemnify owners according to law. The compensation is not an extravagant one—two-thirds of the appraised value of each animal at the time when the death is effected—but such as it is, the obligation is peremptory, and cannot be postponed or evaded without the consent of the parties. Gen. Patrick went to Albany and laid the circumstances before the Governor, asking him to transfer to the use of the commission an unexpended balance from another fund. The time was inauspicious, however. In the midst of an excited political canvass such a transfer might have been quoted by political enemies, and, as between votes and cattle, a well-regulated Gubernatorial candidate usually prefers the former.

This project having failed, Gen. Patrick, accompanied by Dr. Hopkins, returned to Putnam County on Tuesday, and that night a large mass-meeting of the citizens was held at Brewsters for the purpose of taking counsel upon the situation, which is, in reality, a rather desperate one. At this meeting Gen. Patrick addressed the people of the county, explaining the imminence of the peril as based upon American and European experience with the disease, and advising that the Board of Supervisors should meet at the earliest practicable moment, passing a resolution pledging the county to indemnify owners, and take such other measures as might be considered necessary to the extirpation of the pest. Mr. John D. Borden, who participated in the meeting, immediately arose and offered to advance $10,000 to the county officers to be expended under the advice of Gen. Patrick in uprooting the disease, and others came forward with smaller amounts. It was finally concluded to call the Board of Supervisors together, and they met at Carmel yesterday. Some of them expressed doubts as to the legal right of the board to pledge the credit of the county in such an emergency, but all agreed, in conversation with the representative of "The Times," that something must be done, some responsibility taken, and that there was no other practicable remedy except for the county to become security for the compensation and trust to the State to be reimbursed by special appropriation. The board met late in the afternoon, all the members being present. It is composed as follows: J. E. Taylor, of Paterson; Wellington Kent, of Kent; Daniel Baker, of South-east; Jackson Perry, of Putnam Valley; A. Hazen, of Carmel, and G. Spaulding, Phillipstown. Dr. Hopkins was present at the meeting, which was a very harmonious one, and resulted in a resolution to co-operate with the State Commissioner in any measures that he might deem most efficient to prevent the further progress of the pestilence. Yesterday morning Gen. Patrick, with Dr. Hopkins, Sheriff Doune, and others, proceeded to the farm of Freeman Sprague, in the town of Kent, about 10 miles from Brewster, and slaughtered six infected cows. Twenty-seven

Q 2337.

animals had either died of the disease or had been slaughtered previous to yesterday's raid upon Sprague's herd, and there are probably 50 in the various stages of the disease among the several infected herds, while from 150 to 200 have been exposed to the contagion. Indeed, the number of exposures cannot be stated with any degree of certainty. The plague was in Sprague's herd at the date of the county fair held at Carmel on September 17, and as Mr. Sprague was one of the exhibitors, and the period of incubation in contagious pleuro-pneumonia varies from 10 to 12 days to as many weeks, how widely its *semina* were scattered on that occasion the experience of the next few weeks can alone determine. The origin of the disease is a matter of doubt, but it appears to have radiated from three centres in as many different towns. It broke out about the middle of July in the herd of Mr. Sprague in Kent, but he pooh-poohed the suspicion that it was contagious, and commenced doctoring the victims on his own responsibility. Out of a herd of little more than 40 he had lost 15 by the disease. Its origin in this quarter is attributed to a strange herd of cattle which Mr. Sprague sheltered over night early in June. They came from across the river, but neither their destination nor from what point they came has been ascertained. Mr. Sprague is very reticent respecting the disease in his herd, and gives information piece-meal.

Mr. G. W. Patrick, living on the extreme eastern border of Paterson, had a case about the middle of January. The animal had been in his possession eight months without showing any signs of disease, and was originally bought from a farmer residing near by. He bought three cows a few days before this case occurred, but neither of the three has shown any symtoms of pleuro-pneumonia, and he is loath to believe that the seeds of the plague were brought into his barn by them. His cattle, so far as he knows, have had no contact with strange cattle. His herd numbers between 40 and 50. In the herd of Mr. Alvah Hyatt, in the town of Carmel, the disease was first observed some two weeks ago. His herd numbered about 40, among which a few deaths have already occurred. Mr. Hyatt and Mr. W. J. Robinson, also a large owner, have tried inoculation in about 20 cases, but sufficient time to determine its value as a prophylactic has not yet elapsed. The process was the same as that used in the great Australian epidemic two years ago, by Prof. Coleman, now of the New York College of Veterinary Surgeons—namely, by making an incision in the tail and introducing into the wound a pellet of cotton saturated with the sputa of the sick animal. Further experiments in this direction have been forbidden by Gen. Patrick, on the ground that ample experience has discredited the value of the measure, and that it may possibly tend to spread the disease.

The preceding review of the circumstances under which the disease made its appearance leave one altogether in the dark as to the mode of introduction. There are those, however, who state very positively that it originated from some Western cattle which had been herded at Buffalo and arrived in the neighbourhood some months since by way of Albany. The first animal that was taken sick in Mr. Patrick's herd came from the town of South-east, where there are now cases among the herds. Of the animal's previous history he is not informed, nor was there at the date of the transaction any disease, so far as he knows, on the farm from which it was taken. But, as one of the supervisors remarks, the contagion must have been introduced from some quarter without the limits of the county, for no cases of it have occurred there for years, and it is not self-developing. Perhaps the official inquiries of Gen. Patrick, Prof. Law, and Dr. Hopkins, may ultimately bring out this important point. It is very unlikely that the two earliest centres of infection—the one situated in Kent near the western border of the county, and the other in Patterson near its eastern—had a common origin; the two points being many miles apart, and the intervening tract having been comparatively free from the disease until very recently. Contagiousness is demonstrated beyond a doubt by the progess of the disorder in the herds where it has appeared, and by its travelling from herd to herd, in the slow but irresistible manner so familiar to veterinary experts. While Mr. Sprague has been very severely blamed for not having consulted a competent practitioner at the inception of the plague in his herd, it is true that the first sporadic cases of pleuro-pneumonia are usually too insignificant to attract the attention of a busy man. The animal often effects an apparent recovery spontaneously after more or less prolonged illness, and no suspicion as to the deadly nature of the disease is raised. In such cases the disorder re-appears under peculiar circumstances in the same animal. She aborts with calf early during the period of gestation, fever sets in, and pleuro-pneumonia developes itself. On post-mortem the lung is found to be a mass of putrid matter encysted. This termination occurs weeks or months after the first sickness, and contagion has already affected the whole herd.

The symptoms of the present disease are distinctly those of contagious pleuro-pneumonia. The victim commences dripping at the nose an abundant and rather glairy secretion, stands with her feet wide apart and braced and her head depressed. The breathing is rapid and laboured; the eyes are dull and filmy, and senses stupefied. The cause of death is either suffocation or asthenia. On autopsy, one lung, and generally the right one, but sometimes the left, and sometimes both, is found either to have undergone complete hepatization or to have become a mass of encysted gangrene. The colour is occasionally mottled, but usually a deep liver red. The gastric cavity in severe cases is filled with a glairy secretion resembling that seen in yellow fever, and putridity of all the tissues follows rapidly upon death. All these are points too significant to be mistaken. In its reception in the county the disease showed a marked tendency to attack tuberculous animals, and the autopsy demonstrated frequent tuberculous complications: but since it has approximated the epidemic or epizootic form it attacks sound and tuberculous with the same virulence. As, however, according to Prof. J. M. Heard, who speaks on the concurrent testimony of personal reflection and careful inquiry, the average of tuberculous cows is about 15 in every 100, the material for spread is abundant at the beginning. From Putnam County experience, the mode of propagation appears to be by means of the specta. The grass in pastures becoming covered more or less with the diseased secretion, the healthy animal receives it into the system with its food, and is thus solely impregnated with it. Tubercular disease passes from animal to animal in the same way, according to Fleming. Vigorous measures have been instituted, but one of the supervisors said yesterday that they were working more in the hope of saving the adjacent counties from attack than from any prospect of arresting the disease in their own county. It is believed that the best measures would be to quarantine the whole tract represented by the Putnam County, and thus save its neighbours from infection.

No. 25.

No. 21 Consular.

LETTER from the ACTING BRITISH CONSUL, at Philadelphia, to the MARQUIS OF SALISBURY.

British Consulate, Philadelphia,
October 11, 1879.

My Lord,

I HAVE the honour to report to your Lordship that for the month of September there have been but few cases of pleuro-pneumonia or other contagious disease among cattle discovered in this Consular district.

In the State of Pennsylvania the Special Commissioner appointed by the Governor has, during the past summer, placed 17 infected herds in strict quarantine under the care of competent veterinary surgeons, and 60 of the animals infected were killed at the expense of the Commonwealth. In most instances this prompt action has prevented further infection, and I believe in no case has the disease spread beyond the herd infected after the quarantine was enforced.

Pleuro-pneumonia has prevailed to some extent in the counties of Chester, Montgomery, Delaware, Lancaster, and Bucks, the infected herds, as soon as discovered, being placed in quarantine. In three herds 48 animals have been lost, and it is now believed that the surgeons have the disease under control. The prompt action in killing the diseased animals appears to have the desired effect.

I have no reports from the States of Illinois, Indiana, Ohio, Michigan, Wisconsin, or Iowa, and it is the general belief that there are no cases of contagious diseases in these States.

I have, &c.

The Right Honourable   (Signed)   GEORGE CRUMP.
    The Marquis of Salisbury, K.G.
        &c.   &c.   &c.

No. 26.

LETTER from the FOREIGN OFFICE to the CLERK OF THE COUNCIL.

Immediate.

Sir,

Foreign Office, October 21, 1879.

WITH reference to your letter of the 6th instant, I am directed by Her Majesty's Secretary of State for Foreign Affairs to transmit to you to be laid before the Lords of Her Majesty's Privy Council the accompanying note and its enclosure, which has been

Nos. 1, 2, and 3. received from the United States Chargé d'Affaires at this Court, relating to existence of disease among sheep imported from Boston, and I am to request you to move their Lordships to cause Lord Salisbury to be informed what answer should be returned to Mr. Hoppin, and to return the enclosed papers with your reply.

I am, &c.

The Clerk of the Council,   (Signed)   T. V. LISTER.
    Veterinary Department.

Enclosure 1 in No. 26.

LETTER from the UNITED STATES CHARGÉ D'AFFAIRES, LONDON, to the MARQUIS OF SALISBURY.

Legation of the United States, London,
My Lord,   October 20, 1879.

I HAVE the honour to acknowledge the receipt of your letter of the 7th instant informing me that foot-and-mouth disease has been detected by the Inspectors appointed by Her Majesty's Privy Council among five cargoes of sheep imported into Liverpool from Boston, and intimating that should any further consignments of diseased sheep arrive from the United States, the Lords of the Privy Council would feel themselves compelled, however reluctantly, to issue an Order in Council treating sheep in the same manner as cattle and swine from the United States are now treated; and I have to acquaint your Lordship that I lost no time in transmitting to Mr. Evarts the contents of your Lordship's letter.

Meanwhile I ask your Lordship's attention to the copies of two letters written to Mr. Packard, the United States Consul at Liverpool, by Messrs. Leyland & Co. and G. Warren & Co., the managing owners of the steamships which brought the five cargoes of sheep mentioned in your Lordship's letter. It appears from the letters that the percentage of diseased sheep is very small, that a portion of the sheep came from Canada, and that the period for shipment being now nearly over, the new restrictions proposed by the Privy Council may be properly postponed, at any rate, until the next season.

I have, &c.

The Most Honourable The Marquis of Salisbury,   (Signed)   W. J. HOPPIN.
   &c.   &c.   &c.

Enclosures.

Copies of letters.—Frederick Leyland & Co., to the United States Consul at Liverpool, October 11, 1879.
      George Warren & Co. to the same, October 15, 1879.

Enclosure 2 in No. 26.

LETTER from Messrs. LEYLAND AND COMPANY to the UNITED STATES CONSUL, LIVERPOOL.

Sir,   Liverpool, October 11, 1879.

YOUR favour of the 9th instant received. Our steamers have brought over from Boston 18,310 sheep during the present year of 1879. We do not think it probable we shall bring across any more this year. The sheep, ex "Bulgarian," 19th September, were Canadian. We understand the inspector considered seven sheep to be infected with foot-and-mouth disease of the consignment per "Bulgarian," 3rd July, and 11 of the consignment September voyage. These were the only cases of disease during the year that we are aware of.

We are, &c.,

S. B. Packard, Esq.,   (Signed)   *p.p.* FRED. LEYLAND & Co.,
   United States Consul, Liverpool.   FRED. W. LEYLAND.

Enclosure 3 in No. 26.

LETTER from Messrs. GEORGE WARREN AND COMPANY to the UNITED STATES CONSUL, LIVERPOOL.

Dear Sir,   Liverpool, October 15, 1879.

WE beg to hand you herewith a statement of sheep imported by our line of steamers from Boston during the present year to date, showing a total of 30,036.

The sheep by the last three steamers, viz. :—

"Pembroke," 24th September - - - - 1,293 head
"Palestine," 26th September - - - - 212 „
"Brazilian," 3rd October - - - - 421 „

were all slaughtered at point of disembarkation by order of the Inspector of the Privy Council in consequence of discovery (as alleged by him) of foot-and-mouth disease or scab. As far as our information goes the number of diseased animals discovered by him in these cargoes were—

8 cases of foot-and-mouth disease by the "Pembroke."
3 cases of foot-and-mouth disease by the "Palestine."
2 cases of foot-and-mouth disease ⎫
16 cases of scab - - - ⎬ by the "Brazilian."

or a total of 29 cases of disease out of 30,036 imported.

We may mention that a portion of the sheep ex "Pembroke" came from Canada. We may also add that the season for bringing live stock from America is now virtually ended, and we are not likely to carry many, if any, more until next spring.

Trusting these particulars will be of service to you.

We are, &c.
S. B. Packard, Esq., (Signed) GEO. WARREN & Co.
   United States Consul, Liverpool.

No. 27.

LETTER from the CLERK OF THE COUNCIL to the UNDER SECRETARY OF STATE, FOREIGN OFFICE.

Veterinary Department, Privy Council Office,
44, Parliament Street, Westminster, S.W.,
SIR, October 25, 1879.

I HAVE submitted to the Lords of the Council your letter of the 21st instant, transmitting a note and its inclosure which had been received from the United States Chargé d'Affaires at this Court, relating to the existence of disease among sheep imported from Boston.

In reply, I am directed to state, for the information of Lord Salisbury, that their Lordships regret that, having regard to the health of the live stock of this country they cannot make any exception in favour of animals from the United States, and that they will feel themselves compelled, in the event of another cargo arriving with sheep affected with foot-and-mouth disease from that country, to issue an Order of Council placing sheep under restrictions similar to those which now apply to cattle and swine.

I am, &c.
The Under Secretary of State, (Signed) C. L. PEEL.
  &c. &c. &c.
  Foreign Office.

No. 28.

LETTER from the BRITISH CONSUL-GENERAL AT NEW YORK to the MARQUIS OF SALISBURY.

(No. 50.) British Consulate General, New York,
MY LORD, November 8, 1879.

REFERRING to my Despatch (No. 48) of the 9th ultimo, I have the honour to report to your Lordship that pleuro-pneumonia still prevails to a considerable extent among cows in Putnam county in this State.

In the State of New Jersey, an improvement has taken place in the sanitary condition of cattle, owing to the energetic action of the Government inspectors in dealing with the disease so soon as it manifests itself in any part of the State.

I have, &c.
Her Majesty's Principal Secretary of State (Signed) E. M. ARCHIBALD.
  Foreign Affairs, London.

46

No. 29.

LETTER from the ACTING BRITISH CONSUL, at PHILADELPHIA, to the MARQUIS OF SALISBURY.

No. 24 Consular.
My Lord,
British Consulate, Philadelphia,
November 18, 1879.

I have the honour to report to your Lordship that there have been but few cases of pleuro-pneumonia in Pennsylvania during the past month of October, the Special Commissioner of Governor Hoyt having successfully continued his exertions for the suppression of the disease within the State.

Pleuro-pneumonia has not up to this time extended to the Western States of this Consular district, because no eastern cattle go westward. The breeding cattle imported for those States come direct from the Channel Islands, where pleuro-pneumonia, I believe, does not exist.

Mr. Vice-Consul Warrack, of Chicago, reports that in a recent visit throughout the West he did not hear of any cases of the disease in Illinois, Iowa, Michigan, Indiana, or Wisconsin.

Farmers now see the necessity of action by the National Government for the prevention of the spread of pleuro-pneumonia and other contagious cattle diseases to fresh districts. It is proposed to petition the United States Congress from every State in the Union in favour of a stringent national law for the suppression of contagious diseases and the establishment of a bureau with plenary powers. A convention of veterinary surgeons from all the States will shortly be held in New York for the purpose of encouraging this movement.

I beg to enclose for your Lordship printed copy of the proceedings of the American Short Horn Breeders Convention, held at Chicago on the 29th ult. Pleuro-pneumonia was discussed at some length by the members of the Convention. Attention is called to the opinions expressed by a red ink mark made on the enclosed copy, which is the only one I have been able to obtain.

I have, &c.
(Signed)   GEORGE CRUMP,

The Right Honourable
The Marquis of Salisbury, K.G.,
&c.   &c.   &c.

Enclosure in No. 29.

Proceedings of the American Short-horn Breeders' Convention.

At 10.15 a.m., on October 29th, President Christie called a small, but select body of short-horn breeders to order in the club-room of the Grand Pacific Hotel in this city, and the seventh annual convention of American Short-horn breeders commenced its session. It is a matter of regret that this meeting should have occurred at just that date, as was evidenced by the light attendance. But while the attendance was small compared with previous years, it made up in character what it lacked in number, representative men were present, from Canada, and from about a dozen different States.

The unfortunate proximity of the great fat stock show resulted in the absence of many breeders, who could not attend both events. Had the meeting been held during the November show, or had there been a few months of intervening time, there would undoubtedly have been a much larger turnout. However, this was a matter which was beyond the power of the secretary to remedy, as the byelaws of the association itself had fixed the date of meeting. We give below the President's opening address, and an abstract of the discussions.

Upon calling the meeting to order, the Honourable David Christie, of Canada, President of the Association, addressed the meeting as follows:

Gentlemen, As you are aware, at the last meeting of the association it was resolved that the next meeting should be held at Nashville, Tennessee, but owing to the prevalence of that terrible scourge, yellow fever, and in consequence of the urgent remonstrances of many members of the association, the meeting was postponed. The same difficulty occurred this year; in these circumstances, it was deemed proper to consult the directors of the association as to what should be done. The responses were unanimous in naming Chicago as the place of meeting, and certainly, since a wise discretion rendered a change of place necessary, there could be no more fitting place than this great

---

* Printed within brackets [ ]. See pp. 49 to 54.

city, easy of access from all parts of the continents; a great cattle mart, the first in the world, and also the leading city in one of the great cattle States of America, a state not surpassed for fertility and for short-horn cattle.

When we last met, the storm of adversity had compassed the length and breadth of the land, and it extended to every branch of business and to each industrial pursuit. The breeders of short-horn cattle felt the full force of the blast. Prices receded to a degree unprecedented in short-horn history. In England, last year, the average of the 64 sales was 57*l.* 5*s.* 9*d.*; 56 of these comprised 39 per cent. of the whole, and averaged 37*l.* 0*s.* 7*d.* One thousand and thirty-one animals averaged less than 30*l.* One animal, Baroness Oxford 5th, brought 2,660 guineas, or more than the individual proceeds of 51 of the 64 sales recorded. So said the *Mark Lane Express.* Our American averages were not much better. Now the storm has passed, and already we have seen the harbinger of prosperous times. A recent short-horn sale in Chicago has given a better average than we have had in America for two years past, and better than the average in England last year. The lesson taught by adversity should not be lost.

> "Sweet are the uses of adversity,
> Which, like the toad, ugly and venomous,
> Wears yet a precious jewel in her head."

Men of the present generation are not likely again to be tempted to over speculation, or to give excessive prices. Another important lesson is not to place unreasoning reliance on mere pedigree, whether of this or that family or tribe, without giving due weight to personal qualities. Pedigree is very important, because it gives a reasonable degree of assurance of the transmission of valuable qualities from parents to progeny; but how can an animal be expected to transmit qualities not possessed by it, but which, according to tradition, may have been the characteristic of some one or more remote ancestors. The old adage, that "Like produces like," commonly holds true; the principles of pedigree is based on it, and rest assured, gentlemen, that the day has come when the presentation of "long pedigree" will not cover the want of distinguished personal qualities. Both together, but neither singly, will satisfy future purchasers. The demand for good animals, of good pedigree, will increase year by year. The demand for a superior quality of beef for export to the British market will compel breeders and feeders to use only good and well-bred animals; because it will neither pay to breed nor to export inferior cattle. With all due deference to the opinions and statements of our Hereford friends, there is no race of cattle which, for early maturity and aptitude to produce, with profit, really first-class beef, can compare with the short-horn. It is one of the promising features in the future of American agriculture, that a line of demarcation is being drawn between the business of breeding and of feeding cattle for beef. The lands in the east, and as far west as the Missouri, are too high-priced to enable farmers to raise beef cattle with profit. On lands worth from $50 to $100 per acre beef cattle cannot be raised with profit. In ordinary circumstances a steer cannot be ready for market until he is three years old, during which period he will cost more than he will bring in market. In Great Britain this is well understood. English and Scotch farmers purchase, at the great fairs, cattle bred in Wales and the Highlands of Scotland, where they can be raised cheaply, and then feed them. They know well that all the profit of stall feeding does not consist in the extra quantity and quality of beef, but in the large quantity of valuable manure produced, and in the better cultivation of the soil for root crops, which, in due time, result in larger returns of grain per acre in succeeding crops. The farmers of Illinois, Indiana, and Ohio, who feed cattle, act on the principle that it is more profitable to purchase than to raise stock for that purpose. They know that they cannot compete with breeders living on the cheap lands of Kansas, Nebraska, and Colorado, and, therefore, they repair to the great cattle marts of Kansas City, St. Louis, and Chicago; at which, any day in October and November, they can purchase all the stock they need for feeding purposes. A few years ago it was difficult to get as many well-bred steers as were needed, therefore recourse to the lean and ill-favored Texan was a necessity, the descendants of the old Andalusian cattle—a race unprofitable to feed, and sometimes bringing with them, as in 1868, "Texan fever," a scourge which desolated large districts of country. Fortunately, during the past ten years, a better race of cattle has taken their place. From the extensive dissemination of short-horns among the western herds, the supply of good cattle is yearly becoming more abundant, and promises soon to keep pace with the demand. This is a most encouraging fact to the breeders of short-horns. Many of the western herds require the services of 60 to 100 bulls, which of course must be replaced by the purchase of others every third year.

If you will permit me to trespass a little on your time, I wish to quote from a report by Professor Brown, of the Ontario Agricultural College, at Guelph, the narrative of an experiment made at the college, last year, in feeding short-horn steers. Professor Brown says: " During the past winter, our school made two experiments in the fattening of " steers. 1st, with four steers of our own breeding, *fore-fifths* prime fat, and nine " tenths bred short-horns. Secondly, with six steers bought in, half-fed, and two thirds " bred short-horns. All the animals were entered on the 8th December, and withdrawn " on the 6th of March, being 87 days—say three months—average age of all 35 months " and 15 days, at latter date. The food consisted of, daily, 90 lbs. of pulped Swede " turnips, 12 lbs. of cut straw, of sorts, and 12 lbs. of crushed Indian corn, given in two " forms—turnips and straw, put in a heap in alternate layers, so as to slightly ferment, " and corn mixed with them when served; and other pulped turnips direct from the " machine. The four steers averaged, on entry, 1,512 lbs., and 1,754 when finished— " thus gaining 242 lbs. in 87 days, being 2 8-10 lbs. per day, or 16 per cent. on their " weight. The six steers, on entry, averaged 1,260 lbs., and 1,492 lbs. when withdrawn " —thus gaining 232 lbs. in 87 days—being 2 7-10 lbs. per day, or 18½ per cent. on " their weight."

So we can make the following balance sheet, according to current market prices, attendance, and manure, to meet each other for safe figuring:

1st example:—
    Cost of straw, $5 per ton - - - - - $2.61
    Cost of corn, 50 c. per 56 lbs. - - - - - 8.70
    Value of animal when entered, 1,512 lbs., at 5½ c. - - 82.16
                                                                                         93.47
1,754 lbs. sold for 6 cents - - - - - 105.24

    Balance to credit - - - - - - 11.77

2nd example:—
    Cost of food as above - - - - - 11.31
    Value of animal when entered, 1,260 lbs., at 3¾ c. - - 47.25
                                                                                         58.56
1,492 lbs. sold for 5¼ cents - - - - - 78.33

    Balance to credit - - - - - - $19.77

(Or a difference in favour of the half-fed steers of $8 per head.)

There is material here for some very nice discussion and comparisons. Let me approximate the conclusions. That well-bred steers, nearly prime fat, gain 3½ per cent. more on the same food than others that are not so well bred, and that were also 6 per cent. less in weight when put in competition; that, in proportion to weight, the half-fed steers gave 58 per cent. more profit than the others; that, according to weight, the half-fed steers gave 2½ per cent more increase than others almost prime; that, in proportion to weight, the half-fed steers ate 18 per cent. more food than the others; that, as an investment, without reference to manure, the matured animals returned fully 9 per cent., and the half-fed ones 40 per cent. on the original cost, being a difference of 31 per cent. in favour of the leaner animals. No doubt there are circumstances for and against each of these conclusions, which it may be well to notice. The previous treatment of our own bred cattle was likely more favourable. The change of place and food was against the others. Their inferiority of breeding might be against them. Note how much fat, heat, and flesh substances of food was required to produce a certain quantity of beef. One animal, in 87 days, ate, flesh, fat, and heat producers:—

Turnips.	Straw.	Corn.	Total.
574 lbs.	441 lbs.	831 lbs.	1,846 lbs.

In the case of the animals, therefore, the 1,846 lbs. of fat, heat, and flesh-forming substances in the three sorts of food seem to have been required to make 236 lbs. of probably the same things in the animal's frame. This we find was one of flesh to seven of fat. There is, then, under proper management, proper food, and with the proper animal, a large profit in growing beef.

It may be remarked, in reference to the foregoing statement, that the profit would have been much larger, had all the steers in question been bred where they could have been produced, at the proper age, at less cost.

I have alluded to the large increase in the trade in beef with Great Britain. From small beginnings, it has grown to large proportions. In 1876, the total domestic exports from the United States were:—

Live cattle	$1,110,703
Salt beef	3,186,304
Sheep	171,101
(No fresh beef.)	$4,368,108

These figures include the total exports to all countries from the United States.

In 1877, the reports of live cattle, sheep, fresh beef, and salt beef to Great Britain, were:—

Live cattle	$546,829
Salt beef	1,200,000
Sheep	22,578
Fresh beef	4,552,523
Fresh mutton	36,480
An aggregate of	$6,358,410

To Great Britain alone, as against $4,552,523 to all foreign countries during the previous year; being an increase in the items named of $1,989,382.

In 1878, the United States domestic exports to Great Britain were:—

Live cattle	$2,408,843
Sheep	109,777
Swine	69,395
Hams and bacon	38,241,651
Beef salted	2,118,992
Beef, fresh	4,906,152
Mutton, Fresh	8,272
Lard	10,175,475
Meats preserved	4,284,512
	$62,305,969

Thus, the aggregate exports in meats and cattle, sheep and pigs, to Great Britain alone, in 1878, amounted to nearly as much as the total exports to all foreign countries in 1877, while the total exports in those classes to all foreign countries were to the value of $104,272,552; showing an increase from the previous year of $46,983,794, or more than double the export trade in 1876, which amounted to $49,592,834. I could not obtain the statistics of the trade for the present year, but it has been stated that the exports of live stock this year have reached the value of $11,487,754. It is clear, therefore, that the demand keeps pace with the supply, so that short-horn breeders have good cause to believe that their trade will be prosperous. The exports of live stock for food from Canada, are also very encouraging. In 1878, in cattle, sheep, and swine, they amounted to $1,937,365, and in 1879, to $3,342,006—an increase of $1,404,741.

[Amid these indications of prosperity, we must not conceal from ourselves the fact that great danger threatens the whole trade in live stock. It is beyond doubt that contagious pleuro-pneumonia exists among the cattle of several States of the Union. At this date, it is unnecessary to inquire into the truth of the statements as to the existence of the disease among the cattle composing the cargo of the "Ontario," and which led to the scheduling of American cattle. There is grave reason to doubt the correctness of the conclusions arrived at by the veterinary examiners of the Privy Council. We have high authority for stating this. Professor Williams has, in very plain terms, denied that they were correct; and it will not do to impugn the professional status of Professor Williams, in order to get rid of his statements. He is well known to be one of the first veterinary pathologists of the day; and the best proof of this is, that on the 27th of May last, at a special meeting of the Council of the Royal College of Veterinary Surgeons of Great Britain, he was elected President of that body, by a vote of more than two to one over his competitor, who had been one of the examiners on behalf of the Privy Council, of the cattle brought by the "Ontario," and who had given a different opinion from that of Professor Williams. But, as has been stated, we know that contagious pleuro-pneumonia does exist among cattle in some Eastern States, and the imperative duty of every American breeder and professional man is to urge, with determination which cannot be misunderstood, that the Government of the United States shall take such action as shall effectually "stamp out" this dire scourge, and prevent its reintroduction among the cattle of America. Had the Government heeded the warnings given when we were threatened with an invasion of rinderpest, much of the difficulty would have been avoided, and a proper system of quarantine and veterinary inspection would have been instituted. This Association, at its last meeting, at Lexington, two years ago, sent a memorial to the Government on this subject, to which little attention was paid. Last spring, when the existence of the disease was ascertained, the officers of the Association sent a memorial to the Government, urging the appointment of an international veterinary commission for the purpose of ascertaining where the disease existed, and for advising measures for its suppression, and, until that should be accomplished, for preventing its spread. The result was, that nothing was done, no commission was appointed, and Congress was allowed to adjourn without an appropriation being made for the purpose of getting rid of this terrible disease. Shall the interests of the agricultural portion of this country be unheeded, and shall no adequate measures be taken to protect them?

There is no public question at this moment of greater importance to the people of this country than the extirpation of contagious pleuro-pneumonia. The legislature of the State of New York, at their last session, made an appropriation of $35,000 towards this object; a rigid system of quarantine has been instituted, and by the able and efficient officers appointed by the State Government much has been done. But no mere State legislation and expenditure will do the work. There must be Congressional legislation and a large appropriation by Congress, or all other merely local efforts will fail. The Order of the Treasury Department, issued on the 10th of July 1879, falls far short of what is necessary. To the quarantine of 90 days there is the exception: "Where State " or municipal laws provide for the quarantine of such cattle; and in such cases col-" lectors will permit them to quarantine them in such manner as the State or municipal " authorities require." The "Order" or law should be made to apply to every State in the Union alike. The matter is national in its character, and the laws or orders relating to it should be national in their character, otherwise there can be no certainty as to the suppression or exclusion of the disease. We have a signal illustration of this in the case of an importation of cattle which arrived in New York during the week before last. I quote from the *Country Gentleman* of October 23rd: "We observe by the papers that the contemplated importation of Channel Islands cattle, by Mr. P. H. Fowler, Watford, England, was landed at New York last week by the steamship Cornwall, *and from thence they were transferred by rail to the Messrs. Herkness & Co.'s Bazaar, Philadelphia*. Although in a healthy condition, they will be subjected to rigorous quarantine regulations, and until released will be in charge of Thomas I. Edge, Secretary of the Board of Agriculture and State Commissioner, and Dr. Bridge, Veterinary Inspector. The stock comprises 38 Jersey cows and calves, and two Guernsey bulls.

Now, mark what follows: "Since the foregoing was in type, Messrs. Herkness and Co., of Philadelphia, send the announcement of the sale of these cattle which appears on our first page, *it will take place* on Thursday morning, November 6th." The advertisement referred to states that the cattle were "*direct from the Channel Islands, viâ Bristol, England, to New York per steamer Cornwall and thence by rail to Philadelphia.*" Could there be a stronger illustration of the utter inefficiency of the "Treasury Order" to prevent the importation and spread of the disease. From anything known to anyone, these cattle may all be diseased. The period for the incubation of the disease may not have expired, and although apparently healthy, they may have contracted it, and thus be the means of carrying contagious pleuro-pneumonia into the very heart of the country; for, be it observed, they came from an infected country, and in passing from New York to Philadelphia they were carried through a country where disease exists. It is pleasing to observe that at a meeting of the United States Veterinary Medical Association, held in New York, on the 16th of September 1879, a committee was appointed to take action in the matter, and " to draw up a set of resolutions to be presented to Congress in relation to the investigation and prevention of contagious diseases of domestic animals." I beg to recommend the appointment of a similar committee by this association.

I have pleasure in stating my belief that the Government of Canada will co-operate heartily with the Government of the United States in the adoption of measures calculated to prevent the importation of the disease.

The address was listened to with careful attention by his audience, and was received with every evidence of approval.

Upon its conclusion the Hon. L. F. ALLEN moved that the thanks of the Convention be tendered the President, and that the address, pending discussion, be laid on the table.

Carried

JUDGE JONES stated that the President had touched upon a subject of more than ordinary importance. He alluded to the matter of contagious pleuro-pneumonia. He had drawn up a Bill last year, looking to the appointment of a Commission by Congress, to investigate the subject of sanitary regulations, and providing for an appropriation for the expenses of such a committee. He took his Bill on to Washington and placed it in the hands of his Congressman, who presented the same to the House of Representatives. But it was hurried out of sight. At the short session the Bill was not reached, and it finally perished in the extra session for want of log-rolling and lobbying. The trouble is, our members of Congress do not read the agricultural papers; they do not know what pleuro-pneumonia is. State legislation on the subject is insufficient; there must be Congressional action, and the short-horn breeders of America should bring their influence to bear upon the General Government to effect that rseult.

PRESIDENT CHRISTIE here suggested that the Convention should appoint a special committee to press this matter upon Congress.

JUDGE JONES thought it a good idea; but where would the funds to do the "log-rolling" come from? The great difficulty is the want of knowledge on the part of members of Congress. If they understood the matter, it would not be necessary for us to be discussing it here to-day.

PRESIDENT CHRISTIE then read from the proceedings of the American Veterinary Association, showing that Dr. Liautard had then moved that a special committee from that organization be appointed to petition Congress concerning veterinary regulations. This had been carried, and Mr. Christie thought that this association should supplement the action of the Veterinary Association by the appointment of a similar committee.

MR. ALLEN inquired: Who knows anything about the American Veterinary Association.

DR. MCEACHRAN explained that it was an organization of the Veterinary Surgeons of America; and added that if the Short-horn Association would appoint such a committee as had been suggested, it would be a material aid and reinforcement to the veterinary committee. He had understood that this subject would come up here, and he had attended the Convention in order to throw what light he could upon the matter. He had been employed by the Canadian Government to investigate the sanitary condition of cattle in the Eastern States, and so could appreciate the importance of action on the subject. It was of the utmost importance that the breeders of America should be aroused to the magnitude of the question which is now being presented to them. The neglect and delay by the Government and people of England to recognise the enormity of ravages by contagious diseases was the beginning of the downfall of English agriculture; and to this folly he attributed a great share of the distress now prevailing in England. Pleuro-pneumonia has a long period of incubation, say two or three months; and hence we see that in cattle shipped to Australia, altough the voyage takes from 60 to 90 days, the disease does not break out in some cases for several weeks after landing. There are many different ways in which the disease may be transmitted other than by direct contact; the clothes of attendants, the pens where diseased animals have been confined, their bedding, etc.; and wherever infected animals have been killed, the slaughter-houses should be destroyed. White-washing, as is the usual custom, will not suffice. If Pennsylvania tries to stamp out the plague, it is futile and barren of results unless the neighbouring States co-operate. Great care must be taken in drawing up the proposed memorial to Congress; it must not be done hastily; a clear statement of all the facts must be made, and the General Government must appropriate a large and sufficient sum.

MR. ALLEN didn't know much about the matter at present. When the Texas fever raged, some years ago, he served on a committee appointed by the State of New York to control the passage of infected cattle though the State, and by having them slaughtered at Buffalo, and other points, they succeeded in protecting the State. This association began in 1872, with some 120 or 130 members; now he saw 25 or 30 present. More interest must be shown. He reproached the breeders of Illinois for not turning out to the Convention. We may pass resolutions, but how are we to defray the expenses of a Committee at Washington? It is such a hard job to get Congress interested in this subject, that he had grave doubts as to whether the Association could do anything or not.

MR. CLINTON BABBITT said, "popular sentiment" was a thing to be made. We must press this thing upon the people, and we will effect the desired result. This is no mere sectional question, but one in which the people of the whole country is deeply interested. We should appoint a committee whose business it should be to bring the subject squarely before the country, and with the influence of such men as Judge Jones and Hon. David Christie we can and will make ourselves heard. Congress cannot resist popular sentiment when it is once aroused.

COLONEL SCOTT thought this question had a magnitude far beyond mere short-horn interests. It directly affected the whole agricultural interest, and was of vital importance to the millions of people, in our own and foreign countries, who are depending upon us for beef. We stand here in the character of philanthropists. There may be difficulties in the way, but they are not insurmountable. It is a most fortunate feature of this great scourge that it begins to poison the stream at its mouth. It has not reached the source, and it behoves us to see that it does not reach the source. We must grapple with the plague and act promptly and energetically. I am unwilling to sit here and hear it said that we can do nothing. I should feel ashamed if the Iowa men in this Convention could not control the votes of their 11 members of Congress! [Applause.] Kentucky will not stop on any mere petty State rights. My friend Babbitt assures me Wisconsin will be on the right side, and so it will be with all the States. If, as Mr. Allen asserts, this Convention is small in numbers, as compared with the earlier ones, I would say that the association has undergone a winnowing process. We have lost the chaff, and the grain is here. [Applause.] This question belongs to us as men, not as short-horn breeders, and I trust this association will take hold of it and meet it squarely. I do not say short-horn men have no interest in this matter, but it is not confined to them alone; we must throw ourselves into this business in the great cause of common humanity.

MR. ALLEN explained that he had not intended to discourage this movement, but he questioned the ways and means to be used. His Congressman was a patent-medicine man, and he did not believe any amount of talking would arouse him to a sense of his duty in this matter, and he did not believe that Colonel Scott and his colleagues could influence the eleven Iowa votes.

JUDGE JONES said: We must not overlook, of course, the difficulties to be encountered, but Mr. Allen lacks faith. From his zeal he should say that Colonel Scott was a Methodist. (Laughter.) This question does affect all the agriculturists of America; and as this Association is the only representative of the farming interest of the nation, its action would have its influence. I am most heartily in favour of appointing a committee of, say five members, to memorialise Congress on this subject.

Mr. COOMBS stated that, as far as Senator Beck of Kentucky was concerned, he knew that that gentleman appreciated the importance of the question, and was willing to do all in his power towards aiding national legislation on the subject.

JUDGE JONES moved that the Chair appoint a committee of five to press the matter before Congress.

Messrs. BABBITT, PARSONS, and CHRISTIE favoured appointing one member from each State to urge the matter upon the several State Legislatures.

JUDGE JONES also favoured legislative memorials; but he thought such a large committee would prove rather unwieldy, and that five men could press the subject with greater facility than a larger number could.

Motion carried.

PRESIDENT CHRISTIE then announced the following as the members of the Committee: Hon. T. C. Jones, Ohio; Hon. Emory Cobb, Illinois; Mr. Claude Matthews, Indiana; Hon. T. J. Megibben, Kentucky; and Hon. L. S. Coffin, of Iowa.

Upon motion the name of Hon. David Christie was added.

JUDGE JONES moved that the election of officers be made the special order for the afternoon session.

Carried.

Mr. CLAUDE MATTHEWS, the treasurer, then read his regular report, which showed a balance of $37 24 in the treasury. He also moved that the membership fee be fixed at $2.

Carried.

Some suggestions were made regarding the publication of the proceedings of the Lexington Convention, and the current session, but no formal action was taken.

Mr. ALLEN moved that State Agricultural Societies be requested to memorialise the Legislatures of the States to petition Congress on the subject of sanitary regulations concerning live stock.

Carried.

On motion, adjourned to 3 p.m.

Afternoon Session.

The first thing in order being the election of officers, Dr. Sprague moved that Hon. T. J. Megibben, of Kentucky, be elected President, which motion was unanimously adopted. For vice-Presidents, Colonel John Scott, of Iowa, and Hon. M. H. Cochrane, of Canada, were chosen. For secretary, S. F. Lockridge, Greencastle, Indiana. For treasurer, Claude Matthews, of Clinton, Indiana. For directors, J. R. Page, of New York; Leslie Coombs, junior, of Kentucky; T. C. Jones, of Ohio; David Christie, of Ontario; Clinton Babbitt, of Wisconsin; H. Winslow, of Illinois; Pliny Nichols, of Iowa; S. C. Duncan, of Missouri; T. C. Hammond, of Indiana; C. W. Howell, of California; D. W. Crane, of Kansas; M. S. Cockrell, of Tennessee; J. C. Sanborn, of Michigan; T. L. McKean, of Pennsylvania; N. Gates, of Connecticut; A. W. Moore, of Texas; C. Parsons, junior, of Massachusetts; F. W. Russell, of Rhode Island; Le Grande B. Cannon, of Vermont; J. B. Dodge, of New Hampshire; J. G. Cowan, of Virginia; C. A. De Graff, of Minnesota; Charles Shaw, of Maine; John Westfaldt, of North Carolina; J. C. Tremble, of Colorado; J. C. McBride, of Nebraska; W. C. Blinn, of Washington Territory; S. G. Reed, of Oregon; J. M. Browning, of Quebec; H. J. Thornstadt, of Dakotah; H. W. Brewer, of South Carolina; M. B. Helyard, of Mississippi; W. D. Wing, of Montana; and R. H. Allen, of New Jersey.

Judge Jones moved that the next Convention be held at La Fayette, Indiana.

Carried.

President Christie then read the following communication from Professor Law, of Cornell University:—

Hon. D. Christie.

Dear Sir, Cornell University, Ithaca, N.W., October 4, 1879.

My constant absence from home must be my excuse for this late response. I had hoped to have sent you an illustrated article of 100 pages on the "Contagious Pleuro-Pneumonia," now in press, but it will be issued too late for your meeting. It will be mailed as soon as issued. At present I have only time to say that the "lung-plague" has been extinguished in Richmond, Suffolk, and Orange counties in this State. It is almost extirpated from New York, Westchester, and Putnam counties, and now only prevails to any extent in King's county. We have been compelled to delay effective measures, and this last by lack of means, and are now only waiting for further supplies to crush the pestilence in every part of the State. As New York and Brooklyn (King's county) were about equally infested last February, it may interest the meeting to know what measures have been so effective in the former—and the more so that it illustrates how the most stringent measures are by far the best and most economical.

"1st. We got new yards, to which only healthy cattle, from districts known to be sound, were admitted. All stock from infected counties or States, or that had been in cars, yards, or boats open to stock from such States, were rigidly excluded.

"2nd. No animal was allowed to leave the new yards until sold, and then only after examination, and with permit, stating destination, route, and time allowed.

"3rd. Cattle going to any stable in the city, dealer, or milkman, could not leave such stable again, except to an abattoir, for immediate slaughter, and with a permit. We thus abolished dealers' stables, which were simply pest-houses, and stopped the baleful system of peddling cattle from stable to stable, which came to be simply a peddling of disease.

"4th. Dealers were placed on their good behaviour, by our withholding permits from all that broke our rules.

"5th. The co-operation of the police was secured to stop moving of cattle without license, and to impound the same.

"6th. An inspector went every night to the offal dock, where all carcasses are sent, and opened all cattle found there, and traced to their street and number any showing the lesions of the plague.

"Besides these particular measures we had the general rules enforced elsewhere, including systematic inspection of herds, the abolition of pasturage on highways and open lots; of the herding of the stock of different owners together or successively on the same lots; the granting of butter licenses to healthy herds only; for reporting sickness, inspection, condemnation, appraisement, slaughter, indemnity, disinfection, quarantine of infected herds, registration of the same by personal marks, and disposal of fodder, litter, manure, &c.

"The system has been fully enforced in New York for three montht only, and the city and county is now all but sound, whereas, in Brooklyn, where local obstruction hindered its application, the disease still prevails widely.

"I regret that I cannot possibly visit Chicago at present, though it would give me much pleasure to meet with the 'Association of Short-horn Breeders.' I am at present alternating between 'Cornell' and New York, and have not a spare moment at either place.

"Yours very faithfully,
"James Law."

Dr. McEachran then gave a short sketch of the history of contagious pleuro-pneumonia in America, describing the result of his recent investigations in the service of the Dominion Government, and dilating upon the apathy shown by the United States authorities in the premises.

Upon the conclusion of his remarks, Judge Jones rapped the doctor across the knuckles for having made a hasty and ill-timed report to the Canadian Government, which had done the United States a great injury in affecting our live-stock export trade.

Dr. McEachran explained that all that he was required to do was to see if the disease existed in the States; and after he had personally examined various sections and witnessed thousands of infected animals, he made his report to that effect. Was there anything hasty in that? And further, his report was not the cause of the scheduling of the United States cattle in English ports. The Privy Council received their information from an entirely different source.

President Christie came to the doctor's rescue, and gave the United States authorities a merciless scoring, denouncing them in unmeasured terms; charging Secretary Sherman and others with criminal negligence in trifling with such a vital question.

This aroused the patriotism of the honourable gentleman from Delaware, and throwing himself into the breach with flashing eyes, he informed the gentlemen from the Queen's dominions that when they came here to tell us of our misfortunes they should be a little more careful in their statements.

He insisted that it was unjust that simply because a narrow belt of country on the Atlantic slope was infected with this disease, the great West should have to suffer scheduling at the hands of the British Government; intimating that the gentlemen from Canada had helped to bring this about. He thought much more could be accomplished by approaching our Government with kind words, than by making bitter attacks upon those in power.

Dr. McEachran denied the allegation, and stated that they had asserted all along that the West was free from the plague; but the Privy Council recognised no geographical divisions of the United States. The mere fact that pleuro-pneumonia existed in this country was sufficient reason for them to schedule the nation at large.

Mr. Coffin said that since the plague exists along our sea-board, it is a wonder that any of our cattle reach England in a healthy condition. And it is the purest good luck that the disease has not been carried West.

At this point Dr. N. H. Paaren was called for and made a few well-pointed remarks upon the duty of the Government in treating the subject; also avowing that the West was absolutely free from the scourge.

After various other informal observations by Messrs. Parsons, Hayward, Sanders, and others, Mr. Coffin moved that the Director in each State be requested to urge his State Legislature to petition Congress.]

Carried.

On motion, adjourned until 7.30 p.m.

Evening Session.

Mr. G. Sprague, of Iowa, read a paper on Feeding Cattle, which was attentively listened to, and which will appear in our next issue. After the reading of Dr. Sprague's paper, the Convention adjourned to meet at Lafayette, Ind., the last Wednesday of October 1880.

No. 30.

LETTER from the BRITISH CONSUL-GENERAL at NEW YORK to the MARQUIS OF SALISBURY.

No. 51.   British Consulate-General, New York,
My Lord,   December 2, 1879.

I have the honour to report to your Lordship that contagious pleuro-pneumonia among cattle still exists in this city and in Putnam county in this State; also in New

Jersey, as before reported by me. The number of animals affected is, however, not so large as heretofore, the result being doubtless due to the continued efforts of the State authorities to extirpate the disease.

I have, &c.

Her Majesty's
  Principal Secretary of State
    For Foreign Affairs, London.

(Signed)   E. M. ARCHIBALD.

No. 31.

LETTER from the ACTING CONSUL-GENERAL at PHILADELPHIA to the MARQUIS OF SALISBURY.

British Consulate, Philadelphia,
December 9, 1879.

My Lord,

I have the honour to report to your Lordship that a few cases of pleuro-pneumonia among cattle continue to exist in the State of Pennsylvania, notwithstanding the exertions of the State authorities to eradicate the disease. In the county of Philadelphia, among the dairy herds, a few new cases have been discovered, and repressive measures will at once be resorted to.

The Commissioner appointed by the Governor of the State about six months ago has, up to the date of my last report, placed in quarantine twenty-seven herds containing four hundred and eight head of cattle, which were found liable to infection. Of these herds eight have since been released from quarantine and pronounced safe from another outbreak, except by infection from outside cattle.

As soon as the Commissioner learns of the existence of the disease in any district the herd in which a case occurs is inspected by a veterinary surgeon, employed by the State, and the herd at once placed under quarantine, and the diseased animals, after appraisement, are killed.

The history of the infected herds above referred to is as follows:

No. 1. (in York county). Infected by steers bought in Baltimore. Six head were either lost by death previous to quarantine or were killed for the purpose of checking the disease.

No. 2. Contained 20 cows, two bulls, and 10 calves. The herd was quarantined June 12th. Four head died previous to the quarantine, and whilst in quarantine 14 head were killed.

All the animals except one were affected, and a number of them are now useless to the owner. It is apparent in this case that the owner conveyed the disease to his herd after assisting in the care of an adjoining infected dairy.

No. 3. (Delaware county.) The herd contained fifty head, a number of which died previous to being placed in quarantine. In this case the disease was supposed to have been introduced by the purchase of cattle. Eleven head were killed by the State Commissioner.

Nos. 4, 5, and $5\frac{1}{2}$ were herds adjacent to each other, and the farms were traversed by a small stream of water, at the head of which the disease would appear to have orginated, an animal dying in the stream and was buried close to its banks. In No. 4 one animal died and one was killed, and No. 5 the first animal attacked was promptly killed. Isolation was immediately adopted; No. $5\frac{1}{2}$ is still infected. No. 6 having 11 head was quarantined. No. 7 (Lancaster County) had 42 head, and when discovered was infected throughout by two afflicted animals running with the herd. Seven animals were killed in one day, and never placed in quarantine. Subsequently eight more were killed, and the disease effectually eradicated. The infection was taken from an adjoining herd, which, in its turn, was infected by stock from New York.

No. 8. This herd is supposed to have been infected by the owner of No. 2 administering medicine to the animals after attending to his own. Seven animals were lost in this herd and the rest are not yet out of danger.

No. 9. A herd of 31 animals. In this case the disease was checked by the prompt killing of one animal and the immediate isolation of the others. The herd has been released from quarantine.

Nos. 10, 11, and 12. Small herds, in two of which every animal exhibited symptoms of disease, but by prompt measures and the sacrifice of a few head, the contagion was checked.

Nos. 13 to 20 inclusive are recent cases, and the herds have suffered little loss in consequence of the measures immediately adopted.

No. 21. This herd was infected by six cows purchased in the Philadelphia market, the disease showing itself within 10 days after the purchase. Of the six cows five have died or been sacrificed. The cows came from the Philadelphia drove yard, but beyond that place the origin of the infected animals could not be traced.

No. 22 (Montgomery County). This herd was infected by a cow purchased from a drover. When purchased she was coughing, and when examined by the official surgeon, one week subsequently, was so far gone that the owner consented to have her killed as worthless, exacting no compensation.

No. 23. This herd was infected by contact with herd No. 16 previous to its being placed in quarantine. The animals are still under treatment. Sulphur fumes appear to have been effectual in preventing a spread of the disease. All the animals were more or less affected.

No. 24. Containing 30 head, caught the disease from No. 7, as, by accident they got into the inclosure which had previously contained the former herd for a short time.

No. 25. This herd was allowed to graze alongside of No. 7 with no separation other than that afforded by a stream and an open fence. Before the disease was reported to the State Commissioner most of the steers had been sent to market.

All the stock brought into the State of Pennsylvania from Europe is under the control of the State Agent or Commissioner, and the animals are placed in quarantine after inspection by an official veterinary surgeon. After the quarantine they are again inspected and, if found healthy, a certificate is granted permitting their removal to any part of the State. The incoming animals are thus subjected to rigid examinations; first, at the European port of shipment; second, on arrival; and, third, on the termination of their quarantine. In these exactions the interests of the importers are duly considered when they do not in any way conflict with the general interests of the commonwealth.

As far as it has been in my power to learn, there would appear to be no pleuro-pneumonia or other contagious diseases among cattle in the western states of this consular district. It is to be remembered, however, that in the shipments to England from Philadelphia, eastern cattle may be occasionally included, as at the stock-yards the animals are gathered in from all quarters, and the labours of the State Commissioner, detailed in this despatch, show the continued existence of pleuro-pneumonia in various counties of Pennsylvania. It is not improbable that the present Congress of the United States will be called upon to pass a cattle disease Act for the repression of all contagious diseases throughout the country, as the stock raisers are now alive to the incalculable losses that must ensue should pleuro-pneumonia extend to the Western States. Uniformity of regulations throughout the country is absolutely necessary for the aid of those who labour for the repression and the extinction of contagious diseases among cattle. Doubtless strong opposition will arise from the dealer and the skipper, whose interests will not be enhanced by legislative enactment, and they may prove no inconsiderable obstacles to the passage of such a law.

It is apparent, however, that the only safe course to be pursued at home is the continuation of the present order for the slaughter of all cattle for food at the port of debarcation.

I have, &c.
(Signed) GEORGE CRUMP.

The Right Honourable
   The Marquis of Salisbury, K.G.
    &c.   &c.   &c.

No. 32.

LETTER from the BRITISH CONSUL-GENERAL at NEW YORK to the MARQUIS OF SALISBURY.

(No. 6.)   British Consulate General, New York,
MY LORD,   January 5, 1880.

I HAVE the honour to report to your Lordship that since the date of my last report pleuro-pneumonia has made its appearance among some herds of cattle in the county of West Chester in this State, and still prevails there.

As regards other parts of my consular district, I have nothing to add to my last report to your Lordship.

I have, &c.
Her Majesty's Secretary of State   (Signed) E. M. ARCHIBALD.
   for Foreign Affairs.

No. 33.

LETTER from the ACTING BRITISH CONSUL at PHILADELPHIA to the MARQUIS OF SALISBURY.

(Sanitary, No. 1.)
British Consulate, Philadelphia,
January 20, 1880.

My Lord,

I HAVE the honour to report to your Lordship that since my Despatch No. 26 of December 9th, relating to contagious diseases among cattle in this consular district, two fresh outbreaks of pleuro-pneumonia have occurred in the State of Pennsylvania. One in Lehigh county, in a herd of 30 head introduced by a cow purchased in the city of Baltimore, State of Maryland. Ten head were killed at once, and several others since. The contagion spread to adjoining farms by the cattle intermingling before the disease was discovered. The other occurred a fortnight ago in Montgomery County adjoining the city of Philadelphia in a herd of 30 head; four cattle were lost, two having died and two were killed. Eight weeks since a few head of cattle were purchased in the Philadelphia market for this farm, and it is believed the disease was introduced by them.

In the lower section of the city of Philadelphia, where the disease broke out as reported in my Despatch No. 26, it was effectually cured by the prompt killing of all the infected animals.

Pleuro-pneumonia is daily awakening increased attention among stock raisers and dairymen throughout the country. The demand for a national intervention in lieu of State or local regulations for the extirpation of the disease is growing, and the prompt attention of the Congress of the United States is called for. It is necessary to engraft a public confidence in sanitary measures before a complete extinction of the disease in this country can be expected. The following reasons are put forth by the skilled in cattle diseases why the National Government should take the matter in hand:—

1. The disease is an exotic, and if once suppressed would never reappear unless reimported.

2. The plague is slowly extending to the western and southern parts of the United States, and if neglected must lay the entire continent under contribution.

3. If the plague once reaches the unfenced cattle ranges of the South and West it would be impossible to eradicate it.

4. The State wealth of many of the Western States is largely made up of live stock, and the spread of the contagion to those States would be a national calamity.

5. The disease is more violent and fatal in warm climates than in cold. The relative mortality therefore in the Gulf States and in the Mississippi Valley would be greater than in the eastern sections of the country.

6. The infection of the Southern and Western States would inevitably spread the disease over the whole of the Middle and Eastern States, as the Western and South-Western States are the source of the cattle traffic, and the shipments are made in railway cars, which, once infected, would become active *media* of the poison.

7. As the seeds of this disease remain latent in the system for a period varying from ten days to three and a half months, and only become manifest by their effects at the end of this time, infected cattle may be carried from ocean to ocean or from the lakes to the gulf, and remain there often for weeks in apparent health, and yet spread pestilence and destruction in the end.

8. If to avoid this danger it is proposed to quarantine all cattle passing from State to State, safety would require a quarantine of at least three months. Suppose a quarantine of this kind were to be attempted at Buffalo, New York, the regular daily shipment is five trains of 30 cars each, representing 3,000 head of cattle. Detain these for 90 days there would be accumulated 270,000 head of cattle. Any such system would speedily break down by its own unwieldiness. This estimate is far beneath the real numbers, and the number of cattle trains passing east is frequently double or treble that quoted.

9. Chronic cases of lung plague, in which a large mass of lung has become encysted, may carry this for months or even a year before all can be liquified and absorbed, and at any time during this period such cases may become actively infective by the escape of materials from this pent up virulent mass. Against this no quarantine on a large scale can guard; and as even a careful professional examination will not in all cases suffice to reveal the presence of the smaller masses, infection by animals in this condition becomes inevitable wherever a large traffic is carried on.

10. No State can be rendered secure unless all the States are cleared of the contagion.

11. Smuggling of diseased cattle from one State to another can only be prevented by a national executive sanitary administration applying to all the States in the Union.

Q 2337.

12. With different authorities in adjacent States it becomes difficult or impossible to trace infected stock smuggled from State to State; and if the second State has no sanitary administration the smuggled animals may be distributed at will and the area of infection indefinitely extended.

13. With different authorities in different States, and with different systems and measures, mistakes and losses will accrue to both State and purchaser which would be altogether obviated if the system and control were one.

14. Uniform action by one authority in all the States would remove the source of much irritation among dealers who have now to inform themselves as to the restrictions imposed in the different States.

15. It has been decided by the Supreme Court of Illinois that any State forbidding the introduction of cattle from a neighbouring State, on the ground of suspected infection, is unconstitutional. It would, therefore, appear that no State has the power to exclude the infected cattle of a neighbouring State, but must wait for their entry and kill or quarantine them on its own soil. This would require an impracticable system of quarantine, and it devolves upon the United States to give the necessary protection on the principle of controlling and regulating inter-state commerce.

16. Three of the States now infected have shown no tendency to act for the extinction of the disease, and unless the United States pass a general law for its suppression it cannot be eradicated from the country.

The subject can hardly be exaggerated in its importance, and action by the Congress of the United States should not be delayed in any attempt to pass a general law applicable to the entire country for the suppression of infectious and contagious diseases in the United States.

No. 1. The State of Ohio, one of the western states of this consular district, has had a statute on the subject since 1867, and measures are now about to be taken with a view to its rigid enforcement, I have the honour to enclose your Lordship a copy of this Act marked No. 1.

No. 2. The Philadelphia Society for the Promotion of Agriculture and the Academy of Natural Sciences have taken an interest in the question of the suppression of cattle diseases, and I have the honour to enclose your Lordship a copy of the proceedings at those institutions within the past few days, marked No. 2.

No. 3. The quarterly report of the Pennsylvania Board of Agriculture for the quarter ending December 31, 1879, contains the report of the special agent of the governor of the State on contagious pleuro-pneumonia and an interesting report by the veterinary surgeon of the board, two copies of which I have the honour to enclose your Lordship, marked No. 3.

I have, &c.
(Signed) GEORGE CRUMP.

The Right Honourable
The Marquis of Salisbury, K.G.
&c. &c. &c.

Enclosure 1 in No. 33.

STATUTE OF THE STATE OF OHIO, 1867.

Section 1. Be it enacted by the General Assembly of the State of Ohio, that it shall be unlawful for any person to sell, barter, or dispose of, or to permit to run at large, any horse, cattle, sheep, or domestic animals, which are infected with contagious or infectious disease, or have been recently exposed thereto, unless he shall first duly inform the person to whom he may sell, barter, or dispose of such horse, cattle, sheep, or other domestic animal of the same; and any person so offending shall, on conviction thereof, before any court having competent jurisdiction, be fined of any sum not less than $20 or more than $200, with costs of prosecution, or be confined in the jail of the county for not more than 30 days at the discretion of the court.

Section 2. That any person being the owner or having the charge of any horse, cattle, sheep, or other kind of stock, knowing the same to be infected with contagious or infectious disease, shall knowingly permit it to come in contact with any other persons horses or stock, without such persons knowledge or permission, shall be fined in any sum not less than $50, nor more than $500, with costs of prosecution, or be confined in the jail of the county for not less than 10 nor more than 50 days, at the discretion of the court.

Enclosure 2 in No. 33.

PROCEEDINGS of the PHILADELPHIA SOCIETY for the PROMOTION of AGRICULTURE and the ACADEMY OF NATURAL SCIENCES.—The "LUNG PLAGUE," its RAVAGES among the CATTLE, SOUTH and WEST.—The PHILADELPHIA SOCIETY to petition the GENERAL GOVERNMENT to take such ACTION as will PREVENT the TRANSPORTATION of CATTLE from INFECTED DISTRICTS.

At the annual meeting of the Philadelphia Society for the Promotion of Agriculture, held yesterday morning at the rooms of the society, Dr. Charles R. King presiding, Dr. J. W. Gadsden presented the sixth quarterly report of the Pennsylvania Board of Agriculture. He referred to pleuro-pneumonia, and stated that Mr. James Law, professor of veterinary medicine in Cornell University, had traced the disease from place to place to infected herds.

Professor Law asserts the disease is slowly spreading southward west from Alexandria, and it will be as impossible to eradicate it as from the Steppes of Russia. It would be appropriate for the agriculturists of the different States of the South and West to petition Congress to take this matter up and adopt such measures as would for ever rid our country of this most insiduous of all animal plagues. At all hazards this work ought to be done, and that speedily. It is folly, and worse, to quarrel about the means until the plague shall have passed beyond control. Action is wanted of a prompt and decisive nature by the general government or with its assistance, and those who are most deeply interested in the subject should press this upon the government until such action shall have been secured.

Dr. Gadsden requested the Agricultural Society to petition Congress through the Commissioner of Agriculture, Hon. William G. LeDuc, to adopt such measures as would rid this country of the contagious disease in cattle, known as "the lung plague," or pleuro-pneumonia.

Dr. Gadsden referred to a recent case in Lehigh County, where a herd of 30 was infected by a cow brought from Baltimore, and another case of a similar nature, within the past week, at Elm Station, on the Pennsylvania railroad. He stated there had never been a case in this country except as the result of contagion. Massachusetts stamped it out, and has not known it since 1865.

Professor Booth was confirmed in his views that the disease can be stamped out and should be. A petition to Congress on the subject could do no harm, and might result in good.

Mr. Blight suggested the passage of a resolution on the subject, and forwarding a copy of the same to Mr. Le Duc.

Mr. Burnett Landreth offered the following, which was adopted:

Whereas it is patent that the ravages of the "lung plague," or pleuro-pneumonia, can only be arrested by heroic measures, be it

Resolved, by the Philadelphia Society for the Promotion of Agriculture, that the General Government be urgently requested to take such action as will prevent the transport of cattle from infected districts in the seaboard states to the interior, which will certainly be infected unless decisive action be taken by the United States Board of Health or other proper department.

Mr. Peter B. Long presented, through Mr. George Blight, to the Society a copy of the "Freeman's Journal and Philadelphia Mercantile Advertiser," of July 3, 1822, containing an account of the exhibition of the Society, held in June of that year.

An election for officers of the society to serve the ensuing year was held, with the following result:

President.—Dr. Charles R. King.
Vice-President.—Burnett Landreth and W. Heyward Drayton.
Treasurer.—George Blight.
Recording Secretary.—Archibald R. Montgomery.
Assistant Recording Secretary.—J. E. De La Motta.
Chemist.—Professor J. B. Booth.
Librarian.—Archibald R. Montgomery.
Library Committee.—David Landreth, Archibald R. Montgomery, George Blight.
Executive Committee.—The President, Secretary, and Treasurer, also Burnett Landreth, John S. Haines, Dr. Alfred Elwyn, Dr. A. L. Kennedy, Frank A. Comly, and Joseph E. Gillingham.

ACADEMY OF NATURAL SCIENCES.—PLEURO-PNEUMONIA not caused by the PRESENCE of PARASITIC WORMS—A BLIND CAVE INSECT.

At the last meeting of the Biological and Microscopical section of the Academy, Dr. Turnbull read a paper on the peculiar round-worm or strongylus infesting the air-passages, of calves, which Dr. McCoart had recently been reported in the daily papers to have assigned as the cause of the supposed contagious disease of cattle, known as pleuro-pneumonia.

Dr. Turnbull gave a very full and satisfactory account of the parasite, tracing its life history through its various phases, some of which were supposed by eminent authorities to be passed in the intestine of the common earth-worm. From this intermediate host they were supposed to find their way to the grass and herbages eaten by the cattle, and thus be taken into their mouths, stomachs, and air-passages, causing a great amount of irritation, and consequent expectoration when they have attained their adult state, and giving rise to the disease known as parasite bronchitis, husk, or hoose.

It most frequently affects animals pasturing in low, wet, grounds; the relation between the parasite and abundance of earth-worms and its allies being evident.

Dr. Gadsden being introduced, said he was not a little surprised to read, in a report of the proceedings of the last meeting of the section, that these parasites were the cause of the disease known as pleuro-pneumonia. He thought it had been demonstrated, beyond all possibility of doubt, by some of the most distinguished veterinarians, that the disease was specific and malignant, and was spread by the infection of healthy animals, through the medium of a specific virus derived from diseased ones. Many authorities were cited by the speaker, besides cases of his own in this country and England, to prove that such was the case. If this is not the case then it is certainly to be considered a great waste of money by the State and General Governments to have appointed inspectors and established a system of quarantine over herds of cattle known to be affected, in order to prevent the spread of the disease. Not only does the anti-contagious doctrine reflect upon the wisdom of the policy of the State and General Governments, but also upon a large and intelligent class of veterinarians, such as Professors Law and Gamgee. The fact of the existence of the disease in this State, which the authorities are trying in every way to stamp out by the means already referred to, with every hope of success, interferes greatly with our export trade in live meat with England, whose House of Commons recently prohibited the importation of American cattle, which on the authority of one of our Government reports, were said to be diseased.

Dr. McCoart being present, stated that he was very sorry indeed to have been misunderstood, and said that he did not mean to imply that the filariæ were the causes of pleuro-pleumonia, as he had been reported to have said. What he meant to convey was that parasitic bronchitis or hoose no doubt was often mistaken by amateurs for real pleuro-pneumonia. In reply to a question by Dr. Gadsden, Dr. McCoart replied that he did not consider that it had been proved that the disease was contagious.

Dr. Gadsden left some specimens of the diseased and healthy lungs of cattle for microscopic examination by the members. It was remarkable that in pleuro-pneumonia but one lung was affected, the one on the other side remaining healthy. The diseased one is filled up almost to solidity with lymph, and weighs as much as fifty, whilst a healthy one weighs but three and a half pounds.

After further discussion by Drs. Seller, Turnbull, Messrs. Potts, Perot and others, the discussion was closed, the Chair considering it inexpedient to continue the committee appointed at a previous meeting.

Mr. Ryder briefly described a new scale insect, or spring-tail, from a cave in Oregon, where it had been found last summer by Professor Cope. The creature belonged to a genus common in our park, under stones, in moss, etc., known to science as Orchesella. It differed from the species found here mainly in the almost total absence of eyes, these being represented by the faintest black points. The disappearance of eyes was supposed to be due to the prolonged existence of its race in the darkness of the cave for many generations. He proposed to call the new form Orchesella cæca, in reference to its nearly blind condition.

ROUND WORM OR STRONGYLUS.

At the last meeting of the Academy of Natural Sciences, Dr. Turnbull read a paper on the peculiar round worm or strongylus infecting the air passages of calves. It had been reported that Dr. McCoart, of this city, had assigned as the cause of pleuro-pneumonia, the presence of these worms. This was shown to be erroneous. Dr. Turnbull gave a very full and satisfactory account of the parasite, tracing its life history through its various phases, some of which were supposed by eminent authorities to be passed in the intestine of the common earth-worm. From this intermediate state they were supposed to find their way to the grass and herbage eaten by the cattle, and thus be taken into the stomachs and air passages, causing a great amount of irritation, and giving rise to the disease known as parasitic brohchitis, husk, or hoose. It most frequently affects animals pasturing in low wet grounds, the relation between the parasite and its allies being evident.

Dr. Gadsden said he was not a little surprised to read, in a report of the proceedings of the last meeting, that these parasites were the cause of the disease known as pleuro-pneumonia. He thought it had been practically demonstrated beyond all possibility of a doubt by some of the most distinguised veterinarians, that the disease was specific and malignant, and was spread by the infection of healthy animals, through the medium of a specific virus derived from diseased ones. If this is not the case, then it is certainly to be considered a great waste of money by the State and General Government, to have appointed inspectors and established a system of quarantine over herds of cattle known to be affected, in order to prevent the spread of the disease. The fact of the existence of the disease in Pennsylvania, which the authorities are trying to stamp out, and with every hope of success, interferes greatly with our export trade in live meat with England, whose House of Commons recently prohibited the importation of American cattle, which on the authority of one of our Government reports were said to be diseased. The doctor exhibited specimens of diseased and healthy lungs. Generally but one lung is affected. It solidifies, presenting a marbled appearance, and is frequently found to weigh forty and even fifty pounds, while a healthy one weighs three and a half pounds.

Enclosure 3 in No. 33.

From the SIXTH QUARTERLY REPORT of the PENNSYLVANIA BOARD of AGRICULTURE for September, October, and November, 1879.

The LUNG PLAGUE (Contagious Pleuro-pneumonia), by the Special Agent of the Governor.

For several years past there has been a growing desire upon the part of the stock breeders and stock owners of the State, that, if possible, something might be done to prevent, or at least mitigate the losses they have each year experienced from the disease known as pleuro-pneumonia. At meetings of our farm clubs and granges, the subject was discussed and committees appointed to take it into consideration and report.

The immense loss which must result from the infection of the large herds of the West and South-west, was plainly pointed out. It was shown that England, with only 6,000,000 animals, had lost more than $500,000,000 by this disease since its introduction from Holland, and that, in the same ratio, the introduction of the disease among our 28,000,000 cattle, would cause a loss of $2,000,000,000 in an equal time. That in our own State, the loss would in a short time, seriously impair an important interest, and would prove eminently more fatal in the West, where all interests are more or less intimately connected with that of stock raising, and where all interests thrive or languish in sympathy with it.

Massachusetts, by prompt and vigorous action, eradicated the disease from her borders, and last year expended less than $50 for this purpose. It is true that the struggle cost her nearly $68,000, but her stock-owners well know that an immunity from the disease was cheaply purchased at this price. The disease had insidiously crept from dairy to dairy, from farm to farm, from one stock-yard to another, until four of the leading dairy counties of the eastern portion of our State were infected. In these counties the entrance of the disease into a herd was considered as tantamount to a loss of from 20 to 50 per cent., and sometimes exceeded even the latter rate. Dairies were broken up, the business abandoned, and, in many cases the surviving animals sold and scattered, thus forming centres of further contagion. All practical men admitted the presence of the disease. Our agricultural papers discussed its spread and its probable results. Our veterinary surgeons had, in a measure, become familiar with it, and most of them recognised the fact that treatment was of but little avail. With the disease a matter of comment in our daily papers, it was not at all surprising that the British Government, whose farmers had lost millions by this and similar imported diseases, and had spent immense sums in attempts to stamp out this very disease, should direct its attention to the presence of the disease here, and the possibility of the infection being conveyed by cattle imported into

English ports. The agents of the British Government, accompanied by competent veterinary surgeons, who were familiar with the disease during its ravages in England, starting from Canada, found it in all the Atlantic States, from Massachusetts to Carolina, and, reporting its presence to the home Government, a quarantine was ordered on all American cattle. They failed to recognise the fact that the cattle thus imported did not come from infected districts, and that they did not come in contact with infected cattle; but, finding *supposed* cases of contagious lung plague (pleuro-pneumonia) in the cargo of the "Ontario," at once issued the edict which practically stopped the importation of live American cattle, at least for a time. It is now rendered very probable, if not almost certain, that the stock in the "Ontario" were only affected with common or sporadic pneumonia, caused by injuries sustained by the vessel during a severe storm, and the consequent drenching with cold sea water, which the cattle afterwards sustained; yet this furnished the needed excuse, and had not this been found, another would have soon taken its place. Whether this action of the British Government was due to a desire to protect British cattle or arose from a fear of competition, rather than contagion, it is not for us to discuss, but such are the facts of the case.

A number of our best veterinary surgeons and most enterprising cattle breeders and dealers had, for a long time, been anxious that our national Government should quarantine *all* imported cattle; and, if possible, by this inexpensive precaution, prevent the introduction among our stock the much-feared rinder-pest, foot-and-mouth disease, or the many other contagious diseases to which the horned stock of Europe are liable; but their advice and request has not met with appreciative action on the part of the general Government, until after the passage of such an act would assume the appearance of retaliation, and, of course, came too late to have any effect upon the disease which we have under consideration.

By legislative action, the State of Massachusetts had, at least four years before, not only admitted the existence of the disease, but had, also, by legislation, decreed an attempt to eradicate it by what has been styled the "Stamping out process;" and, after a few years of active work, the sought-for result has been attained, and the State, except from cases brought in from neighbouring States, has been pronounced clear from the disease. Connecticut, New York, and New Jersey, by similar legislative enactments, had also recognized the disease in an official way, and had made appropriations and passed laws necessary for its attempted eradication, on a plan similar to that adopted by Massachusetts, and had asked the co-operation of Pennsylvania in a common and concerted attempt to accomplish this purpose, and, if possible, prevent the further progress of the disease westward.

At this stage of the proceedings, the worst injury which could be inflicted upon our export trade in live stock had its effect, and the shipments in live cattle had practically stopped on account of quarantine regulations. The farmers of our State were aroused to the imminent danger resulting from the permanent location of the disease in this country. Several States, for mutual help and protection, had joined in an endeavour to stay the pest, and the assistance of our State was asked. Our past losses were estimated at from $500,000 to $750,000, and good judges placed the amount even higher, and it was impossible to estimate the loss, if nothing was done to prevent its further spread.

Legislation and its Results.

Recognizing all these facts, and being in possession of many more which might be enumerated, a meeting of dairymen of Delaware, Montgomery, and adjoining counties held in Philadelphia, early in March, appointed a committee to wait upon the Secretary of the Board of Agriculture, and urge the importance of legislative action. The veterinary surgeon of the Board, with this committee, visited herds supposed to be infected. Veterinary surgeons who had had years of experience with the disease in England, were called in; post-mortem examinations were made, and the existence of the disease established beyond a reasonable doubt.

The Legislature being then in session, the Secretary of the Board of Agriculture laid all the evidence before the joint Committee of Agriculture of both Houses, consisting, on the part of the Senate, of Senators St. Clair, Seamans, Kauffman, Roberts, Craig, Ross, and Beidelman, and on the part of the House of Representatives, of Messrs. Kincaid, Matlack, Greenawalt, Magill, Ackerly, Miller, Stephens, Hill, McConnel, Landis, Walker, Burton, Eberly, Fullerton, Lowing, Nicholls, Bowman, Hallowell, Schaeffer, Davis, Fabel, Gammel, Newbaker, Eldred, and Morris.

After discussion, this committee decided that it would be proper that the State should adopt a line of precautionary and preventive action not only for the benefit of its own citizens, but also out of respect to the action of adjoining States, and a sub-committee was appointed to consult with the Governor, and if deemed expedient, prepare a draft of an act providing for the desired action. After consultation, the following resolution was offered by Senator Kauffman, and adopted by both branches of the Legislature:

" Whereas, the States of New York and New Jersey, by recently enacted laws to prevent the dissemination among live stock of the disease known as pleuro-pneumonia, now invite this State, by a concert of action, to assist them to eradicate this contagion; therefore,

" Resolved by the Senate (if the House of Representatives concur), that the Governor be and is hereby authorised to take such preliminary action as may be necessary to prevent its further spread."

This resolution was approved by the Governor, March 27, 1879.

At the same time the draft of the Act, as adopted by the committee, was introduced by Senator Kauffmann, and after amendment, passed both branches, and was approved by the Governor, May 1, 1879:

AN ACT to prevent the Spread of Contagious or Infectious Pleuro-pneumonia among the Cattle in this State.

Section 1. Be it enacted, &c., That whenever it shall be brought to the notice of the Governor of this State that the disease known as contagious or infectious pleuro-pneumonia exist among the cattle in any of the counties in this State, it shall be his duty to take measures to promptly suppress the disease and prevent it from spreading.

Section 2. That for such purpose, the Governor shall have power and he is hereby authorised to issue his proclamation, stating that the said infectious or contagious disease exists in any county or counties of the State, and warning all persons to seclude all animals in their possession that are affected with such disease or have been exposed to the infection or contagion thereof, and ordering all persons to take such precautions against the spreading of such disease as the nature thereof may in his judgment render necessary or expedient; to order that any premises, farm, or farms where such disease exists or has existed to be put in quarantine, so that no domestic animal be removed from said places so quarantined, and to prescribe such regulations as he may judge necessary or expedient to prevent infection or contagion being communicated in any way from the places so quarantined; to call upon all sheriffs and deputy-sheriffs to carry out and enforce the provisions of such proclamations, orders, and regulations, and it shall be the duty of all the sheriffs and deputy-sheriffs to obey and observe all orders and instructions which they may receive from the Governor in the premises; to employ such and so many medical and veterinary practitioners and such other persons as he may from time to time deem necessary to assist him in performing his duty as set forth in the first section of this act, and to fix their compensation; to order all or any animals coming into the State to be detained at any place or places for the purpose of inspection and examination; to prescribe regulations for the destruction of animals affected with the said infectious or contagious disease, and for the proper disposition of their hides and carcasses, and of all objects which might convey infection or contagion (provided that no animal shall be destroyed unless first examined by a medical or veterinary practitioner in the employ of the Governor as aforesaid); to prescribe regulations for the disinfection of all premises, buildings, and railway cars, and of objects from and to which infection or contagion may take place or be conveyed; to alter and modify, from time to time as he may deem expedient, the terms of all such proclamations, orders, and regulations, and to cancel or withdraw the same at any time.

Section 4. That all the necessary expenses incurred under the direction or by authority of the Governor in carrying out the provisions of this Act, shall be paid by the treasurer upon the warrant of the auditor general, on being certified as correct by the Governor; provided that, animals coming from a neighbouring State that have passed a veterinary examination in said State, and have been quarantined and discharged, shall not be subject to the provisions of this Act.

During the passage of this Act the existence of the disease in the State had been denied. Hence, immediately after its approval, his Excellency Governor Hoyt appointed a commission to " examine and determine whether infectious or contagious pleuro-pneumonia exists among cattle in any county or counties of this commonwealth, and report the same to the Governor without unnecessary delay." This commission consists of Hon. Samuel Butler and Hon. H. C. Greenawalt, on the part of the Legislature; Thomas J. Edge and C. B. Michener, on the part of the Board of Agriculture; Hon. John C. Morris and George Blight, on the part of the Pennsylvania Agricultural Society; and George S. Garrett, on the part of the dairymen of Philadelphia and vicinity. At the first meeting of this commission Hon. John C. Morris was elected president, and Thomas J. Edge, secretary.

At a meeting held in Philadelphia May 16, a large number of practical dairymen and veterinary surgeons were examined, and their evidence taken down by a stenographic reporter. As a result of this meeting Messrs. Morris, Butler, and Greenawalt were appointed a committee to report to Governor Hoyt, on behalf of the commission, that the disease did exist in at least two counties in the State, and that the decision of the commission was unanimous.

Under authority of the Act before quoted, and based upon the report of the commission, his Excellency Governor Hoyt appointed a special agent to take charge of the matter, to whom he issued the following commission:

"It having been ascertained that an infectious and contagious disease of neat cattle, known as pleuro-pneumonia, has been brought into and exists in certain counties of this State, I hereby appoint you as my assistant to carry out the provisions of the Acts of 1866 and 1879, for the prevention of the spread of this disease. As such assistant you are hereby authorised:

"To prohibit the movement of cattle within the infected districts, except on license from yourself, after skilled veterinary examination, under your direction.

"To order all owners of cattle, their agents, employés, or servants, and all veterinary surgeons to report forthwith to you all cases of disease by them suspected to be contagious; and when such notification is received, you are directed to have the case examined, and to cause such animals as are found to be infected with said disease to be quarantined, as also all cattle which have been exposed to the infection or contagion of said disease, or are located in an infected district; but you may, in your discretion, permit such animals to be slaughtered on the premises, and the carcases to be disposed of as meat, if upon examination they shall be found fit for such use.

"You may prohibit and prevent all persons not employed in the care of cattle therein, kept from entering any infected premises. You may likewise prevent all persons so employed in the care of the animals, from going into stables, yards, or premises where cattle are kept, other than those in which they are employed. You may cause all clothing of persons engaged in the care, slaughtering, or rendering of diseased or exposed animals, or in any employment which brings them in contact with such diseased animals, to be disinfected before they leave the premises where such animals are kept. You may prevent the manure, forage, and litter, upon infected premises from being removed therefrom; and you may cause such disposition to be made thereof as will, in your judgment, best prevent the spread of the disease. You may cause the buildings, yards, and premises, in which the disease exists, or has existed, to be thoroughly disinfected.

"You are further directed, whenever the slaughter of diseased animals is found necessary, to certify the value of the animal or animals so slaughtered, at the time of slaughter, taking into account their condition and circumstances, and to deliver to their owner or owners, when requested, a duplicate of such certificate. Whenever any owner of such cattle, or his agent or servant, has wilfully or knowingly withheld, or allowed to be withheld, notice of the existence of said disease upon his premises, or among his cattle, you will not make such certificate.

"You are also directed to take such measures as you may deem necessary to disinfect all cars or vehicles or movable articles by which contagion is likely to be transmitted. You will also take such measures as shall insure the registry of cattle introduced into any premises on which said disease has existed, and to keep such cattle under supervision for a period of three months after the removal of the diseased animal and the subsequent disinfection of said premises.

"You are further authorised and empowered to incur such expenses in carrying out the provisions of the foregoing orders as may, in your judgment, appear necessary, and see to it that all bills for such expenses be transmitted to this department only through yourself, after you have approved the same in writing.

(Signed)   HENRY M. HOYT,
    Governor.

"Attest: J. R. McAffee,
  Deputy Secretary of the Commonwealth."

The agent of the Governor has issued the following notice:—

To all owners of cattle, their agents, servants, or employés; to all common carriers by land or water; to all veterinary surgeons, and to all others whom it may concern.

His Excellency Governor Hoyt having decided to co-operate with the executive officers of the States of Massachusetts, Connecticut, New York, and New Jersey, in a united effort to eradicate the disease known as pleuro-pneumonia from the herds of the State, it becomes my duty, under the foregoing commission, to request that you will promptly report to me all cases among neat cattle by you suspected to be contagious or infectious. Without your co-operation and assistance this attempt can only result in partial success; with it the result can scarcely be doubtful, and the work thus far accomplished gives us assurance of good results.

His Excellency is anxious that all owners of cattle, and others interested, should be fully impressed with the belief that this commission, as well as the laws of 1866 and 1879, for the prevention of the spread of the disease, are in their interest as well as that of the State. It is also the wish of his Excellency, that while the provisions of these laws are fully enforced and made most effective, and their purposes promptly and fully accomplished, it shall, at the same time, be so managed as to cause the least possible inconvenience and injury to all concerned, and with a minimum of expenditure to the State.

I would particularly call your attention to the language used by his Excellency in relation to the line of action to be pursued when interested parties have concealed the existence of the disease in their herds. This provision is very important, not only to the stock owner, but also to the State, for while the concealment of the existence of the disease will result in pecuniary loss to the owner of the stock, it at the same time greatly increases the danger of infection, and the subsequent expense to the State. With your active co-operation in this respect we may hope for the prompt suppression of a disease which, while it has already caused a great loss to our stock owners will, should it become established in our western States, inflict an incalculable and lasting injury to the stock-raising interests of the whole nation. So far as known, all infected herds in this State have been quarantined, and all diseased animals promptly isolated or killed. In the future, as in the past, it will be our duty to cause as little injury and inconvenience to the owners of stock as is consistent with our duties to the State, and to carry out to the full letter the directions of his Excellency relative to the valuation of all stock condemned and killed.

All reports of supposed infection should be made direct to the office, and all interested are requested to accompany the report with a correct and full account of the location of the herd, and the symptoms, in order that all unnecessary expense to the State may be avoided. No special line of action has yet been marked out for application to cattle in motion from one portion of the State to another, or to those in transit to other States, but it will be the duty of those in charge to cause the least possible inconvenience consistent with the best interests of the State.

Action of the State Authorities.

Under the commission before quoted the agent of the Governor has (up to November 1) quarantined 27 herds, including four hundred and eight animals liable to infection, and distributed in the following counties:—Adams, 1; Lancaster, 4; York, 1; Bucks, 1; Delaware, 4; Montgomery, 5; and Chester, 11. Of these herd 8 (1 in York, 3 in Montgomery, and 4 in Chester) have since been released from the quarantine, and pronounced safe from another outbreak, except from a fresh infection from outside sources.

As soon as the supposed existence of the disease is reported, each animal in the herd is inspected by a veterinary surgeon in the employ of the State, and if the disease is found to exist, is promptly quarantined to prevent its spread to adjoining herds, in order, and if possible, to prevent further contagion in the same herd, all diseased animals are appraised and killed.

The individual history of these herds may be briefly given as follows:—

No. 1. In York county, infected by steers bought in Baltimore market. Six head were either lost by death previous to quarantine or were killed for the purpose of stopping the disease. The whole herd were more or less affected, though a number had a very light attack, and when released from quarantine, September 4, were as well as they probably ever will be. A rigid quarantine, which was very much assisted by the losal surroundings, and the prompt support of neighbouring stock owners, prevented the disease from infecting other stock, and the killing of diseased animals, and the use of disinfectants prevented further loss.

No. 2. Containing 20 cows, 2 bulls, and 10 calves, was quarantined June 12. Previous to quarantine four head had died, and after the enforcement of the quarantine 14 head were killed. With one possible exception all the animals were affected, and a number of them are now in a condition in which they are worse than useless to the owner. In this case the evidence is strongly in favour of the theory that the owner conveyed the

Q 2337.

disease to his herd by assisting in the care of another infected dairy. No spread of the disease to adjoining farms; but it is quite probable that the disease was carried from this herd to herd No. 8 in the clothing or on the person of the owner, who administered medicine to both herds. This herd has furnished an illustration of the disease in one of its worst forms, but is now believed to be clear, but not beyond the danger of infecting other stock.

No. 3. In Delaware county, contained 50 head of stock, and previous to quarantine a number had died. The probability is that the disease was introduced by purchase. After passing into the charge of the State authorities, 11 of the herd were killed. This herd, with Nos. 2 and 7, furnish by far the most stubborn cases we have yet met with. In all three cases every animal had been repeatedly exposed to infection before the existence of the disease was reported, and we may here state that in other herds when the first sick animals were promptly isolated and the case reported the loss by death has been very slight. By allowing the sick and well to run together all are infected before the assistance of the State is asked.

Nos. 4, 5, and 5½. Adjoin one another, and the farms are all traversed by the same small stream. The disease seems to have originated on the upper farm, where the first sick animal died in the stream, and was buried close to its banks. In No. 4 one animal died, and one was killed; and in No. 5 the first one was promptly killed. In both cases the importance of immediate isolation was understood and put in practice. Nos. 4 and 5 have been released from quarantine, but No. 5½ is still infected. Whether, in these cases the stream was the vehicle of contagion or not we cannot say, but the almost simultaneous outbreak on the three farms can be accounted for on no other hypothesis.

No. 6. Had lost 11 head previous to being reported and quarantined. With one doubtful exception, every animal had shown more or less of the effects of the disease, and its owner fully appreciated its contagious nature. Has been released from quarantine.

No. 7. In Lancaster county, was composed of 42 animals, and when reported had been thoroughly infected by two sick animals running with the herd. In this herd seven animals were killed in one day, and seven placed under quarantine; 15 have been killed, and to all appearance the disease has been checked. The infection, no doubt, came from an adjoining herd, which in turn had been infected by stock from New York.

No. 8. Is supposed to have been infected by the owner of No. 2 administering medicine to the animals after attending to his own. Seven head have been lost in this herd, and the others are not clear of the danger.

In No. 9, containing 31 head, the disease seems to have been checked by the prompt isolation and killing of one animal, and has since been released from quarantine.

Nos. 10, 11, and 12. Are small herds, in two of which every animal exhibited symptoms of the disease, but by rigid care on the part of the owners by isolating, and the prompt death of infected animals, the loss has been small.

Nos. 13 to 20 inclusive. Are herds which have been recently reported and quarantined, and, thus far, the losses in them have been slight. By the prompt action of the veterinary surgeon, assisted by care and co-operation on the part of the owner, it is hoped that most, if not all of them, have past the worst point, and that some of them may be released from quarantine as soon as the proper time has elapsed.

No. 21. Was infected by six cows purchased in the Philadelphia market, and showed itself 10 days after the purchase; of the six five have died or been killed, and others are affected. The purchased cows have been traced to the Philadelphia droveyard, but here all further clue to the origin of the disease was lost.

No. 22. In Montgomery county was quarantined October 24, and was infected by a cow purchased from a drover; at the time of purchase she was coughing, and when examined by our surgeon in a week afterwards she was too far gone that the owner was willing to have her killed as worthless and without value.

No. 23. Was infected by contact with the animals in herd No. 16 previous to quarantine; at the request of the owner, who had insured complete isolation, they are being treated by our surgeon. In this case the fumes of burning sulphur seems to have been effective in preventing further trouble, but all the herd were or are more or less affected.

No. 24. Containing 33 head were, no doubt, infected by contact with herd No. 7, as, by accident, they were in the inclosure containing the former herd for a short time.

No. 25. Was allowed by its owner to graze alongside of No. 7 with no separation other than that afforded by a creek and common fence. Before the infection was reported, most of the steers (fat) were sent to market, but one left on the farm has shown all symptoms of the disease.

In addition to the care of stock already in the State, the agent of the Governor has had control of all the stock brought into the State from Europe, and not quarantined by the national authorities or those of other States. The United States Government imposes a quarantine of 90 days upon all such cattle, but in such States as have quarantine regulations already established, they are surrendered to the State authorities for inspection and quarantine. Under these rules now in force in this State, these cattle must present a certificate of clearness from any contagious disease at the point of shipment in Europe, where they are inspected by a government surgeon, must be inspected on their arrival in the State by a veterinary surgeon in the employ of the State and under the control of the Governor's agent, must be quarantine closely at the expense of the importer, under the supervision of the State Surgeon, and must be again examined at the close of the quarantine, and if found clear, are granted a certificate which will authorise the removal to any point in the State. In enforcing this quarantine, care is taken to consult the interests of the importers so far as it is consistent with the interests of the State, and the step is made necessary also only to protect our stock from infection by pleuro-pneumonia, but not with hoof-and-mouth disease, rinderpest, and other contagious diseases.

Name, History, Nature, and Symptoms of the Disease.

It is unfortunate that the common name, pleuro-pneumonia, should have been selected to designate this disease. In the debates in the Legislature during the passage of the Act, in the daily correspondence of the Board of Agriculture, in the agricultural and daily papers, and even in some scientific journals, this name has caused much confusion and needless dispute. By many it has been confounded with common or sparodic pneumonia, which is not contagious, and which may in all cases be traced to exposure, neglect, or to a violation of some law of nature. This common pneumonia will *originate* in a locality, while the lung plague, called pleuro-pneumonia, has never yet been proven to thus originate in any locality in this country; but if its cause can be traced at all it is found to have proceeded from contagion conveyed by another animal, or from the excretion from the bowels, kidneys, skin, or lungs of another animal. No amount of neglect or bad treatment will develope this disease, and we think it may be assured that no bad treatment or abuse will develope a contagious disease of this kind. It is now too late to hope to effect a change of name, but many have been suggested as not only more appropriate, but also more satisfactory to the general reader and average stock breeder. Professor Hertwig, of Berlin, gave it the name of *Lungenseuche*, Haller called it *Viehseuch*, Cathbert styled in *Peri-pneumonia*, in Italy it is known as *Pulmonæ de bovini*. In fact, in different countries, and at different times, it has had names of all lengths and styles, from the "Murie" of Brougelat to the "*Peri-pneumonia exsudation enzootica et contajiosa*" of Gieleu. Throwing aside all technicalities and form, we think that the plain name, "Contagious lung plague" will best suit the case.

When, where, or how this disease first originated (for it must have had an origin) no one can say with any degree of certainty. Delafond quotes Aristotle as writing of his time, that "The cattle which live in herds are subject to a malady, during which the "breathing becomes hot and frequent. The ears droop and they cannot eat. They die "rapidly, and on opening them the lungs are found spoiled." The history of the disease in this country may be thus briefly summed up.

The first notice of its existence was in a cow imported from Germany in 1843, and landed in Brooklyn, and it has been claimed that since then this locality has never been free from the disease, and now forms the main centre of contagion with which the New York authorities have to contend. In 1847, it was brought from England into New Jersey, and in 1850 was again brought into New York by a cow inported from Europe. It was prevalent in Camden and Gloucester Counties, New Jersey, in 1859, and in 1860, broke out among the dairies near Philadelphia. In 1861 it broke out in Delaware County. The Philadelphia cow market served as a centre, and the contagion gradually spread to surrounding counties, and soon Baltimore and the surrounding district was affected, and the disease now threatens to obtain a foothold in southern counties of our State from this centre of contagion.

The dairyman who have lost from 50 to 75 per cent. of his stock, has very little sympathy with any one who will claim that the disease is not contagious. Finding a newly purchased animal sick with an, to him, unknown complaint, which defies all treatment, and soons runs its course in the first animal, and sooner or later attacking every animal of the herd, in some cases proving fatal in more than 50 per cent. of the attacks, and leaving those which *apparently* recover, in many cases, in a condition worse than useless, he discards all fine theories, all fine-drawn arguments of medical men, and assumes that he has to deal with a contagious disease over which he can exercise little or no control.

When, as has been the case in this State since the passage of the law of last winter, he sees seven of his animals all at the same time affected with the same symptoms, each passing through exactly the same stages of disease, and when killed and opened, each presenting exactly the same post-mortem evidence of the same disease, his common sense teaches him that the sick contaminate the well, and that the disease will, in this way, not only spread from animal to animal, but also from herd to herd until the whole country will be infected.

The fact that inoculation will produce all the symptoms of the disease, and when a country becomes thoroughly impregnated with the disease is a last resort, is perhaps sufficient proof of the contagious nature of the disease, but as further proof, we quote as follows from our best authorities on the subject of this and other diseases:

Prof. Williams, of Edinburgh, in "The Principles and Practice of Veterinary Medicine," page 139, when treating of pleuro-pneumonia as contagious, says it is "A contagious "febrile disease peculiar to horned cattle having an incubative period of from two to "three weeks to as many months, at the end of which local complications arise in the "form of extensive inflammatory exudations within the substance of the lungs and upon "the surface of the pleura, finally resulting in consolidation of the pleural surfaces."

In his "Farmer's Veterinary Adviser," Prof. Law, in treating of this disease, says, (page 14–15), it is—

"A specific contagious fever of cattle, with extensive exudations into the chest and lungs. The period of latency of the poison in the system is from four to six weeks, and in exceptional cases perhaps two or three months, or as short as 10 days."

In his "Manual of Veterinary and Sanitary Science and Police," Fleming says (Vol. I., page 408): "This pleuro-pneumonia of cattle is a specific and contagious disease "peculiar to bovine animals, and of a sub-acute or chronic character. It usually appears "as an epizootic or enzootic malady, and in the subtility of its contagion, its general "diffusion, and the great fatality attending it, it is a most serious scourge. In every "country in which it has appeared it has caused an immense destruction."

In his work on "The Diseases of Live Stock," Dr. Tellor styles pleuro-pneumonia "A contagious fever of cattle, accompanied by great prostration, together with local "inflammation, and other diseased changes in the lungs and their envelops. This is no "doubt a specific blood poison."

In his "Four Bovine Scourges," Prof. Walley, of Edinburgh, says: "Zymotic "pleuro-pneumonia is an insidious exudative zymotic disease, due to a specific poison "or ferment, peculiar to the ox, and having its local manifestation concentrated in the "lungs and pleuro. No age, breed, or class, neither sex of bovine species enjoy "immunity from the effects of the virus of this disease. Zymotic pleuro-pneumonia has "a well-defined, though extremely uncertain incubatory stage, and it is alike contagious "(by actual cohabitation) and infectious."

In his report to the National Government (illustrated edition, page 29), Prof. Gamgee, says: "Not only have theories in relation to the cause or combination of causes which "may lead to the development of pleuro-pneumonia been unsatisfactory, but opportunities "are constantly presenting themselves to test the fact that privations, over-crowding, "impure food and water, &c., singly or combined, may help, but never induce the "disease which presents the characteristics of the one referred to in this report. The "malady may be produced at will, by placing an animal suffering from it among healthy "ones, and by direct inoculation. These are the only methods by which it is propa-"gated."

In his official report, Hon. W. C. Le Duc, National Commissioner of Agriculture, states that "Pleuro-pneumonia is a malignant contagious fever, to which, as far as "known, cattle only are only liable, and in them is accompanied by inflammation and "other diseased conditions of the lungs and their membranes, together with great "prostration of the entire system. It proceeds from a poisoned condition of the blood. "How, when, or where this poison was first generated it is impossible to tell. Nor is it "less difficult to determine its specific nature. So far as reliable information has yet "reached, it is never generated spontaneously, but depends entirely on the introduction "of a virus or contagion into the system of a healthy animal. A single animal so "infected infects the herd; the herd, sub-divided and scattered, infects other herds, "until in time large areas of country have been visited and devastated by the fearful "scourge."

69

Symptoms.

In its earlier stages it is very difficult to detect this desease, but in all cases where animals have been recently purchased, or where the affection is plainly one of the lungs, it is safest to assume that it is the so-called pleuro-pneumonia, and at once isolate the animal. If it is the disease it will soon make itself known by its after symptoms; if it is not, no harm is done byond the small amount of additional trouble caused by the isolation.

In its incubatory or first stage the disease is not accompanied by that intense inflammation which afterwards is manifest; yet there is in all cases a slight increase in the temperature, as shown by a thermometer inserted in the rectum. This latter test alone will not prove satisfactory, because a rise in temperature may proceed from other diseases and other causes than pleuro-pneumonia, and as a rule, our surgeons place little reliance upon this test, except when, in addition to other symptoms of a more decided nature, it may be taken as cumulative evidence. While owing to peculiarities in constitution, different animals are affected (in the primary stages) to different degrees and in different ways, we merely take the following as covering a large majority of cases.

In all cases there is more or less shivering, which, in many cases being slight, may pass unnoticed, or which may result from any other cause producing fever. In milking cows, one of the primary results of infection is often an increase in the amount of milk, which naturally results from the unusual excitement of the nervous system, but in a very short time this passes off, and instead of giving a large pail full, as at the previous milking, the amount will often quickly fall off to less than one quart. The animal shows an evident disinclination to associate with the others, and is usually to be found in a fence corner or corner of the yard, by itself. If the herd are accustomed (as is the case with milk cows) to come up to the buildings at certain hours, the infected animal will usually linger behind the others, or will refuse to come in at all. In such cases, if a ditch is to be crossed, it will usually be found upon the bank furthest from the building. The pulse is much increased and the respiration irregular and much disturbed. The animal stands with its back arched, and on applying the ear closely on the diseased side, an unusual and abnormal sound may be detected, similar to that caused by the friction of two thin pieces of dry paper or partially dried hide.

As the disease progresses, the surface of the body and the extremities become cold; the mucous membrane at the external orifices of the body becomes hot, and indicative of the inflammation within; the bowels in a majority of cases become constipated, but in some cases which have come under our notice the reverse has been the case; the skin becomes dry, the coat stares, shivering fits set in, the breathing becomes more hurried, and the pulse reaches 85 to 90 per minute, and an increased harshness or grating is heard in the diseased lung and bronchial tubes. A peculiar dry and husky cough sets in which is heard in no other disease, and which, having once been heard, although it cannot be described, is at once recognised by the surgeons or by the stock-owner who has been so unfortunate as to have the disease in his herd. In the concluding stages all these symptoms are very much intensified; the cough becomes more frequent, and from its increased intensity and the weakened condition of the animal, evidently is more painful, and is usually accompanied by a peculiar grunt or moan, indicative of intense pain. If not so before the bowels become constipated, the skin is more tightly drawn over the protuberances of the body, flesh is lost rapidly, much more so than can be accounted for by the mere abstinence from food; the pulse becomes very irregular, and the animal seeks release from the pain and difficulty of breathing by standing with its elbows thrown out from the chest, and intense pain is shown by a pressure on either side of the spine just back of the shoulders. In the later stages of the disease there is usually a peculiar twitching of the nostrils and corners of the mouth, the exhaled breath is very offensive, and is plainly indicative of the corruption which exists within.

The veterinary surgeon of the Board of Agriculture gives the following summary of the physical symptoms which, after a very little practice, has enabled those who have the disease in their herds, *by a daily examination*, to select the infected animals and at once isolate them, and thus save much loss to themselves and expense to the State:

" By placing your ear at the bottom of the neck, a loud rushing sound of air is heard in the trachæ and bronchial tubes. The same sounds are heard at the top and sides of the chest, just behind the shoulder blade. Below and back of these parts no sound at all is heard, showing that the lungs are consolidated by the fibrous exudations which are being constantly thrown out. At the commencement of an attack, we can often notice what is called the 'friction sound,' from the rubbing together of the thickened and rough membranes during respiration. Should one lung only be affected, the respiratory murmur in the healthy lung is much increased, in consequence of its having to perform double duty. When both lungs are diseased, we expect peculiar effects and sounds, according to the intensity and extent of the lesions. There is increased resonance on percussing the healthy lung, while over the diseased part, a dull, heavy sound is elicited."

In all cases, a post-mortem examination should be made which will indicate some or all of the following conditions, as given by the surgeon of the Board on Agriculture :—

"On exposing the thorac viscera, one of the first indications of epizootic pleuro-pneumonia is the escape of large quantities of fluid from the cavity. This fluid mostly contains large patches of yellow, plastic, or coaguable lymph floating about in it. As a result of the inflammation which has been going on, we find that this plastic lymph has fastened the lungs to the ribs, and formed what we know as 'false membranes,' or 'adventitious tissue.' These false membranes are sometimes fastened to the diaphragm and heart, as wells as the sides of the chest. The lungs are found to be exceedingly heavy, often weighing from fifty to seventy-five, and even one hundred pounds, sink in water, and instead of the bright salmon colour of health we observe a dirty gray colour, mottled, and having the appearance of marble. The surfaces are rough and thickened, and the lung substance hard and firm. The bronchial tubes are frequently found entirely blocked up with fibrinous deposits, thus shutting off the contact of air with the blood, and producing death by suffocation.

This exclusion of the atmospheric air from the lungs accounts for the dark purplish colour of the transuded blood corpuscles, and fibrinous exudations. In some of the more advanced cases, abscesses are found in the substance of the lungs, which either discharge through the bronchial tubes undergo degeneration (the *amyloid* most frequently), or else the discharge takes place within the chest, which give rise to the *amphoric rale*. All the other organs of the body are (as a rule) found to be in a state of health."

Conclusion.

In our dealings with the disease under the immediate direction of the Government, we find many points upon which scientists differ, and which it would be impolitic for a layman like ourselves to endeavour to settle; but of one point we feel certain, and in which we have the indorsement of *every* practical man who has had the disease among his stock, and this is the contagious and dangerous nature of the disease. Whether the disease can only be conveyed from animal to animal by actual contact, or whether it can or cannot be conveyed in the clothing, by the excretion, breath, or animals of another tribe; whether the disease is of ancient or of comparatively recent origin; whether it can be carried from herd to herd by a stream of water; whether it can be intensified in its ravages by bad ventilation or bad treatment; whether a complete separation of a certain specified number of feet of space will or will not prevent infection; whether in its first stages it is or is not contagious; whether it will or will not affect sheep, are all questions for scientists to determine, and which all are lost sight of in the one great question, in the solution of which we are engaged—can the disease be eradicated by prompt and rigid action in the manner proposed? If so, all these questions can be solved in the future; if not then the future of our stockbreeders is indeed precarious. In defense of the proprietory of the action of the joint committne of the Legislature, and of the Legislature itself, as given in the foregoing pages, we have nothing to say, except that the end in view justifies the means. If by the expenditure of a few thousand dollars by the State, we can save hundreds of thousands to her stock breeders and stock owners, and as many millions to the country at large, then we think no one will complain. If the result in New York, New Jersey, and Pennsylvania shall demonstrate that this cannot be done, we may still point with pride to the fact that this action has saved more thousands than it has cost hundreds; has demonstrated to other States that when Pennsylvania is appealed to for co-operation in a good cause, she is not slow to respond; and that when so important an interest is in danger, the State is not slow in her attempt to extend a helping hand.

No. 34.

LETTER from the BRITISH CONSUL-GENERAL at NEW YORK to the MARQUIS OF SALISBURY.

My Lord, British Consulate General, New York, February 4, 1880.

I HAVE the honour to report to your Lordship that the sanitary condition of cattle in this consular district is practically the same as was mentioned in my Despatch (Consular No. 6) of the 5th ultimo on the subject.

I have, &c.

Her Majesty's Principal Secretary of State (Signed) E. M. ARCHIBALD.
for Foreign Affairs, London.

No. 35.

LETTER from FOREIGN OFFICE to the CLERK OF THE COUNCIL.

Sir, Foreign Office, February 20, 1880.

WITH reference to the letter addressed to you from this Department on the 25th of February 1879, on the subject of a circular issued by the United States Secretary of the Treasury ordering the inspection of live cattle shipped from United States ports and the issue of a certificate that they are free from contagious and infectious diseases, I am directed by the Marquis of Salisbury to transmit to you, to be laid before the Lords of Her Majesty's Privy Council, the accompanying Despatch from Her Majesty's Minister at Washington, inclosing a copy of a note from Mr. Evarts, in which he asks for early information as to whether Her Majesty's Government is willing to make such a modification of the regulations upon the subject as would recognize certificates issued by the Customs authorities of the United States, under the above-mentioned circular as sufficient to exempt cattle inspected under its provisions from slaughter upon being landed; and I am to request that you will move their Lordships to inform Lord Salisbury what answer should be returned to Mr. Evarts on this subject.

Nos. 1 and 2.
No. 3.

I am also to request that the enclosed papers may be returned with your reply.

I am, &c.

The Clerk of the Council, (Signed) JULIAN PAUNCEFOTE.
Veterinary Department.

Enclosure 1 in No. 35.

Letter from Sir E. Thornton to the Marquis of Salisbury.

My Lord, Washington, January 26, 1880.

IN my Despatch No. 13 Consular of the 10th of February 1879, I had the honour to enclose copies of a circular issued by the United States Secretary of the Treasury, ordering the inspection of live cattle shipped from United States ports and the issue of a certificate that they are free from contagious and infectious diseases.

In a note of the 23rd instant, which I have received from Mr. Evarts, and copy of which is enclosed, he refers to this circular, and asks for early information as to whether Her Majesty's Government is willing to make such a modification of the regulations upon the subject as would recognize certificates issued by the Customs authorities of the United States, under the above-mentioned circular, as sufficient to exempt cattle inspected under its provisions from slaughter upon being landed.

A copy of my reply is also enclosed. In it I have stated that I would forward to your Lordship a copy of his note by the earliest opportunity; but I thought it my duty at the same time to point out to him that pleuro-pneumonia exists amongst cattle in many parts of the United States, and particularly in the immediate neighbourhood of ports from which cattle are being shipped to England. This is true with regard to Philadelphia and New York. And I observed that whilst the inspection is actually being carried on and the cattle are pronounced sound, they may by contagion be taking the disease which may not develope itself for some weeks later.

I at the same time expressed my hope that such laws would be passed by Congress as would tend to obliterate the disease in this country.

I also called upon Mr. Johnston, a senator from Virginia, who is chairman of the Committee on Agriculture, and represented to him in the most earnest manner of how much importance it was that stringent and uniform measures should be taken throughout the United States for eradicating the disease, and he entirely agreed with me that this could only be done by a thorough inspection, by destroying all such cattle as were found to be diseased, and by indemnifying their owners. He informed me that it was the intention of his Committee to submit to the Senate a Bill which would have this object in view, and making the necessary appropriation for carrying it out. I have spoken to some other senators in the same sense, and I am glad to see that people are awakening to the importance of preventing the great cattle trade which is growing up between the United States and Great Britain, as well as other European countries, from being prejudiced by the well-founded apprehension that the imported cattle may be infected with pleuro-pneumonia.

I have, &c.

The Marquis of Salisbury, K.G.,   (Signed)   EDWD. THORNTON.
&c.   &c.   &c.

Enclosure 2 in No. 35.

LETTER from MR. EVARTS to SIR E. THORNTON.

SIR,   Department of State, Washington, January 23, 1880.

REFERRING to previous correspondence, and particularly to my note to you of the 6th of February last, in which I transmitted to you a copy of a circular of the Treasury Department, dated the 1st of that month, making the inspection of cattle intended for exportation compulsory before shipment, and in which note I at the same time informed you of the desire expressed by the Secretary of the Treasury to do all in his power to prevent the introduction into foreign countries of diseased cattle, and the hope entertained by him that the Treasury Department circular in question would accomplish the object in view, I now have the honour to recall your attention to the subject in consequence of information received through the Treasury Department from exporters of cattle to the effect that the certificate of the Customs officers of the United States given in pursuance of the above-mentioned circular is not accepted as of any force by the officers of Her Majesty's Government in Great Britain.

In view of the importance of the interests involved, and in order that exporters of cattle may not be put to a useless expense for inspection, I would be obliged to you for early information as to whether Her Majesty's Government is willing to make such a modification of the regulations upon this subject as would recognize certificates issued by the Customs authorities of the United States, under the circular of February 1st, 1879, as sufficient to exempt cattle inspected under its provisions from slaughter upon being landed.

I have, &c.

The Rt. Honble. Sir Edwd. Thornton, K.C.B.,   (Signed)   WM. M. EVARTS.
&c.   &c.   &c.

Enclosure 3 in No. 35.

LETTER from MR. EVARTS to Sir E. THORNTON.

SIR,   Washington, January 24, 1880.

I HAVE the honour to acknowledge the receipt of your note of yesterday's date inquiring whether Her Majesty's Government is willing to make such a modification of the regulations respecting the importation of cattle into England from the United States as would recognise certificates issued by the Customs authorities of the United States under the circular of February 1, 1879, as sufficient to exempt cattle inspected under its provisions from slaughter upon being landed.

I shall not fail to transmit a copy of your note to the Marquis of Salisbury by the earliest opportunity. At the same time it is with much regret that I am compelled to admit the fact that fresh outbreaks of pleuro-pneumonia are constantly showing themselves in different parts of the United States, and in some instances in the immediate neighbourhood of the seaports from which cattle are frequently shipped from England.

Cattle arriving from the Western States at these ports are not known to be infected with this destructive and highly contagious disease; but as long as it exists at the ports from which they are shipped there is constant danger of contagion; and at the very moment that the inspectors are examining the cattle and pronouncing them sound, they may be absorbing the germs of the disease, which do not however generally develope themselves for many weeks after their shipment.

By the Circular of the Treasury Department of the 11th July 1879 collectors of customs are instructed not to admit neat cattle from Canada unless they shall be satisfied that they were not imported directly or indirectly from England, or that if so imported they did not arrive in that dominion within 90 days prior to their arrival at a port in the United States. It would, therefore, appear that it is the opinion of the Treasury Department that the incubation of the disease may last for about that time, and that cattle cannot be considered safe until its termination. It is, therefore, justifiable and natural that the same apprehensions should be entertained in England with regard to cattle arriving from the United States in many points of which it is known and admitted that pleuro-pneumonia exists.

I venture to hope, however, in the interest both of Great Britain and the United States that Congress will in its wisdom pass such laws as may have the effect of obliterating the disease in this country, even if it be at the expense of a considerable outlay, though but a trifle compared with the loss of property which would arise from the continuance and spread of this destructive disease.

I have, &c.
The Hon. William Evarts, (Signed) E. THORNTON.
&c.   &c.   &c.

No. 36.

LETTER from the ACTING BRITISH CONSUL at PHILADELPHIA to the MARQUIS OF SALISBURY.

(No. 2 Sanitary.)

MY LORD, British Consulate, Philadelphia, February 21, 1880.

I HAVE the honour to report to your Lordship that the cases of pleuro-pneumonia in Lehigh county and Montgomery county of this State, reported in my Despatch No. 1 Sanitary of the 20th ultimo, have been checked. At these places several additional head were killed, some others have died, and the remainder have been kept in strict quarantine.

Fresh cases have occurred at West Chester, a wealthy farming district of Chester County, Pennsylvania. Five or six head have been killed, and a strict quarantine is exacted by the State Commissioner.

The disease is not likely to spread beyond the farm now affected.

No cases, as far as I have been able to learn, have occurred in any of the Western States of this consular district.

I have the honour to enclose your Lordship copy of the Report of the Board of Agriculture of the State of Pennsylvania for the year 1879, containing an interesting article on lung fever written by the special agent of the Governor of the State. I have applied for additional copies of this printed document, and should I succeed in obtaining them I will forward to your Lordship two more copies.

I have, &c.
The Right Hon. the Marquis of Salisbury. (Signed) GEORGE CRUMP.
&c.   &c.   &c.

No. 37.

LETTER from SIR E. THORNTON to the MARQUIS OF SALISBURY.

(No. 3 Sanitary.)

MY LORD, Washington, February 23, 1880.

I HAVE the honour to inform your Lordship that on the 20th instant the Secretary of the Treasury transmitted a report to Congress relating to the existence of pleuro-pneumonia among cattle in this country. As soon as this report shall have been printed, I shall forward copies of it to your Lordship.

Q 2337.

In the meantime I enclose copies of a précis of the report which has been published in one of the Washington papers, from which it will be seen that the principal conclusions arrived at are as follows:

That the disease is contagious, but may be prevented by inoculation.

That its period of incubation is from nine to 30 days, and not exceeding 40 days.

That the destruction of diseased cattle is the only method of suppressing the disease.

That it does not exist west of the Alleghanies, nor in the United States near the Canadian border, nor in Canada, but is found only in the eastern part of New York, in New Jersey, Pennsylvania, and possibly in parts of Maryland, Virginia, and District of Columbia.

That the general course of the traffic in cattle is from the west to the east, and with proper care and restrictions cattle may pass thence through and out of the eastern ports without danger.

That State regulations do not suffice to prevent and suppress the disease, and that stringent quarantine regulations are essential to protect the country from its importation.

That there should be a Commission to investigate and report upon the disease, and that it should be authorised to co-operate with State and municipal authorities, and to isolate and slaughter diseased cattle, compensating the owners, the necessary funds to be furnished by Congress.

The report was referred to the Committee on Agriculture, and I am not without hopes that Congress is beginning to awaken to the importance of the subject, and that some legislation may be carried through the present session with a view to preventing the further spread of the disease.

I have &c.

The Marquis of Salisbury, K.G. &c. &c. &c. (Signed) EDWARD THORNTON.

Enclosure in No. 37.
Extract "Washington Post," February 21, 1880.

THE CATTLE DISEASE QUESTION.

The Secretary of the Treasury yesterday sent to Congress a communication on the subject of pleuro-pneumonia in cattle. He gave a history of the disease, and some general observations concerning its effect upon commerce. He then proceeds to give a summary of the conclusions arrived at, and his ideas as to appropriate legislation on the subject. These conclusions are embodied 16 distinct propositions, as follows:

First.—Pleuro-pneumonia is a contagious infectious lung fever in neat cattle, as readily communicated among them as small-pox among mankind, not only by actual contact, but by excretions of all kinds.

Second.—In this country it has never developed *de novo*, but has always been introduced by contagion.

Third.—It may be prevented by inoculation, but that remedy is not thought of in this country under present conditions.

Fourth.—It has a period of incubation of from nine to 30 days, not exceeding 40 days, and its symptoms, when developed, are easily distinguished by experts from those of other diseases.

Fifth.—The only proper method of suppressing the disease in the United States is by the destruction of all diseased or exposed cattle and a thorough purification of the buildings where they have been kept.

Sixth.—No contagious pleuro-pneumonia now exists or has existed west of the Allegheny mountains.

Seventh.—It does not now exist in the United States, on or near the Canadian border, and does not now exist in that Dominion.

Eighth.—The disease now exists only in the eastern part of New York, in New Jersey, Pennysylvania, and, possibly, in parts of Maryland, Virginia, and district of Columbia.

Ninth.—The general course of traffic in cattle is from the west to the east. Only a few animals of blooded stock of great value pass westward or into Canada from the east.

Tenth.—At the present time, with ordinary care, cattle may pass from the Western States, which almost exclusively furnish cattle for exportation into Canada, and through Canada, Portland and Boston to foreign ports without danger of infection.

Eleventh.—With proper restrictions against contact with other cattle near the seaboard, cattle may pass from the Western States to the ports of New York, Pennsylvania, and Baltimore without danger of infection.

Twelfth.—State and municipal regulations are not to be relied upon to prevent the importation and spread of the disease, or to effect its extirpation.

Thirteenth.—Stringent quarantine regulations are essential to the protection of this country against its introduction.

Fourteenth.—A veterinary sanitary commission, whose duty it shall be to investigate all reports of the existence of the disease, collect information respecting it, and report to some department that publication is essential to efficient action on the subject.

Fifteenth.—Authority for such a commission to operate with State and municipal authorities in preventing and eradicating the disease. Supplying money out of appropriations by Congress for the purpose would be effective, and is in accordance with Acts of Congress in reference to the National Board of Health.

Sixteenth.—Authority in such board to promptly isolate and slaughter infected and diseased cattle wherever found, and to award compensation to the owners, would be an effective agency in extirpating the disease. It is for Congress to consider the policy and legality of conferring such power.

The document was referred to the Committee on Agriculture.

No. 38.

LETTER from the CLERK OF THE COUNCIL to the UNDER SECRETARY OF STATE, FOREIGN OFFICE.

Sir,　　　　　　　　　　　　　　　　　　　　　　　　　　　　February 28, 1880.

I have submitted to the Lords of the Council your letter of the 20th instant, enclosing a despatch from Her Majesty's Minister at Washington, with copy of a note from Mr. Evarts asking for early information as to whether Her Majesty's Government is willing to make such modification in the existing regulations in regard of live cattle shipped to this country from ports in the United States of America as would recognise certificates issued by the Customs authorities of the United States under the Circular of 1st February 1879 (also enclosed) as sufficient to exempt cattle imported under its provisions from slaughter after being landed.

In reply, I am directed to call the attention of Lord Salisbury to my letter No. 61226 of February 27th, 1879, in which it was stated that their Lordships had carefully considered the orders which had been issued by the American Government in the Circular dated February 1st, 1879, for the inspection of cattle previous to exportation, but that their Lordships were aware from their own experience that no system of inspection at the port, however perfect, affords complete security against the introduction of pleuro-pneumonia. These views, which their Lordships then expressed as to the impossibility of relying upon inspection, have been confirmed by the results of post-mortem examinations of cattle from American ports which have been landed at foreign animals wharves in this country for slaughter.

It appears that during 1879 there were 57 cargoes of American cattle in which pleuro-pneumonia was detected, the total number of animals in which the disease was found to exist was 137, a number far in excess of that which has been received during any year from all other exporting countries put together.

Between January 1st and February 20th of the present year 84 cattle affected with pleuro-pneumonia have been landed in this country.

Under these circumstances it must be evident that their Lordships could not make such modifications of the existing regulations on the subject as would recognise the certificates referred to in Mr. Evart's letter as sufficient to exempt American cattle from slaughter on being landed in this country.

I beg to return the enclosures as requested by you.

I am, &c.

The Under Secretary of State,　　　　　　　(Signed)　　C. L. PEEL.
　　Foreign Office.

No. 39.

LETTER from the BRITISH CONSUL-GENERAL at NEW YORK to the MARQUIS OF SALISBURY.

(Sanitary, No. 2.)   British Consulate General, New York,
My Lord,   March 8, 1880.

I HAVE the honour to report to your Lordship that it has been publicly announced to carry out the provisions of the Pleuro-pneumonia Act which was passed last year by the Legislature of the State of New Jersey; that the Act in question has been repealed, to take effect on and after the 10th instant; and that the quarantine against the State of New York has been raised, so that in future all cattle will be allowed to enter New Jersey without permit.

This action on the part of the New Jersey State Legislature is no doubt attributable to the improved sanitary condition of cattle, not only in the States of New York and New Jersey, but also in other States in this consular district.

     I have, &c.
Her Majesty's Principal Secretary of State   (Signed)   E. M. ARCHIBALD.
     for Foreign Affairs, London.

No. 40.

LETTER from SIR E. THORNTON to the MARQUIS OF SALISBURY.

(Sanitary, No. 6.)
My Lord,   Washington, March 23, 1880.

I HAVE the honour to enclose copy of two Despatches which I received on the 20th and 21st instant respectively from the Acting British Consul at Baltimore, informing me that he has learnt that pleuro-pneumonia exists to a great extent amongst the cattle in some of the counties of Maryland, especially Harford county.

<small>No. 1.
Nos. 2, 3, and 4.</small>

He states further that two steamers have left Baltimore on or about the 18th instant with cattle, one for Bristol and the other for London, and he inquires whether he should be justified in informing your Lordship by telegraph of the appearance of the disease, with reference to the cargoes of the two steamers.

In his second Despatch Mr. Lawford expresses his opinion that the reports in question are not well founded.

<small>No. 5.</small>

In my answer, copy of which is also enclosed, I have instructed him to make further and particular inquiries as to the existence of pleuro-pneumonia amongst the cattle in certain parts of Maryland, and with regard to the place of origin of the cargoes of the two steamers in question; and that on the receipt of his answer I would consider whether it would be expedient to telegraph to your Lordship upon the subject.

It is probable, however, that I shall feel it my duty to telegraph to your Lordship to-morrow or the next day with regard to the cargoes of the two steamers; for it is said in the newspapers that one of the infected counties in Maryland is Baltimore county, in which the city of Baltimore is situated. I should imagine, too, that there is good ground for believing that the disease exists, for the matter is being discussed in the State Legislature by members who themselves are the owners of herds of cattle said to have been attacked by it, and Mr. Williams has introduced a Bill into the State Senate giving great powers to the Governor, when the existence of pleuro-pneumonia shall have been brought to his notice, for ordering the seclusion of deceased cattle, precautions for preventing the disease from spreading, and the destruction of deceased cattle, granting compensation to the owners. It is not probable that such a bill would have been brought before the State Legislature if there had been no truth in the assertion that pleuro-pneumonia exists amongst the cattle in certain parts of Maryland.

     I have, &c.
The Marquis of Salisbury, K.G.   (Signed)   EDWARD THORNTON.
     &c.   &c.   &c.

77

Enclosure 1 in No. 40.

LETTER from the ACTING BRITISH CONSUL at BALTIMORE to SIR E. THORNTON.

(No. 7.)

Sir,
Baltimore, March 20, 1880.

WITH reference to my Despatch, Sanitary No. 2, of the 1st instant, to Lord Salisbury, through Legation, I now have the honour to report that I learn that pleuro-pneumonia exists largely amongst the cattle of some of the counties of this State, especially Harford county.

Two steamers within the past couple of days, the "Riversdale" for Bristol, with 130 head of cattle, and the "Indus" for London, with 136 head on board, have cleared, bearing Customs certificates as to the health of the cattle, and "that no cattle disease exists in this Customs district." On inquiry at the Custom House I learn that Harford county is within the Custom District of this port. These certificates have been certified by me to the effect that the deputy collector's signature and seal were genuine, and that the official is entitled to credence.

The surgeon inspector certified as to the health of the cattle, and the absence of contagion; the collector attaches to that a certificate authenticating the signature of the former, and I, in turn, am called upon to attest the fact of the collector's having signed the second document, which, of course I cannot refuse to do, though the collector's certificate covers an incorrect premise.

As the deputy collector has issued the certificates for the above-named steamers I pointed out to him the existence of an infectious disease amongst the cattle within the Customs District, but he stated that inasmuch as the cattle so shipped were directly from the West, and not from the infected districts, that he did not think the printed clause in the surgeon's certificate, as to the absence of infection in the district, would make much difference.

I have written to Harford county for some information regarding the outbreak which may prove useful to the Government.

The immediate object of this Despatch is to learn whether you think I would be justified in sending a cablegram as to the appearance of pleuro-pneumonia in my district so as to have a bearing upon the two outward cargoes now on their way.

Beyond the regular monthly reports as to cattle disease I have no further instruction from the Foreign Office in the premises.

I have, &c.

The Right Hon. Sir E. Thornton, K.C.B. &c. &c. &c.

(Signed) J. W. LAWFORD, Acting-Consul.

Enclosure 2 in No. 40.

LETTER from the ACTING BRITISH CONSUL at BALTIMORE to SIR E. THORNTON.

(No. 7.)

Sir,
Baltimore, March 20, 1880.

SINCE posting my Despatch, No. 7, of this date to you, I have the honour to state that I have received a letter from Mr. T. W. Baker, the editor of the "Ægis and Intelligencer," of Harford county, a copy of which I have the honour to enclose.

From this letter it will be seen that the newspaper paragraph, on which I based my previous Despatch, and which clipping I also enclose, does not appear to be well founded.

Besides this, the deputy collector of customs called in to say that his inquiries into the matter had been fruitless, and that he has had no official notification of the existence of the contagion as is usual wherein infection is known to exist. He emphasizes strongly that the recently shipped cattle came directly from Illinois, and none from any port of this State.

The second newspaper paragraph would seem to have bearing upon pleuro-pneumonia amongst cattle some months ago, which must have escaped my observation at the time, though I endeavour constantly to note its appearance. I am under the impression that the maladies are, to some extent, kept *sub rosa*, perhaps in the interests of breeders or stock-drovers.

I have, &c.

The Right Hon. Sir E. Thornton, K.C.B., &c. &c. &c.

(Signed) J. W. LAWFORD.

Enclosure 3 in No. 40.

LETTER from the EDITOR of the "ÆGIS AND INTELLIGENCER," of HARFORD COUNTY, to the BRITISH CONSULATE, BALTIMORE.

MY DEAR SIR, Bel Air, M.D., March 19, 1880.

I DOUBT the correctness of the report that pleuro-pneumonia exists amongst Harford county cattle. No information of that character has been received at this Office.

I expect to meet the "Deer Creek Farmers Club" to-morrow, and will inquire particularly in relation to the matter among the members, all of whom are largely engaged in breeding and grazing cattle.

On Monday next I shall be prepared to give you some definite information, and will do so with pleasure.

(Signed) F. W. BAKER.

British Consulate, Baltimore, M.D.

Enclosure 4 in No. 40.

Extract from the Baltimore "Sun" of March 18, 1880.

(Special Despatch to the Baltimore "Sun.")

THE CATTLE DISEASE.—PROPOSED LEGISLATION.—THE PEARRE INVESTIGATION.

Annapolis, M.D., March 17.

Considerable uneasiness is felt on account of the reported existence of a disease said to be pleuro-pneumonia, in some of the counties of this State, especially in Harford. Two of the senators have cattle sick of the disease. One senator has it in a herd of very fine Alderneys, and a government agent has gone to inquire into the matter. A bill has been introduced authorising the Governor to take all necessary steps to suppress the disease should there be occasion in his judgment to do so; to issue proclamation, order quarantine or slaughter; to call on sheriffs of counties to help in the premises, and employ veterinary practitioners and fix their compensation; to examine all incoming cattle, and providing penalties for violations when the Governor has declared a necessity to exist for enforcing the regulation. The State treasury is to be placed at the disposal of the Governor for the necessary funds, and to pay for animals ordered to be slaughtered.

Extract from the Baltimore "Sun" of March 20, 1880.

MARYLAND STATE AFFAIRS.

(Correspondence of the Baltimore "Sun.")

Annapolis, M.D., March 19, 1880.

SUPPRESSION of CATTLE DISEASE.—TESTIMONY of JUDGE PEARRE.—FAVOURABLE REPORT on the SUNDAY LAW BILL.—The PROPOSED GAS COMPANY COMBINATION.—POLICE.—BRIBERY in ELECTIONS.—EMBEZZLEMENT of CARGOES.—BALTIMORE and NORTH-EASTERN RAILROAD, &c.

Cattle Disease.

Senator Williams, of Baltimore county, called the attention of the Senate to-day very plainly to the cattle disease and the need of prompt and stringent measures for its repression in this State. He said his barnyard in Harford county had been swept; President Stump, of the Senate, who is from Hartford county, has lost three; Senator Vanderford, from Carroll, says the disease is rife in his county; Governor Hamilton has received a letter from a veterinary surgeon stating that six or eight cases have been reported within three miles of Frederick city. The Secretary of State of Maryland has received a letter from the Board of Agriculture of Pennsylvania, written in December last, as follows:—

"Dear Sir,—I find my work in suppressing pleuro-pneumonia among horned stock, under a special commission from Governor Hoyt, very much increased by the introduction of stock from Maryland, and especially from Baltimore and the adjacent districts. This morning my surgeons report a herd of 30 infected by a cow from Baltimore. Several have died, and 12 more will probably have to be killed; the herd will be broken up and worse than lost. Is your State taking any action in this matter? If so, what, and with what result? Is co-operation possible, which will prevent this trouble? If so, how and with whom? Massachussetts, New York, New Jersey, and Pennsylvania are engaged in a shoulder-to-shoulder struggle with the infection, and in our case much of the trouble comes from Maryland. Will you please communicate with Governor Hoyt in the matter?

"THOS. J. EDGE,
"Commissioner on Pleuro-Pneumonia."

This communication was answered negatively on the 20th of December by Secretary of State Hollyday, since which time nothing has been done by the Maryland authorities until Mr. Williams introduced the Bill, heretofore referred to, giving the Governor sweeping authority to stamp out the plague within our borders, which Bill is now pending in the Legislature. It has been since learned that the Pennsylvanian Commission is preparing to quarantine Maryland cattle, and place an embargo on shipments from Baltimore and other parts of our State.

Enclosure 5 in No. 40.

LETTER from SIR E. THORNTON to the ACTING BRITISH CONSUL at BALTIMORE.

(No. 4.)

SIR, Washington, March 21, 1880.

WITH reference to your Despatches Nos. 7 and 8 of yesterday's date, I beg to say that I think it would be very advisable that you should make the most particular inquiries, 1, as to whether pleuro-pneumonia exists in some counties in Maryland, and which; and 2, whether the cattle shipped in the "Riversdale" and "Indus" really came direct from the West, or whether they may have been exposed to contagion at Baltimore, or may have been mixed with cattle from Maryland, also shipped on board of those steamers.

I have to request you to give me the best information you can obtain on these two points as soon as possible, and on its receipt I will decide whether it will be expedient for me to telegraph to England upon the subject.

I am, &c.
T. W. Lawford, Esq. (Signed) E. THORNTON.
&c. &c. &c.

No. 41.

LETTER from SIR E. THORNTON to the MARQUIS OF SALISBURY.

(Sanitary, No. 8.)

MY LORD, Washington, March 29, 1880.

WITH reference to my Despatch, No. 6 of this series, and of the 23rd instant, Nos. 1 and 2. I have the honour to enclose copy of a further Despatch and of its Enclosure, which I have received from the Acting Consul at Baltimore, relative to the existence of pleuro-pneumonia among cattle in the State of Maryland. It will be seen that Mr. Lawford doubts as to the truth of the reports upon the subject, and states that the cattle shipped on the steamers "Riversdale" and "Indus" came directly from the West, where no infection existed.

But as he also says that they remained two days in Baltimore, and as there are reasons for suspecting that pleuro-pneumonia does exist amongst cattle in Maryland, I thought it more prudent to telegraph to your Lordship with respect to the cargoes of those two steamers, with a view to their being carefully inspected.

My suspicions that the disease does really exist in that State are strengthened by an article in the "Baltimore Sun" of the 27th instant, which I have the honour to enclose. No. 3. Your Lordship will perceive that, although a committee appointed by a farmers' club did not find the cattle on Senator Williams' farm affected by the disease, a veterinary surgeon, who visited it, declared that one of the cattle, which he received permission to slaughter, undoubtedly had pleuro-pneumonia. The fact that Senator Williams himself admitted that it was so, and proposed a Bill in the Maryland Legislature for the suppression of the disease, convinces me of its existence.

On the receipt of your Lordship's Despatch, No. 2 of this series, and of the 12th No. 4. instant, I addressed to Mr. Hay, acting secretary in the absence of Mr. Evarts, a note, copy of which is enclosed, conveying the substance of the letter of the 28th ultimo, from the Veterinary Department of the Privy Council Office to your Lordships' Office, with regard to the slaughtering of cattle from the United States on their arrival in England, although they brought with them certificates of having been inspected on this side and declared free from disease.

I had two days before observed in the newspapers that the Treasury Department had modified its Order of February 1st, 1879, so that the inspection of cattle on being exported should be no longer compulsory.

The motive of this modification was stated to be that the cattle were slaughtered on their arrival in England, notwithstanding their being provided with certificates of health.

In my note to Mr. Hay, I have requested him to inform me whether this change has actually been made, for I have received no official notification of it.

I have, &c.

The Marquis of Salisbury, K.G. &c. &c. &c. (Signed) EDWARD THORNTON.

Enclosure 1 in No. 41.

Letter from the Acting British Consul at Baltimore to Sir E. Thornton.

(No. 8.)

Sir, Baltimore, March 24, 1880.

I have the honour to acknowledge the receipt of your Despatch, No. 4, of the 21st instant, having reference to cattle plague within this consular district.

I now have the honour to state that I have delayed this Despatch in the hope that I should hear from a Mr. Baker, of Harford county, who promised to write me on Monday. Up to the present time, however, I have not heard from him.

There is quite a division of sentiment as to whether pleuro-pneumonia really exists in any part of this State, and after careful inquiry I fail to find the report confirmed. The infection, if any exists, might be concealed in the interests of interested parties, as mentioned in my last Despatch upon the subject.

I have the honour to enclose herewith clippings from the "Sun" newspaper of this city upon the subject.

Upon careful inquiry I find that the cattle shipped hence by the steamers "Riversdale" and "Indus" came directly from the West—where no infection existed—and that both cargoes were detained at the city for two days only, prior to shipment, no disease having appeared amongst them.

I have, &c.

The Right Hon. Sir E. Thornton, K.C.B. &c. &c. &c. (Signed) J. W. LAWFORD.

Enclosure 2 in No. 41.

Extracts from Baltimore "Sun" of March 24, 1880.

THE PLEURO-PNEUMONIA QUESTION.

We print elsewhere another communication on the subject of pleuro-pneumonia among certain herds of cattle in Maryland. The writer takes issue with the doubt expressed by "Farmer" in our columns yesterday as to the existence of the disease in Maryland, and cites the fact that as late as Monday last two skilled veterinary surgeons found a marked case of the disease in another of the cattle on the farm of Senator Williams, in Harford county, and that the animal was at once slaughtered. At present it is admitted that the cases are very few in point of number, are widely separated, and the total extinction of the disease by slaughtering those who are suffering from it, and isolating the remainder of the herd, can be very easily effected. The extremes of temperature that cattle have passed through this season, the frequent rains to which they have been exposed, and perhaps want of care on the part of some of those who have had charge of them, have probably had much to do with these occasional outbreaks of pleuro-pneumonia. The fact that the disease rarely attacks native cattle, and has never yet appeared among the western herds, which constitute the great bulk of the cattle exported, would seem to indicate the limited range of the disease, except under circumstances where contact with it in its most contagious form cannot be avoided. Since the unusual prevalence of the disease in Massachusetts for six consecutive years after its first appearance in Mr. Chenery's herd, the outbreaks everywhere else have been sporadic, and in no instance known to us has assumed the form of an epidemic. Nevertheless the security of our herds can only be assured by vigilant watchfulness over them, and by the inexorable slaughter of every animal taken down by the disease. The suggestion made by " Farmer," yesterday to provide by law for an unpaid commission of five well-known farmers from different parts of the State, who shall be authorised to employ some eminent veterinary surgeon, and whose duty it shall be to make a thorough examination of diseased cattle, appears to us to be a good one, if such a commission would consent to give its services gratuitously, and especially if it were empowered to order the killing at once of every animal declared to be stricken with pleuro-pneumonia. We see no reason at present for alarm, provided proper steps are taken to examine and deal promptly with cattle alleged to be suffering with the disease. This can only be done by the enactment of a law to that end; and in justice to our farmers and cattle breeders, as well as to quiet any apprehensions in respect to the condition of cattle shipped from Baltimore abroad or sold into other States, such a law should be put on the statute book.

(For the " Sun.")

PLEURO-PNEUMONIA.

MESSRS. EDITORS,

THE writer on pleuro-pneumonia, signing himself "Farmer," in your issue of yesterday, makes a plain issue as to the existence of the disease in Maryland. Referring to the statements of Senators Williams, Stump, and Vanderford, that the contagion is present in the counties they represent, he says, unequivocally, " They are mistaken." It will be useful information to him who thus speaks, evidently without possessing knowledge or seeking to gain it, and perhaps to other sceptics, to know that Monday morning an inspection was made of the herd of cattle owned by Senator Williams, in Harford county, and not only were the proofs plain by external observation, but an animal was slaughtered of pleuro-pneumonia. This animal would have the spot, and disclosed the well-marked lesions undoubtedly furnished a thoroughly good point of contagion of all fresh cattle with which he might have come in contact, the diseased portion of the lung breaking down without even the protection of a cyst wall, and the pus unusually offensive. The examiners were skilled veterinary surgeons, one a member of the Royal Veterinary College of England and the other a graduate of the Veterinary College of Montreal. Further, I believe these gentlemen could find, if deemed necessary, on twelve hours' notice an acute case within the city limits, and I would undertake to pay the value of the animal, if on slaughtering it the disease was not found.—S.

Enclosure 3 in No. 41.

Extract from Baltimore " Sun" of March 27, 1880.

PLEURO-PNEUMONIA IN MARYLAND.—THE QUESTION of its EXISTENCE HERE DISCUSSED.— VIEWS OF PRACTICAL MEN.—HOW IT MAY BE STAMPED OUT.

(Reported for the Baltimore " Sun.")

IN connexion with the Bill now before the State Legislature, introduced by Senator George H. Williams, of Baltimore county, and which has passed the Senate, looking to the prevention or spread of lung fever or pleuro-pneumonia among the cattle in this State, the " Belair Ægis and Intelligencer" has a long article. Mr. Williams, in presenting the Bill, said that his barnyard in Harford county had been swept by the disease, and it was also stated that Senator Stump, of the same county, had also lost three cattle from the same cause. The " Ægis" says, that " the subject was brought forward at a " meeting of the Deer Creek Farmers' Club, held last Saturday, at the residence of Mr. " R. Harris Archer. The members of this club own together at least a thousand head " of cattle. A thorough inquiry at the meeting established the fact that not a single " case of pleuro-pneumonia or other dangerous disease exists among the cattle owned

Q 2337.

"by the members of the club, and none of the gentlemen present knew or had heard of any cases of disease of any kind among stock in any part of the county.

"In view of the reports, however, the club appointed a committee, consisting of Messrs. A. M. Fulford, Thomas A. Hayes, Dr. James M. Magraw, William Munnikhuysen, John Moores, and William F. Hayes, to investigate all the facts upon which the reports were based. This committee ascertained, in the first place, that no cattle have died on Senator Stump's farm. The committee state that all of Mr. Stump's cattle are healthy, showing no signs of disease of any kind.

"The committee next visited Senator Williams' farm. There they found some cause for apprehension, but nothing upon which to base a positive assertion that pleuro-pneumonia existed among Mr. Williams's cattle. The committee were informed that two years ago a steer was brought to the farm from Baltimore city. This animal did not thrive as the other cattle, and died last summer. During last winter two cows also died, but the manager of the farm expressed a decided belief that their death was occasioned by old age. In February of the present year another cow was taken sick and was killed. No postmortem examination was made of the steer or the cow, and no one familiar with the symptoms of pleuro-pneumonia saw them. On Monday of the present week a veterinary surgeon from Baltimore city visited Mr. Williams's farm, and upon examing the cattle selected one, a yearling, and pronounced it unsound. He could not positively pronounce it a case of pleuro-pneumonia without making a post-mortem examination, and the animal was accordingly slaughtered. The lungs which are the parts immediately affected, were taken by the veterinary to the city to be subjected to microscopic examination. The remainder of Mr. Williams's cattle, 12 or 14 in number, are to all appearances healthy and in fine condition. We have ourselves made the most diligent inquiry among farmers from all parts of the county, and have been unable to discover the existence of disease of any kind among the cattle anywhere in Harford county. Pleuro-pneumonia, if it exists here at all, is confined exclusively to the farm of Mr. Williams."

In opposition to these assertions the veterinary surgeon who visited Senator William's farm states that he found three cattle with all the external evidence of pleuro-pneumonia. Permission was given to slaughter one of them, and it disclosed the well-marked lesions of pleuro-pneumonia. It would undoubtedly have furnished a thoroughly good point of contagion for all fresh cattle with which it came in contact, the diseased portion of the lung breaking down without even the protection of a cyst wall, and the pus being unusually offensive. He says that the symptoms were too plain to need any microscopic examination being made; that he found three cattle with all the external evidences of pneumonia. Permission was given to slaughter one of them, and the lungs were found to be badly affected. He states, that in company with another surgeon, who has had much experience of the disease, he has found in several parts of the State fully developed cases of the disease, some of them within the city limits of Baltimore. It is true that all of these cases are isolated ones, but they will form a centre from which, under favourable circumstances, the disease may be disseminated. The greatest danger will be found a few weeks from now, when cattle which have been confined to the stable all winter are turned out to grass. When once an animal has had the disease, even if it seems to recover, the seeds remain, and may under certain conditions be communicable. Besides the danger of infection from the animal itself, the car in which it is housed while sick can also become a medium for conveying the disease. The State board of agriculture of Pennsylvania have decided that all the cases of pneumonia in that State can be directly traced to infection from Maryland cattle, and they have called a meeting for Friday next, in Harrisburg, at which New Jersey will be represented, to take some action in the matter. They threaten that unless Maryland adopts some measures of prevention against the spread of the disease they will establish a 90 days' quarantine against all Maryland cattle, an action which would naturally injure the commercial interests of the State. Those who claim to be informed say, that if the disease should once past west of the Alleghany mountains no power could stop its spread, and that the only plan for Maryland to adopt is to kill all sick cattle and isolate the rest, and thus stamp out the disease in a few weeks. Pleuro-pneumonia is not an exaggerated type of pneumonia, but a separate and distinct disease. Neither is it indigenous, like hog cholera, but has been imported. Massachusetts succeeded by vigorous measures in stamping it out in 1859, and now that England has freed herself from it, she will guard against its reintroduction from any of the Atlantic States.

Enclosure 4 in No. 41.

LETTER from SIR E. THORNTON to MR. HAY.

SIR, Washington, March 27, 1880.

IN my note of the 24th of January last I had the honour to inform the Secretary of State that I would forward to the Marquis of Salisbury a copy of his note of the 23rd of that month, relating to the circular of the Treasury Department, dated the 1st February last, making the inspection of cattle intended for exportation compulsory before shipment, and inquiring whether Her Majesty's Government would be willing to make such a modification of the regulations upon the subject as would recognise certificates issued by the Customs authorities of the United States under the above mentioned circular as sufficient to exempt cattle inspected under its provisions from slaughter upon being landed.

His Lordship has now instructed me to state that he has been in correspondence upon this subject with the Lords of the Privy Council, who have reminded him that, in a letter of February 27, 1879, it was stated that their Lordships had carefully considered the orders issued by the Government of the United States in the circular of February 1st, 1879, for the inspection of cattle previous to exportation, but that they were aware from their own experience that no system of inspection at the port, however perfect, could give security against the introduction of pleuro-pneumonia. Their Lordships add that these views which they then expressed as to the impossibility of relying upon inspection, have been confirmed by the result of post-mortem examinations of cattle from American ports which have been landed at foreign animals wharves in the United Kingdom for slaughter.

It appears that, during 1879, there were 57 cargoes of American cattle in which pleuro-pneumonia was detected, the total number of animals in which disease was found to exist being 137, a number far in excess of that which has been received during any year from all other exporting countries put together.

Between January 1st and February 20th of the present year, 84 cattle affected with pleuro-pneumonia have been landed in the United Kingdom.

Under these circumstances it must be evident that the Lords of the Privy Council could not make such modification of the existing regulations on the subject as would recognise the certificates referred to in Mr. Evarts' note of the 23rd of January last, as sufficient to exempt American cattle from slaughter on being landed in the United Kingdom.

I have recently observed a statement in the newspapers that the order of the Treasury Department of the 1st of February 1879 has been modified, so that the inspection of cattle intended for export is no longer compulsory, and I should feel obliged if you would inform me whether an order to that effect has actually been issued by the Treasury Department.

I have, &c.

The Honourable John Hay. EDWARD THORNTON.
&c. &c. &c.

(Sanitary, No. 3.) No. 42.

LETTER from the CONSUL-GENERAL at NEW YORK to the MARQUIS OF SALISBURY.

MY LORD, British Consulate General, New York, April 2, 1880.

I HAVE the honour to report to your Lordship that the sanitary condition of cattle in this consular district is practically the same as was mentioned in my last Despatch on the subject, Sanitary, No. 2, of the 8th ultimo.

I have, &c.
Her Majesty's Principal Secretary of (Signed) E. M. ARCHIBALD.
State for Foreign Affairs.

(Sanitary, No. 10.) No. 43.

MY LORD, Washington, April 5, 1880.

WITH reference to my Despatch No. 8 of this series and the 29th ultimo, I have the honour to transmit herewith copies of the circular mentioned in that Despatch No. 1.

addressed by the United States Treasury Department to Collectors of Customs, by which it is ordered that henceforth the inspection of cattle exported from the United States will not be compulsory, but may be made upon the request of the shippers at their expense.

No. 2.

I also enclose copies of the letter addressed by the Secretary of the Treasury to the Speaker of the House of Representatives, of which I transmitted a précis in my Despatch No. 3 of this series and of the 23rd February last. At page No. 7 of this document it will be seen that the Secretary of the Treasury admits that it is hardly just, whilst no effective measures are adopted in the United States to even systematically ascertain the extent of the cattle disease in this country, and much less to adopt efficient measures for its suppression to complain that the British Government adopts effective means to prevent the spread of the disease in the United Kingdom.

Nos. 3, 4, and 5.

I also have the honour to transmit herewith a despatch addressed to your Lordship by the Acting Consul at Baltimore, enclosing copy of the Bill to prevent the spread of pleuro-pneumonia among the cattle of Maryland, to which I have alluded in previous despatches of this series.

It is stated in this morning's newspapers that this Bill was passed by both Houses of the Maryland Legislature before its adjournment, which took place on the 3rd instant.

I understand that the Secretary of the Treasury has within the last few days addressed a letter to Mr. Evarts, requesting that he would endeavour to obtain from Her Majesty's Government that cattle coming from the west of the Allegheny Mountains, going though Canada, and exported from Canadian ports, and from Portland and Boston in the United States, should be exempt from slaughter on arriving in England.

It is claimed, and I believe with truth, that pleuro-pneumonia does not exist amongst the cattle to the west of those mountains, and that, if they are transported direct from the Western States to the ports above mentioned, there will be no danger of infection. For my own part, I should be inclined to except Boston, for though of late no cattle disease has been reported from Massachusetts, there is no doubt that pleuro-pneumonia existed in that State some years ago, and that if immunity from slaughter were granted to cattle shipped at that port, an attempt might be made to send cattle from the States of New York to be shipped at Boston.

Mr. Evarts has not made any mention to me of the letter addressed to him upon this subject by the Secretary of the Treasury, and I therefore conclude that he will transmit instructions thereupon to the United States Minister in London.

I have, &c.

The Marquis of Salisbury, K.G. &c. &c. &c.

(Signed) EDWARD THORNTON.

Enclosure 1 in No. 43.

Circular.

Exportation of Cattle to Great Britain.

1880.—Department No. 24, Secretary's Office.

Treasury Department, Washington, D. C., March 18, 1880.

To Collectors of Customs and others:

The Department's Circular Order of February 1, 1879, requiring the inspection of neat cattle, with reference to the question whether they were free from contagious diseases, is hereby revoked.

That order was issued upon information that an inspection and certificate by officers might prevent the United States from being included in the Order of the Government of Great Britain that cattle from certain countries must be slaughtered at the ports of that country within ten days from arrival. By an Order of the Privy Council of Great Britain cattle from the United States are now included in the above-named Order, and are required to be thus slaughtered.

Hereafter, therefore, inspection of cattle shipped from the ports of the United States will not be made compulsory, but inspection may be made upon request of the shippers and at their expense, under Order No. 139, of December 18, 1878, and the regulations and instructions now in force.

Collectors of Customs are requested to forward to this Department any information which they may be able to obtain of the presence of pleuro-pneumonia or other contagious or infectious diseases prevailing among neat cattle in their vicinity.

(By order) H. F. FRENCH,

Assistant Secretary.

85

Enclosure 2 in No. 43.

PLEURO-PNEUMONIA IN NEAT CATTLE.—Letter from THE SECRETARY OF THE TREASURY, relative to Pleuro-pneumonia or Lung-plague in Neat Cattle.

February 20, 1880.—Referred to the Committee on Agriculture.

March 4, 1880.—Recommitted to the Committee on Agriculture, and ordered to be printed.

Treasury Department, Office of the Secretary,
Washington, D. C., February 19, 1880.

Hon. Samuel J. Randall,
Speaker, House of Representatives.

SIR,

The Department of the Treasury has been long embarrassed with several questions arising from the prevalence of the disease known as pleuro-pneumonia or lung-plague in neat cattle. These questions relate (1) to the extinction and prevention of the disease in the United States; (2) to our commerce with nations beyond the seas, especially with Great Britain; (3) to our trade in cattle with the Dominion of Canada.

With a view to such legislation as circumstances may seem to require, it seems proper at this time to submit to Congress some brief remarks upon the nature of the disease in question, the history of its prevalence in other countries and the United States, with a statement of the provisions of law now in force and of the various orders issued by this department relating to it, and some suggestions as to what measures may be properly enacted by Congress for the suppression and prevention of the disease.

Pleuro-pneumonia, or, as it is usually called in England, lung-plague, appears to be a malignant contagious lung fever in neat cattle, communicated by contagion from excretions from the bowels, kidneys, skin, and lung of other neat cattle. It has never originated in this country, all cases of it having been clearly traced to foreign sources.

Neat cattle are subject to pneumonia or common lung fever originating in them, as in man, from exposure to cold or similar causes, which is not contagious, and this disease is sometimes confounded with the true pleuro-pneumonia. A disease also prevails in Texas known as the "Texas fever," sometimes as the Spanish or splenic fever, which, although it is bad enough, is not in the strictest sense of the terms, either contagious or infectious. In Texas, it is said, cattle of all ages are afflicted with this malady in a somewhat latent and mild form. It is communicated to other cattle by feeding upon the ground over which the Texas cattle have been driven. This disease, though sometimes destructive, has no symptoms in common with pleuro-pneumonia, from which it may readily be distinguished.

The Disease in other Countries.

Pleuro-pneumonia is indigenous in Asia, and first appeared in Europe, into which it was introduced from Eastern Russia, at the end of the 17th century; until at the beginning of the present century outbreaks were occurring every few years over all parts of the continent.

According to the statement of Rev. Daniel Lindsey, a missionary in South Africa, before a legislative committee of Massachusetts in 1860, the disease was introduced into South Africa about 1854 by importation of a bull from Holland. The wealth of the inhabitants of that country consists in cattle and sheep, and herds of cattle numbering from five hundred to fifteen hundred wander over large tracts. The disease had spread through these herds in about six years over twelve hundred miles. The disease had become so general that there was no possibility of suppressing it by slaughter of the animals exposed, and inoculation was generally resorted to, and had brought it somewhat under subjection.

The disease first entered Holland in 1833. It was imported into Ireland, where the losses by the disease have been enormous, between 1839 and 1841, with some Dutch cattle, and appeared in Scotland in 1843. At about the same time it was committing great ravages in England. All the large towns containing dairy cows suffered, especially in the neighbourhood of the large cities—London, Manchester, Birmingham, and Liverpool. It is stated that the losses by pleuro-pneumonia during the past twenty-seven years have amounted to as much as ten millions of dollars per annum in the United Kingdom of Great Britain and Ireland. It is doubtful whether the disease has ever entirely disappeared in that country.

The disease was imported into Australia in 1858, by the importation of a short-horn English cow. It soon spread to the open country, and the mortality increased at an alarming rate. "Vigorous measures," says Dr. Law, "for its suppression were adopted; "thousands of infected or diseased cattle were slaughtered, but all proved of no avail. "Not only were the free roaming herds infected, but so many places were contami-"nated that it was soon perceived that help from this source was not to be expected. "Destroy a whole infected herd, and you still left the infection in the station, from "which, in its unfenced state, other herds could not be excluded, and where they were "certain to take in the germs of the malady. After enormous losses had been sustained "by the combined operations of the pest and poleaxe, it was concluded that the remedy "was worse than the disease, and the colonists reluctantly fell back on the expedient of "inoculation."

From England and Holland the disease was propagated in 1847 and 1848 in Sweden and Denmark.

The Disease in the United States.

The first notice of pleuro-pneumonia in the United States was in 1843, when a German cow imported direct from Europe and taken into a cattle shed in Brooklyn, N. Y., communicated the disease which has prevailed, more or less, in King's county, Long Island, ever since.

In 1847 the disease appeared in Delaware, imported in cattle from England by Mr. Thomas Richardson, and his whole stock, valued at $10,000, was slaughtered to prevent the spread of the disease.

The disease appeared in Delaware in 1861, and for three years prior to 1870 its ravages were quite extensive in the district of Columbia and adjacent parts of Maryland and Virginia.

In 1859 the disease was imported by Mr. Chenery, of Belmont, Mass., into that commonwealth. An extra session of the legislature was called to take measures to eradicate the disease, and a commission was appointed with full power to slaughter all cattle which had been exposed. After the slaughter of some 1,200 animals in addition to those which died of the disease, it was apparently exterminated. In 1863, however, Mr. Flint, secretary of the board of agriculture, in a letter to Governor Andrew, stated that the disease still existed in 12 or 15 towns in Massachusetts.

From the report of the Pennsylvania board of agriculture for September, October, and November, 1873, it appears that during that year 27 herds of cattle, including 408 animals, had been quarantined on account of the disease, and the greater part of them slaughtered. The disease seems to have been limited to six counties on the east of the Alleghenys; and was traced to cattle bought in the Baltimore, New York, and Philadelphia markets.

Cases of the disease have appeared, from time to time, in the State of New York, especially near the seaboard; but the legislature of that State, and the efficient action of its commissioners, have in every instance promptly prevented the spread of the disease by extermination of all cattle infected or exposed.

This statement as to the history of the disease in America is taken mainly from Professor Gamgee's report to the Commissioner of Agriculture, published in 1871.

A letter addressed by the Commissioner of Agriculture to the chairman of the Senate Committee on Agriculture, on the 14th of February 1879, states that the disease had prevailed during the previous summer in Burlington county, New Jersey, where it had also been prevalent for some years; that it had existed along the Potomac for a distance of about 45 miles in the years 1877 and 1878; that it had prevailed in Baltimore county, Maryland, for 12 or 15 years; that the report of the New Jersey board of agriculture for 1876 showed that 19 different herds of cattle suffered from this disease in Burlington county of that State during that year. In the same paper it is stated that Professor Gadsden of Philadelphia, who had recently made an examination of infected and deceased cattle on Long Island, wrote, under date of January 29, 1879, that the contagious disease known as pleuro-pneumonia then existed to a frightful extent among the cows near Brooklyn, Long Island.

It is important to observe that in all the reports to which reference has been made there is no indication whatever that a single case of pleuro-pneumonia has ever existed in any State west of the Allegheny Mountains. The importance of this point will be seen when we enter upon the discussion of the proper restrictions upon the trade in cattle between this country and the Dominion of Canada.

Prevention of the Disease.

Early in the year 1879 the department received information that pleuro-pneumonia had appeared in Hull and other parts of England. Hull is a port on the north-eastern coast of England, between which and New York a regular line of steamers plies, touching at Southampton, where cattle from the Channel Islands are taken on board and brought to the United States; and the department was strongly urged by the secretary of the New York Agricultural Society and others, to take precautions against the importation of infected cattle from that quarter. By a letter of February 10, 1879, from Mr. Packard, our consul at Liverpool, and by extracts from the London "Times," it appeared that pleuro-pneumonia had broken out in dairies near Liverpool, and that several cows had been then slaughtered by order of the Privy Council. It was in consequence of this information that an order of this department of February 26th, 1879, prohibiting the landing of cattle imported from England was issued.

In this connexion it is proper to allude to the statement, widely published in this country and Great Britain, that certain cattle shipped from Portland, Maine, early in the year 1879, by the "Ontario," had been found to be diseased with pleuro-pneumonia on their arrival at Liverpool, and were condemned to be slaughtered. It was stated in the London "Times" that of 197 cattle landed at Liverpool by the "Ontario," all had been slaughtered, and 13 of the number found to be infected. Upon inquiry it has been found that this shipment consisted of two herds, one said to have been from the West, and one from Canada. From the best evidence to be obtained, however, it is quite clear that these cattle were not infected with contagious pleuro-pneumonia, but only with common-pneumonia, which is not contagious.

In a letter from Andrew Smith, dated Ontario Veterinary College, Toronto, March 7, 1879, speaking of the cattle shipped by the steamer "Ontario," he says:

"Prof. Williams, of Edinburgh, who is justly recognized as one of the first pathologists of the day, had an opportunity to see over a hundred of these cattle slaughtered, and saw almost all of the deceased ones. He maintains that the cattle were only suffering from sporadic pneumonia, the result of exposure during a long and stormy voyage; but states that the changes in the lung tissues were very different from those which take place in contagious pleuro-pneumonia."

Mr. J. B. Sherman, superintendent of the Chicago Union Stock Yards, under date of February 4, 1879, says:

"The most important blow struck at the interests of this city, State, and the North-west, is the report in circulation relative to the prevalence of the cattle disease in the North-west; and these reports are absolutely false."

From the most reliable information that can be obtained it is safe to conclude that no case of contagious pleuro-pneumonia was carried from the Western States to Liverpool by the "Ontario;" and further, that no case of such disease has ever existed in the North-western States.

In considering what measures are necessary for the prevention of this disease, it is necessary always to bear in mind one fact with regard to it, namely, that it has a period of incubation, varying probably from 10 to 60 days. Animals exposed to the disease have sometimes developed symptoms of it in as short a period as 9 or 10 days; while others exposed in a like manner have developed no symptoms of the disease for nearly 6 days.

In a series of experiments carefully conducted in France in 1851, where diseased animals were distributed among healthy ones, symptoms of the disease were manifested by the healthy animals in from 9 to 57 days after exposure, about 20 per cent. of them escaping contagion altogether.

It does not follow, however, from the fact that symptoms of the disease first appeared in the healthy animals so long after their first exposure that the disease lay dormant in them during all that period, because it is evident that many of them may not have contracted the disease at all until they had been exposed to it during a long period. Again, in cases where cattle have been on shipboard fifty or sixty days, and the disease attracted no attention until the close of the voyage, it cannot be inferred that the disease had not developed itself long before, because it is evident that cattle would not be subject to such careful inspection on board ship as would lead to the detection of the early symptoms. Indeed, in the case of Chenery's cattle imported into Massachusetts from Holland, two of them were in such a condition of weakness that they were unable to walk when landed from the ship, and were carried on waggons some six or eight miles to their destination. By the Order of the Privy Council of England forty days seems to be regarded as the usual period of incubation of pleuro-pneumonia.

Inoculation as a Preventive.

Allusion has already been made to the practice of inoculation as a preventive of the pleuro-pneumonia as practised in South Africa and in Australia. There seems to be no doubt that all cattle are, in general, subject to the disease in question, but that inoculation is a preventive to the disease in its natural form.

Professor Gamgee gives some experiments made by Dr. Willems in Belgium in 1850-51. They are interesting as bearing upon several important points. In those experiments inoculation was introduced at the tip of the tail of the neat cattle, and it was found that symptoms of the disease were usually manifested, in the first group of observations, in from nine to eleven days. In another group of observations no symptoms of the disease were manifested until from twenty-two to twenty-seven days after the inoculation, thus indicating that there is no regular limit to the incubation of the disease.

Dr. Willems also, in the years 1851-52, performed various experiments on animals of different species with a view to ascertaining whether any animals except neat cattle could be infected by the disease. Among the animals subjected to these experiments were rabbits, pea-fowls, chickens, dogs, goats, sheep, and pigs. None of the animals thus treated showed any signs of the disease; and one of the conclusions of Dr. Willems is that the bovine race alone is infected by inoculation with this disease, while other animals of other races inoculated with the same liquid experienced no ill effects.

A recent statement has appeared in the newspapers that more than twenty thousand cattle have perished by pleuro-pneumonia in the island of Mauritius, and that more than a hundred deer had been infected by the same disease. It may be observed that no deer were included in the list of animals subjected to experiment by inoculation by Dr. Willems. While there is no sufficient evidence that other animals except neat cattle are subject to the pleuro-pneumonia, it is evident that there is great danger that the disease may be conveyed mechanically in the fleece of sheep, as it is known to be conveyed in the bedding, and by the executions of neat cattle; and as it also communicated by the stalls and cars in which diseased cattle have been kept. It is safe to conclude that this disease is as contagious and infectious as small-pox, and transmissible in the same manner among animals as that disease is among mankind.

From the experiments of Dr. Willems and from the extensive practice of inoculation in South Africa and Australia, it is fair to conclude that inoculation is a preventive of the disease in its natural form; but the objections to it are so many and so grave, that the practice of it cannot be advised in this country under present conditions.

"The great objection to inoculation," says a writer already quoted, "is that it can "only be practised at the expense of a universal diffusion of the poison, and of its "maintenance in a state of constant activity and growth. With such a universal "diffusion of the virus, the stock-owners are virtually debarred from introducing any "new stock for improving the native breeds, or infusing new vigor or stamina, inasmuch "as such new arrivals would almost certainly fall early victims to the plague. Australia, "therefore, now suffers from the permanent incubus of the lung plague, and can only "import high class of cattle at great risk."

In dairy regions, where the lands are inclosed and cattle are kept under daily supervision, it might be possible to make use of inoculation as the preventive, but not where the disease has broken over all bounds, and become general in a considerable section of country. Such, however, is not the case, and it is hoped never will be in any part of the United States; and inoculation is not to be regarded as any part of the remedy at present to be considered.

Value of Neat Cattle and of the Cattle Trade.

It is estimated that there were in the United States, 1879, something more than 33,000,000 of neat cattle, valued at more than $586,000,000. It is difficult to estimate the loss that would ensue by the prevalence of the pleuro-pneumonia throughout our country. It would evidently far exceed the present value of all the neat cattle of the country, because it would impair the productive capacity of the country for all future time.

In the article already cited, Dr. Law says:

"Thus England, with her 6,000,000 head of cattle, has lost in deaths alone from lung fever in the course of forty years over $500,000,000. We, therefore, with our 28,000,000 should lose not less than $2,000,000,000 in the same length of time, allowing still a wide margin for the lower average value per head in America; and this terrible drain is for deaths alone, without counting all the expenses of deteriorated health in the survivors, of produce lost, of loss of progeny, of loss of fodder no longer safe to feed to cattle, of diminished harvests for lack of cultivation and manure, of quarantine and separate attendants whenever new stock is brought on a farm, of cleansing and disinfection of sheds and buildings, &c., which become absolutely essential in the circumstances.

In this view the general introduction of this disease thoughout our country would impose a loss in forty years of an amount equal to that of the present national debt. With this danger imminent at the present time, it is the duty of every department of the Government to exercise its powers in the prevention of so great a national calamity.

In this connexion it may be proper to give a statement showing the improvement of our trade in neat cattle with other nations, and to call attention to its rapid increase within the past few years. The exports of horned cattle during the first five months of the current fiscal year, ending June 30, 1879, amounted to $4,414,000—being $517,182 in excess of the value of the same during the entire preceding year. Of the cattle exported in 1878, about 62 per cent. went to Great Britain.

The following table gives the number and value of cattle exported from this country from 1873 to 1880.

It is interesting to observe that notwithstanding the restrictions upon the introduction of cattle from the United States into Great Britain, the number and value of cattle thus introduced during the fiscal year ending June 30, 1879, were nearly three times as great as of those introduced in the fiscal year 1878.

STATEMENT showing the NUMBER and VALUE of CATTLE EXPORTED from the UNITED STATES to the UNITED KINGDOM and all other COUNTRIES from July 1, 1872, to December 31, 1879.

Fiscal years ended June 30.	United Kingdom.		All other countries.		Total.	
	Number.	Dollars.	Number.	Dollars.	Number.	Dollars.
1873	-	-	35,455	695,957	35,455	695,967
1874	123	113,800	55,944	1,037,057	56,067	1,150,857
1875	110	73,000	57,101	1,030,085	57,211	1,103,085
1876	244	31,220	51,349	1,079,483	51,593	1,110,703
1877	5,091	546,829	44,910	1,046,251	50,001	1,593,080
1878	24,982	2,408,843	55,058	1,487,975	80,040	3,896,818
1879	71,794	6,616,114	64,926	1,763,086	136,720	8,379,200
Six months ending Dec. 31, 1879	45,556	4,144,304	32,020	827,028	77,576	4,971,332

Treasury Department, Bureau of Statistics,
February 13, 1880.

(Signed) JOSEPH NIMMO, Junior,
Chief of Bureau.

These figures by no means show the full value of our unobstructed trade in neat cattle with foreign nations. Great Britain has suffered so much and so long from the pleuro-pneumonia that she is compelled to adopt stringent measures to prevent its introduction into her territory. Those measures consist at present of orders that cattle shall be slaughtered at or near her principal ports of entry. The British Government has established at the ports "lairs" where animals can be safely housed, and slaughter-pens sufficiently extensive to accommodate the business.

Great complaints have been made by American exporters of cattle to England of these restrictions on the part of the British Government. It is hardly just, however, while no effective measures are adopted in the United States to even systematically ascertain the extent of the cattle disease in this country, and much less to adopt efficient measures for its suppression, to complain that the British Government adopts effective means to prevent the spread of the disease in that country.

The principal export of cattle to Great Britain has been heretofore and perhaps will continue to be of fatted cattle intended for immediate slaughter, and the injury to this branch of traffic by the restrictions referred to is by no means fatal. It is believed, however, that in future an extensive trade in what are known as store or lean cattle, intended to be driven inland in Great Britain and there fattened for the market, will naturally grow up if the traffic be unrestricted by such orders as now exist for the slaughter of cattle at the ports of importation. The British Government, as well as our own, is deeply interested in this question and appears to be disposed to encourage the the trade in question so far as may be consistent with its own safety. Indeed, much correspondence has occurred between the British Minister and the Department of State upon this subject.

Q 2337.

In a letter of January 24, 1880, referring to the correspondence with regard to the recognition of certificates issued by customs officers of the United States, which has been referred to this department, the British Minister says:

"I venture to hope, however, in the interest both of Great Britain and of the United State, that Congress will, in its wisdom, pass such laws as may have the effect of obliterating the disease in this country, even if it be at the expense of a considerable outlay, though but a trifle compared with the loss of property which would arise from the continuance and spread of this destructive disease."

Existing Laws and Regulations on the Subject.

The only authority which any of the departments of this Government has to deal with the disease in question, is found in sections 2493, 2494, 2495, which are as follows:

"Sec. 2493. The importation of neat cattle and the hides of neat cattle from any foreign country into the United States is prohibited: Provided, that the operation of this section shall be suspended as to any foreign country or countries, or any parts of such country or countries, whenever the Secretary of the Treasury shall officially determine, and give public notice thereof, that such importation will not tend to the introduction or spread of contagious or infectious diseases among the cattle of the United States; and the Secretary of the Treasury is hereby authorised and empowered, and it shall be his duty to make all necessary orders and regulations to carry this law into effect, or to suspend the same as therein provided, and to send copies thereof to the proper officers in the United States, and to such officers or agents of the United States in foreign countries as he shall judge necessary."

"Sec. 2494. The President of the United States, whenever in his judgment the importation of neat cattle and the hides of neat cattle may be made without danger of the introduction or spread of infectious or contagious disease among the cattle of the United States, may, by proclamation, declare the provisions of the preceding section to be inoperative, and the same shall be afterward inoperative and of no effect from and after thirty days from the date of said proclamation."

"Sec. 2495. Any person convicted of a wilful violation of any of the provisions of the two preceding sections shall be fined not exceeding five hundred dollars, or imprisoned not exceeding one year, or both, in the discretion of the court."

Under these provisions it seems to have been assumed that the law conferred no authority upon the Secretary of the Treasury to make special orders in particular cases, or to impose any conditions whatever. Upon a critical examination of the provisions in question, under the present Secretary, it has been held that the power to suspend the prohibition of importation implies the power to suspend it upon proper conditions imposed by regulation; and it is under this construction that the annexed order of the department providing for a quarantine for cattle imported from foreign countries was issued. It will be seen by the explanation which will now be given of the orders issued by this department, that the Secretary has exercised to the fullest extent all authority vested in him by law for the suppression of pleuro-pneumonia.

On the 18th of December 1878, a despatch was received by cable from Liverpool, through the Department of State, stating that unless cattle shipped from the United States had a government health certificate when embarked, they would probably be slaughtered on landing; and suggesting that Minister Welch be cabled of an assurance that veterinary officers would be appointed at the seaports. Upon receipt of this despatch the department issued an order to collectors of customs and others, authorising the inspection of neat cattle proposed to be shipped to Great Britain, and the issuing of a certificate that such cattle were free from disease.

A copy of this order, marked A., is herewith transmitted.

On the 1st of February 1879, a second order was issued modifying the order of December 18, 1878, and making inspection at the ports, which before had been voluntary only, compulsory in all cases. By the same order collectors of customs were requested to promptly forward to this department any information which they might be able to obtain of the presence of contagious or infectious diseases prevailing among live animals in their vicinity.

A copy of this order, marked B., is transmitted.

On the 26th of February 1879, an order addressed to collectors of customs was issued, stating that the department had learned that pleuro-pneumonia had recently been found to exist among neat cattle at Hull, England, and prohibiting the landing of neat cattle from England at ports of the United States until further orders.

A copy of this order, marked C., is transmitted.

This order was issued partly in consequence of a letter from the secretary of the New York Agricultural Society, addressed to the Secretary of the Treasury, calling attention to the fact that cattle from the Jersey Islands were brought to the United States frequently and in considerable numbers, by steamers sailing from the port of Hull, touching at Southampton, where they received cattle from the Channel Islands; and epecially that the steamer "Lepanto" was to arrive from England at New York, bringing a herd of cattle from Southampton to be sold at auction in New York.

The department had also been informed that two herds of cattle, one being from the United States and the other from Canada, shipped from Portland by the "Ontario," had been found to be diseased with pleuro-pneumonia on their arrival; and, further, that the Dominion of Canada by the order of February 6, 1879, had prohibited the importation of cattle into that dominion from the United States for a period of three months. This order, by an order of October 14, 1879, was made perpetual until dissolved, and is now in force. A letter had also been received from Dr. Law, of the Brooklyn Board of Health, urging either the absolute prohibition of the importation of cattle from Europe, or of placing them in quarantine, as absolutely necessary for the protection of our country from the disease in question.

It was understood that there were companies in Philadelphia and New York, regularly engaged in importing cattle from the Channel Islands for sale at auction in those cities; and it was ascertained that by these auction sales cattle were distributed throughout all parts of the country.

On the 19th of July, 1879, the order prohibiting the importation of neat cattle from England was revoked, with the proviso—

" That all neat cattle from any part of Europe arriving at ports of the United States shall be kept in quarantine for not less than ninety days, under direction of the customs officers, and at the expense of the parties interested, except when State or Municipal laws provide for a quarantine of such cattle, and in such cases collectors will permit the proper officers to quarantine them in such manner as the State or municipal authorities require."

The department in that order reserved the right to consider special cases, and to decide whether in such cases cattle might be delivered at a period shorter than ninety days. The reasons for issuing this order are obvious enough without explanation. The reason why an order for quarantine was not issued at an earlier period is that, as above stated, the provisions of the statute before cited had been construed to allow only the free importation or the utter prohibition of the importation of cattle from abroad. Under urgent representations from several quarters, the question was reconsidered, and upon consultation with leading officers of other departments, the conclusion was adopted that the Secretary, under the provisions referred to, had, under the authority to prohibit or admit at his pleasure, the power to impose conditions upon the importation of cattle in the nature of quarantine regulations. The correctness of this construction may possibly admit of some doubt; and if Congress shall be of opinion that the Secretary has not the power to establish quarantine regulations, it is respectfully submitted that such authority should be given to him or some other department of the Government to do so.

A copy of this order, marked D, is transmitted.

On the 27th of December 1879, this department published an order modifying the order of July 19, 1879 [Exhibit D.], and requiring that in all cases a quarantine of not less than ninety days shall be enforced, including any term during which cattle shall be quarantined under State or municipal authority; and providing that cattle from Australia and New Zealand shall be regarded as embraced in the order of July 19, 1879.

It was found that under the order of July 19, which allowed State and municipal authorities to quarantine cattle according to their own regulations, a much shorter period than ninety days was often required. Under present regulations, a quarantine of ninety days is required in all cases.

On the 3rd of November 1879, the department issued the following order :—

" *To Collectors and other Officers of Customs:*

" To aid in preventing the introduction in the United States of contagious diseases among cattle, it is hereby ordered, that, in pursuance of the authority contained in section 2493 of the Revised Statutes, the importation of neat cattle from the Dominion of Canada is prohibited until otherwise directed.

" This order will take effect on the first of December next."

A copy of this order, marked F., is transmitted.

It became necessary to issue this order, because it was found that after the publication of the order of July 19, imposing quarantine upon cattle imported directly into the United States, cattle were imported into Canadian Ports and driven across the border into the United States, thus avoiding any quarantine whatever.

It may be proper to state in this connexion that this department has been notified that, by an order of the privy council of Canada, issued on the 6th of December 1879, a quarantine of foreign cattle imported into the Dominion of Canada of ninety days has been established. If it shall be found upon further inquiry, that our opinion that no pleuro-pneumonia exists in Canada is correct, and that a quarantine at the ports of Canada is rigidly enforced, it is in contemplation by this department to rescind the order prohibiting the importation of cattle from Canada into the United States.

It is hoped that the purpose of this Government to dispense with all restrictions upon the importation of cattle from Canada into the United States will be met with a corresponding purpose on the part of the Government of Canada to dispense with all restrictions upon importations of cattle from the United States into that dominion not absolutely necessary to its own protection.

This department is fully satisfied from reports under its order of February 1, 1879 [Exhibit B.], and from other correspondence, and from careful inquiry of members of Congress and others, that contagious pleuro-pneumonia has never existed in any of our territory west of the Alleghany Mountains, and that the importation of cattle from the Western States, through Buffalo and points west of that port, into the Dominion of Canada can be attended with no danger of carrying infection into the Dominion of Canada.

It is hoped that arrangements may be made that the great line of traffic through the posts of Buffalo, Detroit, and Port Huron, over the Grand Trunk Railway through Canada, may be resumed. Extensive cattle yards are in existence at Sarnia, the western terminus of the Grand Trunk Railway, from which cattle crossing from Port Huron were shipped upon that railway for transportation to the Atlantic coast for shipment abroad. That traffic is now entirely suspended by the Canadian order of non-importation. It is of great importance to the United States, to the Dominion of Canada, and also to Great Britain. If proper regulations can be established by Congress, or otherwise, for security against infection at or near the ports of exportation, it is believed that the British Government will gladly rescind the order which now requires the immediate slaughter of cattle imported from the United States into Great Britain at the ports of importation, as already suggested.

With the removal of those restrictions a large exportation of store cattle from the United States to Great Britain might be made to the advantage of both countries.

Althought many complaints were at first made of the order compelling immediate slaughter of cattle imported from the United States into Great Britain, a careful consideration of the position of both countries, with regard to the disease in question, leads to the conclusion that the order was made in perfect good faith to prevent importation of the disease, and not with any view to embarrass the traffic in neat cattle between the countries. The supposed importation of the pleuro-pneumonia by the "Ontario," and the reports of the existence of the disease in several of the Atlantic States, furnished reasonable ground for the action of the British Government, and it is not doubted that the Government will be as ready to rescind the restrictions upon the traffic as it was to impose them, whenever it is convinced that it may do so without danger of introducing the much-dreaded disease.

It is all important, not only with reference to our own protection, but to our commerce with Great Britain in neat cattle, that effectual measures shall be taken by our own Government to guard in general against the spread of the disease in this country, and in particular against its possible introduction into Great Britain, through the shipment of cattle from our own ports.

Measures to Prevent and Suppress the Disease.

Among the measures suggested to prevent the spread of the pleuro-pneumonia, isolation of the infected cattle is naturally suggested. This method, however, has been, and no doubt will be found to be entirely impracticable. The disease, as we have seen, is readily transmissible, not only by contact with the diseased animals, but by contact with buildings, hay, bedding, or excretions of any kind which have been in contact with diseased animals. Neat cattle are short lived, and when once infected by the disease in question, even if they recover, are of very small value either for breeding, for fattening, or for labour. Although a large percentage of the cattle diseased may apparently recover, yet, upon dissection, the lungs will be found to be seriously affected, so that it may be fairly said that cattle once infected with the disease are worthless for any purpose.

Added to this, isolation is very expensive, is attended with great risk to the neighbourhood, and the infected herd must be always suspected, and therefore unsaleable. In no view can the isolation of the cattle be recommended further than for the mere purpose of ascertaining definitely whether or not the disease actually exists.

Inoculation is, as has been before stated, another method practised in some countries to prevent the spread of the disease; but this has never been employed except in countries where the disease had broken through all restraint, and as a last resort to preserve sound cattle from the general infection which surrounds them. Besides the expense and inconvenience of the practice, it is often attended with the mutilation of the cattle by the loss of their tails or otherwise, and sometimes by the loss of their lives. It is not to be thought of as a remedy under any conditions such as exist at the present time in this country.

The only effectual method of eradicating the disease is by prompt slaughter of all infected and exposed cattle. By this method, energetically administered, the disease has been thoroughly stamped out in several places in Massachusetts, New York, Pennsylvania, and other States. To effect this, however, prompt and energetic measures are requisite. Several States have adopted such measures, and are ready to prevent, to attack, and exterminate the disease wherever it may appear within their borders. Most States, however, have adopted no such measures; and it seems absolutely necessary that some measures should be adopted by the general Government to prevent the prevalence of a disease, which, as we have seen, would amount to a national calamity. It is for Congress, and not for this department, to devise the measures necessary for this purpose. It may not be improper, however, to make some general suggestions upon the subject for the consideration of Congress.

The legislature of Massachusetts has recently sent to Congress a memorial requesting prompt action for the prevention and suppression of this disease; and from all quarters a cry is heard that it is time that the general Government should intervene in the matter.

The most obvious method of meeting the emergency is, perhaps, the appointment of a veterinary sanitary commission, whose duty it shall be to promptly investigate all reported cases of pleuro-pneumonia in any part of the country, to collect information with regard to the disease from all parts of the world, and to report the results of their investigation to some department of the Government for publication.

It would be necessary that such commission should be composed, principally at least, of veterinary surgeons or experts in the diseases of cattle. The commission might be small, consisting of from three to seven members, with authority to employ assistants or agents, who should be responsible directly to the commission. From such a commission, even with no greater powers than have been above indicated, much good might result. Owners of suspected herds and their neighbours would at once be informed whether the contagious disease was really present or not. If it were found to exist State and municipal authorities might be invoked for its suppression. If found not to exist, publication of that fact would be of very great value, not only to the suspected neighbourhood, but to the country and world in general.

Going a step further, Government might invest such commission with authority, in proper occasions, to aid municipal and State authorities in the suppression of the disease, and, by means of appropriation for the purpose, grant proper indemnity to the owners of cattle condemned to slaughter. Such proceedings would be in a close analogy with the methods adopted for the prevention and suppression of the yellow fever in the Acts establishing the Board of Health.

Under the provision found in the third section of the Act of June 2, 1879, entitled "An Act to prevent introduction of Contagious and Infectious Diseases into the United States," it is provided that—

"The National Board of Health shall co-operate with, and, so far as it lawfully may aid State and municipal boards of health in the execution and enforcement of the rules and regulations of such boards to prevent the introduction of infectious or contagious diseases into the United States from foreign countries, and into one State from another."

It is understood that this Act does not apply to diseases in animals.

Under this provision large amounts of the appropriation contained in the Act have been expended in co-operation with the authorities of several cities and States infected or threatened with infection by yellow fever; and it is not doubted that, through similar agencies, appropriations by Congress might be properly and effectually used for the prevention and suppression of pleuro-pneumonia among cattle.

As suggested by the British minister, the most obvious method of dealing with the disease would be by the appointment of a commission of some kind, with full power to prevent and eradicate the disease, in any manner they think proper, in any part of the territory of the United States, such power as is exercised by the Privy Council of Great Britain. Without expressing any opinion whether, under the power to regulate commerce, Congress has authority to send its agents into the States and destroy, upon the judgment of a commission, herds belonging to citizens which may be found to be dangerous to inter-State or national commerce, it is somewhat doubtful whether measures apparently so arbitrary would meet with hearty co-operation from State or municipal authorities.

The disease is not in existence in any of our Western States or territories. Indeed, it has existed and is known in only a few States of the Union, and the propriety of so energetic a movement on the part of the general Government might not be appreciated in those States where the disease has not been known. Some scheme for the prevention and prompt eradication of the disease seems to be demanded, and it is for Congress to define the limits both of policy and legality in its enactment.

Inspection of cattle upon railway trains on our great line of transportation has been suggested as a precaution against the conveyance of the disease. The objections to this proposition are based upon the fact that contagious pleuro-pneumonia is not indigenous to this country, that it has never existed in our Western States, whence cattle found upon such lines of transportation are brought, and that therefore such inspection is unnecessary.

Again, the disease has an incubation of from 9 to 60 days, during which the seeds of the disease would not be obvious to any inspector, however skilled. The interest of all shippers of cattle is clearly against the shipment of cattle infected with this disease. The delay of trains for such inspection would be expensive, and would be a great obstruction to business. Such inspection, as a general proposition is not recommended, while there is no practical objection to the inspection of cattle by authorized commissioners in particular cases where the disease is reported to exist.

Conclusions.

Having thus given a brief sketch of the history and character of the disease and a statement of existing laws the orders of this department under them, with some suggestions as to the effect of the disease upon our commerce with other nations, and with some remarks as to appropriate legislation by Congress on the subject, it may be convenient to state in this place, in the form of propositions, the conclusions at which this department has arrived. They are as follows:

1. Pleuro-pneumonia is a contagious infectious lung-fever in neat cattle, as readily communicated among them as small-pox among mankind, not only by actual contact, but by excretions of all kinds.

2. In this country it has never developed *de novo*, but has always been introduced by contagion.

3. It may be prevented by inoculation; but that remedy is not to be thought of in this country under present conditions.

4. It has a period of incubation of from 9 to 60 days, usually not exceeding 40, and its symptoms, when developed, are easily distinguishable by experts from those of other diseases.

5. The only proper method of suppressing the disease in the United States is by the destruction of all diseased or exposed cattle, and a thorough purification of buildings where they have been kept.

6. No contagious pleuro-pneumonia now exists or has ever existed in any State west of the Alleghany Mountains.

7. It does not now exist in the United States, on or near the boundary of the Dominion of Canada, and that it does not now exist in that dominion.

8. The disease now exists only in the eastern part of New York, in New Jersey, Pennsylvania, and perhaps in parts of Maryland, Virginia, and the district of Columbia.

9. The general course of traffic in cattle is from the west to the east. Only a few, and those of blood stock of great value, pass westward or into Canada from the east.

10. At the present time with ordinary care, cattle may pass from the Western States which almost exclusively furnish cattle for exportation into Canada, and through Canada, Portland, and Boston to foreign ports, without danger of infection.

11. With proper restrictions against contact with other cattle near the seaboard, cattle may pass from the Western States to the ports of New York, Philadelphia, and Baltimore for exportation, without danger of infection.

12. State and municipal regulations are not to be relied upon to prevent the importation and spread of the disease, or to effect its extirpation.

13. Stringent quarantine regulations are essential to the protection of this country against its introduction.

14. A veterinary sanitary commission whose duty it shall be to investigate all reports of the existence of the disease, to collect information respecting it, and report to some department for publication, is essential to efficient action on the subject.

15. Authority in such commission to co-operate with State and municipal authorities in preventing and eradicating the disease by supplying money out of appropriations by Congress for the purpose would be effective, and is in accordance with the Acts of Congress in reference to the National Board of Health.

16. The authority in such board to promptly isolate and slaughter infected and diseased cattle wherever found, and to award compensation to the owners, would be an effective agency to extirpate the disease. It is for Congress to consider the policy and legality of conferring such power.

Very respectfully,
(Signed) JOHN SHERMAN,
Secretary.

EXHIBIT A.

CIRCULAR.—*Exportation of Cattle to Great Britain.*

1878—Department No. 139, Secretary's Office.
To Collectors of Customs and others:
Treasury Department, Washington, D. C., December 18, 1878.

The following Despatch has been received by cable, through the Department of State, from Liverpool:

"Unless cattle shipped from United States have Government health certificates when embarked, slaughter probably compulsory on landing paralyzing trade. Can you cable Welsh assurance appointment veterinary officers at sea ports."

You are authorised to cause an inspection to be made of all neat cattle proposed to be shipped from your port to Great Britain, and to issue your certificate that such cattle as shall be shipped are free from all disease, and that there is no known disease in cattle at your port or in its neighbourhood.

In States in which there are officers authorised by law to examine into the diseases of cattle, the collector may avail himself of their services, as the basis of his action, at the expense of the shippers.

(By Order.)
Very respectfully,
(Signed) H. F. FRENCH,
Assistant Secretary.

EXHIBIT B.

CIRCULAR.—*Information in regard to Cattle Diseases.*

1879.—Department No. 23, Secretary's Office.
To the Collectors of Customs and others:
Treasury Department, Washington, D. C., February 1, 1879.

By department's circular of December 18, 1878, it was directed that live cattle shipped from the ports various of the United States might be examined with reference to the question whether they were free from contagious diseases, and that if found to be free from such diseases, a certificate to that effect should be given.

By that circular such inspection was not made compulsory, but the certificate was to be issued only upon the application of parties interested.

As the export trade in live cattle from the United States is of vital importance to large interests, every precaution should be taken to guard against the shipment of diseased animals abroad, and such a guarantee given as will satisfy foreign countries, especially Great Britain, that no risk will ensue from such shipments of communicating contagious or infectious diseases to the animals in foreign countries by shipments from the United States.

Collectors of customs are, therefore, instructed that in no case will live animals be permitted to be shipped from their respective ports until after an inspection of the animals with reference to their freedom from disease, and the issuance of a certificate showing that they are free from the class of diseases mentioned.

Notice of rejected cattle should be promptly given to this department.

In order that this department may be fully informed in regard to such diseases in any part of the United States, collectors of customs are requested to promptly forward to this department any information which they may be able to obtain of the presence of contagious or infectious diseases prevailing among live animals in their vicinity.

It is probable that if the disease prevails to any considerable extent it will be noticed in the local press, and collectors are requested to send copies of any such notices to this department for its information.

(Signed)   JOHN SHERMAN,
Secretary.

EXHIBIT C.

Treasury Department, Office of the Secretary,
Washington, D. C., February 26, 1879.

SIR,

The department learns that the disease called pleuro-pneumonia has recently broken out or been found to exist among neat cattle at Hull, England, and you are hereby instructed not to permit the landing of neat cattle at your port from England, until otherwise instructed, this order being based upon section 2493 of the Revised Statutes.

Very respectfully,
(Signed)   H. F. FRENCH,
Assistant Secretary.

Collector of Customs, New York.

EXHIBIT D.

CIRCULAR.—*Importation of Neat Cattle.*

1879.—Department No. 126, Secretary's Office.
To Collectors of Customs and others:

Treasury Department, Washington, D. C., July 1879.

The order of the 26th of February last, prohibiting the importation of neat cattle from England, is revoked.

By authority of section 2493 of the Revised Statutes, it is ordered: That the operation of the first clause of that section, which prohibits the importation of neat cattle from any foreign county into the United States, be suspended as to all ports of Europe, the Secretary having officially determined that such importation will not tend to the introduction or spread of contagious or infectious diseases among the cattle of the United States. Provided, that all neat cattle from any port of Europe arriving at any port of the United States, shall be kept in quarantine for not less than 90 days, under the direction of the customs officers, and at the expense of the parties interested, except when State or municipal laws provide for the quarantine of such cattle, and in such cases collectors will permit the proper officers to quarantine them in such manner as the State or municipal authorities require.

The department will, upon application, consider special cases where it may be claimed during such quarantine, that the cattle came from entirely healthy localities direct to the United States, and will decide in such cases whether they may be delivered at a period shorter than the 90 days before mentioned.

In any case where, during quarantine not under control of State or municipal authorities, the animals shall exhibit evidence of infectious or contagious disease, the facts will be reported to the department for instructions.

(Signed)   H. F. FRENCH,
Acting Secretary.

Exhibit F.

Circular.—*Prohibiting Importation of Neat Cattle from Canada.*

1879.—Department No. 160, Secretary's Office.

Treasury Department, Office of the Secretary,
Washington, D. C., November 3, 1879.

To Collectors and other Officers of the Customs:

To aid in preventing the introduction into the United States of contagious diseases among cattle, it is hereby ordered that, in pursuance of the authority contained in section 2493 of the Revised Statutes, the importation of neat cattle from the Dominion of Canada is prohibited until otherwise directed.

This order will take effect on the 1st of December next.

By order of the Secretary.

H. F. French,
Assistant Secretary.

Exhibit E.

Circular.—*Importation of Neat Cattle.*

1879.—Department No. 179, Secretary's Office.

Treasury Department Washington, D. C., December 27, 1879.

To Collectors of Customs and others:

The circular published in Decision No. 4104, of July 19, 1879, provided as follows:

"That all neat cattle from any port of Europe, arriving at any port of the United States, shall be kept in quarantine for not less than ninety days, under the direction of the customs officers, and at the expense of the parties interested, except when State or municipal laws provide for the quarantine of such cattle, and in such cases collectors will permit the proper officers to quarantine them in such manner as the State or municipal authorities require."

Collectors of Customs are hereby instructed that in all cases a quarantine of not less than 90 days shall be enforced, including any term during which such cattle shall be quarantined under State or municipal authority.

Cattle from Australia and New Zealand will be regarded as embraced within Order No. 4104, as hereby amended.

H. F. French,
Assistant Secretary.

Enclosure 3 in No. 43.

Letter from the Acting British Consul at Baltimore to the Marquis of Salisbury.

Sanitary, No. 3.

My Lord Marquis,   Baltimore, April 1, 1880.

With reference to my Despatch, Sanitary No. 2 of the 1st ultimo, I have the honour to inform your Lordship that during the past month there were some rumours of the existence of cattle plague in some of the counties of the State of Maryland, and that I at once took measures to ascertain the truth of the reported infection. With a view to the prevention of the landing of the live-stock cargoes of two British steamers, which cleared hence for London and Bristol, I communicated all the facts of which I was informed to the Right Honourable Sir Edward Thornton, Her Majesty's Minister at Washington, asking that I would be instructed to telegraph to your Lordship, if he thought the facts would warrant that course.

Later information, however, did not seem to justify this step, as upon careful inquiry I found that the cattle so shipped came directly from the West, where contagion did not exist, nor did they pass through the counties of this State which were said to have been infected.

The true status of cattle disease in this State is not an easy matter to develop, as the farmers, brokers, and shippers would seem to have a direct interest in the concealment of a pest amongst the cattle.

I have the honour to enclose herewith a paragraph from the "Sun" newspaper of this city, which will show the conflicting reports as to the disease.

Q 2337.

I have also the honour to enclose the printed copy of a Bill now pending before the Legislature of this State, having for its purport the prevention of the spreading of infectious cattle diseases.

I have, &c.
(Signed) J. W. LAWFORD,
Acting Consul.

The Most Honourable
  The Marquis of Salisbury, K.G.
  &c. &c. &c.

Enclosure 4 in No. 43.

A BILL entitled An Act to prevent the SPREAD of INFECTIOUS or CONTAGIOUS PLEURO-PNEUMONIA among the CATTLE of this STATE.

Section 1. Be it enacted by the General Assembly of Maryland, that wherever it shall be brought to the notice of the Governor of this State that the disease known as contagious or infectious pleuro-pneumonia exists among the cattle in any of the counties of this State, or in the City of Baltimore, it shall be his duty to take measures to promptly suppress the disease and prevent it from spreading.

Section 2. And be it enacted, that for such purpose the Governor shall have power to issue his proclamation, stating that infectious or contagious disease exists in any county or counties of the State, or in the City of Baltimore, and warning all persons to seclude all animals in their possession that are affected with such disease, or have been exposed to the infection on contagion thereof, and ordering all persons to take such precautions against the spreading of such disease as the nature thereof may in his judgment render necessary or expedient; to order that any premises, farm or farms, or stables, where such disease exists or has existed, be put in quarantine, so that no domestic animal be removed from or brought to the premises or places so quarantined, and to prescribe such regulations as he may judge necessary or expedient to prevent infection or contagion being communicated in any way from the places so quarantined; to all upon call sheriffs and deputy sheriffs to carry out and enforce the provisions of such proclamations, orders and regulations, and it shall be the duty of all sheriffs and deputy sheriffs, to obey and observe all orders and instructions which they may receive from the Governor in the premises; to employ such and so many medical and veterinary practitioners, and such other persons, as he may from time to time deem necessary, to assist him in performing his duty as set forth in the first section of this Act, and to fix their compensation; to order all or any animals coming into the State, to be detained at any place or places for the purpose of inspection and examination, provided that animals coming from a neighbouring State, that have passed a veterinary examination in said State, and have been quarantined and discharged, shall not be subject to the provisions of this Act; to prescribe regulations for the destruction of animals affected with infectious or contagious disease, or of those in direct contact with such, and liable to spread the disease, and for the proper disposition of their hides and carcasses, and of all objects which might convey infection or contagion; provided, that no animal shall be destroyed unless first examined by a medical or veterinary practitioner in the employ of the Governor as aforesaid; to prescribe regulations for the disinfection of all premises, buildings and railway cars, and of all objects from or by which infection or contagion may take place or be conveyed; to alter and modify from time to time, as he may deem expedient, the terms of all such proclamations, orders and regulations, and to cancel or withdraw the same at any time.

Section 3. And be it enacted, that any person who shall transgress the terms or requirements of any proclamation, order or regulation, issued or prescribed by the Governor, under the authority of this Act, shall be deemed guilty of a misdemeanor.

Section 4. And be it enacted, that any person who shall sell, or otherwise dispose of, an animal which he knows or has reason to believe is affected by the disease, or has been exposed to the same, shall forfeit to the State not less than $50 nor more than $100.

Section 5. And be it enacted, that all the necessary expenses incurred under direction or by authority of the Governor, in carrying out the provisions of this Act, shall be paid by the treasurer, out of any moneys not otherwise appropriated, upon the warrant of the comptroller, on being certified as correct by the Governor.

Section 6. And be it enacted, that in the event of its being deemed necessary by the Governor, or any agent duly appointed by him under the provisions of this Act, to prevent the spread of contagion or infection, to cause any animal or animals not actually diseased to be slaughtered, the value of such animal or animals shall be fairly appraised, and a record kept and a report made thereof, to the General Assembly at its session next ensuing, with a view to the reimbursement of the owners of such animals so killed, should provision therefor be made by law, it being provided that the carcasses of animals so killed and found entirely free from disease, shall, if practicable, be sold, and the proceeds of such sales shall be paid over to the respective owners of the cattle, and the amounts so received and paid over noted against the appraised value thereof.

Section 7. And be it enacted, that this Act shall take effect from the date of its passage.

Enclosure 5 in No. 43.

BALTIMORE "SUN," Newspaper, March 27, 1880.

PLEURO-PNEUMONIA IN MARYLAND—THE QUESTION OF ITS EXISTENCE HERE DISCUSSED—VIEWS OF PRACTICAL MEN—HOW IT MAY BE STAMPED OUT.

(Reported for the Baltimore "Sun.")

IN connexion with the Bill now before the State Legislature, introduced by Senator Geo. H. Williams, of Baltimore county, and which has passed the Senate, looking to the prevention or spread of lung fever or pleuro-pneumonia among the cattle in this State, the Belair "Ægis and Intelligencer" has a long article. Mr. Williams, in presenting the Bill, said that his barnyard in Harford county had been swept by the disease, and it was also stated that Senator Stump, of the same county, had also lost three cattle from the same cause.

The "Ægis" says that

"The subject was brought forward at a meeting of the Deer Creek Farmer's Club, held last Saturday, at the residence of Mr. R. Harris Archer. The members of this club own together at least a thousand head of cattle. A thorough inquiry at the meeting established the fact that not a single case of pleuro-pneumonia or other dangerous disease exists among the cattle owned by the members of the club, and none of the gentlemen present knew or had heard of any cases of disease of any kind among stock in any part of the county.

"In view of the reports, however, the club appointed a committee, consisting of Messrs. A. M. Fulford, Thomas A. Hayes, Dr. James M. Magraw, William Munnikhuysen, John Moores, and William F. Hayes, to investigate all the facts upon which the reports were based. This Committee ascertained, in the first place, that no cattle have died on Senator Stump's farm. The committee state that all of Mr. Stump's cattle are healthy, showing no signs of disease of any kind.

"The committee next visited Senator Williams's farm. There they found some cause for apprehension, but nothing upon which to base a positive assertion that pleuro-pneumonia existed among Mr. Williams's cattle. The committee were informed that two years ago a steer was brought to the farm from Baltimore city. This animal did not thrive as the other cattle, and died last summer. During last winter two cows also died, but the manager of the farm expressed a decided belief that their death was occasioned by old age. In February of the present year another cow was taken sick and was killed. No post-mortem examination was made of the steer or the cow, and no one familiar with the symptoms of pleuro-pneumonia saw them. On Monday of the present week a veterinary surgeon from Baltimore city visited Mr. Williams's farm, and upon examining the cattle selected one, a yearling, and pronounced it unsound. He could not possibly pronounce it a case of pleuro-pneumonia without making a post-mortem examination, and the animal was accordingly slaughtered. The lungs, which are the parts immediately affected, were taken by the veterinary to the city to be subjected to microscopic examination. The remainder of Mr. Williams's cattle, twelve or fourteen in number, are to all appearances healthy and in fine condition. We have ourselves made the most diligent inquiry among farmers from all parts of the county, and have been unable to discover the existence of disease of any kind among the cattle anywhere in Harford county. Pleuro-pneumonia, if it exists here at all, is confined exclusively to the farm of Mr. Williams."

In opposition to these assertions, the veterinary surgeon who visited Senator Williams's farm states that he found three cattle with all the external evidences of pneumonia. Permission was given to slaughter one of them, and it disclosed the well-marked lesions of pleuro-pneumonia. It would undoubtedly have furnished a thoroughly good point of contagion for all fresh cattle with which it came in contact, the diseased portion of the lung breaking down without even the protection of a cyst wall, and the pus being unusually offensive. He says that the symptoms were too plain to need any microscopic examination being made; that he found three cattle with all the external evidences of pneumonia. Permission was given to slaughter one of them, and the lungs were found to be badly affected. He states, that in company with another surgeon, who has had much experience of the disease, he has found in several parts of the State fully developed cases of the disease, some of them within the city limits of Baltimore. It is true that all of these cases are isolated ones, but they will form a centre from which, under favourable circumstances, the disease may be disseminated. The greatest danger will be found a few weeks from now, when cattle which have been confined to the stable all winter are turned out to grass. When once an animal has had the disease, even if it seems to recover, the seeds remain, and may, under certain conditions, be communicable. Besides the danger of infection from the animal itself, the car in which it is housed while sick can also become a medium for conveying the disease. The State Board of Agriculture of Pennsylvania have decided that all the cases of pneumonia in that State can be directly traced to infection from Maryland cattle, and they have called a meeting for Friday next, in Harrisburg, at which New Jersey will be represented, to take some action in the matter. They threaten that unless Maryland adopts some measures of prevention against the spread of the disease they will establish a 90 days' quarantine against all Maryland cattle, an action which would naturally injure the commercial interests of the State. Those who claim to be informed, say, that if the disease should once pass west of the Alleghany mountains, no power could stop its spread, and that the only plan for Maryland to adopt is to kill all sick cattle and isolate the rest, and thus stamp out the disease in a few weeks.

Pleuro-pneumonia is not an exaggerated type of pneumonia, but a separate and distinct disease. Neither is it indigenous, like hog cholera, but has been imported. Massachusetts succeeded by vigorous measures in stamping it out in 1859, and now that England has freed herself from it, she will guard against its re-introduction from any of the Atlantic States.

No. 44.

LETTER from the ACTING BRITISH CONSUL at BALTIMORE to the MARQUIS OF SALISBURY.

Sanitary, No. 4.
My Lord Marquis,   Baltimore, April 8, 1880.

With reference to my Despatch, No. 3, of the 8th instant, upon cattle disease in this State, I now have the honour to report that the Bill then pending before the State Legislature, a copy of which I have enclosed, being No. 2 for the provision of the spreading of pleuro-pneumonia amongst cattle, has now become a State Law.

This is regarded here as being an important item, and I shall endeavour later, to bring to your Lordship's notice any cases of its workings or evasions.

I have, &c.
(Signed)   J. W. LAWFORD,
Acting Consul.

The Most Honourable
  The Marquis of Salisbury, K.G.
   &c.   &c.   &c.

No. 45.

LETTER from the ACTING BRITISH CONSUL at PHILADELPHIA to the MARQUIS OF SALISBURY.

No. 3, Sanitary.
My Lord,   British Consulate, Philadelphia, April 16, 1880.

I have the honour to report to your Lordship, with reference to contagious diseases among cattle in this consular district, that during the months of February and March but few new cases of pleuro-pneumonia have occurred in the State of Pennsylvania, and that no cases, as far as I have been able to learn by careful inquiry, in the six Western States of this consular district have been discovered. These States, namely, Illinois, Ohio, Wisconsin, Michigan, Indiana, and Iowa, all west of the Allegheny mountains, receive no eastern cattle, and import but few of the finest English breeds direct from the eastern sea-board.

It can, therefore, be taken for granted that the disease pleuro-pneumonia has not extended from the Eastern States, where it has more or less prevailed, across the mountain belt to the extensive cattle raising districts of the western portion of the United States.

The Government of Pennsylvania are increasing, month after month, their efforts for the eradication of the disease which has been discovered, since the stringent investigations made during the past year, to be so disastrous to the dairy farmers of the Commonwealth. Particular attention is at the present time directed to the promiscuous shipment of live stock from the Baltimore (Maryland) stock yards to the open markets of Philadelphia, and it is expected that in a short time a strict quarantine will be enforced on the railways entering the borders of this State. The State of New Jersey, which adjoins Pennsylvania on the east, but is not within this consular district, will forcibly encourage the authorities of this Commonwealth in repressing the importation of unhealthy cattle from Maryland, where it is now well established, pleuro-pneumonia prevails to a considerable extent.

As applicable to this subject I have the honour to enclose your Lordships copies of a report of a paper read at a special meeting of the farmers and cattle breeders of Maryland, by Mr. John W. Gadsden M.R.V.C., a very able veterinary surgeon practising in this city, and who has taken a deep interest in, and continuously laboured for, the crushing out of the disease in this part of the country. The State of Maryland, in consequence of Mr. Gadsden's representations, is about to pass an Act for the prevention of the spread of pleuro-pneumonia among cattle within its limits, copies of which are herewith enclosed.

No. 1.

A deep interest continues to prevail throughout the Western States in the passage of a general Act by the Congress of the United States applicable to the entire Union with full powers invested in a body of Commissioners for the suppression of the disease. Three Bills have been brought in, differing more or less in particulars, for the purpose. No doubt one of them will be enacted during the present session.

I beg to enclose your Lordship a copy of two articles upon this subject, just published, the authors of which are practical men, and deeply interested in the matter.

I have, &c.

The Right Honourable,
  The Marquis of Salisbury, K.G.
    &c. &c. &c.

(Signed)   GEORGE CRUMP.

Enclosure 1 in No. 45.

PLEURO-PNEUMONIA.—PAPER read by Dr. JOHN W. GADSDEN, M.R.V., COLLEGE OF ENGLAND, at the MASS MEETING held at the COURT HOUSE, TOWSONTOWN.

"Pleura-pneumonia," better known to us as the "lung plague of cattle," is a malignant fever, introduced into the system of a healthy animal by contagion. This is a specific disease different from all other diseases of man or beast—not influenced by exposure to inclement weather, bad ventilation, changes of temperature, &c., which might cause ordinary inflammation of the lungs. Of all cattle diseases this, in the long run, is the most destructive, because the most insidious and the least likely to rouse a people to united action for its suppression. It has a period of incubation which is variable. There is often an interval of from one to two months from the reception of the contagion to the first general symptoms of this disease, but the usual time it remains latent in the system appears to be from ten days to two months. In many cases the disease creeps on very slowly, the only symptom being a slight cough, but of a peculiar character, which is often not noticed by the owner. The coat looks dull and staring. When the animals are made to move briskly they commence to cough. I will not detain you with all the symptoms unless you wish them, as that would take up too much of your time.

I quite agree with Professors Gamgee, Law, McEachran, and Laintard, that this disease never originates in this country, but as the result of contagion; therefore it can be prevented. We have no proof that any other than bovine animals will receive the infection. Whenever it appears it spreads in proportion to the opportunities for transmission. The long period of incubation renders its conveyance to great distances perfectly possible. In winter, when the cattle are confined to the stables, and but little communication with other herds takes place, the malady diminishes in severity;

but in fine weather, when grazing commences and different herds meet, if there is a diseased animal among them, it soon spreads. This fact is noticed every summer in Alexandria, Virginia, where the cattle are turned out on the commons together. A suspension of cattle traffic and movement in an infected country quickly reduces the number of attacks. This was proven beyond the possibility of a doubt during the past six months in Pennsylvania, as in localities where the disease had been for years it cannot now be found, owing to the strict quarantine of stock where the disease existed. Up to the 1st of November last the special agent of the Governor had quarantined 27 herds, which included 408 animals, distributed in seven counties of the State. Now they would not be able to find the disease if fresh diseased animals had not been sent in from other States. They still keep to the three months quarantine, but have only now four centres of contagion. Calves are often affected, and become carriers of the contagion. I have seen this fact several times proved in my practice in England. About 18 years ago, in Berkshire, I remember a large dairy of fine cows swept away by this disease through buying one sick calf, and employing an ignorant '' cow doctor'' who did not believe in contagion or infection. We traced out and found the calf came from a diseased herd in another county.

This disease was first introduced to this country in 1843, through a German cow imported direct from Europe, and taken from shipboard into a Brooklyn cattle shed. Here it was communicated to other cattle, and is said and believed to have prevailed in King's county, Long Island, more or less ever since. The authorities of New York have been vigorously engaged during the past year in stamping out the disease. In a valuable work written by Professor Law, of Cornell University, the progress of the disease is accurately traced from moving infected animals from one part of the State to another. It also contains valuable information which should be read with interest by all who raise or deal in cattle.

Professor Gamgee, in a paper written in 1871, and published in the report of the Commissioner of Agriculture, on the disease of cattle in the United States, traces the history of pleuro-pneumonia in this country from 1843 to 1868. As the professor is a man thoroughly versed in all diseases of animals, and spared no pains or expense to make his report perfect in every respect, the symptoms of the disease and post mortem appearance being particularly explicit and accurate, the paper is a very valuable one.

I have personally examined cattle with this disease, both before and after death, in the States of New York, Pennsylvania, and Virginia, and have no hesitation in declaring the disease there prevailing to be the same which occasioned such great losses in England, having made many post-mortems in that country of that specific disease.

Now I will give you as briefly as possible the opinions, published to the world, of some thoroughly scientific men who have made this disease a study for a number of years.

Professor Law, Cornell University, New York, says, "It is a specific contagious " disease peculiar to cattle, and manifested by a long period of incubation, (ten days to " three months,) by a slow insidious onset, by a low type of fever, and by the occurrence " of inflammation in the air passages, lungs, and their coverings with an extensive " exudation into the lungs and pleura."

Professor Laintard, New York Veterinary College, says, "Contagious pleuro- " pneumonia has at last forced itself upon the American public. This great danger has " been lurking in our midst, gaining strength day by day, as it quickly spreads from " numerous foci of propagation, waiting only for the opportunity to spread like wild-fire " throughout our land."

Professor Simonds, Principal of the Royal Veterinary College, London, says, that " pleuro-pneumonia in cattle is traceable to the introduction of newly-purchased animals, " who often bring the disease in a latent state with them, and which, on its declaring " itself, extends by ordinary infection to those with whom they are located. The same " fatality which marks the progress of the disease here attends it everywhere, and " throughout the continent it is looked upon as an incurable disease, and dealt with " accordingly."

Professor Walley, Principal of the Edinburg Royal Veterinary College, says, "pleuro- " pneumonia is an insidious, exudative, zymotic disease, due to a specific poison or " ferment peculiar to the ox, and having its local manifestations concentrated in the " lungs and pleura. No age, breed, or class, neither set of bovine species enjoy " immunity from the effects of the virus of this disease. It is one of the most insidious " diseases with which we are acquainted, and I do not hesitate to assert that it has been " the cause of greater losses to British stock owners and dairymen than any other single " disease to which animals are subject. No estimate, not even an approximate one,

" could possibly be made of the losses sustained by it, for the simple reason that
" thousand of cases never come under the cognizance of the authorities. It is alike
" contagious (by actual cohabitation) and infectious. The period of incubation is more
" indefinite than in any other zymotic disease, with the exception of glanders and rabies,
" while the average period may be stated at from three weeks to three months. It very
" frequently happens that it is prolonged to four or six months."

Professor Williams, Principal of the New Veterinary College, Edinburgh, says, " Pleuro-pneumonia is a contagious, febrile disease, peculiar to horned cattle, having an
" incubative period of from two to three weeks, to as many months, at the end of which
" local complications arise in the form of extensive inflammatory exudations within the
" substance of the lungs and upon the surfaces of the pleura, finally resulting in con-
" solidation of some portions of the lungs and adhesion of the pleural surfaces. In some
" cases there is extensive and rapid destruction of lung tissue, with death from
" suffocation, but most commonly the disease is of a lingering character, with symptoms
" of great prostration."

Mr. George Fleming, F.R.G.S., &c., says in his most valuable works on veterinary science :

" Pleuro-pneumonia of cattle is a specific and contagious disease peculiar to bovine animals, and of a sub-acute or chronic character. It usually appears as an epizootic or enzootic malady, and in consequence of its insidious invasion, the subtlety of its contagion, its general diffusion, and the great fatality attending it, it is a most serious scourge in every country in which it has appeared. It has caused an immense destruction, perhaps greater on the whole than cattle plague (Rinderpest) as in very few countries have any active steps been taken to eradicate it."

In the annual report of the Commissioner of Agriculture to the President, dated Washington, D.C., November 15th, 1878, is the following :

One of the most dreaded contagious disease known among cattle is that of pleuro-pneumonia or lung fever. It was brought to this country as early as the year 1843, and has since prevailed to a greater or less extent in several of the Eastern and a few of the Southern States. It made its appearance about a century ago in Central Europe, and has since spread to most European countries. With the exception of rinderpest it is the most dreadful and destructive disease known among cattle. Unlike Texas cattle fever, which is controlled in our northern latitude by the appearance of frost, this disease " knows no limitation by winter or summer, cold or heat, rain or drought, high or low " latitude." It is the most insidious of all plagues, for the poison may be retained in the system for a period of one or two months, and even for a longer period, in a latent form, and the infected animal in the meantime may be transported from one end of the continent to the other in apparent good health, yet all the while carrying and scattering the seeds of this dreaded pestilence.

Since the appearance of this effection on our shores it has prevailed at different times in the States of Massachussetts, Connecticut, New York, New Jersey, Maryland, Delaware, Virginia, and in the district of Columbia. It has recently shown itself at two points in Virginia (Alexandria and Lynchburg) where it was recently prevailing in a virulent form.

At present the disease seems to be circumscribed by narrow limits, and could be extirpated with but little cost in comparison with the sum that would be required should the plague be communicated to the countless herds west of the Alleghany mountains. This disease is of a such a destructive nature as to have called forth for its immediate extirpation the assistance of every European government in which it has appeared, many of them having found it necessary to expend millions of dollars in its suppression. The interests involved in this case are of so vast a character, and of such overshadowing importance, both to the farming and commercial interests of the country, as to require the active intervention of the Federal Government for their protection, and for this reason the considerate attention of Congress is respectfully asked to this important matter.

It is of vital importance, not only to stock raisers and dealers, but also to capitalists and those interested in shipping and steamship companies, that this disease should be stamped out of this country as soon as possible. England having lost cattle by this disease valued at about $10,000,000 per year, is making vigorous efforts to eradicate it ; therefore dreads its re-introduction and placed an embargo on the importation of American cattle where she will not remove until this country is free from the disease.

It is time that our people had awakened to the importance of this subject, for Canada is now endeavouring to secure the cattle trade of this country.

The following telegram will show the effort she is now making :

"By Atlantic Telegraph, London, December 3, 1879.

"The 'Times,' discussing the appointment of Sir A. T. Galt, as Canadian Minister, resident in London, says, 'The Home Government consider it highly desirable that the 'Dominion should be represented in England by a Cabinet Minister, who can give 'expression to the views and policy of the Canadian Government of the day. It con- 'cerns the interest of Canada that the embargo placed upon United States cattle 'imported into this country should be removed, for at present a large source of profit 'to the Dominion railways, shippers, and middle men is lost owing to its existence. It 'is not unreasonable to expect that cattle from certain divisions of the United States 'which are far removed from the districts where pleuro-pneumonia exists, might be 'permitted to pass through Canada on conditions of effective inspection at ports of 'entry and landed in this country on the same terms as Canadian cattle. The sole 'reason for maintaining the embargo is to prevent the importation of the contagious 'disease, and it may be possible for the Canadian Minister resident here to submit a 'scheme of safeguards which will obviate the necessity for this country applying 'prohibition to the whole of the United States.'"

Now, if they can succeed in releasing that portion of the United States west of the Alleghany mountains, and in which at present there is no disease, the western cattle can be transported on Canadian railways to Canadian ports and shipped on Canadian steamers to England, and Canada will reap the benefit and obtain the trade which should seek Boston, New York, Philadelphia, and Baltimore as its natural outlets.

In Philadelphia alone the American Steamship Company had made arrangements last spring to ship 700 head of live cattle per week, which was to have been increased to 1,000 weekly during the summer months, but the entire trade is now stopped by reason of the embargo.

We can rest assured of one fact, that England wants cheap beef, and offers an excellent market for our cattle, but she will not have them so long as this disease continues, and shipping them is attended with the risk of introducing pleuro-pneumonia.

Enclosure 2 in No. 45.

CONTAGIOUS CATTLE DISEASES.—WHAT HAS BEEN DONE BY THE STATES.

The present status of legislation on cattle disease is far from satisfactory, and is calculated to create the greatest apprehensions on the part of all having special acquaintance with the matter. A year ago, when England shut her ports against American cattle, New York, as the largest exporting State, took prompt action, and was followed by New Jersey and Pennsylvania. But in not one of these States has the work been carried out in the spirit in which it was begun.

In New York, as successive developments showed that the lung plague was far more widely prevalent than had been at first supposed, it soon became clear that the appropriation made by the Legislature was most inadequate to pay for the work demanded. Concerning "infectious disease affecting domestic animals," it was, by the law of 1878, "the duty of the Governor to make measures to suppress the same promptly, and to prevent the same from spreading." But the Governor, who had established a special reputation for economy, refused absolutely to exceed the appropriation by a single dollar, preferring to let the Veterinary Sanitary Staff disband, and to allow the plague to spread once more over the ground that had been conquered, the money that had been expended to be worse than thrown away, and the moral effect of the success to be lost rather than incur any appearance of personal responsibility, or add to the indebtedness of the State.

To obviate the probably irremediable results of an entire suspension of work, the acting officials had to reduce the force, give up most of the effective suppressive work, and confine their efforts mainly to preventing any renewed spread of the disease; and this they have maintained for seven months, until the Legislature should come together and find time to make a new appropriation. This has now been obtained and active suppressive measure recommenced, which it is to be sincerely hoped will not again be interferred with, from any cause whatever, until the last trace of infection has been driven from the State, and until the danger of infection from other adjacent States has been entirely removed.

In *New Jersey*, where the law provided for the payment of all necessary expenses out of the State Treasury without any special appropriation, and where, accordingly, there should have been no hindrance to the most prompt, extensive, and effective work, the opposion of political enemies, unfortunately, drove the official into a temporising policy, which has only brought them a double defeat. To avoid the imputation of extravagant expenditure, the officials virtually abandoned the principle of compulsory slaughter, and killed only such animals as the owners were willing to sell to the State at a very low price. When the owner was indisposed to part with his stock on these terms, they were quarantined on the premises, all ingress and egress of cattle being forbidden; and as the disease usually leaves encysted masses of dead lung in the chest for months, and even for a year and more, the duration of such quarantine necessarily became practically endless, and the only resort for the owner was to fatten as many as possible, and sell them to the butchers and to give up the rest to the State. Meanwhile his milk, cheese, or breeding business was stopped, so that his losses were by no means confined to the sacrifice of his stock. The system naturally developed much dissatisfaction among the owners of stock, and entailed a very considerable outlay for the prolonged quarantine under *expert* supervision, and of these the enemies of the measure made good use in the present Legislature, and secured not only the discharge of the officials, but the repeal of the law. A movement is on foot to have the same law re-enacted, or another passed; but with the inimical elements in the way, it remains to be seen whether anything can be accomplished.

In *Pennsylvania* a number of diseased cattle have been killed, and Mr. Edge appears sanguine that the plague has been in the main suppressed; but, to one who has had an extended experience with the malady, it does not appear that his confidence has a sufficiently stable basis. From the printed report it appears that in certain herds the acutely sick have been killed, and after a short interval the herd has been released from quarantine as sound animals. In such circumstances it cannot be doubted that many cattle bearing encysted masses of infecting matter in the chest must have been turned loose upon commerce. Moreover, in the Philadelphia as in the Jersey City stock-yards, no sufficient pracautions are taken to prevent the contact of healthy and sick, of store and fat cattle; and these yards are thus made pestilential centres from which infection is widely distributed. To show that this is not overstated, it need only be named that the inspectors on the New Jersey frontier of Pennsylvania, in a short time, turned back into the latter State over fifty head of cattle affected with the lung-plague. Dr. Gadsden, of Philadelphia, writes us: "We have several fresh outbreaks clearly traced to diseased "cattle from the Baltimore cattle market. *The authorities here have not taken any* "*steps to prevent the sale of such animals in the cattle markets of this city.* * * "Am afraid Baltimore will do nothing in the matter. They send, on an average, 400 "head of cattle from that market to Philadelphia every week, and I am informed on "good authority that there are from 100 to 150 diseased animals with pleuro-pneumonia "in the vicinity of Baltimore; also, that there is no law in the State to prevent the "spread of the disease, and that every week 2,000 cattle change hands. So you see "how we stand."

The Baltimore cattle market is very largely supplied from Virginia, where, on the occasion of our visit, a year ago, we ascertained that the lung-plague was extensively prevalent.

Connecticut has had cattle diseased with the lung-plague in the town of Greenwich for a year past, and, after continuous efforts that would have discouraged any man who was less enthusiastic and determined, Hon. H. E. Hyde has succeeded in advancing, in both houses, a most effective bill, which, it is hoped, will soon become a law.

A showing such as the above is by no means encouraging as to a speedy extinction of the lung-plague, and is largely calculated to create many and painful doubts as to the probability of our reaching any such extinction at all. Out of seven infected States, three only have attempted anything, and not one of the three has accomplished anything like what it might and ought to have done. Meanwhile, the whole political horizon is beclouded with the smoke of the battle waged for success in the Presidential campaign, and the indications are only too strong that the question of averting the calamity of this plague from the country will be quite lost sight of in the question, so much more congenial to the partizan mind, of who shall next occupy the White House.

PROBABLE COST OF STAMPING OUT LUNG-PLAGUE.

Well sustained and properly directed efforts for the extinction of the lung-plague should rid the United States of the incubus in the course of two years, and the expense would probably not exceed $2,000,000. This estimate is based on the supposition that the plague does not extend beyond the limits of the seven seaboard States known to be

Q 2337.

infected, and that the money appropriated would be honestly applied to the work, under efficient officers, and not applied to create sinecures for political hacks. The country cannot afford the misapplication of such a fund. The success of this effort in animal sanitation involves much more than the suppression of the lung-plague of cattle, though even this would far exceed in its benefits the extinction of the entire debt created by the civil war. The successful extinction of the lung-plague will give a reasonable hope of the future extinction of the swine-plague, and of most of the other animal contagions that now devastate our flocks and herds. It means the ultimate saving of scores or hundreds of millions yearly to the stock raisers of America. It means the suppression of contagions and parasites that now destroy our farm animals, and are by them conveyed to the human being. It means the preservation of human health and the lengthening of human life, the enchancement of the value of labour, and of the wealth and power of the Nation.

Present Losses from Lung-Plague.

To many, and no doubt to legislators, the estimate of $2,000,000 as the cost of eradicating this plague, will be startling. But a correct statement of our present losses, if such could be obtained, would be more astonishing still. To take but one item of such losses as were caused by the closure of England against our cattle. One of the most extensive exporters of cattle estimates the difference between the returns from cattle that must be slaughtered at the docks at Liverpool, and those than can be taken inland to be killed when and where they may be wanted, to not less than half a cent per pound, live weight, or $1 per hundred pounds net. On an average this would make a difference of not less than $7 per head. Other exporters have set the average as nigh as $10 per head. The exports from the port of New York alone, during 1879, were 95,370 head of cattle. The loss on these, at $7 per head, caused by the English embargo, is $667,590; at $10 per head it would amount to $953,700 or close upon $1,000,000 for the year. Add to these the exports from Boston, Philadelphia, and Portland, and the depreciation of our exports of cattle from this cause alone cannot be less than $1,500,000 per annum.

Then, if we consider the losses from this disease in our herds, we set it low at $500,000 more. Thus year by year we are taxed to the extent of $2,000,000 by this plague alone; and yet it seems probable that the outlay of a similar sum, once for all, in the work of extinction, would permanently rid us of the pestilence. We need not adduce the scores of millions which a general extension of the plague would cost us, the bulk of humanity do not care to provide against prospective evils, and judge that they have enough to do in taking care of the present; but when we can demonstrate that even at present we are squandering every year, through our shiftlessness, $2,000,000, which, if once rightly expended, would permanently remove the pestilence, surely no policy of "let well enough alone" can find a moment's acceptance with citizen or statesman.

No. 46.

LETTER from SIR E. THORNTON to EARL GRANVILLE.

(No. 12, Sanitary.)

Sir, Washington, April 26, 1880.

With reference to my Despatch No. 9 of this series and of the 3rd instant, I have the honour to state that a report on contagious pleuro-pneumonia among cattle has recently been transmitted by Mr. Le Duc, United States Commissioner of Agriculture to the Committee on Agriculture of the House of Representatives. The report is the result of investigations made by Dr. Lyman in different parts of the United States.

As it has not yet been printed, and it may be some weeks, or even months before it will appear, I have the honour to enclose a synopsis of its contents as published recently in the "New York Herald."

From this report, it appears that the disease has shown itself, and now exists in some parts of the State of Connecticut, Westchester County, New York City, and Long Island in the State of New York, and in several counties in the States of New Jersey, Pennsylvania, and Maryland.

It is supposed that the disease also exists in the District of Columbia, and in Virginia, but no investigation has yet been made in these parts.

It would seem from this report that many cattle have died of the disease in the above-mentioned States, that others have been slaughtered, that regulations made to prevent the spread of the disease are not attended to, and are sometimes wilfully evaded, and that there are quite enough infected cattle to cause the disease to spread over a large extent of territory unless stringent measures are adopted and vigorously enforced for its suppression.

I have, &c.
(Signed)   EDWARD THORNTON.

Her Majesty's Principal Secretary of State
for Foreign Affairs.

Enclosure in No. 46.

PLEURO-PNEUMONIA.—CHARACTER and EXTENT of the DISEASE.—AN OFFICIAL REPORT to CONGRESS.—INTERESTING FACTS and FIGURES for HOUSEKEEPERS.—RAVAGES of the PLAGUE.—INFECTED HERDS in NEW YORK, NEW JERSEY, and other STATES.

Washington, D. C., April 17, 1880.

Mr. William G. Le Duc, Commissioner of Agriculture, has transmitted to the chairman of the Senate Committee on Agriculture an interesting report on the subject of contagious pleuro-pneumonia or lung-disease of cattle. It was prepared by Dr. Charles P. Lyman, under the instructions of the department. Dr. Lyman began his investigations in the city of New York early in February last. He says that on his arrival in that city he visited Dr. Liantard, from whom he learned that the disease still prevailed to some extent in Eastern New York and on Long Island, and that there was a reported outbreak at Haverhill, N. H. The New Hampshire State Commission had pronounced this outbreak as of a sporadic character, yet the circumstances attending it were of a suspicious nature, at least sufficiently so as to throw doubt on the decision arrived at by the State Commission, and a further investigation was regarded necessary in order to positively determine the matter.

The Disease in Connecticut.

Dr. Lyman says :—

In the course of my investigations in Connecticut the following facts were gleaned :— An outbreak of contagious pleuro-pneumonia, says Mr. E. H. Hyde, chairman of the commission, had occurred at Greenwich, occasioned by exposure to a calf which had been brought from New York and placed in the herd of Mr. B. Livingstone Mead. This farm is located on the State line, a part being in the State of New York and a part in Connecticut. This herd consisted of 20 head. The buildings are in Connecticut. From seven to nine animals have died, the last one about the 18th of March 1879. The remainder are unaccounted for. These animals were at one time examined by Professor Law.

The herd of Daniel M. Griffin, on an adjoining farm, contracted the disease from Mr. Mead's herd. He had 27 head, eight of which died. With the exception of one animal Mr. Griffin sold the remainder of the herd to dealers in New York for slaughter. The one he retained remains with his tenant, and will soon be slaughtered on the place.

Joseph B. Husted, of Greenwich, took some cattle to New York for slaughter, among them two cows. They were all landed at the infected Sixtieth street yard. The cows were not sold, and, after some hesitation on the part of the New York Commission, they were allowed to be returned to Connecticut, the Commissioners of the last-named State being notified of the fact. The State authorities at once ordered them quarantined, but before the letter reached Mr. Husted he had sold them, and they are still untraced. They were taken away from Greenwich on or before July 11, 1879.

Mr. Curtis Judson, of Watertown, near Waterbury, keeper of the Gramercy Park Hotel, bought two cows from Mr. Hedge, a dealer in New York, and placed them in an excellent herd of his own at Watertown. They proved to be effected with contagious pleuro-pneumonia, and soon affected the herd with which they had been placed. The herd was quarantined, by order of the State Commissioners, but the owner, on the 8th of March 1879 broke quarantine and took them to New York. This fact coming to the knowledge of the authorities in time, they were enabled to be in New York on the arrival of the animals, where they were at once killed by order of the New York Commission. Mr. David D. Hawley, of Danbury, had an outbreak of disease in his herd on October 27, 1879. They were visited by Dr. Hopkins, of New York, who made an autopsy of a calf and pronounced the disease tuberculosis. The calf came from New York, and had been with the herd but a month.

Mr. Porter, of Waterbury had an outbreak among his cattle on the 13th of November, which the attendant veterinarian feared might prove to be contagious pleuro-pneumonia. The herd was visited by the State Board on November 18, and the decision arrived at was that the animals were suffering simply from sporadic disease. No post-mortem examination was made, and they are now reported as doing well.

Some trouble was reported among cattle at Hartland and Milford, but on examination by the Commissioners the disease was decided to be sporadic. I visited the herd of B. L. Mead, of North Greenwich, which I found suffering from contagious pleuro-pneumonia. Although the trouble was of long standing some of the cows certainly were in a condition to convey the disease to healthy or non-infected animals. There were 10 cows, one pair of oxen, one yearling, and six calves in this herd.

The herds of Daniel M. Griffin, Joseph B. Huxted, David D. Hawley, and Mr. Porter were visited, but no cases of the plague were found. Reports from Watertown, Waterbury, North Bradford, Hartland, and Milford were of such an assuring character that I did not deem it necessary to visit those points.

New York.

I am indebted to the New York Commission for the following statement, made February 12, 1880:—

Putnam County.—On the line of the Harlem Railroad there have been lately slaughtered 176 animals; of these, forty were acute cases. The others, having been exposed to the contagion, were killed to prevent the spread of the disease. The beef was marketed.

In the town of Kent, Joseph R. Sprague has an infected herd of 60 head of cows, steers, and calves. They are now in quarantine.

Westchester County.—In Yonkers, Mr. Austin had a herd of twenty-seven head, which had been reduced by the ravages of the disease to eight animals. Mr. Pierpoint had a herd of eleven head which had been exposed to infection; two of these had been killed. Mr. Cheever, on Odell's farm, has a herd of twelve head that had been infected. Mr. Cayl has one animal infected.

In Croton Falls, Bedford township, Mr. Butler who generally keeps about fifty animals, has lost by death and slaughter, his entire herd, with one exception.

New York City.—In the city there are believed to be but five infected stables left. These are in quarantine and are located as follows:—

No. 1.—West Seventienth Street, old chronic cases.
No. 2.—West Seventy-eighth Street, acute cases.
No. 3.—East Ninetieth Street and Madison Avenue, acute cases.
No. 4.—One hundred and twentieth Street and Fourth Avenue, acute cases.
No. 5.—One hundred and twenty-first Street and Fourth Avenue, acute cases.

Long Island.

The whole western end of this island, as far back as Jamaica, is more or less infected. The stables of Gaff, Fleischmann, & Co., of Blissville, originally the hotbed of the disease, are now perfectly free from all contagion. Jamaica is located some ten and a half miles back, therefore the infected district includes Brooklyn, New Utrecht, Flatbush, Gravesend, Flatlands, and New Lots, in King's County, and Long Island City, Newtown, Jamaica, Flushing, and Creedmoor, in Queen's County.

Suffolk County.—At the extreme eastern end of the island are extensive unfenced ranges used as common pastures. The plague prevailed among herds grazing on these ranges, but it is now believed they are thoroughly freed from it, as the last known cases were destroyed at Montauk, August 28, 1879, and at Bellport, August 11, 1879. This portion of the island has been subjected to numerous examinations, and is now regarded as entirely free from the plague.

Staten Island.

A year ago one case of the plague was discovered on this island. The animal was killed. No case has since appeared, and the island is now regarded as absolutely free from the disease.

On the 12th and 13th days of February, in company with one of the New York inspectors, I visited several stables in Brooklyn. I found several chronic cases in the stables, but no acute ones. At Johnson avenue slaughter-house I was shown a portion of a characteristically diseased lung which had been taken from an animal killed a few hours previously.

On February 14 I visited the stables of Mr. Lang, 109th Street and Fourth Avenue, New York, where I found three cows suffering with the plague. One of these was a very acute case, and I was informed, had been afflicted but three days. This, and one of the others, had been condemned to the offal dock. Mr. Foudre, a neighbour of Mr. Lang's lost a cow on the 12th day of February by the disease. A week before he had bought a cow from a dealer named Louis, and the cow that died was taken sick on the day that this cow came to his stable. The nearest stable to Mr. Foudre's place is on 112th Street and Fourth Avenue. Mr. Foudre had owned the cow he had for eight months. Lang purchased his sickest cow from a dealer named named Franke some five or six weeks previous. She was a "two titter," and on that account Franke knocked off $5 on her price. She never did well. The other two commenced coughing three or four days before my visit.

On the afternoon of the same day I visited the offal dock and witnessed the autopsy of Lang's cows, alluded to above. Both cases revealed well-marked lesions of acute pleuro-pneumonia contagiosa. One of the animals, which showed a temperature of 105 degrees Fahrenheit, and thirty-six respirations per minute, had the whole posterior lobe of the left lung consolidated and strongly adherent to the costal pleura. The right lung was healthy. The pericardium was thickened to half an inch. In both lungs of the second cow were found a number of small isolated spots of the characteristic lesions of the disease, the largest being about the size of a double fist. Their borders were well defined, and the intermediate portions of the lung tissue appeared perfectly healthy to the naked eye. On February 16th, at 120th Street and Fourth avenue, I found three cows which had been exposed to infection and were in quarantine. They appeared healthy, and one had just been sold to a butcher named McEvoy.

In Fremont, at the stable of Mr. Bohle, I found two cows, one of which had been put into an infected stable on Christmas. Her temperature was 101 degrees Fahrenheit, and she was breathing at the rate of thirty respirations per minute. The other animal was a Jersey cow. Both animals had been ordered slaughtered as soon as they could be got ready for the butcher. A Mr. Cannons, a neighbour, had had some trouble with his herd, but they were quarantined and seemed to be doing well. The infection to this herd of Mr. Bohle's was communicated by a cow that was pastured with ten others on a common lot. She developed contagious pleuro-pneumonia and was killed in the month of August. Three months and nineteen days thereafter the second animal was attacked and sent to the offal dock, where she was slaughtered. At the end of three weeks a third, and at the end of four weeks a fourth animal was taken sick and both were slaughtered. The first one of these animals belonged to Mr. B. Jorkman, other three to Mr. Bohle, who, as has been before stated, bought a fresh cow on Christmas and put her in with one remaining from his original herd. This was in direct violation of the law and his instructions. She is now diseased and has been ordered to be killed. These ten animals were strictly isolated as soon as the first cow was killed, and no other infection was then possible. Two of them have since been fattened and sent to the butcher in a healthy condition. The remainder, with the exception of those belonging to Mr. Bohle, are still free from disease.

On the 17th day of February, in company with Professor Law and Dr. Hopkins, I visited the farm of Mr. Joseph Sprague, in Kent, Putnam County, whose herd was infected and had been in quarantine for some time. The herd consisted of fifty-three head, and were sold during the day by the State Commission to butchers who had been notified to attend. The animals brought an average of $6 per head, which was regarded as a low price. Three of the animals were considered too badly diseased for beef, and on being killed showed well-marked lesions of the disease in its different stages. This herd was infected by a cow purchased from a dealer named Robinson.

On February 18, in company with the same gentlemen, I visited Croton Falls, Westchester County. We found here a gentleman by the name of Butler, who had lost thirty-one animals out of a herd of thirty-two by the plague. His remaining cow was in quarantine, with no symptoms of the disease manifest. On the 15th of June last Mr. Butler bought seventeen cows of Mr. Robinson the dealer above referred to, and they were delivered to him on the 17th of the same month. They had been pastured all the the summer on "Hyatt's Lower Farm," with a cow that had been sick but had recovered. The first animal on Butler's farm sickened on September 16 and soon died. The remaining thirty head were either slaughtered for beef or killed diseased.

On February 19, in company with the same gentlemen, I visited the farm of Mr. Daniel Austin, in Yonkers, Westchester County. Originally this gentleman had a herd of twenty-seven head, eighteen of which had either died of the plague or had been killed for beef in the incipient stages of the disease. Five of the animals were killed for beef and showed no lesions of the disease. Of the four remaining, two are well-marked chronic cases—*i.e.*, having portions of encysted lungs. This herd was infected by a cow that had pastured on an infected range called "Hog Hill," in the town of Yonkers. She wandered into a field near Mr. Austin's place, where she died on the 27th or 28th of July, and was not buried for some days after. The disease appeared among Mr. Austin's cattle on October 21. The herd of Mr. Odell, on whose farm this cow died, was no doubt infected by the same animal. His herd consisted of some valuable Jerseys, among which the plague appeared on August 28. We killed three of his animals, and they all showed well-marked lesions of the disease.

On February 20 we visited Mr. Tice, of Newtown, which is a suburb of Brooklyn, L.I. This herd was infected about the middle of October. Eight of his animals died, and he had continued to fill their places with fresh animals. We found twelve of his animals suffering with the plague. Two cows were killed—one an acute and the other an older case—and both showed well-marked traces of the disease. His herd was infected by a cow sent him about the 20th of September.

A Mr. Grady, whose stables are in Blissville, a portion of the suburbs of Brooklyn, had lost eleven head of cows out of a herd of fourteen since the middle of September.

Pennsylvania.

I arrived in Philadelphia on February 24, and during the evening visited and had a conversation with Dr. J. W. Gadsden relative to the prevalence of the plague in Pennsylvania. Dr. Gadsden showed me a private telegram giving him the information that the British Government contemplates raising the embargo on cattle transported from the western and south-western States, through Canada and shipped to Great Britain from ports of the Dominion Government. On the morning of February 25, in company with Dr. Francis Bridge, I visited the farm of Mr. J. F. Taylor, located near the town of Marple, Delaware county, Pa. We found this gentleman's herd suffering with the disease. Having selected and paid for four acute cases the animals were slaughtered and examined. The post-mortem examination revealed all the lesions of the disease in its acute stage. This herd was infected by a cow purchased by Mr. Taylor in the Philadelphia stock yard. She was in very good condition, and when she arrived on the farm seemed very tired. Next morning she refused to eat and seemed sick. She died a few days thereafter with all the symptoms exhibited by those that have since died of contagious pleuro-pneumonia.

On February 26 I visited the farm of Mr. Wynne, near Philadelphia. His herd originally consisted of 34 head. Ten of these had already been killed, and two had died of the disease. An examination of those left developed the fact that the disease was still present in both an acute and chronic form. The owner objected to the slaughter of any of the animals. His herd was infected by some cows he purchased in the Philadelphia stock yards. The disease broke out about the 1st of June last.

On the 27th day of February I visited Messrs. Martin, Fuller & Co., who have charge of the Philadelphia stock yards. They offered me every facility for an examination of the premises. During my interview with these gentlemen Mr. Fuller said something ought to be done to relieve the dealers in stock from the oppression of the English embargo; that the European trade is now carried on at a positive loss, and that this loss is clearly traceable to the embago on our live cattle. He further stated that he was in Europe last season and found the market flooded at Liverpool. His stock was detained 15 days in quarantine before it could be slaughtered. Besides the expense of feeding all this time his animals were positively shrinking in weight; that when they were finally slaughtered he was compelled to accept any price offered. He found dealers there who said they could afford to give him from $15 to $20 per head more for the animals if they were allowed to drive them back into the country and slaughter them only as needed. During the day I met by appointment Secretary Edge, special agent of the Governor. He seemed to appreciate the fact that more thorough and active measures than those heretofore used are necessary for a complete suppression of the plague. He thinks the better plan would be to pay a good price for all exposed animals, and that in the country all exposed and infected animals should be slaughtered, as well as those acutely diseased. Under existing circumstances he does not think it would be politic for the State of Pennsylvania to thoroughly eradicate the disease; indeed, he does not think this possible so long as the southern border of the State is unprotected from importations from Maryland. Until quarantine measures are established against this State, or the State itself takes some action for the suppression of the disease within its borders, the State of

Pennsylvania cannot hope for success. The farmers of Pennsylvania will go the Baltimore stock yards to buy "frames," and in this way new cases are continually being brought into the State. Under the present construction of the law sufficient means to pay a fair indemnity cannot be obtained, and to kill even diseased animals without funds to pay for them the secretary believes would result disastrously, as it would prejudice the farmers against a better law which is hoped for in the near future. His policy is simply an effort to keep the disease within its present limits, with the destruction of as few animals as possible. Up to January 1, 1880, the secretary had expended but $2,700 in repressive measures.

On February 28, while examining some cows at the stock yards, I found an acute case of contagious pleuro-pneumonia. The affected animal was in a yard with some 20 other milch cows, and all were being offered for sale. This animal was seen also by Dr. Bridge. On March 1, while examining lungs of slaughtered animals at the Philadelphia abattoir, I found one showing the well-marked lesions of the plague. The butcher said the animal came from Illinois, but it was afterwards traced to Cecil County, Md. On the 2nd day of March I visited Camden, and learned some facts relative to the extent of the plague in New Jersey. On the 3rd inst. I attended a meeting of the farmers and stock raisers in the infected district. The meeting was held in Philadelphia and was called for the purpose of devising means for the extirpation of the plague. During the day I visited Elm station, Montgomery County, and assisted in selecting six diseased animals from Mr. Wynne's herd for the purpose of post-mortem examination. On the 4th and 5th days of March I was engaged in examining lungs of slaughtered animals at the Philadelphia abattoir. I found no traces of the disease, but, on the 4th inst., while examining some cows at the stock yards, I found a second case of the plague in an animal that came from near Gettysburg, Adams County, Pa.

The following are the sources of infection and locations of diseased herds in Pennsylvania:—

Philadelphia County.—The Philadelphia stock yards are infected. These yards are constantly receiving and sending out to different localities diseased and infected animals.

Chester County.—Mr. M. Covning, of Chester Valley, has a herd of 27 head, among which the disease has appeared. The herd was infected by a cow purchased from a drover, and the infection could not be traced.

Mr. J. Dickinson, of Chester Springs, has a herd of 28 head. These animals were infected by the owner, who brought the contagion from a neighbouring farm where he had administered medicine to a diseased animal.

Mr. G. V. Rennard, Chester Valley, had a herd of 18 animals infected by his neighbour's cattle (Mr. Covning's).

Mr. Rennard's cattle had infected a herd of 14 head, owned by Mr. J. W. Wilson, his near neighbour.

Mr. C. Holland Frazer, of the same neighborhood, had a herd of 26 head infected by a purchased animal, which he was unable to trace.

Mr. W. Pugh, of Chester Springs, had his herd infected by Mr. Dickinson, alluded to above, who visited this herd for the purpose of administering medicine to a sick animal.

W. J. and H. A. Pallock, Downington, had a herd of 30 head infected by a purchased animal.

Mr. W. Reid, Westchester, herd of five head. Chronic cases; source of infection unknown.

Mrs. Hermann, Westchester, herd of 12 head. Infected from neighbouring cattle.

Mr. W. E. Pennypacker, Cambria, herd of 14 head. Probably infected from neighbouring herd.

Holmes and Bunting, Oxford, herd of 35 head. Infected by Mr. Turner's cattle on adjoining farm.

Mr. M. Young, Bradford, herd of 36 head. Infected by Mr. Turner's cattle.

Between the herds of Holmes and Bunting and Mr. Turner was a large meadow. The bulls broke down the two intervening fences and the herds mingled in the meadow. The herds were separated as soon as men on horseback could separate them, but not soon enough to prevent infection.

Montgomery County.—Messrs. J. L. and A. S. Reiff, Worcester, herd of 15 head. Jacob L. Reiff had bought of five different dealers during May and June, and it was impossible to tell from which one the disease came. Two animals have died and two others have been killed by order of the State inspector. Five others had been slightly affected, but had recovered. A. S. Reiff purchased a cow of his son in July, about the time of the outbreak. One animal died, and a second one was condemned and killed by order of the State inspector. Five other animals were affected, but all had recovered, and had been released from quarantine.

Joseph Tyson, Worcester, herd of 13 head. Mr. Tyson purchased a cow of a man who had previously purchased her at the Philadelphia stock yards. She was killed on September 24, 1879, by order of the State inspector, but as she had been isolated on the appearance of the first symptoms of the disease only one other animal was infected.

Charles T. Johnson, Lederachsville. This gentleman's herd was infected by an animal purchased from a dealer. Up to the date of the first inspection in October last five animals had died. One was afterwards condemned and killed. Five out of the remaining 10 were affected, but had recovered.

Peter M. Frederick, Lansdale. Herd quarantined January 29, 1880. The infection was communicated by a cow purchased in the Philadelphia stock yards. Two animals had been condemned and killed. The remainder, 10 animals, were free from disease on March 4.

Jacob D. Wisler, Worcester. Herd quarantined February 6. Three animals had been condemned and killed, and three others were sick.

John C. Blattner, Worcester, herd of 16 head. The plague had prevailed in this herd in a mild form for the past four months. None of his animals died, and he did not suspect the nature of the disease. His cows were greatly reduced, and he had been feeding at a loss. One of his animals had commenced to lay on fat, and all were free from disease except the altered structure of the lungs, the natural result of the disease. This herd was infected by Mr. A. S. Reiff's cattle, mentioned above.

W. W. Latrobe, Merion, herd of 14 head.

W. Wynne, Elm Station, herd of 28 head. This gentleman had lost several animals. The infection came from a cow purchased at the West Philadelphia stock yards.

Bucks County.—Aaron Yoder, Dublin. This herd was quarantined September 25. The first to sicken was one that he purchased two weeks previously. As she had passed through the hands of three different parties, it was impossible to trace her back satisfactorily. Three out of the four were affected, but had recovered.

Isaiah Kletzing, Dublin. This herd received its infection from Yoder's cattle before they were quarantined. Three animals had recovered.

Lehigh County.—Charles Krauss, East Greenville. This herd was quarantined December 13. The infection came through a cow purchased at the Baltimore stock yards. Two animals died, and 11 were condemned to be killed. Thirty animals remain and are thought to be free from disease.

Cumberland County.—Samuel Hess, Ebersley's Mills. Herd quarantined March 20, 1879. Infected by cattle coming from Baltimore stock yards. This herd is in York County.

Delawere County.—R. L. Jones, Upper Darby, herd of 49 head. Infected by purchase from Philadelphia stock yards.

Thomas Cunningham, Upper Darby, herd of 21 head.

J. G. Haenn, Darby, herd of 14 head.

J. Lickens, Ridleyville, herd of 15 head.

J. F. Taylor, Marple, herd of 36 head. One-third of his animals had died, and the disease was still present.

Lancaster County.—J. F. Turner, near Oxford, Chester County, herd of 52 head. Infected by the adjoining herd, into which the disease had been introduced by some calves brought from the State of New York.

David Williams, Colerain. This herd had come in contact with the diseased Oxford herd, and was quarantined before any symptoms of the disease appeared.

Lane Gill, Colerain, herd of five head, adjoining above.

Adams County.—J. Redding, Gettysburg, herd of 13 head. Infected by purchase from Baltimore stock yards.

New Jersey.

The following are the locations of some of the diseased herds in New Jersey at the time of my investigations in February:

Atlantic County.—Benjamin Gibberson, Port Republic, herd of 11 head. This herd was quarantined October 29, and again on November 28, as chronic cases. Eight animals had been affected by the disease.

H. A. Johnson and William Ramsay, both of Port Republic. The herds belonging to these gentlemen were diseased and in quarantine.

Gloucester County.—Charles B. Leonard, of Paulsboro, has two farms, upon one of which, he has a herd of 22 animals, six of which are suffering with the plague. He has 28 animals on the homestead farm, only one of which has shown symptoms of the disease. Both herds are in quarantine.

Benjamin J. Lord, of Woodbury, herd of 25 head. On June 13, six of these animals were suffering with the plague. October 27, there were 21 of these animals sick. On November 25, the same number were suffering with the disease, and were all in quarantine. Of the first lot of 25 animals six were attacked and three died. He then bought four or five fresh animals. These remained in good health for five months and 12 days, but of the original animals 21 had suffered with the contagion.

Camden County.—An occasional case of contagious pleuro-pneumonia had been found here, but no great amount of the disease had ever existed. A most thorough system of inspection of cattle coming from Philadelphia had been established here, and its rigid enforcement had undoubtedly been of great service in preventing the importation and spread of the contagion. From August 28 to December 15, 217 animals, known to have been exposed to infection, were returned to Philadelphia. 41 head of these were suffering with plain and unmistakable symptoms of the malady.

Burlington County.—Howard Stakes, West Hampton, herd of 11 head. Quarantined June 20, but does not obey quarantine regulations.

Job Evan, Mount Holly. Herd quarantined July 11. One acute case.

D. Mullone, Recklesstown. Lost one animal on January 20.

William Murray, Jacksonville, herd of 14 head. There have been four acute cases in this herd, and two animals have died. He will probably lose others. The herd was quarantined July 11.

Ocean County.—E. H. Jones, Forked River, herd of 29 head. There have been 27 acute cases in this herd. Six animals were killed on October 2nd, and on the 15th of the same month the balance were slaughtered. The infection to this herd was brought in some calves purchased in Fortieth Street, New York City. From October 1878 to October 1879, Mr. Jones lost 32 animals by this disease.

At the same place as above, Moses Street has one animal, Captain Wilson three, and James Holmer 23, all of which are infected and quarantined.

Mercer County.—G. E. Neunamaker, Pennington. On November 17 three of his animals were suspected. On the 20th of the same month two acute cases had developed, and the herd was quarantined. One animal was slaughtered on January 17. Two animals recovered and are still on the place.

William Walton, Dutch Neck, herd of 32 head. On May 5 one acute case appeared. On May 15 the animal was very sick, and as other cases were developing, the herd was quarantined. The owner did not believe his animals were affected with the plague, and failed to observe the quarantine regulations, until one of the animals was killed, in order to prove the fact. The herd becoming seriously affected, Mr. Walton sold, on October 29, all his animals to a butcher. This herd was infected by a cow purchased in New York. She calved, and her offspring at five weeks' old showed the well-marked lesions of contagious pleuro-pneumonia.

Monmouth County.—D. C. Robinson, West Freehold. One cow died of the plague on May 13. On the 19th of the same month another cow showed symptoms of the disease, and the herd was quarantined. On June 11 three more animals were sick, one of which has since died, and a second one recovered. The quarantine is continued.

A. D. Voorhees, Adams' Station, herd of five head. One of the animals was found sick on October 13, and the herd was quarantined. On the 16th of the same month another animal showed symptoms of disease. One of the afflicted animals was killed. On November 19 a third animal was taken sick. The herd is still in quarantine.

Piny Parks, who resides on an adjoining farm, had a herd of eight animals infected. One was killed, and the remainder quarantined on October 16.

D. W. Watsons, Perth Amboy, herd of 13 head. His herd was quarantined March 29, 1879. October 13, nearly six months after, he still had 11 head. On February 5, 1880, having added to his herd, he had 13 animals, three of which were sick, and the others reported as well (?). The three sick animals were quarantined and the remainder set at large.

Isaac Morris, Metuchen, herd of 14 head. The first case of the plague was discovered in this herd on May 22. The animal was taken to the butcher and killed, and the herd quarantined, which is still continued.

Hunterdon County.—Joseph Exton, Clinton, herd of 51 head. On June 9, 18 of the animals were found suffering with the disease, and were quarantined. The quarantine is still continued.

Morris County.—D. Frank Carl, Sterling, herd of 13 head. On March 26, 11 head were sick. On February 20 but five animals remained, one of these showing old lesions. They are in quarantine.

Benjamin Runion, Millington. Herd of 20 head, 12 of which were sick on June 13, when the animals were quarantined, two animals were killed, and on the 26th of June eight animals were sick out of the 18 remaining. Two new cases had occurred, but the others were improving. The herd is still in quarantine.

Mary Smith, Chambers Street, Newark, herd of five head. On October 24 one animal was reported sick. On the 28th of the same month a second one was attacked, and two were killed. On January 14 the others were reported as "recovered," but were still quarantined.

Alice Kennedy, Roseville, had one animal affected with the plague, which was killed August 14.

Union County.—C. E. Winans, Salem, herd of nine head. Had lost two animals up to August 5. The remainder were sick and in quarantine.

Louis E. Meeker, Salem, herd of thirteen head. Five animals were sick on August 1, when the herd was quarantined. On January 2, having purchased another animal, he had fourteen head. Three of these were chronic cases, and were ordered quarantined for thirty days longer.

J. O'Callighan, Salem, on August 26 had a herd of nine head, with but one animal sick. Up to November 12 he had lost five animals, and had but four left. On January 20 he was visited by the State Inspector, but refused to drive his cattle in from the field for examination. The officer, on threats of personal violence, ordered him to keep up the quarantine, and left without making the examination.

E. A. Bloomfield, Salem, herd of four head, one sick; quarantined August 26. Had one chronic case on January 1; quarantine continued.

F. Saltzman, Raselle, herd of three head; two sick; quarantined September 3. On January 20 one animal was sick, and the herd was still in quarantine.

Bergen County.—C. McMichael, Leonia, herd of 21 head; five sick quarantined April 1. On July 11 had two animals sick, and on January 21 had but five animals left, two of which were sick; quarantine continued.

Christian Freund Closter, herd of ten head; five sick; quarantined November 11. The same report of this herd was made on November 19; it is still in quarantine.

Hudson County.—The disease exists in the following localities:—

Stables Nos. 133 and 144 Essex Street, Jersey City.

Jersey City Heights.—Mary Mullin, No. 106, Thorn Street; J. Lewis, corner Hutten and Sherman Streets; J. Platz, No. 899, Montgomery Street; J. Gurrey, Hopkins Street; Martin Staunton, Hopkins Street; George Reed, No. 87, Germania Avenue; J. Leddy, Nelson and Charles Streets; J. Ryan, No. 25, Laidlaw Avenue; Jonathan Meyer, No. 22, Gardner Street; John Bosch, Congress and Hancock Streets. These localities are all in quarantine.

Greenville.—B. O'Neil, Brittain Avenue; William Shaw, opposite cemetery; Mrs. Corcoran. All quarantined.

Hoboken.—Benjamin Engle, No. 200, Newark Avenue; John Torpey, No. 172, Grand Street; V. Cohen, old small-pox hospital. (Mr. Cohen, having diseased animals, desired a permit to put a fresh cow in his stable. He was refused, but he stated to the officers he should put her in anyway. This he did and I afterwards saw this cow in his stable suffering with the disease in its acute stage.) Michael Reynolds, No. 165, Grand Street.

West Hoboken.—J. Claude, Cortlandt Street; Harris Aaron, Newark Street; H. M. Nass, Hallingen; Mrs. Schmidt, Hackensack Plank Road; B. Benjamin, Cusset Street; Kuntzle, Blume Street; Mrs. Schlooler, Blume Street; Ernest Weiss, Demot Street, and Oldmeyer, Boulevards.

Secaucus.—Latenstein, county road; H. Fisher, Secaucus Road; Loeffle, race course; Bryan Smith, race course; N. Wohlker, race course; H. Block, North Bergen.

Delaware.

The only information I have as to the prevalence of the disease in Delaware I received in the course of a conversation with Mr. George G. Lobdell, president of the Wilmingtod Car Wheel Company. His farm is located in New Castle Hundred, about two miles from Wilmington. In 1858 he had a valuable herd of animals. During this year contagious pleuro-pneumonia broke out among some cattle on a farm about three miles from his place. Fearing the infection of his herd he commenced to sell off his cattle as he could find purchasers, but before this was accomplished, and perhaps within four months, it reached his farm, and by spring he had but one animal left. For two years after this he was without cattle, but at this time he commenced to stock his farm again. About six years ago the disease was introduced into a herd kept on a farm about two miles from his place. His own cattle remained exempt until about two years ago, when they were again infected. Since then he has been using the fumes of burning sulpher and has had no fatal cases. Mr. Lobdell informed me that some sort of a law had been passed by the State looking to a suppression of the disease, and that three commissioners had been appointed by the Governor to superintend and enforce its provisions.

Maryland.

Although it has long been known in a general way that contagious pleuro-pneumonia existed among the cattle of this State, no effort on the part of the authorities has ever been made to ascertain with any exactness the localities of the diseased herds. On the 8th of March I proceeded to Baltimore, where I at once called upon Mr. William B. Sands, editor of the " American Farmer," a gentleman who had greatly interested himself in this matter, and who gave me all the information in his possession as to the localities and extent of the plague in the State, as well as kindly furnishing me with letters of introduction to the officers of the different agricultural societies throughout the State. On the 9th March I visited Hagerstown, the county seat of Washington county, where on the next morning I called upon P. A. Witner, Esq., secretary of the County Agricultural Society. He said he did not believe there was any disease in the county; that upon the day before there had been a meeting of the Board of Agriculture, at which there had been a good representation from all the different sections. Those present agreed that they had never known or heard of a case of lung plague in any part of the county.

I was next introduced to Mr. J. B. Bausman, a cattle dealer of this place. In the pursuit of his business he had been all over the county repeatedly, but had never known of a case of the disease. The drift of cattle in this place was entirely from Western Virginia through to Baltimore—never, so far as he knew, from Baltimore here. In his trade he feels very much the evils of the English embargo. It makes a difference to him of at least $10 per head in the price of his cattle. I then saw Dr. H. J. Cossens, an English veterinary surgeon, who has been located here for the past 15 years, and whose practice extends over the entire county. He had a considerable experience with the lung plague in England, but had never seen but one case in this country; that was many years ago in Virginia. He is sure there is none in this county, nor has there ever been. Several other gentlemen from different localities were seen, but always with the same result. One farmer had a cow, which he had recently bought, that was coughing and not doing well. I visited her and found her suffering from tuberculosis. In the afternoon I proceeded to Frederick city, the county seat of Frederick county. Here, upon the 11th of March I called upon Mr. J. W. Baughman, secretary to the Local Agricultural Society. He did not know of any diseased animals, but took me out to the Court House, where we saw and questioned a number of gentleman from different parts of the county. None of them knew of any cases of this disease; they were very sure that had there been any unusual sickness they would have known of it.

I next saw Dr. P. R. Courtenay, an English veterinary surgeon. He had been here but a comparatively short time and had heard of nothing that caused him to think that there was any of this disease in the county. He kindly offered to bear the matter in mind and if any cases of the disease came to his knowledge he would let me know at once. Here, as in Washington county, the whole drift of cattle is from west to east. In the afternoon I went to Westminster, the county seat of Carroll county, and called upon Colonel W. E. McKillip, president of the county Agricultural Society. He was sure there was no disease of the kind in the county, but he said that it was quite a common thing at certain seasons of the year for cattle to be brought here from Baltimore. This I regarded as a very suspicious circumstance, and so asked for an introduction to some cattle dealers in town. This was kindly granted, and I proceeded to call upon Mr. Edward Lynch. He said:—" Farmers hereabout generally make milk for the
" Baltimore market, and procure their cows from among themselves; but from the
" time that grass comes up until late in the fall of the year some of them are in the habit
" of feeding cattle; that the cattle for this purpose are generally bought at the ' Scales '
" in Baltimore; that in this way last fall Mr. Samuel Cover, of Silver Run, this county,
" procured some stock which, after having been on his place for a short time, developed
" disease of some sort; some died and some that were sick got well. Also a Mr.
" Beacham, of Westminster, had had trouble of a similar nature for some time past. In
" a general way he knew that the farmers hereabout were somewhat frightened about
" contagious pleuro-pneumonia." On March 12 I drove to the farm of Mr. Samuel Cover above referred to, at Silver Run, and found there three cases of chronic contagious pleuro-pneumonia. This gentleman stated that he had got the disease last fall through some steers that came from South-western Virginia, but which had stopped at the Baltimore stock yards for some little time, at which place he had bought them. Some

Q 2337.

four or five weeks after he got them the disease broke out among them. He had at the time some 80 head of neat stock. Of these 15 were sick. When the disease first showed itself he put all the sick animals in a building by themselves, and had all his stables thoroughly disinfected. This was kept up all the time, and the places repeatedly whitewashed. In all four animals died—two of them the Baltimore steers; the other two were cows which he had had for some time. Mr. Coven further says that now, when he gets cattle, he always puts them by themselves in a building entirely away from his regular cow stables, and hopes in this way to avoid any further outbreak among his herds.

Returning to Baltimore on March 7 in company with Dr. Le May, a veterinary surgeon, I visited a herd of milch cows kept in a dairy in Woodbury near Baltimore. Here we found one acute and two chronic cases of the plague. The man in charge said that he had got through with the disease, from which he had suffered greatly some two months ago, by selling out all his sick animals. From here we went to another large dairy in the same neighbourhood. The gentlemanly owner here informed us that he had had none of the disease for some time; that his plan was to buy often and sell often. In this way he found he could keep up his milking stock and keep rid of disease. From here we visited a near neighbour living on the direct road to the city. In answer to questions this man said that he did not know if his neighbour (the one from whom we had just come) called it having the disease or not, but that he drove many a sick one past his house on his way to the Baltimore market. He (our present informer) was free to say that he followed the same practice himself, and had done so ever since he lost his first eight animals. He supposed this was not right, but his neighbours did it, and so he did. Summer was invariably the worst time thereabouts. The next place visited was about two miles distant and on a different road. The dairyman here had suffered greatly in the past, but thought that now by selling the sick ones he had nearly rid himself of the plague.

March 18.—We drove in several directions around city and found the disease or its effects in all the herds except one that we visited.

March 19.—To-day we examined a number of the cow stables in the city itself, in which many chronic and a few acute cases were found.

March 22.—I went to Harford county, where the disease was reported as existing in a number of different directions. However, we concluded to visit the farm of Senator George A. Williams, whose herd of fine Alderneys have been suffering more or less from the scourge for the past two years. Here among several chronic cases was one that, although he had been sick for some time was making no progress towards a good recovery. This animal the overseer consented to let us kill. The autopsy showed, well marked, the lesions of the disease. The infection here, as with all the other outbreaks hereabouts, came from Baltimore. At this point further investigations were given up for the present, and it still remains, in order to properly finish this report, to make an examination of the remainder of this State, the District of Columbia, and Virginia, in all of which places it is believed that contagious pleuro-pneumonia of cattle exists to a greater or less extent.

What the Investigation shows.

As a result of my investigations thus far I find this ruinous foreign plague actually existing among cattle in the following States:—

Connecticut.—In Fairfax county.

New York.—In New York, Westchester, Putnam, King's and Queen's counties.

New Jersey.—In Atlantic, Gloucester, Camden, Burlington, Ocean, Mercer, Monmouth, Middlesex, Hunterdon Morris, Essex, Union, Bergen, and Hudson counties.

Pennsylvania.—In Philadelphia, Chester, Montgomery, Bucks, Lehigh, Cumberland, York, Delaware, Lancaster, and Adams counties.

Maryland.—In Carroll, Baltimore, Harford and Cecil counties. The middle and south-western portions of this State have not yet been visited.

No examination has as yet been made in the district of Columbia or of the infected territory of Virginia; but as the plague prevailed quite extensively in both of these localities last season, it will no doubt be found still in existence when the investigation takes place.

117

No. 47.

LETTER from the BRITISH CONSUL-GENERAL to EARL GRANVILLE.

Sanitary, No. 4.

My Lord, British Consulate General, New York, May 1st, 1880.

I have the honour to report to your Lordship in reference to the sanitary condition of cattle in the State of New York, that it appears by the statement just published of Professor Law, one of the State inspectors, that contagious pleuro-pneumonia among cattle is now practically confined to Brooklyn and its suburbs.

In regard to other States in this consular district, I have no further information to communicate to your Lordship beyond that already reported by me.

I have, &c.
(Signed) E. M. ARCHIBALD.

Her Majesty's Principal Secretary of State
for Foreign Affairs, London.

No. 48.

LETTER from the ACTING BRITISH CONSUL at BALTIMORE to EARL GRANVILLE.

Sanitary, No. 5.

My Lord, Baltimore, May 1st, 1880.

I have the honour to report that since my Despatch, Sanitary, No. 4, of April 8, to Lord Salisbury informing his Lordship that a Bill (copy previously enclosed) for the prevention of pleuro-pneumonia amongst cattle in this district, had become a law, some few cases of cattle disease made its appearance and was dealt with by the provisions of the new law. I have the honour to enclose a newspaper paragraph which fully shows how this law went into operation.

I have also the honour to state that owing to the rigour with which the law under which all cattle are slaughtered on arrival at ports in the United Kingdom is carried out, the United States Customs Authorities at this port have discontinued cattle inspections by surgeons who have, until recently, certified as to the health of cattle intended for export.

Cattle for export are brought by railway directly from the west, where pleuro-pneumonia is unknown.

I have, &c.
The Right Hon. the Earl Granville, K.G. (Signed) J. W. LAWFORD,
&c. &c. &c. Acting Consul.

Enclosure in No. 48.

Extract from "Baltimore Sun," April 27, 1880.

Stamping out Pleuro-Pneumonia.

Correspondence of the "Baltimore Sun,"
Belair Md., April 26, 1880.

Slaughter of Cattle in Harford County; Prompt Suppression of the Disease;
How it was nipped in the Bud; Interesting Particulars, &c.

At a meeting of the Deer Creek Farmers' Club of Harford County, on Saturday last, the subject of pleuro-pneumonia was considered, in connexion with other matters of interest to farmers. The meeting was held at the house of the president of the club, Mr. Jas. Lee, and was largely attended. The farmers present were as follows: James Lee, Benjamin Silver, junior, R. H. Archer, B. H. Barnes, G. R. Glasgow, Thos. A. Hays, Wm. Hays, Johns H. Janney, W. D. Lee, Thos. Lochary, John Moores, Wm. Munnikhuysen, George E. Silver, Silas B. Silver, S. M. Lee, Judge J. D. Watters, Herman Stump, R. E. Morgan, W. S. Forwood, M. T. Murphy, Parker H. Lee, Dr. J. M. Magraw, and F. W. Baker, editor of the "Ægis."

These names comprise some of the most influential and snbstantial farmers of the county, owning some of the richest lands under tillage, and representing a wide area of country. It was stated that the members of the club own collectively upwards of a thousand head of horned cattle, so that they are of course deeply interested in the protection of their stock from any and all contagious diseases. The Deer Creek region is considered the richest as well as the best cultivated part of Harford county; it certainly possesses beautiful lands, which are under the highest cultivation. The country is gently rolling; the homesteads are excellent and give exterior as well as interior evidences of the thrift and prosperity of an energetic and affluent race of people.

One of the preliminaries of the club meeting was to inspect the farm and barnyard of Mr. Lee, who is known to be one of the most successful agriculturists of this State, in order that the committee might report and the meeting discuss any particular subject suggested by the inspection. It was ascertained that Mr. Lee devotes much attention to stock raising. He has two short-horn cows, "Mary Leslie" and "Lady Hendleston," which are models, perfect in form and condition. He has also two fine bull yearlings of the same blood, besides other short-horn cattle originally derived from L. H. Long, of Kentucky. Besides other stock he has upwards of sixty horned cattle, chiefly short horns. Besides the blooded stock the stalls were found filled with beef cattle, which have been fed all the winter and are now ready for market. Corn used for winter fattening of cattle realizes greater profit to the producer than if sold as grain. Probably the most satisfactory inspection of Mr. Lee's farm was made in the dining-room, however, where the table demonstrated most agreeable excellence, which all the guests knew how to appreciate as well as the points of the short horns.

So far no pleuro-pneumonia has manifested itself among the cattle of the Deer Creek region, which is not far from the Pennsylvania line. Each member of the Farmers' Club was questioned by the president on the subject, and they all answered that no disease of the kind had appeared among their cattle or in their immediate neighbourhood. That contagious and fatal pleuro-pneumonia had existed in other portions of the country is incontestable, but that the surest means have been employed to stamp it out is also equally true, so that at this time it may be truly said none is known to exist in Harford. The wisdom of the act of the Legislature at its late session, providing the means of controlling the murrain, is acknowledged on all sides, and the power vested in the executive has been most wisely exercised.

Governor Hamilton commissioned Honourable Herman Stump, President of the Senate, six days after the expiration of the late session of the Legislature, to investigate the pleuro-pneumonia in Harford. Subsequently, Captain E. W. Gallup, tenant of the Dairy Farm property, belonging to the Citizens' Bank of Baltimore, and situated about nine miles from Belair, reported to the Governor that pleuro-pneumonia had appeared on his premises, and he asked for the application of the remedies which the law prescribes.

Senator Stump designated Dr. James M. Magraw to inspect the cattle at the "Dairy Farm." Dr. Magraw is a well known and skilful practitioner of medicine, who also possesses veterinary knowledge and the well-placed confidence of the community where he practices. After a careful examination of Gallup's cattle he reported the existence of pleuro-pneumonia in the herd. The fact was telegraphed to Annapolis, and the slaughter of the cattle on the place, twenty-two in number, was sanctioned. Four other cattle, which had herded with these, were traced up, two were killed, and two others will share the same fate, though neither of them betrayed any signs of actual disease.

Preliminary to the extirpation of the Gallup herd, Dr. Magraw had one of the diseased cows slaughtered for dissection. The lungs were found to be solidified, and, as in the case of pleurisy, adhering to the sides. Among the witnesses of the post-mortem were Hon. Herman Stump, James Lee, John Moores, Alexander M. Fulford, Dr. James T. Billingslea, W. Smithson Forwood, Joseph A. Price, E. A. Gallup, John C. Davison, Henry Fulford, Wm. P. Trimble, Gabriel Christy, R. Emory Taylor, G. W. Hanway, W. R. Cunningham, Thomas A. Hays, John B. Price and others. No doubt existed in the minds of these gentleman as to the true nature of the malady.

While the Act of Assembly does not provide compensation for diseased cattle which may be killed, those not actually diseased, slaughtered to prevent the spread of the contagion, are to be appraised and reported to the next General Assembly, with the view of reimbursing the owners, should provision be then made for that purpose by law. For all other expenses the Governor has immediate and ample authority. The appraisers for the Gallup cattle were Messrs. John Moores and James Lee.

Dr. Magraw, after due examination, reported at the farmers' meeting that there is now no evidence of pleuro-pneumonia among the Alderneys at Ranger's Lodge, the farm of State Senator George H. Williams. Dr. Magraw said the disease may have shown itself there, but he has seen no evidence of it. Before this visit to the premises, a steer had been killed by a veterinary surgeon, and the lungs were carried away to Baltimore, but he only saw the hide and carcass, so that there was nothing left by which to form a judgment. No cases of *actual disease* have been discovered in the county, except on the Dairy Farm and the Ranger's Lodge estate, and in both cases every precaution has been taken at a favourable time to prevent the spread of the contagion. The Dairy Farm is isolated in a great measure. It contains nearly one thousand acres, and is bounded on the south by Bush river, on the east by Church creek, and on the west the farm of Mr. Charles A. McGaw separates it from Bush creek. There is no disease upon Mr. McGaw's farm. No public road passes through it, and the nearest thoroughfare is the old post-road along which, in olden times, four-horse stage coaches conveyed passengers between Baltimore and Philadelphia. This road is several miles distant from the field where Gallup's cattle were kept, and separated therefrom by a large body of Woodland. It is therefore not at all probable that it has spread, and now that the cattle are destroyed, of course all danger is over from that quarter.

It was realized in good time that everything depended upon stamping out the disease while it could be controlled, and while the cattle were yet herded in the barn-yards before they were turned out to pasture, where the chances would be greater of its wide dissemination.

Following up the enforcement of the law on Gallup's herd, the Secretary of State wrote to Senator Stump, April 23rd, to the effect that on account of complaints received from the Governor of Pennsylvania Governor Hamilton had directed such other action to be taken in Harford county as the exigencies of the case demanded, within the limitation of instructions heretofore given. But as all the cases of pleuro-pneumonia that could be discovered in Harford have been disposed of, and suspected cattle have been placed under surveillance and in quarantine, very little now remains to be done so far as this county is concerned.

Details of the operations of the commission in Harford county are reported officially as follows:—On the 21st of April instant Dr. Magraw slaughtered 22 cattle belonging to E. W. Gallop, of which five were diseased and 17 healthy animals. Those considered sound were in bad condition and looking thin. Those affected when slaughtered were four cows and one steer. The animals exempt from disease which were killed included five cows, one bull, two oxen, two steers, and four yearlings.

Mr. Gallup reports that he bought 30 steers at the Calverton stock yards, Baltimore, September 19th, 1879. One Steer died November 24th, 1879; five or six were slightly affected at the same time with cough and other symptoms, but pleuro-pneumonia was not suspected until the steer died. Another steer died December 20, the symptoms being the same as in the case of the steer which died November 24. Two cows seriously affected were killed about the same time. All the affected cattle were treated with turpentine and other counter irritants. Two recovered. Thinking the disease had subsided, Mr. Gallup sold 28 head of steers at Calverton, December 21, 1879. The disease disappeared from the Dairy Farm precincts until January 24, 1880, when one cow died. No other cases appeared until about three weeks ago. Since January 24, four head of cattle have died or were killed. Four cows were sold to Taylor Pyle, in Chester county, Pa., a dealer, who lost a number of animals.

Mr. Gallup states that since September 19, 1879, he has lost 17 head of cattle by death or slaughter, not including the 22 despatched under the provisions of the law. Three steers were also sold from this place to Thos. Morgan, by whom they were sold to Philadelphia butchers.

On the 21st instant Dr. Magraw slaughtered two cows belonging to William E. Cromwell, coloured, which were exempt from disease, but had herded with the Gallup stock. Two others, belonging to Wesley Gallion, had also wintered with Mr. Gallup's cattle, and were removed three or four weeks ago. Dr. Magraw has examined one of them at Abingdon, and finding it apparently sound, ordered it to be quarantined for two weeks to await results. The other, at Aberdeen, will be killed.

No. 49.

LETTER from the ACTING BRITISH CONSUL at BALTIMORE to EARL GRANVILLE.

Sanitary No. 6.

My Lord, Baltimore, June 1st, 1880.

I have the honour to report that since my Despatch, Sanitary No. 5 of the 1st ultimo, some few cases of pleuro-pneumonia appeared amongst the cattle of this city, but every precaution was adopted by the authorities under operation of the new law, to check the spread of the disease. The affected cattle were found to be in stables of bad condition, poorly ventilated, and dirty, and the animals continually confined to the stable, fed on grain and swill slops from the breweries.

The disease was generally of a mild type, and did not necessitate the slaughter of the cows, and the fresh pasturage ordered to them proved beneficial.

The great trouble in managing this disease is owing to the owners of the cattle. As soon as they are found to be affected, they sell off their stock and thus spread the disease. Men are known to have sold milk from diseased kine, and in numerous cases the buyers were aware of the condition of the stock, but, as they purchased at cheap rates they took the risk with the expectation of curing them.

Cattle from this vicinity are never taken for export to the United Kingdom, but are brought on directly from the Western States where pleuro-pneumonia is comparatively unknown. The stock thus brought on have no delays in transit until they are driven on shipboard.

I have the honour to enclose herewith a newspaper paragraph giving the full text of the law upon this subject as adopted by the late legislation of this State, and which has been published according to law for the guidance of those interested and concerned.

I have, &c.

The Right Hon. the Earl Granville K.G.   (Signed)   T. W. LAWFORD,
&c.   &c.   &c.   Acting Consul.

Enclosure in No. 49.

The Baltimore "Sun" newspaper of May 5, 1880.

PLEURO-PNEUMONIA AMONG CATTLE.

AN ACT to prevent the SPREAD of INFECTIOUS or CONTAGIOUS PLEURO-PNEUMONIA among the CATTLE of this STATE.

Section 1. Be it enacted by the General Assembly of Maryland, that whenever it shall be brought to the notice of the Governor of this State that the disease known as contagious or infectious pleuro-pneumonia exists among the cattle in any of the counties of this State or in the City of Baltimore, it shall be his duty to take measures to promptly suppress the disease and prevent it from spreading.

Section 2. And be it enacted, that for such purpose the Governor shall have power to issue his proclamation stating that infectious or contagious disease exists in any county or counties of the State, or in the City of Baltimore, and warning all persons to seclude all animals in their possession that are affected with such disease or have been exposed to the infection or contagion thereof, and ordering all persons to take such precautions against the spreading of such disease as the nature thereof may, in his judgment, render necessary or expedient; to order that any premises, farm or farms, or stables where such disease exists or has existed, be put in quarantine, so that no domestic animal be removed from or brought to the premises or places so quarantined, and to prescribe such regulations as he may judge necessary or expedient to prevent infection or contagion being communicated in any way from the places so quarantined; to call upon all sheriffs and deputy sheriffs to carry out and enforce the provisions of such proclamations, orders and regulations, and it shall be the duty of all sheriffs and deputy sheriffs to obey and observe all orders and instruction which they may receive from the Governor in the premises; to employ such and so many medical and veterinary practitioners and such other persons as he may from time to time deem necessary to assist him in performing his duty as set forth in the first section of this Act, and to fix their compensation; to order all or any animals coming into the State to be detained at any place or places for the purpose of inspection and examination; provided, that animals coming from a neighbouring State, that have passed a veterinary examination in said State, and have been quarantined and discharged, shall not be subject to the provisions of this Act; to prescribe regulations for the destruction of animals afflicted with infectious or contagious disease, or of those in direct contact with such and liable to spread the disease, and for the proper disposition of their hides and carcasses, and of all objects which might convey infection or contagion; provided, that no animal shall be destroyed unless first examined by a medical or veterinary practitioner in the employ of the Governor as aforesaid; to prescribe regulations for the disinfection of all premises, buildings and railway cars, and of all objects from or by which infection or contagion may take place or be conveyed; to alter and modify from time to time, as he may deem expedient, the terms of all such proclamations, orders and regulations, and to cancel or withdraw the same at any time.

Section 3. And be it enacted, that any person who shall transgress the terms or requirements of any proclamation, order or regulation issued or prescribed by the Governor, under the authority of this Act, shall be deemed guilty of a misdemeanor.

Section 4. And be it enacted, that any person who shall sell or otherwise dispose of an animal which he knows, or has reason to believe, is affected by the disease, or has been exposed to the same, shall forfeit to the State not less than $50 nor more than $100.

Section 5. And be it enacted, that all the necessary expenses incurred under direction or by authority of the Governor in carrying out the provisions of this Act shall be paid by the treasurer out of any moneys not otherwise appropriated, and upon the warrant of the comptroller, on being certified as correct by the Governor.

Section 6. And be it enacted, that in the event of its being deemed necessary by the Governor, or any agent duly appointed by him under the provisions of this Act, to prevent the spread of contagion or infection, to cause any animal or animals not actually diseased to be slaughtered, the value of such animal or animals shall be fairly appraised and a record kept, and a report made thereof to the General Assembly at its session next ensuing, with a view to the reimbursement of the owners of such animals so killed, should provision therefore be made by law, it being provided that the carcasses of animals so killed, and found entirely free from disease, shall, if practicable, be sold, and the proceeds of such sale shall be paid over to the respective owners of the cattle, and the amounts so received and paid over noted against the appraised value thereof.

Section 7. And be it enacted, that this Act shall take effect from the date of its passage.

HERMAN STUMP, Jr.,
President of the Senate.
HIRAM McCULLOUGH,
Speaker of the House of Delegates.

Approved April 10, 1880.

WM. T. HAMILTON,
Governor of Maryland.

We hereby certify that the aforegoing is a correct copy of an Act of the General Assembly of Maryland, passed at the January Session, 1880.

EUGENE HIGGINS,
Secretary of the Senate.
MILTON Y. KIDD,
Chief Clerk of the House of Delegates.

No. 50.

LETTER from the ACTING BRITISH CONSUL GENERAL at NEW YORK to EARL GRANVILLE.

Sanitary No. 5.

British Consulate General, New York,
June 1st, 1880.

MY LORD,

I HAVE the honour to report to your Lordship that since the date of my last Despatch (Sanitary, No. 4, of the 1st ultimo) pleuro-pneumonia has again manifested itself among cattle on Staten Island, in New York Harbour. Measures have, however, been taken by the State inspector which it is hoped will effectually prevent the spread of the disease.

The sanitary condition of cattle in other parts of this consular district is about the same as previously reported.

I have, &c.,
(Signed) PIERREPONT EDWARDS,
Acting Consul General.

Her Majesty's Principal Secretary of State
for Foreign Affairs, London.

122

No. 51.

LETTER from the BRITISH CONSUL-GENERAL at NEW YORK to EARL GRANVILLE.

Sanitary, No. 6.

British Consulate General, New York,
July 1st, 1810.

My Lord,

I HAVE the honour to report to your Lordship that the sanitary condition of cattle in this consular district, as reported by Acting Consul General Edwards Despatch (Sanitary, No. 5) of the 1st ultimo, remains practically unchanged.

I have, &c.,

Her Majesty's Principal Secretary of State (Signed) E. M. ARCHIBALD.
for Foreign Affairs, London.

LONDON:
Printed by GEORGE E. EYRE and WILLIAM SPOTTISWOODE,
Printers to the Queen's most Excellent Majesty.
For Her Majesty's Stationery Office.

CATTLE DISEASE (UNITED STATES OF AMERICA).

REPORT ON TEXAS FEVER

BY

PROFESSOR BROWN;

AND

FURTHER CORRESPONDENCE RELATING TO DISEASES OF ANIMALS

IN THE

UNITED STATES OF AMERICA.

Presented to both Houses of Parliament by Command of Her Majesty.

LONDON:
PRINTED BY GEORGE EDWARD EYRE AND WILLIAM SPOTTISWOODE,
PRINTERS TO THE QUEEN'S MOST EXCELLENT MAJESTY.
FOR HER MAJESTY'S STATIONERY OFFICE.
1880.

[C.—2693.] *Price 5d.*

CATTLE DISEASE (UNITED STATES OF AMERICA).

REPORT ON TEXAS FEVER

BY

PROFESSOR BROWN.

In a country so vast in extent as the United States of America, it is not perhaps remarkable that a malady with absolutely unique characters should exist among the herds of certain States and from time to time commit extraordinary ravages without attracting much attention on this side the Atlantic.

From the reports of various investigators who have studied the subject it appears that Texas fever is indigenous to some of the districts on the Gulf Coast, and does not originate above the thirty-fourth degree of north latitude, although it may be communicated to cattle in higher latitudes by association with Texan cattle. The following extract from a Report of the Veterinary Surgeon to the Pennsylvanian Board of Agriculture, published in 1879, includes the chief facts in the history of the disease:—

"Texas or splenic fever has existed ever since cattle of the Gulf States have come in contact with herds of northern and higher countries. There can be but little doubt that if the Indians ever drove the cattle which were native to the States bordering on the Gulf of Mexico, or cattle which had become acclimated to those States northward to higher latitudes, even before the settlement of the States, that Texas fever must have followed in their wake wherever they came in contact with other cattle. The reports which came to us for a long time from Kansas and Missouri of the existence of this disease among cattle in those States failed to be noticed until, by the better facilities for transportation, numbers of Texan cattle were landed in Illinois, Indiana, and Ohio, where they infected vast numbers of native stock. A general fear now took the place of passive indifference, and the existence of Texas fever became a fact—a startling fact—to the owners of the large herds which graze on the extensive prairies of the west, as well also as to eastern shippers and buyers.

"Dr. James Mease speaks of this disease, in 1814, as having 'long been known,' and hints that possibly the 'long-leaf pine country is the seat of the infection.' In 1866 splenic fever existed in southern Kentucky and Kansas and south-western Missouri, and by 1867 it was reported as having made its appearance in Arkansas, parts of Tennessee, North Carolina, Illinois, and the hills of South Carolina and Georgia; and in all these outbreaks the passage through or presence of Texas cattle was traceable as the direct source of the malady.

"In 1868, in addition to the States already mentioned as infected, we find added to the list, Ohio, New York, New Jersey, Pennsylvania, Virginia, and some parts of New England."

In reference to the character of the disease, the same writer remarks:—

"Texas or splenic fever is an enzoötic whose special poison is generated only in certain localities, and only capable of transmission through the medium of the excretions, and that during the warm months. It is indigenous to Texas, Florida, and certain other parts of the Gulf Coast States below the thirty-fourth degree of north latitude.

"Although some able authorities have classed this as an anthrax disease, I am forced to take exception to this view, for the following reasons.

"Cattle do not die in large numbers in the locality where the disease is spontaneous as they do from anthrax diseases.

"There can be no inoculable virus detected in cases of Texas fever.

"Anthrax shows a decided preference for the best and fattest cattle of the herd, which splenic fever does not.

"The flesh of anthrax cattle eaten by man develops malignant pustule, but this never arises from eating cattle which have been slaughtered while affected with Texas fever. Splenic fever is characterised by the absence of bacteria. Nor is Texas or splenic fever analogous to malignant typhus or typhoid fever. Its origin, development, and progress

Q 2761. Wt. 8107.

are essentially different. We do not see its counterpart in any of the diseases which affect the human family, although it is developed in the same countries where malarial diseases attack man."

In the Report of the Transactions of the New York State Agricultural Society for 1867, Dr. Moreau Morris gives the following account of the symptoms and post-mortem appearances of the disease:—

"Animals suffering with this disease present the following obvious symptoms: Generally standing apart from their fellows, listless, indifferent to surrounding objects, restless, evidently desiring to lay down, but fearing to do so until compelled to yield by rapidly waning strength; the head hanging low down, frequently within an inch of the ground, or occasionally pressed firmly against some unyielding object; the base of horns hot, the ears drooping, the eyes dull and staring, the spine or back peculiarly arched, the hinder feet been drawn under the body and placed in a bracing attitude; a tremulous creeping over the flank muscles, with frequent efforts at voiding fæces which are generally small, hard, and rounded and covered with bloody mucous, though there is sometimes considerable looseness of the bowels during some stages of the disease, frequently passing urine of a dark bloody appearance. The pulse is rapid, very soft and feeble, respirations frequent, and during hot weather panting without exertion. The temperature, both externally and internally, increased. Flies are also observed to adhere to the animals who seem to be unconscious of their presence or too feeble to drive them off.

"Upon opening the animal the muscular tissue is seen of a dark red colour; the fat is of a deep brown yellow, having in intense cases a green bronzed tinge.

"The spleen is found enlarged, more or less engorged with dark coloured blood softened frequently to a pulpy mass.

"The abomasum, or fourth stomach, upon its inner tubular pyloric portion invariably presents sloughs, erosions, and deep excavated ulcers of various forms and extent. There is usually accompanying these, more or less inflammatory appearances of the larger and more vascular portion of this stomach (gastritis). The ulcerations, or rather the peculiarities, that were found in the tubular portion of the rennet, or fourth stomach, and at the base of the longitudinal folds in that stomach, finally appeared to be a surer guide to a recognition of the disease than was the mere appearance and size of the spleen or the liver; the absolute tests by the minute examination of the liver, bile, and spleen-pulp by the microscopist, and the historical and symptomatic history of the animal before death being of course preferred to all other kinds of evidence. Yet to the practised eye these ulcerations, sloughs, and erosions served as trustworthy guides in deciding the nature of any case in which for the moment the other kinds of evidence were not accessible.

"Kidneys generally enlarged, darker in colour than normal, congested with blood, and the cortical substance usually softened.

"The liver enlarged, increased in weight, generally fatty or waxy; its bile-ducts and radicals fully injected with bile, its colour changed to a yellowish-brown.

"The gall bladder filled with a dark, thick, tarry or flaky bile.

"The bladder distended with dark, bloody urine.

"The intestinal canal in its various portions, the ileum cœcum, and rectum, frequently presenting congested vessels under its mucous coat, its epithelium softened and easily scraped off with the finger.

"The heart muscular tissue sometimes found softened.

"The lungs generally in a healthy condition; in some intense cases interlobular emphysema.

"The brain in same cases congested and softened."

Professor Law, of the Cornell University, remarks in reference to the disease:—

"There seems to be an incubation of four or five weeks, ending in elevated temperature (103° to 107°) and followed in five to seven days by dullness, languor, drooping head till the nose reaches the ground, arched back, hind legs advanced under the belly and bent at the fetlocks, cough more or less frequent, muscular trembling about the flanks, jerking of the neck muscles, heat of horns, ears, and general surface (limbs cold in exceptional cases), and impaired appetite and rumination. Soon weakness compels lying down, by choice in water, eyes are glassy and fixed, secretions lessened, dung hard and coated with mucus, or with clots of blood, and the urine changes to a deep red or black and coagulates on boiling. The mucous membranes are of a deep yellow or brown, that of the rectum seen in passing dung is of a dark red, as in rinderpest.

"All these symptoms become aggravated, weakness becomes extreme, and the patient dies in a state of stupor, or sometimes in convulsions.

"The disease usually passes unnoticed in the Texan cattle, but is exceedingly fatal in northern beasts."

Professor Gamgee investigated the disease in Texas in 1868, and his elaborate report on the results of his inquiry is published in the Report of the Commissioners of Agriculture on Diseases of Cattle in the United States in 1871.

The following are the conclusions at which Professor Gamgee arrived:—

"That southern cattle, especially from the Gulf Coast, are affected with a latent or an apparent form of the disease.

"That they become affected in consequence of the nature of the soil and vegetation on which they are fed, and the water which they drink.

"That their systems are charged with poisonous principles which accumulate in the bodies of acclimatized animals that enjoy an immunity.

"That southern cattle may be driven so as to improve in condition, and yet for some weeks, and probably not less than three months, continue to excrete the deleterious principles which poison the cattle of the States through which the herds are driven on their way north or west.

"That all breeds of cattle in States north of those on the Gulf Coast, without regard to age or sex, if they feed on grass contaminated by southern droves, are attacked by the splenic fever; that the disease may be, but is very rarely, propagated through the feeding of hay.

"That the disease occurs mainly during the hot months of summer and autumn, and never after the wild grasses have been killed by frosts, until the mild weather in spring returns; that then the grasses are healthy, and continue healthy, unless fresh droves of Texan or of Florida cattle are driven over the land.

"That heat and drought aggravate the disease in individual animals.

"That there is not the slightest foundation for the view that the ticks disseminate the disease.

"That the splenic fever does not belong to that vast and deadly group of purely contagious and infectious diseases of which the rinderpest, the lung-plague, and eruptive fevers are typical.

"That it is an enzoötic, due to local influences, capable of only a limited spread, analogous to or identical with the "black water," of various parts of Europe.

"That, however warm the weather may be, cattle affected with splenic fever have not developed in their systems any poison like the anthrax poison; and that the flesh, blood, and other tissues of animals are incapable of inducing any disease in man or animals.

"That splenic fever is not malignant typhus or typhoid fever. That it has no analogue among human diseases, but is, however, developed under conditions which prevail where the so-called malaria injuriously affects the human health."

The following are the conclusions arrived at by the Cattle Commissioners of the several States who met at Springfield in December 1868:—

"The disease is communicated by southern cattle.

"The cattle communicating the infection, though showing signs of splenic enlargement or evidence of once-existing disease, when slaughtered are apparently well and actually increasing in weight and vigour.

"Infection is not usually communicated in winter, and fields may be safely depastured in spring which have been occupied in winter by southern cattle. In a single case reported an apparent exception is presented.

"Animals receiving the infection from southern cattle do not communicate it to other natives. This exemption is a rule so undeviating that probably not one farmer in one hundred, whose stock has suffered by this disease, would fear a dollar's loss by communication of their unaffected with sick animals.

"Southern cattle removed to localities characterised by the same climatic conditions (as from one portion of the Gulf Coast to another, or upon the same parallel of latitude) do not communicate disease to local stock.

"The virus appears to be eliminated from the system after a stay of a few weeks or months in a northern climate, so that no infection is communicated to the cattle with which they come in contact.

"A preponderance of testimony tends to establish the theory that the infection is conveyed through the voided excrements.

"It does not appear that the disease has ever been communicated, 'except to animals 'that have fed upon pastures, or in lots soiled by the excrements of the southern 'cattle.'

"The period of incubation is not of uniform length. From causes which may be left for medical investigation to determine the potency of the virus is variable. Sometimes a week intervenes between the exposure and the attack; frequently a period of ten days or two weeks elapses; sometimes two, three, or six weeks intervene, and in one case in Washington County, Arkansas, the time of incubation was three months. In portions of Arkansas, in which the climatic conditions are similar to those of the region from which the migrating cattle come, no infection occurs; and in proportion as a section assimilates in climate to such region, it is reasonable to suppose the liability to the disease is lessened, and probably the period of its incubation extended.

"The disease runs a brief course of a few days, generally three or four, often but one or two, and proves fatal in nine cases of every ten.

"Liability to infection is so imminent that few exposed animals escape. When circumstances favour the greatest virulence of the disease whole herds have often been destroyed, and the cattle of entire districts nearly all swept away, while behind the line of exposure, distinctly marked as the boundary of a sweeping conflagration or resistless tornado, not a herd nor an animal has been touched.

"Medication has been of little service, though the testimony gives colour to the probability that a slightly reduced mortality might be secured by skilful medical treatment and feeding with soft mashes.

"The loss from this disease for a few years prior to the war, and for years since its close, cannot be accurately stated, but undoubtedly amounts to several millions of dollars. The greatest fatality has been in Missouri and Kansas. In 1858 the loss in Vernon County, Missouri, was 200,000 dollars. Losses were widely distributed and severe throughout southern Kansas and south-west Missouri in 1866 and 1867; in 1868 there were less in these States, as the result of general enforcement of restrictive laws, but were heavy and alarming in eastern Illinois and western Indiana, when the prairie pastures of those States were for the first time occupied by cattle direct from Texas. The deaths numbered about 5,000 in Champaign County, Illinois; 1,500 in Warren, 600 in Benton, and 400 in Jasper, in Indiana; and many counties in these and other States were involved to a less extent. The mortality of 1868, reported by our returns, amounts to at least 15,000 cattle, involving a loss of not less than 500,000 dollars.

"While meat of diseased animals can never be deemed wholesome food, the milk and flesh of cattle affected with this disease do not generally cause immediate sickness." *

The microscopic characters of the diseased tissue and fluids were closely investigated by J. S. Billings, Bot. Lt.-Col. and Asst. Surg., and Edward Curtis, Bot. Maj. & Asst. Surg. U.S. Army, and these savants report as follows :—

"From the specimens that we have had the opportunity of examining, it would appear that in the blood, bile, and urine of cattle slaughtered in Texas, apparently healthy while alive, but presenting after death the appearances considered characteristic of the splenic fever, there are present minute bodies corresponding to the micrococcus of Hallier, which exhibit the same behaviour with reagents as the spores of fungi.

"In the bile and urine bacteria and cryptoccus cells also occur. The micrococcus granules, however, have no specific characteristics, and cannot be distinguished from similar bodies which are to be seen in any blood in an incipient stage of putrefaction. Thus, on the 4th of June, vacuum tubes were filled with blood from a healthy sheep, slaughtered near Washington, and this blood, examined 60 hours afterwards, contained in equal abundance these same bodies (micrococcus) that were found in the blood of the Texas cattle. The attempt to give these micrococcus molecules a special and important character by the 'cultivation' in various ways of the blood containing them also failed. In all cases the fungous growth that appeared upon the cultivated material was composed of the commonest moulds, and, instead of being unique as to species or even genus, comprised various forms and sizes of cryptococcus, torula, penicillium, coremium, mucor, and the so-called schzosporangia of Hallier, of all forms and sizes; these various fungi being either simultaneously or successively developed. Moreover, all these varieties of fungi can be also developed by a similar cultivation of healthy blood, though not so rapidly nor in so great luxuriance.

---

* Of the testimony bearing upon this point, that of Mr. Eaton, in charge of the Broadland farms of Mr. Alexander, in Champaign County, Illinois, is very strong. He states that 140 head of native cattle died there in 1868 from Texas fever, and among them nearly all the cows on the place, whose milk was used with apparent impunity until they ceased to give milk; the calves sucked as long as their mothers could stand, and, in one instance, a calf sucked three cows alternately until each died; and in some cases the hogs consumed the carcases of dead cattle. Not a single case of disease or injury resulted from the use of meat or milk.

"The fact that in our cultivations we never obtained any growths of ustilago, coniothecium, or tilletia, which were so frequently produced in Hallier's experiments, is probably due to the circumstance that no specimens of those fungi were ever brought into the room where our experiments were conducted.

"In cases of splenic fever of cattle our experiments, therefore, fail to establish the presence of any peculiar or special cryptogamic germs in the blood, and instead of supporting the notion that the micrococcus granules which are present in any way cause the disease, tend rather to show that their occurrence should be considered as an effect of the malady, whether constant and inherent, or altogether fortuitous, for since these granules, if fungous in their nature, must be as indicated by the cultivations, forms of the very commonest moulds, it is certainly a much more probable hypothesis that the disease so destroys the vitality of a part of the blood as to render it capable of supporting and nourishing a low form of these ubiquitous fungi, which perish when introduced into a healthy subject, than it is to imagine a deadly disease, occurring only under certain rigidly prescribed conditions, as caused by the presence, in the economy of the germs of fungi notoriously harmless and of univeral occurrence.

"It is, of course, possible that these fungi, developed in the fluids of a diseased animal, may become the carriers of contagium. This can be determined only by a series of inoculations upon healthy cattle."

It is clear from the summary which has been given of the conclusions of medical and veterinary authorities in the United States of America that the splenic fever of Texan cattle is not the same disease as the splenic fever of this Kingdom. In fact the two affections, although possessing certain common features, notably the engorgement of the spleen with dark blood and extravasations of blood in different parts of the body, are distinguised the one from the other, not only by well-defined pathological characters which are appreciable by experts, but also by facts in their life history which are evident to ordinary observers. These specialities may be briefly stated in separate columns for the purpose of facilitating comparison.

Texas Fever. Affects Cattle only.	Splenic Fever. Affects different Animals.
Is indigenous to Texas, Florida, and some other parts of the Gulf Coast States of America, and only extends to other States by the movement of diseased cattle from the infected districts.	Is not confined to any particular climate or latitude, although more prevalent in some localities than others, and appears in districts without the movement of diseased animals.
The disease never survives the frosts of winter, and even Texan cattle during the winter months do not transmit it.	When introduced into fresh districts, usually retains its vitality, and re-appears at uncertain intervals.
Texan cattle suffer very little from the disease, but communicate it readily to Northern cattle, which are said to be incapable of again transmitting the disease.	No partial immunity to any animals known, and all affected animals seem capable of transmitting the poison.
No inoculable virus has been discovered, the blood, flesh, and milk of the diseased animals are harmless, and do not produce disease in man or animals.	The blood and tissues contain a virus which certainly produce disease in man and animals by inoculation.
The excrement of the diseased animals left on the pastures is most probably the infecting material.	The carcases of the diseased animals most dangerous, and probably one of the principal means of spreading the disease.
All cattle taken from other States into Texas and Florida suffer more or less from the disease, and it is stated that from one third to one half of the cattle imported into Texas die of the malady before they are acclimatized, calves being more readily acclimatized than older animals.	No general extension of disease occurs among animals which are taken into splenic fever districts, as in the case of Texas fever. And no period of time is sufficient to acclimatize animals or confer immunity from attacks of splenic fever.
A prolonged period of incubation, well-defined symptoms of illness lasting several days before the animal dies.	Period of incubation extremely short. No well-defined symptoms observed. Animals usually die very suddenly.

Texas Fever—*cont.*	Splenic Fever—*cont.*
Enlargement of spleen, and often also of liver, with fatty degeneration of latter organ. Hæmorrhage, erosions, and ulceration in different parts of the mucous membrane of the digestive organs.	Enlargement of spleen, with great increase of weight. Hæmorrhagic patches on serous and mucous membranes without ulceration.
Absence of the *Bacillus Anthracis* in the blood.	Presence of the *Bacillus Anthracis* in the blood and spleen after death.

In 1868 the attention of the Veterinary Department was called to the subject of Texas fever by the publication in the "Pall Mall Gazette" of an extract from the "New York Times" of May 23rd, 1868, to the effect that a very subtile and terribly fatal disease was raging among the cattle in some portions of Illinois. Over 100 head had fallen victims to the disease in a few days. The disease kills in a few hours, and yields to no remedy or treatment, and is fatal in every instance.

In consequence of this intelligence a letter was addressed to the Foreign Office, requesting that an inquiry might be made respecting the nature of the disease referred to, and on August 19th, 1868, the following reply was received:—

British Consulate, Chicago, U.S., July 31, 1868.

My Lord,

I have the honour to acknowledge the receipt of Mr. James Murray's despatch of the 6th ult., transmitting a copy of a letter and its enclosure from the Veterinary Department of the Council Office respecting a fatal disease reported to be raging among the cattle in some parts of Illinois, and instructing me to furnish your Lordship with all the information upon this subject which I may be able to obtain.

I now have the honour to send to your Lordship an original letter I have received from the Honourable Sharon Tyndale, Secretary of State for the State of Illinois, enclosing the printed reports of Dr. George T. Allen, of Springfield, and Dr. H. C. Johns, Special Commissioner upon Diseases of Cattle for the Illinois State Agricultural Society, extracted from the "Illinois State Journal" of the 22nd and 27th May ultimo.

I have delayed writing this despatch in order to enclose reports from Decatin, Quincy, and other places in this State, in which localities I was informed that the same disease had shown itself, but to-day I ascertained from reliable authority that there was no cause for alarm from this particular disease in those vicinities.

The heaviest live-stock dealers in Chicago can afford me no information in the matter. They say that reports have reached them from time to time that there has been some disease among the cattle in the country, but that the cattle received at this market for some time past could not have been in a healthier condition.

From the various inquiries I have made, I find that the breaking out of this disease at Springfield has been assigned to different causes by different persons, but that so far, they have not decided upon any particular one.

A disease called the Spanish fever has broken out lately in several portions of Illinois and Indiana caused by the importation of Texas cattle.

A meeting was held at Tolono, in this State, on the 28th instant, in order to see that the State law was put in execution against every offender.

I have the honour to enclose an extract of the "Chicago Tribune" of yesterday in relation to the cattle disease, which embodies the State law in regard to Texas cattle.

Any further information I can gain upon this subject I shall at once communicate to your Lordship.

I have, &c.
(Signed) T. Frederick Wilkins,
Acting Consul.

The Lord Stanley, M.P.

State of Illinois, Secretary's Office,
Springfield, June 30, 1868.

Dear Sir,

To your letter of (27th June instant) inquiry concerning diseased cattle, I have the honour to reply by sending you the accompanying newspaper and slip, and to say, besides being personally long and well acquainted with Dr. G. T. Allen, that with other gentlemen I had the honour to accompany him in his post-mortem examinations, and can therefore testify as well to the exactness and truthfulness of the statements made in Dr. Allen's report as to his high standing as a gentleman of attainments.

The information given in the communication of Dr. Allen is about all we were able to gather at the time of, and upon the ground where, the fatal ailment was raging apparently endemic.

The manner of the action of the different cows, their appearance after death, &c., were reported to us in about the same way by their various owners, who conveyed essentially the same details which are not considered important except in the general features mentioned by Dr. Allen, viz., inability or indisposition to eat or drink or ruminate, though standing near or over the feed tub, stupidity of appearance, sloth of action, quick and difficult breathing, with final inability to stand, followed by complaints in moaning and moving the head in apparent desire to regain their feet, but in every instance without ability to even half rise (at least without success) and falling back in groans.

In most of the cases death occurred within 12 hours from the first outward indication of disease.

I will add that no case (of disease or death) among cows or other cattle has been reported to us since the 20th day of May, nor have we been able to discover any case since that day.

So far as we have been able to trace *all* the deaths, from the same apparent symptoms, the number, I think, has not exceeded thirty (30) and they all died in the same ten days (10 days).

We discovered only one case of recovery, and that was a heifer one year old, having apparently the very same symptoms, upon the appearance of which her owner immediately took her up (into his own inclosure) and gave her one pint of linseed oil, which he repeated in about ten (10) hours; when we saw her she had been affected about sixteen (16) hours and was yet quite stupid, though still upon her legs and beginning to nip the grass again.

Very respectfully, &c.
(Signed)   SHARON TYNDALE,
Secretary of State,
Illinois.

T. Frederick Wilkins, Esq.,
H.B.M. Acting Consul, Chicago, Illinois.

In the "Standard" of August 24th, 1868, the following paragraph appeared:—

A serious disease among our cattle we have, if not the rinderpest with which you have had so much trouble. This disorder has made its appearance in nearly all the Western States, at the great cattle yards, as well as in New York and Rhode Island. It is traceable, in all cases, to animals brought from Texas, which have infected droves of Northern and Western cattle. Mr. John Gamgee, who has resided in the States since last year, says that the disease is spread by the excreta of Texas cattle, and is due to the feeding by the cattle upon a peculiar plant. Mr. Gamgee asserts that the disease does not affect the animals feeding upon this plant, but only others with which they may be brought in contact. But this explanation is rejected by many drovers, who say that the disease is due to the carapato, an insect of a greenish colour, and about the size of a finger-nail. The carapatos bury themselves in the flesh wherever the skin offers least resistance; on the parts covered by the thicker skin, however, they swarm by thousands. Another theory is that the affection is due to the fever bred in the animals in their long journeys, both by railway and across the plains and prairies, without water. Many of the droves received in New York are kept forty-eight hours on the passage from the West without water. Perhaps all the causes enumerated combine to produce the disease. It is curious that the Texas cattle should be only the disseminators of the plague, and not themselves the sufferers. Active efforts are made to check the pest. In Pittsburg 34 carloads of cattle have been killed by order of the authorities. In Jersey City and Communipaw, where the droves for the New York market are landed, cattle to the number of about 1,000 have been killed since the 1st of August by the officers of the Health Board. Several herds have been slaughtered at different railway stations between New York and the Western States. The disease is very fatal, killing more than half the cattle attacked. Something of a panic exists in New York; beef has largely advanced in price, while consumers fancy all sorts of horrors.

On August 28th, 1868, Professor Ferguson, of the Irish Veterinary Department, addressed the following letter to the English Veterinary Department:—

Veterinary Department of the Privy Council Office,
Dublin Castle, 28th August 1868.

SIR,

I AM directed by Government (in Ireland) to request the favour of being informed if any consular reports have been received relative to the cattle disease stated to have broken out on the American Continent, and mentioned in the annexed extracts copied from the "Times" and "Morning Herald," and that, should any such reports have been received, to beg you will kindly direct copies of them to be transmitted to me for the information of the executive in Ireland. I am also directed to bring under your notice the great danger of infection being brought to Great Britain by the importation from America of undressed hides, should the epizoötic at present raging in parts of that continent be infectious or contagious. According to a private communication received from a veterinary practitioner at Chicago the malady is eminently so.

Apologising for giving so much trouble,

I have, &c.
(Signed)   HUGH FERGUSON,
H.M.V.S.

To Dr. A. Williams, Veterinary Department,
Privy Council Office, Princes St., Westminster, S.W.

CATTLE PLAGUE IN AMERICA.

The Philadelphia correspondent of the "Times" writes: "The American public are having a very "disagreeable sensation just now, in the presence of a cattle disease, which, though not the rinderpest "that has afflicted Europe, seems to be equally fatal in its effects. This scourge is the Spanish or "Texan fever, and it has been imported into the Northern States with herds from Texas. It first "appeared in Indiana and Illinois a few weeks ago, and still rages in those States. During May and "June some 15,000 cattle were brought from Texas to Champaign County, Illinois, and driven by easy "stages over the prairies, pasturing as they went. In less than five days the native stock grazing on "the prairies where the Texan herds had grazed were all sick or dead, while those grazing where the "Texan cattle had not appeared remained healthy. In the first two weeks of the disease 235 cattle "died, after which the mortality increased, one farmer losing 55 out of 70 cows in a few days. No "animal attacked seems to have recovered. The excitement in some of the diseased localities was so "great that the farmers formed vigilance committees to prevent the introduction of any more Texan "cattle. Many of the animals found their way to Chicago, where they communicated the disease to "the stock in the drove yards, and some of these infected cows were slaughtered and sold in the "markets. The disease spread to the adjoining State of Indiana, where thousands of cattle are still "dying from it."

The correspondent of the "Morning Herald" says: "In New York, Rhode Island, New Jersey, "Massachusetts, Connecticut, Vermont, Pennsylvania, Ohio, Illinois, Indiana, and Missouri, the State

Q 2761.

"and local authorities are examining droves and cars, slaughtering cattle, disinfecting yards, and
"taking other steps to stamp out the pest. In the Dominion also some alarm prevails, the Govern-
"ment have prohibited importations of cattle from the State into Quebec and Ontario. Introduction
"of cattle into New Jersey from the West has been prohibited by the State authorities; this cuts off
"the chief source of supply for the New York market. After advancing to a high figure the price of
"beef in New York has materially declined; at first the butchers took advantage of circumstances to
"increase prices, but now the consumers, themselves affected by panic, as a rule, abjure beef. I have
"already described the peculiarities of the disease now carrying off our cattle. It is now generally
"thought that the pest is not due to the feeding of Texas cattle upon a peculiar plant, but to that
"hideous green insect, the carapato. The Chicago journals describe Mr. Gamgee, who puts forth the
"first-named theory, as a humbug. As the interests of tens of thousands of people in the West are
"involved with the trade in cattle, it may easily be supposed that the excitable Hoosiers are in great
"trouble. In Champaign County, Ohio, a great rendezvous and feeding ground for cattle from Texas
"and the Western States, widespread panic prevails, since not less than 30,000 cattle are turned out
"to grass in that county alone. A similar alarm is observable in certain great grazing counties in
"Illinois, where the mortality among cattle has been very heavy. On the south-western borders of
"Missouri a small civil war exists. Drovers from Texas and the Indian country have collected vast
"herds of cattle, which the Missourians will not permit to pass. The drovers threaten violence, and
"the border men promise bloodshed if the threat be made good. The Governor of Missouri has issued
"a proclamation commanding these belligerents to keep the peace. The cattle disease runs its course
"in about three days, it is attended by loss of milk from the first in the cows, by terrible emaciation,
"by violent inflammation of the bowels and kidneys, and occasionally by pustulent eruptions, and by
"great discharge of water and mucus from the mouth. It is now said that instead of 50 per cent.
"nearly all the cases end fatally."

The following letter was addressed to Her Majesty's Customs:—

Privy Council Office, Veterinary Department, Princes Street,
Sir,   Westminster, S.W., September 1, 1868.

WITH reference to the importation of undressed hides from America I have the honour to request that you will be good enough to inform me, for the information of the Lords of the Council, whether the hides so imported are limed or otherwise prepared.

I have, &c.
The Secretary, Custom House.   (Signed)   C. EARDLEY-WILMOT
                                                                    for Secretary.

On September 3rd, 1868, the following statement appeared in the "Standard":—

The cattle disease has broken out in Paris and Dundas, Canada. It was communicated to the Canadian cattle by a drove sent over the Great Western Railway. The Canadian authorities have sent commissioners to the States to examine the infected cattle, and, if possible, trace out the cause of the disease. In the Eastern States the panic has materially subsided, the West is still thoroughly alarmed. A quarantine for cattle has been established in Chicago; the necessity for this is apparent in view of the fact that sometimes not less than 130,000 head of cattle are collected in the yards of that city.

And on September 7th, 1868, the following dispatch was received from the Colonial Office:—

Sir,   Downing Street, September 5, 1868.

I AM directed by the Secretary of State for the Colonies to transmit to you, for the information of the Lords of the Privy Council, acting as a Board of Health, copies of the under-mentioned documents.

I am, &c.
The Clerk of the Council.   (Signed)   FREDERIC ROGERS.

No. 156, 15th August 1868. Despatch from the Governor of Canada, enclosing a copy of an Order in Council prohibiting the importation of horned cattle from the United States into the Dominion.

VISCOUNT MONCK to the DUKE OF BUCKINGHAM.

MY LORD DUKE,   Quebec, Canada, August 15, 1868.

I HAVE the honour to transmit, for your Grace's information, a copy of an Order in Council by which the importation of horned cattle from the United States into Canada is temporarily prohibited in consequence of the prevalence of contagious disease amongst the cattle of the former country.

I have sent a copy of this order to Her Majesty's Minister at Washington.

I have, &c.
His Grace the Duke of Buckingham and Chandos.   (Signed)   MONCK.

GOVERNMENT HOUSE, OTTAWA, Thursday, 13th day of August 1868.
Present:
His Excellency the GOVERNOR GENERAL in Council.

Whereas by an Act passed in the 29th year of Her Majesty's reign, entitled "An Act to provide against the introduction and spreading of disorders affecting certain animals," authority is given to the Governor in Council to take such measures as may appear to be necessary, in order to prevent the introduction of contagious or infectious disorders affecting cattle and other animals, and to check such disorders from spreading if introduced.

And whereas a contagious disease or epidemic affecting horned cattle prevails in many parts of the United States of America, and is increasing and extending its ravages; and whereas it is expedient in order to prevent the introduction of the same into the provinces of Quebec and Ontario, heretofore constituting the Province of Canada, that the importation of horned cattle from the United States of America should be prohibited.

His Excellency in Council, on the recommendation of the Honourable the Minister of Customs, and under the authority given by the said Act, has been pleased to order, and it is hereby ordered, that from and after the date hereof, and until this Order shall have been altered or revoked, the importation from the United States of America or introduction therefrom into the Provinces of Quebec and Ontario heretofore constituting the Province of Canada, or into any part thereof, of horned cattle be and the same is hereby prohibited.

Certified,
(Signed)   W<small>M</small>. H. L<small>EE</small>,
Clerk, Privy Council.

A despatch, dated 22nd August, 1868, was received from the Foreign Office on September 10th, relating to the same disease:—

M<small>Y</small> L<small>ORD</small>,   British Consulate, Buffalo, August 22, 1868.

I <small>HAVE</small> the honour to report that a species of cattle plague, which is generally assumed to be identical with the European rinderpest, has recently made its appearance here.

Symptoms of the disease were first detected among a drove of about 50 head, imported by rail from Illinois on the 10th instant. The infected animals were at once picked out and slaughtered, and the remainder transferred to a quarantine pasture outside the city limits, where they are gradually being killed off as the first symptoms declare themselves.

The Board of Health physician informs me that these cattle are ascertained to have been fattened upon a pasture which had previously been grazed over by a herd from Texas. It is, I am assured, under these precise conditions that the disease has been invariably developed in this country. Texan cattle import the germ of infection to other pastures, but, strange to say, show themselves no symptoms of the plague.

With reference to this singular fact, I beg to state that the Report of the United States Department of Agriculture for April contains an article, the writer of which insists that the disease thus propagated is not the European rinderpest, but a much less formidable epidemic, properly named "Spanish fever." He bases his arguments specially on the fact that in genuine rinderpest the poison is fatal to the animal communicating it, as well as to all others through which it successively passes, while in Spanish fever the communicating animal—as in the case which forms the subject of this despatch—may be in apparent health, and may even constantly improve in condition.

The disease in Buffalo has, so far, been strictly limited to the imported herd referred to above.

I have, &c.
(Signed)   H. W. H<small>EMANS</small>.

The Lord Stanley, M.P.,
&c.   &c.   &c.

On September 10th, 1868, a letter was received from the Commissioners of Her Majesty's Customs, in response to inquiries which had been addressed to them in accordance with the terms of Professor Ferguson's letter of August 28th:—

S<small>IR</small>,   Custom House, September 10, 1868.

H<small>AVING</small> laid before the Board of Customs Mr. Eardley Wilmot's letter of the 1st instant, requesting to be informed whether undressed hides imported from America are limed or otherwise prepared, I am desired to transmit, for the information of the Lords of Her Majesty's Privy Council, copies of the Reports of the Controller of the Out-Door Department in London, and of the surveyors at the ports of Liverpool and Bristol, whom the Board directed to make inquiry on the subject, those being the ports into which hides are principally imported.

I am, &c.
(Signed)   J. W. H<small>ALE</small>.

Dr. Williams,
&c.   &c.   &c.

H<small>ONOURABLE</small> S<small>IRS</small>,   Custom House, London, September 9, 1868.

I <small>BEG</small> to forward reports from the surveyors stating that the hides imported from North America are tanned, and that those from South America are either salted or dried in the sun.

(Signed)   C<small>HARLES</small> H<small>UNT</small>,
Contr. of O. D. Department.

The Honourable Commissioners
of H.M. Customs.

                                                        Bristol, Out-Door Department, Water Guard,
S<small>IR</small>,   September 3, 1868.

I<small>N</small> obedience to the Honourable Board's Order of the 2nd inst., No. 91, I beg to state that from inquiry I have made that all the undressed hides imported into this port from America are not limed, but salted and pickled for the preservation thereof in the country from whence imported, and that they do not undergo any subsequent process on their being landed in this country.

I am, &c.
(Signed)   J. J<small>ONES</small>,
Acting Inspector, Water Guard.

The Collector.

G<small>ENTLEMEN</small>,   Custom House, Liverpool, September 4, 1868.

B<small>Y</small> the within reports of the surveyors at the several docks it will be seen that undressed hides imported into this port from America are not limed or otherwise prepared on importation or subsequently, to their knowledge.

From inquiries I have made of one of the largest importers of hides into this port, I find that hides from North America come in a dried and half-tanned state, and are subsequently tanned and curried in this country; those from Central America and the West Indies are imported in bundles in a dry state and principally limed, and hides from South America are generally imported loose, wet, and salted only, and occasionally in bales in a dried state, but neither tanned nor limed, but are subsequently tanned and curried in this country; hides limed being rarely imported from South America, and when so, not amounting to more than one hide in a thousand.

Respectfully,
The Collector and Comptroller,   (Signed)   EDWARD ARMSTRONG,
Liverpool.   Surveyor.

On September 9th, 1868, the Hon. Wilbraham Egerton, M.P., Knutsford, Cheshire, wrote to the Vice President of the Council regarding the importation of American hay:—

DEAR LORD ROBERT,   Rostherne Manor, Knutsford, September 9, 1868.

CONSIDERABLE fear exists in some parts of this county that a species of rinderpest will be introduced by the sale of hay in the Liverpool market coming from America, where it is known that a new cattle disease is spreading. Can the Privy Council take any steps either to allay the alarm by proving that it is groundless, or forbid the importation, if any real danger is shown to exist? Farmers here are very sensitive on the matter, and I hope that you will be able to do something which will reassure them or remove their fears.

Believe me, &c.
The Right Hon. Lord R. Montagu.   (Signed)   WILBRAHAM EGERTON.
&c.   &c.   &c.

And on September 12th, 1868, Mr. John Tollemache, M.P., wrote on the same subject:—

MY DEAR SIR,   Beaumaris, September 12, 1868.

OUR poor farmers in Cheshire are naturally very sensitive on the subject of cattle plague of any kind, and entertain fears on account of the quantities of hay imported into Liverpool from the United States, where it is said that a sort of rinderpest, or some fatal plague, is now raging.

I acknowledge that no such apprehensions are entertained by me, but you will greatly oblige me by writing me a few lines to assure us that these fears are groundless.

I should not trouble you with this letter had I not been pressed to write to the Authorities of the Privy Council on the subject.

I remain, &c.
Dr. Williams,   (Signed)   J. TOLLEMACHE.
Privy Council O

In consequence of these representations, an Order of Council was passed on September 15th, 1868, restricting the landing of hay from America:—

(247.)

At the COUNCIL CHAMBER, WHITEHALL, the 15th day of September, 1868.
By the Lords of Her Majesty's Most Honourable Privy Council.

Present:
LORD STANLEY. | MR. DISRAELI.

THE Lords of Her Majesty's Most Honourable Privy Council, by virtue and in excercise of the powers in them vested under the Contagious Diseases (Animals) Acts, and of every other power enabling them in this behalf, do order, and it is hereby ordered, as follows:—

1. This Order shall take effect on and after the twenty-fifth day of September, one thousand eight hundred and sixty-eight.

2. Hay which shall have been shipped at, or imported from, any port of the United States of America, and which has been brought to or arrived at any port or place in the United Kingdom, shall not be removed out of or from the ship or vessel in which the same shall have been so brought, or shall have so arrived and landed in any port or place of the said United Kingdom.

3. Provided that, notwithstanding anything in this Order contained, it shall be lawful for the captain or other person in charge of a ship or vessel to land hay which shall have been shipped at or from any port of the United States of America, and which shall be intended to be consumed in the United Kingdom, by horses only, upon obtaining a licence, under the authority of the Lords of Her Majesty's Privy Council, authorising the landing of the hay which shall so have arrived in such ship or vessel, or of such part of such hay as by the said licence shall be permitted to be landed, and the transmission thereof to such person or persons, or place or places, as in the said licence shall be mentioned in that behalf.

And the Right Honourable the Lords Commissioners of Her Majesty's Treasury are to give the necessary directions herein accordingly.

(Signed)   ARTHUR HELPS.

Interference with the trade in American hay caused a great deal of complaint among importers, and it was deemed advisable to revoke the Order on January 15th 1869:—

(253.)

At the COUNCIL CHAMBER, WHITEHALL, the 15th day of January 1869.
By the Lords of Her Majesty's Most Honourable Privy Council.

Present:
LORD PRESIDENT. | MR. FORSTER.

THE Lords of Her Majesty's Most Honourable Privy Council, by virtue and in exercise of the powers in them vested under the Contagious Diseases (Animals) Acts, and of every other power enabling them in this behalf, do hereby revoke their Orders bearing date the fifteenth day of September, one thousand eight hundred and sixty-eight, and the nineteenth day of October, one thousand eight hundred and sixty-eight, relating to hay which is shipped at, or imported from, any port of the United States of America, and which is brought to, or arrives at, any port or place in the United Kingdom; provided that nothing herein shall be deemed to invalidate or make unlawful anything done under the said Orders before the date of this revocation, or interfere with the institution or prosecution of any proceeding in respect of any offence committed against, or any penalty incurred under, the said Orders, or either of them.

(Signed) ARTHUR HELPS.

On November 27th, 1868, a letter was received from the Foreign Office in reply to our letter of August 18th:—

MY LORD,
British Consulate, Chicago, U.S.,
November 9, 1868.

WITH reference to my despatch to your Lordship, No. 7 of the 31st July ultimo, I have the honour to enclose herein the Report of the Commissioners on the Texas Cattle Disease to the Pork Packers Association of Chicago.

I have, &c.
(Signed) T. FREDERICK WILKINS,
H.B.M. Acting Consul.

The Right Honourable the Lord Stanley,
Her Majesty's Secretary of State for Foreign Affairs,
Foreign Office, London.

SPLENIC FEVER, or BLACK WATER of TEXAS.

REPORT of COMMISSIONERS on the TEXAS CATTLE DISEASE to the PORK PACKERS ASSOCIATION of CHICAGO, October 1868.

To the Pork Packers Association of Chicago:—

AT various times in the history of this and other countries alarming diseases among cattle have existed, and at times taken the shape of epidemics. Fortunately, in our own country, the extent of these maladies has not been very great or disastrous. Many of these diseases have been of a local character, generally understood and yielding to skilful treatment.

With the tide of emigration and centre of population tending westward, the production of neat stock to supply the wants of the older settled portions of the country has necessarily followed or gone with them to cheaper lands, all the time rapidly increased in volume.

In early days, Ohio was the Far West, where cattle were raised, gathered in droves, and passed over the mountains into Pennsylvania, and then fed for the sea-board markets.

With the opening up of Illinois, its immense and rich prairies offered superior advantages to the stock raiser. The stock at about three years old or over was then driven into the older State of Ohio and East, to be fed and fitted for market. Illinois at once took the lead as a stock State, and for many years has held that position, much the larger portion of the live stock reaching the Eastern markets quoted as Illinois stock having been fed by our citizens. As our State has rapidly increased in population, ranges have become more contracted, our largest feeders having gone farther west, into Missouri and Iowa, purchased and pastured, during the summer, large herds of cattle, and then brought them to this State to fatten upon our immense fields of corn. The bulk of production of cattle, in this manner, has been kept in a measure on the frontiers, where the range is largely on the public domain, and expenses are comparatively light. Herds have increased from a few score to hundreds and thousands.

Occasional or periodical seasons of excessive losses have occurred among cattle by diseases, such as incident to a new country, with rank vegetation and increase of herds—varying very much in magnitude and extent with different seasons.

But no disease has been wide-spread, or very disastrous. That which has attracted the most attention was the pleuro-pneumonia, which for a time raged in Massachusetts, and threatened to become general, but by prompt and efficient measures adopted in that State the disease was stayed.

In 1865, when this country became so much exercised by the terrible ravages of the cattle plague in Europe, precautionary measures were adopted by several States and by Congress to prevent the importation of the disease here. The Illinois State Agricultural Society appointed a commission to gather all the information possible, and carefully watch the course of the disease, the history of which is now familiar to all. The Society also appointed commissioners, early in August, who have been pursuing their investigations in various parts of the west with reference to this disease.

As emigration pushed west and south-west, Texas and the Indian country naturally drifted into the production of stock on a large scale. Those countries afforded superior advantages for the business, as no care of stock was needed the year round, except to occasionally herd and brand them.

As early at least as 1849, this class of stock sometimes found its way in small herds as far north as Missouri. About this time there also appeared a new disease among the native cattle, following where these droves of southern cattle had been herded and pastured. It was at that time considered that it was in some way attributable to the presence of these cattle, but how communicated or what the particular nature of the disease was, no one seemed to have investigated at that time. For ten years the trade in those cattle was continued on a small scale, some years the peculiar disease appearing and others nothing being seen of it. About 1858 the volume of the trade had gradually increased to considerable proportions, and the greater prevalence of the new disease began to attract general attention, creating in various localities on the frontier in south-western Missouri and southern Kansas, great excitement. Legislation was had in Kansas in 1861, to regulate the handling of this stock.

During the war but little was heard or known of the disease, as comparatively few of this class of cattle found their way north. With the close of the war, however, the cattle which had been accumulating in vast herds in the south-west, again commenced coming north, only to repeat the disasters that had so frequently followed in their trail in previous years. So great were the ravages of the disease that the State of Missouri passed stringent laws, approved March 13, 1867 (see appendix), regulating the handling of the stock in the State. Kansas, also, remodelled its legislation on the subject, laws approved February 1886 (see appendix), the more perfectly to guard against the spread of the disease. The Legislature of Illinois, at the session of 1867, also passed the present prohibitory laws (see appendix) against the introduction of these cattle into the State. Other States have also passed laws on the subject.

Notwithstanding all this legislation, and the knowledge of the dangerous character of the stock, there were many men who either disbelieved in the injurious character of the stock, or for love of the gain the trade in these cattle promised, disregarded the laws, or evaded the officers, and continued to bring in cattle during the year 1867.

As the risks and dangers of trying to force cattle through the south-western portion of Missouri and south-eastern Kansas increased, the traders sought other routes. One was established through Kansas, west of the sixth principal meridian, up to a point or points on the Union Pacific Railroad (east division), where, during the fall of 1867 and spring of the present year, some 2,000 carloads of them were shipped east, some to the prairies of Illinois and Indiana, and others into the markets, both east and west. Another route was established by the gulf coast to New Orleans, and thence up the river to Cairo, St. Louis, &c. Still another was to drive to the mouth of the Red River, and thence up the Mississippi river. Other lots still found their way on foot, crossing the Mississippi below St. Louis, and then reaching the prairies of our State.

Early in the spring a brisk business began on all these routes, and cattle were started in immense droves by the various channels, their arrival commencing in this State about the last of April.

So far as we are aware no effort was made to check the importation of these cattle—even the men, in some instances, who were foremost in obtaining the passage of our law, being engaged in the handling of them. The result was the disease appeared late in July in various localities in the State. In view of this, and a desire on your part to know more of this somewhat mysterious disease, I accepted from this Board a commission to proceed to the localities where it existed to investigate it, with authority to employ competent associates. I accordingly employed Professor John Gamgee, a noted veterinary surgeon from London, England, who happened to be stopping in Chicago, and Dr. J. V. Z. Blaney, an eminent chemist of this city, to accompany me in the investigations.

We left Chicago July 20th for Tolono, a point on the Illinois Central Railroad, where a large number of these Texas cattle had been unloaded, and where we were informed the disease had appeared. On arriving there and making inquiry, we had no difficulty in finding numerous cases of sickness and death among the native stock. Close examination of different animals gives the following:

Symptoms of the Disease.

The symptoms which the ordinary observer would notice would be indications of an intense fever, with pulse ranging, as we found it, from 60 to 120 per minute; breathing often laboured and generally frequent; loss of appetite; in cows, the almost entire suspension of milk secretions; head drooping when standing, and when lying the nose thrust hard onto the ground, sometimes turned back over the side, and pressed against it; the ears drooping, back arched, flank hollow, hind legs drawn up under the body; frequent knuckling over of the hind fetlocks; disposed to lie down and get up again, which it does with difficulty. When made to move, it is often with a staggering, unsteady gait. Occasionally an animal appears delirious; at others, sleepy. The coat becomes rough. At times frequent twitching of the muscles appear about the shoulders and other parts of the body.

Careful post-mortem examinations of several animals, some killed for the purpose, and others that had died, gave the following:

Post-mortem Appearances.

The post-mortem appearances are blood-staining, petechia or ecchymoses of the internal membrane of the body, especially in and around the heart, sometimes but rarely over the lungs, in a few cases over the lining membrane of the belly, and very generally over the mucous lining of the stomach and intestines. The respiratory passages are found healthy—the lungs sometimes very partially congested, and were commonly blown up with air between their lobules, constituting what is known in medicine as interlobular emphysema.

The three first stomachs are usually healthy, and especially the third, which has been described as impacted, does not differ materially in the great majority of cases from that state which we are so well accustomed to see in the healthy cattle we slaughter. The fourth stomach is intensely congested at its upper end, less so near the intestines, but all over may be seen, in some cases, spots of blood extravasation, in others greyish, granular deposits, and in almost all erosions of the lining membrane.

The intestines are with rare exception congested and blood-stained, more or less, throughout their whole extent.

The liver often congested, is not materially implicated in the disease. The gall-bladder has its coats sometimes thickened by a gelatinous-looking fluid, and its contents are dark and viscid. Its internal coat is sometimes congested.

The spleen is always enlarged. It should usually weigh from one to one and a half pounds, but it is found in this disease as high as five, six, and even eight pounds in weight. It is dark coloured, and its structure broken up.

The kidneys are congested, and the mucous membrane within them often blood-stained. In a small percentage of cases the bladder contains clear urine. In the great majority this organ is greatly distended by bloody urine, and its internal lining is dotted with small, bright pin-point-like extravasations.

The brain and spinal cord is congested, more or less, and even the seat of blood extravasations according to the extent of paralysis and other nervous symptoms during life.

Professor Gamgee proposes to call the disease *splenic fever*, or Black Water of Texas—from its similarity, or identity with a malady known in the old world as Black Water, or enzoötic hematuria.

From Tolono our next stop was at Farina, in Effingham County, where the Commission was joined by Mr. H. D. Emery, one of the editors of the "Prairie Farmer," who after that time became one of the Commission.

Here we learned that about 18 carloads of Texas cattle (some 250 head) were unloaded and placed in charge of Mr. E. Richardson, about a mile south-west from the railroad station. The cattle were a part of a lot of about 1,100 that were received at Cairo, and destined for Iroquois County. Those unloaded here were in poor condition, many of them said to be suffering from wounds and bruises received in the journey up the river on crowded boats, and were left behind on that account, while the balance went forward to their destination. These cattle remained in charge of Mr. Richardson until about the 16th of June, when they were sufficiently improved to travel, and were again loaded on the cars and shipped north. During their stay there some 15 head died, it was thought from the injuries they had received. While on this place they were allowed the same range with a lot of 50 native steers and one milch cow of Mr. R.'s. The cows of the village residents in that part of the town were also allowed the same range. About the 1st of July Mr. R.'s cattle commenced dying, with all the symptoms of the disease known as Texas or Spanish fever, and the same as seen at Tolono, and at the time of our visit he had lost, of his 51 head, no less than 48, and most of the cows in that part of the town which had been allowed the same range were either dead or sick, while on the opposite side of the railroad, where the cattle had been isolated from the common range, not a case of the disease had appeared. Here we made several post-mortem examinations, showing the same conditions as found at Tolono.

Our next point was at Cairo, August 2nd. We here learned that the first shipments of cattle were received by the river April 23rd, 250 in number; on the 26th another 250; then followed other lots, until we were informed by the railroad officers that about 16,000 head had been received and shipped up the I. C. R. R., the larger proportion of them going to Tolono. From gentlemen who had much to do with these cattle while at Cairo having furnished the hay and fed them in the yards, we learned that the earliest receipts were in excellent condition and apparent good health; that as warm weather came on some lots showed symptoms of disease, and it was not uncommon to find 10 to 15 dead in the yards in the morning, after unloading from the boats; and frequently six or eight dead were found on the boats when they were unloaded.

We would here remark that it is customary to load these cattle at New Orleans on the boiler decks. They are often crowded as close as they can be packed, and all the food they have is hay, thrown in among them from above; we were told that many of them make the whole passage without water, as it is impossible to get it to them. The only wonder to us is that no greater number of them die. The fatigue and heat would, no doubt, tend to the development of any disease there might be in them; and we cannot doubt but many of the deaths were from disease, developed by the conditions surrounding them.

It was the usual custom to yard, feed, and water the cattle, allowing a rest of about 24 hours, when they were loaded on the cars for shipment. If any animals were unable to travel they were usually sold, for a small sum, to such as were ready to buy. These were taken to the shambles or, in some cases, turned out on the limited range about the city.

Upon careful inquiry and personal interviews with several persons about the city, it was found that many cattle had died, showing all the outward symptoms we had observed at other points. The first death having occurred about the 25th of May, and many others following in a short time. One dairyman had lost 16 head out of 22 at the time of our visit, and had more that were suffering. Upon further inquiry, we found that the losses were mostly of cows belonging to the labouring population, whose range was on the commons and over the same grounds where a few of the southern cattle had from time to time ranged; also that the cattle had access to the feeding yards at the transfer yards when emptied, where they picked up the hay left in them. The gentleman who lost the 16 head referred to, stated that his cows had frequently been in those yards; that he had often seen the Texas cattle in the yards and while being unloaded from the boats; that he had seen them with the same symptoms observed in his own cattle when sick, and that he had examined them after death and found them diseased, showing the same appearance of organs as his own.

While at Cairo a shipment of these cattle was received from a boat, but the excitement up the road being so great, the Ill. Cent. R. R. refused to transfer any more of that class of cattle. These cattle we carefully examined in the yards, without detecting any outward symptoms of disease. They were all in fair condition, eating heartily and appeared well. We saw this same lot of cattle in Chicago market, some three weeks afterward, to which place they had been shipped, viâ St. Louis, having remained in that city, in the stock yards, for several days. They still retained their healthy appearance, but had lost flesh for want of proper food, &c.; none had died or given out on the journey.

During this part of the trip a powerful microscope was frequently brought into use, in carefully examining the tissue of the organs found diseased, and the contents of stomach, intestines, and bladder, and the blood, milk, and meat of the animals.

Returning up the road we again stopped at Tolono, August 3rd, found that cattle were still rapidly dying—235 head having been reported dead to the vigilance committee up to the night of the 1st, the first death having occurred about the 20th of July. At this point we left the railroad, passing east about 15 miles to the large stock farm of J. T. Alexander, where a large number of these Texan cattle had been driven. On the way out we passed many persons places where all the native cattle had died, and others had lost a large proportion of their stock. In all of these cases these cattle ranged over the same ground where the Texan cattle had been driven. Where cattle were found that had been isolated and kept under fence, without access to these ranges, no losses had occurred. We learned that there had been about 15,000 head of this class of stock unloaded at Tolono, and distributed in various directions, extending into the western counties of Indiana. Following up many of these trails for long distances, found the disease appeared upon these lines of travel and nowhere else, and that complete isolation, if only by a road fence, seemed in all cases to be a perfect protection to the native stock. During this trip we saw a large number of the Texan cattle, and carefully examined them for any symptoms of disease, without finding any that gave any appearance of suffering from this or any other cause. They showed great vitality and were doing well on the rich pastures, while the native stock were dying in all directions.

At this point of the investigation, your Commission, considering it would require more time than anticipated, and further preparation, to pursue the matter, returned to Chicago, when Prof. Gamgee and Dr. Blaney made verbal reports of progress to this Board. At this time, Hon. Horace Capron, Commissioner of Agriculture, arrived in Chicago, and made arrangements with Prof. Gamgee to pursue the investigation for, and report to the Department at Washington; and it was arranged that the investigations should go on as begun, myself and Mr. Emery reporting to your body, while Prof. Gamgee reported to the Department of Agriculture; Dr. Blaney not being able, from other duties, to further accompany the Commission.

We again left Chicago, August 5th, stopping off at Tolono, and going east as far as Mr. Alexander's farm, where we met several parties who had lost stock by the disease, and learned more of the extent of the same. On Mr. Alexander's farm, Mr. C. L. Eaton, the manager, did all in his power to assist the Commission, by placing as many cattle at our disposal as we chose, both native and Texan, for examination; as did also Mr. J. M. Sullivant, living in the same neighbourhood. Being desirous of examining more critically some of the Texan animals, the herds were looked over, and an animal selected that seemed to be ill, and had been down for two days. The animal was quite emaciated, breathed hard, and was evidently near death. It was killed and most critically examined throughout, without presenting appearances of any disease at all analagous to that afflicting the native cattle; in fact, there seemed to be no disease, but a wasting away of the animal, and dying of poverty. The fatty tissues had all been absorbed in sustaining life, and the system did not seem to have vitality enough to rally from the fatigues the animal had undergone on the journey to the farm. We found Mr. Eaton had isolated all the native cattle remaining on the farm, from the ranges of the Texas cattle, and was feeding them on a field of green corn. Under this treatment, the disease seemed to be abating. Among the cattle that had died of the disease were some Texas work oxen that had been on the place three years, showing that they were not exempt from it, after having become thoroughly acclimated to this region.

From this point we visited Sadorus, a village on the railroad west of Tolono, where it was said several horses had died of the disease. On arriving there inquiry was made regarding the matter. The gentleman, James Miller, who was said to have lost them, we found, and learned from him, that he had lost horses, but had never attributed it to the cattle disease; one had died from a snake bite; another was overheated, and died with her colt; another died suddenly, after eating very heartily, cause not known. At this point we found quite a large number of the Texan cattle had been driven and distributed to points further west and north; and that large numbers of native cattle had died, estimated by some to reach 400 or 500 within a few miles. All who had lost cattle, so far as we could ascertain, had allowed their stock on the Texas range. Here we found one peculiar case; a cow belonging to G. F. Byers had died during the night previous; it was considerably bloated. We carefully dissected it, found all the digestive organs, liver, intestines, gall, &c. in nearly normal condition; the heart somewhat blood-stained on both inside and outside, and undergoing decomposition; the spleen considerably enlarged, and structure destroyed. Hemorrhage had occurred from it, flooding the cavity of the body; the animal's death evidently being immediately caused by this hemorrhage, although it would probably have died had it not occurred.

At this place we met Dr. I. G. Wisner, who was in Taxes during the war in 1864, who stated he was familiar with what is called Spanish fever in that country. That it affects horses only, and that many died during the war; also that he had seen many cattle that had died, during his service there; had seen on one journey of 40 miles on the Rio Colorado as many as 40,000 dead; had examined them frequently, found the lungs affected, but nothing like the appearances found here. He attributed the deaths of these great numbers to the gathering of very large herds, without sufficient water, and the excessively warm weather prevailing at the time. From Sadorus several droves of cattle were taken west as far up as the forks of the Sangamon, some 24 miles.

Champaign, Aug. 7th.—Here we examined three head of cattle, belonging to P. Harris, which had died; finding the same appearances as at other points. His cattle had been exposed to the range where he had pastured some Texas cattle purchased at Tolono.

Aug. 8th.—Six miles west of Champaign in Scott Township, we examined a herd of cattle belonging to several parties, which had been fed on the range over which the Texas cattle had passed from Sadorus; the disease was killing many animals. Here we made several post-mortem examinations with no new developments.

J. A. Harris at this place purchased last fall a drove of 85 herd of south-western cattle, and placed them on his farm with his native stock, 38 in number; these were wintered and fed together up to the time of our visit. Previous to July 15, they had been out of the range of the new importations of cattle. The whole herd had done well, no disease having appeared among any part of them. On July 15th, the whole lot were removed to the range over which the new Texas cattle had lately been driven, and remained there some 12 days. August 3rd, the native cattle began to die, and at the time we were there 20 of the 38 were then dead, and the balance all ailing. The Texans with them that had been wintered over were apparently well and healthy, and gaining rapidly in flesh.

We further obtained information of not less than five lots of southern cattle that were brought into that neighbourhood, during the falls of 1866 and 1867, from which no injury has occurred to native stock the following summer.

We here learned that the disease prevailed considerably further north, as far as the Texas cattle had been driven, and westward as far as the main line of the Ill. C. R. R., through Piatt and Macon counties.

August 13th, visited Benton and other counties in Western Indiana. On the farm of Fowler and Earl, at Hickory Grove, we found a large number of Texan cattle, 1,000 head of which were purchased in the fall of 1867, in Chicago, and wintered on the farm. A small shipment was received from New Orleans about the 1st of June of the present year. About the 12th of July and 8th of August there were brought on to the place some 2,000 head, which had come on by the way of Abilene, in Kansas. So far as it has been possible to distinguish there seems never to have been any disease communicated by the 1,000 head brought on to the place last fall and wintered over; and not until sufficient time had elapsed after the fresh importations had been made did the disease appear on their track.

In this neighbourhood for several miles around we visited several farms where cattle had died, and were dying. Several of the losers were owners of Texas cattle; others were sufferers without having handled them, their stock passing and feeding on the same range of the fresh importations of Texas cattle.

While at the farm of Fowler and Earl, we learned of a lot of 300 southern cattle that were purchased in the fall of 1866, brought in by the way of Quincy. These cattle were kept over winter on this farm, and herded on the prairies during the whole summer of 1867 without doing any harm.

August 14th.—Made careful post-mortems of several animals on the farm of J. Heath, without showing any new features. The first Texas cattle were received on the place 20th of June, second lot 2nd of July; the first case of sickness noticed was August 8th, soon terminating in death, and several others had died previous to our visit.

August 15th.—Visited Reynold's Station on the New Albany and Chicago Railroad. First Texas cattle received 27th of May; first case of sickness early in June. One gentleman had 73 head of native stock, which fed on the range over which the Texas had been driven; at the time of our visit 55 to 60 of them were already dead and others sick.

On returning to Chicago we visited the vicinity of the stock yards, where a large number of cattle, especially milk cows of the fifth ward had died, and ascertained the following facts: Cattle coming into the yards and remaining unsold are frequently turned out for a short time to range on the prairies west and south-west of the yards; sometimes are placed in inclosures where they remain for days. The cattle that died had so far as could be learned, without exception, been allowed to run on the open prairie over which the Texas cattle had been. The precise time of exposure previous to death could not be ascertained, as many fed up to the time of death.

Again, the proprietor of the Hough house has kept through the summer over 30 head of milch cows in a fenced lot adjoining the stock yards on one side, on two other sides joining lots in which Texas cattle had been, nearly every day of the season—the division fence being only a common board one—not a case of sickness or death had occurred among these cattle up to the time of our visit, or since, as we are informed. Another gentleman, near by, had several cows which had been similarly isolated and had lost none.

A careful post-mortem examination was made of a cow which was suffering and was killed for the purpose, showing the usual appearance found elsewhere; from close investigation there was no chance to doubt the disease being the same that had affected the cattle at other places.

We could not learn that the mere passage of native cattle through the same shipping yards, or the transportation in the same cars previously occupied by the Texas cattle, had ever produced the disease.

St. Louis, August 21st.—On our arrival at East St. Louis we learned that some 10,000 head of the Texas cattle had been received there, mostly forwarded by the Chicago and St. Louis Railroad to Green, Sangamon, and Morgan Counties. Some had been shipped by the other roads running east, to the central part of the State, and eastern markets. Surrounding the village there had been many deaths of native cows which had fed on grounds temporarily occupied by the Texans.

Passing over into St. Louis City we visited the various stock yards, and found all transactions in stock at a standstill, as the railroads refused to handle the Texas cattle. Boats coming up the river loaded with cattle were not allowed to land them, and in some instances, we were informed, went up the river and landed them at obscure landings, from whence they were driven into the interior of Illinois.

Calling at the Health Office, the officer (Dr. Clemens) informed us that considerable sickness and many deaths had occurred among the native cows of the citizens in the suburbs of the city, with symptoms indicating the presence of this disease. He kindly furnished conveyance, and accompanied the Commission to a part of the city where several animals had died, and more were sick. Here we found unmistakable symptoms in several animals. One cow that was apparently in the last stages of the disease was killed, and a careful post-mortem examination showed all the general appearances found elsewhere.

These cattle were allowed free range of vacant lots about the outskirts of the city, across which frequent droves of Texas cattle had been driven during the summer. They had also drank from the pond holes about the same regions.

We also visited, near St. Louis, an extensive dairy, where some 50 cows had suddenly died not long before our visit. The owner described their symptoms, which corresponded in the main with what we had seen in this Texas disease. The cows had been purchased only a short time before from the stock yards in St. Louis, and were said to have been brought from Illinois, but further particulars we could not learn.

From St. Louis we went to Kansas City in Missouri, a point where large numbers of the Texas cattle are transferred from the Pacific Railroad to the different railroads running east from there. We could learn of no disease having appeared in the neighbourhood this year. The arrangements for the transfer of these cattle are so well perfected and guarded that the native cattle do not come in contact with them at all.

Deeming it desirable to see the condition of the Texas cattle on their first arrival at the shipping points, we took the cars of the Pacific Railroad, intending to stop at Abilene. On our way out, however, we had conversation with several stockmen and farmers, from whom we learned that no disease had appeared in that region during the season; but on arriving near Junction City, we were informed that the disease had appeared there within a few days among a lot of native cattle. We stopped at that point August 24th, found a drove of work-oxen that had been driven from Salina, some 80 miles west, having crossed the trail of the Texas cattle in several places. The gentleman in charge had just returned from St. Louis, where he had taken 36 head of the lot, four of them having died while in the yards there; of those remaining at home we found several sick, and 16 had died. The temperature of rectum and pulse were taken of many that were yet apparently quite well, but indicating the certain presence of the disease. We here made careful post-mortem examinations without any new developments.

Our next point was at Abilene, where extensive arrangements for handling and shipping this class of stock had been made by J. G. McCoy & Co. These yards were completed and ready for use

Q 2761.

September 5, 1867, after which time, in that year, about 1,000 carloads of Texas cattle were received and shipped east from them. From all we could learn there was no disease communicated from any of the cattle received at that point to the native stock of the neighbourhood. The disease not following these cattle, in a measure threw people off their guard, and with the early spring of the present year active preparations were commenced by the drovers for a large business in this class of stock. The journey overland was made with more than usual expedition in many cases, to take advantage of an early market.

The first shipments being made June 10th, and up to the time of our visit over 900 carloads had been shipped east.

We found on our arrival at that point that the disease had recently broken out among the native stock, and scarcely an owner was found who had not lost more or less. Post-mortem examinations showed the same we had found elsewhere.

We found the excitement east had put an entire stop to the forwarding of these cattle, and scores of Texan drovers were camped with their herds immediately about the town and back on the trail on which they came, for 20 miles. We are met by many of these gentlemen in the most cordial manner, and every facility was afforded us for the examination of their herds. We were accompanied by several of them to their herds, and travelled over 20 miles back on the trail, never out of sight of these cattle, which were estimated to number from 25,000 to 30,000 head. Much time was spent in riding through and examining the cattle, and quite a number were caught with the lasso and their temperature and pulse taken and their feet examined (as it was thought by some that the disease was communicated through their sore feet). Two days were thus spent without finding any animal that could be called sick.

Many were lame in some droves, but from careful examination there seemed to be nothing of a contagious character; the sores were evidently caused by travelling over stony ground and rough stubble where fires had run; occasionally a temperature was found to be higher than perfect health would indicate. The fatigues of these long journeys (from 400 to 600 miles) is great, and unless the driving is done with good judgment, the cattle are apt to fall away and many of them give out, but when driven slowly, and sufficient time allowed for forage and rest, the herds come through in good order and constantly improve. Some droves we saw were in prime condition, while the others were not. There was also a noticeable difference in the lots from different regions of Texas—those from the central or northern portions showing to the best advantage. On passing over the Smoky Hills we came to a herd of cattle, where we found a Texas steer which had died during the night previous, not yet cold. The animal was carefully examined, showing the same general appearances that had been seen elsewhere in the native stock. There was the absence of bloody urine. There is no doubt that the animal died of the same disease that has affected the native stock.

The animal had appeared perfectly well the previous day, but towards night broke away from the herd, and it was hard run to bring it back. This unusual excitement, no doubt, immediately developed the disease, which might otherwise have remained latent. This animal was driven from the south of Texas, about 40 miles from the Gulf Coast.

From conversation with many of the drovers (who of course are interested) it would seem that for several years past there has been but little sickness among the cattle in Texas, and that generally there is but a small per cent. of losses by sickness in driving them from that country.

One gentleman, however, who had driven these cattle for several years, informed us that some seasons his losses had been considerable, and that he had frequently shot diseased animals in by-places, to prevent their being seen when passing through portions of Missouri.

Thus we found on the borders in Kansas, the disease developed in the Texas stock, which we failed to find in the whole of our trip previously, through Missouri, Illinois, and Indiana.

On our return from Kansas we stopped at Quincy, the transfer point of stock coming east over the Hannibal and St. Joseph R. R. The arrangements for this purpose are admirably planned. The ferry boats run to the upper part of the landing where the yards are between the railroad track and the river. The cattle never cross the track, nor are city cattle ever allowed access to the transfer yards. Diligent inquiry failed to bring to our knowledge a single case of sickness at this point.

After our return to Chicago, we found the disease still existing to some extent. Cool weather checking it, while hot spells seemed to give new impetus to it. The same thing has occurred at most of the points where the disease has prevailed.

We also learned of a drove of Texas cattle that were taken from the Chicago stock yards and driven west of Kendall County in July. At many points on this route we have heard of the appearance of the disease, which has been quite destructive. The exposure of the native cattle was from four to five weeks before the first deaths, and cases have been reported up to the first weeks in October.

As soon as stock are known to have been exposed, they should at once be isolated and fed on green succulent food, and have plenty of good pure water; slops made of linseed have been recommended. There seems to be little use to treat them after the disease has advanced so far as to be outwardly apparent, with the present knowledge of the immediate causes affecting the Texas cattle at home.

In some cases cattle have seemed to recover from the disease, but remain for a long time in an unthrifty condition. One gentleman, a large loser, in Champaign County, informed us, October 21st, that he had several that had apparently recovered, but were now failing and dying.

CATTLE ON THE FRONTIER.—While in the west, we made careful inquiry in order to ascertain the number of Texas cattle on the frontier, ready to come into market, and should place the number about Salina, Abilene, Junction City, Fort Scott, and south-western Missouri, at the time we were there, at not less than 100,000 head, while very large numbers known to be on the route from Texas had not arrived. Many estimated the number much higher, and we are fully satisfied we are under rather than over the amount.

CATTLE BROUGHT INTO THIS STATE.—From the best information we have been able to gather from railroad books and those who have handled this stock, we should estimate the number received into this State for feeding, slaughter, and in transit would considerably exceed 100,000 since the opening of the trade in the spring.

19

The following letters and statements have been furnished us giving some additional facts to those already given.

HISTORY of the CATTLE DISEASE, as it prevailed in the Vicinity of Francesville, Ind.

The first Texas cattle introduced into this section of the State were brought hither by Lyman Blair, in the winter of 1867, who purchased them at the Union Stock Yards, Chicago. The cattle were driven directly from Texas, grazing as they came. They were 180 in number, and in very poor condition. They were placed upon the farm of Mr. Pharos, brought into immediate contact with his native cattle, mingling and intermingling with them while feeding. The winter was extremely severe upon them, yet they did remarkably well, considering them as natives of a warm climate. About ten of their number died during the winter. Having received the best of care and attention during the extreme cold months, they were turned out upon the green grass of the prairie at the opening of spring, as early as possible, from which time they have made most astonishing improvement. No cattle have ever done better than they have done, or are now doing. No disease was propagated by them, notwithstanding their immediate connexion with the native cattle upon the farm, being inclosed in the same pound or inclosure at night.

Mr. Blair having a most excellent and powerful artesian well upon his farm, his cattle have all enjoyed the purest and most healthful water; while their pastures have also been of the finest quality.

In the spring of 1868 Mr. J. J. Fairchild, a prominent cattle dealer of this section, went to New Orleans with the object of purchasing Texan cattle. After some days, he, in connexion with Mr. Raub, of the Fowler and Earl Farm, Benton Co., Ind., succeeded in purchasing a lot of 440 that had been wintered, some two seasons, others one season, in the parish of St. Mary La., where they were grazing at the time of purchase. They were driven to New Orleans, where, upon the 9th and 11th of May, they were shipped upon steamers and started northward, up the river. They were four and five days upon the river, when they arrived at Cairo, where they were re-shipped upon the Illinois Central, and brought to Chebanse, where they were unloaded, May 18th. They were brought through this long journey in the finest possible condition, only 11 having died on the way, and but few being bruised or crippled. From Chebanse they were driven to this point, grazing leisurely along where opportunity offered, as they were driven. They arrived upon the farm of Mr. Fairchild, on the 26th of May, in fine condition. About seven were left along the way, as being unfit to drive; they suffering from injuries, &c., sustained upon the boats and cars. Of this number, six died; the remaining one recovered. These cattle, 211 in number, were also brought in immediate contact with the native cattle upon Mr. Fairchild's farm, where they were allowed to mingle and intermingle in grazing, for about six weeks, no disease making its appearance.

At about this time Mr. Blair purchased, at the Union Stock Yards, another lot of 377 Texan cattle, which were immediately driven to his farm in this county. They were also from the frontier, and were in excellent condition. Like the others, they were placed upon the old grazing ground, and native cattle were permitted to mingle with them, and to graze upon the same ground with and after them. This herd was placed, for quite a number of days, in a large pasture which was reserved for milch cows. After they were removed therefrom, the milch cows were immediately returned thereto, and have been grazing therein ever since, and no disease has made its appearance in their midst, as yet.

On the 1st of July, this herd was moved on a ground opposite to that on which Mr. Fairchild's herd were grazing, a small creek, which becomes nearly extinct in dry weather, only intervening. These grounds are located upon a broad stretch of open prairie, upon and over which the native cattle belonging to over 20 small farms were allowed to graze, and, as a consequence came into immediate contact with both of the above herds of Texas cattle, having been in contact, especially at the creek where they procured water, with Mr. Fairchild's herd, from the day of their arrival upon the prairie, the 26th day of May. About two weeks after Mr. Blair's cattle had been placed upon this ground, the weather became extremely hot; and the season having previously been very dry, the water was speedily dried up in the creek, except where it stood in stagnant pools, from which the cattle had to drink it, and the grass became dry and parched, unfit for food. Cattle suffered greatly from the extreme heat, and received but little nutriment from the dried grass which they ate, and the stagnant water which they drank. Their systems being thus depressed by these adverse causes were rich resorts for any disease, the germs of which might be present.

On the 27th day of July the stock belonging to Frederick Cruger, a German, began to manifest symptoms of disease. A number of them died very suddenly, others lingered for six or eight days. On the succeeding day the same dreaded symptoms began to manifest themselves among the cattle belonging to Jacob Garling, and, as in the former case, a number died very shortly after the first symptoms of disease appeared, while others lingered for six or eight days. The above cattle, at the time of taking sick, and for two weeks previously, were in immediate contact with Mr. Blair's most recent herd. From the day on which the disease first manifested itself on the farm of Mr. Cruger, it appeared successively among all the cattle that were allowed at any time to wander and graze over the ground whereon the Texan cattle were kept. The most intense excitement was now awakened amid the people. Remedy after remedy was administered, but nothing could save after the fearful symptoms of the disease had made their appearance. The only positively safe remedy was soon found to be a preventive, namely—confining the Texan cattle closely upon their grounds, not allowing them to be moved about from one place to another, and to carefully prevent all native cattle from coming into contact with them or the pastures upon which they had grazed. This judicious course, together with several fine heavy rains, followed by a cooler atmosphere, better water and pasture, occurring about two weeks after the first appearance of the disease, had the happy effect of checking the prevalence of it. No new cases occurred, excepting upon the farms where it already existed. Even amid the cattle most severely afflicted, a marked change for the better was immediately observed. Many of them began to recover slowly, and have finally reached a complete recovery. F. Cruger has nine head upon his farm that were very sick with the disease, but are now well. Jacob Garling, eight; St. Clair Range, ten; J. J. Fairchild, eight; E. E. Smith, one; J. C. Slatery, one; Henry Crumb, ten, and quite a number of other instances might be given. Keeping native cattle from coming in contact with the herds and pastures of the Texan cattle is the only safe method of preventing the disease or guarding against its spread. We have had numerous proofs here that the disease is not a contagious one, and that it is absolutely necessary to graze upon the ground or eat of the remains of food on which Texan cattle have been feeding. Calves that were confined to the pound and never permitted to graze on the infected pastures sucked their dams regularly while sick, and in several instances after death; while calves that were permitted to graze upon the ground were the first to grow sick and die. In another instance, the Texan cattle were allowed to graze on all sides of a pasture in which a number of native cattle were inclosed. They communicated with each other through the fence every day, yet no disease has made its appearance among these native cattle.

Cattle have been dying along the route pursued by Mr. Fairchild's herd from Chebanse, wherever the native cattle were allowed to graze upon ground upon which the Texan cattle were allowed to graze.

About a week before the appearance of the disease, on account of the filthy and stagnant condition of the water, Mr. William Jones, the overseer of Mr. Blair's cattle, considered it prudent to move the herd above noticed from the ground upon which they were grazing in close proximity to Mr. Fairchild's to a grazing ground about three or four miles westward, where they have been ever since. Several lots of native cattle have come in contact with the pasture since they have been there, but no disease has made its appearance as yet.

About the 20th of August the disease began to abate, and, as before stated, many cattle that were afflicted fully recovered. No new cases manifested themselves until within the past few days (Sept. 21 and 22). Owing to six or eight days of extreme heat, the disease has again appeared upon the farm of Elijah Rees. Mr. Rees' cattle have associated with Mr. Fairchild's herd and grazed upon the same ground from the first arrival of the herd, and have been in closer and longer continued connexion with the same than any other cattle in this section, yet he lost but a single head when the disease was so prevalent a few months ago. A good number are sick now, and it is impossible to tell when the disease will again abate. Mr. J. C. Slatery has also lost two cows within the past few days. His cattle were exposed to Mr. Fairchild's herd when they were first brought here, and have not been in contact therewith since, yet the disease has again made its appearance in their midst. He lost one cow when the disease prevailed so badly before.

About one hundred and fifty head of native cattle have died from the disease in this immediate vicinity up to this date, and perhaps as many more along the route between this point and Chebanse.

A few weeks ago the disease manifested itself with great virulency upon the farm of Mr. Van Patten, near San Pierre, upon the route traversed by Mr. Blair's last herd, which were, as you are already aware, purchased at Chicago. Mr. Van Patten, when last heard from, had lost 27 head. Thus you can readily perceive that the disease has followed in the wake of both herds, those which were brought here in the spring, and that it did not manifest itself in the last-named three instances until nearly four months after the first exposure.

J. G. W.

Francesville, Ind., Sept. 23rd, 1868.

STATEMENT of V. T. CHILTON.
[Made to Capt. Brown, one of the Commissioners of the Ill. State Ag. Society.]

DEAR SIR, Smith City, Mo., October 4, 1868.
I HAVE been well situated to make observations in regard to the Texas or Spanish fever (so called) usually following in the track of Texas cattle, having lived on one of the most publicly travelled roads in Missouri for many years before the introduction of Spanish cattle into this country, and on the one that they have mostly travelled, and having been three times loser by them, caused me to give some attention to the subject. I have been well situated for making observations, there being several small prairies near me, separated from each other by farms, enabling me to note the effects resulting from Texas cattle herding on them at different times. My observations date back to the first introduction of southern cattle to this country, having been the first to sustain losses from them, but since the war I have given the subject but little attention, having previously satisfied my own mind in regard to it, and having learned a prevention, I ceased to trouble myself about it.

Without troubling you with details, I will just state the conclusions at which I have arrived. First and most important is, How is the disease communicated? Beyond a doubt from contact, or rather from feeding and watering with or after Texas cattle, as I have never yet known a case that could not be traced directly to this cause, nor have I known a case in which disease was communicated when a fence intervened between the healthy and infected stock.

I have had my own cattle separated from large herds of Texas cattle by a fence, without any evil result, and of the immense number that have died on this road, none have died on pastures from which Texas cattle have been excluded. The instances to sustain this view are so numerous that I will not undertake to give them. My opinion is, that the poison is taken into the stomach with their food or water; the greatest danger being in watering in stagnant pools after infected stock, the known habit of cattle when watering leaving much fetid and feverish matter in the water. In very hot, dry weather, it is not safe to let cattle to ground that has been used by diseased cattle for at least eight weeks after they have been removed, as I have twice known the disease contracted nearly that length of time after they had vacated it, and immediately after hard rains when it was thought the disease had been swept off by the water, but it was only washed into the water pools with their droppings, and new energy given to the virus.

I am not prepared to say whether native cattle when diseased will communicate the infection or not, as we usually keep them apart from healthy ones; though I once had a native bull to jump in with my herd and die without harming my stock, but one case is not sufficient to establish a theory, so it is safe to keep them apart.

We have no specific for the disease, though many things have been tried; when not too far gone green corn has effected more cures than anything else we have tried, and when the first symptoms are discovered, herds have been turned on green corn fields with good results. There is one certain preventive, that is to keep your cattle from Texas cattle and from their feeding grounds, and they will never have it. I have not had a case since I adopted the plan, though tens of thousands have passed my yard. We never had the disease with us until the Texas cattle came, and then it was confined to their walks, and as the people drove them from one road to another, they carried the disease with them, until the war put a stop to their introduction, from which time there was not a case in the country until it came with them after peace was restored.

Most persons believe that all Texas cattle communicate disease, but my impression is that only deseased droves impart a disease; nearly all the cases that I have known have been traced directly to infected stock, but it usually affects them so slightly that it is difficult to detect it, consequently it is best to avoid them all; indeed but a small portion of the droves that pass leave disease, but one is sufficient to inoculate the entire route of their travel.

It is not necessary to bring Spanish stock to this country to kill our stock, that is, the change of climate is not what does it, for it has been known in this country for many years, even before our terrible experience with them, that our cattle when taken to Texas all die, so soon as they come in contact with their herds. The Gulf cattle are much worse than those from northern Texas. The change to this climate, after a short stay, appears to have a disinfecting influence with them, so it would seem not to result from travel as some suppose; if so you would have had more of the disease in former years than we.

This thing of Gulf cattle travelling north, spreading disease, is no new thing; near 50 years back, when Mississippi and Florida were territories, there was just such an excitement as this, caused by the long-horned or Cherokee cattle passing through North Carolina and Virginia, on their way to the northern markets, and diseasing the cattle as they passed, and were only stopped by legislative enactment in the States suffering from them. I think my native State, Virginia, has never repealed her laws in regard to them.

Cattle that have been here a few months seldom impart the disease, hence the cause that you have had but little of the disease until you commenced receiving them by rail, they having heretofore undergone the necessary acclimation in travelling to your State.

I have never known but one herd that was wintered here that was diseased the next summer, and they may have taken it from other droves that were passing through the country.

The fatality with cows appear to be greater than with steers. The first symptom with cows is their failure to secrete milk.

They have been passing us now for 12 or 14 years, and we feel no danger if cattle are kept from them, we do not even remove ours from the pastures adjoining the roads when they are passing.

The disease is much more virulent some seasons than others—the excessive heat of this summer causing it to be worse than usual.

Your people may discard all fears of its spreading a fearful epidemic like the cattle disease of the old country, for you will hear no more of it after cool weather.

Captain J. N. Brown, Berlin, Ill.

STATEMENT of JOHN H. TICE.

DEAR SIR,   St. Louis, August 21, 1868.

In answer to your inquiry to furnish such information as I possess relative to the Texas cattle disease, I will make the following statement of facts:—

The first cases I saw were in 1858, occurring on the premises adjoining my land at Cheltenham, in this county, five miles west of the court house. There was a drove of cattle, perhaps 180 head, about three-fourths of which were from Texas, judging them by their horns, and the remainder appeared to be native stock. In a few days a disease broke out amongst them. The first died on Saturday evening; by Monday morning there were 12 dead, when the drove were taken away; all the dead were native cattle. The disease did not spread. The pasture was isolated on all but one side, where it adjoined the turnpike. There was a spring in the pasture furnishing water enough for the cattle, but none of it flowed out at that time, as it was during the driest season of the year.

In 1860 there was a large drove of Texas cattle put in a pasture opposite to above and south of the road. There is a sluggish stream running through this pasture, below which the neighbourhood cattle, feeding on the common, drank. Some of the drove died; how many I do not know, nor whether the dead were Texas cattle. The disease soon appeared in the neighbourhood cattle, which were nearly all cows. In 10 days 35 cows and a Galloway bull had died, besides a few heifers. There was scarcely a cow left in the neighbourhood. I lost all I had, three cows, and only saved a heifer which had never come in contact with the Texas cattle, being kept up, as she accidentally had lost her muzzle. She during the day was in the pen where the cows were sick, and one had died, but never became affected. This is the only fact that I know bearing upon the question, whether the infection can be communicated from one to another by the native cattle. But from an isolated case we are not justified to draw the inference that it is not so communicable; but this, however, is the general opinion in this State. If the infection was not in this instance communicated by the water, I know of no other way; except that some 30 mules belonging to the drovers broke through the fence one night and ranged over the commons.

The last case I know of occurred in my neighbourhood in October 1866. About the middle of October some derangement in the machinery of a cattle train occurred opposite to my house, and the train was detained somewhere about three hours. On the train were Texas cattle, and as some Irish people employed on the road lived there, and who during the morning and evening pastured their cows within the inclosed railroad, I went and advised them not to let their cows in. One of them did and one did not. The cow let in was a very valuable one, he having paid a short time before 80 dollars for her. In about 10 days she sickened with the Texas fever, and died in a few hours. She pastured on the commons, when taken sick, with the neighbourhood cattle. But the day after she died (on the 30th of the month) we had the first killing frost of that season. No further disease was developed.

Wherever the cattle were driven the disease soon after has sprung up along their track, but never has spread into adjacent neighbourhoods, as far as I know. I have no knowledge whether Texas cattle wintered in this climate will spread infection afterwards. I live in the suburbs of the city, and the cattle brought there are for the shambles, and are soon after butchered; I know not of a single instance where any have been held over winter for the next season.

Yours respectfully,
JOHN H. TICE.

W. E. Richardson, Esq., Chicago, Ill.

STATEMENT of L. ASHBROOK & Co.

St. Louis, September 12, 1868.

DEAR SIR,
Yours of the 11th was received this morning. We will to give you our experience in handling Texas cattle. In the fall of 1866 we bought 320 head in New Orleans, and shipped them to St. Louis during the first half of September. They were thin in order. We grazed them until November, and fed through the winter on corn. We put them on grass in May, and kept them until October, 1867. We never had a lot of cattle to fatten and do any better than they did.

During the spring and summer of 1867 they were grazed in the same pasture with 200 native cattle, and we did not lose one; nor did we have a sick steer during the whole time they were in our possession; and we are fully convinced that cattle shipped from Texas after the fall season commences, or cattle that have been wintered in this State, or Kansas, will not communicate disease to our native cattle, as our experience in the trade has proved it up to our entire satisfaction. We have some 500 head on hand at present; 300 of them were wintered in this State. They are now on pasture near Springfield, Ill. We have had several native cattle running with them since the 1st of June, and nothing has gone wrong with any of them—no disease whatever; and we also have a lot that were brought through last spring, that are running with eight or ten milch cows in the same pasture, and all is well with them.

Very respectfully,
L. ASHBROOK & Co.

Mr. W. E. Richardson.

STATEMENT of C. L. EATON.

"Broadlands," near Homer, Ill., September 12, 1868.

DEAR SIR,
Agreeable to your request for my experience in handling Texas or Cherokee cattle here in former seasons, I beg to inform you that on January 1, 1867, we received on this farm 247 Texas cattle that had been brought from Texas the previous summer. On the 4th of May following, we received another lot of 300. This lot had been purchased in Texas in the spring of 1866, driven to southern Missouri, there wintered, and brought on here in May. Both of these lots were grazed on this farm through the spring, summer, and fall of 1867, intermixed with some 3,500 native cattle. We had no disease of any kind; our percentage of deaths of cattle on the farm that season was less than one-half of one per cent. from all causes.

Several of our neighbours had herds of Texas cattle that season that had been wintered here, varying from one to five hundred; they all did remarkably well, and I heard of no disease of any kind amongst them.

My experience and observation would go to show that there is no danger whatever of disease from southern cattle brought here during the season of frosts.

Respectfully yours,
C. L. EATON.

W. E. Richardson, Esq., Chicago.

STATEMENT of E. L. HUFFMAN.

Louisville, Ky., August 27, 1868.

DEAR SIR,
You ask my views about Texas cattle. I am just from the cattle pens of N. York, and am the first man that shipped that kind of stock to Kentucky. I am like all other cattle men, I have an opinion and think I am correct. I kill from 100 to 300 cattle a month to supply boats. I grazed over 2,000 head all the summer of 1866 in the blue grass pastures of Kentucky. I kill the Texas cattle winter and summer, and have taken great care and pains to find out the cause of this disease. I find the cattle that come around by sea, or that come from Galveston or Powder Horn, when brought here in winter, their livers and bladders are all right; but when brought in the summer, the bladders are inflamed and filled with yellow or bloody water. I find the cattle are affected in this way that come from where they have "mosquito" grass. The cattle that come from northern Texas are all sound, and don't kill native cattle.

I handled 600 head brought here in May from Grayson, Dallas, and Cook Counties, and they never diseased any cattle and were quite healthy themselves. I find all the Texas cattle fatten very well on Kentucky blue grass. I have grazed the nueses cattle for months on adjoining pasture or small fence between, and found no damage, but when any native cattle ate the grass or walked over the road where they urinated it was death. I am sure it was not the breath, as some think. Some say it is the ticks. I have killed thousands, and have killed some since I got your letter. I have examined them closely and I find at the end of the bladder a knot, and it is inflamed. Livers all bad, but fat, and meat fine.

I am sure it is the cattle that come from the "mosquito" region.

I handled some Texas cattle in company with Gen. R. W. Gano, Centerville, Bourbon County, Ky. Mr. Joseph Scout at Paris, Bourbon County, Ky., brought a large lot here from New Orleans in March last.

I am confident it is the urine and the cattle come from the "mosquito" grass country.

I brought 300 here in April from Northern Texas, they are getting fat. Have grazed them with native cattle and no damage.

Yours,
E. L. HUFFMAN.

23

STATEMENT of SECRETARY of MISSOURI STATE BOARD OF AGRICULTURE.

The following extracts are from the Report of the Secretary of the Missouri State Board of Agriculture for 1866, and the reports furnished that fall :—

"Mr. William Montgomery, of Stockton, Missouri, writes: 'We are at a loss as to how the disease is communicated, as there is no apparent disease among the Texas cattle, but wherever they are herding any length of time, our cattle take some disease similar to dry murrain, and the actions of the animal with the disease are similar to a horse with the botts or colic. They seem to suffer severely with inward fever. When dissected, they appear to be dry and scorched with inward fever. Nearly all that take the disease die unless treated immediately. Our remedy is to drench them with lard, or slugs of fat bacon. It does not look reasonable that the Texas cattle could communicate disease when they have no disease themselves, but the general opinion is that the disease is communicated by the breath.

"'As to an amendment of the laws, we think it would be well to have them so amended as to prohibit Texas cattle from passing through the State, except during the cool season of the year, as we have noticed no disease similar to Texas or Spanish fever, except during warm weather, mostly contracted near ranches and watering places.'

"Another gentleman of south-west Missouri writes as follows: 'I have lost very heavily this season by the "Texas fever," and although it is very strange to me how an animal that is healthy itself can impart so dangerous a disease to other healthy cattle, I am nevertheless satisfied it can be done, as I have lost about one hundred and fifty head by the disease. They show the first symptoms by standing perfectly still in the position that they take to hold back, head down, fore feet thrust a little forward, ears dropped down, and are neither hungry nor thirsty. Their bowels become very costive, in fact it seems as if their intestines became entirely dry, and unless an operation can be obtained they die. Our most successful mode of treatment was to make them swallow a piece of fat meat (bacon), and force another one up their posterior (rectum) with the arm, as large as admissible and as far as possible. We saved about sixty after we adopted this mode of treatment, but the hair came off in spots from one to five inches in diameter. I doubt whether it can be cured in every case.

"'There is another fact that cannot be gainsaid; that is, since 1861 there has not been a single case of Texas fever in south-west Missouri, neither has there been any Texas cattle. Until the past spring and summer we have had Texas cattle and Tevas fever. I have been dealing in cattle all the time since 1861, and in the time did not lose a brute until the past summer; so I say it is the southern cattle, and they ought not to be allowed to enter the State from the 15th of April to the 1st of October.'

"Mr. Huron Burt, of Williamsburg, Callaway County, says: 'We have had some experience with the disease on the Nine Mile Prairie. Last spring, early in April, a lot of oxen passed through our county on their way west for some overland freighters, that had been shipped from New Orleans to St. Louis. The grass was just starting forth, and the cattle were occasionally stopped to bite at it. Wherever they grazed the virus of the disease was left, and all cattle that fed on the same ground on which the Texas oxen grazed were afflicted with the disease—nine-tenths of all the cattle affected dying.

"'The disease was communicated for several months—in fact, during the whole season, until the unusually heavy rains in September, which seemed to have washed away the seeds of the disease that had been so fatally implanted all along their route. It was necessary for an animal to feed on the self-same ground to contract the disease—those feeding up to the very verge of the poisoned ground, with only a fence intervening, were unharmed; and I am further informed that the disease is only communicable from Texas cattle—stock feeding after our home cattle that are diseased escape unaffected.

"'This has proven to be the most fatal cattle disease, and the most destructive to the stock-growing interest ever known in Callaway. If the intervention of law was ever required in any case for the protection of stock growers, it is in this instance, and I am heartily glad to see the movements made in this direction. Four and a half or five months should be the extreme limit allowed for passing this kind of Stock through our State, and I am not sure but a shorter limit would be justifiable, say from November 15 to March 15.'

"Dr. Albert Badger, of Vernon County, writes: 'This disease was first recognized as having been propagated by cattle driven from Texas some 12 or 13 years ago; the disease having been in the county some two seasons previous to its having been traced to the Texas cattle.

"'From the first breaking out of this fever it was found to be confined to the large roads or highways running through the county from south to north, and finally was centred on the Texas cattle, I believe, in the year 1853, by its being confined to one highway through the county over which these cattle passed in that year. On this road the disease was quite fatal, killing about 50 per cent. of all the cattle on the road, and persons living near the watercourses over which the road crossed lost as high as 90 per cent. Captain Freeman Barrows and Peter Colley, the one living at the ford of the Osage river, the other near by, lost the latter per cent.—one of them owning about 100 head, while the former had considerably above that number; Mr. Collins, living at the ford of Clear creek, south of the above, lost an equal proportion.

"'The disease being in no other part of the county that year satisfied the people, on this road at least, that they had found the true origin, as it had been among the cattle in the country for two summers past. In a season or two after, almost every settler of the county was convinced that the Texas cattle in some way communicated this fever to our stock, although a few persons living secluded from the great highways were unbelievers, and still remain so. In fact, the way this disease is propagated, the obscurity surrounding it for want of a defined cause, together with the different conflicting opinions of almost every citizen familiar with it, gives them at least a reasonable excuse for believing no one's opinion. Two things only, the symptoms of the fever and its fatality, are agreed to by every one, the latter being much greater in a warm, dry summer than in a cold, wet one; the disease always ceasing when the frosts and freezes have killed the vegetation.'"

Regarding the causes of the disease, we have met and conversed with the advocates of many theories, and the obscurity that has existed concerning the manner of communication has led to much speculation upon the matter. That it is a species of vegetable poison introduced into the system through the stomach seems the most rational conclusion, based upon the pathological appearances of the animal, and the course and termination of the disease, and the fact that it is analogous to several diseases well known in Europe and treated of by various veterinary authorities under the names of "Wood Evil," "Moor Ill," the "Darn of Aberdeenshire," "Melæna," "Wald Krankheit," "Holz Krankheit," and "Maladie de bois." A disease has also been known in Ohio for many years called the "Buckeye" disease, resembling this in most particulars in symptoms and appearances, and is known to be produced by the cattle eating the young shoots of the buckeye tree in the spring, and the fruit in the fall.

It was well known also many years ago that the cattle coming from Florida and Mississippi during certain months of the year communicated a disease, believed to be identical with this one, and it has been well established that it was caused by the cattle there eating certain species of oak in the early spring and leaving their native country in hot weather, and under the fatigue occasioned by the journey, they throw off the poisonous properties that are in a measure dormant as long as they remained in their natural climate and condition.

The fact of the Texas cattle being the cause of the disease, we think now no one can for a moment doubt, and the abundant testimony furnished, shows that (with rare exceptions, if ever) cattle must graze on the grounds over which the Texas cattle have passed, or must drink from stagnant pools, where the Texans have drank and urinated, and to our minds it seems perfectly plain that it arises from poison imbibed through or from the excrement, or urine, or both of the Texan animals.

There is a limit to the time when these cattle can communicate the disease after leaving their native state, which time we have no doubt varies very much with the condition the animal is kept in and the character of the seasons. From what we have seen we are inclined to believe the time quite short after their arrival here, for it is rarely, if ever, that any Texas stock coming into the country in August or September have ever been known to communicate the disease. But the injury done by stock coming in early in the season is permanent, and no cattle should ever be allowed on their ranges for three or four months after their occupation by the Texans, and safer yet, if not occupied until after hard killing frosts have occurred.

The sooner the Texans reach this country after leaving Texas in the *early* spring, the more dangerous their character; hence the necessity of their remaining on the frontier for a considerable length of time, or not allowing them to come into the State at all, between certain fixed times, which times should be regulated in common by the several State Legislatures of the States particularly interested in the matter.

The question of supply of stock for feeding in this State is now one of very great importance, and the fact that cattle can be raised in the south-west to three or four years old, and sold for $8 to $10 each at a profit to the growers, offers, in a business light, one of the greatest opportunities for profit to our feeders.

We would not, however, recommend the abandonment by our farmers the rearing of all the stock their facilities will allow them to grow, as the extra quality of stock produced will fully compensate for the extra outlay of care necessary to produce it. We deprecate the wholesale slaughter of calves that so generally prevails all over our State, and would urge upon our farmers the rearing of every one they can, which at one, two, or three years old, will always find a ready market at paying prices.

If we observe the native cattle now found in our markets it will be seen that they are placed there at least a year younger than should be done to realise the greatest profit from them, and younger than has been the rule in years gone by. This has in a measure resulted from the excessive demand during the war and the natural increase of consumption; and the only way to remedy this will be to stimulate production at home, and adopt safe ways to avail ourselves of the cheaper stock of the south-west, for the bulk of our supply.

The only safe and feasible way now to handle this south-west stock for *grazing* and *feeding* in our State seems to be to bring it here in the fall and winter, say between November 1st and March 1st. This of course will require more care, risk, and capital, than to bring it in in the spring and turn it off in the fall; but the extra quality of beef produced will fully pay for all this, and better yet, if the cattle can be kept two seasons here before slaughter, as there is but a small portion of the stock brought in and fed for only a single season, that will furnish the best grades of packing beef.

What remains now to be done seems to be, to so modify our State legislation with regard to this stock, that we shall never have a repetition of what our State has suffered the past season, and we would urge a hearty response to the call for a convention of State's Commissioners to meet at Springfield, early in December, to perfect some uniform laws to be adopted by all the States interested.

The losses of cattle in this State this year have been very great in the single county of Champaign, estimated to reach 7,000 head. These losses have led to immense trouble and litigation, wherever the injury has been done; hundreds of suits have been commenced against those who owned and handled this stock. While some of these gentlemen have come forward and honourably compromised and settled with their neighbours, others resist all claims, and defy the loosers. It seems no more than right that the innocent sufferers should have their pay for stock destroyed, and it would seem that policy alone, among the owners and carriers of these cattle (which are comparatively few) would dictate some prompt and liberal compromise and settlement of the difficulties, without waiting for legal decisions.

W. E. RICHARDSON.
H. D. EMERY.

APPENDIX.

Missouri Laws.

An Act creating a Board of Cattle Inspectors, and preventing the spread of the so-called Texas or Spanish fever among Cattle.

Be it enacted by the General Assembly of the State of Missouri, as follows:

Section 1. The county courts of the several counties of this State are hereby authorised to appoint three competent and discreet persons in their counties, to form and constitute a board for the county, for the inspection of cattle supposed to be distempered or affected with a disease called the Texas or Spanish fever; and such board, or a majority of them, shall have the powers and authority, and shall perform the duties herein-after mentioned. Said board shall be called Board of Cattle Inspectors.

Sec. 2. Whenever the county court of any county in this State shall appoint a board for the inspection of cattle under this Act, the clerk of the county court of such county shall, without delay, make out a commission to each member of said Board, under the seal of said court, which commission shall be signed by the president of said court, and countersigned by the clerk; and it shall be the duty of such clerk to deliver such commissions without delay, and said inspectors shall take the oath of office required by law.

Sec. 3. The board thus appointed in any county shall meet immediately after receiving their commissions, and being qualified select one of their number president of their board, and the president of said board shall, upon his personal knowledge, or receiving information from others that any Spanish, Mexican, Texas, or Indian cattle are roaming or feeding at large, or are herded in the county, or are being driven or about to be driven into or through the county, under any pretext whatever, without delay give notice to the other members of the board, of such information or knowledge; and they, or a majority of them, shall proceed to the place where such cattle may be in the county, and the president of said board shall notify the person or persons having such cattle in charge, that the board will proceed to an examination of said cattle, and also hear proof, and to determine whether said cattle are liable to be condemned and adjudged to be affected with what is commonly known as Texas or Spanish fever, or capable of imparting the same, and killed under the provisions of this Act; and if the person or persons having charge of said cattle desire to produce any evidence that such cattle are sound and not capable of imparting said disease, said board shall appoint some day, not exceeding 10 days, to hear such testimony, and in the meantime such cattle shall be impounded and remain under the control of said board.

Sec. 4. Said board, or any member thereof, shall have power to administer oaths to any witness brought before them, and the president of said board, or any other member thereof acting as such, may, whenever they deem it necessary, call upon the sheriff or any constable of their county, who shall, when required to do so, assist them, and furnish a sufficient posse to stop any drove of cattle being driven or about to be driven through their respective county, and enforce all orders of said board necessary to carry out the provisions of this Act.

Sec. 5. If upon an examination of such cattle, and receiving evidence in relation to such cattle, the board find, adjudge, and decide said cattle to be diseased or distempered, or in a condition to communicate any contagious or infectious disease or distemper called or known as Texas or Spanish fever, the president of said board, or other member acting as president, shall, in writing, order and command the person or persons having such cattle in charge, to remove such cattle without delay from the county, upon the same route upon which they came in, if practicable; which order shall be delivered to the person or persons having such cattle in charge, and said board shall retain a copy of said order, and cause it to be filed in the office of the clerk of the county court.

Sec. 6. If any person or persons having in charge such cattle ordered to be removed from the county, under the provisions of the preceding section, shall do so upon the same route and track, as near as may be, upon which they came in, and in other respects comply with the order or command of the president, then, and in that event, said cattle and the owners of them, or persons having them in charge, shall not be further liable in any county under the provisions of this Act; and upon the production of the written order delivered to them, under the provisions of the preceding section, their said cattle shall not be subjected to any other inspection in any other county on such routes, provided such cattle be driven out of the State without unnecessary delay.

Sec. 7. If, after receiving such order from the president, the person or persons having such cattle in charge, such person or persons shall wilfully delay, refuse, neglect, or fail to remove them from said county, according to the order of the president, the president shall issue under his hand a writ directed to the sheriff or any constable of the county, commanding him to proceed without delay to remove such cattle, driving said cattle out of the county upon the same route, as near as may be, upon which they came in, or to kill all of such cattle, if such board should think it necessary to prevent the imparting of the Texas or Spanish fever to other cattle.

Sec. 8. Any person or persons who shall knowingly and wilfully obstruct, resist, oppose, assault, beat, or wound any officer while executing any writ, or performing any of the duties required by this Act, shall be arrested, and, upon conviction, shall suffer all the pains and penalties now prescribed by law, in case said officer had been engaged in the execution of any writ or order from any court.

Sec. 9. The officer executing a writ issued under this Act shall make a return thereon within five days thereafter to the president of said board, stating in full and in what manner he executed such writ, how many cattle were killed, if any; and the president of the board shall cause said writ, with the return thereon, to be filled in the office of the clerk of the county court.

Sec. 10. If the president of the board shall die, resign, or refuse to serve, or be absent, any other member of said board may act as president, and a majority of said board are hereby authorised to act and perform any duty imposed upon said board under this Act, and the county court may fill any vacancy in said board.

Sec. 11. Each person appointed inspector under this Act shall hold his office for two years, and until his successor shall be appointed and qualified.

Q 2761.

SEC. 12. No such inspector, or any officer acting under the authority of said board of cattle inspectors, shall be liable to any action or to pay any damages for executing or carrying out the provisions of this Act, or any writ or process issued in pursuance thereof.

SEC. 13. The inspectors appointed under the provisions of this Act shall be allowed two dollars per day for each day they may be actually employed, to be audited by the county court, and paid as other county expenses. All officers executing writs under or by virtue of any of the provisions of this Act shall be allowed the same fees as are allowed by law, for similar services in other cases, to be paid out of the county treasury.

SEC. 14. Whenever any cattle shall be ordered to be removed or killed, as provided in this Act, then and in all such cases the party owning, and also the party or parties driving such cattle shall be liable for all the costs that may accrue in any such case of examination, removal, and killing. The president or person acting as president of said board of cattle inspectors shall issue an execution for the amount of said costs against the owner or owners, and driver or drivers of such cattle, directed to the sheriff or any constable of the county, which execution shall have the same force and effect as any other execution which is now by law directed to such officer, and shall be made returnable to the president of said board. If such execution is returned not satisfied, or returned satisfied in part, the county shall pay the amount not satisfied.

SEC. 15. Nothing contained in this Act shall be so construed as to prevent the transportation of such cattle through this State on railroads or steamboats, or to prohibit the driving through any part of this State such Texas or Southern cattle as have been wintered at least one winter north of the southern boundary of the State of Missouri.

SEC. 16. All Acts and parts of Acts inconsistent with this Act are hereby repealed.

SEC. 17. This Act to take effect from and after its passage.

Approved March 13, 1867.

KANSAS LAWS.

AN ACT for the Protection of Stock from Disease.

Whereas a disease, both contagious and deadly, commonly known as "Spanish fever," is almost invariably communicated to the native and other cattle of the State of Kansas, by contact with cattle raised in and brought from the Indian country south of Kansas and the State of Texas, where said disease exists among the cattle in virulent form; and

Whereas said disease is most contagious in the spring and summer months; therefore, as a sanitary measure for the protection of the cattle of the State from the ravages of said disease,

Be it enacted by the Legislature of the State of Kansas:

SECTION 1. No person or persons shall be allowed to drive or cause to be driven into the State of Kansas, or through any part thereof, any cattle from the Indian territory south of Kansas, or from the State of Texas, that may have come into the State between the first days of March and December of each year, except as provided for in section 12 of this Act, and any person or persons violating the provisions of this section shall, on conviction thereof, be deemed guilty of a misdemeanor, and for the first offence be punished by a fine of not less than 100 nor more than 1,000 dollars, and by imprisonment in the county jail not less than 30 days nor more than six months, and for every subsequent offence the penalty shall be double that for the first offence, and continuing to drive said cattle through the State shall be deemed a subsequent offence.

SEC. 2. Justices of the peace within their respective counties shall have exclusive jurisdiction of all cases arising under this Act; and upon affidavit of any householder of his county filed with or made before him, setting forth any violation of the preceding section of this Act, it shall be the duty of any justice of the peace to forthwith issue a warrant for the arrest of the offender or offenders, which warrant shall be executed by the sheriff of the county, or by any constable thereof, or by some competent person specially deputed by the justice for that purpose; and the officer or person so authorised to execute said warrant shall have power to call to his aid a *posse comitatus* sufficient to arrest and bring before the justice such offenders.

SEC. 3. When any person shall be brought before a justice of the peace under the provisions of this Act, it shall be the duty of the justice to hear and determine in a summary manner the complaint alleged against the defendant, and if said person or persons so arraigned shall be found guilty of violating the provisions of this Act, it shall be the duty of the justices to issue an order to the sheriff or any constable of the county or any other competent person to be deputed by him for that purpose, directing him to drive said cattle out of the State over and on the same route whence they came in, and the said sheriff, constable, or other person is hereby empowered to drive said cattle in or through any county through which said cattle may have been driven on their way into the State, or through any portion of it, and the officer or person so authorised to execute said warrant shall have power to call to his aid a *posse comitatus* sufficient to drive said cattle as directed in the order of the justice.

SEC. 4. That in the examination of any person or persons charged with violations of the provisions of this Act, it shall be necessary only to prove before the court or jury that said cattle are from the State or territory lying south of the State of Kansas, by their general description and appearance, and by their undomesticated habits.

SEC. 5. That any person violating any of the provisions of this Act shall be liable for all damages that may be done by said cattle by imparting disease, and the evidence for the trial of actions for damages shall be the same as is provided herein for the trial of criminal cases, and that the justice may, when the evidence is clear or presumption great, hold the offender to bail or fine as in other criminal cases.

SEC. 6. All trials before a justice of the peace under this Act shall be by a jury of six competent men residents and householders of the county, to be by the said justice empannelled, as in civil cases, forthwith upon the arrest and appearance of the offender or offenders before him, who, if they find the defendant or defendants guilty, shall assess the fine to be paid and the imprisonment to be inflicted, subject to appeal to the District Court, but an appeal shall not operate as a stay of proceedings under the third section of this Act, unless the defendant or defendants give bonds in the usual manner in double the value of the cattle, that the cattle will immediately be driven out of the State upon the same route upon which they came in, or until they are ten miles from any settlement or settler, and that they shall not be allowed to range within ten miles of any settler during the pendency of said suit.

Sec. 7. No continuance shall be granted or appeal be had from the judgment of the justice in cases arising under this Act, and no exceptions taken to the decision of the court upon matters of law shall operate as a stay of execution or order of imprisonment; before obtaining a writ of error the defendant shall execute a bond with three good and sufficient sureties, to be approved by the justice, in twice the amount of the fine imposed, conditioned for the prosecution of his writ, to abide the judgment of the court.

Sec. 8. One fourth of the fine collected under this Act shall go to the complainant and the other three fourths to the common school fund of the county.

Sec. 9. It shall be the duty of the prosecuting attorney of the proper county to appear on behalf of the State in all cases arising under this Act, and when the prosecuting attorney is absent it shall be the duty of the justice before whom the prosecution is had to employ counsel for the prosecution, to be paid by the county.

Sec. 10. In cases where judgment is rendered against defendant it shall be the duty of the justice to assess at costs a sum sufficient to cover all expenses of driving cattle out of the State, as provided in the third section of this Act.

Sec. 11. That upon the arrest of any person or persons charged with violating the provisions of this Act, all cattle found in their charge shall, during the arrest and trial of the offenders, be stopped and taken charge of by the officer or person executing the warrant of arrest, to abide the judgment of the justice before whom the offender shall be tried.

Sec. 12. The provisions of this Act shall apply to all that portion of the State east of the sixth principal meridian; also, to all that portion of the State north of township nineteen (19), but shall not apply to that portion of south-west Kansas west of the sixth principal meridian and south of township eighteen (18), as above provided; and provided further, that all persons herding or driving the description of stock mentioned in the first section of this Act in that portion of Kansas west of the sixth principal meridian and south of township eighteen (18), within five miles of any public highway or any ranche, or other settlement, without the consent of the settler or owner of such ranche, shall be liable as provided for in the first and fifth sections of this Act; and provided further, that any person, association, or company may, upon execution of a bond in the penal sum of 10,000 dollars, payable to the State of Kansas, approved by the Governor and filed with the Secretary of State, conditioned to pay all damages that may be incurred by any citizen of the State of Kansas, select a route from some point in south-west Kansas west of the sixth principal meridian, and south of township eighteen, to some point on the U. P. R., E. D., west of the first guide meridian west from the sixth principal meridian where such cattle may be shipped out of the State, but in no case unloaded within the State; and provided further, that said person, association, or company shall not locate said route or drive said stock, or allow them to range on any persons premises, or within five [miles] of any settler without his or her consent in writing, and shall not drive said cattle along, or allow them to feed on or near any public road or highway, and any person violating any provisions of this section shall be liable to all the penalties provided in the first and fifth sections of this Act.

Sec. 13. All fines imposed under the provisions of this Act shall be collected on execution as provided by law in civil cases.

Sec. 14. That any person who shall drive into or through the State, or any portion thereof, any of the class of stock herein-before mentioned, between the 1st day of December and the 1st day of March in each year, shall be liable, to the party injured, for all damages, in the same manner as is provided for in section five of this Act.

Sec. 15. Sections four and five of an Act to provide for the protection of stock from contagious diseases, approved May 1, 1861, are hereby repealed.

Sec. 16. This Act shall take effect and be in force from and after its publication once in the "Leavenworth Evening Bulletin."

Approved, February 26, 1867.

S. J. Crawford,
Governor.

I hereby certify that the foregoing is a correct copy of original enrolled law on file in my office, and that the same was published in the "Leavenworth Bulletin," March 11, 1867.

R. A. Barker,
Secretary of State.

Illinois Laws.

An Act to prevent the Importation of Texas or Cherokee Cattle into the State of Illinois.

Section 1. Be it enacted by the people of the State of Illinois represented in the General Assembly, that it shall not be lawful for any one to bring into this State or own or have in possession any Texas or Cherokee cattle.

Sec. 2. Any person who shall violate the provisions of this Act shall, for every such violation, forfeit and pay into the treasury of the county where the offence is committed a sum not exceeding 1,000 dollars, or be both fined and imprisoned in the county jail, at the discretion of the court, though such time of imprisonment shall not exceed one year; and such person or persons shall pay all damages that may accrue to any one by reason of such violation of this Act.

Sec. 3. This Act shall not apply to any Texas or Cherokee cattle now on hand within this State, but persons having such shall be compelled to keep them within the bounds of their own premises or separate from other cattle; and any damage that may accrue from allowing such cattle to run at large, and thereby spreading disease among other cattle, shall be recovered from the owner or owners thereof, who shall be liable to all the pains and penalties, as provided for in section second of this Act.

Sec. 4. This Act shall be deemed a public Act, and shall be in force from and after its passage.

Approved, Feb. 27, 1867.

KENTUCKY LAWS.
CHAPTER 1,571.

An Act to prohibit the Importation and Sale of Texas Cattle in this Commonwealth.

Whereas it appears to this General Assembly that cattle imported into this State from the State of Texas spread among our native herds a dangerous and fatal disease; now, therefore, for the purpose of preventing the introduction and spread of this disease:

Be it enacted by the General Assembly of the Commonwealth of Kentucky, Sec. 1: that it shall be unlawful for any person after this Act takes effect, during the time between the first day of March and the first day of November, in any year, to import into this State from any other State, any of that breed or kind of cattle known as Texas cattle; and it shall also be unlawful, after the first day of October 1867, for any person to buy or sell any such cattle within the limits of this State, or to drive them from one point to another over the public highways; and any person who violates any of the provisions of this section shall be guilty of misdemeanor, and shall be subject to a penalty of not less than 500 and more than 5,000 dollars: Provided, however, that the prohibition of sales and transit of cattle in this section shall not be held to apply to cattle imported into this State between the 1st day of November and the 1st day of March at any time thereafter.

Approved, Feb. 28, 1867.

CHAPTER 636.

An Act to amend an Act entitled "An Act to prohibit the Importation and Sale of Texas Cattle in this Commonwealth," approved February 28, 1867.

Be it enacted by the General Assembly of the Commonwealth of Kentucky, Sec. 1: That an Act approved February 28, 1867, entitled "An Act to prohibit the importation and sale of Texas cattle in this Commonwealth," be and the same is so amended that it shall be lawful to import said cattle into the State at any time between the first day of November and the first day of April in each year.

Approved, February 28, 1868.

Nothing further transpired in reference to Texas fever at the time, and it may be remarked that twelve years ago no one contemplated the possibility of a regular cattle trade being carried on across the Atlantic. The extraordinary development of that trade in the last few years has not been unattended with risk of importation of disease, and the danger of introducing Texas fever has more than once been hinted at by the agricultural press. This danger assumed a palpable form when on August 4th, 1880, the inspector of the Privy Council stationed at the port of Liverpool detected five cases of splenic fever among cattle from Boston brought over in the "Iowa."

As splenic fever is one of the names given to the Texan malady, it was to be expected that a suspicion of the existence of Texas fever would arise, and in view of the serious issues involved in the question, I immediately telegraphed to the inspector at Liverpool to detain the manure in order that it might be destroyed, and to inform the sanitary authorities of the existence of the disease among the cattle, in order that they might exercise their powers in regard to the passing or condemning of the carcases of the animals as fit or unfit for human food, the inspector of the Privy Council having no power under the Contagious Diseases (Animals) Act to interfere with the disposal of carcases unless he is of opinion that they may introduce disease.

Information of the outbreak of disease was also sent to all the inspectors at ports where American cattle may be landed.

I also instructed the Assistant Inspector of the Department, Mr. Duguid, whose intimate knowledge of the history and character of splenic fever as it is known in this country, peculiarly fitted him for the inquiry, to proceed to Liverpool and investigate the matter.

Mr. Duguid reported as follows:—

August 17th, 1880.

In accordance with your instructions, I went to Liverpool on Monday, August 9th, and made inquiries in reference to a cargo of American cattle landed at the Woodside Foreign Animals Wharf, Birkenhead, on August 5th, ex S.S. "Iowa," from Boston, among which some cases of splenic fever were detected by Mr. Moore, the inspector stationed at the port of Liverpool.

There were shipped at Boston 848 cattle on board the "Iowa." Of these 43 died and were thrown overboard on the voyage, one was landed dead, and 804 landed alive. On landing, five were observed ill, and at once slaughtered, and the inspector, on examining them the following morning, found they had been affected with splenic fever, and reported the fact by telegram to this Department. Meanwhile the dressed carcases of these animals had been removed in the usual way for sale by the consignee.

By Monday, the 9th, four days after landing, eight more cases of the disease were discovered, and the animals slaughtered. Mr. Moore, the inspector, then gave information to the Local Authority, and these carcases were examined by the Sanitary Inspector and Medical Officer, and removed by their orders from the Foreign Animals Wharf. A magistrate's order was afterwards obtained for the destruction of these carcases as unfit for human food.

I had an opportunity of making an examination of the whole of these carcases on Tuesday, August 10th, before they were destroyed, and found them in good condition as regarded the amount of fat, not only round the internal organs, but throughout the body, showing that the animals had not been ill a sufficient length of time to cause any marked wasting of the body. The most marked post-mortem lesion I observed was an enlarged condition of the spleen which in some cases weighed over 9 lbs., and was much altered in structure; instead of finding the ordinary red appearance with the white fibrous bands passing through the tissue when the capsule was divided a thick dark red material escaped which to the naked eye presented no trace of tissue, but appeared like feebly coagulated blood.

On the mucous membrane of several portions of the intestines I found patches of congestion and also of extravasation. These were most marked in the cœcum and rectum.

The kidneys showed a few extravasated spots, and the traces of fluid in the pelvis of the kidney was highly coloured, but not blood-stained in those I examined. In the fat in different parts of the body there was evidence of blood-staining and extravasation, but as decomposition had already set in the appearances were somewhat altered.

On making a microscopic examination of the blood, and also of the spleen, I found a considerable number of small bright spherical bodies or spore-like objects, but no other kind of organism was present at the time of my first examination, but on the following day my specimens were full of the organisms usually accompanying putrefaction.

I had no opportunity of observing the symptoms in the animals while alive, as no cases of the disease were seen after my arrival in Liverpool; but from the description I received it would appear that the animals became suddenly ill, and in a few hours, without any very well-defined symptoms, became collapsed. Some that appeared healthy at night were almost dying in the morning.

I examined all that remained alive of the cargo, about half the original number, and found them in good condition, certainly not below the average of the American cattle I have seen landed at Liverpool. They were apparently healthy, and as the greater part of these were slaughtered during my stay in Liverpool, I had an opportunity of making a post-mortem examination, and found no trace of splenic fever lesions in any of them.

At the time I left Liverpool on Monday, August 16th, 47 cattle of the cargo were still alive and healthy, 11 days after landing. I obtained the following information respecting the animals that were found affected by this disease: They formed part of one consignment of 297 sent by Messrs. Hathaway and Jackson, marked with H clipped on the side. Of this consignment 11 were thrown overboard on the voyage, one was landed dead, and of the 285 landed alive, 13 were found affected with splenic fever. The other consignment of the cargo showed no disease after landing, although 32 of these had died and been thrown overboard during the passage.

The few remaining cattle of the cargo were shut up in one section of the lairage which was locked, and was also the portion of it where the diseased cattle had been. This will not be again used till after it has been thoroughly cleansed and disinfected.

The portions of the lairage occupied by the healthy consignment of the cargo have been thoroughly cleansed. The manure from these animals has been kept separate and mixed with lime, but as the contents of the viscera and the third stomachs are usually put in the manure, it appeared necessary that special precautions should be taken to destroy it. The traffic manager to the Mersey Docks and Harbour Board has undertaken to have the manure destroyed, and also the remainder of the fodder landed from the vessel. Mr. Moore, the inspector stationed at Liverpool, will see that none of the manure or broken fodder is utilised, and the places where the manure and fodder have been kept will be thoroughly cleansed and disinfected under the inspector's directions.

I have, &c.
Professor Brown, (Signed) W. Duguid.
&c. &c. &c.

Another cargo of cattle, among which splenic fever was detected, was landed from Baltimore ex. steamship "Edwards" on August 23rd, and on examination of the morbid parts which were sent by the inspector led to the suspicion that the disease had still further points of resemblance to Texas fever; especially in respect of the deep erosions or ulceration in the mucous membrane of the digestive canal. No signs of Bacillus Anthracis were detected in the blood, and the inoculation of guinea-pigs with the blood gave negative results, whereas inoculation of these animals with the blood of an animal affected with splenic fever is uniformly fatal in a few hours.

No opportunity has yet been afforded for the examination of the blood of an American animal which had died of the disease, and as the Bacillus Anthracis is not found until after death has occurred, the inquiry cannot be said to be complete.

On August 31st, the inspector of the Privy Council at the port of Cardiff reported that 109 cattle had been landed at Cardiff from New York ex. S.S. "Rhiwindda," of which three had died on board the day before. Two of the cattle were slaughtered on arrival, and one of them showed indication of splenic fever.

The sanitary authority was communicated with, and all necessary precautions were taken. The matter is still under investigation.

It has been asserted that Texas fever is not contagious, and the pathologist will at once admit that it does not belong to the pure contagia, of which cattle plague and foot-and-mouth disease are examples; but it is also beyond dispute that Texas fever is communicable from Texan cattle to cattle of other breeds with which they may come in contact, or which may feed on pastures contaminated with the excreta of the

Texan beasts. Animals which are thus infected suffer and die at the rate of 90 per cent., but they are not capable of infecting other cattle. This peculiarity in the infective character of Texas fever places it in a class by itself, and to the stockowner in this kingdom the matter will be rendered more easily intelligible if it be assumed as a possibility that a herd of infected Texan cattle shall be landed in this country, and in the natural course of trade be carried by rail or driven from one market to another until they are all disposed of. All along the route home-bred cattle will contract Texas fever and die; but the owners of the stricken herds will have the consolation of reflecting that they alone will be the sufferers; their neighbour's stock, although in the next field, separated from the dying cattle by a wire fence, will be safe. The poison is rendered harmless by entering the system of any but a Texan beast, or probably it may be more correct to say that only Texan cattle have the power of excreting the poison of the disease.

G. T. BROWN.

Veterinary Department,
    Privy Council Office,
        August 31, 1880.

FURTHER CORRESPONDENCE

RELATING TO

DISEASES OF ANIMALS

IN THE

UNITED STATES OF AMERICA.

No. 1.

LETTER from the BRITISH CONSUL at BOSTON to EARL GRANVILLE.

(Sanitary, No. 3.)

My Lord, Boston, July 6th, 1880,

I have the honour to report that this consular district has continued free from cattle plague during the past month, with the exception of two places called Fairfax and Georgia, in the State of Vermont, where a disease appeared temporarily at the beginning of the month amongst some herds of cattle, the symptoms of which were described as follows: "First, signs of weakness and drooping, then violent trembling " and difficulty of breathing, swelling of the throat, followed by a whitish mucous " discharge from the mouth and nose, and death."

No report has been received here since the 11th of June of the continuance of the disease amongst the herds in which it made its appearance, or of its spread to others.

I have, &c.

Her Majesty's Principal Secretary of State for Foreign Affairs. (Signed) C. A. HENDERSON.

No. 2.

LETTER from the COLONIAL OFFICE to the CLERK OF THE COUNCIL.

Sir, Downing Street July 22, 1880.

I am directed by the Earl of Kimberley to transmit to you, for the information of the Lord President of the Council, a copy of a despatch from the Governor-General of Canada, with enclosures, relating to an application made by the United States Government for the free importation into Canada of cattle raised west of the Alleghany Mountains.

Nos. 1, 2, 3, and 4.

A copy of this despatch, with the Minute of the Privy Council of the Dominion, has been communicated to the Foreign Office.

I am, &c.

The Clerk of the Council. (Signed) JOHN BRAMSTON.

Enclosure 1 in No. 2.

Letter from the Marquis of Lorne to the Earl of Kimberley.

(No. 196.)

My Lord, Canada, Ottawa, June 23, 1880.

I have the honour of forwarding to you a copy of a despatch which I have received from Her Majesty's Minister at Washington, enclosing a copy of a note from the Secretary of State of the United States stating that several Canadians wish to purchase cattle in Kentucky for breeding purposes, if arrangements can be made to allow them to be brought to this country.

I also enclose a copy of a report of Council which contains the views of my Government on the subject, and which has been communicated to Sir E. Thornton for the information of the United States authorities.

	I have, &c.
The Right Hon. the Earl of Kimberley,	(Signed) LORNE.
&c. &c. &c.	

Enclosure 2 in No. 2.

LETTER from Sir E. THORNTON to the MARQUIS OF LORNE.

(No. 42.)

MY LORD,   Washington, June 9, 1880.

I HAVE the honour to transmit herewith, for the consideration of your Excellency's Ministers, a note which I have received from Mr. Evarts respecting the wish of several Canadians to purchase cattle in Kentucky for breeding purposes, provided arrangements can be made to allow them to be taken into Canada.

I have received a deal of information at various times from different parts of the United States with regard to the condition of cattle, and I have never heard of pleuro-pneumonia or other contagious disease being prevalent among them to the west of the Alleghany Mountains.

	I have, &c.
His Excellency The Marquis of Lorne, K.T.,	(Signed) EDWARD THORNTON.
&c. &c. &c.	

Enclosure 3 in No. 2.

LETTER from Mr. EVARTS to Sir E. THORNTON.

                                         Department of State, Washington,
SIR,   June 8, 1880.

I HAVE the honour to state that Mr. Thomas C. Anderson, of Kentucky, an extensive breeder of short-horned cattle, has brought to the attention of this Department the fact that a number of citizens of Canada have expressed a desire to visit Kentucky this season for the purpose of purchasing cattle there for breeding purposes, providing arrangements could be made to allow them to be taken home. Mr. Anderson suggests that as the region west of the Alleghany Mountains is free from cattle disease, the Canadian authorities could without risk grant the desired privilege. He says, moreover, that there are now in the western States nearly 3,000 short-horned cattle advertised for sale, many of which would be bought by Canadians if they could take their purchases home.

In view, therefore, of the important mutual interests involved in this matter, I beg to submit to Her Majesty's Government to consider the practicability of so modifying the rules regulating the importation of cattle into Canada as to permit short-horned cattle raised west of the Alleghany Mountains to enter the Dominion unobstructed, for breeding purposes.

I have, &c.
(Signed)   WM. W. EVARTS.

The Right Hon. Sir E. Thornton, K.C.B.,
    &c.   &c.   &c.

Enclosure 4 in No. 2.

COPY of a REPORT of a COMMITTEE of the HONOURABLE THE PRIVY COUNCIL FOR CANADA, approved by his Excellency the GOVERNOR GENERAL on the 21st day of June 1880.

THE Committee of Council have had under consideration a note, dated 8th June 1880, transmitted by Sir Edward Thornton from Mr. Evarts respecting the wish of several Canadians to purchase cattle in Kentucky for breeding purposes, provided arrangements can be made to allow them to be taken into Canada.

The Honourable the Minister of Agriculture, to whom said note has been referred, reports that the action of the Canadian Government is to a very large extent influenced by the Imperial Act respecting diseases of animals, and the action under it which has been taken by the Veterinary Department of Great Britain.

That the consideration of Canadian interests, in view of the Imperial Law and Orders in Council, is to prevent Canada from being scheduled and Canadian cattle from being slaughtered at the port of entry in England.

That the difficulty in the way of carrying out the request of Mr. Evarts is the fact that the orders issued under the "Imperial Contagious Diseases (Animals) Act," treat the United States as one country, without making any provision for lines of demarcation between the eastern and western States.

That the whole of the United States is, therefore, treated in England as a diseased country, and importations into Canada from any part are inconsistent with the privilege now enjoyed of allowing the ports of Great Britain to remain open for the entry of Canadian cattle alive—the great importance to Canada of the unimpeded continuance of the trade in cattle makes the prohibition complained of, if not a necessity, at least a paramount interest.

That the cattle shipped from Canada among which pleuro-pneumonia was found to exist were taken on board the railway train at Buffalo, New York.

That if a line, however, were drawn between the infected States of the east and those of the west, which are believed to be free from disease, and regulations framed of such a nature as to prevent cattle from the east going to the west, he, the Minister, is of opinion that provisions might be adopted to admit of the importation into Canada of cattle from the western States.

That any action in this direction, however, would be dependent upon a relaxation of Imperial orders under the Act referred to of such a nature as not to make the scheduling of Canada a consequence.

The Committee submit the views above stated for your Excellency's approval, and recommend that a copy of this minute, when approved, be transmitted to Sir Edward Thornton, for the information of the Government of the United States.

Certified,
(Signed)   J. O. COTÉ,
Clerk, Privy Council, Canada.

No. 3.

LETTER from the BRITISH CONSUL-GENERAL at NEW YORK to EARL GRANVILLE.

(Sanitary, No. 7.)   British Consulate General,
MY LORD,   New York, August 2nd, 1880.

I HAVE the honour to report to your Lordship that since the date of my last despatch (Sanitary, No. 6) pleuro-pneumonia has made its appearance among the cattle in the lower section of Elizabeth, a town in the State of New Jersey, and it is stated that several cows have died from the disease. With this exception there have been no further cases reported in this consular district.

I have, &c.
Her Majesty's Principal Secretary of   (Signed)   E. M. ARCHIBALD.
State for Foreign Affairs, London.

No. 4.

LETTER from the ACTING BRITISH CONSUL at BALTIMORE to EARL GRANVILLE.

(Sanitary, No. 8.)
MY LORD,   Baltimore, August 2nd, 1880.

I HAVE the honour to report that since my Despatch No. 7 (Sanitary) of the 1st ultimo, some few cases of pleuro-pneumonia was developed amongst the cattle in the vicinity of this city. The animals were promptly slaughtered and the infection was thus checked in its earliest stage. None of these cattle were intended for exportation, but belonged to small farms in the suburbs.

I have, &c.

The Right Honourable The Earl Granville, K.G. &c. &c. &c. (Signed) T. W. LAWFORD.

No. 5.

LETTER from the CLERK OF THE COUNCIL to the UNDER SECRETARY OF STATE, COLONIAL OFFICE.

SIR,   August 5th, 1880.

I AM desired by the Lord President of the Council to acknowledge the receipt of your letter of the 22nd July enclosing a copy of a despatch from the Governor General of Canada on the subject of an application made by Mr. Evarts, on behalf of the United States Government, for a modification of the rules regulating the importation of cattle into Canada so as to permit short-horned cattle raised west of the Alleghany Mountains to enter the Dominion unobstructed for breeding purposes.

The difficulty in the way of carrying out the request of Mr. Evarts is stated in the report of the Committee of the Privy Council for Canada to be that, under the orders issued under the Imperial Contagious Diseases (Animals) Act, the United States are treated as one country without any provisions for lines of demarcation between the Eastern and Western States: that the whole of the United States is therefore treated in England as a diseased country; and that importations into Canada from any part are inconsistent with the privilege now enjoyed of allowing the ports of Great Britain to remain open for the entry of Canadian cattle alive.

This statement, so far as the Imperial Government is concerned, is perfectly correct, and the circumstances under which the Lords of the Council were reluctantly obliged to withdraw the exemption originally granted to United States animals, with the consequent action of the Canadian Government were fully explained in a letter addressed to Mr. Langevin on the 2nd May 1879, a copy of which is enclosed.

As Lord Kimberley is aware, since the date of that letter special arrangements have been made with the Canadian Government by which, under very stringent regulations, cattle are allowed to pass through Canada in closed trucks from one frontier of the United States to the other, and these arrangements are now in operation.

The Lord President has fully considered the whole question, and sees no possibility, in the existing state of affairs as regards disease in the United States, of departing from the course which has hitherto been pursued.

The prevalence of contagious pleuro-pneumonia in the United States is admitted by the highest American authorities, and is confirmed by the frequent arrivals in this country of cargoes of cattle from America affected with the disease.

It does not appear that there is any sufficient security against the spread of disease from one part of the United States to another, or that there is any legal line of demarcation between the Eastern and the Western States which would prevent the movement of animals from the one to the other.

This view of the case is fully borne out by a letter from the Secretary of the (United States) Treasury laid before the House of Representatives, dated February 19th, 1880, in which the writer, after calling attention to the existence of pleuro-pneumonia in the country, and to the serious losses which that disease has entailed upon other nations, observes, with reference to the action of Her Majesty's Government, that "great complaints have been made by American exporters of cattle to England, of these restrictions on the part of the British Government. It is hardly just, however, while no effective measures are adopted in the United States to even systematically ascertain the extent of the cattle disease in this country, and much less to adopt efficient measures for its suppression, to complain that the British Government adopts effective means to prevent the spread of the disease in that country." Mr. Sherman adds that "State and municipal regulations are not to be relied upon to prevent the importation and spread of the disease or to effect its extirpation," and that " it is for Congress to consider the policy and legality of conferring such power."

A similar view is evidently taken by a number of veterinary surgeons of the United States, who, in a petition to Congress published in the newspapers at the beginning of this year, state:

"that different animal plagues prevail to a disastrous extent among the live stock of the United States."

"that the unfenced stock ranges of the West and South are at the source of the traffic in live stock, and their infection must determine the infection of all the channels of the traffic (cars, boats, yards, &c.) and of the Middle and Eastern States."

"that it is not probable that all of the infected States will of themselves go to the trouble and expense of stamping out these pests in which they have so much less pecuniary interest than other States which are as yet unaffected."

and "that in view of the urgent necessity for the eradication of the lung-plague of cattle from the United States, the restriction of the Texas fever of cattle to those Southern States in which it is already domiciled, and the protection of our flocks and herds against pestilences that may be imported with foreign stock, Congress is further respectfully requested to appropriate a sufficient sum of money to enable the Veterinary Sanitary Organization to deal at once and effectually with these three important matters."

Whatever opinions may be entertained in America as to the disease being at present confined to certain districts, there can unfortunately be no doubt that it is very frequently imported into this country from the United States.

In the six months January to June of the present year, no less than 182 cases of contagious pleuro-pneumonia have been detected in cargoes from the United States,—a number which far exceeds the number of cases detected amongst foreign animals from all countries imported into this country during the six years which next preceded the passing of the Act of 1878.

It may be observed that a system of inspection which was at one time adopted by the United States Government at the port of shipment only increases the danger to the importing country when a disease exists in the exporting country the incubation of which may extend over a period of two or more months. The effect of such an inspection is that every animal which exhibits the slightest symptom of disease is withdrawn from the cargo, whilst the apparently healthy animals are allowed to proceed, carrying with them the seeds of the contagion, which may not be developed till many weeks after their landing in the importing country.

Under these circumstances the Lord President regrets to be obliged to arrive at the conclusion that if Canada allows the introduction of any kind or class of cattle from any part of the United States, it will be necessary to omit Canada from the list of countries now excepted from the ordinary provisions of the Act of Parliament, and to place Canada in the same position as the United States.

The Lord President hopes that Lord Kimberley will be disposed to impress on the Canadian Government (in case they think such a measure as that suggested by Mr. Evarts desirable) the necessity of urging the Federal Government at Washington to obtain legislative powers for the enforcement of such regulations for the whole of the Union as will provide for the health of cattle in the States now free from disease, and prevent the spreading to them of disease by transit of cattle or otherwise.

It is only by the adoption of such measures as these that the disease now existing in the United States can be eradicated, and the general health of animals in that country be rendered satisfactory for the purposes of the Imperial Act of Parliament.

When that result has been attained it will be the pleasure, as it will be the duty, of the Lord President to advise the removal of the restrictions which the law at present imposes upon an important trade, of the value of which to this country the Lord President is fully sensible.

I am to add that in the present circumstances the Lord President has not thought it necessary to enter into the consideration whether the Privy Council are legally entitled under the Act of 1878 to except from the provisions as to slaughter and quarantine animals from any particular part of a country which as a whole does not satisfy the conditions of the Act.

I have, &c.
The Under Secretary of State,   (Signed)   C. L. PEEL.
&c. &c. &c.
Colonial Office.

Enclosure in No. 5.

LETTER from the CLERK OF THE COUNCIL to the Honourable H. L. LANGEVIN.

Veterinary Department, Privy Council Office,
SIR,   44, Parliament Street, Westminster, S.W., May 2nd, 1879.

I AM directed by the Lords of the Council to acknowledge the receipt of your letter of the 25th ultimo, enclosing a memorandum on the subject of the transit of cattle from one part of the United States to another through Canada, in which arrangements are proposed for isolating the cattle in transit in such a manner as to ensure complete security against any chance of cattle within the Dominion becoming infected with disease. The adoption of these arrangements is proposed on the grounds that Her Majesty's Government would thus be enabled to continue the present system under which Canadian cattle are allowed to be landed without being subject to slaughter or quarantine under Part IV. of the 5th Schedule to The Contagious Diseases (Animals) Act, 1878, and that at the same time an important improvement in the condition of the carrying trade in Canada would be effected.

This proposal has received the most careful consideration of the Lords of the Council, who have also had before them a suggestion submitted by Mr. Pope, through Sir J. Rose, on April 21st, to the effect that under certain conditions the present restrictions on the introduction of cattle from the United States into Canada might be removed.

Their Lordships observe that both these proposals proceed on the view that no contagious disease of cattle exists in the western parts of the United States, and that there is no movement of cattle there from east to west (except in the case of expensive animals for breeding) and that therefore, if the proposed transit were allowed, there would be little or no danger of diseased cattle being brought into or moved through Canada.

I am, however, to point out to you that the action which the Lords of the Council can take with reference to the importation of animals into the United Kingdom is strictly limited by the terms of the Act of Parliament.

The general rule which applies to all foreign animals (which term by section 5 of the Act includes animals brought from any country out of the United Kingdom) is laid down in the 5th Schedule to the Act. Such animals can only be landed at a foreign animals wharf, defined for that purpose by an Order of Council, and are not to be moved alive out of the wharf.

The provisions under which Canadian cattle are at present exempted from slaughter or quarantine are contained in Part IV. of the same schedule, which provides that if and so long as the Privy Council are satisfied with regard to any foreign country (that is, any country out of the United Kingdom) that the laws thereof relating to the importation and exportation of animals, and to the prevention of the introduction or spreading of disease, and the general sanitary condition of animals therein, are such as to afford reasonable security against the importation therefrom of diseased animals, then from time to time the Privy Council by general or special Order shall allow animals or any specified kind of animals brought from that country to be landed without being subject to slaughter or quarantine.

By The Foreign Animals Order, as originally issued, animals from the United States and from the Dominion of Canada were admitted under this exceptional provision, but in consequence of the discovery of contagious pleuro-pneumonia in cattle from the United States, the Lords of the Council were reluctantly compelled to withdraw the exemption accorded to cattle from that country, and the same course would have been adopted with regard to Canadian cattle but for the prohibitory order passed by the Dominion Government on February 1st of this year.

Application has been made to Her Majesty's Government by the United States Government for the restoration to the United States of the privilege to land their cattle under Part IV., but under existing circumstances it has been found impossible to accede to this request, and the Lords of the Council have been unable to draw any distinction between different parts of the United States territory.

With reference, therefore, to the proposals now made on behalf of the Canadian Government, the Lords of the Council regret to have to inform you that if cattle from the United States are admitted into or allowed to pass through Canada they would not be justified under the Act of Parliament in continuing the exemption from slaughter at the port of landing which has been hitherto extended to Canadian cattle.

I am, &c.

The Hon. Hector L. Langevin,   (Signed)   C. L. PEEL,
    Alexandra Hotel, Hyde Park, W.

No. 6.

LETTER from HER MAJESTY'S CHARGÉ D'AFFAIRES AT WASHINGTON to EARL GRANVILLE.

(Sanitary, No. 21.)

My Lord,
Rye Beach, August 10th, 1880.

With reference to questions asked lately in the House of Commons respecting the desired modification of Cattle Quarantine Regulations, I have the honour to enclose herewith an extract from the "Boston Herald," giving a very succinct account of what has been gathered respecting pleuro-pneumonia in this country, and of the remarks made by Doctor Lyman sent specially by the United States Department of Agriculture to the United Kingdom to examine cattle from America reported to be infected with pleuo-pneumonia, and to endeavour to obtain some modification of the restrictions imposed by England on the importation of cattle. He was, it appears, also instructed to represent to the Privy Council and to persons of influence, that cattle embarked at Boston were entirely free from infection, and to show that a modification of the restrictions in favour of Boston would work no injury to English herds.

On Saturday last, the 7th instant, however, the Agricultural Department at Washington received a letter from Doctor Lyman declaring that he could ask no more for Boston than for other ports, as he found that three-fourths of the cases of pleuro-pneumonia amongst cattle landed in England from America came from western cattle exported from Boston.

Thus, Doctor Lyman corroborates the danger which Mr. Mundella showed still to exist from the infection of imported American cattle without the present restrictions.

I have, &c.
(Signed) VICTOR DRUMMOND.

Enclosure in No. 6.

Special Despatch to the "Boston Herald."

Washington, D.C., August 9, 1880.

In February last, when legislation regarding pleuro-pneumonia in American neat cattle was mooted, Assistant Secretary French of the Treasury proposed an exhaustive communication on the subject, which was submitted to Congress. In it the nature and history of the disease and the means of its prevention and cure, the value of the neat cattle and of the cattle trade in the United States, and the existing laws and regulations of the subject of pleuro-pneumonia were set forth. Among the conclusions of Assistant Secretary French were—"No contagious pleuro-pneumonia now " exists, or has ever existed, in any State west of the Alleghany Mountains. It does not " now exist in the United States over or near the boundary of the Dominion of Canada. " It does not now exist in the Dominion. It now exists only in the eastern part of " New York, in New Jersey, Pennsylvania, and perhaps in parts of Maryland, Vir- " ginia, and the district of Columbia. At the present time, with ordinary care, cattle " may pass from the western States, which almost exclusively furnish cattle for " exportation into Canada, and through Canada, Portland, and Boston to foreign ports " without danger of infection. With proper restrictions against contact with other " cattle near the seaboard, cattle may pass from the western States to the ports of " New York, Philadelphia, and Baltimore for exportation without danger of infection." In April 1880 Commissioner Le Duc transmitted to Congress the report of Dr. Charles P. Lyman, veterinary surgeon, upon the

Location and Extent of the Disease,

embodying the result of personal investigation from January to April 1880. He stated that the disease existed in Fairfield County, Ct., in New York City, and four counties in New York, in 14 counties in New Jersey, in Philadelphia, and in nine counties in Pennsylvania, and in several counties in Maryland. Since then he investigated the district of Columbia and Virginia, finding pleuro-pneumonia in both. In June the Department of Agriculture sent Dr. Lyman to England to examine cattle imported from America reported infected with pleuro-pneumonia, with a view to ascertaining its extent, and to endeavour to secure some modifications of the restrictions imposed by England upon the importations of American cattle. He was instructed to represent to the Privy Council and to members of Parliament that Boston was absolutely free from pleuro-pneumonia, and that western cattle brought through Canada or northern New York to Boston, and thence exported would be found uninfected, and that therefore a modification of the burdensome quarantine restrictions as to the port of Boston at least would work no injury to the English herds. On Saturday last the Agricultural Department received a letter from Dr. Lyman, dated the last week in July, announcing his failure to accomplish the object he had in view. He asserts that he has examined infected American cattle arriving at Liverpool since he came; that he finds many infected with what is known here and in England as pleuro-pneumonia (although, he adds, Professor Williams of Edinburgh does not consider it pleuro-pneumonia); that the disease was in most cases fresh; that the lungs were but slightly affected; and that three-fourths of the cases were western cattle exported from Boston. He points out the

INEVITABLE AND STARTLING INFERENCE

that pleuro-pneumonia exists either in the west of Boston, both hitherto confidently pronounced exempt from it. He adds that the cattle imported last winter from Canada viâ Portland were infected, although both are considered free from the contagion. He thinks nothing can be done either in England or America until the locality wherein this pleuro-pneumonia exists is definitely ascertained. All is uncertainty until this is done. He has made his Liverpool examinations carefully, and preserved in pickle infected lungs, so that definite conclusions relative to the character of the disease may be reached. There is a difference of opinion in England with the preponderance of authority in favour of its being genuine contagious pleuro-pneumonia. When Dr. Lyman reached England the time before Parliament was to consider the subject was so short that he hastily carried out his instructions. He represented to members of Parliament, the Privy Council, and the health authorities that cattle exported from Boston were uninfected, and that a modification of quarantine as to that port would be beneficial rather than injurious.

The Liberal members of Parliament accepted his statements, and at the time he wrote, had invited him to aid them with facts and figures in support of his assertions. On August 6, when the question was to come up in Parliament, he regretfully admitted that he could not, in the light of his personal examinations, respond to this appeal. He could ask no more for Boston now than for any other port. He concluded his letter by saying that all we could ask of England is, that should non-infection of any port and of the cattle shipped from it be hereafter demonstrated, a modification of her quarantine restrictions as to that port. The Department of Agriculture are profoundly impressed with the importance of Dr. Lyman's discovery. It practically deprives the United States of the only port of exportation hitherto unsuspected. It will materially affect our foreign exportations of western cattle, which, in 1879, to England alone aggregated in value $6,616,114, and to all other countries $1,768,086.

No. 7.

LETTER from the COLONIAL OFFICE to the CLERK OF THE COUNCIL.

SIR,   Downing Street, August 12th, 1880.

I AM directed by the Earl of Kimberley to acknowledge the receipt of your letter of the 5th instant, with its enclosure, respecting the application made by the United States Government for the free importation into Canada of cattle raised west of the Alleghany Mountains.

Copies of your letter have been communicated to the Governor-General of the Dominion and to the Foreign Office.

                                        I am, &c.
The Clerk of the Privy Council.   (Signed) JOHN BRAMSTON.

No. 8.
LETTER from SIR E. THORNTON to EARL GRANVILLE.

My Lord, London, August 14th, 1880.

In compliance with your Lordship's desire, and with reference to the letters from the Veterinary Department* which I return herewith, I have the honour to state that it does not appear to me that I can add anything to the observations which I took the liberty of making in my letter of the 13th ultimo.

The ground which I then took was that contagious disease among cattle was not known to exist in the States west of the Alleghany Mountains, that in a country of such extent as the United States that portion of it might well be considered as a separate country with regard to the export of cattle, and that if the latter should be conveyed to the eastern coast for export through Canada and those of the States in which it is believed that no contagious disease exists, it might be possible to relax the regulations now in force in the United Kingdom with regard to the importation of cattle from the United States.

But as it appears that the Lords of the Privy Council cannot consent to draw any distinction between different parts of the United States, I am unable to offer any further argument in favour of the relaxation of the rules, and can only hope that the Congress of the United States will pass such laws as will enable the Executive Government to take energetic and general measures for preventing the spread of pleuro-pneumonia and any other contagious diseases which may exist among cattle, and for stamping it out completely in the States where it is now known to prevail. For the last year I have been urging these measures upon members of Congress and the United States Government.

I have, &c.

The Right Hon. Earl Granville, K.G. (Signed) EDWARD THORNTON.
&c. &c. &c.

No. 9.
LETTER from the CLERK OF THE COUNCIL to the FOREIGN OFFICE.

Veterinary Department, Privy Council Office,
Sir, 44, Parliament Street, Westminster, S.W., August 20th, 1880.

I am directed by the Lords of the Council to state that considerable alarm has been created in this country by the rumour that a disease, resembling Texan fever, has been introduced from America into the port of Liverpool. It appears that on the 5th instant, the steamship "Iowa," from Boston, landed a cargo of American cattle at the Foreign Animals Wharf, Birkenhead, among which some cases of splenic fever were detected by the Inspector of the Privy Council stationed at the port of Liverpool. The animals affected were found to be part of one consignment of 297 cattle sent by Messrs. Hathaway and Jackson, marked with H clipped on the side. The total cargo embarked at Boston consisted of 848 cattle; of these, 43 were thrown overboard, one was landed dead, and 805 were landed alive. Of the 43 thrown overboard, 11 belonged to this consignment.

I am directed by the Lords of the Council to request that you will have the goodness to move Lord Granville to give instructions to Her Majesty's Consul at Boston to trace, if possible, the consignments on board the "Iowa," more especially that consignment marked H, above referred to, and to ascertain whether any and what disease exists at the places where they were respectively fed or reared, for the information of their Lordships.

I am, &c.

The Under Secretary of State, (Signed) C. L. PEEL.
&c. &c. &c.
Foreign Office.

---

* The letters referred to are the same as those forwarded to the Colonial Office. See pages 34–6.

40

No. 10.

LETTER from the CLERK OF THE COUNCIL to the FOREIGN OFFICE.

Veterinary Department, Privy Council Office,
Sir,   44, Parliament Street, Westminster, S.W., August 30th, 1880.

REFERRING to the despatch (with enclosure) of Mr. Drummond, (Sanitary, No. 21), of the 10th instant, addressed to Earl Granville, I am directed by the Lords of the Council to request that you will have the goodness to move Earl Granville to direct that application may be made to Mr. Drummond to obtain a copy of the letter addressed by Mr. Lyman to the Agricultural Department at Washington, referred to in the above-mentioned despatch, returned herewith.

I am, &c.
The Under Secretary of State,   (Signed)   C. L. PEEL.
    &c.   &c.   &c.
        Foreign Office.

LONDON:
Printed by GEORGE E. EYRE and WILLIAM SPOTTISWOODE,
Printers to the Queen's most Excellent Majesty.
For Her Majesty's Stationery Office.

CORRESPONDENCE

RESPECTING

THE MANUFACTURE OF OLEOMARGARINE

IN

THE UNITED STATES.

Presented to both Houses of Parliament by Command of Her Majesty.

LONDON:
PRINTED BY GEORGE EDWARD EYRE AND WILLIAM SPOTTISWOODE,
PRINTERS TO THE QUEEN'S MOST EXCELLENT MAJESTY.
FOR HER MAJESTY'S STATIONERY OFFICE.

1880.

[C.—2502.] *Price 6d.*

CONTENTS.

	Page
No. 1.—Despatch from Foreign Office to Board of Trade, 9th October 1879	3
„ 2.—Despatch from Consul General Archibald to Foreign Office, 16th September 1879	3
„ 3.—Extract from "New York Advertiser" of 2nd February 1878	5
„ 4.—Extracts from "American Dairyman" of 6th June 1878.—Oleomargarine by John Michels	6
„ 5.—Extract from "New York Times" of 27th June 1878.—Oleomargarine Butter	8
„ 6.—Extract from "American Dairyman" of 3rd April 1879.—Caul Fat by R. M. Piper	13
„ 7.—Prospectus of Commercial Manufacturing Company of New York. Manufacture of Oleomargarine	18
„ 8.—Copy of Act of New York State Legislature of 5th June 1877, and of Resolutions of the New York Board of Health in reference to Oleomargarine	20
„ 9.—Extract from Report of Commissioners of Agriculture for 1878, p. 135. Chemist's Report on Examination of American and Foreign Butters and Oleomargarine	21

CORRESPONDENCE.

No. 1.—DESPATCH from FOREIGN OFFICE to BOARD OF TRADE, 9th October 1879.

SIR, Foreign Office, October 9, 1879.

WITH reference to your letter of the 13th of August last (S. and C., 1986) I am directed by the Secretary of State for this Department to transmit to you, for the information of the Lords of the Committee of Privy Council for Trade, a Despatch with its enclosures from Her Majesty's Consul-General at New York, reporting on the exportation of oleomargarine from that city.

I am, &c.

The Secretary to the Board of Trade, (Signed) T. V. LISTER.
&c. &c. &c.

No. 2.—DESPATCH from CONSUL GENERAL ARCHIBALD to FOREIGN OFFICE, 16 September 1879.

MY LORD, British Consulate General, New York, September 16, 1879.

I HAVE the honour to acknowledge the receipt on the 12th instant of Mr. Lister's Despatch, of the 22nd ultimo, instructing me to furnish your Lordship, for the information of the Board of Trade, with any particulars I may be able to obtain with regard to the exportation to the United Kingdom from New York of a certain article made to resemble butter, and known commercially by the name of "bosch," "buttarine," or "oleomargarine," and more particularly in regard to the quantity exported, and the designation under which it is exported.

In reply, I have the honour to report to your Lordship the information which I have obtained on this subject, which is as follows:—

The only establishment in this consular district for the manufacture of "oleomargarine" or "oleo-margarine butter," under the license of the proprietors of the patent of the process, is that of the "Commercial Manufacturing Company," whose premises are situated in this city. The president of the Company is Mr. H. K. Thurber, of the firm of Thurber and Co., wholesale grocers, of New York, who have, as I am informed, opened a branch house in London. The above-named Company have the exclusive right of manufacture in the State of New York under a license granted them by the American Dairy Company, which Company possesses the sole right from Mons. Mège, of France, the inventor and patentee of the process, to issue such licenses for the United States. Similar licenses have been recently granted by the American Dairy Company to parties in other States, and there are at present in operation the following factories:—

Two in Pennsylvania; one being in Philadelphia, and one at Pittsburg.
One at Baltimore, Maryland.
One at Chicago, Illinois.
One at Cincinnati, Ohio; and
One at New Haven, Connecticut.

The business, however, of these establishments, compared with that of the Commercial Manufacturing Company, is of a limited character.

Besides the Commercial Manufacturing Company, one or two other "outside" manufacturers have since largely engaged in the business in this city, in alleged infringement of the Mège patent, the quality of whose articles is said to be inferior to those made by the licensees.

The Commercial Manufacturing Company commenced operations in 1876, and their business soon attained considerable proportions, as much as 500,000 lbs. of fat per week having been converted by them into oleomargarine or oleomargarine butter, which, at the rate of 2½ lbs. of fat to 1 lb. of oil, would produce 200,000 lbs. of oil or butter. This rate of production was maintained up to the middle of 1877, when it fell off owing to two causes; one being the passage of an Act of the New York State Legislature forbidding the sale of "oleomargarine butter" as butter, and the other the generally lower prices which have prevailed for butter during the past two years which, at times, have rendered the manufacture of oleomargarine butter unremunerative. For, it is stated that, when the retail price of genuine butter falls below 23 cents. a pound, it does not pay to manufacture the imitation butter. The average wholesale price procured here for oleomargarine oil and butter since 1876 has been 13 cents per lb. for the oil, and 15 cents a pound for the butter.

During the last two years the quantity of fat manufactured into oleomargarine and oleomargarine butter by the Commercial Manufacturing Company has been, it is stated on reliable authority, about 200,000 lbs. per week, yielding 80,000 lbs. of oil and butter. Of this about 75 per cent. or 60,000 lbs. per week was the *oil* product, "oleomargarine," all of which was exported in barrels or tierces, for the most part under the name of "oleomargarine," but sometimes as "butter fat," or simply as "oil." This would give a yearly exportation by this Company alone of about 3,000,000 lbs.; but it is estimated that nearly an equal quantity is now being made by the outside manufacturers, so that the total quantity of oleomargarine exported from this port may be stated in round numbers as about 6,000,000 lbs. annually. The shipments of the outside manufacturers are made to Hamburg, Bremen, and other German ports, and also to Rotterdam, but none, as I am informed, to the United Kingdom. In the case of the Commercial Manufacturing Company, their shipments are chiefly to Rotterdam, whence the oil is sent to a place called "Oss," and possibly to other towns in Holland, where it is mixed with a certain proportion of milk (to give it a butter flavour) and colouring ingredients to perfect its resemblance to butter, and is then churned and converted into butterine. It is then reshipped to France and England, but chiefly to England, but under what designation I am unable to ascertain.

In the warm months the oil is the main export, although the butter product is also shipped by steamers in refrigerators. But during the winter months both oil and butterine are exported, the butterine being chiefly shipped to the United Kingdom under the designations of "butterine," "oleomargarine," "butter fat," "butter grease,' or, *possibly*, as butter itself. The quantity of butterine exported to England, compared with that of the oil to German ports and to Holland, is comparatively small, and during the past few months little, if any, has been shipped. The manufacture of the articles being almost a monopoly, and the exports being in the hands of one or two firms who are naturally interested in disposing of their substitute as the genuine article, it is not easy to ascertain if shipments of the imitation article are sometimes made as genuine butter. From inquiries I have made of some of the steamship companies, I have ascertained that the consignments of the butter products are chiefly made by their steamers under the designation of "butterine." The article is put up in half tubs or firkins in precisely the same way as butter, and the tubs are enclosed in crates to protect them from injury on the voyage. It is also made up into 1 lb. "pats" covered by muslin or thin cotton wrappers, stamped as genuine butter is stamped, and packed in boxes for shipment.

"New York Commercial Advertiser," Feb. 2, 1878; "American Dairyman," June 6, 1878, and Apr. 3, 1879; "New York Times," June 27, 1878.

I transmit, herewith enclosed, extracts from local publications in reference to the manufacture of oleomargarine, and to its healthfulness as an article of food; I also enclose a copy of the prospectus of the Commercial Manufacturing Company, and of the Act of 1877 of the New York State Legislature above referred to, together with a copy of the resolutions of the Board of Health of this city reporting on the subject of this imitation article.

According to the statement in the "New York Commercial Advertiser" of February 2nd, 1878, it will be observed that there are "numerous factories of oleomargarine "butter in France, Holland, Germany, England, and Ireland," as well as in the United States.

I have, &c.

Her Majesty's Principal Secretary of State for Foreign Affairs, London.

(Signed) E. M. ARCHIBALD.

No. 3.—EXTRACT from "NEW YORK ADVERTISER" of 2nd February 1878.

Analyzed.—Oleomargarine Butter identical with Milk Butter.—The future of the Dairy Interest.—Coming Changes.

THE great industry recently introduced into this country by the establishment of oleomargarine butter factories has grown into large dimensions in Europe. There are numerous factories in France, Holland, Germany, England, and Ireland, employing many thousands of men, and involving investments of capital to the amount of millions of dollars. In Vienna one establishment employs 500 men, and its annual production of butter is equivalent to that of 30,000 cows. An order was received in this city by the Commercial Manufacturing Company, a few weeks ago, for five tons of oleomargarine oil for Ireland. The same Company has also shipped 10,000,000 gallons of the oil to fill orders from England and France, and has refused orders amounting to hundreds of thousands of pounds.

The rapid growth of the business in this country indicates very clearly that the discovery made by M. Mège, who established the identity of the limpid and odourless oil of fresh beef fat with the oily element of cow's milk, came in time to meet a present want—just as petroleum was discovered when the whale-fishery began to languish, and gold when the world's supply of the precious metal was running short. The processes through which M. Mege arrived at his extraordinary results, have been vividly described by M. Felix Bondel in a paper published in the "Moniteur Scientifique." At his farm in Vincennes, M. Mège placed several milch cows on a strict diet, found that they soon decreased in weight and in the yield of milk; but their milk always contained butter. This led to the conclusion that

THE BUTTER WAS PRODUCED

from the fat of the animal, which being re-absorbed and carried into the circulation, was deprived of its stearine by respiratory combustion, and furnished its oleomargarine to the udders, where, under the influence of the mammary pepsin, it was changed into butyric oleomargarine, that is to say, into butter. The way was then opened to the production of an article precisely the same as milk-butter. Tests with fresh beef-fat, from which the pure oil was expressed at a low and uniform temperature, produced the desired result, as exhibited in the following comparative analyses made by Drs. Brown and Mott since the introduction of the new product into the United States:—

ANALYSES of ARTIFICIAL and MILK BUTTER.

Constituents.	Artificial Butter. By Dr. Brown.	Artificial Butter. Average of Two Analyses. By Dr. Henry A. Mott.	Butter made from Cream. By Mott.	Same as III. Calculated to 5·225 per Cent. of Salt.
	I.	II.	III.	IV.
Water	11·25	12·005	12·29	11·827
Butter, solids	88·75	87·995	87·71	88·173
	100·00	100·000	100·00	100·000
Fats: oleine, palmitine, stearine, butterine, &c.	87·15	82·025	86·01	82·765
Caseine	·57	·745	·19	·183
Salt	1·03	5·225	1·51	5·225
Colouring matter	Trace	Trace	—	—
	88·75	87·995	87·71	88·173

Dr. Mott points out that the difference in the per-centage of fat in his analysis and either of the others is owing to the greater per-centage of salt, as will be seen by comparing No. 3 with the last analysis; but the proportion of salt, he adds, may be reduced or augmented in the manufacture to suit taste and requirements.

It was confessed at the Cleveland Convention of American Dairymen, by Mr. Eastman Reader, of New Hope, Pa., who read a paper on "Oleomargarine v. Butter," that the new product had "already become a serious competitor in the market for anything but the finest grade of butter." The foregoing analyses tell the reason why. When severe chemical tests produce such results as these, the dairymen's confession of defeat follows as a natural consequence.

This point suggests another, namely, the absolute necessity now pressing upon the dairy interest to withdraw from the market all but the finest quality of milk butter, for what are called the "fancy brands" will always find a market, even if the price be 50 or 75 cents. per pound. It is inevitable that the inferior qualities of butter which are produced cheaply and sold dear, under the false pretence that they are Orange County or other prime brands, will be entirely displaced by oleomargarine butter as soon as the public thoroughly understand what the latter product really is. The dairy interest represents an enormous trade, it is true—some six hundred millions of dollars a year—and nothing is more natural than that that interest should revolt at the introduction of a product which threatens to take its market. But it is the lesson of history that the changing tides of human demands are promptly met by fresh invention and fresh discovery. The spinning jenny, the sewing machine, the reaping and mowing machines did not destroy industry; they only stimulated it, and their introduction established new enterprises that have grown to fabulous proportions. If our dairymen, therefore, are compelled, as they will be, to make less butter and to produce more cheese, or

TO KILL FEWER CALVES,

and raise more beef, they will merely be turned aside into other channels of industrial pursuits quite as profitable as, and a good deal more reputable than, that of putting inferior butter upon the market and demanding top prices for it.

Apropos of this, the following extracts from a letter written by Mr. Thomas R. Downes, one of the largest provision brokers in London, are interesting. Speaking of the new butter, which he considers one of the most important discoveries of the day, and one that will year by year gain favour with the public, he says, "Miller and Hall " and other agents, of London, are receiving some from America of so fine a quality " that competent judges have pronounced them good butter." Alluding to the factories of America, he says, "They are on a scale of magnitude equal to the produc- " tion of 5,000 packages weekly of so fine a quality that it will drive Canadian and " common American off this market. I write as a disinterested party, desiring to see " justice done to the article, and to induce others to try it who have hitherto felt " prejudiced against it."

THE MAGNITUDE OF THE NEW INDUSTRY

in this country is a surprise even to those who introduced it with sanguine expectations of success. The books of the Commercial Manufacturing Company (Room 57, Coal and Iron Exchange, Cortlandt Street), which holds the exclusive patent right for the States of New York and New Jersey, show that during the past 10 or 12 months the total amount of prime beef fat used for making oleomargarine oil and butter was 20,000,000 lbs. in the New York factory alone; besides proportionate amounts in half-a-dozen other factories, which are worked, like the one in this city, under the general Mege patent bought by the United States Dairy Company, but are scattered at different points nearest the great sources of cattle supply. Orders for oil and butter have been filled at the New York factory to the amount of millions of pounds during the period indicated, and the demand is constantly growing.

No. 4.—EXTRACTS from "AMERICAN DAIRYMAN" OF 6th June 1878.—OLEOMARGARINE by JOHN MICHELS.

Oleomargarine.—Its true nature.—Is it likely to become dangerous to life and health?—A startling view respecting this substance.

EDITOR, "AMERICAN DAIRYMAN,"

THE close resemblance of oleomargarine to butter suggested to me the propriety of making a microscopical examination of both substances, for the simple reason of testing if they could be readily distinguished by such means.

For this purpose I placed a small portion of oleomargarine, purchased at a depôt in Vesey Street, upon a glass slide, covered it with a thin glass, and pressed it out to a fine film. A sample of butter from a leading New York house was treated in the same manner. Both were then examined with a $\frac{4}{10}$th objective, and drawings made direct with the camera lucida. A scale of $\frac{1}{100}$th of an inch, divided into 10 parts, was also drawn under the same conditions. The sketches I subjoin give the results.

It will be noticed that the large feathery crystals are characteristic of oleomargarine, and that the general appearance of the sample is different from that of butter, which merely shows the fat globules observed in milk, with here and there a crystal of chloride of sodium or common salt.

It is important in estimating the dietetic value of oleomargarine as a substitute for butter, to take into account that it is manufactured from the fat of animals, and that during the whole process, from first to last, this fat is *never submitted to a higher temperature than* 120 *degrees Fahrenheit.*

The fat oils are, therefore, merely liquefied or set free, and manipulated to have the general appearance of butter, but they are virtually still in a raw state when thus offered for human consumption. It would appear to follow that germs of disease (or

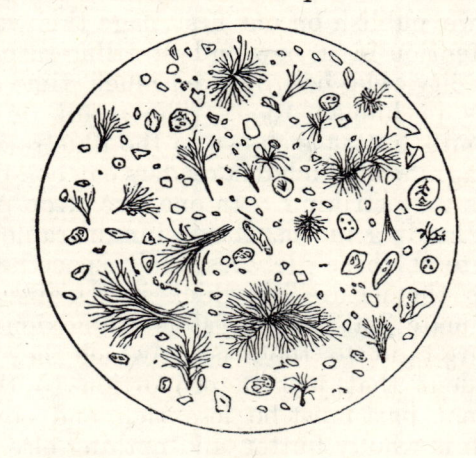

APPEARANCE OF OLEOMARGARINE UNDER THE MICROSCOPE.

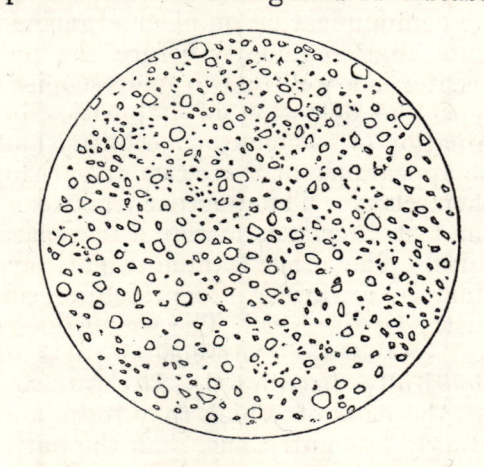

APPEARANCE OF BUTTER UNDER THE MICROSCOPE.

their equivalent), morbid secretions and embryos of parasites, are thus liable to be transferred in a living condition into the systems of those who make use of this substance.

The necessity for giving full weight to this view of the case will be admitted by all physicians and those who have studied recent investigations in regard to contagion. It is well known that a large number of diseases can be reciprocally communicated between man and animals, and that small-pox, scarlet fever, and measles, which are the worst forms of epidemics, probably took their origin from the lower animals.

Animals used for food are also subject to the attack of internal parasites, that lodge in countless multitudes in all parts of their bodies. Some of the most dangerous forms of these pests will also live and thrive in man. The trichinæ, which enter the body, at once breed by the million, and invade the whole system from head to foot.

But one protection exists by which man can guard himself from the contagion of these pests that annually carry off millions of the brute creation, and this is the practice of *thoroughly cooking all animal substances intended for food.*

The Germans, who disregard this rule and eat raw ham and meat, suffer in consequence. Cases of the trichina in the human system are now not uncommon in this city. I have in my possession a portion of the muscle from the neck of a woman, honeycombed with *trichinæ spiralis*. Probably from twenty to thirty millions of these parasites were present in her body. In this case, the simple act of eating a little raw ham probably brought her to the dissecting table of Bellevue Hospital.

For these and other reasons, I view with some anxiety the introduction of an article of food which, however disguised in appearance, is substantially raw fat, or fat oil; especially as I find in it parts of the tissue of the animal, with fragments and cells of a suspicious character.

The prospectus of the companies states that the caul fat of the ox only is used for making oleomargarine, but I have reason to believe that the refuse fat of at least one pork-packing establishment is used. Thus already a departure is made from the programme, and as the trade increases fat of every description will probably be offered for sale, and even that from the carcases of diseased animals may be purchased without guilty knowledge by the managers.

For cooking purposes oleomargarine appears to be an excellent substitute for any

---

* Scale of measurement 1—100 of an inch.

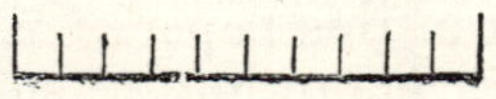

fat previously used, but I consider considerable risk is attached to its use in a raw state as table butter, and as such it should be rejected.

My object is to direct attention to this special view of the case, which, I believe, has not hitherto been placed before the public.

(Signed) JOHN MICHELS.

New York, June 1, 1878.

Oleomargarine in a new Light.

The communication on oleomargarine which we publish on our first page this week, presents that commodity before the public attention in a new and startling aspect. The writer is a well known microscopist of this city, who has devoted much time and study to the detection of impurities in liquids in human food. The result of his examination of oleomargarine butter and pure milk butter is shown in the illustrations of the appearance of those two articles highly magnified, which our readers can compare for themselves. The difference between them is very striking. In one, the drop used for the test, is seen as merely a transparent film holding in suspension innumerable fat globules. The other is almost entirely destitute of these globules, their space being supplied by a variety of crystalline substances the nature of which it remains for chemistry to discover. The writer does not intimate that these crystals are noxious or hurtful, or that their presence imparts any impure taint to the mass in which they are so plentifully distributed. It, however, is evident that just in proportion to their extent the mass of which they form a component part must be less rich, and correspondingly less nutritious, than the butter which is wholly butter and nothing else.

The further point suggested by Mr. Michels is more significant, and will, undoubtedly challenge close and widespread attention. If adequate experiment fail to overthrow the proposition that animal fats rendered at a temperature of not over 120 degrees Fahrenheit remain so substantially uncooked as to retain unimpaired any poisonous elements or living parasites which might have been contained in the fatty tissues of the living animal, the oleomargarine business will receive a severe shock. The public will require very strong assurance of cleanly selection and preparation before they will admit such a substance into use as a universal article of diet. The theory is not unlikely to be verified. Animal life is known to withstand high temperature sometimes. Professor Brewer, of Yale College, while connected with the geological survey of the State of California, took living organisms from several of the boiling lakes of that State, the temperature of which was in no case under 190 degrees Fahrenheit, and frequently was as high as 200 degrees. The field of inquiry opened out by our correspondent is one of superlative importance, and we shall watch for its solution with anxious interest.

No. 5.—EXTRACT from "NEW YORK TIMES" of 27th June 1878.—OLEOMARGARINE BUTTER.

Oleomargarine Butter.—Recent Microscopic Tests.

PROF. MOTT'S REPLY TO JOHN MICHELL.—Comparative Purity of Dairy Butter and the New Article of Commerce.

PROF. MOTT has recently made microscopic tests of samples of dairy butter and oleomargarine butter. The result of his labours will be found in the subjoined communication. He shows the grade of purity attainable in the new article of commerce, and in what particulars it excels certain grades of dairy butter.

To the Editor of the "New York Times."

In a recent number of a dairy organ there appeared an article on oleomargarine by one John Michell, the object of which was evidently an attempt to damage the oleomargarine industry. The writer presents two microscopical plates illustrating oleomargarine butter and natural butter as they appear under the microscope to him. I do not hardly know how to express myself with respect to Mr. Michell, but one thing is certain, that the plate representing to be oleomargarine butter was either intentionally originated to create a sensation, or that Mr. Michell himself is a person perfectly incompetent to make microscopical investigations. This I think will be clearly demonstrated to any fair-minded man further on in this paper. Mr. Michell states in his article that the close resemblance of oleomargarine to butter suggested to him the propriety of making a microscopical examination of both substances, to see if they could be distinguished by such means. This suggestion was a good one, and had he carried it out conscientiously, science would be at least benefited by the examination. Seeing the importance of a thorough microscopical investigation after such gross misrepresentations as have been presented by Mr. Michell, I visited Prof. J. W. S. Arnold, Professor of Histology and Microscopy in the University Medical College of this city, who is acknowledged to be one of the leading microscopists of this country, and engaged him to make the investigation.

Not being satisfied with a microscopical examination of the butter alone, I determined to have examined caul-fat, stearine, oleomargarine (before churned), and oleomargarine butter, and compare the same with natural butter, both pure and rancid.

The samples examined by Prof. Arnold were obtained from the Commercial Manufacturing Company by myself in person and given to him.

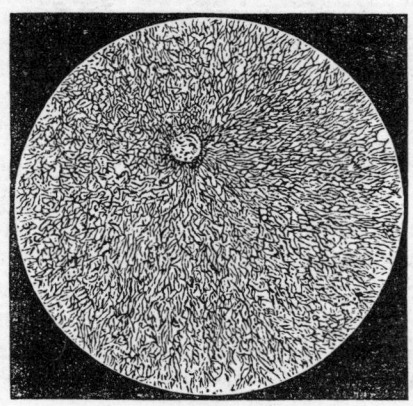

FIGURE 1. 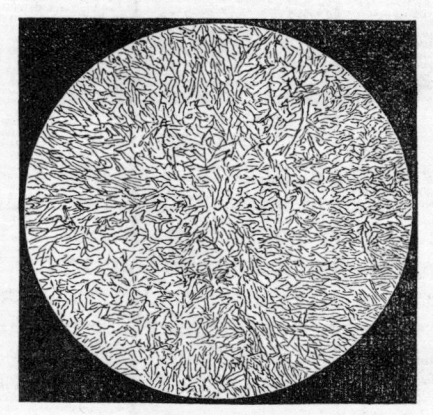   FIGURE 2.

Figure 1 represents caul-fat under the microscope, the crystalline nature and adipose tissue being clearly seen, as also a globule of oil.

Figure 2 represents oleomargarine before it is churned, or what is known as "oleomargarine oil." It will be seen from this plate that oleomargarine before churned is entirely in a crystalline condition. It will be necessary before proceeding to a description of the other plates to explain the cause of the crystallization. When oleomargarine butter was first introduced into this city, several years ago, it had a very gritty consistency, which was easily detected by the tongue; this was entirely due to the fact that the product was allowed to crystallize, that is, to cool slowly from a fluid condition to a solid state. This objectionable feature was not removed until I discovered that by rapid chilling it would solidify so suddenly that crystallization would be entirely prevented, and the product would then have the fine texture of natural butter. So the crystalline condition of oleomargarine oil is due to the fact that the oil is allowed to cool gradually, and then crystallize to a solid condition. To demonstrate this point most emphatically to your readers, I directed Prof. Arnold to melt a sample of natural butter, allow the same to cool slowly to a solid condition, and then make a microscopical examination, the result of which is illustrated in Figure 3. From this figure it will at once be seen that the mass is entirely crystallized and in no way differs from oleomargarine oil, as shown in Figure 2.

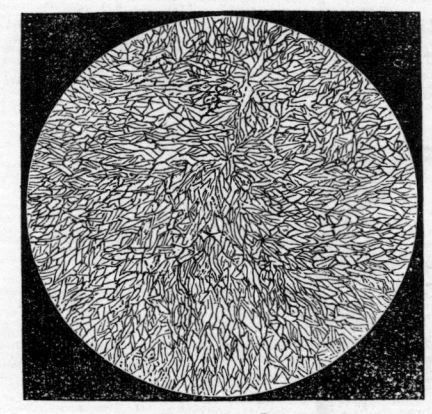

FIGURE 3. 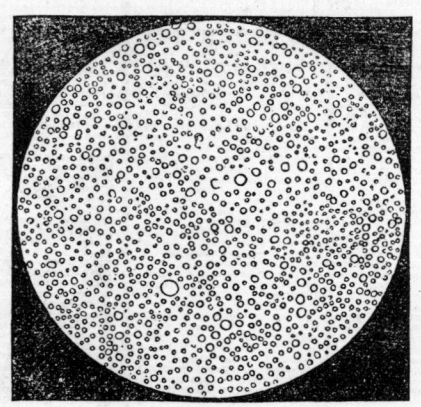   FIGURE 4.

Figure 4 represents oleomargarine butter, and Figure 5 natural butter. It will be seen by examination of these two figures that they consist only of an innumerable

O 889.

number of minute globules of varying size, but not a trace of a crystal appears in either, nor is there to be seen any contorted shape, imaginary figures or bodies, as represented in Figure 6, which is Michell's representation of oleomargarine butter. I quote the

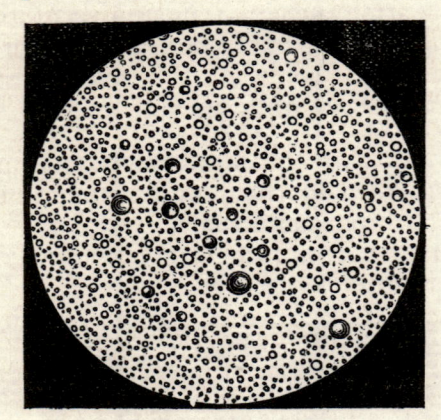

FIGURE 5.   FIGURE 6.

following paragraph from an article published by Michell on the "Microscope and its Misrepresentations." "The fact that the most skilful microscopists of the age all " differ upon the true appearance of a common and not very minute object, and the " microscope itself presenting to the vision the most opposite appearances of one and " the same object, should act as a caution to those who accept too readily theories " based upon microscopical researches." If this remarkable spontaneous effusion is true about skilful microscopists, how much more important it is to receive with the very greatest of caution the inaccurate or manufactured results of an amateur microscopist.

The remarkable illustration by Michell shown in Figure 6, when compared with the accurate illustration by Prof. Arnold, shows at once that the former was obtained by a person perfectly incompetent to make a microscopical examination. If Michell did obtain under the microscope any such illustration as shown in Figure 6, it only demonstrates more clearly how incompetent he is to make the examination—for the contorted-shaped bodies can only be explained (if at all) by the glass cover pressing too hard on the butter under examination—and the crystals to carelessness in placing the slide in some hot place so that the butter would melt, and after solidifying (crystallizing) again, examining the sample as if the slide were properly prepared, and had undergone no change.

In either case it is the result of the ignorance of an amateur, or a gross misrepresentation of the facts.

In the editorial notice on Mr. Michell's article I find the following:—"The writer " does not intimate that these crystals are noxious or hurtful, or that their presence " imparts any impure taint to the mass in which they are so plentifully distributed. " It, however, is evident that just in proportion to their extent, the mass of which they " form a component part must be less rich, and correspondingly less nutritious, than " the butter which is wholly butter and nothing else." The last part of this paragraph is so absurdly ridiculous that I hardly think it requires answering; but fearing that your readers might accept the same without giving thought to it (as it was undoubtedly written without the proper thought or consideration), I think it may be well to answer it, and in the shortest way possible, which I will do by asking a simple question. Is crystallized sugar "less rich, and correspondingly less nutritious," than powdered sugar? If you think so, just powder some of the crystals and try it.

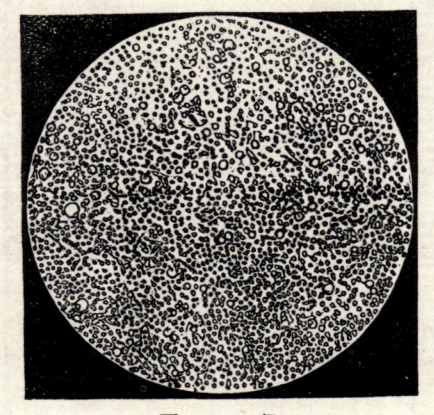

FIGURE 7.

Figure 7 represents a sample of rancid butter bought on Eleventh Avenue, the retail price being 20 cents. a pound. It will be seen on examining this figure that dark black indentations are to be seen in most of the globules, showing that decomposition is in progress. This decomposition is the first stage of putrefaction, which can only take place by the growth and development of multitudes of minute organisms. All of the soluble fats which give the aroma and delicate flavour of butter are by the growth of the organisms decomposed into rancid acids, which, when taken internally, bring about a general disorder of the system, producing "violent cramping and purging, and " often setting up putrefaction in the tissues." There can be no doubt that a very large per cent. of the sickness among the poorer classes is due to the use of rancid butter, who, before the introduction of oleomargarine butter, were compelled to buy it, owing to the high price of a better article. I say owing to the high price of a better article; this statement is not altogether correct, for if they had the inclination to buy a pure, sweet article free from rancidity, it would be, under the present condition of things, an impossibility to supply their demand. It is the admission of the Secretary of the American Dairymen's Association that only five per cent. of the 800,000,000 lbs. (the annual production of butter) is a perfect article. Mr. Curtiss, to explain this statement, says that the five per cent. means "strictly fancy" butter, and that at least 25 per cent. will be pronounced fine, while 50 per cent. of the butter is sweet and palatable, and also wholesome. This explanation, although somewhat more favourable to dairymen, is certainly not saying very much. To think that, by their own admission, 400,000,000 lbs. of butter sold in this country is offered at a somewhat lower price than the price of good butter, because it is in a state of decomposition, tainted by rancid acids, and swarming with minute organisms, and because of its cheapness the poor people had to purchase it before the introduction of oleomargarine butter. Does this speak well for the dairymen? No! It only speaks for the filthiness of the dairy, for cleanliness is nine-tenths of the secret in making a pure, sweet butter. One drop of milk left in the milk-pail, the milk-pan, or the churn, soon becomes the proper medium for the growth and development of the numerous germs of life which float in our atmosphere—fermentation and putrefaction of this little drop of milk soon takes place. Add now to either of these different apparatuses fresh milk or cream, and that which was fresh and sweet before adding is now tainted and itself in the process of decomposition. From such conditions no pure sweet butter can be obtained.

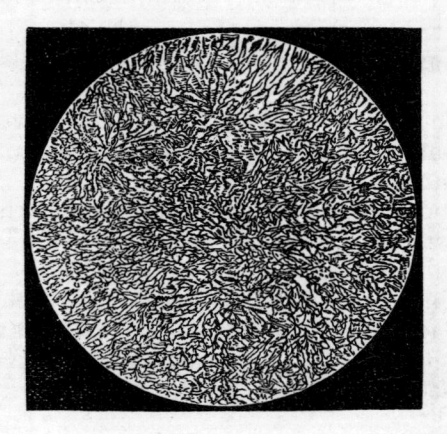

FIGURE 8.

Figure 8 represents stearine, which will be seen to be in an entirely crystalline condition.

The following is the report of Prof. J. W. S. Arnold on the samples examined by him, all of which I carefully examined myself, and can verify to the accuracy of his investigation:—

Physiological Laboratory,
Medical Department, University of New York,
June 17, 1878.

MY DEAR SIR,

I HAVE made a careful microscopical examination of the sample of caul fat, stearine, and oleomargarine which you placed in my hands. These substances are entirely free from any impurity or injurious material detectable by the microscope. I have also submitted the oleomargarine butter to a similar examination, comparing it with natural butter, and find the oleomargarine butter to consist of exceedingly clear and beautiful oil globules, a sufficient proof of its purity.

The specimen of rancid butter shows very nicely the granular and irregular oil globules characteristic of decomposing fat.

I send you a series of photo-micrographs of the various fats and butter examined. The magnifying power equals a four-tenths objective and "A" eye-piece.

Very truly yours,

Dr. H. A. Mott, Jr. (Signed) J. W. S. ARNOLD, A.M., M.D.

Further reference to Mr. Michell's article almost seems a waste of time, but as he makes some sensational remarks about finding in the butter " parts of the tissue of the " animal, with fragments and cells of a suspicious character," and then, in connexion with these remarks, speaking of trichinæ, and of diseases which can be communicated from animals to man, although there is not the least foundation for his imaginary speculations, I think it well to answer a few of the more prominent ones. In the first place, if Mr. Michell understood how to prepare a slide with oleomargarine butter for microscopical examination, he would have obtained results which could not be distinguished from the result obtained when natural butter is examined, as demonstrated by Figures 4 and 5.

Then he would not have discovered any tissue and remarkable cells; but not knowing how to examine a sample, he obtained any number of distorted shaped bodies, which were entirely the result of ignorance, or, as before stated, intentional misrepresentation. Again, Michell calls attention to the fact that, as the fat is never submitted to a higher temperature than 120° Fahrenheit, that it is merely liquified, and that " it " would appear to follow that germs of disease (or their equivalent), morbid secretions " and embryos of parasites, are thus liable to be transferred in a living condition into " the system of those who make use of this substance." The best answer to these remarks is, probably, a confession which Mr. Michell made to me personally, when he stated that in all his examinations, and in all his reading, he had never seen or heard of germs of disease or embryos of parasites in caul fat. And still, acquainted with those facts, he was unprincipled enough to insinuate directly to the contrary.

I give below a few paragraphs from some correspondence which has been carried on respecting this subject by two of the highest authorities in this country on any subject connected with parasites. The first is from a letter by Prof. A. E. Verrill, A.M., S.B., of Yale College:—

" In regard to ' worms ' in beef fat, I will state definitely that no such instances are known to occur. Nor has trichinæ been observed either in the fat or flesh, except when the embryos have been purposely fed to the animals before killing them (for experimental purposes)."

The second is from two letters by Prof. William H. Brewer, also of Yale College:—

" The idea that oleomargarine is more dangerous than butter, because heated to only 120° Fahrenheit, is simply nonsense."

Prof. Brewer also gave the following written answers to the questions cited below:—

First.—Do parasites infest the bovine race that could find their way into the human system through the use of oleomargarine as food?

" To this I answer, not that I have ever heard of; if such exist, science has not yet found them. The bovine race, like most other creatures, have parasites, but no species has yet been described which would be transmitted to man in that way."

Second.—Can the microscope be relied on to distinguish between the butter fats, whether natural or artificial?

" On this I cannot speak with certainty. My belief is that it cannot, so far as the mere fats are concerned, but that it would be an aid to chemistry in the hands of a skilful expert to distinguish between butter and other compounds of which such fats are ingredients."

Third.—Is not oleomargarine, as made by the Mege patent, as wholesome and nutritious as cream butter?

" So far as chemistry and common sense suggest, I see no reason why it should not be as wholesome and as nutritious as cream butter, and will so believe unless its actual use demonstrates to the contrary."

The microscope, then, demonstrates oleomargarine to be entirely free from " any " impurity or injurious material," and shows that oleomargarine butter, instead of consisting of " crystals and tissue of animals with fragments and cells of a suspicious " character," consists of " exceedingly clear and beautiful oil globules," the same as the purest natural butter. Although this investigation has taken a great deal of time, with the assistance of the ablest scientific men of the country, to refute the gross misrepresentation of Mr. Michell, it will have two effects: One to more publicly establish the remarkable purity of oleomargarine butter, and the other to influence the public in the future to hesitate to accept the imaginary results of an ignorant amateur. The microscope, then, establishes the absolute purity of oleomargarine butter. What now can chemical analysis say? The result of a careful qualitative analysis conducted by myself has demonstrated that every constituent found in natural butter is to be found in the artificial products. This being the case, let us turn our attention to quantitative analysis and see how each constituent compares with each other as to quantity present.

The following analyses, which I have just conducted of natural and artificial butter, are the most elaborate that have as yet been made:—

ANALYSES of NATURAL and ARTIFICIAL BUTTER, by DR. H. A. MOTT, Jr.

Constituents.		No. 1.* Natural Butter.	No. 2. Artificial Butter.
Water		11·968	11·203
Butter solids		88·032	88·797
		100·000	100·000
Insol. fats	Olein	23·824	24·893
	Palmitin Stearine Arachin Myristin	51·422	56·298
Sol. fats	Butyrin Caprin Caproin Caprylin	7·432	1·823
Casein		·192	·621
Salt		5·162	5·162
Colouring matter		Trace	Trace
		88·032	88·797

* No. 1 is calculated to the same per-centage of salt as No. 2.

By examining the above true analyses it will be seen that the artificial butter contains a somewhat larger per-centage of butter solids. The per-centage of soluble fats which was determined by Herner's new method in artificial butter is somewhat less than in the natural product; quite sufficient though to give to the product a good flavour and aroma, but hardly sufficient when decomposed to render the product rancid, and it is for this reason that oleomargarine butter keeps so much longer than natural butter.

Chemical analysis joins, then, with the microscope to prove the identity of natural and artificial butter and demonstrate the absolute purity of the latter. It is to be hoped, then, in the face of these facts, especially when the Board of Health pronounce it a pure and wholesome article of food, that all further controversy is at an end for ever. It will be so to science and also to all honest and fair-minded dealers, but not to men whose avarice is paramount to principle so long as they can realise their 5 and 10 per cent. on the 400,000,000 lbs. of impure, rancid butter. Just so long will they endeavour to hunt up Michell in every shape and form, having no regard whatever for the health of the great masses of people to whom such impurities are dealt out.

(Signed) H. A. MOTT, Jr, Ph.D., E.M.

No. 6.—EXTRACT from "AMERICAN DAIRYMAN" of 3rd April 1879.—CAUL FAT by R. M. PIPER.

Caul Fat.—Its vile and sickening character.—The compound full of living organisms. Complete corroboration of the " Dairyman's " position.

THE "American Dairyman" in its issue of June 13, 1878, set forth the proposition that animal fat rendered at a low temperature was liable to retain in the oil any living organisms or parasitic germs that might have been in the animal from which the fat was taken. It is a well-known fact that oleomargarine must be rendered from animal fat at the lowest practicable temperature, in order that it shall be devoid of the disagreeable odour and flavour which would otherwise inevitably attach to it. As a consequence this much-vaunted product of caul fat is accordingly liable to contain any living germs which may perchance have been in the animal to which the fat originally pertained. We did not then assert that oleomargarine or its product, butterine, necessarily contained such detrimental and unwholesome creatures, but only that they both probably would do so if the material out of which they were made was so infected. Our statement made a great sensation at the time. The caul fat manufacturers were highly incensed, and threatened condign vengeance upon the "American Dairyman," which to this date has consisted solely in the withdrawal of their advertising patronage, material which long ere this we should have rejected from our columns as being hostile to the dairy interest, in whose service this paper is published. But time has fully demonstrated the accuracy of our prediction. Scientists in various parts of the country

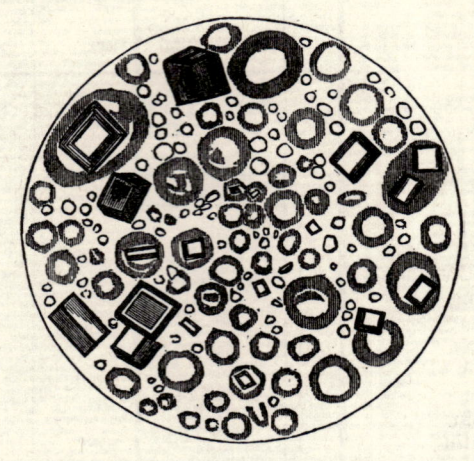

FIG. 1.—PURE BUTTER MAGNIFIED 564 DIAMETERS.

have investigated the caul fat compound, and, whenever they were not retained or bribed by the manufacturers thereof, their verdict has unanimously sustained the presence of living creatures in the stuff as an incontestible fact. We republish below the latest testimony from the pen of Prof. R. U. Piper, a Chicago microscopist, whose address on this subject before the recent Convention of the Butter, Cheese, and Egg Association we have already discussed. Prof. Piper, writing to the "Western Rural," of Chicago, says in corroboration of the position of Mr. Michels in the "Dairyman" above referred to :—

About a year since my attention was called to the new compound which is now being introduced as a substitute for butter. Up to October 1878, I made a few examinations of the substance with the microscope, with a view to finding out whether it could be distinguished from butter, under the name of which it was said to be often put upon the market. At this time Mr. Michels' paper was put in my hands, and also some papers from Professors Verrill and Brewer, of Yale College, taking direct issue with Mr. Michels. To this may be added a certificate of Professor Arnold, of the University of New York, published in the "New York Times" in connexion with a communication signed by Dr. Henry Mott, purporting to be a review of Mr. Michels' report on oleomargarine. Mr. Michels says that on applying to the "New York Times" office he was candidly told by the editor-in-chief that the letter to which Dr. Mott had signed his name was nothing but an advertisement from the oleomargarine factory; that in fact they had received hundreds of dollars for its insertion, and that therefore no reply would be permitted to me." How much the learned professors got for their certificates is not stated. But Mr. Michels goes on further to say: "I state these facts and leave them " without comment, for if honoured names and great institutions can thus be used to " advertise a grease factory, abuse rather than praise must be welcome from such a " source." It seems that Dr. Mott is the chemist for one of these "grease factories."

Since receiving these papers I have made it my business, whenever I have had the leisure to do so, to make examinations of oleomargarine, comparing it with genuine butter, getting my samples of this compound from various sources, so that I must have had, I think, specimens from nearly or quite all of the manufactories. The result of these many examinations is embodied in the drawings I send you (and which are published in this issue), which I shall endeavour to describe in words in the present paper.

The claims for this compound cannot, perhaps, be better set forth than by quoting from Prof. Brewer's statement as published in the "New York Times" of June 27, 1878.

The paper cites Prof. Brewer as saying: "The idea that oleomargarine is more dangerous than butter because heated only to 120° Fahrenheit is simply nonsense." Prof. Brewer's answers to the following questions are given as quoted:

"First. Do parasites infect the bovine race that could find their way into the human system through the use of oleomargarine as food?"

"To this I answer not that I have ever heard of; if such exist, *science has not yet found them.* The bovine race, like most other creatures, have parasites, but no species has yet been described which would be transmitted to man in that way."

"Second. Can the microscope be relied on to distinguish between the butter fats whether natural or artificial?"

"On this I cannot speak with certainty. My belief is that it cannot, so far as the mere fats are concerned, but that it would be an aid to chemistry in the hands of a *skilful* expert to distinguish between butter and other compounds of which such fats are ingredients."

"Third. Is not oleomargarine as made by the Mege patent as wholesome and as nutritious as cream butter?"

"So far as chemistry and common sense suggests, I see no reason why it should not be as wholesome and as nutritious as cream butter, and will so believe unless its actual use demonstrates to the contrary."

The first statement of Prof. Brewer practically resolves itself into this, in order to cover the whole ground, as I shall proceed to show: Is there anything in the animal tissues (if you please the "bovine animal tissues") inimical to human life ("dangerous"), either in the spore or perfected form which a temperature of 120° will not destroy? Now, Messrs. Editors, you will remember that the specimen of oleomargarine which I exhibited to you under the microscope, which was crowded with active wriggling forms, had been exposed twenty-four hours previous to the heat of boiling distilled water, in a test tube, and then allowed to cool, the grease forming a coating impervious to outside spores. When making the examination in your presence, I thrust the glass pipette through this grease crust into the water beneath, and from thence obtained the myriads of moving objects you saw. That spores or eggs are there is pretty well proven; if not by this one experiment, at least by the hundreds of like

FIG. 2.—OLEOMARGARINE MAGNIFIED 564 DIAMETERS.

experiments which I have tried, and which have resulted in the production of similar living organisms. The cases which I have given would seem to furnish sufficient proof of the resistance of these organisms to the action of high temperatures. I will merely add to this the testimony of Rev. W. H. Dallinger, the English microscopist, who is certainly the greatest living authority on this subject. He says that the germs of this series of organisms require at least 212° to 231° Fahr., for their destruction in fluid, and he goes on to say that their introduction, or that of their eggs, into the human intestinal track is quite a serious matter, which will probably impress itself upon the public in an unwelcome manner.

The answer to the third question in this series is involved in the word "dangerous," in Prof. B.'s first statement, and may be put thus: Are these organisms dangerous, or is there in oleomargarine, or can there be any spores or eggs, or substances whatever coming from the animal whose fat is used in the manufacture introduced through this process, which under any conditions will develop into agents inimical to human life? Are the organisms which you saw, Messrs. Editors, thus inimical? They are present in all decaying, putrifying animal matter, and at least by their presence show this condition in the substance under examination. If found in oleomargarine in so short a time after it has been thus cooked, it would certainly seem that the process of manufacture had but little if any tendency to prevent the putrefactive process. Let any one thus boil good, fresh, healthy beef, and protect it as I did in my experiment from the outside air, it may go months, and years even, and remain sweet. Meat from diseased cattle I have seen show this spore life in from two to ten hours. Who shall say that in all cases the fat of healthy animals is used in this manufacture? In order to insure this, of course every animal must undergo the most careful examination. Do the oleomargarine manufacturers ever see any of the cattle from whom they obtain their grease? Respectable butchers whom I have consulted tell me that a single piece of diseased meat put in a barrel of good meat will cause them to lose the whole, no matter how careful they may be in the process of salting; and that with all their care they frequently "get caught" in this manner. May it not now and then happen that the fat of such an animal will get into a batch of oleomargarine? Suppose it should so chance that while the watchers of the oleomargarine manufactories were asleep, the fat of a single over-driven animal should get converted into butter. Morand tells us that "if the blood or raw flesh of "such animals be applied to the unbroken skin of a human being, a dangerous, and often "a fatal inflammation is excited." He tells us also that an eruption of gangrenous boils is produced by eating this flesh. The writer himself has seen a strong, healthy young man die in a few hours after handling the blood of an animal which was said to have exhibited no signs of disease. But this is not all; the wise Professor tells us that "science has not yet found parasites which could find their way into the human system "through oleomargarine." Indeed, has he not heard of some species of tapeworm which

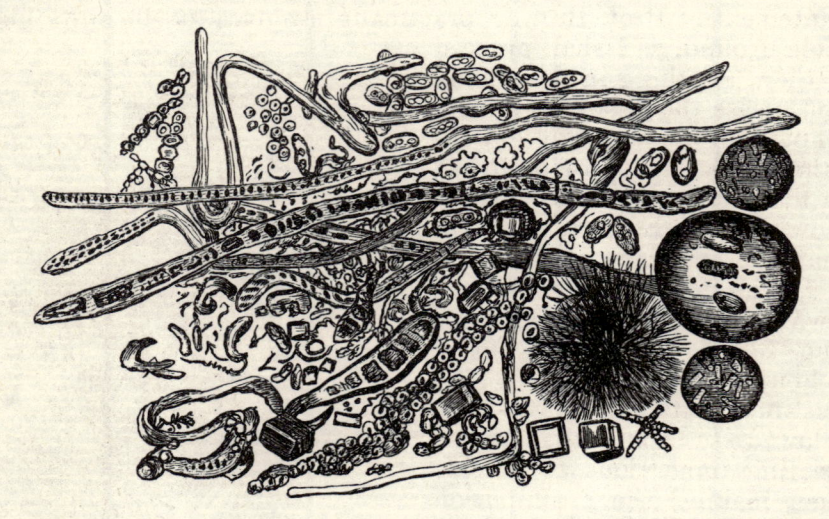

FIG. 3.—OLEOMARGARINE MAGNIFIED 564 DIAMETERS.

could be thus introduced through the flesh of animals of the bovine family? Suppose such flesh should chance to be present in a given specimen? He will perhaps answer that these organisms are only found in the lean meat, and that this is not used in this manufacture. Are we sure of this last fact? You will bear me out, Messrs. Editors, in the statement, that in a single examination of each of two specimens of different manufacturers of this substance, I found sufficient lean muscular fibre in which to lodge eggs enough to people the body of one individual, at least. I have these samples preserved on microscopic slides. They might carry *trichinæ spiralis*, as who shall say that some of the flesh of hogs may not get into oleomargarine, spite of the honesty and vigilance of the manufacturers? Certainly it is possible for this to happen, and the very samples of lean flesh on my slides may, for aught we know, be veritable swines' flesh. This, it will be well to bear in mind, is the result of but a single examination of two specimens of imitation butter put in my hands for the purpose.

But what has " chemistry and common sense," in the language of the Professor, to do with the results of such examinations? Can chemistry or common sense tell us anything about the relations of organised bodies to each other? Can it tell us why the *living yeast plant* will do one thing, while the *dead yeast plant* will produce no such effect? Can chemistry or common sense even tell us that oil of orange and oil of savin, which are chemically precisely alike (C10, H16), are so widely different as is known to be the fact in their effects on the human system, the one a pleasant flavouring substance, while the other is a most dangerous poison? In 1839 at a fête day in Zurich, Switzerland, six hundred people were badly poisoned by the meat used on the occasion. The symptoms in these cases were as follows: Shivering, giddiness, headache, burning fever, diarrhœa, and vomiting. Some had delirium, others a fetid salivation and ulcers of the mouth, and in other cases collapse, involuntary stools and great prostration preceded death. Now suppose the fat of such an animal should by any chance get converted into oleomargarine, will "chemistry and common sense" say that it would be a safe article for human food? In this case chemistry and common sense both found only incipient putrefaction in the meat, precisely what I find in all of the samples of oleomargarine, either when first submitted to examination (as in Fig. 2), or some time after cooking as seen in the sample exhibited to the editors of the "Western Rural" and others.

As to the second question, and Prof. Brewer's answer to the same, I am not quite clear. He speaks of distinguishing by means of the microscope between "butter fats" whether *natural* or *artificial*. It is to be inferred that a scientific professor in such a college as Yale would speak in *specific language*, and it may be that some *artificial fats* which we have not heard of in the benighted West have been invented by the savants of the college, and are in use in this manufacture. If so, I have certainly failed to discover them. But if he means to say that animal fats cannot be told from butter fats, he may well put this statement on the grounds of belief or of guessing, for the veriest tyro in microscopy who has studied the matter at all, would be able to meet him with a positive denial.

In comparing the keeping qualities of tallow or lard with these same fats as found in oleomargarine, it will be remembered that when properly prepared both lard and tallow are submitted to high temperatures, and are, moreover, free from "the cells of suspicious "character and fragments of tissue and muscle" which Mr. Michels tells us he found in every specimen of oleomargarine he examined, and which has also been my experience in all of my many examinations. Now, as every one knows the slight salting such shreds of animal tissue undergo in the preparation of the artificial butter can have but little effect in preventing putrefaction, and this, as we have seen, takes place whenever the substance is brought under the proper conditions. Thus in the oleomargarine itself, when sealed from the air by the coating of fat, when there is left any moisture from the milk or water used in the process of manufacture, in contact with these particles of meat or other animal tissue, this process goes rapidly on; and also under various conditions of cooking when left standing for a few hours, as in my experiments.

To sum up the whole matter, spores or eggs of living organisms, and sometimes these organisms themselves, some of them known to be inimical to the human system, may be introduced into it through oleomargarine, as we find this substance contains in all cases fragments of animal tissue; that, moreover, if this tissue is perfectly healthy in the first instance, and does not contain these spores or organisms, it is like all other animal flesh when dead—sure, sooner or later, to pass into the putrefactive process when exposed to the ordinary conditions of moisture and warmth; and we have already seen how dangerous such putrefying meat may become to the human economy.

2. That good butter has none of these organisms, nor indeed can the very *worst* article of the kind carry in it the eggs of the tapeworm or trichinæ, which oleomargarine is very liable to do in the fragments of animal tissue constantly being found in it.

3. Mr. Michels tells us that "there can be no doubt that fats and grease of every "description are used to make oleomargarine, because all the caul fat of oxen brought "to New York city in a week would not be sufficient for one manufactory for four days, "and there are seven oleomargarine manufactories in the city." Thus it will be seen that every variety of vile grease is used in this compound. A recent foreign scientific authority says that such grease used in soap is often found to be dangerous. Is it safe, then, to take such substances into the human stomach?

4. The saddest and most dangerous thing in all this, however, is not in the words of Mr. Michels, "that honoured names and great public institutions can thus be used to "advertise a *grease factory*," but that they could be used either knowingly or ignorantly on their part thus to misstate facts in order to deceive the public and aid unprincipled men in flooding the market with an article which, to say the least, is a fraud and deception, inasmuch as the most of it is sold under a false name. Herbert Spencer says of such transactions that they are no less fraudulent than theft or robbery, and that they are far more dangerous to society, inasmuch as they seem to justify the idea that science itself is the friend and ally of falsehood.

As it regards the effect this manufacture may have on the farmers, the producers of the legitimate article, it is hardly necessary for me to speak. If, as is stated, a single manufactory in New York is producing 100,000 lbs. a day of the unwholesome compound (and there are seven of these concerns in that city, to say nothing of others in different localities), how long will it take to drive genuine butter out of the market, especially if, as is claimed, the bogus stuff can be so scented and flavoured as to prevent its being distinguished by the taste or by other means than a scientific examination?

O 889.

The following are explanations of the plates which are herewith published:—

Plate 1. Genuine clean butter as seen under the microscope. The circular globules are composed of butter fats. The prismatic and cubical forms represent salt crystals. Sometimes the butter fats present irregular or oval outlines.

Plate 2. This is from a specimen of New York oleomargarine, bought of a regular dealer and sold as such. Here are seen fat crystals such as are shown under the microscope in animal fats, *e.g.*, cattle, sheep, hogs, human fats, &c. Pieces of animal tissue are also present in this drawing, together with salt crystals, suspicious rounded forms of various kinds, &c.

Plate 3. This drawing was made from a specimen sent me for examination by the keeper of a respectable eating house in this city. I have made a number of like examinations for this gentleman, who has shown himself specially anxious to furnish his customers with a good and pure article of butter. This plate is made up of drawings from several examinations of the specimen mentioned. When placed on the slide in the first place the shreds of animal tissue, salt and fat crystals and spores were seen, and also a peculiar form which I have frequently met with in foul water. The other objects, many of which were active living forms, together with the fungi, were found after the material had been boiled in water, as before described, and also after it had been dissolved in sulphuric ether. As I have said in another place, many of these forms are such as are present in all putrifying animal matter, while others are perhaps the bacteria of special diseases, or the strange, silent workers whose office it may perchance be to prepare the system for the accession of such cruel maladies, for illustration, as we are told by the authorities resulted in England from eating the flesh of animals afflicted with the "cattle disease."

The drawings are all made with the utmost care, under the camera lucida, and are faithful transcripts of the objects represented.

(Signed)   R. U. PIPER.

No. 7.—PROSPECTUS OF COMMERCIAL MANUFACTURING COMPANY OF NEW YORK. MANUFACTURE OF OLEOMARGARINE.

The attention of butter dealers and the public generally is called to the following:—

"Report of the judges of the American Institute Fair, held in the city of New York, October and November 1878.

"OLEOMARGARINE BUTTER.

"Commercial Manufacturing Co., 635–653, W. 48th Street.

"The oleomargarine butter (Mège process) has the general appearance of the usual style of good dairy butter. The texture presents some slight difference to the eye of an expert. The absence of some of the elements which give the peculiar aroma to the best quality of spring grass butter tends to prevent the approach of any unpleasant change in this article, and it is thus enabled to resist the effects of time, as upon a long sea voyage.

"We have examined the process of manufacture, and find the product clean and wholesome.

"While the best quality of dairy butter must still maintain its superiority, any departure from the most perfect manufacture will make the oleomargarine a dangerous rival.

"This process utilizes valuable animal products, and makes useful in the kitchen and upon the dining-table much that was formerly used for less important purposes, and for this and its keeping qualities it should receive some recognition by the Institute.

"The medal of excellence awarded.

"A true copy of the report on file.

"(Signed)   JOHN W. CHAMBERS,
Secretary."

Also, to the appended card which appeared in the New York daily papers of December 5th, 1878, during the holding of the International Dairy Fair in this city. Concerning which we beg to state that the managers of the dairy fair, in their strenuous efforts to discover the lots referred to, held under lock and key and employed a chemist to analyse, a large number of tubs of choice dairy butter supposing them to be the oleomargarine butter exhibited. Nevertheless the entire number of parcels exhibited by the Commercial Manufacturing Co. are now in its possession, bearing all the marks of exhibition and examination, and not a single parcel was identified by the judges as being oleomargarine butter! The oleomargarine butter thus tested was placed in competition with the finest samples of dairy butter made especially for the exhibition.

We leave these facts to speak for themselves, merely adding that the use of oleomargarine is conducive to health and economy. It is absolutely pure, can be sold at much lower prices than good dairy butter, and for culinary purposes three quarters of a pound of oleomargarine will accomplish as much as one pound of dairy butter, as shown by the following report of the officers of the French Government:—

"According to French official reports, artificial butter goes much further as food than the genuine article, and forms a perfectly wholesome dietetic material. The Parisian *octroi* officials have recognised the efficiency of the substitute by imposing on it the same duties which are chargeable on ordinary butter. The company established for the manufacture in France had in 1874 seven manufactories, in which 400 men were employed. There can be no doubt that a pure, sweet fat, such as is manufactured by the process of M. Mège-Mouriès, is a safer and more wholesome article than the unsavoury rancid butter, which is sold so freely among the poorer classes."—"*Encyclopædia Britanica*," 9th Edition," article "Butter."

It is packed in cases holding 60 one pound prints, and in attractive tubs holding 28 and 50 lbs. each.

The following are to-day's quotations:

Large tubs, 15 cents per lb.; small tubs, 16 cents per lb.; prints, 17 cents per lb.
New York, January 27, 1879.

Ask your grocer for it.

Orders from dealers, addressed as below, will receive prompt attention.

Commercial Manufacturing Co., 635 to 653, West 48th Street, New York, only legalised manufacturers of oleomargarine butter and oleomargarine, for the States of New York and New Jersey. Also for sale by grocers and butter dealers.

Caution.—Any parties infringing upon the rights or trade marks of this Company, or manufacturing or dealing in either of the above-mentioned products, without license from the patentee, will be liable to prosecution and damages to the full extent of the law.

Below is the card referred to.

A challenge.

The International Dairy Fair and Oleomargarine.

Oleomargarine, which has become one of the most important industries of the United States, having been refused admission to the International Dairy Fair in this city by the executive committee, in consequence of the fears entertained by the commission dealers in the dairy interest that it will interfere with their commissions, the following correspondence is submitted to the public:—

Dear Sir,   New York, October 23, 1878.

This Company proposes to make exhibit, at the coming fair, of its oleomargarine butter, and we will be obliged if you will send us the necessary blank applications, rules, &c.

Respectfully yours,
T. Mortimer Seaver, Esq.   The Commercial Manufacturing Co.,
A. S. Patterson, Secretary.

Reply.

Dear Sir,   New York, October 26, 1878.

Your communication, making application to exhibit oleomargarine butter at the International Dairy Fair, has received the attention of our committee, and is respectfully declined for the reason that it is not a deemed dairy product.

Very respectfully,
A. S. Patterson, Esq.,   T. Mortimer Seaver, Secretary.
Secretary Commercial Manufacturing Co.

Nevertheless, oleomargarine butter has been placed on exhibition in the fair, surrounded by the choicest exhibits of dairy butter of this nation and that of others. "Not being a dairy product," by the decision of said committee, it will be an easy matter, of course, to detect and single out the same.

Therefore, with a view to aid the fund for the prosecution of dealers in unbranded oleomargarine, we offer $50 if a majority of the judges of the fair will select and specify the oleomargarine exhibits which are now on exhibition, and were manufactured by the Commercial Manufacturing Co., by subjecting them to the same tests as dairy butter, namely, texture, taste, and smell.

THE COMMERCIAL MANUFACTURING CO.,
Office, 643, West 48th Street, New York.

December 5, 1878.

No. 8.—COPY of ACT of NEW YORK STATE LEGISLATURE of 5th June 1877, and of RESOLUTIONS of the NEW YORK BOARD OF HEALTH in reference to OLEOMARGARINE.

CHAP. 415.

AN ACT for the protection of Dairymen, and to prevent deception in sales of Butter.—Passed June 5, 1877.

The People of the State of New York, represented in Senate and Assembly, do enact as follows:

Sect. 1. Every person who shall manufacture for sale, or who shall offer or expose for sale, any article or substance in semblance of butter not the legitimate product of the dairy, and not made exclusively of milk or cream, but into which the oil or fat of animals not produced from milk, enters as a component part, or into which melted butter, or any oil thereof has been introduced to take the place of cream, shall distinctly and durably stamp, brand, or mark upon every tub, firkin, box, or package of such article or substance the word "oleomargarin," and in case of retail sale of such article or substance in parcels, the seller shall in all cases deliver therewith to the purchaser, a written or printed label bearing the plainly written or printed word "oleomargarin," and every sale of such article or substance not so stamped, branded, marked, or labelled, is declared to be unlawful, and no action shall be maintained in any of the Courts of this State to recover upon any contract for the sale of any such article or substance not so stamped, branded, marked, or labelled.

Sect. 2. Every person who shall knowingly sell, or offer to sell, or have in his or her possession with intent to sell, contrary to the provisions of this Act, any of the said article or substance required by the first section of this Act to be stamped, marked, or labelled as therein stated, not so stamped, marked, or labelled, or in case of retail sale without delivery of a label required by Section 1 of this Act, shall, for each such offence, forfeit and pay a fine of one hundred dollars, to be recovered with costs in any of the Courts of this State, having cognizance thereof, in an action to be prosecuted by the district attorney, in the name of the people, and the one-half of such recovery shall be paid to the informer, and the residue shall be applied to the support of the poor in the county where such recovery is had.

Sect. 3. Every person who shall knowingly sell, or offer or expose for sale, or who shall cause or procure to be sold, or offered or exposed for sale, any article or substance required by the First Section of this Act to be marked, branded, stamped, or labelled, not so marked, branded, stamped, or labelled, shall be guilty of a misdemeanor, and on trial for such misdemeanor proof of the sale or offer or exposure alleged shall be presumptive evidence of knowledge of the character of the article so sold or offered, and that the same was not marked, branded, stamped, or labelled as required by this Act.

State of New York,
Office of the Secretary of State,

I HAVE compared the preceding with the original law on file in this office, and do hereby certify that the same is a correct transcript therefrom, and of the whole of said original law.

Given under my hand and the seal of office of the Secretary of State, at the city of Albany, this eighth day of June, in the year one thousand eight hundred and seventy-seven.

[SEAL.]

EDGAR K. APGER,
Dp. Secretary of State.

21

The Board of Health on Oleomargarine.

The following is the response of the New York Board of Health to the inquiry of the State Senate relative to the healthfulness of oleomargarine, for which we are indebted to Dr. Chandler, President of the Board of Health.

To the Honourable the Senate of the State of New York.

The Board of Health of the Health Department of the City of New York, having been requested to report upon the subject of oleomargarine by the following resolutions of the Honourable the Senate of the State of New York:

"Resolved. That the Board of Health of the City of New York, be requested to report to the Senate, at as early a day as possible.

"1st. Whether in the opinion of said Board 'oleomargarine' is a good and wholesome article of food.

"2nd. That if it is not, what legislation is required to effectually prevent its manufacture and sale.

"3rd. That if it is, what additional legislation is necessary to prevent its imposition upon the public as pure butter, the product of the dairy."

Has given to the subject due consideration and is of the opinion—

1st. That oleomargarine is a good and wholesome article of food.

2nd. That no legislation is necessary to prevent its imposition upon the public as pure butter, the product of the dairy, additional to Chapter 415 of the Laws of 1877.

All of which is respectfully submitted.

By order of the Board,
(Signed)   CHARLES F. CHANDLER,
President.

(Signed)   EMMONS CLARK, Secretary.

No. 9.—EXTRACT from REPORT of COMMISSIONERS of AGRICULTURE for 1878, p. 135. CHEMIST'S REPORT on EXAMINATION of AMERICAN and FOREIGN BUTTERS and OLEOMARGARINE.

Examination of American and Foreign Butters and Oleomargarine.

The examination of the American and foreign butters was made with a view of discovering if American butter could not be shipped to South America and arrive there in as good condition as foreign made butters.

The butters analyzed included the following, viz.:—One specimen each of Danish, Swiss, and French butter, received from J. B. Thompson, of 54, Broad Street, New York city; one specimen each of Iowa butter of second quality, New York dairy butter, and oleomargarine bought in Washington markets. To these are added the analyses of two specimens of oleomargarine received from House Committee for District of Columbia.

No.		Fats.	Casein.	Salt.	Sugar.	Water.	Total.
1	Danish	90·94	1·46	2·75	·52	4·17	99·84
2	Swiss	87·73	1·91	2·50	·65	6·35	99·14
3	French	87·36	·86	4·74	·18	6·80	99·94
4	Iowa	86·09	1·82	2·76	·13	9·05	99·85
5	New York	83·92	2·23	4·10	1·82	7·66	99·73
6	Oleomargarine	84·92	1·19	6·65	·60	5·89	99·25
7	Oleomargarine	84·72	·69	6·21	1·33	7·19	100·14
8	Oleomargarine	86·28	·59	5·05	1·26	6·85	100·03

In animal fats the fatty acids insoluble in water form 93·5 to 96 per cent., while in true butter the insoluble fatty acids average from 85·5 to 87·5 per cent. of the butter fat, and never exceed 89·6 per cent. Hence, since in the sample of oleomargarine, No. 6, the fatty acids equal 95·96 per cent. of the fats, it will be seen that this sample of oleomargarine was made from animal fats to which had been added a little milk in the process of manufacture.

In washing a true butter with water the water becomes milky, and a portion of these washings under the microscope shows a vast number of fat globules present in the buttermilk contained in the butter. The specimens of oleomargarine, Nos. 7 and 8, on the contrary, give a nearly clear water by washing, and this water is almost entirely destitute of fat globules, except that, since milk is used in their manufacture to a limited extent, there was found a comparatively small number of fat globules in the washings of these specimens of oleomargarine.

The sugar present in analyses, Nos. 5, 7, and 8 indicates beyond doubt the addition of this substance to the butter and the samples of oleomargarine. The small quantity in the other samples may be due to the products of decomposition in the butter analyzed, which products deported themselves in a manner similar to sugar in their effects upon the reagents used in the analysis.

These analyses show the American butters to be fully as good as the foreign butters, and, in fact, the specimens of French, Danish, and Swiss butters were in such condition of rancidity when received that they would hardly count as third rate butters in our markets.

There appears to be no reason to doubt that good American butters could compete favourably in the South American market with either of those examined.

REPORTS OF MR. CLAY, JUN.

My Lord,   Bow Park, Brantford, Ontario, December 17, 1879.

I RECEIVED a communication from your Secretary, Mr. Peel, asking me to send in a preliminary report as an assistant commissioner.

Before going further I have to thank you as President of the Commission for the honour you have done me. It shall be my earnest endeavour to act to the best of my ability.

So far my work has been in conjunction with Messrs. Read and Pell. I accompanied them during their stay in the province of Ontario; they found, however, that it would be impossible for them to overtake the whole dominion of Canada, and they have left that part of the American continent to my sole care.

As yet I am not in a position to send home a report upon such a wide and varied country. After this date I will be steady at work getting up information on the various subjects mentioned in my instructions, more especially upon feeding and shipping of cattle, dairy farming, hop growing (both very important industries), and other branches of agriculture. Mr. Read has also suggested in his last letter to me that I should make a systematic inquiry into immigration, both from a practical and theoretical point of view, and to direct those inquiries more especially to the great North West. At the same time he thinks it would be as well to arrive at some understanding about the increase of railroad building to be carried out in that region within the next few years. Perhaps no part of America is destined to exercise such an influence upon the wheat markets of the world as the vast prairies which stretch away on either side of the Saskatchewan river. What the states of Texas, Colorado, Kansas, and Nebraska are to the stock feeders, so will that " great lone land " in British North America be to the grain buyers of the world. Its progress will depend in a great measure upon the policy of the Canadian Government, whether by judicious action they encourage a legitimate and healthy immigration, and the flow of it will be prompted in such a rich and magnificent country by bold and decisive railroad schemes. Upon the instructions I have already received from home, and those left by Messrs. Read and Pell, I will endeavour to act. Be so good as to instruct me further if you wish any particular information, as during winter and spring I have considerable spare time.

After my fellow commissioners had left Ontario they went to Manitoba. Being at that time very busy, attending agricultural shows and sales, I did not accompany them. It was arranged that I should meet them about the 20th October in the west, but from our letters being miscarried I did not join them until about the 8th or 10th of November. We then went through Indiana, Kentucky, and Ohio, and at present I am busy preparing a report upon the shorthorn, and its influence upon the beef trade of America, which I will send to Mr. Pell.

While travelling there an order was published in Washington putting an embargo upon all Canadian cattle entering the States after 1st December. Having under my charge one of the largest shorthorn herds in the world, composed of between 300 and 400 head of pedigreed cattle, and as our principal trade is with the Western States I had to hasten home in order to ship 50 head suitable for the spring trade over to the States before the embargo came into force.

Having got this business satisfactorily settled I was hurrying back again so as to join my colleagues when a fire took place at the farm we keep our cattle upon, and eight large buildings were burned. I was unable to join Messrs. Read and Pell again, as they will probably explain to you. I am busy settling with insurance companies, and after I am finished with them I will be able to continue my report upon Canada.

Q 6574.

From a strange run of unexpected occurrences I have as yet done far too little. It is to be hoped that all those difficulties are over, and that I will be able to fulfil with credit the position in which I have been placed. Having once put my hand to the plough I do not care to turn back.

I remain, my Lord,
Your obedient servant,
(Signed) JOHN CLAY, Jr.

To His Grace the Duke of Richmond,
London.

Brantford, Ontario,
November 9, 1880.

DEAR SIR,

By same mail as this letter I forward to you my Report upon California. In the face of the adverse criticism which Messrs. Read and Pell's Report has met with at the hands of various parties, the writing of a report upon California, the greatest wheat-producing State of the Union, has been a work requiring considerable time, more especially as I have to take an entirely opposite line from the majority of writers upon this subject.

Let me state briefly my position in regard to writing upon trans-Atlantic agricultural questions. I am an Anglo-American having interests in both countries. Of late years my attention has been directed to this continent, and I am not only engaged in practical agriculture, but I am constantly consulted in regard to land questions of various kinds, which along with the demands of regular business leads me into nearly every State in the Union. While seeing the show places of the States and Canada, I have lived and visited among many of the ordinary farmers. My intercourse with them is not that of a day or a week, but it goes on from one year's end to the other. While I see the lights, I also look upon the shadows of the American farmer's life. Notwithstanding the glorious climate, crops are much more uncertain here, and when depression does come it is a heavier burden than at home. In England the question generally resolves itself into one of rent, which apart from some unfortunate legislation is a question betwixt landlord and tenant; but here, when the evil day comes, as come it will in every country or clime, it is almost impossible to say how far matters will go. To show the depression which took place in Canada some three years ago, land could only be sold at half its former value, and western lands which now are readily taken up were absolutely unsaleable at any value.

Agriculture just now on this continent is fairly prosperous and more especially in the Western States, the result of an improved trade, of great crops, and of almost total failure in Europe. On this continent the wave of depression flowed over the country long before it struck Great Britain, and it recovered sooner, which along with the circumstances stated above made farming a profitable business. So in England the prospects of agriculture, I am glad to see, improve with the first flicker of commercial prosperity we have had for years.

After a great deal of thought and examination I have come to the conclusion that wheat cannot be produced so cheaply as it is generally supposed. In my report I have tried to bring this out, but to be brief, I wish to crystallize a few thoughts for the benefit of his Grace the President, and the other members of the Commission.

The causes which will operate against production are:—

1. Great crops, such as Providence has blest America with for three years past, cannot be reasonably expected to continue.
2. With the revival of trade freights will increase; they have done so very materially within the last twelve months.
3. Labour will rise, and the cost of production will visibly increase in this department.
4. Machinery will also increase in value, but probably this account will be balanced by improvements and simpler methods.
5. The wheat producing regions are constantly receding from the sea-board, which means enhanced cost of transit.

In regard to stock, it is more difficult to give a definite opinion, as the trade of exporting is yet in its infancy. It will perhaps be information to many, that for two years past beef has steadily risen in price, and perhaps never in the history of America were fat cattle so scarce and difficult to buy as to-day. This does not seem as if the British markets were to be swamped, while at the same time it speaks volumes for the stock feeders of America.

These remarks are respectfully submitted for your consideration.

I remain, &c.,
(Signed) JOHN CLAY, Jun.

W. A. Peel, Esq.,
8, Richmond Terrace, Whitehall,
London.

REPORT by JOHN CLAY, jun., on the STATE of CALIFORNIA, with some GENERAL REMARKS on AMERICAN AGRICULTURE.

Of the various States in the American Union, perhaps there is not one so interesting as California. There is a variety about it, a continual change of scene and manners, that is not to be found in any other part of North America. It is a cosmopolitan State, peopled by representatives of every race, who seem to thrive equally well within its confines, excepting the Red man, who here, as elsewhere, is doomed to extinction. Attracted by its golden illusions, thousands have been drawn here from all points of the globe. But apart from its hidden treasures amid the gulches of the Sierra Nevadas, the salubrity of its climate draws many a wanderer. In this respect it is a wonderful country. Through winter and summer, during spring and fall, the variations in temperature are not very marked, while the hottest day is never oppressive, owing to the dryness of the atmosphere. In summer time, during the afternoon, a cool breeze springs up, and the evenings and nights are most enjoyable. In such a climate the people are vigorous and full of that nervous energy which overcomes all difficulties. Men's spirits are ever buoyant and hopeful, and the motto of every one is—Excelsior. To glance briefly at the subject of climate, it is difficult to get reliable information. The State has done nothing towards gathering reliable data, and if it had not been for the kindness of one of the officials of the Central Pacific Railroad, no details could have been given. Observations have been made at their stations for several years past, and they afford a great deal of curious information. From these records it will be found that the rainfall in the Sacramento Valley averages annually 20 in. or thereabouts. The highest reading at any one spot is 29 in., and the lowest 16 in. In the San Joaquin Valley they have much less moisture, the highest reading there being 9½ in., and the lowest 4 in., while it is believed that at many points, more especially in the Mojave Desert, there is even less than the above small quantity. It may be said that certain sections of California are rainless, and unless irrigation is brought into play no vegetation will exist. From April till October, all over the State, little or no rain falls, and the sky is almost cloudless. Day after day of the most perfect weather is experienced, while the earth becomes parched, and the dust is fearful, making travelling most disagreeable. When rain does come it is in storms of two or three days. The mean temperature of the State, as stated above, varies very little; that of the inland counties is about 65 degrees, while on the coast it is a little lower; but to avoid any mistakes the actual figures will speak for themselves in regard to rainfall and temperature.

Climate.

Stations.	Latitude.	Longitude.	Height above Ocean.	Extent of Series.	Annual Mean of Rain in Inches.
	° ′	° ′	ft.		
Fort Reading	40 30	122 05	674	1852–1856	29.11
Red Bluff	40 10	122 15	307	1872–1877	18.41
Tehama	40 0	122 08	222	1870–1877	16.30
Chico	39 40	121 50	193	1871–1877	21.99
Marysville	39 21	121 30	67	1871–1877	17.46
Sacramento	38 34	121 28	30	1849–1877	18.75
Stockton	37 57	121 17	23	1854–1857 / 1871–1877	13.23
Modesto	37 40	120 55	91	1871–1877	9.60
Merced	37 20	120 26	171	1871–1877	9.36
Borden*	36 55	120 0	274	1875–1877	3.32
Tulare	36 14	119 18	282	1875–1877	4.83
Delano	35 43	119 12	313	1875–1877	4.03
Sumner	35 23	118 58	415	1875–1877	3.92

* Fort Miller, 25 miles north-east from Borden with a greater elevation of 128 feet, from a record of nearly seven years, receives an annual average of 18.99 inches.

MR. CLAY'S (JUN.) REPORT.

The Mean Annual Temperature of

Redding is	-	-	-	-	64 degs. 14–100
Red Bluff is	-	-	-	-	66 ,, 22 ,,
Chico is	-	-	-	-	62 ,, 46 ,,
Marysville is	-	-	-	-	63 ,, 62 ,,
Sacramento is	-	-	-	-	60 ,, 48 ,,
Stockton is	-	-	-	-	61 ,, 99 ,,
Modesto is	-	-	-	-	63 ,, 68 ,,
Merced is	-	-	-	-	63 ,, 16 ,,
Borden is	-	-	-	-	66 ,, 37 ,,
Tulare is	-	-	-	-	64 ,, 09 ,,
Delano is	-	-	-	-	68 ,, 64 ,,
Sumner is	-	-	-	-	68 ,, 29 ,,

CALIFORNIA CLIMATE.

The following table shows the mean temperature of January and July in various portions of California and other States and countries, taken from reliable sources :—

Place.	Jan.	July.	Difference.	Latitude.
	°	°	°	° ′
San Francisco	49	57	8	37 48
Monterey	52	58	6	36 36
Santa Barbara	54	71	17	34 24
Los Angeles	52	75	23	34 04
Jurupa	54	73	19	34 02
San Diego	51	72	21	32 41
San Luis Rey	52	70	18	33 15
Sacramento	45	73	28	38 34
Stockton	49	72	23	37 56
Humboldt Bay	40	58	18	40 44
Sonoma	45	66	21	38 18
St. Helena	42	77	35	38 30
Vallejo	48	67	19	38 05
Antioch	43	70	27	38 03
Millerton	47	90	43	37 00
Fort Jones	34	71	37	41 40
Fort Reading	44	82	38	40 28
Fort Yuma	56	92	36	32 43
Cincinnati	30	74	44	39 06
New York	31	77	42	40 37
New Orleans	55	82	27	29 57
Naples	46	76	30	40 52
Jerusalem	47	77	30	31 47
Honolulu	71	78	7	21 16
Mexico	52	65	13	19 26
Funchal	60	70	10	32 38
London	37	62	25	51 29
Dijon	33	70	37	47 25
Bordeaux	41	73	32	44 50
Mentone	40	73	33	43 41
Marseilles	43	75	32	43 17
Genoa	46	77	31	44 24
Algiers	52	75	23	36 47

Eastern and European readers can compare this general climate with theirs, and at once discover the difference :—

Places.	Jan.	Feb.	March.	April.	May.	June.	July.	August.	Sept.	Oct.	Nov.	Dec.	Average.
San Francisco	49	51	52	55	55	56	57	57	58	57	54	51	54
Vallejo	47	52	53	57	59	67	67	66	64	62	54	47	58
Sacramento	45	48	51	59	67	71	73	73	66	64	52	45	59
Millerton	47	53	56	62	68	83	90	83	76	67	55	48	66
Fort Reading	44	49	54	59	65	77	82	79	71	62	52	44	62
Fort Yumo	56	58	66	73	76	87	92	90	86	76	64	55	73
St. Helena	42	49	56	57	66	70	77	70	66	59	54	51	
Vacaville	43	53	55	62	66	72	74	73	72	66	60	43	52
Meadow Valley	34	37	41		61	66	71	68	57	52	44	36	
Fort Jones		37	43	49	51	61	71	68	62	51	41		
Grass Valley	27	37	38	44	49	52	63	58	53	53	43	36	46
New York	31	30	38	47	57	67	73	72	66	55	45	34	51
New Orleans	55	58	64	70	75	81	82	82	78	70	62	55	69
Steilacoom	38	40	42	48	55	60	64	63	57	52	45	39	50
London	37	40	42	46	53	58	62	62	57	50	44	40	49
City of Mexico	52	54	61	63	66	65	65	64	64	60	55	52	60
Naples	46	47	51	56	64	70	76	76	69	61	53	49	60
Funchal	60	60	62	63	64	67	70	72	72	67	64	60	65
Honolulu	71	72	72	74	76	77	78	79	78	76	74	73	75
Jerusalem	47	53	60	54	66	71	77	72	72	60	58	47	62
Canton	52	55	62	70	77	81	83	82	80	73	65	57	69
Nagasaki	43	44	50	61	69	77	80	83	75	66	53	47	62

Q 6574.

Such a climate distinctly divided into periods has much to favour as well as a great many disadvantages as regards the agriculturist. Once get the crops and there is no danger of harvesting. The difficulty is to get them. At some points a rainfall of 12 inches, or even less, will secure a good crop of wheat, but as a rule it takes 17 to 20 inches to produce an average yield. When irrigation is in vogue, no climate is so suitable as that of the State, and the most marvellous results follow the use of water while the management is thoroughly understood and well regulated. It is, however, believed that vast improvements will take place in this line, and at present most interesting experiments are being made to find out the character of the various soils so as to regulate the amount of water that they can absorb. Grand as the methods are, and notwithstanding the perfection of the system, it is believed by many of the most intelligent men in the State that irrigation is yet in its infancy, and that modern science will devise means of economising water to a large degree, so that the greater portion of the State may have the advantages which only a few districts at present enjoy. The climate seems to be naturally adapted to this style of agriculture and husbandry, and it seems as if providence will make the barren yet in reality fruitful plains of the San Joaquin Valley blossom under the influence of artificial moisture. Not a few persons (enthusiasts they are called) prophesy that the clear waters of the Sacramento River will some day or other spread a genial influence over the valley, which at present it drains. Those are conjectures which time can only fulfil.

California is a narrow strip of land lying alongside the Pacific Ocean. It is intersected by a chain of mountains called the Coast Range, the valleys of which run down to the coast, and are very prolific, possessing good soil and a temperate climate. Betwixt the Coast Range and the Sierra Nevadas lies a great valley, which is really the agricultural portion of the State. Two great rivers drain it, discharging their waters into the bay of San Francisco, the Sacramento, flowing from the North, and San Joaquin from the South. The former is navigable to Red Bluff; while it depends upon the winter rains how far the latter can be navigated. During a great part of the year it has not enough of water for carrying large steamers or barges. The above valley terminates on the north side at Mount Shasta, where the Sacramento rises, and on the south side at the Tejon Pass, where the Sierras and Coast Range join. South of this lies the Mojave Desert, and then passing through that arid plain the traveller comes into a fruitful country lying around Los Angelos and along the sea coast. The mountains are exceedingly rough and wild, being covered with wild grass and bush, and they afford excellent grazing for sheep and cattle, more especially during the winter, when the herbage is most succulent and feeding. Granite is the prevailing rock, and the soil of those valleys is simply pulverised stone probably brought down from the mountain sides and deposited there by glacial action. That soil is of a very rich description. It is better adapted to the growth of cereals than any other class of soil in America. It is full of potash, a chemical which does more to supply plants with life than any other substance. It is to this fact, this immense amount of potash, that the State of California has gone ahead of all others as a wheat producing country. But it is gradually being worked out, and the evidence we have collected tends to show that the fertility of the soil, is steadily decreasing. But apart from its climate and soil the general configuration of the State well adapts it for being commercially a grand success. In addition to those rivers which intersect its great central valley, railways have been run through it and carry the grain down to the sea board. They bring it to the wharves and store houses on the bay of San Francisco, without doubt one of the greatest harbours in the world. The navigator passing through the Golden Gate for the first time will scarce imagine that beyond its narrow channel lies an immense inland sea, in which all the fleets of the world might ride at anchor safe from the greatest storm. To this point comes all the wheat and produce of the State, and from thence it finds its way to all parts of the world. As a commercial centre San Francisco has no rival on the Pacific Coast; it commands the whole trade, and its growth, along with that of Chicago, is unparalleled in the history of the world. Thirty two years ago it was a mission station. To-day its population numbers, roundly speaking, 250,000 souls. Strange to say it is the only large city on the American Continent whose population has decreased during the last five years. The heathen Chinee and the disciples of Dennis Kearney have driven thousands away.

Thirty-two years ago the world was startled with the news of gold discoveries in California. A wanderer

General configuration.

The rise of agriculture.

detected the precious metal. Another Eldorado had been found. In the river beds, among the canyons and gulches, deep-bedded in the rocks, was the precious ore, and in search of it came many an adventurous spirit. Long, however, before those discoveries, the agricultural resources of the Pacific slope had been tested. In 1769, the missionaries of Spain had travelled on from Mexico. There in the choicest spots they had planted their vineyards, and out on the plains they kept their flocks and herds. The Redmen, half Mongolians, and of the lowest type, became in a certain degree their slaves, or at least were under their influence and control.

Combining the salvation of souls along with more earthly pursuits, those men met for many years with a certain measure of success; and while they taught the untutored savage many virtues, his mind became impregnated with an equal number of vices. The missions had been founded, reached the zenith of their power, and had almost sunk into oblivion ere the golden days of California began. A new world was opened as if by a magician's hands, and not even the imagination of the eastern mind could picture the wealth which was lying dormant there. Years of terrible excitement followed. The idol of Mammon became the god of the Pacific slope. But the great golden era came to an end. It was followed by that of silver. To-day both interests are far from flourishing. The spirit of olden times is not dead, but it has not so much to exist upon, for the precious ore is harder to get, and when won from its rocky fastness or sandy bed is not nearly so rich. In those early years, even in the midst of untold difficulties, the rush of immigration was tremendous. Thousands, regardless of the future, never dreaming of a collapse in the mining districts, flocked to the country. From the port of disembarkation they marched past a beautiful land, one flowing literally with milk and honey, and started into the barren mountains, lived like pigs, became worse than heathens, all for the love of gold. After years of prosperity came the decline of mining interests. Then in reality began the era of agriculture. The men were there, they did not wish to go back to their homes; so, forced in a large measure by stress of circumstances, they settled down to the more peaceful and less exciting pursuits of agriculture.

To-day agriculture is the leading industry in the State, and the wealth of California lies more in its farms than its mines. Gold gave it prestige, but grain will give it stability, and from the ranches will come the people who will build up and sustain the country, who will give it character and moral tone, for while the attraction of gold brought many an adventurous spirit, it also drew together an unprincipled lot of villains who have been, and are, a curse to one of the fairest spots on earth.

The Spaniard supplanted by the Anglo-Saxon.

During the reign of the missionaries numbers of Mexicans found their way up the coast or across the deserts towards this country. Many of them either bought or forcibly possessed themselves of vast tracts of land. Those their families held when the great rush took place. To-day scarcely a Mexican landowner remains. They have sold out to the more sturdy and pushing Anglo-Saxon.

The evils the landed system

In the eastern and western States we find the land divided into farms of medium size. It enables a country to be equally and fairly populated. Although the land does not produce larger crops the people are more contented. Villages stud the country, schools and churches become necessary leavening in a degree the dwellers around them. While this has been the policy of the East, that of the Pacific slope, from the force of circumstances, has been the opposite. Vast tracts of land are held by individuals which economically is fatal in most respects to the prosperity of the State. This is the rock upon which Californian agriculture has split: too much land for the capital employed. It is extraordinary with what tenacity a man will hold on to landed property. The merchant when hard pressed lets his goods go, and tries to make the best of it, but the possessor of lands catches at the last straw before he will yield his rights. In this manner the growth of the State has been dwarfed; for, while in the backwoods of Canada, and amid the prairies of the great West the policy of the different Governments laid the foundation of a magnificent people by sub-dividing the land into small properties, no such line of action could be followed in this State. As stated above, before it became the property of the American union its vast and fertile valleys had been taken possession of either by Mexicans or adventurers from other nations who, straying far from the haunts of civilization, had as they imagined buried themselves in this wonderful country. Here there is no land for the landless. For the poor man) that is, the man who has to earn his living by the sweat of his brow, there is a grand harvest or time of plenty for a few months, followed by hungry days during the remaining ones. The want of constant labour is the greatest enemy of the working man, and in California this is eminently the case, and sooner or later not only agriculture, but every interest in the State must suffer severely.

From the above facts, aided by the adverse manipulations of a vast railway corporation, which drains the pocket of the producer to the last extremity, and assisted by the excitement periodically more or less marked in all mining countries, the agriculture of California is in a very precarious position. Wheat growing has now become in many instances a gambling transaction upon a leviathan scale. The steady, old-fashioned yeoman of England would be considered little better than a mummy in California. When passing through the country on our tour of inspection, we often heard of men who, with scarce one sixpence to rub against another, had essayed to rent and cultivate 5,000 or 10,000 acres of land. They bought everything on credit, and paid their men's wages with borrowed money, raised at a ruinous rate of interest. With a good crop and high prices all went well, but when the day of adversity came, when drought or hot winds reduced their receipts by half, then the grand scheme collapsed. Castles in the air vanished into space. Driving one afternoon across the mighty fields of the Sacramento Valley the history of my driver told its own tale. Starting with a capital of 6,000 dollars, he had made money by renting land and producing wheat. Gradually his operations extended. The spirit of ambition and excitement of money-making led him deeper and deeper. A bad crop occurred, little cash came to hand, interest ran up at a fearful rate, compounded in genuine western fashion, till his creditors closed on him. "That broke me, sir," are the words still ringing in my ears. And what is the state of the wheat producers to-day, looked at from a financial point of view? Nearly every man engaged in this industry is poor and loaded down with debt, in the hands of outsiders, who control his actions. Theoretically, all over America wheat growing is a paying business, but practically it is the opposite. True it is that during the last few years men with large possessions have made considerable sums in this business, owing to the poverty of the crops in Europe, assisted by cheap land, cheap labour, and low freights; but go back on the history of American agriculture, and the result of investigation proves that immense landholders who follow the pursuit of wheat growing have in most cases made miserable failures. The majority of English writers who have made this the subject of investigation are led into the most extraordinary statements as to the cost of production; in fact many people believe that wheat can almost be produced for nothing. To meet this argument it is of no use going into figures; we produce a stronger refutation. If wheat can be produced at 50 cents a bushel, and delivered at Chicago or San Francisco, say, at 75 cents, one would naturally expect that the men who sell it at prices ranging from a dollar to a dollar and a half would become millionaires in a short time, as the quantities they produce are simply enormous. The cry of cheap produce is in a great measure a myth. The fact that most of the men who are supposed to produce so cheaply make but little money, considering their capital employed, tells its own tale.

The precarious position of the agriculturist.

California is the greatest wheat producing State in the Union. The quality of the grain is excellent, probably the finest in the world. The Sacramento Valley is one vast wheat field, one mass of grain of a golden colour, through the summer months. Nothing in our experience has astonished us so much as those vast plains devoted by man to one grand object, wheat raising. Occasionally the eye meets belts of wood, or vast vineyards or orchards, rich with some semi-tropical fruit, but the staple production is wheat. In fact the people talk of nothing but wheat. It is wheat from dawn to dewy eve, and from the persistency with which many stick to this subject a stranger would almost believe that wheat was to be the salvation of their souls when they passed over to the great majority. Your commissioners had the good fortune to see California under the most advantageous circumstances. There had been a season of great plenty and prosperity; perhaps the crops on the whole were the finest that the State had ever produced. After staying a few days in San Francisco, we started up the Sacramento Valley, which, as mentioned before, is by far the richest portion of the State. Nature has provided it with a navigable river, and on each side of this runs a railway, thus giving the wheat producers great facilities of sending grain to the seaboard, if the competition was not checked by the railways belonging to one corporation. In an extended tour through this district we visited many of the finest farms in the Valley. After examining them carefully any impartial observer must admit that the soil is the most prolific, so far as cereals are concerned, in the world, and that, taking advantage of its natural capacity, the wheat raisers are taxing it above its power.

Its wheat producing powers.

The ranches, as they are called, vary in size from 60 acres to 60,000. To manage such a farm as the latter requires the skill of a general, and immense executive power. But as a rule no such thing exists. There is an utter want of management. Most of the places are conducted upon principles in which the first idea of order is wanting. On those vast farms we expected to find everything carried on as if they were commercial establishments. We thought we should meet the owners in their offices with a staff of managers and foremen, who were trained to economise and work out details. Instead of such a state of things, you would see the proprietors, or renters as the case might be, driving wildly from place to place, relying on their own individual exertions for carrying forward the work. In fact, "they are penny wise and pound foolish." On farms so vast in extent as those Californian ranches, the management lies not in a personal superintendence. It is brains working and guiding the assistants; it is keen insight into the state of the markets; it is the calculating mind, which can keep track of details without seeing much of them, which are the elements of success in such gigantic enterprises.

When three to five hundred men are employed and all boarded, as is the custom in the State, the work of the commissariat is a heavy one. Scarcely a ranche man could tell us the cost of keeping his men. In some cases the leakage appeared to be enormous and most exhaustive. In this line alone a good living might be made on some farms by saving. We had occasion to talk with some lumber-men a few days ago. They conducted a business alike in some degree to the above, employing a large staff of hands. They had the average cost per man exactly calculated. It was the low figure of 23 cents per day. From only one firm in California could we get statistics on this point, and the daily cost per man was 37½ cents. At this point we copy from our diary a few remarks penned one evening at a country hotel. They are not exactly complimentary, but they state the case of the Californian agriculturist as it appears to our mind. "The most striking feature of California is the energy of the people. No idle persons are seen, all are working as if it were their last efforts; under the burning sun they toil on from morning till night, resting only when the sun goes down beyond the mountains. More especially is this the case with the farmers. As a class they are poor. Many of them, owning in name vast tracts of land, are miserably involved and loaded down with debt. In summer life is little better than slavery, the man who owns almost a kingdom is seen with his coat off doing the work of a two-dollar-a-day hand. With such a class of men farming can never be a grand success, as it should be on this Pacific slope. If the Californian ranche-man would sit down and think, if he would, when time is not so scarce, travel about and find out what improvements are going on in the other parts of the State or Union, if he would systematise his labour, if he would study the lines of commerce and gain a knowledge of the best way to market his grain or get advances on it, then there would be more comfort and ease. What do we find? In this land, one of the richest in the world, the farmers are ignorant, conceited, and self-opiniative, conducting their business in the most slip-shod manner, cropping their lands year after year with wheat, no rest for the weary in their system, and when they have got the grain they waste it during cutting and threshing in the most lavish manner. In fact, in all our travels in either Europe or America we have never met anything so destructive as the system of agriculture pursued in the rich valley of the Sacramento. It is not a lack of energy, it is a want of foresight and system." These ideas are the result of personal observation as well as being opinions gathered from some of the most intelligent farmers of the State, who see with alarm the great damage that is being annually wrought on the country at large through a reckless and foolish system.

Practical management. Leaving this subject, let us turn to the practical part of wheat growing as followed in the valleys of California. Ploughing begins in the fall as soon as the rain comes and moistens the ground sufficiently, which generally happens about the middle of October. The ploughs universally used are double-mould-boards drawn by four to six horses or mules, the driver sitting on the plough. Seeding commences at once and continues till February, when it stops. The very first defect in farming is noticeable here. It is shallow ploughing. Second comes careless sowing and poor harrowing or cultivation. In good seasons the growth of wheat is enormous. Harvest commences about the middle of June and continues for at least four months. In this country grain will stand in the fields for this long period without any harm or much loss, except that it becomes very dry and loses much of the natural sap which belongs to it. So great is the evaporation that grain in its shipment to Europe will sometimes gain 15 or 20 per cent. of weight on the voyage round the "Horn." The universal system of cutting is to use a header, an implement about 16 ft. wide and which can be regulated to cut any height, the general custom being to leave 3 feet of straw on the ground and take about 18 inches along with the grain. This clumsy looking machine is pushed by six mules. The grain as it is cut falls on to an endless canvas and is carried by it into immense waggons which travel alongside. Four of those waggons drawn by a pair of mules are necessary to keep a machine in full play. When full, they are driven to a point some 200 hundred yards away, and the short straw is emptied on to a rick. These ricks are about 20 yards square and 8 feet high, always standing in pairs with an open space of 6 or 8 feet between them. Day after day those headers go on, no stop on account of the weather. Very often a threshing machine is placed at some convenient point, the headers begin to cut round and round it, and the grain is threshed right off. An ordinary machine keeps four headers going, each of those requires four waggons, so it can be imagined that the scene is a very lively one and full of interest. On the large ranches most of the grain is manufactured in this way, but modern invention has produced an implement which combines both header and thresher, and at one point we had the pleasure of seeing such a machine at work. It was a header 17½ feet in width with a small threshing machine placed on a platform behind. The grain was elevated by an endless canvas into the machine and a constant stream of wheat run into bags which were sown up, slipped off and picked up by a man with a waggon behind. This enormous machine is pushed by 20 mules, and four men are employed upon it; one drives the mules, another steers, a third sews up the bags, and the fourth looks after the belts, &c. Thirty acres per day fall before this mammoth implement. The price is at present $2,000, and we must say it is a marvel among many marvellous sights. Except at the large ranches, reaping is finished first and then threshing commences.

As we drove over the country, flat as a pancake in most places, the traveller observes endless piles of straw, always in pairs. A steam engine, often a portable but sometimes drawn by horses, and as a rule a straw burner, along with a separator, are placed alongside those ricks. The latter is placed exactly opposite the division of those mounds. Into the opening a waggon is drawn on which is placed a derrick. From its top hang two pulleys, through which ropes run attached at one end to immense forks. The other ends of those are fastened to a light two-wheeled machine drawn by horses. A man handles each fork. It is so constructed that it catches a large quantity of the straw. The horses are moved forward, the forks are drawn up with their load near to the top of the derrick, the attendant jerks a rope, and the grain, loosed from the fork, falls on to the waggon platform. Two men are standing on it with hand forks, and from where they are placed a framework, with an endless canvas, spans the distance betwixt them and the separator. On to this they fork the straw; a mechanical arrangement placed above this feeder regulates the amount, so that careless feeding does no harm. In goes the headed grain; chaff and straw pass out at one end, and at the side, grain, ready for market, runs into bags. As soon as one of those is filled it is sewn up and placed in a pile near by, and left there till it is teamed to a depôt or warehouse. Two ordinary piles of straw will generally yield 250 bags containing over two bushels each, and a machine will average about 1,000 bags a day. They have thus to move four times a day; no time is lost; as soon as the place is cleaned up, the belt which connects the engine is thrown off, the endless canvas is slid on to the derrick waggon with its forks and rope, horses are hooked to the various machines, and away they go to the next point, generally less than 200 yards distant. All goes on like clockwork, every man knows his own post, and in 12 to 17 minutes the machine is in working order. Thrashing is very often done by contract. The price last season was 11 cents. a bag, the contractor doing everything except boarding his men. The cost of labour and horses is over 50 dollars per day. After paying interest on machine wear and tear, a considerable profit is realised if an average of 1,000 bags per day can be reached. At this rate piles of bags filled with wheat soon accumulate. Left with a slight covering of straw to protect them from the sun, those remain undisturbed till the teamster comes to haul them to the shipping point. At all the depôts and wharves large warehouses may be seen either of wood or brick. Many of those are built by companies of farmers, others are run by private individuals. The general charge for storage is a dollar a ton of 2,000 lbs., a paying price, as the buildings are put up at little cost, and the expense of handling is very little, as in all cases the railroad runs alongside the building. When the grain passes into the store a receipt is given, and upon this guarantee of weight it is sold, so that a farmer or merchant has nothing else to do but trnsfer his receipt at time of sale. Parties not wishing to selean borrow money on this receipt to at least two-thirds of its value. Last year money was lent up to 200 dollars a ton at the rate of 8 per cent., a decline of about 4 per cent. in one year. For some time previous the regular rate had been 1 per cent. a month, and in old days 1½ was often charged. Nothing indicates returning prosperity to any agricultural country so much as a low rate of interest. Under the old system of 20 per cent. per annum no industry could thrive.

The average production. The average production of wheat per acre is exceedingly difficult to estimate. In the Surveyor-General's report we find the estimate for 1878 put at 10 bushels per acre, while the agricultural report of the United States places it at 17 bushels per acre. There is a great discrepancy here, and one not easily accounted for, except that those statistics are very much the result of random calculation. The report of the Surveyor-General is derived from figures supplied by the county assessors, and it is likely that farmers will put their average yield as low as possible when they are to be rated at the value of their property. The official returns of the United States Government place the average wheat yield at 12·2 bushels per acre. Very few practical men believe that it is so low. In the worn out lands of the Eastern States it may be somewhat near the average, but if it is true of the whole continent, Great Britain would have little cause to fear competition. In the west, the great producing region of America, it is much higher. The prairie farms of Minnesota and Dakota produced 16 to 18 bushels, and in some cases more. Certain it is, if the average production is nearly what it is stated to be, the American wheat producer is in a much worse plight than his English brother. In California it is much more difficult to get at the correct data than any other State in the union, so varied in a sense is the climate. The whole success of wheat growing there depends on the rainfall, otherwise the surroundings, both as to quality of soil and situation, with a long period of rainless days, are unequalled. In the San Joaquin Valley, where irrigation is not employed, they reap fair crops about three years out of five. On some of the ranches there we estimated the yield at about 15 bushels per acre, but on irrigated lands it is much higher, the average being about 26 to 28 bushels to a certainty. In the Sacramento Valley drought and hot winds, while the wheat is in the milk, are also the great enemies. 12 inches of rain in the latter valley means a failure, 17 insures a crop, and 20 produces an average, or about it.

The conditions are therefore very unfavourable for a correct calculation. For the past year many of the ranch-men place the average production at 18 bushels per acre, and we are inclined to think they have not overstepped the mark. The crop was an enormous one; in fact, the country was overflowing with wheat of the very best quality. Threshing would not be finished before the rains set in, and granaries were rising up at every depôt in anticipation of the great surplus, while the amount of shipping in sight was very small in comparison to the amount required to carry this food to the various countries where it is needed. The San Francisco shippers expected to export at least 850,000 tons this year. Allowing a very liberal quantity for home consumption, the whole amount would not come up to the above average, considering the number of acres cultivated or supposed to be in cultivation.

The cost of production. Taking the calculation of the farmers themselves, and placing the average yield for this season, considering the enormous crop, at 18 bushels, the gain to the cultivator will not be large if he has to sell at 85 cents a bushel, delivered at San Francisco, equal to about 72 cents at home, for it takes about one sixth on an average to send it to this point. The average cost of cultivation, delivery, &c., as taken from statistics derived from farmers, is eight dollars per acre. Thus:—

18 bushels at, say, 72 cents - 12.96
Cultivation - - 8.00

Gain - - 4.96 dolls.

We may ask, at this price where is the great gain to the farmer if he pays a rent for his land valued at 50 dollars per acre, or if he calculates interest at 8 per cent. on that amount. We are putting the working expenses at the lowest rate. Then it must be kept in mind that much of the land, generally one third on every ranche, lies idle or is fallowed, and of course rent or interest must be charged against it, which raises the cost of production; but place this item against the less cost in getting a volunteer crop, which needs neither seed nor labour, and it is probable that the above will just cover the various expenses. Then we must consider that this calculation is based on a very high average production. Suppose it declines to 15 bushels, which is considered a fair yield for the State, the profits will be reduced to nil. Go further still, reduce the average to 12 bushels as may happen some year. What then is the result? But the most practical point of the case lies in the fact that all the wheat growers, large and small, with few exceptions, have made no headway, and are loaded down with debt. From the enormous sums handled by those parties we would naturally have expected to find most of them capitalists, but it is not the case. This is the best proof that wheat has been produced at figures just touching cost or a little above it. Our experience among the ranch-men teaches us that they cannot afford to place wheat year after year on board ship at San Francisco below a dollar per bushel, which means from 48s. to 50s. in England, say:—

	s.
Eight bushels at 4s.	32
Freight at the rate of 14s. per qr.	14
Charges in Liverpool, &c., say	2
	48

There is every probability it will be above than below that point. At present prices in California wheat can be delivered in England at less than 45s. per quarter, but it does not pay, and wheat at present is below an average price. From 1863 to 1878 the average price of wheat in the States was 1$\frac{20}{100}$ dollars a bushel, but during the last eight of these years the average only reached 1$\frac{03}{100}$ dollars, and that low price was in our opinion the result of great depression, which reduced the consumption and also cheapened the production. It was an occurrence well worthy of note that the price of wheat fell just about the same percentage as other materials. During the first three of the latter years, just before the great wave of commercial distress swept over the States, the average price was 1$\frac{21}{100}$ dollars per bushel. Last season, both in Chicago and San Francisco, the price ranged about that figure, and as we write at present, wheat in the former city is selling freely for one dollar, in the face of the largest crop we have had throughout the world for many years. When wheat is selling in Chicago for a dollar a bushel, it will bring over 45s. per quarter in Liverpool. This year, perhaps, the production of wheat per head in America has reached its height for some years to come. Forced by hard times from Europe and the Eastern States, men have absolutely rushed to the West, but immigration will decline with the return of prosperity in commerce and trade. In this respect the tide is fairly turned. The Western farmer and the Californian ranch-men will have enhanced prices to pay for everything they use. Machinery will be dearer, freights will be higher, and the land will produce less under the unfortunate system forced upon them by circumstances, but all tracing to the want of capital. In California at least the days of cheap wheat are past. Land has become too valuable; the stock-raiser and the fruit-grower intrude upon this territory, once virgin soil and producing fabulous crops. Nothing distresses the farmer of those fair valleys so much as the steady decline per acre of the wheat product. What they want is a mixed system of husbandry, one that feeds as well as draws from the land.

The annual export. The export of wheat from the State of California for the last eight years has been as follows:—

The following table shows the number of vessels engaged in the direct wheat and flour trade, and the tons and value of the flour and wheat carried by them:—

	Vessels.	Tons.	Value.
			$
1872–73	339	531,800	19,166,000
1873–74	247	455,300	19,400,000
1874–75	265	508,800	16,134,300
1875–76	174	373,300	14,751,800
1876–77	307	604,100	21,335,100
1877–78	109	259,200	11,580,100
1878–79	269	580,100	19,842,900
1879–80	273	600,000	21,538,200
Totals	1,983	3,912,600	143,748,400

MR. CLAY'S (JUN.) REPORT.

The following are details as to the nationality and tonnage of ships engaged in the wheat trade.

CALIFORNIA WHEAT FLEET for eight years.

National Flag.	1872-73. Vessels.	1872-73. Tons.	1873-74. Vessels.	1873-74. Tons.	1874-75. Vessels.	1874-75. Tons.	1875-76. Vessels.	1875-76. Tons.	1876-77. Vessels.	1876-77. Tons.	1877-78. Vessels.	1877-78. Tons.	1878-79. Vessels.	1878-79. Tons.	1879-80. Vessels.	1879-80. Tons.
American	136	161,300	91	121,200	62	87,800	82	115,100	94	133,000	50	84,100	83	127,800	113	170,000
British	162	137,600	123	124,000	179	124,400	83	101,000	178	208,400	55	67,800	162	198,300	140	174,000
German	26	15,700	9	7,500	8	7,100	3	2,900	13	11,400	2	2,200	11	10,100	6	5,000
French	8	3,700	20	11,200	12	7,100	4	2,700	12	7,400	1	800	7	4,200	7	3,900
Hawaiian	3	1,900	—	—	—	—	—	—	1	500	—	—	1	900	—	—
Dutch	2	1,000	1	1,700	—	—	—	—	—	—	—	—	—	—	—	—
Italian	1	700	2	1,200	—	—	1	800	4	3,500	—	—	2	1,500	—	—
Norwegian	1	500	1	200	1	800	—	—	3	2,600	1	600	3	2,900	4	4,300
Austrian	—	—	—	—	1	400	—	—	—	—	—	—	—	—	—	—
Peruvian	—	—	—	—	2	2,100	—	—	—	—	—	—	—	—	—	—
Swedish	—	—	—	—	—	—	1	1,100	2	1,900	—	—	—	—	1	600
Nicaraguan	—	—	—	—	—	—	—	—	—	—	—	—	—	—	1	300
Honduras	—	—	—	—	—	—	—	—	—	—	—	—	—	—	1	500
Totals	339	322,400	247	267,000	265	229,700	174	223,600	307	368,700	109	155,500	269	345,700	273	358,600

This year, as we said above, it is expected to reach the enormous total of 850,000 tons, by far the largest amount ever sent out, but it is not likely we shall ever see such an abundance again, except under extraordinary circumstances. With all the land it is possible to place under cultivation, with an enormous yield consequent on a favourable season, we may expect that the state has reached the zenith of its greatness.

As it had gold and silver eras, both of which declined, it is not unnatural to suppose that with wheat it will be the same. Now that the virgin soil has been nearly all broken up, the decline may be slow, but it will be sure and steady. In the Prairie States the same rule holds good. Illinois, one of the older of those States, and in former days exporting large quantities of wheat, has almost stopped doing so. Further west, virgin soils send in their vast increase, and swell the staple production every year. But even in America virgin soil will run out, while the longer we live the great wheat-producing tracts are removed further from the seaboard. Every mile away from water carriage means an enhanced price, and gives the home producer the advantage. If the valley of the Genessee, and many other famous portions of the Eastern states, and Canada produced as much wheat as they did when the forest was first cleared away, it would be a sorry day for the British farmers. Nature seems to give compensation in all those matters. The labour of clearing the backwoods is over; the primeval forest is almost a thing of the past in the cultivated regions, but while the wheat is more easily produced, the freight is greater, and many scourges unknown in the days of old make the profits of production much more uncertain.

To conclude this portion of our report, we are not afraid of the vast wheat fields of California. There the wheat raisers are not any better off with their vast possessions than those at home. The shadow of the distressed agriculturist rises up in that golden land with as much emphasis and reason as at home. Why? Simply for the reason as we stated before, a general depression of trade, a lack of confidence among the ranks of commercial men, made havoc with business. Even with low rates for shipping, with average crops and other things in their favour for the last few years, the money lender has been the great money maker, and the farmer has just been able to keep his head above water. If wheat cannot be produced in California and laid down in Liverpool at less than 45s. to 50s. per quarter (it is impossible to calculate very closely), it is not at all probable that any other part of the United States or Canada can do it for any length of time.

Of the other cereals, barley is the only one grown to any extent. A very large acreage of it is annually sown, but it is almost entirely a low quality, only suited for feed purposes, and on this grain all the horses and mules of the country are fed. In certain favoured portions of the State, notably on the shores of the Bay of San Francisco, some of the very finest malting barley is produced. It is perhaps the best we ever saw, but the production is so limited that it does not visibly have any outside effect. The total export for some years back has been about 20,000 tons per annum, and that amount cannot be much increased. If the price of barley demanded it, perhaps double the quantity might find its way to Europe, but at present there is not much prospect of this being the case.

The stock-raising interest of the Pacific slope is an immense one. Vast herds of cattle and countless flocks of sheep roam not only over the State of California but also among the hills and valleys of Oregon and Washington territory. Unlike the wheat interest, it does not affect the British farmer, but it has, of course, indirectly, an influence upon him. The Surveyor-General's Report gives the following figures :—

	Horned cattle.	Sheep.	Hogs.
1878	525,565	4,655,543	372,642
1879	595,933	3,755,781	322,650

The figures are also collected by the assessors of the various counties, and from what I can gather, they are far from correct. In the item of sheep there is nearly a decrease of a million in a single year, which is a very large number to dispose of in a single season along with the produce of these flocks, although there is little doubt but what there was a large actual decrease on account of the low price of wool, which made ranch-men turn their attention to cattle as a more profitable investment. Thousands of those sheep were sent over the mountains to the Prairie States, from whence they find their way to the eastern markets. The value of cattle and sheep had risen greatly just previous to our visit, or at least within 12 months. Good four year old steers were worth 35 to 40 dollars, and wethers were making $2\frac{25}{100}$ dollars, while the best class of wool was worth 30 cents. The average of wool would be about 24 cents. As we said above, no beef or mutton finds its way to the English market directly except it is packed, and nearly the whole of the wool is shipped to Boston, so that, as a fact, the competition is not great; but stock-raising is a growing business, only yet partially understood on the Pacific slope. The State of Oregon possesses, perhaps, the most remarkable climate in the world. It is thoroughly temperate and suited to the production of cereals, and it is a most remarkable grazing region. With the decline of the wheat interest there will be a gradual uprising of stock-raising till it is likely the latter will overtop the former. Already most of the wheat growers have vast herds of sheep. Through the summer they graze them on the foot-hills and mountains, which produce during the spring months a splendid herbage. Then they drive them down to the stubbles and alfalfa pastures of the plains, where they graze on the wheat straw left standing, and the natural grazing which springs up after the crop is cleared. The future of the stock-raisers on the Pacific slope is much brighter than that of the wheat grower. Under the present system, which the latter pursues, the result is ruin sooner or later, but the former has an almost illimitable field in the way of improvement. The fostering influence of the climate matures rapidly all classes of stock. Lean kine are never seen. Even during the driest days of the long summer the cattle and horses are fat and flourishing. They need, however, to improve the quality of their stock. To this fact they have given little or no attention. No State needs pure-bred cattle more than California. Doubtless there are a few herds of shorthorns in the State, but they are a mere drop in the bucket. They must cater to the demand for first-class beef before they can compete with our English market, for it is certain that some day or other the surplus cattle of California will find their way to England. In such an era as the present, when no one can conjecture what improvements or inventions will take place, it is impossible to say by what means they will reach it, but certain is is they will come, and the cattle men of California, and those other States, will be wise in their generation if they commence at once to improve their cattle, which are of every imaginable breed, size, and colour—a heterogeneous lot, with neither character nor quality. Of such native cattle those in California are by far the best as a class, without doubt the result of the fostering climate.

<small>The beef trade of the States and Canada.</small>

The supply of good shipping steers here as elsewhere is far below the demand. Just now in Canada there is scarce a fat steer for sale. In Chicago any thing of a fair quality is at once bought up for the Eastern and English markets. The real fact is, that while Great Britain was more than ready to take American beef, that country was not ready to supply it. There was more than enough of an inferior quality, but none to spare of the superior, and in New York to-day good beef commands almost as much as it does in London. With an immense and yearly increasing consumption in America itself, and also an increased demand for Europe, we are confident that it will take all the efforts of the stock-raisers to cope with the demand. Nearly every portion of Amercia suitable for grazing purposes is covered with cattle and sheep. In some of the States, such as Colorado, they have more than enough. What is wanted is a better class of cattle. Quick returns are the motive of the farmer in these days, and it takes capital to produce this result. In this very respect the British farmer is ahead of his transatlantic competitors. In the older States the production of cattle will not be much above the consumption. It is those Prairie States which have to give our home markets their supply. Some three years ago the western graziers began to see this demand arising, and "as coming events cast their "shadows before them," the most enlightened and shrewdest began to prepare as rapidly as possible. Thousands of Short-horns and Hereford bulls are now upon the plains, improving their quality and impressing their forms upon the scrubs of the prairies, but as Rome was not built in a day, as the tree takes years to grow, it is impossible to convert scrubs into even high grades in a short space of time. We shall need to wait for years till we see even a decent class of stock upon those ranches. In California, assisted by the climate, they can attain those results quicker than in any other portion of the Union, and it is likely that their distance from market will be balanced by the superiority of their cattle and early maturing propensities, nurtured by their soil, grasses, and climate, and if California be far removed from the centre of consumption she gains more than her loss in this respect by the superior quality of her products. In a former report, I took occasion to impress the immense competition we should need to meet in this respect, but I think the British farmer can so far modify it by turning their serious attention to the improvement of their stock, most of which can stand a large measure of improvement. The ranch-men of the plains are making gigantic efforts to improve their stock. They are hunting the whole country for pure-blood bulls, and it is no uncommon occurrence for one party alone to ship a couple of hundred to improve one herd. Not a few of those western stock-raisers own from three to five hundred pure-blood bulls. Those will work a wonderful renovation if we calculate that each bull will get at least thirty calves per annum. It is almost impossible to define how far this business may be carried. It is a mere question of how fast pure-bred animals can be bred. In the west at any rate the supply is far below the demand, for although parties may purchase them wholesale, they cannot be bred very rapidly. For the last three years there has been a steady increase in the value of pure-bred bulls. Three years ago a stock-raiser informed us that he had purchased all his bulls at 70 dollars each, next season they were 85 dollars, and last year they cost upwards of 100 dollars each, while next spring, so great is the present demand, he may have to again raise his price to 120 or 130 dollars, at which price farmers can raise this class of cattle very profitably. Within the last 12 months all classes of stock have risen considerably in the States and Canada, and good steers, instead of being cheaper, can scarcely be bought. These facts bear out the general tone of our arguments as regards wheat. With an increased supply comes an increased and seemingly never failing demand. There is a bottom price at which everything can be raised at, and that price was evidently reached some two years ago in America. While it lasted English landlords and tenants justly got scared; but ere another 12 months pass away we shall not be so much afraid of American competition. It would be a bad thing for the British farmer if he had no one to stir him up. The severity of the ordeal will do him good; necessity will become in this, as in other cases, the mother of invention, and new modes and more liberal management will enable the home agriculturist to stand up against the world.

Near the head of the San Joaquin Valley, right in view of the Tejon Pass, where the Sierra Nevadas and Coast Range join in the form of a horse shoe, lies the Haggin and Carr Ranche, an immense property, some 330,000 acres in extent. It is, properly speaking, a vast commercial enterprise conducted on the most enlightened principles, guided by judgment and great administrative ability. So far as the management of a farm is concerned, it was by far the most striking case we met in California, in fact we do not know of any other place equal to it in size, where all the operations of arable and stock farming are carried forward on such a magnificent scale. The estate is divided into various ranches, each used for a distinctive purpose. Thus one place is devoted almost to horses, where a most beautiful lot of thorough-bred brood mares are kept, and, like the wild horses of the prairies, a stallion runs with the mares which are being bred to him. Next come the head-quarters of great flocks of sheep; and at another point we came across an immense herd of fat cattle brought in from the outlying portions of the estate, which are used as vast runs for sheep and cattle. Away in the mountains we saw a cattle ranche, from whence the bands of steers are drafted to be fed on the alfalfa pastures. To work and conduct this place from three to five hundred men are employed. The proprietors do not live upon it. Away in an office in San Francisco sits the master mind, but an able superintendent, a general in his way, stays at one of the ranches. Under him are able overseers; all men of experience, with little to say. Expert book-keepers are employed, and from early morning till the sun goes down work goes on with clockwork regularity. It is very unlike other Californian farms in this respect. As a usual occurrence all is hurry-scurry. The farmer tries to be everywhere, and as a consequence is seldom at the right place when required. At this ranche it is different. Dr. Thorton, the able manager, drives about the estate quietly and calmly. There is alway time to be civil and courteous to the lowest of the employés, and a grin of uncommon satisfaction comes over the Chinaman whom he may happen to meet. The first rudiment of a Celestial's education here seem to be able to salute the chief of the ranche with the words, "How do you do, big bossie." The employés also work steadily, and they are well paid. Wages range from a dollar a day with board up to five dollars for skilled workmen, while the overseers and foremen are also generously treated. The wages book is a marvel of neatness and skilfully kept, as the firm act in a certain degree as bankers to many of their workmen. A large number of Chinamen are employed. They make excellent workmen and receive a dollar a day, but they board themselves. Three surveyors find employment in this place, and a regular force of canal builders are kept. The work of improvement goes on all the time, and neither labour nor expense is spared to make the place complete. All crops are grown by irrigation, and about 40,000 acres are kept in regular cropping. Of wheat there are 20,000 acres, about 8,000 in barley, and the remaining 12,000 are devoted to Alfalfa. The water is drawn from the Kern River, and is conducted by large canals to the various points on the estate. It is led from those into ditches of various sizes, and passing through sluices whole fields are flooded at a time. The water is guarded by checks which retain it till enough is put on, when another sluice is opened and the over-flow passes on to the next field. To attain proper and economical systems of irrigation the most accurate surveys are necessary. It is not too much to say that they are perfect on this estate, and at one point one man can irrigate 1,000 acres in a week. For cereals, flooding land once a year is sufficient, but for Alfalfa it requires more frequent watering. On land that is almost an arid desert, without irrigation, the average yield of wheat is 26 bush. per acre, about 30 bush. of barley, and 12 to 14 tons of hay over and above grazing. The most wonderful crop is Alfalfa, or Lucerne. It luxuriates in hot weather, as it sends its roots deep into the soil. It can be cut three or four times a season and be grazed all fall and winter. If the water is turned on, say first day of the month, a crop of hay can be cut, drawn, and stacked before the first of the following month. The rapidity of growth is enormous, and the amount of feed is larger than from any other crop we know of. Much of this Alfalfa is also grazed, and all of it is pastured by cattle or sheep during the winter, while the hay is fed off by cattle also. They get fat on it alone. The stubbles are also economised. No sooner is the grain threshed than sheep are brought in from the ranches and allowed to pasture most part of the winter. They clean off the straw and manure the land. Over the pasture land roam about 12,000 cattle, 75,000 sheep, and 2,000 horses, along with a number of hogs, the census of which had not been taken lately. The

<small>The Haggin and Carr ranches.</small>

cattle, &c. are tended by Mexicans. Chinamen do the cooking, while representatives of all nations are employed at other work. The average cost of keeping a man per day is 37½ cents, equal to about 10s. per week. Twenty cents a day keeps a mule or horse, and land can be ploughed at about one dollar per acre. Fencing cost 500 dollars per mile. 2,000 cattle, 10,000 sheep, 5,000 lambs are annually sent to the market; up to this time the horses have been allowed to breed up. This year 350,000 bushels of wheat will be disposed off. The taxes are at the rate of $1\frac{67}{100}$ per cent, and the place is rated at about ⅓ of the actual cash invested, which amounts to between three and four million dollars.

Another noticeable feature here, as on many of the large Californian farms is the vast workshops which are situated at the principal places of the estate. Carpenters and smiths are busy at work, and turning-lathes, and saws are running constantly. Waggons are built, and much of the machinery, if it is not actually made, is kept in splendid order. The grand idea is to live as much as possible within themselves, and on such a place as the Haggin and Carr Ranche, they can afford to do it. As elsewhere in California, the buildings and barns are miserable both in architecture and usefulness. They may be suited to the country but there is a want of taste displayed throughout. The magnificent climate does not call for expensive erections and the country is too new for the agriculturists to indulge in too many luxuries of this kind.

It will pay any traveller, whether he be agriculturist or not, to spend a day or two at such a place as this. It is most interesting to watch the various operations and the modes of procedure practised. Machinery of the most improved kind is used. No improvement takes place but it gets a fair trial, and it is really wonderful to see how implements take the place of manual labour. Nothing can equal the rapidity with which a load of hay is hoisted on the stack, and away goes the waggon to get reloaded. It makes an old country farmer feel ashamed, and stirs up a spirit of ambition in every practical man. Nor is the possession of this immense ranche a mere hobby. Business men own and control it, and they have put their money into it to realise a fair interest. Looking ahead, the parties saw that the future wealth of California was in her land rather than in her mines, they invested their money in the belief that while gold and silver may vanish, or at least the profits of finding them may decline, land is certain and sure to maintain a fair value, higher or lower as the trade and commerce of the world increases or decreases. Up to this time, it has been a case of putting in capital year after year, but this season a return is expected, and it is hoped to make the estate a great and lasting success. Certain it is that having once put their hands to the plough, the proprietors have never turned back.

But farming upon a leviathan scale is not the only result. Colonisation has been tried with considerable success. A large number of Italians and Portuguese who are well adapted to this climate, have been induced to settle down and become cultivators of the soil. Sections of 200 to 500 acres have been laid off, and neat houses and commodious barns have been built. The tenants are provided with, horses and implements and all other necessaries. The rent consists of ¼ of their whole produce. To begin with all those men are poor, but many of them have done well, and are gradually clearing of their indebtedness to the proprietor. As the grain is threshed by machines belonging to the firm the exact amount is easily obtained. The charge for doing this part of the business is 7 cents. a bushel. Of course everything is raised by irrigation. Small though the percentage of the rent seems to be for the advantages given, the system is an exceedingly profitable one. Another profit is derived from supplying those parties with stores of various kinds, in fact something like the truck system of Great Britain prevails, but in a modified degree.

The custom of renting land in California is very prevalent. Vast tracts are hired by the year, generally without lease, only short agreements being used, and the rent is almost invariably paid in shares, that is, a percentage of the grain grown. As a rule the farmer gives land and buildings, while the tenant provides teams and machinery. At other times, as at the Haggin and Carr ranche, the proprietor supplies everything necessary to start a farm. In the Sacramento Valley we came across a good specimen of a rented farm. Many years ago the present proprietor had taken it up as a sheep ranche, never dreaming of raising wheat upon it. For several years sheep and cattle ranged freely over the whole of this country. When the wheat rage began, the owner turned his ranche of 10,000 acres into cultivation, and bought a large sheep run among the mountains which bordered for a considerable distance with his lowland property, still sticking to his flocks and herds, and owning a warehouse for storing grain which is a business in itself; the arable land has been rented to another party, and a system of agriculture commenced, which is at once suitable to wheat growing and stock raising. Thus 3,300 acres are ploughed every fall, and seeded down with wheat, this is headed, next summer, and allowed to volunteer, that is, no seed is sown. A splendid growth of wheat springs up from that which falls while it is being cut. Next summer this is again headed, and the sheep from the mountains come down and pasture it as soon as threshing is completed. Here they will graze from August till late in the fall, or even all winter if it is necessary. Such a system suits admirably, as the grass upon the mountains gets very dry and scanty during summer. After being grazed off, this land is ploughed and summer fallowed, so that the whole farm goes through a course of summer fallow once in three years, thus:—

  3,333 acres in seeded wheat.
  3,333 „ volunteer „
  3,334 „ summer fallow.

  10,000, altogether.

Supposing the average to be only 15 bushels per acre the net produce of this place, over and above grazing, would be about 100,000 bushels, so that if the proprietor got a quarter of produce as rent he would have 25,000 bushels of first-class wheat to dispose of. By this system of grazing and summer fallow the fertility of the land is in a certain degree kept up. It is a cheap system of management, and well adapted to the country in the present circumstances.

In glancing thus imperfectly at the agriculture of this wonderful State it would be unfair not to say a few words about the coming interest of this portion of the Pacific slope. While gold and silver and other precious metals have produced and are producing, their millions of dollars per annum, while wheat and wool have so far reached the maximum of their production, the wine and fruit interest has till within a year or two only received slight attention. But its day is coming, and though last, it shall not be least, in fact the writer is thoroughly impressed with the idea that wine growing will be the coming interest of California. Many reasons convince the impartial observer of this fact. While the valleys of the Sacramento and San Joaquin grow magnificent grapes, it is likely that there culture will reach the greatest perfection among the hills and vales which lie at the base of the mountains, which, in fact, form a debateable land, and which are watered by clear sparkling streams fed by the snows of winter, lying deep in mid-summer among the gulches of the mountains. In brief the indications which lead us to form a favourable impression of this industry are as follows:—

Wine and fruit.

1st. A rich and almost inexhaustible soil largely charged with lime and phosphates and suitable in every way to grape culture.
2nd. An absolutely certain climate, never less than five months of dry weather, in fact a rainless season from May till October.
3rd. Rare opportunities to irrigate. Thus producing enormous crops, and driving away any fear of phylloxera, for it is proved that this insect can be drowned out.
4th. An ever increasing demand for light wines, and the constant decrease of those in the great producing districts of France and Germany.
5th. The comparative ease and economy with which grapes can be grown. This season the average in the Napa Valley would be from 6 to 8 tons per acre, value 5l. per ton, and the total cost of culture, rent of land, &c., is calculated at 4l. per acre.
6th. It is argued that Californian wines are not equal in quality to those of Europe. But as wine improves with age so will the race of wine growers. Granted that it is not so good, it is getting so much better every year that the day is not far distant when it will rival the very finest European brands. The progress within the last few years in the process of producing claret and hocks has been very great.

The wine makers followed for several years the ways in which they had been reared while in France and the Rhine Land, but they have a different climate, a richer soil, a more fruity grape than there, and they are gradually adopting plans more suitable to the variation of soil and climate. Every day we learn something, and there are men of observation among those viniculturists of the Pacific Slope, who will perfect rapidly their system of winemaking.

Closely allied to wine-making is fruit-raising. California produces magnificent specimens of all classes of semi-tropical fruit, and no one who has wandered through the beautiful orange groves of the San Gabriel Valley, or visited the great vineyards of Napa or Sonoma counties, can doubt the greatness of its future production in all kinds of fruits; some very large establishments have been started for the manufacture of dried fruits, notably raisins, which are of the finest quality, and are spreading over all America, entering into competition with those of Europe, and other parts of the world. Not far from Daviesville, near to the city of Sacramento, we visited a vineyard about 300 acres in extent devoted entirely to the production of raisins. For the last two years, although not at full-bearing, the profits have been very large. Here it may be observed that while all wheat growers were murmuring, there was a happy smile on the face of the fruit grower. Wheat is a precarious crop, most kinds of fruit a certainty. The peculiarity of this vineyard, apart from its size, is the manner of irrigation, called the "seppage" system. As water cannot be got by gravitation at this point except at great expense, a steam engine has been placed by the side of a creek which pumps water into a tank at the rate of 2,600 gallons a minute. The water from this tank is lead in main pipes 8 inches in size across various parts of the vineyard. From those main conduits smaller pipes are laid lengthways at intervals of every 16 feet. Those get so much water from the large pipe, and small apertures, also at distances of 16 feet distribute it. It is very much like our system of drainage at home, only on a reverse scale. While our leading drains take away the water, here they distribute it. The pipes are about 2 feet under ground, and as the slope of the field is gentle and equal, the distribution takes place very equally in quantity, but the calculation as to the amount to escape at the holes of the lesser pipes had been a little astray; too much was escaping, and parts of the field at the furthest points from the mains were receiving no moisture. Those vines that had received a fair share of the water were much better than the others, and both the amount of fruit and the healthy foliage proclaimed the benefits of the system. If this plan is a success, it will revolutionise the whole system of irrigation, and make the watering of plant-life easy and certain. The pipes are made of cement and gravel. The cost of laying those we saw, including the distributing, tanks, engine, &c., was about $70 per acre for about 100 acres, but it is believed that it can be done for $40 per acre, not a large sum considering the benefits which follow it.

He would be a bold man indeed who would predict the future of the Pacific Slope from an agricultural point of view. The State of California is fully developed in a sense, but Oregon and Washington Territory are as yet practically lying dormant. Vast tracts of land, great valleys full of the alluvial deposits of ages, have yet to feel the influence of the plough. When the whistle of the locomotive is heard in those remote regions, away as it were from civilization, a change will come over the scene, and the granaries of the world will feel the pulsation of a new region pouring out its riches. But the day is not yet at hand when the fullness of those regions will send forth their surplus. There, as east of the Rocky Mountains, virgin soil will supply the decrease of the over-cropped and older portions of the country. Just as in a future day the valley of the Saskatchewan, that great "loneland" will fill the multitudes of Europe who are asking for bread. But the man who would prophesy of the year or even the decade when necessity will lead producers to those regions would need a wonderful second sight. Further we should not like to go on this subject than merely to say that, as the demand calls for it, then, and only then, the undeveloped countries of the world will open up their hidden treasures.

The future of the Pacific slope.

In conclusion, your Commissioner has to thank one and all of the gentlemen he met during a lengthened sojourn through the State for the great trouble they took to help forward his work. To Mr. Forman, of the firm of Balfour, Guthrie & Co., and to Mr. Walker, of Falkner, Bell & Co., many thanks are due for information given directly and indirectly, and the writer will never forget the kindness he experienced at the beautiful home of General John Bidwell, one of California's oldest and foremost pioneers.

JOHN CLAY, Jr..

Bow Park, Brantford, Ont.
10th Nov. 1880.

LONDON:
Printed by GEORGE EDWARD EYRE and WILLIAM SPOTTISWOODE,
Printers to the Queen's most Excellent Majesty.
For Her Majesty's Stationery Office.

CATTLE DISEASE (UNITED STATES OF AMERICA).

FURTHER CORRESPONDENCE

RELATING TO

DISEASES OF ANIMALS

IN THE

UNITED STATES OF AMERICA.

Presented to both Houses of Parliament by Command of Her Majesty.

LONDON:
PRINTED BY GEORGE EDWARD EYRE AND WILLIAM SPOTTISWOODE,
PRINTERS TO THE QUEEN'S MOST EXCELLENT MAJESTY.
FOR HER MAJESTY'S STATIONERY OFFICE.

1881.

[C.—2787.] *Price* 3½*d.*

No. 1.

LETTER from the ACTING BRITISH CONSUL-GENERAL at New York to EARL GRANVILLE.

Sanitary, No. 8.

British Consulate-General, New York,
September 1, 1880.

My Lord,

I HAVE the honour to report to your Lordship that no further outbreak of pleuro-pneumonia among cattle in this Consular District has been reported during the past month; the sanitary condition of the cattle remaining practically the same as at the date of Mr. Consul-General Archibald's last report on this subject.

I have, &c.
(Signed) PIERREPONT EDWARDS,
Acting Consul-General.

Her Majesty's Principal Secretary of State
for Foreign Affairs, London.

No. 2.

LETTER from the ACTING BRITISH CONSUL at Portland, Maine, to EARL GRANVILLE.

Sanitary, No. 8.

British Consulate, Portland, Maine,
September 2, 1880.

My Lord,

I HAVE the honour to report to your Lordship that according to information received from the local sanitary authorities, with the following exception, there has not been any appearance of contagious disease among animals within this Consular District of the State of Maine during the month ended 31st ultimo.

The town of Northfield, in the western part of Washington county, in this State, has lately lost 21 head of cattle. No surgical examination has been made to discover what the disease was, but it is supposed to be "black leg," and to have originated from bad ventilation and want of drainage.

I have, &c.
(Signed) GEORGE H. STARR,
Acting Consul.

The Right Hon. the Earl Granville, K.G.,
&c. &c. &c.
Foreign Office.

No. 3.

LETTER from the SECRETARY OF THE BRITISH LEGATION at Washington to EARL GRANVILLE.

Sanitary, No. 22.

My Lord,

Lenox, September 6, 1880.

I HAVE the honour to enclose herewith an extract from one of the New York daily papers, expressing fears lest Texan fever amongst the herds forwarded to the eastern markets here should spread, and advising that precautionary measures be taken.

I have, &c.
(Signed) VICTOR DRUMMOND.

The Right Hon. the Earl Granville, K.G.,
&c. &c. &c.
Foreign Office.

Q 4854. Wt. 17652.

Enclosure in No. 3.

Newspaper Extract.

DISEASED AMERICAN CATTLE.

WHILE the attention of that portion of the public interested in the live stock trade of the country is just at the moment directed to the fear of pleuro-pneumonia becoming prevalent throughout the herds of the West, little notice is taken of Texas fever, a worse disease, and one requiring the strict enforcement of prohibitory and precautionary laws. For some weeks past and for several weeks to come the Spanish herds of Texas have been and will continue to be forwarded to the Eastern markets. At all times the herds, when grass-fed, are dangerous and unprofitable; at the present time those sent to our local markets are extremely poor in quality and are largely infected with tick, a loathsome parasite which adheres to the hide of the beast, and plainly shows the poverty of the animal's system. These herds are now most wisely prevented from being driven, and, according to a law recently enacted, arrive by train direct from the Western Plains. As the export trade in beeves is already hampered by quarantine in Great Britain, the authorities would do well to guard against further annoyance to exporters.

No. 4.

LETTER from the CLERK OF THE COUNCIL to the FOREIGN OFFICE.

Veterinary Department, Privy Council Office,
44, Parliament Street, Westminster, S.W.,
September 20, 1880.

SIR,

THE attention of the Lords of the Council has been drawn to a telegram which appeared in the London papers of the 9th instant, that Texan fever had occurred on a farm in Oswego county, in the State of New York, among cattle which had been brought from Texas, and I am directed by their Lordships to request that you will have the goodness to move Earl Granville to give instructions that inquiry may be made as to the truth of the telegram in question.

I am also directed by the Lords of the Council to request that instructions may be given to Her Majesty's Consul at Baltimore to endeavour to trace, if possible, the origin of the consignments of cattle arriving at Liverpool on the 23rd of August last from Baltimore by the steamship "Edwards," among which splenic fever occurred; and to Her Majesty's Consul at New York, similarly, as to origin of cattle arriving at Cardiff on the 30th of August last from New York by the steamship "Rhiwindda," among which there were also cases of splenic fever.

I have, &c.
(Signed) C. L. PEEL.

The Under Secretary of State,
&c.   &c.   &c.
Foreign Office.

No. 5.

LETTER from the BRITISH CONSUL-GENERAL at New York to EARL GRANVILLE.

Sanitary, No. 9.

British Consulate-General, New York,
September 27, 1880.

MY LORD,

I HAVE the honour to report to your Lordship that pleuro-pneumonia is stated on reliable authority to again exist in an aggravated form among the cows stabled in Brooklyn and its vicinity in this State, and that many animals are suffering from the disease.

The disease has also broken out in a malignant form among the cattle at Westbury, in Queen's county, Long Island, at Jericho, and at other places on Long Island.

The cattle will doubtless be quarantined, as heretofore, to prevent the disease spreading into other districts, and the animals badly affected will be slaughtered.

I have the honour further to report that Texan fever has recently made its appearance among cattle on a farm at Oswego, in the North-western part of this State, the fever having been contracted from Texan cattle slaughtered at the place. The locality has been visited by Dr. James Law, of the Cornell University, who has been on several occasions associated with the State Cattle Inspector in his inspection of infected districts. Mr. Law has certified that the disease is Texan fever, and not pleuro-pneumonia.

In regard to other localities in this Consular District no further reports of outbreaks of pleuro-pneumonia have come under my observation.

I have, &c.

Her Majesty's Principal Secretary of State for Foreign Affairs.   (Signed)   E. M. ARCHIBALD.

No. 6.

LETTER from the BRITISH CONSUL at Boston to EARL GRANVILLE.

Sanitary, No. 6.

MY LORD,   Boston, September 30, 1880.

ON receipt of Mr. Lister's Despatch marked Sanitary, No. 1 of the 31st of August, I made every effort to ascertain the particulars referred to in that Despatch in regard to the consignment of cattle which arrived at Liverpool on the 5th of that month by the steamship "Iowa."

Amongst the persons from whom I sought information, the only ones from whom I obtained any bearing on the subject were Mr. James A. Hathaway, of the firm of Hathaway and Jackson, superintendent of the cattle yards of this city, and Mr. Albert N. Monroe, superintendent of the stock yards of the Boston and Albany Railway Company.

These gentlemen are the principal dealers here in cattle for consumption and exportation, have many years' experience in cattle in all parts of the country, and appeared to be perfectly willing to give me all the information in their power.

With regard to the consignment by the "Iowa," above referred to, Mr. Hathaway could not, however, tell me anything more definite than that it was a portion of different lots collected together from various parts of Indiana and Illinois, but in this, as in the majority of cases, he could not, he said, tell the exact locality in which such of the cattle as died or became sick had been reared or fed.

What, he said, he could state with certainty was, that the cattle were at the time of purchase and of shipment in excellent condition, and, as far as could be judged from close and careful inspection, perfectly healthy. As an argument in favour of the utmost care being taken to ship none but healthy animals, Mr. Hathaway observed that it was obviously against the interests of the shipper to pay a heavy freight on such as appeared likely not only to become sick and die, but, in the opinion of some, to cause infection amongst those which were originally healthy.

Both Mr. Hathaway and Mr. Monroe expressed their conviction, based on their own knowledge and experience, that whilst pleuro-pneumonia has occasionally made its appearance, notably in one case in which it was imported into New Jersey from England, it has always been killed out before it has spread to any dangerous extent, and that, practically, it may be said that no contagious disease exists amongst cattle throughout the country.

The only disease which, they say, is general at certain times, and presumably ineradicable, is what is termed by some Texas fever, but more generally known here by the name of "Red water." It is, according to them, the same thing as murrain, is not contagious, and only makes its appearance in an intensified form in seasons of severe drought, either as a result of atmospheric influence, or insufficient and bad water, or both combined.

They assert that it is as incorrect to call it Texas fever as it is absurd to pretend that it is communicated by healthy Texas cattle to those reared in other States, or in fact by diseased cattle to such as are healthy, and are not exposed to the peculiar climatic influences which produce the disease. It has, they say, been found by them in cattle which have never been in the vicinity of those from Texas, and, contrary to a general impression, in Texas cattle as well.

Whilst admitting that the disease is not likely to be contracted during the railway journey or the sea voyage, Mr. Monroe, who is not himself a shipper, said that it was sometimes slow in developing itself, and was as liable to make its appearance during the voyage as before shipment, and Mr. Hathaway maintained that the number of cases occurring on board were comparatively few, the majority of deaths being caused by suffocation or injury during bad weather, and not by disease. As a proof of this he referred to a suit brought by him in the Supreme Court of this State against one ship in which he has just obtained a verdict for the value of 67 head of cattle which died on the voyage.

Whatever may be the value of these gentlemen's statements, it appears to me proper to report them as they were given to me, for the event of its being deemed expedient to test them by a minute and full inquiry, a proceeding which does not appear so far to have been undertaken by the authorities of the country, notwithstanding the vast and increasing importance of the subject.

Meanwhile the inspection of cattle shipped to England, which was ordered by the United States Government in the year 1878, and which was made by the State Cattle Commissioners, whose certificates were authenticated by this office, was discontinued in the early part of this year, and shippers are now free to export cattle without official supervision of any kind.

I have, &c.
(Signed) C. A. HENDERSON.

Her Majesty's Principal Secretary of State
for Foreign Affairs.

No. 7.

LETTER from the ACTING BRITISH CONSUL at Portland, Maine, to EARL GRANVILLE.

Sanitary, No. 9.

British Consulate, Portland, Maine,
October 1, 1880.

MY LORD,

I HAVE the honour to report to your Lordship that according to information received from the Local Sanitary Authorities, with the exception of a general prevalence of the epizootic in a mild form among horses, there has not been any appearance of contagious disease among animals within this Consular District of the State of Maine during the month ended on the 30th of September last.

I have, &c.
(Signed) GEORGE H. STARR,
Acting Consul.

To the Right Hon. the Earl Granville, K.G.,
&c. &c. &c.

No. 8.

LETTER from the BRITISH CONSUL at Baltimore to EARL GRANVILLE.

Sanitary, No. 10.

MY LORD,
Baltimore, October 1, 1880.

I HAVE the honour to report that since Mr. Acting Consul Lawford's Despatch, Sanitary, No. 9, of the 1st ultimo, 17 head of cattle in Harford county of this State are reported to have died of pleuro-pneumonia.

This disease appears to be local and confined to one farm, and cattle intended for exportation to the United Kingdom are not transported through the infected district.

I have, &c.
(Signed) DENIS DONOHOE.

The Right Hon. the Earl Granville, K.G.,
&c. &c. &c.

No. 9.

LETTER from the BRITISH CONSUL-GENERAL at New York to EARL GRANVILLE.

Sanitary, No. 10.

British Consulate-General, New York,
October 2, 1880.

MY LORD,

I HAVE the honour to report to your Lordship that the disease known as the epizootic has made its appearance among the horses in this city and Brooklyn, as well as in other parts of this Consular District. It is similar in all its features to the disease which prevailed here in 1873.

Its symptoms are a deep-seated cough, running at the nose, great debility, feeble pulse, affection of the eyes, disinclination for food, and general muscular languor. At first it was in mild form, and did not interfere with the working of the horses, and was limited to but a few stables. But within a few days past it has become very general, and more severe in its character. Thus far I have not learned of any death among horses, but the disease is becoming so much more dangerous that this cannot long be the case.

Owing to the suddenness of the appearance of this disease, I have deemed it prudent to send the following telegram to your Lordship:

"Epizootic among horses in this city and neighbourhood becoming very general, with increasing severity.

"ARCHIBALD."

I have, &c.

Her Majesty's Principal Secretary of State   (Signed)   E. M. ARCHIBALD.
for Foreign Affairs.

No. 10.

LETTER from the FOREIGN OFFICE to the CLERK OF THE COUNCIL.

Foreign Office, October 3, 1880.

LORD TENTERDEN presents his compliments to the Clerk to the Council, and begs to inform him that the following telegram, dated the 2nd instant, has been received from Her Majesty's Consul-General at New York:

"Epizootic among horses in this city and neighbourhood becoming very general, with increasing severity."

No. 11.

LETTER from the BRITISH CONSUL at Baltimore to EARL GRANVILLE.

Sanitary, No. 11.

MY LORD,   Baltimore, October 5, 1880.

I HAVE the honour to acknowledge the receipt of Mr. Lister's Despatch, Sanitary, No. 1, of the 25th ultimo, instructing me to endeavour to trace the origin of the consignments of cattle shipped from here on the 9th August by the Spanish steamer "Eduardo," and landed in Liverpool on the 23rd of August.

I have obtained the information required by your Lordship personally from the skipper of the cattle, as well as from the head man in charge of them on the passage to Liverpool.

The number of cattle shipped was one hundred and thirty (130) head, ninety-six (96) head were purchased in open market at Chicago, and came from the States of Illinois and Iowa, and were forwarded from Chicago to this port by rail.

Seventeen (17) head were sent from Fauquier county, Virginia, and seventeen (17) head were bought in the Baltimore market and came from southern Ohio.

Thirty-five (35) head were lost on the voyage, having died of the so-called Texan fever, and these thirty-five (35) belonged to the lot purchased in the Chicago market.

I have, &c.

The Right Hon. the Earl Granville, K.G.,   (Signed)   DENIS DONOHOE.
&c.   &c.   &c.

No. 12.

LETTER from the BRITISH CONSUL-GENERAL at Baltimore to EARL GRANVILLE.

Sanitary, No. 12.

MY LORD,   Baltimore, October 7, 1880.

WITH reference to my Despatches No. 27 of October 31st, No. 29 of November 21st, and No. 30 of December 17th, 1872, relative to the outbreak of a disease amongst horses, and the latter Despatch containing a full report upon the disease, I have the honour to report that a similar disease has appeared here amongst the horses, but so far it is of a very mild form.

The disease made its appearance in Boston about a month ago, and has gradually extended south, the symptoms being similar to those noted in 1872, viz., "a coughing, "sneezing, and wheezing on the part of the animals attacked, and later a running of the "nose, a dulness of the eyes, loss of appetite and necessarily of strength, which, unless "the victim was given rest and attention, soon unfitted him entirely for service."

The weather is very fine at present; but the managers of the tramways state that if wet weather should set in, they apprehend serious trouble with their horses.

I have, &c.

The Right Hon. Earl Granville, K.G.,   (Signed)   DENIS DONOHOE.
&c.   &c.   &c.

No. 13.

LETTER from the BRITISH CONSUL-GENERAL at New York to EARL GRANVILLE.

Sanitary, No. 11.

British Consulate-General, New York,
My Lord,   October 11, 1880.

I HAVE the honour to acknowledge the receipt of Mr. Lister's Despatch, Sanitary, No. 1, of the 25th ultimo, stating that your Lordship's attention has been called by the Council Office to a telegram which appeared in the London papers of the 9th ultimo, reporting that Texan fever had occurred on a farm in Oswego county, in the State of New York, among cattle which had been brought from Texas, and instructing me to inquire into the truth of the telegram in question; also instructing me to endeavour to trace the origin of a consignment of cattle which arrived at Cardiff on the 30th ultimo from New York by the S.S. "Rhiwindda," among which there were cases of splenic fever.

In reply, I have the honour to confirm the statement in the telegram referred to in regard to the Texan fever having made its appearance at Oswego. The fact of some cattle in the locality in question having contracted the fever from others which had been imported from Texas, and that the animals had been specially inspected by Professor Law of the Cornell University, who had certified to the character of the disease, had already been reported in my Despatch, Sanitary, No. 9, of the 27th ultimo, which doubtless has reached the Foreign Office before this. Dr. Law has not, as far as I am aware, made any further report on this subject.

In reference to the other matter mentioned in Mr. Lister's Despatch, I have the honour to state that I am making inquiry for the purpose of ascertaining where the cattle consigned by the S.S. "Rhiwindda" came from, and will report to your Lordship so soon as I shall have obtained definite information.

I have, &c.

Her Majesty's Principal Secretary of State   (Signed)   E. M. ARCHIBALD.
for Foreign Affairs, London.

No. 14.

LETTER from the BRITISH CONSUL-GENERAL at New York to EARL GRANVILLE.

Sanitary, No. 12.

British Consulate-General, New York,
My Lord,   October 19, 1880.

I HAVE the honour to report to your Lordship that a new disease among cattle is reported to have broken out at Providence, Rhode Island, which is briefly described in one of this mornings newspapers as follows:—

"Providence, Rhode Island, October 18th. A disease has just been discovered in this State in a herd of 47 cattle recently imported from New York.

"This is its first appearance in these parts. Small worms infest the air passages, multiplying so rapidly that respiration is stopped. At the same time the digestive organs fail to work, and the animals pine away and die in fifteen days after inoculation.

Forty of the herd are already dead, and the rest will not live more than a day or so. The disease is not epidemic, but contagious only from close contact, so the worms can pass from one animal to another. Once in the animal's body death is sure to follow. The infested herd has been isolated."

I have written to Vice-Consul Ashley, instructing him to make inquiries into the truth of this statement, and report the result.

The epizooty, or influenza among horses, referred to in my Sanitary, No. 10, of the 2nd instant, is now prevalent in all parts of the country. Thus far it has been by no means so severe as the like disease which prevailed here seven years ago; and but few fatal cases have been reported in the newspapers.

I have, &c.
(Signed) E. M. ARCHIBALD.

Her Majesty's Principal Secretary of State
for Foreign Affairs, Foreign Office, London.

No. 15.

LETTER from the BRITISH CONSUL-GENERAL at New York to EARL GRANVILLE.

Sanitary, No. 13.

British Consulate-General, New York,
October 19, 1880.

My Lord,

REFERRING to my Despatch, Sanitary, No. 11, of the 11th instant, I have now the honour to transmit herewith enclosed copies of letters of the 13th and 19th instant received by me from Messrs. Daniel Toffey & Co., agents for Messrs. Gillett and Toffey, of Jersey City, by whom the cattle forwarded to Cardiff from this port on the 14th of August last were shipped, giving such information as they are enabled to afford in regard to the origin of the consignment in question.

In their second letter Messrs. Toffey state that owing to the absence in Europe of their employé, who had charge of the shipment of the cattle per "Rhiwindda," they are unable to indicate from which particular place the cattle found on arrival at Cardiff to be diseased came; but that on the clerk's return, in the course of two or three weeks, they will endeavour to furnish me with the needful information.

I have, &c.
(Signed) E. M. ARCHIBALD.

Her Majesty's Principal Secretary of State
for Foreign Affairs, Foreign Office, London.

Enclosure 1. in No. 15.

Sir,
Jersey City, New Jersey, October 13, 1880.

IN reply to your letter of October 8th inquiring about cattle shipped per steamer "Rhiwindda" on the 14th of August last, I should state that we bought the cattle at the central stock yards of Jersey City, and that they were examined by Morice and Preston's bureau of inspection and by ourselves, and were pronounced by us a very healthy lot of cattle. We understood that two or three of the cattle were pronounced unhealthy in Cardiff, and our agents, Johnson and Miles, sent them to London and had them inspected by an authorised agent of the British Government, who pronounced them healthy; they were then sold by them, and we heard no more of it.

35 cattle came from Chicago, Ills., and were bought of Samuel Shuster, 11th August.
29 cattle were bought of Newton and Holmes, August 11, and came from State of Ohio.
30 cattle were bought of J. F. Sadler and Co., August 13, and came from State of Kentucky.
16 cattle were bought of J. Shamberg and Co., August 13, and came from Chicago, Ills.

110 cattle; number shipped by s.s. "Rhiwindda," August 14th.

As near as we can ascertain, the cattle arrived here by the Pennsylvania and Erie railroad. We do not know exactly how long they were in transit. We do not know of any disease on the line of the above-named railroads or between here and where they were shipped.

Yours, &c.
(Signed) DANIEL TOFFEY AND CO.,
For Gillett and Toffey.

E. M. Archibald, Esq.,
H.B.M. Consul-General, New York.

Q 4854.

10

Enclosure 2. in No. 15.

Sir,　　　　　　　　　　　　　　　　　　　　　Jersey City, New Jersey, October 19, 1880.

Yours of the 14th instant, wishing to know if we are in a position to indicate in which lot of cattle those found unhealthy at Cardiff were included, I duly received.

We have to state, in reply, that it is impossible for us to give you the desired information at present, owing to the young man who had charge of the "Rhiwindda" cattle being in Europe with cattle now, but when he returns, which will be in the course of two or three weeks, we shall endeavour to obtain from him full particulars.

　　　　　　　　　　　　　　　　　　　　　　　　　　Yours, &c.
E. M. Archibald, Esq.,　　　　　　　　　(Signed)　　Daniel Toffey and Co.
　H.B.M. Consul-General, New York.

No. 16.

Letter from the BRITISH CONSUL-GENERAL at New York to EARL GRANVILLE.

Sanitary, No. 14.

British Consulate-General, New York,
My Lord,　　　　　　　　　　　　　　　　　　　　October 23, 1880.

With reference to my Despatch (Sanitary, No. 12) of the 19th instant, I have now the honour to transmit herewith enclosed for your Lordship's information, a copy of a letter of yesterday's date from Mr. Ashley, Vice-Consul at Providence, Rhode Island, confirming the report in regard to the fatality of the disease which had broken out among cattle in Cumberland, near Providence, and furnishing also a full description of the disease, and its effects upon the animals.

　　　　　　　　　　　　　　　　　　　　　　I have, &c.
　　　　　　　　　　　　　　　　　(Signed)　　　E. M. ARCHIBALD.
Her Majesty's Principal Secretary of State
　for Foreign Affairs, Foreign Office, London.

Enclosure 1. in No. 16.

Sir,　　　　　　　　　　　　　　　　　　　　　　　Providence, October 22, 1880.

I have to acknowledge the receipt of letter from your office dated 19th instant, relative to a new and fatal disease which has broken out among cattle in Cumberland, near this city, and to state in reply that I have had conversation with Dr. Fisher, Secretary of the State Board of Health, who is investigating the disease.

Dr. Fisher returned from Cumberland this p.m., and he informs me that the extract which I enclose herewith (from the "Providence Journal" of the 19th instant) gives a correct account of the facts in relation to the disease and its introduction into this State up to the 19th instant. Since that time a number of cattle have died, and three of the cows with which the herd were pastured show signs of infection. One of these was killed yesterday, and upon examination worms were found in its lungs and air passages; 39 out of the 47 purchased at Brighton have died, including two which were killed. It is expected that all of the cattle purchased will die, as they are probably all infected.

Dr. Fisher also informed me that he has taken pains to ascertain whether the disease has appeared in other localities, and has examined cattle in various places for miles around, but has not heard of a single case either in this or any other State existing at the present time.

A meeting of the Board of Health has been called for the purpose of thoroughly investigating the disease and taking such action as may be necessary to prevent the spreading of the same.

Dr. Fisher kindly promised to give me such further facts in relation to the disease as may be obtained, and I will forward the same to you.

　　　　　　　　　　　　　　　　　　　　　Very respectfully,
　　　　　　　　　　　　　　　　　　(Signed)　　E. C. Ashley,
E. M. Archibald, Esq., C.B.,　　　　　　　　　　　　　Vice-Consul.
　H.B.M. Consul-General, New York.

Enclosure 2. in No. 16.

Providence Journal, 19*th October* 1880.

Cattle Disease in Cumberland.

The State Board of Health was notified on Saturday that a disease among cattle existed in Cumberland in the herd of Mr. John P. Jencks. Dr. Charles H. Fisher, secretary of the State Board of Health, and Dr. C. H. Peabody, a veterinary expert, went to Cumberland on Saturday for the purpose of investigating the disease and its causes. The facts as given by Dr. Fisher are as follows:—On the 25th of August, Mr. Jencks purchased 47 head of young stock, mostly calves, in Brighton. Mr. Jencks understood that these calves came from New York. On the 29th of the same month, the calves were driven to Cumberland. After going about a mile, one of them, which appeared weak at starting, gave out entirely and was carried the rest of the journey. The others were driven without difficulty. On September 2nd the one that was taken ill on the road died. On the 14th of the same month two more died, and between that time and the 1st of October there were four other deaths. Since then more have died, and two in the last stages of the disease were killed for *post mortem* purposes. The after-death examination disclosed the fact that the symptoms of the affected animals, as they occurred in regular order, were as follows:—

In the first place there was a cough, short, harsh, gradually becoming hoarse, and finally having a muffled sound, hardly characteristic of a cough. The animals affected had the appearance of great fatigue, their breathing becoming more rapid, gradually more laboured. All were more or less constipated, and with respect to some, diarrhœa set in. The affected animal would eat up to within 24 hours of death, but emaciation gradually went from the incipient stages to the death. The time of the duration of the disease is from 15 to 20 days. In all advanced cases it was found that the pulse was weak and irregular, that respiration was rapid, being from 70 to 112 per minute. With every breath there was a slight catch or groan. Respiration was attended by much more abdominal expansion and contraction than of the chest, and with great apparent oppression. The animal stood with head down, back arched, hind feet drawn under the body, fore feet separated with toes turning inward. A copious secretion flowed from the nostrils, the coat was staring, skin shrivelled, and eyes dull and heavy. In some cases there was considerable secretion of saliva.

In the very last stages of the disease the pulse became slower, scarcely perceptible, and breathing, not much more frequent than natural, was performed with great difficulty, and every breath was attended by a groan. Upon casual inspection the symptoms indicated pleuro-pneumonia, with congestion or solidification of the lungs; but upon listening to the respiration, and upon percussion of the chest, it was discovered that the disease could not be pleuro-pneumonia. A *post mortem* examination was then made in two animals that had recently died, and upon two that were killed in the advanced stages of the disease. The examination disclosed the fact that disease was caused by lung worms (*filaria bronchœ* or *filaria pulmonalis*). These worms were hair-like, varying from one half to one and one half inches in length. When once introduced into the air passages they multiply with great rapidity, and by the irritation of their presence excite some degree of fever and cause an increased secretion of mucus, with which and with the increased number of worms respiration is obstructed and the system suffers in proportion; derangement of all the organic functions ensues; digestion and assimilation of food is interrupted, and emaciation gradually follows. The presence of the worms causes also the cough; they crawl into the farthest extremities of the air passages and block them in great numbers, so that the use of the lungs is gradually destroyed. The disease is contagious only when the parasites find their way from one animal to another. With proper precautions the disease may be confined to the farm of Mr. Jencks. Dr. Fisher has given such orders and directions as will restrict the disease to that herd. The disease is much more likely to attack young stock, particularly calves, than stock three or more years of age. It is hoped and expected that Mr. Jencks's older stock, of which there are 20 valuable animals, may be saved from the disease. Doubtless all that were bought at Brighton will die. Samples of the diseased lung have been sent to Professor Liautard, of the American Veterinary College of New York, and an account of the condition and appearances, as revealed by a *post mortem* examination, will be furnished the "American Veterinary Review" by Dr. Peabody. Dr. Peabody has seen the same disease in New York, but as far as known this is its first appearance in this vicinity.

No. 17.

LETTER from the CLERK OF THE COUNCIL to the FOREIGN OFFICE.

Veterinary Department, Privy Council Office,
44, Parliament Street, Westminster, S.W.,
October 29, 1880.

SIR,

I AM directed by the Lords of the Council to request that you will have the goodness to move Earl Granville to give instructions that inquiry may be made of Her Majesty's Consul at Chicago as to the alleged existence of Texas fever in Illinois and Indiana, as hitherto no official report on this subject has been received by their Lordships.

I am, &c.

The Under Secretary of State, &c. &c. &c.
Foreign Office.

(Signed)   C. L. PEEL.

No. 18.

LETTER from the BRITISH CONSUL-GENERAL at New York.

Sanitary, No. 16.

British Consulate-General, New York,
November 1, 1880.

MY LORD,

I HAVE the honour to report to your Lordship with reference to my Despatch of the 27th September last (Sanitary, No. 9.) that the measures taken by the authorities of the city of Brooklyn for preventing the spread of pleuro-pneumonia among the cows stabled in that city have had a beneficial effect, a recent inspection by veterinary surgeons deputed by the City Board of Health having shown that the condition of the animals has generally improved, and that the disease is gradually diminishing.

On the re-appearance of the disease in the latter part of September, in one stable especially, that of Nicholas Elers, it is stated that out of 39 cows, nine were sick. This stable, with others, was immediately quarantined, and will remain so until all signs of disease shall have been eradicated.

In the other localities referred to in the above-mentioned Despatch an improvement has been exhibited in the condition of the animals.

The "epizooty" among horses is still prevalent in all parts of this Consular District. In this city and in Brooklyn, however, the number of horses now sick and under treatment is not nearly so large as heretofore; and the fatality in these cities, notwithstanding the very large number of animals affected, has been exceedingly small. But in the southern part of the State of New Jersey, the disease has been prevalent in almost every town. In Ocean and Monmouth counties, especially in the towns skirting the coast, the malady is as violent as it was in 1873.

It is stated that wild onions are being used by the farmers as a cure for the disease with much success.

I have, &c.
(Signed) E. M. ARCHIBALD.

Her Majesty's Principal Secretary of State
for Foreign Affairs, Foreign Office, London.

No. 19.

LETTER from the ACTING BRITISH CONSUL at Portland, Maine, to EARL GRANVILLE.

Sanitary, No. 10.

British Consulate, Portland, Maine,
November 1, 1880.

MY LORD,

I HAVE the honour to report to your Lordship that according to information received from the local Sanitary Authorities, there has not been any appearance of contagious disease among animals within this Consular District of Maine during the month ended on the 31st of October last, with the exception of a general prevalence of the epizootic among horses in a mild form, which has now about disappeared.

I have, &c.
(Signed) GEORGE H. STARR,
Acting Consul.

To the Right Hon. the Earl Granville, K.G.,
&c. &c. &c.
Foreign Office.

No. 20.

LETTER from the BRITISH CONSUL at Baltimore to EARL GRANVILLE.

Sanitary, No. 13.

MY LORD, Baltimore, November 1, 1880.

WITH reference to my Despatch, Sanitary, No. 10, of the first ultimo, I have the honour to report that I have heard of no cases of cattle disease since the date of that Despatch.

In my Despatch, Sanitary, No. 12, of the 7th ultimo, I had the honour to report the appearance of a disease amongst horses in this city; I now beg to state that this disease has been prevalent since that date, but of a very mild type, and that but few horses are now suffering from it.

I have, &c.
The Right Hon. the Earl Granville, K.G., (Signed) DENIS DONOHOE.
&c. &c. &c.

No. 21.

Letter from the FOREIGN OFFICE to the CLERK OF THE COUNCIL.

Sir,
Foreign Office, November 3, 1880.

I have laid before Earl Granville your letter of the 29th ultimo applying for information respecting the alleged existence of Texas fever in Illinois and Indiana, and I am now directed by his Lordship to acquaint you that he has caused the Acting British Consul at Philadelphia to be instructed to procure, through the British Vice-Consul at Chicago, a report on this subject.

I am, &c.

The Clerk of the Council, &c. &c.
Veterinary Department.

(Signed) T. V. LISTER.

No. 22.

Letter from the ACTING BRITISH CONSUL at Philadelphia to EARL GRANVILLE.

Sanitary, No. 4.
British Consulate, Philadelphia, November 9, 1880.

My Lord,

I have the honour to report to your Lordship that the cattle disease pleuro-pneumonia has been eradicated from the dairy herds of the State of Pennsylvania, no cases having recently occurred.

The State authorities by stringent measures succeeded in stamping out the disease, paying the dairymen and herdsmen a fair price for all afflicted cattle killed by order of the State Commissioners, and continuing a strict quarantine on all cattle coming within the State for 90 days.

In the Western States of this Consular District there appear to be no cases of pleuro-pneumonia, Illinois, Indiana, Michigan, Iowa, and Wisconsin being singularly free from any disease of the nature of pleuro-pneumonia.

It was reported that many head of western cattle on arrival in England were afflicted with the disease. Should this report, attributed to Dr. Lyman, be correct, it can only be accounted for by the supposition that the cattle took the disease en route from the West to Boston, at some point east of Chicago, at Buffalo, Cleveland, or Albany, or while awaiting shipment at Boston.

I have, &c.

The Right Hon. Earl Granville, K.G., &c. &c. &c.
Foreign Office.

(Signed) GEORGE CRUMP.

No. 23.

Letter from the BRITISH CONSUL at Boston to EARL GRANVILLE.

Sanitary, No. 8.

My Lord,
Boston, November 15, 1880.

I have the honour to report that, as far as direct information has been received here, this Consular District has been free from cattle plague during the past month.

I have nevertheless seen a newspaper reference to a published report of the Department of Agriculture at Washington for the past year, stating that foot-rot and other minor diseases have prevailed amongst sheep in the State of New Hampshire.

I have, &c.

Her Majesty's Principal Secretary of State for Foreign Affairs.

(Signed) C. A. HENDERSON.

No. 24.

Letter from the BRITISH CONSUL-GENERAL at New York to EARL GRANVILLE.

Sanitary, No. 17.
British Consulate-General, New York,
December 1, 1880.

My Lord,

I have the honour to report to your Lordship that since the date of my last Despatch on the subject (Sanitary, No. 16) of the 1st ultimo no further outbreak of pleuro-pneumonia of importance has been reported in this Consular District.

The disease, however, still exists in certain localities but to a smaller extent than heretofore.

In regard to the "epizootic" among horses, I have the honour to report that the disease has continued to spread throughout this State, and has also made its appearance in numerous localities in other States in my Consular District, and it has been the cause of much solicitude on the part of owners of horses. While, however, the disease has been widely prevalent, it has, as I have heretofore reported, been on the whole of a much milder form than that of 1873.

In Syracuse, in this State, 25 per cent. of the horses have had the disease, and others have been affected by a new disease termed the "pupura hemorrhagaie," a malignant kind of fever which has broken out there.

The horses' legs swell, they are taken as with a colic, and this is followed by general debility and prostration.

I have, &c.
(Signed) E. M. ARCHIBALD.

Her Majesty's Principal Secretary of State
for Foreign Affairs, London.

No. 25.

Letter from Sir E. THORNTON to EARL GRANVILLE.

Sanitary, No. 29.
Washington, December 13, 1880.

My Lord,

I have the honour to transmit herewith copies of a set of resolutions agreed to by a meeting of owners of live stock held at Chicago, with respect to the existence of pleuro-pneumonia among cattle. They urge that measures may be taken by Congress to prevent the spread of the disease, and to secure its extermination they recommend that one or two veterinary inspectors should be appointed to ascertain definitely and designate the infected localities. They refer to a Bill presented to the House of Representatives during its last session by Mr. Keifer, a member from Ohio, proposing a supervision of contagious and infectious diseases among cattle on the part of the general Government.

Copies of this Bill I have also the honour to enclose.

It is to be hoped that this appeal to the House of Representatives, to which the enclosed resolutions were submitted on the 10th instant, may induce that body to take this important subject into its serious consideration.

I have, &c.
(Signed) EDWARD THORNTON.

The Right Hon. the Earl Granville, K.G.
&c. &c. &c.

Enclosure 1. in No. 25.

At a meeting of the live-stock growers of the United States, held in Chicago, Illinois, November 17, 1880, the Hon. S. R. Scott, of Champaign, Illinois, was called to the chair, and General George E. Bryant, of Madison, Wisconsin, was chosen secretary. The meeting, after a lengthy discussion, passed unanimously the following preamble and resolutions:

Whereas the contagious pleuro-pneumonia of cattle exists in several of the States of the Union bordering on the Atlantic seaboard; and

Whereas it is evident that, so long as unrestricted traffic in live cattle is permitted between these infected States and those not infected, the live-stock interests of all sections of our country are menaced by a terrible danger; and

Whereas the state of things above indicated has resulted in the adoption of regulations by the British Government which materially interfere with our export trade in live cattle with that country, thereby entailing great damage to all cattle raisers and feeders in the United States; and

Whereas in view of the decision of our States and Federal courts the States acting as such are powerless to protect themselves from infection from an adjoining State, and for the same reason an infected State is powerless to stamp out the contagion as long as it exists on its borders in an adjoining State: Therefore,

Resolved, That it is the imperative duty of Congress to enact such a law as shall effectually prevent the spread of this disease into States not already infected, and which shall result in its entire extermination at the earliest practicable date.

Resolved, That as an important preliminary step we heartily second the recommendation made by Judge Jones, of Ohio, to the President of the United States for the appointment of one or more veterinary inspectors, who shall definitely ascertain and designate the infected regions.

Resolved, That we recognise the Bill introduced into the House of Representatives at its last session by General Keifer, of Ohio, as embodying the essential features necessary to an intelligent and efficient supervision of contagious and infectious diseases of live-stock generally on the part of the Federal Government, and that we heartily recommend its passage, with an additional provision which shall clothe the Commission with authority to prescribe rules and regulations under which the live stock of any infected State, territory, or district may be transported or taken therefrom, and under which live stock may be transported through such infected State, district, or territory, or in their discretion to prohibit absolutely the transportation of live stock from or through such infected district when in their opinion the same shall be essential to the general safety.

Resolved, That we further recommend that petitions be prepared and circulated in all parts of the country and forwarded to Congress calling attention to this subject, and urging favourable consideration for the measures proposed in the foregoing resolutions.

Resolved, That these resolutions be engrossed and a copy of the same delivered to the chairman of the Committee on Agriculture of the Senate and House of Representatives of the United States.

A true copy.
Attest:

GEO. E. BRYANT, Secretary.

Enclosure 2. in No. 25.

In the HOUSE OF REPRESENTATIVES, February 9, 1880. Read twice, referred to the COMMITTEE ON AGRICULTURE, and ordered to be printed.

Mr. Keifer, by unanimous consent, introduced the following Bill: To create a Commission of Inquiry into the causes and for the prevention of Contagious Diseases among Domestic Animals.

BE it enacted by the Senate and House of Representatives of the United States of America in Congress assembled, that the President of the United States shall nominate and, by and with the advice and consent of the Senate, shall appoint a board consisting of three commissioners, to be known as the Commission of Inquiry into the causes and prevention of Contagious Diseases among Domestic Animals; that at least one of the said commissioners shall be a competent and experienced veterinary surgeon, one shall be a practical stock raiser, and one an experienced business man, familiar with questions pertaining to commerce in live stock; that said commissioners shall be appointed for the term of three years, unless sooner removed by the President, by and with the advice and consent of the Senate, and they shall each receive compensation during their term of service at the rate of 4,000 dollars per annum. There shall be one clerk to the commission who shall be paid at the rate of 2,000 dollars per annum.

SEC. 2. That it shall be the duty of said commission to institute a thorough, searching, and continued inquiry, with a view to ascertaining the origin, discovering the most effectual remedy, and acquiring information as to the possibility and means of preventing the introduction and dissemination of contagious disease of all kinds among domestic animals; and it shall be the further duty of said commission to submit annually to the Secretary of the Treasury a detailed report of its labours and investigations and the results thereof, and to report from time to time, through the Secretary of the Treasury, such measures as may be deemed essential for Congress to adopt to prevent the importation and to stay the spread of such diseases.

SEC. 3. It shall be the duty of the Secretary of the Treasury to make and establish such rules and regulations for the government and guidance of said commission, under the provisions and within the scope of this Act, as shall seem to him necessary and advisable, to make all necessary orders for carrying the decisions of said commission into effect, to send copies of such decisions, and the rules and regulations made by him in pursuance thereof, to the proper officers of the United States, and to such officers and agents of the United States in foreign countries as in his judgment shall be necessary.

SEC. 4. That there be, and hereby is, appropriated, out of any moneys in the Treasury not otherwise appropriated, the sum of 20,000 dollars for the purposes of this Act, and the same shall be immediately available in the discretion and under the direction of the Secretary of the Treasury.

SEC. 5. So much of section 2,493 of the revised statutes of the United States as is inconsistent with the provisions of this Act is hereby repealed.

No. 26.

LETTER from the BRITISH CONSUL at New Orleans to EARL GRANVILLE.

Sanitary, No. 13.

British Consulate, New Orleans,
December 8, 1880.

MY LORD,

I HAVE the honour to enclose two newspaper slips, containing a paper read before the American Public Health Association (now in cession in this city) by Dr. J. R. Smith, of the United States Army, upon the subject of Texas cattle fever.

I have, &c.
(Signed) A. DE G. DE FONBLANQUE.

Her Majesty's Principal Secretary of State
for Foreign Affairs, Foreign Office, London.

Enclosure in No. 26.

TEXAS CATTLE FEVER.

By Jos. R. Smith, M.D., surgeon, United States army.

THE opinion exists among many persons that disease prevails extensively in Texas cattle; that a disease prevails, epidemic and contagious, to such an extent as to raise the suspicion that Texas is or soon may become, unsafe as a source of supply of beef for the market of the Northern States.

The correctness of this opinion I have endeavoured to test, and with this end in view have talked on the subject with cattle breeders and drovers, as many as I could meet.

I have also written to various persons (medical men and others) in different sections of the country, whence it seemed probable that definite information on the subject might be obtained, and have asked answers to the following questions:—

1. What is the age of the animals slaughtered at your post or in your neighbourhood? (Age of each for a period of time.)
2. The age of the oldest animal of whom you can learn in your vicinity, and the cause of death, when they have died.
3. Does the pericardium contain bloody serum?
4. Are there any ecchymoses on the outer or inner surface of the heart?
5. The weight of the liver.
6. Does the liver show any signs of fatty degeneration?
7. Does the gall-bladder show any reddening?
8. What are the length, breadth, and weight of the spleen?
9. Its colour and consistence?
10. Do the pelves of the kidney show a bright red colour, a dark colour, or are they streaked with blood?
11. What is the colour of the lining membrane of the bladder, and does it show any traces of hemorrhage?
12. What is the colour of the lining membrane of the fourth or true stomach? Is it flaccid, or stained, or spotted with petechia?
13. What is the rectal temperature of the animals, or a few of them? (This can be obtained by throwing them just before they are killed.)
14. Do you notice any pathological appearances other than those suggested above?
15. Do you know or learn of any disease prevailing or epidemic among the cattle in your vicinity?
16. Have any northern cattle been imported in your vicinity, bulls or cows? If so, did any become sick after emigration, and were any special precautions taken to preserve their health?
17. So far as you can learn, what is the annual mortality among herds in your vicinity, and the cause of death among them?
18. Any facts you may be able to obtain bearing on the life, disease, fitness for food of beef cattle, either while in pasture or being driven to northern markets.

Other letters in reply to my inquiries are on the road, or have been received at too late a date to embody in this paper.

In comparing among themselves the replies herewith presented, very great discrepancies will be seen, the most striking referring to the pathological appearances

The age of cattle slaughtered ranged from two and a half years at Fort McKavett to a little over seven years at Corpus Christi.

The weight of the liver varied from $5\frac{1}{2}$ pounds in a yearling to 15 pounds in a beef slaughtered at Corpus Christi. As a general rule the weight of the liver increased with age.

The liver and gall-bladder are reported generally as healthy.

Of the spleen, the size is reported at Fort Duncan as eight inches to a foot in length by two to three inches broad, the thickness not being given, while at Corpus Christi it is reported as $19\frac{1}{3}$ inches in length by $5\frac{2}{3}$ to $4\frac{9}{10}$ inches in breadth, the thickness not being given. The average weight reported is 1 pound $5\frac{1}{2}$ ounces at Corpus Christi and 2 pounds at San Felipe. The extremes are not reported. Its colour is reported respectively as white, dark red, and mottled, and mottled blue or grayish externally and dark red internally, and its consistence is described as soft, brittle, easily broken down, and very vascular; as firm in consistency, and as more inclined to flabbiness than the human spleen.

The pelves of the kidney are described as light red, not streaked; as white with blush of pink; as of dark colour, and bright red, by two observers.

The lining membrane of the bladder is generally described as of yellowish hue, one only describing it as faint pink. The colour of the lining membrane of the abomasus is represented as greenish drab, as dull red, as pinkish white, and as bluish white. The organ itself is further represented by two observers as flaccid, by two as not flaccid, and by one simply as "normal." By only two observers is the rectal temperature reported. Dr. Hanner, at San Felipe, reports it as 98°, and further says, "The "operation was performed as carefully as possible. I think the observations are correct."

Dr. Davis, of Corpus Christie, reports the average temperature of five animals as 103° 88′, with maximum 105° 2′, and minimum 101° 4′. He further reports: "Owing to the wildness of the cattle and the "want of proper facilities, it was found impracticable to carry out the suggestions offered relative to "the manner of making the observations. The mode of slaughtering is by severing the spinal cord in "the cervical region by means of a sharp lance thrust into the neck of the animal from above, and in "four of the above cases the observations were made immediately after the animals had been stricken "down. They were labouring under intense excitement and terror, and were with great difficulty "driven into the slaughter cage, which, doubtless, affected the range of temperatures. The minimum "case records above was that of a comparatively gentle animal, and the temperature was taken before "being slaughtered.

Some of these differences, as seen in the reports, are doubtless to be ascribed to the greater or less familiarity with the pathological appearances presented. Some may be due to more or less imperfect sense of colour, colour blindness, and some to the personal equation of the observer; the same consistency, for instance, appearing as "flaccid" to one and "not flaccid" to another.

To the question, however, whether any epidemic prevails among the Texas cattle, there is but one answer; No. While the figures given are insufficient to furnish answer to the question as to the annual mortality, the answers are sufficiently definite to show that the mortality is small, and that ordinarily death only ensues from injury, exposure to inclement weather, starvation or old age. This is true, however, only of Texas bred cattle. The improved stock of Northern cattle imported into the State have met with a sad fate, by far the greater number dying within a few months of their arrival. To illustrate, I will quote from an exceedingly interesting letter written by Mr. B. F. Gooch, a stock-raiser living near Mason, Texas: "In 1874 I purchased in Kentucky and Kansas 53 head of "short-horn Durhams, 18 females and 35 males, ranging from six months' to six years' old, all "thoroughbred, pedigreed animals but three, and arrived at Mason, Texas, with them the 13th day of "December. When within two and a half miles of this place one of my yearling bulls died with the "Spanish or Texas fever, and from that time on for 35 days they continued to die until I had but 16 "of the 53 living. I tried about all the remedies recorded in 'Clater's Cattle Doctor,' 'American "Cattle,' by Allen, besides many other remedies that all the 'Dicks, Toms, and Harrys' who came "along knew, all to no avail. In fact, it looked as though every one I doctored at all died, "but one yearling bull, to which I gave copperas in corn meal gruel. I imagine it did him "good; and one heifer was made to swallow freely, at different times, raw eggs, and she got well, and "is living to day. But just here, let me say to the credit of Dr. Clater, referred to above, that just "what he says in his work, pages 262-3, about drenching cattle, was experienced in nearly every "instance with my patients. The poor cattle were suffocated by the medicines being poured down "their wind-pipes and entering their lungs instead of their stomachs. When I had read him on the "subject of drenching, I opened the lungs of one that had died, and found a considerable portion of "the medicine in the lungs, and I confidently believe a number of my cattle that died would have lived if "nothing had been done for them. * * * The sixteen head that lived all had the fever, and "with the exception of the two alluded to, got well without any treatment. Out of the 18 females "brought here in 1874, I saved three yearling heifers, from which I have had 17 increase, 14 of which "are living."

Similar are the mortality reports from every other cattle breeders whom I have questioned. Captain Richard King, of Santa Gertrude's ranch, the largest ranch in Texas, who numbers his acres by hundreds of thousands, and his cattle by tens of thousands, informs me that among the fine cattle, Durhams, imported by him, the mortality within the first year was fearful; while among those bred by him on his ranch, death from disease, that is, from any cause other than those above named, was of the rarest occurrence. It is not certain whether the cause of this mortality is climatic or dietetic. Some maintain that the Spanish or Texas fever is nothing but a process of acclimation; that it is due to new conditions of sunshine, moisture and temperature, and that it affects all animals, human beings as well as the four-footed.

On the other hand some maintain that the sickness is caused by change of food, not only different grasses and grains, but the pastures in these latitudes are full of larvæ and insects of various kinds, noxious when taken into the stomach.

I am told that one or two varieties of distoma have been recognised, and the embryo of taenia saginata, it is well known is found in the flesh of the cattle, whence occurs the prevalence of this variety of tapeworm among the people of Texas, and it is a fact that tapeworm is more prevalent in this State than anywhere else that I have ever been stationed. These are simply popular beliefs as to the cause of the prevalence of mortal diseases among imported stock in this State.

The question, then, must still be regarded as "sub judice."

As bearing on this question, I may state that in the special report from the Department of Agriculture for 1879, being an investigation on diseases of swine and infectious and contagious diseases incident to other classes of domesticated animals, appear reports from 30 counties of Texas as to the prevalence of diseases among domesticated animals.

In 24 counties it is either stated that little or no disease prevails among cattle, or inferentially it is made so to appear by the failure to mention such prevalence. Six counties report as follows:—

Austin county.—A strange disease has been prevailing among cattle in the northern part of the county, and every animal attacked has died.

Q 4854.

Hopkins county.—And cattle (are affected) with bloody murrain.

Kerr county.—Fifty-four cattle have died during the present year of dry murrain. The condition of all farm animals, however, is a little better than the average.

Titus county.—Cattle are affected with murrain and black tongue, and nearly all die that are attacked by these diseases. Many also die from feeding on acorns.

Upshur county.—A good many cattle and hogs have died in this county during the past year of diseases peculiar to these classes of farm animals.

Uvalde county.—And cattle (die) of lung fever and spinal diseases.

In the report on the same subject for 1880 appear statements from 32 counties. Of these 2 report freedom from disease, the same as the report for 1879. Eight counties report as follows:—Camp county: "Several cattle have died of bloody murrain." Chambers county: "I am led to believe " that the losses * * * from disease in this county for the last year will amount to * * * at " least 20,000 dollars (of cattle)." Eastland county: "A few calves and yearlings died in this county " last spring of a disease called black-leg." Gillespie county: "Some eight or ten head of calves " recently died here of black tongue. Horses, cattle, and sheep are in a healthy condition." Kerr county: "A good many calves and yearlings are now affected with a disease known as black-leg." Lamar county: "A great many diseases have prevailed among farm animals in this county during the " past season, and the losses have been heavier than usual. I estimate the losses * * * of cattle at " 10,000 dollars." Uvalde county: "Cattle here are mainly afflicted with some kind of slow fever, " known generally as Spanish fever." Walker county: "Murrain is prevalent among cattle, and but " few attacked recover." These reports are too indefinite to warrant the formation of precise conclusions; but in the absence of definite statements as to numbers, and as to whether the affected cattle are imported or home-bred, they are far from proving the prevalence of epidemic disease among the Texas cattle.

In regard to cattle driven from this State to the northern markets, the assertions of all drivers with whom I have communicated are perfectly positive, viz., except from starvation or over-fatigue or exposure, they lose no cattle on the road. I have this day (December 1) conversed with a Northern dealer in cattle who buys thousands in Texas every year and drives them to his northern ranch, where they are either bred from or fattened for the market. He says he has now about 5,000 Texas cows on his ranch, and no disease exists among them or has ever followed their arrival at their new home from the road.

In this connexion I insert a quotation from the letter before quoted of Mr. B. F. Gooch:

"It is so seldom that an animal dies on the route north from any disease that it would not be worth mentioning. Starvation kills a great number in some herds. When men from their great anxiety to make money have brought up in the fall of the year large numbers and thrown them into small pastures (large pastures in acres but small in grass compared with the number of cattle) during the winter, and by reason of having overstocked the pasture they are forced to take them out in the latter part of the winter, before grass, and start them on the trail, they have often met with heavy losses; but where cattle have had a reasonable pasturage during the winter, and not placed under close herd before grass in the spring, and are then started on the road north, although they may be poor at the time of starting they increase in flesh and strength from the very first until they reach Kansas or Nebraska, and there is no loss by death unless killed in a stampede or drowned in swollen watercourses in the drover's haste to get to market."

I am aware that the facts I have here given are not in conformity with the opinions which have been entertained and promulgated by some others.

Thus Dr. Salmon, in his report to the Commissioner of Agriculture, defines "the southern cattle " fever" under its different synonyms as "an exceedingly fatal epizootic, specific, communicable fever " of cattle, at present confined to regions south of the 37th parallel of north latitude, except as com-" municated to cattle north of this line by cattle brought from south of it," &c. &c."

The whole of Texas is included by this boundary. Dr. Salmon further says: "Not very much is " known of the disease in Texas, except that it is very difficult to acclimate thoroughbred cattle on " account of it." Mr. Mark Huselby, of Fort Elliott, Texas, in a letter to the National Live Stock Journal (1879, p. 258), says: "It is much more extensive than you seem to be aware of, for in the " section of the country known as the Panhandle of Texas, I might make a fair estimate by saying that " 1,000 head of stock die annually from that disease. * * * We suppose it to be contagious in Texas, " though cattle seldom die of it. What are known here as American, Colorado, and Mexican cattle, " when brought in contact with Texas cattle almost invariably suffer severely."

Mr. Huselby's description does not conform to Dr. Salmon's definition, certainly as to mortality, and seems to confirm the statements in the first part of this paper that the disease rather affects the imported and not the Texas-bred cattle. Further on, in the same report, reference is made to certain post-mortem appearances in Texas cattle, which seem to show that a disease of some kind affected native Texas cattle driven north, and that the pathological appearances in a large number of apparently healthy Texas bullocks were similar to those found in cases of Spanish fever. If these observations are confirmed they prove too much—at least, their interpretation is doubtful.

This paper does not profess to be an essay on the diseases of cattle in general; and I, therefore, make no mention of them save to say that to my inquiries of stockmen and butchers the reply is made, that, of course, individual cases of very many cattle diseases occur, and that whenever cattle are crowded in comparatively small pastures, or stockyards, or stables, for fattening, as they mostly are in the vicinity of large towns, more frequent cases of disease occur.

As far as my inquiries extend, they seem to lead to the conclusion that no epidemic disease prevails among the Texas-bred cattle living and grazing in that State, but that imported cattle soon after their arrival are affected by a disease called Texas or Spanish fever, which is very fatal to them alone.

I regret that I am not able to present a larger number of precise answers as to the pathological appearances in the cattle killed. These, however, I hope to obtain during the coming year, and embody in a more complete report, to be offered at the next meeting of the Public Health Association.

To acquire exhaustive information on the subject, researches should be prosecuted from both ends of the line, from the breeding places and pastures, and from the slaughter-houses, the history of all animals found diseased in the northern slaughter-houses being carefully traced back to their homes.

No. 27.

LETTER from the ACTING BRITISH CONSUL at Philadelphia to EARL GRANVILLE.

Sanitary, No. 5.

British Consulate, Philadelphia,
December 21, 1880.

MY LORD,

I HAVE the honour to acknowledge the receipt of Mr. Lister's Despatch No. 1, Sanitary, of the 3rd ultimo, instructing me to obtain through the British Vice-Consul at Chicago a report on the alleged existence of Texas fever among cattle in Illinois and Indiana, and in reply to inclose your Lordship copy of a Despatch received from Mr. Warrack, wherein he states that he has not been able to find an authenticated case of Texas fever since October 1879.

I may venture to state to your Lordship that the farmers and cattle dealers are averse to giving information upon the subject, supposing that pecuniary losses will follow publicity, especially in the exportations of cattle to England.

From a sanitary point of view, it may not be impertinent to call your Lordship's attention to the immense mortality among swine by a disease known as "hog cholera," of which about 700,000 head have died this year in Illinois. Immense quantities of pork are annually shipped to the United Kingdom, and as the disease "trichina spiralis" seems to be on the increase in this country the subject is not unworthy of attention. Two persons recently died in Milwaukee and one in Chicago. In the latter city several people are ill with it at the present time, and one entire family attacked about a month ago are not yet out of danger. A case just reported from Kansas describes the symptoms of the disease when it attacks the human family. In this case the victim is a farmer. He had been ill for some time and became much reduced in flesh. Upon consulting a physician, trichinæ were found, worms were in his flesh by the millions, being scraped and squeezed from the pores of the skin. They are felt creeping through his flesh and are literally eating up his substance. The disease is thought to have been contracted by eating sausages.

Trichina spiralis may be conveyed to human beings, it is thought, by the gross adulterations used in the manufacture of butter and cheese, of which there is some exportation to England. The former is adulterated with lard and grease, which in many cases are taken from the places where hogs die of diseases and then rendered into grease, glue, &c., and the latter by a commodity called "anti huff."

I have, &c.

The Right Hon. the Earl of Granville, K.G., &c. &c. &c.
Foreign Office.

(Signed) GEORGE CRUMP.

Enclosure in No. 27.

British Vice-Consulate, Chicago, Dec. 17, 1880.

SIR,

IN reply to your letter of 16th ult., directing me to report to you, for the information of Earl Granville, upon the alleged existence of Texas fever in Illinois and Indiana, I beg to say that, after due inquiry, I have not been able to find an authentic case of this disease since early in October 1879, when 11 out of 12 native cattle purchased by a farmer in the stock yards here, and taken to his farm, 25 miles west of Chicago, to be fed during the winter, died of what was generally admitted to be Texas fever, and undoubtedly was so. In September 1880, "The National Live Stock Journal," a respectable periodical published here, professes to have seen references to several cases in its exchanges published in some of the Western States, and in the October number printed the following editorially:—

"The summer drive from the South has brought its usual freight of disease to the Northern States, and already many isolated outbreaks have taken place on land where the southern cattle have temporarily sojourned. The half or the whole of a herd has been suddenly cut off, and a district has become panic-stricken in view of what seems to threaten a great public calamity; but when the true cause is shown the losses are borne silently, under the idea that there can be no help, and that even individual States are debarred from self-protection in this matter, &c. &c."

On applying to the editor of the "Journal," he was unable to name any of the cases referred to, and said that the article was written in consequence of his having seen several references to the appearance of the disease in many of the newspapers issued in the Western States.

I have, &c.
(Signed) J. WARRACK,
British Vice-Consul.

George Crump, Esq., British Consulate, Philadelphia.

No. 28.

LETTER from SIR E. THORNTON to EARL GRANVILLE.

Sanitary, No. 30.
MY LORD, Washington, December 27, 1880.

I HAVE the honour to transmit herewith copies of a Bill which was submitted to the House of Representatives on the 6th instant, by Mr. Ryan, a member from Kansas, to provide for the prevention and suppression of infectious and contagious diseases of domestic animals.

It proposes to impose fine and imprisonment upon persons transporting infected live cattle from one state or territory to another, and to establish a commission, who, with the assistance of a veterinary surgeon, shall make rules and shall have power to purchase and slaughter infected animals. The different states and territories are to be invited to adopt the rules made by the commission, and those who do so will benefit by the grants made for carrying out the provisions of the Act, for which purpose it is proposed to appropriate the sum of $200,000.

The Bill, which goes into a good deal of detail, was referred to the Committee on Agriculture.

Another Bill, having a similar object, copies of which are also enclosed, was submitted to the Senate on the 14th instant, by Mr. Williams, a senator from Kentucky. This Bill, however, would throw the power and responsibility of taking steps for the suppression of contagious diseases among cattle into the hands of the National Board of Health, and to meet the expenses to be incurred it proposes a grant of $1,000,000.

Unfortunately the session of Congress will end on the 4th of March next, and it is very doubtful whether it will have time to do more than pass the necessary appropriation bills.

I have, &c.
(Signed) EDWD. THORNTON.

The Right Hon. the Earl Granville, K.G.
&c. &c. &c.

Enclosure 1. in No. 28.

In the HOUSE OF REPRESENTATIVES, December 6, 1880.—Read twice, referred to the COMMITTEE ON AGRICULTURE, and ordered to be printed.

Mr. THOMAS RYAN introduced the following bill: To provide for the prevention and suppression of infectious and contagious diseases of domesticated animals.

BE it enacted by the Senate and House of Representatives of the United States of America in Congress assembled, that no railroad company within the United States whose road forms any part of a line of road from one state or territory to another, or from a state into the district of Columbia, or the owners or masters of any steam or sailing or other vessels or boat, shall receive for transportation or transport from one state or territory to another, or from any state into the district of Columbia, any live cattle affected with any contagious or infectious disease, and especially the disease known as contagious pleuro-pneumonia. Nor shall any person, company, or corporation deliver for such transportation to any railroad company, master or owner of any boat or vessel, any live cattle affected with any contagious or infectious disease; nor shall any person, company, or corporation drive on foot or transport in private conveyance from one state or territory to another, or from any state into the district of Columbia, any live cattle affected with any contagious or infectious disease, and especially the disease known as pleuro-pneumonia.

SEC. 2. That any company or persons operating any such railroad, or master or owner of any boat or vessel, or owner or custodian of, or person having control over, such live cattle, who shall violate the provisions of section one of this Act, shall be guilty of a misdeameanor, and, upon conviction, shall be punished by a fine of not less than 100 nor more than 5,000 dollars, or by imprisonment for not more than one year, or by both such fine and imprisonment.

SEC. 3. That it shall be the duty of the several United States district attorneys to prosecute all violations of Section 1 of this Act, which shall be brought to their notice or knowledge by any person making the complaint, and the same shall be heard before any circuit court of the United States or any district court of the United States holden within the district in which the violation of this Act has been committed, or the person or corporation resides or carries on or has his or its place of business.

SEC. 4. That the Commissioner of Agriculture, the Second Assistant Secretary of State, and the Second Assistant Secretary of the Treasury be, and they are hereby, constituted a commission, to be known and designated as "The National Board of Commissioners for the Suppression of Infectious and "Contagious Diseases of Domesticated Animals."

SEC. 5. That the Commissioner of Agriculture shall be president of said Board. All meetings of the Board shall be called by the president, and any two members of the same shall constitute a quorum for the transaction of business.

SEC. 6. That no member of said Board shall receive any compensation for his services as a member of this commission, except the president thereof, who shall receive from the funds hereinafter appropriated the sum of 100 dollars per month in addition to his present salary.

SEC. 7. That said board shall elect a secretary, who shall perform all the duties usually pertaining to such officer, and such other duties as may be required by the Board of Commissioners.

SEC. 8. That said Board shall also appoint a veterinary surgeon, who shall superintend, under the direction of the Commissioners, all measures for the prevention and suppression of infectious and contagious diseases of domesticated animals; he shall draft such rules and regulations as he may deem necessary for a speedy suppression of the outbreak under consideration, and upon approval by the board of said rules and regulations, the same shall be certified for acceptance to the Governor and Veterinary Surgeon of the State wherein said disease prevails.

SEC. 9. That on notification by the Governor of the acceptance of the rules and regulations framed by the veterinary surgeon of the Board, a meeting of the Board of Commissioners shall at once be held, and such sum as may be deemed necessary for the purchase and slaughter of all diseased or infected animals in the State or territory in which the outbreak has occurred shall be awarded from the fund hereinafter appropriated for this purpose, Provided, however, that a sum not exceeding two-thirds the market value of a healthy animal shall be allowed for an infected or diseased one; and a sum not exceeding 100 dollars may be made in special cases, but no animal shall be considered of special value unless he be purely bred, and the pedigree found duly recorded in a well-established herd book. Provided further, that should the first award not be sufficient for the complete eradication of the disease in said State, an additional sum may be allowed; and should the first award prove larger than necessary, the unexpended balance shall be covered into the general fund.

SEC. 10. That any state or territory may adopt the regulations forming the concluding portions of this Act, and designated as articles from one to eight, inclusive, and all states and territories adopting the same shall be entitled to such portion of the appropriation hereinafter provided as may be deemed expedient by the Board of Commissioners for the suppression of any outbreak of any infectious or contagious disease amongst domesticated animals therein.

SEC. 11. That all states and territories failing to adopt the articles mentioned in the preceding Section shall be debarred from the benefits of any portion of this appropriation, except as hereinafter provided.

SEC. 12. That on the acceptance or adoption by the Legislature of any state or territory of the articles mentioned in Section 10 of this Act, it shall be the duty of the Governor of said state or territory to forward to the President of the Board of Commissioners a certified copy of the same; said copy, with the certificate of the Governor, shall be recorded by the Secretary of the Board in a book kept for that purpose, and the original shall then be forwarded to the Secretary of State, who shall be the custodian of the same.

SEC. 13. That whenever the Governor of any state or territory, the Legislature whereof has complied with the provisions of this Act, has notified the President of the Board that an infectious or contagious disease prevails among any class of domesticated animals within said state or territory, the President of the Board may, if he deem it expedient, dispatch the veterinary surgeon to the locality of the outbreak Said veterinary surgeon shall then make a thorough examination as to the nature, extent, and infectious and contagious character of the malady, and at once report the results of his investigation to the Board of Commissioners. Should the said report confirm the infectious and contagious character of the disease, and the Board of Commissioners deem it expedient to institute repressive measures, the veterinary surgeon shall, in conjunction with the state or territorial authorities, proceed to form and promulgate such rules and regulations as may be deemed necessary.

SEC. 14. That no diseased or infected animal shall be paid for out of any funds hereinafter appropriated unless the same shall have been condemned and slaughtered on the authority of the veterinary surgeon of the Board, and no bill for condemned and slaughtered animals shall be allowed or paid by said Commissioners unless the same shall have been receipted for by the owner and certified as correct by the veterinary surgeon of the Board, and the veterinary surgeon of the state or territory wherein the animal or animals may have been condemned.

SEC. 15. That no part of the sum hereinafter appropriated for the suppression of infectious and contagious diseases of domesticated animals shall be expended except in payment for such animals as may have been condemned and slaughtered by authority of the National and State veterinary surgeons, the additional salary of the President of the Board and the disbursing officer thereof, the salary of the Secretary of the Board and the veterinary surgeon of the same, printing, stationery, postage, office furniture, and the necessary travelling expenses of the members and officers of the board.

SEC. 16. That during the prevalence of extensive epidemics among domesticated animals the Board of Commissioners may employ additional veterinary surgeons and such other assistants as the exigencies of the case may require; and said additional employées shall be paid from the same fund and in the same manner as other servants of the Board.

SEC. 17. That the salary of the secretary and veterinary surgeon, and all other employées of the Board, shall be fixed by the Board of Commissioners, and paid monthly, except that of the disbursing officer, who shall be paid quarterly, out of the appropriation hereinafter provided, at the rate of two hundred dollars per annum, in addition to his present salary as disbursing officer of the Department of Agriculture.

SEC. 18. That salaries, and all other indebtedness of whatsoever character, shall be paid by draft on the United States Treasurer, signed by the President of the Board and countersigned by the secretary of the same; and no moneys shall be paid by said Board of Commissioners except on receipted vouchers, showing the nature of the obligation and the character of the services rendered.

SEC. 19. That said Board of Commissioners shall annually make a report to Congress, giving full detail of the work performed during the year, the amount expended for all purposes, the character of the epidemic treated, and the amount expended in each state and territory respectively.

SEC. 20. That the President of the Board shall furnish office room in the Department of Agriculture for the transaction of the business of the Board of Commissioners, which room shall be used for the meetings of the Board and for the transaction of all business of said Commission save that relating to the disbursing officer of the Board.

SEC. 21. That the sum of two hundred thousand dollars is hereby appropriated out of any money remaining in the Treasury and not otherwise appropriated for the purpose of carrying out the provisions of the foregoing Act.

SEC. 22. That until the disease known as contagious pleuro-pneumonia of cattle shall have been extirpated no part of the sum appropriated under the provisions of this Act shall be used for the suppression of any other disease.

SEC. 23. That upon approval by the Board of Commissioners of such laws and regulations as may now be in force in any state or territory infected by contagious diseases of domesticated animals, and upon acquiescence of the executive of said state or territory, the Board may proceed to enforce the provisions of this Act in lieu of the supplemental articles accompanying this Act : Provided further, that in case any animal or animals in any state or territory having no law on the subject shall have been exposed by proximity or otherwise to a diseased or infected animal, or to a centre of infection, the veterinary surgeon of the Board may be authorised to purchase and kill the same, payment to be made only upon a proper certificate of the facts, which certificate shall be signed by the veterinarian of the Board and the owner of the cattle thus taken or destroyed.

SEC. 24. That whenever any infectious or contagious disease affecting domestic animals, and especially the disease known as pleuro-pneumonia, shall be brought into or shall break out in the district of Columbia it shall be the duty of the Commissioners of said district, in conjunction with the National Board of Commissioners, to take measures to suppress the same promptly and to prevent the same from spreading ; and for this purpose the said Commissioners are hereby empowered to order and require any premises, farm, or farms where such disease exists, or has existed, to be put in quarantine ; to order all or any animals coming into the district to be detained at any place or places for the purpose of inspection and examination ; to prescribe regulations for, and to require the destruction of, animals affected with infectious or contagious disease, and for the proper disposition of their hides and carcasses; to prescribe regulations for disinfection, and such other regulations as they may deem necessary to prevent infection or contagion being communicated.

SEC. 25. That the Secretary of State shall, as soon as convenient after the passage of this Act, forward a certified copy of the same to the governors of each of the states and territories of the United States.

SEC. 26. That it shall be the duty of the President of the Board of Commissioners to call a meeting of the same for the purpose of organisation within ten days after the passage of this Act.

SEC. 27. That this Act shall be in force from its passage.

SUPPLEMENTAL ACT FOR ADOPTION BY STATES AND TERRITORIES.

ARTICLE 1. In the event of an outbreak of any infectious or contagious disease among domesticated animals in other states or territories so connected by railways or navigation with this state that animals may be transported into or through it in a comparatively short time, it shall be the duty of the Governor, upon the presentation of undoubted evidence of such fact, to issue a proclamation prohibiting the importation into the state of all animals belonging to the class affected ; said proclamation shall declare the penalties prescribed for the doing the acts which are prohibited by it. And it shall be the further duty of the Governor, upon satisfactory proof that any class of domesticated animals in any other state or territory would by their presence in this state, or any part thereof, be reasonably certain to impart to any domestic animal of this state a disease commonly known as the Texas cattle fever, or any other dangerous disease, to issue his proclamation prohibiting the importation into this state, or any part of it he may designate, of all animals belonging to such class, except at such times and upon such conditions as he may in his proclamation specify ; and said proclamation shall declare the penalties prescribed for the doing the acts which are prohibited by it.

ARTICLE 2. As soon as any case of disease or death occurs among any class of domesticated animals within the state of a malady supposed to be of an infectious or contagious nature, the owner thereof shall forthwith inform the Governor, whose duty it shall then be to appoint and dispatch a competent veterinary surgeon to investigate and report upon the nature of the disease ; and the owner must not slaughter or dispose of any such animal until the nature of the malady has been determined by the veterinary surgeon of the state. Until such investigation has been made by the veterinary surgeon the sick and infected animal or animals must be so kept that men and uninfected animals liable to spread or contract the disease shall not have access to them. On failure to comply with the provisions of this article the owner or owners, on conviction thereof in the proper court of the county in which the offence occurs, may be fined in a sum not exceeding dollars, or imprisoned in the county jail for a period not exceeding thirty days, or both, at the discretion on the court.

ARTICLE 3. The veterinary surgeon, after a thorough examination as to the nature and cause of the disease, shall make a full report in writing to the Governor, whose duty it shall then be to issue a proclamation prohibiting the removal and transportation of all animals of the class affected from the locality in which the outbreak has occurred, and shall authorise such quarantine measures, under such penalties as he may deem expedient for a strict observance of the same, as will most effectually prevent the spread of the contagion.

ARTICLE 4. Immediately upon the receipt of the report of the veterinary surgeon, the Governor shall notify the President of the National Board of Commissioners for the Suppression of Contagious and Infectious Diseases of Domesticated Animals, and ask the co-operation of said Board in such manner as may be deemed expedient for the speedy suppression of the disease.

ARTICLE 5. All measures for the suppression of infectious and contagious diseases of domesticated animals shall be determined by the veterinary surgeon of the National Board of Commissioners and the veterinary surgeon appointed by the Governor of the State. They may prepare such rules and regulations as they may deem expedient for the most speedy suppression of the disease. A copy of said rules and regulations shall be filed with the clerk of the county court in the county in which the outbreak has occurred, and shall be accessible to all persons interested.

ARTICLE 6. The Governor shall employ a properly qualified veterinary surgeon, and his salary, and the salaries of such assistants as the Governor may deem necessary to appoint or employ for the speedy suppression of the disease, shall be fixed by the Governor and paid from the fund of the State Treasury. All travelling and other extraordinary expenses incurred by the veterinary surgeon and his assistants or employées while in the performance of their duty shall be paid by the State out of any funds not otherwise appropriated.

ARTICLE 7. The Governor shall, on the presentation of satisfactory evidence of the complete suppression of an infectious or contagious disease previously existing among any class of domesticated animals, by and with the advice and consent of the National Board of Commissioners for the Suppression of Infectious and Contagious Diseases of Domesticated Animals, issue his proclamation suspending all quarantine measures respecting the removal and transportation of animals belonging to said class. The Governor may also, by proclamation, whenever he may deem it expedient, remove all restrictions and prohibitions against the importation and transportation of such class of domesticated animals and their products as previously prohibited by authority given in article 1.

ARTICLE 8. If any person shall import, transport, or drive, or cause to be imported, transported, or driven, into or through this state any domesticated animals of the class or classes mentioned in article 1, the importation, transportation, or driving of which shall have been prohibited by the Governor by proclamation, as herein-before provided, or shall transport or drive, or cause to be transported or driven, in violation of the rules and regulations prescribed by the proper officers, as hereinbefore provided, any infected domesticated animals from the place within this State where an infectious or contagious disease may have broken out among domesticated animals, each person so offending shall, upon conviction thereof, be fined in any sum not exceeding one thousand dollars, or be imprisoned in the jail of the proper county not exceeding sixty days, or both, at the discretion of the Court.

Enclosure 2. in No. 28.

In the SENATE of the United States, December 14, 1880. Mr. Williams asked, and, by unanimous consent, obtained leave to bring in the following Bill, which was read twice and ordered to lie on the table.

A Bill to prevent the introduction and dissemination of Epizootics or Communicable Diseases of Domestic Animals in the United States.

Be it enacted by the Senate and House of Representatives of the United States of America in Congress assembled, that it shall be unlawful to import or introduce into the United States from foreign countries, or into one state, territory, or district from another, any animal affected with a communicable, infectious, or contagious disease, or any animal conveying in its system the poison of splenic or Texas cattle fever, except in accordance with the provisions of this Act and all rules and regulations adopted by the National Board of Health, or any state or territory or the district of Columbia made in pursuance of this Act; nor shall any person, company, or corporation offer for sale or sell any domestic animal affected with an infectious or contagious disease, such as the lung plague or contagious pleuropneumonia of cattle, the splenic or Texas cattle fever, foot and mouth disease, hog-cholera, trichinosis, farcy, and glanders, and so forth, in violation of the provisions of this Act.

SEC. 2. That the National Board of Health, or in the interval of its sessions its executive committee, shall report to the President of the United States whenever any place in the United States is considered by it to be dangerously infected with communicable diseases of domestic animals, and that upon the official publication by the President of such report, the removal or transportation therefrom of animals from such place into another state shall be unlawful, unless such removal or transportion shall be carried on in accordance with rules and regulations made by the National Board of Health and approved by the President.

SEC. 3. That any person, company, or corporation having control over such live animals who shall violate the provisions of sections 1 and 2 of this Act shall be guilty of a misdemeanour, and, upon conviction, shall be punished by a fine of not less than 100 nor more than 5,000 dollars, or by imprisonment for not more than one year, or by both such fine and imprisonment.

SEC. 4. That it shall be the duty of the several United States district attorneys to prosecute all violations of Sections 1 and 2 of this Act which shall be brought to their notice or knowledge by any person making the complaint; and the same shall be heard before any district or circuit court of the United States, holden within the district in which the violation of this Act has been committed, or the person or corporation resides, or carries on or has his or its place of business.

SEC. 5. That the National Board of Health shall, and is hereby authorised to, investigate, record, and report on the diseases of animals prevailing in the United States, or in countries from which the United States may import domestic animals for breeding or other purposes, and also draft such rules and regulations as they may deem necessary for the arrest or prevention of any infectious or communicable disease, in accordance with the provisions of this Act.

SEC. 6. That the National Board of Health shall be, and is hereby, authorised to appoint a duly qualified veterinary supervisor, who shall be ex officio member of said Board, and such other veterinary surgeons as inspectors or investigators of animal diseases as may be required to co-operate with any duly appointed officers of district, state, or territory, acting under the sanction of the governor or any state law in operation for this purpose, or to act independently in accordance with the provisions of this Act.

SEC. 7. That the National Board of Health may, and is hereby empowered to, elect special officers or clerks to perform all duties required under this Act apart and beyond the special work of veterinary supervision and inspection, and to publish weekly or monthly bulletins, if necessary, illustrated by a map or maps relating to the distribution of communicable diseases in animals, with special reference, but not necessarily restricted, to the diseases named in section 1.

SEC. 8. That the National Board of Health is authorised to detail as inspectors duly qualified persons to serve in the office of the consul at any foreign port, for the purpose of recording and reporting on the diseases of live stock passing to and fro across the ocean : provided that the number of officers so detailed shall not exceed at any one time four.

SEC. 9. That the National Board of Health shall, and is hereby authorised to prepare such rules and regulations applicable to the prevention and suppression of communicable or infectious diseases of animals, including rules for compensation of owners for the slaughter of infected or sick animals, as may be carried out in conjunction with, or with the approval of the authorities of any state or territory, or the district of Columbia, where an epizootic may prevail or manifest itself.

SEC. 10. That any district, state, or territory may adopt the methods and rules adopted by the National Board of Health in the suppression of disease within the limits of such district, state, or territory; and all districts, states, and territories adopting the said regulations shall be aided pecuniarily, as may be deemed expedient by the National Board of Health, for the eradication of any infectious or communicable disease.

SEC. 11. That the President is authorised, when requested by the National Board of Health, and when the same can be done without prejudice to the public service, to detail officers from the several departments of the government, for temporary duty, to act under the direction of the said Board in carrying out the provisions of this Act; and such officers shall receive no additional compensation except for actual and necessary expenses incurred in the performance of such duties.

SEC. 12. That to meet the expenses to be incurred in carrying out the provisions of this Act the sum of one million dollars, or so much thereof as may be necessary, is hereby appropriated, to be disbursed under the direction of the Secretary of the Treasury on estimates to be made by the National Board of Health, and to be approved by him. Said National Board of Health shall, as often as quarterly, make a full statement of its operations and expenditures under this Act to the Secretary of the Treasury, who shall report the same to Congress.

No. 29.

LETTER from the BRITISH CONSUL-GENERAL at New York.

Sanitary, No. 18.

British Consulate General, New York,
December 29, 1880.

MY LORD,

I HAVE the honour to report to your Lordship that since the date of my last Despatch (Sanitary, No. 17, of the 1st instant), many cases of pleuro-pneumonia have been found in certain of the cow stables in the city of Brooklyn and at other places on Long Island. The veterinary surgeons deputed by the Brooklyn Board of Health to inspect the stables report that in one stable, containing 14 animals, 10 were found to be affected with pleuro-pneumonia, the other four being very emaciated.

In another city stable 10 sick cows were discovered; and at Penny Bridge, on Newtown Creek, Long Island, 10 cows were also found to be suffering from pleuro-pneumonia. All the sick animals were immediately quarantined.

An inspection has likewise been recently made by the veterinary surgeon to the State Cattle Commission of cattle at Hempstead, Long Island, at which place there exists a large establishment for fattening sick cows and calves on the refuse food and swill of hotels for sale in the New York and Brooklyn markets. I transmit, herewith enclosed, an extract from a local newspaper on the subject. 78 cows, one bull, and 189 calves are reported as having been found at this place, four of them having pleuro-pneumonia, and many of them chronic tuberculosis. All the diseased cattle, 75 in number, have since been slaughtered, and the owner has been convicted and fined under the law for the prevention of cruelty to animals.

The epizootic disease among horses, which I have referred to in my previous reports as being prevalent in different parts of my Consular District, has now practically disappeared.

I have, &c.
(Signed) E. M. ARCHIBALD.

Her Majesty's Principal Secretary of State
for Foreign Affairs, London.

Enclosure in No. 29.

A PEST HOLE.

DISEASED CATTLE ON LONG ISLAND.

Fattening sick cows and calves for the New York and Brooklyn markets; report of a veterinary surgeon to the State Cattle Commission; nearly 200 sick animals kept in a filthy manner and fed on swill from New York hotels.

AN extensive feeding station for sick cattle has been discovered on Long Island by the officers of the State Cattle Commission, which is in charge of General Patrick. Mr. J. Howard Rushmore, who is the agent of the Commission for Queen's County, while on a tour of examination recently through that county, found on the farm owned by Sidney W. Hendrickson, at Hempstead, 78 cows, one bull, and 189 calves, all in a starving and sick condition. One of the animals was suffering from acute tuberculosis, 12 from chronic tuberculosis, and four from pleuro-pneumonia. Veterinary Surgeon James D. Hopkins was sent on Wednesday last to make a thorough examination of the animals and premises on which they are kept, and yesterday made the following official report of the condition of affairs :—

"These animals are fed exclusively on soup, made from the refuse of New York hotels, and as the food is unnatural they take very little of it. This is one of the many feeding stations located in the vicinity of New York for fatting calves for market. This is the most extensive of its kind, and the most filthy place I have ever seen. Here animals in the last stages of disease may be slaughtered and the carcass carried to the sausage maker, and no meat inspector can detect the inhuman practice. This is one of the pest holes that should be blotted from the face of the earth.

"JAS. D. HOPKINS."

Dr. Hopkins and the other attachés of the State Cattle Commission say that Mr. Hendrickson, the owner of the farm, would only tell the name of one of the owners of the cattle, Moses Heilman, of First Avenue, near Forty-fifth Street, New York. Mr. Hendrickson professed not to know the names of the other owners, but from information obtained of other parties it is expected that all the owners will be discovered shortly. The cows and bull were kept in an open yard and the calves in a cellar which was flooded from four to six inches in depth with liquid filth. The cows and calves which were badly diseased were killed and the entire stock yard has been put under quarantine. Sheriff Alonzo Wright, of Queen's County, is in possession of the yard, and the most efficient measures will be taken to prevent the diseased stock being taken away.

At General Patrick's head-quarters to-day it was learned that on November 13th last Moses Heilman obtained a permit to remove 100 head of cattle, which were in poor condition, from the Central Stock Yard in New York City to the cattle yard in Jersey City, and it is presumed that some of the 100 cattle, as they became sick, were smuggled to the Hendrickson farm. In fact, the authorities know, they say, much more than they choose to reveal at present of the mode by which the animals were smuggled to the farm at Hempstead. General Patrick's subordinates complain bitterly of the lack of funds at their disposal, which prevents them at once slaughtering all the animals affected and afterward indemnifying their owners. These officials have called upon the New York and Brooklyn health authorities for aid in the discovery and punishment of the numerous persons who have recently been engaged in the transportation of sick cattle to feeding farms in the country adjacent to the two cities.

Dr. Hopkins is authority for the statement that all the swill used as food for the cattle on Hendrickson's farm was cooked in a large cauldron, and the mass of refuse in the cauldron was of such a character that he has not been able to purify his hands since he put them in the cauldron to discover the ingredients of the cattle soup then being cooked. He also states that he has reason to believe that a sick and dying cow had its throat cut just prior to his arrival at the farm, and that the attendants there were preparing to cut up the cow and place its flesh in the cauldron when his arrival caused them to desist from doing this. Dr. Hopkins also reports that all the animals at the farm are suffering from diarrhœa, the effect of the harmful food given them, and that none of them are fit for human food.

No. 30.

EXTRACT from Annual Report of the Secretary of the Treasury (Washington) on the State of the Finances for the Year 1880.

EXPORTATION AND IMPORTATION OF CATTLE.

IN a letter of February 19, 1880, from this Department to the Speaker of the House of Representatives, the attention of Congress was called to the prevalence of the disease known as pleuro-pneumonia, or lung-plague, in neat cattle, and some recommendations were made as to the proper legislation on the subject.

It may be assumed that this disease has never existed in this country west of the Alleghany mountains; and that it has not for a long time existed in Canada, or in this country near the line of Canada. The exportation of live horned cattle from the United States is very large, and is rapidly increasing, the cattle going mostly to Great Britain. For the eight months ended August 31, 1880, the value of such animals exported was 12,462,837 dollars, which is nearly double the value of the exportation for the same period in 1879.

By an order of the Privy Council of Great Britain all American cattle must be slaughtered at the port of arrival within ten days. The effect of this order is to prevent the shipment of any but fat cattle, and it entails great loss as to that class of animals by compelling the immediate slaughter of such as are injured or become sick upon the voyage, and therefore of little value for food. It also prevents the owners from driving the cattle from the port of importation to a better market, or from keeping them until the market improves. Furthermore, there is a large demand in England for store or stock cattle, to be fed and fattened in that country for its own markets, a demand which this country could supply to an unlimited extent. It is believed that this trade, if unrestricted, might far exceed the trade in fat cattle. The losses and embarrassments by reason of the order for immediate slaughter are, commercially considered, very great. The British Government, however, is ready to rescind it when it may be done without danger of spreading pleuro-pneumonia in their country through importations from the United States.

The question of the rescission of the order has been the subject of official discussion between this Government and the Government of Great Britain, as well as in Parliament. It is believed that whenever Congress makes provision for the extinction or prevention of the disease, or for such security of the great routes of travel from the West to the seaboard as will make it reasonably certain that the cattle shipped from our ports, or any of them, will not carry infection with them, the Order of Council requiring immediate slaughter will be rescinded.

The recommendation that a Commission be created, whose duty it shall be to investigate reports of the existence of the disease, and to collect information respecting it, reporting the results to some Department for official publication, is renewed. It is further recommended that such Commission be authorised to co-operate with State and municipal authorities and corporations and persons engaged in the transportation of neat cattle, and establish regulations for the safe conveyance of such cattle from the interior to the seaboard, and the shipment of them, so that they may not be exposed to the disease; and that such Commission, also, may establish such quarantine stations and regulations as may be deemed necessary to prevent the spread of the disease by importations from abroad. It is believed that the legislation thus indicated, properly executed, will induce the Government of Great Britain to rescind its order for immediate slaughter, and thus promote a very large increase in the exportation of neat cattle from this country. Whether Congress should go further, and undertake the extirpation of the disease in the States where it now exists, is a question of more difficulty, and it is deemed best to leave that part of the subject for independent consideration.

No. 31.

LETTER from the BRITISH CONSUL at Baltimore to EARL GRANVILLE.

Sanitary, No. 1.

MY LORD, Baltimore, January 1, 1881.

I HAVE the honour to enclose a copy of a Report made by the Sanitary Inspector of this State to the Governor on the subject of the cattle disease.

The only cases reported by the Inspector are those that have appeared in some dairy-farms, and he further states that the disease has almost disappeared in the State of Maryland.

I have heard of no cases in other States within the district of this Consulate since my Despatch, Sanitary, No. 14, of the 1st ultimo.

I have, &c.
The Right Hon. the Earl Granville, K.G., (Signed) DENIS DONOHOE.
&c. &c. &c.

Enclosure in No. 31.

From Baltimore "American," of December 25, 1880.

PLEURO-PNEUMONIA.

A GRATIFYING REPORT from the STATE INSPECTOR OF CATTLE.

AT the last session of the State Legislature a law was passed relating to the killing of cattle affected with pleuro-pneumonia, and providing certain quarantine regulations to prevent the spread of the disease. The appointment of a sanitary inspector was authorised, and means suggested to stamp out the disease in the State. Governor Hamilton appointed Mr. Daniel Lemay, veterinary surgeon, an inspector under this law, and he yesterday handed in the following gratifying report of his work:—

"To his Excellency WILLIAM T. HAMILTON, Governor of the State of Maryland.

"MY DEAR SIR, "Baltimore, December 24, 1880.

"I HAVE the honour herewith to transmit my report upon the condition of the cattle I have examined in this State relative to the pleuro-pneumonia which prevailed to so great an extent not long ago. I take pleasure in announcing to your Excellency that the disease has almost entirely disappeared in the State, and the law in regard to its prevention and suppression has been so thoroughly enforced that this favourable and encouraging disappearance is the result. Of all the farms and dairies which it has been necessary to hold under quarantine regulations since you placed me on duty but a few have still doubtful chronic cases in their stables, the balance having been discharged from the quarantine; the only localities in which the disease now exists being Woodberry, Highlandtown, and Lower and Upper Canton. All other sections of the city and State where the disease was known to exist are now entirely free from it, and I hear no more rumours of its existence even in isolated cases.

"It is my custom to regularly inspect the stock yards at Calverton, by which means all or nearly all the cattle arrive in Baltimore, and I am glad to be able to report that thus far I have not encountered a single case. How far this pleasing result may be owing to the numerous placards relative to the disease and the law in regard to its suppression, I cannot say, but a satisfactory proof of the successful results accomplished by the efforts made to stamp out pleuro-pneumonia is plainly illustrated by the fact that during my inspection tour of last week I visited nearly 1,000 cattle, and found, in Highlandtown, a place where the disease has prevailed for years, but 22 distinctly chronic cases, and 25 which were suspicious, and not one single acute case in the whole number. In addition to the efforts made by the State to eradicate the disease, cattle owners themselves have become educated to the necessity of self-protection, and their efforts have aided in the disappearance of the disease from the State.

"On the 15th instant I wrote your Excellency for assistance in inspecting certain ries. This I thought necessary for my personal protection, as threats had been made by cattle ow. hat I would not be allowed to inspect their stock. While I received no injuries in these places, s, however, subjected to abuse and insult, which was far from pleasant; and I would again re that your Excellency will empower me to call upon a deputy sheriff when I find his services necess , for my own protection.

"In reference to the grave accusation made by the Pennsylvania authorities, to the effect that one-third of the pleuro-pneumonia in that State is imported across the borders from Maryland, I have no hesitation in saying that it is a gross exaggeration. While I am willing to admit that some cattle in the period of inoculation may have got over the border either one way or the other, and the number coming into the State is fully as great as that going out (I mean in regard to cows), the charge that one third of the whole number sick in Pennsylvania is due to Maryland is without foundation. All cattle shipped direct from the stock yards in Baltimore to Philadelphia or New York are inspected. Those passing through in transit I do not deem it necessary to inspect, as they remain here but a few hours, for food and water.

"From the repeated complaints of Mr. Thomas J. Edge, special agent of the Governor of Pennsylvania, I deemed it necessary, and did make a thorough investigation in order, if possible, to get at the grounds of his complaints. My investigation proves conclusively that Mr. Edge has been misinformed and deceived. I have been unable to find any party by the name of Millar who had shipped cattle to Philadelphia at the time mentioned by Mr. Edge, October 1880. Mr. B. Miller, of the firm of Miller and Brewer, did ship a load of cattle in the latter part of November, but they were properly inspected and sold under a certificate to Mr. James Duffy. The Mr. Millar mentioned by Mr. Edge is said to have sold his cattle to a Mr. A. Burns, who had them taken to Delaware county, where they were sold at public auction. If Mr. Edge was not misinformed, he must settle with himself to believe either that the inspector gave a fraudulent certificate, which is not probable, or that the cattle were infected after the sale in Delaware county. Trusting, sir, that my report may be satisfactory to you, I have the honour to be,

"Very respectfully, your obedient servant,
"Daniel Lemay,
"Veterinary Surgeon."

LONDON:
Printed by GEORGE E. EYRE and WILLIAM SPOTTISWOODE,
Printers to the Queen's most Excellent Majesty.
For Her Majesty's Stationery Office.
[17652.—1625.—2/81.]

FURTHER CORRESPONDENCE

RESPECTING

THE MANUFACTURE OF OLEO-MARGARINE

IN THE

UNITED STATES.

(*In continuation of* C.—2502 *of* 1880.)

Presented to both Houses of Parliament by Command of Her Majesty.

LONDON:
PRINTED BY GEORGE EDWARD EYRE AND WILLIAM SPOTTISWOODE,
PRINTERS TO THE QUEEN'S MOST EXCELLENT MAJESTY.
FOR HER MAJESTY'S STATIONERY OFFICE.

1880.

[C.—2767.] *Price* 2*d.*

CONTENTS.

			PAGE.
REPORT FROM Mr. A. E. BATEMAN TO BOARD OF TRADE			3
APPENDIX No.	1.	Price of Butter at New York in 1879	6
,,	2.	Extract from "American Dairyman" of 7th October 1880: Butter on a Soapstone Basis	6
,,	3.	Extracts from "American Dairyman" of 1st April 1880: New Bill relating to Oleo-Margarine, before New York State Legislature	6
,,	4.	Extracts from "American Dairyman" of 8th April 1880: The Issue Joined; the Butter Market	8
,,	5.	Extract from "American Dairyman" of 22nd April 1880: Oleo-Margarine	9
,,	6.	The New Article of Commerce: Oleo-Margarine	10
,,	7.	Extract from "American Dairyman" of 7th October 1880: Exports of Butter versus Oleo-Margarine	13
,,	8.	Return of Exports of Oleo-Margarine from New York, 1879 and 1880	14
,,	9.	Return of Exports of Butter from Holland, 1876 to 1880	14

THE
MANUFACTURE OF OLEO-MARGARINE
IN THE
UNITED STATES.

TO THE SECRETARY OF THE BOARD OF TRADE.

SIR,

As I was lately staying in New York for a week, I took the opportunity to make some inquiries into the oleo-margarine question, with special reference to its progress during the past year since Mr. Consul-General Archibald's despatch on the subject was written $\frac{(C.\ 2502)}{1880}$.

In making these inquiries I received valuable assistance from Mr. Archibald in introductions to the officers of the New York Produce Exchange, the Commercial Manufacturing Company who are the principal makers of oleo-margarine, and in many other ways. I had thus the privilege of seeing the whole process of manufacture of the oil and butter under the Mége patent, and of tasting both these products. I also tasted a new artificial butter made at Chicago entitled "Suene," to which I shall make further reference.

I visited the Commercial Manufacturing Company rather late in the afternoon, so as to see the premises in their least attractive aspect, when the day's work was nearly done; but I am bound to say that, beyond the floors being very slippery in places with spilt oil, there was nothing to disgust the eye, and all possible attention seemed to be given to the cleanliness of the plant and utensils of the manufactory.

The process of making the oil is, stated briefly, as follows: the beef suet on arriving at the factory from the abattoir is first weighed, and then thrown into tanks of tepid water and allowed to stand a short time, it is then washed several times in cold water, when it is disintegrated or separated from fibre by passing through a "meat hasher" worked by steam, and is then passed through a fine sieve. It is now ready for melting, which is effected by "jackets" containing hot water surrounding the tanks of fat, but the temperature is not allowed to exceed 120 degrees Fahr., for fear of giving a flavour of tallow to the oil. Continual stirring is maintained for some time, and afterwards the adipose membrane of the fat called "scrap" separates and settles to the bottom of the tank and a clear yellow oil is left above, covered by a film of white oily substance with the water contained in the fat. The scrap having settled the film is skimmed and the yellow oil is drawn off and allowed to stand and granulate in wooden cars. The refined fat, as it is now called, is next taken to the press room—kept at 85 or 90 degrees Fahr.—and there packed in cotton cloths and placed in galvanised iron plates in a press, and being then subjected to some pressure, the oil flows out and leaves cakes of pure white stearine, which are sold for candle making.

I tasted the oil at this last stage, and did not find it unpleasant, being nearly tasteless. The oleo-margarine, as it is now called, is next packed in barrels if for sale or export, but if it is to be manufactured into butterine 10 per cent of milk is first churned, the oil is then added and churned with it. It is next coloured with annatto, and rolled with ice; the ice, or rather water, is then extracted, and the last process is the addition of the salt, after which the butterine is packed in kegs or tubs or made up in 1 lb. "prints." The taste of butterine is very much like that of second-class butter, but it is rather salt, and has not the peculiar "bouquet" of the best butter, from which it appears to differ in the much smaller proportion of the soluble fats, "butyrine," "caprine," &c.

Dr. Mott's chemical analysis, quoted at p. 13 of last session's Oleo-Margarine Correspondence, gives 7·432 as the percentage of these fats in natural butter, and only 1·823 in butterine, and I have not seen any contradiction of these figures. The supporters of oleo-margarine butter state that the absence of these fats increases largely the keeping qualities of their artificial butter, and I was shown and invited to taste some butterine that had been made two years ago, but as I was in bad health I declined, although I could not detect by smell any rancidity in the specimen.

The average yield of oleo-margarine is about 35 per cent. of the beef caul fat used, the percentage being more in a very fat animal and less in a lean one. The present retail price of butterine in New York is about 25 cents, or one shilling, per lb.

The manufacture of oleo-margarine proper, *i.e.*, under the process I have described, appears to have largely increased during the past year, in spite of the continued opposition of the dairy interests of the Eastern States.

The importance of these interests is shown by the fact that the cows in New York State are a million and a half in number, and in the other Eastern States nearly two millions, and the exports of butter from New York last year amounted to 38 million pounds as compared with 4 million pounds in 1874, 14 millions in 1876, and 26 millions in 1878. The new competition of the Western States in growing grain has doubtless stimulated the production of butter and cheese in the East.

It is almost impossible to obtain accurate figures of the production of oleo-margarine and butterine, or even of their export, but from the information with which I have been favoured by Mr. H. K. Thurber, of the Commercial Manufacturing Company, and others, the present production of oleo-margarine and butterine in the Eastern States under the Mége patent appears to be at the rate of nearly 10 million pounds per annum, the manufacture having increased very considerably in the last nine months. The rise in the price of natural butter, which occurred in the autumn of 1879 (see Appendix, No. 1), doubtless gave a great impetus to the production of the counterfeit article, and as this rise has been fully maintained up to the present time, there is no reason to anticipate an immediate falling off in the manufacture of oleo-margarine.

As regards the export of oleo-margarine and butterine, I found great difficulty in obtaining reliable figures, in consequence of butterine not being separately distinguished in the United States Customs accounts. It is true that by the New York State Act, 1877 (see p. 20 of C. 2502), the tubs, &c. containing oleo-margarine or any other artificial butter, when manufactured for sale, must be stamped with the word "Oleo-margarine," but I was informed that this law is constantly evaded, and, moreover, is only operative in the State of New York. The Commercial Manufacturing Company appear to carry it out with great care, and are in favour of general Customs regulations compelling the separate registration of these products. They are thus in accord with the dairy interest and the New York Produce Exchange, and it seems probable that in the next few months some action will be taken in the matter. The manufacturers under the Mége patent are doubtless influenced towards this by the numerous infringements of their patent and other imitations of oleo-margarine butter which are made at Chicago and in the West. As I mentioned above, I had the privilege of inspecting and tasting an artificial butter called "suene," which is made at Chicago, and is stated by Mr. Thurber to contain 50 per cent. of lard and 50 per cent. of Western dairy butter. It was coloured to resemble butter, and the smell and taste were not unpleasant, though the texture was inferior to (so-called) genuine oleo-margarine. As lard costs about 8 cents per lb., and Western butter 17 cents, it is evident that "suene" can be very cheaply produced, and may before long become a very dangerous rival to "butterine." Further, I am informed by Mr. Thurber that much oleo-margarine oil is sold to the farmers who prefer to churn their own butterine.

A good deal of Western butter is also found to be adulterated with a substance called soapstone, and I subjoin in the Appendix an extract from the "American Dairyman" on this subject. (See Appendix No. 2.)

Mr. Thurber is of opinion that in artificial butter, as in most other preparations, such as condiments, sauces, &c., the manufacturer or merchant of repute will in time sell under his own name or trade mark, which will be a guarantee that the butterine is made under the Mége or some other approved process. Anyhow, it is certain that without some such guarantee, this new preparation is particularly open to fraud and danger to the consumer, even though the statements of the dairy interests as to the risk of using it may be highly coloured. With regard to this, I subjoin in the Appendix some correspondence, articles, &c. that have appeared in the "American Dairyman," respecting oleo-margarine, and also a communication from the New York Board of Health which has been much circulated by the supporters of the new substance.

Again, with reference to the registration on export question, I may mention that the members of the New York Produce Exchange have lately been in communication with the Treasury Department at Washington, and Mr. Nimmo, the chief of the Statistical Department, informs them in his reply (Appendix No. 7) that oleo-margarine is already distinguished in the trade accounts, and he states the export to have been nearly 19 million pounds, in the year ended 30th June last. The New York Produce Exchange rejoins, however, that no account is here taken of the churned butterine, and they contend that a large amount of this article is entered under the head of butter. I have been favoured by Messrs. Walter Carr & Co., an eminent firm belonging to the Exchange, with an approximate account of the exports of butterine in the three months, July, August, and September, which amounted to more than $3\frac{1}{4}$ million pounds, and it is noted that the winter export has hitherto been much larger than the summer.

It will be noticed that the amount of oleo-margarine and butterine exports greatly exceeds the estimated production under the Mége patent, and from this some idea may be formed of the numerous infringements of the patent that are going on in the Eastern States, in addition to the many imitations and admixtures of suene and soapstone at Chicago and in the West.

Table No. 8 of the Appendix contains the exports of oleo-margarine from the port of New York in 1879 and in the first nine months of the present year, and the export this year is shown to have reached $15\frac{3}{4}$ million pounds, $12\frac{1}{2}$ million pounds having gone to Rotterdam and Antwerp, presumably for churning into butterine in Holland. We should therefore expect some increase in the butter exports from that country, and this is shown to be the case in Table 9 of the Appendix (compiled from the Dutch Customs Accounts), from which it appears that the exports of butter increased from 23 million kilogrammes in 1877 to 36 million in 1879, five-sixths of such exports being to this country.

To sum up, then, the chief points I have noticed, besides describing the process of manufacture under the Mége patent, are—

1st. The increase of production of oleo-margarine in the past year owing to the higher prices of natural butter;
2nd. The present large export of both oleo-margarine and butterine to Holland and the United Kingdom, being double the production under the Mége patent; and
3rd. The large quantity of artificial butter that must now be manufactured under other processes, such as "suene," soapstone butter, &c., owing to which the manufacturers of *real* oleo-margarine desire the separate registration of their product.

I have the honour to be,
Sir,
Your most obedient servant,
A. E. BATEMAN.

Statistical and Commercial Department,
Board of Trade, November 10, 1880.

APPENDIX.

APPENDIX No. 1.

AVERAGE PRICES of BUTTER at NEW YORK in each Month of 1879.

Months.	Cents.
January	16 to 20 per lb.
February	16 ,, 20 ,,
March	14 ,, 18 ,,
April	13 ,, 16 ,,
May	13 ,, 15 ,,
June	13 ,, 15 ,,
July	13 ,, 15 ,,
August	13 ,, 15 ,,
September	17 ,, 20 ,,
October	20 ,, 25 ,,
November	28 ,, 33 ,,
December	26 ,, 30 ,,

APPENDIX No. 2.

EXTRACT from "AMERICAN DAIRYMAN" of 7th October 1880.

BUTTER on a SOAPSTONE BASIS.

THE recent article about *butter on a soapstone basis* moves me to send for your inspection a small piece of the stone as it appears before it is ground. You will see by scraping it with a knife that it forms a fine light powder, something like flour in appearance, and it is just about the same weight as flour. It is largely manufactured in this country, principally at Gouverneur and Hallesborough, goes by the name of "talc,' and is sent to market in sacks, similar to flour-sacks. It is taken out of the bed and has to be piled up to season and dry before it is ground. It pays a very large profit to the manufacturer—probably not less than 10 dollars per ton—even when the price is not more than 20 dollars in market. I know of no legitimate use for ground-talc or soapstone, unless it may be necessary to the manufacture of paper, though I have heard that even then it is more a filling to make weight than anything else. It may be looked for in all articles that are worth more than 3 or 4 cents a pound. Flour, sugar, starch, soap, and other articles may be made to hide this new adulterating material; in fact, butter is about the last place I should have thought of looking in for it. The problem will soon be whether the "honest farmer" can sell the "honest" merchant the most stone in the products of the farm or be forced to take the most in the goods he receives for his own consumption, while the poor human stomach will be forced to take "stone," though it calls ever so loudly for bread.—A Subscriber, St. Lawrence Co., New York, in "New York Tribune."

APPENDIX No. 3.

EXTRACT from "AMERICAN DAIRYMAN" of 1st April 1880.

NEW BILL relating to OLEO-MARGARINE now before the STATE LEGISLATURE at ALBANY.

CONSIDERABLE interest has been aroused here within the last few days about a bill regulating the sale of that peculiar product known as "oleo-margarine." Two or three enterprising lobbyists have, too, come in the field in opposition to the bill, which is considered a fair and necessary proposition in not alone protecting the public from deception, but also in regulating the laws of trade as to the sale of butter and "oleo-margarine." Two of the lobbyists seem to differ as to the methods of "handling" the Legislature in connexion with this measure. As the whole community is more or less interested in this matter, we give the full text of the bill as follows:—

SECTION 1.—Section 1 of Chapter 415 of the Laws of 1877, entitled "An Act for the protection of "dairymen, and to prevent deception in sales of butter," is hereby amended so as to read as follows:—

SEC. 1.—Every person who shall manufacture for sale, or who shall offer or expose for sale by the tub, firkin, box, or package, any article or substance in semblance of butter, not the legitimate product of the dairy, and not made exclusively of milk or cream, but into which the oil of fat of animals not produced from milk enters as a component part, or into which melted butter or any oil thereof has been introduced to take the place of cream, shall distinctly and durably stamp, brand, or mark upon the top and also upon the side of every tub, firkin, box, or package of such article or substance, the word "oleo-margarine,' where it can be plainly seen, the letters of which shall be burned on or painted thereon with permanent black paint, and shall not be less than one-half inch in length ; and in case of retail sales of such articles or substance in parcels, the seller shall in all cases sell or offer or expose the same for sale from a tub, firkin, box, or package, stamped, branded, or marked as herein stated, and deliver therewith to the purchaser a written or printed label bearing the plainly written or printed word "oleo-margarine," and every sale of such article or substance by the tub, firkin, box, or package, not so stamped, branded or marked, and every sale of such article or substance, at retail that shall not be sold from a tub, firkin, box, or package, and labelled as above stated, is declared to be unlawful and void, and no action upon any contract shall be maintained in any of the courts of this State to recover upon any contract for the sale of any such article or substance not so stamped, branded, marked, labelled, or sold.

Sec. 2.—Section 2 of said chapter is hereby amended so as to read as follows :—

Sec. 2.—Every person who shall knowingly sell or offer or expose for sale, or have in his or her possession with intent to sell, by the tub, firkin, box, or package, any of the said article or substance required by the first section of this Act to be stamped, branded, or marked, as therein stated, that shall not be so stamped, branded, or marked, contrary to the provisions of this Act, or in case of retail sales in parcels, without selling the same from a tub, firkin, box, or package, stamped, branded, or marked, as in said first section stated, or without delivery of a label as required by section 1 of this Act, shall for every such offence forfeit and pay a fine of 100 dollars, to be recovered with costs in any of the courts of this State having cognizance thereof in an action to be prosecuted by any district attorney in the name of the people, and the one half of such recovery shall be paid to the informer and the residue shall be applied to the support of the poor in the county where such recovery is had.

Sec. 3.—Section 3 of said chapter is hereby amended so as to read as follows :—

Sec. 3.—Every person who shall knowingly sell or offer or expose for sale, or who shall cause or procure to be sold, offered, or exposed for sale by the tub, firkin, box, or package, any article or substance required by the first section of this Act to be stamped, branded, or marked as therein stated, not so stamped, branded, or marked ; or in case of retail sales in parcels, every person who shall knowingly sell or offer or expose for sale, or who shall cause or procure to be sold, offered, or exposed for sale any article or substance required by the first section of this Act to be sold, offered, or exposed for such sale from a tub, firkin, box, or package not stamped, branded, or marked, and without labelling the same as therein stated, shall be guilty of a misdemeanor ; and on trial for such misdemeanor, proof of the sale or offer or exposure alleged shall be presumptive evidence of knowledge of the character of the article so sold, offered, or exposed for sale, and that the same was not stamped, branded, or marked as sold from a tub, firkin, box, or package, and labelled as required by this Act.

Sec. 4.—This Act shall take effect immediately.

To the Honourable O. J. Curtis, Senator, having in charge the above Bill, relative to Oleo-Margarine, before the Senate of the State of New York.

Dear Sir,

We noticed in Saturday's "Herald" full text of bill in relation to oleo-margarine. No objection to the bill, so far as it goes, but it occurs to us that it omits one very important point, which it might easily be made to cover.

For instance, the Commercial Manufacturing Company of this city sell largely of adulterated butter for export, and it is supposed by many that such sales are made at the factory, and that the packages are not marked or branded "Oleo-margarine" at all, but the goods first being put up in exactly the same style as the natural product, they are lightered direct to steamships and *go among the clearances as genuine butter*.

If you will pardon us, we would suggest an additional section, making it obligatory that the "stuff" sold for export shall be branded as in section 1st, and also that it shall be cleared through the Custom House as " oleo-margarine."

We are led to believe that thousands of packages have been shipped to Europe through fall and winter—and all substantially as butter, being cleared as such with the genuine article. You can easily see that, if branded when sold, such brand may easily be erased by the shipper, who may substitute others instead ; as, "Best N. Y. State Dairy Butter," etc., thus making use of terms which have value as connected with the genuine product of the respective sections where such is most largely identified with superior quality and quantity.

The penalties so far as small sales are concerned may answer, but a party buying 1,000 packages or more for shipment would be but slightly disturbed if he did have to pay 100 dollars fine—it would only be 10 cents per package—while the change of brand, carrying the impression that it was genuine butter, would, no doubt, cause the stuff to bring fully one dollar more per tub than if branded "oleo-margarine."

Relating to this "bastard grease," the export question is perhaps of much greater importance than the home trade. American butter within the past few years has gained a footing, not only in Great Britain, but also on the Continent of Europe, very largely so in Germany. This unnatural mixture going in there has operated very injuriously to the legitimate traffic in genuine butter—changing the entire status of values, restricting the demand, and contributing to put the genuine product of this country in dubious repute. In fact, it bids fair to kill the export trade in the genuine article entirely, unless proper laws can be enacted to protect the latter. There are already many complaints from abroad, and foreign dealers ordering American butter are beginning to demand certificates that the article is genuine.

We quote the following from a London circular dated February 1880 :—

"A Parliamentary Paper issued this week on the subject of the manufacture of oleo-margarine in the United States has greatly added to the difficulties of the situation, some buyers now requiring a guarantee that the article sold is pure butter."

Of course there is a good deal of this beef oil exported, which is no doubt cleared as oleo-margarine, but of the adulterated butter exported, *we do not suppose that one tub out of one thousand goes out under the brand of oleo-margarine,* but more likely under some of the following marks or brands, which have an established value, having long been associated with our better grades of genuine butter, viz.: "Choice Goshen," "Selected Orange Co. Butter," "Gilt-edged Chautauqua Butter," "Finest St. Lawrence Dairy," "Choice Delaware Butter," "Premium Madison Co. Creamery," "Fresh Courtland Co. Dairy," "Chemung Dairy XXX," "Sweet Clover Dairy, Otsego Co." "Choice Chenango Valley Creamery," "Chenango Co. Dairy XXX," etc. Is it possible that those representing the dairy interests of this State are willing that the reputation, which many counties have been nearly a century in establishing, for their dairy products, shall be prostituted to advance the interest of the vilest adulteration ever foisted upon the people, and at the same time permit their constituents to furnish the material with which to disguise and shield their deadly enemy—being thus made to destroy their own cause, to impoverish themselves, and to render their farms comparatively worthless—as everyone knows that the lands of New York State are of much greater value for dairying than for any other purpose. We will take occasion to add, in conclusion, that all legislation relative to oleomargarine which cannot find, (1), a good and proper cause for *prohibiting* its manufacture and sale, on the grounds that it is deleterious as an article of food; (2), to *prohibit* its use, *in being adulteriously mixed with milk product,* under the disguise and character of which *only* can it be made to appear like butter, or pass as a substitute for it; or (3), to tax it the same as whiskey, and many other manufactured articles, will, in our opinion, be incomplete.

That oleo-margarine, as presented in the form of butter, is an adulteration—a counterfeit—we think can be clearly established.

That it is deleterious to health, we think can be scientifically proven.

That it is working ruin to one of the most important industries of the country, is beyond question.

Respectfully,
WALTER CARR & Co.

New York, March 31, 1880.

APPENDIX No. 4.

EXTRACTS from "AMERICAN DAIRYMAN," of 8th April 1880.

THE ISSUE JOINED.

THE dairymen, farmers, and dealers in butter and cheese in all parts of the country are awakening to the loss the dairy industry has sustained, and is still threatened with, by the fraudulent sale of that bastard compound, oleo-margarine, and with one voice demand relief and protection from the Federal and State Governments. They have been wronged, and consumers have been imposed upon until forbearance has ceased to be a virtue, and they now demand the passage of laws that will extirpate the plague. Temporising has been indulged in by those who have assumed to represent the cause of the dairy too long already. Dairymen have been indifferent and dealers have contented themselves with an arrest now and then of a retailer under a law which, from its conservatism and incompleteness, has proven a failure for all practical purposes, both in Pennsylvania and New York. They have fought oleo-margarine only to promote its sale, by advertising it. They have argued for its legitimacy and commercial rights until they have been effectually whipped with their own weapons. Now let the dairymen and the dealers of all markets be heard through Congress and the State Legislatures. They are preparing to speak, and their utterance will be in tones of such volume and force that it will be heard and respected. Live, active, earnest friends of the dairy industry have taken hold of the matter. The International Dairy Fair Association, through its new President, Mr. Francis D. Moulton, has come to the rescue just when its services are most needed, and will exhaust its utmost powers to crush out the plague. Mr. Moulton has taken command in person, and will direct the fight. He has the facilities and the ability to accomplish the most valuable results, and with the support he is receiving from all parts of the land, he will wage a warfare which already causes the enemies of the dairy to tremble.

He has trusty agents in all parts of the country. In the north-west, Col. R. P. McGlincy, the secretary of the North-western Dairymen's Association, and the Hon. Geo. P. Lord, mayor of Elgin, are doing excellent work. Col. Littler, the efficient secretary of the National Butter, Cheese, and Egg Association, is a host in himself. In Baltimore, A. A. Kennard represents the movement. In Philadelphia, J. B. Myers, president of the Produce Exchange, John J. Macdonald, Francis Weldy, and J. J. Hitschler. In Pittsburgh, Pa., O. H. Head marshals the forces against the fraud. In St. Louis, M. M. McKean and S. R. Udell. In Chicago, Geo E. Gooch, A. H. Barber, and W. W. Dexter. In Boston, G. W. Simpson has conducted a successful fight. And thus throughout the country the best men have come to Mr. Moulton's support. In this city Walter Carr, Esq., the well-known commission merchant, has been working indefatigably for a long time, spending his time and money to save the dairymen; and Geo. S. Hart, Jno. S. Martin, Capt. Hunter, J. H. Seymour, W. Winsor, J. H. Groht, Webb, Evans, & Co., and others, have done noble service. We say Amen to their efforts, and commend their labours. Let each continue and the number of workers increase until an end is made of the gigantic swindle. Dairymen, organise in every district. Call upon your representatives in Congress to support the measures proposed by the International Dairy Fair Association. Avoid patronising any firm or individual who buys, sells, or encourages the sale of oleo-margarine. Make the trade odious, as it is dirty and unfair. Ostracize all connected with it, and then the laws you secure will be the more easily made effective. The issue is—oleo-margarine or no oleo-margarine. Either it must be crushed out or it will crush out the natural product of the dairy. Don't be humbugged by the assertion of the adulterators that oleo-margarine only affects poor butter. They are not engaged in the business of improving the product of the dairy. They would stop the production of the finest creamery and the finest dairy butter as quick as they would the commonest kind. We don't want to destroy the dairy industry to raise the quality of butter.

THE MARKETS.
Wednesday Evening, April 7.

Butter:—The market has been dull, lower, and unsettled. Creamery butter is in supply beyond requirements and accumulating. Stock is offered freely, and the tendency is still downward; very little business above 30 cents. The finest grades of State dairy are largely being used in place of creamery. Receipts of new State dairy are larger, and prices have declined heavily. Few choice lines, without selection, exceed 26 cents, though 27 cents is occasionally reached for nice lines of half-firkin tubs; good lots of Welsh are selling down to 25 cents. The demand has been generally very dull until to-day, when there is rather more activity. Old State dairy is in very light stock; prices irregular and scarcely quotable longer. Western dairy and factory butter is much lower in sympathy with creamery and State dairy. Receipts have been moderate, but trade has been very quiet. A sale of prime factory to an exporter is said to have been made at 22 cents. Low grades of all kinds are relatively less plenty than fine. *The chief cause of the dulness and declining tendency in butter is thought to be the extensive sale of oleo-margarine. This article has attracted the attention of buyers by its cheapness compared with recent prices of butter, and its sale has increased to an alarming extent. It is reported that one house in this city has been recently selling oleo-margarine at the rate of 1,200 packages per day at 18 to 19 cents per lb.*

APPENDIX No. 5.

EXTRACT from "AMERICAN DAIRYMAN," 22nd April 1880.

OLEO-MARGARINE.

EDITOR "AMERICAN DAIRYMAN."

JUST at this time it is interesting to glance at a few facts in relation to this product. To hear the remarks of some of the butter dealers one would think that dairy butter was about to be wiped out of existence by a new and iniquitous compound akin to arsenic and nitro-glycerine. The quantity of oleo-margarine made is greatly magnified; the natural downward course of the butter market which comes at this season every year, almost without exception, is held up as a warning, and according to these prophets nothing but dire disaster is in store for dairymen. Let us see what facts we have to go by. Oleo-margarine has been manufactured to a considerable extent in this country for four years; last year, in the face of its manufacture, prices of butter advanced one hundred per cent., and held the advance as well as in any former year. In Europe oleo-margarine has been largely manufactured for ten years, during which there have been the usual fluctuations in the market, but full average quotations for fine butter have ruled, and this in the face of a very largely increased production of the better qualities, caused by the competition of oleo-margarine with poor butter. What does this prove? Simply that, as the production of fine butter increased, the consumption also increased (people eat more butter when the quality is good). The poorer classes ate oleo-margarine because it is better than poor butter, and the middle and higher classes also obtained a better quality of dairy butter and increased their consumption accordingly. Thus all classes were benefited, and we believe our experience will be the same in this country. Prices of butter may not rule so high during the next ten years as they have during the last ten, but people should remember what the prices were before the war, when the quantity produced was vastly less than now. Then dairying in the great West was unknown, and in the East was restricted to a comparatively limited area.

There are now oleo-margarine factories at Boston, Providence, New Haven, New York, Philadelphia, Baltimore, Pittsburg, Cincinnati, Louisville, Indianapolis, Chicago, St. Louis, and New Orleans. Their maximum of production has probably been nearly reached, yet they have hardly made an impression upon the butter market. Their product is sold by a majority of wholesale grocers and butter dealers on its merits, for precisely what it is, and it will probably not be long before nearly everybody will be handling it, and that it will assume a recognised place in the list of food products, as it has in Europe, where it is sold at retail as well as wholesale upon its merits. There is it exhibited at dairy fairs, and even sold within these precincts. How does this compare with the rediculous attitude of American dairymen and dealers in dairy products who have heretofore treated it as if it were an epidemic disease?

The "Scientific American," in a recent article sensibly remarks:

"The complaints of farmers against oleo-margarine are unfounded in fact, and are kept up only by appeals to unthinking prejudice. Oleo-margarine is as much a farm product as beef or butter, and is as wholesome as either. It is as legitimate a commercial product as tallow or lard, which might be as well proscribed as oleo-margarine. The only argument advanced by its opponents which has any validity is that it is sometimes sold as butter; this practice, however, has been greatly exaggerated; wholesale dealers sell it for what it is, and the number of retail dealers who do the same is daily increasing. Oleo-margarine chiefly interfered with the sale of common grades of butter to which it is far superior, and it is mainly dealers in this grade of butter who raise an outcry against the new product; although the outcry has been taken advantage of by parties outside of the dairy interest to curry favour with dairymen and serve their own selfish ends."

Some people may consider it enterprising for a salt house to bolster up a declining brand of salt by becoming alarmists upon the oleo-margarine question, and it might have worked if they had not overdone the business of instigating meetings, sending out circulars, and generally undertaking to use

Q 3641.

everybody who would consent to be blinded by their apparent zeal and to grind their little business axe; but will this pay in the end? Do dairymen or dealers serve their own interests by accepting such champions and their statements?

"COMMISSION MERCHANT."

APPENDIX No. 6.

The New Article of COMMERCE, OLEO-MARGARINE; perfectly Pure and Wholesome.

Reply of the Board of Health of New York City to a Congressional Inquiry.

Hon. Morgan R. Wise, of Pennsylvania, Chairman of the Committee on Manufactures, of the House of Representatives, addressed a letter to Professor Charles F. Chandler, President of the New York Board of Health, informing him that the Committee has under consideration a bill in relation to adulterations in food and drink, and asking whether the article known as oleo-margarine or butterine is wholesome or unwholesome, and for such other information as might be in the possession of the Board. The following is Professor Chandler's response:—

MY DEAR SIR,   Health Department, 301, Mott Street, New York, March 27, 1880.

IN reply to your letter of inquiry, I would say that I have been familiar with the discovery of Mége Mouries and its application in the manufacture of artificial butter, called "butterine" or "oleo-margarine," since the date of its first publication.

I have frequently seen it manufactured, witnessing all the operations, and examining both the material and the product.

I have studied the subject with special reference to the question of its use as food in comparison with the ordinary butter made from cream, and have satisfied myself that it is quite as valuable as the butter from the cow; that the material from which it is manufactured is perfectly fresh beef-suet; that the processes are harmless; that the manufacture is conducted with great cleanliness. The product is palatable and wholesome, and I regard it as a most valuable article of food, and consider the discovery of Mége Mouries as marking an era in the chemistry of the fats.

Butterine is manufactured of uniform quality the year round, and can be sold at a price far below that at which ordinary butter is sold. It does not readily become rancid, and is free from the objectionable taste and and odour which characterise a large proportion of the butter sold in this market.

I am informed that there are at present 13 factories in the United States licensed under the patents to manufacture this butter. The Commercial Manufacturing Company of New York is making at the present from 30,000 to 40,000 lbs. daily. In addition to this industry, there is a large manufacture of what is known as "oleo-margarine oil," which is shipped as such to Europe, to be there converted into butter, so that this product has become an important article of export to foreign countries.

The beef-suet which was formerly converted into common tallow, only suitable for the manufacture of soap, is, by this beautiful discovery, now manufactured into oleo-margarine oil and stearine of double the value of the tallow formerly produced. The following analysis made by Drs. Brown and Mott sufficiently illustrate the composition of the butterine:—

Constituents.		No. 1. Natural Butter.	No. 2. Artificial Butter.
Water		11,968	11,203
Butter solids		88,032	88,797
		100,000	100,000
Insol. fats	{ Olein, Palmatin, Stearine }	23·824	24·893
	{ Arachin, Myristin }	51·422	56·29
Sol. fats	{ Butyrin, Caprin, Caproin, Caprylin }	7·432	1·823
Casein		·192	·621
Salt		5·162	5·162
Coloring matter		Trace.	Trace.
		88·032	88·797

Last winter a resolution was adopted by the Legislature of the State of New York, requesting the Board of Health of the city of New York to investigate the subject, and report whether in its opinion the butterine is a wholesome article of food. In response to this resolution, the Board of Health stated that in its opinion there is no sanitary objection whatever to the unrestricted manufacture and sale of this substance.

In support of my opinion herein expresssd, I enclose the statement to the same effect made by Professor George F. Barker, of the University of Pennsylvania; Dr. Henry A. Mott, jun., of New York; Professor S. C. Caldwell, of Cornell University; Professor S. W. Johnson, of Yale College; Professor C. A. Goessmann, of the Massachusetts Agricultural College; Professor Henry Morton, of the Stevens Institute of Technology, of Hoboken; Dr. Chas. P. Williams, of Philadelphia; Professor W. O. Atwater, of the Wesleyan University at Middletown, Conn.; and Professor J. W. S. Arnold, of the Medical Department of the University of New York.

Hoping that this, my reply, contains all the information you desire, I remain,

Very respectfully yours,
CH. F. CHANDLER, Ph.D.,
President of the Board of Health.

To Hon. M. R. Wise,
   Chairman of the Committee on Manufactures,
      House of Representatives, Washington, D.C.

University of Pennsylvania,
Philadelphia, March 22, 1880.

GENTLEMEN,

In reply to your inquiry, I would say that I have been acquainted for several years with the discovery of Mége Mouries for producing butterine from oleo-margarine fat. In theory, the process should yield a product resembling butter in all essential respects, having identically the same fatty constituents. The butterine prepared under the inventors' patents is, therefore, in my opinion, quite as valuable a nutritive agent as butter itself. In practice, the process of manufacture, as I have witnessed it, is conducted with care and great cleanliness. The butterine produced is pure and of excellent quality, is perfectly wholesome, and is desirable as an article of food. I can see no reason why butterine should not be an entirely satisfactory equivalent for ordinary butter, whether considered from the physiological or commercial standpoint.

Respectfully yours,
GEO. F. BARKER.

The United States Dairy Co.

Stevens Institute of Technology,
Hoboken, New Jersey, March 16, 1880.

GENTLEMEN,

During the last three years I have had occasion to examine the product known as artificial butter, oleo-margarine, or butterine, first produced by M. Mége, of Paris, and described by him in his patent of July 17th, 1869.

I have also frequently witnessed the manufacture of this material, and with these opportunities of knowing exactly what it is, I am able to say with confidence that it contains nothing whatever which is injurious as an article of diet; but, on the contrary, is essentially identical with the best fresh butter, and is very superior to much of the butter made from cream alone which is found in the market.

The conditions of its manufacture involve a degree of cleanliness and consequent purity in the product, such as are by no means necessarily or generally attained in the ordinary making of butter from cream.

Yours, &c.
HENRY MORTON.

The United States Dairy Co.

Sheffield Scientific School of Yale College,
New Haven, Connecticut, March 20, 1880.

GENTLEMEN,

I AM acquainted with the process discovered by M. Mége, for producing the article known in commerce as oleo-margarine or butterine.

I have witnessed the manufacture in all its stages, as carried out on a large scale, and I can assert that when it is conducted according to the specifications of M. Mége, it cannot fail to yield a product that is entirely attractive and wholesome as food, and one that is for all ordinary culinary and nutritive purposes the full equivalent of good butter made from cream.

Oleo-margarine butter has the closest resemblance to butter made from cream in its external qualities—colour, flavour, and texture. It has the same appearance under the microscope, and in chemical composition differs not in the nature, but only in the proportions of its components. It is therefore fair to pronounce them essentially identical.

While oleo-margarine contains less of those flavouring principles which characterize the choicest butter, it is, perhaps, for that very reason, comparatively free from the tendency to change and taint which speedily renders a large proportion of butter unfit for human food.

I regard the manufacture of oleo-margarine or butterine as a legitimate and beneficent industry.

S. W. JOHNSON,
Professor of Theoretical and Agricultural Chemistry;
Director of the Connecticut Agricultural Experiment Station.

The United States Dairy Co.

Chemical Laboratory, Cornell University,
Ithaca, N.Y., March 20, 1880.

I HAVE witnessed, in all its stages, the manufacture of "oleo-margarine" and of oleo-margarine butter or "butterine."

The process for oleo-margarine when properly conducted, as in the works of the Commercial Manufacturing Co., is cleanly throughout, and includes every the reasonable precaution necessary to secure a product entirely free from animal tissue or any other impurity, and which shall consist of pure fat made up of the fats commonly known as oleine and margarine. It is when thus prepared, a tasteless and

Q 3641.

inodorous substance, possessing no qualities whatever that can make it in the least degree unwholesome when used in reasonable quantities as an article of food.

In the manufacture of butterine, since nothing but milk, annotto, and salt, together with perhaps a little water from clean ice, are added to this oleo-margarine, to be intimately mixed with it by churning and other operations, I have no hesitation in affirming that this also, when properly made accordingly to the Mége patent and other patents held by the United States Dairy Co., and when used in reasonable quantities, is a perfectly wholesome article of food; and that, while not equal to fine butter in respect to flavour, it nevertheless contains all the essential ingredients of butter, and since it contains a smaller proportion of volatile fats than is found in genuine butter, it is, in my opinion, less liable to become rancid.

It cannot enter into competition with fine butter; but in so far as it may serve to drive poor butter out of the market, its manufacture will be a public benefit.

S. C. CALDWELL.

Amherst, Mass., March 20, 1880.
GENTLEMEN,

I HAVE visited, on the 17th and 18th of the present month, your factory, on West Forty-eighth Street, for the purpose of studying your mode of applying Mége's discovery for the manufacture of oleo-margarine butter or butterine. A careful examination into the character of the material turned to account, as well as into the details of the entire management of the manufacturing operation, has convinced me that your product is made with care, and furnishes thus a wholesome article of food. Your oleo-margarine butter or butterine compares in general appearance and in taste very favourably with the average quality of the better kinds of the dairy butter in our markets. In its composition it resembles that of the ordinary dairy butter; and in its keeping quality, under corresponding circumstances, I believe it will surpass the former, for it contains a smaller percentage of those constituents (glycerides of volatile acids) which, in the main, cause the well-known rancid taste and odour of a stored butter.

I am, very respectfully yours,
C. A. GOESSMAN, Ph.D.,
Professor of Chemistry.

United States Dairy Co., New York.

Laboratory, No. 912, Samson Street,
Philadelphia, March 22, 1880.

DURING a period of upwards of two years I have been practically familiar with the details of the manufacture by the Mége method of oleo-margarine butter or "butterine." From my experience and observation of the care and cleanliness absolutely necessary in the manufacture of this product, together with my knowledge of its composition, I am satisfied that it is a pure and wholesome article of food, and in this respect, as well as in respect to its chemical composition, fully the equivalent of the best quality of dairy butter.

I will add further, that, owing to the presence of a less quantity of the volatile fats, the keeping qualities of the oleo-margarine butter are far superior to those of the dairy product.

CHARLES P. WILLIAMS, Ph.D.
Analytical Chemist; late Director and Professor
Missouri School of Mines, State University.

H. A. Mott, Junr., Ph.D., E. M., Analytical and Consulting Chemist,
Office, 117, Wall Street, New York, March 12, 1880.
GENTLEMEN,

HAVING been acquainted for the past six years with the process of the manufacture of the product called oleo-maragarine butter or butterine, and having made numerous microscopical and chemical examinations of the product, I am clearly of the opinion that the product called oleo-margarine butter is essentially identical with butter made from cream; and as the former contains less of those fats which, when decomposed, render the product rancid, it can be kept pure and sweet for a much longer time.

I consider the product of the Mége discovery a perfectly pure and wholesome article of food, which is destined to supplant the inferior grades of butter, and be placed side by side with the best product of the creamery.

Respectfully,
HENRY A. MOTT, Jr., Ph.D.

United States Dairy Co.

University Physiological Laboratory,
410, East 26th Street, April 2, 1880.

THIS is to certify that I have carefully examined the "Mége Patent Process" for the manufacture of oleo-margarine butter or butterine; that I have seen and tasted at the factory each and every ingredient employed; that I have made thorough microscopical examinations of the material used and of the butter; and I consider that each and every article employed in the manufacture of oleo-margarine butter or butterine is perfectly pure and wholesome; that the oleo-margarine butter differs in no essential manner from butter made from cream; in fact, the oleo-maragarine butter possesses the advantage over natural butter of not decomposing so readily, as it contains fewer volatile fats. In my opinion, oleo-margarine is to be considered a great discovery, a blessing for the poor, and in every way a perfectly pure, wholesome, and palatable article of food.

J. W. S. ARNOLD, A.M., M.D.,
Prof. Physiology and Histology, Med. Dep. Univ. New York.

13

Wesleyan University, Middletown, Conn., March 29, 1880.

I HAVE carefully looked into the theory and the practice of the manufacture of butterine (oleomargarine) by the "Mége process," and examined the product. A consideration of the materials used, the process of manufacture, and the chemical and microscopical character of the butterine, seem to me to fully justify the following statements:

As to its qualitative composition, it contains essentially the same ingredients as natural butter from cow's milk.

Quantitatively it differs from ordinary butter, in having but little of the volatile fats which, while they are agreeable in flavour, are, at the same time, liable to rancidity. I should, accordingly, expect butterine to keep better than ordinary butter. The best evidence within my reach indicates that just such is the case. The butterine is perfectly wholesome and healthy, and has a high, nutritious value. The same entirely favourable opinion I find expressed by the most prominent European authorities— English, French, and German—who are unanimous in their high estimate of the value of the "Mége discovery," and approval of the material whose production has thereby been made practicable.

I am very truly yours,
W. O. ATWATER.

APPENDIX No. 7.

EXTRACTS from "AMERICAN DAIRYMAN" of 7th October 1880.

EXPORTS of BUTTER v. OLEO-MARGARINE.

A communication was recently addressed to Secretary of the Treasury Sherman by the President of the New York Produce Exchange, at the request of merchants in the butter trade, asking that clearances of oleo-margarine should be distinguished in Custom House returns from those of butter. The following reply has been received:—

Treasury Department, Bureau of Statistics,
DEAR SIR, September 28, 1880.

YOUR letter of the 23rd inst., addressed to the Secretary of the Treasury has been referred to this bureau. Recognizing the importance to the dairy interests of the country of correct statistics of actual butter, as distinguished from oleo-margarine and other substitutes, I have already given attention to the matter, and will in due time inform you of what has been done. The statistics of our domestic exports now give the quantities and values of butter separately from those of oleomargarine. I find that there were returned to this bureau, as exported from the port of New York during the year ended June 30, 1880, of—

	Lbs.	Value.
Butter	31,061,610	$5,179,071
Oleo-margarine	18,833,330	2,581,317

* * * * * * *

A complaint similar to yours was found in a circular of Mr. Lloyd I. Seaman, dated New York, August 28, 1880, stating that the reported exports of butter by the United States Clearing Department in the Custom House were false, one half of it being oleo-margarine. This statement being referred to the collector at New York for investigation and report, that officer, under date of the 14th instant, reports "that the report to the press for the period in question has been verified by a re-examination of the manifests on file as sworn to by the shippers." The difficulty appears to be, not in a want on the part of the Customs officers to co-operate in the furnishing of correct export statistics, but in the fraudulent description of oleo-margarine as butter in the sworn manifests. You will greatly facilitate my endeavour to secure to us data of the butter export if you will kindly send to me copies of any State laws, or city ordinances, or rules adopted by the New York Produce Exchange in regard to distinguishing between oleo-margarine and butter. I shall be happy also to receive from you any suggestions as to the best practical methods by means of which the Customs officers may discover false entries of oleo-margarine in the outward manifests.

* * * * * * *

I am, Sir, very respectfully,
JOSEPH NIMMO, Jr.,
Chief of Bureau.

P. H. Parker, Esq.,
President New York Produce Exchange,
New York City.

The "Bulletin" states that the contents of the above letter were communicated by Mr. Parker to several leading members in the butter trade, and they all expressed their gratification at the attention given to the matter at Washington. It was stated that measures would be taken to procure the data called for by Mr. Nimmo, and to furnish him with all the additional information necessary in order to bring about the desired reform.

APPENDIX No. 8.

Return of the Exports of Oleo-Margarine from Port of New York, in the Year 1879 and in the first Nine Months of 1880.

Cleared for	Year 1879.	Jan. 1st to Sept. 30th, 1880—9 months.
	Pounds.	Pounds.
Rotterdam	11,931,174	11,127,574
Antwerp	173,537	1,367,526
London	188,426	58,639
Liverpool	1,091,266	590,974
Glasgow	274,023	1,399,694
Other ports	222,438	1,215,246
Total	13,880,864	15,759,653

APPENDIX No. 9.

Return of the Exports from Holland to various Countries in each of the Years 1876, 1877, 1878, and 1879, and in the first Eight Months of 1880. (Domestic Produce only.)

Years.	To United Kingdom.	To Germany.	To Belgium.	To other Countries.	Total.
	Kilogrammes.	Kilogrammes.	Kilogrammes.	Kilogrammes.	Kilogrammes.
1876	19,942,070	288,772	1,296,881	1,391,717	22,919,440
1877	19,682,780	464,885	1,513,036	1,449,991	23,110,692
1878	22,657,000	—*	1,593,000	1,917,000	26,167,000
1879	30,572,000	—*	4,236,000	1,626,000	36,434,000
1880 (first 8 months)	19,540,000	—*	3,283,000	1,323,000	24,146,000

* Included in other countries.

LONDON:
Printed by George E. Eyre and William Spottiswoode,
Printers to the Queen's most Excellent Majesty.
For Her Majesty's Stationery Office.

ROYAL COMMISSION ON AGRICULTURE.

REPORTS

OF THE

ASSISTANT COMMISSIONERS.

FURTHER REPORT BY MR. CLAY, JUNR.,

ON

AMERICAN AGRICULTURE.

Presented to both Houses of Parliament by Command of Her Majesty.
August 1882.

LONDON:
PRINTED BY GEORGE E. B. EYRE AND WILLIAM SPOTTISWOODE,
PRINTERS TO THE QUEEN'S MOST EXCELLENT MAJESTY.
FOR HER MAJESTY'S STATIONERY OFFICE.

1882.

[C.—3375.—VI.]   *Price* 2*d.*

ROYAL COMMISSION ON AGRICULTURE.

Supplementary Report by Mr. John Clay, Jun., on American Agriculture, showing its Influence on that of Great Britain.

To His Grace the Duke of Richmond and Gordon, President.

ROYAL COMMISSION ON AGRICULTURE, LONDON.

My Lord Duke,

Since Messrs. Read and Pell reported upon the aspect of American agriculture just two years ago, there have been such changes that it will be necessary for me in this report to go over much of the same ground as they did. Twelve months ago, under your instructions, I prepared a report upon the agriculture of California, more especially referring to its bearing upon the work of the husbandman at home, and while writing particularly upon the Pacific Slope I ventured to assert that it was more than probable that we had seen wheat at its lowest point for some years to come, and so fully has that assertion been borne out for this year that I venture to state the ideas I have gathered in all parts of the United States and the Dominion of Canada more boldly and with greater confidence than heretofore.

Men living in this country, and more especially those farming in it, have seen within the last two years a great increase in the value of land, equal at least to 20 per cent., in the Middle and Western States. In some portions of the west it has been over 100 per cent.

Three years ago, west of the Mississippi it was impossible to sell western lands at any price. Now they are readily taken up at prices varying from three to six dollars per acre. It is almost impossible to say positively what has been the rise, for you had a class of goods in the shape of title deeds to land which were almost unsaleable at any sacrifice; while following in the train of that we have an immense increase in the value of all live stock and of every product connected with agriculture. It is safe to say that for the last two years the agriculture of America has been at the very flood tide of its prosperity. How long that tide will flow till it begins to ebb, it is not my province to speculate upon; but as certain as the sea breaks over the rock-bound shore, so surely it recedes again and leaves dry ground behind it. Thus in agriculture, as prosperity floods upon us, some have to meet an evil day.

The agriculture of this country had reached a low ebb during the years 1874, 1875, 1876, and 1877. In 1878 a change began to come; the price of labour was exceedingly low, all classes of live stock were sold at ruinous prices, and the cost of living was exceedingly moderate. Those circumstances, with cheap land, had insured cheap production. Both beef and bread were produced at very low figures. All classes, both in town and country, began to feel that another day of prosperity was beginning to dawn after a long night of commercial and agricultural depression. Confidence was restored, and as if all the elements were in favour of a great stride in the upward path of national improvement, there came an era of most prolific crops.

During those years of depression, from 1873 to 1878, a silent revolution had been going on. In the east, where the times were exceedingly hard, and more especially in the manufacturing districts, whose prosperity was partly owing to protection, there had been a gradual movement of people to the west. It went on almost unseen, this grand emigration. If it had been in Ireland or among the Scotch crofters, the population would have held on with iron tenacity to their poverty, but the adaptability of the American mind solved the problem in an easier, less bloody, and more beneficial manner.

R 3331.

Every country has its proverbial silent workers, men who do great deeds, the effect of which are not immediately seen, but which live long after their conception and accomplishment. The silent workers of this period on the American continent were the emigrants who gradually moved out to the Western States, relieving the closely populated cities of the east to people up a great western country, full of hidden wealth and vast riches.

Not but that there is a constant emigration to that great country, but it drifted on faster and almost unseen through those years of commercial depression.

Every year vast tracts of land were broken to the plough, and consequently in 1878 and 1879 a grand extent of fresh land lay ready for the husbandman. Then, as if to cap the whole thing, there came a run of favourable seasons scarce ever experienced before. For four years the granaries of America ran over with grain, and that grain produced at a cheap rate, produced on cheap land with cheap labour. And as if to fit into this circumstance, the English farmer had had to meet a course of most unfavourable years. Who can forget 1877, 1879, and now 1881? Wheat poured into Great Britain at an alarming rate, so alarming that the British farmer almost gave up hope; and perchance if the uneducated eye of the British agriculturist had seen the full extent of the country on which this vast plethora of beef and bread was raised, he would have given up the last thread that bound his hopes together.

When matters are at their blackest there are always any number of alarmists to heap coals on the fire.

It was prophesied by high authorities that wheat was to be laid down for all time to come, or for a generation at least, at marvellously low prices. One party writing to the leading journal of England said that it was more than probable that for many years we should have American wheat placed in England at 40s. per qr.

There is a limit, of course, to low production as well as high, and of one thing I am sure, that this season at least the American farmer cannot possibly lay down wheat at the above with anything like a suitable compensation. The agriculturists of this continent, more especially those who farm in the Western States, are not going to be satisfied with a price which will only repay them for their labour.

A pioneer's life, the earlier part of it spent in semi-civilisation, needs some compensating power to induce men to venture upon it, so we shall need to allow the producer of American wheat a very liberal profit upon his investment and hard work.

The rigour of a pioneer life had to be borne by those parties who ventured out to the prairie, and the experiences they had were more hard to bear than is the usual lot of those who engage in a frontier life.

They had little money for the first few years; their products brought almost nothing, for the railway had yet to come, so that they could ship their grain.

Few of them had been brought up at the school of agriculture; they did not realise what a life of toil it is. Men from England take some time to realise the slavery to his business that an American farmer has to endure. The spring, summer, and autumn are one long day of intense toil, from morning till night ceaseless work; and then comes a hard, cold winter, when the overworked man can get rest. If you go through Canada and look at the old men, the generation who went into the trackless forest and felled it, you will find them bent, broken down, and racked with rheumatism, the result of tremendous labour.

People on this side who have given some attention to the land question in Great Britain think that the result of American competition lies not in the fact that farmers on this side of the Atlantic produce at too low a rate, but they think that the cost of production has grown to an abnormal height in England. There is immense justice and hard truth in this idea. The writer emphatically shares it. The land of Great Britain has at the very outset to support three classes, while in America the proprietor is very generally also a farmer and labourer. The circumstances are, of course, a little different, but it is clear that if the land of Great Britain is to compete with the cheap lands of America, its value must be modified. Wealth is accumulating in England, notwithstanding hard times, but the increase is not among the classes connected with land.

It cannot possibly be. What we need is more work, more capital, more energy in the management of our farms at home, a close attention to business, so that we may produce grain and live stock at an increased rate. Cheap wheat means national prosperity eventually, so the British farmer will need to lower the standard of his expenses and raise that of his husbandry, so that the millions whom he has partially to support may eat their bread and butter at a moderate rate. The crisis to which British agriculture is now drawing nigh and has almost come to at the present moment is eventually to fall on the heads of the landlords. The farmers have had a hard time of it, but it is clear that the men who own the land will have the heaviest burden to bear. As long as the tenants had capital to work upon, and their leases bound them with adamantine chains to their farms, the days passed away in comparative security for the landlord and his agent. Time wears on, leases come to an end, and the farmer follows his son, who has started a year or two before, to some foreign land, where the bone and sinew, and perchance a little capital saved from the wreck of former prosperity, make a new home, of which he is landlord and farmer and performs most of the manual labour with his own hands and the assistance, perchance, of his family. Thousands and thousands of those men are coming to America. How are their places to be filled? by whom is the land to be cultivated? That is the problem which those who have left their native land and see and hear of the continual stream of emigration wish to have solved. I appeal to the honourable members of the Commission as a British subject, as an Anglo-American farmer, and as one deeply interested in the welfare of Great Britain, one who wishes to see her institutions reformed, not pulled down, to suggest some idea to the legislators of our country to stay this tide of emigration, to make the people contented at home, and to raise her agriculture to a pinnacle not yet reached in the history of husbandry.

It is no false feeling or jealousy of the American people, it is the welfare of thousands and thousands of British subjects that you must protect. British agriculture is wasting under some terrible disease, whose direful effects are intensified by disastrous seasons.

Providence will provide a cure for the latter, but the former must be seen to by the representatives of the farmers and our legislators, and the Commission is placed in a position to do much that is good, and to it the eyes of the British farmers are turned. Let us take a lesson from the past. France drove the Huguenots from her shores, and her loss was England's gain, a gain that has planted in her cities vast industries which have made her glorious and great.

People of all countries have turned their eyes towards England as the Mecca of manufactures, and side by side her agriculture has kept pace with her leading industries. But drive away from her shires and counties the best of her yeomen, plant them on American soil, and the very men who might have led the van of improvement are placed in competition against her.

Let this suicidal policy go on for a year or two longer, and what is to be the result?

Leaving, therefore, generalities, let us take up the question of wheat in detail, and look first at

Its position on this continent.

The growth of the American wheat trade is a perfect study in itself, and the developments it has made are one of the wonders of the world. In 1850 the total production of the United States was about 100 millions of bushels. Last year it reached the enormous aggregate of 480 millions of bushels, an increase of 500 per cent in thirty years. More marvellous still is the increase in the export of the staff of life. From a small beginning in the former year of ¾ of a million of bushels it grew up last year to nearly 180 millions, a growth almost incredible. Those figures refer to the United States and do not include the British possessions, which would swell the amount of American exportation to some extent. For many years after an English speaking race devoted their energies to the soil of America the culture of all crops was a hard process. Trees had to be felled and stumps taken out, and not till after a period of 8 or 10 years at least did the husbandman reap his reward. Previous to railways, canals and rivers provided the sole outlet for wheat, and as such accommodation was only limited, the growth of this great industry was necessarily slow. With the introduction of railways came a great change. New fields were opened up as if by magic. The forest belt was passed and the prairie regions reached. In 1850 the country was just emerging from its sleep. That greatest of pioneers, the steam-engine, had fairly got loose among the unbroken tracts of undeveloped country. The engineer had got to a country where railroads could be made far easier than good macadamized roads. The tracklayer could lay his rails on the open prairie, scarce any grading being required at all. To-day, at favourable points, a road can be laid at the rate of 2,500l. per mile. With such advantages, with no trees to interfere with the plough, with the soil enriched by the fires of countless years, the time had arrived for great events in the produce markets of the world. The Eastern States had slowly but surely developed the business, but it was not till 1850 that its influence was felt outside. Since then the march of the wheat crop has been steadily moving westward and latterly west by north. Gradually it went from the rich valleys of New York, the New England States and Canada to Ohio, Indiana, Michigan and Illinois. Then in a few years, when it had spread over those countries, it travelled on to Missouri, Kansas, Iowa, and Wisconsin. Later still it pointed towards the north to Minnesota and Dakota, and eventually it will reach its limits in the Canadian north-west, where its greatest development will take place, as we have attempted to show in another portion of this report. Ten miles every year is the computed march of this cereal from the seaboard. Ten miles more of carriage every year, 100 miles in ten years and 200 in twenty, if the march is not arrested, and it will not be for half a century at least if the style of American farming does not change for the better. Wheat after wheat tells on the best of soil, and as it is easier to fell a tree than to wait for one growing, so it is a much simpler process to impoverish land than to replenish it.

Thus a few of the Western States produce over 60 per cent. of the whole wheat product of America, or to be more correct, take the following statistics.

SUPPLEMENTARY REPORT BY MR. JOHN CLAY, JUN.

The Wheat Crop in the United States.—For the Year 1879.
As per Returns of the U. S. Agricultural Department.

STATE.	Aggregate Product, Bush.	Acreage.	Average Yield per Acre.	Average Value per Bush.	Acreage Value per Acre.	Total Value
				$ ct.	$ ct.	$
Maine	488,000	30,500	16.0	1 44	23 04	702,720
New Hampshire	159,120	13,600	11.7	1 50	17 55	238,680
Vermont	494,000	32,500	15.2	1 39	21 13	686,660
Massachusetts	15,300	850	18	1 50	27 00	22,950
Rhode Island	—	—	—	—	—	—
Connecticut	39,600	2,200	18	1 50	27 00	59,400
New York	10,746,000	716,400	15	1 40	21 00	15,044,400
New Jersey	1,783,500	145,000	12.3	1 38	16 97	2,461,230
Pennsylvania	22,307,400	1,458,000	15.3	1 32	20 20	29,445,768
Delaware	1,012,700	77,900	13	1 38	17 94	1,397,526
Maryland	6,999,840	486,100	14.4	1 42	20 45	1,939,773
Virginia	8,851,320	962,100	9.2	1 27	11 68	11,241,176
North Carolina	3,223,500	460,500	7	1 28	8 96	4,126,080
South Carolina	1,140,720	135,800	8.4	1 57	13 19	1,790,930
Georgia	3,617,100	401,900	9	1 26	11 34	4,557,546
Florida	—	—	—	—	—	—
Alabama	1,502,760	178,900	8.4	1 32	11 09	1,983,643
Mississippi	417,600	58,000	7.2	1 36	9 79	567,936
Louisiana	—	—	—	1 00	—	—
Texas	3,454,200	454,500	7.6	1 15	8 74	3,972,330
Arkansas	1,384,000	173,000	8	1 07	8 56	1,480,880
Tennessee	11,852,800	1,481,600	8	1 09	8 72	12,919,552
West Virginia	4,351,100	334,700	13	1 08	14 04	4,699,188
Kentucky	7,681,800	548,700	14	1 08	15 12	8,296,344
Ohio	36,591,750	1,876,500	19.5	1 20	23 40	43,910,100
Michigan	28,773,120	1,498,600	19.2	1 17	22 46	33,664,550
Indiana	43,709,960	2,153,200	20.3	1 17	23 75	51,140,653
Illinois	44,896,830	2,400,900	18·7	1 07	20 01	48,039,608
Wisconsin	20,565,720	1,632,200	12.6	1 04	13 10	21,388,349
Minnesota	31,886,520	2,592,400	12.3	94	11 56	29,973,329
Iowa	32,786,830	3,214,400	10.2	92	9 38	30,163,930
Missouri	26,801,600	1,914,400	14	1 01	14 14	27,069,616
Kansas	18,089,500	1,644,500	11	89	9 79	16,099,655
Nebraska	13,043,590	1,554,300	11.3	84	9 49	10,956,616
California	35,000,000	2,500,000	14	1 23	17 22	43,050,000
Oregon	8,188,800	511,800	16	98	15 68	8,025,024
Nevada, Colorado and the Territories	16,900,000	1,300,000	13	1 06	13 78	17,914,000
Total 1879	448,756,630	32,545,950	—	—	—	497,030,142
„ 1878	420,122,400	32,108,560	—	—	—	326,346,424
„ 1877	364,194,146	26,277,546	—	—	—	394,675,779
„ 1876	289,356,500	27,627,021	—	—	—	300,259,300
„ 1875	292,136,000	26,381,512	—	—	—	294,580,990
„ 1874	309,102,700	24,967,027	—	—	—	281,107,895
„ 1873	281,254,700	22,171,626	—	—	—	323,594,805
„ 1872	249,997,100	20,858,359	—	—	—	310,180,375

Summary by Geographical Divisions.—For the Year 1879.

	Aggregate Product.	Acreage.
New England States	1,196,020	72,650
Middle States	35,849,600	2,397,300
Southern States	54,476,740	5,675,800
Western States	284,101,880	18,927,100
Pacific States	56,232,390	4,166,100
Territories	16,900,000	1,300,000

New York State produces now but 10 to 12 millions of bushels of wheat, while Indiana and Illinois each gives us over 43 millions. Ohio still produces largely, about 36 millions. California 35 millions. Kentucky produces but seven millions, while Minnesota and Iowa have a grand total of 30 and 32 millions respectively.

Those figures refer to 1879. In 1880 an increase took place in nearly every State, as far as quantity was concerned, but the production per acre is less: while in 1881 the number of bushels per acre will still further decline. 1879 and 1880 were extraordinary prolific years for wheat. The average crops of the States is a little over 12 bushels per acre, but during those years it nearly touched 14 bushels per acre. The present year will probably show an average of a little over 10½ bushels per acre.

The computed average of the State of Minnesota, made from careful inquiries, was a little over 11 bushels per acre. Illinois, by far the richest of the States, popularly known as the Garden State, produces an average of 16½ bushels per acre. This year it will be far below that amount, as many of the fields were a failure. But while Indiana and Illinois still lead the van, new districts are being so rapidly developed that they will likely take a secondary place. In a few years, a decade or more, and the Canadian north-west will show forth its increase.

In 1879 Iowa had more acres under wheat than any other State, probably on account of its dry, free soil; and while it headed the list in acreage, it shows the worst return per acre of the Western States. In such a favourable year as the above its average was but 10 bushels per acre. This is owing, not so much to the poverty of the land in Iowa as to the fact that wheat is emphatically the crop of the poor man, and as Iowa received within late years an enormous emigration, we find that her lands, regardless of their nature, have had to produce this cereal irrespective of its capabilities.

Iowa is a stock-raising and corn-growing State, and in

time will come into its proper place in the agriculture of America; and those remarks lead us to say that sooner or later the continent of America will be as sharply defined in regard to its products as what different parts of England are at present.

Gradually the cost of producing will be calculated so nearly that farmers will find what soil and climate best suits the different classes of stock and system of culture. Wheat will be a universal crop, but its prominent location will be the north-west, further north than at present away towards the land of the Saskatchewan and Peace Rivers, while the Red River country will be also its peculiar stronghold. Other regions will compete with those, but the granary of this continent will be there, and in other parts we shall find a race of farmers adopting their separate systems, one will breed and another feed cattle. Many will raise beef and mutton, the ubiquitous hog will flourish in every section; while the cheese factory and creamery will have each their grazing lands and well-manured wheat fields around them. Those changes will be gradual, but we shall find the details worked out slowly and surely, and when that period is reached the mad management of present times will cease, necessity will bring it, and the science of agriculture, fostered by education, specially directed to it, will thrive and wax very great.

There are already signs of those changes coming about. Fifty years ago the valley of the Genesee was the proverbial granary of the world. From its barnyards came the golden wheat. Years ago it declined, and this beautiful section of country, with its glorious landscapes and beautiful homesteads was almost forgotten. A wanton and wasteful system had reduced its fertility, just as Virginia and Carolina have suffered from tobacco culture, so did this portion of New York State bear the burden of wheat after wheat. The product declined, western competition cheapened the article, and the dwindling crops did not pay.

But as the years rolled on, new systems were adopted. Dairy stock made its appearance. The cheese factory, planted by some pleasant stream, rose up, and with it came wealth in many ways; but it brought over and above a grand renovator, farmyard manure. Seven years ago, passing through this beautiful country, the writer saw their fields of grain with heads blasted like Pharoah's.

But a transformation has come over this country. The old homesteads have brightened up, the barns are repaired, the fences are renewed, and the wheat-fields are waving glorious and green when we passed through in summer of this year.

The reign of law has already begun, just in the same measure as the British farmer has to change his system and improve on old ways, so we find in this portion of America the change begun which must eventually transform the whole agriculture of America.

The process of reformation will not be fast, but it will come; and while there may not be so many acres in wheat the product per acre will gradually increase, for land undergoes a system of recuperation very fast in such a climate as America, with its sub-arctic winter and semi-tropical summers; and while it is plain to every one that the virgin soils of the western prairie are wasting under a false system of agriculture and would eventually give out if there were no more worlds to conquer in this line. Still when the whole of those vast regions have yielded their first great increase the wave of an improved husbandry will follow on the track of the worn-out soil. This is the hope of American agriculture.

It may be long years till it is accomplished, but it is the inevitable way it shall go.

Production: Its Cost and Limit.

When we consider that in 1879 the United States exported to various countries 717 million dollars worth of goods, such as stock, bread stuffs, and manufactured materials, and of that amount 604 millions belonged to its agriculture, or nearly 85 per cent. of the whole, we can realise what reason there is to consider this question. Of this enormous amount 210 millions of dollars is charged against bread stuffs, so that we have to face this enormous competition in England, which country takes of this amount as much as she needs, varying from five to seven-tenths of the whole amount.

We have chosen this year on account of the statistics being reliable, but during 1880 the increase was very great, about 288,000,000 dollars, while in 1881 it will decline. In 1880 the United States exported 160,000,000 bushels of wheat or its equivalent, as about 15 per cent. of this amount goes as flour.

This year they will not export much over 100,000,000, an immense decline. It is accepted by the best authorities that the crop of 1881 is short from 125 to 140 millions of bushels, and we shall have probably about 380 millions of bushels against 480 last year. We allow an increase in acreage, so that probably the exact product will be 100 millions of bushels less, with an increase of one million people to feed. The production per capita will be reduced from 9$\frac{1}{2}$ bushels to about 7$\frac{1}{2}$, and if we allow 5$\frac{1}{2}$ bushels per capita for home use, the total export will be a little over the amount, but we must remember there is a surplus of last year's crop to work upon.

In a former report your Commissioner ventured to assert that probably the production of wheat per capita was reached in America during the year 1880.

An extraordinary fruitful year might increase it, but it will be some years before the circumstances arise again which shall force so many men to become producers, nor is it likely that we shall have such a period of favourable seasons all in close succession, which by their glorious allurements, and at the same time substantial gains, drew thousands upon thousands of sturdy men to the western prairie.

Wages were exceedingly low in 1877 and 1878, but now things have changed, and while immigration still flows on, the march to the west is somewhat allayed. The prospect for the labourer in the eastern and other cities is sufficient to keep him there, and the producers are more than counterbalanced by the consumer. Be that as it may in theory, this year is a practical proof of the statement we ventured to make. Perchance 5, 10, or 15 years from this date a series of hard years and commercial depression may force the surplus population of the cities to move out on to the unbroken prairie, but at present there are no signs of such a social exodus. If this be true we shall also have higher prices. The following table is interesting, and affords much information:—

Average Prices of Wheat, Monthly and Yearly, at New York.—For the Year 1880.

Month.	No. 2. Red Winter, per bushel.	No. 2 Milwaukee Spring, per bushel.	No. 2. Chicago Spring, per bushel.
January	1 48$\frac{1}{4}$ @1 49	1 41$\frac{1}{2}$ @1 42$\frac{1}{4}$	1 42$\frac{1}{4}$ @1 47
February	1 48$\frac{1}{4}$ 1 49$\frac{1}{8}$	1 40$\frac{3}{4}$ 1 41$\frac{1}{4}$	1 39 9–10 1 40 7–10
March	1 45 9–16 1 46 9–16	1 40$\frac{1}{2}$ 1 42$\frac{1}{8}$	1 38 3–16 1 42$\frac{1}{8}$
April	1 33$\frac{3}{8}$ 1 34 5–16	1 25 1–5 1 28	1 26 7–16 1 27$\frac{1}{2}$
May	1 32 1–16 1 33$\frac{7}{8}$	1 22 1 23	1 21 15–16 1 22 13–16
June	1 25 1–16 1 26 1–16	1 14$\frac{3}{4}$ 1 16 1–16	1 14 1 20
July	1 14 13–16 1 15 15–16	1 10$\frac{1}{8}$	107$\frac{1}{8}$
August	1 08 1–16 1 08 9–16	1 05 15–16 1 06 15–16	1 04 7–16 1 05$\frac{1}{4}$
September	1 06 1–16 1 06$\frac{1}{2}$	1 04 1–16	1 03$\frac{1}{4}$ 1 04$\frac{5}{8}$
October	1 14$\frac{1}{8}$ 1 15	1 12 15–16	1 12$\frac{3}{8}$
November	1 21 1 22$\frac{1}{8}$	1 19$\frac{3}{4}$	1 18 1–5
December	1 18$\frac{3}{4}$ 1 21$\frac{3}{4}$	1 19$\frac{3}{8}$	1 19$\frac{1}{4}$
Range of Daily Prices	1 14$\frac{1}{8}$ 1 49$\frac{1}{8}$	1 04 1–16 1 42$\frac{1}{4}$	1 03$\frac{1}{4}$ @1 47
Yearly average 1880	1 26$\frac{1}{4}$ 1 27$\frac{3}{8}$	1 21$\frac{3}{8}$ 1 28$\frac{1}{2}$	1 20$\frac{5}{8}$ 1 26$\frac{1}{4}$
Range Daily Prices, 1879	1 08 1 60$\frac{1}{4}$	1 00 1 50	96 1 50
Yearly average, 1879	1 21 9–10 1 22 15–16	1 13$\frac{1}{4}$ 1 20$\frac{1}{8}$	1 12$\frac{1}{2}$ 1 22$\frac{1}{2}$

Average Prices of Flour and Corn, Monthly and Yearly, at New York.—For the Year 1880.

Month.	Flour.		Corn.			
	Common Ex. State, per barrel.		Steamer Mixed, per bushel.		No. 2 Mixed, per bushel.	
January - - -	5 59	@5 78	$59\frac{1}{8}$	@ —	$60\frac{3}{4}$	@$61\frac{1}{8}$
February - -	5 48	5 69	$57\frac{3}{4}$	58 1–16	60	60 15–16
March - - -	5 36	5 55	$57\frac{5}{8}$	$58\frac{1}{8}$	58 1–5	59 5–16
April - - -	4 68	4 94	52 13–16	53 9–16	$53\frac{1}{4}$	54 3–16
May - - -	4 45	4 69	52	52 7–16	$52\frac{3}{4}$	53 7–16
June - - -	3 95	4 11	$50\frac{1}{4}$	—	51 15–16	$52\frac{1}{2}$
July - - -	4 24	4 38	49 9–16	49 9–16	48 9–16	48 13–16
August - -	4 03	4 23	—		49 11–16	50
September - -	3 84	3 98	—		$50\frac{7}{8}$	$51\frac{1}{8}$
October - - -	4 34	4 46	—		54 5–16	54 13–16
November - -	4 79	4 92	57 15–16	$58\frac{1}{2}$	58 15–16	$59\frac{3}{4}$
December - -	4 50	4 69	56 1–16	56 3–16	58 3–16	59
Range of Daily Prices -	3 84	5 78	47 9–16	$59\frac{1}{8}$	48 9–16	$61\frac{1}{8}$
Yearly average 1880 -	4 60	4 78	54 9–16	55 1–16	54 13–16	55 7–16
Range Daily Prices 1879	3 60	6 40	$41\frac{1}{2}$	$63\frac{1}{2}$	43	67
Yearly average 1879 -	4 42	4 58	$48\frac{1}{2}$		49 3–10	$50\frac{3}{8}$

Average Prices of Oats, Rye and Peas, Monthly and Yearly, at New York.—For the Year 1880.

Month.	Oats.		Rye.		Peas.
	Western No. 2, Mixed, per bush.		Canada in bond, per bush.	State, per bush.	Canada Field in bond, per bush.
January - - -	$48\frac{1}{4}$	@48 11–16	$96\frac{1}{2}$	93	$86\frac{1}{2}$
February - - -	47 15–16	$48\frac{1}{8}$	96 5–16@97	$95\frac{3}{8}$ @96 5–16	85 @ 86
March - - -	$45\frac{3}{8}$	$45\frac{5}{8}$	$95\frac{1}{4}$	$96\frac{1}{4}$	85
April - - -	$41\frac{1}{4}$	42	89	89 15–16	85
May - - - -	$43\frac{3}{4}$	$44\frac{1}{8}$	92	$91\frac{1}{2}$	$83\frac{1}{4}$
June - - -	$38\frac{1}{8}$	38 9–16	96	$96\frac{5}{8}$	82 to 109 free
July - - - -	35 13–16	36 7–16	—	—	109 ”
August - - -	39	39 7–16	81	$85\frac{1}{4}$	81
September - - -	42 13–16	44	$93\frac{1}{2}$	93 5–16	81
October - - -	$39\frac{1}{8}$	$39\frac{3}{4}$	1 00	1 $01\frac{1}{2}$	$81\frac{5}{8}$
November - - -	42 5–16	$42\frac{7}{8}$	1 $06\frac{1}{2}$	1 03 9–16	83 7–16 $85\frac{1}{8}$
December - - -	43 13–16	$44\frac{1}{4}$	99	98 7–16	86 9–16 88
Yearly Average 1880 -	42 5–16	@42 13–16	95 @ 97	95@96 5–16	83 11–16@$86\frac{3}{8}$

It conveys in plain terms the information that in round numbers the price of wheat at New York was about 40*s*. per quarter. The average rate for freight during 1880 was close upon 5*s*. per quarter. So if we add insurance, dock charges, and other items it will not reach the British miller at less than 47*s*. to 48*s*. per quarter.

While, at the same time we write, wheat in Chicago is worth about 45*s*. per quarter, and in New York it stands at 48*s*. per quarter. With rates at an exceedingly low point wheat is finding its way to England at prices not much above those rates, while actually for some weeks past the prices in New York and Chicago have almost been on a par with those of London and Liverpool. Thus in Chicago on the 14th October 1881 wheat was carried from Chicago to Liverpool at 21 cents. a 100 lbs. Suppose then wheat in Chicago at

Original cost - - - -	45*s*.
Freight - - - - -	4*s*.
Insurance and handling - -	3*s*.
	52*s*.

But the usual rate, and the one that will pay the railway company and shipper is from 10*s*. to 12*s*. per quarter.

A railway and steamship company must live as well as other people, and we should therefore have wheat at 60*s*. per quarter in Liverpool just now if freights were at a paying point. It would not be at all fair to calculate the cost of freight from the above rates which are the result of a railway war, unequalled in the history of America. Those who live on this side of the Atlantic know well what the conscience of a great railway corporation is.

They have none, in fact, and while the writer saw a contract made to carry 100 lbs. of wheat from Chicago to Liverpool *viâ* rail to New York, a distance of 800 miles, and other 3,000 by sea, at the above rate of 21 cents. per 100 lbs., he had to pay one of the railway companies who contracted to carry this grain part of the way, and must have got about 1 cent. per 100 lbs. for every 100 miles, at the rate of 10 cents. per 100 lbs., and the distance was 30 miles. Get grain once to the great centres and you are comparatively safe, but away on a line where no competition exists and then the charges are about commensurate with the ability of the producers to pay.

As an instance of this fact take the rates of a railway company just published. We do not state names, as we only use this for illustration :—

	Miles.	Rate per 100 lbs.
A. to B. - -	457 -	$53\frac{1}{2}$ cents.
B. to C. - -	1,252 -	$20\frac{1}{2}$ cents.

We have all along contended that the actual cost of production far out upon the prairie had little to do with the influence of the wheat trade upon the English farmer. The real matter to contend with was and is the price at the great leading markets, such as Chicago and New York. From those points we can calculate with some certainty the exact cost of transportation, as, for instance, we are well aware 5*s*. or 6*s*. will carry a quarter of wheat from New York to England, or about 12*s*. to 14*s*. from Chicago to Liverpool will pay all charges, but he would be a man of no ordinary ability who could analyse the rates of American railway companies where they have no competitors, or where they pool together if in opposition. This subject of transportation is one of the greatest problems of this continent. When rates can decrease from say 60 cents. a 100 lbs. to one-third of that amount there is something radically wrong. Every citizen of the United States and of Canada has an interest of the strongest nature in this business. Gradually the great railways are being concentrated into fewer hands.

Vanderbilt, Gould, and lesser lights stand up against the great crowd of humanity, who are for ever travelling to and fro, or sending goods from one point to another, and at their will they can dictate as they please. Day after day, month after month, and year after year, a band of monopolists mightier than European princes, richer and more powerful than British peers, are welding together in a few great systems the whole transportation interest of this continent.

The little fish are gradually being devoured by the leviathans who hold control.

It is an old saying that " when thieves fall out honest " men get their own," so we find the great railway corporations enter into conflicts with one another, time and again. The public for the time of the warfare reaps a great benefit, but those struggles only lead to a period when the weaker parties having lost all give up their rights, and the producers and consumers have eventually to pay richly for the license they have enjoyed. No person who is acquainted with the American continent can but foresee great trouble looming up in the future on this very question. It is one of vital interest to the English farmer.

Its present effect in America is one of concentration.

Cities grow up at favoured points with mushroom rapidity, while the great country districts which should receive and would benefit by thriving towns and smiling villages are left out in the cold.

Vast regions under the control of one railway have to bend to the laws of its dictator, and as its whole interest is producing beef or bread for home and foreign use, its very life and prosperity depend upon its means of transport. We have given an instance of this, but take another: The rate on wheat from the point where the writer resides is sometimes greater than what it is at Chicago, 500 miles further from the seaboard. To the English farmer it means enhanced prices with extreme fluctuations.

With a poor crop in America this season we have cheap freight, but in a month or two they may turn round and go as far the other way. The tendency is to have low freights with dear grain, and high freight when the crop is abundant and prices moderate.

Looking at the subject from this point, and to our ideas, the only just way of looking at it, we cannot but consider the cost of production on the farm as a secondary consideration. In regard to this business we have to look at the reality. If, as many standard authorities maintain, wheat upon the prairies can be produced and laid down at a profit in England at 40s. per quarter, the gain of the American wheat grower must have been almost fabulous when we consider that during 1880 American wheat sold at an average of 48s. per quarter, then we have a gain of 8s. per quarter over and above the legitimate profit of the producer.

Now we are perfectly certain that no such handsome returns have come to the wheat growers of this country. The average wheat grower makes but little money. He clears a fair return, but seldom makes a fortune. I know of large wheat farms on the prairies which with all those stories of cheap production and great prices, have scarcely paid interest and expenses, instead of making their owners gigantic fortunes, as they should have done at the above figures. The evidence in California, where the most leviathan wheat farms in the world are met with, is conclusive on this point, and I venture to say that most of the large wheat farms on the prairie will eventually fail, as nearly all large farms have done in this country. There are men of course who can carry through gigantic operations of any kind, but the average result will be failure. If the American farmer can get no more than 40s. per quarter for his finest wheats in the Liverpool markets, it will be a sad day for him. It is his only stronghold; the British farmer, when wheat fails him, has other strings to his bow. Our experience of farming is that the principal products of the farm, and more especially wheat, are delivered to the consumer at a little over cost of production. Rarely the price goes below par; there may be no profit, and just as seldom does the husbandman reap an enormous advantage; and we imagine that when the price of wheat was delivered in England at 48s. per quarter it allowed the American grower a very liberal return for his labour and capital.

Proceeding more immediately to the question of production on the farm, it is universally admitted that it takes at least

Ten dollars to produce an acre of wheat.

In 1878 the cost would be about 8½ dollars per acre, but as wages have risen at least 25 per cent. since, as wheat lands have gone up in the same ratio, as well as all other articles, the estimate of 10 dollars is a very low one, and we make this estimate of 10 dollars upon wild lands valued at 5 dollars per acre in their unbroken state, but if we take the whole American continent and allow a fair rent for land we shall have to raise our estimate far above that figure. Probably it will be nearer 12 dollars.

But, for the sake of argument, place the production of an acre of wheat at the above sum, we should find the figures thus:

1 acre of wheat costs	10 dollars.
1 acre average 12½ bushels per acre, cost per bus. at railway depôt	80 cents.
Average rail and ocean freight from the West	55 ,,
Total in Liverpool	135 ,,
Price per quarter	45s.

It may be argued that 12½ bushels is too low for the average of the Western States. But while some favoured localities may produce much more, we have got to average the Continent, for we are not treating of individual cases, we argue from a general point of view.

The crops of Minnesota this season are estimated at 11 bushels per acre while the crops of Illinois will decline from 16¾ bushels to about the same amount, and it is likely that the whole product of the Continent will decline from an average of 13⅓ bushels in 1880 to about 10½ bushels in 1881, which will still give the United States close on 400 millions of bushels, and then we shall have the products of Canada into the bargain. With very low wages, with implements cheap, and all the necessaries and luxuries of life moderate in price, wheat may be delivered at lower rates and still give the grower a living profit, but at the present prices of everything it cannot be done. With an average crop and favourable seasons it is more than probable that whatever American wheat makes above 45s. per quarter in the Liverpool markets is extra profit to either the grower or the shipper. More than likely the railway companies will manage to take most of it.

A rate, including insurance and commission, of 45 cts. per bushel from Chicago to Liverpool pays well, so that we only allow 10 cts. from outside points to Chicago, but as a large proportion of grain will come from other parts on this side of that great port, the allowance of an extra 10 cts. per bushel will be ample. It is from the West where the surplus wheat comes from.

The Eastern States do not supply themselves.

Thus in 1880,

New York State, with 5,000,000 people, produced only 12,000,000 bushels of wheat, less than half what she required.

Massachusetts, with 1,783,000 people, produces but 15,606 bushels wheat.

Virginia almost meets her own demands.

On the other hand we find

Illinois, with 3,000,000 of people, produces 53,000,000 bushels wheat. (This was an unprecedented crop. The estimate for 1881 is only 32 to 35 millions of bushels.)

Minnesota, with 780,000 people; gives this Continent 40,000,000 bushels at an average value, at the railway depot of 88 cents.—(This season is estimated at about 30,000,000.)

Missouri, with over 2,000,000 people, produces 30,000,000 bushels wheat.

Indiana, Ohio, Michigan, Wisconsin, Kansas, Iowa, Dakota, &c., are very large producers of wheat. Much of their extra produce has to supply the Eastern States, and we may safely say that our English market is supplied from points west of Chicago; and as the wheat product is gradually coming from points further west we shall find that the total supply will be from regions west and north-west of Chicago. The price of wheat last year in Minnesota, as stated above, was 88 to 90 cts. per bushel at the railway depôt. Add to this an average rate of 55 cts. for freight, insurance, commission, &c. we have wheat in Liverpool from this great wheat-growing State at 143 cts. or 145 cts. per bushel, or 48s. per qr. And we must calculate that this price was maintained in the face of the largest crop America ever produced. At the present moment such wheat is worth 54s. to 55s. per qr. in England, and if freights had not been excessively low we should have had it selling at 60s. per quarter.

In my report upon California, I took occasion to state that the probabilities were that the average wheat production of the States about 12·2 bushels per acre, which is the official return, was too low.

Unwilling as I am to admit this for the sake of the American agriculturist, I am inclined to accept it, after seeing how crops can decline in one year.

I have calculated the average yield at 12½ bushels, a little above the official estimate.

LIVE STOCK.

The writer has a very large business in live stock of all kinds, and could fill many pages upon this subject, but I deem it better to concentrate the leading facts connected with this important branch of the subject as it bears on Great Britain. I shall endeavour to treat this portion of my report as concisely as possible.

At the very outset, I take an entirely opposite view of the live stock business to that of wheat and corn growing. Every acre of wheat raised under the present system of American farming is so much loss of capital, while every beast raised and fed is so much addition to the farmer's account. The one deteriorates, the other enriches the soil, and thus while the difference of profit may be on the side of wheat in its early stages the grand success of the farmer is stock.

Wheat growing at present is mere speculating, a great gambling transaction in the Western States at least, but cattle, sheep, and hogs add wealth to the land, and consequently to the farmer's purse. When we consider that to make 100 tons of meat, about 600 of grain is used, the advantages of the stock farmer over the wheat grower are enormous, for he is returning a vast quantity of this amount back to the soil. Take the export of Indian corn for instance. Less than 10 per cent. is exported, the remaining 90 per cent. kept at home, some of it is used for household food, but the great proportion made into beef, mutton, and pork.

The American stock farmer has in reality far more advantages than his brother wheat grower, and while at present the British farmer may fear the import of wheat, he shall eventually have more to complain of when the stock raising interest of America has emerged from its infancy. Great though the strides have been of the last 50 years, the practical agriculturist is well aware of the crude state of agriculture in so far as the stock of the farm is concerned.

We have quantity but no quality, nine-tenths at least of the whole cattle and sheep of the United States are inferior and not fitted for export. The constant cry of the exporter is for good grades, great grand bullocks such as we have got in England, after long years of patient improvement. We know how long and perseveringly the British stock farmer has worked at the improvement of his stock, and what a spirit of emulation has existed among cattle breeders and sheep raisers. The pioneers in this business have added millions by their efforts to the wealth of Great Britain, and the great work still goes forward more slowly, in days of depression when actually it is most needed; but it revives again, and the fire of improvement blazes forth as bright as ever. This great work, so far as America is concerned, has yet practically to come.

What have the efforts of breeders of blooded stock accomplished so far when we look at the annual product of both cattle and sheep in the North American continent. They have but trodden on the borderland of improvement. When we think that the present stock of cattle in the United States aggregates the enormous number of 33 millions, and that since the introduction of shorthorn cattle, some fifty years ago, about 50,000 bulls have been registered in the herd books, we can see how little has been done.

Thousands of bulls, such as shorthorns, Herefords, polled Angus, &c., have of course done good service, and no record of their pedigree, a criterion of pure blood, been kept. In England comparatively few bulls are entered in the herd book, but here in America, a large number previous to this time have been recorded on account of their scarcity. Of late years when so many young bulls have gone to the plains, so correct a record has not been kept, but the above figures prove to many a one that as yet but very little has been done in improving the native cattle of this country, and as a fact up to the time when the exportation of cattle to Europe became thoroughly founded, little or no attention had been paid to the improvement of their stock by the ordinary farmer of America.

At rare intervals you would meet cases of individuals who for years had used in their herds nothing but pure bred bulls. Even in Kentucky, the primary home of the American shorthorn, the great majority of the cattle are little better than scrubs, while in Canada there is the most miserable class of cattle on this continent, so far as the semi-cultivated regions are concerned. The farmers of Ontario have had in their midst some of the very finest herds of cattle on this continent, and of late years they have gradually driven the breeders of shorthorns out of the country, or at least made them seek other markets. It is safe to say that in the above province, not one farmer in a hundred has a pure bred bull, whereas even for necessary purposes the proportion should be one for every ten farmers.

This is the rock upon which the stock raising interest of America has been stranded ever since the export of cattle began. They have found themselves unable to meet the demand.

First came the export business, which swallowed all the best steers, and thousands were shipped before they were prime, so great was the margin between the producer's price in this country, and that of the consumer is Great Britain. Second, there followed an increased home demand, which has grown so great within the last twelve months, that certain we are that at the present time this continent could swallow all the first class cattle that are put out of the American feeders' hands. This may seem a strange statement, yet it is true. Butchers complain in every town that they cannot find cattle adequate to the demand in regard to quality. As people become richer, they wish a better article, and it is not likely that the American people will tamely see all their best cattle shipped to foreign lands, and not get a taste of it.

People will not tolerate the leather beef-steaks of olden time. Their taste is educated for something better. Nothing corroborated those statements better than the fact that prices in Chicago stock yards on the 14th of October 1881 ranged from 2·50 to 7·25 per 100 lbs. It shows the demand for good beef, and it is also consoling in some measure that at present the best classes of American beef can only be laid down in Liverpool and delivered to the butcher at a rate of 8d. per lb. more or less according to freight. Those are the present prices.

What with a short supply of good cattle, a short supply of feed, and an ever increasing demand from the manufacturing districts in America, we cannot say what will be the figure next Spring. The tendency, however, is strongly upwards.

There are 33 millions of cattle in the States, over 40 millions of sheep, and 34 millions of hogs.

While sheep are increasing within the last two years, it is calculated that cattle and hogs have materially decreased. The former through the fierce winters of 1878–79 and 1880–81, while the price of the latter went so low that the production was stopped to a great extent, but as the fecundity of the sow is great they can be increased to a great number in a year's time. It is beef we have got principally to deal with, for we may safely take for granted that pigs can be raised cheaper in America than at home.

The American farmer is a hog-raiser upon the most scientific principle, while the British yeoman does not take so kindly to them. More perfectly than any other animal the hog meets the requirements of a western farm. They are easily raised without care or attention, and can find food for themselves, as they are omnivorous. The habits of the pig are so far changed in America that we may call him a grazier; and of all breeds the Berkshire is the most superlative. He fattens and grows and does all the scavenger work.

Before entering on the beef question let us take some statistics on this subject. Taking mess pork at the standard, we find that in Chicago on

		$	ct.		$	ct.	
16th October	1878, price	7	50	to	7	55	p. barrel.
,, ,,	1879, ,,	10	00	,,	10	50	,,
,, ,,	1880, ,,	18	00	,,	18	25	,,
14th ,,	1881, ,,	16	60	,,	16	90	,,

Following this increase in price is a vast increase in numbers. Thus in the western or packing States, while 1878–79 produced a total of 9 millions of hogs packed, we find that in 1880 and 1881 12 millions were packed, an increase of 33 per cent., with an increase of over 100 per cent. in price. The number of hogs slaughtered yearly increased, while the numbers on the farm decreased. Production did not meet the demand. The high prices, however, have turned the special attention of the breeders to pigs, and probably the next returns will show an increasing number. The average weight of the hogs killed in 1878 was 217 lbs., those of 1881 equalled 207, a decrease of 10 lbs. per hog. This diminution is probably owing to the hogs being sent earlier to market. Next spring will show whether there is to be any increase or not in the number slaughtered. Corn has increased in price over 30 per cent. this season, and it must make a vast difference in the price of pork, as it is the principal food used for fattening. We may take it for granted, however, that the Americans will produce pork either in the raw material or the manufactured article at a cheaper and more profitable rate than can be done in England. They have got this business so thoroughly under their control. The animals are so well graded up, and the climate so suitable, that I am certain they will always hold this market under their control. In a new country full of riches, where the soil is prolific, where dear labour often hurries the husbandman over his work, and when much is left behind that might economically be placed in the barn yard. These circumstances favour the hog. On the great cattle farms where corn is fed the practice is to feed this indigestible grain in a whole state, that is not crushed. Much of it passes through the animal in its original state. We find, however, that the pig, whose organs of digestion are exceedingly powerful, following up the steers and making use of the offal.

The ultimate end of the beef trade will probably be something of the same, though not to such a degree, nor is it likely that such a consummation will speedily arrive. The great obstruction is the uncertainty of the climate in the regions where the great mass of the cattle are raised away in Texas, Colorado, Wyoming, and Montana, and the kindred States. Already it is claimed that many of the best ranges for cattle in those countries are overcrowded, and that the death-rate of last year was as much the result of too many cattle as the hard winter. Still the great fact remains that all through those regions we have a great country which is liable to either severe drought or terrible winters, which make the raising of cattle and sheep a somewhat precarious business. The cost of raising steers of first quality on land which can be used for all agricultural purposes, will leave but a small margin for export. The competition we need seriously to look at is that which originates far out on western wilds where cattle are raised for their herding expenses, but so far the quality of this class of stock has been so poor that we have little or no reason to fear it. Let them once improve the quality of their young stock, then there are places upon the vast feeding farms of Illinois and its sister States where they can put on to the frames any quantity of beef.

We hear a great deal about the vast herds of the Western States, but when seen they are a miserable class of scalawags, an unthrifty race, and their effect upon British agriculture is small indeed. They, of course, fill up a gap. They supply a certain class of the population, and allow the better class of stock to be exported, and of course this is sufficiently serious, but it will be plain to all parties who have studied the tastes of the beef-eating races of the world, that there is an insatiable craving after a better quality of meat. In the halcyon days of the British mining interest, some ten years ago, it was marvellous how quickly the miners became perfect connoisseurs in this respect. Now we are going through the same operation in America. Within two years it is wonderful how the home demand has grown for a better class of meat, and the prices quoted above tell their own tale in this respect. Notwithstanding the strenuous efforts of the breeders and feeders, they have been totally unable to cope with the demand, and the consequence has been an enormous rise in the price of all butcher's articles.

If the British farmer will not improve his stock and keep pace with the demand for better grades of all classes of beef and mutton, he will surely lose the day ; but if he goes ahead and does all that lies in his power to maintain his reputation as THE cattle raiser and feeder of the world, justly proud of his preeminent position, then he need not fear American competition so much. Almost boundless though the territory of the trans-Atlantic stock raiser may be, we must ever remember that on the very best grazing lands of America it will take more than two acres there to do the work of one at home ; while out on the prairie, on the arid plains of Colorado and Wyoming, it will often require the grass product of 50 to 100 acres to keep an animal, while in good wild land it is estimated that a steer will need 10 to 15 acres to carry it through the year.

There is, of course, room for expansion on the plains, but the great stride, if it is made, is in producing not a greater quantity of cattle, but in grading up and improving the quality of those that are already there. This can only be done by using a better class of bulls, and by giving the stock a more generous supply of food, that is extending the range. It is easy to diminish even a well-bred class of cattle by poor feed. We have seen shorthorns within a generation or two change almost into Ayrshires through neglect and poor feeding, and so it is upon those western plains. It will need skilful management to keep up the standard of excellence. Rapid though the movements and great the force with which an American acts upon his ideas, yet they have not the means to accomplish any great transition in their stock of cattle. The improvement will be slow and gradual, but it will be much faster than it would be in Great Britain.

The exports of cattle and sheep from the United States and Canada for the last five years are as follows :—

UNITED STATES.

	Cattle.	Sheep.
1876	392	—
1877	11,538	13,120
1878	68,450	43,940
1879	76,117	119,350
1880	154,814	66,722

CANADA.

	Cattle.	Sheep.
1876	2,557	1,862
1877	7,649	10,275
1878	17,989	40,132
1879	25,185	73,913
1880	48,103	78,074

Another account places the Canadian export thus :—

1879.

26,176 Cattle
78,780 Sheep
386 Horses   Value - $2,681 000
74 Mules
3,391 Hogs

1880.

50,817 Cattle
81,547 Sheep
700 Hogs   Value - $4,738 700
49 Horses

Those figures show a remarkable increase in one year, but when we consider that there are over 35 millions of cattle on the continent, and far above 40 millions of sheep, the amount shipped is infinitesimal, yet the complaint is that the shippers cannot get cattle to make up their contracts. In June of this year we saw large numbers of third class cattle shipped, and when asked what was the reason, the reply from the shipper was that he had a contract to fill and he had to send what he could get. Those cattle were costing the shipper 7 cts. per lb. live weight on board ship at New York, and were losing money at a ruinous rate. Over and above those cattle shipped in a live state, nearly as many go over as dead meat. Canned meats and pork make up a grand total of dead meat and live, about 100,000,000 lbs. were shipped. When we consider that in 1879 the United States exported of animals and animal matter a grand total of 146,641,233 dollars worth, we can see how small this export of live cattle and sheep amount to. Taking altogether in round numbers, Britain imported in cash value of such animals from the United States and Canada about 20,000,000 dollars. Of bacon and hams the United States exported in 1880 to the amount of 60,000,000 dollars ; pork, 7,000,000 dollars ; fresh beef 9,000,000 dollars ; salt beef, 2,000,000 dollars. We can therefore see how much we have to fear in England this great growing business.

It may increase to tremendous proportions. Of the above amounts all did not reach England, but a very large per centage did. Of the hog products alone of the United States Great Britain took 52¼ per cent.

We might go ahead giving endless statistics, but as the actual facts of personal observation are of more value for the present, we turn to the value of the animals exported and the question of transportation. We may dismiss the subject of the hog, as we said above. With 34,000,000 of hogs in America, we may say that the 3,000,000 in Great Britain will stand but a small chance, so we pass on to the subject of cattle. There are just about four times as many cattle in the United States and Canada as in Great Britain, and as we said above, the home farmer's safeguard lies in the superior quality of his product. Although a cattle raiser myself, I have been unable to procure any definite average price of raising a steer for the English market. You will find so many different classes of stock and such a variety of soil and climate that the average cost of raising a steer in America is a difficult matter to handle. Canadian breeders and feeders agree that steers of the best quality can be sold at home with a fair profit at 5 cents per lb. live weight when they are prime. At that price, with feed at a moderate rate, they can do so; but during this winter I do not see that they will be able to turn them out of their stable at such a price. The ruling price for a Canadian steer has been above that figure for a year past. Last spring feeders realised 6 cents at home easily. About the month of June the trade was partially demoralised through heavy losses of shippers, who had contracted cattle in the spring months, shipping them in May to England and meeting adverse markets. Thus in June prices had declined to about 5 cents, and a steer bought at this price in Canada would be landed in Liverpool at the following price:—

Three Years old Steer.

Live weight, 1,400 lbs. at 5 cents	70.00
Average freight from interior	3.00
Feed and attendance on cars	.75
Feed on board ship	3.50
Expense of loading and attendance on ocean trip	1.50
Average insurance	2.50
Ocean freight, Montreal to Liverpool	20.00
Commission and expenses in Liverpool	4.00
	$105.25
Equal to about	£22 0 0

If this bullock dressed 784 lbs. of dressed meat, we have meat laid down in Liverpool at less than 7d. per lb., or say at that rate, because it is more than likely, with one risk and another, it will need to realise this price. Nor have we allowed any commission or profit for the Canadian middleman, for he is an important personage in this trade and has to realise a very considerable profit, as his work is hard and tedious, the roads being bad and the distances long.

If we calculate this steer at 6 cents per lb., equal to about 25l. in England, we shall find that he is worth about 7¾d. per lb. To calculate nearly we must allow the Canadian shipper about 7½d. per lb. for his beef in Liverpool, or 8s. 9d. per stone of 14 lbs. Canadian cattle are often poor shippers, as many are fed at the large distilleries which are found at many points in the Dominion, and they are consequently soft and produce a poor quality of meat. The supply of good cattle is also exceedingly limited, and the least increased demand sends up prices. Consequently Canadian shippers have, on the whole, had a poor time of it.

At the above date the same class of bullock shipped from New York would stand thus:—

Three Years old Steer.

Live weight, 1,400 lbs. at 6½ cents per lb.	91.00
Freight	12.50
Expenses and feed	5.00
Insurance	2.50
Selling	2.00
	$113.00
Equal to about	£23 10 0

Such beef would only be delivered to the butcher at 7¼d. per lb. in Liverpool. There again we shall need to calculate 7½d. as a remunerative rate.

Shippers were losing money at that time, and prophesied lower rates; but since then they have gone up and are higher, while there has been a steady decrease in the quality of the cattle, owing to the dry summer.

While in June 1881 such cattle were purchased in New York or landed at that rate from western points at prices equal to that figure, we find in June 1880 cattle of the same size and quality could be purchased at 5¼ cents per lb. The present prices of first-class cattle will not allow either New York or Chicago cattle to be landed at profit at less than 8d. per lb. We are talking, of course, of first-class cattle. They are by far the most profitable shippers. During this summer, however, a large number of second-class cattle have been sent across to complete steamboat contracts made in spring, and the result has been a loss. Many shippers had made contracts at the rate of 20.00 dollars per head, and as the business was not paying at the above rate, those who had made contracts on such a basis were in a bad way. Messrs. Read and Pell computed very fairly that during the autumn of 1879 beef could be sold in Liverpool at 6½d. per lb.; but notwithstanding that freights have decreased very materially since then, the price of the raw material has increased so much on this side of the Atlantic that it cannot be placed in England with a fair profit at less than 7½d. per lb. At the present time I see no prospect of that price being materially lessened.

The tendency, so far as my observation goes, is upwards with freights at 2l. to 2l. 10s., such rates are liable to increase at any moment. Sheep follow the price of cattle very nearly, and may be classed alongside of them. The freight and other expenses of a sheep across the ocean is about 1s.

As a rule they are more easily handled and give a better return.

To show the loss in stock on board ship we quote the ruling rates of Insurance.

January and February	10	per cent.
March „ April	4	,, ,,
May	¾	,, ,,
June and July	1	,, ,,
August	2	,, ,,
September and October	4	,, ,,
November and December	4 to 5	,,

But as most of the cattle are shipped in the summer months we have an average rate of 2 to 2½ per cent.

The question of dead meat really lies in the above which we have discussed. The only difference is that at times large quantities of second class material flood the English market which have to be sacrificed and give a very bad reputation to the whole trade.

CONCLUSION.

In conclusion, I have tried to treat this subject of American competition in as narrow limits as possible, and have no hesitation in saying that its influence upon British agriculture has been exaggerated. I have only treated the main issues of beef and bread, as I think the other questions of dairy produce, &c., are but secondary and really hang upon the above.

Put British Agriculture upon a fair basis, give it the justice it is entitled to with even average crops, and I am certain that so far it can stand up against the world and fight its own battle.

If it cannot stand on its own feet without protection, both internally and externally, better let it sicken and die, and let a new system take its place.

I will be ready at any time to appear before the Commission and give whatever information is needed in regard to American Agriculture.

I remain,
My Lord Duke,
Your obedient Servant,
Bow Park, Brantford.　　　　　　　　　JOHN CLAY, JUN.
20 January 1882.

APPENDIX I.

EMIGRATION.

To America.—Emigration means wealth, with it comes gold and silver, bone and sinew, and inventive power. Putting aside the two former, we have the exact article that is wanted in a country full of raw material and which can be used to a great extent without much capital.

For years there has been a steady drain from the so-called overcrowded countries of Europe to this land on the other side of the Atlantic, whose vast natural facilities draw to its confines alike the farmer and the mechanic. Call the countries crowded as we may it is clear that properly cultivated the lands of Europe could carry all the population that they have without fear of famine, but it is also clear that if no population had come to America, and the people who left there had increased as fast as they have done, there would have been too dense a population, more especially in our cities. Just as the darkness of the middle age was closing, Columbus steered for the west and brought back news of the glorious land that lay towards the setting sun. A land which for years enriched the coffers of Spain, but which eventually has become populated with an English speaking people, a great hybrid race full of energy, power, and indomitable perseverance, a grand people rising up by gigantic strides, possessing one language and imbued with the same religious feeling. A nation of inventors, nothing too hard for their brains to master in the way of manufacturing cheaply, or overcoming the greatest problems of modern engineering. A nation full of egotism, but who never allow it to interfere with their welfare or business.

This is the nation whom the British farmer, the husbandman of an old Conservative country, have to compete with, and who having almost bridged as it were the Atlantic appear in the home market with them.

This great growing country, battling in its infancy through countless difficulties, has at last reached the stage of youth. Men who live in it and travel over its length and breadth think that it is just emerging from its childhood. Its foot-falls are on the region of wild extravagance.

England and Europe have passed that. They are matured and their greatness depends upon their Governments and their economy. Even as they grow older they may improve if they put back into their land what they take away, and by mining deep into the ground they will find fertilizers that for long years to come will keep up the standard of the soil. Strange though it may seem, and in startling antagonism to the richness of American soil, it is still a fact of vast importance in this great controversy of American competition to know that it takes two acres in America, so far as wheat is concerned, to produce as much as one in England, while I am also certain that in regard to grazing the same holds good. But the American agriculturist gets land almost for nothing, at least in the great wheat growing states. He is not as good a farmer as those of the old country, while labour is dear he can do with less, for he has a better climate and his implements are far handier and more perfect, and then he can turn round and change his system while whose at home would be considering the matter. Nor does he spend much on houses, on barns or fences. These will come in good time, and consequently as far as houses are concerned, the British labourer is better housed than the American farmer. Strange how a man changes in this respect when he touches American soil.

Once breathe the transatlantic air and the voyager seems to get a new life, and well it is, for the conformation of the country and the climate change a man's ways of life and means of getting a livelihood. This American country is a world of change, a man changes his business and thinks little of it, and gathers experience as he goes along. Thus you will find men who have almost done everything under the sun. There runs through the society of the whole States both north and south, and the infection spreads to Canada, a sort of nervous anxiety to be continually working. There is no idle class. The country is too young, it cannot afford it, and though there are loafers by the score, they soon drop out of existence, and thousands of them through drink are swept into an early grave.

As the question of emigration is a most important one in regard to agriculture, let us present a few facts and statistics, showing its power and place upon the continent of America, and consequently upon the agriculture of the world.

The population of the United States in round numbers is 50 millions of people, that of Canada about five millions, so that on the North American continent we have over 55 millions of souls of an English speaking population. Those people have been gathered from every conceivable part of the globe. Of the 50 millions who compose the people of the States, about 10 millions have immigrated and settled down within the last 100 years, most of the people in the prime of youth, and consequently exceedingly reproductive. As a rule about 25 per cent. are under 15 years of age, and about 10 per cent. over 40, so that the whole number are mostly people who came at an age when they can benefit a country to their farthest degree. It is a subject of common remark that the climate of America is exceedingly favourable to reproduction in the case of new comers.

Perchance there is some truth in the remark, but the marked increase among immigrants is due to the remarkable strength and health of the class who emigrate. Probably another reason may be found, that the average American woman is blessed with few children. Be that as it may, the immediate progeny of the new population are the healthiest class we have. Tracing up this question, we find that since 1783 to 1880, nearly 100 years, 10,616,056 people have come from other countries to the United States, and that number is divided as follows :—

IMMIGRANTS FROM 1783 TO 1880.

Chief Nationalities.	Number.
England	953,898
Ireland	3,137,364
Scotland	172,187
Wales	19,066
Not specified	560,242
Total British islands	4,842,757

[The "not specified" includes the 250,000 arriving before 1820.]

CONTINENTAL EUROPE.

Germany and Austria	3,159,072
Scandinavia	420,369
France	318,013
Switzerland	89,815
Italy	79,098
Holland and Belgium	72,138
Russia	42,882
Spain and Portugal	37,802
Poland	17,008
Hungary	10,448
Other countries and not specified	403,410
Total	4,650,055
British islands	4,842,757
All Europe	9,492,812

APPENDIX TO SUPPLEMENTARY REPORT BY MR. JOHN CLAY, JUN.

	Number.
Asia (eight-tenths Chinese)	233,876
British America	703,703
West Indies	64,558
Mexico	25,224
Central and South America	19,099
Africa	1,554
Pacific islands and not specified	75,230
Grand total	10,616,056

If we add the arrivals up to the 1st of June 1881, and allow for many thousands who have come in from Canada and Mexico, of whom no record was made, the aggregate of immigration will reach more than 11,000,000. This does not include about a million "annexed" in our acquisitions of territory—first, by the purchase of Louisiana, then Florida, then Texas, then California, and lastly Alaska.

The statistics in this article are taken from the Government returns and from the pages of the "New York Herald."

This year will bring the grand total up to 11,000,000. It will be seen that the British islands contribute about half of the grand total, or rather more if those who have gone from British North America were counted in, so that we have half, or more than half, English speaking. Gradually the others have changed their tongue and habits, and we have the whole, both in language and manners, turned into an Anglo-Saxon race. In the separate countries Germany leads the van, but Ireland follows quickly on her heels, and from this very fact, that Ireland should send such a contribution of people from such a small country, we may well draw a lesson. To produce such an emigration something must be wrong, both with the people and their mode and style of life. Those two countries produce a people whose characteristics are entirely opposite. We have the fiery Celt and the calm, plodding Teuton. One a fighter, the other a man of peace. One a drawer of water and hewer of wood, the other a quiet, unassuming farmer, who settles far out on the prairie, and does his daily work day after day away from the maddening crowd and the scenes of the city. One a politician, the other a family man given up to his children and watching their welfare.

Both have their places. Turbulent though the Irishman is, he builds the railways and makes the canals, does most of the hard work of America, and while an inveterate grumbler, his admixture with the people of America softens his nature, and his children grow up good citizens. The bad qualities disappear in the second generation. Yet few of those Irishmen take to farming. You will find them scattered here and there, but their dwelling place is the city and its confines. They are the great consumers, while the German element is the great producer.

It is however worthy of note that the flow of emigration from Ireland has decreased materially in the last decade, as will be seen from the following figures.

Decade.	Irish.	German.
1820–30	57,278	7,729
1830–40	198,233	152,454
1840–50	733,434	434,626
1850–60	936,665	951,667
1860–70	774,883	831,405
1870–80	436,871	781,191
Aggregates	3,137,364	3,159,072

In the face of existing facts it shows that the inhabitants of the Emerald Isle must in a certain degree be more contented, but it is probably due to the fact that the emigration was so great in former years that there are fewer people to come. Since the present agitation began the increase is exceedingly large. Thus in—

1877 there came	13,991
1878 "	17,113
1879 "	27,651
1880 "	84,799

During the first of those years business of all kinds was exceedingly dull, and the flow of emigration was rather from America than towards it.

Whenever prosperity came fairly back we find all classes as well as the Irish flowing like a mighty maelstrom to this country. So that no mistakes may be made we subjoin the following interesting table:—

	1861.	1862.	1863.	1864.	1865.	1866.	1867.	1868.	1869.	1870.
England	8,976	10,947	24,065	26,096	15,038	2,770	11,100	11,107	55,046	59,048
Ireland	32,274	35,859	96,088	89,442	77,370	83,894	108,857	59,997	79,030	75,514
Scotland	767	657	1,940	3,476	3,037	672	1,420	1,949	12,415	11,820
Wales	461	536	706	628	146	23	150	103	1,225	672
Total British Islands	43,472	47,920	122,799	116,951	112,237	131,620	125,520	107,582	147,716	151,089
Germany	31,711	27,640	33,247	57,506	83,846	115,985	134,118	123,465	127,311	96,963
Scandinavia	840	2,550	3,119	2,961	7,258	14,495	8,491	22,439	46,115	27,406
Europe, except British Islands	37,728	35,720	40,935	62,282	101,811	147,302	158,231	158,273	187,648	137,498
Total Europe	81,200	83,710	163,734	185,233	214,048	278,022	283,751	265,855	335,364	288,587
China	7,518	3,633	7,214	2,975	2,942	2,385	3,863	10,684	14,902	11,943
Total Asia and Islands	7,528	3,640	7,216	2,982	2,947	2,415	3,961	10,701	15,000	12,058
Total Africa and Islands	47	12	3	37	49	33	25	63	31	24
British North America	2,069	3,275	3,464	3,636	21,586	32,150	6,014	10,894	30,921	53,340
West Indies	358	585	492	719	851	895	817	858	3,016	1,109
Mexico	218	142	96	99	193	239	292	275	371	461
Central America	21	27	2	2	—	4	4	3	8	25
South America	47	146	96	152	148	294	224	145	67	84
Total America	2,673	4,175	4,150	4,608	22,778	33,582	7,357	12,175	34,833	55,019
Pacific Islands	312	34	188	468	620	374	392	311	488	602
All other Countries	73	254	924	84	8,610	3,165	2,878	8,110	10,656	22,506
Aggregate for year	91,923	91,825	176,215	193,412	249,052	318,491	298,358	297,215	395,922	378,796

(*Continued.*)

	1871.	1872.	1873.	1874.	1875.	1876.	1877.	1878.	1879.	1880.
England	61,174	72,810	69,600	43,396	30,040	21,051	18,124	19,581	40,997	64,190
Ireland	61,463	69,761	75,848	47,688	29,969	16,506	13,791	17,113	27,651	84,799
Scotland	12,135	14,565	13,008	8,765	5,739	4,383	3,408	3,700	8,728	14,495
Wales	1,348	755	868	558	419	294	232	311	1,046	948
Total British Islands	143,937	157,905	159,355	100,422	66,179	42,243	35,556	40,706	78,424	164,438
Germany	111,971	160,695	140,084	63,881	42,604	37,370	31,795	36,839	49,790	152,272
Scandinavia	25,312	28,750	34,553	14,105	12,447	12,859	10,724	14,080	29,679	78,555
Europe, except British Islands	152,819	223,555	110,232	107,637	78,000	72,306	59,239	70,677	105,787	277,659
Total Europe	296,756	381,460	369,487	208,059	144,179	114,549	94,795	111,383	184,211	442,097
China	6,030	10,642	18,154	16,651	19,033	16,879	10,379	8,468	9,189	7,011
Total Asia and Islands	6,071	10,687	18,221	16,704	19,088	17,055	10,407	8,518	9,218	7,098
Total Africa and Islands	54	78	44	80	42	100	10	25	20	15
British North America	39,929	40,288	29,508	30,596	23,420	21,218	22,123	30,102	53,267	139,761
West Indies	1,228	1,301	1,974	1,749	1,530	1,568	1,010	923	1,312	1,866
Mexico	493	604	473	442	682	532	486	473	550	437
Central America	10	13	34	21	14	14	46	18	27	42
South America	110	123	168	129	139	135	78	61	90	119
Total America	41,774	42,329	32,159	32,938	25,786	23,467	21,743	31,577	55,246	142,225
Pacific Islands	1,288	1,914	1,050	1,467	1,080	1,281	745	635	837	1,125
All other countries	995	1,282	1,584	1,566	1,056	988	826	1,069	1,033	1,143
Aggregate for year	346,938	437,750	522,545	260,814	191,231	157,440	130,526	153,207	250,565	593,703

It may well be asked what is the influence of this mighty flood of human beings upon the agriculture of Great Britain, this half million of stalwart men and women with few children and fewer aged people, all workers and driven mostly by untoward circumstances from home, come determined to do their best, for it is their last chance. A man who cannot swim in this country with the ocean of prosperity is not likely to do it in any place else, so here we have year after year a class of people coming who were naturally consumers at home, but once on wing, the majority turn into producers. The effect of this is likely to be very great and has already acted on our markets at home, but we do not deem it at all fatal to home agriculture.

It has certainly struck a violent blow at the work of the husbandmen at home, but while with favourable seasons it injures home agriculture by reducing prices, we must remember that when a poor crop comes, there is an immensely increased population to feed, and such made improvident by plenty are very wasteful in their habits. This great flow of emigration has helped to work evil in another way and it is altogether not such a blessing. It has helped to force the price of land up very materially so that the rate of production is very much increased.

Speculation is rife, and though the population of America is increasing fast the price of labour is enormous, in fact to show this clearly we quote a Chicago authority, who some days ago said that bricklayers were earning 14s. per day, carpenters 12s. per day, and labourers 8s. per day, while a man and team could readily command 24s. per day. It is clear to all impartial parties that those figures cannot stand, and consequently much of the work performed at those prices will not, in a year or two, be remunerative; or to simplify the case, a house built with wages at the above rate over and above the prices of all the other articles, such as brick, lumber, and lime, comparatively as dear, will not be let or sold at a figure to pay interest on the money. It is upon this basis that we argue that wheat cannot be produced at anything like the rates we have had a year or two ago. In this country, notwithstanding the great influx of foreign labour and foreign capital, everything within the last 12 months has increased 15 to 25 per cent., labour has done so, all raw material feels the increase. Wheat has bounded up with a great stride, while beef has closely followed.

To close this subject we may infer that while such an emigration as we are having to this American Continent is a great and glorious blessing, a rich heritage both for those who come and are coming, it is not without its evils, and we notice that following upon the vast flow of emigration to this country in 1872 and 1873 there came a period of terrible depression which is liable to repetition. The truth is that this great flood of prosperity has come upon the States faster than it could receive it, and the price of everything has gone up too rapidly, and we are approaching a time when even upon the comparatively cheap lands of the prairie the cost of production is getting too high.

APPENDIX II.

THE NEW NORTH-WEST.

Two hundred years ago, before the age of railways or telegraphs, and when the present territory of the United States was in an almost undiscovered state, the land which now bears the above title and forms by far the largest portion of the dominion of Canada attracted the attention of some British merchants and others.

It would be useless here to trace the history of the various companies and like undertakings up to the year 1870.

Suffice it to say that just two centuries after the first charter had been granted, the territory, so vast in extent that few people can grasp the idea of its dimensions, was fairly opened up to settlement.

The Hudson's Bay Co., by far the largest and most influential, and with which all other companies merged, did not advance the interest of agriculture.

Their policy was against it, as settlement was likely to spoil their peculiar trade. Here then in 1870 lay a vast ocean of land, full of lakes and rivers, abounding in coal, and whose mountains were full of minerals, all was lying dormant as if it had been a glacier solitude so far as the world of agriculture was concerned. Ten years have passed since it threw open its doors, and as yet the plough of the husbandman has scarcely crossed the threshold.

True it is that for years past a solitary colony with a few stray settlers have guided their oxen and teams behind the all-powerful ploughshare, but up to this time we may call it a virgin country, and strange though it may seem no such land on the American Continents can either produce quantity or quality of the wheat which is raised on the black loamy land, the products of the annual fires which for ages have swept across the country, leaving behind them an aggregation of wealth which within the next 50 years is to produce the largest portion of the wheat that is used both here and in Europe. What would have been the results on the wheat product of the world if this country had been opened up half a century ago it is not in our province to speculate upon. We have to face the fact that to-day another country as great as the western states of America is bing opened up fairly for settlement.

Till this spring a real vigorous and sound emigation did not take place. The half-hearted and weak railway policy of two successive Governments did not encourage or give confidence to the class of people who make a country prosperous. But when business men, men who had been tried in the balance and not found wanting, took hold of the contract to connect ocean with ocean across Canadian territory, and when settlers saw some distinct and sure hope of a railway to fetch supplies and take back wheat and stock, then came the rush to those vast unbroken prairies. It is said, and not without truth, that the Syndicate who control this contract, notwithstanding all rumours to the contrary, have done more for the country in five months than the Government did in five years. The rush of emigration, and the constant clinking of hammer and trowel in the cities, testify to the truth of this statement.

To our mind this railway is going to have more influence upon the agriculture of the world than any other single line that we have ever seen. On the American side, in the Western States, the railways were pushed just ahead as it were of civilisation. They went forward in the van, and in fact stray settlements had very frequently been the precursor of the road, but here you have a railway pushed through a region by far the most fertile of this continent with not a soul but an Indian or a trapper in its van. No wonder that the price paid for the accomplishment of such an undertaking was thought to be extravagant, but it took courage and determination, and above all strong faith in the future of the country's destinies to undertake the work at any price.

As the months roll on feeders will be run from the main line to the best districts, and the whole of the country, or as much of it as will be cultivated, can pour in its vast wealth to the grannaries of the world.

Granting then that the settlement of this great region has fairly begun, let us look at the effect it is to have upon the future agriculture of the world. It would of course take a prophet to scan the mist that covers mortal eyes in order to tell the exact effects that are likely to arise from the development of this country. We shall not attempt such a course, but we shall endeavour to point out a few of the inevitable results which shall follow the rise of agriculture in this country. But before doing so let us look back upon the agriculture of the American continent as it has progressed for the last hundred years. Then the great West, as it is now termed, was a great unknown wilderness. The producing portion of this continent lay in the eastern provinces.

Backwoodsmen had to fell the forest and carve out a home for themselves amongst stumps and brush.

Wheat was produced with great labour and expense, for though the soil was rich the price of clearing it was very great. In a new country, money is generally scarce and hard to get among the agricultural classes, and so the new settlers in every country were forced to grow wheat year after year, till the soil, weary of one crop, began to show signs of giving out. Take for instance the Genesee valley, the richest of the many wheat producing regions of the State of New York. For years it poured forth vast quantities of wheat, and so in certain portions of Ontario, but after constant cropping for years we find that about 20 years ago the cultivation of the wheat plant became in these portions of the American Continent very unprofitable, not only from the decrease in quantity, but the plant was subject to so many enemies and scourges that its cultivation, apart from the yield, became a very precarious operation.

If the American people had had to depend upon those Eastern States, they would have been in a bad way for bread, but gradually as those lands stopped producing, and as population increased they discovered westward that grain of all kinds was much more easily cultivated, and the pioneers pushed past the old settlements till by-and-bye they reached the prairie where man can plough without using his hatchet, and where the increase is greater than in the old woodland states.

For a 100 years this gradual movement westward has taken place. Twenty years ago the current turned towards the north-west, and the flow of emigration to this new north-west is but a continuation of the movement which is settling up Minnesota and Dakota. But just as surely as the march of emigration flowed towards the west, so did the wheat growing fields begin to show signs of decay as the years rolled. Thus it is that we find the great wheat producing regions gradually come westward, and now many of the fairest countries whose granaries once overflowed with grain, produce but small and infinitesimal quantities. The force of circumstances, as well as the promise of more prolific and profitable crops, has forced the wheat growers of this country to such a course.

For some years back the upper valley of the Red River has given promise of being the greatest wheat producing region of this continent, but in a few years it will be destined to eclipse by those regions drained by the Assiniboine, the Saskatchewan and Peace Rivers. But on this theory, in less than half a century, the great wheat producing regions will have given out, but a remedy is already in view.

Men who have watched the course of events discern a better system of agriculture rising up and giving place to the old crude ways which grew wheat after wheat. Take as an instance the very valley of the Genessee where the farmers have improved their ways, built barns, sowed manure, introduced rotation of cropping, and we find that the average of their wheat product per acre has been steadily gaining for 10 years past, and indicating that we may look forward to a large surplus of wheat from this region at no distant day. It is not too early to anticipate this state of affairs. Men who live and farm in one or two regions all their lives do not see the change. It comes almost imperceptibly, and they scarcely realise it; but those who are travelling from day to day see this system of evolution gradually but surely covering its cycle of time.

In a climate such as England, without artificial manure, the land would take long years to recuperate, if it was run down to the same extent as those wheat lands were. But on the American continent, where the climate is more generous, where a sub-arctic winter is followed by a semi-tropical summer which pulverizes and returns the best qualities to the soil, the system of recuperation goes on much faster than in Great Britain. Thus we expect to see at no late day the worn-out wheat lands once more pour forth their increase, and when the time comes the New England and New York States with the province of Ontario, and many other portions of the continent will again help to fill the ways of commerce with an abundance of grain. In the north-west States the land is holding out longer and standing more severe cropping on account of the climate, and it is likely the Canadian north-west with its rich and fertile lands, lying in a comparatively temperate zone will not so easily be worn out. But it will come, for no soil is inexhaustible.

It is probable that in 1880 the wheat product of America reached its maximum point in the ratio to its population. It may go higher if the crop is a very good one, but such a result is not likely.

The vast tract of lands which year by year are going into cultivation would apparently double up the product of wheat, but happily for the British farmer the decrease in the average yield of some States is so great that it almost meets this vast increase in another direction. Thus the State of Minnesota is only expected to yield this season about an average of 11 bushels per acre. This is an unprecedented small average, and at that rate some other system of farming must be instituted to make it pay.

In the Canadian north-west the average crop is much higher. The exact amount we cannot say, but it will probably average 17 or 18 bushels per acre with only the choicest selection of land under crop. More than likely it will maintain such an average when it is fairly tried. Of course we meet with many cases where 25, 30, or 35 bushels per acre are obtained, but we have got to deal with the general estimate, and not the individual returns.

Scarcely any grain finds its way out of the country up to the present moment. It is all needed in home consumption. But in talking of agriculture in America and its bearing on British husbandry we have got to bear in mind and look to the future of this vast country. Any estimate of the acres in it which can produce wheat, and that of the best quality, has never yet been thought of. A transient glance at an ordinary map will show a vast country lying north of the line which divides British territory and the States as far north as the Peace River, and guarded on either side by the

Nelson River and the Rocky Mountains. In this country there is scarce a piece of waste land. All is ready for the railway, that great pioneer of settlement.

The wave of emigration is flowing towards the north-west. It will advance across the winding Assiniboine, stay for some years on the banks of the Saskatchewan, and then strike out for the unknown regions drained by the Athabasca and Peace Rivers. In those regions there will grow up a hardy race of people, inured by climate to stand intense cold, but whose vigorous system will have in it a vast amount of work and energy.

Towards it, for a century to come, the eyes of hungry multitudes will be turned, and though it be far from the great centres of civilization, human skill helped by the grand natural highways of water will send the vast volume of wheat to the markets of the world. There, perchance, grain may be produced at less cost per bushel than in any other region of the world, because your Commissioner believes the country to contain the richest soil and more of it than any other in the world.

But the transit will always act upon the profit of the husbandman. Just now America looks to Great Britain as the market for her surplus grain, and notwithstanding the croakers who prophecy the decline of British skill and manufactures, still all statistics and facts show that no other country has passed the rubicon of depression so easily as Great Britain, and already the tide of prosperity is flowing upwards. This great region, then, will need to look to England as the purchaser of its surplus grain. But we must consider that the interest of the home farm will always be protected by the great distance this product has to travel before it reaches Great Britain. Except an outlet is found by the Hudson's Bay, nearly 6,000 miles will lie betwixt producer and consumer, a vast distance by rail, lake, and sea.

In such a region, far away from supplies, it is not likely that an acre of wheat can be produced much below twelve dollars per acre. If it takes 10 dollars to cultivate an acre as a general average over the States, in this remote region it will be considerably more. Even if the average were 20 bushels per acre, the cost per bushel of production would be 60 cents per bushel, which means 20s. per quarter on the spot. Then in most cases it will take a considerable sum to haul it to market, after which comes in the middleman's profit at the home market; next the charge to Liverpool, which will be fully equal to the original price, after which will come landing charge, &c., raising it from the original price to something like the following:

	£	s.	d.
Cost of 1 quarter wheat	1	0	0
Hauling to market	0	0	6
Profit of buyer	0	0	3
Cost of transit	1	0	0
Charges in Liverpool	0	2	0
	2	2	9

But we must allow that it is not likely that an average of 20 bushels will be reaped, probably two or three bushels less. The average of the American continent is only about 12, and if we allow this rich region six bushels more, the limit will be reached.

Then transit will be exceedingly cheap. If a quarter of wheat can be taken from a point, say, on an average 500 miles west of Winnipeg, at 20s. per quarter, when for some years past the average cost from Chicago has been about 14s. per quarter, and the rates from Dakota at present are about 10s. per quarter, calculating at present rates, and suppose the facilities for transport were all in running order at present, it is not likely that a quarter of wheat could be placed in England at much less than 50s. from such a remote place.

But suppose we place it at 46s., no one is going to make a great deal of profit, while the British farmer will be tolerably safe at this rate, that is to say, if rents are kept in proper order, while also the consumer will have no reason to complain. We have taken up this subject to try to disabuse the minds of parties at home who suppose, or at least preach the doctrine, that British agriculture will be swamped with cheap wheat. Even in this great north-west it takes time, capital, and skill to produce the raw material, and it must be borne in mind that railways and steamboats must have also handsome profits, while the all-powerful middleman has to get his commission.

LONDON:
Printed by George E. B. Eyre and William Spottiswoode,
Printers to the Queen's most Excellent Majesty.
For Her Majesty's Stationery Office.

CATTLE DISEASE (UNITED STATES OF AMERICA).

FURTHER CORRESPONDENCE

AND

REPORTS

RELATING TO

DISEASES OF ANIMALS

IN THE

UNITED STATES OF AMERICA.

Presented to both Houses of Parliament by Command of Her Majesty.

LONDON:
PRINTED BY GEORGE EDWARD EYRE AND WILLIAM SPOTTISWOODE
PRINTERS TO THE QUEEN'S MOST EXCELLENT MAJESTY.
FOR HER MAJESTY'S STATIONERY OFFICE.
1882.

[C.—3200.]   *Price* 1s. 4d.

CONTENTS.

		PAGE
CORRESPONDENCE	- - - - - - -	3
REPORTS	- - - - - - -	45

CORRESPONDENCE.

No. 1.
LETTER from the CLERK OF THE COUNCIL to the FOREIGN OFFICE.

Veterinary Department, Privy Council Office,
44, Parliament Street, Westminster, S.W.,
January 11, 1881.

SIR,

I AM directed by the Lords of the Council to request that you will have the goodness to move Earl Granville to give instructions that the Government of the United States of America may be informed by telegraph that the S.S. "France" with ten Alderney cows on board left England for New York on the 7th instant; that the "France" brought cattle affected with foot-and-mouth disease a few days ago to England; and that this vessel had not been cleansed and disinfected before her return voyage.

I am, &c.

The Under Secretary of State,   (Signed)   C. L. PEEL.
&c. &c. &c.
Foreign Office.

No. 2.
LETTER from SIR E. THORNTON to EARL GRANVILLE.

Sanitary, No. 4.

MY LORD,   Washington, January 24, 1881.

ON the receipt of your Lordship's telegram of the 12th instant, directing me to inform the United States Government of the fact that the steamer "France" which had left England with ten Alderney cows on board, was infected with foot-and-mouth disease, I addressed to Mr. Evarts a note to that effect, copy of which I have the honour to enclose.

In his answer, copy of which is also enclosed, he offers his thanks for your Lordship's courteous action in regard to this matter.

I have, &c.

The Right Hon. the Earl Granville, K.G.   (Signed)   EDWARD THORNTON.
&c. &c. &c.

Enclosure 1 in No. 2.

SIR,   Washington, January 13, 1881.

IN compliance with an instruction which I have received by telegraph from Earl Granville, I have the honour to inform you that the S.S. "France" left England for New York on the 7th instant with ten Alderney cows; that the foot-and-mouth disease was already on board of that vessel; and that she had not been cleansed nor disinfected.

I have, &c.

The Hon. Wm. M. Evarts,   (Signed)   EDWD. THORNTON.
&c. &c. &c.

Enclosure 2 in No. 2.

SIR,   Department of State, Washington, January 14, 1881.

I HAVE the honour to acknowledge the receipt of your note of the 13th instant, advising me that on the 7th of this month the S.S. "France" left England for New York, having on board the foot-and-mouth disease, and to inform you in reply that I at once communicated the contents of your note to my colleague, the Secretary of the Treasury.

With thanks for the courteous action of Earl Granville in regard to this matter, which I beg to say is fully appreciated by this Government,

I have, &c.

The Right Hon. Sir Edwd. Thornton, K.C.B.,   (Signed)   W. M. EVARTS.
&c. &c. &c.

R 679.   Wt. 19205.

CORRESPONDENCE.

No. 3.

EXTRACT from LETTER from SIR E. THORNTON to EARL GRANVILLE.

Sanitary, No. 5.

Washington, January 24, 1881.

MY LORD,

In my Despatch, No. 30 of this series, and of the 27th ultimo, I had the honour to transmit copies of a Bill which was submitted to the Senate on the 14th of that month by Mr. Williams, a senator from Kentucky, for the suppression of contagious diseases among cattle.

On the 19th instant Mr. Williams found an opportunity of calling the serious attention of that body to the object of the Bill. He showed what great losses were suffered by stock owners from the ravages of cattle-plague, and how much more valuable the trade with Europe, and particularly with Great Britain would become if vigorous measures were taken to prevent the spread of the disease, and finally to exterminate it. Mr. Williams proposed that the Bill should be referred to the Select Committee on Epidemic Diseases, but Mr. Johnston, a Senator from Virginia, who is much interested in the subject, and with whom I have had some conversation upon it, moved that a Committee of five Senators should be appointed by the President, to which should be referred all Bills relating to pleuro-pneumonia and other infectious and contagious diseases among cattle and other domestic animals, and which should be allowed to report by Bill or otherwise.

This resolution was agreed to, and I hope that in due time a Bill may be drawn up by the Special Committee, though I fear that considering the short time which this Congress has still to sit, and the great amount of necessary business which it has to get through, there is but little chance of any Bill of the nature of that proposed by Mr. Williams being discussed and passed during the present session.

I have, &c.

The Right Hon. the Earl Granville, K.G., &c. &c. &c.

(Signed) EDWARD THORNTON.

No. 4.

LETTER from the BRITISH CONSUL-GENERAL at New York.

Sanitary, No. 1.

British Consulate General, New York, January 29, 1881.

MY LORD,

I HAVE the honour to acquaint your Lordship that since my last despatch (Sanitary, No. 18) of the 29th ultimo, pleuro-pneumonia has made its appearance on two more farms in Queen's County, Long Island, and another case of this lung disease has been also reported at Yonkers, a town about 17 miles from this city. Both localities have been officially inspected and the usual precautions taken to prevent the spread of the disease.

I have the honour also to report that some cattle, comprising four bulls and eight heifers, consigned to this country from London for breeding purposes, by the S.S. "France," of the National Line, which arrived here on the 20th instant, were, some days after they had been landed, found to be affected with the foot-and-mouth disease. The animals were at once quarantined and will be kept so until all danger of infection shall be over.

I transmit, herewith enclosed, an extract from the "New York Herald" of the 25th instant in reference to this matter, from which it would seem that there is a suspicion that the disease may have been contracted on board the steamer, some of the cattle which she had carried on her last voyage from this port having died on the passage.

The steamer will be thoroughly fumigated before she again leaves New York.

The Governor of this State has sent in the following message to the Assembly, urging suitable provision for arresting the progress of pleuro-pneumonia in the State:—

"To the Legislature.

"At the annual meeting of the State Agricultural Society, resolutions relating to the disease of cattle, known as pleuro-pneumonia, were adopted, a copy of which, togethe with a letter from the Secretary of the Society, is herewith transmitted.

CORRESPONDENCE.

"The prevalence of this contagious and fatal disorder seriously menaces agricultural and dependent interests in this State, and in the country at large, and disastrous consequences may be expected unless timely and vigorous steps be taken to prevent its spread into the grazing districts.

"A subject of such great importance demands, and will no doubt receive your prompt attention and co-operation. The hope is expressed that Congress will ultimately establish appropriate measures for the suppression of this disease among animals, but meanwhile suitable provisions should be made by the State to arrest its progress.

"ALONZO B. CORNELL."

The message has been referred to the Committee of Ways and Means to report.

The Assembly subsequently passed a resolution which had been introduced by Mr. Skinner, one of its members, calling upon Congress to take some steps in the direction of staying contagious cattle diseases.

Mr. Skinner, in support of his resolution, remarked " that the State of New York had " done all in its power to stamp out pleuro-pneumonia among cattle, but that the State " acting alone in this matter is not sufficient. Cattle from neighbouring States had " access to the herds within the borders of the State of New York," and that it was consequently necessary that some federal action should be taken in the premises.

The whole subject is now under the consideration of Congress.

I have, &c.
(Signed)   E. M. ARCHIBALD.

Her Majesty's Principal Secretary of State
for Foreign Affairs, London.

Enclosure in No. 4.

Extract from the "New York Herald," January 25, 1881.

EPIZOOTIC-APHTHA.

Appearance of the English Cattle Plague among Mr. Easton's Jersey Stock on the Steamship "France."

Since the introduction of pleuro-pneumonia among the cattle of the United States by the importation to Brooklyn in 1843 of a single diseased cow from England no discovery more startling to cattle owners has been made than that of the existence of epizootic-aphtha on board the steamer "France." This discovery has been made within two days past by Veterinary Surgeon Hopkins, who was called on to inspect the Jersey cattle brought over last week on that steamer. It will be remembered that the cattle are a part of a valuable consignment of blooded stock to Mr. W. Easton, a full description of which was published in the "Herald" last week. The entire consignment, with the exception of three horses which died on the voyage of non-infectious diseases, arrived in port, it was supposed, in good condition. It was only after some days had elapsed that the disease named was detected in the cattle, but after it had been once discovered other veterinaries confirmed the diagnosis, and it is no longer doubted that one of the great English cattle plagues is present on these shores.

The Disease described.

The cattle, comprising four bulls and eight heifers, are of the pure Jersey stock, bred by Mr. Tattersall at Old Oak Farm, Shepherd's Bush. They are beautiful specimens of the stock, and the herd is valued at about $6,000. They were intended for breeding in this country, and were selected especially with reference to their fine points. A reporter visited them yesterday in company with Dr. Hopkins, and was greatly impressed with their beauty, even in their condition. They were still standing in the stalls in which they had made the voyage, and were carefully blanketed, but seemed alert and almost unconscious of their disease, which is still in an incipient stage.

"What is epizootic-aphtha?" asked the reporter.

"It is one of the great cattle plagues of Europe," replied Dr. Hopkins, "of which there have " hitherto been no cases in this country. It is commonly called the foot-and-mouth disease, affecting, " as it does, the hoof as well as the mouth. It is a blood disease, but what the specific poison is that " affects the blood no man has yet been able to tell, any more than the specific poisons in various " human diseases are known. It is contagious, never arising spontaneously, so far as is known, but " being acquired by mediate or immediate contagion. If you put other cattle with these they would " all be affected, or if you removed these and placed others in the same quarters without a thorough " disinfection, the new comers might, and probably would, catch the infection."

"How were these cattle infected?"

"I do not know. The shippers declare that they were in first-rate condition when they were put on " board, and the people connected with the ship say they have never had the disease aboard. They " do not make any very strenuous declarations, though," he added with a half smile, "for they lost " 15 head of cattle on this same ship on her last voyage."

"How did they lose them?"

"They don't know, for there was no veterinary surgeon on board. All they know is that the cattle died. I should think that the value of 15 head of cattle would pay the expense of a veterinary. But we do not know where these cattle caught their disease; all we know is that they have it and that these quarters are now infected. It is a very fortunate thing that the disease was discovered before the cattle got out among others in this country, for the spread would probably have been as great as that of pleuro-pneumonia has been, and that has spread so in less that 40 years that it will cost the Government $50,000,000 to stamp out the diseases if they try it as is now proposed."

"Is this disease as dangerous as pleuro-pneumonia?"

"In one sense it is not. The danger of infection is not as great, because the disease breaks out sooner after infection. The period in pleuro-pneumonia is sometimes as long as 90 days, which is long enough for a beast to travel to San Francisco and back twice over. In epizootic-aphtha it is from two to six days usually, although it has been known to be as long as three weeks. Of course, during the period of incubation the disease cannot be detected. It is, however, a dangerous disease when developed."

Precautions against the Contagion.

"Will these cattle die?"

"I cannot tell yet. It will depend perhaps on whether the disease assumes a benign or a malignant type. I shall remove them at once to a horse stable in New York, where they will be under medical treatment at any rate until the danger of infection is thoroughly done away. The ship also is to be thoroughly fumigated and will take no cattle on board till I sign, as General Patrick's assistant, a certificate that she is entirely free from danger."

When the reporter left the floors of the stalls and all the slighter woodwork of the cattle deck were being torn away, preparatory to washing, fumigating, and whitewashing the entire deck.

No. 5.

Extract from Letter from the BRITISH CONSUL at Philadelphia to EARL GRANVILLE.

Sanitary, No 1.

British Consulate, Philadelphia,
February 4, 1881.

My Lord,

I have the honour to report to your Lordship that there have been no fresh cases of pleuro-pneumonia among cattle in the State of Pennsylvania, and the farms where there were a few cases, according to Mr. Crump's last report, have been relieved of a strict quarantine.

The quarantine under the laws of the State is enforced for three months, the Government inspector visiting the infected district about once a fortnight, keeping a strict record of the number and description of the cattle. Should any be found missing since the last visit, the proprietor is subjected to a rigid examination, and if he should be found guilty of violating the rules of the quarantine he is subject to a penalty. In executing the laws regulating the quarantine, the inspector must necessarily depend largely on the integrity of the farmer or cattle raiser in his reports of the condition of his stock and the disposition of any number found missing.

I have not been able to definitely settle the question of the existence of pleuro-pneumonia in the Western States of this Consular district. Inasmuch, however, as large numbers of young cattle are sent West from the Eastern States for breeding purposes to fill up the gap made by the exportation to England, it is but a question of time, perhaps, for the disease to reach the vast cattle-raising districts west of the Allegheny mountains.

Mr. Vice-Consul Warrack has forwarded to me a copy special despatch from Bedford, State of Iowa, addressed to the "Chicago Tribune," and published in that journal on the 30th ultimo, copy of which I herewith enclose, wherein it is stated that several cases of pleuro-pneumonia have recently occurred in Taylor County.

I have, &c.
(Signed) ROBT. CHAS. CLIPPERTON,
Her Majesty's Consul.

The Right Hon. the Earl Granville, K.G.,
&c.   &c.   &c.

CORRESPONDENCE.

Enclosure in No. 5.

COPY SPECIAL DESPATCH to "CHICAGO TRIBUNE," dated Bedford, Iowa, 29th January, and published on 30th January 1881.

PLEURO-PNEUMONIA.

THERE are several cases of contagious pleuro-pneumonia in this (Taylor) county. As yet the fact is known only to a few, but notwithstanding over 60 deaths have occurred. It was introduced by Eastern calves; 20,000 of the latter are scattered through the State of Iowa. In Taylor County five car loads of these Eastern calves were brought in on 4th September by Edward Moss, of Birmingham, Iowa, and taken to Bedford, where all were sold to one man, Mr. S., who lives 10 miles east of this place. Mr. S. so far has lost 65 head; and not only most of the rest, but also a great many of his other native cattle are coughing and show symptoms more or less plain. On September 27th Mr. Moss brought in some more Eastern calves, and sold them to other parties. He represented those calves to be from Michigan, but this is doubted. They very likely are from New York or other parts in the East. The existence of contagious pleuro-pneumonia in this part of Iowa is established beyond a doubt, and it probably has spread much further than yet known, because, as said before, 20,000 Eastern calves have been distributed all over the State. A great many have also gone to Illinois, and no doubt exists that the disease has invaded that State. A true copy.

(Signed) JAMES WARRACK,
British Vice-Consul, Chicago.

No. 6.

LETTER from the CLERK OF THE COUNCIL to the FOREIGN OFFICE.

Veterinary Department, Privy Council Office,
44, Parliament Street, Westminster, S.W.,
February 9, 1881.

SIR,

I AM directed by the Lords of the Council to request that you will have the goodness to move Earl Granville to give instructions that the attention of the Governments of Germany, France, the Netherlands, and the United States of America may be drawn to the great injury which English stockowners have recently sustained from the introduction of foot-and-mouth disease into this country through the agency of diseased animals which have been imported from the countries above named.

I am to append a list showing the number of vessels (and the ports of the respective countries from whence they have come between the 20th September last and the 6th instant) which have brought disease to this country. It will be seen that two infected cargoes have arrived from Germany, five from France, three from the Netherlands, and five from the United States of America within the periods above mentioned.

I am to add that until very shortly after the 20th September last the whole of the United Kingdom of Great Britain and Ireland had been for some time, so far as the Veterinary Department of the Privy Council were able to ascertain, free from foot-and-mouth disease; that Ireland and Scotland are still unaffected, and that the strongest evidence exists that this disease was introduced from Deptford and abroad.

The Lords of the Council are of opinion that the adoption of strict measures of sanitary police, and a more effective system of inspection at the ports of embarkation, would have the effect of preventing the exportation of diseased animals, and of those which had been herded with them.

Their Lordships are aware that a mere cursory inspection which results only in the withdrawal of the actually diseased animals from a cargo is no protection; but they are satisfied that if it were clearly understood that no cargo would be allowed to leave the foreign port if any disease were found amongst it, the effect would be to induce greater care on the part of shippers, and to deter owners from sending for exportation any animals that had been exposed to contagion.

I am directed also to request that reference may be made to the pressure which is now being brought to bear on the Privy Council to act under the powers conferred on them by The Contagious Diseases (Animals) Act, 1878, for the purpose of prohibiting the importation of animals from countries where foot-and-mouth disease exists, and to the difficulty which the Privy Council will have in resisting such pressure, unless foreign Governments will take effectual measures to exterminate the disease within their countries, and, as far as possible, to check the exportation of either diseased animals, or of those which have been in contact with them.

I have, &c.
(Signed) C. L. PEEL.

The Under Secretary of State,
&c. &c. &c.
Foreign Office.

CORRESPONDENCE.

Enclosure in No. 6.

CASES of FOOT-AND-MOUTH DISEASE detected in FOREIGN ANIMALS landed in GREAT BRITAIN from September 20, 1880, to February 6, 1881.

Date when landed.	Name of Vessels.	Brought from	Landed at	Number Diseased.		
				Cattle.	Sheep.	Swine.
1880.						
September 20	Swallow	Havre	London	30	—	—
November 8	Hamburg	,,	,,	2	—	—
December 17	Osprey	Hamburg	,,	—	—	15
,, 30	Bohemian	Boston	Liverpool	18	—	—
1881.						
January 1	France	New York	London	59	—	—
,, 6	City of Liverpool	,,	,,	267	—	—
,, 18	City of London	,,	,,	12	—	—
,, 28	Concordia	Boulogne	,,	21	—	—
,, 28	Rochester	Boston	,,	42	—	—
,, 29	Cologne	Boulogne	,,	7	—	—
,, 30	Rhine	,,	,,	16	—	—
February 2	Fyenoord	Rotterdam	,,	7	—	—
,, 4	Tiger	Hamburg	Hull	—	10	—
,, 6	Alford	Rotterdam	London	5	—	—
,, 6	Wansbeck	Amsterdam	,,	3	—	—
,, 6	Moselle	Boulogne	,,	71	—	—
			Total	560	10	15

No. 7.

LETTER from DR. CHARLES P. LYMAN to PROFESSOR BROWN.

Department of Agriculture, Washington, D.C.,
February 9, 1881.

SIR,

I AM happy to be able to inform you that the outbreak amongst cattle at Bedford, Iowa, recently reported through the newspaper to have been one of contagious pleuro-pneumonia is not that disease.

This I have from the report by telegraph of Drs. McLean, of Brooklyn, and Detmers, of Chicago, who were recently sent to the localities for the purpose of examining the herd in question.

The detailed report of this examination has not yet reached me.

Yours, &c.

Professor G. T. Brown,
Veterinary, Privy Council,
London, England.

(Signed) CHARLES P. LYMAN,
V.S. to U.S. Department of Agriculture.

No. 8.

EXTRACT from LETTER from the BRITISH CONSUL at Philadelphia to EARL GRANVILLE.

Sanitary, No. 2.

British Consulate, Philadelphia,
February 10, 1881.

MY LORD,

DR. GADSDEN, who has been of great service in furnishing information to this Consulate as well as to the Agricultural Department of the United States upon this subject, has instituted a series of questions addressed to the principal veterinary surgeons in the State of Iowa, requesting replies as to the existence of pleuro-pneumonia in the Western States. Two answers were received this morning, copies of which I herewith enclose your Lordship. They both state that the disease does not exist in their respective localities. On receipt of further letters upon this subject from the West, Dr. Gadsden will place them at my disposal.

I have, &c.

(Signed) ROBT. CHAS. CLIPPERTON,
Her Majesty's Consul.

The Right Hon. the Earl Granville, K.G.,
&c. &c. &c.

CORRESPONDENCE.

Enclosure 1 in No. 8.

Dear Sir,   Tipton, Iowa.

Yours of the 26th to hand. In reply I beg to state that the community here is entirely free from that contagious disease. It has been reported several times that there are cases, but a careful examination proved the contrary, or at least I have not met with any. Some people imagine when one or two animals in a herd become ill that it is pleuro-pneumonia contagion. My opinion is, that when it does break out it will create considerable havoc, but this Western country is entirely too healthy for such diseases. It requires cities, where stables are crowded, to have it originate spontaneously.

Yours, &c.

To Dr. Gadsden, Philadelphia.   (Signed)   U. S. S. Springer, V.S.

Enclosure 2 in No. 8.

(Extract.)   Detroit, January 22, 1881.

I have heard nothing of pleuro-pneumonia in the West, but considering your statement that several thousand store calves and yearlings were sent from New York and New Jersey, it seems very probable that pleuro-pneumonia would be carried wherever those cattle were taken. I have heard nothing of it in this State, nor have I seen any reference to any unusual disease among cattle of the other Western States. Having no positive evidence of the existence of pleuro-pneumonia in the Western States, I incline to regard its existence as at least doubtful.

I will make all the inquiry that I can as to the prevalence or non-prevalence of pleuro-pneumonia in the West, and if I ascertain anything confirmatory of its existence I will at once let you know, as I am very much interested in the matter.

Yours, &c.

To Dr. Gadsden, Philadelphia.   (Signed)   A. J. Murray.

No. 9.

Extract from Letter from Sir E. THORNTON to EARL GRANVILLE.

Sanitary, No. 7.

My Lord,   Washington, February 21, 1881.

I enclose copies of a Bill [S. 2097] which was submitted to the Senate on the 25th ultimo, by Mr. Johnston, a Senator from Virginia, as Chairman of the Select Committee on Diseases of Animals, for the suppression and prevention of such diseases.

The first section proposes the establishment of a "Bureau of Animal Industry," which, with the assistance of a veterinary surgeon, shall report upon the causes of contagious diseases among cattle, and the means for their prevention and cure.

Section 2 provides that special investigation shall be made as to the existence of pleuro-pneumonia or other contagious cattle disease along the usual lines of transportation of live stock for export.

Section 3 directs that the Commissioner of Agriculture and the Commissioners provided for by this Act shall co-operate with the State and municipal authorities and corporations engaged in the transportation of live stock, for their safe transportation to the sea board, and in the suppression of disease amongst them.

Section 4 proposes the establishment of quarantine stations for cattle on being imported.

Section 5 makes it illegal to import into the United States or any State thereof any animal affected with contagious disease, or which "has been exposed presumably thereto," except in accordance with the provisions of the Act.

Section 6 instructs the Commissioner of Agriculture, with the Chief of the Bureau and the National Board of Health, to prepare the necessary rules and regulations for the suppression and extirpation of the diseases in question.

Section 7 provides for the purchase and slaughter of infected or suspected animals.

Section 8 directs the Commissioner of Agriculture to report to the President whenever he finds any place dangerously infected, and that upon the publication of such report the removal of animals susceptible of said diseases from that place into another State shall be illegal, except in accordance with the regulations.

Section 9 assigns $200,000 for carrying out the Act.

Sections 10 and 11 impose penalties for violations of the Act, and instructs the United States district attorneys to prosecute them.

A somewhat similar Bill was submitted to the House of Representatives on the 14th instant; but it has less detail, is less complete, and would, in my opinion, be less effective than the Bill now before the Senate.

The latter Bill has been discussed in the Senate on three or four different occasions, but although several amendments have been proposed and adopted, it does not seem in general to have found favour in the minds of Senators, and I understand that the Select Committee has consequently determined to withdraw it, and to recommend as a substitute for it a Bill, of which copies are enclosed [S. 1893], and which was submitted to the Senate on the 13th of December last by Mr. Rollins, a Senator from New Hampshire. This provides for the appointment of a Commission of three to be appointed by the President and confirmed by the Senate. They are to have power to investigate all cases of disease among cattle, and to prescribe rules and regulations to be approved by the Secretary of the Treasury. The State authorities are to co-operate with the Commission, and power is given to establish quarantine and to slaughter diseased cattle. The Commission is also to inspect the lines of transportation between this country and Canada with reference to the export of diseased cattle.

I much doubt, however, whether there will now be time to pass any Bill upon the subject through both Houses during the short remainder of the session.

I have, &c.
(Signed)   EDWARD THORNTON.

The Right Hon. the Earl Granville, K.G.,
&c.   &c.   &c.

Enclosure 1 in No. 9.

46th Congress, 3rd Session. S. 2097.

In the SENATE of the United States, January 25, 1881, Mr. Johnston, from the Select Committee on the subject of pleuro-pneumonia and other contagious and infectious diseases of cattle and other domestic animals, reported the following Bill, which was read the first and second times by unanimous consent and re-committed.

January 28, 1881, reported by Mr. Johnston with amendments, viz.: omit the parts struck through and insert the parts printed in *italics*.

A Bill for the establishment of a Bureau of Animal Industry, and for the suppression and prevention of contagious diseases among domestic animals.

Be it enacted by the Senate and House of Representatives of the United States of America in Congress assembled, that the Commissioner of Agriculture shall organize in his department a Bureau of Animal Industry, and shall appoint a chief who shall be a competent veterinary surgeon approved by the National Board of Health, and whose duty it shall be to investigate and report upon the *number*, value, and condition of the domestic animals of the United States, their protection and use, and also inquire into and report the causes of contagious *and communicable* diseases among them, and provide *the means* for the prevention and cure of the same, and to collect such information on these subjects as shall be valuable to the agricultural and commercial interests of the country. The Commissioner of Agriculture is hereby authorised to call to his aid in investigating contagious *said* diseases in animals, and in providing means for the prevention and cure of said diseases *thereof*, the National Board of Health, whose duty it shall be to render such aid and to employ such means as they deem necessary to obtain all information in regard to said diseases, their prevention and control; he is also authorised to employ two commissioners, one of whom shall be a practical stock-raiser, and one an experienced business man, familiar with questions pertaining to commercial transactions in live stock, whose duty it shall be to advise with regard to the best methods of treating, transporting, and caring for animals, and of providing against the spread of contagious *said* diseases; he is also authorised to employ an agent in each State and Territory, whose duty it shall be to collect all facts and statistics belonging to the animal industry, and to the diseases of animals in such State or Territory, and report to the Commissioner of Agriculture. The compensation of said commissioners, agents, and of the members of the National Board of Health while employed in this service shall be at the rate of *not more than ten* dollars per diem, with all necessary travelling expenses while engaged in the performance of their duty under this Act. The salary of the chief of bureau shall be three thousand dollars per annum; and the Commissioner of Agriculture shall appoint a clerk for said bureau with a salary of two thousand dollars per annum.

SEC. 2. That in order to promote the exportation of cattle *live stock* from the United States the Commissioner of Agriculture, through said chief of bureau, shall make special investigation as to the existence of pleuro-pneumonia, or any contagious *or communicable* disease, along the dividing line between the United States and the Dominion of Canada, and along the lines of transportation from all parts of the United States to ports from which cattle *live stock* are exported, and make report of the results of such investigation to the Secretary of the Treasury, who shall establish such regulations concerning the exportation and transportation of cattle *live stock* as the results of said investigation may require.

SEC. 3. That the Commissioner of Agriculture, through said chief of bureau, acting with the National Board of Health and the commissioners provided for in section one of this Act, when deemed necessary, shall co-operate with and aid State and municipal authorities, and corporations and persons engaged in the transportation of neat cattle *live stock*, by land or water, in establishing regulations for the safe conveyance *transportation* of such cattle *stock* from the interior to the seaboard, and the shipment thereof, so that such ~~cattle~~ *stock* may not be exposed to said disease, and shall also co-operate with State and municipal authorities in the suppression of ~~the disease~~ *said diseases* by aiding in carrying into effect their laws and regulations, by advising or assisting them in establishing regulations for the isolation of any cattle suspected of having ~~the disease~~ *said diseases* and the slaughter of those ascertained to be so diseased, and shall provide, *by the appointment of inspectors, to be approved by the National Board of Health,* for the inspection of all cattle passing from the United States or shipped for exportation to a foreign country, and for giving proper certificates of health. *But the provisions of this Act shall not apply to cattle shipped from the Gulf States, or any of them, to the West India Islands.*

SEC. 4. That ~~whenever the Commissioner of Agriculture, acting in the manner prescribed in section three of this Act, shall find that there is a necessity for quarantine stations, he shall report the facts to~~ the Secretary of the Treasury, ~~whose duty it~~ shall ~~be to~~ establish quarantine stations at such ports or other points as may be necessary for any ~~cattle~~ *live stock* that may be imported from foreign countries, and may establish and carry into effect such regulations, consistent with State laws, as may be necessary to prevent the spread of ~~the disease~~ *said diseases* by importations from abroad; and ~~he~~ is authorised to employ officers of the Customs and vessels of the Revenue Marine Service in carrying out and enforcing such regulations.

SEC. 5. That it shall be unlawful to import or introduce into the United States from foreign countries, or into one State, Territory, or District from another State, Territory, or District, or to sell or offer for sale any domestic animal affected with ~~an infectious or contagious disease~~ *such diseases, or has been exposed presumably thereto,* except in accordance with the provisions of this Act and the rules and regulations adopted in pursuance thereof.

SEC. 6. ~~That the Commissioner of Agriculture shall direct said chief of bureau, in connection with the National Board of Health and the commissioners provided for in this Act to superintend all measures for the suppression of infectious and contagious diseases of domesticated animals, and to draught such rules and regulations as they deem necessary for a speedy suppression of said diseases; and said rules and regulations shall be certified for acceptance to the executive authority of the State or Territory wherein said diseases prevail.~~ *That it shall be the duty of the Commissioner of Agriculture, through said chief of bureau, in connection with the National Board of Health, to prepare such rules and regulations as they may deem necessary for the speedy and effectual suppression and extirpation of said diseases, and to certify such rules and regulations to the executive authority of each State and Territory; and whenever any State or Territory shall accept the same, then it shall be the further duty of the Commissioner of Agriculture, through the said chief of bureau, and the commissioners and agents authorised by this Act, in connection with the National Board of Health, to assist in such State or Territory in the execution of such rules and regulations.*

SEC. 7. That when the Commissioner of Agriculture is notified by the executive of ~~the~~ *any* State or Territory of the acceptance of said rules and regulations, such sum as may be deemed necessary for the purchase and slaughter of all diseased or infected animals, *or animals suspected of disease,* in the State or Territory in which the outbreak has occurred shall be awarded from the fund herein-after appropriated for this purpose: *Provided, however,* That a sum not exceeding two-thirds the market value of a healthy animal shall be allowed for an infected or diseased one, and a sum not exceeding one hundred dollars may be paid in special cases, but no animal shall be considered of special value unless he be purely bred, and the pedigree found duly recorded in a well-established herd-book: *Provided further,* That should the first award not be sufficient for the complete eradication of the disease in said State, an additional sum may be allowed; and should the first award prove larger than necessary, the unexpended balance shall be covered into the general fund.

SEC. 8. That the Commissioner of Agriculture shall report to the President of the United States whenever he finds any place therein is dangerously infected with ~~a contagious~~ *any such* disease among domestic animals; and that upon the official publication by the President of such report the removal or transportation of animals *susceptible to said diseases* from said place into another State, Territory, or District shall be unlawful, except in so far as such removals shall be made in accordance with the rules and regulations for which provision is made in section six of this Act.

SEC. 9. That to meet the expenses that may be incurred in carrying out the provisions of this Act the sum of two hundred thousand dollars, *to be immediately available,* is hereby appropriated, out of any money remaining in the Treasury and not otherwise appropriated, to be disbursed under the direction of the Commissioner of Agriculture, *who shall annually report to Congress his proceedings under this Act, with an itemised account of expenditures.*

SEC. 10. That any person, company, or corporation ~~having control over live animals affected with any contagious or infectious disease~~ who shall knowingly violate the provisions of this Act~~, and the rules and regulations made in pursuance thereof,~~ shall be guilty of a misdemeanour, and upon conviction, shall be punished by a fine of not less than one hundred nor more than five thousand dollars, or by imprisonment for not more than one year, or by both fine and imprisonment.

SEC. 11. That it shall be the duty of the several United States district attorneys to prosecute all violations of this Act which shall be brought to their notice or knowledge by any person making the complaint; and the same shall be heard before any district or circuit court of the United States holden within the district in which the violation of this Act has been committed, or the person or corporation resides, or carries on or has his or its place of business.

Enclosure 2 in No. 9.

46th Congress, 3rd Session.   S. 1893.

In the SENATE of the United States, December 13, 1880. Mr. Rollins asked, and, by unanimous consent, obtained leave to bring in the following Bill, which was read twice and referred to the Committee on Agriculture.

A Bill for the suppression and prevention of the Pleuro-pneumonia in neat Cattle.

Be it enacted by the Senate and House of Representatives of the United States of America in Congress assembled, that there shall be established a national commission for the suppression and prevention of pleuro-pneumonia in neat cattle, which shall be known as the National Cattle Commission, to consist of five members, to be appointed by the President, by and with the advice and consent of the Senate, and whose compensation during the time when actually engaged in their duties under this Act shall be ten dollars each per diem and actual necessary expenses. Such commission shall meet in Washington within thirty days after the passage of this Act, and in Washington or elsewhere from time to time, upon notice of the president of the commission, who shall be chosen by the members thereof, or upon its own adjournments, and shall form all rules and regulations authorised or required by this Act, and shall make or cause to be made such special examinations and investigations at any place or places within the United States as they may deem best to aid in the execution of this Act and the promotion of its objects. The duties of the commission shall be to obtain information upon all matters relating to the disease in question ; to investigate all cases of the disease the existence of which shall be reported to them ; to advise the several Departments of the Government, the executives of the several States, and the Commissioners of the District of Columbia on all questions relating to said disease submitted by them, or whenever, in the opinion of the commission, such advice may tend to the prevention and suppression of said disease.

SEC. 2. That in order to promote the exportation of cattle from the United States to foreign countries, said commission shall make special investigation as to the existence of pleuro-pneumonia along the dividing line between the United States and the Dominion of Canada, and along the lines of transportation from all parts of the United States to ports from which cattle are exported, and make report of the results of such investigation to the Secretary of the Treasury, under such regulations as he may prescribe.

SEC. 3. That said commission shall co-operate with and aid State and municipal authorities and corporations and persons engaged in the transportation of neat cattle, by land or water, in establishing regulations for the safe conveyance of such cattle from the interior to the seaboard, and the shipment thereof, so that such cattle may not be exposed to said disease. Said commission shall also co-operate with State and municipal authorities in the suppression of the disease by aiding in carrying into effect their laws and regulations, by advising or assisting them in establishing regulations for the isolation of any cattle suspected of having the disease, and the slaughter of those ascertained to be so diseased, and shall provide for the inspection of all cattle passing from the United States or shipped for exportation to a foreign country, and for giving proper certificates of health.

SEC. 4. That said commission may establish quarantine stations at such ports or other points as may be necessary for any cattle that may be imported from foreign countries, and may establish and carry into effect such regulations consistent with State laws as may be necessary to prevent the spread of the disease by importation from abroad.

SEC. 5. That all regulations adopted by said commission shall be approved by the Secretary of the Treasury, who is authorised to employ officers of Customs and vessels of the Revenue Marine Service to aid in carrying out such regulations.

SEC. 6. That the Secretary of the Treasury is authorised, upon the nomination of said commission, to appoint a secretary of said commission, who shall act as disbursing agent thereof, and shall give bond, conformably to section one hundred and seventy-six of the Revised Statutes, for the faithful performance of his duties, and whose compensation shall be   dollars per annum and necessary travelling expenses, which shall be in full for his services as secretary and disbursing officer ; and said commission is authorised, with the approval of the Secretary of the Treasury, to procure suitable offices in the city of Washington for the transaction of its business, and the necessary office furniture, stationery, and postage, payable out of such appropriation.

SEC. 8. That said commission may temporarily employ veterinary surgeons and such other assistants as the exigencies of each case may require, who shall be paid such compensation as shall be fixed by said commission, with their necessary travelling expenses from such appropriation.

SEC. 7. That to meet the expenses to be incurred in carrying into effect the provisions of this Act the sum of   dollars, or so much thereof as may be necessary, is hereby appropriated out of any money in the Treasury not otherwise appropriated, to be disbursed under the direction of the Secretary of the Treasury on estimates to be made by said commission and to be approved by him. Said commission shall as often as quarterly make a full statement of its operations and expenditures under this Act to the Secretary of the Treasury, and shall make to the Secretary of the Treasury an annual report of its operations for transmission to Congress, with such recommendation as it may deem of public interest,

CORRESPONDENCE.

No. 10.

Letter from the FOREIGN OFFICE to the CLERK OF THE COUNCIL.

Foreign Office, March 7, 1881.

Sir Julian Pauncefote presents his compliments to the Clerk of the Council, Veterinary Department, and is directed by Earl Granville to transmit to him, for the information of the Lords of the Council, a copy of a telegram from Her Majesty's Minister at Washington, relative to the alleged existence of hog disease in Cincinnati.

Enclosure in No. 10.

(Telegram.)

March 6, 1881.

Cincinnati Chamber of Commerce denies Crump's report of December last on hog cholera,* and declares that the hogs of the whole West have been during last year singularly free from disease of all kinds.

No. 11.

Letter from SIR E. THORNTON to EARL GRANVILLE.

Sanitary, No. 8.

My Lord,

Washington, March 7, 1881.

I received on the 4th instant from Her Majesty's Consul General at New York a telegram, copy of which is enclosed [Enclosure 1], to the effect that Her Majesty's Consul at Philadelphia had telegraphed to England that seven hundred thousand Ohio hogs had died of cholera, the consequence of which was a stagnation in the trade. I at once telegraphed to Captain Clipperton, asking whether there was any truth in the report. But at the same time it occurred to me that the rumour must refer to Mr. Acting Consul Crump's Sanitary Report to your Lordship, of December 21, 1880, an extract from which was published in "The Times" of the 19th ultimo. I therefore sent to Mr. Archibald the telegram of which a copy is enclosed [Enclosure 2], informing him that the statement with regard to the mortality in hogs was made in Mr. Crump's report, for which I presumed he had good grounds.

On the same day I received from Mr. Archibald the despatch, of which a copy is enclosed, and a telegram from Captain Clipperton, a copy of which is also enclosed [Enclosures 3 and 4], in which he states that the information was received from Chicago, and was based upon what was believed to be authority.

In the evening of the same day I received from the Cincinnati Chamber of Commerce, the telegram, of which I enclose a copy [Enclosure 5], transmitting a resolution adopted by that Chamber, which refers to the report as to the mortality among Ohio hogs, and declares that it was unfounded, and that the hogs of the State of Ohio and of the whole of the West have for the past year been singularly free from disease of all kinds, and that the reports must have had their sole origin in mercenary motives.

I also enclose copy [Enclosure 6] of a letter from Messrs. Fowler & Co., of New York, upon the same subject.

To the Cincinnati Chamber of Commerce I replied that the report of the Consul at Philadelphia, referred to hog cholera in Illinois, not in Ohio.

But, as their resolution declared that the whole of the West had been singularly free from disease of all kinds, I thought it right to telegraph to your Lordship that statement.

At the same time I thought it right to address to Captain Clipperton the despatch, copy of which is enclosed [Enclosure 7], in which I have stated that I think it desirable that the authority upon which Mr. Crump had made his report should be known, and requested him to inquire upon what data it was founded. This morning I received, from Mr. Evarts, the note, a copy of which is enclosed [Enclosure 8], in which he states that the concurrent testimony of the authorities, both federal and State, of the Western States, leads his department to regard the rumour "as not only without good basis, but as absolutely false."

In my answer, copy of which is also enclosed [Enclosure 9], I have stated that Mr. Crump's report referred to Illinois and not to Ohio, and that Her Majesty's Consul at

---

* See Parliamentary Paper [C.—2787] of 1881.

CORRESPONDENCE.

Philadelphia had stated, in reply to a telegram from me, that there was good authority for the contents of that report.

March 8. I have this moment received from Captain Clipperton the despatch, of which and its enclosure I transmit a copy [Enclosures 10 and 11], in which he states that the information given by Mr. Crump was obtained direct from Illinois. In view of the charges made with regard to the incorrectness of the report, I think that Mr. Crump should furnish further details, and I shall request Captain Clipperton to direct him to do so.

I have, &c.
(Signed) EDWARD THORNTON.

The Right Hon. the Earl Granville, K.G.,
&c. &c. &c.

Enclosure 1 in No. 11.

Telegram to Sir Edward Thornton from Mr. Archibald, March 4, 1881.

"Consul Clipperton is stated to cabled to England that seven hundred thousand Ohio hogs have died of cholera. Trade consequently in stagnation. I am assured by members of Produce Exchange that reported cholera is unfounded."

"British merchants here and at home demand immediate denial by cable."

Enclosure 2 in No. 11.

Telegram en clair.   Washington, March 5, 1881.
To E. M. Archibald, Esq., C.B., New York.

Statement respecting seven hundred thousand Illinois hogs having died of hog cholera, was made in Mr. Crump's report of 21st December last, for which I presume he had good grounds.

(Signed) EDWD. THORNTON.

Enclosure 3 in No. 11.

Sir,   British Consulate General, New York, March 4, 1881.

I have the honour to report to you, that I was called upon by Messrs. Fowler Brothers, British merchants, here very largely engaged in the provision trade with the United Kingdom, who showed me a cablegram from their correspondents, Fowler Brothers, of Liverpool, as follows:—British Consul, Philadelphia, cabled 700,000 Ohio hogs died cholera."

"Business since complete stagnation. Make thorough inquiry, enlist trade influence to get "Government to contradict officially, cabling promptly."

On receipt of this information, Consul Edwards went with Mr. Fowler to the Produce Exchange, where he was introduced to several of the leading shippers of pork and other provisions, who assured him that there was no foundation for the cablegram attributed to the Consul at Philadelphia, and they could not believe any British Consul had sent such a telegram.

The merchants interested have been urgent with me to telegraph these circumstances to you, and to request that a denial of the statement said to have been cabled by the Consul at Philadelphia may be promptly telegraphed to England. I have accordingly just transmitted to you the following message. (See Enclosure.)

I have, &c.
The Right Hon. Sir Edward Thornton, K.C.B.   (Signed) E. M. ARCHIBALD.
&c.   &c.   &c.

Enclosure 4 in No. 11.

Telegram en clair.   Philadelphia, March 5, 1881.
To Sir Edwd. Thornton, British Legation, Washington.

Crump reported in his Sanitary for December, that seven hundred thousand hogs died of cholera in Illinois in 1880, information from Chicago. The Trichina Spiralis was also in same report, and based on what is believed authority.—CLIPPERTON.

Enclosure 5 in No. 11.

Telegram from the Cincinnati Chamber of Commerce to Sir Edward Thornton, dated March 5, 1881.

We have the honour to transmit the following resolution, unanimously adopted by the Cincinnati Chamber of Commerce to-day:

Whereas it is currently reported that the British Consul at Philadelphia has sent a despatch to England completely false in character, to the effect that 700,000 Ohio hogs have died from cholera:

CORRESPONDENCE.

Therefore resolved; that the Cincinnati Chamber of Commerce hereby gives to the official representatives of Great Britain in this country the most positive assurances that the hogs of the State of Ohio and of the whole West have been during the past year singularly free from disease of all kinds, and respectfully asks that the members of the Legation do take such action as will immediately correct the effect of the reports which are calculated to inflict great damage on the provision trade of both United States and Great Britain, and which doubtless have had their sole origin in mercenary motives.

                        (Signed)   HENRY C. URNER, President.
                                „   J. H. FOOTE, Secretary.
                                „   SIDNEY MAXWELL, Superintendent.

Enclosure 6 in No. 11.

DEAR SIR,   17, Broadway, New York, March 4, 1881.

THERE has been a panic in England, and stagnation in the provision trade on accounts of reports emanating from France, and also from the United States, that on account of disease in the hogs in America the product was injurious to health.

The provision trade in England appointed Messrs. Fowler Bros., John Sinclair and Co., and John Hargraves, of Liverpool, a committee to investigate these reports, and after a careful inquiry, this committee was fully satisfied that there were no grounds for such reports, but the panic still continues among the British public on account of a despatch from the British Consul at Philadelphia saying that 700,000 hogs had died of Cholera in Illinois. We enclose copy of telegrams passed between us and your consul at Philadelphia on the subject.

It is of the utmost importance to the trade on both sides of the Atlantic that these reports should be officially contradicted immediately.

It is well known to all the trade that disease has been less prevalent among hogs this season than during any former year.

We shall be glad to give you any information you may require on this subject, as we represent the largest interests in the American and English provision trades.

                                                                                   Yours, &c.
To Sir Edwd. Thornton,   (Signed)   FOWLER BROS.
   &c.   &c.   &c.

Enclosure 7 in No. 11.

SIR,   Washington, March 6, 1881.

I ENCLOSE copy of a telegram and a despatch I have received from Her Majesty's Consul General at New York [Enclosures 1 and 3], of a letter from Messrs. Fowler Brothers, of New York [Enclosure 6], and of a telegram from the Cincinnati Chamber of Commerce [Enclosure 5], all of which, though they speak of a telegram sent by you to England on the subject of hog cholera, evidently refer to the report made by Mr. Acting Consul Crump, on the 21st of December last. I cannot doubt that Mr. Crump's statements were made on good authority, and that he believed them to be true; but under the circumstances of their being now contradicted, it is advisable that they should be known, and I have therefore to request you to inquire of him what data he had for making the report in question.

                                                                                   I am, &c.
Captain Clipperton,   (Signed)   E. THORNTON.
   &c.   &c.   &c.

Enclosure 8 in No. 11.

SIR,   Department of State, Washington, March 7, 1881.

I HAVE the honour to call your attention to the report which reaches this department that the Consul of Her Majesty at Philadelphia has recently cabled to his Government that excessive mortality has prevailed among western swine during the past season, and that over 700,000 had died of hog-cholera in Ohio alone.

The injurious effects which such a statement could not fail to cause to a large and profitable branch of American industry, if substantiated, has led this Government to take the most active measures to investigate the truth of the rumour. The concurrent testimony of the authorities, both federal and state, of the Western States, covering all the districts where swine are raised for a market, leads this department to regard the rumour as not only without good basis, but as absolutely false. Neither infectious disease nor unusual mortality from epidemic causes are known to have prevailed during the past two years. On the contrary, I receive the most positive assurances from all sources that the condition of the hogs in the West was never healthier than during that period.

In view of the natural alarm caused by the unverified statements of the Consul at Philadelphia, and of the irreparable damage which may ensue to wide-spread interests without its immediate and positive contradiction, I hasten to bring the matter urgently to your attention, to the end that the denial of this hasty assertion may be so prompt and authoritative as to undo the harm already done.

                                                                                 I have, &c.
The Right Hon. Sir E. Thornton, K.C.B.,   (Signed)   WM. M. EVARTS.
   &c.   &c.   &c.

CORRESPONDENCE.

Enclosure 9 in No. 11.

Washington, March 7, 1881.

Sir,

With reference to your note of to-day's date, I have the honour to inform you that the statement to which you refer concerning the mortality among swine, must have arisen from a report which was made on the 21st December last by Mr. Crump, then Acting Consul at Philadelphia, and which was published at London in "The Times" of the 19th ultimo. You will perceive that it refers to Illinois and not to Ohio. I have already made inquiry upon the subject by telegraph of Her Majesty's Consul at Philadelphia, who has informed me by the same means that the statement was made upon good authority; but I expect to receive a further report from him to-morrow.

I have, &c.
(Signed) E. Thornton.

The Hon. William M. Evarts,
&c. &c. &c.

Enclosure 10 in No. 11.

British Consulate, Philadelphia, March 7, 1881.

Sir,

I beg to acknowledge the receipt of your despatch No. 6 dated yesterday, with its enclosures, relative to the emotion created in New York and Cincinnati by Mr. Acting Consul Crump's despatch of the 21st December last, on the subject of hog cholera.

I now beg to enclose a copy of a memorandum which I gave to a committee from the New York Produce Exchange, who attended at this Consulate to-day on the same matter.

I have &c.
(Signed) Robt. Chas. Clipperton,
Her Majesty's Consul.

The Right Hon. Sir Edward Thornton, K.C.B.
&c. &c. &c.

Enclosure 11 in No. 11.

Memorandum Furnished to Committee of the New York Exchange, March 7, 1881.

The reports of the mortality among swine in the State of Illinois in the year 1880, as furnished the British Government by the Acting Consul at Philadelphia in his Sanitary Despatch of December last, and said to amount to 700,000 head, was obtained by the Acting Consul direct from Illinois. Should the figures quoted prove to be an error, Captain Clipperton, Her Majesty's Consul, will at once make the necessary correction.

It is believed that the mortality in 1880 was no greater than it was in 1879 in the State of Illinois.

No. 12.

Letter from the CLERK OF THE COUNCIL to the FOREIGN OFFICE.

Veterinary Department, Privy Council Office,
44, Parliament Street, Westminster, S.W.,
March 10, 1881.

Sir,

Referring to Mr. Crump's despatch (with enclosure) of the 21st December last, and to Sir Edward Thornton's telegram of the 6th instant, relating to hog cholera in Illinois, I am directed by the Lords of the Council to request that you will have the goodness to move Earl Granville to cause inquiry to be made of Mr. Crump as to the grounds for his statement that during the past year 700,000 head of swine died in Illinois of hog cholera.

I beg to return Mr. Crump's despatch.

I am, &c.
(Signed) C. L. Peel.

The Under Secretary of State,
&c. &c. &c.
Foreign Office.

No. 13.

LETTER from Sir E. THORNTON to EARL GRANVILLE.

Sanitary, No. 9.

My Lord,

Washington, March 11, 1881.

With reference to my despatch No. 8 of this series, and of the 7th instant, in which I transmitted copy of a despatch which I had received from Her Majesty's Consul at Philadelphia relative to hog cholera in Illinois, and stated that I intended to request him to furnish further details, I have the honour to enclose copy of the Despatch [Enclosure 1] which I addressed to him in that sense, and of his answer [Enclosure 2]. In the latter Captain Clipperton states plainly that the report of 700,000 hogs having died of cholera in Illinois in 1880, was sent by the British Vice-Consul at Chicago.

Mr. Crump does not himself appear to have had access to any statistics from Illinois, but to have relied on the information given him by Mr. Warrack. I therefore thought it right to address a further despatch to Captain Clipperton, copy of which is also enclosed [Enclosure 3] instructing him to call upon Mr. Warrack to give the basis of of calculation, and the authorities upon which he relied.

This morning I received a further communication from Captain Clipperton, copy of which is also enclosed, transmitting newspaper articles [Enclosures 4, 5, and 6], and stating that persons interested in the hog trade desire to let the matter rest, lest it should appear that the mortality was really greater than they supposed. But in my answer, copy of which is also enclosed [Enclosure 7] I have pointed out that, as doubt has been raised as to the correctness of Mr. Crump's report, it is desirable that Mr. Warrack should state upon what he founded the information given by him.

On the evening of the 9th instant I received from Mr. Blaine the note of which I have the honour to enclose a copy [Enclosures 8, 9, and 10] in which he expresses regret that that I should not yet have communicated a further report upon the subject from Her Majesty's Consul at Philadelphia. He again denies the truth of Mr. Crump's report, and expresses the opinion that he must have been imposed upon.

In my answer, copy of which is also enclosed [Enclosure 11] I have forwarded a copy of Captain Clipperton's despatch of the 9th instant, and have shown him that, although Mr. Crump's report may have been exaggerated, it was not wholly unfounded; for in the report of the Agricultural Department of Illinois, it is stated that the loss by disease among hogs during the year 1880, was 227,259 head.

Although there is no doubt that in some recent years, the loss among swine of the United States has been very great, I am inclined to think from what I hear, that, though still considerable, it has not been so great, taking the whole of the United States, during the year 1880, as in some previous years.

I have, &c.
The Right Hon. the Earl Granville, K.G., &c. &c. &c. (Signed) EDWARD THORNTON.

Enclosure 1 in No. 13.

Sir, Washington, March 8, 1881.

I HAVE received your despatch No. 14, of yesterday's date, which is satisfactory as far as it goes; but I beg to state that, considering the charges which have been made by the United States Government, the Cincinnati Chamber of Commerce, and certain merchants, I think that Mr. Crump should furnish further details, and let me at least have the data upon which he founded his report, and the authority which supported them.

I am, &c.
Captain Clipperton, &c. &c. &c. (Signed) EDWARD THORNTON.

Enclosure 2 in No. 13.

Sir, British Consulate, Philadelphia, March 9, 1881.

I HAVE the honour to acknowledge the receipt of your despatch No. 7, of the 8th instant, and with reference to your despatch No. 6, of the 6th instant, relating to Mr. Crump's Sanitary Report to Her Majesty's Principal Secretary of State for Foreign Affairs, for the month of December last, and in reply, to inform you that the report of about 700,000 hogs having died in the State of Illinois in the year 1880 was sent to him by the Vice-Consul stationed at Chicago.

Upon further inquiry upon this subject, I learn that the reports furnished the public are more or less of an estimated character, and should be accepted in that light. In the Report of the Agricultural Department of the State of Illinois for 1878, vol. 16, pp. 377 and 8, under the head of "Hog Cholera," the number of hogs in the State is assessed at 3,334,920, and the losses by disease at 474,758 head or 14 per cent. of the whole stock, and the pecuniary loss laid down at $1,438,589. Volume 17, p. 383, of the same publication, quotes the number of hogs and pigs which died of cholera from May 1st 1878 to May 1st 1879 to have amounted to the enormous figure of 1,391,422. In one county alone (Warren) 59,544 head died. At pages 544 and 5 the mortality to the 1st May 1880 is placed at 182,577. There appear to be no later published reports, at least, I have not been able to procure any.

When it is taken into consideration that hundreds of thousands of young pigs are littered after the taking of the census (in April) amongst which there must be more or less mortality from swine disease,

R 679.

and that the figures are so very large, 1,391,422, for the previous year, it is not improbable that the number quoted for 1880, viz., 700,000, is very little, if any, in excess of the actual mortality.

I beg to call your attention to the remarks of the Commissioner of Agriculture in his Report for 1878, (p. 24), which are as follows: "for less than half the territory of the United States they show "annual losses amounting to $10,091,483 in swine. These figures indicate that the losses of farm "animals throughout the United States annually aggregate the sum of $30,000,000 or more. As at "least two-thirds of this amount seem to be sustained in the loss of swine from affections which "appeared to be but little understood by the farmer and stock raiser, I regarded the subject of "sufficient importance to call for an appropriation, &c. In addition to the saving of so vast an amount "of property, the health of our people demands the completion of this work, as it is a noteworthy but "lamentable fact, that many herds of hogs are shipped to the nearest markets, or slaughtered by the "owner for marketable purposes as soon as the disease makes its appearance among them."

I have, &c.

The Right Hon. Sir Edward Thornton, K.C.B. &c. &c. &c.

(Signed) ROBT. CHAS. CLIPPERTON, Her Majesty's Consul.

Enclosure 3 of No. 13.

SIR, Washington, March 10, 1881.

I HAVE received your despatch No. 15, of yesterday's date, and as it appears that the Vice-Consul at Chicago was the author of the statement that 700,000 head of swine had died of hog cholera during the year 1880, and as this has been so positively denied by the United States authorities, I think that you should at once call upon Mr. Warrack to give you the basis of his calculation and the authorities on which he has relied.

In the "Illinois Crops for 1880," issued by the Illinois Department of Agriculture, it is stated at p. 35 that the loss of hogs by disease during that year was 227,259. It is very possible that the number was understated, because from various motives farmers frequently endeavour to conceal the numbers of their losses; but, no one supposes that the loss can have exceeded 300,000, which is very different from the number given by Mr. Warrack.

It is stated in the document above-mentioned, at page 79, that the number 227,259, is an increase of 44,682 head over the loss in 1879.

I am, &c.

Captain Clipperton, &c. &c. &c.

(Signed) E. THORNTON.

Enclosure 4 of No. 13.

SIR, British Consulate, Philadelphia, March 10, 1881.

WITH reference to my despatch No. 15, of yesterday, I beg again to refer to the matter of "hog cholera."

The "Times" of this city published yesterday a leading article with reference to the issue of a document to Foreign Governments by the State Department at Washington, a copy of which I herewith enclose. I also enclose a statement published in the "Public Record," telegraphed from Washington.

I am informed that the persons interested in the hog trade are desirous of letting the matter rest rather than ask for a thorough investigation to be made in the State of Illinois, as, if it is decided to have one, the result may prove quite different to what is so strongly alleged by the Produce Exchanges, i.e., the pork dealers in New York, Philadelphia, St. Louis, Chicago, Indianopolis, Cleveland, and other centres.

It appears that some of the Chicago Committee have been to Springfield, Illinois, and it is not unlikely that the statistics they discovered there have satisfied them that there is and has been a great mortality among hogs in the State.

I believe that so far as the reports are concerned they are bonâ fide statements prepared from documents and evidence, of which there can be no suspicion, and I feel sure that should an investigation be made, and the figures given are found to be incorrect, the fault will not be attached to this Consulate but to the statistics from which these reports have been prepared.

I have, &c.

The Right Hon. Sir Edward Thornton, K.C.B. &c. &c. &c.

(Signed) ROBT. CHAS. CLIPPERTON.

Enclosure 5 of No. 13.

Extract from the "PHILADELPHIA TIMES," of March 9, 1881.

LAWYER EVARTS found resolution during the last days of his tenure to send out a document to Foreign Governments that his department, having examined the hogs of the West, found them full of healthful fat and no signs of trichina spiralis. How rash a statement this is any farmer from Maine to Iowa could tell Lawyer Evarts. The fact is that the trichina parasite is as inseparable from pork as his bristles. Medical science does not leave a loophole for dispute on this point. The Foreign Governments that have forbidden hog importation know perfectly well that lush flesh of swine cannot resist the intrusion of these hideous parasites, and the edict against pork is not probably against the trichina so much as against the fetid preparations of the flesh sent out by greedy speculators in the West, who think more of the temporary profits of the day than the permanent traffic which an honest article would build up. Hog flesh can be made perfectly safe for those who care to eat it by thoroughly cooking it. Sufficiently boiled the most active principle of trichinoisis is destroyed and the parasite rendered as innocuous as the active principle which makes water under a glass a microcosm of incredibly active vitalism. Prepared meats in scores of forms are exported and devoured in Europe, where live meat is a luxury if not a rarity, save among the very rich. Therefore, the policy of this country should be to send abroad articles of unimpeachable purity. At best, the Continental nations import with reluctance, and the Governments which hold the American protective system in abhorrence naturally seize every opportunity that comes to hand to discourage trade upon terms so unequal. This sentiment has found expression in France in the discussions of the Assembly. As to the trichina outbreak, the French Academy of Medicine has virtually sanctioned the theory of the celebrated Dr. Declat, which assigns all disease to the presence of a parasite. This physician, after the application of a life devoted to the study of the germ or atomic theory in disease, has given the most startling evidences of the probability of this claim. A more fascinating or terrible chapter is not to be found in pathology than the results of Declat's experiments. Every form of organism was in turn submitted to his acute analysis and every form of life presented its peculiar and ineradicable parasite. Having found what he demonstrated to the Academy the germinant source of disease, the doctor set to work to discover a force which should destroy the appetant life of the animal without at the same time injuring the sane tissue. This, he claims, has been accomplished by powerful mingling of carbolic acid with some unknown active agent, which in practice appears to have satisfied the Academy. Experiments on a disease so terrible as yellow fever have shown that the doctor is not an empyric, and tests now going on by order of the French Government in its African and Indian possessions are awaited by the Medical Academy to crown the doctor's life-work. If this shall prove a panacea for human parasites, and it has been used with effect on dogs, and calves, and sheep, it may be made to strip the lushious pork of its fermentative terrors and make it a dish fit for Jews as well as Gentiles.

Enclosure 6 of No. 13.

EXTRACT from the "PHILADELPHIA PUBLIC RECORD" of March 10, 1881.

Washington, March 9.

THE Secretary of State to-day addressed a note to the British Legation in Washington on the subject of the false reports sent by the Acting British Consul at Philadelphia in regard to the prevalence of disease among the swine of the Western States. The Secretary reiterates the statements made in Mr. Evart's note of the 7th of March, that all the means of information at the resource of the department concur in showing the late published report as wholly without foundation, and sends copies of the resolutions of the Merchants Exchange of St. Louis and of the Chamber of Commerce of Cincinnati explicitly denying the reports of disease among swine, and showing that the condition of the stock in the States of Ohio and Illinois is exceptionally healthy. The statement of Mr. Crump in regard to the prevalence of disease in Ohio is emphatically and fully denied.

The Secretary of State sent also the substance of a communication received from the Secretary of the Treasury conveying an explicit denial of the report published in England, and asking that the character and source of the information on which Mr. Crump's despatch was based be ascertained. In answer to the British Minister's statement that the Consul at Philadelphia made his report upon what appeared to be good authority, the Secretary of State says that all this Government can learn, after searching inquiry, leads irresistibly to the conclusion that the good faith of Her Majesty's representative at Philadelphia has been imposed upon by designing speculators to their own selfish interests and the incalculable injury of legitimate commerce.

The Secretary further expresses his trust that the British Minister will concur with him in the opinion that no steps can be too urgent or too imperative to overtake and contradict this false statement, and that this Government confidently looks to Her Majesty's Legation for an authoritative denial.

New York, March 9.

A meeting of the provision trade was held this afternoon at the Produce Exchange to consider the hog cholera scare. The chair was filled by Mr. F. H. Parker, who in a speech said that the exports of hog products rank third in importance in this country, exceeding 1,300,000,000 pounds in quantity and $100,000,000 in value. "On Saturday," he said, "we were enabled to cable to our correspon-
" dents at Liverpool contradicting and disproving the alarming reports on the authority of Commis-
" sioner of Agriculture Le Duc, and to assure all interested in foreign countries that they could
" consume the products of the hog manufactured in this country with impunity. I desire to add that
" to the British Consul General Archibald and Vice-Consul Edwards, of this city, we are under many
" obligations for their hearty assistance and co-operation."

During 1879 the exports of hog products to all parts of the world from the United States aggregated 1,181,892,318 lbs., valued at $77,356,947. This trade had increased to 1,326,157,330 lbs. in 1880, valued at $100,798,914. The exports to the United Kingdom of Great Britain alone during 1880 aggregated 670,890,839 lbs., worth on the market $50,432,786.

The report of the committee sent to Philadelphia to confer with the British Consul there, consisting of Messrs. Orr, Fowler, and Sinclair, was then presented and read to the meeting.

Enclosure 7 of No. 13.

SIR, Washington, March 11, 1881.

I HAVE received your Despatch No. 16 of the 10th instant, and in reply beg to state that the question with regard to hog cholera is not as to what the persons who are interested in the trade in this country may happen to wish. The question is as to the doubt of the correctness of the reports made by Her Majesty's Consulate, for which in this instance the Vice-Consul at Chicago seems to be responsible. I have given you the loss, as stated in a statistical document prepared at Springfield, Illinois, of 227,259 from all diseases during 1880, which is very different from 700,000 from hog cholera given by Mr. Warrack, and I must repeat that you should call upon Mr. Warrack to report to you for my information what were the statistics upon which he founded his statement

I am, &c.

Captain Clipperton,
&c. &c. &c.

(Signed) E. THORNTON.

Enclosure 8 in No. 13.

Department of State, Washington, March 9, 1881.

SIR,

I HAVE the honour to acknowledge the receipt of your note of the 7th instant, addressed to my predecessor in response to his note of the same day to you on the subject of the alleged prevalence of hog cholera in the Western States. While most fully appreciating your promptness and courtesy in taking such energetic steps to investigate the authority for the strange announcement made by Mr. Crump, late Acting Consul of Her Majesty at Philadelphia. I regret that the further report on the subject looked for by you from the Consul at Philadelphia should not have yet been communicated to this Department, in view of the urgency of the matter.

Confirming the statement in Mr. Evart's note of the 7th, that all means of information at the resource of the Department concurred in showing the late published report as wholly without foundation, I hasten to transmit copies of resolutions of the Merchant's Exchange of St. Louis, and of the Chamber of Commerce of Cincinnati. The latter explicit denial, as you will perceive, covers the State of Ohio to which, as you remark, Mr. Crump's statement refers, and not to the State of Illinois.

I am also, to-day, in receipt of a communication from my colleague, the Secretary of the Treasury, conveying explicit denial of the report published in the "Times," and asking that the character and source of the information on which Mr. Crump's despatch was based be ascertained. It may be that, as stated in the telegram you have received from the Consulate at Philadelphia, credence has been given to what appeared to be "good authority;" but all this Government can learn, after searching inquiry, leads irresistibly to the conclusion that the good faith of Her Majesty's representative at Philadelphia has been imposed upon by designing speculators, in their own selfish interests and to the incalculable injury of legitimate commerce.

Should this be so, I trust you will concur with me that no steps can be too urgent or imperative to overtake and contradict this false statement, and that this Government cannot too confidently look to Her Majesty's Legation for an authorative denial thereof.

I have, &c.

The Right Hon. Sir Edward Thornton, K.C.B.
&c. &c. &c.

(Signed) JAMES G. BLAINE.

Enclosures:
1. Resolution of the St. Louis Merchants' Exchange.
2. ,, ,, Cincinnati Chamber of Commerce.

Enclosure 9 of No. 13.

St. Louis, March 7, 1881.

THE Board of Directors of the Merchants Exchange of St. Louis to-day adopted the following:—

Whereas a report has been made public to the effect that a disease of a malignant character is prevalent among the swine of this country, tending to intimidate foreign and local buyers of the product, and whereas all experience and knowledge of this year's packing warrant the opinion that never before in the annals of the pork-packing trade was there comparatively less disease among swine, or less cause for apprehension on the part of the consumer than at present; therefore resolved that in the opinion of the Directors of the Merchants Exchange of St. Louis, the alarm caused by said reports is entirely without foundation, and the assurance is given that the hog product of this season is more free from disease, and more healthful generally than ever before.

(Signed) MICHAEL McENNIS, President.

Enclosure 10 in No. 13.

Cincinnati, March 5, 1881.

THE Cincinnati Chamber of Commerce to-day unanimously adopted the following resolution:—

Whereas it is currently reported that the British Consul at Philadelphia has sent a despatch to England completely false in character, to the effect that 700,000 hogs have died from cholera; therefore resolved, that the Cincinnati Chamber of Commerce hereby gives to the official representatives of Great Britain in this country, its most positive assurance that the hogs of the State of Ohio, and of the whole West, have been during the past year singularly free from disease of all kinds, and respectfully asks the members of the Legation to take such action as would immediately correct the effect of the reports which are calculated to inflict great damage on the provision trade of both the United States and Great Britain, and which doubtless have had their sole origin in mercenary motives.

(Signed) HENRY C. URNER, President.
,, J. H. FOOTE, Secretary.
,, SIDNEY D. MAXWELL, Superintendent.

CORRESPONDENCE.

Enclosure 11 in No. 13.

Sir,   Washington, March 10, 1881.

I HAVE the honour to acknowledge the receipt of your note of yesterday's date, upon the subject of the report made by the Acting Consul at Philadelphia concerning hog cholera. As there still seems to be a misunderstanding, I am obliged to repeat that the report in question referred to Illinois and not to Ohio.

A soon as I heard of the alleged incorrectness of the statements made by Mr. Crump, I directed Her Majesty's Consul at Philadelphia to inquire into the matter, and to inform me upon what authority the assertion was made that 700,000 hogs had died in Illinois during the year 1880.

Captain Clipperton replied first by telegraph, and then by post, that the report was made on good authority from Chicago. I was not satisfied with this explanation, and called for further details. I have now the honour to enclose copy of a letter which I have just received from Captain Clipperton. [Enclosure 2 in No. 13.]

In the meantime I have had access to a pamphlet entitled "Illinois Crops for 1880," published by the Illinois Department of Agriculture, from which it appears that the loss of hogs by disease in Illinois during 1880 was 227,259. It is evident therefore that Mr. Crump's report of the loss was greatly exaggerated, though in view of the loss above-mentioned it can hardly be said that it is wholly without foundation.

I received on Saturday night the resolution of the Cincinnati Chamber of Commerce, of which a copy was enclosed in your note of yesterday. On Sunday morning, I despatched a telegram to Earl Granville, informing him that the Cincinnati Chamber of Commerce had denied Mr. Crump's report of December last, and declared that the hogs of the whole West have been during the last year singularly free from disease of all kinds.

The Hon. James G. Blaine,   I have, &c.
    &c.   &c.   &c.   (Signed)   EDWARD THORNTON.

No. 14.

LETTER from the FOREIGN OFFICE to the CLERK OF THE COUNCIL.

Sir,   Foreign Office, March 14, 1881.

I HAVE laid before Earl Granville, your letter of the 10th instant, and I am directed by his Lordship to state to you for the information of the Lords of Her Majesty's Privy Council that he has instructed Her Majesty's Consul at Philadelphia to ascertain from Mr. Crump the grounds on which the latter reported that 700,000 head of swine had died in Illinois of hog cholera.

                                                I am, &c.
                                              (Signed)   JULIAN PAUNCEFOTE.
The Clerk of the Council, Veterinary Department.

No. 15.

LETTER from the BRITISH CONSUL at PORTLAND to EARL GRANVILLE.

Sanitary, No. 2.   British Consulate, Portland, Maine,
My Lord,   March 14th, 1881.

A PARAGRAPH having to-day appeared in the newspapers of this town (of which I beg leave to enclose a copy extracted from the "Portland Argus") with reference to the excitement prevailing amongst British and other European importers of American meat, I have the honour to report to your Lordship that, upon my making inquiries at once into the truth of the report referred to in the enclosed newspaper extract, viz., that diseased carcases are shipped from this port, I find that there are no grounds whatever for the truth of such a statement.

The report in question may, however, perhaps have arisen from a fact lately quoted by an agricultural journal of the State of Maine (called the "Maine Farmer,") the correctness of which has to-day been confirmed to me by a reliable authority, viz., that a short time ago a firm in the village of Castine, near Belfast, in Maine (engaged in preserving and exporting "canned" meat and fish), exported a certain number of cases containing mutton in tins, which was found by the buyers to be of such inferior quality that the entire quantity was returned. My informant, however, states that this mutton was not sent to England, nor was it actually *diseased*; but it was unfit for human food, as it consisted merely in skin and bones.

                                                                                       I have, &c.
The Right Hon. the Earl Granville, K.G.,   (Signed)   WILLIAM WARD.
    &c.   &c.   &c.

CORRESPONDENCE.

Enclosure in No. 15.

EXTRACT from the "Portland Argus" Newspaper of March 14th, 1881.

New York, March 13th.

A London despatch says the statements from Chicago and New York contradicting reports of hog cholera appears in all the papers, but the mischief has been done, and it will be slow work to undo it. Several wholesale dealers in London say the scare has frightened away nearly all their customers.

Stories are now appearing as to danger of eating American canned meats. It is alleged that diseased animals are put up, and the statement is supported by quotation from a Maine farmer that diseased carcases are shipped from Portland.

No. 16.

LETTER from the BRITISH CONSUL at Philadelphia to EARL GRANVILLE.

Sanitary, No. 3.

MY LORD, British Consulate, Philadelphia, March 21, 1881.

I HAVE the honour to report to your Lordship that the sanitary condition of cattle in this Consular District is good, with the exception of a few cases of pleuro-pneumonia which have occurred in the small herds of dairy farmers near this city. The State Government inspector has placed the herds so afflicted in strict quarantine, killing such as have taken the infection, burying the carcasses and re-imbursing the farmer at an average price of 6l. per head.

Pennsylvania would be entirely free from the disease were it not occasionally an infected animal is brought within its border from an adjoining State, especially Maryland, where young milch cows are sold in the open market.

Dr. Gadsden, the well-known veterinary surgeon, has recently addressed a letter to the "Farmers Journal" giving three additional reasons why the United States Congress should enact a law for the total eradication of the disease, a copy of which I beg to enclose. Pleuro-pneumonia has not so far as investigation extends as yet reached the enormous herds of cattle in the Western States.

Alderney and other blooded stock recently imported by the Messrs. Heikness of this city to the value of 10,000l. is now undergoing the State quarantine of 90 days.

I have, &c.
(Signed) ROBT. CHAS. CLIPPERTON,
The Right Hon. the Earl Granville, K.G.,   Her Majesty's Consul.
&c. &c. &c.

Enclosure in No. 16.

EDS. FARMER :—I will give you at least three additional reasons why Congress should now be urged to pass a law to eradicate the disease known as "pleuro-pneumonia in cattle" from this country, where it does not belong.

1st. There has already been a loss to the sellers (breeders and dealers) in this country of over $2,000,000, caused by the restriction placed on fat cattle by the British Government, (known as compulsory slaughter at the port of entry), which they will not remove until this Government stamps out the disease from the Atlantic or Eastern States, where it exists at the present time.

2d. There is now great danger of the spread of this contagious pleuro-pneumonia to the Western States from the infected dairy districts of New York and New Jersey, as thousands of calves were sent from New York cattle markets to the Chicago stock yards during the past five months, and there sold to the farmers for grazing purposes, as they were in poor condition.

3d. This State would now be entirely free from this disease if other States did not send us a fresh supply of diseased animals. All the late outbreaks have been traced directly to cattle that have arrived from Maryland; they have been placed in quarantine by the State authorities.

Now, sir, I must ask you to urge your readers to petition Congress to enact such laws (before it is too late) that will eradicate this disease from our land, or at least prevent its spread into the States not already infected.

Very respectfully,
(Signed) JOHN W. GADSDEN, V. S.

CORRESPONDENCE.

No. 17.
Letter from Sir E. THORNTON to EARL GRANVILLE.

Sanitary, No. 10.

My Lord, Washington, March 21st, 1881.

With reference to my despatch No: 9 of this series and of the 11th instant, I have the honour to inform your Lordship that on the 19th instant, two gentlemen from Chicago, Mr. Atkinson and Mr. Fowler, called upon me for the purpose of giving me information with regard to hog cholera, which they thought might remove some of the objections which have recently been raised in England to the importation of American pork. They informed me that they were British subjects residing in Chicago, and that about half of the pork-packing trade was in their hands.

They complained of the effect which had been caused in England by Mr. Crump's Report of December 1880, stating that 700,000 head of swine had died of cholera in Illinois during the year 1880, and that trichinosis prevailed to a great extent among swine in that State. It was not so much of the incorrectness of that statement that these gentlemen complained, as that it was made to appear that there had been a sudden increase of hog cholera during the past year, whereas they claimed that throughout the United States there had been less disease than usual.

With regard to Mr. Crump's statement, they themselves showed me figures which convinced me that the Vice-Consul at Chicago, who had supplied Mr. Crump with the data upon which he founded his Report, had good grounds for those data, which he appeared to have extracted from the returns made by the Illinois Assessors. My visitors, however, asserted that these returns were incorrect. They maintained that the officials in question procured them for the purpose of deciding upon the amount of taxation; that the farmers were fully aware of their object, and always understated the number of swine they owned and overstated the number they had lost by disease and other causes. They could not, however, but admit that Mr. Warrack was fully justified in the statements he had derived from the returns of the Assessors, and that if they were incorrect, it was the latter who were to blame.

Messrs. Atkinson and Fowler further stated that it was impossible that hogs which had died of or were affected with cholera could be used for preserving or packing, because the flesh of such animals would immediately turn black, and they further declared that the authorities rigorously prohibited dead or diseased animals from being sent to the packing establishments, and took care that they should be used only for being boiled down for lubricating grease and oil.

With regard to trichinosis, they said that it was a well-known fact that the trichinæ were universally found when they did exist in what is here called the "tender loin," being the under part of the ribs or fillet; and that this part was never packed for exportation, but was always sold at home. I should doubt the certainty of the fact that trichinæ are only found in that part of the animal; but everyone seems to admit the truth of their further statement that, when subjected to a certain amount of heat, the worm is destroyed and the meat is rendered safe as food.

Yesterday morning I received from Her Majesty's Consul at Philadelphia copy of a letter and its enclosure from the Vice-Consul at Chicago, giving the authority from which he had derived the data furnished to Mr. Crump. I have the honour to enclose copy of these documents [Enclosures 1, 2, and 3], which appear to me fully to justify the statements made by Mr. Warrack, and I have accordingly addressed to Mr. Blaine a note, copy of which is also enclosed [Enclosure 4], transmitting Mr. Warrack's explanations, and pointing out that, even if the returns of the Illinois Assessors are incorrect, no blame can attach to Mr. Warrack for appealing to and basing his calculations upon official documents such as those described above.

To show, however, how little these statistics are to be relied upon, I enclose a statement [Enclosure 5] of the loss of swine by disease during the years 1877, 1878, and 1879, as given on the one hand by the Agricultural Department of Illinois, and on the other hand as furnished to that Department by the Assessors of that State.

I have, &c.
(Signed) EDWARD THORNTON.

The Right Hon. the Earl Granville, K.G.,
    &c. &c. &c.

CORRESPONDENCE.

Enclosure 1 in No 17.

Extract from Sanitary, No. 4.
British Consulate, Philadelphia,
March 21st, 1881.

My Lord,

With reference to Mr. Crump's Sanitary Report of December 21st last, I beg to inform your Lordship that its publication in England occasioned severe comment in this country, and has, in some measure tended to cause a stoppage of a rise in the prices of pork, but has not, according to the best information at my command, occasioned a decline. The report was received from Mr. Vice-Consul Warrack, of Chicago. That gentleman has forwarded to this Consulate, under instructions from Sir Edward Thornton, the bases of his statement. Mr. Warrack says:—

"I beg to say that the statement, as forwarded by me to Philadelphia on 18th December last, was founded on official documents in my possession, and other data as more particularly set forth in the enclosed memorandum."

I have deemed it my duty to continue the inquiry and lay before your Lordship the actual condition, so far as I have been able to learn it, of the diseases among swine in the State of Illinois, especially, and in the hog breeding States of the country in general. I have not confined my inquiries to the single year 1880, but have gone back for two or three previous years, and have used only the figures as published by the Illinois State Agricultural Society and the Reports of the Commission of Agriculture at Washington.

It is quite true that all statistical calculations upon the subject of diseases among animals are more or less approximate, as I am told there is no department of the Government, State, or National, devoted exclusively to this particular service. The figures are obtained by the Agricultural Department at Washington, and the agricultural societies of the respective States under much difficulty. Doubtless, selfish motives engender a tendency to withhold information that would prove very valuable to the public at large.

In volume 16 of the Transactions of the Department of Agriculture of Illinois for 1878, pages 377–8, under the head of "Hog cholera," the number of hogs is assessed in Illinois at 3,334,920, and the loss by disease 474,758 head, or 14 per cent. of the entire stock. The pecuniary loss is laid at $1,438,589. In volume 17 for 1879, page 383, the number of hogs which died of swine diseases is reported to have been 1,391,422, and the weight, at an average of 100 lbs. per head, 139,853,508 pounds, with a pecuniary loss of $1,438,589. In one county alone (Warren) 59,544 head perished.

ILLINOIS STATE DEPARTMENT OF AGRICULTURE.

	No. of Hogs.	Value of Product.	Deaths by Diseases.	Pecuniary Losses.
		$		$
1877	2,961,366	22,738,881	1,445,268	1,583,415
1878	3,334,920	16,724,384	1,391,422	1,438,589
1879	2,799,051	16,640,061	679,738	588,487
1880	3,133,557	22,137,461	*227,259	*937,293

Special Table of the Losses, Value, &c., of Deaths by "Hog Cholera," in the State of Illinois.

	No. of Hogs Assessed.	Per cent. died.	No. Died.	Average Weight.	Value.
					$
1876	2,665,935	17	452,208	103	1,577,012
1877	2,961,366	12	358,844	104	1,853,415
1878	3,334,920	14	474,758	108	1,438,589
1879	2,799,051	6	182,577	98	588,487
1880	3,133,557	7	†227,259	104	937,293
Average	2,978,965	12	339,129	103	1,224,759

It would appear that these figures for the year (ending May 1st) do not take into account the fact that hundreds of thousands are littered after the month of April, among which there is more or less mortality by swine disease. In Circular No. 70, page 79, issued August 20th, 1880, the report continues:

"The loss to the farmers of the State resulting from so-called 'hog cholera' the last five years has averaged nearly a million and a quarter of dollars ($1,224,759). The number of hogs reported as having died the past season from disease is 227,259 head, an increase of 44,682 head over 1879.

---

* Applies to deaths by "hog cholera" only.
† Fourteen counties out of 102 did not render any returns of deaths by hog cholera. It is distasteful to many hog breeders to report the number of deaths by this disease.

"The value of hogs lost in 1880 is $937,293, or $348,806 more than last season. The amount of loss the farmers have sustained during the last five years from so-called 'hog cholera' is $6,123,796, a sum that would pay off the mortgages on more than a thousand farms and largely add to the material prosperity of the State."

That "hog cholera" exists and has for some years existed in this country there would appear to be no doubt. Mr. Le Duc, Commissioner of Agriculture of the United States Government, refers to the matter in his Report for the year 1878, pages 24-5, in the following language :—"During the past 20 years, or more, the spread of infectious and contagious diseases among domesticated animals in this country has been very rapid and unceasingly malignant and destructive. So widespread and fatal had many of them become that I determined a year ago or more to institute a preliminary investigation looking to a discovery of the cause and a remedy for some of the more virulent and destructive of these maladies (p. 24, Agr. Rep. for 1878). For less than half the territory of the United States they show annual losses amounting to $10,091,483 in swine alone. These figures indicate that the losses of farm animals throughout the United States annually amount to the sum of $30,000,000 or more. As at least two thirds of this amount ($20,000,000) seemed to be sustained in the loss of swine from affections which appear to be but little understood by the farmer and stock raiser. I regarded the subject of sufficient importance to call for an appropriation, etc. In addition to the saving of so vast an amount of property the health of our people demands the completion of this work. As it is a noteworthy but lamentable fact that many herds of hogs are shipped to the nearest market, or are slaughtered by the owner for marketable purposes as soon as disease makes its appearance among them (pp. 24-5 Report for 1878)."

A circular from the Agricultural Department of Illinois, No. 51, dated Springfield, December 3rd, says :—

"The so-called hog cholera involves such a large annual loss on the produce of the State as to seriously cripple the efforts of the largest class of our citizens, who are not in a condition to sustain such enormous drafts upon the small margin of profits received under the most favourable conditions from the farm. The extent of the loss each year to the farmers of Illinois can only be estimated, as the larger proportion of the losses sustained by diseases among swine is not reported. To avert the serious loss and ruin in many instances resulting from hog cholera, many more of our farmers will be compelled to abandon the breeding and feeding of swine until some remedy or preventive is discovered. The disposal at a fair profit of surplus corn, heretofore fed to hogs, will then be a difficult problem to solve."

With reference to the contagious character of the disease known as "hog cholera," Dr. Detmers, the Veterinary Surgeon of the United States Agricultural Department, states :—

"The contagion or the infectious principle is and has been disseminated through the whole country in a wholesale manner, as I shall show immediately. Champaign, Ill.: I stopped at the Doane House, a hotel belonging to the Illinois Central Railroad Company, and constituting also the railroad depot. Every night car loads of diseased hogs destined for Chicago passed my window. Only a very short time ago, on one of the last days of October, a farmer, J. T. M., living near Tolono, sold 67 hogs (some, if not all of them, diseased, and a few of them already in a dying condition) for two cents. a pound to be shipped to Chicago. I could cite numerous instances, but I think it is not necessary, because these facts are known to everyone where swine-plague is prevailing. Besides, in every little town in the neighbourhood of which cases of swine-plague are of frequent occurrence, there is a rendering establishment to which dead hogs are brought. These establishments pay one cent. a pound, and the farmers have their dead hogs sent sometimes 10 or 15 miles in open wagons past farms, barns, and hog lots, and disseminate thereby the germs of the disease through the whole country. The transportation of dead hogs by wagon I admit might be stopped by State laws; but these prove usually to be ineffective where railroad companies (interstate and international traffic) are concerned."

Dr. Detmers throughout his report demonstrates the fact "that swine-plague or 'hog cholera' is an infectious and contagious malady, and that it is easily communicated from one animal to another by direct inoculation, by way, or food, and drinking water, and that a fluid so innocent as milk will produce the disease with just as much certainty as an inoculation with pulmonal exudation from a diseased or dead hog, and that the contagion is transmitted from herd to herd, and from farm to farm." (Special Report of the Department of Agriculture, No. 22 of the year 1880.)

Mr. Robert Hudson, in Oquawka, has made the following statement :—"I have a farm on the banks of Henderson River, and last year kept quite a herd of hogs; one morning I found lodged at my hog-lot which joins the river, a dead hog, which had come down stream and had probably been thrown in some distance above. My hogs discovered it earlier than I, and were feeding on the carcase when I came. Ten days later they commenced to die; my loss amounted to fully $1,500." (Special Report Agricultural Department No. 22 of 1880.)

"On Mr. Miller's farm near Prairieville, Illinois, in the year 1877, in a herd of 240, no less than 237 died. The disease soon spread from this farm in all directions in 1878. Mr. Miller having three hogs left bought 32. These commenced to die at the rate of one, two, and three a day. Another farmer, Patrick Murphy, near Gap Grove, had 10 hogs. They took the disease, and rapidly died off. The disease spread around his place. A neighbour named Hadeler lost 100 head, and saved nine." (Special Report No. 22 of 1880.)

"A radical extermination is the only thing that will be effective unless it can be proved that a spontaneous development is taking place or can take place within the borders of the United States. Fortunately, the low temperature of the winters in our principal pork-producing States facilitates a stamping out if undertaken at the proper time, in winter and spring, because a low temperature (frost), and especially snow interrupts very essentially the diseased germs and the spreading of the disease. But the measures of extermination or stamping out must be thorough. Anything undecided, doubting, hesitating, or wavering, and fraternizing will be of no avail, but will only tend to prolong the existence of the plague and increase the cost. Although not called upon to propose any law or legislation, I consider it my duty to lay before you a plan which, if executed, will lead to a

CORRESPONDENCE.

" prompt and effective suppression, and the final extinction of that terrible plague which costs the
" country every year many millions of dollars, and undermines the prosperity not only of individual
" farmers but of whole States." (Special Report No. 22 of 1880, p. 33.)

I have, &c.
(Signed) ROBT. CHAS. CLIPPERTON,
H.M. Consul.

Enclosure 2 in No. 17.

SIR, British Vice-Consulate, Chicago, 16th March 1881.

I BEG to acknowledge the receipt of your despatch of 12th, enclosing copy of one from Sir Edward Thornton to you of 10th instant, and inquiring as to the bases on which I formed my calculations, &c., when reporting to Mr. Vice-Consul Crump on the mortality among swine in the State of Illinois in the year 1880, and in reply I beg to say that the statement as forwarded by me to Philadelphia on 18th December last was founded on official documents in my possession and other data as more particularly set forth in the enclosed memorandum.

I have, &c.
(Signed) J. WARRACK,
British Vice-Consul.

Enclosure 3 in No. 17.

MEMORANDUM referred to in annexed Letter.

Illinois Agricultural Department's Circular 70, dated 20th August 1880, and the latest available at date of my letter of 18th December 1880, states the number of hogs and pigs died of cholera as follows:—

1877.	1878.	1879.
1,445,268	1,391,422	676,738

These are the "figures" returned by "Assessors." Years 1878 and 1879 are verified by showing in detail the loss in each county, vide for 1878, page 383 of the 17th vol. Transactions of Departments of Agriculture, Illinois, and for 1879, see page 107 of Circular 70. For the year 1878, 13 counties do not appear to have reported, and there are three missing in 1879. The numbers of hogs assessed per reports of Assessors, see page 50 of Circular 70, are in—

1879.	1880.
2,799,051	3,133,557

At this date, 20th August 1880, the per-centage of deaths of the assessed hogs in 1880 had not been ascertained, but in Circular 72 of 31st December 1880, it is given as 6 per cent. in 1879 and 7 per cent. in 1880, and on page 80 of Circular 72, the following figures appear:—

Year.	No. of Hogs Assessed.	Per-Cent. Died.	No. Died.	Average Weight.	Value.
					$
1877	2,961,366	12	358,844	104	1,853,415
1878	3,334,920	14	474,758	108	1,438,589
1879	2,799,051	6	182,577	98	588,487
1880	3,133,557	7	227,259	104	937,293

This shows an increase of 12 per cent. in the number of assessed hogs, and a further increase, viz., 1 per cent. in the rate per cent. of those which died. That there were more swine in Illinois in 1880 than in 1879 is corroborated by the following statistics taken for the regular "Board of Trade" Circular, issued daily from the best and most trustworthy sources accessible to the publishers.

	1880.	1879.
*Receipts of hogs at Chicago for 10 months to 1st November	5,222,495	4,888,309
Shipments, same period	1,285,993	1,509,840
Number packed, including city consumption, from 1st January to 1st November 1880	3,936,502	3,278,469
Number packed from 1st November 1880 to 17th December 1880, the date of my advice being 18th December	1,505,050	1,300,000
Total	5,441,502	4,578,469

Increase of hogs killed in Chicago from 1st January to 17th December 1880, 863,033 or 19 per cent.

---

* These are not all Illinois swine, but also come from adjoining states.

CORRESPONDENCE.

The increase in the number assessed as reported by the State Assessors being the difference between 2,799,051 for 1879 and 3,133,557 is 334,506 or 12 per cent.

It will be observed that the figures dealt with by the parties interested in attacking the accuracy of Mr. Crump's Report, are the deaths of the *assessed* hogs, and they do not appear in any of their numerous published communications to refer to the figures as given by the only authorised State Assessors of Illinois, and published in the Illinois reports of the deaths of the total so-called "hog crop" of the State.

Something has been said by the parties who ignore the *total* deaths, to show that the light weights of the *assessed* hogs, say an average of 108 lbs. in 1878, 98 lbs. in 1879, and 104 lbs. in 1880, prove these to have been among young "shoats" and pigs, but turning to the reports of the Assessors as detailed on page 81 of Circular No. 70, dated 20th August 1880, we find that the gross weights of the "hogs and pigs which died of cholera," and the number in the following years, are as under:—

	1877.	1878.	1879.
"Number of hogs and pigs died of cholera"	1,445,268	1,391,422	676,738
"Total gross weight of swine died of cholera"	106,949,832	139,853,508	49,326,591
These give average weights in these years of	74 lbs.	100 lbs.	73 lbs.

as against 108 lbs. and 98 lbs. already quoted as the average weight of the swine which died in these years (1878 and 1879) out of the assessed numbers.

The figures, 700,000, given by me was purposely put low, and was based mainly on the statistics as published, and also on the general information one gathers from dealers and farmers. Had the circular of 31st December 1880 been available at the time I reported, or rather had I reported after its issue instead of before, I would have made the loss at least 750,000, perhaps 800,000. For if a loss of 182,577 accrues in 1879 from a 6 per cent. rate on 2,799,051 assessed swine, and the total loss in the same year is 676,738, then it is clear that if the death rate in 1880 is 7 per cent. and the deaths of assessed hogs 227,259 out of 3,133,557, then the total deaths for 1880 of all the swine raised in the State will be about 842,000.

(Signed) J. WARRACK.

Chicago, 16th March 1881.

Enclosure 4 in No. 17.

Sir, Washington, March 21st, 1881.

With reference to my note of the 10th instant, relating to the Report made by the Acting British Consul at Philadelphia in December last, I have the honour to inform you that as the statement that 700,000 head of swine had died in Illinois, of cholera, during the year 1880 had been transmitted by the British Vice-Consul at Chicago, I instructed Her Majesty's Consul at Philadelphia to request that Vice-Consul to furnish the data and authority upon which he had founded the statement in question.

I have now the honour to transmit herewith copy of a letter and an accompanying memorandum sent by Mr. Warrack to Captain Clipperton, showing upon what authority the former made the statement which has given rise to so much bitter and even unjust comment.

You are doubtless aware that Her Majesty's Consular officers are in possession of peremptory instructions from Her Majesty's Government to make periodical reports of the sanitary condition of the domestic animals in this country, so many of which are now contributing towards the supply of food to the inhabitants of Her Majesty's Dominions. In performing this duty they naturally endeavour to obtain the most correct data, and I know not where they are so much justified in looking for them as in the statistics collected by the authorities, whether of the individual States, or of the United States. In this instance Mr. Warrack appeals to statistics collected and furnished to the Agricultural Department of Illinois by the Assessors of that State, and he shows that the statement which has been the subject of so much complaint is borne out by the figures given by the Assessors.

It is admitted by the Agricultural Department of Illinois that the loss of hogs by disease in that State was greater in 1880 than in 1879. The Assessors declare that the number of pigs and hogs which died of cholera in 1879 was 676,738. It is therefore probable that Mr. Warrack, in stating that 700,000 had died in 1880 was rather under than over the mark.

It may be that the returns made by the Assessors were incorrect, and they are certainly not in accord with those published by the Agricultural Department of Illinois, but no blame can certainly attach to Mr. Warrack for giving credit to the statements of such officials as the Assessors of Illinois.

I have at the same time the honour to invite your attention to the report of the United States Commissioner of Agriculture for 1879, page 24, where, in speaking of hog cholera, it is stated that "careful returns from correspondents of the department show these losses to be at present from "$15,000,000 to $20,000,000 annually." It is added that it is not unusual to receive intelligence from some of the large hog growing localities in the West that the losses in single counties will reach the large sum of from $50,000 to $80,000, and in some instances as high as $150,000 in one season, through the devastating operations of this disease.

I have, &c.
(Signed) Edwd. Thornton.

The Hon. James G. Blaine,
&c. &c. &c.

CORRESPONDENCE.

Enclosure 5 in No. 17.

STATEMENT.

	1877.	1878.	1879.	1880.
Hogs died of cholera according to the Agricultural Department.	358,844	474,758	182,577	227,259
Hogs died of cholera as returned by the Assessors.	1,445,268	1,391,422	676,638	No return as yet.

No 18.

EXTRACT from LETTER from the BRITISH CONSUL-GENERAL at NEW YORK to EARL GRANVILLE.

Sanitary, No. 3.

British Consulate General, New York,
March 31, 1881.

MY LORD,

I HAVE the honour to report to your Lordship that since the date of my last Report (Sanitary, No. 2 of the 1st instant) I have not received any information in regard to further outbreaks of pleuro-pneumonia among cattle in this Consular District.

A report appeared in one of the local papers of yesterday that a fatal disease had attacked the pigs in Ulster County in this State, but the nature of the disease is not stated. I will make inquiry in reference to this, and report further to your Lordship.

I have the honour to transmit herewith enclosed, for your Lordship's information, copies of an editorial article which appears in the "New York Times" of this date, upon the subject of trichinæ in pork.

I have, &c.

Her Majesty's Principal Secretary of State for Foreign Affairs.

(Signed) E. M. ARCHIBALD.

Enclosure in No. 18.

EXTRACT from the "NEW YORK TIMES" of 31st March, 1881.

FACTS ABOUT TRICHINÆ.

THE report on trichina spiralis which is soon to issue from the office of the public printer at Washington will, no doubt, be a valuable and instructive work. Its author, the late Passed Assistant Surgeon Glazier, is said to have studied deeply the history and habits of this parasite, and to have availed himself of the fruits of the studies of others so far as they are accessible in the literature of the subject. The Treasury Department considers the report a highly important official publication, and is proud of it. But will the work be useful? Will it do anything to prevent the spread of infection among swine or to check the sale of trichinosed pork? Or will it serve merely as a work of reference to other medical men who wish to write further books on trichinæ? This is a practical question. Everybody knows the important place which pork and hog products hold in our domestic food consumption and in our export trade. It is known, too, that half a dozen European countries, including France, have forbidden the importation of American pork, alleging as a reason the fear of trichinosis. One of the chief branches of our export trade—bringing in $84,838,502 during the year ending June 30, 1880—is threatened with destruction. There is urgent need of practical measures to check or exterminate the pest where it exists, and, secondly, to determine to what extent it does exist. A firm and probably well-founded belief prevails that the French Government has been unnecessarily alarmed about American pork; but it does no good to say that our hogs are as free from trichinæ as those of any other country. The assertion must be backed up by evidence of an official character, or it will be regarded in foreign markets as nothing but trade puffing.

Dr. Glazier's report, however exhaustive, will serve neither of these purposes well. Like most Government publications, it will never be read by those who would chiefly profit by it. A clear and simple treatise of half a dozen pages, concisely stating the dangers to human life and to commerce arising from trichinæ in pork, explaining the method of detecting their presence, and giving directions for preventing the spread of the disease, would have been far more useful, because it might have been scattered by thousands in every Congressional district where hogs are raised for the market. No doubt Dr. Glazier's report contains all this information, but there is too much else. Farmers, butchers, and pork-packers do not read big books, yet they are the classes who must be reached. Nor is the country so great as to make it impossible to reach them. A well organised agricultural bureau ought to be able to put its publications into the hands of the leading farmers of every school district in the Union. The trouble is that our Government is ponderous and ungainly in its attempts to be paternal. The Government printing-office issues every year a large amount of valuable information; but, outside of certain classes who know how and where to find what they want, most of it is thrown away.

CORRESPONDENCE.

In the matter of trichinosis there is dense and wide-spread ignorance to be overcome, and the task is one of no small difficulty, for it concerns one of the common affairs of life, in respect to which the mass of people are tenacious of habit and hard to teach. There is hardly a newspaper in this country or in Germany which has not at some time, or a dozen times, published the fact that trichinæ are killed by cooking, and that pork which has been fried, boiled, broiled, or in any way subjected to heat above 176° is perfectly harmless; yet the Germans of the Fatherland and those who have come over here persist in eating raw ham, and their folly and ignorance have occasionally fatal consequences. There have been alarming epidemics in Germany owing to this revolting habit, as, for instance, at Hedersleben, a town of 2,000 inhabitants, where there were 327 cases of trichinosis in 1866, of which 82 were fatal. The disease is common in Sweden, too, from the same cause. In France, where, as might be supposed, the food of even the poorest classes is generally well cooked, it is said that but a single instance of trichinosis has ever been known. At Crépy-en-Valois, in 1878, 17 persons were taken violently ill after eating of fresh pork. One, a girl, died, and an autopsy revealed the presence of innumerable encysted trichinæ. It is worthy of remark that it was a French and not an American pig which caused this outbreak, the only one which has ever been reported in France.

By excluding American pork the French Government inflicts a hardship upon its people, but does not prevent trichinosis; the people themselves do that by cooking what they eat. The imperfect statistics we have, seem to show, however, that trichinæ are more common in American swine than in those of any other country, except, perhaps, Sweden. Out of 1,400 animals examined at Chicago, 28—1 in 50—were found infected; out of 210 hams sent in one cargo to Sweden, 8—1 in 26—were infected. A German professor publishes the following results of microscopic inspection in various cities: In Brunswick trichinæ were found in 1 hog in 5,000; in Halle the proportion was 1 in 1,500; Gotha, 1 in 1,800; Schwerin, 1 in 550; Copenhagen, 1 in 465; Stockholm, 1 in 266; in Kiel, Prussia, 1 in 260, and in Lieukeping, Sweden, 1 in 63. In many German cities the microscopic examination of the flesh of every hog slaughtered is obligatory, and experts are appointed for the purpose. In other cities the butchers and marketmen, sensibly recognising their interest in the matter, have formed societies, of which every member is provided with a good microscope, and knows how to use it. Microscopic examination, however, is a safeguard which, in order to be efficient, must be applied to every animal, either slaughtered in a country or imported into it, and it would be a manifest impossibility to thus inspect every carcase which goes out of the great abattoirs of Cincinnati and Chicago. Legislation can do very little with trichinosis, except by aiding to diffuse information. If swine-raisers can be taught that feeding their hogs on the flesh of animals of any kind helps to spread and perpetuate trichinosis, one important step will have been taken toward the extermination of the pest. Another fact which everybody should know is that well-cooked pork never produces trichinosis in human beings.

No. 19.

EXTRACT from a DESPATCH from the BRITISH CONSUL at Philadelphia.

April 7, 1881.

THERE have been no new cases of pleuro-pneumonia in this State during the month of March, and in the Western States of the Consular district the disease has not been found. It may be mentioned, however, that Dr. Detmers, Special Agent of the Agricultural Department at Washington, has been sent to the State of Iowa to investigate disease amongst cattle.

No. 20.

LETTER from the BRITISH CONSUL-GENERAL at New York to EARL GRANVILLE.

Sanitary, No. 4.   British Consulate General, New York,
MY LORD,   April 12, 1881.

WITH reference to my despatch, Sanitary, No. 3, of the 31st ultimo, I have the honour to report to your Lordship that, having made inquiry in regard to the disease among pigs which was reported in the New York papers, to have broken out in Ulster County in this State, I am informed, on reliable authority, that the facts have been much exaggerated; that the disease, instead of being hog cholera, as was reported here, was merely a case or two of simple diarrhœa in the city of Rondvict, New York.

I have also made inquiry in reference to the disease among cattle since reported at Watertown, New York, and find that a small herd of well-bred cattle on a farm in the vicinity of that city has been attacked with a disease which is pronounced by the veterinary surgeon who attended the animals, and who is my informant, to be murrain; and that the disease has also manifested itself on other neighbouring farms, on one of which a large number of cows is stated to have been affected. At present, however, but two fatal cases are reported.

I have, &c.
Her Majesty's Principal Secretary of State   (Signed)   E. M. ARCHIBALD.
     for Foreign Affairs.

CORRESPONDENCE.

No. 21.

LETTER from SIR E. THORNTON to EARL GRANVILLE.

Sanitary, No. 11.

MY LORD, Washington, April 23, 1881.

IN compliance with the instruction contained in your Lordship's despatch, No. 6, Sanitary, of the 22nd of February last, relating to foot-and-mouth disease among cattle I addressed a note to the United States Secretary of State, communicating to him the substance of that despatch and of its enclosure.

I have now the honour to enclose a copy of Mr. Blaine's answer, in which he states that the subject shall receive the careful consideration of his Government.

I have, &c.

The Right Hon. the Earl Granville, K.G., (Signed) EDWARD THORNTON.
&c. &c. &c.

Enclosure in No. 21.

SIR, Department of State, Washington, April 22, 1881.

I HAVE the honour to acknowledge the receipt of your note of the 7th ultimo, inviting the attention of this Government to the injury which it is alleged English stock owners have recently sustained from the introduction of foot-and-mouth disease through the agency of diseased animals said to have been imported from the United States and from certain other countries, and suggesting the adoption of strict measures of sanitary police, and a more effective system of inspection at ports of embarkation with a view of preventing the exportation of diseased animals.

I beg to inform you that the subject of your note shall receive the careful consideration of this Government.

I have, &c.

The Right Hon. Sir E. Thornton, K.C.B., (Signed) JAMES G. BLAINE.
&c. &c. &c.

No. 22.

EXTRACT from a Report by MR. DRUMMOND to SIR E. THORNTON.

Washington, April 25, 1881.

REPORTS show a fair condition of farm animals. In the West and Texas much loss was caused amongst horses owing to cold and inattention. Epizootic and distemper prevailed in all sections of the country, but the type has been of a mild form, and in most States is disappearing or has disappeared entirely. There was a large mortality in Texas and Arkansas from black leg, blind staggers, and farcy.

The condition of sheep is reported as poor. Suffering and death for want of shelter during the past severe winter occurred. There were complaints from North and South Carolina, together with the Gulf States, except Texas, that numbers of worthless days had prevented the breeding of sheep in these States. Scab has been prevalent in California. The condition of cattle is reported as good. Feeding and proper shelter have led to good results. With respect to diseases, the authorities in Pennsylvania have been successful in eradicating the disease of contagious pleuro-pneumonia. On the 14th of March last there were only three infected herds in that State; all were quarantined; the State is now paying full value for infected animals. There are a few cases of this disease in the States of New York and New Jersey; in Maryland cases are reported, and the veterinary surgeons report it in an acute form in a number of stables and farms, and that some dairymen in the vicinity of Baltimore practise inoculation.

In Virginia and the Southern States there have been cases of black leg, distemper, and murrain, but there is no mention of pleuro-pneumonia or other disease of like importance, nor in any other of the States or territories.

Swine show rather a poorer condition than last year. Lack of sanitary conditions, defective and improper food, and general lack of cleanliness have caused quinsy, lung fever, and measles; but their range is narrow and loss insignificant. Swine plague is largely reported, as it was last year, but does not assume any more, if as malignant a type, or as great a ratio of loss; this appears to be more especially the case in the South Atlantic and Gulf states; in those States deaths also occurred from starvation, from too many acorns, and from too much cotton seed. In Illinois and Iowa, nearly one half of the reports mention cholera as present in some herds in their counties; while in Ohio, Michigan, Wisconsin, and Minnesota there is hardly any.

CORRESPONDENCE.

No. 23.

LETTER from the BRITISH CONSUL-GENERAL at New York to EARL GRANVILLE.

Sanitary, No. 5. British Consulate General, New York,
MY LORD, April 27, 1881.

I HAVE the honour to report to your Lordship that since my last despatch, in regard to the sanitary condition of cattle, &c. in this consular district, pleuro-pneumonia has made its appearance among cattle on a dairy farm in Patterson, Putnam County, in this State. The disease is stated to have been communicated to the rest of the cattle on the farm by a cow and a bull which the proprietor had purchased in Maryland. Six of the animals have been slaughtered, and the farm has been quarantined to keep the disease from spreading to other herds in the locality.

A strange disease is also reported to have broken out among the cattle in Denning, Ulster County, in this State—several of the farmers in the neighbourhood having lost stock by reason of it. When first attacked the animals appear to be in much pain, and they refuse to eat. They are "seized with trembling and bloating," and blood sometimes flows from the nostrils. Death is said to ensue in a few hours.

A statement appeared recently in one of the local newspapers that cattle disease was "quite prevalent" at Fairhaven, New Jersey. On making inquiry, I found that the report was groundless.

I have, &c.
Her Majesty's Principal Secretary of State for (Signed) E. M. ARCHIBALD.
   Foreign Affairs.

No. 24.

LETTER from the BRITISH CONSUL-GENERAL at New York to EARL GRANVILLE.

Sanitary, No. 7. British Consulate General, New York,
MY LORD, May 28, 1881.

I HAVE the honour to report to your Lordship that there has recently been a fresh outbreak of pleuro-pneumonia among the cattle on Staten Island, New York. A dozen cows on a farm at Northfield have died from the disease, and several others are still suffering from it.

A farm has also been quarantined at East Willeston, near Hempstead, Long Island, on which some cattle have died from pleuro-pneumonia.

I have, &c.
Her Majesty's Principal Secretary of State for (Signed) E. M. ARCHIBALD.
   Foreign Affairs, London.

No. 25.

LETTER from the BRITISH CONSUL at New Orleans to EARL GRANVILLE.

Sanitary, No. 7. British Consulate, New Orleans,
MY LORD, June 27, 1881.

I HAVE the honour to report that charbon has appeared amongst the horses, mules, and cattle on the lower coast of this State, and that precautions have been taken to prevent its introduction and spread in New Orleans.

No cattle are being exported at present.

I have, &c.
(Signed) A. DE G. DE FONBLANQUE.
The Right Hon. the Earl Granville, K.G.
   &c.   &c.   &c.

CORRESPONDENCE.

No. 26.

LETTER from the BRITISH CONSUL-GENERAL at New York to EARL GRANVILLE.

Sanitary, No. 8.
My Lord,

British Consulate General, New York,
June 30, 1881.

I have the honour to acquaint your Lordship that, with the exception of a reported outbreak of disease among hogs in the town of Oyster Bay, Long Island, no reports of contagious disease among cattle or other stock, have come under my observation since the date of my last despatch, Sanitary, No. 7, of the 28th ultimo.

On inquiry as to the alleged sickness among the pigs at Oyster Bay, I find that the matter has been greatly exaggerated, and that it is unnecessary for me to further refer to it.

I have, &c.

Her Majesty's Principal Secretary of State for Foreign Affairs, London.

(Signed) E. M. ARCHIBALD.

No. 27.

LETTER from the BRITISH CONSUL at New Orleans to EARL GRANVILLE.

Sanitary, No. 9.
My Lord,

British Consulate, New Orleans,
July 28, 1881.

REFERRING to Mr. Lister's circular (Sanitary) of June 18th, I have the honour to state that no report has reached me respecting the existence of disease amongst animals within this consular district, of the classes enumerated in the enclosure, and which are the subject of legislation in Great Britain.

At the same time I beg to add that the disease called charbon, reported by me on the 27th June 1881, to be affecting animals on the lower coast, has spread, or appeared in other parts of this State and of Mississippi.

If information be required respecting this disease—which is highly contagious and fatal—it can be obtained from the writings of M. Pasteur, of Paris, who has made it a special study.

I have, &c.
(Signed) A. DE G. DE FONBLANQUE.

Her Majesty's Principal Secretary of State
for Foreign Affairs,
&c. &c. &c.

No. 28.

LETTER from the BRITISH CONSUL at Charleston to EARL GRANVILLE.

Sanitary, No. 9.
My Lord,

British Consulate, Charleston, South Carolina,
August 1, 1881.

I have the honour to report that no complaints, other than the newspaper paragraph herewith inclosed, of the existence of any cattle plague within the limits of my Consular District, have reached me since the date of my last return.

I have, &c.

Her Majesty's Principal Secretary
of State for Foreign Affairs.
&c. &c. &c.

(Signed) W. PINCKNEY WALKER

Enclosure in No. 28.

EXTRACT from the "CHARLESTON, SOUTH CAROLINA, NEWS AND COURIER" of July 19, 1881.

There is a disease among the calves in some places in Colleton County, of which four out of five attacked die. The symptoms are swelling under the throat and weakness. The disease runs its course in a week or ten days, when it either culminates in the death of the animal or its rapid recovery.

CORRESPONDENCE.

No. 29.

LETTER from the BRITISH CONSUL at New Orleans to EARL GRANVILLE.

Sanitary, No. 10.
My Lord,
British Consulate, New Orleans,
August 3, 1881.

REFERRING to my despatch No. 7, Sanitary, of June 27, 1881, I have the honour to report that charbon still prevails on the lower coast and in some portions of North Louisiana, and also in Yazoo County, State of Mississippi.

I have, &c.

Her Majesty's Principal Secretary
  of State for Foreign Affairs.
&c. &c. &c.
(Signed)   A. DE G. DE FONBLANQUE.

No. 30.

LETTER from PROFESSOR JAMES LAW to PROFESSOR BROWN.

DEAR SIR,
Cornell University, Ithaca, N.Y., August 13, 1881.

"THE Treasury Cattle Commission" have decided to mark with eartag and number all cattle bought at the Great Western marts for the export trade, provided you will instruct your inspectors to apprize me at once by cable if any of our cattle so marked are condemned on arrival as affected with pleuro-pneumonia. Many will still be shipped without marks, as it would be useless to go to this trouble with stock selected at the port which it would be impossible to trace to their former home. Our eartags will bear a letter and number, both of which must be sent as being essential to identification, together with the vessel's name and the date of her arrival. It may be addressed Professor Law, Ithaca, N.Y. As a commission we shall do all we can to discover any possible centre of contagion in the West, and this is one important means of inquiry.

I have already taken steps to secure the transmission of cable messages to be paid on arrival. The Commission meets again on August 31st, too soon for a letter, therefore please cable me "yes" or "no" as soon as you may have reached a decision. Your first message will require prepayment, which I shall remit when I hear from you by mail.

I have, &c.

Professor George Brown.
(Signed)   JAMES LAW.

No. 31.

LETTER from the BRITISH CONSUL-GENERAL at New York to EARL GRANVILLE.

Sanitary, No. 11.
My Lord,
British Consulate General, New York,
September 1, 1881.

I HAVE the honour to report to your Lordship that since Mr. Acting Consul-General Edwards' despatch (Sanitary No. 10) of the 1st ultimo, the sanitary condition of cattle and other live stock in this consular district has been, and is now, generally satisfactory.

I have, &c.

Her Majesty's Principal Secretary of
  State for Foreign Affairs, London.
(Signed)   E. M. ARCHIBALD.

No. 32.

LETTER from the CLERK OF THE COUNCIL to the FOREIGN OFFICE.

Veterinary Department, Privy Council Office,
44, Parliament Street, Westminster, S.W.,
SIR,   September 19, 1881.

I AM directed by the Lords of the Council to transmit copy of a letter, dated the 13th ultimo, received by this department from Professor James Law, Cornell University, Ithaca, United States of America, and to request that you will have the goodness to move Earl Granville to communicate to the American Minister at this Court, that their

Lordships have given the necessary instructions to the Inspectors at the ports where animals from the United States are landed to secure, as far as practicable, the carrying into effect of Professor Law's request.

I am to add that a reply (yes) has been sent by cable to Professor Law as he desired.

The Under Secretary of State,
&c. &c. &c.
Foreign Office.

I am, &c.
(Signed) C. L. PEEL.

No. 33.

LETTER from the FOREIGN OFFICE to the CLERK OF THE COUNCIL.

SIR, Foreign Office, September 23, 1881.

I HAVE laid before Earl Granville your letter of the 19th instant, with its enclosure, from Professor James Law, of Cornell University, United States of America, relative to the marking of cattle intended for exportation to this country; and I am now directed by his Lordship to state to you for the information of the Lords of Her Majesty's Privy Council that he has addressed a communication in the sense of your letter to the United States Minister at this Court.

The Clerk of the Council,
Veterinary Department, Council Office.

I am, &c.
(Signed) J. PAUNCEFOTE.

No. 34.

LETTER from Dr. CHARLES P. LYMAN to PROFESSOR BROWN.

Department of Agriculture, Washington, D.C.,
DEAR SIR, September 30, 1881.

I HAVE to inform you that contagious pleuro-pneumonia has recently invaded again the district of Columbia, and that therefore this place must now be added to our "infected district," no other change in the general condition of that district has come to the knowledge of this department.

Prof. G. T. Brown, Veterinary Department,
Privy Council, London, England.

I have, &c.
(Signed) CHARLES P. LYMAN,
V. S. to Department of Agriculture.

No. 35.

LETTER from the BRITISH CONSUL at Philadelphia to EARL GRANVILLE.

Sanitary, No. 9. British Consulate, Philadelphia,
MY LORD, October 7, 1881.

I HAVE the honour to report to your Lordship that pleuro-pneumonia has again been discovered in three different herds of cattle in Delaware County, State of Pennsylvania.

The herds have been placed in strict quarantine, and every step taken by the State authorities to prevent any spreading of the disease.

It is not believed that the disease will extend to other herds, as the three afflicted are in near proximity to each other, not being one mile apart, and distant from all railway communication with the Western States.

The Government of Pennsylvania is now paying but half of the assessed value of the cattle afflicted with pleuro-pneumonia, and slaughtered by the order of the State Commissioner.

I beg also to inform your Lordship that veterinary surgeon, Mr. Gadsden, who is commissioned by the United States Government to investigate all matters connected with pleuro-pneumonia in this district, reports to me that he examines, from time to time, hundreds of the lungs of Western cattle slaughtered in this city, for consumption in

CORRESPONDENCE.

Philadelphia markets, and that he has failed, up to the present time, to find any trace whatever of contagious pleuro-pneumonia amongst them.

No reports of contagious diseases among cattle in the Western States of this consular district have been made to me by the persons with whom I am in correspondence.

I have, &c.

(Signed) ROBT. CHAS. CLIPPERTON,
The Right Hon. the Earl Granville, K.G.,   Her Majesty's Consul.
&c.   &c.   &c.

No. 36.

Letter from the BRITISH CONSUL at New Orleans to EARL GRANVILLE.

Sanitary, No. 14.   British Consulate, New Orleans,
My Lord,   October 10, 1881.

I have the honour to report that a disease popularly known as "pink eye" as appeared amongst the horses and mules in this city, and is said to be spreading rapidly.

Mr. Emmett, a veterinary surgeon of repute, describes it as follows:—

"The primary symptoms are those of fever, rigors, and dulness, succeeded by swelling of the eye-lids, discharge of tears from the eyes, pain in the limbs, and tumefactions more particularly around the articulations. The pain in the limbs is manifested by restlessness, shifting of the feet, and irritability; the succeeding swellings are superficial, involving the subcutaneous areola tissue, and their occurrence gives relief to the pain. At first they are limited, but soon extend upwards and downwards, embracing the greater extent of the limb or limbs affected. The pulse is hard in this disease, and the impulse strong, the temperature of the body elevated to 103 degrees or 104 degrees, and when blood is withdrawn, it coagulates firmly and manifests the presence of an increased quantity of fibrine. The condition of the intestinal canal is disordered. There is a constipation, the faeces generally covered with much mucus, and their colour frequently indicates the absence of billiary secretion, or the presence of altered bile being tinged or stained with coffee-coloured streaks, the rectum is irritable and the passage of faeces causes some degree of pain, hence the term muco-enteritis.

"The colour of the conjunctive is altered to a pink, hence the term 'pink eye.' There is often a loud cough, at first dry, but often becoming moist without any signs of serious pulmonary complications. The disease runs its course and terminates favourably in from four to six days, leaving the animal but little altered.

"There is not the debility as in influenza, nor is the recovery so prolonged as when an animal has suffered from inflammation of an important organ. In some instances the pulse, at first strong, becomes gradually feeble, the horse at the time presenting no other bad symptoms; the pain having left the limbs, the appetite returning, the swellings having diminished, and the secretions having gained their normal conditions.

"Several instances of this kind have come under my observation, and all but a careful veterinarian have been confident of the animal's recovery. The horse has suddenly died and the post-mortem has revealed the presence of thrombi in the cavities of the heart, while the heart and its members show no trace of the disease. In other instances the animal has recovered and resumed work, continuing well for weeks when death has occurred from rupture and degeneration of the liver. In some horses signs of cerebral disturbances have become evident, the patients dying from coma and general paralysis.

"The post mortem examination of all these instances has brought to light that there has been pligging of the blood-vessels of supply—the hepatic and cerebral arteries.

"Now, if we inquire how this has been brought about, we shall find that in the first place the disease is one attacking the areolar tissue; and the inflammation of connective tissues, like of the more truly fibrous, causes the development of the fibrinous erasis; the coagulating properties of the blood are thus increased, and owing, perhaps, to some local but undemonstrated fault in the blood-vessel or heart, coagulation has taken place in the living body, ultimately leading to a fatal termination.

"It is necessary to bear in mind, in order to overcome this tendency to death, and such medicaments as have the property of preventing this liability to coagulation are to be administered.

CORRESPONDENCE.

"By carefully watching this disease it will be observed that spontaneous diarrhœa sometimes occurs, which immediately relieves the symptoms. In some cases looseness of the bowels occurs on the second day, to the manifest relief of the animal. But all cases do not thus terminate."

I have, &c.
(Signed) A. DE G. DE FONBLANQUE.

Her Majesty's Principal Secretary of State
    for Foreign Affairs,
&c.   &c.   &c.

No. 37.

LETTER from the BRITISH CONSUL-GENERAL to EARL GRANVILLE.

Sanitary, No. 13.   British Consulate General, New York,
                                     October 17, 1881.
MY LORD,

I HAVE the honour to report to your Lordship that the disease known as "pink-eye" has, during the past few days, broken out among horses, principally those in car stables, in this city and vicinity, and it is stated that between five and six hundred animals are affected by it, but as yet there have been no fatal cases. The disease is also reported to be prevalent in some of the Western cities, especially Chicago, Illinois, and Denver, Colorado.

The outbreak of this disease is no doubt attributable, primarily, to sudden changes in the temperature. In this section of the country a fall of nearly forty degrees recently occurred in a single day.

I beg leave to enclose an extract from a local newspaper in regard to the symptoms and treatment of this disease.

I have, &c.
(Signed) E. M. ARCHIBALD.

Her Majesty's Principal Secretary of State
    for Foreign Affairs,
&c.   &c.   &c.

Enclosure in No. 37.

The STATEMENT of a VETERINARY SURGEON:—SYMPTOMS OF THE DISEASE and HOW IT SHOULD BE TREATED.

AN impression exists that the horse disease known as "pink-eye" is epidemic, but such is not the case, said veterinary surgeon Samuel S. Field to a telegram reporter this afternoon. On the contrary, he continued, it is endemic. It originates in certain stables, and its causes and effects are confined to the stables where it appears. The disease became known as "pink-eye" about ten years ago. In 1871 it was very prevalent, and has not raged here since until it broke out two weeks ago. There are now between 500 and 600 cases in this city. I have had 70 patients, and there are nearly 50 now on my list. When it strikes a stable it affects on the average seven-tenths of the horses in it. The disease is a catarrhal fever. Its primary cause is a sudden atmospheric change from heat to cold, and it is most apt to develope in crowded stables, where a large number of animals breathe and rebreathe the same air.

Symptoms of the Disease.

The symptoms are:—Loss of appetite; pulse almost imperceptible; temperature elevated from 98, which is normal, to 106 or 107. All the mucous membranes are affected and there is great muscular debility. A horse may be working to-day and to-morrow morning both of his eyes will be tightly closed; the membrane under the eyelids will be inflamed and discharge profusely, sometimes more freely than the nostrils do. In 12 hours the legs become stiff and swollen and very sore to the touch. The fever reaches its height in three or four days, and convalescence begins on the tenth or twelfth day. Ten days thereafter the horse is as well as ever he was. If proper treatment is applied in time, not more than one case in a dozen proves fatal. It may be likened to the hay fever in man, or a mild form of the epizootic, but the latter is epidemic and dangerous. "Pink-eye" only becomes serious when it breaks out in a stable where there are several hundred green horses. Having been weakened by railroad travel, subjected to a change of diet and water, and not being acclimated, they are predisposed to develop the disease.

The Treatment.

Veterinary surgeons expect equine sickness from this cause every spring and fall, and are prepared to meet it. I have not lost a patient so far and none of my colleagues has so far as I know, but I have heard of fatal cases where proper treatment was not resorted to in the first stages. The first essential thing to be done is to reduce the temperature: the next thing is to increase the strength. I do not propose to make my recipes public through the telegram, but will say this much—I use no quinine unless the temperature goes above 102 or 103, for the drug is too expensive, but use other medicines to allay the fever and bring down the temperature. When a horse loses his appetite his vitality gradually sinks and stimulants are necessary to keep up the strength, but great care must be taken not to give them in quantities that have intoxicating effects. Prevent the vital powers from sinking and reduce the fever and the disease is under control.

No. 38.

LETTER from the BRITISH CONSUL-GENERAL to EARL GRANVILLE.

Sanitary, No. 14.
MY LORD.
British Consulate General, New York,
November 1, 1881.

I HAVE the honour to report to your Lordship that since the date of my last sanitary despatch, no cases of contagious disease among cattle or other live stock have, so far as I can ascertain, been reported in this consular district.

The disease known as "pink-eye," with which, as I informed your Lordship in my despatch of the 17th ultimo, a number of horses in this city and neighbourhood were affected, has now considerably abated, and will probably soon disappear altogether.

I have, &c.

Her Majesty's Principal Secretary of State
for Foreign Affairs, London.
(Signed)   E. M. ARCHIBALD.

No. 39.

LETTER from the BRITISH CONSUL at Savannah to EARL GRANVILLE.

Sanitary, No. 11.
MY LORD,
British Consulate, Savannah,
November 2, 1881.

I HAVE the honour to report to your Lordship that a disease called "pink-eye," has appeared amongst horses in this State, and has spread rapidly. So far as I can ascertain it has proved fatal in two cases only.

I have, &c.

Her Majesty's Principal Secretary of State
for Foreign Affairs.
(Signed)   LEWIS JOEL.

No. 40.

LETTER from the BRITISH CONSUL at New Orleans to EARL GRANVILLE.

Sanitary, No. 16.
MY LORD,
British Consulate, New Orleans,
November 2, 1881.

I HAVE the honour to state that no other cases of cattle plague than that of "pink-eye" reported in my Number 14, of October 10, 1881, have been heard of in this consular district during the past month.

"Pink-eye" is dying out here, but I understand it is making its appearance further north.

I have, &c.
(Signed)   A. DE G. DE FONBLANQUE.

Her Majesty's Principal Secretary of State for Foreign Affairs,
Foreign Office, London.

No. 41.

LETTER from the BRITISH CONSUL at Baltimore to EARL GRANVILLE.

Sanitary, No. 12.
MY LORD,
Baltimore, November 8, 1881.

A DISEASE has broken out here amongst horses, which appears to have made its first appearance in the Western States some three months ago.

The name it goes under is "pink-eye," and at present there is a large number of horses suffering from it. Upon most of the tram-car lines only half the usual number of cars are running.

The disease is described in the newspaper clipping which I have the honour to enclose.

I have, &c.
(Signed) DENIS DONOHOE.

The Right Hon. the Earl Granville, K.G.,
&c. &c. &c.

Enclosure in No. 41.

Extract from The "BALTIMORE AMERICAN," November 7, 1881.

THE PINK-EYE PEST. TWO HUNDRED HORSES KILLED BY THE DISEASE IN THIS CITY.

Something about the Origin and Characteristics of the Malady. The Three Stages of Development. Talks with Veterinary Surgeons. An Interesting Review.

The disease known as pink-eye, now prevailing among horses all over the country, threatens to prove as epidemic in character as the epizootic of nine years ago, and equally as disastrous in its consequences. It first made its appearance in the Western cities, and was not long in spreading, until now horses in almost every village and hamlet in the country are more or less affected by the disease. Since it first appeared in this city, some six weeks ago, it has steadily increased, and although many horses have by skilful and humane treatment recovered, no less than 200 have died. The passenger railway companies and livery stables are the greatest sufferers. Of the former the Citizens line was the first to feel its effects, and at one time this company had 100 of its horses affected with the disease. Forty of these are said to have died. The remainder have recovered, and are again in harness. During the past week the Blue line of the City Passenger Company was compelled to take off eight cars, the Green line three, and the other lines found it necessary to reduce the working time of many horses to one trip a day. Almost every third car has a sick horse coupled with one that is free of the disease. There is hardly a sales, livery, or private stable in the city entirely free from the disease, and dealers in horses find their business anything but remunerative. At the present time there are between 600 and 700 horses under treatment by the veterinary surgeons. The surgeons are having a busy time of it. During the past three days their services have been constantly in demand, causing one prominent surgeon to remark, Saturday, that he was completely broken down from overwork. A number of stable keepers have adopted the excellent plan of turning over their entire stock to the care of a doctor, and acting under his instructions no horse is allowed to do any work.

THE ORIGIN AND CAUSE OF THE DISEASE.

Surgeons differ somewhat as to the origin and cause of pink-eye, but are generally unanimous as to the effect and necessary cure. Dr. Thomas Barron, who was called on in reference to the matter, said with [that proper treatment a horse could be easily cured. He had already had a number of cases, and of those brought to him in time not a single animal had died. He thought that pink-eye was due to the inhaling of an atmospheric germ, which enters the system and poisons the blood. There are four stages. At first, the horse experiences a heavy, languid feeling, and is noticeably weak. In the second stage, the eyes become inflamed and discharge a watery substance. During the third stage the animal loses its appetite, and in the advanced stage his limbs and body begin to swell, until death relieves his suffering. A horse should not be put to any work while sick, but should be kept in a clean and well-ventilated stable. The medicine which is given is intended to work on the liver and kidneys, it being the object of the surgeon to carry off the surcharged watery matter, which would otherwise undoubtedly end in a dropsical affection. If care is, therefore, taken, both as far as sanitary and physical measures are concerned, the horse will recover in almost every instance. Dr. Barron showed the reporter a stable where, on the floor, lay a large white horse, which had been brought to him after it had reached an advanced stage. The animal's limbs and body were greatly swollen, while his groans testified to his suffering. Opposite to him stood a large bay horse, who was also in an advanced stage, but more likely to recover than his neighbour. The reporter also visited the stables of Dr. R. P. Lord, on Pennsylvania avenue, who was also at work on his horses. In reply to the question as to the origin of pink-eye, he said, he attributed it to an excess of bile on the liver. superinduced by feeding the animals on too much rich food, combined with the excessive heat during the past season. Unless this bile was carried off the system, and the horse given tonics the blood would eventually be poisoned. The pinkish colour of the eyes, he thought, was due to the effusion of the red particles of the blood under the mucous membrane. The disintegration of the blood is the cause of the dropsical swelling all over the body. Dr. Lord also expressed himself strongly against the practice of allowing horses to work while affected with the disease. They were not fit to be in harness, and would undoubtedly recover if placed in comfortable quarters. The disease might be contagious, nevertheless he kept his own stock in the same stable with the diseased horses. He mentioned a number of stables of which he had charge, and in which hardly a horse escaped the attack.

DIFFERENCE BETWEEN PINK-EYE AND EPIZOOTIC.

"The disease" said he "seems to be misunderstood in New York, where they compare it with the "epizootic. The latter is altogether different, it being a catarrhal disease, and affects the lungs, while "pink-eye affects the liver and kidneys." He called attention to a young colt in the stall, which was just recovering. It was Sadie Bell, by Basha, and well known in sporting circles.

CORRESPONDENCE.

No. 42.

LETTER from the CONSUL-GENERAL at NEW YORK to EARL GRANVILLE.

Sanitary, No. 15.   British Consulate General, New York,
MY LORD,   November 15, 1881.

I HAVE the honour to report to your Lordship that a fresh distemper among horses has lately made its appearance, and within the past week has been widely prevalent in this city and elsewhere in this consular district.

In some respects it resembles the disease called "pink-eye," heretofore reported by me, and under timely treatment is not fatal.

I enclose copies of a report of the disease published in a morning newspaper of this day furnishing a description of the distemper, and a statement of the extent to which it prevails; but private inquiries lead me to believe that this statement is somewhat exaggerated.

I have, &c.
Her Majesty's Principal Secretary of State   (Signed)   E. M. ARCHIBALD.
for Foreign Affairs, London.

Enclosure in No. 42.

EXTRACT from the "NEW YORK TIMES."—November 15, 1881.

ANOTHER HORSE DISTEMPER. ONE EIGHTH of the HORSES in the CITY prostrated.

A DISTEMPER is prevailing among the horses in New York which the veterinary surgeons are unable to find in books treating of diseases peculiar to these animals. It made its appearance about three weeks ago) and spread so rapidly that scarcely a horse has escaped. Working horses more frequently than carriage horses seem to have been affected. The hospitals of nearly all the street car companies are filled with sick animals and many have died. The disease is not necessarily fatal, and prompt and careful treatment generally effects a cure. The horses of the Fourth Avenue line are suffering quite severely from the affection. At present, 160 of the 762 owned by the company are in the hospital. Dr. Samuel Whelpley, the surgeon in charge, detailed the symptoms of the distemper to a reporter o "The Times" yesterday afternoon. The eyes matterate, the nose discharges profusely, the legs swell to abnormal proportions, and every organ appears to be affected. Unless treated in time it will develop into pneumonia. It is very debilitating, and renders the animal attacked so weak that it can hardly stand. Dr. Whelpley said that he had heard no name applied to it, but he regarded it as a form of typhoid-pneumonia. Horses have died within 16 hours after exhibiting the first symptoms. Some animals recover in a few days and others not in weeks. In their stalls the horses stand in a position to favour their weakening condition and keep their heads down. They eat very little and apparently have no appetite. Frequently cases are attended with coughing and strangling. The only remedy for the disease appears to be relief from work, good care, and the free use of stimulants and tonics. If taken in time, veterinary surgeons say, no case need prove fatal, but owners and drivers do not generally know the serious consequences, and so neglect the animals too long. The mortality among horses since the distemper appeared has been very large. A horse owner said yesterday that in going from Fourteenth Street to Central Park, a day or two ago, he saw five horses that had died in the street from the disease. There is this peculiarity about the disease, that when a horse is seemingly almost recovered it may suddenly fall down dead. The surgeons all agree that the distemper is due to atmospheric conditions, and think that it will prevail only in the damp seasons—the Spring and Fall. It is not contagious, and it is expected that it will disappear when the cold weather and frosts set in. If a horse in perfect health were isolated it would be just as likely to be attacked, the surgeons state, as if it were among animals sick with the disease. The distemper seems to have taken the place of epizooty, though "pink-eye," or scarlatina, still prevails to a great extent. Horses once prostrated with the affection, as far as can be learned, do not suffer a second attack. Very few of the labouring horses have escaped, and since the distemper made its appearance the street car, omnibus, express, and truck companies have been greatly crippled. The Fourth Avenue Street Car Company have bought a great many horses in the country and brought them to the city to make up the loss sustained by the fire at its stables. These were the first to be prostrated with the disease, and the symptons were more severe than in horses accustomed to the work and climate. The Third Avenue line has 1,850 horses, the Sixth Avenue, 1,200, the Seventh Avenue and Broadway 700, and the Eighth Avenue 800. In the stables of these companies the disease has raged with more or less severity. The loss to each company has ranged from 6 to 25 horses. A surgeon on the West Side with whom the reporter talked said that he considered the distemper a catarrhal influenza, and he believed that it required hygienic care rather than anything else. He had administered a mild form of quinine with excellent results. At the sale and boarding stables on East Twenty-fourth Street, between Lexington and Second Avenues, nearly every horse has been sick, and several valuable animals have died from the disease. Mr. J. H. Dahlman, whose stables contain 350 fine horses, thought the disease was virulent sore throat, accompanied by blood poisoning. The inflammation, he said, settled in the legs very often, but he did not regard the disease as so serious as epizooty. The treatment in the Twenty-fourth Street stables differed from that in the car stables. Ale and milk punches were used, and in many instances nitre was mixed with the feed. C. H. Hayward, Oakley and Smith, Fiss and Doerr, and Isaac Mehrbach, who keep from 100 to 150 horses, had tried these remedies with success. Mr. Dahlman said he first heard of the distemper in the West. It travelled from Missouri to Illinois, Indiana, and thence to New York. He had been informed by a horseman in Boston that it had reached that city. At present it is raging in the lower part of New York to a greater extent than elsewhere. It is estimated that at least one-eighth of all the horses in the City are suffering from the disease. The symptoms of "pink-eye," from which the City is by no means exempt, are sore eyes and throat, swollen legs, nose, lips, and tongue. Often the hind legs crack open. Sometimes "pink-eye" terminates in hemorrhoida.

No. 43.

LETTER from the BRITISH CONSUL at Savannah to EARL GRANVILLE.

Sanitary, No. 12.
MY LORD,
British Consulate, Savannah,
December 1, 1881.

I HAVE the honour to report to your Lordship that the epidemic amongst horses in this State called "pink-eye" still continues, though in a mitigated form.

I have, &c.

Her Majesty's Principal Secretary of State,   (Signed)   LEWIS JOEL.
    for Foreign Affairs.

No. 44.

LETTER from the BRITISH CONSUL-GENERAL at New York to EARL GRANVILLE.

Sanitary, No. 16.
MY LORD,
British Consulate General, New York,
December 1, 1881.

REFERRING to my despatch (Sanitary, No. 15) of the 15th ultimo, I have the honour to report to your Lordship that the horse distemper which was then prevalent in this city to a considerable extent, has greatly abated, and but a comparatively small number of animals in this city and in Brooklyn are now affected.

No reports of contagious disease among cattle in this consular district have come under my notice of late. A report was recently published in one of the New York newspapers of a disease among pigs having broken out in certain localities in Queen's County, Long Island, but I have not succeeded in obtaining any reliable confirmation of it, and it has not been further alluded to in the press.

I have, &c.

Her Majesty's Principal Secretary of State   (Signed)   E. M. ARCHIBALD.
    for Foreign Affairs, London.

No. 45.

LETTER from the BRITISH CONSUL at Galveston to EARL GRANVILLE.

Sanitary, No. 13.
MY LORD,
British Consulate, Galveston,
December 1, 1881.

I HAVE the honour to report that a disease confined to horses and prevalent in this country commonly termed "pink-eye" has lately appeared in this State.

The characteristics of this disease are a slight fever, great depression of nerve power, particularly in the lumbar regions, swelling of the pasterns, mucous discharges from the nostrils and eyes, the latter being invariably suffused with blood and from which symptom the disease has derived its name.

By some it has been designated as a typhoid fever, by others, spinal-meningitis.

The attack yields readily to careful treatment such as rest and a change of food from hay and corn to grass and mashes of bran, but if neglected, the animal suffers from super-purgation and dies.

The disease has been confined chiefly to working, stall-fed horses, those that are pastured in the open prairie are reported to have been free from the malady.

With the above exception the animals throughout the State continue free from the diseases which are legislated for under the Contagious Diseases (Animals) Act of 1878.

I have, &c.

Her Majesty's Principal Secretary of State   (Signed)   ARTHUR T. LYNN.
    for Foreign Affairs.

CORRESPONDENCE.

No. 46.

LETTER from the BRITISH CONSUL at Boston to EARL GRANVILLE.

Sanitary, No. 12.
MY LORD,　　　　　　　　　　　　　　　　　　　　Boston, December 12, 1881.

I HAVE the honour to report that, as far as information has been received here, this consular district has continued free from cattle plague during the past month, and no contagious or infectious disease exists among animals in this district, an epidemic having, however, spread during the month amongst horses, which, though fatal in some cases, has generally ceded to proper care and treatment.

This epidemic is described as a catarrhal affection, accompanied with fever, redness about the eyes, and great debility, and is known here by the name of "pink-eye."

I have, &c.
Her Majesty's Principal Secretary of State　　　(Signed)　　C. A. HENDERSON.
　for Foreign Affairs.

No. 47.

LETTER from the BRITISH CONSUL at Portland, Maine, to EARL GRANVILLE.

Sanitary, No. 15.　　　　　　　　　　　　British Consulate, Portland (Maine),
MY LORD,　　　　　　　　　　　　　　　　　　　December 31, 1881.

I HAVE the honour to report to your Lordship that, according to information furnished to me by the Maine Agricultural Society, there has been no case of infectious or contagious disease amongst cattle, sheep, or pigs, throughout this State during the month of December ended this day.

I am, however, further informed that a disease known here under the name of "pink-eye" has been prevalent of late, and continues to prevail amongst horses in some parts of Maine; but that hitherto only a few cases of this disease have ended fatally.

I have, &c.
The Right Hon. the Earl Granville, K.G.,　　(Signed)　　WILLIAM WARD.
　&c.　　&c.　　&c.

No. 48.

LETTER from the FOREIGN OFFICE to the CLERK OF THE COUNCIL.

SIR,　　　　　　　　　　　　　　　　　　　　Foreign Office, January 17, 1882.

WITH reference to your letter of the 19th September, I am directed by the Secretary of State for Foreign Affairs to transmit to you to be laid before the Lords of Her Majesty's Privy Council a copy of a note from the United States Minister in this country stating that no action has yet been taken as to the marking of cattle destined for exportation from the United States.

I am, &c.
The Clerk of the Council, Veterinary Department.　　(Signed)　　T. V. LISTER.

Enclosure in No. 48.

MY LORD,　　　　　　　　Legation of the United States, London, January 10, 1882.

REFERRING to your Lordship's letter of the 23rd September last, in relation to the marking and numbering of cattle intended for the export trade from the United States, I have the honour to acquaint you that having sent a copy of that letter to the Department of State, and a copy of Professor Law's letter having been afterwards forwarded to that Department, at the request of Mr. Blaine, I have now received a despatch from Mr. Davis, the Assistant Secretary of State, in which he desires me to observe that the Government of the United States has as yet taken no action with reference to the matter. It appears by a letter from the Secretary of the Treasury to Mr. Blaine, dated on the 15th December last, a copy of which was inclosed in Mr. Davis' despatch that Professor Law states that no circulars have been issued by the American Cattle Commission upon the the subject of marking cattle, and none have been issued by the Department of the Treasury.

I have, &c.
The Right Hon. the Earl Granville,　　　　　　(Signed)　　J. R. LOWELL.
　&c.　　&c.　　&c.

R 679.

CORRESPONDENCE.

No. 49.

LETTER from the BRITISH CONSUL at Philadelphia to EARL GRANVILLE.

Sanitary, No. 1.　　　　　　　　　　　　　　British Consulate, Philadelphia,
MY LORD,　　　　　　　　　　　　　　　　　　　　January 17, 1882.

In this series I beg to report to your Lordship that the disease, pleuro-pneumonia among cattle in the State of Pennsylvania, up to the present time has not been entirely eradicated, there being eight herds now in quarantine, under the laws of the State of Pennsylvania, namely, three herds in Delaware County, numbering about 35 head; one herd in Montgomery County, numbering about 16 head; one herd in Philadelphia, numbering about 40 head; and three herds in York County, numbering in all about 20 head.

These herds were placed in quarantine last week, four or five head having been previously lost among these herds by this disease, and two head were killed, and their carcases burned to avoid contagion.

The quarantine will last during three months from the date of the last case. The laws, however, do not prevent farmers from buying cattle, and placing them among the herd in quarantine.

The disease was brought from the adjoining State of Maryland, a cow having been purchased in the city of Baltimore, and taken to the herdman's farm in York County. From this cow and another purchased in Maryland the disease spread to the before-mentioned districts.

A disease of a mysterious nature broke out in November last in the State of Iowa, which has proved very fatal. The animal when attacked extends the neck full length, and is seized with paroxisms which speedily end in death.

The carcase of a dead animal left unburied breeds contagion, although in the strict meaning it is not a contagious disease.

This disease has been found to be the well-known "black leg," or malignant anthrax. In the State of Iowa it is more frequent among young and rapidly-thriving cattle. Recoveries are very rare, and it is no doubt brought on by the cattle eating large quantities of corn which they obtain from the stalks when turned into the corn fields after harvest time. The disease has of late subsided in consequence of removing the cattle from these fields.

In the month of November the Government of the State of Illinois issued a proclamation, copies of which are herewith enclosed, prohibiting the importation into the state of cattle from any of the counties of Connecticut, New York, Pennsylvania, New Jersey, Delaware, and Maryland, where pleuro-pneumonia had existed. A violation of this order is declared to be a misdemeanour, and the offender is liable to a fine of not less than $1,000 nor more than $10,000 for each offence.

In Pennsylvania the State authorities have renewed the payment of indemnity for animals killed by order of the inspector, the valuation of the animal being fixed by the inspector, and in the event of discontent on the part of the owner, two neighbouring farmers are called in to decide the price.

In this State the animals are now burned upon piles of wood. The plan is considered to be a great improvement upon the old system of burial.

　　　　　　　　　　　　　　　　　　I have, &c.
　　　　　　　　　　　　(Signed)　　ROBT. CHAS. CLIPPERTON,
The Right Hon. the Earl Granville, K.G.,　　　　Her Majesty's Consul.
　　&c.　　　&c.　　　&c.

Enclosure in No. 49.

STATE OF ILLINOIS:—PROCLAMATION by the GOVERNOR.

　　　　　　　　　　　　　　　　Executive Department, Springfield, November 1, 1881.

IN pursuance of the Act of the General Assembly of Illinois, entitled "An Act to suppress and "prevent the spread of pleuro-pneumonia among cattle," approved May 31, 1881, I, Shelby M. Cullom, Governor of the State of Illinois, do hereby proclaim that I have good reason to believe that pleuro-pneumonia among cattle has become epidemic in certain localities in the States of Connecticut, New York, Pennsylvania, New Jersey, Delaware and Maryland, viz.: In the county of Fairfield, in the State of Connecticut; in the counties of Putnam, Westchester, New York, Kings and Queens, in the State of New York; in the counties of Lehigh, Bucks, Berks, Montgomery, Philadelphia, Delaware, Chester, Lancaster, York, Adams, and Cumberland, in the State of Pennsylvania; in the counties of Bergen, Hudson, Morris, Essex, Union, Somerset, Hunterdon, Middlesex, Mercer, Monmouth, Ocean, Burlington, Camden, Glouster, and Atlantic, in the State of New Jersey; in the county of Newcastle, in the State of Delaware, and in the counties of Cecil, Hardford, Baltimore, Howard, and Carroll, in the State of Maryland; and I do hereby, as required by said Act, prohibit the importation of any domestic animals of the bovine species into this State from the aforesaid counties in the States of Connecticut, New York, Pennsylvania, New Jersey, Delaware and Maryland, after the 10th day of November inst., unless accompanied by a certificate of health, properly signed by a duly authorised veterinary inspector.

"Any corporation or individual who shall transport, receive, or convey such prohibited stock, shall be "deemed guilty of a misdemeanour, and upon conviction thereof, shall be fined not less than one "thousand dollars ($1,000), nor more than ten thousand dollars ($10,000), for each and every offence, "and shall be liable for any and all damage or loss that may be sustained by any party or parties by "reason of the importation or transportation of such prohibited stock." (Section 4 of Act approved May 31, 1881.)

In testimony whereof I hereto set my hand and cause the great seal of State to be affixed. Done at the city of Springfield, the day and year above written.

S. M. CULLOM.

By the Governor :
Henry D. Dement, Secretary of State.

An Act to Suppress and Prevent the Spread of Pleuro-Pneumonia among Cattle.

Section 1. Be it enacted by the people of the State of Illinois, represented in the General Assembly, that the Governor of this State is hereby authorised and instructed to appoint a competent veterinary surgeon, who shall be known as State veterinarian or inspector, and whose duty it shall be to investigate any and all cases of contagious or infectious disease among domestic animals of the bovine species in this State, which may be brought to his notice by a competent veterinary surgeon or practising physician in the locality where such infectious or contagious disease may exist, and it shall be his duty to make visits of inspection to any locality where he may have reason to suspect that contagious or infectious disease may exist.

Section 2. In all cases of pleuro-pneumonia among cattle in this State, the State veterinarian shall have authority to order the quarantine of infected premises, and in case such disease shall become epidemic in any locality in this State, the State veterinarian shall immediately notify the Governor of the State, who shall thereupon issue his proclamation forbidding any animals of the kind among which said epidemic exists from being transported from said locality, without a certificate from the State veterinarian, showing such animals to be healthy. In case of epidemic, as aforesaid, the State veterinarian shall order the quarantine of infected premises, and shall order the slaughter of diseased animals thereon, and in cases of pleuro-pneumonia among cattle, he shall, as herein-after provided, order the slaughter of all cattle upon the premises which have been exposed to contagion ; but before doing so he shall call in consultation with two (2) reputable veterinarians or practicing physicians residing within ten (10) miles of the infected premises, and shall not order the slaughter of any animals not actually diseased without a written order signed by one (1) or both of the said veterinarians or practicing physicians.

Section 3. Whenever it becomes necessary, as herein provided, to order the slaughter of animals, the State veterinarian shall notify the nearest justice of the peace, who shall thereupon summons three (3) disinterested freeholders of the neighbourhood as appraisers of the value of such animals. Said appraisers, before entering upon the discharge of their duty, shall be sworn to make a true and faithful appraisement, without prejudice or favour. They shall, after making their appraisement, return a certified copy of their valuation to the justice of the peace by whom they were summoned, who shall, after entering the same upon his record, and making an endorsement thereon, showing the same to have been properly recorded, return it, together with the order of the State veterinarian, to the person or persons owning live stock ordered slaughtered.

Section 4. Whenever the Governor of the State shall have good reason to believe that such disease has become epidemic in certain localities in other States, or that there are conditions which render such domestic animals liable to convey disease, he shall thereupon, by proclamation, schedule such localities and prohibit the importation of any live stock of the kind diseased into this State, unless accompanied by a certificate of health, properly signed by a duly authorised veterinary inspector. Any corporation or individual who shall transport, receive, or convey such prohibited stock, shall be deemed guilty of a misdemeanour, and, upon conviction thereof, shall be fined not less than one thousand dollars ($1,000), nor more than ten thousand dollars ($10,000), for each and every offence, and shall become liable for any and all damage or loss that may be sustained by any party or parties by reason of the importation or transportation of such prohibited stock.

Section 5. If any person or persons shall have upon his premises any case of pleuro-pneumonia among cattle, and shall fail to immediately report the same to the State veterinarian, or if any person or persons shall wilfully and maliciously obstruct or resist the State veterinarian in the discharge of his duty, as herein-before set forth, he shall be deemed guilty of a misdemeanour, and, upon conviction of either charge, shall be fined not less than fifty dollars ($50) nor more than five hundred dollars ($500) for each and every such offence, and upon conviction a second time shall, in addition to the above-named fine, be liable to not less than thirty (30) days nor more than six (6) months imprisonment.

Section 6. The State veterinarian shall annually make a report to the Governor of all matters connected with his work, and the Governor shall transmit to the Department of Agriculture such parts of said report as may be of general interest to breeders of live stock, to be published with the proceedings of the State Board of Agriculture.

Section 7. All claims against the State arising from the slaughter of animals, as herein provided for, shall, together with the order of the State veterinarian, and the award of the appraisers in each case, be submitted to the Governor, and he shall, after having examined each case, if satisfied of the justice of the same, endorse thereon his order to the State auditor, who shall thereupon issue his warrant on the State treasurer for the same so ordered paid by the Governor.

Section 8. The state veterinarian shall be entitled to receive for his services the sum of eight dollars ($8) per day for every day actually employed under the provisions of this Act, together with his necessary travelling expenses. He shall make an itemised account to the Governor, properly signed and sworn to, of the number of days he has served, and of the expenses which he has paid, and the Governor shall, if satisfied that the same is right and proper, endorse thereon his order on the State auditor for the amount. The appraisers, heretofore provided for, shall be entitled to receive the sum of one dollar ($1) each for their services, to be paid out of the treasury of their respective counties, upon certificate of the justice of the peace summoning them. The justice of the peace shall be entitled to receive the ordinary fee for issuing summons, to be paid out of the town fund in counties under township organisation, and out of the county fund in counties not under township organisation. The physicians called in consultation shall be entitled to receive for their services the sum of two dollars ($2) per day, and mileage at the rate of ten cents (10 cents) per mile one way; such compensation and mileage to be paid out of the veterinarian contingent fund. The State veterinarian shall have at his disposition the sum of two thousand dollars ($2,000), to be expended in disinfecting infected premises and other incidental expenses connected with his work, for which he shall, before entering upon the discharge of his duties, give bond with good and sufficient security, in the sum of five thousand dollars ($5,000), and shall make a sworn statement to the Governor of the amounts he disburses. Any part of said two thousand dollars ($2,000) not used shall lapse into the State treasury.

Section 9. For the purpose of carrying out the provisions of this Act, the sum of eight thousand dollars ($8,000), or so much thereof as is necessary, is hereby appropriated out of the State treasury, to be paid as hereby provided out of any funds not otherwise appropriated.

(Approved May 31, 1881.)

REPORTS.

LIST OF REPORTS.

	Page		Page
Second Report by Dr. C. P. Lyman, F.R.C.V.S.	45	Reports by Drs. W. B. E. Miller, D.V.S., and J. C. Corlies, D.V.S.	82
Third Report „ „ „	54	Report by Dr. J. W. Gadsden, M.R.C.V.S.	85
Extract from Annual Report of the Department of Agriculture, Washington	65	Report by Dr. W. H. Rose, D.V.S.	87
Fourth Report by Dr. C. P. Lyman, F.R.C.V.S.	67	Report on American Pork: Result of an Investigation made under Authority of the Department of State of the United States	96
Report by Dr. J. D. Hopkins, D.V.S.	81		

No. 50.

SECOND REPORT by Dr. CHARLES P. LYMAN, F.R.C.V.S., to the COMMISSIONER OF AGRICULTURE, Washington.

SIR,

IN my last report to you upon contagious pleuro-pneumonia, I pointed out, as thoroughly as any means for investigation which I then had would enable me to do, the States and counties wherein animals affected with this disease could be found. It was thought at that time, and no investigation since then has been able to show differently, that these counties, or those lying very close to them, contained all the cases that could be found in the United States. Supposing I had succeeded in thus mapping out the whole of our infected district, I began pushing inquiries in a new direction, and for this purpose the following letter was written to one of the most prominent veterinary surgeons and authors in England:

DEAR SIR,   Springfield, Mass., May 10, 1880.

I MAIL you herewith a copy of my report to the Commissioner of Agriculture on pleuro pneumonia contagiosa. From it you will be able to see *exactly* to what extent we are infected. The facts to which I especially call your attention are these:

1st. That our ports of Portland, in the State of Maine, and Boston, in the State of Massachusetts, are not in or anywhere near the infected districts; no nearer in fact, I believe, than are some of the free continental ports or provinces to some of the infected ones.

2d. That the cattle coming to those ports for shipment, and indeed for all uses, come entirely from the West—one, two, and even more thousands of miles away from our infected districts.

3d. That the lines of rail over which these cattle are carried going to these ports do not pass through or go anywhere near the infected districts.

4th. That our Western States are free, luckily for us, and always have been, of this scourge.

Now, under these circumstances, is there any method which suggests itself to you by which the Government of Great Britain can be induced to raise the embargo against our cattle coming to her from these free districts, and through these free ports? If you think there is any chance for the matter being arranged the Commissioner of Agriculture will, I think, be very glad to enter into negotiations upon the subject.

Very truly,
C. P. LYMAN.

George Fleming, F.R.C.V.S.,
Veterinary Surgeon, Second Life Guards, London, England.

To which, in due time, the following answer was received:

DR. CHARLES P. LYMAN,   London, June 24, 1880.

PLEASE excuse my delay in replying to your two letters. I have been away on a tour of army inspection, and only returned yesterday. Very many thanks for your report on contagious pleuro-pneumonia. I very much fear there is not the slightest chance of the embargo on American cattle being raised in this country until the States are entirely free from the malady, notwithstanding the fact you point out that there is an immense extent of country uninfected. So long as only one State, or one portion of a State, is contaminated, so long, depend upon it, will the present law continue. Even the present goverment, which when not in office strenuously opposed the law brought into office with regard to United States cattle, is now most determined to carry it out. If it were relaxed in the case of the United States it would have to be so also in the case of Russia and Germany, with respect to cattle plague, and then this country would certainly not be safe. Commerce spreads these diseases. The feeling here is to keep this country free from infectious animal diseases, after we have stamped them out at an awful cost and trouble; and to allow live stock to enter from anywhere where these diseases exist would not be heard of. Whenever the United States is certified to be a clean country, the embargo will be raised. Your government is not taking active steps to free the States from pleuro-pneumonia, and there is no knowing how far it may spread. So long as the government is indifferent to this matter, so long will your people suffer from the embargo. The losses from contagious diseases here have been so terrible, through a similar apathy, that the authorities are now fully aroused.

With regard to the transit of American cattle, I cannot say anything which would be of much value to you; but I would recommend you to write to Professor Brown, Veterinary Department, Privy Council Office, London. He knows everything pertaining to the shipment and carriage of cattle, and will, I have no doubt, afford you every information.

As for myself, I shall only be too glad to assist you all I can, and in offering to do so I take once more the opportunity of renewing a paper friendship, which I trust will be converted into something more substantial should you visit England.

Believe me to be, yours, very truly,
GEORGE FLEMING.

Before this answer was received, however, the department was in receipt of the report of the Veterinary Department of the Privy Council of Great Britain for 1879, when, as you will remember, I addressed to you the following communication:

SIR, Washington, D.C., June 12, 1880.

In the report of the Veterinary Department of the Privy Council of Great Britain for the year 1879, which report has just been received, on page 7 appears the following:—"The most notable "event of the past year in connexion with the trade in foreign animals was the removal of the United "States of America from the list of countries from which cattle could be imported as healthy, owing "to the landing at different times during the year of animals affected with pleuro-pneumonia." The first known such importation is said to have been made from the steamship "Dominion" from Portland, Me., about January 14. Next, the detection of the same disease in the cargo of the "Ontario" afforded further evidence of its existence among cattle in the United States. "Cargoes of cattle, "among which pleuro-pneumonia was detected, continued to arrive," until finally an order was passed (February 10) the effect of which was to cause the slaughter of all cattle from the States at the place of landing in Great Britain. It is perhaps worth noticing in passing that Professor W. Williams, of Edinburgh, one of those called upon by the authorities to examine the "Ontario" lungs, says:—"Since "first arrival of 'Ontario' with cattle others have arrived at Liverpool, and I have examined the lungs "said by Privy Council Inspectors to have pleuro-pneumonia, and satisfied all who have seen them "that no pleuro-pneumonia has arrived here from America; indeed, every one is surprised that such a "gross mistake should have been made." (Same report, p. 9.)

As you will remember, my recent investigation into this matter shows that our ports of Baltimore, Philadelphia, Jersey City, and New York are the only ones that are in our infected districts. In this report of the Privy Council the only ports referred to by name as having sent diseased cattle are Portland and Boston. This is most strange, and if true means that we have pleuro-pneumonia among our western herds, as the animals shipped from the two ports come in every case from the West, not passing through or anywhere near the district which we know is infected.

During my recent investigation every means at command was used to ascertain if this disease had an existence among our western herds. Every inquiry possible was made, and hundreds of lungs from slaughtered animals coming from all parts of the West were examined, and the result seemed to show that there was not, nor never had been, any pleuro-pneumonia in that part of our country.

Here, then, are two seeming facts which are in direct antagonism. The English examinations show, beyond doubt, that our western cattle upon being landed there exhibit unmistakable signs that pleuro-pneumonia exists among them. My own investigation, on the other hand, conducted with the greatest thoroughness, shows that pleuro-pneumonia does not exist West.

And now, as the determination of this question, one way or the other, is a matter of great importance to the immense cattle interests of our country, it would seem to be right that the investigation already commenced should be carried to the other side, and an American inspection be made of the cattle coming into Liverpool; then, having found there a few of these numerously reported cases, to trace them back by means of the way-bills, &c., over their course of travel to their original starting point in the West, or as near to it as possible.

Very respectfully,
CHARLES P. LYMAN.

Hon. William G. Le Duc,
Commissioner of Agriculture.

The result of this communication was that, at your direction, on the 23rd of June last, I left New York for Liverpool, and arrived there on the 4th day of July; proceeded at once to Edinburgh, Scotland, and called upon Professor W. Williams, F.R.S.E., and principal of the new veterinary college, who, you will remember, was one of the three experts originally selected to examine the diseased lungs taken from the American cattle which had been landed from the "Ontario" on January 26, 1879, and the only one of them who positively declared in public that the affection was not contagious pleuro-pneumonia. Professor Williams stated, that during the six months succeeding the arrival of the "Ontario" he had examined portions of the lungs of fully three-fourths of all the animals that had been found diseased, and that he has still not the slightest hesitation in saying that in no case has he found them to exhibit the characteristic lesions of contagious pleuro-pneumonia. He said that Mr. Welsby, a veterinary surgeon living in Derby, near Liverpool, was employed by the steamer people, Messrs. Warren & Co., to examine these animals, in company with Mr. Moore, veterinary surgeon to the Privy Council and inspector of the port of Liverpool, whose procedure was, as soon as an affected lung was found, to make a section of the most diseased portion, which was sent up to London for the inspection of the chief of his department. Mr. Welsby would at the same time secure a similar piece and send to Professor Williams; therefore he believed that he had an equal chance with the London authorities for a good examination. He also made several trips to Liverpool and examined the beasts and their lungs while they were being slaughtered. The correspondence with Mr. Welsby was then shown me. A letter of March 16, 1879, accompanied portions of lungs from three different animals, which were condemned by the port inspector as showing the lesions of pleuro-pneumonia contagiosa. These pieces were shown to me, and presented simply the lesions of bronchitis with collapse. In a letter of March 17, he writes:

Dear Mr. Williams, West Derby, Liverpool, England.
By the time you receive this, the portions of lung I am forwarding will have come to your hand, and which I fear you will declare true cases. Each piece is from a separate animal, and these have arrived per the "Ontario," the vessel that brought the cattle you were in Liverpool about a short time since. In examining fifty-five lungs to-day twelve were found similarly affected (some a little more) to the specimens sent you. I should be glad if you will wire me by 10.30 a.m. to-morrow * * what your opinion is * * *

In haste, yours faithfully,
J. WELSBY.

These portions of lungs were shown me, and exhibited, as did the others, simply the lesions of bronchitis with collapse. On March 18, he writes: "I have not agreed with " the opinion expressed here about any of them, but am doubtful about a piece of the " last lot sent you. In London, they have *no doubt*." On March 24: "With regard " to the animals when living, I had opportunities of seeing them daily; they appeared " well; no cough; breathing and temperature normal, and eating well." On April 21: "No more specimens are wanted in *London*." On May 19: "Have sent to Professor " Walley also specimens from cattle received by steamship 'Minnesota'; he agrees " with us in this, but says that it was zymotic pleuro-pneumonia on 'Ontario.'" On June 7 he writes: "I am commencing to direct attention to the Canadian cattle instead " of Western States. Mr. Moore sent a piece of lung from a Canadian ox to London on " Thursday and informed me it was typical of contagious pleuro-pneumonia, and " expected Professor Duguid down, but instead, a telegram came, ordering their release " if no further disease was found; two others were then slaughtered, and I was requested " to be present; they were perfectly healthy. I was sorry that I could not send you " a piece of the lung that went to London, but no doubt shall have an opportunity of " doing so before long." Here I was given a piece of lung which certainly showed lesions resembling those of contagious pleuro-pneumonia more than did any other specimen that I saw in the Professor's possession; it was said to be from the Canadian case above referred to, but had been in spirits so long that a satisfactory examination could not be made. Professor Williams, however, declared that in his opinoin even it was not the disease, but that it looked more like it than did anything else he had seen from our side of the water.

In the new edition of his book on Veterinary Medicine Professor Williams has gone into the matter thoroughly, not only in the text, but by coloured lithographic plates which are said by all who saw the pieces of lung which were sent to Edinburgh to be remarkably like them. In the appendix the whole of this matter will be found reproduced.

I next saw Professor Walley, principal of the Edinburgh Veterinary College, who holds an appointment in Edinburgh under the Veterinary Privy Council, and was one of those who went to Liverpool and examined as an expert the lungs from some of the "Ontario" cattle. He said: "I was called to Liverpool, and there shown animals together " in a building which I was told came per steamship 'Ontario' from America; a few " of them were coughing, I should judge giving the pathognomonic cough of contagious " pleuro-pneumonia. I examined them; they gave no elevation of temperature that " amounted to anything as a sign, they varied a little; some would be a degree higher " than others, but nothing remarkable in any. While this examination was going on, " and before we had finished to my entire satisfaction, a man came to say that we were " wanted in the slaughter-house, where we went at once, and found two animals, that " we were told had been taken hap-hazard from this cargo of the 'Ontario,' hanging " partially dressed, and from these I saw lungs taken that exhibited to me, without " any doubt, the well-known lesions of contagious pleuro-pneumonia. I was not at " the place for more than an hour, and Professor McCall, principal of the Glasgow " Veterinary College, was the only veterinarian with me. Mr. Hall, the consignee, or " his agent was there, and said there was no doubt about this: 'that it really was pleuro.'" In answer to questions the Professor said the animals were in as good a condition as any of the others—*i.e.*, about half fat; that there were several diseased spots in their lungs, and that the largest was about the size of the crown of a Derby hat; that the diseased portions were "marbled," and the parenchyma varied in colour from deep red to pink, but it was mostly of a pinkish shade; that there was no attempt towards the formation of a cyst-wall around any of the diseased portions, because the disease had not been of sufficient standing.

Being asked if he did not think it strange that contagious pleuro-pneumonia should exist to so great an extent and the animal be as fat as any of the rest, and still have no elevation of temperature, and no encysted portion of lungs, he answered that he had had no opportunity of examining *these* animals before death as to temperature or anything else, and could give no idea as to how they looked when alive. He regretted that no one had saved a piece of these lungs—it ought to have been done. Since that, which was the only time he had been in Liverpool on this business, he had examined several *pieces* of lungs said to be from American cattle, and they had *not* exhibited to him lesions of contagious pleuro-pneumonia, but of broncho-pneumonia, and the coloured plate in Professor Williams's book was a fairly good representation of their appearance, but it did not represent *at all* the appearance of the lungs that he had examined in Liverpool said to be from the "Ontario" cargo. He was told that these two cattle that he saw in the Liverpool slaughter-house had been drafted at random from the cargo of the "Ontario" by Mr. Hall.

From Edinburgh I proceeded to London and the office of the Veterinary Department of the Privy Council. In the absence of Professor Brown, the chief of the department, I saw Mr. Cope, the chief inspector, who kindly showed me what specimens they had of "American pleuro." They were few in number, and very small in size, and had been in preservative fluid so long that they were very much altered. They were very different from those I had been shown in Edinburgh—said to be the same—(see p. 5, Mr. Wellsby's proceedings) having very much more the appearance of the contagious pleuro-pneumonia, of which the former showed *nothing*. "Animals affected with " pleuro-pneumonia," said Mr. Cope, "come to us from the ports of Baltimore, " Philadelphia, New York, Boston, and Portland, and we are now (July 12) receiving " more than ever of it. You can see it for yourself by going either to Deptford or " Liverpool, but Liverpool would be the best place." I was informed by this gentleman that formerly the Privy Council had power to release from the restriction a part of any country that they saw fit; but now it must be a whole country, if any, and that could not be until the whole of that country was absolutely free from disease. Anything else would need the action of Parliament. There is absolutely no option in the matter—the rule or law must govern. In answer to a question Mr. Cope said that they had never had a suspicion of Canadian cattle. Subsequently I was fortunate enough to see Professor Brown, veterinarian-in-chief to the department.

I asked him, supposing drafts of cattle were made from our healthy western districts, transported over lines of rail which were entirely away from our infected districts, in cars used for these and no other cattle, if inspectors could guarantee that they had not been in the same yard, or mixed with any other cattle on the route, or at the port of embarkation, and were healthy at time of shipment, and inspection at the port of debarkation should show that cargo after cargo coming under these regulations could be landed free from pleuro-pneumonia, would the embargo be raised in favour of cattle so inspected from such a port? To this Professor Brown answered that even if England were disposed to remove the restriction from any one port under certain methods of inspection, as he understood it, the United States were not, as matters now stood, able to prevent cattle coming to said port from any point that people chose to send them. I told him that I thought the matter could undoubtedly be arranged with the State authorities and railroad companies so as to be perfectly safe. He intimated that this would be too loose an arrangement to give England much confidence, and further said that he did not know what there was to prevent a diseased or infected animal from being sent at any time from the infected eastern district directly to the parts in the West from which these drafts were being made. The Government of the United States, as a government, had not as yet shown the slightest interest in the matter, and that, in the absence of any national laws relating to the movements of animal exposed to or infected with contagious diseases, he should not advise any change from their present methods. Here a representation was made setting forth the sovereignty of States and their powers—that a State could make any laws upon the subject that she thought proper, providing it did not conflict with the Constitution of the United States. In answer to this the opinion given was that decidedly, in this matter, these could not take the place of national laws; that it would be highly impracticable for Great Britain to recognise independent State governments while dealing with the United States.

Following is a list, which was kindly furnished me by the Veterinary Department, giving the cargoes of cattle among which pleuro-pneumonia had been detected, and which had

SECOND REPORT BY Dr. C. P. LYMAN.

arrived from our ports of Boston and Portland (thought to be free from disease) since January 1, 1880:

Date.	Steamer.	From	To	Number of Cases of Pleuro pneumonia.
January 11	Milanesian	Boston	London	12*
,, 16	Massachusetts	,,	Liverpool	9
February 4	Palestine	,,	,,	2
,, 7	Bavarian	,,	,,	3
,, 10	Lake Nepigon	Portland	,,	2
,, 12	Brazilian	Boston	,,	10
,, 12	Iowa	,,	,,	16
,, 17	Canopus	,,	,,	1
,, 20	Salerno	,,	Hull	2
,, 21	Bulgarian	,,	Liverpool	3
,, 26	Lake Winnipeg	Portland	,,	1
,, 27	Bohemian	Boston	,,	3
March 4	Massachusetts	,,	,,	7
,, 4	Illyrian	,,	,,	7
,, 20	Palestine	,,	,,	3
,, 24	Iowa	,,	,,	4
,, 27	Egypt	,, (?)	,,	1
,, 30	Glamorgan	,,	,,	3
April 18	Massachusetts	,,	,,	5
,, 30	Iberian	,,	,,	1
May 5	Lake Nepigon	Portland	London	1
,, 19	Bohemian	Boston	Liverpool	4
,, 20	Illyrian	,,	,,	13
June 2	Victoria	,,	,,	4

* Two died.

At Deptford, which is the foreign animals' wharf for London, I at this time saw some twenty-seven hundred head of American bullocks tied up waiting slaughter; they had been received mostly from New York, a few from Baltimore. From the ocean steamers these beasts are landed some distance down the river, and from there reshipped in a transport, which brings them directly to the landing-stages for this wharf. This transport boat is thoroughly disinfected after each cargo.

From London I proceeded to Liverpool, arriving there on the 13th of July. Cattle from the United States arriving in this port are allowed to land at three different places, namely, the Huskisson Branch Docks, No. 2, on the Liverpool side of the river, at Woodside and Wallasey landing-stages on the Birkenhead side, and at these places only. For their reception, and the accommodation of the trade, under the present restrictions, the dock company have fitted up on the wharves fine buildings to serve as stables for the cattle while alive, also slaughter-houses and cooling rooms.

The law allows the animal to remain alive not longer than 14 days after debarkation, during which time he must remain in this building, subject to a certain daily charge, payable to the dock company. After each cargo has been disposed of, the whole of the premises are most thoroughly cleaned before being again filled, and if any such contagious malady as foot-and-mouth disease has been found they are thoroughly disinfected, and if thought necessary all the manure and other litter with which they may have been in contact is destroyed, under the direction of the Veterinary Department, but at the expense of the dock company.

With the credentials furnished me from the Privy Council Office I called upon the Veterinary Inspector of the port, Mr. J. W. T. Moore, F.R.C.V.S., and requested to be allowed to accompany him for a time in his daily inspections. To this he kindly assented, and during the whole of my stay showed me every attention and rendered me every assistance within his power. His method of inspection is to make an examination of the live animals within as nearly as possible 12 hours after the landing of a cargo. For this purpose the beasts are driven into the stables and tied up facing a passage way. Down this the inspector passes, noticing carefully each beast. If anything unusual is observed in any one case, the animal is made the subject of a minute examination, when, if found particularly diseased, he is either put by himself or slaughtered at once. This examination being completed and the cargo "passed," the owners are at liberty to commence slaughtering as soon as they wish. In the slaughter-house the men have orders not to allow any lung or *portion* of it to be taken way until it has been inspected by Mr. Moore. For the purposes of this lung inspection this product of the whole day's killing is hung up, and once each day every slaughter-house where killing is going on is visited by the inspector, and every lung carefully examined by him. If any one is found which he considers exhibits the lesions of pleuro-pneumonia it is destroyed, and an inquiry made which soon shows beyond a doubt exactly to what cargo the affected animal belonged.

On July 14, 210 bullocks, the cargo of the steamship "Carolina," from Baltimore, were examined, and four of these were condemned by the inspector as being "suspicious" of pleuro-pneumonia. However, upon *post-mortem* examination, nothing of the sort was found.

On July 15, the steamship "Federico," from Norfolk, Virginia, landed 128 bullocks and a carcass. A *post-mortem* examination of this carcase showed that the animal had been trampled to death; seven of the ribs were broken. During the lung examination to-day two pairs were found that were condemned as showing the lesions of pleuro-pneumonia. One pair showed plainly and plentifully the peculiar lesions of tuberculosis, and in addition contained several small spots in which the changes supposed to be peculiar to pleuro-pneumonia could be plainly seem, and upon which they were condemned. The history of these animals, so far as it could be procured in Liverpool, was that Mr. Smith bought Mr. Roddick 194 bullocks, *ex* steamship "Brazilian," from Boston, July 7. These were consigned to the seller by J. and C. Coughlin, of London, Canada, but were from the United States; there were 200 of them; five died on the passage. The inspector here saw the lungs of some of these that were landed dead, and found death to have occurred from causes other than pleuro-pneumonia.

July 16.—A case of pleuro-pneumonia was reported by Mr. Moore as coming on the "Iberian" from Boston, but the lung lesion was so very small (scarcely as large as a filbert), and its appearance was such that it seemed to me very doubtful if even the semblance of the disease was present.

July 17.—Examined *ex* steamship "Malta," from Boston, 397 bullocks. Five were landed dead, and one was killed on landing. One of the five landed dead was so much decomposed as to prevent a satisfactory examination. The lungs of the other four were emphysematous only.

July 19.—Two lungs from beasts which came on the steamship "Victoria," from Boston, were reported as showing pleuro-pneumonia, the largest "spot" being about $1\frac{1}{4}$ inches in its largest diameter, and situated exactly at the root of the lung, indurated to the touch, and upon being cut into exhibited the usual "marbled" appearance of pleuro-pneumonia, but in the centre of the "spot" appeared a small, rounded body not larger than $\frac{1}{4}$ inch in diameter, the exact nature of which future microscopic examination will probably determine. This was surrounded by a layer scarcely a line wide of what seemed to the naked eye to be a thin pus of a grayish colour; this, in its turn, by a thin membranous wall; this, again, by the "marbled" appearance already referred to, the interlobular effusion and thickening being well marked. The lungs of one of these beasts had one, the other three, of these "spots." These animals were sent by Timothy Coughlin, London, Canada, but were animals from the United States.

July 20.—At Canada Docks were examined 222 cattle, *ex* steamship "Texas," from Montreal. One of these animals, a fat cow, was breathing rapidly and had a temperature of 104° Fahr. She was killed and the lungs examined, but no indication of pleuro-pneumonia was found. Inspector Moore assured me that he had repeatedly had this done, always with the same result.

July 23.—To-day was found a good specimen of what the port inspector regards as showing the lesions of pleuro-pneumonia in the lung of a beast from the cargo of the "Aleppo," from New York. These animals were shipped by Charles Kalm, of New York, and by their look did not seem to be "westerners."

I have thought best to make these few extracts from my diary, as they refer to all the cases that were condemned during my stay, and also as they help to show the manner in which the work is done. I have also prepared a table which will show the number of animals landed in Liverpool from the United States from the 2nd of July to the 13th of August, most of which I had the privilege of examining alive and dead during my stay. You will observe that the percentage reported by Mr. Moore as affected with pleuro-pneumonia is very small indeed, there being only six such out of 10,670 animals examined.

The animals coming from Canada are landed at wharves entirely separate from those used for the trade with the United States. The animals coming off shipboard are tied up in houses furnished for the purpose, and after a 12 hours' rest and quarantine are subjected to a not very close inspection by the veterinary officer of the port, when, if no contagious disease is found—and there never has been as yet—they are allowed to go inland on the hoof without any further restriction. In this way they become scattered to such an extent before being slaughtered that it was impossible for me to see the lungs as I

SECOND REPORT BY Dr. C. P. LYMAN.

did those of our own cattle; and, indeed, no officer gives them *any* examination except in so far as has already been stated.

TABLE showing NUMBER of ANIMALS LANDED in LIVERPOOL from the UNITED STATES, from JUNE 2nd to AUGUST 13th.

Steamship.	From Port of	Date landed.	Cattle.	Sheep.	Hogs.	Remarks.
Olympus	Boston	July 2	391	—	—	—
Saint Albans	New York	„ 9	392	239	—	—
Palmyra	„	„ 13	296	288	—	—
Bulgarian	Boston	„ 7	434	—	522	—
Carolina	Baltimore	„ 13	210	—	—	—
Iberian	Boston	„ 14	434	—	—	1 case condemned as pleuro-pneumonia; 6 very small centres of disease.
Brazilian	„	„ 7	569	1,314	—	2 cases condemned as pleuro-pneumonia; centres very small.
Federico	Norfolk	„ 14	129	—	—	—
Victoria	Boston	„ 15	597	—	—	2 cases condemned as pleuro-pneumonia; very small centres.
Cella	New York	„ 15	98	306	375	—
Malta	Boston	„ 16	398	—	—	—
Aleppo	New York	„ 18	282	719	—	1 case condemned as pleuro-pneumonia, and by far the best lesion found.
Massachusetts	Boston	„ 19	519	230	483	11 cases swine fever.
Minnesota	„	„ 21	416	860	—	—
Palestine	„	„ 26	366	815	—	—
Bavarian	„	„ 25	441	—	—	—
Pembroke	„	„ 28	294	561	287	7 cases swine fever.
Bohemian	„	„ 30	435	—	—	3 cases foot-and-mouth disease in cattle.
Tuscany	Philadelphia	„ 30	224	—	—	—
Illyrian	Boston	Aug. 1	437	—	—	—
Istrian	„	„ 5	438	—	—	—
Iowa	„	„ 5	805	—	207	13 cases resembling splenic apoplexy; 5 cases swine fever.
Enrique	Norfolk	„ 6	122	—	—	—
Gracia	Baltimore	„ 8	130	—	—	—
Canopus	Boston	„ 9	444	—	—	—
Bulgarian	„	„ 10	427	—	—	—
Brazilian	„	„ 13	660	618	363	10 cases sheep-scab.
Sicily	Philadelphia	„ 13	282	—	—	—

Total number of animals landed:
- Cattle - 10,670
- Sheep - 5,960
- Hogs - 2,237
- Number condemned as having pleuro-pneumonia - cattle - 6
- Number condemned as having foot-and-mouth disease - „ - 3
- Number condemned as having scab - sheep - 10
- Number condemned as having swine fever - hogs - 23

RÉSUMÉ.

About February 1, 1880, the Department of Agriculture, under the Act providing for an inquiry into the contagious diseases of domesticated animals, commenced an investigation, the result of which should declare, if possible, the *exact* extent of territory in which there existed any cattle affected with contagious pleuro-pneumonia, on account of which the Government of Great Britain has placed a restriction upon all cattle coming from the United States.

After due time and a thoroughly conducted investigation, this territory was defined to be one extending (at that time) from Fairfield County, in Connecticut, over New York City and portions of the State of New York lying just north of it; Brooklyn, Long Island, and parts of the island lying just east of it; Jersey City, and over a considerable portion of the State of New Jersey; Philadelphia, and some of the more south-easterly counties of Pennsylvania to Baltimore, and over portions of the more north-easterly counties of Maryland. Further than this, in any locality it was impossible to find a case of the disease, although efforts were made in all directions, and especially among the cattle coming from the same parts of the West as did most of the cattle going to Europe.

Reports were constantly being received, however, from England that cattle affected with pleuro-pneumonia were being frequently landed there. A very short investigation on this side demonstrated clearly that these animals came directly, in nearly all cases, from the West, and oftentimes over lines of rail that were entirely away from any point at which the disease could be located. The next step, therefore, seemed to be to carry the investigation to the other side, to see the diseased cattle as landed there, and by means of manifests, way-bills, &c., to trace them back to their original starting points in the West, and thus establish the object of the investigation, namely, to find *all* the infected territory.

This was done, and out of nearly 11,000 beasts landed and examined in Liverpool during parts of July and August, in no one of which could pleuro-pneumonia be detected in the *living* animal, the inspector of the Veterinary Department of the Privy Council condemned, after *post-mortem* examination of the lungs, six cases. These six cases have been traced back, and in all except one it has been found that the animals undoubtedly came from the West, and over lines of rail which are entirely north of any localities that are known to be contaminated, the fact being that a part of their journey eastward was generally made through portions of Canada. This of course means that we have this dreaded cattle scourge established among our western herds; that Chicago, Buffalo, Albany, Boston, or Portland are diseased centres, or else the disease is not pleuro-pneumonia at all.

If pleuro-pneumonia exists in the West, or there are diseased centres in or about the points named through which the cattle pass on their journey eastward, the information now in possession of this department will insure its exact location after a little further time for examination.

In relation to the last phase of the matter, all that can at present be said is, that the particular lungs exhibited present *in their fresh state* and to the naked eye, ALL the lesions of the contagious disease, but on a VERY SMALL SCALE, and in addition there is another lesion that is *constantly* present in these condemned lungs which has never been described by any authority or noticed by any of our veterinarians to be a constant or even a known accompaniment of the disease in question. What bearing this fact may have upon this part of the question a further and more minute investigation of the subject alone can decide. Professor William Williams, of Edinburgh, a comparative pathologist of world-wide celebrity, asserts that the lungs examined by him previous to my visit did not show the lesions of the disease, but that the changes noticed were caused by bronchitis.

Whether these cases are or are not due to true contagious pleuro-pneumonia is a matter which does not in the mean time have much bearing upon the question of the removal of the English embargo upon our cattle. While we have pleuro-pneumonia in *any* part of our country, and certainly while we have no national legislation looking in any way towards restricting its spread, and its eventual total suppression, just so long the embargo must and will continue to operate against one of our best commercial interests, and to lay that portion of our agriculturists in the West who are engaged in the raising and feeding of fine beef bullocks under a very severe and unmerited tax, one which, in the estimation of a very good judge of the matter, has reached, during the present year, a sum rising $2,250,000. What are the actual losses sustained from the presence of the disease, by the farmers and dairymen of the East who are unfortunate enough to be located in the midst of a contaminated centre, it is very hard to say; but that the annual losses by death alone can be no very light tax to them is a safe conclusion.

Then, again, while it is still possible to exterminate this ruinous foreign plague, because it is, we most certainly believe, confined to animals that are kept upon fenced farms, should it *once*, by any misfortune, be carried among the great herds that breed, grow, and feed upon the unfenced ranges of the West, its extirpation would become IMPOSSIBLE. The whole Western country, from Texas northward, would become infected; notwithstanding all efforts that *then* might be made to remedy the evil, this great and growing national interest would be perpetually mortgaged, and there would be an almost incalculable annual loss from deaths alone.

The one remedy *now* for all of this is plain, and of comparatively easy accomplishment, viz.: Let Congress enact such measures, and authorise such an execution of them, as shall immediately restrict the movements of cattle out from and within infected districts, and in time eradicate every case of lung plague.

SOUTHERN CATTLE FEVER.

This disease, widely known as "the Texas cattle fever," although it has never as yet reached Great Britain, and, therefore, has never been put upon the schedule as one of the contagious diseases coming from the United States, and requiring restriction, is one that, for a short time in each year, causes such immense losses among the animals belonging to Western, Northern, and Eastern cattle-growers, dealers, and shippers, that its mention in connexion with this report seems to be quite in place.

Beginning, generally, towards the last of July, and extending with increasing destructiveness, until the time of frost, Western and Northern cattle that have been in contact, in certain ways with some of the cattle coming from several of the more southerly portions of the country (these seeming perhaps to be in perfect health), contract this fever, which to them is much more fatal than it seems to be among the Southern animals, often killing a proportion as high as 90 per cent. of those affected.

A very curious, but still undoubtedly true, feature of the malady is, that these sick Northern animals are not able in any way to communicate the disease to other animals. Its incubation may be from 15 to 40 days. During this period the beast may be shipped from the West, and slaughtered in the East for human food; or it may be placed on board ship and started for the English market, where it is destined seldom, if ever, to arrive, for dying in mid-ocean its carcass is thrown overboard and becomes a total loss to the owner or those insuring its safe arrival.

Heavy losses from this cause are also sustained each season by the farmers and dealers in all parts of the North, West, and East; but, perhaps, the greatest sufferers of all are the breeders and growers of cattle who are so unfortunate as to be located in the States through which the Texans pass on their journey to market, and the States suffering more particularly in this way this past season have undoubtedly been Missouri and Illinois, although nearly every other State into which the Texans were shipped, from Kansas to Massachusetts, have suffered to a greater or less extent.

How these losses in connexion with the foreign trade occur and how they are divided up can readily be seen from the following:—

In June 10,642 animals were shipped to Liverpool; 114 died—loss about 1 per cent.

In July 12,137 animals were shipped to Liverpool; 110 died—loss less than 1 per cent.

In August 9,464 animals were shipped to Liverpool; 272 died—loss over 2 pe cent.

In September 10,826 animals were shipped to Liverpool; 619 died—loss over 5 per cent.

This shows a loss in September over June of, say, $67,662.50, which excess of loss is considered by the insurance people to be due entirely to Texas fever, and to verify this we have the following quotations of the rates of Insurance:—

In August, 1880, the Canadian and English companies charged $2\frac{1}{4}$ to $2\frac{1}{2}$ per cent from Montreal. At the same time the rates on American cattle from Boston were from 3 to 6 per cent., the highest rates obtaining against Missouri and Illinois beasts.

During September the Canadian and English rates were $2\frac{3}{4}$ to 3 per cent. from Montreal. The rates on American cattle during the first half of this same month were 5 to 7 per cent.; during the second half, from $5\frac{1}{2}$ to 10 per cent.; that is Ohio cattle could be insured at from 5 to $6\frac{1}{2}$ per cent., Missouri from $6\frac{1}{2}$ to 10 per cent. These differences in insurance make a total on a cargo of, say, 300 beasts, of $2,635 against Missouri, $1,312 against Ohio, as the *extreme* Canadian cost of such insurance is but $1,125. This, on the September shipment to Liverpool alone, gives a loss of from $45,000 to $85,000, which loss, in the end, comes probably out of the agriculturists.

Of course these "rates" are based upon the actual results of experience. This being so, the question at once suggests itself, what is the cause for this great *difference* of experience between Boston and Montreal? To this the unqualified answer is that it is due to a properly maintained veterinary inspection carried on systematically under proper laws and upheld by the Canadian Government while we have nothing of the sort. To substantiate this it will perhaps be well to quote here from a letter recently received from Messrs. Endicott and Macomber, insurance agents, of Boston, Massachusetts, who have this year employed an inspector, and who would accept no "risks" on cattle unless they had been "passed" by this examiner. On October 27, 1880, they write "We have made this list of ours to include the whole sickly season. It shows a loss of $1\frac{1}{4}$ per cent., and would show much less had we not taken a small line on Brazilian, which ran into a gale on first day out. The loss on uninspected cattle during the same time has been upward of 6 per cent." When it is remembered that this inspection is only undertaken during the "sickly season," and to prevent the ill results arising from Texas fever alone the facts are full of significance.

As affecting the breeders of Missouri and Illinois, it may be said that in Boston, October 5, 1880, cattle for shipment were selling at the following prices: Ohio cattle, among which there is considered to be no risk of Texan contamination, 6 cents to

6¼ cents; Illinois steers, 5¾ cents; Missouri steers, 5½ cents. That is, the Missouri farmer, besides having to pay more freight, loses about $15 per head on his steers, and he has to stand not only this severe loss, but in addition, during these months, the constant risk of having his herd contaminated, which invariably results in a heavy death loss.

The absolute remedy for this is plain, and in view of the facts as related, suggests itself, viz.: let there be enacted proper laws, with a provision for their proper execution by properly qualified persons, which can be done without injustice to the Southern breeders, and the Western, Northern, and the Eastern breeders, traders, and shippers will be protected from this source of danger to the very large commercial interests which they together represent.

Foot-and-Mouth Disease.

Has been landed in Great Britain in several instances among cargoes of sheep, and once in a cargo of bullocks from the United States. This is a scheduled contagious disease, and our animals are now under restrictions because of it, which, of course, as long as the contagious pleuro-pneumonia restriction remains, does not really make any difference, and probably any measure that will provide for a *properly conducted* inspection of our cattle previous to shipment will prevent further trouble from this cause.

Sheep Scab.

Has also been landed from the United States. A proper inspection before shipment will stop this, and thus prevent future trouble.

Swine Fever.

Hogs arriving from the United States are restricted on account of this disease. To devise a perfect method for preventing this needs further time and consideration.

Very respectfully,
Hon. Wm. G. Le Duc,   CHARLES P. LYMAN, F.R.C.V.S.
   Commissioner of Agriculture.

No. 51.

Third Report by Dr. CHARLES P. LYMAN, F.R.C.V.S., to the COMMISSIONER OF AGRICULTURE, Washington.

Sir,

Although my recent examination of American cattle, as landed and slaughtered in England, had for its chief object the detection of the contagious pleuro-pneumonia so frequently reported by the English governmental authorities as existing among them, and the subsequent location, as nearly as possible, in the United States of the herds from which these animals had been taken, I made my last report to you upon this subject before having had sufficient opportunity to examine as thoroughly as seemed to me desirable, the details connected with this direct investigation, because I considered that, incidentally, matters of the greatest importance connected with our cattle export trade had come to my knowledge, and that under the circumstances it was very important that these facts should come to the knowledge of Congress early in the session, so that, if they deemed them of as much importance as they seemed to me, they might have time to take such action as they deemed necessary.

Therefore the second report was made, and I was obliged to content myself, at that time, with the statement that if pleuro-pneumonia existed in the West, or if there were diseased cattle in or about the points through which the animals passed on their journey eastward, the information already possessed would, after a little further time, insure its location. That time I have now had, and in this report I intend to discuss simply the facts bearing upon these two points of the inquiry. First, by tracing back the condemned animals, so far as I have been able, from England to the States wherein they were raised, and to show what likelihood there is that contagious pleuro-pneumonia exists in any of these States. Second, by submitting to you the report of Dr. W. F. Whitney, the microscopist, whose services were engaged for the special purpose of examining the diseased portions of lung brought home by me from Liverpool; and, third, by discussing, in addition to this, which may be called the direct testimony in the case, the circumstances connected with the marketing, transporting by rail, and shipping of cattle through our uninfected districts and ports to England, *i.e.*, that part of the matter which may be called the indirect testimony, or in reality a putting together of *facts* connected with this shipping business, and drawing from them what seems to me to be reasonable deductions.

The lungs condemned in my presence were six in number, and were from animals coming from Boston to Liverpool in the following named steamers, and in the numbers given: "Iberian," one; "Victoria," two; "Brazilian," two; and from New York to Liverpool in the steamer "Aleppo," one.

The history of these animals, as I have been able to learn, is as follows: Mr. Smith, butcher, bought of Mr. George Roddick, cattle salesman, at Liverpool, 194 bullocks from the cargo of the steamer "Brazilian," landed at Birkenhead, July 7, 1880. These animals were consigned to the salesman by Messrs. J. and C. Coughlin, of London, Ontario, Canada, who bought them in Boston, to which place they had been shipped direct from the Chicago market *viâ* the Grand Trunk Railway of Canada to Buffalo, thence *viâ* the New York Central to Albany, thence *viâ* the Boston and Albany to Boston. The lot consisted of steers from the States of *Missouri, Iowa,* and *Illinois*.

Mr. Alfred Dawson, butcher, bought of Mr. George Roddick, cattle salesman, at Liverpool, several bullocks from the cargo of the steamer "Victoria," landed at Birkenhead, July 15. These animals were consigned to the salesman by Mr. Timothy Coughlin, London, Canada, who bought them in Boston, to which place they had been shipped direct from the Chicago market *viâ* the Grand Trunk Railway of Canada to Buffalo, thence *viâ* the New York Central to Albany, thence *viâ* the Boston and Albany to Boston. This lot, as in the last case, consisted of steers from *Missouri, Iowa,* and *Illinois*.

Since leaving Liverpool, I am advised that up to the 21st of November, seven more animals were condemned, as follows: On September 5, from the cargo of the steamer "Palestine," three animals. These were from a lot consigned to Messrs. Utley and Sons, of Liverpool, by Messrs. T. and F. Utley, of Boston; 44 of them were *Missouri*, and 100 *Iowa* animals. They were bought in the Chicago market and came to Boston *viâ* Buffalo and Albany over the Grand Trunk, New York Central, and Fitchburg railroads.

On November 9, from the cargo of the steamer "Victoria," one animal. This was from a lot consigned to Mr. Ramsden, cattle salesman, Liverpool, by Messrs. Wales and McLeavitt, of Boston, all of them being *Illinois* steers, bought in Chicago market and shipped to Boston over the Michigan Central, Grand Trunk, Vermont Central, and Fitchburg railroads.

On November 18, from the cargo of the steamer "Bohemian," one animal. This was from a lot consigned to Mr. Hewlett, cattle salesman, Liverpool, by Mr. William Hawksworth, Brighton, Mass. They were *Illinois* steers, one half purchased in Albany, coming to Boston *viâ* Boston and Albany railroad. They had been brought to Albany from Chicago over the Lake Shore and Michigan Southern route. The other half were bought in Brighton market, Boston, and had been brought from Chicago *viâ* Grand Trunk, New York Central, and Fitchburg railroads.

On November 18, from the cargo of the steamer "Brazilian," one animal. This was from a lot consigned to Mr. William Carroll, Liverpool, by Messrs. Hathaway and Jackson, of Boston, and were all *Ohio* cattle, bought especially for this shipment in that State, and were shipped *viâ* Buffalo, and from there over the New York Central to Albany, thence over the Fitchburg railroad to Boston.

On November 21, from the cargo of the steamer "Iowa," one animal. This was from a lot consigned to Messrs. Utley and Sons, Liverpool, by Messrs. T. and F. Utley, of Boston. Fifteen or twenty of them were *Ohio* cattle, and came direct from London, Ohio, by way of Buffalo, Albany, and Fitchburg, to Boston. The remainder were *Missouri* and *Illinois* steers, and came from Chicago by Grand Trunk road.

With one exception this traces, I believe, all the condemned animals that have arrived at Liverpool from Boston from July 7 to November 21, 1880. (The one not traced was from the cargo of the steamer "Iberian," landed July 14; the reason for this will be described further on in this report.) From it will be seen that the native States of the condemned animals are Missouri, Iowa, Illinois, and Ohio; that the only markets through which they have passed are Chicago, Buffalo, Albany, and Boston; that the lines of rail that have been used are the Lake Shore and Michigan Southern, Michigan Central, Grand Trunk line of Canada, New York Central, Vermont Central, Boston and Albany, and the Fitchburg, or, as it is sometimes called, the Hoosac Tunnel route.

Cattle from the United States, upon being landed in Liverpool or at Birkenhead, are driven into stables erected for the purpose upon the wharves upon which they are landed, and are tied up in rows facing each other between which there is a passage way. After they have remained here, resting and feeding for at least 12 hours, they are examined by the veterinary inspector of the port, and after they have passed this examination, the salesman to whom they are consigned is at liberty to sell them, and the butcher who buys them to drive them into the shambles, also situated upon the same wharf, where they are killed under the restriction that all *lungs* must be laid aside until they have been examined by the inspector, when those not condemned may be disposed of in any way that the owner sees fit. This examination is made by clasping, one at a time, the lungs between both hands, and in this position passing them over their entire surface, when, if anything peculiar is *felt*, it is cut down upon and examined. In this way the slightest variation from the normal becomes at once apparent; in fact, it is surprising how quickly the smallest change in them may be located. In this connexion I also wish to have the fact borne in mind that in no one of these cases condemned in my presence did the inspector discover the disease before the animal was killed, although every animal was closely inspected in the way described, and in no one case was there any appearance about any one of these condemned animals that caused the slightest question to be raised as to his healthfulness, notwithstanding he had but very recently passed the scrutiny both of the port inspector and the butcher who had bought him; nor was there one of them that was not fully up to the average of his fellows in flesh.

The microscopic appearances of these six lungs in their fresh state were as follows:—

"*Brazilian*" No. 1.—This lung contained, in about its centre, a large hardened object that could be both seen and felt, and would measure, perhaps, about 6 inches through its largest diameter. This, upon being cut into, appeared to be an abscess containing nothing but a pure, rather thick, creamy pus, and, although any portion of dead tissue that might be contained within this cavity was thoroughly searched for, nothing of the sort could be found. The cavity was surrounded by what seemed to be a rather thick cartilaginous wall, this again by a considerable amount of "marbled" tissue in which the parenchymæ was of an even pinkish colour, with the interlobular thickening well marked, white, hard, and firm. This, in its turn, passed almost imperceptibly, the parenchymæ becoming gradually more and more areable, and the interlobular thickening growing narrower and narrower into the healthy lung tissue surrounding the whole.

"*Brazilian*" No. 2.—This lung, with its fellow, upon its surface presented to the eye no indication of disease, but upon being handled in the way described above, several small nodules within its substance at once became apparent; these, upon being cut down upon, in the one lung disclosed the unmistakable lesions of tuberculosis, and in the other, where these indurations felt were much fewer and smaller, the nodules showed the peculiar lesions upon which it was condemned. There were several small nodules situated in the periphery of the extreme posterior portion of the large lobe of the right lung, the larger of which was about ½ inch in diameter; in its centre there appeared to be a cheesy deposit; this was surrounded by a very thin layer of a thin greyish coloured pus; outside this a very thin membrane; outside this again, a very limited amount of marbled tissue which, near the centre, was well marked, but more indistinct toward its outer margin. Of these nodules there were some four or five perfectly isolated from one another, but all being, to the unaided eye, of the same description.

"*Victoria*" lungs.—There were two pairs of these, condemned from the same lot at the same examination. One lung showed one and the other three indurated spots upon which the lungs were condemned. The largest of these "spots" was about the size of an English walnut, and was situated exactly at the root of the lung; the remaining three were situated in various isolated positions in the substance of the lung. Upon being cut down upon they all exhibited the same general appearance as those of the Brazilian No. 2 lung already described, except that in the case of the largest specimen there was a fair amount of sub-plural thickening, although there had been no adhesion between these surfaces. Of this portion of lung Dr. Whitney says: "The size and appearance of the "diseased portion after a clean cut had been made through it is represented on Plate IV.* "The disease involves about one-half dozen lobules, representing about 50 to 75 cubic "centimeters in bulk (Plate IV. *a*). These are quite homogeneous in appearance, and "within them are seen one are two small irregularly rounded cavities containing a cheesy "material. The interlobular tissue between them and the more healthy portion of the "lung (Plate IV. int. tis.) is very thick and dense." In its fresh state this cheesy

---

* The plates referred to in the Report are not printed in this Return.

deposit was surrounded by a thin layer of what appeared to be a thin greyish pus; this again by a thin membraneous wall, this by the "marbled" tissue, limited in extent, and surrounded on three sides by healthy tissue.

"*Aleppo*" *lung.*—The lung from which this specimen was taken was from a bullock, killed in Liverpool, July 23, and which the inspector said he considered a fine specimen of contagious pleuro-pneumonia, and, as will be seen by reference to Plate VII., which is copied from a painting made by a leading firm of photographers in Liverpool, from the lung itself, on the same day upon which it was taken from the animal, and is a most perfect representation of its appearance, has very much the look of that disease; indeed so close is its resemblance that no one would be warranted in saying that it was not it until a most thorough examination had been made of the specimen.

Plate VII*a*. represents the point at which adhesion had taken place between the two pleural surfaces, and at which, upon being broken down by the fingers, there was left a small rounded eminence of loosely formed connective tissue *b*, the diseased nodule showing the discoloured lobules and the greatly thickened interlobular tissue; *c, c*, healthy lung tissue.

After getting this portion of lung to Boston, another cut was made into the nodule parallel to the first, and at a point directly through the centre at *a*. The surface thus exposed had a very different appearance. At about the centre of the nodule was a small irregularly shaped cavity surrounded by a mass of material having a greyish cheesy look; in fact giving precisely the appearance noticed in all of the specimens except the Brazilian No. 1.

Iberian.—This specimen was not retained by me, nor were any inquiries made about it that would enable me afterwards to trace the animal in the United States, because at the time it was discovered by Mr. Moore, the inspector, and shown to me, I did not think that there was the slightest indication of pleuro-pneumonia about it, and so told Mr. Moore, who, I thought, agreed with me at the time, and so the lung was not retained. Two days afterwards, however, I found, much to my surprise, that it had been condemned and reported to the London authorities as having been a case of pleuro-pneumonia. My recollection of its appearance is that it contained seven or eight nodules isolated from one another, consisting of a small cheesy deposit no larger than a pea, surrounded by a thin membrane, and showed *no* marbled tissue whatever.

In addition to this description I may say that every specimen described in this report was seen and examined by Inspector Professor Duguid, of the London office, and pronounced by him to be undoubtedly pleuro-pneumonia. Also that each and every one of them were shown in August last to Professor Williams, who declared that, in his opinion, none of them were pleuro-pneumonia unless it was the "Aleppo" specimen, upon which he would give no opinion without a chance for a more minute examination of it.

Microscopic Examination.

All of the specimens of lungs which I have endeavoured to describe were given by me to Dr. W. F. Whitney, of Boston, Mass., curator of the Warren Anatomical Museum, and assistant in Pathological Anatomy in the Medical Department of Harvard University, who made a most thorough microscopical examination of them, and whose report upon the subject I have the honour to herewith submit:

Dear Sir,   Boston, Mass., December 30, 1880.

At your request I have examined the portions of lungs coming from American cattle killed in Liverpool, said to be affected with contagious pleuro-pneumonia.

From a careful study of those specimens in comparison with others obtained from an unquestionable case of that disease, and from the description of its characteristics as given by Williams, Yeo, Roy, and others, it appears that the changes seen in those specimens are caused by *chronic inflammatory processes, especially of the interstitial tissue, in some cases combined with miliary tuberculosis which, reasoning from analogous processes found in the human lung, are not contagious.*

In proof of the above statement I send your herewith the preparations upon which it is based, with drawings, and in explanation of them will call your attention, first, to the relations of the healthy lung, then to the changes seen in a lung affected with contagious pleuro-pneumonia, and, finally, to the manner in which the changes seen in the specimens sent for examination differ from those of that disease.

The lungs of cattle differ from those of man, in that each lobe is distinctly sub-divided into numerous lobules (each occupying the space of from 10 to 30 cubic centimeters) joined to each other by fine bands of connective tissue, which also forms the walls of extensive lymph spaces, connecting on the one hand with those lying in the pleura, and on the other with the lymph canals, which nearly surround the blood-vessels accompanying the bronchus into the lung tissue. These relations are shown in the preparation marked " normal lung of bullock, lymph spaces injected with blue," and from which Plate I. has been drawn. Fig. 1 represents a section through the whole of one and part of an adjoining lobule with the uniting bands of connective tissue inclosing lymph spaces. The extreme

B 679.

thinness of this band is especially to be noticed. The walls of the alveoli, which form the lung tissue proper (Fig. 1, lung tis.), are fine, and have a slightly wavy crinkled outline, and in them are a few scattered lymph and epithelioid cells. One or more small bronchi are usually to be found in each lobule. A more highly magnified view of one of these is represented in Fig. 2. In this can be distinguished three coats, a mucous or inner coat, a muscular or middle coat, and an external coat. The mucous coat (Fig. 2, muc. ct.) is formed by a layer of columnar epithelium, its inner surface resting upon a narrow zone of connective tissue (sub-mucous coat) which is thrown into folds when the bronchus is contracted. The muscular coat (Fig. 2, mus. ct.) is composed of unstripped fibres arranged concentrically. Outside of this is the external coat, composed, for the greater part, of a collection of round cells, probably of a lymphoid character, separating it from the accompanying artery and vein (Fig. 2, art. and v.), which are almost surrounded (in some places entirely so) by the lymph canals (Fig. 2, lym. sp. c.).

In the diseased lungs the changes occuring in the connective tissue, including the lymph spaces in the alveoli with their walls, and in the bronchi will be considered and compared with each other.

Contagious Pleuro-pneumonia.

Contagious pleuro-pneumonia presents three stages (designated as A, B, and C), dependent upon the degree to which these tissues are affected.

In the earliest or stage A (see preparation marked contagious pleuro-pneumonia, stage A, from which Plate II. has been drawn) the most marked changes are in the lymph spaces. Those in the pleura are in a great measure obliterated by the growing together of its two layers, and such as remain (Plate II. lym. sp. A) are filled with young round cells, leaving only a narrow passage close to the wall. The interlobular spaces (Plate II. lym. sp. B), are filled with a semi-gelatinous fluid, which in hardened specimens becomes coarsely fibrilated and in which are a few scattered round (lymphoid) cells. The bands of connective tissue forming the walls of the lymph spaces are but slightly thickened. In the lymph canals about the versels are a few clumps of lymph cells. The opening of the canal is in general free (Plate II., Figs. 1 and 2 lym. sp. c.)

The walls of the alveoli have no longer a crinkly outline, but a slightly stiff appearance, giving the alveoli a much rounder look. This is partly due to an engorgement of the vessels and partly to an increase of lymph and epithelioid cells in and upon the walls (Plate II., Fig. 1, lung. tis.).

In the small bronchi the changes are confined to the mucous coat (Plate II., muc. ct.), which is thickened from a proliferation of the epithelium, the cells next the free surface having a tendency to degeneration as shown by a slight detritus.

In the second stage (see preparation contagious pleuro-pneumonia, stage B) the exudation in the interlobular lymph spaces is firmer and there are a greater number of cells. The walls of the spaces are but little changed from the preceding stage. The canals about the vessels are more extensively filled with cells, and here and there a vessel is plugged.

Most of the alveoli are filled with an exudation, in places resembling that in the interlobular lymph spaces in stage A, and similar to that found in cropus pneumonia of the human lung, in places consisting entirely of lymph and epithelioid cells. The contents of certain of the alveoli take colouring matter badly, showing that a degeneration has taken place in the cells.

The mucous membrane of the bronchus is much thickened, and in the opening of the tube is to be seen detritus of exfoliated and degenerated epithelium.

In the third stage (see preparation marked contagious pleuro-pneumonia, stage C, and from which Plate II. has been drawn) the interlobular exudation is a little firmer and more fibrillated, the original walls of the lymph spaces are still to be distinguished as moderately thickened bands (see Plate III., Fig. 1, lym. sp. B). The canals about the vessels (Fig. 1, lym. sp. C) are completely filled with lymphoid cell, the vessels are usually plugged, and a more or less extensive hemorrhage may take place into the surrounding tissue (see Fig. 1, art).

The alveoli are filled with lymph and epithelioid cells, in many cases degenerated and retracted from the walls into little granular clumps. The walls themselves are much thickened in some places from an hypertrophy of the fibres of unstripped muscular tissue, which is normally present in small amount, especially at the place where the bronchus passes into the alveoli (see Fig. 2, mus. hyp.)

The bronchi in this stage are only distinguished with difficulty, and the explanation lies in the fact that the mucous membrane has become entirely degenerated and cast off from the walls (see Fig. 1, br. muc. ct.), the cells reduced to a detritus which, together with lymph and blood cells, completely occlude the opening, leaving no characteristics by which to distinguish it from any other plugged vessel.

Upon grouping together the appearances as presented in the different stages, it is manifest that the lymph spaces are at first filled with a coagulable material, and the increased density of this in the later stages of the disease are due to an increase in the number of cell elements and not to a material increase in the thickness of the walls of the spaces. With the increasing firmness of this exudation the alveoli are filled with cells and exuded material, as are also the lymph canals about the vessels; and when this has reached a marked degree, the mucous coat of the bronchus, which in the earlier stages of the disease has taken part by a proliferation of its epithelium, is cast off and the tube is filled with its detritus and an exudation similar to that in the neighbouring lymph canals. The muscular coat of the bronchus resists longer and can be clearly distinguished after the mucous coat is destroyed. With this filling of the lymph canals the vessels are occluded and hemorrhage may take place into the surrounding tissue.

Diseased Lungs from Liverpool.

The one first examined was marked "Steamer 'Victoria,' from Boston, July 19, 1880, Liverpool," and will be referred to as the "Victoria" lung.

The size and appearance of the diseased portion after a clean cut had been made through it, is represented in Plate IV. The disease involves about one-half a dozen lobules, representing about

50-75 C. C. in bulk (Plate IV. A). These are quite homogeneous in appearance, and within them are seen one or two small, irregularly rounded cavities, containing a cheesy material. The interlobular tissue between them and the more healthy portion of the lung (Plate IV., B.) is very thick and dense (Plate IV., int. tis.)

The whole has a resemblance to contagious pleuro-pneumonia in that the lobules and interlobular tissue are involved, but differs in the small amount of tissue implicated when considered in relation to the *degree to which* the interlobular tissue is affected. What the cause of these changes is, will be understood from the preparation marked S.S. "Victoria," &c., and from which Plate V. has been made.

Looking first at the interlobular spaces it will be seen that there is no longer any trace of the lymph spaces, but that the lobes are joined by a firm band of connective tissue, rich in young cells. (Plate V., int. tis.) The earlier stages of this are seen in that part of the preparation which shows no changes to the unaided eye (this is not shown in the drawing), and there it appears that this tissue results from a thickening of the walls of the lymph spaces. Later, when this has become dense, an accumulation of cells takes place in the contracted spaces and the whole becomes fused into the firm mass shown in the drawing.

From the action of this connective tissue the alveoli are compressed, and the walls are slightly thickened from the presence in them of large numbers of young cells. There is but little tendency, however, to exudation or accumulation of cells within the alveoli.

The greatest changes within the lobules are seen about the bronchi and their accompanying vessels. It will be remembered that there is normally a narrow zone of connective tissue, rich in cells surrounding the bronchus and separating it from the adjacent vessels. These cells have proliferated to such an extent as to form a wide band about the bronchus, involving the blood-vessels, which are, however, still pervious, but compressing the lymph canals to such an extent that their presence is with difficulty made out. The coats of the bronchi are also affected, but in the reverse order from what they are in contagious pleuro-pneumonia, viz., the muscular coat has almost disappeared (see Plate V., mus. ct.), while the mucous coat (see Plate V., muc. ct.) remains quite distinct, and the opening of the bronchus (contrary to the case in pleuro-pneumonia, when the cellular exudation is as extensive as here) is patent and even slightly dilated (condition known as bronchiectasis). This proliferation about the bronchi (known under the name of peribronchitis) may become degenerated finally, and thus give rise to the small cavities filled with cheesy detritus noted in the description of the specimen (Plate IV., A.).

The commencement of such a degeneration may account for the appearance seen in the middle lobule of the preparation (see also Plate V., tbl.), or it may be due to a secondary tuberculosis.

The whole process can be classified as one of chronic interstitial pneumonia, with peribronchitis and bronchiectasis with the formation of cavities.

Steamship "Brazilian," from Boston.

The next two specimens examined were both marked S.S. "Brazilian," from Boston, and will be described as "Brazilian" lung No. 1 and No. 2.

"*Brazilian" Lung No.* 1 consisted of several pieces forming part of the wall of a large abscess. The side of the specimen which lay next to the cavity of the abscess was quite smooth, and the tissue immediately adjoining was firm, dense, and quite homogeneous, so that the outline of the lobules could only be made out with difficulty. This very dense portion extended for about 1–2^{cm}, when the tissue began to assume more the appearance of normal lung; only that between the lobules were firm bands connecting directly with the dense tissue near the edge.

Two preparations were made from this, one from the dense portion and the other from the more healthy looking part.

Upon examining the former (see preparation marked S.S. "Brazilian" No. 1, near abscess wall, and from which Plate VI. has been drawn) it will be seen that the great increase in density is principally due to an increased thickening of the interlobular tissue (see Plate VI., int. tis.), and upon comparing this with the preparation made from the more healthy portion (see preparation marked S.S. "Brazilian," recent disease), it will be found that this increase is due, as in the case of the "Victoria" lung, to a thickening of the walls of the lymph spaces rather than to an organisation of a material filling the lymph spaces.

In the thick bands of connective tissue traces of small vessels are seen, showing that the process has been of long duration. The bronchi lying in their midst are still open and to be distinguished by their epithelial lining, but their muscular coat has almost disappeared.

In the recent preparation the alveoli show simply the results of compression, with an increase of round cells in their walls. Near the abscess wall the lobule is quite solidified, but this is due not to an exudation into the alveoli, but to the effects of the compression of the connective tissue and to a thickening of the walls by a round cell infiltration. Scattered throughout the alveoli lobules, replacing one or two alveoli, in the walls of the smaller bronchi and in the bands of new formed connective tissue are small circular collections of round cells, having a tendency to degeneration with a sharp line between them and the surrounding tissue (see Plate VI., tbl.); these are probably minute points of chronic purulent inflammation, but may belong to the class of tubercles, although only about half the size of those bodies and lacking in giant cells and stroma.

The changes found in this lung are those of chronic induration, which are entirely explained by the proximity to the large suppurating cavity, and have nothing in them indicative of what may have been the cause of it.

"*Brazilian" Lung No.* 2.—In the second specimen from the "Brazilian" there were two nodules from different parts of the lung, showing different stages of disease, the one more advanced than the other.

In both of these nodules there were only a few lobules which presented any changes from the normal, and in the more recent specimen it was only in a single lobule that these changes reached a marked degree.

In this the lobule, which was the centre of the disease, was quite homogeneous, except in the middle, where a portion of the tissue was separated from the rest by a distinct line of irregularly indented outline. In this portion were numerous small losses of substance, giving to the whole a slightly necrosed look. This central lobule was separated from the adjoining ones by a firm, broad band of tissue, while in the more remote interlobular spaces the walls of the lymph spaces were seen to be thickened and lying in the spaces thus reduced in diameter by this thickening of the walls, were firm, fibrous-looking masses, which were only slightly adherent to the walls, and could in consequence be withdrawn intact. In contagious pleuro-pneumonia, it will be remembered, the substance filling the interlobular spaces is perfectly continuous from side to side, and cannot thus be withdrawn.

From this specimen three preparations were made, two from the recent nodule, and one from the more advanced.

The first of these (see preparation marked S.S. "Brazilian" No. 2 (A.) Recent disease) was taken from the recent nodule in the tissue from the neighbourhood of the central diseased lobule, and presented to the eye only a thickening of the interlobular tissue with masses in the lymph spaces. Under the microscope it was found that the walls of the lymph spaces were thickened in the same way as in the previous cases, and that the masses lying in the spaces were composed entirely of cells, having none of that peculiar loose, meshed, fibrillated network characteristic of contagious pleuro-pneumonia. About the small bronchus, with its accompanying vessels, a dense cellular infiltration is seen. The muscular coat is quite degenerated, while in one portion of the wall of the bronchus the cells have assumed an indistinctly circular outline about a centrally degenerated point (tubercle?). The changes in the alveoli with their walls are very slight, consisting only in an increase of cells.

The second preparation was made through the central lobule, in which, as described above, was a circumscribed necrosis.

The thickening between the lobules (see preparation marked S.S. "Brazilian," No. 2 (B), recent disease) is due, as in the previous cases, to a thickening of the walls of the lymph spaces, with here and there narrowed lymph spaces filled with cells more or less adherent to the walls. In the preparation coloured by hæmatoxylon the necrosed portion is brought sharply out by a deep blue line, lying just within its border, and due to the presence of a large number of cells and nuclei. Within this line the alveoli are filled with yellow, finely granular detritus, in which lie scattered nuclei and cells in the process of degeneration. Very few nuclei or cells are seen in the alveolar walls, and the whole looks dead. Within the centre of this necrosed portion are seen the blood vessels still pervious, surrounding which is a zone of cell infiltration as shown by the deep colour. The bronchus lies between the vessels, but can only be distinguished with difficulty, since the external and middle coats are almost obliterated, the mucous coat destroyed, only one or two projections of the submucous coat remaining to mark its character, and the opening of the tube filled with round cells and nuclei.

The walls of the alveoli of the tissue bordering this necrosed portion are very much compressed, and, together with the new cells, which have been inflated, form a sort of wall. The remaining alveoli are comparatively free, although a few are filled with the same yellow, finely granular detritus, as are those within the necrosed portion.

Within the nodule or more advanced decease was a cavity $\frac{1}{2}$ to 1 centimeter in diameter, surrounded by a thick wall, and the lobule containing it was separated from its neighbours by thick bands of tissue, which could be followed for some distance among the more healthy lobules.

Under the microscope (see preparation marked S.S. "Brazilian," No. 2, Advanced disease) it appears that the interlobular tissue is composed of the same connective tissue, only rather firmer than marks the preparations already examined, and has apparently been formed in the same way. The wall about the cavity is also composed of a similar fibrous tissue rich in cells, and passes insensibly into the walls of the alveoli which are compressed and slightly thickened, but otherwise comparatively open. Surrounding the bronchi and vessels are an accumulation of cells which have infiltrated the bronchus from without inwards, leaving still a remnant of the epitheleal lining.

The general outline of the cavity is such as to indicate that it had been formed by a necrosis of a circumscribed portion of the lung, as in the more recent specimen. This necrosed portion has been gotten rid of, and the slight wall of separation seen in the recent specimen has been thickened and condensed.

The whole process is one of chronic interstitial pneumonia with peribronchitis and necrosis of the lung tissue.

Steamship "Aleppo," from New York.

The specimen was a portion of lung about half the size of the palm of the hand, in which was a firm wedge-shaped nodule, the base of which measured 22.5^{cm}, and was at right angles to the pleural surface, which was slightly thickened all over the portion of lung. The nodule was quite homogeneous in appearance, with broad bands of tissue separating the lobules. In one of the lobules there were small losses of substance, giving to that part a honeycombed look, and in another lobule there was a small cavity.

The bands of interlobular tissue (see preparations marked S.S. "Aleppo" from New York, From diseased nodule, and S. S. "Aleppo," &c., Section of entire nodule) are composed, as in the previous cases, of firm connective tissue quite well vascularized, showing here and there the presence of masses of cells in the narrowed lymph spaces.

The lung tissue is compressed and the alveolar walls are thickly studded with round cells and nuclei. In the honeycombed tissue mentioned above (see preparation marked From diseased nodule) these cells are collected together in little round groups, which were often degenerated in the centres, causing the little losses of substance referred to. The alveoli themselves were filled with exuded masses, detritus, and cells.

The section through the lobule containing the cavity (see preparation marked Section of entire nodule) shows that the cavity is surrounded by a thick wall having a slightly reticulated appearance, and here and there giving the outline of a circular body. In the remaining parenchyma of the lung are two or three round bodies of a similar size with a rather broad meshed stroma, in which lie round cells (miliary tubercles).

The bronchi and vessels are surrounded by accumulated cells.

Many of the alveoli of the lobules bordering upon the diseased nodule are filled with blood corpuscles, which, however, lie freely within them, and have not uniformly infiltrated all the tissue as is the case in the hemorrhagic infarction of the contagious pleuro-pneumonia.

The whole process can be classifield as one of chronic interstitial pneumonia, combined with tuberculosis and the formation of cavities.

Conclusion.

Looking at the cases as a whole, it will be seen that they are the results of inflammations of different parts of the constituents of the lungs, there also being indications in all the specimens that tuberculosis may take part in producing some of the changes.

The antecedence of one process over the other cannot be exactly determined, but judging from the thickness of the interlobular connective tissue, and the fact that it can be distinctly traced among the apparently unaffected lobules, it is probably implicated among the first, and from the fact of the thickness of this tissue as compared with the small amount of lung involved, the processes must be placed among the chronic ones, which require weeks or months rather than days for their accomplishment, and as such are probably not contagious.

Yours truly,
W. T. Whitney.

Chas. P. Lyman, F.R.C.V.S.,
Veterinary Surgeon, Department of Agriculture.

Therefore, if we may place *any* value upon facts as evidenced by the microscope—and who will say that we cannot?—the absolute fact is well shown that not only were the lungs condemned in my presence as being affected with pleuro-pneumonia *contagiosa* not affected with that disease, but that the changes noticed in them, in all but one case, were due to a chronic interstitial pneumonia with peribronchitis, with necrosis and the formation of small cavities at and within the lung tissue proper; and further, there are evidences amounting to a certainty, in one case at least, that the disease known as tuberculosis, probably plays a more or less prominent part in the etiology of these changes. The other lung (Brazilian No. 1) that cannot be included in this class of cases, was, however, very distinctive, in that the lung contained the large abscess, already described, and the microscope shows the changes in the lung tissues upon which the condemnation was made to have been chronic induration of these tissues, caused by the pressure upon them of the large abscess found to exist in their immediate neighbourhood; in fact just the condition that under the circumstances we would expect to find. I think that, without pursuing the history of the beasts from which these lungs came, it may be safely stated that they were not affected with contagious pleuro-pneumonia. The next thing, therefore, will be to consider these cases that have been reported as being diseased with contagious pleuro-pneumonia since the time I left Liverpool, and up to the 21st of November last, of which there were seven, as has been already stated. As the lungs or diseased portions of them, were not obtainable for examination, it will be possible only to show by negative evidence what the probabilities are respecting them. As you will remember they came to Liverpool by various steamships from Boston; to Boston they came from Missouri, Iowa, Illinois, and Ohio, and none of them were at at any time in any of the cattle markets except those of Chicago, Buffalo, Albany, and Boston, and the only lines of rail over which any of these passed were the Grand Trunk of Canada, New York Central, Fitchburg, Michigan Central, Vermont Central, Boston and Albany, Lake Shore and Michigan Southern.

It will be shown further on that there cannot be any disease in Chicago or Buffalo, and the same argument will be as true regarding Albany as Buffalo. In the case of Boston I may say that ever since the "stamping out" of pleuro-pneumonia from Massachusetts in 1867 there has always existed, and does to-day, in this State a most efficient board of State Cattle Commissioners, composed, amongst others, of the same veterinarian (Dr. E. F. Thayer) under whose administration the disease was "stamped out," and that although this board has, during all these years, kept a most lively look-out for any cases of the disease within their State, and although thousands of animals have been examined in Brighton Market, alive and dead, by Dr. Thayer, not one single case of pleuro-pneumonia has been discovered within that State within the last 14 years.

Regarding the native States of these cattle, it may be said that in Missouri this department has 104, in Iowa 84, in Illinois 86, in Ohio 83 correspondents, whose particular duty it is to inform themselves as to the nature of any disease that may at any time show itself among the animals within their district, and that these correspondents have not at any time reported the existence of any disease the symptoms of which at all similated those of contagious pleuro-pneumonia, although every special effort possible has been made to discover it should it exist there. So far as is known, and equally strenuous efforts have been made to discover the facts, pleuro-pneumonia does not exist in any region of country through which the lines of rail over which these animals have been carried passes. This, then, leaves as the only possible source of contamination the cars in which the animals have been conveyed. That the disease may have been contracted in this way is possible, but not at all probable, and as bearing upon this point it may be said that cattle going to Boston for local uses are conveyed in exactly the same way, and oftentimes in the same cars as the animals going from thence to Great Britain; and that, although I myself have examined many hundreds of these, alive and dead, I have never yet found a single case of contagious pleuro-pneumonia; and this is the fact, as I have before stated, regarding the very extensive examinations made of these same animals by the Massachusetts State Board of Cattle Commsisioners.

In considering this question in all its phases I am naturally led to a review of the circumstances attending the landing and examination of the cargo of animals *ex* steamship " Ontario," which arrived at the port of Liverpool on the 26th of January 1879, consisting of 195 cattle and two carcases; 87 head of cattle had been thrown overboard on the voyage, thus making the original shipment 284. These animals were shipped from Portland, Me., but of their origin Mr. Welsh, Minister of the United States at London, says:—" From reliable parties in Liverpool I learn that while a part of the
" cattle by the " Ontario " came from Chicago, and a part from Buffalo, at least 45 head
" of them came from Toronto, and were so mixed with the others that the Canadian
" and United States cattle could not be distinguished. It is also beyond dispute that
" those which came from the United States passed for several hundred miles over the
" Grand Trunk Road through the Dominion of Canada; that all the cattle were
" exposed to weather of unusual severity; that they remained for a considerable time in
" Portland without food or water, and they had undergone an exceptional amount of
" hardship and bad usage before entering upon a voyage which was made at an inclement
" season and during excessively rough weather." In a memorandum on the subject, Professor Brown of the Veterinary Department of the Privy Council, says:—" On
" examining one of the carcases the inspector at Liverpool found evidence of pleuro-
" pneumonia, and forwarded portions of the lung to the Veterinary Department. This
" specimen was found to represent the characteristic indications of the contagious pleuro-
" pneumonia of cattle so well known in this country. By direction of the Lord President
" I immediately instructed Mr. Duguid, one of the inspectors of this Department, to
" proceed to Liverpool and report as to the condition of the animals which had been
" detained there. Mr. Duguid remained at Liverpool and superintended the slaughter
" of the cattle and in the course of the *post-mortem* examination he detected 13 cases of
" pleuro-pneumonia *in various stages*." Now take the statement of Professor Walley made to me in Edinburgh in July 1880, in regard to this matter. He says:—

" I was called to Liverpool and there shown animals together in a building which, I was told, came per steamship ' Ontario' from America ; a few of them were coughing, I should judge giving the pathognomonic cough of contagious pleuro-pneumonia. *I examined them ; they gave no elevation of temperature that amounted to anything as a sign;* they varied a little; some would be a degree higher than others, but nothing remarkable in any. While this examination was going on, *and before we had finished to my entire satisfaction*, a man came to say that we were wanted in the slaughter-house, where we went at once, and found two animals that we were told had been taken haphazard from this cargo of the ' Ontario' hanging partially dressed, and from these I saw lungs taken that exhibited to me, without any doubt, the well-known lesions of contagious pleuro-pneumonia. I was not at the place for more than an hour."

In answer to questions, he further said :

"The animals were in as good condition as any of the others ; that there were several diseased spots in their lungs ; that the deceased portions were ' marbled,' and the parenchyma varied in colour from deep red to pink, but it was mostly of a pinkish shade ; that there was no attempt towards the formation of a cyst-wall around any of the diseased portions, because the disease had not been of sufficient standing."

I have made these extracts because they seem to me to embrace the entire evidence tending to show that the disease on the " Ontario " was contagious pleuro-pneumonia ; and I think it worth while to put in contrast with them here what may be called the circumstantial evidence tending to show that there may have been some mistake.

The fact seems to be beyond dispute that so far as the animals came from the United States they came from Chicago and Buffalo *viá* Canadian Grand Trunk Road to Portland. Since 1877 the Department of Agriculture has had, all through the West, regular correspondents, whose duty it is to collect and forward evidence relating to any disease, contagious or otherwise, that may prevail to any extent in the different localities in which they are located. In this way nearly every disease that animal flesh is heir to has received some sort of mention, but in no case has any description been received that could in any way be construed into a description of contagious pleuro-pneumonia of cattle. Besides this, the Department kept Veterinary Surgeon H. J. Detmers at the Chicago live-stock yards, examining cattle with the single view of ascertaining whether any trace of this disease could be discovered in that great depôt for western cattle. This examination, which was made in 1879 and continued for some time, showed that it was unknown there. The market of Buffalo is in the State of New York, and therefore came directly under the examination of Prof. James Law, Veterinarian-in-Chief to the State of New York, whose particular business, under a special law, was to find and get rid of, so far as any means at his command would allow of its being done, this very disease—pleuro-pneumonia of cattle—and with the splendid system of detecting its existence in any cattle within the State, and with the great facility which he had for tracing any diseased animals that were found to their starting point, he was never able, in any way, to locate the disease in Buffalo or at any point in the State within 400 miles, or thereabout, of that market. Neither has this Department, although every means at its command has been tried, ever been able to find that it had any existence at any time nearer to Buffalo than the points indicated by Professor Law. Now we have in evidence that these animals passed for several hundred miles over the Grand Trunk Road. To do this and get to Portland after leaving Buffalo, they would not again enter the States until they had reached Vermont, where they cross a small portion of the extreme north-easterly corner of the State; thence across the extreme northerly portion of New Hampshire; thence for a short distance across the southerly portion of Maine to Portland; and at no time would they be nearer than Portland to the infected district, the nearest point of which is something over 300 miles away. It may be stated to a certainty that contagious pleuro-pneumonia of cattle does not exist in either Vermont, New Hampshire, or Maine. How then could these animals have become infected? So far as the territory through which they travelled on their way to the seaport lies within the United States, it can safely be said that no pleuro-pneumonia exists along, or anywhere near, their line of route. The cars in which they travelled could scarcely have been previously contaminated, for presumably they were those of this Great Northern Trunk line, and would never be sent down into the neighbourhood of New York, Philadelphia, or Baltimore for the conveyance of local cattle freight. The only way, then, would seem to be that the disease was contracted on board ship during the voyage. But ships that have carried cattle are, on their return to Liverpool, required by law to be *thoroughly disinfected*, so that unless the "Ontario," on her out voyage, brought to this country from England cattle affected with contagious pleuro-pneumonia, she could scarcely convey it to other and hearty beasts on the return trip.

That pleuro-pneumonia did exist among these cattle we have the evidence of, first, Mr. Moore, the inspector, who discovered it; second, that of Professor Duguid, who was sent down from London for the express purpose of inspecting this cargo; third, that of Professor Walley, who came from Edinburgh for the same purpose, all of them gentlemen who are particularly well qualified to judge of the matter, and give a valuable opinion regarding it. But it certainly does seem that Professor Duguid and Mr. Moore were undoubtedly mistaken as to the lungs condemned by them in my presence last July and August. May it not be that pleuro-pneumonia *contagiosa* is, after all, not so distinctive in its appearance as has always been supposed, or rather that changes are produced by certain other diseases, the lesions of which resemble so closely those of contagious pleuro-pneumonia that in the absence of any history of the animal would require a much more careful examination to detect its difference than veterinarians have heretofore supposed to be necessary?

The other gentleman, Professor Walley, says that he should judge that these animals were giving the pathognomonic cough of pleuro-pneumonia, but that he examined them, and even with the thermometer (a most delicate aid in these cases) he could get no indication that amounted to a sign that they were diseased; but still, *before he had finished his examination to his entire satisfaction*, he was called away to the slaughter-house, where he saw lungs removed from two beasts that to him presented "without any doubt " the well-known lesions of pleuro-pneumonia." These lungs were marbled and the parenchyma varied in colour from deep red to pink, but it was mostly of a pinkish shade; that the largest diseased spot was as large as the crown of a Derby hat; that there was no attempt at the formation of a cyst wall, because the disease had not been of sufficient standing; that the animals were in as good condition as any of the others, and that they had been selected haphazard from among the cargo in question. Is it not remarkable that although so large a portion of lung was affected there was no sign or symptom by which the animal could be selected out from among the others, which on the testimony of this gentleman showed no sign that "amounted to anything" of their being diseased and that the only way of finding its presence was by a critical examination of the lung itself after the animal had been killed? Was ever such a case of acute contagious pleuro-pneumonia with this amount of lung implicated heard of before? I think not; and still this gentleman, who has had great experience with this disease, who knows that in Edinburgh the existence of "pleuro" is generally discovered by an examination made of the live animals in the byre, and not of the dead ones made in the abattoirs, and before he has had sufficient time to finish his examination to his own entire satisfaction, says that without a doubt these animals were affected with contagious pleuro-pneumonia! Now, I submit, are there not in this *evidences* of a hurried examination? Has it not obviously been taken for granted that the detection of contagious pleuro-pneumonia, *post mortem*, was a thing requiring a knowledge only of a most superficial sort? And I ask the authorities in this case if, in view of all the facts, it is not possible, nay, even probable, that a disease of not a sufficiently pronounced character to interfere with the well-doing of these animals may exist that shall give to the naked eye, upon examination of the lung *post mortem*, the exact appearances of contagious pleuro-pneumonia, but which is not that disease, but the result of some chronic process, the nature of which, in the absence of all history of the animal, may require a most careful and minute examination to detect its real differences?

The only gentleman engaged in the affair who seems at that time to have been of my present opinion and to have realised its importance is Professor Williams, of Edinburgh, who was called to Liverpool in precisely the same manner as was Professor Walley. This gentleman, who spent more time in the examination, who has had at least as large an experience as have any of the others, said, when he had finished the examination in Liverpool and was asked for his opinion, "I have as yet no opinion to give, and shall "have none until I have been able to make a more thorough examination of the lung." For this purpose he took with him to Edinburgh portions of the lung, and he received from Mr. Wellsby, a veterinary surgeon in the employ of Messrs. Warren & Co., the steamship owners, for the next six months, portions of the diseased lungs which were condemned by the inspector at Liverpool, all of which received a most careful examination by himself and Dr. Hamilton, pathologist to the Royal Infirmary, and demonstrator of morbid anatomy in the University of Edinburgh, and after all this he declares that he has "not the slightest hesitation in saying that in no case has he found them to "exhibit the characteristic lesions of contagious pleuro-pneumonia." Therefore it seems to me that there is, *at least*, fair reason to doubt whether the disease noticed among this cargo of the "Ontario" was really contagious pleuro-pneumonia. I have not gone into the discussion of this question in any captious spirit of criticism, neither do I mean for a moment to call into question the professional ability of any of those gentlemen, which I believe to be of the highest quality, and I most thoroughly believe that their decisions were given in accordance with their honest convictions; but if these convictions were arrived at too hastily, and before proper, and, in view of the gravity of the question, sufficiently exhaustive examinations of the facts were made, it is certainly my privilege to comment upon them, and show, if possible, that it was so. And if any statement or argument that I have advanced seems to be of sufficient consequence to really throw a doubt upon the decision of the authorities of Great Britain in this matter, I would most respectfully suggest that in fairness to the great interests of the United States, which are by this decision very severely prejudiced, that the judgment should at least be reconsidered.

My own opinion, arrived at after a most thorough and careful investigation and consideration of the facts, is that the lungs which were condemned by the Inspector of the Privy Council at Liverpool during my stay there in parts of July and August last, as being affected with contagious pleuro-pneumonia, were in reality not affected with that disease. And further, I do not believe that a single case of contagious pleuro-pneumonia has ever existed in the West or has been landed in England from our ports of Boston or Portland, unless, indeed, it may have been communicated to the animals after they were placed on board the ocean steamer, from various contamination of the vessel, by transportation in it of diseased animals from Great Britain to America, an event which I must say that in the case of pleuro-pneumonia I think to be very unlikely.

Respectfully submitted,

Hon. Wm. G. Le Duc,   CHARLES P. LYMAN, F.R.C.V.S.
Commissioner of Agriculture.

REPORT OF THE DEPARTMENT OF AGRICULTURE

No. 52.

EXTRACT from the ANNUAL REPORT of the DEPARTMENT OF AGRICULTURE, Washington, for the Year 1881.

CONTAGIOUS DISEASES OF DOMESTICATED ANIMALS.

On assuming control of the Department of Agriculture I found that my predecessor had provided for a continuation of the investigation of contagious diseases of domesticated animals by assigning to duty those previously employed and the appointment of an additional number of veterinary surgeons. This additional force seems to have been made necessary by the increased duties imposed by Congress in making an appropriation for the purpose of determining the extent to which the disease known as contagious pleuro-pneumonia exists in the States heretofore reported as infected with the malady. Agents for this purpose had been appointed in the following named States: New York, New Jersey, Pennsylvania, and Maryland. Two surgeons had been appointed in New Jersey, one of whom had been directed to make examinations also in Delaware.

The agent in Maryland had been directed to extend his investigations into the district of Columbia, and such counties on the eastern border of Virginia as he might be able to visit. As these agents were engaged in an active prosecution of the investigation, it was thought best to continue them until the work was completed, or at least until satisfactory evidence was obtained as to the prevalence or non-existence of this destructive disease in the territory above named.

Notwithstanding the many disadvantages under which these agents have laboured, being without either State or governmental authority for making inspections, their reports indicate the existence of contagious pleuro-pneumonia among cattle in the above-named States and in the district of Columbia. While but comparatively few acute cases of the disease were discovered, many chronic cases and numbers of infected stables, premises, &c., were found in a majority of the localities visited.

The reports of these veterinary surgeons will be submitted in detail hereafter.

In addition to further experiments for the purpose of more accurately determining the nature of the diseases known as swine plague and fowl cholera, Dr. D. E. Salmon had been instructed to institute and carry out as thorough an inquiry as possible into the nature and peculiar characteristics of the fatal disease among cattle known as Spanish fever. This inquiry was regarded as necessary for the purpose of more definitely determining the nature of the virus or infecting principle of the disease, the part of the body in which this virus multiplies, and the manner in which it is excreted and conveyed to healthy animals.

To properly understand this disease it would seem necessary to know how an animal, apparently healthy, can be the means of so widely disseminating so fatal a malady, and why those actually affected with it in its most destructive type are unable to transmit it to other animals.

Another equally important point to be determined is, as to how the virus of this disease can become acclimated and resist a temperature much lower than was formerly possible, and to what extent this accumulation may continue, and consequently what danger there may be of the Northern States becoming permanently infected in the future. These points once clearly and definitely established, much more effective measures for the prevention of the disease may be devised than are now possible.

The past season has been rather an unfavourable one for the successful prosecution of this investigation, owing to the fact that the disease has prevailed to a much less extent than in former years. Dr. Salmon has, however, made some important discoveries in regard to the transmission of the malady, having already successfully inoculated several. He is still engaged on this branch of his work, and as soon as the result of his experiments are more definitely determined, a detailed report of his investigation will be transmitted for the consideration of Congress.

Dr. A. J. Detmers was instructed to continue his experiments with the disease known as swine plague, with special reference to ascertaining what agents seem to offer the best results when used as prophylactics. He was advised to put to a practical test, on a large scale, the subjects selected for experiment. By studying the disease in large herds, and watching closely the effects of the agents used, it was thought that a cheap, simple, and efficient preventive of this destructive disease might be discovered and a lasting benefit thus conferred on the farming community and the nation generally. A full report of the results of his experiments will be submitted hereafter.

In addition to the above-named diseases, which requires still further experiments to definitely determine all their peculiar characteristics, there are many other destructive

R 679.

contagious maladies which, as yet, have received no consideration at the hands of this department.

The most important, because the most fatal and destructive of these diseases, is that of anthrax or charbon. Many classes of our domesticated animals are subject to this disease, and perhaps the annual losses from this malady are heavier than from any other single disease now prevalent among our farm animals. While the investigations referred to were going on in this country, Dr. Lyman, a veterinary surgeon, who had been employed for that purpose, was pursuing his investigations in England with regard to the alleged existence of pleuro-pneumonia and foot-and-mouth disease among cattle landed in that country from the United States. He was accompanied by Professor Whitney, the accomplished microscopist, and the results of his scientific inquiry and of his conferences with the privy council are interesting and valuable. He was instructed by my predecessor to continue the investigations undertaken by the Department in England the previous year. In an interview with the Privy Council, Dr. Lyman requested that an examination of portions of diseased lungs taken from the cattle condemned last year might be made by the veterinary surgeon of the council and himself unitedly, at the same time assuring them that no pleuro-pneumonia had been found West, and that this Department had employed competent officers to inspect all suspected districts along the Atlantic coast. As the result of the examination, the British veterinary surgeon, Dr. Brown, expressed the opinion that there need be no occasion for alarm in the future with regard to condemning cattle, and that "if the United States " was entirely free from pleuro-pneumonia no condemnations would be made upon lungs " presenting the appearances only of those that were condemned last year." It appears that out of 32,000 animals imported into English ports, outside of Liverpool, in six months ending June 25, 1881, only 35 have been condemned even under the suspicion of having contagious pleuro-pneumonia. And Dr. Lyman remarks that—

As a result of my conference with the authorities of Great Britain upon this subject, I think it may safely be stated that the impressions which they held regarding the health, in this respect, of our western herds, have been materially changed, and that lungs, having a certain appearance, heretofore condemned as being of contagious pleuro-pneumonia, will not be so considered in the future.

Between January 1 and May 31, 1881, large numbers of American cattle landing at London, Liverpool, and Glasgow were considered as having foot-and-mouth disease. Careful investigation shows that the disease, if it existed, was caused by infection communicated to the cattle after they were shipped from American ports, and is to be attributed to exposure to the virus imported into England from France, and spread abroad from Deptford market, where it was first discovered. It is considered possible that the disease may be imparted to American cattle by the use of the head-ropes, which are often taken from diseased European animals and used on board American vessels employed in the cattle trade, and also by taking on board these vessels articles for shipment from wharves where diseased cattle have been landed. If this theory is true, legislation will be required to remedy the evil. Dr. Lyman reports that during his stay in Great Britain no diseased hogs were landed from the United States. He quotes from the report of the Veterinary Department of the Privy Council for the year 1879 a statement showing that out of 279 portions of swine flesh taken from American hogs that had been condemned and slaughtered on account of swine fever, only three were found to contain living trichinæ. The British report, after giving as a reason why the direct importation of American pork was not prohibited, that " such a measure would " have damaged the trade without producing any satisfactory results," continues: " Besides, trichinosis among swine is known to exist in Germany, and it probably exists " in other exporting countries, so that nothing short of prohibition of swine flesh in all " forms from all foreign sources would have been effectual." " In view of the recent " total embargo placed by some of the foreign governments upon the imports of our hog " products on account of the alleged existence in them of trichinæ," it is recommended that measures be taken to ascertain more definitely what percentage of American hogs are thus diseased, the geographical distribution of the disease in this country, and all other information which may aid in devising such means as shall decrease to a minimum their existence in American pork products.

With regard to the transportation of cattle to the European markets, I am happy to say that American cattle, shipped from American ports, " arrive at their destination " with fewer bruises and in better condition generally than do those from some of the " neighbouring European ports."

The losses of cattle on ship-board from January 1 to September 30, 1880, exceeded 5 per cent. In the corresponding months of 1881 the losses were about $2\frac{1}{2}$ per cent.

FOURTH REPORT BY Dr. C. P. LYMAN.

No. 53.

FOURTH REPORT by Dr. CHARLES P. LYMAN, F.R.C.V.S., to the COMMISSIONER OF AGRICULTURE, Washington.

SIR, Washington, D.C., November 15, 1881.

CONGRESS, at its last session, appropriated the sum of $15,000 for the purpose of enabling the Department of Agriculture to ascertain, as accurately as possible, all facts in relation to the existence of contagious pleuro-pneumonia among cattle in the United States. For this purpose there were appointed in March last, several veterinarians of experience with this disease, who were located at various points throughout the entire infected region, and directed to collect all information which should enable them to point out the exact location of all herds of cattle within a certain prescribed district, for each one, that might be affected with the disease. They were also ordered to report the general drift of the movement of cattle within such district, so that, in case evidence might be found that such animals were being collected for shipment, or were being shipped out from the district, early knowledge of the fact, together with information relating to their probable destination, might at once be communicated to this department. Much of this work has been accomplished, and the result of their investigations will be found detailed in the accompanying reports which I have the honour of presenting to you herewith.

While in this way it was thought that statistics of value as to the number of diseased animals and the distribution of the malady over the infected area might be gained, it was well understood that the reports would not, in the nature of the circumstances under which the data must necessarily be collected, be anything more than approximations of the truth, and as such, simply, they are offered, with the hope and in the conviction that they will prove to be of service to any who may desire to make computations which shall show the probable number of cattle that would have to be paid for in case "stamping out" with remuneration was decided upon as a means of ridding our country of this foreign disease. And, further, it was thought that it would show what became of dangerous cattle, more especially of the calves from such districts, for, within the past year, much has been very properly said and written as to the danger of transplanting this disease into the great herds of the West by means of a trade to them of Eastern-bred calves, a danger which it seemed to be of great importance to have accurate knowledge concerning, that restrictive measures, were they found to be necessary, might at once be undertaken. While the examinations by these inspectors are more thorough than any heretofore made by the Government, still I must confess to a disappointment; for when it is borne in mind that whatever inspections are made, whatever advice concerning the disposition of diseased and infected animals is followed, that, in fact, whatever knowledge of any kind regarding the absolute condition of these herds was to be had only by and through the courtesy of the cattle owners themselves, many of whom, I am sorry to say, have thrown unexpected obstacles in the way, it will be seen that the reports cannot be as full and complete as the necessity demands. These remarks do not apply, however, to the States of Pennsylvania and New Jersey, where the secretary of the State Board of Agriculture, Hon. Thos. J. Edge, in the former, and the secretary of the State Board of Health, E. M. Hunt, M.D., in the latter, have rendered such cheerful and powerful assistance that the reports from these two States should be looked upon as being more than approximately correct.

From the Honourable the Commissioner of Agriculture I received in May last the following instructions:—

"You will, on or about the 10th day of June, proximo, take passage for Great Britain, and having arrived there you will continue your investigations undertaken for the Department of Agriculture, in England, last season. These examinations may be pursued by you during the summer months or such a part thereof as may be found necessary, at such port or ports of Great Britain as the circumstances existing from time to time may seem to demand.

"It will be well if you can persuade the veterinarians employed by the Government of Great Britain to join you in making a thorough examination of any animals, or lungs thereof, arriving from the United States, that may appear to them to show symptoms or lesions of contagious pleura-pneumonia, with a view to the settlement, if possible, of the present contested question as to whether the animals now so freely condemned by them as showing the presence of this disease really do have it, or if the lesions of some other disease have been mistaken for it, as is shown by the result of your own examination of the lungs of animals that were pronounced by the British authorities to be unmistakably affected by pleuro-pneumonia *contagiosa*.

68 FOURTH REPORT BY Dr. C. P. LYMAN.

"As a part also of your duties you will, so far as possible, examine in a proper manner the hogs arriving in Great Britain from the United States during your stay there, with a view of ascertaining to how great an extent they are diseased or are infected with trichinæ.

"You will also investigate, so far as possible and as circumstances may seem to demand, the question of the existence of any other contagious diseases that may be present or alleged to be present among any animals arriving in Great Britain from this country."

In accordance with these instructions, I have the honour to report that upon June 24 I arrived in London, and the next day called upon the Right Hon. Mr. Mundella, Vice-President of the Privy Council, to whom I presented my credentials and stated the objects of my mission. He said that the matter seemed to him to be of great importance, and that it had best be laid at once before the Lord President of the Council, and for this purpose he appointed so early a time as 1 o'clock the following Monday, June 27.

At the hour designated, in company with his Excellency Minister Lowell and Dr. Whitney, pathologist, I proceeded to the Privy Council Office, where we were received by the Lord President, Earl Spencer, the Vice-President, the Right Hon. Mr. Mundella, the secretary, Mr. Peel, and the Veterinary-in-Chief, Professor Brown. Mr. Lowell introduced us and briefly stated the object of our visit, saying that, as the particular request we had to make to the Council had been reduced to writing, with his Lordship's permission he would proceed to read it. Dr. Whitney then read the following paper:—

"MY LORD SPENCER AND GENTLEMEN: We have ventured to ask this conference of you to-day in order to call your special attention to this, the third report upon contagious pleura-pneumonia, recently issued by the Department of Agriculture of the United States, and to the fact that the conclusions arrived at therein are at variance with those of your inspectors.

"In order that a more thorough understanding of this difference of opinion may be reached, we respectfully ask that the question may be reconsidered.

"For this purpose specimens of condemned lungs, upon which this report is based, have been brought to London, and we respectfully ask leave to submit them to you, or to experts selected by you, at any time and place that may be most convenient. And we further hope that you will allow us, together with these same gentlemen, to examine the lungs of any Western cattle now coming to Great Britain from the ports of Boston or Portland, which may be condemned by your inspectors as affected with contagious pleuro-pneumonia. As the Government of the United States have undertaken to carry out measures which must eventually result in the extermination of the disease, and hope before long to be able to show a country entirely free from this scourge, it is of the utmost importance that the finer appearances of the disease should be clearly recognised; for even after the country is entirely free it is very possible that lungs may be found from time to time, similar to those condemned last summer, that present grossly the appearance hitherto ascribed to contagious pleuro-pneumonia, but which, in reality, result from chronic inflammatory processes entirely unconnected with contagion. And these appearances, unless the authority of precedent is corrected, might cause insurmountable restrictions to be imposed."*

---

* *Minute by Professor Brown.*—This paper was presented by Dr. Whitney and Dr. Lyman, who were received by the Lord President on June 27th. The American minister was also present. In accordance with the Lord President's instructions the specimens referred to, which are sections of lungs mounted and stained for observation under the microscope, have been examined by Dr. Yeo, of King's College, and also by the Chief and Assistant Inspectors in this department. (See the Chief Inspector's Report below.) There is no probability that, if the United States are ever entirely free from pleuro-pneumonia, restrictions will be imposed on the cattle trade on any but the clearest evidence of disease in the animals landed at our ports.—G. T. B. 12.7.81.

SIR, July 7, 1881.

I HAVE to report that a meeting which took place this day at King's College, between Dr. Whitney, Dr. Lyman, and myself, the specimens which were brought from America by the former gentleman, were submitted to the observation of Dr. Gerald Yeo, professor of physiology at King's College, who expressed it as his opinion that they presented microscopical appearances identical with those which he has frequently observed in pleuro-pneumonia, and that they did not show changes characteristic of any other disease; and further that in some of the specimens the peculiar characteristics of pleuro-pneumonia were so well marked, that they could be easily recognised by the unaided eye.

Should any cases of pleuro-pneumonia be landed in this country from the ports of Boston or Portland, I have arranged to have the lungs of the animals sent up to London for examination.

I have, &c
(Signed) ALEXANDER C. COPE.

Professor Brown,
&c. &c. &c.

Following the reading of this paper, questions were asked by his Lordship and other members of the Council present, which developed the fact that the Department of Agriculture had already established throughout the infected districts a corps of inspectors, all of them veterinarians of experience with pleuro-pneumonia, whose duty it was to know and report to their department the location and numbers of diseased herds, their movements, and the movement of all calves from among them; that Mr. L. McLean, M.R.C.V.S., had, in its interest, travelled extensively through the West, visiting all of the Iowa, Missouri, and Illinois herds, among which it was at one time reported, by irresponsible persons, that the disease had been introduced by eastern calves; that he had visited all of the large stock yards from Kansas City to Chicago, many of the large feeding stables in and about the larger cities of the West, and certain other isolated herds; in fact, that all intimations coming to the knowledge of the department which seemed to indicate in any way that pleuro-pneumonia might have an existence in the West or anywhere outside of the known infected district, had been and would continue to be thoroughly investigated. As yet no such disease had been found; in the event of its making its appearance in any new locality, most certainly the department would have and make public early and positive information concerning it. That I could, as a result of these examinations, together with much reliable information gleaned from other sources, most emphatically state that pleuro-pneumonia had no existence in the West, or along certain lines of rail leading to Boston and Portland, or in or about these ports, nor did I think it possible that calves from diseased herds could go West without the fact being known to inspectors of the department.

As a result, both our requests were very cordially granted; the question was ordered reopened and the Veterinarian-in-Chief was directed to examine, with us, both the specimens of last summer's condemnation that we had brought with us, and the lungs of any of the designated animals that might be condemned during our stay in that country.

On June 28 we called by appointment upon Professor Brown with specimens from *all* of the lungs that were condemned for pleuro-pneumonia at Liverpool, during my stay there last summer.* These were carefully examined by Professor Brown, who said that before giving an opinion he should very much prefer that the whole pathological part of the question should be gone into by Professor Yeo, pathologist at King's College, and that he would arrange that we meet the professor for this purpose as soon as possible.

As a result of this desire, on July 7 we visited King's College, where we met Professor Yeo, who, after a rather hurried examination of the specimens, said he would not absolutely say that these changes were due to contagious pleuro-pneumonia; he could only do so in any case after seeing the *fresh* specimen, as he considered it impossible to make an absolute diagnosis without noting carefully the entire relation of the diseased portions of lung to the healthy tissues of the same organ. He was rather inclined to the belief that there is no change resulting in the lungs of cattle, from either an acute or chronic inflammation, which may not be, so far as its appearances under the microscope are concerned, duplicated by the action of the disease known as contagious pleuro-pneumonia.

The only positive thing that he did state in relation to the specimens was that he considered the changes shown in them to be the result of a disease of at least two to three months' standing. Unfortunately for us during the whole of our stay, which was until the 16th of August, no condemnations for pleuro-pneumonia were made, therefore we could not furnish to Professor Yeo the fresh specimens demanded, and the matter, so far as he was concerned, ended here.

Before we left, Professor Brown assured me that he did not think there need be any occasion for alarm in the future; *that if our country was entirely free from pleuro-pneumonia*, no condemnations would be made upon lungs presenting the appearances only of those that were condemned in my presence last year.

The following tabulated statement contains the particulars of all of the condemnations of American animals for pleuro-pneumonia that have been made in Great Britain this year, so far as I am informed. If others are to be added they have arrived there since August 16:—

---

* See Senate Ex. Doc. No. 5, 46th Congress, 3rd session, p. 9.

Name of Steamship.	From port of—	To port of—	Date landed.	Number condemned.
			1881.	
Milanese	Boston	London	Jan. 4	4
Greece	New York	London	Jan. 12	5
Utopian	New York	London	Jan. 13	2
Schleswig	New York	London	Jan. 16	2
Assyrian Monarch	New York	London	Jan. 19	12
Rochester	Boston	London	Jan. 28	2
Australia	New York	London	Jan. 29	1
City of Bristol	New York	Liverpool	Feb. 1	1
Minnesota	Boston	Liverpool	Feb. 4	1
France	New York	London	Feb. 9	1
Sumatra	Boston	London	Feb. 27	1
Edinburgh	Boston	London	April 15	4
Devon	New York	Bristol	June 16	1

Making a total of 37 animals from January 1, 1881.

Of these there were condemned in London from New York, 23; London from Boston, 11; Liverpool from New York, 1; Liverpool from Boston, 1; Bristol from New York, 1.

There were landed in Liverpool, from January 1 to August 12, 30,310 cattle, from which two only were condemned. Exactly what number were landed in London and at other British ports during this time, I have as yet been unable to ascertain; but during the six months ending June 25, 1881, there were landed in Great Britain from the United States, 56,721 head. This would make at all the other ports except Liverpool, during the six months, about 32,000 animals, of which one was condemned in Bristol, and 34 in London, as suffering from contagious pleuro-pneumonia.

In this connexion I feel it my duty to report to you as a result of my two seasons' inspections in England, that while the Governmental examinations at Liverpool are conducted so carefully and methodically that there is no danger of a wrong credit being giving for a case of disease found, there is, in my opinion, every chance that in London a diseased lung found in the slaughter-houses at Deptford foreign animals market, may be returned as coming from a port in the United States through which the animal never passed; or even that an animal landed there from France or other European country, the lung of which is condemned as showing lesions of pleuro-pneumonia may be returned to the Privy Council Office as coming from the United States, or *vice versá*.

On the 20th of July last, in the course of a conversation on this point, the inspector at Deptford stated to me that this method of detecting pleuro-pneumonia was when he did not diagnose it in the living animal (and he acknowledged that his accommodations for such examinations were inadequate) to have all the lungs reserved and afterwards examine them carefully, and when a nodule of any kind was discovered to cut down and examine it critically. He further remarked that when he found a diseased lung and had not previously condemned the animal, *there was scarcely any mark upon the carcase by which diseased animal could be identified*. When asked how he reported such a case to the Privy Council, he said he simply reported it as one case of pleuro-pneumonia. To the further question as to what country, or what cargo the diseased animal was credited, whenever animals from two or three different countries or ports were being slaughtered by the same person at the same time, as was very often the case, he answered that *he never had any difficulty in identifying the animal*.

As a result of my conference with the authorities of Great Britain upon this subject, I think it may safely be stated that the impressions which they held regarding the health, in this respect, of our Western herds have been materially changed, and that lungs having a certain appearance, heretofore condemned as being that of contagious pleuro-pneumonia, will not be so considered in the future.

Still the fact remains that we, as a country, are not free from this disease, that it continues its ravages to some extent among the herds in a narrow strip of country extending from about New York City to and including the District of Columbia, and the district about Alexandria in Virginia, and that so long as this state of affairs is allowed to exist it will be impossible to obtain any relief whatever from the present burdensome restrictions placed upon all our cattle going to Great Britain. Nor shall we in any way be able to prevent the ultimate spread of the disease to our Western herds, and their consequent destruction, unless restrictive measures are at once adopted.

FOURTH REPORT BY Dr. C. P. LYMAN.

As a remedy against present loss and future danger from this source, I cannot do better than to ask your consideration of my recommendation of last year, viz : Let Congress enact such measures, and authorize such an execution of them, as shall immediately restrict the movement of cattle out from and within infected districts, and in time eradicate every case of lung plague.

Inasmuch as there are at present two very important questions, both of them having a very material bearing upon the methods to be adopted for ridding a country of pleuro-pneumonia, I would suggest the propriety of undertaking, in addition to the present work of the Division, a plan of experimental study with a view of ascertaining:

1st. Whether pleuro-pneumonia contagiosa can be communicated in any way except by actual contact of the healthy with the diseased living animal; and

2nd. Whether or not unprotected animals can safely be introduced into a stable in which the disease has formerly existed, but into which no animal but those that have been properly inoculated and have recovered have been allowed to enter for some time, and in which it is known that the disease in its pure form has not existed for at least six months.

There is very much that might be said upon these two questions, but probably the statement will be sufficient here that high English authority, including that of the Privy Council, assert an unbelief in the mediate contagion theory of spread, while other and perhaps as good authority both in England and in the United States say that their own actual experience causes them to hold opinions exactly the reverse.

In regard to the second proposition, while the practice of preventive inoculation is by no means new, it is a fact that recently its management has seemed to be better understood in some ways, and the results of its systematic practice in the Netherlands and in certain parts of Great Britain, as well as upon isolated diseased premises within our own districts, seem to show a rather easy way of possibly ridding ourselves of the scourge especially in our larger infected city dairies. While such eminent authority as Fleming asserts that it can be done, the fact still remains that no country has as yet in this way rid itself of the plague.

Foot-and-Mouth Disease.

In January of this year the Veterinary Division of the Department of Agriculture was notified by the Veterinary Department of the Privy Council that 59 cattle affected with foot-and-mouth disease had been landed at Deptford (London) from New York by the steamship "France." This warning was followed in a few days by a notification that at the same place 267 cattle from the steamer "City of Liverpool," from New York, had been similarly condemned. These notifications continued to arrive at frequent intervals, all of them relating to condemnations made at London, until on March 23, with the condemnation of 371 cattle from the steamship "City of Liverpool," the manifestations of the disease among our animals at this port stopped as suddenly as it had begun.

In the meantime, however, notice had been received that on the 17th of March the disease has been found at Liverpool, when on that day, 208 animals from Portland, by the steamship "Lake Manitoba," were condemned as suffering from it. From this time, notably on May 11, when 694 such condemnations were made from the cargo of the "Iowa" from Boston, until June 9, notices of its arrival at this port continued to be received, when it subsided as suddenly as it had done at London, with the condemnation of 137 animals by the steamship "Istrian," from Boston. Before this desired end was reached, however, notice had been received that a cargo had been landed at Glasgow from the steamship "Phœnician," from Boston, among which 235 bullocks suffering from foot-and-mouth disease had been condemned. Here its appearance began and ended with the landing of this cargo.

Immediately upon the receipt of this information, means were undertaken which it was hoped and supposed would lead to the source of this new and threatening danger. Careful inspections of animals going abroad were made at the ports of debarkation; certain cattle that had been condemned upon reaching England were traced to the Eastern yards and from thence to Chicago, to which place Mr. McLean, M.R.C.V.S., was sent. From there he successfully traced them on to other stock yards, and in a number of instances even into the stables where they had been feeding for weeks; notwithstanding all of which, no indications of the presence of the disease could be discovered. This being the unsatisfactory state of the affair at the time it was determined to send a representative to England in connection with the pleuro-pneumonia inquiry, the added instruction was given me as already detailed, in the hope that some solution of the problem might be reached.

Therefore, upon landing in Liverpool, and before proceeding to London, I at once visited the wharves upon the Birkenhead side of the river, upon which animals from the United States are landed. Here I found but few cattle, and they appeared to be in a perfectly healthy condition. Great precautions had been taken to render the buildings and premises free from the contagion of foot-and-mouth disease; small brick furnaces, in which sulphur had been burned, were placed within short distances of one another in the buildings; a very large quantity of strong lime-wash, in which, I was told, had been dissolved 20 per cent. of crude carbolic acid, had been used upon all the walls of the buildings, both inside and out; also upon all runs, fences, out-buildings, &c., about the place, small boxes had been arranged into which, before being allowed to leave the inclosed premises, all men that had been in contact in any way with the condemned animals were obliged to go and receive a thorough fumigation. These sanitary and preventive measures were established by the inspector, Mr. Moore, F.R.C.V.S., and were carried out in a most thorough and praiseworthy manner.

As no disease offering opportunity for examinations existed here at this time, I decided to go immediately to London and there ask permission of the proper authorities to prosecute my investigations upon premises under their control. During the meeting with the council on June 27, to which I have referred in the report upon pleuro-pneumonia, some conversation regarding the landing of foot-and-mouth disease took place, and in answer to questions put to me by Lord Spencer I stated that so far as I knew and believed, and that much time and effort had been used to demonstrate the truth, the disease had no existence among the animals in the United States. This, of course surprised them, and they were at as great a loss as myself to account for its appearance, and immediately offered to do all in their power to help ascertain the facts. Afterwards I told Professor Brown that if he would send an inspector with us, that we might together investigate the matter, I should be glad to have him do so. This proposition, however, he failed to accept.

At the Veterinary Department I was furnished a list of the names and dates of landing of all the steamers from which American animals had been condemned as suffering from foot-and-mouth disease upon arrival, as follows:

Name of Steamship.	From port of—	To port of—	Date of landing.	Number condemned.
			1881.	
France	New York	London	Jan. 1	59
City of Liverpool	New York	London	Jan. 6	267
City of London	New York	London	Jan. 18	12
Rochester	Boston	London	Jan. 28	42
France	New York	London	Feb. 9	56
Faraday	New York	London	Feb. 13	339
Greece	New York	London	Feb. 23	23
Lake Manitoba	Portland	Liverpool	March 17	208
City of Liverpool	New York	London	March 23	371
Palestine	Boston	Liverpool	March 27	186
Lake Nepigon	Portland	Liverpool	April 7	113
Iowa	Boston	Liverpool	May 11	694
Phœnician	Boston	Glasgow	May 31	235
Istrian	Boston	Liverpool	June 9	137
		Total		2,742

I concluded to begin this investigation by calling upon the owners, or those representing the various steamers from which condemned animals had been landed. At the office of the National Line, represented in the above list by the "France" and "Greece," the statement was made that all of the vessels of this company upon arriving at the port of London with cattle tranship them some distance down the river on to a tender, which takes them from there to Deptford. Sometimes this change is made in the stream, at others the transport boat goes with the vessel into the dock, in which case there must be a detention of at least one tide. These transport boats are provided by the London General Steam Navigation Company under contract to the Veterinary Department of the Privy Council; they are of good size, and there is never more than one provided at a time, although at various times there have been a number of different ones used. It is understood that this tender is thoroughly disinfected between each cargo.

FOURTH REPORT BY Dr. C. P. LYMAN.

Steamship "France."—First Diseased Cargo.

The vessel on her outward trip sailed from London on November 27, 1880 having among her cargo manufactured goods only. On the homeward voyage she arrived in London January 1st 1881. The animals were transhipped without delay, and although no one on board had any knowledge of the existence of disease among them, there were condemned, four hours after landing at Deptford, 59 head as affected with foot-and-mouth disease.

Steamship "France" Second Diseased Cargo.

This ship sailed again from London, January 7, having among her cargo 21 bales Marseilles wool, two bales goat skins, 11 bags English wool 32 bales of skins from Bombay, 15 casks of salted skins from England 50 bales unwashed Australian and 200 bales Russian wool. This wool was stored in No. 1 orlop and No. 5 steerage deck (she also carried two bulls and eight heifers, consigned to the "American Horse Exchange, Limited," in New York, when upon arrival, January 21, 1881 they were found to be affected with foot-and-mouth disease and quarantined for 90 days). On her return trip all cattle were carried on the main deck. She arrived in London again on February 9, when the following telegram was received from the captain: "'France' arrived at 12 o'clock; lost 18 cattle on the voyage." She was not docked until 10 o'clock next morning. Upon the examination of the cattle at Deptford, 56 head were condemned for foot-and-mouth disease.

Steamship "Greece."

This vessel sailed from London on her outward trip January 20, 1881, having among her cargo one bale rabbit skins, 30 bales raw skins, 23 bales dry English skins, and 50 bales Russian wool. This wool was stored in the steerage where the cattle were carried on the return voyage. She arrived back on the 23rd of February, and the captain telegraphed: "Arrived at 2.45 p.m., and cattle now going out." Upon being examined at Deptford 23 head were condemned for foot-and-mouth disease.

Because these vessels dock some distance down the river, it is believed that no head-ropes, grain bags, pails, or other articles used about the cattle during the voyage, and which are all landed with them at Deptford, under the law, are re-shipped, as the expense of transportation and dockage rates would be very high. The cattle fittings are all retained, but are thoroughly disinfected after each voyage. No live cattle have ever been carried as stores. The presence of the disease had never been "logged." Mr. Brook's visiting agent for the company, was very sure that none of the disease in question had been noticed on any of their boats. At the time the "France" had landed her second "diseased" cargo, he had gone to Deptford to see the cattle, and found them sick, as he was told, with foot-and-mouth disease; that they were sick he was satisfied. Just afterward (February 23), on the arrival of the "Greece," he went on board and made a careful examination of the animals in Company with the first officer and Mr. Pilling, representing the consignee, Mr. Bell (who had come to the steamer especially for this purpose) and the head cattleman. As a result, they all agreed in declaring that there was no sickness whatever among them.

Captain Pierce, of the "Greece," said that he did not notice any disease among the cattle on this voyage; it is his habit during a voyage to go below and among the animals. Whenever cattle die on board he logs the fact; he has never logged an outbreak of sickness because he has never yet had one.

We next called upon Messrs. William Ross & Co., agents of the City Line, represented in the list by the City of Liverpool and City of London. These steamers never go to Deptford, but tranship their cattle in precisely the same manner as do those just described.

Steamship "City of Liverpool"—First Diseased Cargo.

This vessel sailed from London on the outward voyage November 28, 1880, having among her cargo five bales wool, 18 tons salted hides, and 19 bales dry skins. On the homeward voyage she arrived in London, January 6, 1881. The cattle were transshipped at once; of these, after being landed at Deptford, 267 head were condemned as suffering from foot-and-mouth disease.

R 679.

STEAMSHIP "CITY OF LIVERPOOL."—SECOND DISEASED CARGO.

On this voyage the ship sailed from London, February 11, 1881, having among the cargo 22 tons salted hides and skins, 5 bales wool, 214 bales "greasy" wool (probably Australian), and 12 bales skins.

On the homeward voyage she arrived in London on March 20, when, because the steamer had not been telegraphed from Gravesend, there was no transport ready to receive the cattle, she therefore docked with them still on board, and it was not until the second day after that they were transhipped, and on the 23rd, 371 head were condemned as suffering from foot-and-mouth disease.

STEAMSHIP "CITY OF LONDON."

This vessel, on her outward trip, sailed from London, December 11, 1880, having among her cargo 35 tons salted hides, 4 tons salted skins, and 2 tons dry skins. On the homeward voyage she arrived in London, January 17, 1881, where, on account of the state of the tide, and to save time, the transport accompanied her into the dock, as is very often done under such circumstances. This caused so much of a delay that the animals were not examined until the next day, at which time 12 head were condemned as suffering from foot-and-mouth disease.

These vessels have never carried any live stores, nor have they, so far as known, ever carried back to America any head-ropes, bags, pails, &c. that had been in the Deptford lairages. The cattle fittings are permanent, thoroughly disinfected after each voyage, and whenever repairs upon them are needed it is done in America, and with lumber procured there.

We next saw Messrs. Adamson and Ronaldson, who made the following statements regarding steamers under their control:

STEAMSHIP "ROCHESTER."

This vessel, on her outward voyage, sailed from London on December 8, 1880, having among her cargo 131 bales of wool (probably Australian unwashed). On her homeward trip, after a long and stormy passage, she reached London, January 28, when, at a considerable distance down the river, the cattle were put on board the transport boat. This was not the common practice, but was in fact the only time she had not gone alongside at Deptford to discharge. Upon being examined, all that were left of the original shipment, viz., 42 head, were condemned as suffering from foot-and-mouth disease. Concerning this shipment I was told that the animals, before going on board, were detained on the railroad four days over time by snow storms, during which they were probably neither fed nor watered. Upon reaching Boston they went immediately on board ship; seemed very tired and laid down *at once;* shortly after, two died; soon they commenced dying in large numbers, and the carcasses were thrown overboard. Owing to the unprecedented roughness of the passage, the cattle arrived very much bruised and exhausted, and, in the opinion of the owners of the vessel, this was the only cause for their condemnation. The practice of the steamers of this line is to go alongside the landing stages at Deptford and discharge the cattle direct, simply because it is convenient for them to do so, as they berth at the Millwood docks, which are just across the river. They never carry any live stores, and the cattle fittings are put up at Boston, and when repairs are necessary they are made there. When asked if they ever carried back to America any head-ropes, bags, &c. from the premises at Deptford, they at first said "No," but, upon looking into the matter, found that the steamer "Milanese," sailing from London, October 2, 1880, the steamer "Sumatra," sailing from London, June 16, 1881, the steamer "Housa," sailing from London, June 27, 1881, had done so, and they now thought it more than possible that upon other occasions other steamers had carried to Boston bundles of such ropes, which had been brought to the ships by watermen's boats directly from the Deptford lairages.

STEAMSHIP "FARADAY."

This vessel is owned by the Messrs. Siemen Brothers, but at the time of the voyage in question was chartered to Messrs. Adamson and Ronaldson. In 1878 she was employed in carrying cattle; later she was engaged in laying telegraphic cable, and, towards the close of the year 1879, she was laid up in Millwood dock, where she remained empty for more than a year. She had carried live stores while laying cable, but not when engaged on these other voyages.

FOURTH REPORT BY Dr. C. P. LYMAN.

The cattle fittings were put up partly while she was in Millwood docks, and partly during the outward voyage, of lumber obtained in England; she has never carried any provender, head-ropes, pails, or grain-bags. This vessel, on her outward trip, sailed from London in November 1880, with a cargo among which were 2,848 bales of Russian wool loaded into the tanks, at the bottom of the vessel, generally used for storing the cable. The combings of the hatches are raised about 4 feet above the level of the docks, so that it was thought if a bale had been broken while being hoisted out the wool would have fallen back into the tank, and not have been scattered over any of the decks upon which cattle were afterwards carried. Going into New York, when off Sandy Hook, she broke her propeller, and was obliged to lay up in Brooklyn for several weeks before taking on board her live cargo, which she did at the Henderson docks in New York. The passage home was a very long one, some 21 or 22 days, and it was not until the consignee of the cattle, Mr. Bell, or his agent, went on board the ship upon her arrival home that there was thought to be any disease among the cattle; he, however, discovered it then. She went alongside the landing stage at Deptford on February 13th, and discharged her cattle, from which were condemned 339 head as suffering from foot-and-mouth disease.

Steamship "Lake Manitoba" and Steamship "Lake Nepigon."*

Although the representatives of the Beaver Line, to which both these steamers belong, were personally seen, they, for their own reasons, preferred to answer my questions regarding them by letter, as follows: "In reply to your inquiries as to cattle by the " above steamers from Portland, Me., arriving here on the 16th March and 7th April " 1881, I have to inform you that 208 head were landed affected with foot-and-mouth " disease from the 'Lake Manitoba,' and 113 head from the 'Lake Nepigon.' The " outward cargoes by each steamer were the usual general cargoes, and contained no " hides, skins, head-ropes, pails, &c. The disease did not develop during the voyage " sufficiently to come under the notice of the captain and officers of the steamers, and " no entries were made in the log-book respecting it. On the voyage in question the " 'Lake Manitoba' left Portland the 5th of March, and the 'Lake Nepigon' the 22d " of the same month, but had no live stock on ship's account on board. The shippers " of the cattle were Messrs. R. Craig & Co. and D. H. Craig, ex. 'Lake Manitoba'; " Messrs. R. Craig & Co. and D. H. Craig, ex. 'Lake Nepigon.'"

Calling upon Messrs. George Warren & Co., representatives of the steamers "Palestine" and "Iowa," I received the following information:

Steamship "Palestine."

The steamer left Liverpool on her outward voyage February 24th, having among her cargo four casks skins. Although there was no mention of there being any head-ropes, &c. on board, I was assured that possibly there might have been some, as they often take them. On the homeward voyage she left Boston, March 12th, and arrived in Liverpool and discharged her animals by going alongside the landing stage (as all vessels do at this port) on the 27th of March, when 186 head were condemned as suffering from foot-and-mouth disease.

Steamship "Iowa."

This vessel, on her outward voyage, left Liverpool, April 12th, having among her cargo four casks wet skins, 328 bags hide cuttings, *four bundles corn-bags and four bundles head-ropes from the lairages to R. Craig & Co.*, 83 coils old rope, 500 salted hides, 21 bales dry hides, and 125 bags Yorkshire wool. She left Boston on the homeward trip April 30th, at noon, with about 849 cattle shipped by Thomas Crawford & Co., S. W. Clark, C. M. Acer & Co. (which, the gentlemen remarked, is the same as Craig), R. Craig & Co., John S. Fraser, D. Coughlin, F. R. Lingham, and T. and F. Uttey. The first disease, said by one of the cattlemen to be foot-and-mouth, was, says the ship's log, noticed at 8 a.m. on the 6th of May, among animals belonging to C. M. Acer & Co., on the port side of the after steerage; on the 7th of May, at 8 a.m., the same trouble was showing among cattle by the forward hatch, belonging to R. Craig & Co.; on the

---

* Mr. J. W. T. Moore, Inspector of the Privy Council at Liverpool, states with reference to the "Lake Nepigon," which brought animals affected with foot-and-mouth disease, that the master of the vessel informed him that every head-rope carried on this voyage was brand new, and that the vessel had never had foot-and-mouth disease on board previously.

9th, at 4 a.m., it was discovered among other cattle occupying space in the after steerage, forward steerage, main deck, and starboard alley-way; on the 10th, at 4 a.m., it is recorded that foot-and-mouth disease is still spreading among the cattle all over the main deck, and on the 11th of May, at 6 a.m., at which time they were landed in Liverpool, the disease had spread throughout the ship, and 694 head were condemned as being affected with the disease.

The "Iowa" has never carried to America from England any cattle, calves, sheep, or pigs; neither do any vessels of this line carry live stores. The cattle fittings are put in and repaired at Boston.

Steamship "Phœnician."

This vessel is of the Allan Line, and of that division of it having its headquarters at Glasgow. From the firm there I have the following information concerning her: On the two previous voyages, that is, since the 20th of September, 1880, she was employed in the River Plate trade, where she carried no cattle. Upon the outward trip, of the voyage in question, she had simply the ordinary general cargo, not having among it any articles that could with reason be supposed to have been in any way in contact with diseased animals of any kind. On the return voyage she left Boston at 1.45 p.m., on the 17th of May. The cattle, 239 head in all, were shipped by J. McShane, jun., of Montreal. The first symptoms of sickness among them were noticed three days after the vessel had left port, "on an old bull;" from him the infection speedily spread through the rest of the cattle, until, upon the 31st of May, when she landed them at Glasgow, 235 head were condemned as suffering from foot-and-mouth disease. Her cattle fittings were put in and all repaired in Boston. She did not carry any live stores, nor was there anything about her which could have given rise to the disease. In a letter on the subject the Messrs. Allan say, "We are satisfied that the aliment originated with " the old bull, and was brought from America; he however, had recovered before the " end of the voyage."

Concerning this shipment, I had learned early in June, from the Messrs. Allan, at Boston, that of the 239 animals shipped on this vessel by Mr. McShane, six car-loads, consisting of 103 head, were Canadian cattle, and 137 head were Western States *steers*. These *steers* were bought of Munroe, of Brighton (Boston), and the lot was made up as follows:—

Thirty-head lot, averaging 1,331 pounds, bought of R. Strahom & Co., Chicago, May 7.

Thirty-seven head, of a lot of 127 head, averaging 1,302 pounds, bought of R. Strahom & Co., Chicago, May 7.

Sixteen-head lot, averaging 1,400 pounds, bought of R. Strahom & Co., Chicago, May 7.

Five head, of a lot of 30 head averaging 1,224 pounds, bought of Reynolds, Enoch & Co., Chicago, May 7.

Four head, of a lot averaging 1,685 pounds, bought of Robinson, Chicago, May 7.

Forty-five head, of a lot of 82 head, averaging 1,329 pounds, bought of Daly, Miller & Co., Saint Louis, May 6.

Giving the total of 137 animals, making, Mr. Munroe assured me, a nice straight lot of steers.

I afterwards learned that Mr. McShane had frequently shipped cattle to Liverpool during the existence in the lairages there of foot-and-mouth disease, and I was told by another shipper, who has had more or less to do with him, that it was McShane's practice, as well as that of nearly all exporters, to bring back and use their old head-ropes.*

Steamship "Istrian."

I am indebted to Messrs. Frederick Leyland & Co., the owners of this steamer, for the following particulars: She left Liverpool on the outward voyage May 12, having among her cargo 9 bales wool waste, 2 bales hair, 3 casks salted skins, 350 bundles salted calf skins, 272 coils old rope, 31 bales wool, 11 casks salted skins, 868 wet salted hides, 3 bundles calf skins, and 259 bales wool. On the homeward voyage

---

* James McShane, junr., shipped cattle from Boston to Liverpool as follows; January 27, 177 head, on the "Pembroke"; February 18, 100 head, on the "Glamorgan"; February 23, 80 head, on the "Pembroke"; April 6, 130 head, on the "Pembroke"; April 13, 175 head, on the "Glamorgan."

she left Boston on the 29th May. Although the log makes no mention of any disease among the cattle, it does mention in several instances sickness and death among the sheep on board, which fact carries the inference that had anything wrong been noticed with the cattle, it, too, would have been "logged." She discharged the cattle in Liverpool at 4.40 p.m., June 9, when 137 head were condemned as having foot-and-mouth disease. The sheep were not mentioned as being affected.

This vessel, as well as others of this line, have frequently carried back head-ropes; they are brought from the lairages and taken charge of during the voyage by the servants of the owners of the cattle who return upon the steamers.

The shippers of the cattle were Messrs. Swift Bros. & Co., and Messrs. J. and C. Coughlin, who are regularly engaged in the trade between Boston and Liverpool. Afterwards, in an interview with one of the Messrs. Coughlin, I learned that their practice was to collect their head-ropes in the lairages and re-ship them for use in America, and that he would rather use a new rope with every animal than have this disease appear among them, and he thought other shippers entertained the same views. The investigations so far seemed to point to the fact that from whatever source the infection had reached the American animals, the vessels themselves in their general cargoes and management, should be held blameless, and that notwithstanding a few instances in which its appearance might reasonably be due to other causes, notably in the second cargoes of the steamers "France" and "City of Liverpool," the outbreaks were directly chargeable to the self-same infection that had already caused so much trouble in Great Britain, conveyed by the indiscriminate use of the head-ropes, &c., coming from the foreign animals' wharves at Deptford and Liverpool, which were, at that time, hotbeds of the disease. It remained, then, to ascertain how these premises became infected; how this infection could have been conveyed to these articles; how they, having become impregnated with the virus, could have come in contact with the cattle in such a way as to cause the outbreaks which undoubtedly had taken place in mid-ocean, and not at the same time have been introduced to our various seaboard markets.

INTRODUCTION AND SPREAD OF THE DISEASE IN THE DEPTFORD MARKET.

In the report of the Veterinary Department of the Privy Council office for 1880, Professor Brown writes:

"In the middle of September last, the inspector of the Privy Council at Deptford had his attention called to the existence of the signs of foot-and-mouth disease in the tongues of some French cattle which had been slaughtered in the market; no symptoms of the disease had been seen in the animals during life, but the morbid appearances were characteristic, and left no room for doubt as to the nature of the infection. Soon afterwards, on September 20, a cargo of cattle from Havre were landed at Deptford from the ship 'Swallow,' and on inspection the second day after landing some of them were found to be affected with foot-and-mouth disease.

"The disease thus introduced into Deptford foreign-cattle market continued to spread among the animals which were landed there, and as the lairs at that time were over-crowded with animals from America as well as from Europe, no opportunity was afforded for the effectual disinfection of the places where disease had existed, and consequently animals which were perfectly healthy on landing became infected soon after entering the lairs."

From the assistant inspector, in relation to the same matter, I have it that "foot-and-mouth disease was brought to Deptford by the steamship 'Swallow' from Havre, September 20, 1880; she had on board 57 cattle, 30 of which were affected with the disease; other cargoes with foot-and-mouth disease were landed at Deptford from France, November 8 and December 17, 1880."

In a conversation upon the subject, the inspector of the Privy Council at Deptford said to me that if he remembered rightly their first real trouble was during the latter part of September, 1880, and was caused by some animals coming from France; from these, foot-and-mouth disease spread over the entire premises. From that time onward it had caused them much trouble, and they have taken a number of extra precautions as to disinfecting, and so on. He further said that upon going into the lairages animals are necessarily greatly mixed, and in a number of instances he remembered that there had been cattle landed from the United States in a healthy condition which had afterwards contracted foot-and-mouth disease on these premises through coming in contact, either directly or indirectly, with those from other countries already diseased. Alterations were then under *consideration*, which, when carried out, it was hoped would overcome this evil. The lairages were not then (July 20) nearly as badly infected as they had been, but still it was not improbable that even then some of the infection might remain about the premises; in fact, quite recently he had discovered its existence in animals that had been landed healthy, and that could have contracted it only from their contaminated surroundings.

Introduction and Spread of the Disease in the Liverpool Markets.

The history of the introduction and spread of foot-and-mouth disease into and through the Liverpool lairages is in some respects remarkable, and inasmuch as it has never yet, to my knowledge, been given publicly, it will, perhaps, be worth while to give it here at length. For my ability to do so I am greatly indebted to Mr. Moore, the local inspector of the Privy Council, whose exact methods of preserving the various data in connexion with his inspections were invaluable to me in this case.

Very early in January, 1881, the steamship "Brazilian," bringing cattle from Boston to Liverpool, upon entering the River Mersey, grounded, and in trying to get off became disabled to such an extent that it was found to be necessary to take the cattle from her where she lay. Engaged in this work were several small boats as follows:—

	Head.
January 4—	
The tug "Cruiser" brought up	111
The tug "Wrestler" brought up	111
The tug "Rover" brought up	65
The tug "Knight Templar" brought up	53
The tug "Knight of Malta" brought up	33
The tug "Fury" brought up	1
The tug "Republic" brought up	3
Ferry-boat "Sunflower" brought up	224
Flat-boat "Mersey" brought up	32
The tug "Lord Lyons" brought up	1
The tug "Ajax" brought up	4
Flat-boat "Mersey" (two cargoes) brought up	24
"Mudhopper B" brought up	2
Crane barge "Ironsides" brought up	1

In all, 665 animals were thus landed at the Woodside lairage. There were 10 others landed, part at Wallasey and part at Huskisson No. 2 lairages, and one swam ashore and was killed on the beach. Of the health of these animals, Mr. Moore says: "I examined them all on the 5th and found them free from disease. On the 9th a bullock, one of those landed at Woodside, was found sick. He was slaughtered, and the *post-mortem* examination revealed recent foot-and-mouth disease. There were vesicles in the mouth and on the tongue, but none on the feet. On the 10th three cases more were discovered in the same lot, and on the 11th two more were found." It seems that these animals, as soon as the disease was discovered, were killed very quickly, for, while at midnight of the 8th 452 of them were still alive, there were on the 11th but nine head remaining. This probably accounts for the fact that no more cases were discovered among them. On the morning of the 11th the premises with the remaining nine animals were locked up, and no one but the attendants allowed to enter. The animals were quickly killed, and disinfection of the place they had occupied commenced.

There were on the other half of the wharf eight bulls remaining from a cargo of 32 animals landed healthy on the 7th of January, from the steamship "England," from New York. On the 10th, or eight days after the Brazilian outbreak was first noticed, four of these were found diseased. They were killed, the premises disinfected, and the wharf was not again used until after January 29. It could not be ascertained to be a fact that any of the boats engaged in this transhipment, except the "Mersey," were in the habit of carrying home-cattle about the river. She undoubtedly was, and there was also some little indication that the ferry-boat "Sunflower" had done the same thing. To one of these two boats then conveying infection contracted from English animals, previously carried to those brought by it from the disabled steamer, must be ascribed the honour of introducing foot-and-mouth disease into this lairage, for when the history as related is considered, and when it is remembered what a short time is necessary for its incubation, any other explanation of the occurrence seems impossible.

FOURTH REPORT BY Dr. C. P. LYMAN.

Nothing more was seen of foot-and-mouth disease here until on the 17th of March, more than two months afterwards, the steamship "Lake Manitoba," from Portland, landed a cargo of 259 head, among which were found 208 cases. They were landed at Woodside, and were all slaughtered by the 19th. The portion of the wharf occupied by them was disinfected and closed up, remaining so until the 29th.

On the 27th of March the steamship "Palestine" landed at Wallasey 240 oxen, among which were 186 cases of foot-and-mouth disease. They were all slaughtered by the 29th, and the wharf was closed for 11 days.

On the 7th of April the steamship "Lake Nepigon," from Portland, landed at Woodside 141 oxen, among them 113 cases of the disease. All of these were soon slaughtered, and the wharf closed for a time. On May 11 the steamship "Iowa," from Boston, landed at Wallasey 859 oxen, among them 694 cases of the disease. All of these were slaughtered by the 16th, and the wharf was closed from then until the 31st. On the 9th of June the steamship "Istrian," from Boston, landed at Woodside 371 oxen, among which were found 137 cases of foot-and-mouth disease. These were slaughtered by the 19th, and the wharf was closed until the 3rd of July.

Regarding the spread to healthy animals in the buildings, Mr. Moore made to me the following statement: "On January 4, oxen ex steamship 'England,' from New York, " were infected in the Woodside lairages by the 'Brazilian' lot. Oxen which were " landed healthy from the steamship 'Canopus' on the 23rd, from the steamship " 'Pembroke' on the 20th, and from the steamship 'Bavarian' on the 22nd, were " found on the 27th of April to have contracted the disease. The steamship 'Illyrian,' " from Boston, landed her cargo of 346 oxen on the 26th of April, all healthy. These " animals were examined carefully every day, and on the 30th foot-and-mouth disease " was found among them.

" The steamship 'Lake Manitoba,' on the 27th of April, landed 338 oxen, all healthy. " They were carefully watched, and the disease made its appearance among them on the " 1st of May.

" On the 28th of April the steamship 'Minnesota' landed a cargo of 406 oxen, all " healthy. On the 1st of May foot-and-mouth disease appeared among them.

" On the 4th of May the steamship 'Massachusetts' landed 565 bullocks, all healthy. " They were examined every day, and on the 7th one case only had been discovered. " They were not 'mouthed,' and the butchers may have removed and killed cases that " were not seen, but, so far as is known, only 16 of this whole lot became diseased.

" On the 8th of May four cases were found among previously healthy cattle that had " been landed from the steamship 'Ontario,' May 4.

" On the 9th of May foot-and-mouth disease was found among previously healthy " animals that were landed on the 4th from the steamships 'Bulgarian' and 'Palestine.'

" On the 11th of May, at 7.50 a.m., the steamship 'Iberian' landed a cargo of 352 " oxen. They remained healthy up to the 16th, when the disease was found to be " among them.

" On the 18th of May the steamship 'Toronto' landed 251 cattle. The first evidence " of the disease among these animals was observed on the 24th.

" On the 26th of June six cases of foot-and-mouth disease were found among oxen that " had been landed healthy from the steamship 'Palestine' on the 17th. This infection " was supposed to have been from the cargo of the 'Istrian,' which landed the disease " on the 9th of June."

GLASGOW.

From any information that is at present in possession of this Department, I think that it can scarcely be said that the premises at Glasgow have ever become infected, for, although it is true a cargo of condemned animals from the steamship "Phœnician" were landed there, they were so quickly killed, and the premises so thoroughly disinfected, that it seems not to have gained any foothold. The appearance of the diseased cargo there seems to be entirely explained by the evidence already given.

Mr. McShane, the shipper, had 130 cattle on the steamship "Pembroke," which left Boston for Liverpool on the 6th of April. The "Pembroke" landed all her cattle in a perfectly healthy condition in Liverpool on the 20th of April; on the 27th, however, they were unfortunate enough to contract the disease in the Woodside lairages. Twenty days afterward, or on the 17th of May, we find Mr. McShane making a shipment of 239 cattle on the steamship "Phœnician," from Boston to Glasgow, from among which, upon her arrival at that port, 235 head were condemned as suffering from foot-

and-mouth disease. It is also in the evidence that Mr. McShane was in the habit, as were others, of bringing back and using again head-ropes that had done previous service upon animals in the contaminated Liverpool lairages.

It would seem, therefore, that the "Phœnician" outbreak is chargeable to infection brought direct from Liverpool. All cattle shipped from America to Great Britain are, after going on board the steamer, tied to stanchions by ropes which have been placed around the base of the horns, technically known as "head-ropes." Upon their arrival at the port of destination, the end that was made fast to the fixture on the vessel is untied, and the animals, with the ropes still hanging, are driven into the lairs, where they are to remain until taken out for slaughter. At Deptford these ropes are sometimes removed from the heads in the lairages when they are sold; at others they accompany them to the shambles. In Liverpool, so far as I have observed, they always remain on the animals until they are slaughtered. In this way every chance is given for their thorough impregnation with the virus of any contagious disease that may be present in either the lairs or the slaughter-houses. To show how thorough this chance is, I may say that in London I saw a lot of Dutch bulls tied "head on" to the same rail with a lot of American bullocks; also a lot of Spanish head-ropes hanging over a rail to which American animals were tied at the time; and in the shamble pens were some cattle with the original head-ropes on, some with ropes supplied by the butchers, and others without either, mixed indiscriminately with Spanish and Dutch cattle, all awaiting slaughter. In several instances the animals in one pen were tied facing those in the next, all to the same rail.

It was told by the inspector at Deptford that no head-ropes had been returned to America for two years, but I think he must have been mistaken in this, for not only were dates given me by the steamship owners, upon which they had received and shipped them, but on several occasions while at Deptford I saw large bunches of them hanging over the cross-rails, which, upon inquiry from the workmen collecting them, I was told were being got ready for re-shipment to the United States.

At Liverpool, Mr. Moore assured me that old ropes were constantly returned, and that he, realising the danger from such a practice, had done what little he could to prevent it. From inquiry and personal observation I find that, as a rule, cattle going abroad are "roped" either after the car load arrives at the dock, when a man goes into the car for the purpose, or else not until the animal has been driven from the car on to the steamer. To this fortunate circumstance, and for no other reason probably, is it that the animals in our home markets have so far escaped foot-and-mouth disease.

Although following the movements of contagion is, as a rule, not the most certain of all pursuits, it does seem as if this investigation into the causes of the appearance of this disease among some of our cattle landed in Great Britain during the past year had been attended with success, and that while certain dangerous practices are allowed in the matter of unsafe articles of import, such as unwashed wools, green hides, skins, &c., there is no one cause among them all sufficiently constant to be regarded with anything more than suspicion. On the other hand, the evidence plainly shows that to an article not looked upon or imported as cargo, but simply sent back to accommodate the cattle shippers, and used by them without a thought of danger, must be ascribed the cause of the outbreaks, and when the evidence is read the transmission of foot-and-mouth disease by the head-ropes seems so simple and easy of accomplishment that the wonder is that any one conversant with the practice of the trade need for a moment have had any doubt as to the true source of the infection.

To prevent future outbreaks of the kind I shall recommend for your consideration that Congress be asked to pass a law prohibiting, under certain penalties, the introduction of all articles from the foreign animals' wharves of Great Britain, and that Custom officers be directed to enforce such law.

Trichinæ in Swine.

In relation to that part of my instructions directing me to examine the hogs arriving in Great Britain from the United States, with a view of ascertaining to how great an extent they are diseased, or are infected with trichinæ, I have to report that during my stay no such animals were landed. But as tending to give some idea of the percentage of animals thus affected (and it will not probably be found to be in excess of these figures), I will call your attention to the following extracts from the report of the Veterinary Department of the Privy Council Office for the year 1879:

"The slaughter of large numbers of American swine at the port of landing, on account of swine fever, afforded an opportunity of obtaining specimens of flesh for examination, with a view to ascertain what proportion of the animals were infected with trichinæ. The inspectors of the Veterinary Department examined 279 separate portions of swine's flesh which were sent from Liverpool, and detected living trichinæ in three specimens ; * * * but it was not deemed expedient to prohibit the introduction of American pork into this country, for the reason that such a measure would have damaged the trade without producing any satisfactory results. A large proportion of the objectionable meat would have been sent to this country by a circuitous route, and thus the object of the restriction would have been defeated, *besides which, trichinosis among swine* is known to exist in *Germany*, and it probably exists in other exporting countries, so that nothing short of total prohibition of swine flesh in all forms from all foreign sources would have been effectual."

In view of the recent total embargo placed by some of the foreign Governments upon the imports of our hog products into their countries, on account of the alleged existence in them of *trichinæ*, I would suggest that an inquiry be established which shall point out, first, the actual percentage of American hogs that are infected by this parasite; second, the portion of the country in which the largest percentage of animals so affected are found to exist: third, the nature of the food, if there is any difference, that these pigs receive; fourth, whether animals that are kept around the home buildings are more subject than are those kept in the field to the invasion of this entozoon, and all other matters relating to the question which may aid in devising such means as shall decrease to a minimum their existence in American pork products.

Condition of Animals arriving in Great Britain.

The losses occasioned by death and injury to cattle while being shipped abroad have been greatly reduced, and they are now landed at the various ports of Great Britain in a much better condition than formerly. Indeed, notwithstanding the much greater distance they are necessarily carried, they arrive with fewer bruises and in better condition generally than do those from some of the neighbouring European ports. This gratifying condition of affairs is due to the good care and improved methods of ventilation, &c., adopted by the owners of steamships. Experience in the trade, and the requirements of the insurance companies, have compelled many improvements for the comfort and safe transport of these animals. More light and space are given them, and by means of various ventilating devices an abundance of fresh air is furnished throughout the entire voyage. In most of the vessels a method of drainage into the bilge has been arranged, which may be pumped out as often as desirable. While much has been done in this direction by the steamship owners alone the managers of the insurance companies interested have not been idle, but so great has been the care exercised by them in the selection of animals for transportation and the provident provisions made for them during the voyage that the losses which amounted to more than 5 per cent. from January 1 to September 30, 1880, have been reduced to about $2\frac{1}{2}$ per cent. during the same months of this year. Notwithstanding this great improvement, the weather during some parts of the past season has been the most severe ever known to the trade.

Very respectfully,
Hon. George B. Loring,   CHARLES P. LYMAN, F.R.C.V.S.
 Commissioner of Agriculture.

No. 54.

Report by Dr. JAMES D. HOPKINS, D.V.S., to the COMMISSIONER OF AGRICULTURE, Washington.

Contagious Pleuro-Pneumonia in New York.

Owing to circumstances over which the department had no control, the investigation in the State of New York was brought to a close on or about the 20th May last. The examinations made in that State by James D. Hopkins, D.V.S., from April 8 to May 17, will be found recorded below. From information received from the highest authority in such matters in this State, it would seem that contagious pleuro-pneumonia prevails to about the same extent that it did prior to the recent efforts of the State authorities to stamp it out. Dr. James Law, in writing to the Commissioner of Agriculture, under date of October 10 last, says :—

"Putnam County, which was purged from the plague in the early part of last year, has been infected (one herd at least) for the whole past summer; Westchester County contains at least two centres of infection, and Richmond (Staten Island) two, though both these counties had been purged of the infection; New York City, which was all but rid of the plague, harbouring it only in places known and circumscribed, is again suffering; and finally, the east end of Queen's County, which had been long clear, has been extensively infected."

NUMBER and LOCATION of DISEASED HERDS examined by DR. JAS. D. HOPKINS.

Name of Surgeon.	Name of Owner.	State.	County.	Day Examined.	Number in Herd.	Number Sick.	Number Died.	Name of Disease.
Jas. D. Hopkins, D.V.S.	Michael Tierney	New York City, 23rd Ward.	New York	1881. April 8	17 head (a)	Not given	6	Contagious pleuro-pneumonia.
Do.	-	New York City	Do.	Do.	24 cows (b)	Do.	(Killed)	Do.
Do.	David Titus	Do.	Queens	April 22	13 cows (c)	Do.	5	Do.
Do.	Ann N. Titus	Do.	Do.	Do.	21 head (d)	Do.	7	Do.
Do.	Valentine Willets	Do.	Do.	Do.	14 cows (e)	Do.	5	Do.
Do.	C. C. Willets	Do.	Do.	Do.	13 cows (f)	1	1	Do.
Do.	Fred. Willets	Do.	Do.	Do.	9 cows and 6 calves (g).	Not given	1	Do.
Do.	Jas. A. Hayt	Do.	Putnam	April 27	Not given (h)	7 head	6	Do.
Do.	D. P. Titus	Do.	Queens	„ 28	7 head (i)	3 head	2	Do.
Do.	Richard C. Hubbs	Do.	Do.	Do.	12 head (j)	Not given	11	Do.
Do.	M. R. Hines	Do.	Do.	Do.	10 head (k)	1 acute and 6 chronic cases.	2	Do.
Do.	Philip Seibert	New York City, Blissville.	Do.	May 12	22 head (l)	2 acute cases	-	Do.
Do.	J. S. Daugherty	Do.	Do.	Do.	16 head (m)	1 chronic case	-	Do.
Do.	Joseph Stevenson	Do.	Do.	Do.	30 head (n)	3 chronic cases	-	Do.
Do.	W. H. Cutter	New York City, Port Richmond.	Richmond	May 17	24 head (o)	1 chronic case	10	Do.

(a) These animals died between October, 1880, and March 1, 1881.
(b) These cows were bought at the Central Stock Yards, and conveyed by regular cattle boat to Eisness' slaughter-house, Forty-fourth Street.
(c) These cows died since January 2, 1881; the last one died February 24.
(d) There are seven chronic cases. This herd was inoculated by cattle on adjoining farm of R. H. Robbins, who had lost seven or eight cows out of a herd of 20.
(e) Inoculated by cow bought from dealer in October last.
(f) Killed diseased cow and inoculated remainder in October, and has had no disease since.
(g) He sent three cows to the butcher and inoculated the remainder. Inoculation seems to give satisfaction to the people in this locality.
(h) Has lost six valuable animals up to date, and has seven still suffering with the disease. His place has been quarantined.
(i) These animals died last winter, and he now has three chronic cases.
(j) These animals died last fall. No sick animals at present.
(k) These two cows were lost about a month ago; thinks his animals were infected by Hubbs' cattle. His place has been quarantined.
(l) Swill stables.
(m) Swill stables.
(n) Swill stables.
(o) The disease appeared here about the 1st of March last, since which time 10 animals have died.

No. 55.

REPORTS by DR. W. B. E. MILLER, D.V.S., and DR. J. C. CORLIES, D.V.S., to the COMMISSIONER OF AGRICULTURE, Washington.

CONTAGIOUS PLEURO-PNEUMONIA IN NEW JERSEY.

SIR, Camden, N. J., October 31, 1881.

In accordance with your request I have the honour herewith to forward you a brief summary report of the work done upon the veterinary staff of the Department of Agriculture since the date of my appointment, May 12th last, until the present time.

My first official act, after receipt of proper authority, was to establish a border quarantine between Philadelphia and Camden, and other points on this side of the river, in order that cattle passing over the ferries should be detained for the purpose of inspection.

To facilitate the transportation and examination of the same, cattle pounds were erected at each ferry yard into which all stock were ordered to be driven and detained until such time as they could be seen and inspected.

Owing to the distance of some of the ferries from a central locality, much delay must sometimes be necessarily imposed, and I very soon found it absolutely imperative to employ a proper person to watch and assist at the yards in order to prevent some of the drivers from removing their stock prior to examination. The person so employed was invested with authority to arrest any person or persons unwilling to comply with the order of quarantine and inspection. I am happy to state that no arrests have thus far been required, as I have endeavoured to accommodate all parties as far as was in my power as rapidly as possible, and in order to do so have very frequently had to employ the assistance of Dr. Zuill, D.V.S., of Philadelphia, to visit a number of the ferry yards while I was engaged at others.

Since the establishment of the quarantine order, 7,164 cattle have been examined. Many of them have been sick with the ordinary diseases of cattle, and quite a number have been found to be infected with diseases of an infectious or contagious character. But I am glad to inform you that but very few cases of contagious pleuro-pneumonia (the disease for which I was instructed to examine) have been found in comparison to the number of cattle examined. All of them, however, have been carefully reported to the department, and the source of the disease traced whenever it was possible to do so.

The first case was discovered June 29, 1881, and the animal traced back to Wilmington, Del., where she was reported as one of a lot that came from Baltimore, Md. Another case, on July 6, in a lot of four calves from Marple, Delaware County, Pennsylvania, all of which were slaughtered at the abattoir, and two of which showed lung lesions. The next case, on July 12, that of a cow and calf in a lot of eighteen from West Philadelphia stock yards. The cow was ordered to be killed by the State Board of Health, and a *post mortem* examination revealed the disease well marked in both lungs; lesions were also plainly seen in the lungs of the calf. On July 22 a calf brought from Guineatown, Bucks County, Pennsylvania, was detected by Dr. Zuill, and the case referred to me, which I immediately condemned to be slaughtered, when a *post mortem* examination fully confirmed our diagnosis.

On the 14th of September two cases were ordered into close quarantine as very suspicious. A proper history was afterwards obtained, stating that they originally came from West Virginia to Baltimore, where they were resold and shipped from Baltimore stock yards to West Philadelphia. Being fat, they were ordered to the abattoir for slaughter, and a *post mortem* examination showed the suspicions to be well founded.

On the 22nd of September two cows were discovered in a herd that came from Glendale, Northampton County, Pennsylvania. On the 29th two others, in a lot that came from Bethlehem, Pa., all of which had been herded together at the New Jersey State Fair, in charge of A. S. Shimer, and which were affected with lung trouble. A subsequent investigation made by Dr. Gadsden, of Philadelphia, would seem to indicate that the animals had no contagious disease. He did not, however, see the cattle at the time of his visitation, but did see others of the same herd. Almost daily cattle affected with *Phthisis Pulmonalis Verminalis* (hoose or husk) are seen at the ferry yards, and in view of the fact that this affection has been alarmingly fatal in young animals in this State during the last two or three years, it would seem as if some legal measures should be adopted to prevent its spread. Other diseases of animals, such as swine plague, glanders in horses, chicken cholera, foot-rot in sheep, &c., are existing throughout the whole State, and call for some action on the part of government.

During the time that has elapsed since the date of my appointment, especially during the latter part of July and the month of August, I made weekly visits to the State of Delaware as instructed, and found many cases of infected farms and several acute and chronic cases of pleuro-pneumonia. That part of the State immediately bordering upon Pennsylvania and the eastern shore of Maryland is certainly an infected locality, and the section surrounding Wilmington had suffered from the ravages of the disease. The law in that State is inoperative, and no measures are taken to prevent the spread of disease.

From my investigations thus far, I must conclude that contagious pleuro-pneumonia of cattle exists in New York, New Jersey, Pennsylvania, Delaware, and Maryland; that other diseases of animals, especially swine plague, glanders, and chicken cholera, are to be found in every section of the country. From my personal experience, of the last two years particularly, I believe that the only way to exterminate these diseases is to stop the interstate traffic in animals from infected States, to thoroughly examine all cattle crossing from one State to another, whether from infected States or not, and to destroy all diseased and exposed animals at sight.

Since the system of inspection was adopted at this point a very decided change has taken place in the general appearance of the animals crossing these ferries. Instead of poor, delicate looking half-starved animals, or sick or almost disabled, as was formerly the case, none now appear for inspection but the very best, and it certainly has proven a source of great benefit to this section particularly. No suspicious or unhealthy cattle are allowed to pass when they do appear. As a result, dealers and drovers do not attempt to pass inferior animals over if they can possibly avoid it. Occasionally, however, a stranger will come with a lot driven directly from the country, or some parties will go to the stock yards, and purchase a poor class of animals simply because they can buy them cheap, and I invariably subject them to a thorough examination and inspection.

The work has been vigorously and thoroughly accomplished, and great good has been derived therefrom.

Respectfully submitted,
WM. B. E. MILLER, D.V.S.

Honorable George B. Loring,
 Commissioner of Agriculture.

REPORTS BY Dr. MILLER AND Dr. CORLIES.

Sir,   Newark, N. J., October 11, 1881.

I have the honour to submit the following report of the work done by me since acting as agent for the Department of Agriculture in investigating, inspecting, locating, and reporting the existence of contagious pleuro-pneumonia among cattle in this State. On March 21, 1881, I received my appointment and letter of instructions, and immediately proceeded to visit localities that were known to have been infected by the malady in the past. My previous connection with an organisation that existed in this State a year prior to this time, made me somewhat familiar with such places. I also prepared, and had printed two thousand circulars, which I caused to be circulated among stock raisers in different parts of the State, requesting those having the malady, or reasons to believe they had it in their herds, to report the same to me at my office without unnecessary delay, and I am happy to state a number responded to it. Upon investigation, however, a majority of cases proved to be some other form of disease resembling contagious pleuro-pneumonia in its symptoms. I however found, as a rule, the farmers were difficult to approach, and in a number of cases tried to cover up the existence of the disease as much as possible. This difficulty may be overcome by arming those whose duty it is to make inspections, with authority to enter any premises where they suspect the malady to exist. Being at liberty to exercise my own judgment in adopting the best means to find where the disease existed, I consulted the State board of health through its secretary, and made a proposition to go personally to all reported infected places, make the necessary inspections, and furnish a duplicate report to them free of expense, if they would acquaint me with cases reported to them.

The movement of cattle out of the State is limited to high-bred stock, and from farms that are so well managed that contagious diseases cannot get a foothold. There are, however, a large number of young calves moved from New York for slaughter, through the abattoir building at Jersey City, to various parts of the State, and as there are no restrictions imposed they may be a means of conveying pleuro-pneumonia to other localities. The most of the calves raised in the State are fattened and disposed of to the butchers.

The annexed tabulated report cannot be relied upon as showing the actual extent of contagious pleuro-pneumonia in the State at the present time. Enough, however, has been gained to show that it has an actual existence, but not to the same extent as it did at the time of the going into effect of the first act approved March 13, 1879.

Number and Condition of Herds examined.

Counties.	Herds.	Number.	Sick.
Atlantic	2	40	—
Burlington	5	76	—
Camden	—	—	—
Cumberland	—	—	—
Bergen	3	29	5
Essex	10	139	15
Gloucester	3	54	—
Hudson	10	120	12
Hunterdon	2	76	—
Middlesex	15	132	8
Mercer	5	73	5
Monmouth	9	131	—
Morris	6	85	2
Passaic	3	33	2
Sussex	2	92	—
Somerset	3	36	1
Ocean	9	141	—
Union	6	132	2
Warren	4	60	—
Cape May	—	—	—
Total	97	1,449	52

Honorable George B. Loring,
   Commissioner of Agriculture.

Respectfully submitted,
JAMES C. CORLIES, D.V.S.

No. 56.
REPORT by DR. JOHN W. GADSDEN, M.R.C.V.S., to the COMMISSIONER OF AGRICULTURE, Washington.

CONTAGIOUS PLEURO-PNEUMONIA IN PENNSYLVANIA.

SIR, Philadelphia, October 31, 1881.

In accordance with instructions from your department, I herewith submit a statement of the extent to which "contagious pleuro-pneumonia" has prevailed recently in this State, and the efforts made by the State authorities for its extirpation.

The disease has existed in the State of Pennsylvania to a greater or less extent for a number of years; and although the legislature, by Act of April 12, 1866, endeavoured to prevent its extension and prescribed penalties for those disposing of or removing infected animals, no systematic attempt seems to have been made looking to the eradication of the disease by the destruction of affected animals, until the spring of 1879, when, alarmed by the fact that the ports of Great Britain had been closed to cattle shipped from the United States, and it being learned that in several counties of the State the disease at that time existed, a bill was introduced in the legislature providing for the stamping out of the contagion. This measure met with most vigorous opposition, caused mainly by the declaration of certain veterinary surgeons, that the disease was not contagious. By the earnest efforts, however, of Mr. Thomas J. Edge, secretary of the State Board of Agriculture, who was in possession of the testimony of dairymen and farmers who had suffered from the ravages of the disease, and of veterinary surgeons who had had actual experience with it both in this country and in England, and consequently were well aware of its contagious character, the Act of May 1, 1879, passed both branches of the legislature, and was approved by the Governor.

Immediately after its approval the Governor appointed a commission to " examine " and determine whether infectious or contagious pleuro-pneumonia existed among cattle " in any county or counties of this commonwealth, and report the same without un- " necessary delay." After hearing the testimony of a number of practical dairymen and veterinary surgeons, the commission decided unanimously and reported to the Governor that the disease did exist in at least two counties in the State.

Upon the receipt of this report, the Governor appointed Mr. Thomas J. Edge his special agent and assistant, to carry out the provisions of the Acts of 1866 and 1879, for the prevention of the spread of this disease, and issued to him a commission and instructions for his government.

Too much praise cannot be given to this gentleman for the energetic manner in which he has fulfilled the duties of his appointment, and the great results he has accomplished at a comparatively trifling expense. He immediately appointed, in the several counties of the State, 450 persons as official reporters, with instructions to communicate to him at once the existence of any infected animals, or those supposed to be infected; and upon receipt of such information a veterinary surgeon was at once sent to examine the animals, and if the disease was found to be that of contagious pleuro-pneumonia, the entire farm was placed in quarantine, the animals appraised, those diseased killed and paid for by the State, and the others kept under surveillance until three months after the last trace of disease was discovered, when the quarantine was removed.

From May 1, 1879, to the present time, 64 herds, numbering 1,252 animals, have been placed in quarantine, 324 animals have been killed, of which 257 were paid for by the State, the entire cost to the State being only $10,750, of which $4,325 was paid for animals destroyed.

The disease has been confined to nine counties in the eastern and southern sections of the State, the herds quarantined being distributed among the counties as follows:—

Adams - - - 1	Montgomery - - - 17
York - - - 2	Bucks - - - 3
Lancaster - - - 2	Lehigh - - - 1
Chester - - - 15	
Delaware - - - 17	Total - - 64
Philadelphia - - - 6	

In many of these herds the cause of infection has been traced directly to diseased animals brought from Maryland and placed among healthy cattle, numbers of which were infected by them. In other instances the disease was communicated from chronic cases that had apparently recovered; in others, by the contact of persons who had been attending diseased animals, and afterwards went among healthy ones without first disinfecting their clothing. In still other instances it was communicated from one farm to another by means of streams of running water, or by healthy animals being allowed to graze in fields adjoining those in which diseased ones were pastured.

REPORT BY Dr. J. W. GADSDEN.

At the present time the disease is confined to the counties of Delaware, Montgomery, and Philadelphia; in the former of which three herds numbering 36 animals, in Montgomery one herd numbering 19 animals, and in the latter one herd numbering 41 animals, are now in quarantine.

The disease at present in Delaware County was introduced to one herd by cattle from Baltimore, Md., and communicated from this herd to two adjoining farms. The existence of the disease was discovered by Dr. Bridge, the State inspector, by the meat of diseased animals being exposed for sale in the Philadelphia markets.

There is no question that the State of Pennsylvania would be entirely free from infection to-day were it not for the fact that no precautions are taken by the Maryland authorities to prevent the spread of the contagion; diseased animals from that State are constantly brought into this and thus infect healthy herds.

Since my appointment by the Department of Agriculture, I have been in constant communication with the State authorities, and they have always co-operated with me in all measures for the discovery of the disease, and have laboured faithfully to prevent its spread.

The calves in all infected districts are slaughtered by direction of the State inspector, and are not allowed to be removed into other portions, or out of the State, for fear of spreading the infection.

By official statistics the number and value of cattle in Pennsylvania, last year, was:—

Cows	851,790	$18,625,000
Oxen and other cattle	674,000	14,962,000
	1,525,790	$33,587,000

When the amount of money invested in cattle is considered, the sum expended by the State for stamping out the disease seems very insignificant; yet the State officers were very much crippled in their operations by a decision of the auditor-general, made in June 1881, that the payment for cattle destroyed was not a necessary expense within the meaning of the Act, and refusing to allow any claims for such payment; and it was not until October 15, 1881, that he was induced to reconsider his decision and allow such claims, and only then provided the total amount expended for the year should not exceed $5,000.

In the meantime some diseased animals had been introduced from Baltimore, and we have learned of instances where the owners of them concealed the fact, knowing that the State had ceased payment.

In conclusion, from personal observation and the reports received from those actively engaged in its suppression, I am convinced that the disease can never be effectually eradicated without—

First. A more efficient quarantine;

Secondly. The killing of all chronic cases, no matter how *apparently* healthy the animals may be; and

Thirdly. The adoption of stringent regulations for the proper inspection of all animals removed from one State to another, the inspector to have full power to cause the instant destruction of all diseased animals.

The present system of quarantine seems to be almost a farce. The animals are allowed to roam at will over a whole farm, and are placed in fields bordering on public roads, and divided from neighbouring farms only by an open fence. In this way the disease has been communicated in a number of instances. The only effective way would be to confine all animals that have been subjected to infection in an inclosure remote from other cattle, separating the sick animals from the healthy ones, and allowing no one who has had access to the diseased animals to approach the healthy without first thoroughly disinfecting their clothing.

Chronic cases, although the animals may be apparently healthy, are but moving centres of contagion, for from the nature of the disease the lungs once affected never resume their normal state, and we have several instances where these chronic cases have affected herds, and the animal communicating the disease has outlived those infected by it.

From the experience of this State, the necessity of preventing the transmission of the disease from one State to another cannot be overestimated, and until a law looking to this end is enacted, it will be impossible to rid the country of the disease, for, one State refusing action, may endanger all those lying contiguous to it, even though they may be using every endeavour to rid themselves of the plague.

Respectfully submitted,

JOHN W. GADSDEN, M.R.C.V.S.

The Hon. George B. Loring,
   Commissioner of Agriculture.

REPORT BY Dr. W. H. ROSE.

NUMBER and LOCATION of DISEASED HERDS examined by Dr. J. W. GADSDEN.

Name of Surgeon.	Name of Owner.	State.	County.	Day Examined.	Number in Herd.	Number Sick.	Number Died.	Name of Disease.
J. W. Gadsden, M.R.C.V.S.	Jacob K. Ulrich	Pennsylvania	Delaware	1881. March 31	(a) 24	Not given	3 killed	Contagious pleuro-pneumonia.
Do.	Ed. Krider	Do.	Philadelphia	Do.	(b) 31	Do.	15 killed	Do.
Do.	James Milner	Do.	Bucks	Do.	(c) 8	Do.	4 killed	Do.
Do.	Jacob K. Ulrich	Do.	Delaware	April 7	(d) 21	Do.	-	Do.
Do.	Ed. Krider	Do.	Philadelphia	Do.	(e) 16	Do.	-	Do.
Do.	James Milner	Do.	Bucks	Do.	(f) 4	Do.	-	Do.
Do.	David P. Forney	Do.	York	June 2	(g) 11	1	-	Do.
Do.	Do.	Do.	Do.	„ 23	(h) 11	3	-	Do.
Do.	M. Worral	Do.	Delaware	Do.	(i) 31	4	-	Do.
Do.	Do.	Do.	Do.	June 30	(j) 30	12	1	Do.
Do.	Do.	Do.	Do.	July 14	(k) 29	11	1	Do.
Do.	Alonzo Parker	Do.	Do.	Aug. 25	(l) 12	2	2 cows killed	Do.
Do.	Do.	Do.	Do.	Sept. 8	(m) 11	1	1 killed	Do.
Do.	Do.	Do.	Do.	Sept. 15	(n) 10	4	1 killed	Do.
Do.	M. Worral	Do.	Do.	Do.	(o) 24	Not given	-	Do.
Do.	Nicholas Bowden	Do.	Do.	Do.	(p) 15	2	-	Do.
Do.	Alonzo Parker	Do.	Do.	Sept. 22	(q) 9	3	1 killed	Do.
Do.	M. Worral	Do.	Do.	Do.	(r) 21	Several	-	Do.
Do.	Nicholas Bowden	Do.	Do.	Do.	(s) 15	1	-	Do.
Do.	John H. Webster	Philadelphia, Pa	Philadelphia	Oct. 20	(t) 42	5	2	Do.
Do.	John S. Andrews	Pennsylvania	Montgomery	„ 9	(u) 19	2	2 killed	Do.

(a) Twenty-one animals have been quarantined by order of State authorities. (b) Sixteen animals in quarantine by order of State authorities. (c) Remaining animals in quarantine. (d, e, f) Four animals belonging to Mr. Ulrich's herd were, a few days after this report was made, slaughtered for beef and showed no evidences of disease. During the month Mr. Milner's herd, having developed no symptoms of disease, were ordered from quarantine. No evidences of disease having appeared in the herds of Messrs. Ulrich and Krider, they were also released from quarantine early in June. (g) This animal was infected by a cow purchased in Baltimore, which was suffering with chronic contagious pleuro-pneumonia; quarantined. (h) Herd still in quarantine. (i) Infected by stock from Baltimore. Quarantined by order of State authorities. (j, k) At the foregoing date this herd is represented as being in a sad plight; one animal died July 12, another August 4, and still another August 17. The herd was properly quarantined. (l) The two cows killed on August 23 were in the last stages of the disease; animals were infected by Worrals herd on adjoining farm; quarantined. (m) This animal was killed by order of State authorities. (n) A second animal was killed by order of State authorities on September 14. (o) The State inspector regards 15 of these animals as chronic cases. (p) Infected by adjoining herd belonging to Mr. Worral; quarantined. (q) This animal was killed by State inspector. (r) The animals sick are chronic cases, and are doing well. (s) No changes since last report. (t) These animals died but recently. The owner was of the opinion that the State had ceased to pay for condemned cattle, and hence made no report. (u) On November 8, when again examined, two more animals in this herd were found sick. The herd is still quarantined.

No. 57.

REPORT by DR. W. H. ROSE, D.V.S., to the COMMISSIONER OF AGRICULTURE, Washington.

CONTAGIOUS PLEURO-PNEUMONIA IN MARYLAND, THE DISTRICT OF COLUMBIA AND VIRGINIA.

SIR, Baltimore, M.D., November 1, 1881.

BY request I forward you a report of my investigations throughout the State of Maryland and the District of Columbia, as inspector of contagious pleuro-pneumonia in cattle. It will be necessary to subdivide my report, in order to impress upon the minds of those who may read it the fact of the existence of such a terrible malady; also to what extent it has been transmitted, and the amount of virulence contained in each infected stable and district. It is my intention to give you a report of the past as well as of the present, and for this purpose I have kept a complete record of those who have lost stock during the existence of this disease. I am satisfied, however, that I have missed many stables where the disease previously existed, which fact I attribute to the fear of owners of neat cattle who have experienced the ill effects of the disease among their stock. One point to be remembered is the non-existence of this disease on some farms where it was reported by the owners to have previously prevailed. It is true that some people have confounded this disease with the southern cattle fever, which may be very readily distinguished by the general observer during the existence of either of these diseases; but in making a diagnosis of a certain disease of the past, with an imperfect history to guide us, we are compelled to reserve our decision. This I found to be the case about Alexandria, Va., and in some parts of Maryland. The majority of intelligent people who read the symptoms, course, and termination of contagious pleuro-pneumonia in cattle, generally quote the remarks given by our standard authors of the very malignant form of the disease. It appears deeply impressed upon their minds that all cases must show these severe symptoms. It would be well if such was the case; more of them would die. This would lessen the spread of so contagious and infectious a malady. But all cases do not die (unfortunately); convalescents transmit the disease to other animals, especially if removed from the infected stable to a healthy herd of cattle in some other locality. Again, some animals do not show any symptoms of the disease, although others about them may die. I wish to impress upon the minds of cattle owners the necessity of watching these cases with care; oftentimes they are the means of transmitting the very worse form of the disease to other animals. They are often affected but slightly, resolution having taken place before any external symptoms are observable. Although these remarks are well understood by yourself, still I think them very necessary for the benefit of cattle owners, especially in Maryland.

INFECTED LOCALITIES IN BALTIMORE CITY AND COUNTY.

I commenced my investigations as Inspector of Cattle in the State of Maryland for the Department of Agriculture, March 28, 1881. In beginning my report of this city and county, and before alluding to the ravages of the malady in the past, it will be necessary to mention the stables in which the disease existed at the time of my investigations. April 7, 1881, I found an infected stable 4 miles north of Baltimore city, belonging to Judge D. M. Perine. He owned at this time some valuable stock. I found several of them sick with contagious pleuro-pneumonia. No history relating to its origin among his cattle could be obtained until the hired man spoke of a bull which belonged to a neighbour named J. B. Manning. This bull was allowed to enter the barnyard of Judge Perine at all times. Being suspicious of this animal, I made inquiry regarding his whereabouts during the past six months. I found, by further inquiry and careful examination of other herds in this locality, that he had infected animals belonging to Mr. Thos. R. Jenkins and Mr. J. W. Ward. The former had six cows, one of which I examined and found the left lung consolidated in its middle and upper portions; hydrothorax was present; temperature 104$\frac{2}{5}$° F.; died April 10. Precautions were taken to prevent its spread if possible. Mr. Ward, who owned four cows, was less fortunate. He wintered the animals belonging to Manning. I found one of this herd sick with the disease. Temperature 104° F.; slight dullness on percussion over the right lung, with the characteristic cough. This cow died one month later, but previous to her death another one of the four was attacked. Owing to the lack of power to destroy these infected animals, I was compelled to allow them to roam about the farms, to further disseminate the disease. Manning's place has been infected for the last 10 years. He has lost cows at different periods, sometimes one, at other times two or three animals, and has thus kept up a constant supply of virus sufficient to infect animals entering his stables at any season of the year, or that might come in contact with his recovered cases.

About the middle of April last I visited a section of Baltimore county called Long Green and Delaney Valley, distant 17 miles north-east of Baltimore city. Most of these farmers have valuable stock in the line of milch-cows. Thos. Pierce claims to have had the first outbreak of the disease in his section of Baltimore county this spring. His farm consists of 1,000 acres of land, most of which has been used of late as a pasture field. Cattle come here from all parts of this county to graze. He could not tell me how his cattle contracted the disease. I found a herd consisting of 30 cows and two bulls. Four of the cows were sick with the disease, and five others had died previous to my visit. His neighbour, who owns the adjoining farm, lost nine cows with the same malady, while others were suffering with it during my visit. I was not satisfied with the history given me by the hired man on the latter place, which is owned by General Trimble, but the General admitted that one of his animals jumped the fence into the pasture field belonging to Mr. Pierce. Three weeks after he noticed this outbreak among his cows. I went from this place to Long Green, which is two miles east of Delaney Valley, to examine a herd of cattle consisting of 10 cows and one bull, belonging to John A. Conklin. Mr. Conklin allowed two of his cows to winter on the Pierce farm. Hearing of this outbreak, he had his cows returned to his own farm, but shortly after the disease appeared in his herd. Five animals were attacked at different periods, and during the months of March and April two died. No disinfectants were used, and great negligence was manifested, and I was not surprised to find on a second visit towards the close of April that other animals were affected. In the barn one case was found. Calling again about the same time at Mr. Conklin's place I found no change in his animals, except that, in the interim, he seems to have used disinfectants freely. Two sick animals were allowed to roam at will over his entire farm.

On May 4th and 5th I visited a place called Glencoe (Northern Central Railroad), situated on the Baltimore and Yorktown turnpike. Here I found four gentlemen, owning adjoining farms, who had experienced heavy losses in cattle. Dickinson Gorsuch, who lives 1 mile west of Glencoe, had the first outbreak of contagious pleuro-pneumonia in this neighbourhood. Many head of cattle have died with the disease on his place since 1876. It was transmitted from this farm to that of T. T. Gorsuch, a relative, who lives one-half mile east. On the same turnpike, opposite the former place, lives another relative, Joshua Gorsuch, whose cattle also contracted the contagion. The latter sold a cow affected with the disease to a man named Jessup who lives in this locality, which soon infected his stock, ultimately causing a heavy loss. I recite this history simply in order to explain the transmission of the disease from one place to another. I found two chronic cases on the farm of T. T. Gorsuch. Adjoining lives another relative named Alfred Mays, on whose place I found three cows out of five sick with the disease. A cow had died previous to my visit. I advised the owner not to permit his cows to go to other pastures. He paid no attention to my advice, but allowed the sick animals to leave his place to graze on his father's farm distant 1$\frac{1}{2}$ miles north. I followed the animals to his father's (Jno. P. Mays), where I found the disease prevailing among his cattle. He has lost 12 head of fine Ayrshires and Alderney cows during the past six weeks. I saw four others suffering with the disease. The first animal to infect this locality was brought from Baltimore City.

On March 30, I visited a dairy stable near Cathedral Street, Baltimore, belonging to Jno. McCormack. I found a case of contagious pleuro-pneumonia among this herd of seven cows; recovered, but right lung affected. On May 16, another cow in this stable showed symptoms of the disease.

On April 1, the stable of Herman Breakman, Highlandtown, contained five cows, one of which was suffering with the disease.

About the same time I visited the stables of Mr. Douglas, Upper Canton, 1½ miles east of Baltimore. This stable contained 52 cows, all of which had been inoculated with the virus of contagious pleuro pneumonia. I have made repeated visits to this place for the purpose of studying the effects of inoculation. But owing to the continual exchange of cattle, I have gained but little information. I could detect no cases although the disease existed here last summer.

On April 12, I visited the dairy farm belonging to Chas. P. Harrison, of Pikesville. This and the Douglas farm are the only farms on which inoculation has been practised in the State to my knowledge. Mr. Harrison says he has been exempt from the disease since 1873, and claims inoculation as a great preventive measure.

On April 2, I visited the dairy of Mr. Jeokel, 1 mile east of Baltimore. This herd consisted of 50 cows. In his stable I found five recovered cases. This gentleman lost a great many cattle last summer by the disease; but could not, or would not, tell how many.

On April 5, I visited South Baltimore. I found this section of the city also infected. Wm. Hamburger (dairyman), Hanover Street, had 18 cows, among which was one chronic case of contagious pleuro-pneumonia. This place has been infected for at least 6 years. There are other dairies in close proximity to this one. If one of them remains free of the disease for a short period the others will have one or more cases to contend with. I have made many visits in this section of the city, and I have invariably detected at least one case of the acute type of the disease. Recently I explained to Dr. Lyman the condition of this locality, and on visiting it pointed out to him two acute and one chronic case of the disease. I found also one dead animal on the commons near these stables. We had the dead cow removed to the bone yard, and the post-mortem examination revealed all the characteristic lesions of the disease. I may safely say that the diseased lung weighed at least 35 pounds. The diseased animals on the commons were allowed to commingle with the healthy ones. This man has lost by contagious pleuro-pneumonia at least 35 head of cows within the past 6 years. In all such infected localities I find the people attribute all this trouble to dealers in cattle. A majority of fresh cows purchased of these dealers are healthy at the time they enter these infected stables, and they develop the disease sooner or later afterwards. Edward Saches and brothers keep separate dairies, but occupy the same stable, which is separated only by a partition wall in its centre. They usually have 30 or more head of cows, among which I have occasionally found a diseased one.

Cornelius Frostler (dairyman, same locality), owns 13 cows, and tries to keep that number on hand. I found three chronic cases of contagious pleuro-pneumonia in this stable on April 5. I have made several visits here each month, but have failed to detect an acute case. Animals are not often exchanged in this stable, which has a tendency to lessen the number of acute cases. On June 10 one of his cows died with the malady.

John Hillar (dairyman, same locality). This stable contains 13 cows and has been infected for a long time. On June 8, after lingering some time with the disease, one cow died. On June 10 I found two others suffering with the disease. On June 23 one of the sick animals, which I found on the 10th instant, was missing. The other one was still lingering. On July 27 I found two more of these cows sick with contagious pleuro-pneumonia; four others had been removed from the stable and new cows placed in their stalls.

On April 7 I visited a dairy belonging to David Stevens, at Woodbury. Here I found seven recovered cases from the outbreak which he experienced last year. He lost at least 20 head of cows at that time from the effects of the disease. One cow died the day previous to this visit. The lungs were shown to me. The right lung was completely consolidated throughout its anterior lobe. Since then I have been unable to detect any more affected animals in this stable. Mr. Stevens has decided to part with every cow which shows the slightest symptoms of the disease.

R 679.

REPORT BY Dr. W. H. ROSE.

Infected Localities in Baltimore City and County prior to 1881.

Name of Owner.	Localities of infected Stables and Premises.	No. died.	Year.
Laurence Weimbeck	Highlandtown, one-half mile east of Baltimore, Baltimore County.	6	1880.
Mr. Michaelman	Ditto	4	1880.
Mr. Kiefer	Ditto	3	1880.
Mr. Doran	Ditto	Unknown	1880.
Mr. Douglas	1½ miles east of Baltimore, Baltimore County	,,	1880.
R. Brooks	Canton, east of Baltimore, Baltimore County	20	1880.
John Sweeny	East of Baltimore, Baltimore County	3	1880.
John Baumgartner	Northeast of Baltimore, Baltimore County	Unknown	Unknown.
Patrick Holland	Philadelphia Road, east of Baltimore, Baltimore County.	35	1871.
Mrs. Hartman	Ditto	Unknown	Unknown.
George Furley	Canton, east of Baltimore, Baltimore County	,,	,,
Mr. Zorn	Ditto	,,	,,
Mrs. Clay	Ditto	8	1880.
B. Miller	Patapsco Neck, 2½ miles east of Baltimore, Baltimore County.	Heavily	1880.
Henry Hughs	North end of Baltimore, Baltimore County	3	1879.
Mr. Lenne	Ditto	5	1879.
James M. Davis	Huntington Avenue, north end of Baltimore, Baltimore County.	Unknown	1871.
A. S. Abell	4 miles north of Baltimore, Baltimore County	1	1880.
J. R. Manning	3½ miles north of Baltimore, Baltimore County	22	Since 1861.
William Hamburger	South of Baltimore, Baltimore County	35	Since 1875.
George and Edward Sachs	Ditto	(*)	—
Mrs. Sweigert	Ditto	2	1880.
Cornelius Frostler	Ditto	4	Since 1878.
John Hillar	Ditto	Unknown	—
George Klein	Ditto	,,	—
John Rugall	Washington Road, near Baltimore, Baltimore County.	17	Since 1871.
John Bair	Ditto	Unknown	—
Mr. Rogan	Washington Road, near Baltimore, Baltimore County.	Unknown	—
Mr. Fogal	Ditto	60	Since 1870.
Mrs. Kinny	Ditto	4	1880.
Thos. Langhor	Frederick Road, west of Baltimore, Baltimore County.	37	1872.
John Glenn	Catonsville, 6 miles west of Baltimore, Baltimore County.	4	1873.
Aug. Lurman	Ditto	6	1874.
Nicholas Boary	Sterrett Street, Baltimore, Baltimore County	15	1880.
Ross Winans	Baltimore Street, Baltimore, Baltimore County	Unknown	1864.
Hayfield Merryman	Ditto	,,	1864.
Mr. Shipley	Ditto	35	1866.
Mr. Ridgely	Towsontown, 7 miles north of Baltimore, Baltimore County.	1	1880.
Dr. Piper	Ditto	1	1880.
John Smith	2 miles north-east of Towsontown, Baltimore County.	20	1880.
Jacob Wisner	1 mile east of Towsontown, Baltimore County	8	1880.
Samuel E. Parks	Ditto	10	1879.
William Williams	Govanstown, 4 miles north of Baltimore, Baltimore County.	5	1876.
P. McGreever	Ditto	5	1879.
William Anderson	Hillen Road, near Govanstown, Baltimore County.	20	1880.
Charles P. Harrison	Pikesville, 6 miles north-west of Baltimore, Baltimore County.	Heavily	1873.
Dr. B. E. Wood	Hillen Road, near Govanston, Baltimore County	6	1880.
John W. Wagner	Pikesville, 6 miles north-west of Baltimore, Baltimore County.	1	1880.
Slade & Scribner	1¼ miles from Pikesville depôt, Baltimore County.	10	1879.
C. L. Rogers	1 mile from Pikesville depôt, Baltimore County	12	1876.
James Lyon	Ditto	Unknown	—
McDonough Institute	Near Pikesville depôt, Baltimore County	6	1880.
— McCauley	Ditto	Unknown	—
James Vaughan	Mount Washington, Baltimore County	(†)	—
Charles Baker	Ditto	Unknown	—
David Stevens	Woodberry, Baltimore County	20	1880.
Dennis Mathews	Dulaney's Valley, Baltimore County	3	1880.

* Not willing to tell their loss.   † Impossible to tell, constantly changing.

REPORT BY Dr. W. H. ROSE.

Name of Owner.	Localities of infected Stables and Premises.	No. died.	Year.
William P. Hagan	2 miles east of Long Green, Baltimore County	5	1879.
D. Gorsuch	1 mile west of Glencoe, Baltimore County	—	1876.*
T. T. Gorsuch	Ditto	8	1879.
Eli Mathews	1 mile west of Monkton, Northern Central Railroad, Baltimore County.	3	1879.
Mr. Russell	Mount Winans, Baltimore County	1	1880.

* Infected since 1876.

REMARKS.

I cannot give you accurately the aggregate loss sustained by the owners of dairy cows in this city and its suburbs on account of so many having retired from the business. Many cases of contagious pleuro-pneumonia are hidden from me, not only by the owners of such animals, but many dealers about here make a practice of exchanging such animals. I have repeatedly visited stables in the eastern and southern part of Baltimore, fully expecting to find some acute cases. Occasionally I have succeeded, but not to that extent which I should have done. Some cases which are mild in character are allowed to remain in these stables, providing they assume convalescence. I must confess that these people are very shrewd in their prognosis of such cases. All those that assume the colliquative type of the disease are disposed of prior to death. No later than last year the malady existed in the eastern part of the city to an alarming extent. Very few of the dairy stables escaped its ravages. I have found it a universal fact, not only in this but in other States, that periodical outbreaks of the disease are to be looked for wherever its destructive elements have become imprisoned. In South Baltimore I have noticed isolated cases among the different dairy stables ever since March last. Too much buying and selling is done in both of these sections to ever rid the stables of the disease. They allow a cow to remain in them long enough to develop the malady and then she is hurried off by the dealers to other quarters. This practice is the cause of the transmission of the disease into the outlying counties of Maryland as well as into the States of Pennsylvania and New Jersey. I am convinced that many people have experienced serious losses among their stock from such sources of infection, and yet they seem indisposed to acknowledge the fact. This accounts in a great measure for the many infected farms throughout the interior of Maryland. We have still another source of transmission, that is from those animals called recovered cases. Their tissues are stamped with the virus for an indefinite period of time after convalescence, and where such animals are allowed to exist the virulency of the disease is only reserved for the infection of healthy animals. Many stock-owners in this State have confirmed opinions as to the poor quality of food given and regard this as the cause of disease. This is an absurdity. No matter how an animal may be fed, it must come in contact with a diseased one or enter some infected stable before the contagion can generate in its system. To illustrate this fact we can have no better example than the history of this disease as shown throughout this county.

During my investigations I have been very careful in trying to trace the malady to its origin, but as yet I am unable to find any stable where it existed prior to 1864. At that time most of the cows were sent from the Middle States into Baltimore and Washington, the war having stopped the supply. At this time the disease was known to but few people. Ross Winans, of Baltimore, who was among the first to experience the disease, tried his utmost to prevent the public from knowing of its existence among his cows. A few persons fix the date of its appearance in his stable as early as the year 1863. However, other dairy stables in the vicinity commenced to lose cows with the disease, when it was traced to Washington (see report of Washington). In 1866 Mr. Shipley succeeded Ross Winans in the dairy business. He used the same stable, having been told by Winans that no disease of any kind had ever existed on his premises. Shortly after taking possession Mr. Shipley noticed a few of his cows coughing, while others became short of milk and lost appetite. Eventually, 35 head of cows died. Mr. H. Merryman sustained a loss in this stable about the same time. Other dairymen commenced to suffer from its ravages. Outside of this city, all along the line of the Western Maryland Railroad, in Baltimore county, can be found stables where the disease has existed, and since the above time it has been transmitted from one section of the county to another. This was caused, generally, by buying infected animals at the Baltimore stock-yard, and by allowing animals from infected stables to pasture with healthy ones. We are now able to point out sections in different parts of not only this but other counties of Maryland where periodical outbreaks of the disease occur annually. Sometimes these outbreaks are of a mild and at other times of a most malignant form. Baltimore city and its surroundings furnish infecting material for a wide extent of country.

CECIL COUNTY.

On May 9 I commenced my investigations of this county. Elkton is its county seat. The following day the members of the Cecil County Agricultural Society held a special meeting, which gave me an opportunity to converse with men who are anxious to aid the officers of your department in checking the spread of contagious pleuro-pneumonia. From Mr. A. R. Magraw, president of the society, I gained considerable information regarding the hygienic condition of cattle throughout the county. Elkton I consider free from the disease at present, although many cattle are brought here in the early fall from Baltimore to be wintered by farmers, and after being fattened are sent to Philadelphia and elsewhere for human consumption. A great many milch-cows are also sent here from the eastern counties of Maryland and from Virginia, thus avoiding to a great extent the infection which prevails about Baltimore. When we remember to what extent this city and vicinity is infected it seems miraculous that any locality in the State should be so exempt as this. Mr. James Yates, three miles north-east of Elkton, informed me that, in 1879, he lost three cows with the disease, and from the history he gave me I concluded that such was the case.

On May 11 I visited a place called Brick Meeting House, where I found a recovered case of contagious pleuro-pneumonia, belonging to Levi Mearns, who bought some cattle at the Baltimore stock-yard, in company with a neighbour, Mr. Thomas Stevens, in 1879. Shortly after the arrival of these animals the disease developed itself among them, four head dying on Stevens', and three on Mearns' farm. A few recovered on each place, which were afterwards sold to a butcher, who took them to Philadelphia. This small village is situated but a short distance from the State line between Pennsylvania and Maryland. From here I went to Rising Sun, which is still nearer the line, but could find no sign of the disease, although it had recently existed near this place in Pennsylvania, where it had been stamped out by the authorities of that State.

On May 12 and 13 I visited all the principal towns along the county line from Rising Sun to Perryville. During this investigation I visited many fine dairy farms and inspected a number of valuable herds, each herd consisting of from 20 to 30 head of milch-cows, but could detect no signs of disease among any of them. At Perryville I found a gentleman named John Stump, who, in 1879, lost 11 head of cattle by the disease. The disease was brought to his place by cattle purchased at Baltimore.

May 25, 26, and 27 I concluded the investigation of this county by visiting all of that portion lying south of the Philadelphia, Wilmington, and Baltimore Railway, commencing at Fredericktown and working north to Chesapeake. I failed, however, to detect a single case of contagious pleuro-pneumonia in this section of the county. At Chesapeake I found a few gentlemen who deserve great credit for the energy which they display in trying to exclude from this place all cattle from infected districts. Mr. John A. Harriot, member of the Cecil County Agricultural Society, seems to be the most active in this good work.

I will mention here that I visited a portion of Kent County called Galena. I made this visit because steamboats ran daily between Baltimore and Fredericktown. The two counties are separated by the Sassafras river. Thinking that an occasional infected animal might enter the county by these boats, I made a close observation of the cattle in this place, but I failed to detect the existence of any disease.

HARFORD COUNTY.

During the early part of June I visited this county, of which Bel Air is the county seat. I met prominent citizens who informed me of the existence of contagious pleuro-pneumonia among their cattle in former years. I visited all the towns and many farms, but failed to find a single case of the disease in the entire county. I was well pleased with the preventive means adopted by Colonel Stump and Dr. Magraw. In 1880 they received authority from the Governor to appraise all animals infected with the disease, with authority to destroy them. Early last year Eldridge Gallop, who occupies the large farm belonging to the Citizens' Banking Association of Baltimore, brought a large herd of cattle to his place from the Baltimore stock-yard. Shortly after their arrival disease appeared among them, and four died in a few weeks. Not knowing the nature of the disease at that time, he commenced to treat the sick cows. Those which showed no symptoms of ailment were sold. Four such were sent into Pennsylvania, where they soon infected cows belonging to Mr. Pyle. This fact becoming known to the Pennsylvania authorities, they destroyed every sick cow and quarantined the stable. Mr. Gallop sold others singly to different parties in Abingdon, in this county. As soon as Colonel Stump and Dr. Magraw learned of the condition of these animals, they proceeded to kill every one of the cows that came from Gallop's infected herd. They then visited the infected stables and killed 22 head. Some animals had been sent to Baltimore previous to this slaughter, a fact unknown to these gentlemen at the time. In this herd 17 animals in all died from the effects of the disease. Since this transaction no further trouble has been experienced in this locality. I visited other sections of the county, where many herds of cattle are raised, and where large tracts of land are used for pasturing and wintering fat cattle. I think this latter pursuit is carried on to a greater extent in this county than in any other county in the State. The most of this grazing county lies along Deer Creek. Farmers in this locality frequently winter from 75 to 100 head each. The cattle pass through the Baltimore stock-yard previous to their arrival here. In the early spring they are sent to the Philadelphia markets. I was told that a Mr. Amos and Son, who lived in the northern part of this county, had lost cattle from contagious pleuro-pneumonia. I visited their farm on the 7th of June, but from the history of the disease given me by the owner, I am satisfied it was southern cattle fever, a disease which prevails here occasionally, and generally causes heavy losses.

Carroll County.

During the latter part of June I visited the different towns in this county, but I failed to find any case of contagious pleuro-pneumonia, either acute or chronic, until I reached a place called Manchester. After travelling a few miles north of this place I found a farm belonging to Barney Zepp, where the disease has existed since April 30. A short time previous to this he bought three cows from a dealer in this place, who buys cattle in all the different counties of Maryland and Pennsylvania, and sells them in most instances at the Baltimore stock-yard. At the time mentioned contagious pleuro-pneumonia broke out among them. Two showed the severe symptoms of the disease and soon died. The remaining cows were taken sick at different periods, and two died. I think the last two cases will recover. In 1875 they had an outbreak of the disease a few miles west of this place, in Bachman's Valley; cows from Baltimore stock-yard caused this infection. The movement of cattle in the fall of each year from Baltimore here is similar to the movement of cattle into Harford County, only to a less extent. In the spring and summer months dealers drive most of the cattle to the Baltimore stock-yard, from which very few of them return during the latter period.

Frederick County.

On July 14 I visited Frederick City (county seat). The disease does not exist in this county at present. The most of the cattle brought here come from Virginia. The only place where the disease ever existed in this county is Woodboro', 12 miles north of this city. George Smith lost 11 head from its effects last year. None of those affected recovered. I am satisfied that Frederick County will remain free from the extreme ravages of the disease so long as such men as Dr. Fairfax Schley is at the head of the Agricultural Society. He is well versed in the nature of the disease, and is therefore enabled to explain to the members of his society the precautions necessary to prevent its spread.

Anne Arundel County.

I visited the principal city (Annapolis) and most of the small places in this county. No disease has existed in any of these places during the last three years. On the dairy farm of Mrs. Berry, $1\frac{1}{2}$ miles north-west of Annapolis, a few animals died previous to the death of her husband, which occurred three years ago. Very few dairy stables that contain over five or ten cows are to be found in this city. On its outskirts are a few farms stocked with valuable cattle. I was surprised not to find more of the disease here, because boats make daily trips to and from Baltimore, and often bring cows from the stock-yard in that city. Since the outbreak of the disease in Baltimore last year, however, most of the people in this county are very careful where they purchase their stock.

Prince George's County.

During the early part of August and the latter part of September I made investigations in this county. Near the line of the district of Columbia, I found the disease had existed in previous years. I could detect no cases at present. In the year 1879, David

Campbell, dairyman, 3¾ miles south-east of Washington, in this county, contracted the disease among his cows by purchasing an animal affected with it from Mr. McDowell, of Washington. A veterinarian was sent from the latter place, who advised Mr. Campbell to destroy his cows. Two of them were killed, two others died, and the remainder were sold. A man named Brooks, who lives one mile south of this infected stable, lost two cows by the disease. They were infected by Mr. Campbell's cattle. I found other farms where the disease had existed in the district of Columbia, near the county line, which I shall mention in my report of the district. All of that section of this county bordering on the eastern line of the district of Columbia has been liable to more or less of the disease among the dairy cows since its appearance within the district. This is especially so as regards the dairy cows along the Baltimore and Ohio Railroad. A few miles from Washington, near Benning's Bridge, I found a farm where the disease existed in 1878. The place belongs to W. B. Lacey, who lost 13 head of cows at that time. Those that recovered were sold. There is no disease on his place at present.

MONTGOMERY COUNTY.

On August 10 I visited Rockville, the county seat. I could find no one here who ever heard of the existence of the disease, except near Sandy Springs, which is situated near the border line between this and Howard County. I have been in most of the towns of the county, but I have failed to detect a single case. At Sandy Springs, in the year 1876, Dr. Thomas and his brother Edward, who have adjoining farms, experienced a mild form of the malady among their cattle. The disease was communicated by a cow purchased in Washington. Other owners of cattle in this locality also suffered losses among their stock, among them Philip Stabler and Wm. Moore. The latter's farm is located 2 miles west of Sandy Springs. All of that portion of land lying west of the Metropolitan Railroad, and bordering on the Chesapeake and Ohio Canal, is used as pasture for fattening cattle. Since the termination of the war a great many cattle have been bought from men in south-west Virginia and afterward pastured in this locality until they were fit to send into the market. Very few come from either Washington or Baltimore, and the danger of infection is therefore greatly lessened.

DISTRICT OF COLUMBIA.

I consider the district of Columbia and a portion of Virginia as liable to periodical outbreaks of contagious pleuro-pneumonia. It has existed in this locality since 1864, and is in about the same condition as Baltimore city and county. I made repeated visits to this section in the months of August and September, and found one or more cases during each visit. On August 11th I visited the north end of Washington, a locality commonly called "Cowtown," where I found a small portion of inhabitants owning a greater or less number of dairy cows. Near by is a large common where most of these animals are pastured. During one of my visits in this locality I detected a cow with all the symptoms of an acute form of the disease. It was owned by Mr. Hollidge, who lives on Sherman Avenue. In the same stable I found a chronic case. This animal formerly belonged to his brother, who kept a dairy stable, two months previous to this time, on Spring Road, about 1½ miles north of the boundary line of the city. This gentleman became disheartened by the loss of cows affected with the disease, and sold out. Those bought by his brother showed no symptoms of the disease at the time of purchase, but it developed itself in this cow after her arrival. This man lost heavily in cows in the year 1871.

Mr. McKay, who keeps a dairy stable on Ninth Street, one half mile north of Boundary Street, bought seven cows from Mrs. Seidenberger, who was anxious to sell as she lost four cows by the disease last February. Her stable is located near the infected stable on Spring Road, which was used by Mr. Hollidge. McKay denied the existence of the disease among his cows, but three of them have disappeared in some way unknown to me. I wish to mention here that it is useless for me to watch any of the stables where I find the disease so long as we have no power to destroy the affected animals.

Mr. Harman lives at Mount Pleasant, about one mile north of Washington. On the 30th of September I found a cow in his stable suffering with the disease. Previous to my visit Dr. C. P. Lyman had visited this stable and found a heifer calf suffering with the disease in an acute form. It died the same day. An autopsy was made and a portion of the right lung preserved. On the same day I visited a stable owned by Robert Brown (coloured) who lives a short distance south of Mr. Harman's. I found one of his cows sick with the disease. This man says that the disease has been on his place since 1875, and that he has lost several cows by it.

On October 1, I was refused admittance to the stable of Mr. Shugrew, which is located a few hundred feet south of Mr. Hollidge's. One of his animals was undoubtedly sick. The rest of them, 14 in number, were running at large. As I was unable to see the sick animal I could not decide as to the nature of the disease. Since 1871 this man has lost 30 cows by the malady.

On October 3, I visited the commons about Mount Pleasant. Among a large herd of cows which belonged to different owners, I found several recovered cases. I also discovered a very acute case in a field adjoining these commons, which I learned belonged to Robert Hays. Six other cows were with her. I thought it important to make this case known at once to the department, in order that some one else would go and examine it. From the time of the discovery of this animal until my return in company with a representative of the department, which was but two or three hours, the cows had been removed to their stables in "Cowtown," near Seventh Street and Boundary, and the sick animal exchanged for a healthy one. When questioned the owner could not give the residence of the dealer with whom he had exchanged the cow. He acknowledged that he had lost 30 cows by the disease since 1871.

On the same day I visited the stable of Captain Viall, Meridian Hill, north-western boundary of Washington. This place has been infected since 1876. During this period he has lost 28 cows. Two have died since last June. One animal is still living, and has been running at large for the last two months. She is liable to spread the disease among other animals.

October 7, I walked over the commons on the eastern part of the district of Columbia where most of the cows in this section graze. I detected one cow among them sick with the disease, and concluded to follow her to the stable situated on D Street between Eighth and Ninth, north-east. Mr. Callahugh, the owner, acknowledged having had four cows affected with the disease. Whenever they commenced to grunt or showed severe symptoms he disposed of them to the butchers. He said he intended to dispose of this cow in the same way if her appetite did not soon return. I found her temperature to be $103\frac{1}{5}°$ F. He noticed his first sick cow in the month of June, and has been troubled with the contagion among his cows up to this date. At the beginning of this outbreak he owned seven cows, five of them have been affected. Other people in this locality have lost a few cows lately. L. Obenstein, who lives one square east of Callahugh's stable, lost one affected with the disease last week. Mr. Bresnaham, C Street, between Eighth and Ninth, north-east, lost one cow affected with the disease during the month of September; also Mrs. Clancey on Fifth Street, between North A and East Capitol Street, lost an animal in the month of August. Since 1870 this lady has lost 60 cows by the disease.

The DISEASE in the DISTRICT of COLUMBIA prior to 1881.

Name of Owner.	Locality of infected Stables.	Number of Deaths.	Year.
Mrs. Keefe	910, Twentieth Street, near K Street, Washington.	4 cows	1864
Michael White	Seventh Street, near Boundary	20 ,,	1869
Mr. Hollidge	Sherman Avenue, Boundary, Washington	Unknown	1871
Owen Shugrew	Ditto	30 cows	1871
Mrs. Morrisy	Seventh Street, near Boundary, Washington	14 ,,	1871
Robert Hays	Boundary Street, near Seventh, Washington	30 ,,	1871
Mrs. Clancey	Fifth Street, between North A and East Capitol Streets, Washington.	60 ,,	1871
William Davis	Corner of T and Twenty-seventh Streets, Washington.	23 ,,	1873
Mr. Harrington	3418, First North Street, Georgetown	20 ,,	1875
Mr. Ray	2 miles south-east of Washington, Marlborough Road.	28 ,,	1875
Mr. Holden	2 miles south-east of Washington, Marlborough Road.	Unknown	1875
Mrs. Schench	Corner of Seventh Street and Rock Creek Road, Washington.	40 cows	1875
Mr. Andries	Tenallytown, near Washington	12 ,,	1876
Mr. Bangerter	Ditto	Unknown	1876
Captain Viall	Meridian Hill, north-west of Boundary Street, Washington.	28 cows	1876
Mrs. Blagden	Fourteenth Street, 2 miles north of Washington	5 ,,	1877
Benjamin Green	Ditto	2 ,,	1877
Mrs. R. Hamilton	Fourteenth Srteet, 1 mile north of Washington	5 ,,	1877
Mr. Nehman	Tenallytown, D.C.	14 ,,	1877
Mrs. Kelly	Corner of G and Twenty-fifth Streets, Washington.	16 ,,	1879

SUMMARY.

The result of my investigations enables me to give the following summary:

Number of cattle examined since March 1881	11,270
Number of acute cases of disease found since March 1881	110
Number of chronic cases of disease found since March 1881	41
Total number of diseased animals found since March 1881	151
Number of deaths that have occurred since March 1881	67
Number of deaths reported as having occurred since 1864	1,029

Respectfully submitted,
W. H. ROSE, D.V.S.

Hon. George B. Loring,
  Commissioner of Agriculture.

No. 58.

REPORT ON AMERICAN PORK.—Result of an Investigation made under Authority of the Department of State of the United States.

Sir,   Department of State, Washington, April 26, 1881.

In compliance with your instructions that I should visit the cities of Chicago and Cincinnati and report on the pork industries of those great centres of the trade, I left Washington on the 23rd ultimo, and arrived in Chicago on the 25th.

Following your directions that I should spare no pains to render my investigations of the various phases of the pork industry, from the raising of the hogs until the product is ready for consumption as complete as possible, I have the honour to state that I have visited (generally accompanied by stenographers and experts) representative hog-raisers, buyers, shippers, packing-houses, stock-yards, rendering establishments, forwarding agencies, and all others nearly or remotely connected with the pork trade, as well as health offices, and to submit the following report, with accompanying papers, as the result of my investigations.

The statistics and testimony herewith presented were obtained from various sources, and are of such a nature as should for ever set at rest all fears or suspicions respecting the sanitary condition of American hogs and the quality of the American pork-product, and at the same time entitle the trade to immunity from the attacks of those whose interests might be subserved by injuring the reputation of American pork and lard.

The Hog and Hog-Products of Illinois.

Hog Cholera.

The recent alarm in England consequent upon published reports concerning the prevalence of "hog-cholera" in Illinois, reports said to be based upon published returns of the Department of Agriculture of that State, made it my first duty to visit Springfield, the capital, to seek an explanation thereof.

Having waited upon Governor Cullom and explained my mission, his Excellency gave me a letter to Mr. Fisher, Secretary of the Agricultural Department of the State, who has the supervision of the publication of all agricultural reports.

The Agricultural Department, it would seem, published two sets of returns, one set supplied by the State assessors and the other by correspondents of the department.

The discrepancy between these returns is very marked, and their publication, without an accompanying explanation, has afforded a seeming official foundation for reports of a very misleading character. For example, in the returns of the "farmer correspondents" the number of hogs which died of hog cholera in the State of Illinois during the year 1879 is given by the Department of Agriculture as 182,577, while the number of deaths for the same year, as reported by the assessors, is given by the department as 676,738. It was the publication of these last figures which caused so much needless alarm in England.

I submit herewith an official report from the secretary of the department of Agriculture concerning the losses in the State of Illinois from "hog cholera," and his explanation of the apparent discrepancy in the returns above noted.

State of Illinois.

Department of Agriculture, Secretary's Office,
Sir,   Springfield, March 28, 1881.

I have the honour to acknowledge the receipt of your favour of the 26th instant asking for information concerning the extent of loss of hogs in this State from "hog cholera."

The following table gives the per-centage of loss of hogs from so-called "hog cholera" during the past five years, as well as the average weights of the diseased hogs, and the figures are taken from the

REPORT ON AMERICAN PORK: 1881.

official reports received by this department. Said reports were made by farmers of experience, selected by this department by reason of their high standing and thorough knowledge of the actual state of affairs in their several localities:—

Year.	Per-centage of hogs died from hog cholera.	Average weight of hogs died of the cholera.
		Pounds.
1876	17+	103
1877	12+	104
1878	14+	108
1879	6+	98
1880	7+	104

The foregoing figures conclusively prove that there is no foundation for the exaggerated statements in circulation concerning the increase in numbers of hogs dying in this State from so-called hog cholera.

There has been a large and steady decrease in the loss of hogs in the State from so-called hog cholera, from 17 per cent. of the entire number of hogs assessed in 1876 to 7 per cent. of the number assessed in 1880.

The number of deaths from so-called hog cholera, as returned by assessors, is given below for the years 1877, 1878, and 1879, which also shows that there is a decrease of over 50 per cent. in the numbers of hogs dying of this disease in 1879 when compared with the previous year. The apparent discrepancy in the return of assessors in the following table is partially accounted for by the fact that spring pigs are not as a rule included in the returns of assessors for taxation, and the principal loss by disease is among young pigs.

The table gives the number of hogs assessed for taxation, number marketed, and the number died of cholera for the years 1877, 1878, and 1879, and conclusively proves that the great majority of hogs reported as having died from so-called cholera were pigs not considered of sufficient age and value to be listed for taxation.

Year.	Number of hogs assessed.	Number of hogs marketed.	Number of hogs died of cholera.	Number marketed and died of cholera.	Number marketed and died exceeds assessment.
1877	2,961,366	2,455,573	1,445,268	3,900,849	939,475
1878	3,335,550	2,273,493	1,391,422	3,662,915	327,365
1879	2,799,051	2,543,278	676,738	3,220,016	421,065

During the years named above there were not less on an average than 600,000 brood sows in the State, which number added to the figures in the last column will approximate the total number of hogs and pigs in the State in 1877, 1878, and 1879.

The decrease in numbers of hogs dying from so-called hog cholera from 1,391,422 in 1878 to 676,738 in 1879 is about 50 per cent., and the percentage of loss by disease the past year (1880) is about the same as in 1879.

All diseases of hogs are included under the caption of hog cholera so called.

Your attention is invited to the difference between the average live weight of hogs marketed, 252 pounds, and the average weight, during the past five years, of hogs dying from so-called hog cholera, of 103 pounds, and this difference shows that the deaths occur chiefly among young hogs and pigs.

In view of the above fact there seems to be very little occasion to question the healthy condition of mature hogs when ready for market.

The production of pork has been one of the leading industries of this State for many years, and the various conditions affecting this interest have been thoroughly investigated by intelligent men of extensive practical experience for years, with a view of obtaining the best results as to economy of production and quality of product.

The improvement in the quality of swine in Illinois has probably received as much if not more attention than in any of the States, and it is a well established fact, confirmed by packers of many years' experience, that for superiority of quality the hog products of Illinois are not surpassed.

The increased attention given to the sanitary management of swine has doubtless had much to do with the decrease of mortality.

I have, &c.
(Signed)   S. D. FISHER, Secretary.

Michael Scanlan, Esq.,
   Chief of the Bureau of Statistics, Department of State, Washington, D. C.

It will be observed by Secretary Fisher's report that the lesser figures are from "farmer correspondents selected by the department by reason of their high standing and "thorough knowledge of the actual state of affairs in their several localities." It would

R 679.

appear that these farmer correspondents did not include in their returns *† the deaths of pigs among which the principal losses by disease occur, as being of no present marketable value, while the assessors included all.

Taking either statement into consideration, it is apparent that the loss of hogs by cholera in the State of Illinois has decreased from 17 per cent. in 1876, to 7 per cent. in 1880. It should be borne in mind that all deaths of hogs, whether from disease or accident, are "placed under the caption of hog ' cholera.' " It appears from the official returns that the number of hogs assessed in the State of Illinois, during the year 1880, was 3,133,557, while the number of deaths from hog cholera and all other diseases as well as accidents was 227,259.

It should be borne in mind that no attempt whatever is made, either in Illinois or Ohio, to deny the existence of the disease known as "hog cholera." Hog cholera, or disease similar thereto, and equally fatal, prevails in all hog-raising countries as is fully verified by various statements hereto attached. But the prevalence or absence of "hog cholera" may be shown to have no bearing on the quality of the hogs which enter into the market nor on the quality of the meats produced therefrom, it being naturally impossible for hogs which have died from disease or any cause whatever to enter into consumption.

Having visited and conversed with some of the principal hog raisers and well known experts, in Illinois and Ohio, I submit the following statement, fully substantiated by the annexed papers, to show the manner in which the American hog is raised for the market.

Hog Raising in Illinois and Ohio.

The hogs of Illinois and Ohio (and doubtless the same statement would be true in respect of the hogs of the other Western States) are of various improved breeds, mainly high-grade Berkshire and Poland-Chinas and, as fully attested by Mr. Foster, a well known British expert, in his letter herewith ‡ are unsurpassed for purity by the hogs of the best British fancy breeders.

The pigs are generally farrowed in April and May, and as soon as they are able to do so, are allowed to follow corn-fed cattle, with the range of grass pasture and pure running water during the summer and fall. When not following corn-fed cattle, the pigs are fed with corn until the spring grass and their age makes it possible for the animals to subsist and thrive on grass alone.

Formerly hog-killing was all done during the winter, and the farmers consequently had a special season for preparing their hogs for market; but now that summer killing, especially in Chicago, has attained proportions nearly as large as the winter killing, the farmer can find a market for his hogs at any time during the year, and has only to consult his own convenience as to the time for fattening, being sure of finding a market whenever he has a car load ready for transportation.

When the hog reaches the age of six months or more—and it is previous to this age and while he has no present marketable value to the farmer that the principal deaths from "hog cholera"—he is put into pens and well fed upon corn and is also given access to pure spring water. Should the hog be attacked with cholera during this period, he is immediately separated from his fellows, and the disease being fatal, the dead animal must be disposed of by burial or utilised as a fertiliser. The suddenness with which this disease affects the hog is shown in the accompanying statement of Dr. Stetson,§ who observes that "it destroys life almost at once," and adds that "it is impossible to "make good meat of such a hog by any process whatever, decomposition setting in "before the death of the animal in most cases."

It may, in fact, be stated as beyond a doubt, that all rumours or reports that American hogs dying of disease, or even by accident ever enter upon any market in the shape of meat or lard,‖ are founded wholly upon malice and ignorance, for it is not in the power of the hog meat curer or lard refiner, whatever his inclination, to utilise the meat of hogs which have died of cholera, in any edible form that could pass the most superficial inspection.

Mr. Morrison, one of the leading packers of Cincinnati, of thirty years experience in the business says:

---

* It is more than probable that much confusion has been caused in Europe by the term "pig" as applied in the United States. Here the animal is called a "pig" until it arrives at the age of about six months; and it is not called a hog until it has reached maturity. In Europe the word "pig" is applied in the same sense as the word "hog" is applied in the United States. Hence, when the Europeans read of so many "pigs" dying of cholera in the United States, they give the word its European application.

† See in connection, statement of Morrison & Co., page 117.

‡ Page 106. § Page 109. ‖ See statement of J. C. Black, Esq., page 116.

I was brought up as a farmer in Europe, and know that the chances of getting diseased hogs into the American market are as one to a thousand in getting the old world hogs into the old world markets, for the simple reason that in Europe the hogs are generally killed by the farmers, who, when they find a hog getting sick, send for the butcher at once, while in America all the killing, for foreign marked especially, is done in certain central localities—three or four days' journey from the feeding ground—rendering it impossible for hogs attacked by disease to be disposed of as in Europe.

A hog that dies from disease or accident cannot be cured; he will betray himself immediately. The discoloration of the flesh and skin is such that no art of the curer can remove. Such a hog could be detected at sight in a thousand boxes of meat.

Dr. Ezra Stetson of Neponset, Illinois, a well-known stock-raiser and scientist, remarks as follows:

It makes no practical difference whether Mr. Crump's (the British vice-consul at Philadelphias estimates are too high or too low. That quite a large percentage of young pigs and a few old hog die of a disease known as hog-cholera all are willing to admit. The loss falls on the producer and not on the consumer, except in the enhanced price paid for the product. It is simply a loss of numbers. It has no effect whatever upon those that survive. The ranks of the human family are being constantly depleted by contagious diseases, but those that escape or survive are in no way injured in their bodily health. Hogs that die of this or any other disease do not find their way to market; those only that are healthy are used in commerce. Since the disease has been known and recognised, no case has ever been reported, or, for that matter, ever can be reported, where swine's flesh has been the cause of human disease.

There is no pork made anywhere in the world that can compare in cleanliness, healthfulness, and all that goes to make a delicious article of swine's flesh with our American corn-fed pork.

The farmer having a drove of hogs ready for the market sells them to the buyers, who are continually going through the country for this purpose, or he ships them direct to the stock-yards at Chicago or Cincinnati.

Whatever the mode of shipment may be, the shipper knows that it would be useless to forward anything but the very soundest and best animals, for none else could possibly pass the inspection to which they are sure to be subjected, as will be seen further on. As the hogs are from two to five days in railroad transit, and as this transit could not be made by unsound animals, it would prove unprofitable to ship any but the best.

One good effect of the scrutiny which the animals now undergo before being accepted by the packer or exporter, has been to completely check the careless handling of hogs which prevailed some years ago.

Instead of driving the hogs to the railroad, as in former times, the farmer, to insure their good condition, now generally hauls them in sleighs or wagons—the mark of a whip-lash, prodding, &c., being sufficient cause for the rejection of a hog by the packers.

They are shipped in well-ventilated cars, fed and watered at regular intervals, and handled with all possible care en route. All that arrive dead or maimed at the stockyards are almost a complete loss to the shipper.

Upon arrival at the stock-yards* the commission salesman sees to the feeding and watering of the hogs, in order to preserve them in the best possible condition for market.

The dead hogs (for, notwithstanding all precautions, deaths occur in the cars from suffocation, fatigue, omission to water, &c.), are taken possession of by the employés of a company empowered by charter with the exclusive right to seize all dead animals found within the yards. This company fixes an arbitrary price to be paid to the owners of such dead hogs—a price so profitable to the company as to insure the watchfulness of its employés.

That a dead hog could escape the vigilance of these interested parties is, at least, not probable. The disposition made of these dead hogs will be shown further on.

Purchasing, Killing, and Curing.

One of the most experienced buyers at the Union Stock-yards at Chicago, whose statement is annexed hereto,† says:

As proof of the health and soundness of American hogs, it may be mentioned that the number of dead hogs which arrive at the stock-yards will not average one hog to each car-load, although the cars frequently contain between 90 and 100 hogs each, and will average 70 hogs to the car on the receipts the year round. It must also be borne in mind that some hogs are on the railroad for four, five, and even six days in making the journey to Chicago from points of shipment in the far West, and even these come to hand after all the delay in excellent condition.

I have seen hogs arrive at Birmingham and Wolverhampton, from Liverpool, after being eight or ten hours in transit, and the average of dead hogs to the car was many per cent. more than the average

---

* Particular reference is here had to the Union Stock-yards at Chicago. The subsequent description of the purchasing, killing and curing has reference to Chicago packers. It may be said, however, that in all essentials, surveillance, inspection, curing, &c., what applied to Chicago is equally applicable to Cincinnati.

† See statement of Mr. Foster, page 106.

on hogs that I have seen arriving at the Union Stock-yards from the Missouri River, after a three or four days' run.

Mr. Williams, secretary of the Union Stock-yards at Chicago, in his communication annexed hereto,* remarks as follows:

The great bulk of hogs arriving at this market are raised in Illinois, Kansas, Missouri, Wisconsin, Ohio, and Indiana.

They are generally well fatted, weighing from 150 to 450 pounds per head. Upon arriving at these yards they are placed in covered pens, fed with the best of corn, and good pure water given them. If any are crippled in transit they are sold to the cheap markets in the city. Dead hogs are taken possession of by the Rendering Company and made into grease and fertilizer. As to the health of the hogs arriving here, I will say that I have been familiar with this market and have been located in the yards for about twenty-six years, and during all those years I have never known the hogs to be in such excellent condition, so healthy, as they have been during the past year.

It is proper to observe here that this report gives full details, from the farrowing of the pig until the meat product is placed upon the local and foreign markets, and that the various details which follow of purchase, inspection, weighing, driving to the slaughter-house, and the process of manufacture for export are the result of a personal examination made by me, accompanied by a stenographer and experts.

The house at which the examinations were made is one of the largest in the world, and kills and cures both for the English and the home markets. As my visit was unexpected, there was no opportunity for any special display on the occasion, even were it possible or necessary to vary the regular course of business of such a vast establishment, where more than a million of hogs are annually slaughtered. Indeed the packers and hog dealers of Chicago and Cincinnati were only too anxious for the fullest and severest investigation, feeling confident that through such investigation they could refute calumny and correct erroneous opinions in regard to their trade in the most direct and positive manner.

Upon the arrival of the hogs at the Union Stock-yards† at Chicago, the trains are run alongside a platform and unloaded, the animals passing down an inclined plane into pens. The hogs belonging to each owner being collected into large separate pens, the buyers of the different packers examine each lot with a view to purchase. All purchases are made with the understanding that the purchaser has the right of selection and rejection.

After the lot has been purchased and a selection made out of the general drove, the selected animals are removed to what is known as a sorting-pen, where each hog is inspected by the packer's expert, called a sorter. The severity of this "sorting" is such that no animal can pass unless in the best condition.

As no diseased or crippled animal can *reach* this stage, all those rejected are rejected for reasons not connected with disease or injury.

The rejected consist of sows, stags, rough hogs, hogs having any marks from whips or sticks, &c.

After this careful examination, the selected hogs are driven to the scales of the Union Stockyard Company and weighed, and an official certificate issued.

The price originally agreed upon is paid by the purchaser on the basis of this official weight.

Up to this point the hogs are subject to the rules and regulations of the Stockyard Company, and the owners and purchasers must conform to said rules.

Considering the transportation of the hogs by rail from the farm to the yards, and the handling, selecting, and driving to which they are subject from their unloading until they are weighed in the company's scales, it is apparent that neither diseased nor inferior animals can possibly pass the ordeal.

From the company's scales the hogs may be said to come fully into the possession of the purchaser.

The hogs are then driven up an inclined plane, carefully prepared, into the chute which leads to the packing-house. These chutes are elevated covered-ways, connecting the scales and packing-houses, and running over sheds, pens, and roads, thus facilitating the passage of the hogs to their destination. These chutes are from a quarter to half a mile in length, according to the position of the packing-houses. In winter they protect the animals from storms, and in summer (while they get plenty of air, and fresh water being sprinkled from time to time as they slowly move forward), from the heat of the sun. Should any of the hogs become tired they are lifted into vehicles contrived for the purpose, and hauled along after the drove to the resting pen.

---

* Page 111.
† See in this connection, page 114, statement of John H. Porter, Esq., of Cincinnati.

Arrived at the packing-house the drove is allowed to rest, in well-constructed builings, from 24 to 48 hours, according to the season, so that the hogs may be thoroughly cooled and in suitable condition for killing.

At the slaughtering place is a pen which is generally supplied with about a dozen hogs at a time.

A chain is fastened around one of the hind legs of the hog, and the animal is hoisted head downwards, and passed on by machinery to the sticker. It is asserted by experts, that this is the speediest and best method of killing the hog, preparing him for quick and complete bleeding when stuck. The noise and struggles of the animal when hoisted have almost entirely ceased by the time the sticker is reached, and when it is considered that as many as eight or ten hogs are killed in the short space of a minute, in the large houses, during their busy seasons, it is evident that the time for struggling must be very short.

After being stuck, the hog is passed along by the same machinery which hoisted him, and is allowed to hang until he is thoroughly bled and life is extinct.

With the perfection of their machinery and the expertness and number of their employés, the large houses of Chicago can kill and handle 4,000 hogs in a day, with perfect ease and precision.

All the hogs killed are fully and thoroughly bled, and life is extinct before they have passed from the hanging position into the tank of boiling water, preparatory to their being scraped and relieved of hair and bristles, which latter operation is generally done by an ingenious machine through which each hog is drawn.

After passing through this machine the work of scraping is completed by hand.

The hog is next suspended by the hind legs from a rail, opened, the intestines taken out, the head severed from the body and the inside thoroughly washed with cold water.

The hog is then split down the back, the spine removed, and the two sides moved along into a room, where the temperature is always maintained at 32° (Fahrenheit). Here it is allowed to hang between 48 and 72 hours for the purpose of removing all animal heat and to prepare it for cutting up.

From this preparatory room the hogs are taken to the cutting-room, where each is examined to ascertain what his weight and quality fit him for. The lightest and choicest are set aside and carefully cut into sides and hams to suit the English market; the sides and hams being most carefully and scientifically trimmed by expert knivesmen into cuts suitable for the different English districts, viz., Staffordshire, Yorkshire, Cumberland, Wiltshire, &c.

The hams and sides are then conveyed to the cellar and assorted into different piles, according to weight. They are here carefully powdered with English refined saltpetre which gives them the fine colour so much admired by the English buyer; the fleshy parts are sprinkled with a mixture of Liverpool salt and the best granulated sugar. They are then carefully laid one upon another, to a height of about four feet, in which position they are kept for 10 days. They are then changed, sprinkled with the same preparation, salt and sugar, and the sides which were at the bottom placed on top, and *vice versâ*. The cellars where these operations take place are flagged and are kept scrupulously clean, all light being excluded. Here, at a temperature of 40° (Fahrenheit), the meats are kept undergoing the process of curing for 16 to 30 days, according to the weight of the pieces, and are then removed to the packing rooms. Here they are thoroughly scraped, cleaned, and retrimmed, and the meat minutely inspected for imperfections, such as bruises, taint, &c. The perfect pieces are carefully sorted into uniform sizes, and according to thickness and weight; and are then weighed and packed in boxes containing about 500 lbs. each. Each piece before being placed in the box is rolled in fine Liverpool salt, and salt is also sprinkled between the layers.

The boxes are made of the best quality of lumber, grooved and tongued, the aim being to have them as air-tight as possible. The boxes are made of various sizes to suit the different cuts of meat. Each box is branded with particulars of contents and the packer's and company's names.

The meats are now ready for shipment to Europe. They are shipped in special refrigerator cars, built for the purpose, which in summer are kept at a temperature of 45° (Fahrenheit).

The houses which kill and cure for the English market ship their goods in special trains to the port of shipment, where the meats are immediately transferred to the steamer.

They have special agents at the port of shipment, to insure prompt transfer from the cars to the steamer, and branch houses on the other side to take charge of the meats upon arrival, and give them the careful handling which is so necessary, and for lack of which, as will be told further on, meats, originally good and pure, may become unsaleable.

The foregoing process of curing, it will be remarked, is the special process of curing for the European markets, both for the Continent and the British Isles.

The same care is taken in the inspection and killing of the hogs for home consumption, but the sides and hams are cut into shapes to suit the American market, and are cured in American salt, without any addition of saltpetre or sugar. The pieces are handled with as much nicety and precision as for the English market, fresh salt being added at intervals of ten to fifteen days.

Although not cured, sized, and cut in the same style, the home meats are in general fully equal to those cured for the English market; and the entire process of buying, inspecting, killing, curing, and packing home meats is the same, except in some details, as that which characterizes the handling of meats for the English markets, so similar indeed that a description of the process of killing and curing for the American market would be almost a repetition of the foregoing remarks.

The preparation of "mess pork" for the home market is as follows: the sides of the hog, exclusive of the hams and shoulders, are cut into strips of from six to eight inches in width, and packed fresh into barrels, with Turk's Island salt. The barrels are then filled with pickle.

Domestic hams are cured in sweet pickle, composed of salt, saltpetre, molasses, and water, in which they are allowed to remain for sixty days, when they are taken out, dried, smoked, and canvassed ready for the market.

In this connexion I can do no better than refer you to a communication, hereto annexed, from one of the largest and most experienced curers and dealers in the West (see statement* by William Henry Davis, Esq., of Cincinnati, entitled "American "ham-curing for the home and foreign markets," which gives a clear and succinct account of the curing of American hams, both for home and foreign consumption). I had the pleasure of going through the establishment, and of seeing the care and expertness with which the hams were handled until they were packed ready for export, and as this house may be said to represent ham curing in the United States it appears to me that no hams in the world can surpass the American for purity, cleanliness, and flavour.

In continuation of the disposition of the hogs by the packers, for everything is utilized and nothing allowed to go to waste, it seems necessary to make some statement respecting the lard product.

Leaf-lard and the fat trimmings from the sides and hams are rendered in iron tanks with steam, at a pressure of from 35 to 40 pounds, and cooked continuously from twelve to sixteen hours, after which the tanks are allowed to settle, when the lard is drawn off into tierces containing about 350 pounds each.

In this condition the lard is an article of commerce, but before reaching the consumer it generally passes through the hands of the refiner. The settlings of the tanks are valued as a fertilizer.

The lean meat trimmings from the hams and sides are made into sausage; the feet are sold to the glue manufacturers; the tenderloins and spare-ribs are sold fresh to local consumers; the blood, when dried, is used as a fertilizer; the intestines and salt trimmings collected at the time of preparation for packing are rendered in specially prepared tanks, and made into soap-grease; the refuse of these tanks is also used as a fertilizer.

How Hogs dying of Disease or Accident are disposed of.

In view of the reports of our consuls during the last few years of the recklessness with which statements tending to injure the reputation of American lard have been disseminated through Europe, and the skilful manner in which interested parties have played upon the fears of the consumers as to the probability of "lard" manufactured from hogs dying of cholera or other disease, or even dying from accidental causes, being shipped from the United States and sold to Europeans as a good article, special pains were taken to investigate this part of the hog-product question.

Consul Potter, of Stuttgart, Germany, transmitted to this Department, in the latter part of 1880, a translation, from a leading German journal, of a communication from a correspondent in Chicago, of which the following is a paragraph:

You are perhaps not aware that in the stink factories at Globe Station, near Chicago, large quantities of lard are produced from animals which have died from disease, and that much of this lard is exported to England and Germany. It is said that it is only used for lubricating purposes, but who can tell what disposition is made of it by the dealers? This lard is as white as snow and is odourless;

---

* Page 112.

and it is possible that many poor persons employ it for culinary purposes who have not the remotest idea of how it is manufactured.

The manner in which this paragraph, by its extravagance, overleaps all probability would render it unworthy of serious consideration or refutation were it not for the fact that the fears of the masses in Europe are excited by all such published statements in regard to American lard. No matter how absurd they may seem to us they gain a certain amount of credence in Europe, and their refutation consequently becomes a duty.

All hogs found dead in the cars upon arrival at the Union Stock Yards at Chicago, or dying therein, are taken possession of by the Union Rendering Company,* a Company chartered by the legislature of Illinois for this purpose, and shipped to their rendering works at Globe Station, on the Indiana State line.

The company pays the owners of dead hogs an absolute price fixed by itself, which, as was the intention of the legislature when granting the charter, makes the business so profitable as to excite the watchfulness of the employés of the company to such a degree that no dead or diseased animal can escape detection.

Accompanied by a stenographer I visited the rendering works at Globe Station, and was shown through the establishment by its very intelligent foreman, a German, who has had twenty-five years' experience in the business. In passing through, this foreman described, in detail, the process of extracting the grease from the dead animals and converting the residue into a fertilizer.

Upon receipt of the dead hogs from the Union Stock Yards they are run up an inclined plane, by steam power, to the top of the building, and then put into the cooking tanks. After the animals are thoroughly cooked the grease is drawn off and the residue is treated as a fertilizer.

The grease is then barrelled and branded according to quality, "White grease" and "Brown grease."

The time occupied in converting the dead animals into these products is but twenty-four hours.

The grease, both white and brown, is principally sold to soap manufacturers.

Upon being interrogated as to the possibility of any of this grease being sold in Europe as lard,† the foreman of the establishment said:

There is a smell from this grease, after our severest refining, which renders it impossible to be palmed off as lard. The hogs dying a natural death decompose so rapidly that it is impossible to convert them into meat or lard.

In Cincinnati the same care is taken to seize and send to the rendering houses all dead and diseased hogs. Mr. Thompson,‡ the very efficient city contractor for the removal of dead animals, says:

It would seem to be impossible that diseased hogs could be converted into human food in Cincinnati. Our very efficient board of health would render the opportunity to do so almost impossible, even were there persons bad enough to attempt it. The hogs are inspected as they are unloaded from the cars, and if there is anything wrong with them they are immediately taken possession of by the employés of the city contractor, who renders them down for the grease, which is marked "Dead hog grease," and which is wholly used for soap and other manufacturing purposes, and nothing else. No person could possibly mistake this grease, in any form, for lard.

TRICHINÆ.

In addition to the testimony which is presented herewith, from gentlemen whose professional duties brought this subject within the line of their special supervision and investigation, the general testimony of all intelligent and practical men with whom I conversed concerning trichinæ in pork, is, that in all the West not the slightest fears are entertained in this regard.

Of course this general testimony assumes that pork shall not be eaten without being well cooked. All persons, scientists, farmers, packers, consumers, &c., were unanimous in the assertion that all cases of trichinosis, or suspected trichinosis, coming within the range of their observations, were caused by eating pork in a raw state, generally in the form of sausage, and the very inferior scraps which were rejected as unfit for human food.

The people of the United States may be said to be the greatest pork eaters in the world, the agricultural classes eating thereof two or three times a day during the greater portion of each year, and the subject of trichnæ never troubles them.

---

* See statement of the foreman of this company, page 115. Also statement of Dr. Dewolf, Commissioner of Health of the city of Chicago, page 118.
† See paper headed "Ohio Hogs and Hog Products," page 119.
‡ See Mr. Thompson's further statement, page 115.

In the cities pork also constitutes the meat food of the working classes almost altogether; and when it is taken into consideration that those portions of the hog not cured by the packers, (and so never entering at all into the export trade), such as the tenderloin and spare-rib, are considered by scientists as the portions most likely to be infested with trichinæ, and that such portions are sold to the local dealers for local consumption, the few cases of deaths from trichinosis in Chicago, and these the result of eating the raw and inferior scraps, afford conclusive evidence of the purity and wholesomeness of American pork. It may be doubted whether any other animal food, if subjected to so much suspicion and inspection, would show so clean a health record.

In regard to the great pork-eating city of Cincinnati, Dr. A. J. Mills, health officer, says:

In reply to your inquiry in regard to the prevalence of *trichinæ spiralis* in this city, I beg to state that there has not been a single case of this disease during my term of office; and the records do not show a single case occurring in this city at any time previous to that time.

Thus it would appear that no case of trichinosis has ever been reported as having occurred in Cincinnati. All outside testimony, so far as the investigations went, fully corroborated the statement of Dr. Mills.

Dr. John H. Rauch, secretary to the Illinois State Board of Health, prepared at my request, the following official statement:

Since 1866 11 deaths have occurred in the State of Illinois of trichinosis, and those deaths, in every instance, resulted from eating raw ham or sausage.*

As a sanitarian, I regard the danger of life from this source as practically amounting to nothing, it being so easily prevented by thorough cooking. No doubt more deaths occur from many other articles of diet that are regarded as harmless, no record of the same being made.

Dr. Oscar C. De Wolf, commissioner of health for the city of Chicago, says:

Our mortality in this city for the last four years ranged from 8,000 in 1877 to 10,000 in 1880, and only two cases of trichinæ have been reported during that period;† and the fact that the meat rejected by the packers is consumed locally, and is more likely to be infected than that exported, adds materially to the importance of this statement.

Dr. Ezra Stetson, of Neponset, Illinois, a scientist and practical stock-breeder and farmer, upon being questioned concerning trichinæ, considered the subject as scarcely worthy of consideration, remarking as follows:

I suppose you will eat pork with us at dinner to-day. We eat it ourselves continually. We have neither fears nor scruples in this regard so long as it has been well cooked. Trichinæ is not confined to the hog alone; horses, cows, and rabbits are subject thereto; that is the true parasite. This parasite is effectually destroyed and rendered innocuous by thorough cooking. Just as soon, and no sooner, as all flesh, and even fish, is cooked before eating, trichinæ will cease to be a bugbear.

Conclusions arrived at.

The conclusions arrived at in this report are as follows:

1. That the swine of America are of the best and purest breeds,‡ and are fed and fattened for market on corn. It is not believed that swine are thus fed in any other country.
2. That the reports published in Europe concerning the deaths of American hogs from hog cholera are gross exaggerations.
3. That the percentage of deaths among American swine from disease is no greater than the percentage of deaths among European swine from similar diseases.
4. That American hogs which have died or may die of cholera, or from any cause whatever, can have no relation to the meat product (except to decrease it), as such animals cannot by any possibility pass the severe scrutiny and inspection to which hogs destined for killing and curing are subject; that, even if it were possible to pass such inspection, no art of the curer could convert such animals into meat which could pass the inspection, in the words of a leading curer, "even of a blind man."
5. That the fears excited and fostered in parts of Europe by interested persons, that any portion of hogs, which have died or may die of cholera, or from any other cause, is or can be converted into merchantable lard, are founded on the grossest ignorance, for merchantable lard cannot be produced from such dead animals.
6. That every pound of the product rendered from diseased hogs, except that part used as a fertilizer, is plainly marked "brown grease," "white grease" or "dead hog's

---

* During this period the average population of Illinois was over two and a half millions.
† This shows only two cases of trichinosis in nearly 40,000 deaths, whose causes are here reported.
‡ See statement of Charles F. Mills, page 116; also statement of J. H. Cunningham, page 122.

grease," and sold as such largely to soap manufacturers and that its colour and odour preclude it from being mistaken for lard.

7. That the same care is taken in the handling and manufacture of American lard which is taken in the handling and curing of American meats; and that, as the corn-fed American hog* is the cleanest of its species anywhere, it is undeniable that American lard is the purest lard in any market.

8. That the percentage of American hogs infected with trichinæ (though this question is thus far largely one of supposition) is in all probability, by reason of the superiority of the breed and feed, much less than that among the hogs in any other country.

9. That the freedom from trichinosis of the two great pork-consuming centres of the West, Chicago and Cincinnati, furnishes the strongest possible evidence of the purity of American pork. In Chicago, for a series of years in which 40,000 deaths were reported with their causes, only two cases of trichinosis were reported. In Cincinnati during the same period not one case was reported.

10. That the reported cases of trichinosis have resulted from eating uncooked meat,† shown to be inferior or rejected, and that thorough cooking entirely destroys this parasite and removes all danger, in this regard, from eating pork.

11. That the selection, inspection, and killing of American hogs, and the subsequent handling and curing of the meat, are not surpassed, if at all equalled, for care, precision, and understanding, by the packers or meat-curers of any other country.

12. That, as a rule, the hogs selected for foreign trade are in all respects equal to the very best disposed of in our home market.

13. That the great exaggerations so industriously spread in regard to diseased pork have been aided by the different significations attached to the word "pig." In Europe it is used as the synonym of hog, whereas in America it means the young swine under six months, and generally refers to those only a few weeks old. The number of "pigs" that die from various causes compared with the numbers of "hogs" that die is very large, and grossly erroneous conclusions are formed by confounding the two words.

As an earnest of the conclusions to which it is hoped and believed the governments of Europe which have excluded American pork, as well as other governments, may arrive; and in view of your suggestion, Mr. Secretary, that its publication is due to the candid spirit in which the Government of His Majesty the King of the Belgians has met the charges made against the pork product of the United States, I have the honour to add that, as appears by a circular addressed on the 28th April last by the Belgian Minister of the Interior to the governors of His Majesty's provinces, the question of excluding American pork from that country has been decided in favour of the United States.

The charge against our product, under which it had been excluded from France, is disposed of in this circular by conclusions, the substance of which is—

That disease generated by trichinæ is unknown in countries where, as in Belgium, pork is sufficiently cooked; and that it has been demonstrated by many experiments that the trichinæ cannot resist a temperature of 56° Centigrade, and that they are invariably killed at a temperature of 75° to 100 C.

This report also says:

It is important to make known the fact that pork well cooked, whatever trichinæ it may contain, is entirely inoffensive, and consequently no one need suffer from this cause, unless he wishes to, and nothing is necessary except scrupulous persistence in the use of needful precautions of the kitchen.

Remarking that these conclusions of the Belgian Minister of the Interior are based on a careful report of the Belgian Official Council of Public Health,

I have, &c.

(Signed) MICHAEL SCANLAN,
Chief of the Bureau of Statistics,
Department of State.

Hon. James G. Blaine,
    Secretary of State.,
&c. &c. &c.

---

* See report headed "Pork-packing in Cincinnati," page 121.
† See statement of Morrison & Co., page 117.

R 679.

APPENDIX to REPORT on AMERICAN PORK.

[In addition to the gentlemen who prepared the following statements, special thanks are due for valuable services rendered in the investigations necessary to the preparation of this report, to Charles Randolph, Esq., Secretary of the Board of Trade of Chicago; John A. Atkinson, Esq., and Mortimer Scanlan, Chicago; Col. Sidney D. Maxwell, Secretary of the Chamber of Commerce of Cincinnati, and Hon. J. W. Fitzgerald, of the same city.]

AMERICAN and BRITISH HOGS and HOG PRODUCTS COMPARED.—STATEMENT by MICHAEL FOSTER, Esq., of CHICAGO.

SIR,
Having heard that you are out here collecting information and figures relating to hog raising and pork packing in the West, I take the liberty of addressing you on the subject, and stating some facts in this connexion that may possibly throw some light on this very much misrepresented though all-important question. I am aware that the agitation of the public mind on this subject at present, in both the Old and New World, renders it absolutely necessary that a matter of such international importance should be approached with caution, and touched only by those whose experience and observation have gained them a knowledge on the subject of such an extent and character as may be deemed reliable. With this view I therefore wish to say that whatever I here state are facts, and not mere assertions; and when I state that my experience with hogs and hog product runs back over a quarter of a century in the leading marts of the world for these two articles of merchandise, I may be allowed the privilege of claiming a certain reliability if not authority for what I state.

I have before me a letter lately received from a friend in Ireland. It is dated "Limerick, "February 16, 1881," and contains the following passage:

"The pig trade is very bad at present, in consequence of a scarcity, and the price of pigs here just now is 65s. per hundredweight."

To explain this more fully, I will say that the price for the *dressed weight* for the hog in Limerick is equal to about $16 per "long" hundred, or 112 pounds of dressed pork, making it necessary to obtain on the London Market no less than 80s., or say $20 per 112 pounds for the manufactured article out of the Limerick hog, in order to remunerate the packer or "bacon curer" for his investment.

Taking this fact alone simply proves the market price of Irish bacon in London; but when I tell you that at about the same time 80s. to 83s., or say $20 to $21 per hundredweight was being paid for this Limerick cured bacon you could select the finest brands of Chicago bacon in Liverpool at from 45s. to 52s., or $11 to $13 per hundredweight. You will naturally ask "What is the cause of "this great difference in price? Is the American hog so far inferior to the Irish or English hog?" In answer to this last query I say emphatically "No"; and I will undertake to prove not only that such is not the case, but that the reverse condition to that implied by this question is the actual position of the hogs of the two countries in any comparison as to quality that may be instituted between them. I have handled in large numbers hogs raised and fed in every county in Ireland from 1857 to 1871; as a member of the live stock firm of Thomas Foster and Sons, Smithfield, Birmingham, I handled 50 per cent. of the imported hog supply for the great manufacturing midland counties of England; I have bought hogs out of the crack pedigree droves of England, including that of William Looker, Esq., Clenchwarton Hall, King's Lynn, Norfolk, one of the most celebrated breeders of pedigree hogs in England; I have handled hogs from the royal farms and from the Smithfield Club Show, London, and the Bingley Hall Show at Birmingham; and in all my Irish and English experience I *never saw* finer or purer-bred hogs than I have seen and handled at the Union Stock Yards, Chicago.

I make these statements, knowing well that the "hog question" is at present receiving keen attention from numerous interested parties on both sides of the Atlantic, and therefore to take up any position from which one may have to back down is not alone impolitic but unwise.

In Ireland, generally speaking, the hogs are bred promiscuously, unless in exceptional cases where the landlord or large bacon curer introduces fine-bred stock for the free use of the peasantry, which is notably the case in the counties of Waterford and Tipperary, and parts of the counties of Kilkenny, Wexford, Cork, and Limerick; but strict adherence to the principles of pure breeding from pedigree stock is "honoured more in the breach than in the observance," and hence the diversity of breeds to be found in the national hog of Ireland. In England, likewise, the different breeds of swine are not kept as pure as they are in a general way in America, though of course there are many "fancy" breeders in England who are as fastidious regarding the "pedigree" of their "prize pig" as if the ultimate climax of the hog's earthly career was to be the Two thousand Guineas or the Derby, instead of making sausage and pork pies and boiling with cabbage for the sturdy Britons.

Before leaving the subject of breeding I will give some general impressions you very readily get in moving among hogs in the three countries. In Ireland and England you have to hunt up fine-bred hogs if you wish to see any, and even then, as I before stated you only find them in "spots," the principal portion of the hogs showing unmistakable evidence of the utter lack of care in breeding from any one particular stock. But in Western America, as represented at the Union Stock Yards, your attention is frequently arrested by the singular purity of the breeding of whole car loads of hogs, and even passing over these cases where exclusive breeding seems to have been rigidly observed, you cannot help remarking how uniformly first-class pedigree shows through most of the hogs that arrive to supply the demands of the day. It is not an unusual occurrence to see all the hogs of one train of, say from 20 to 30 cars, exhibiting such strong signs of having sprung from the same original stock as to indicate to the most casual observer that they had all been raised in and shipped from the same section. Now as to the question of feeding, I will state that the American hog is the best fed, simply because he feeds and fattens on Indian corn, the finest grain that grows out of the earth, while "slop" butchers' garbage, brewers' grains, distillery swill, and vegetable matter of various kinds enter largely into the diet of hogs in both Ireland and England, with of course a considerable portion of damaged Indian corn, barley, meal, and poor oats. There is this difference, that as a rule food of all kinds, except oats, is cooked for the hogs in Ireland and England, thereby eliminating any "oily" or greasy property in the food, while in America the hog gets the corn "neat" or raw, and as there is 8 per cent. more oil in Indian corn than in any other grain, the "oily" or "greasy" condition is present in a more or less degree in American pork and bacon, though the same amount of care in preparation for market as is given to Irish or English bacon, and a little more age than is generally accorded to it by the trade in this country, would certainly free it from this one detrimental though not unhealthy quality.

I will give a very pointed example here to prove that grain in a "raw" state is apt to make "soft" pork if constantly fed to hogs. In parts of Connaught the hogs are chiefly fed on black oats, and first-class bacon curers discriminate so sharply against them that they are unwilling to buy them even at a large reduction from what they pay for hogs from other parts of Ireland, simply because they are apt to be "soft" in the fat. If any proof were necessary to show that Indian corn is the best food in the world for fattening I would call attention to the fact that while the best beeves in Great Britain are "forced" and pampered with "oil-cake" and other artificial food the mammoth steer of the Western plains is brought up to the splendid condition and huge proportions of a prize winner on the pure "golden grain." In this connexion I will recite one more case relating to corn as an article of sound healthful food for hogs. I once bought hogs for a packing firm that was engaged in putting up fancy cuts of meat for the English market, and we were desirous of getting a test as to the relative merits of hogs from the different sections of the country tributary to Chicago. In fact, it took the form of a test between Michigan and Missouri, because the one (Missouri) represented the "pure corn-fed" hog and the other (Michigan) the "mixed-fed" hog; for be it known that Michigan is supposed to feed in no meagre proportion such vegetables as pumpkins, melons, squashes, and other similar "truck," with a small modicum of corn to her hogs. There were accordingly bought for this purpose two droves of hogs on two different days, but of an equal number and weight, and as even and nearly alike in every respect as it was possible to get them. They were killed, cut, and cured separately with the following results: the Missouri hogs yielded 71½ per cent. product and shrank 1½ per cent. in the curing process, while the Michigan hogs yielded 67½ per cent. product and shrank 3½ per cent. in the curing process, thereby proving most conclusively that "corn was king." The idea suggests itself right here that corn should be cooked for hog feeding in this country, but the labour and expense attending such a system precludes all probability of it ever coming into general practice in the West, where hogs are fed in such large droves.

Given that the hogs in Western America are well bred and well fed, does it follow that they should be more subject to disease than the hogs of any other country? I think this question admits of no answer but the one suggested by reason and common sense, which clearly establishes the negative in any unprejudiced mind. You will remember one thing, that the circumstances surrounding the case admit of no comparison whatever between the relative mortality among hogs and cattle in this country, for the reason that a farmer having a cow on the eve of calving takes particular care that the welfare of the cow just then shall be assiduously looked after, as he can realize from $5 to $10 for the calf after having fed it with the cow's milk for, say, from two to four weeks, whereas the sow under similar circumstances is allowed to take care of herself, because her offspring are more numerous, and will, under favourable conditions, take from eight to ten months to put on the 200 pounds of solid pork required at present price of hogs in the country to realise $10.

Thus it will be seen that very young pigs have no present, but a prospective value, and that only on the farm where they are raised. A sow generally will have from 7 to 12 pigs at a farrow, and the death, through accident or otherwise, of any of the brood causes little if any notice from the farmer as there is no feeling of present loss, so that the reports of deaths among the very young swine are taken pretty much as a matter of course, especially on farms where the fruitful and healthy sows are constantly increasing the porcine population. At the age of three or four months the pig begins to have a commercial value, and also begins to attract some notice from the farmer, but even then he is expected to get his own living in some shape or other around the farm, and as he instinctively understand the maxim "root, hog, or die," he will do some "tall" rooting in pursuit of his sustenance. It is at this stage of his existence that his troubles come on him, and he may possibly be called on to help swell "cholera reports" and "mortality statistics," but I don't see why it should be matter of surprise if a young pig has to encounter sickness and every other trouble incidental to extreme youth when it is an established fact that all animals, both rational and irrational, undergo a continual struggle for life during the period of passing from immaturity to maturity.

Generally about the age of six months the pig is penned up in the feed lot and is fed with all the corn he can eat until he becomes ripe and fit for market, and at this stage disease seldom claims him for a victim. Now it is monstrously unjust to try to circulate the belief that the American hog selfishly claims a monopoly of the "hog cholera" when the hogs in Ireland and England suffer to a much greater extent proportionately from the same disease, but under different names. What the scientific name of the disease is I do not know, but it is popularly known in Ireland as the "sudor," and in England as the "purples," and as I have seen hogs affected with the disease in all three countries, I unhesitatingly say that it is one and the same, both in regard to its epidemic nature, its symptoms, and its results.

But to assume that "hog cholera" cuts any figure or in any way enters into the manufacture of cured meats for home or foreign consumption argues a very imperfect knowledge of the pork-packing business of the present day. Certainly "hog cholera" exists in a more or less degree among American swine, as it also does among the porkers of Great Britain, and it will so exist as long as hogs are bred, but then in America it only represents the "waste" of the industry of hog raising, in the same manner that the broken vases, the cracked crockery, the faulty fire-arm, the false mirror, the tainted bacon, and the locomotive wheel with a flaw in it are the "waste" of the business in which the several makers of these articles are engaged.

With the manufacturers here alluded to, the "waste" occurs at the workshop generally during the early stage of the process of making the goods and in like manner the "waste" occurs with the farmer at a similar stage in his production of live pork, so that "cholera hogs" rarely find their way into the hands of a pork packer, who, in fact, is doubly guarded, as I shall show, against such an unwished-for visitation. Drovers who travel through the country in pursuit of their calling are not easily imposed upon and are therefore not very likely to buy sick hogs from a farmer. In studying their own interests they ship their stock in good condition, and so it invariably arrives at the stock-yards unless delayed on the road by storm or some other untoward circumstance. Arrived at the stock-yard the hogs are taken in charge by a commission salesman, who is particular to have them well fed and watered before putting them on the market for sale, or at all events before they are weighed to the party who has purchased them. The dead hogs, should there be any in the car, through suffocation, the fatigue of travel, or other causes, are taken by the agents or employés of a company having a charter from Springfield, Ill., for the exclusive right to purchase all dead animals within the premises of the Union Stock Yard and Transit Company, so that no packer, butcher, or outside dealer can have an opportunity, if so disposed, to convert the fat or any portion of the dead hog into an article of human food.

As proof of the health and soundness of American hogs, it may be mentioned that the number of dead hogs which arrive at the stock-yards will not average one hog to each car-load, although the cars frequently contained between 90 and 100 hogs, and will average near 70 hogs to each car on the receipts the year round. It must also be borne in mind that some hogs are on the railroad for four, five, and even six days in making the journey to Chicago, from points of shipment in the far West, and even these come to hand after all in excellent condition. I have seen hogs arrive at Birmingham and Wolverhampton from Liverpool, after being about eight or ten hours in transit, and the average of dead hogs to the car was many per cent. more than the average on hogs than I have seen arrive at the Union Stock-yards from the Missouri river, after three and four days' run. I have said that packers were doubly guarded against "sick" or unmerchantable hogs in their operations at the stock-yards, and in doing so I simply stated a fact that admits of no contradiction. Every packer doing business at this point has one or more buyers as the extent of his business may require, and each buyer has an expert assistant whose duty it is to select from a drove the grade of hogs suitable for the house for which the purchasing and assorting is done, and as the "sorter" is quite a factor in the manipulations of the hog business at the stock-yards, I will here quote from an article on the subject I published some time ago in a local live-stock paper:

"Take, for instance, the grading of hogs, or what is known to the trade as 'sorting,' which is very little understood, except by persons actually engaged in the business. The newspapers may state, as they frequently do, that, for some specified reason, the buyers of certain grades of hogs got a 'good sort' or 'bad sort,' a 'close sort' or a 'liberal sort'; but, no matter what variations the 'sort' may assume, the phrase is Greek, and the meaning a perfect mystery, to the untutored in the classic language of 'swinedom.' We will suppose a case where the buyer for a packing-house engaged exclusively in putting up English meats buys one or more car-loads of hogs from a salesman on the condition that they are to be 'sorted' to suit the requirements of the house for which the purchase is made. To facilitate this 'sorting' there are several 'sorting' pens, popularly called 'mills,' established in close proximity to each scale, and it is here in these 'mills' that the really important branch of the hog business is carried out, for it is certainly here that good or bad, prime or inferior, hogs are ground out by the man who does the 'grinding business in the 'mill' in the capacity of 'hog sorter.'"

With the arrangements so elaborate and perfect for selecting just such hogs as the packer wants, it is difficult to see how he can get any but the primest hogs for use in his trade, and having got them by the systematic methods I have just described, it is not likely that he will relax any of his wonted vigilance in having the hogs converted into the choicest cuts of meat, either for foreign or domestic trade.

It may appear strange to that portion of the public who are not aware that pork-packing ranks third in importance in the industrial records of this country—I say it may appear strange that all this fineness of detail is observed in what is popularly supposed to be a very rough and ready, common-place business, but nevertheless such is the fact, and furthermore the principle on which several pork-packers here at the stock-yards and throughout the West run their business is to "shut their eyes on expenses," and endeavour by every means that the skill and ingenuity of experienced workmen can devise to get up an article that will be a credit to their houses and satisfactory to their customers. The majority of the packing-houses located here pay their skilled hands from $3 to $5 a day, and generally hire them for a season at these figures. Foremen over the different departments of the house get from $1,500 to $1,800 a year, according to their knowledge of the trade, and generally superintendents are paid from $1,800 to $2,500 a year.

The work is divided into gangs as follows: The killing gang, the cutting gang, the cellar gang, the packing gang, and the "roustabout" or "shoo-fly" gang. Each gang is under the direction of a "boss," who is accountable to the foreman of his department for the work performed by the men under him, and the foreman in his turn is held responsible for the running of the section of the house over which he is placed. This I should say is pretty good discipline for a packing-house, or indeed for any enterprise where organised labour is brought together for the prosecution of a class of work that depends mainly on skill and unremitting care for a successful result.

To describe the working of a large packing-house in detail is not necessary here; therefore I will confine myself to a brief mention of the cutting, curing, and packing. I have always found that the operations of the cutting gang have had more interest for strangers and even old habitues of a packing-house than any other section of the work. There is something almost akin to fascination in watching how deftly a well-trained knifesman carves a picture in pale pink and white out of the rough side of fresh pork that is placed before him on the cutting bench. It looks like exaggeration to call a side of bacon a picture, but when the "trimmer" puts it out of his hands ready for the cellar his enthusiasm may well be excused when the symmetry, squared ends, and fine lines of the work give it the appearance of having been cast in a mould, and though not a picture in the artistic sense it certainly is a masterpiece from the hands of a mechanic. From the cutting room the meat is sent down through a chute into the cellar, where it is subjected to an ice-cooling process to drive out the last remaining particle of animal heat, after which it is very lightly sprinkled with saltpetre or some other mixed "cure," of which, however, this last-named article is the principal ingredient. After this it is thoroughly salted and piled one on the other with as much mathematical precision as if the work were done under the guidance of a plumb-line. After it has lain in salt for a week or so, it is again "overhauled," though overhauling is not looked upon with favour by packers who want to get a fine "cherry-red" colour on their meat.

Packing day comes around in due time and the meat is shipped out under the inspection of an inspector belonging to the house or one who has been sent to get out some order that has been bought from the house for shipment. In either case the strictest attention is paid to the quality of the meat, its age, and condition; and everything that does not rank first-class is re-inspected and will ultimately be packed and shipped to the pineries, the mines, the plains, the fisheries, the collieries, and the South, or any other market where they wish a second-class article at hard-pan prices and where epicurean tastes are not cultivated as they are with the over-fed Briton or the dainty Gaul.

With this showing, it is not an unreasonable assumption to contend that the American pork-packer equals the manufacturer or merchant of any country in his desire to put before the public an honest article of food; and when it is considered that his wishes in that direction are backed by proverbial enterprise, unfaltering liberality, and unlimited means, it may safely be stated that he has achieved a genuine success which will surely overwhelm the obstacles that jealousy has ineffectually thrown in his way.

In this review of the hog trade at this point I have not as much as once mentioned trichinæ, the prime cause of the present great outcry against American pork. I have omitted this purposely to avoid a purely scientific question that I am incapable of handling, but I can nevertheless give my ideas on the subject from a practical man's standpoint. I do not know whether it is known to the American public, but at all events it is well known to the people of Ireland and England, that measles exist to a very great extent among the hogs in both the countries named, and when packers or "bacon-curers" happen to get some of them in their purchases they simply "dock" the seller of such pig 4s. or $1 per hundredweight on the measled pig. In England they are more severe in their dealing with measly pigs; they sell the fat to the tallowchandler and destroy the lean meat.

I believe the trichinæ of America and the measles of Great Britain are analogous from the many similar features they present, but I never knew of any one being injured from eating "measly" pork in either England or Ireland, because they cook pork and all other white meat to the point where it is certainly "overdone," and if it had not been for the cannibalism of some of the people in this and some European countries, who persist in eating raw pork, we perhaps would never have heard of trichinæ outside the laboratory of the chemist or the lecture room of the scientist. How can you protect a man who will go deliberately and eat raw pork, heedless of its condition and in direct opposition to every dictate of reason and every degree of civilization? We claim a superiority over the Fiji islanders, forgetful that we have cannibals in our midst who eat raw pork of every conceivable age and quality, and then express holy horror at the Fiji man eating "raw missionary."

American pork is sound and wholesome, and vastly superior to what it was fifty years ago, and yet the number of deaths from eating it during the past half century is not enough to be even remembered by the ordinary run of mankind, and is only made matter of record in some bureau of extraordinary causes of mortality. A mere observance of the most primitive laws of civilized life, which demand that we make a distinction in the matter and manner of taking our food between the cannibal and ourselves, would be the surest safeguard for American or European pork in the provision markets of the world.

I remain, yours, faithfully,
MICHAEL FOSTER.

Michael Scanlan, Esq.,
  Chief of Bureau of Statistics, Department of State,
    &c.   &c.   &c.

HOG RAISING, HOG CHOLERA, AND TRICHINÆ.—STATEMENT by Dr. EZRA STETSON, of Neponset, Ill.

I was educated a physician, but for the last twenty to fifty years have been extensively engaged in farming here. The statistics of the losses among swine show that the dead hogs never found their way to Europe. They imagine in Europe that the dead animals enter into the Chicago slaughter-houses.

I contend that American corn-fed pork is the best pork that is made in the world anywhere. I have been on the other side of the "pond" and have seen their hogs; there can be no better article of pork made than is made from corn, grass, and cold water; it is the most healthy feed in the world. We raise on our farm a great many hogs—from three to five hundred a year. I eat our own pork, I am not afraid of trichinæ; only barbarians eat raw pork or raw meat of any kind. So far as hog cholera is concerned, where hogs are kept together in large numbers and get infected, it is because sanitary regulations are not complied with.

You have heard of men talking about typhus fever—for it is now almost a matter of history. Where men in great numbers have huddled together, on shipboard, in camps, where armies were gathered together, they had the fever—the plague they called it in olden times. It is simply typhus fever. It has the name of hog cholera, and it will go by that name, and all creation cannot stop it now. At the beginning of the disease, where old and young are not separated, the weak ones are affected, and the larger the herd of swine the greater the intensity of the virus or poison. This disease gathers intensity by numbers.

Is the attack sudden?

It becomes so potent that it almost destroys life at once.

Your experience is that the hog affected with it will not make good meat?

It is impossible to make good meat by any process; that hog is not made into meat; the decomposition sets in before the death of the hog in most all cases.

What is the process of raising hogs; are they allowed to run loose, and how long?

We raise our pigs, and we sell them at any age we think we can make the most money; but our pigs that are dropped in March, April, and May, if not disposed of, are most always kept eighteen or twenty months, sometimes two years, before being disposed of. The sows are fed on corn, grass, and cold water.

Don't you think that many cases of so-called hog cholera are from exposure?

Occasionally. The loss of numbers is the best evidence in the world to show the disease; it has the name of hog cholera; there are very few hogs that are perfect, and they are more likely to die of pneumonia than almost any other disease.

Where the deaths are very sudden the hogs die of paralysis of the heart; it arrests the circulation of the blood. There are probably a thousand hogs raised in this State where one was raised fifty years ago. We convert all our corn into pork to beat the railroads; we cannot afford to pay transportation; we must consume our coarse grains on our farms, and our meat is certainly better than could be made in Europe.

The hog is the most prolific animal we have; they have from six or eight to twelve and fifteen at a litter. Of course the mortality among small pigs is large; the young pigs do not enter into the reports, they enter into no sort of calculation whatever. We have lost from six to thirty pigs, but those are never included in the count. The loss during the cold season and inclement weather is much greater than in warm weather.

I have felt that we needed quarantine regulations between the States, as well as in the States. For instance: If I have cholera among my hogs it is against public policy for me to remove them from my place, because I may communicate the disease to my neighbour. If they are diseased hogs I have no business to ship them. I would have local inspectors in every township, and no man should be allowed to remove his hogs from his own place unless they were in perfect condition. That would be public policy anyway. It would be a matter of economy to do that.

What is your opinion, as a scientist, of trichinæ?

The trichinæ scare is one of the silliest things ever invented, even though there is an occasional case found. I suppose you will eat pork for dinner to-day; we eat it ourselves; we have no scruples of conscience about eating pork when it has been well boiled. Trichinæ is not confined to the hog alone; horses, cows, and rabbits are found with trichinæ; that is the true parasite.

What have been the very worst kind of scarecrows are the scientific theorists; they have been imagining all sorts of things to sustain their theory. Now this man ———— has been exercising a horrible influence in animal products, and he has a sort of quasi authority from our government, as having been appointed by Commissioner Le Duc. I had designed to give Secretary Blaine my views to show them the pernicious effects in regard to our commerce.

I claim, and I have so written and published for a good many years, that hog cholera is an unnecessary disease; it is produced by bad sanitary arrangements. I would assist sanitary laws, as men do under like circumstances; I have used carbolic acid for the last fifteen years among my swine. I commenced at first by sprinkling their sides. I have also used crystallised carbolic acid and carbonates of lime; and for the last eight or ten years I have been giving my hogs carbolic acid every time they drink, and if they had the disease it has been in so mild a form and they have been so healthy that I did not know anything about it. My attention was first called to this from a report of the Commissioner of Great Britain investigating pleuro-pneumonia.

Now, some assert that corn-fed hogs are fatter, but that there is less substantial meat than on pea-fed hogs; what is your opinion?

Well, if we could raise pease I would feed them with mixed feed; pease are nicer feed than corn is, but our climate does not raise pease. You cannot develop a hog much better on pease than on corn.

Then the corn-fed hog is a clean good hog?

He is the best hog in the world.

Do you think there is an interest among farmers to keep improving the breed of the hogs?

Some claim that by too much breeding the hog lost vitality, that he had been improved so much that he had lost his vitality. Naturalists tell us that hogs have been derived from the wild boar of Europe and the wild boar of Asia. Now, the hog of India is one that takes on flesh remarkably fast, and these two races have been crossed together. As they approximate the hog of India they are all fat, and as they approximate the wild boar of Europe they are all bone and gristle. The happy medium is in combining the two distinct races of the hog, and that of the Poland-China hog combines more points of profit than any other breed of hogs at the present day.

How are the hogs transported from the farm to the railroad car?

No fault can be found in the way they are transported to the cars. At this day nine-tenths of the hogs are taken to the trains on wagons and sleighs; they are not worried so much as formerly, but are carefully handled. They are carried in double-decked cars, but there is hardly surface room enough.

What do the farmers do with their dead hogs?

The hogs, like a dead man, should be removed as a nuisance; although it is not fashionable, yet all the dead hogs should be cremated, and no owner of the dead hogs should be allowed to sell them. I would prohibit it by statute law, making it a nuisance to traffic in dead or diseased hogs.

Could it not be possible for farmers to turn them into fertilizers?

No, sir; we are not suffering for fertilizers; we never bought any; it might be tried out into grease.

As to the necessity of this sanitary regulation, Secretary Blaine will doubtless make a recommendation; * * * it should have been done, now it must be; each State, at any rate, can make its own law. There must be uniformity in the laws; there ought to be a general sanitary law. There should be State supervision, and there should be national supervision. * * *

The water furnished to the hogs is medicated every month, or oftener if necessary, with crude carbolic acid. The object of this medication is to promote the porcine appetite and prevent disease; and that object is achieved. By supplying his swine constantly with fresh water medicated in this manner, and by constructing their pens and lots so that they are never in want of pure air, and by other hygienic instrumentalities, Dr. Stetson effectually prevents hog cholera on his farm. He is never troubled by it, even in the seasons during which it rages most destructively around him. His methods with respect to this matter are the result of his knowledge of comparative physiology and pathology, and are well worth the careful study of hog breeders and raisers through th country.

REPORT ON AMERICAN PORK: 1881.

Extract from an article prepared for publication by Dr. Stetson.

Since the foregoing was written some new-fangled notions have come to the surface that demand attention. First comes France, with an edict prohibiting the importation of American pork; their savans have just discovered that there may be trichinæ in American pork, which would render it unfit for human food. Since this edict has been promulgated an attack of trichinous disease has broken out in their own country, and from eating the raw flesh of French fattened swine. The truth of the matter is, that trichinæ are occasionally found in swine and other animals in all parts of the globe. Now the remedy, or specific rather, is well understood by all civilised people. This parasite is effectually destroyed and rendered innocuous by submitting meat containing them to the boiling point of water. This cooks the parasite, and no flesh of any kind is safe to be used as human food until its temperature has thus been raised. Trichinæ have been found in the flesh of the ox, hare, sheep, and particularly in the rabbit, of which the French are noted consumers. Just as soon, and no sooner, as the people practice the cooking of all flesh, and even fish, trichinæ will cease to be a bugbear.

There is no country in the world where government supervision of food and drinks is so strict as in France. While I do not complain of this being an evil in itself, if their supervision was extended to the manner of fattening their domestic animals for the butcher, this supervision would be much more satisfactory. With the exception of their veals all other meats are very mediocre if not execrable. Their beef is scraggy, mutton insipid, and horse-flesh blue—of their pork, bah?

No person after seeing their swine fattened, as I have done, would ever hanker after French pork. A few miles from Havre I had occasion to pass a pit of a few acres in extent where the human excreta of this large city was daily deposited. In this pit, at the time I saw it, were somewhere from 50 to 100 hogs, rooting and smelling for their daily bread. Here were all the parasites of the human system deposited in this cesspool for the hog to eat and grow fat upon, and be eaten in their turn by the very Frenchmen who turn up their noses at American corn-fed pork.

It is a matter of natural history that the ova of the tinea (tape-worm), if eaten by swine, will in them produce a disease called measles. Now, this same measly pork contains the ova of the tapeworm, and will reproduce itself in the human family when swine's flesh not thoroughly cooked is eaten by man

Next comes Mr. Crump, the British Vice-consul at Philadelphia, with his statistics of the mortality of the hog in America. It makes no practical difference whether this man's estimates are too high or too low. The slaughter of the innocents began before St. Bartholomew's day, and will continue to the end of time. That quite a large percentage of young pigs and a few old hogs die of a disease known as hog cholera all are willing to admit. This loss falls on the producer, and not on the consumer, except in the enhanced price paid for the product. It is simply their depletion. The ranks of the human family are constantly being depleted by contagious disease, but those that escape or survive are in no way injured in their bodily health. Hogs that die of this or any other disease do not find their way to market, and only those that are healthy are used in commerce. Since the disease has been known and recognised no case has ever been reported, or, for that matter, ever can be reported, where swine's flesh has been the cause of human disease.

This sensational story has only been gotten up in the interest of parties who are trying to depress the price of one of the great staples of American produce, and one that the labourers of the Old World cannot and will not see destroyed. There is no pork made anywhere in this world that can compare, in cleanliness, healthfulness, and all that goes to make a delicious article of swine's flesh, with our American corn-fed pork. Corn, maize, grass, and cold water are the chief factors in making the American hog. In contradistinction to the slop and garbage-fed animals of Europe, we have a decided advantage in a sanitary point of view. Having eaten pork for very nearly threescore and ten years, a large proportion of the time a practitioner of medicine, I can affirm in all good conscience that I have never seen a case or had reason to suspect a case of trichinous disease. Aside from a few cases reported in the "Journal of Medicine" and the secular press, cases of trichinæ are more rare in America than the deaths from the bites of mad dogs. I do not believe that a single American citizen ever ate, or contracted this disease from eating raw meat. It is only barbarians that eat raw flesh of any kind.

ARRIVAL AND HANDLING OF HOGS IN CHICAGO.—STATEMENT by GEO. T. WILLIAMS, Esq.

Union Stock Yard and Transit Company,
Chicago, April 9, 1881

DEAR SIR,
Your letter of inquiry respecting the live hog business of the North-west, their conditions, manner of handling the same, &c., is before me. In reply will say that the principal part of the hogs raised and fatted in the North-western States come to this market, both for packing here and shipment East. The receipts of hogs at this point for year 1880 were 7,059,355; the number of head packed here for the year was 5,664,366; the number shipped alive to Eastern markets were 1,394,990; the number of head packed during the winter packing from November 1, 1880, to March 1, 1881, was 2,781,064; there are packed during the summer, from March 1, 1879, to November 1, 1880, 2,971,127. The great bulk of hogs that arrive at this market are raised in Illinois, Iowa, Kansas, Missouri, Wisconsin, Ohio, and Indiana, and usually reach this market from 5 to 48 hours from the time they are collected in country. They are generally well fatted, weighing from 150 to 450 pounds per head. Upon arriving at these yards they are placed in covered pens, fed with the best of corn, and good pure water given them. If any are crippled in transit they are sold to the cheap markets in the city Dead hogs, if there are any, from being overloaded, are sold to the rendering company, and made into what is called grease. The hogs that are in fine healthy condition are sold to the packers or eastern shippers. Those sold to packers go into mess-pork, hams, shoulders, long and short clear sides, short rib and various other cuts, and lard, all of which is nicely handled, passing into cooling rooms before placed in pickle, or dry-salt cure.

As to the health of the hogs arriving here, will say that I have been familiar with this market, and located in the yard business for about 26 years, and in all those years I never knew the hogs to be in such an excellent condition, so healthy, as they have been during the past year. There never was a crop packed in Chicago more healthy, and that made so fine hog product, as the past year. I have not heard of a single case of trichinæ pork or an unhealthy condition of hogs or hog meat at any packing house in the city during the past year; and you will find this to be the universal answer, inquire of whom you will, that in no year has the hog and the quality surpassed the year of 1880 and 1881.

Respectfully yours,
GEO. T. WILLIAMS,
Secretary.

Michael Scanlan, Esq.,
State Department, Washington, D.C.

AMERICAN HAM-CURING for the HOME and FOREIGN MARKET.—STATEMENT by WILLIAM HENRY DAVIS, Esq., of the house of S. Davis, Jun. & Co.

DEAR SIR,   Cincinnati, April 20, 1881.

The founder of the house began business in provisions in this city in 1835. Then the packing of pork and beef was chiefly in the winter months, and the greater portion of it was for account of dealers in the Eastern cities. The transportation of the product of that section of the country was by steam and flatboats to New Orleans, thence by vessels to Eastern ports; this required six to ten week's time on way. Later in the season bacon for Philadelphia and Baltimore was taken up the river to Pittsburgh, thence by canal and rail. Now provisions are carried from this city to New York by rail in six and eight days.

Changes as great as this is in matter of transportation can be cited in the curing of hams in the West. In early years many hams were cured in country towns with plain salt; they were long and roughly cut. While the city hams were trimmed better, most of them were cured in bulk with a slight use of saltpetre.

In 1841 the former senior of the house cured a moderate number of what were termed fine hams.

With many people in the West there was quite a prejudice against hams cured other than in a plain way.

Until about 1845 there was but a small fraction of the hams cut from the hogs, then put up for the Western and Southern markets, that were cured in pickle.

It had been the custom with Eastern provision dealers to place their hams in pickle and forward them in tierces and hogsheads. But those hams were not equal in quality to the hams prepared to-day by the leading curers of the West, whose markets are now almost all over the world.

Instead of a small portion of the hams prepared in the West being of fine cure, as was the case 35 years ago, it can now be stated that quite a small number are plain cured. This change has greatly increased the consumption of hams, for all classes now realise the economy and advantage in many ways of a well-cured ham, *which is well cured and not too salt.* For the trade of our own country short-cut hams are preferred. There is an advantage in a long-cut ham if kept many months; the butt protects and prevents a too rapid drying of the better portion of the ham.

Hams are cut from hogs well cooled, but they are usually spread upon floors or racks with a small quantity of old dry salt* for a day or two. The hams are examined before salting and before being placed in pickle, to see that there are none that show any outward signs of bruises, and very coarse hams are set aside, and often the sizes are assorted. Hams are then placed in large vats or casks and pickle added. In the use of sweets dry sugar is the best. The hams are changed over from three to four times when in pickle; this is done to give more even cure. The number of times in changing hams varies as the desire of curer may be for more quickly curing, and somewhat depends upon the weather. The time taken to cure rests upon the size of the hams and the weather; the curing process being quicker in mild weather than cold. It may be said that the most successful seasons for curing are when there is steady moderately cold weather. Hams are kept in pickle from six to ten weeks; they are taken out, washed, and drained with the shanks down, then the hams are hung by the leg in smoke-houses, and sometimes left to dry before the smoke is placed upon them.

Afterwards they are taken from smoke-houses and carefully tried; even a ham that may only be considered, by an expert, prospectively bad, is set aside. The ham is then branded, papered, and placed in muslin closely sewed. For the home markets hams are dipped in a wash, labelled, and then hung up in racks in a cool, dry place, ready for packing.

For the foreign markets hams are usually of small or medium sizes. Generally they are hung to dry before canvassing. Of late, the hams after being dried are covered with very light muslin, followed by thin paper, and a heavy muslin is sewed upon them. We do not place wash upon the covers of these, unless it be late in the season, and then it is a white wash.

Winter shipments are sometimes in tierces; as the season advances hams are placed in partially open crates. There are more labour and cost in the preparation of hams for foreign shipment than for the domestic market. The modes referred to are more applicable to shipments to France. The demand from that country the past three years has greatly increased, and dealers have reported that American hams have been steadily gaining the favour of their customers. Trade now though is seriously interrupted, as the inspection of meats in France, with its delays, confiscations, costs, and the order the hams are left in after inspection, deters further orders.

Something may be stated about hams found with bruises inside, without any surface indications or means of detection by curers, and only to be discovered when cut. It seems strange to state, but there are probably more to be found in proportion to the number of hogs packed than was the case 30 years ago. And yet hams are better for consumers now than then. Why? The hogs are of better breeds. Feeders many years ago found market for their hogs chiefly in the winter; this caused hogs to be older when killed than now. With the ice-curing and increased growth of cities the demand is for every month in the year, so that hogs are fattened at an earlier age and quicker; their frames and

---

* Salt free from bitter water, not fresh from licks.

bones are not as strong as the old-time hog, and slips and bruises in transportation are more likely to affect them in the joints.

More care in driving and transportation should be used. The proposed improved stock-cars will greatly remedy all this. A pattern of the new cars was recently exhibited here, and you probably have drawings of same. This is mentioned to counteract the feeling with many consumers of hams that reddish colouring, and sometimes bruises and breaks in meat at joints (which are more likely to be found in heavy hogs), are often mistaken for bad condition of the animal.

The keeping of hams and their cooking, if well understood, would greatly increase their use. The chief fault is that few persons boil, bake, or roast a ham sufficiently, and, when boiled, know how essential it is to have hot coals to cook with, and serve when hot.

Perhaps these are more details than you may have desired, but we respectfully submit the above for your perusal.

Very respectfully yours
WM. HENRY DAVIS.

Michael Scanlan, Esq.,
Bureau of Statistics, Department of State, Washington, D.C.

How to Keep and how to Cook Hams.—Inclosure in Mr. Davis's statement.

Selecting Hams.

There is no article of food about which so little is really known as the ham. The consumer is puzzled to pick out a good ham or piece of breakfast bacon, and even subtle judges of hams—ham experts—are unable to tell a good ham from a poor one when they see it; therefore the only safe guide for the general consumer is to trust to some standard brand, which for years has been pronounced excellent in all climates, and at any age—one, two, or even four years.

Hams should be taken out of casks on receipt, *and hung up in a cool, dry place.*

When mold appears it should be brushed off.

Hams a year old are often preferable, and the same ham can be kept safely two, three, or four years, each year adding to its richness.

Although the trade demands a short-cut ham, the long-cut hams have their advantages. The advantages of this cut are that the centre of the ham is protected from the strong acid of the smoke and does not dry as quickly as the short-cut.

To boil Hams.

If early in the season boil the ham as it is; if later, it should be scraped and washed.

If the ham is six or eight months old it should be *soaked* in cold water 24 hours, and longer in proportion to its age; then boil it slowly, the water being kept at a quiet, low, scalding heat; it should not boil violently, only simmer.

A ham weighing 13 to 14 pounds should boil slowly or simmer *eight* or *nine* hours. After boiling it may be placed in ice water to prevent the escape of its natural juices, or it may cool in the same vessel.

An old ham may be boiled with a moderate amount of course fresh beef placed in the water; this imparts a delicate freshness to the ham, though when cooked this way it should not be kept too long.

To roast or bake Hams.

A ham to be baked or roasted should be *first boiled*, but not so long as directed above. After boiling, take off the skin, baste the ham with soft powdered crackers or bread crumbs, and place it in the oven until it changes to a dark yellow colour; or before baking it may be dressed with flour and cloves, or with sugar.

One of the simplest ways of cooking is to take a ham and soak it two or three hours, even if of recent cure, much longer if an old ham, or according to age; and place it in the improved roaster and baker—a deep pan for roasting or baking with a cover. A medium-sized ham is cooked in three or four hours, and requires very little attention. Served hot or cold it will be found richer than when boiled.

The *dry part* of a cooked ham may be trimmed off, chopped fine, and warmed up with butter, eggs, and flour, making a palatable dish, and thus economically consuming the whole ham. It also makes good sandwiches.

Broiling.

A broiling ham should be good-sized. Strip canvas off and keep ham in a large thick muslin sack; tie closely for protection and to prevent drying. Cut thin slices from the butt end with a sharp knife and saw (there is no economy in cutting a ham in the middle, as you leave the two cut sides to dry at once); then place the slices over bright hot coals, turning quickly two or three times until the fat is browned. Eat while hot, or, to be brief, "If 'twere done when 'tis done, then, 'twere well it were done quickly."

Some cooks recommend the separation of the lean from the fat, broiling the former and frying the latter, then serving both together.

Breakfast bacon may be broiled or boiled. If late in the season it should be placed in water a short time and dried before broiling.

R 679.

ARRIVAL AND HANDLING OF HOGS IN CINCINNATI.—Statement of JOHN H. PORTER, Esq., Secretary and Treasurer of the United Railroad Stock Yards.

United Railroad Stock Yard Company, Cincinnati, April 13, 1881.

DEAR SIR,

In reply to your inquiry as to the live hog business of the country supplying Cincinnati, their condition, the manner of handling, in transit and after reaching the stock yards, would say that much of the hogs raised in Kentucky, Ohio, Indiana, and Southern Illinois are brought to this market, reaching here in from five to thirty hours of transportation by the several railroads centring here. This stock yard company, acting as the live-stock agent for those railroad companies, have made all needed preparation for the receiving and shipping and all proper care of all live stock that may be brought here, having a large number of clean, well-paved pens, mostly roofed over, each provided with troughs for watering, hydrant for each pen supplied with water from city waterworks, and a full and large supply of water supplied to the stock while in pen. Feed houses with stock of fresh corn and other feed on hand to answer all demands of owners of stock for feed. A sufficient force of men on hand to promptly care for all stock in receiving and delivering—of night men that are on duty all night to unload and pen all stock received at night; similar force for the same work during the day. Men and teams for prompt delivery of feed, as ordered, and carts for the daily use of the cleaning force to clean up pens as stock is taken from them.

The several divisions of the yard are supplied each with a scale house, with scales to weigh the stock in any number, from three or four head to one and two car loads at once, each scale permanently under charge of a competent and intelligent weigher, and all needed force for the prompt handling of stock. The stock trains arrive at yards at various hours of night and day, and are at once hauled to the unloading chutes, the hogs driven out of cars into the pens, and from these into the sale pens; in these the hogs and all other stock remain under the care and control of the company until the owners, or those having them for sale, have made sale, when they are driven to the scales, weighed, and then delivered to the purchaser here; they are then driven by purchaser to the packing houses, or to the slaughter houses of the market butchers. If sold to shippers they are driven to pens in the yard adjacent to the railroad tracks, from thence loaded by the employés of the company on the cars.

From the overloading or crowding too many hogs into a car by the owners at the feeding places in the country, hogs are found dead in the car on arrival at these yards. Such dead stock is at once taken to the platform of the fertilizer company in the yard, are there weighed, receipt for weight and price given to owner of stock and paid for. Any hogs dying in the pens from effects of such overloading, or any other cause, are invariably dealt with in same way. These all are daily taken by the fertilizer company to their works and are rendered into grease, oil, or used for manufacturing purposes. By ordinance the fertilizer company are the only purchasers of such stock. The city, by its Board of Health, keep at this yard at all times a regular inspector of live stock, whose duty is to examine daily all hogs and other stock arriving here, and if any diseased animals are found in pens or cars, to notify owners of same of their condition and to see that such stock is not disposed of here in any way by which it can be used as food. It can only be sold to the fertilizer company. The company have always given every facility for full and free exercise of such inspection, believing that it is always the wish as well as to the interest of all shippers and owners of live stock, and of packers and curers of meat, that any diseased stock brought here should be quickly removed from the vicinity of the healthy stock; our experience is that it is seldom such is sent here. The hogs sold in this market are fed when young on corn and clover and then fattened on corn. This feeding is altogether in the fields, pasture and cornfields, where there is a plentiful supply of fresh water, and to be suitable for packers' and curers' purposes and to be considered merchantable, must so be fed; this manner of feeding must make healthful and wholesome meat. Hogs fed on garbage or any foul feed, as may be the case in vicinity of large towns, are unmerchantable and show their condition. These may develop the disease of trichinosis, which is of rare occurrence, and such feeding is quite exceptional.

The half dozen cases of trichinosis that have occurred in the past 25 years in the country from which our hogs come have always been traced to the eating of the uncooked meat from hogs so fed. The country adjacent, which supplies the receipts of live stock here, has been very free the past year from any kind of disease among hogs. The receipts at the yards show this by the quality of hogs received. The percentage of loss in hogs in shipment from country to this place is less than one per cent. in dead hogs.

By a law of the National Government it is unlawful to run a train of live stock more than 28 hours without unloading for rest, food, and water. In the shipment of hogs in summer it is the habit after loading car to have each car of hogs well drenched with water from the water-plug by hose. Of the hogs sold at these yards from March 1 to November 1, or the summer receipts, those killed here are used for the daily market supply or cured for the domestic trade; the rest sold for shipment to Boston, New York, Philadelphia, Baltimore, and Cleveland, &c. The larger proportion of hogs received here between November 1 and March 1 are slaughtered and cured here, and of this product much is exported.

The receipts of hogs at this yard for the year 1880 were 823,789 head. Number slaughtered for same year, 566,410 head; number shipped to other markets east, 257,379 head. These hogs are generally well fattened, weighing from 150 to 400 lbs. and upward.

This statement of the manner of receiving and handling hogs at this point will, I think, plainly show the improbability of diseased hogs in any amount or number getting into the cured hog products of this city.

Very respectfully, yours,
JNO. H. PORTER,
Secretary and Treasurer of United Railroad Stock Yard Company.

Michael Scanlan, Esq.,
Chief of Bureau of Statistics,
State Department, Washington, D. C.

REPORT ON AMERICAN PORK: 1881.

How dead Animals are disposed of in Chicago.

1.—Statement of the Foreman of the Union Rendering Company at Globe Station, near Chicago.

We receive the animals from the city and stock yards. We run them inside the building under cover, and make connexion with our steam hoisting apparatus. We run the carcasses on a small car up an inclined plane on to our floor; we run them up by steam power. We skin the horses and cattle, not the hogs; the dead animals were received last night, and are put in this morning; we have 12 tanks here for receiving and cooking the animals; we chop them through once to have them put into the tank. After the carcasses are cooked in the receiver, we draw off the grease first, and then we run the meat into large vats of water, straining the water 11 times before the river receives it. We keep back the animal refuse by strainers and press it by high-pressure presses—there are five presses—taking the animal stuff off dry. This stuff, after being pressed and half dry, is then run through drying machines. The dry fertilizer is the result of the animal meat. We have two drying machines, which we can work up every 24 hours.

We work up all the stuff from the beginning to the end within 24 hours after receiving it, if there is no accident to the machinery.

The grease is then barreled and shipped. There are two qualities of grease, and the best grease is sold and branded as *white grease*, and the poorer brown grease is also sold to soap makers, branded as *brown grease*. Much of the grease is sold to Cincinnati soap men. This grease cannot be sold as lard in Europe; there is a smell to the grease which renders it impossible to be palmed off as lard; the blood of a dead hog that dies a natural death ferments, and it is impossible to get the blood out of the flesh.

Men at this railroad station eat raw pork, German working men; they claim it has more strength than the cooked.

The Union Rendering Company is the only establishment that gets the dead hogs in this county; we get all the dead animals from the stock yards and city.

Question: Have you more dead hogs in summer than in winter?
Answer: In the real hot weather, or real cold weather, we have more, but at other times the stuff comes regularly. Dead cattle and sheep are rendered together to make tallow; horses separate.
Question: Where do you generally sell this grease?
Answer: All over; it is shipped to the South, shipped East, and some in this State; the most of the fertilizer goes to Baltimore.

2.—Statement of the Editor of the "Drovers' Journal," Chicago Union Stock Yard.

Dead hogs come in the cars with the live ones, sometimes one, sometimes as many as 15 in a car. They are taken from the car, put on a platform, and then taken from the platform by carts or trucks for that purpose, to an establishment at the corner of the yards for receiving such carcasses, and from there they are taken to the rendering establishment some miles out in the country, and in that they are entirely separated from the stock-yards and all the operations here. There is no reputable packer, that I have ever heard, would ever have anything to do with them, all being rendered into what is called grease. There are a very considerable number of crippled hogs coming in, that is, partially disabled, that cannot travel to the packing houses; there is a class of buyers all the time purchasing them, and they are slaughtered for the city trade and almost exclusively used up in that way. The dead hogs are sent to the rendering establishments. There are occasionally a small lot of crippled hogs here, but the packers won't have anything to do with them; the packers, unless they were imposed upon, would not deal in such hogs; on the contrary, the packers are cautioned about them. They are bought by these city dealers that purchase inferior or refuse hogs, and they are used in the city; they are used for the city trade. It is a notable fact in the hog trade that hogs have never been more healthy than during the past year.

How dead Hogs are disposed of in Cincinnati.—Statement by George Thompson, Esq.

Sir, Cincinnati, April 16, 1881.
In reply to your request for information in regard to the manner in which dead and diseased hogs are disposed of in this city, I submit the following statement. I beg to premise this statement by saying that I have had an experience in this connexion of 25 years in raising and feeding hogs, and for the last 15 years have occupied my present position as contractor of the city of Cincinnati for the seizure and removal of dead animals and animal matter unfit for human food.

In regard to what is termed "hog cholera," my experience is that hogs attacked thereby invariably die. The class of hogs generally attacked are young—too young for marketing—weighing only from 50 to 100 pounds.

I never heard of any hogs attacked by hog cholera or dying from any disease or accident being used, or attempted to be used, for human food. Even if there were parties mean enough to attempt such a thing, the officers and employés of our Board of Health would at once have them arrested and punished. So that such a thing as using diseased or dead hogs for human food may be set down as having not the least foundation in fact.

The hogs are all inspected as they are unloaded from the cars, and if there is anything wrong with any of them they are condemned and turned over to the city contractor and sent to the rendering works, where they are converted into grease, which is plainly branded "dead hog grease," the residue being converted into fertilizer.

Yours, very respectfully,
George Thompson,
City Contractor for the removal of Dead Animals and Animal Matter, &c.

REPORT ON AMERICAN PORK: 1881.

AMERICAN MEATS AND LARD IN EUROPE.—EXTRACTS* from a STATEMENT by J. C. BLACK, Esq., of the House of Armour & Co., Chicago.

* * * * * *

SHIPPING.

After the meat is cured, at the proper time the buyer sends his inspector to the packing house to inspect, receive, and pack the meat. The man we sell to has his own expert who tries every piece of meat and sees it weighed. The meat is perfectly sweet, but he is compelled to be there and see to it. A soft hog they throw that out; that is soft, they don't want it. He tries it with his trier and says it is a little sour, he don't want it. He rejects everything that is not proper, and goes off. It is plain to be seen that what is sour in the shoulder, or sour near the shoulder, has not been salted thoroughly. It is easy to be seen, there cannot be any deceit about it. This man does nothing but inspect meat and buy hogs; he is an expert in his business. The meats are then packed into boxes, salt being sprinkled upon it. We cure by salt altogether. The box is then put under a screw and screwed tight, nailed and strapped, made as strong as possible, put aboard the cars, and is shipped.

One great trouble with the meats in Europe is that they do not take any care of the meats after they get there. In Havre, for instance, they lie in the rain, no care being taken of them. They are not put into the warehouse; the rain gets in. These boxes are not watertight.

In Havre there is a proposition to build some warehouses on all the docks where they can handle these meats. They pile it up four or five boxes high. You cannot do anything with your own meats. Different cuts of meat go into the home market. I want even more careful handling than at the home market; the American never finds any fault whatever.

LARD.

It is impossible to render a dead hog into lard; decomposition has already set in. We cannot get away with the bad smell of lard after decomposition; it cannot be done. You cannot render it and have it sweet lard, it is an utter impossibility; it is not in the possibilities. They do a great many of these things for spite across the water. You will see the impossibility of being cheated; there is no possible object in trying to cheat. The manufacturers' names are on the tierces of lard. The refiner would not receive anything but choice lard. It is called refining; it is a hardening process, the lard being dropped until it is whitened—it is only handling it—and then they send the lard to Europe. It stands transportation better. You cannot sell lard in the raw state; it is first refined. They have extensive refineries in Berlin.

TRICHINÆ.

We examined 5,000 hogs and found no trichinæ; then the Health Department sent a man; he tried the eyes and sides, and he was unable to find any. We tried the hams and sides. A man came here some time ago, a German who served a long apprenticeship in Europe, and in speaking about the matter said he knew of his own knowledge that their pork was infected more than the American pork. For curiosity we allowed him to spend a week in our yard; he was an expert in his business; he had a microscope; he inspected 5,000 pieces of ham, and then tried 10,000 hogs as they were killed, after they had been fully cut up, and he found nothing.

We had in Europe (at the time this edict was promulgated) 500 boxes of meat, and 200 boxes of shoulders; they did not find a single case of trichinæ in the whole lot.

HOG CHOLERA.

Regarding the hog cholera I think it is an entirely mistaken idea about the hog. If a young hog is out exposed to the cold, and has taken cold as we do, it is called hog cholera; a young pig may take cold from being exposed to the rain and storm and die; you know, of course, the sow has nine pigs, and they smother some of them. For that reason I am under the impression myself that we must have more intelligent reports about the disease. The trade which has grown has stumbled along; the Europeans positively wanted our meats, and wanted them to sell.

AMERICAN vs. WESTPHALIAN HAMS.

I went to Hamburgh at one time to get them to take hold of it; their hams were selling for 90 marks a hundred, and ours for 50 marks. I went back in less than a month after, and those Westphalian hams were 70 marks, and our hams were 60 marks per hundred.

HOG RAISING in ILLINOIS.—STATEMENT by CHARLES F. MILLS, Esq., Breeder and Importer of Berkshire Pigs.

Elmwood Stock Farm, Springfield, Ill.,
March 28, 1881.

SIR,

In compliance with your request I have the honour to call your attention to the general management of the swine fed in this State for market.

[* Those portions of Mr. Black's statement omitted referred wholly to the purchasing, inspection, and killing of the hogs, and to the curing of the meat, and as those points are fully covered both in the body of my report, as well as in the report of Mr. Foster, it would be only simple repetition to insert them in the above statement.—M. S.]

There is such a very limited number of hogs confined in pens and fed slop or swill in this State as to be worthy of no consideration.

The hog product of Illinois is made from hogs of the various improved breeds or swine, mainly high-grade Berkshires and Poland-Chinas.

Pure-bred boars are generally used, and the brood sows are the result of so many crosses by well-bred boars as to readily pass inspection at the hands of the majority of hog-breeders and dealers as very nearly pure-bred hogs.

The pigs are farrowed in April and May, and as soon as old enough to get about are allowed to follow corn-fed cattle, with the range of blue-grass pasture during the summer and early fall. When not running after cattle, pigs are fed on some corn, in addition to pasturage, until the growth of grass in spring and the age of the pig makes it possible for the animal to subsist and thrive on grass alone.

The range of pasture, pure air, and the healthful exercise necessary for hogs to obtain subsistence develops the growth of muscle and lean meat, and the quality of this meat when finished off on corn in the fall months is not to be compared with the soft, greasy, fat meat resulting from feeding slop and swill to swine in small, ill-ventilated pens, as is the general custom abroad.

The "pork products" of Illinois are not approached in excellence by the far-famed "Irish bacon" when firm, well-marbled meat is considered, and it is a well-known fact that the highest-priced fancy pork products sold in Ireland by Limerick dealers are put up in Chicago, and by special instruction marked with the private brands of Limerick dealers who have for years past been selling Illinois pork products on the continent as Irish bacon-hams, &c.

The mortality among hogs and pigs in this State, resulting from disease, is comparatively trifling considering the vast number of hogs raised annually, and the insignificant value placed on young pigs.

When the neglect of young pigs and indifference manifested by the average hog-breeder as to the number of pigs that survive "pighood" is taken into account, the vitality and power of swine to resist the effects of exposure to the elements and rough treatment is the more remarkable, and is one of the strongest arguments that can be used as to the hardy and vigorous constitution of swine raised in this State.

In early times, when pork would hardly pay the expense of driving the hogs to market, and when hogs were turned out on the open range and expected to hunt their own living, the old maxim of "root, hog, or die," was considered orthodox, and the prevailing sentiment of the present is to the effect that a hog to be worthy of any consideration must be able to "weather the storm," and do well with sufficient corn, grass, and water.

It has been my experience that the mortality among pigs can be reduced one half by providing shelter and giving reasonable attention to the comfort of the sow and her litter the first month after farrowing.

Absolute neglect and exposure is the cause of the loss by disease of three-fourths of the hogs reported as dying each year in this State from so-called hog cholera, which name is given to all diseases affecting swine.

Yours, &c.
(Signed)   CHARLES F. MILLS.

Michael Scanlan, Esq.,
   Chief of the Bureau of Statistics,
      Department of State, Washington, D. C.

PORK PACKING IN CINCINNATI.—STATEMENT prepared by MESSRS. JAMES MORRISON & Co.

DEAR SIR,   Cincinnati, April 12, 1881.

We have for the past 30 years been actively engaged in the packing and preparation of pork meats for European consumption. In all our experience we can safely say we have never known the hogs of the West to be freer from disease or in a more healthy condition than at present, or during the past two or three years. Cholera, or kindred diseases have always existed among hogs, not only in America, but in Europe, wherever the animal is raised and cultivated. Cholera, as is well known, attacks the young pigs, ranging from one to three months in age, the matured and fattened hogs enjoying almost complete immunity from its attacks. In America, the great distances of the feeding fields from the packing centres, and the necessary time consumed in forwarding hogs to the packer, is a thorough and complete protection against any hogs affected with the disease ever reaching the slaughterers' pens. Hogs when attacked with the disease are so prostrated that it would be impossible to move them to market. Three to seven days is invariably required to move hogs from the feeding grounds to the packers' establishments; all of which time the hogs must be active and lively. To pass inspection at the sale pens, all hogs, to be merchantable, must be able to walk on the weighing scales. It will thus be clear to the uninitiated the possibility of hogs attacked with disease to undergo the days of exhaustion, exposure, and fatigue necessary in forwarding them to market. Again, a diseased hog is easily detected by the discolouration of the meat and skin of the carcass, which the process of curing and all the curers' arts cannot restore to the natural colour, and would instantly be detected by the inspector or consumer. All meats prepared for foreign shipment undergo a rigid inspection before leaving the packing houses.

Since the introduction of summer or ice curing, much meat has been spoiled while in transit. This is the result of too early exposure to the high summer temperature and before the meat has been thoroughly cured, but this is by no means owing to the original quality of the meat. As to the general healthfulness of the products of the hog, the millions of people who are and have been consumers of the meat both in America and Europe and grow healthy and thrive upon it can testify.

As to trichina, we understand not a single case of it has ever been identified in man or woman in Great Britain, the greatest of all pork-eating nations. Isolated cases of it having been reported in America, but we assert the cause cannot be traced to the consumption of fairly-cured or cooked pork.

That the people of Continental Europe, both at home and in this country, are in the habit of eating uncooked food and sausages, concocted of material too vile to be mentioned, and in rare instances suffer unpleasant consequences, should not frighten or deter consumers of regularly-cured and properly-cooked meat of the hog.

Trusting this plain statement of facts, as they have come under our observation, will be of service to you in your investigations.

We remain, &c.
(Signed) JAMES MORRISON & Co.

Michael Scanlan, Esq.,
  Chief of Bureau of Statistics of the
    Department of State at Washington, D. C.

INSPECTION OF HOGS AND HOG-PRODUCT IN CHICAGO.—Statement of Dr. Oscar C. Dewolf, Commissioner of Health of the City of Chicago.

Under the ordinance we have five meat inspectors on duty; two of them on duty at the stock-yards, and three in the city markets.

Technically we have no right to exercise police power at the stock-yards; nevertheless the stock-yard proprietors, and commission men dealing in animals, find it to their interest to permit our meat inspectors to exercise their functions at the yards, because, if we condemn an animal as unfit for food in the yards, they retain the carcass for fertilizing purposes, while if it is put on the markets outside the yards, we confiscate the carcass when condemned, and make no return to the owner for the material confiscated. I regard that as the sharp and sure method of punishing the dealer. There is a company at the stock-yards, chartered by legislative enactment, known as the "Union Rendering Company." One of the enactments of this charter provides that all dead animals found in the yards, and that implies coming in on the trains dead, or dying after arriving at the yards, as well as animals condemned by our inspectors as unfit for food, shall be turned over to this company for rendering purposes. These dead or deceased animals condemned by our inspectors as unfit for food are turned over to this company for rendering purposes. These dead or deceased animals are removed from the stock-yard inclosure by this Union Rendering Company on their own trains, running to the Indiana line, about 29 miles. There they have extensive facilities for the extraction of grease, and conversion of the residue into commercial fertilizers. During the year 1880, 480,000 pounds of meat found in our city markets by our inspectors, and unfit for use by cause of the emaciation of the carcass, bruising of the carcass, or taint after slaughter, had been condemned and thrown into the rendering tanks as above described.

HOGS.

The supply of hogs brought to the yards for the purpose of packing is not critically inspected by our meat inspectors (for reasons above stated) outside our lines, and I am only interested in protecting the citizens of Chicago. I have, however, for scientific purposes and other reasons, kept a very sharp eye upon the condition of the hogs received at the stock-yards since February 1877. I believe, and indeed I positively know, that the stories and reports current near Chicago, and far from us, touching the disposition of packers to slaughter deceased or emaciated hogs for packing purposes, are maliciously and wickedly false.

The larger packing houses employ buyers for their pens, of great experience, and to whom they pay large sums. Mr. Armour, for example, and the "Anglo-American Packing Company," I have understood, employ three men, to each of whom they pay $5,000 a year. The hogs are scrutinized with the greatest care, &c. However that may be, a hog infected with trichinæ cannot be detected by any general appearance of the animal.

I have seen hogs suffering from trichinosis in the most perfect condition of physical health. The only possible means of detecting this condition is by the examination of the carcass with the microscope.

I have been consulted by the packers several times touching the propriety of organizing a corps of scientists, for the purpose of inspecting the carcasses packed at the yards.

The impracticability of any such move will appear to any one who recalls the fact that more than five millions of hogs per annum are slaughtered for packing here. A single individual, no matter how expert, could hardly cover more than 10 or 12 carcasses a day.

In September 1878, I requested two gentlemen, recognised as authority in microscopical work in this city, to undertake an examination of the pork supply which the packers were using. We have been accredited with a pork supply from 3 to 5 per cent. of which is declared to be infected with trichinæ. It is true that some seasons this per cent. of infection has been discovered, and I am inclined to believe that a similar extent of disease would have been discovered in the domestic supply of France and Germany had the same care been taken in investigation; for example, it was necessary on some occasions to examine 50 specimens from one hog before trichinæ were discovered.

Do you not see how readily such carcasses might be regarded as sound and perfectly free from infection, if you made an examination simply from two or three specimens from the carcass?

In the investigations made by these gentlemen, and by the State microscopical society a few years previous (see report of Chicago health department for 1878, page 21), a number of specimens examined from each carcass showed a thoroughness of work altogether beyond that declared as necessary by foreign examiners.

Our supply of pork this year is more free from trichinæ than for any year, certainly during the last six or eight years previous.

This fact I assert because I have kept for the past month an accomplished microscopist at work in the yards, and he has failed to find a single case of trichina.

Another matter of interest in this connexion, our mortality in this city for the last four years ranges from 8,000 in 1877 to 10,000 in 1880. Only two cases of trichinæ have been reported in the city of Chicago during that period. This is an important statement in view of the fact that our markets, without great watchfulness on the part of the health department, are supplied with meat rejected by the packers.

The supply of meat, therefore, distributed to the city has a much greater probability of infection than that used by the packers.

Ohio Hogs and Hog Products.

At a meeting of the pork dealers, raisers, and packers of Cincinnati and vicinity, held at the pork room of the Cincinnati chamber of commerce on April 13, 1881, the following information was given concerning American pork products, and the care taken to prevent deceased or unmerchantable pork from entering the trade.

The meeting was called to order by the chairman, Mr. McKeehan, who introduced Mr. Scanlan, Chief of the Bureau of Statistics of the Department of State of the United States, and the secretary of the Cincinnati chamber of commerce, Colonel Maxwell, read a letter from Secretary Blaine, which also introduced Mr. Scanlan, and stated the object of his visit to Cincinnati.

Mr. Scanlan then said:

There is scarcely any necessity for me to explain the feeling which exists in many countries in Europe in regard to American pork. Rumours of the most derogatory character in this regard have been circulated broadcast in the Old World, as you all know. This erroneous idea about American pork first started in Germany. Some time ago a man in Chicago sent a statement to Germany that all dead hogs, horses, and other animals dying from disease or accident were rendered into lard. To you it would seem impossible that such a statement could receive any public credence, but it has met with sufficient to injure the trade somewhat in Germany. That outrageous statement was taken up in France and then in England, together with the more recent exaggerated reports of this hog cholera. What seems preposterous here seems possible there. Only the other day I read an extract from an English scientific publication in which it was seriously stated that they were not sure what became of the hogs that died of cholera and other diseases in the United States; whether they entered into the trade or not. I, therefore, want to know from you, gentlemen, what sort of hogs you pack, where they come from, how they are received here, what is done with the dead animals, what care is taken to prevent dead animals from entering into the trade, &c., in order that this whole question may be definitely settled.

I would therefore request your chairman to select some of you gentlemen, experienced in this matter, to give me the necessary information in this connexion, commencing with hog-raising and following the subject up until the product is ready for export giving me all the details. Then I want to know what is done with the dead hogs. I will then go to the rendering company's works myself and get a report therefrom.

Mr. LIPPINCOTT.—Allow me to remark that the hogs marketed here are marketed under exactly similar circumstances to that in Chicago. We are but a small affair alongside of Chicago, though packers here think, probably, they handle their stuff with more care; but if you have all the statistics with regard to Chicago, I think it will be about the same here.

Mr. SCANLAN.—While I am satisfied of that, I would like to have whatever you can give me, and I will lay the matter before Secretary Blaine, and it will form a part of my report, giving these facts from you.

Mr. MICHAEL RYAN.—I would like to ask if you want the statement of individuals, or a statement made over the signatures of the officers of this association, this being the pork packer's association?

Mr. SCANLAN.—I would like to get a report from some gentleman to begin with upon hog-raising.

Mr. CUNNINGHAM, of Middleton, Ohio.—Mr. Maxwell has a written report from me which he will hand you. [This report will be found annexed hereto.]

Colonel MAXWELL.—Do you understand that all the hogs marketed here are corn-fed? I think if Mr. Cunningham would state how hogs are fed it would aid you very materially to understand the quality of our products here.

Mr. CUNNINGHAM, of Middleton.—I have fed hogs myself for a number of years. The custom in feeding hogs is to turn them in the field where there is plenty of running water. There is a mistaken idea with some that hogs are not taken care of. They are put where there is plenty of running water and they are fed on the best corn the farmer has. The disease known as cholera first attacks the young pig. The older hogs are not very often diseased with cholera; it is among the young and delicate pigs chiefly. After the hog matures so that he takes on flesh he is always in a good healthy condition, and the farmer is just as particular with the hogs as he is with the horse. If a hog is diseased among them, the farmer removes him immediately from the rest, and if a hog dies he is buried so that the other hogs won't partake of the disease at all.

Sometimes the disease will be worse in one neighbourhood than another. I have fed as high as three or four hundred in one inclosure, and never had a hog die. There are no hogs killed in this market at all to my recollection but hogs fed on corn. It is the cheapest and best article the farmer can feed.

Mr. MORRISON.—What is your observation as to the disease the last year or two?

Mr. CUNNINGHAM.—In our neighbourhood it has been less than usual; a great deal less than in former years.

Mr. MORRISON.—What is the action of this disease when it first attacks the hog?

Mr. CUNNINGHAM.—The probabilities are that the hog won't feed at all; he will move off from the rest, and the farmer, the moment he sees that hog, gets him out of the way.

Mr. MORRISON.—Does it prostrate the hog?

Mr. CUNNINGHAM.—Immediately.

Mr. MORRISON.—What is the probability of driving the hog one or two hundred miles after he is attacked?

Mr. CUNNINGHAM.—It could not be done at all. I have seen them die in two hours; sometimes almost instantaneously.

Mr. MORRISON.—Anyone familiar with the trade, and the manner of feeding hogs, knows that almost every hog is three or four days' journey away from the packer's pen. First he must be driven to the receiving pen, and there remains a day to be loaded on the cars; it takes a day or more to bring him to town, and every hog has to walk on to the scale; the rule is that the merchant need not receive him if he cannot walk. From the scales he is driven to another pen before being slaughtered, and he afterwards goes through the process of killing and packing, so that it is utterly impossible that a hog attacked with cholera could be driven from the feeding pen and find his way to the slaughtering pens.

Mr. LIPPINCOTT.—You will find that nine-tenths of the hogs dying from cholera are young pigs weighing from 60 to 100 pounds. Hogs seem to go through their diseases the same as children with the measles, whooping-cough, &c. The average of the hogs killed here last winter I suppose would be 270 pounds gross, and there is no question but that a fat hog is of necessity a healthy hog; it can't be otherwise. The disease of cholera don't, except on rare occasions, get among hogs ready for market.

Mr. FITZGERALD.—How about trichinæ?

Mr. LIPPINCOTT.—That is a myth; we don't know of such a thing. There is not a packer in the city of Cincinnati that has had ocular demonstration of that.

Mr. SCANLAN.—Have there been any deaths here from trichinosis?

Mr. LIPPINCOTT.—Not to my knowledge.

Colonel MAXWELL.—There is not a pound of meat packed in Cincinnati that I would be afraid to eat in my own house.

Mr. LIPPINCOTT.—The dead hogs that our fertilising company get are brought in here during the packing season, shipped in perfect condition, understand, but from being crowded in the cars, the cars being overloaded perhaps, or from being overheated, for the animal heat of a fat pig is intense, and they overlay one another, and occasionally you will find a car with three, four, possibly five or more dead hogs that have been smothered; not dead from disease but from being actually smothered. These comprise the bulk of the receipts of dead hogs by the fertilising company, and these are rendered up, the bones used for fertilisers and the fatty substances used for grease out of which soap is manufactured, and the idea that any of them get into the trade is preposterous.

Mr. SCANLAN.—Would it be possible for a packer to take a dead hog, one that died from disease or accident, and make it into good meat by any means?

Mr. ELMORE CUNNINGHAM.—They dare not do it, sir.

Mr. MORRISON.—A hog that has died from disease or accident, if you hang him up, and attempt to cure him, will betray himself immediately. The discoloration of the flesh and skin is such that no art of the curer can remove. You can detect it in a thousand boxes.

Mr. RYAN.—In regard to the hogs bought by the packers at the scales, every hog must be in a merchantable condition. If a man comes here, and I ask him his price, and he sells to me, it is understood that the hog must not be slop-fed, but corn-fed; he must be merchantable. If any hog can't walk into the scales from any cause, he is not merchantable; so there is no hog purchased here that is not merchantable in every shape, manner, and form. If a hog is not in perfect condition he is rejected by the buyer, and goes to the fertilising company, and is boiled up for grease.

Mr. MORRISON.—It has been found by the packers often that the farmers have got out exaggerated reports about the disease to enhance the price of pork. This generally occurs in the fall of the year, just before the packing season opens.

Mr. MCKEEHAN.—The farmers will also get out the report that they have lost a great many pigs in the spring of the year, in order to influence prices.

Mr. MORRISON.—Yes, in the agricultural columns you will find a long string of items that such and such a man's hogs have been affected by cholera, when, if the statistics were presented, they would show a very small percentage; but they have these reports circulated all over the country to show that the crop will be small, and thus affect the price.

Mr. RYAN.—There is another rumour gotten up by the farmers and raisers of hogs for the purpose of creating public opinion, giving an idea that the hogs are all dead through the country, thereby framing the opinion that the pork will be very high and scarce. For instance, I met one gentleman about one year ago, and he said, "All the hogs in my part of the country are dead; they all died with the cholera; these are my last lot; I don't think you could get a car-load of hogs in four counties.' Two weeks afterwards I met him with two car-loads, and said, "I thought you said the hogs were all dead?" "Well," said he, "these are some I didn't think about!' and, honestly, he came in with forty-seven loads of hogs during the season.

Mr. MORRISON.—Just as soon as the farmers find they are injuring themselves these reports will cease. I was raised a farmer, in Europe, and know that the chances of getting diseased hogs into the American markets are as one to a thousand in the old country, for the simple reason that the hogs are all killed at home in Europe, and if they find a hog sick they don't allow him to walk around long, but send for the butcher and have him killed.

There is no more wholesome food in the world than our corn-fed hogs. The European hogs are fed largely on slops from the kitchen, &c.

Mr. RYAN.—We have some slop-fed hogs, however, but they don't enter into the export trade.

Mr. SCANLAN.—I suppose it is the same in Cincinnati as Chicago; if there is an inferior hog it is kept for the local market, and the best pork is used for exporting?

Mr. MCKEEHAN.—A rejected hog can't be cured here at all, either for the local market or for export.

Mr. SCANLAN.—I do not mean rejected hogs or those that are diseased, but such as are not fit for export.

Mr. MORRISON.—Our house has been engaged in the foreign trade for twenty years or more, and we pursue the same course as Mr. Scanlan says they do in Chicago, only not quite so much. We select out of the hogs we kill the best and soundest—what we call the smoothest—for the foreign trade. Anything that is the least blemished, as for instance a skin bruise, or anything of that kind, is kept for the home market, and I know from my own experience that the choicest meat this country produces goes to Europe. We have an agent in Liverpool who distributes for the three kingdoms, and we have never had a single report of bad consequences from any meat of ours.

Mr. LIPPINCOTT.—How about the summer packing of hogs?

Mr. MORRISON.—I have written a letter for Mr. Scanlan, in which I touch on that. I say that a large amount of this trouble has occurred since the introduction of summer curing. This arises from the packers shipping before the goods are sufficiently cured, and is bound to make trouble, and the consequence is enormous loss from meat perishing on their hands in Europe. It is not from any original defect in the quality of the meat, but from exposure in warm weather.

Mr. MICHAEL RYAN.—I want to say that I was very happy to know that Secretary Blaine has come to our rescue. In three months last winter we packed something over half a million of hogs in this city, and the trimmings, tenderloins, sausage meat, &c., were purchased by all classes of people; and during the whole season, I haven't heard a word of one single case of trouble from this cause. We are not afraid to eat our meat. Every packer in this city has his reputation at stake. We are all engaged in the business, and we are not disposed to risk our reputations for the sake of a few dollars we might make by putting bad meat into a barrel with our brand on it. Packers themselves are interested in seeing that the meat is thoroughly sound and good. We sell a good deal of meat on contracts, and have to hold it for a good while, and we are very scrupulous about seeing that the meat is from good, healthy hogs. Our people have entire confidence in the pork of this city, and there is no man in Cincinnati that is afraid to buy any packer's brand and eat it. I am very glad the Secretary of State has taken this into hand, and hope he will be able to effectually disprove these calumnies.

Mr. SCANLAN.—You must make allowances for the Europeans. You have beaten them so badly that they will take advantage of everything and anything to decry American meats.

Mr. MORRISON.—I think they should assume a manly manner, however, and put an import duty on our pork if necessary, and not calumniate our products.

Mr. SCANLAN.—This thing will all result in raising the value of American pork; it cannot be otherwise.

Colonel MAXWELL.—You understand that much the larger part of our pork is winter packed, while in Chicago it is not so.

Mr. MORRISON.—Summer cure is just as good, however, if properly cured.

Mr. SCANLAN.—What are your regulations in regard to your stock-yards; do they all come into one, or have you more?

Mr. MORRISON.—There are four in Cincinnati; one principal one, and three others.

Mr. LIPPINCOTT.—I would remind Mr. Scanlan that here the Cincinnati Fertilising Company has a contract with the city, and is the only party that can purchase dead animals where they are found within the city limits. We have an ordinance to that effect.

Mr. SCANLAN.—The yards in Chicago are outside the city limits, and therefore are covered and regulated by State law.

Mr. FITZGERALD.—Our city law is the same in effect as the State law in Chicago. The very minute a hog becomes diseased, the fertilising company takes possession of that hog.

Mr. LIPPINCOTT.—Probably the strongest argument a packer could use is the matter of the safety to his own interests, as that interest is the ruling principle of us all.

Mr. SCANLAN.—A great deal of trouble arises from the fact that no care is taken of the meat after it gets to Europe. A Chicago packer had an agent at Havre, to whom he sent a very large amount of meat, upon which he fixed a limit in price. The meat was landed on the quays, and the agent, not being able to get the limit fixed by the owner, left the meat three or four weeks uncovered on the quays, in the rain and snow.

Mr. LIPPINCOTT.—I was told of an instance in which a large Chicago packer sent one thousand boxes of short clear middlings to Havre, fixing a limit on the price, and the commission man not obtaining the price, put that meat in store and waited for the market. He never gave it any attention, and when they came to examine it it was actually a putrid mass, having perished for the want of being overhauled and re-salted. Of course that stuff must find a market for something or other, and people might imagine that was a sample of American hog product.

Mr. MORRISON.—There is not much trouble caused by clean pork. The Germans have a method of manufacturing all sorts of garbage into sausage, and that is where the trichinæ is found more than in clean cured pork. I know I have had fellows come to me to buy stuff for sausage, and I have been compelled to notify them that if they did not pay more attention to cleanliness I would report them to the health officer.

Mr. SCANLAN.—Is your process of saving any different from that of Chicago?

Mr. McKEEHAN.—No; I think there is no particular difference.

Mr. MORRISON.—The people of both Chicago and Cincinnati in a measure sample nearly every carcass, by buying sausage, tenderloin, spare-ribs, &c., so that if there is anything of that kind (trichinæ) they would have it in these cities.

Upon request of Mr. Scanlan, the chairman, Mr. McKeehan, then appointed a committee of three, composed of Messrs. Morrison, Lippincott, and Ryan, to act with Colonel Maxwell, Superintendent of the Chamber of Commerce, to furnish Mr. Scanlan with some official information in addition to the matter given above by the individual members of the Pork Packers' Association; after which the meeting adjourned.

PORK PACKING in CINCINNATI.—Report of a Committee of the Pork Packers' Association.

DEAR SIR,   Cincinnati, April 15, 1881.

Your committee, to whom was referred the preparation of a report to Michael Scanlan, Esq., Chief of the Bureau of Statistics of the Department of State, U.S.A., on the quality of the hogs packed at Cincinnati, and the liability to bad meats cured therefrom, begs to submit the following:

R 679.

1st. The hogs packed in this market are all corn-fed hogs, raised mainly in the States of Ohio, Kentucky, Indiana, and Illinois. They are fatted on corn because it is the most abundant and the cheapest food, and they are usually fed in the fields. They ordinarily have wide range and plenty of water, and are surrounded by entirely healthful circumstances. The rules of the Cincinnati Chamber of Commerce (Rule 23) for the government of the provision trade of this city provide that "all hog "product to be 'regular' must be corn-fed slaughtered hogs."

2nd. These hogs are mostly driven to the railroads, and shipped to some one of the stock-yards of this city, where they are unloaded, placed in clean pens, supplied with water from our city waterworks, and fed with good corn.

3rd. When purchased by our packers they are removed to the packing-houses, which are generally located conveniently to the stock-yards, where, by the most approved methods, they are slaughtered, cleaned, and cut in conformity with the rules of the Chamber of Commerce, and the product cured in apartments constructed and appointed with a view to securing the best possible results.

4th. Skilled inspectors appointed by the board of officers of the Chamber of Commerce, under bonds for the faithful performance of their duties, governed by specific regulations, and accountable to the committee on provision inspection, also appointed by the board of officers of the chamber, hold themselves in readiness to inspect all the hog product they may be called upon to inspect, and the rules are so constructed as to offer the largest possible inducements to buyers to have inspected the product they may purchase.

5th. Under the rules for the regulation of the stock-yards, all animals found dead in the cars, which is not an infrequent occurrence, from suffocation by crowding, pass directly to the fertiliser company, under its contract with the city, and are at once removed to its works to be converted into grease, fertilisers, &c., but in no case into any article of food, neither the owners of the stock nor the managers of the yards having any discretion in the matter. It should also be remarked that there are inspectors appointed by the municipality charged with supervising all stock, so that if there were any inducements to buy any other than sound hogs by the packers, the opportunity would not be afforded.

6th. The best hogs brought to this market are purchased by the packers. Those packed in the past winter averaged 268·37 pounds gross. It will thus be seen that, inasmuch as the hogs which are attacked by cholera are generally the young swine averaging less than 100 pounds per head, by the time the hogs attain the size required by the packers they will have passed the ailments to which young animals are generally liable; and, furthermore, that as a sick hog cannot be fattened, the liability of a packer here to get a sick animal is very remote. Even if a hog of such weight as is usually bought by our packers should be afflicted with cholera when killed, the meat would be so affected in colour as to be at once discoverable, and if put in with sound meat would be liable to impair the quality of the good. Ordinary business prudence would thus prevent any attempt to utilise the product of the sick animal. The hogs freest from bruises, abrasions, &c., are selected for the foreign markets.

7th. As to trichinæ, it is our firm conviction that if any at all exists in hogs packed at Cincinnati it is in such exceptional cases as to reduce the liability to accident from their presence to the infinitesimal. The circumstances under which the hogs marketed here are raised and fed are so unfavourable to the production of this enemy of the hog product under certain conditions as to render its presence the most remote possibility. Doubtless the hogs going into home consumption would, in the very nature of the case, be the most likely to be affected, and yet the existence here of a single well-authenticated case of sickness arising from using pork so affected is unknown.

8th. The packers of this city are generally old, reputable houses, who could not afford to risk their good name nor hazard the reputation of their product, by killing and curing any other than healthy hogs.

9th. From our observation and information the hogs of this locality, and of the entire country, have been, during the past year, unusually exempt from maladies of all kinds.

JAMES B. LIPPINCOT,
MICHAEL RYAN,
THOMAS MORRISON,
SIDNEY D. MAXWELL, Secretary,
Committee.

James McKeehan, Esq.,
President Pork Packers' Association of Cincinnati.

HOG-RAISING in OHIO.—Statement by J. H. Cunningham, Esq.

DEAR SIR,   Middletown, Ohio, April 12, 1881.

IN compliance with your polite request, I beg to say that I reside at Middletown, Butler County, Ohio, and for more than thirty years have been familiar with the business, both in hogs and the meats made therefrom. This locality raises hogs largely, and ships them to foreign countries as well as to various parts of the United States. From my observation I should say that the health of the hogs in this vicinity in the past year has been singularly good, as good as at any time in a period of 20 years.

I might remark, as far as hog cholera is concerned, that the disease, when it prevails, generally attacks the young swine, while the matured hogs are measurably exempt. Not only so, but you cannot get a diseased hog to take on fat. Now, inasmuch as only the well-fatted and grown hogs are used by the packers at Cincinnati, it will be seen that, even in an epidemic, there would be comparatively little danger from bad meat. The hogs of this locality are usually fatted in the fields, away from all unwholesome influences, and since corn is the cheapest article with which to fatten the animal, there is no temptation to use anything else. These hogs generally, after leaving the fields, require three days before reaching the slaughter pens, so that if they were sick before they would reach the slaughterer they would be almost certain to be discovered, and, even if killed, the appearance of the meat would at once condemn it.

I give it as my candid opinion, based on a large observation as a packer and otherwise, that the pork of Cincinnati was never more wholesome than now, and that the danger from disease of all kinds is no greater than from that of any other kind of food. In my judgment there never has been a time when there was less occasion for alarm.

Yours very respectfully,
J. H. CUNNINGHAM.

Michael Scanlan, Esq.,
Chief of the Bureau of Statistics, Department of State,
Washington, D.C.

Hamilton, Butler County, Ohio, April 13, 1881.

My opportunities for observation have been similar to Mr. Cunningham's, and I fully concur in all that he has said on this subject.

W. SHAFFER.

PORK-PACKING in CINCINNATI.—Statement prepared by Col. Sidney D. Maxwell, Superintendent of the Cincinnati Chamber of Commerce.

WINTER SEASON, November 1, 1880, to March 1, 1881.

Whole number of hogs packed	head	522,425
Average gross weight	pounds	268.37
Aggregate yield of lard	do.	20,617,859
Average yield of lard per head	do.	39.46
Aggregate cost		$6,466,288
Average cost per 100 pounds gross		$4.61.19
Total amount of barrelled pork produced	barrels	26,596
Amount of lard produced:		
Tierces		61,009
Barrels		100
Kegs		1,083
Buckets		3,435

Production of cut meats (green weights):

Clear sides	pounds	3,667,127
Clear rib sides	do.	30,379,095
Long clear sides	do.	2,893,957
All other kinds of sides, including rough sides and bellies	do.	3,700,829
Hams	do.	15,758,450
Shoulders	do.	12,980,389
Total production of cut meats	do.	69,379,847

SUMMER SEASON, March 1 to November 1, 1880.

Whole number of hogs packed	head	110,556
Average gross weight	pounds	252.78
Aggregate yield of lard	do.	6,042,121
Average yield of lard per head	do.	54.65
Aggregate cost		$1,266,313
Average cost per 100 pounds gross		$4.53.11
Total amount of barrelled pork produced	barrels	2,065
Total amount of lard produced	tierces	17,814

THE HOGS AND HOG PRODUCT OF THE UNITED STATES.—Statement presented by the Anglo-American Packing Company, Chicago, Illinois.

It is difficult to point out many new or interesting features relative to the trade in general, simply because there are none. The magnitude of the trade, and its value to the commercial interests of the country, are facts quite well established. The Bureau of Statistics at Washington gives the

VALUE OF HOG PRODUCTS EXPORTED

from America for the year 1880, at $100,799,414, against $77,356,947 in 1879. The same authority gives the gross weight of hog product exported for the year 1880 as 1,326,157,330 lbs. against 1,081,892,318 lbs. for the year 1879, an increase of 244,265,012 lbs. Add to this the amounts consumed at home and it is apparent that this is one of the leading industries of the United States. The capital employed in the prosecution of the business, the money paid out for hogs, the immense number of men employed, and it is easily seen that, to the West especially, it is of most formidably necessity. Look beyond this and imagine, if one can, that there is not a farmer in the entire West but looks to the packers to buy his hogs, and it is seen that it is an interest which

PERMEATES THOUSANDS UPON THOUSANDS

of households, for to the packers belongs the credit of having so thoroughly introduced to the Old World the value of the meat of the hog, and having developed an immense demand therefor. Of course they did this more especially for their own profit, but what would the trade have been without their assistance? The business has grown to such immense proportions that it practically controls itself now—has grown to man's estate, and therefore able to take care of itself.

TRICHINÆ.

On the 18th of February 1881, the French Government passed a law prohibiting the importation of American hog products within her borders. This action was peremptory, the law going into effect at once, no word of warning being given either buyers in France or shippers from America. As a result of this, all the product in transit for that country, as well as considerable for which inland and ocean freight-room had been engaged, was practically without a landing point. The decree was an unjust one; the world does not believe, nor is there any justice, in *ex post facto* law. So far as France is concerned, America could have gotten along without her aid, and found a market for whatever of hog products she had to sell; but the action of the hot-blooded French created distrust, fears being entertained that other countries might take similar action on the impulse of the moment, and this caused a bad break in values at all points. There has been some modification of the law as originally passed, and we predict that the Government of France will yet be glad to rescind her unjustified action. But it cost the provision dealers of America thousands upon thousands of dollars, and worked an injury to the trade which it will take time to eradicate.

In this connection, we submit to the world at large a few simple facts in regard to this matter. America produces annually from 33,000,000 to 35,000,000 head of hogs. Each one of these

HOGS REPRESENTS A MONEY VALUE,

and every hog that dies of disease entails an actual money loss. It is not reasonable to suppose that hog producers want to lose hogs, for the hogs represent money; and besides, for the last three years none of the farm productions have paid a greater per cent. of profit on the investment than that of hog raising. The corn crops for three years have been large ones, and prices for the same, in consequence of large crops, have ruled low. For this reason corn has been fed very freely to hogs, for it brought more in this shape than in the berry. In the light of these facts (and they are facts) is it not reasonable and common sense to suppose that hog raisers would take care of their property, and if there was any diseased stock, take it away from the herd and take care of it? There is no healthier food than

AMERICAN CORN FOR HOGS,

and no better meat food than that which has for its foundation corn. It is the sheerest of nonsense, it is foolish, to claim that American bacon is not, on the whole, extremely healthy. The great trouble with France, and some other countries, lies in the fact that it sells cheaper, and is better than their own productions.

It would be idle to claim that there is never any disease among hogs. The law of nature teaches us better. But a little reasoning on the part of our foreign brethren must convince them of one fact, and that is, that the American people cannot afford to allow any disease to gain any hold upon hogs. The interest is too large—there is too much money at stake. The hogs are raised as a matter of business, and strictly for pecuniary gain; the product is made for the same purpose. We do not raise hogs or manufacture bacon for the sake of simply feeding people. Neither the producers nor the manufacturers are foolish enough to work against themselves, and this is just what it would amount to if they should allow any diseased hogs to be sent to market. If the industry was small instead of large, there would not be so great an incentive to be careful as there now is, but where

MILLIONS OF MONEY ARE AT STAKE

the future is not lost sight of. The great trouble is, America's exports exceed her imports; she is growing rich somewhat at the expense of other nations; and, unless we are not mistaken, this disparity in the balance of trade between the Old World and the New has had more to do with raising the cry of trichinæ than the existence of the parasites themselves.

The system of direct shipments, noted for the last two or three years especially, continues an important factor in the provision trade. It is now so complete that through bills of lading are issued to every prominent point in the world, as well as to many minor points. This does away with a great deal of incidental trouble, as well as facilitating the transfer of goods, and assisting in exchanges. All the lines of ocean carriage (or nearly all) have representatives in this city, all of whom are enabled to issue through bills direct. Besides reducing the incidental expenses which would be incurred if product was shipped from here to the seaboard, and reshipped from there, it facilitates a more rapid transfer, and enables shippers to count more readily the number of days required to lay the property down at a given point.

PROSPECTS FOR THE SUMMER SEASON.

The summer season of 1881 promises to be less active than that of 1880 in a manufacturing sense, for the chances are the supply of hogs will be less than then. As there is reason in all things this is our reason for the assertion: From early in 1879 until late in 1880, a period of at least 18 months, there was scarcely a day that hogs would not gain flesh by proper feeding, the winter of 1879-80 being an extremely temperate one, and exceedingly favourable for raising stock. The result was a meagre mortality among the pigs, and a resultant large crop of hogs. High prices ruled throughout the summer and the last winter months, and no doubt hogs were marketed much closer than usual on this account. The winter just closed has been an exceedingly severe one for hog raising, and as the old stock was drawn down lower than usual, there are certainly good reasons for stating that the nucleus for a big crop is lacking, a much larger number than usual of young hogs perishing by virtue of the severe winter. There is plenty of good corn in the country, and there will be a good many hogs gotten ready for market, but not nearly so many as last year, while if the consumption increases in the same ratio as it has in the past, we ought to have a good many more hogs than during the summer of 1880. Ice is plenty and very cheap, and the cost of cure will be reduced in this particular, but it is extremely doubtful if packers will be enabled to secure all the hogs they need, for reasons above noted.

Chicago, March 18, 1881.

REPORT ON AMERICAN PORK: 1881.

Pork Packing in Chicago during the Year ending March 1, 1881.—Statement prepared by Messrs. Davies, Atkinson, & Co., Packers for the English Market.

Packers.	Summer packing, March 1 to November 1.			Winter packing, November 1 to March 1.					Total Hogs packed for 12 Months.
	Hogs packed.	Average net Weight.	Average yield of Lard.	Live Hogs packed.	Dressed Hogs packed.	Total Hogs packed.	Average net Weight.	Average yield of Lard.	
	Number.								
*Agar and Marshall	4,000	240·00	53·00	3,000	2,000	5,000	260·00	57·00	9,000
Allerton Packing Company	69,406	209·00	41·30	69,812	2,145	71,957	257·00	46·13	141,363
Anglo-American Packing and Provision Company.	719,363	170·15	26·00	447,014	—	447,014	179·80	28·00	1,166,377
Armour & Co.	708,555	213·50	31·50	501,537	—	501,537	242·75	43·50	1,210,092
Arnold Brothers	6,000	260·00	120·00	1,000	2,250	3,250	260·00	120·00	9,250
Baldwin, George D., & Co.	52,449	209·00	35·00	31,604	4,706	36,310	243·05	45·00	88,759
Botsford, H., & Co.	128,894	224·68	38·93	118,158	—	118,158	260·76	50·25	247,052
Bush, W. H.	7,800	220·00	50·00	3,990	70	4,060	210·00	40·00	11,860
Carpenter, W. O., and Son	1,082	186·00	30·00	—	7,434	7,434	195·00	31·66	8,516
Chicago Packing and Provision Company.	27,336	237·00	42·00	357,126	—	357,126	241·20	47·36	384,462
Cudahy, John	64,654	208·00	35·48	73,560	—	73,560	239·70	40·21	138,214
Dahmke and Fischer	5,724	223·00	57·00	2,784	160	2,944	257·00	48·40	8,668
Davies, Anderson, & Co.	198,957	164·82	27·00	146,842	—	146,842	162·36	25·00	345,799
Delaney, James J.	800	250·00	90·00	—	3,000	3,000	250·00	90·00	3,800
Doud, L. B., & Co.	111,271	164·00	29·00	117,026	—	117,026	180·40	33·00	228,297
Dupee, Cyrus, & Co.	—	—	—	16,162	—	16,162	238·00	45·09	16,162
Hately, John Craig	74,585	173·00	29·35	48,969	—	48,969	168·00	29·42	123,554
Heeney and Sons	45,781	160·00	23·00	16,221	—	16,221	130·00	16·12	62,002
Higgins, George W., & Co.	60,186	212·00	40·00	149,889	433	150,322	246·00	46·25	210,508
Jones and Stiles	89,509	190·00	30·39	70,875	—	70,875	160·00	24·00	160,384
Latcham, Dawson, and Miller	17,000	190·00	31·00	—	—	—	—	—	17,000
Meyer, E., & Co.	2,600	200·00	40·00	500	2,300	2,800	240·00	60·00	5,400
Moran and Healy	—	—	—	42,991	—	42,991	165·64	26·50	42,991
Murphey, B. F., Packing Company.	99,734	218·40	41·00	108,653	—	108,653	246·90	49·00	208,387
Palm and Schuler	—	—	—	9,873	—	9,873	156·00	24·00	9,873
Ricker Packing Company	41,368	205·00	34·73	50,002	—	50,002	245·30	47·11	91,370
Silberhorn, W. H.	—	—	—	62,782	—	62,782	157·20	23·18	62,782
Small, William	45,883	156·00	25·00	60,047	—	60,047	161·00	25·00	105,930
Teufel and Seiter	25,372	140·70	20·61	—	—	—	—	—	25,372
Teufel, Son, & Co.	55,476	145·00	20·00	48,993	—	48,993	160·00	25·50	104,469
Tobey and Booth	224,048	178·00	26·00	136,245	—	136,245	182·00	25·77	360,293
Underwood & Co.	28,735	150·00	40·00	17,366	—	17,366	170·00	43·00	46,101
Small houses	54,559	205·34	51·12	9,421	34,124	43,545	233·30	60·70	98,104
Total	2,971,127	189·54	30·83	2,722,442	58,622	2,781,064	212·55	37·94	5,752,191
Total season 1879-80	2,155,418	190·77	33·48	2,421,943	103,276	2,525,219	222·77	40·59	4,680,637
Total season 1878-79	2,017,841	194·26	36·72	2,823,743	119,372	2,943,115	225·15	44·44	4,960,956
Total season 1877-78	1,508,026	196·09	32·50	2,381,116	120,169	2,501,285	228·37	39·60	4,009,311
Total season 1876-77	1,315,402	189·79	29·10	1,494,512	123,572	1,618,084	215·97	35·10	2,933,486
Total season 1875-76	728,781	176·19	26·77	1,554,847	37,218	1,592,065	217·32	36·32	2,320,846
Total season 1874-75	446,368	—	—	1,659,436	30,912	1,690,348	212·42	37·30	1,781,896
Total season 1873-74	306,536	—	—	1,461,084	58,940	1,520,024	216·47	37·44	1,581,560
Total season 1872-73	31,571	—	—	1,365,364	59,715	1,425,079	236·25	44·02	1,456,650
Total season 1871-72	10,450	—	—	1,110,557	108,301	1,218,858	232·42	43·73	1,229,208
Total season 1870-71	48,917	—	—	741,723	127,447	869,170	225·75	37·94	918,087

PORK PACKING IN CHICAGO during the Year ending March 1, 1881—continued.

PRODUCT MANUFACTURED—WINTER SEASON.

Packers.	Lard. Tierces made.	Pork, Barrels made. Clear.	Mess.	M. O.	Family and Back.	Prime Mess.	Extra Prime.	Butt and Shoulder.	Rump.	Total Pork.	Sweet Pickled. Tierces.	Hams made. Green. Pounds.	Dry Salted. Pounds.	Long Cut. Pounds.	Stafford-shire. Pounds.	Other Cuts. Pounds.
Agar and Marshall	835	—	—	—	—	—	—	—	—	—	500	—	—	—	—	—
Allerton Packing Company	9,879	—	10,878	—	—	2,844	1,488	—	—	12,366	5,600	266,200	—	46,534	26,702	246,400
Anglo-American Packing and Provision Company.	37,928	—	1,905	—	2,946	—	—	302	—	7,997	19,860	—	16,684	6,618,839	—	1,155,814
Armour & Co.	64,792	1,154	49,838	—	3,158	4,549	1,610	—	—	60,309	51,350	689,425	51,600	—	—	—
Arnold Brothers	1,200	—	—	—	—	—	—	—	—	—	325	—	—	—	—	—
Baldwin, George D., & Co.	5,000	225	3,750	—	—	59	1,085	—	—	5,119	2,800	531,782	—	—	—	—
Botsford, H., & Co.	17,722	385	18,915	—	—	290	2,522	—	—	22,112	8,564	1,590,268	—	26,135	—	279,953
Bush, W. H.	486	—	—	—	240	—	—	—	—	240	400	—	—	—	—	—
Carpenter, W. O., & Son	700	—	1,990	—	115	—	—	—	—	2,105	71	127,313	101,442	—	—	—
Chicago Packing and Provision Company.	50,827	—	55,446	—	36	1,332	—	—	—	56,814	8,585	8,812,989	—	—	—	—
Cudahy, John	9,238	300	12,382	—	—	6,249	—	—	—	18,931	1,241	1,731,396	241,677	74,014	—	—
Dahmke and Fischer	432	—	—	—	—	—	—	—	—	—	—	94,200	—	—	—	—
Davies, Atkinson, & Co.	10,885	—	—	—	—	—	—	—	—	—	—	—	156,359	2,295,216	334,752	1,339,109
Delaney, James, J.	810	—	—	—	—	—	—	—	—	—	300	—	—	—	—	—
Doud, L. B., & Co.	11,702	—	6,500	—	—	250	158	—	—	6,908	900	1,110,000	—	1,109,000	80,000	75,000
Dupee, Cyrus, & Co.	2,193	—	670	—	—	—	78	—	—	748	1,474	87,542	43,439	1,417,790	123,719	—
Hately, John Craig	4,514	—	—	—	—	217	—	—	—	217	322	—	—	194,259	65,537	—
Heeney & Sons	783	—	—	—	—	—	—	—	—	—	4,548	3,250,000	176,000	1,252,700	—	338,700
Higgins, George W., & Co.	20,742	—	28,678	—	15	836	—	—	—	29,529	344	395,000	50,000	—	—	—
Jones and Stiles	5,154	—	—	—	762	50	—	—	—	812	—	—	—	—	—	—
Latehan, Dawson, and Miller	—	—	—	—	—	—	—	—	—	—	280	125,098	—	1,214,543	55,410	—
Meyer, E., & Co.	500	—	—	—	—	—	—	—	—	—	141	—	—	257,452	—	6,812
Moran and Healy	3,445	—	27,191	—	293	840	82	—	—	27,191	1,055	3,210,466	54,000	833,845	—	—
Murphey, B. F., Packing Company	15,887	—	—	—	—	—	—	—	—	—	120	230,000	130,100	2,130,800	—	—
Palm and Schuler	725	—	6,478	—	—	—	—	—	—	6,560	4,880	703,000	—	—	—	—
Ricker Packing Company	7,188	—	—	—	—	—	—	—	—	—	1,448	—	—	—	—	—
Silberhorn, W. H.	4,411	—	—	—	—	—	—	—	—	633	—	—	—	613,832	259,532	64,524
Small, William	4,621	—	—	—	—	—	—	—	—	—	320	—	587,275	2,651,756	1,659,792	—
Teufel and Seiter	3,425	—	—	—	—	—	—	—	—	—	—	302,000	—	23,000	—	—
Teufel, Son, & Co.	10,640	—	76	—	430	1,200	—	—	—	1,706	550	—	—	63,000	—	—
Tobey and Booth	2,260	—	328	—	20	300	—	—	—	673	2,183	510,924	—	—	—	—
Underwood & Co.	8,008	25	—	—	—	—	3,593	—	—	—	—	—	—	—	—	—
Small houses																
Total	316,882	2,089	225,025	—	8,015	18,516	7,023	302	—	260,970	118,161	23,767,603	1,558,576	20,822,715	2,605,444	3,506,312
Total season 1879–80	304,079	187	313,620	—	6,816	4,492	6,719	1,392	—	333,226	108,638	25,983,488	2,799,420	16,897,857	1,710,742	2,534,856
Total season 1878–79	395,659	972	219,802	1,863	8,807	8,579	2,209	—	—	242,232	108,327	19,858,661	3,263,268	11,691,539	2,429,386	24,292,534
Total season 1877–78	295,260	987	324,583	71	3,375	4,452	4,506	528	—	338,431	90,270	34,533,454	1,383,220	12,478,043	1,871,207	—
Total season 1876–77	172,869	1,903	234,056	859	3,774	24,129	22,082	4,457	21	290,693	32,404	25,088,124	—	17,593,061	1,660,103	—
Total season 1875–76	174,572	3,535	200,821	1,337	9,537	15,195	6,167	316	57	236,430	29,107	23,715,834	—	14,932,532	1,830,346	—
Total season 1874–75	197,038	4,286	216,515	1,054	13,703	16,028	9,749	—	806	262,675	49,084	23,364,922	—	12,650,879	1,853,927	—
Total season 1873–74	177,877	1,840	170,307	780	2,852	14,544	4,514	—	426	195,917	36,554	27,299,458	—	8,972,048	1,052,977	—
Total season 1872–73	196,054	2,873	88,385	—	—	8,726	1,796	—	876	102,986	40,726	28,272,469	—	5,263,989	—	—
Total season 1871–72	168,983	425	126,059	1,671	—	19,933	3,048	—	1,912	152,012	25,478	27,702,599	—	2,161,488	—	—
Total season 1870–71	108,885	1,258	98,731	1,819	—	40,837	3,593	—	—	148,150	31,350	18,542,779	—	123,900	—	—

REPORT ON AMERICAN PORK: 1881.

Pork Packing in Chicago during the year ending March 1, 1881.—*continued*.

PRODUCT MANUFACTURED—WINTER SEASON.

Packers.	Shoulders made. Sweet pickled.	Green and dry salted.	Rough.	Cumberland.	Short rib.	Long rib.	Short Clear.	Long Clear.	South Staffordshire.	Stretford.
	Tierces.	*Pounds.*								
Agar and Marshall	440	—	—	—	125,000	—	—	—	—	—
Allerton Packing Company	—	1,836,663	—	6,521	1,875,410	1,394	1,950,759	1,806,161	—	—
Anglo-American Packing and Provision Company.	3,155	4,746,743	—	—	3,505,684	—	3,536,478	3,787,108	—	—
Armour & Co.	5,637	7,478,216	—	—	14,696,446	—	13,815,949	16,566,773	—	—
Arnold Brothers	100	—	—	—	—	—	—	—	—	—
Baldwin, George D., & Co.	184	725,544	—	—	1,831,674	—	635,311	658,027	—	—
Botsford, H., & Co.	313	2,274,768	—	—	3,112,501	—	2,719,274	3,514,607	—	—
Bush, W. H.	320	—	—	—	190,000	—	40,000	—	—	—
Carpenter, W. O., and Son	—	146,610	—	—	151,391	—	—	—	—	—
Chicago Packing and Provision Company.	2,586	7,518,000	—	—	19,039,000	—	4,228,000	8,278,000	—	—
Cudahy, John	309	740,529	25,000	2,740	2,244,532	—	1,133,918	1,694,689	—	—
Dahmke and Fischer	—	77,950	—	—	36,500	—	175,000	—	—	—
Davies, Atkinson, & Co.	—	638,420	—	1,708,525	115,602	106,510	359,487	—	174,490	179,153
Delaney, James J.	280	—	—	—	—	—	—	—	—	—
Doud, L. B., & Co.	—	2,000,000	—	545,400	1,371,100	72,000	853,000	1,046,405	—	140,000
Dupee, Cyrus, & Co.	—	376,679	—	—	586,034	—	546,456	523,045	—	—
Hately, John Craig	—	767,953	—	1,383,507	737,951	6,234	—	134,440	190,750	28,110
Heeney and Sons	—	—	—	112,757	—	76,382	—	45,166	—	55,368
Higgins, George W., & Co.	516	3,228,414	—	—	3,706,200	—	4,499,500	3,240,300	—	—
Jones and Stiles	800	202,600	—	1,261,700	408,300	435,600	280,800	2,701,900	227,800	—
Meyer, E., & Co.	260	—	—	—	25,000	—	—	—	—	—
Moran and Healy	—	230,270	—	1,174,653	193,734	32,557	165,842	562,922	59,827	4,522
Murphey, B. F., Packing Company.	—	2,521,798	—	—	3,061,666	—	1,605,383	2,768,195	—	—
Palm and Schuler	—	29,479	—	142,062	6,649	46,452	61,908	193,242	108,645	52,682
Ricker Packing Company	338	1,015,517	—	—	1,925,120	7,212	740,650	1,853,569	—	—
Silberhorn, W. H.	446	117,647	—	685,846	284,862	458,426	459,872	1,453,484	119,876	—
Small, William	—	474,000	—	2,462,300	743,700	—	—	—	—	186,000
Teufel, Son & Co.	—	182,664	—	514,315	179,333	146,620	187,651	942,630	297,790	—
Tobey and Booth	—	188,271	—	1,312,569	242,956	—	1,728	798,477	5,047,425	—
Underwood and Co.	450	250,000	—	24,000	47,000	7,000	—	—	—	—
Small houses	1,586	397,300	—	36,000	199,500	15,740	108,000	10,000	8,000	—
Total	17,720	38,166,035	25,000	11,372,895	60,642,845	1,412,127	38,109,966	52,579,140	6,234,603	645,835
Total season 1879-80	15,171	43,962,290	52,500	6,772,144	87,512,180	860,666	27,281,460	39,751,783	7,587,763	1,162,714
Total season 1878-79	9,538	50,436,332	294,634	5,633,091	65,355,578	938,601	50,924,356	60,574,293	9,966,843	1,898,225
Total season 1877-78	9,172	34,449,280	330,000	4,946,312	49,173,464	851,826	43,256,893	64,159,504	8,458,727	2,481,551
Total season 1876-77	4,649	17,924,082	157,800	11,921,540	27,042,092	881,770	22,512,665	32,250,203	6,540,864	2,749,295
Total season 1875-76	2,252	25,637,105	539,410	9,678,047	36,749,334	2,005,722	16,089,655	33,465,864	7,483,783	3,151,328
Total season 1874-75	3,225	31,344,345	367,457	7,784,284	32,034,524	1,420,872	24,288,051	25,539,746	8,589,264	3,795,988
Total season 1873-74	3,381	33,961,424	598,110	8,411,539	34,553,010	1,871,561	25,234,501	22,327,558	3,381,369	2,751,788
Total season 1872-73	1,645	35,348,191	731,019	4,639,512	26,251,028	310,048	52,260,549	27,442,320	2,042,397	2,383,039
Total season 1871-72	797	31,827,752	1,730,603	6,235,424	31,700,039	—	24,923,980	18,302,005	412,420	1,209,025
Total season 1870-71	—	21,988,859	4,115,872	5,218,351	30,062,824	—	12,392,937	6,808,832	—	343,600

Pork packing in Chicago during the Year ending March 1, 1881.—*continued*.

PRODUCT MANUFACTURED—WINTER SEASON.

Packers.	Sides, Pounds made. Irish Cut.	Yorkshire.	Birmingham.	Wiltshire.	Other Cuts.	Singed Bacon.	Bellies.	Backs.	Hocks, Barrels made.	Pig Tongues, Barrels made.	Grease, Packages made.
Agar and Marshall	—	—	—	—	—	—	65,000	—	—	—	—
Allerton Packing Company	—	—	—	—	—	—	4,682	9,641	—	—	106
Anglo-American Packing and Provision Company.	—	—	—	—	22,458,637	—	—	—	582	2,032	1,794
Armour & Co.	—	—	—	—	764,400	—	1,423,943	1,123,992	139	—	2,674
Arnold Brothers	—	—	—	—	—	—	78,000	—	—	—	60
Baldwin, George D., & Co.	—	—	—	—	—	—	950	—	—	—	25
Botsford, H., & Co.	—	—	—	—	70,544	—	404,824	776,006	—	—	112
Bush, W. H.	—	—	—	—	—	—	40,000	—	—	—	—
Carpenter, W. O., & Son	—	—	—	—	—	—	42,359	—	—	—	—
Chicago Packing and Provision Company.	—	—	—	—	—	—	30,695	—	274	—	409
Cudahy, John	—	—	—	—	199,428	—	42,084	57,635	114	—	171
Dahmke and Fischer	—	—	—	—	—	—	30,250	—	—	—	—
Davies, Atkinson, & Co.	36,822	1,755,630	3,263,455	—	—	2,310,257	418,201	408,927	—	734	793
Delaney, James J.	—	—	—	—	—	—	70,000	—	50	8	10
Doud, L. B., & Co.	—	53,200	57,000	506,000	—	640,000	336,000	416,000	100	—	100
Dupee, Cyrus, & Co.	—	—	—	—	—	—	—	—	76	81	16
Hately, John Craig	—	178,327	—	—	—	—	126,727	170,982	—	—	—
Heeney & Sons	26,444	—	245,649	655,771	—	—	—	—	18	53	17
Higgins, George W., & Co.	—	—	—	—	—	—	40,000	115,000	—	—	105
Jones and Stiles	—	—	—	642,900	143,800	—	141,500	—	—	—	86
Meyer, E., & Co.	—	—	—	—	—	—	60,000	—	—	—	—
Moran and Healy	22,196	—	—	642,646	1,559	26,909	98,821	143,150	—	—	63
Murphey, B. F., Packing Company.	—	—	—	—	—	—	—	—	80	—	63
Palm and Schuler	—	—	—	—	—	—	2,837	4,713	—	—	15
Ricker Packing Company	—	—	—	—	60,969	—	16,038	24,996	117	—	227
Silberhorn, W. H.	3,602	15,603	—	602,308	436,363	—	38,500	—	—	—	32
Small, William	—	96,000	595,300	—	—	—	81,250	119,550	—	—	—
Teufel, Son & Co.	8,083	46,583	—	291,844	—	1,015,337	—	—	—	—	30
Tobey and Booth	—	81,834	521,760	—	2,550,909	—	52,547	32,685	—	—	875
Underwood & Co.	—	—	—	—	—	—	360,000	370,000	—	125	100
Small houses	7,500	—	—	—	—	—	751,325	—	60	—	112
Total	104,647	2,227,177	5,325,810	2,700,382	26,712,259	3,965,594	4,756,533	3,773,277	1,610	3,033	7,995
Total season 1879-80	1,015,548	1,349,771	1,073,855	2,428,451	26,978,427	2,714,867	4,373,233	1,974,643	1,253	2,243	9,975
Total season 1878-79	813,492	727,470	460,000	911,692	37,503,464	1,155,125	5,106,677	7,120,598	1,915	7,091	9,683
Total season 1877-78	539,084	1,383,801	411,485	1,069,897	22,600,834	2,006,000	2,436,681	2,474,926	2,578	1,998	3,638
Total season 1876-77	1,203,218	1,191,251	701,312	837,289	5,038,701	23,000	2,830,476	1,018,365	2,394	3,556	2,610
Total season 1875-76	1,424,571	2,730,240	1,706,759	1,722,890	—	2,143,000	1,783,487	363,229	1,977	5,778	2,802
Total season 1874-75	1,175,671	1,618,010	1,454,400	1,390,567	—	160,000	2,166,465	443,105	2,204	5,833	3,410
Total season 1873-74	1,719,347	738,480	296,194	439,829	—	74,000	1,682,741	423,269	531	5,080	4,791
Total season 1872-73	—	—	—	225,000	—	—	1,426,606	—	—	—	5,272
Total season 1871-72	—	—	—	—	—	608,191	894,245	—	—	—	3,946
Total season 1870-71	—	—	—	48,377	—	—	—	—	—	—	—

LONDON:
Printed by GEORGE E. EYRE and WILLIAM SPOTTISWOODE,
Printers to the Queen's most Excellent Majesty.
For Her Majesty's Stationery Office.

OLEOMARGARINE.

RETURN to an Address of the Honourable The House of Commons, dated 9 June 1884;—*for*,

"COPY of the CORRESPONDENCE on the Use of OLEOMARGARINE in the Manufacture of BUTTER and CHEESE in the State of *New York*."

Privy Council Office, 15 July 1884.

C. L. PEEL.

(*Mr. Duckham.*)

Ordered, by The House of Commons, *to be Printed,* 16 *July* 1884.

LONDON:
PRINTED BY HENRY HANSARD AND SON,
PRINTERS TO THE HOUSE OF COMMONS.

To be purchased, either directly or through any Bookseller, from any of the following Agents, viz., Messrs. HANSARD, 13, Great Queen-street, W.C., and 32, Abingdon-street, Westminster; Messrs EYRE and SPOTTISWOODE, East Harding-street, Fleet-street, and Sale Office, House of Lords; Messrs. ADAM and CHARLES BLACK, of Edinburgh; Messrs. ALEXANDER THOM and Co., or Messrs. HODGES, FIGGIS, and Co., of Dublin.

275.

COPY of the Correspondence on the Use of Oleomargarine in the Manufacture of Butter and Cheese in the State of *New York*.

— No. 1. —

(No. 84,565.)

Letter from the Clerk of the Council to the Foreign Office.

Agricultural Department, Privy Council Office,
44, Parliament-street, Westminster, S.W.,
31 March 1884.

Sir,

Referring to the enclosed copy of a Question of which Mr. Duckham has given notice, relative to a Report of a Committee of the New York Senate appointed to inquire into the adulteration of dairy products, and to the importation into this country from the United States of America of Oleomargarine and Cheese, I am directed by the Lords of the Council to request that you will have the goodness to move Lord Granville that inquiry may be made of the American Government with a view to obtaining full particulars on the subject of the manufacture of and trade in Oleomargarine, and that the result of the inquiry, together with copies of the Report of the Committee of the New York Senate referred to in the Question, may be furnished to their Lordships.

I am, &c.
(signed)   C. L. Peel.

Enclosure in No. 1.

Question.

Mr. *Duckham*,—To ask the Chancellor of the Duchy of Lancaster whether he has seen the following Report of a Committee of the New York Senate, appointed to inquire into the adulteration of dairy products, as published in the "Standard" of the 24th instant: "Of thirty samples of butter two-thirds were only remotely traceable to milk. The refuse fat of pigs and bullocks was the chief and most savoury ingredient, but often spoiled greases were used which had been deodorized by nitric and sulphuric acids of a strength sufficient to rot a workman's cowhide boots, to cause the finger nails to fall off, and induce various lingering diseases. The material was also found to contain ingredients which are fatal to infants. The doctors, upon oath, declared that the consumption of this compound had a distinct bearing upon the death-rate. The Committee advises the total prohibition of the manufacture of oleomargarine:"

And, seeing that an enormous quantity of oleomargarine and cheese is brought into this country from the United States, whether he will cause an inquiry to be instituted as to the correctness of that report, in order that the public may be assured that such deleterious food is not sold to them.

— No. 2. —

LETTER from the Foreign Office to the Clerk of the Council.

Sir,   Foreign Office, 2 April 1884.

I AM directed by Earl Granville to acknowledge the receipt of your letter, dated the 31st ultimo (84,565), enclosing a copy of a question, of which notice has been given in the House of Commons by Mr. Duckham, M.P., relative to a Report by a Committee of the New York Senate, respecting the alleged importation into this country of adulterated dairy products from America; and I am to state, for the information of the Lords of Her Majesty's Privy Council, that Her Majesty's Minister at Washington has been requested to procure the particulars on this subject desired by the Agricultural Department.

                                                                           I am, &c.
                                                (signed)   *Edmond Fitzmaurice.*

— No. 3. —

DESPATCH from Her Majesty's Minister at Washington to Earl *Granville.*

My Lord,   Washington, 17 April 1884.

I HAVE the honour to acknowledge the receipt of your Lordship's Despatch of the 2nd instant, calling for information respecting the adulteration of dairy products in the United States, and to enclose to your Lordship, herewith, copy of a letter which I have received from the Commissioner of Agriculture, together with the paper which accompanied it. The other document to which the Commissioner alludes will be forwarded to your Lordship as soon as received.

                                                        I have, &c.
                                          (signed)   *L. S. Sackville West.*

Enclosure 1, in No. 3.

Dear Mr. West,   United States Department of Agriculture,
                                                                       16 April 1884.

IN answer to your communication of the 15th instant, I herewith transmit to you the accompanying paper upon the subject of oleomargarine, prepared from various agricultural publications received at this Department; and I shall take pleasure in forwarding to you as soon as obtained a copy of the report of a Committee of the Legislature of New York upon the subject, and of the Bill proposed as a remedy for the evil, also any other like information I may be able to procure.

The Hon. L. S. S. West.   (signed)   *Geo. B. Loring.*

Enclosure 2, in No. 3.

IT is reliably stated that out of 100,000,000 lbs. of butter sold in New York City, between 40,000,000 and 60,000,000 lbs. are bogus. Oleomargarine has cut down the price of average butter ten cents per pound, involving a loss of 4,000,000 dollars annually to farmers. One-half to two-thirds of the receipts at New York of butter is classed as butterine, an article produced by the admixture of lard and good butter, half and half. Suine comes under the head of butterine, and is similarly made, only having a larger proportion of lard. Oleomargarine is, however, manufactured from grease of any and all kinds. For this purpose tallow, lard, cotton seed, pea nut, and other oils are sought for and obtained from all sources and from all countries. These fats are deodorised and neutralised by treatment with nitric acid, mixed with milk, cream, or poor butter, and churned. The acid in this composition is, of course, very deleterious, and, in proportion

to

to its quantity, is the resultant injury. Many of these products can scarcely be told from genuine butter, even by experts, and tests by microscope and sulphuric acid are essential to determine their true character. Laws are in force in many States requiring the manufacturers to brand such articles according to their constituents; but, unfortunately, when they reach the point of distribution the removal of the brands subjects the consumer to deception. The almost universal decrial of these bogus productions is having its effect all over the country, and stringent measures will doubtless be inaugurated to detect and punish those engaged in these deceptions.

Whilst this country may very properly be charged with the odium of sending out these articles, their manufacture is extending to many countries, and it will be well for others to guard against the spread of the evil. It is asserted that "stakes are driven into the sewers at London, from which stakes a fatty deposit, left by the current, is scraped every day, and, after proper treatment, this fatty deposit becomes dairy butter." The manufacture of oleomargarine cheese has almost ceased, owing to the greater profit for the oleo oil when employed in the making of artificial butter. Lard cheese is, to some extent, made, but only to the amount of about half a million pounds per annum. This, too, is "distinctly branded on the box, and on the bandage, 'imitation cheese,' and sells on its merits." There has been no complaint from abroad of this article, and therefore much more could be made and exported, as it materially lessens its expense in those countries where cheese constitutes so large an item of diet. The chief complaint coming from abroad is that we furnish too much skim-milk cheese, and much that is whole-milk cheese is often so characterised.

— No. 4. —

DESPATCH from Her Majesty's Minister at Washington to Earl *Granville*.

My Lord,   Washington, 22 April, 1884.

WITH reference to my Despatch of the 17th instant, I have the honour to enclose to your Lordship herewith copy of the Act* of the Senate of New York referred to in your Lordship's Despatch of the 2nd instant, as well as copy of the speech of the chairman of the Committee on Public Health, which documents have been forwarded to me by the Commissioner of Agriculture.

I have, &c.
(signed)   L. S. Sackville West.

Enclosure in No. 4.

EXTRACT from the "Albany Evening Journal" of 2 April 1884.

Bogus Butter.—Senator Low's startling Analysis of Adulterations.—The Agricultural Interests and the Public Health Insidiously Undermined.—A forcible presentation of Facts and Figures.

ON Friday last Senator Henry R. Lowe, Chairman of the Committee on Public Health, made the following address to the Senate in support of the Bill to prohibit absolutely the manufacture of adulterations of butter. After amendment in a few unimportant details the Bill was ordered to third reading.

Mr. *Chairman.*] The Senate Committee on Public Health was instructed by resolution of the Senate to make an inquiry as the manner of the adulteration of food and dairy products. When the Senate charged the Committee with this duty it had no conception, and, I think, the public had not, of the extent to which adulteration in the different kinds of foods has prevailed, especially the extent to which the adulteration of dairy products is now prevailing. No one, I think, was more astonished at the discoveries than myself. Instead of finding a very limited amount of this counterfeit, or bogus butter and cheese, manufactured and sold in the State of New York, the Committee in their investigations ascertained that nearly one-half of all the butter sold in the State of New York is the product of this counterfeit and vile stuff; that of the hundred millions of pounds that find a market in this State, between forty and sixty millions of pounds is made from the caul fat, principally of hogs, mixed with oils, imported from Italy, and colouring matter; and thus manufactured, as they term it, into an article resembling butter, and

the

* *See* page 12 for the Act referred to.

the better qualities so closely counterfeiting it that it can often only be detected by a chemical analysis.

In order to show the great importance of this question and the manner in which it affects the great interest of this State, I may be permitted to state a few facts as to the farming interests of the State generally. Senators from rural districts know that until within a few years this State was a grain-growing State; that it furnished not only grain for the support of its own inhabitants, but sold outside our borders. When the facilities for cheap travel and cheap freights were opened up to the country we were driven out of the grain-growing business to a large extent, as we could buy grain cheaper from the west than we could raise it, and the consequence was that the farmers who had their values in their lands were driven to find some other source of occupation. The pure water, the fertile soil, and the rich grasses of the State naturally invited them to turn their attention to dairy products. In the Census of 1880 it was discovered that almost the entire farming interests of the State were thus devoted. We now raise only a small portion of the grain we use here, the balance being imported from the west. There are to-day 380,000 farms of the State engaged in raising cattle and producing for consumption butter, milk, and cheese. This business was a few years ago much more profitable than it is to-day. And why? It is simply because we have now a new element, the competition of counterfeit and imitation butter with natural butter. Cheap corn enabled farmers of the west to make butter at the creameries as successfully as we could in the State, and low freight enabled them to bring a larger quantity to market here, and it became a close competing article with the butter of our own State.

The appearance of the Bogus Article.

By great industry, and keeping in the front with all the improvements of the day, we were getting along tolerably well, and, as long as they made and sold upon our markets only the genuine article we had no cause to complain. It was a fair competition, and we had to meet it. But five or six years ago there appeared in our markets a new article, a new element of danger to our dairy products. A Frenchman, during the Franco-Prussian War, in order to feed the inhabitants of Paris, when the Parisians were beleaguered by the Prussians, concocted an article from the fat of beef known as "olio," which was used as a substitute for butter. It was not sold as butter. It was never intended to take the place of it, except during that emergency and under its proper name. That invention found its way to our shores, and companies were formed for the purpose of making this article in our own country. At the outset it was very carefully manufactured. The oil was manufactured at a temperature of 105 degrees to 115 degrees Fahrenheit. It was put in a churn with a considerable quantity of milk or butter and churned and coloured, and thus made into an article called "Oleomargarine." It was at first exported in large quantities under the name, however, of butter. The counterfeit was detected by the foreign buyers and the exportation of it was prohibited and stopped. This article was sold in our own markets as butter, and retail dealers were induced to enter into the sale of it to their customers who did not know it from the natural product. The fraud having been started it was found that a cheaper article could be made from the fat of the hog, costing much less money, mixing it with a little genuine butter and colouring it, and then putting it in the hands of the retailers, and there has been more of it sold during the past year than of the natural butter. It was a fraud upon the wholesale and retail dealers and consumers, resulting in a great injury to the farming interests of the State. Mr. Robinson, of Chicago, admitted before our committee that he employed only a capital of 75,000 dollars in the manufacture, which amounted from six to eight million pounds per year; and at a profit of 10 per cent. he would clear upon this investment the enormous sum of 240,000 dollars. In my own county, in the town of Chester, in a little building not worth over 200 dollars, there is manufactured daily 1,600 lbs. of butterine, displacing 23,000 quarts of milk, the products of one hundred farms, and the outfit would not cost 500 dollars. It requires but little capital and but little is invested. A farmer can make in his cellar, with the milk from two dairies, by mixing with the fats, as the manufacturers do, enough to supply a township. This great wrong affects the value of every cow and every farm in the commonwealth. It lessens the income of every farmer. One-half of the inhabitants of this State are tillers of the soil, and more than one-half of the balance live directly or indirectly through their industry. There are in the State 1,437,000 cows, and the value of the live stock of the State is 117,868,000 dollars. Before this article was brought into the State there was produced in the State 122,000,000 pounds, annually, of butter, and 127,000,000 pounds of cheese (more than one-half of the cheese made in the United States) much of it being exported, and bringing back to us wealth and prosperity.

Extent of the Dairy Interests.

The production of milk in this State, independent of that which goes into butter and cheese, we have no means of ascertaining except in the cities of New York and Brooklyn. We found in our investigation that in those cities there are 500,000 quarts of milk sold daily, and that the whole value of the milk made in this State annually is 23,196,555 dollars, while the value of all the dairy butter in the State amounts to 56,000,000 dollars annually. The value of the farms of the State amounts to over 1,000,000,000 dollars.

All other interests sink into insignificance when we once bring our minds to this subject and look into the effect of this upon the interest of the State.

All the questions we have been discussing here the last month do not compare in importance to this one we now have under consideration. What has been the consequences to our State? Go to any part of the State and ask the farmers how they are getting along; they have but one story; they are growing poorer year by year. Their hard work of 12 and 14 hours per day cannot support their families. It was bad enough to compete with the creamery butter of the West, but how vile and wicked when these rascals poured the product of their slaughter-houses upon us; counterfeiting our butter and palming it off upon unsuspecting consumers. When they did this they committed a fraud and wrong, that should consign them behind the prison bars. Some of the most experienced butter dealers in New York testified before our committee that the actual damage to the value of natural butter has been from 5 to 10 cents per pound, independent of what the decrease is in the value of milk, an average loss of $7\frac{1}{2}$ cents per pound, making a loss to the farmers of the State of nearly 4,000,000 dollars annually; and that the loss in the value of cheese has been about 1 cent per pound, making a loss of about 1,000,000 dollars annually, and the same relative loss on the value of milk; and the committee came to the conclusion that there was a cash loss to the farmers of the State, exceeding 5,000,000 dollars annually; and no one but the swindlers who foist it upon the market and a few retail dealers are in any way benefited. The farmers are made poor, the consumers are swindled and deceived, and through the arts of this fraudulent combination in putting up the price of Western creamery butter, pay about the same price for the counterfeit article as for genuine butter.

I am only giving you, senators, the material loss, the economic loss to the State, typified by a representation which I saw in one of the New York pictorial papers the other day, a representation of the sheriff's notice of sale on the farmer's outer door, and in the distance the cows being driven to the slaughter-house. Perhaps it was a little exaggerated just now, but it is coming to that; and it is only a question of time, unless this dishonest law-defying adulteration of the dairy products of the State is stopped, and that very soon.

The Dangers to the State.

There is another loss, another danger threatens us, more dangerous than this, and I ask the senators to look it well in the face; one of the leading wholesale dealers, and one of the most respectable in the State of New York, said to me last night—and the gentleman sits here in the audience to-day—he said: "If you cannot prohibit this adulteration and imitation, legislation can be of no possible protection to the dairy interests." I asked him what the effect of this would be upon our exports? He said: "If you allow this thing to continue until our name shall be thoroughly bad, as it will deserve to be, you won't send a pound of our dairy products to Europe in the near future!" I now warn you senators if you allow this thing to continue a few years longer this valuable product, that now brings you millions of dollars a year from abroad, will have to remain on our shores for consumption. What are we coming to? There is no nation in the world that has attained the vile reputation we are fast acquiring; we shall soon be known the world over as a nation of "frauds" and "shams" unless there is enough of public virtue left to break down for ever this monster fraud; and our own State, with its great commercial emporium, is leading the van. Half the articles we eat are more or less adulterated, and the enormous profits made in the business has created an organization with such influence and power that the legislature has never been able to deal with this crime as it deserves. Gentlemen, this evil should have been taken by the throat long ago! The iniquitous practice of pouring the refuse products of Western slaughter houses upon our State to the injury of your farmers and the swindling of your own people, should have been throttled at the outset!

Iniquitous Combination.

This iniquitous combination has been strong enough to come here and say to the Legislature and to the Governor on one occasion: "You have no power to prohibit! You are helpless! You can regulate our frauds, but we will defy you! You may pass laws to brand our stuff, but we will brand it as we please, and we will colour it and sell it in defiance of you and your laws!" They have been strong enough and powerful enough to prevent the legislature up to this time from taking hold of this thing and tearing it out by the roots.

Gentlemen ask me if we are going to destroy its manufacture? I say yes; if there is power enough and public virtue enough left in the State it is to be destroyed! Outrages not half so great have overturned empires and brought kings to the block. In the Western States where the evil has never existed to one-half the extent it has here, they have passed laws prohibiting it, as they had the right to do, and enforced them too, and their own State Courts and the Federal Courts have sustained them. Is there not virtue enough in the representatives of the people of this State to prevent this great and growing evil? If we do not wipe out these adulterations and counterfeits I do not know where the thing will end. We owe it not only to our farmers but we owe it to ourselves, to our good name, to common honesty, and to the millions of men and women who are helpless in the hands of these sharpers, to stamp out these iniquities, and put ourselves once

once more upon an honest basis of living and dealing. I was forcibly struck with the reply made by Mr. Bachsen, a dealer of the highest character in New York City, when I asked him what the effect would be if this thing were to continue? His answer was: "Every producer will be a counterfeiter and every retailer a swindler." We have not a single word of proof that any farmer in this State has sold a pound of this adulteration, and they are the only interest in the State affected by the counterfeit that has stood firm against it. But how long will they be able to hold out against this danger? How long will you tempt them? How long if this adulteration is to continue before the Sheriff will sell out their farms, or the farmers be compelled to meet these dealers on their own ground by using the same adulterations? No one can use it so well and as easily as they. The rendered fat and oil is put up in packages and sent all over the world. It can just as easily be sent to the farmers of St. Lawrence, Herkimer, and Chautauqua, as to Chicago, New York City, or to Holland. Do you want to tempt them further? Do you want to take the risk of having this bogus, this unhealthy, counterfeit product mixed with the butter made at the farms of your State which they could so easily put upon the market?

Examining the Butter.

Our Committee caused to be bought in New York City, as you have seen in the published proceedings of our investigations, 30 samples of what was supposed to be pure butter. Our agents asked for pure butter, and bought it as such. Those 30 samples were analysed and the analysis showed that 20 of the samples were bogus, that only 10 of the 30 were pure butter. One-third of those who sold us the pure butter also sold oleomargarine, as we afterward learned, but we happened to get pure butter at the time we bought it. A cry went up against all these people at once from the unsuspecting consumers when they found their grocery men were cramming down their throats this vile concoction of fats, oils, and other unhealthy products! Why did the retailers do this? Simply because most of them were driven to do so by the competition of unprincipled competitors. They were obliged to sell this article to compete with their dishonest neighbour. They were as much opposed to it as you are,—as much opposed to it as the farmer, but their customers were going to their competitors, and many of them were compelled to deal in it or go under. Some of the wholesale dealers from the same pressure dealt in it, but I am glad to say that the great bulk of them never did sell it to any great extent, many of them not at all. I hold in my hand a petition presented to me yesterday, signed by 285 wholesale firms and dealers in butter in New York City, embracing 90 per cent. of all engaged in the butter and cheese trade, and every one of them ask you to prohibit the further manufacture and sale of this fraud within the commonwealth. It is signed by Acker, Mervell & Condit, Park & Telford, John S. Martin & Co., J. H. Seymour & Co., and that class of men who know what they are doing, and were not deceived when they put their names to that paper. And when these gentlemen say to you that the good name of the State and the interest of the farmers and dealers in butter can only be saved from ruin in the way it is proposed, it is time that this country and this Legislature awoke from their slumber and paid some little attention to these warnings. The Senator from the Sixth, Mr. Murphy, made the remark a little while ago that he didn't know whether I "represent the farmers or not." I will say to the gentleman that he will know it before this thing is through! I not only represent the farmers, but I voice the candid, solemn, honest opinion of nine-tenths of all the respectable dealers in the City and State of New York, a majority of whom live in the Senator's own district. The question is asked, first: "Is this product unhealthy?" It is asked, second: "Have you power to prohibit the manufacture of oleomargarine, butterine, lardine, and suine." These interests are represented here by a powerful lobby, and they are willing to be restricted. They are bringing bills here and putting them in the hands of senators asking to be restricted. They are willing you should insert anything but the word "prohibit." They have become very sensitive about the rights of the people, about Constitutional right. These law breakers, who live by counterfeiting, who fatten by deception and dishonesty, have become extremely solicitous about the "poor man's butter." The interests of the working classes who are most imposed upon by their villany, they need not trouble themselves on that score. We have the right to prohibit it just as much as the Government has to prohibit counterfeit money, just as much as you have to say you shall not take 10 per cent. for the use and forbearance of money. You have already passed laws similar to this Bill in principle. This Bill is only going one step further. The legal right of the State is beyond question. The question of justice and honest dealing is the one I am now discussing. Is this product deleterious to health? These gentlemen came before the Committee with reports in which they say they have analysed it and find there is nothing detrimental to health in the mixture. They brought it before the Committee. Now examine it and see what you have. At your breakfast in the morning take a bottle of the lard, or raw fat, pressed out by hydraulic pressure from the gut, or caul, fat of the animal, generally heated to a temperature of 125° Fahrenheit, mix it with a little cotton-seed oil, put in a little salt and annato prepared with potash, or soda, to colour it, and mix together on your plate, add a small percentage of natural butter and a little nitric acid, and you have the whole thing. And if there is a senator who would like to eat it, I would like to have him arise in his place. There is not a man who is not starving to death who would touch it. The poor labouring man, who these gentlemen are so solicitous about, would be the last to use it if he knew what it was. But they say it is greatly improved

when

when you put this in with some butter and milk and mix it and churn it. They claim that a great chemical change takes place. What is the chemical change? We asked the chemists who were examined by our committee, brought there by themselves and ourselves, if any chemical change occurred. They said no possible chemical change occurred in the constituent elements of this stuff. The lard is prepared with nitric acid. We may take very small amounts of this acid into the system without any very noticeable injury, but it is a deadly poison. If a drop of it should fall upon your woollen coat it would burn a hole clear through it; and still it is used in making this product! I know they will bring chemists to say that this thing is not hurtful, that it is wholesome. There was one before our committee who said his family "hankered after it," but no one believed it. The most of them said they never eat it themselves. Of all the dealers before us we found but one who ever used it, and most of them loathe it as they would the most deadly poison. They never feed it to their own family. When asked why they did not eat it themselves, they said "they were able to get good creamery butter from the West, and therefore did not eat it."

The Stuff not Healthful.

It is all nonsense, Mr. Chairman and Senators, to say this stuff is a good substitute for butter or that it is healthful. Why? Milk is a natural food; Nature has prepared it. Our Maker has made it, and when the child or grown person uses it it gives him strength and health. The chemist will analyse it and say the elements are all healthful; but let the chemist go to a drug store and buy those same elements and put them together, what kind of milk would you have and how many children would live on it for a single month. Butter is one of the God-given fruits of the earth, and necessary to our health, strength, and growth. These gentlemen say they have the same thing, that they have the fat, the casine, all the elements that go to make butter. Let the chemist go to the drug store and buy the elements and put them together, what sort of butter will you have? They misconceive this whole question when they attempt to say it is wholesome, good food, because there are not poisonous ingredients shown by chemical analysts. This is not the only kind of food that is bad, made unwholesome by a little change in elements. You can put harmless substances together in chemical compounds, yet they may kill you almost as soon as nitric or prussic acid. In Nature's laboratory good healthful food is made, but when put together by human agencies they are enemies of the system, and will poison and destroy it if you continue the use. Now suppose all these ingredients in themselves are harmless, and that a chemical butter is made by mixing artificially, the compound may still be injurious to health and indigestible, especially to delicate people. But there is another element in this thing that I had no idea of when we commenced the examination. Mr. Robinson, of Chicago, was asked to give the manner of rendering the fat, and he told us how they got the fat from the hog, and how they hashed it up in the hasher, and how they put it in the hydraulic pressure and washed it. I asked him if that was all? He said, "No, there is another ingredient we use." I said, "What is it?" "I decline to answer; it is revealing the secrets of our business." I pressed him again and again and he declined to answer, and he did not answer. Another witness declined to answer. Mr. Robinson found he might be brought before the bar of the Senate, and he called me out alone, and says, "I will tell you. I don't want these fellows around here manufacturing this product to know it, but I will tell you what it is." He said, "We use just a little nitric acid in this work necessary to prevent the fat from decomposing and putrifying. We take the smell away with the nitric acid." You all know what nitric acid is; you can take it in infinitesimal doses and not feel it, but it will in larger doses kill you as soon as prussic acid will. They put the nitric acid in the water, Mr. Lafferty told our Committee, to deodorize the fat and take away the qualities of fat that will putrify and decompose, and the fat as rendered they say has no taste or smell. How much of that prussic acid is likely to remain in this product? The chemist of Columbia College said a very little might adhere to the fat, and added, "it would be a dangerous proceeding in the hands of any person who has not been trained how to use it." I will not detain you, Senators, knowing that you will read the testimony our committee has taken on the subject, and thus obtain all the facts.

Another witness undertook to swear that Lafferty did not tell the truth. I asked him why? He said, "It could not be possible." He said, "It could not be possible when he said there was nitric acid in it." But he said he used colouring matter, and in colouring it he had to use caustic or potash. That was a new article. I have not looked to see whether it was injurious or not, but I would not like it regularly in any considerable quantities.

The fraud does not stop here, Mr. Chairman; they spoil the lard as an article of commerce. We ascertained in our investigation that in taking this oil from the lard that the refuse is packed and sold in the market. How long will we be sending our lard to Europe when these things are found out? How long before our bad name would make us a by-word among the nations of the earth?

I need hardly refer to the adulteration of milk, as it is a notorious fact, and has been greatly discussed, and the fact conceded.

It appeared before our committee that in 1882 about two-fifths of the milk going to the City of New York was watered, or skim milk. The laws that were passed in that year reduced the adulteration of milk sent to the cities about one half. They still adulterated it by putting in about one quart of water to every five quarts of milk. The State

State has made no standard, by legal enactment, for solids and fat to be contained in milk. Massachusetts, New Jersey, and other States have a standard made by these States; any milk that goes to New York City that is up to the standard of the Board of Health is passed, and no prosecution can be maintained against the party who does not put his milk below that standard. The standard made by the Board of Health I say in my report is 8 per cent. I think I made a little error there; I think it is about 9 per cent. The milk in Orange County averages about 14 per cent. of solids, of which about 3½ or 4 per cent is fat. We have about 40,000 samples and tests made on record, and the lowest that has ever been found from a healthy cow fed upon good healthy food exceeds 12 per cent. The New York dealer buys a can of milk in Orange, Westchester, or Dutchess counties, and takes it to New York City; it has 13 or 14 per cent. of solids; it has 4 per cent. of fat. He puts in water enough so that the mixture will be reduced to 9 per cent. of solids, and 2½ per cent. of fat. He can put in 10 quarts of water in a can, and that is now sold all over the City of New York as the pure milk of the city. Even at many of the best hotels there, where they do not get their milk fresh daily, you are more likely than not to get milk adulterated in that way. Sometimes water and sometimes skim milk is put in the genuine article. We have in one Bill fixed a standard of 12 per cent. of solids, of which 3 per cent. shall be fat, so there can be none sold below that standard without being liable for selling adulterated milk. That is 1 per cent. less than the Massachusetts law. The Massachusetts law provides there shall be 13 per cent. of solids in the milk, and if there is not the milk is deemed adulterated, and the person is liable for selling adulterated milk.

Witnesses testified before our committee that three-fourths of all the children in New York City and Brooklyn are brought up upon cows' milk, and the importance of this question will be seen when that fact is realised. The physicians all testified before our committee that this adulterated milk kill thousands of children every year.

The proposed Remedy.

I now come to the proposed remedy. By this Bill we propose to prohibit this. The word prohibit sounds harsh to many at first; I am aware of that. We investigated to see if there was any other remedy by which we could prevent the sale of this adulterated food. We have upon the statute books no less than six enactments in which the ingenuity of man has been taxed to devise some remedy to regulate this traffic, and I defy you to suggest any provision to regulate that is not already in your laws. They are as effective as a rope of sand. You can only stop it as you stop the traffic in counterfeit money, by prohibiting it by law, and if they violate the law incarcerate them in the dungeon; and that is what we propose to do in this Bill. But they say Governor Cornell vetoed a Bill once, because he thought it was unconstitutional. Why was it unconstitutional? Because it was claimed the article was made under a patent issued by the United States. I do not want to talk to lawyers about that proposition, because any lawyer will see how idle that pretension is, but to the layman it may be well to say that the United States Government, in granting the patent, gave the right to manufacture it in pursuance of the laws of the State, and merely guarantees that the party to whom the patent is granted has a monopoly of its manufacture, and that if any others infringe upon it he has his remedy; but in no way, by no possible construction, does it give the party any right to contravene the laws of the State, or sell any article that is forbidden by the laws of the State. Governor Cornell, I understand, vetoed a Bill on that ground, but he afterwards, I think, must have reconsidered it, because he signed another Bill that has precisely the same objectionable features. But, it is said, we have no power to prohibit an *honest industry*, no power to prohibit people from coming into our State from foreign countries or other States, and putting upon our markets an article, an unwholesome product ruinous to our good name and the interests of one whole people. Why have we not the power to prohibit it? You say a man who comes here to loan his money shall not take more than 6 per cent. interest. You have that power. You have the power to say a man shall not sell any unclean or unwholesome article. You say in hundreds of cases that they can only sell under certain restrictions and circumstances, and that in many cases they cannot sell at all, even though the article be not unwholesome. Whenever the exigencies of the case require, whenever great crimes and counterfeits can only be prevented in that way, it is not only the right, but is the sacred duty of the Legislature to prohibit this outrage. They talk about an "industry!" What right has this miserable counterfeit to be called an industry? and this fungus growth upon the industry of the country, this cancer that ought to be cut out by the roots instead of being poulticed until its roots strike to the very vitals of the body politic. It is a travesty upon words to call this an "industry!" You cannot prevent the traffic in this counterfeit butter in any other way than by prohibiting it. You cannot pass any law that will effectively *regulate* it. You have no right to create inspectors under the Constitution of the State. You cannot go to the consumers' rooms and inspect it. But in order to satisfy the doubts of any person who may be overscrupulous or very conscientious in regard to it, I have brought here the decision rendered in the United States Court on this very question.

In order to prevent any ground of cavil I have used the very words of that Missouri law in this Bill here. They are not, perhaps, just the words that you or I, or other lawyers might use, but they have been adjudicated upon, and, therefore, we were safe in taking the exact language. There the dealer was imprisoned. He was brought up on

habeas

CORRESPONDENCE RELATING TO OLEOMARGARINE.

habeas corpus, brought up in the most favourable manner where the power of the court could be exerted in his behalf, and the great talents of Roscoe Conkling were employed by these men to go to Missouri and defend them in this death grapple with this counterfeit product which the people of that State had set the seal of their condemnation upon.

Senator *Plunkitt.*] Did the oleomargarine men lose their case?

Senator *Low.*] They lost in the State Court and in the United States, and there Roscoe Conkling argued it before Judges McCrany and Miller, and they decided in favour of the Missouri law and against these counterfeiters.

Senator *Plunkitt.*] Conkling lost his case?

Senator *Low.*] Yes! And, he was so well satisfied with the decision that he did not attempt to appeal it, and it stands now as the law of the land upon this important question. They did not put it upon the ground that it was unhealthy, but upon the ground that the Commonwealth of Missouri had the right to put their foot upon this vile product and protect their own interests, which were being sacrificed for the benefit of the slaughter-houses of Illinois.

The Fraud must be Condemned.

A year has passed almost since then, and we have now come to the question ourselves, and I appeal to the Senate, I appeal to this Legislature, I need not appeal to the people of the State upon this question, that we shall put the seal of our condemnation upon this fraud, and for ever destroy this business. The farmers have the right to ask, and you, Senators, have no right to stand in their way and say they shall not have it. If there is any doubt about this thing, let the farmers have the benefit of this doubt. They will undertake to enforce this law. One of these manufacturers in New York City who said there was not power enough in New York State to enforce this law, will find out his mistake. You give us this law, gentlemen, and we will show them whether there is not power enough to enforce it. We will soon scatter them out of the State with their vile work. Every honest man should be indignant at the impudence of these rascals who come here and tell you that you cannot enforce a law to protect this great interest of the State.

But the work, I concede, will be no child's play. These men have grown rich by counterfeiting; they have fattened upon their ill-gotten gains, wrung by fraud and deception from the honest consumers, and they, a compact organization, bound together by a common tie, know how to use their gains, and where to put them; but there is no time better to grapple it than now. Every day the fraud is gaining strength, the foul ulcer is sinking deeper into the industrial body of the Commonwealth, and our good name is being more and more imperilled. You have now the great agricultural interest with you. You have every honest dealer and firm in New York and Brooklyn with you, and every consumer among both the rich and the poor, who has been wronged, sickened and outraged by this manufacture and sale within the precincts of our Commonwealth.

The farmers of this State demand the passage of this Bill. They are a slow-moving class of people. They are a conservative class of people. They are, as a class, a long-suffering and law-abiding people. If any other interest in the State had been menaced as the farming interest has been by the vile compound, you would have witnessed in the State a riot, and they would have arisen long ago and protected themselves, if the power of the State had not protected them. The farmers bear more than their share of the burthens of the State. They give you most of that which is valuable to our prosperity and happiness, and they only ask simple justice at your hands, that you shall not permit to be put upon them such vile products of the West, the unhealthy, impure, and unclean products of the hog pens by this wretched business of mixing vile fats, oils, and acids, to counterfeit the great industry of our State.

"The live cow cannot compete with the dead hog."

The highwayman who takes your money by force is less a criminal than he who takes it by fraud, which poisons as well as impoverishes you.

I sincerely trust that this Bill will speedily become a law.

— No. 5. —

LETTER from the Foreign Office to the Clerk of the Council.

Sir,   Foreign Office, 27 May 1884.

I AM directed by the Secretary of State for Foreign Affairs to transmit to you, to be laid before the Committee of Council, copies (received from Her Majesty's Consul General at New York) of an Act of the Legislature of the State, prohibiting the manufacture of Oleomargarine within that State.

I am, &c.
(signed)   *Edmond Fitzmaurice.*

Enclosure in No. 5.

LAWS OF NEW YORK.

By Authority.

[Every law, unless a different time shall be prescribed therein, shall commence and take effect throughout the State, on and not before the twentieth day after the day of its final passage, as certified by the Secretary of State. Sec. 12, title 4, chap. 7, part 1, Revised Statutes.]

Chap. 202.

An Act to prevent Deception in Sales of Dairy Products.

Passed 24 April 1884; three-fifths being present.

The People of the State of New York, represented in Senate and Assembly, do enact as follows:—

Sect. 1. No person or persons shall sell or exchange, or expose for sale or exchange, any unclean, impure, unhealthy, adulterated, or unwholesome milk, or shall offer for sale any article of food made from the same or of cream from the same. This provision shall not apply to pure skim cheese made from milk which is clean, pure, healthy, wholesome, and unadulterated, except by skimming. Whoever violates the provisions of this section is guilty of a misdemeanour, and shall be punished by a fine of not less than twenty-five nor more than two hundred dollars, or by imprisonment of not less than one or more than six months, or both such fine and imprisonment for the first offence, and by six months' imprisonment for each subsequent offence.

Sect. 2. No person shall keep cows for the production of milk for market, or for sale or exchange, or for manufacturing the same, or cream from the same, into articles of food, in a crowded or unhealthy condition, or feed the cows on food that is unhealthy, or that produces impure, unhealthy, diseased, or unwholesome milk. No person shall manufacture from impure, unhealthy, diseased, or unwholesome milk, or of cream from the same, any article of food. Whoever violates the provisions of this section is guilty of a misdemeanour, and shall be punished by a fine of not less than twenty-five nor more than two hundred dollars, or by imprisonment of not less than one or more than four months, or by both such fine and imprisonment for the first offence, and by four months' imprisonment for each subsequent offence.

Sect. 3. No person or persons shall sell, supply, or bring to be manufactured to any butter or cheese manufactory, any milk diluted with water, or any unclean, impure, unhealthy, adulterated, or unwholesome milk, or milk from which any cream has been taken (except pure skim milk to skim cheese factories), or shall keep back any part of the milk commonly known as "strippings," or shall bring or supply milk to any butter or cheese manufactory that is sour (except pure skim milk to skim cheese factories). No butter or cheese manufactories, except those who buy all the milk they use, shall use for their own benefit, or allow any of their employees or any other person to use, for their own benefit, any milk, or cream from the milk, or the product thereof brought to said manufactories, without the consent of the owners thereof. Every butter or cheese manufacturer, except those who buy all the milk they use, shall keep a correct account of all the milk daily received, and of the number of pounds and packages of butter, the number and aggregate weight of cheese made each day, the number of packages of cheese and butter disposed of, which shall be open to inspection to any person who delivers milk to such manufacturer. Whoever violates the provisions of this section shall be guilty of a misdemeanour, and shall be punished for each offence by a fine of not less than twenty-five or more than two hundred dollars, or not less than one or more than six months' imprisonment, or both such fine and imprisonment.

Sect. 4. No manufacturer of vessels for the package of butter shall sell or dispose of any such vessels without branding his name and the true weight of the vessel or vessels on the same with legible letters or figures not less than one-fourth of an inch in length. Whoever violates the provisions of this section is guilty of a misdemeanour and shall be punished for each offence by a fine of not less than fifty nor more than one hundred dollars, or by imprisonment of not less than thirty or more than sixty days, or by both such fine and imprisonment.

Sect. 5. No person shall sell or offer or expose for sale any milk except in the county from which the same is produced, unless each can, vessel or package containing such milk shall be distinctly and durably branded with letters not less than one inch in length, on the outside, above the centre, on every can, vessel or package containing such milk, the name of the county from which the same is produced, and the same mark shall be branded

or

or painted in a conspicuous place on the carriage or vehicle in which the milk is drawn to be sold, and such milk can only be sold in or retailed out of a can, vessel, package or carriage so marked. Whoever violates the provisions of this section shall be guilty of a misdemeanour, and shall be punished by a fine of not less than twenty-five nor more than two hundred dollars, or not less than two months' or more than four months' imprisonment, or both such fine and imprisonment for the first offence, and by four months' imprisonment for each subsequent offence.

Sect. 6. No person shall manufacture out of any oleaginous substance or substances, or any compound of the same, other than that produced from unadulterated milk, or of cream from the same, any article designed to take the place of butter or cheese produced from pure, unadulterated milk or cream of the same, or shall sell, or offer for sale, the same as an article of food. This provision shall not apply to pure skim-milk cheese made from pure skim milk. Whoever violates the provisions of this section shall be guilty of a misdemeanour, and be punished by a fine of not less than one hundred nor more than five hundred dollars, or not less than six months' or more than one year's imprisonment, or by both such fine and imprisonment, for the first offence, and by imprisonment for one year for each subsequent offence.

Sect. 7. No person shall offer, sell, or expose for sale in full packages, butter or cheese branded or labelled with a false brand or label as to county or state in which the article is made. Whoever violates the provisions of this section is guilty of a misdemeanour, and shall be punished by a fine of not less than twenty-five or more than fifty dollars, or imprisonment of not less than fifteen or more than thirty days, for the first offence, and fifty dollars or thirty days' imprisonment for each subsequent offence.

Sect. 8. No person shall manufacture, sell, or offer for sale, any condensed milk, unless the same shall be put up in packages, upon which shall be distinctly labelled or stamped the name or brand by whom or under which the same is made. No condensed milk shall be made or offered for sale unless the same is manufactured from pure, clean, healthy, fresh, unadulterated and wholesome milk, from which the cream has not been removed; or unless the proportion of milk solids contained in the condensed milk shall be in amount the equivalent of twelve per centum of milk solids in crude milk, and of such solids twenty-five per centum shall be fat. When condensed milk shall be sold from cans or packages not hermetically sealed, the vendor shall brand or label such cans or packages with the name of the county or counties from which the same was produced, and the name of the vendor. Whoever violates the provisions of this section shall be guilty of a misdemeanour, and be punished by a fine of not less than fifty or more than five hundred dollars, or by imprisonment of not more than six months, or both such fine and imprisonment for the first offence, and by six months' imprisonment for each subsequent offence.

Sect. 9. The Governor, by and with the advice and consent of the Senate, shall appoint a Commissioner, who shall be known as the New York State Dairy Commissioner, who shall be a citizen of this State, and who shall hold his office for the term of two years, or until his successor is appointed, and shall receive a salary of three thousand dollars per annum and his necessary expenses incurred in the discharge of his official duties under this Act; said Commissioner shall be appointed within ten days after the passage of this Act, and shall be charged, under the direction of the Governor, with the enforcement of the various provisions thereof. Said Commissioner may be removed from office at the pleasure of the Governor, and his successor appointed as above provided for.

The said Commissioner is hereby authorised and empowered to appoint such Assistant Commissioners, and to employ such experts chemists, agents, and such counsel as may be deemed by him necessary for the proper enforcement of this law. Their compensation to be fixed by the Commissioner.

The said Commissioner is also authorised to employ a clerk at an annual salary of not to exceed twelve hundred dollars.

The sum of thirty thousand dollars is hereby appropriated to be paid for such purpose out of any moneys in the Treasury not otherwise appropriated. All charges, accounts, and expenses, authorised by this Act, shall be paid by the Treasurer of the State, upon the warrant of the Comptroller. The entire expenses of said Commissioner shall not exceed the sum appropriated for the purposes of this Act.

The said Commissioner shall make annual reports to the Legislature, not later than the fifteenth day of January of each year, of his work and proceedings, and shall report in detail the number of Assistant Commissioners, experts, chemists, agents, and counsel he has employed, with their expenses and disbursements. The said Commissioner shall have a room in the new capitol, to be set apart for his use by the Capitol Commissioner.

Sect. 10. The said Commissioner and Assistant Commissioners, and such experts, chemists, agents, and counsel as they shall duly authorise for the purpose, shall have full access, egress and ingress to all places of business, factories, farms, buildings, carriages, cars, vessels, and cans used in the manufacture and sale of any dairy products or any imitation thereof. They shall also have power and authority to open any package, can, or vessel containing such articles which may be manufactured, sold, or exposed for sale in violation of the provisions of this Act, and may inspect the contents therein, and may take therefrom samples for analysis.

Sect. 11. Courts of special sessions shall have jurisdiction of all cases arising under this Act, and their jurisdiction is hereby extended so as to enable them to enforce the penalties imposed by any or all of the sections hereof.

Sect. 12. In all prosecutions under this Act the costs thereof shall be paid out of the fine, if one is collected; if not, the same shall be paid in the manner now provided for by law, and the rest of the fine shall be paid to the State Treasurer.

Sect. 13. In all prosecutions under this Act, relating to the sale and manufacture of unclean, impure, unhealthy, adulterated, or unwholesome milk, if the milk be shown to contain more than eighty-eight per centum of water or fluids or less than twelve per centum of milk solids which shall contain not less than three per centum of fat, it shall be declared adulterated, and milk drawn from cows within fifteen days before and five days after parturition, or from animals fed on distillery waste, or any substance in the state of putrefaction, or fermentation, or upon any unhealthy food whatever, shall be declared unclean, impure, unhealthy and unwholesome milk. This section shall not prevent the feeding of ensilage from silos.

Sect. 14. The doing of anything prohibited being done, and the not doing of anything directed to be done in this Act shall be presumptive evidence of a wilful intent to violate the different sections and provisions hereof.

Sect. 15. Chapters four hundred and sixty-seven of the laws of eighteen hundred and sixty-two, five hundred and forty-four and five hundred and eighteen of the laws of eighteen hundred and sixty-four, five hundred and fifty-nine of the laws of eighteen hundred and sixty-five, four hundred and fifteen of the laws of eighteen hundred and seventy-seven, two hundred and twenty and two hundred and thirty-seven of the laws of eighteen hundred and seventy-eight, four hundred and thirty-nine of the laws of eighteen hundred and eighty, and two hundred and fourteen of the laws of eighteen hundred and eighty-two, are hereby repealed.

Sect. 16. This Act shall take effect on the first day of June, eighteen hundred and eighty-four, except as otherwise provided therein.

State of New York,
Office of the Secretary of State, } ss.:

I have compared the preceding with the original law on file in this office, and do hereby certify that the same is a correct transcript therefrom, and of the whole of said original law.

Joseph B. Carr,
Secretary of State.

OLEOMARGARINE.

COPY of the Correspondence on the use of Oleomargarine in the Manufacture of Butter and Cheese in the State of New York.

(*Mr. Duckham.*)

Ordered by, The House of Commons, *to be Printed,*
16 *July* 1884.

[*Price* 2 *d.*]

275.   H.—18.7.84.   *Under* 2 *oz.*

CATTLE DISEASE (UNITED STATES OF AMERICA).

FURTHER CORRESPONDENCE

RELATING TO

DISEASES OF ANIMALS

IN THE

UNITED STATES OF AMERICA,

WITH AN APPENDIX.

Presented to both Houses of Parliament by Command of Her Majesty.

LONDON:
PRINTED BY EYRE AND SPOTTISWOODE.

To be purchased, either directly or through any Bookseller, from any of the following Agents, viz.,
Messrs. HANSARD and SON, 13, Great Queen Street, W.C., and 32, Abingdon Street, Westminster;
Messrs. EYRE and SPOTTISWOODE, East Harding Street, Fleet Street, and
Sale Office, House of Lords;
Messrs. ADAM and CHARLES BLACK, of Edinburgh;
Messrs. ALEXANDER THOM and Co., or Messrs. HODGES, FIGGIS, and Co., of Dublin.

1884.

[C.—3978.]   *Price* 1s.

CONTENTS.

	Page
Correspondence	3

Appendix:—

Proceedings of a National Convention of Cattle Breeders and others called in Chicago, November 15 and 16, 1883, to consider the subject of Contagious Diseases of Domestic Animals	84
Message from the President of the United States, transmitting a Report on the existing restrictions on the Importation of American Neat Cattle into Great Britain	151
Summary of a Report of the Cattle Commission on Pleuro-Pneumonia, directed to be held by a Resolution of the Senate of the United States on February 10, 1882	154
Compilation of the Laws of Different States in reference to Diseases of Farm Stock. From the Report of the United States Treasury Cattle Commission, 1882	158

CORRESPONDENCE.

No. 1.

LETTER from the BRITISH CONSUL at Savannah to EARL GRANVILLE.

Sanitary, No. 1. British Consulate, Savannah,
MY LORD, January 2, 1882.

I HAVE the honour to report to your Lordship that the equine disease called the pink-eye has assumed increased proportions in this city. One line of street tramway cars had to cease running for some days, having but 14 horses out of 40 fit for use, and other lines have been compelled to reduce the number of their daily journeys.

This new disease has been called pink-eye in consequence of the eyes of the animals attacked becoming so surcharged with blood as to present a pink appearance. It causes extreme prostration, high fever, and great swelling of the limbs, particularly the hind legs. When so affected the animal refuses to eat, and in extreme cases breathes with difficulty, and evidently suffers acute pain. The disease is of short duration, lasting five or six days, but it is followed by prostration, from which young animals speedily recover, the aged being much longer in regaining strength.

The veterinary surgeons here have not agreed as to what the disease is, or on any method of cure, though its effects are very similar to the epizooty.

I have, &c.
(Signed)   LEWIS JOEL.

Her Majesty's Principal Secretary of State
for Foreign Affairs.

No. 2.

LETTER from the BRITISH CONSUL-GENERAL at New York to EARL GRANVILLE.

Sanitary, No. 3. British Consulate General, New York,
MY LORD, January 10, 1882.

I HAVE the honour to report to your Lordship that pleuro-pneumonia has made its appearance among cattle in several stables at Westbury, Long Island; and that, to prevent the spread of the disease, the State Commissioner has caused the stables in question to be closely quarantined. No fatal cases are at present reported.

I have, &c.
(Signed)   E. M. ARCHIBALD.

Her Majesty's Principal Secretary of State
for Foreign Affairs.

No. 3.

LETTER from the BRITISH CONSUL at Portland, Maine, to EARL GRANVILLE.

Sanitary, No. 1.   British Consulate, Portland (Maine),
MY LORD,   January 31, 1882.

I HAVE the honour to report to your Lordship that, according to information furnished to me by the Maine Agricultural Society, there has not been any case of contagious or infectious disease amongst cattle, sheep, or pigs in the State of Maine during the month of January ending this day.

The "pink-eye" disease prevailing amongst horses in some parts of this State, as reported in my Despatch No. 15, of the 31st ultimo, still continues to make its appearance; and some cases of this disease are stated to have occurred recently at Portland itself, as well as in a few other localities of Maine.

I have, &c.
(Signed)   WILLIAM WARD.

The Right Hon. the Earl Granville, K.G.,
&c.   &c.   &c.

No. 4.

LETTER from the BRITISH CONSUL-GENERAL at New York to EARL GRANVILLE.

Sanitary, No. 5.   British Consulate General, New York,
MY LORD,   February 1, 1882.

I HAVE the honour to report to your Lordship that several cases of pleuro-pneumonia among cattle, two fatal, have recently occurred on a farm at Elen Head, Long Island. Quarantine has been established there, as also at Westbury, and some other localities on the island where the disease is said to exist.

The spread of this disease on Long Island is attributed to the admixture with the stock on the farms of a poor description of cattle which some of the Long Island dairymen purchase in New York City from a certain class of dealers, who sell cheaply and give a long credit. These cattle when brought home, if not already sick, not infrequently become so, and communicate the disease to others.

Excepting as above reported, I believe the State of New York to be generally free from the disease.

I have, &c.
(Signed) E. M. ARCHIBALD.
Her Majesty's Principal Secretary of State
for Foreign Affairs.

No. 5.

LETTER from the BRITISH CONSUL at Savannah to EARL GRANVILLE.

Sanitary, No. 2.   British Consulate, Savannah,
MY LORD,   February 3, 1882.

I HAVE the honour to report to your Lordship that the equine disease called pink-eye has greatly abated in this district.

I have, &c.
(Signed) LEWIS JOEL.
Her Majesty's Principal Secretary of State
for Foreign Affairs.

No. 6.

LETTER from the BRITISH CONSUL at Philadelphia to EARL GRANVILLE.

Sanitary, No. 3.   British Consulate, Philadelphia,
MY LORD,   February 10, 1882.

WITH reference to the existence of pleuro-pneumonia in this consular district, I have the honour to report that there has been no material change in the cases reported in my Despatch No. 2 Sanitary, excepting that three additional herds have been afflicted, resulting either in death or slaughter, numbering about 12 deceased animals, and the herds placed in quarantine under the laws of the State of Pennsylvania. These cases, like those in my Despatch No. 2 Sanitary, can be traced to cattle brought from the adjoining State of Maryland. Thus far pleuro-pneumonia has not obtained any hold in the States of Ohio, Illinois, Indiana, Michigan, Iowa, and Wisconsin, the western States of this consular district.

I have, &c.
(Signed) ROBT. CHAS. CLIPPERTON.
The Right Hon. the Earl Granville, K.G.,
&c. &c. &c.

No. 7.

LETTER from the BRITISH CONSUL-GENERAL at New York to EARL GRANVILLE.

Sanitary, No. 7.
MY LORD,

British Consulate General, New York,
February 28, 1882.

I HAVE the honour to transmit, herewith enclosed, for your Lordship's information, an extract from a letter recently received by me from Mr. J. Howard Rushmore, one of the Deputy State Cattle Commissioners, in reply to my inquiry as to the prevalence and source of contagious pleuro-pneumonia among cattle in certain localities on Long Island.

In regard to other parts of this consular district, I have no further information to report to your Lordship.

I have, &c.
(Signed) E. M. ARCHIBALD.

Her Majesty's Principal Secretary of State
for Foreign Affairs.

Enclosure in No. 7.

EXTRACT from LETTER from Mr. J. HOWARD RUSHMORE, a Deputy State Cattle Commissioner.

"I AM compelled to state that contagious pleuro-pneumonia exists in several localities on Long Island; mainly in King's County, from which Queen's County receives frequent incursions.

"The cattle killed at East Williston I have traced to a stable in Brooklyn, E.D., from which they had been taken some three months previous. The cattle killed at Glen Head contracted the said disease from a cow purchased at 59th Street Yard in New York; this cow *presumably* came from a city stable, though represented by the dealer as a cow direct from the country.

"I have had a thorough (practical) knowledge of contagious pleuro-pneumonia for over 25 years, and I have yet to meet the first drover who believes that it is among Western cattle. New York and Brooklyn, and several suburban districts, are, and probably will be, infected for some time to come, New York very slightly, Brooklyn and suburbs very considerably.

"I do not feel that the conditions are such as to warrant any alarm abroad, so long as Western cattle are competently supervised previous to shipment."

CORRESPONDENCE.

No. 8.

LETTER from the BRITISH CONSUL at Portland, Maine, to EARL GRANVILLE.

Sanitary, No. 2.   British Consulate, Portland (Maine)
MY LORD,   February 28, 1882.

I HAVE the honour to report to your Lordship that, according to information furnished me by the Maine Agricultural Society, there has not been any case of infectious or contagious disease amongst cattle, sheep, or pigs in this State during the month of February ended this day.

The "pink-eye" disease still prevailing to a slight extent amongst horses in January (as reported to your Lordship in my Despatch No. 1 of the 31st ultimo) is considered now to have disappeared from this district.

I have, &c.
(Signed)   WILLIAM WARD.

The Right Hon. the Earl Granville. K.G.,
&c.   &c.   &c.

No. 9.

LETTER from the BRITISH CONSUL at Boston to EARL GRANVILLE.

Sanitary, No. 3.
MY LORD,   Boston, March 6, 1882.

I HAVE the honour to report that, as far as information has been received here, this consular district has continued free from cattle plague during the past month, and no contagious or infectious disease exists among animals in the district.

I beg to enclose the Report for 1881 of the Massachusetts Commissioners on Contagious Diseases among Cattle, showing the sanitary condition of animals, and proceedings of the Commissioners.

I have, &c.
(Signed)   C. A. HENDERSON.

Her Majesty's Principal Secretary of State
for Foreign Affairs.

Enclosure 1 in No. 9.

SIR,   Boston, January 10, 1882.

I HAVE the honour herewith to transmit to the Legislature the annual report of the Commissioners on Contagious Diseases among Cattle.

I am, &c.
(Signed)   LEVI STOCKBRIDGE.

Hon. Robert R. Bishop, President of the Senate.

CORRESPONDENCE.

Enclosure 2 in No. 9.

COMMONWEALTH OF MASSACHUSETTS.

Annual Report of the Commissioners on Contagious Diseases among Cattle, 1881.

The Commissioners are gratified to be able to report that the year 1881 has been one of general health with the neat stock of the State, and that our stock interests have been unusually prosperous. In our last annual report the attention of the Legislature was called to the fact that contagious pleuro-pneumonia existed in several sections of the country, and that it was alleged in England that cattle exported from the port of Boston had been found infected with it, causing apprehension among our stock-owners lest there might be an outbreak of the disease here, and throwing suspicion upon Boston as a cattle-shipping port. Mention was also made of investigations then in progress by agents of the United States as to the truth of the allegations. These investigations have been continued, and it is now believed that while this disease exists in certain sections of New York, New Jersey, Pennsylvania, Maryland, and Virginia, not a case of it has ever occurred west of the Alleghanies, and that the suspected cattle from Boston were affected by ordinary lung disease, induced by foul air on ship-board. But the apprehension of danger from the disease remains in full force, and, as a result, the Commissioners are frequently notified by private persons and municipal officers of supposed cases of it. In July, the select men of Lanesborough, in Berkshire County, requested us to examine the herd of a farmer of that town who had lost five animals, and had three others sick, the symptoms of which were thought to resemble those of this disease. The herd was examined and a post-mortem made of the animals, and the trouble found to be sporadic pneumonia. There have been other cases of lung difficulty, but none of them of the contagious type. The Commissioners entertain the opinion that there is little danger of the appearance of this malady in localities remote from the great lines of transportation. Inflammation of the lungs, or tuberculosis, may be engendered in the stock of any farm by undue exposure, want of ventilation, or confinement in damp and filthy enclosures. But contagious pleuro-pneumonia, which has symptoms resembling those diseases, is the result of contact with an animal possessing the infection, or with some object he has infected, and is disseminated from animal to animal, like small-pox or measles in the human family. The appearance of lung disease on remote and isolated farms, unless it can be traced to contact with animals from abroad, should cause no alarm, but should prompt their owners to a careful hygienic examination of their premises and methods of stock management. So long, however, as this cattle plague exists in four of our sister States, and their cattle are not forbidden to mingle in the great current of trade, so long there is danger of its dissemination along the lines of transit. Twenty years ago, and when it was widely spread through the State, Massachusetts "stamped" it out at an expense of more than two hundred thousand dollars, and not for the benefit of itself alone, but for the whole country; and it would appear that common interest, and comity between the States, should induce a like action where it now exists. The ravages of this disease in other countries have cost them millions of dollars, and to prevent a like result here is an object worthy the combined action of the State and National Governments.

To prevent the introduction of Spanish fever to our herds, the Legislature of 1876 enacted that no Texas or Cherokee cattle should be brought into the State between the 15th day of May and the 1st of November. Other States in the West, where it had caused great losses, had a similar statute; but, in a contested case before the United States court, in Missouri, it has, during the last year, been declared unconstitutional, because it attempted to interdict or control commerce between the States—a power possessed only by Congress. Assuming a like result would follow in a contested case in this State, and that our enactment was void, representations of the case were made to the Legislature at its recent special session for the revision of the Statutes, and the law complained of was stricken from the code. For it was substituted an Act giving the Commissioners power to take possession of all such cattle when brought within the State, and to confine them to the premises of the railroad transporting them, or to make such disposition of them as to prevent the exposure of our native cattle. Sufficient time has not elapsed to decide the efficiency of the Act, but it is apprehended that railroad interests and convenience will interpose serious obstacles to its enforcement. The dangerous and insidious disease of glanders in horses has not diminished since our last report. The germs of the disease appear to be quite generally diffused through the State, except in the south-eastern section, and in the counties of Berkshire and Franklin. The enactment of 1881, removing the obligation to appraise and pay for animals condemned and killed, has materially simplified the duty of the board, and must eventually diminish its expenditures; it wrongs no man, for the glandered horse is not only valueless to his owner, but a source of constant danger. The municipal officers of the towns or cities have called for the aid of the board in 57 cases; and of these 40 have been condemned and ordered to be killed. The Commissioners are firm in the belief that—as soon as horse-owners are cognisant of the fact that no compensations can be received for condemned animals, and that to call for their aid is simply to ask for an order for the death of the subject if found diseased—the owners or officers will destroy all pronounced cases, and hasten the work of suppression.

On the 25th September the selectmen of Charlemont, in Franklin County, notified the board of the existence of a malignant and apparently contagious disease in the swine of a farmer of that town, and requested us to take control of the same. The locality was visited, and an examination made of the diseased animals then living, and a post-mortem made of one which had died the day of the visit, which established the fact that the disease was hog cholera, or swine plague, and in all important respects identical with the scourge which has made such havoc in this class of stock at the West and South. The circumstances attending the development of the case were very unusual and peculiar; but to guard the public along the lines of rail transportation from the recurrence of a like calamity in the future, should be placed before the public. It appears that on or about the 12th of August a freight train on the Tunnel Railroad was derailed a short distance from the Charlemont depôt. In the train was a car-load of swine billed from the West to some slaughtering establishment near Boston. The animals were released from the cars by the accident; and the State agent of the railroad, to prevent them from straying away, caused them to be driven to, and secured in, the yards of Mr. E. C. Hawkes, a farmer, whose residence was less than a half-mile from the depôt. There were 170 of the animals, about 20 of which indicated sickness, or slight injuries from the accident, supposably the latter. After remaining in the yards of Mr. Hawkes two days, they were all forwarded to their destination, though several were so feeble that it was necessary to carry them to the cars. Mr. Hawkes was a large owner and breeder of choice swine, and at the time of the accident had, in his pens adjoining the yards where the Western hogs were confined, 118 of these animals of different ages. About ten days after the hogs from the railroad were removed, it was noticed that quite a number of them refused their food, appeared sick, and manifested behaviour quite like that of the supposed injured animals. The disease developed rapidly; numbers of them soon died, and it spread to all the pens and enclosures. Various remedies were tried without effect, and at the time the Commissioners were notified, more than half the stock had been lost.

Not knowing the disease with which his swine were troubled, or its cause, and hoping to save some of them, Mr. Hawkes had removed a number to an outlying farm two miles away, and turned them into an open field; but they carried the disease with them, and made another centre of contagion, causing serious alarm throughout the vicinity, to allay which, and remove the difficulty, appeared to require severe repressive measures. As chap. 24 of the Acts of 1878 had extended the powers and duties of the Commissioners for the suppression of contagion among cattle to " the prevention of contagious and infectious diseases among " domestic animals," and as this was surely such, and circumstances made it peculiarly dangerous, it was determined to apply the provisions of the law applicable to herds of cattle infested with contagious pleuro-pneumonia. Accordingly, on the 13th of October, the entire stock alive at that date, 15 in number, were slaughtered. Of these, six, on inspection, were adjudged free from disease, and were appraised and paid for. Measures were taken for the safe disposition of the carcasses of the diseased animals and the disinfection of the premises, and there have been no cases on the adjoining farms. That the disease was the dreaded swine plague of the West, and that it was communicated to Mr. Hawkes' stock by the animals taken from the cars, there is not a shadow of doubt. Through no fault of his own, for the hogs from the cars were taken to his yards in his absence, and without his consent, Mr. Hawkes met with a great pecuniary loss. The result should lead all to great caution against similar exposure. The last appropriation for the purposes of the Commission was $2,000.

There has been allowed and paid bills to the amount of $1,949, and there are now outstanding bills to the amount of $600, leaving a deficiency to be provided for of $549. The expenses incurred by the board the past year have been unusually large; caused by the greater number of calls for aid, the distance travelled, and the peculiar character of some of the cases. The eradication of glanders from one centre of infection at Taunton was effected only by an expenditure of $500. With the facts of the past year before us, if the work of the board is to be continued, we recommend an appropriation for the ensuing year of $2,500 in addition to the deficiency now existing.

(Signed)   LEVI STOCKBRIDGE,
E. F. THAYER,
H. W. JORDAN,
Commissioners on Contagious Diseases among Cattle.

Boston, January 10, 1882.

No. 10.

LETTER from the BRITISH CONSUL at Philadelphia to EARL GRANVILLE.

Sanitary, No. 6.   British Consulate, Philadelphia,
MY LORD,   April 12, 1882.

I HAVE the honour to report to your Lordship that since my Sanitary Despatch No. 4, of the 15th ultimo, upon the subject of diseases among cattle in this consular district, there has been no change either in the increase of pleuro-pneumonia or its diminution. The herds reported in that despatch as undergoing quarantine are still retained.

I have, &c.
(Signed)   ROBT. CHAS. CLIPPERTON.

The Right Hon. the Earl Granville, K.G.,
&c.   &c.   &c.

No. 11.

EXTRACT from LETTER from the BRITISH CONSUL at Philadelphia to EARL GRANVILLE.

Sanitary, No. 7.   British Consulate, Philadelphia,
MY LORD,   May 3, 1882.

I HAVE the honour to report to your Lordship that during the month of April there has been no change in the few small herds of cattle now under quarantine in the State of Pennsylvania affected with pleuro-pneumonia, and that no new cases have occurred.

I have, &c.
(Signed) ROBT. CHAS. CLIPPERTON.
The Right Hon. the Earl Granville, K.G.,
&c. &c. &c.

No. 12.

LETTER from the BRITISH CONSUL-GENERAL at New York to EARL GRANVILLE.

Sanitary, No. 11.   British Consulate General, New York,
MY LORD,   June 1, 1882.

I HAVE the honour to report to your Lordship, in regard to the sanitary condition of cattle, &c. in this consular district, that there has been no fresh outbreak of contagious disease reported during the past month.

The situation is practically the same as when I last reported to your Lordship.

I have, &c.
(Signed) E. M. ARCHIBALD.
Her Majesty's Principal Secretary of State
for Foreign Affairs.

No. 13.

LETTER from the ACTING BRITISH CONSUL-GENERAL at New York to EARL GRANVILLE.

Sanitary, No. 13.   British Consulate General, New York,
MY LORD,   July 31, 1882.

I HAVE the honour to report to your Lordship that, with the exception of Long Island, where cases of contagious pleuro-pneumonia occasionally manifest themselves, and are, as I am informed, at once isolated, this consular district may be considered free from disease among cattle.

I have, &c.
(Signed) J. PIERREPONT EDWARDS.
Her Majesty's Principal Secretary of State
for Foreign Affairs.

No. 14.

LETTER from the BRITISH CONSUL at Portland, Maine, to EARL GRANVILLE.

Sanitary, No. 9.   British Consulate, Portland (Maine),
MY LORD,   July 31, 1882.

I HAVE the honour to report to your Lordship that, according to information furnished me by the Maine Agricultural Society, there has not been any case of contagious or infectious disease amongst cattle, sheep, or pigs in the State of Maine during the month of July ended this day.

Several cases, however, of the "pink-eye" disease have lately occurred amongst horses in this district, and I am informed that this disease is yet prevailing to a considerable degree at Portland itself.

I have, &c.
(Signed)   WILLIAM WARD.

The Right Hon. the Earl Granville, K.G.,
&c.   &c.   &c.

No. 15.

LETTER from the ACTING BRITISH CONSUL at Baltimore to EARL GRANVILLE.

Sanitary, No. 8.

MY LORD,   Baltimore, August 1, 1882.

WITH reference to Mr. Consul Donohoe's Despatch, Sanitary No. 7, of the 23rd ultimo, in which he expressed the hope to be able to send a supplementary despatch containing the Governor's reply to an allegation by the United States Treasury Cattle Commission that pleuro-pneumonia *did* exist in the State of Maryland, the Governor having denied that any cattle disease prevailed in his State during the past six months, I have the honour to report that the Governor entirely ignored the statement of the Commission above referred to, and having made no reply to the same, gives the impression that he was mistaken in making such a sweeping statement.

From the State Cattle Inspector I learn that 10 cases of pleuro-pneumonia in dairy stables had been brought to his notice during the past month, and that the 10 animals were slaughtered to prevent further infection. The disease in this State and Virginia seems to be well under control, and is decreasing. No cattle intended for export are ever taken from either of these two States.

I have also the honour to report the development of some few cases of "pink-eye" amongst horses in this city during the past week. Should the infection increase I shall not fail to report to your Lordship.

The disease "pink-eye" was fully reported upon in Mr. Consul Donohoe's Despatch, Sanitary No. 12, of the 8th November 1881.

I have, &c.
(Signed) T. W. LAWFORD.

The Right Hon. the Earl Granville, K.G.,
&c. &c. &c.

No. 16.

LETTER from the ACTING BRITISH CONSUL at Philadelphia to EARL GRANVILLE.

Sanitary, No. 10. British Consulate, Philadelphia,
MY LORD, August 9, 1882.

I HAVE the honour to report to your Lordship that during the last month there have been no cases of pleuro-pneumonia among cattle within the States composing this consular jurisdiction.

Another disease, however, has shown itself among cattle in Berks County, Pennsylvania, within the past few days, and which proves fatal within a few hours after the animals are attacked. It is reported that in none of the cases so far occurring has a single animal recovered, and a herder engaged in the skinning of an animal became inoculated with the poison by getting some of the animal's blood into a cut upon his hand, and died of lockjaw after terrible agony. It is reported that the blood of the animals dying of this disease rapidly turns black.

A veterinary surgeon of the neighbourhood states that he has noticed slight symptoms of the disease for some time past, and thinks that it starts in the head and then descends to the spleen. He, therefore, terms it apoplexy of the spleen. It is believed to be contagious. The animals drop dead in the field or in the stable after but a few hours' sickness.

In two townships, North Heidelberg and Jefferson, where the disease up to this date is confined, 42 animals have died within a fortnight. The horns of the afflicted animals are burned by the veterinary surgeons, who become sick at the stomach in consequence of the stench emitted. The carcasses swell up immediately after death and throw off a fearful odour.

Pigs are also attacked by this disease, and the farmers lance them by plunging a knife into the back of their necks. It is stated that the disease is destined to prove more fatal than either rinderpest or pleuro-pneumonia. Thus far it is not known where the disease originated. Some assert that it was introduced by imported cattle.

The action of the virus upon the human system is sudden, causing great pain, inability to take food; the arms and lower limbs swell, and dark blotches break out on the skin. The sores are burned with caustic. The dead animals are no longer skinned, but are at once taken to the woods and buried.

The farmers who have lost cattle fumigate and otherwise disinfect their premises, while others keep their herds in the stables as a protection against infection.

I have, &c.
(Signed) GEORGE CRUMP.
The Right Hon. the Earl Granville, K.G.,
&c. &c. &c.

No. 17.

LETTER from the Hon. L. S. SACKVILLE WEST to EARL GRANVILLE.

Sanitary, No. 35.
My Lord, Washington, August 12, 1882.

YOUR Lordship will have been informed by the Acting Consul at Philadelphia of the outbreak of a new cattle disease in North Heidelberg township, Bucks County, Pennsylvania. This epidemic completely puzzles the veterinary surgeons, as the animals show no sign of disease before dropping dead, and it is said that the cows continue to give milk as usual until the last moment of life, a fact which necessitates extreme caution in its usage. Measures will doubtless be taken to prevent the spread of this disease, which seems to have caused a panic in the district.

I have, &c.
(Signed) L. S. SACKVILLE WEST.
The Right Hon. the Earl Granville, K.G.,
&c. &c. &c.

No. 18.

LETTER from the BRITISH CONSUL at Portland, Maine, to EARL GRANVILLE.

Sanitary, No. 10. British Consulate, Portland (Maine),
My Lord, August 31, 1882.

I HAVE the honour to report to your Lordship that, according to information furnished to me by the Maine Agricultural Society, there has not been any case of contagious or infectious disease amongst cattle, sheep, or pigs in the State of Maine during the month of August ended this day.

The "pink-eye" disease, reported in my Despatch No. 9 of the 31st ultimo as prevailing to some extent among the horses in this district, has not yet disappeared; but it would seem that during the past month the number of fresh cases has been inconsiderable.

I have, &c.
(Signed) WILLIAM WARD.
The Right Hon. the Earl Granville, K.G.
&c. &c. &c.

No. 19.

LETTER from the ACTING BRITISH CONSUL-GENERAL at New York to EARL GRANVILLE.

Sanitary, No. 14.   British Consulate General, New York,
MY LORD,   August 24, 1882.

I HAVE the honour to report to your Lordship that Texan fever has recently broken out among cattle in Cayuga County, in the north-western part of this State, originating, as it is supposed, with Texas cattle recently pastured in the district; and that, so far, there have been about 20 fatal cases. The district in which the fever has manifested itself is said to have been strictly quarantined, and it is hoped that the spread of the disease will thereby be prevented.

I transmit, herewith enclosed, an extract from the New York Herald of this day on the subject.

No reports of contagious disease from other parts of this consular district have come under my observation since the date of my last report.

I have, &c.
(Signed)   J. PIERREPONT EDWARDS.
Her Majesty's Principal Secretary of State
for Foreign Affairs.

Enclosure in No. 19.

EXTRACT from the NEW YORK HERALD, August 24, 1882.

Texan Fever prevailing among the Herds of Cayuga County.—Quarantine to be enforced.

(By Telegraph to the Herald.)

Weedsport, N.Y., August 23, 1882.

ABOUT a week ago a peculiar cattle disease was discovered among a herd of native cattle a few miles south of this village. The cattle showed symptoms of Texan fever, and the owners immediately telegraphed to Governor Cornell and Professor Law, of Ithaca, for directions how to act. Mr. Law could not be reached, and the Governor was unwilling to act till satisfied that the disease amounted to a plague. Veterinary surgeons from Syracuse and Auburn made examinations and declared the disease caused by eating dry fibrous grasses, and not contagious. For several days the malady was confined to one pasture, and no particular alarm was felt here. Recently cattle near by have shown signs of disease, and, in answer to several despatches from Dr. Brown, editor of the Cayuga "Chief," John R. Page, and others, Governor Cornell sent Augustus Denniston, State Cattle Commissioner, and Dr. Thomas J. Herr, of New York, to make a full examination of the diseased cattle and take what measures may be required to keep the pest, if such it were found to be, from spreading. This morning these gentlemen arrived at Sennett, accompanied by J. V. Henderson, veterinary surgeon, of Syracuse, and at once went to the pasture where the cattle were first taken with the disease. These were carefully examined, and a cow that had died in an adjoining field the previous night was opened and all the vital organs examined. The surgeons not being willing to give an opinion till further examination, visited the farm of William Sheldon, where a herd of twenty-three were infected. A two-year-old heifer was slaughtered and a post-mortem made, and all the symptoms of Texan fever were plainly discovered. The spleen was found greatly enlarged, inflamed, and congested; the kidneys were in a very unhealthy state; the stomach impaired badly, being of a stony hardness. The lungs, heart, and liver were in an apparently normal condition. Temperature of cattle found to be only two or three degrees above normal. All are covered with countless bugs or ticks, but whether these are the cause of the malady Dr. Herr did not say, but by them he believed it might be transmitted. About twenty have thus far died, and more than thirty more have been directly exposed and show now the first signs of fever. None, however, have been attacked except those pasturing where Texan or Cherokee cattle were turned in early in the spring.

As soon as the surgeons pronounced the disease definitely Texan fever the county sheriff, in accordance with the statute, and by direction of Commissioner Denniston, took the entire control of the matter, charging the owners to establish a strict quarantine, and not allow other cattle to mingle with those already affected, nor these to leave the pastures they are now in. All persons, as far as possible, must be prevented from visiting the contaminated fields. The Board of Health of Auburn are daily endeavouring to prevent beef and milk from the towns of Brutus, Throop, and Sennett from coming into the city. Mr. Denniston stated to the correspondent of the "Herald" that the report of the surgeons would be laid before Governor Cornell immediately, and after careful consultation all necessary measures to prevent the contagion from becoming epidemic would be adopted. He thought it likely that all cattle now sick or that had been exposed would be slaughtered and the owners reimbursed. The neighbourhood of Sennett is noted for its fine cattle, and many herds of thoroughbreds are grazing near by, their owners feeling much alarm for their safety. It is feared, especially, that the disease may be carried to other herds by streams of water that flow through pastures along the banks of which hundreds of cattle are feeding. This is more alarming from the fact that sick cattle seek cool places, and often lie in streams, frequently being found dead there.

o 11711.

No. 20.

LETTER from the BRITISH CONSUL at Baltimore to EARL GRANVILLE.

Sanitary, No. 9.

MY LORD, Baltimore, September 1, 1882.

WITH reference to Mr. Acting Consul Lawford's Despatch, Sanitary No. 8, of the 1st ultimo, I have the honour to report that the State Cattle Inspector informs me that during the month of August there have been in the State of Maryland eight cases of pleuro-pneumonia in Baltimore and Montgomery Counties, and that he considers the disease at a standstill.

The cattle shipped from this port during the past month for Great Britain were 340 head on the S.S. "Thanemore" for London on the 24th ultimo. These cattle came from the west, and were directly put on board the steamer.

I have, &c.
(Signed) DENIS DONOHOE.

The Right Hon. the Earl Granville, K.G.,
&c. &c. &c.

No. 21.

LETTER from the ACTING BRITISH CONSUL-GENERAL at New York to EARL GRANVILLE.

Sanitary, No. 15. British Consulate General, New York,
MY LORD, September 4, 1882.

I HAVE the honour to report to your Lordship that since the date of my last sanitary despatch pleuro-pneumonia has made its appearance among the cattle at the north end of Hudson County in the State of New Jersey. The usual quarantine measures will, it is stated, be adopted by the State Commissioner, to confine the disease to its present locality.

As yet no animals are reported to have died.

I have, &c.
(Signed) J. PIERREPONT EDWARDS.

Her Majesty's Principal Secretary of State
for Foreign Affairs.

No. 22.

LETTER from the ACTING BRITISH CONSUL-GENERAL at New York to EARL GRANVILLE.

Sanitary, No. 16. British Consulate General, New York,
MY LORD, September 12, 1882.

I HAVE the honour to report to your Lordship that Texas fever has broken out among cattle in Schenectady County in this State. The disease is believed to have been contracted from

Texas cattle imported by a farmer in the town of Rotterdam two months ago, and it has spread to neighbouring herds. Two animals have already died, and many others are reported to be affected.

Referring to my Despatch, Sanitary No. 14, of the 24th ultimo, reporting the appearance of the same disease among cattle in Cayuga County, I have the honour to state that, owing to the energetic measures adopted by the State Cattle Commissioners and by the farmers themselves in promptly slaughtering the cattle attacked with the fever, it is believed that the disease has been now effectually stamped out in that locality.

I have, &c.
(Signed) J. PIERREPONT EDWARDS.

Her Majesty's Principal Secretary of State
    for Foreign Affairs.

No. 23.

EXTRACT from LETTER from the ACTING BRITISH CONSUL at Philadelphia to EARL GRANVILLE.

Sanitary, No. 11.   British Consulate, Philadelphia,
MY LORD,   September 13, 1882.

I BEG to report to your Lordship that during the month of August no cases of pleuro-pneumonia have occurred in the State of Pennsylvania, and that for the Western States of Ohio, Indiana, Iowa, Michigan, Illinois, and Wisconsin I have received no reports showing the existence of any contagious diseases among cattle.

With reference to the disease that broke out in Berks County, Pennsylvania, reported in my Despatch No. 10 Sanitary, I have nothing additional to add. Many conflicting statements are circulated as to the nature of the disease which proved so destructive in one or two localities.

I have, &c.
(Signed) GEORGE CRUMP.

The Right Hon. the Earl Granville, K.G.,
  &c.   &c.   &c.

No. 24.

LETTER from the BRITISH CONSUL-GENERAL at New York to EARL GRANVILLE.

Sanitary, No. 17.   British Consulate General, New York,
MY LORD,   September 28, 1882.

I HAVE the honour to acquaint your Lordship that since the date of Consul Edwards' last sanitary despatch, contagious pleuro-pneumonia in a virulent form has broken out among cattle on a farm at Staten Island in this State. Eight cows have died, and the authorities have caused several others to be slaughtered.

The farm in question has been closely quarantined by the State agent, to prevent the communication of the disease to other cattle in the vicinity.

In regard to other parts of this consular district, no further reports of contagious disease among cattle have come under notice since the last report was made to your Lordship.

I have, &c.
(Signed) E. M. ARCHIBALD.

Her Majesty's Principal Secretary of State
    for Foreign Affairs.

No. 25.

LETTER from the BRITISH CONSUL at Portland, Maine, to EARL GRANVILLE.

Sanitary, No. 12.   British Consulate, Portland (Maine),
MY LORD,   October 1, 1882.

I HAVE the honour to report to your Lordship that, according to information furnished to me by the Maine Agricultural Society, there has not been any case of contagious or infectious disease amongst cattle, sheep, or pigs in this State during the month of September ended yesterday.

The "pink-eye" disease prevalent amongst the horses (referred to in my Despatch No. 10 of August 31st last) is considered to be about dying out; and only a very few cases are reported to have occurred throughout this district during the past month.

I have, &c.
(Signed) WILLIAM WARD.

The Right Hon. the Earl Granville, K.G.,
    &c.   &c.   &c.

No. 26.

LETTER from the BRITISH CONSUL at Baltimore to EARL GRANVILLE.

Sanitary, No. 10.

MY LORD,   Baltimore, October 2, 1882.

WITH reference to my Despatch, Sanitary No. 9, of the 1st ultimo, I have the honour to report that the State Cattle Inspector informs me that the total number of cases of pleuro-pneumonia during the past month in the State of Maryland have been nine; the number of these cattle slaughtered has been two, and that he considers the disease as increasing, and that he is unable to control it on account of not having sufficient authority from the Governor of the State.

There has been no export of cattle to the United Kingdom during the past month from this port.

I have, &c.
(Signed) DENIS DONOHOE.

The Right Hon. the Earl Granville, K.G.,
&c. &c. &c.

No. 27.

LETTER from the BRITISH CONSUL-GENERAL at New York to EARL GRANVILLE.

Sanitary, No. 18.   British Consulate General, New York,
MY LORD,   October 30, 1882.

I HAVE the honour to report to your Lordship that, since the date of my last Sanitary Despatch (No. 17, of September 28th), there have been no further reports, which have come under my observation, of contagious disease among cattle in this consular district.

I have, &c.
(Signed) E. M. ARCHIBALD.

Her Majesty's Principal Secretary of State
for Foreign Affairs.

No. 28.

LETTER from the BRITISH CONSUL-GENERAL at New York to EARL GRANVILLE.

Sanitary, No. 19.   British Consulate General, New York,
MY LORD,   November 9, 1882.

I HAVE the honour to report to your Lordship that an outbreak of typhoid fever has occurred during the past few days on a dairy farm at Secaucus, at the north end of Hudson County, New Jersey, which has been attended with considerable mortality among the stock. Out of 92 cows and 5 horses on the farm, 22 of the former and 2 of the latter have died. The Local Board of Health have been notified, and measures have been taken to prevent the spread of the disease.

I have, &c.
(Signed) E. M. ARCHIBALD.

Her Majesty's Principal Secretary of State
for Foreign Affairs.

No. 29.

LETTER from the BRITISH CONSUL at Baltimore to EARL GRANVILLE.

Sanitary, No. 11.

My Lord, Baltimore, November 9, 1882.

WITH reference to my Despatch, Sanitary No. 10, of the 2nd ultimo, I now have the honour to report that the State Cattle Inspector informs me that the total number of cases of pleuro-pneumonia during the past month in the State of Maryland have been 11, besides 4 of Texas fever. The number of diseased cattle slaughtered have been 13; that he considers the disease at a standstill, and that the Governor of the State is doing his utmost to eradicate the disease.

I have, &c.
(Signed) DENIS DONOHOE.

The Right Hon. the Earl Granville, K.G.,
&c. &c. &c.

No. 30.

LETTER from the ACTING BRITISH CONSUL at Philadelphia to EARL GRANVILLE.

Sanitary, No. 13. British Consulate, Philadelphia,
My Lord, November 11, 1882.

WITH reference to my Despatch, No. 12 Sanitary, of October 19th last, I beg to report to your Lordship that the disease among cattle near Lancaster, State of Pennsylvania, has, upon official investigation, been pronounced, not pleuro-pneumonia, but impaction of the rumen. The symptoms of this disease would appear to farmers similar to those of pleuro-pneumonia, having the grunting and cough, caused by pressure on the diaphragm. But one animal died out of a number of cases. The disease is attributed to feeding large quantities of dry food while the animals were in low condition.

No reports of pleuro-pneumonia having occurred in any part of this consular district during the month of October have reached this consulate.

I have, &c.
(Signed) GEORGE CRUMP.

The Right Hon. the Earl Granville, K.G.,
&c. &c. &c.

No. 31.

LETTER from the BRITISH CONSUL-GENERAL at New York to EARL GRANVILLE.

Sanitary, No. 20. British Consulate General, New York,
My Lord, November 29, 1882.

I HAVE the honour to report to your Lordship, that since the date of my last sanitary despatch, No. 19, of the 9th instant, there have not been, so far as I have been able to ascertain, any cases of contagious disease among cattle reported in this consular district.

I have, &c.
(Signed) E. M. ARCHIBALD.
Her Majesty's Principal Secretary of State
for Foreign Affairs.

No. 32.

LETTER from the BRITISH CONSUL at Baltimore to EARL GRANVILLE.

Sanitary, No. 12.
MY LORD, Baltimore, December 1, 1882.
WITH reference to my Despatch, Sanitary No. 11, of the 9th ultimo, I have the honour to report that I have learned from the Cattle Inspector of the State of Maryland that the only cases of cattle disease, pleuro-pneumonia, were four in Baltimore County, of which number one was slaughtered, and that in the dairy districts of the same county there are a number of chronic cases of the same disease.

None of the cattle of this State are ever exported to Europe.

I have, &c.
(Signed) DENIS DONOHOE.
The Right Hon. the Earl Granville, K.G.,
&c. &c. &c.

No. 33.

LETTER from the BRITISH CONSUL at Philadelphia to EARL GRANVILLE.

Sanitary, No. 14. British Consulate, Philadelphia,
MY LORD, December 12, 1882.
I HAVE the honour to report to your Lordship that no cases of pleuro-pneumonia have occurred within this consular district during the month of November.

A report was published in the "Breeders Gazette" as follows:—
"Pleuro-pneumonia has appeared among the cattle at Lan-
"caster, Pennsylvania. S. H. Saunders, of Chicago, Secre-
"tary of the Cattle Commission, pronounces Baltimore and the
"farms adjacent a hot-bed of the disease."

Immediately upon hearing of this report steps were taken to investigate the matter. The Secretary of the Board of Agriculture of the State of Pennsylvania has written to the Veterinary Surgeon, Dr. Gadsden, of this city, stating that the report above referred to related to the supposed cases near the city of Lancaster, reported by Acting Consul Crump in his Despatch, Sanitary

No. 13, and pronounced, not pleuro-pneumonia, but impaction of the rumen. The State Inspector, Dr. Bridge, has started for Hanover, in the interior of the State of Pennsylvania, to investigate a reported case of pleuro-pneumonia. Should he find this to be a genuine case of pleuro-pneumonia, it will be the first that has occurred in this consular district since May of the present year.

I have, &c.
(Signed) ROBT. CHAS. CLIPPERTON.

The Right Hon. the Earl Granville, K.G.,
&c. &c. &c.

No. 34.

LETTER from the BRITISH CONSUL-GENERAL at New York to EARL GRANVILLE.

Sanitary, No. 21.

British Consulate General, New York,
December 30, 1882.

MY LORD,

I HAVE the honour to report to your Lordship that the disease known as the "dry epizooty" has recently broken out in some stables belonging to an Express company in Camden, New Jersey, and has affected a considerable number of horses. So far, however, no fatal cases have been reported, although the disease is said to be of a severe character.

In regard to cattle, no cases of contagious disease in this consular district have come to my knowledge since the date of my last report.

I have, &c.
(Signed) E. M. ARCHIBALD.

Her Majesty's Principal Secretary of State
for Foreign Affairs.

No. 35.

LETTER from the BRITISH CONSUL at Baltimore to EARL GRANVILLE.

Commercial, No. 1.

MY LORD, Baltimore, January 2, 1883.

WITH reference to my Despatch, Sanitary No. 12, of the 1st ultimo, I have the honour to report that I have learned from the State Cattle Inspector that six cases of pleuro-pneumonia have been developed during the past month, but that, generally speaking, the disease is decreasing in this State. Inoculation is now being practised, and results are looked forward to with much interest.

I have, &c.
(Signed)   DENIS DONOHOE.
The Right Hon. the Earl Granville, K.G.,
&c.   &c.   &c.

No. 36.

LETTER from the BRITISH CONSUL at Philadelphia to EARL GRANVILLE.

Commercial, No. 1.   British Consulate, Philadelphia,
MY LORD,   January 4, 1883.

I HAVE the honour to report to your Lordship that no cases of pleuro-pneumonia among cattle have occurred within the State of Pennsylvania during the month of December, nor in any of the Western States of this consular district.

During the past nine months there have been no cases of acute pleuro-pneumonia in Pennsylvania. A few cases of chronic pleuro-pneumonia were discovered, but in all the cases the animals were slaughtered and the farmer paid therefor.

Since the year 1879, when the Act of the Legislature for the prevention of the spread of pleuro-pneumonia and other contagious disease among cattle was passed, the total expenditure by the State authorities was $14,098.61, or 2,800*l.*, disbursed as follows:—

	$	c.
Expenses under resolution, &c.	456	78
Surgeons' fees and expenses	4,017	32
Amount paid for animals slaughtered	4,784	35
Special agent's salary and expenses	4,036	73
Office expenses	803	43
	$14,098	61

I have, &c.
(Signed)   ROBT. CHAS. CLIPPERTON.
The Right Hon. the Earl Granville, K.G.,
&c.   &c.   &c.

No. 37.

LETTER from the INSPECTOR OF THE PRIVY COUNCIL at Liverpool to PROFESSOR BROWN.

SIR,   Birkenhead, January 30, 1883.

I BEG to inform you that the "Kansas," from Boston, landed this morning at Wallasey Wharf 313 cattle and 398 sheep, and that on examining them this afternoon I found 219 cattle affected with foot-and-mouth disease, and six sheep affected with scab.

I am, &c.
(Signed)   JOHN W. T. MOORE.

The diseased animals are being slaughtered as quickly as possible, and all sanitary precautions enforced.

No. 38.

LETTER from the ACTING BRITISH CONSUL-GENERAL at New York to EARL GRANVILLE.

Commercial, No. 2.

British Consulate General, New York,
February 1, 1883.

MY LORD,

I HAVE the honour to acquaint your Lordship that no reports of contagious disease among cattle in this consular district have come under my observation during the past month.

The disease among horses in Camden, New Jersey, referred to in Sir Edward Archibald's Despatch (Sanitary No. 21) of the 30th of December last has also disappeared.

I have, &c.
(Signed)   J. PIERREPONT EDWARDS.

Her Majesty's Principal Secretary of State
for Foreign Affairs.

No. 39.

LETTER from the BRITISH CONSUL at Baltimore to EARL GRANVILLE.

Commercial, No. 4.

MY LORD,   Baltimore, February 1, 1883.

WITH reference to my Despatch, Commercial No. 1, of the 2nd ultimo, I have the honour to report that I have learned from the State Cattle Inspector that eight cases of pleuro-pneumonia have been developed during the past month, that eight cattle have been slaughtered, and that he considers the disease decreasing. All the cases were in Baltimore County, and there were no other cases in the State of Maryland. He also writes as follows:—

"My mode of inoculation is as prescribed by the English authors, Fleming's especially. The result has been very satisfactory. I inoculate in the tail; however, I prefer slaughtering when it is possible or convenient to do so; it saves expense and trouble and there is no danger of its spreading."

I have, &c.
(Signed)   DENIS DONOHOE.

The Right Hon. the Earl Granville, K.G.,
&c.   &c.   &c.

No. 40.

LETTER from the INSPECTOR OF THE PRIVY COUNCIL at Liverpool to PROFESSOR BROWN.

SIR,	Birkenhead, February 9, 1883.

I BEG to inform you that the " Mentmore," from Baltimore, landed this morning at Wallasey Wharf 149 cattle and 482 sheep (18 thrown overboard), and that on examining them this afternoon I found 14 sheep affected with foot-and-mouth disease. The diseased sheep were at once slaughtered, and the usual precautions taken.

I am, &c.
(Signed)	JOHN W. T. MOORE.

No. 41.

LETTER from the INSPECTOR OF THE PRIVY COUNCIL at Liverpool to PROFESSOR BROWN.

SIR,	Birkenhead, February 19, 1883.

I BEG to inform you that the " Norseman," from Boston, landed this day 281 cattle and 727 sheep at Woodside Wharf, and that on examining them I found 13 sheep affected with foot-and-mouth disease. A large number of cattle and sheep have been lost on the passage, and there are still some dead cattle and sheep on board, which will be landed late this evening, so that my examination of these carcases will not be completed till to-morrow when I will report fully. The diseased animals will be slaughtered this evening. I have taken the usual precautions.

I am, &c.
(Signed)	JOHN W. T. MOORE.

No. 42.

LETTER from the INSPECTOR OF THE PRIVY COUNCIL at Liverpool to PROFESSOR BROWN.

SIR,	Birkenhead, February 20, 1883.

IN continuation of my letter of yesterday's date, I beg to report that the " Norseman," from Boston, landed at Woodside Wharf 287 cattle, 14 carcases, and 727 sheep and 8 carcases. There were 58 cattle and 164 sheep thrown overboard. I examined the carcases this morning and found them free from disease. I have arranged with Mr. Proctor for the part of the wharf occupied by the sheep to be closed for one week.

I am, &c.
(Signed)	JOHN W. T. MOORE.

No. 43.

LETTER from the ACTING BRITISH CONSUL at Portland, Maine, to EARL GRANVILLE.

Commercial, No. 2.

British Consulate, Portland (Maine),
January 31, 1883.

MY LORD,

I HAVE the honour to report to your Lordship that, according to information received from the Secretary of the Board of Cattle Commissioners of the State of Maine, there has not been any case of contagious or infectious disease among horses, cattle, or sheep during the month of January 1883.

I am informed, by the same official, that the disease known as hog cholera has, to some extent, prevailed among swine in the county of Kennebec, deaths to the number of 75 or more having resulted from this disease.

I have, &c.
(Signed) GEO. E. BIRD.

The Right Hon. the Earl Granville, K.G.,
&c. &c. &c.

No. 44.

LETTER from the BRITISH CONSUL at Baltimore to EARL GRANVILLE.

Commercial, No. 6.

MY LORD, Baltimore, March 1, 1883.

WITH reference to my Despatch, Commercial No. 4, of the 1st ultimo, I have the honour to report that the State Cattle Inspector informs me that six cases of pleuro-pneumonia have occurred during the past month; that none of these cattle have been slaughtered; that all the cases have been in Baltimore county of this State; that he considers the disease decreasing, but that it is always existing in the dairy district near this city, and that within that district only he resorts to inoculation.

I have, &c.
(Signed) DENIS DONOHOE.

The Right Hon. the Earl Granville, K.G.,
&c. &c. &c.

No. 45.

LETTER from the INSPECTOR OF THE PRIVY COUNCIL at Liverpool to PROFESSOR BROWN.

SIR, Birkenhead, March 15, 1883.

I BEG to inform you that the "Kansas," from Boston, landed last night at Woodside Wharf 416 sheep, and that on examining them this morning I found 55 of them affected with sheep-scab.

There were also landed 456 cattle, and it may be interesting to note that none of the animals showed any symptoms of foot-and-mouth disease. Last voyage 219 out of 313 cattle were diseased.

I am, &c.
(Signed)   JOHN W. T. MOORE.

No. 46.

LETTER from the BRITISH CONSUL at Baltimore to EARL GRANVILLE.

Commercial, No. 8.

My Lord,   Baltimore, April 2, 1883.

WITH reference to my Despatch, Commercial No. 6, of the 1st ultimo, I have the honour to report that I am informed by the State Cattle Inspector that, whilst no new cases of pleuro-pneumonia amongst cattle have been reported during the past month, the disease does still exist, especially amongst dairy cattle in the vicinity of this city, but that it is materially decreasing.

I have, &c.
(Signed)   DENIS DONOHOE.

The Right Hon. the Earl Granville, K.G.,
&c.   &c.   &c.

No. 47.

LETTER from the BRITISH CONSUL at Boston to EARL GRANVILLE.

Commercial, No. 6.

My Lord,   Boston, April 10, 1883.

I HAVE the honour to report that, as far as information has been received here, this consular district has continued free from cattle plague during the past month, and no contagious or infectious disease exists among animals in the district.

In connexion with this subject, I have the honour to enclose the report for the year 1882 of the Massachusetts Commissioners on Contagious Diseases among Cattle to the Legislature of the State.

I have, &c.
(Signed)   C. A. HENDERSON.

Her Majesty's Principal Secretary of State
   for Foreign Affairs.

CORRESPONDENCE.

Enclosure 1 in No. 47.

Senate No. 7.

Sir, Boston, January 9, 1883.

I HEREWITH transmit to you, for the use of the Legislature, the annual report of the Commissioners on Contagious Diseases among cattle.

I am, &c.
(Signed) LEVI STOCKBRIDGE,
Chairman.

Hon. George G. Crocker,
President of the Senate.

Enclosure 2 in No. 47.

COMMONWEALTH OF MASSACHUSETTS.

Annual Report of the Commissioners on Contagious Diseases among Cattle, 1882.

To the Honourable Senate and House of Representatives of the Commonwealth of Massachusetts.

The Commissioners on Contagious Diseases among Cattle, in submitting their annual report, are happy in being able to convey the information that the past year has been one of almost unparalleled prosperity to every department of our neat-stock interest. As in former years, the municipal officers of many towns and cities have notified our board of supposed contagious disease within their jurisdisdiction; but an examination proved in all cases that such was not the fact, and that the diseases, though in some places causing considerable individual loss, were ordinary sporadic complaints, the causes of which were purely local, and with no contagious or even epidemic character. The known fact that contagious pleuro-pneumonia exists in several States of the Union between which and ourselves there is more or less exchange of cattle, and that our railroad connexions are such that Spanish fever may be brought here by any stock-train from the cattle-ranges of Texas, causes a constant apprehension among the owners of neat-stock, especially when their animals are of great value. Therefore, when any distemper afflicts their herds with some symptoms similar to those of the diseases named, alarm takes the place of apprehension, which calls for the services of the Commission, and which it is very difficult to allay. Though for the last three or four years these fears have been groundless, yet the fact remains, that we are in constant danger, and shall continue so, until by the action of the National or State Government, or of both combined, the former of these diseases is eradicated from our territory. Our citizens have enormous pecuniary interests in the cattle-ranges of the Western plains, the stock of which can be preserved from this disease only by untiring vigilance. The losses by it in Australia have amounted to more than a hundred million of dollars; but this loss is small compared with what must ensue if it should make its appearance among the countless cattle of the far West. We cannot refrain from calling the attention of the Legislature to these facts, and intimating that our interests call for some action to awaken the general government to the adoption of a comprehensive plan to ensure the public safety.

The efforts of the Commissioners during the last three years, and the modification of the laws relating thereto, appear to have produced the desired results of diminishing the disease called glanders, and the cost of controlling it. During the year 1881, we were called by municipal officers to take charge of 57 cases, in 40 of which the animals were condemned, and ordered to be killed. The present year we have been called to 12 cases, and have caused seven animals to be killed, in addition to which three have been killed by the selectmen of different towns without the interference of the Commissioners. The Legislature of 1882 appropriated two thousand dollars for the purposes of the Commission that year. Of this sum there has been expended in bills paid or now outstanding six hundred and sixteen dollars and fifty cents ($616.50), leaving an unexpended balance of thirteen hundred and eighty-three dollars and fifty cents ($1,383.50). If by the provisions of law this balance now reverts to the general treasury, it will be necessary that another appropriation be made, and as a measure of safety against emergencies which are liable to occur, it should not be less than that of 1882, though it is hoped there would be no occasion for its expenditure.

(Signed)   LEVI STOCKBRIDGE,
E. F. THAYER,
H. A. JORDAN,
Commissioners on Contagious Diseases among Cattle.

No. 48.

LETTER from the BRITISH CONSUL at Philadelphia to EARL GRANVILLE.

Commercial, No. 3.   British Consulate, Philadelphia,
MY LORD,   April 21, 1883.

SINCE writing Despatch No. 2 Commercial, I beg to inform your Lordship that a case of foot-and-mouth disease broke out on the farm of Mr. Samuel C. Kent, West Grove, Chester County, a county adjoining Philadelphia, in the State of Pennsylvania, and contiguous to two commercial ports, Baltimore and Philadelphia. Eighty-two head, composing the herd, all took the disease, one animal dying. The herd was placed in, and now remains in, strict quarantine. The disease was not communicated to any other animal, and after careful inquiry it can be accepted as a fact that there is not another case of the disease in the State of Pennsylvania.

This case is the only one for the past three years, when a single herd was afflicted, the disease being traced to a single animal, an imported cow from Liverpool at Philadelphia. Previous to the last-mentioned case, the disease was unknown in Pennsylvania.

The herd belonging to Mr. Kent was a direct importation from Liverpool to Baltimore, per S.S. "Nessmore," the animals landing March 18th, and taken directly to Mr. Kent's farm by a herder from England, and under the charge of a United States officer, having come into no contact with any other animals. The animals arrived at the farm on the 19th, and on the following day a large number were found suffering with foot-and-mouth disease. The steamer that brought these animals out was laden on her return voyage with cattle for slaughter in England. It is reported here that these animals were found on arrival in England to have symptoms of the disease among them, and that they took the disease in consequence of occupying the same stalls on board ship.

Particular attention has been called in this country to the motion of his Grace the Duke of Richmond and Gordon in the House of Lords on the 16th instant, with reference to hoof-and-mouth disease as existing in the United States.

A United States Commission was appointed last year to investigate the subject of this disease of foot and mouth in the Western States of this country, and they reported their inability to find a single case, or any evidence of the existence of the disease whatever. I beg to enclose to your Lordship a copy of a letter I have this day received from J. W. Gadsden, M.R.C.V.S., a veterinary surgeon of very extensive practice among cattle, and well known both in England as an inspector under the Diseased Animals' Act and in the United States as a Government Inspector for the prevention of the spread of contagious diseases in cattle.

I have, &c.
(Signed) ROBT. CHAS. CLIPPERTON.
The Right Hon. the Earl Granville, K.G.,
&c. &c. &c.

Enclosure in No. 48.

SIR, Philadelphia, April 20, 1883.

I NOTICED by the published despatches that a statement was made in the House of Lords, England, on the 16th instant, by the Duke of Richmond and Gordon, that a contagious disease among cattle, known as the foot-and-mouth disease, was prevalent to a considerable extent in this country. As I have made a specialty of inquiring into contagious and infectious diseases in animals in this country, and being constantly in communication with veterinary practitioners in different parts of the United States for the purpose of detecting and tracing diseases of this character, I deemed it my duty to contradict this statement, as the disease does not at present exist in this country. The report evidently has its origin from the introduction of the disease into this State from England about a month ago, under the following circumstances:—

The steamer "Nessmore," of the Johnson line, which left Liverpool with a herd of Guernsey cattle, arrived in Baltimore, Maryland, on the 18th of March. The animals, 82 in number at that time, were placed on cars in bond and brought to West Grove, Chester County, Pennsylvania, there to be placed in quarantine for three months, as the laws of the United States require shall be done with all imported cattle. They arrived there on the 19th, and on the 20th, the animals being sick, Dr. Bridge, a veterinary surgeon of this city, and the inspector for the State, was called to examine them, and found them, with hardly an exception, suffering with foot-and-mouth disease. This, except in the case of one animal which died, readily yielded to treatment, and the residue of the herd have entirely recovered, although still kept in strict quarantine. The cars on which they were shipped were thoroughly disinfected with quicklime, and the animals themselves from the time of leaving the ship were kept carefully secluded from all other cattle, so that not another case has been reported. The steamer, however, was at once reloaded with American cattle, and immediately thereafter sailed for England, and it is natural to presume that the infection remaining in the ship contaminated these animals, thus giving rise to the report.

If the disease existed in any other State I would have received information of it through my correspondents.

In former years, in every instance in which the disease has appeared in any part of this country, it has been traced directly to animals imported from England.

From all information which I can gather from the most reliable sources, the disease is entirely unknown in the Western States, from which the great bulk of the cattle exported are brought direct to the port of shipment.

It is an act of simple justice that such a statement should not be acted upon until careful inquiry has been made as to its truth, and I am convinced that if an investigation is ordered, it will be found that the report will be found to be totally unsupported by facts.

I have, &c.
(Signed) J. W. GADSDEN, M.R.C.V.S.

Capt. Robert C. Clipperton,
H.B.M. Consul, Philadelphia.

No. 49.

LETTER from the BRITISH CONSUL at BALTIMORE to EARL GRANVILLE.

Commercial, No. 10.

My Lord,   Baltimore, May 1, 1883.

WITH reference to my Despatch, Commercial No. 8, of the 2nd ultimo, I have the honour to state that the cattle inspector of this district reports that eight cases of pleuro-pneumonia amongst cattle have been developed during the past month, and these cases exist only amongst the dairy cattle in this vicinity, also that every possible means will be resorted to with a view to eradicating the disease in the coming summer.

I have, &c.
(Signed)   DENIS DONOHOE.

The Right Hon. the Earl Granville, K.G.,
&c.   &c.   &c.

No. 50.

LETTER from the BRITISH CONSUL-GENERAL at NEW YORK to EARL GRANVILLE.

Commercial, No. 6.

My Lord,   British Consulate General, New York, May 21, 1883.

I HAVE the honour to state, for your Lordship's information, that it has been publicly announced that the new cattle quarantine station at Plainfield, New Jersey, established by the United States Board of Commissioners for inspecting Foreign Cattle, to prevent the introduction of cattle disease at this port, will be ready for use by the 1st of July next, and that on and after that date all imported animals arriving in New York will be sent there for veterinary examination.

I have, &c.
(Signed)   WM. LANE BOOKER.

Her Majesty's Principal Secretary of State
for Foreign Affairs.

No. 51.

LETTER from the BRITISH CONSUL-GENERAL at NEW YORK to EARL GRANVILLE.

Commercial, No. 7.

My Lord,   British Consulate General, New York, May 31, 1883.

I HAVE the honour to report to your Lordship that the sanitary condition of cattle in this section of my consular district remains generally good. So far as I can ascertain, there have been no published reports of contagious disease during the past month.

I have addressed to the authorities of the Western States and territories in my district an inquiry as to the existence of pleuro-pneumonia among cattle there, and will report hereafter in regard to those States.

I have, &c.
(Signed) WM. LANE BOOKER.

Her Majesty's Principal Secretary of State
for Foreign Affairs.

No. 52.

LETTER from the BRITISH CONSUL at Baltimore to EARL GRANVILLE.

Commercial, No. 12.

MY LORD, Baltimore, June 1, 1883.

WITH reference to my Despatch, Commercial No. 10, of the 1st ultimo, I have the honour to report that I have received a communication from Dr. Lemay that he has given up his position as State Cattle Inspector. The appointment, from what I learn, will be filled up in a few days, and I hope will be given to an experienced Fellow of the Royal College of Veterinary Surgeons, London, who is an applicant for it.

The only cases of pleuro-pneumonia in this district are in the immediate neighbourhood of the city, amongst the "dairy" cattle, and are usually from six to eight each month.

I have every hope that, with the appointment of an experienced man as cattle inspector, it will be stamped out.

I have, &c.
(Signed) DENIS DONOHOE.

The Right Hon. the Earl Granville, K.G.,
&c. &c. &c.

No. 53.

LETTER from the BRITISH CONSUL-GENERAL at New York to EARL GRANVILLE.

Commercial, No. 9.

British Consulate General, New York,
MY LORD, June 18, 1883.

IN reference to my Despatch, No. 7 Commercial, of the 31st May, I have the honour to advise your Lordship that the authorities of the States of Kansas, Nebraska, and Colorado, and the territories of Wyoming, Utah, and Dacotah, report that pleuro-pneumonia has not shown itself among the cattle of those States and territories. Kansas and Nebraska have State boards of agriculture, Utah has an agricultural society, Wyoming has a system of veterinary inspection, which is stated to be very perfect. The inspector reports that during the past year he has personally examined the condition of cattle over the greater part of the territory; that his inspection has covered many thousands, including not only the herds indigenous to Wyoming, but all cattle of both sexes which have been brought in from other States and territories.

I have, &c.
(Signed) WM. LANE BOOKER.
Her Majesty's Principal Secretary of State
for Foreign Affairs.

No. 54.

LETTER from the BRITISH CONSUL-GENERAL at New York to EARL GRANVILLE.

Commercial, No. 10.

British Consulate General, New York,
June 20, 1883.

MY LORD,
I HAVE the honour to enclose copies of a circular which I have received from the Customs authorities of this port, embodying regulations governing the treatment and quarantine of imported cattle.

I have, &c.
(Signed) WM. LANE BOOKER.
Her Majesty's Principal Secretary of State
for Foreign Affairs.

Enclosure in No. 54.

Circular.

REGULATIONS governing the TREATMENT and QUARANTINE of IMPORTED CATTLE.

Treasury Department, Washington, D. C.,
June 8, 1883.

TO COLLECTORS AND OTHER OFFICERS OF THE CUSTOMS:

1. All cattle arriving in the United States from Europe, Asia, Africa, Australia, or New Zealand shall be subjected to a quarantine of ninety days, counting from the date of shipment.

It shall be the duty of the veterinary inspector at each port to see that the cattle imported shall be securely guarded against the risk of transmitting or receiving contagion until they shall have entered the quarantine grounds, and all imported cattle shall be under his control from the time of landing until they reach the quarantine grounds. He shall also be superintendent of the quarantine, and shall have charge of the grounds, buildings, yards, and all property thereto belonging.

Collectors of Customs are requested to co-operate with the veterinary inspectors and health authorities in enforcing these regulations, and will take such action as the facts and regulations may require.

2. Imported cattle shall be examined by the Government veterinary inspector before they leave the wharves, and if any are there found to be suffering from any of the following diseases —lung plague, rinderpest, aphthous (eczematous) fever—they shall not be admitted to the established quarantine grounds, but shall be quarantined elsewhere, at the expense of the importer, or be dealt with in such other manner as the veterinary inspector, in co-operation with the State or municipal authorities, shall determine.

3. In case of imported animals proving to be thus infected, such portions of the cargo of the vessel as have been exposed to the cattle or their emanations shall be subjected, under the direction of an inspector, to fumigation with the gas from burning sulphur, or to such other disinfection as may be considered by the veterinary inspector of the port necessary, before they can be landed.

4. No litter, fodder, or other aliment, nor any ropes, straps, chains, girths, blankets, poles, buckets, or other things used for or about the animals, and no manure, shall be landed, excepting under such regulations as the veterinary inspector shall provide.

5. On moving cattle from the ocean steamer to the quarantine grounds they shall not be unnecessarily passed over any highway, but must be placed on the cars at the wharves, or removed to the cars on a boat which is not used for conveying other cattle. If such boat has carried sheep, goats, or swine within three months antecedent, it must be first cleansed and then disinfected under the supervision of the veterinary inspector, and after the conveyance of the imported cattle the boat shall be disinfected in the same manner before it can be again used for the conveyance of cattle. The expense of such disinfection shall be paid by the United States. When passage across or upon a public highway is unavoidable in the transportation of imported cattle from the place of landing to the quarantine grounds, it must be under such careful supervision and restrictions as the veterinary inspector may, in special cases, direct.

6. The banks or chutes used for loading and unloading imported cattle shall be reserved for such animals, or shall be cleansed and disinfected, as above, before and after being used for such imported cattle.

7. The railway cars used in the transportation of cattle to the quarantine grounds shall either be cars reserved for this exclusive use or box cars not otherwise employed in the transportation of meat animals or their fresh products, and after each journey with cattle to the quarantine grounds they shall be disinfected by thorough cleansing and disinfecting under the direction of the Government veterinary inspector. The charge for such disinfection shall be paid by the United States.

8. While cattle are arriving at the quarantine stations, or leaving them, all quarantined stock in the yards adjoining the alley ways through which they must pass shall be rigidly confined to their sheds.

9. Cattle arriving by the same ship may be quarantined together in one yard and shed, but those coming on different ships shall, in all cases, be placed in separate yards.

10. The gates of all yards shall be kept locked, except when cattle are entering or leaving quarantine.

11. The attendants on cattle in particular yards are forbidden to enter other yards and buildings, except such as are occupied by stock of the same shipment with those under their special care. No dogs, cats, or other animals, except those necessarily present, shall be allowed in the quarantine grounds.

12. The allotment of yards shall be under the direction of the veterinary inspector of the port, who shall keep a register of the cattle entered, with description, name of owner, name of vessel in which imported, date of arrival and release, and other important particulars.

13. The veterinary inspector shall see that water is regularly furnished to the stock, and the manure removed daily, and that the prescribed rules of the station are enforced.

14. Food and attendance must be provided by the owners of the stock quarantined. Employés of such owners shall keep the sheds and yards clean, to the satisfaction of the veterinary inspector.

15. "Smoking" is strictly forbidden within any quarantine inclosure.

16. No visitor shall be admitted to the quarantine station without special written permission from the Collector of Customs of the port, the veterinary inspector, or a member of the Treasury Cattle Commission. Butchers, cattle dealers, and their employés are especially excluded.

17. No public sale shall be allowed within the quarantine grounds.

18. The inspector shall, in his daily rounds, so far as possible, take the temperature of each animal, commencing with the herds that have been longest in quarantine, and ending with the most recent arrivals, and shall record such temperatures on lists kept for the purpose. In passing from one herd to another he shall invariably wash his thermometer and hands in a weak solution (1 to 100) of carbolic acid.

19. In case of the appearance of any disease that is diagnosed to be of a contagious nature, the veterinary inspector shall notify the chairman or other professional member of the Treasury Cattle Commission, who shall visit the station personally or send a delegate, and, on the confirmation of the diagnosis, the herd shall be disposed of according to the gravity of the affection.

20. If the disease should prove to be one of the exotic plagues —lung plague or rinderpest—the animals shall be dealt with in

such manner as the veterinary inspector, in co-operation with the State or municipal authorities, shall determine.

21. The yard and shed in which such disease shall have appeared shall be subjected to a thorough disinfection. Litter and fodder shall be burned. Sheds, utensils, and other appliances shall be disinfected as the veterinary inspector may direct. The yard fence and manure box shall be freely sprinkled with a strong solution of chloride of lime. The flooring of the shed shall be lifted, and the whole shall be left open to the air, and unoccupied for three months.

22. If the contagious disease shall prove to be aphthous fever, anthrax, Texas fever, cow-pox, diphtheria, or scabies, the infected herd shall be rigidly confined to its shed, where disinfectants shall be freely used, and the attendants shall be forbidden all intercourse with the attendants in other yards and with persons outside the quarantine grounds.

CHAS. J. FOLGER,
Secretary.

No. 55.

LETTER from the BRITISH CONSUL-GENERAL at New York to EARL GRANVILLE.

Commercial, No. 11.

British Consulate General, New York,
MY LORD, June 26, 1883.

I HAVE the honour to report to your Lordship that pleuro-pneumonia has recently made its appearance among cattle on a farm near New Dorp, Staten Island, in this State; but at present no fatal cases have been reported. The cattle have been quarantined by the health authorities, with the view of preventing the spread of the disease.

I have, &c.
(Signed) WM. LANE BOOKER.

Her Majesty's Principal Secretary of State
for Foreign Affairs.

No. 56.

LETTER from the BRITISH CONSUL at Baltimore to EARL GRANVILLE.

Commercial, No. 15.

MY LORD, Baltimore, July 2, 1883.

WITH reference to my Despatch, Commercial No. 12, of the 1st ultimo, as to cattle plague, I have the honour to report that there are still a few cases of pleuro-pneumonia amongst the dairy cattle which are kept in stables about the city.

I fear that unless there is some fresh legislation, giving full power to the State Inspector to order the slaughter of animals affected with this disease, it will be impossible to stamp it out in this State.

I have, &c.
(Signed) DENIS DONOHOE.

The Right Hon. the Earl Granville, K.G.,
&c. &c. &c.

No. 57.

LETTER from the BRITISH CONSUL-GENERAL at New York to EARL GRANVILLE.

Commercial, No. 12.

British Consulate General, New York
July 11, 1883.

MY LORD,

REFERRING to my Despatch, Commercial No. 11, of the 26th ultimo, I have the honour to report to your Lordship that, notwithstanding the precautions taken by the local authorities, pleuro-pneumonia among the cattle on Staten Island appears to be steadily increasing in the district comprising the towns of Middleton, Westfield, Castleton, Smithfield, and Northfield. Upwards of 40 cattle are reported to have died of the disease, which is not confined to inferior cattle, but is found to prevail also among the select stock kept for private use. Stringent efforts are being made to stamp out the disease.

I have, &c.
(Signed) WM. LANE BOOKE.

Her Majesty's Principal Secretary of State
for Foreign Affairs.

No. 58.

LETTER from the BRITISH CONSUL at Philadelphia to EARL GRANVILLE.

Commercial, No. 8.

British Consulate, Philadelphia,
July 13, 1883.

MY LORD,

SINCE writing my "nil" cattle disease return for the month of June, I beg to call your Lordship's attention to a telegraphic report, two copies of which are herewith enclosed, that the disease glanders has broken out in 19 counties of the State of Illinois.

As glanders is highly contagious and infectious, as well as fatal, and the State having within its borders 1,023,082 head of horses of all breeds, the existence of this disease within the State is likely to be a public calamity unless the authorities of the Commonwealth take immediate steps to stamp it out.

I have, &c.
(Signed) ROBT. CHAS. CLIPPERTON.
The Right Hon. the Earl Granville, K.G.,
&c. &c. &c.

Enclosures in No. 58.

IF it be true that the horses in 19 counties in Illinois are afflicted with glanders the sooner that all the sick animals are destroyed the sooner all other Illinois horses will be regarded as beasts safe to buy and work. Until the disease is absolutely and wholly stamped out no one will venture to buy a horse from Illinois. It is true economy to kill the comparative few so afflicted.

THE Illinois State Veterinarian reports that glanders is prevalent among the horses in 19 counties in that State. He claims to have been prevented from killing the animals afflicted, the attorneys of the owners contending that he could only resort to this measure after the Governor had issued a proclamation declaring the glanders epidemic.

No. 59.

LETTER from PROFESSOR JAMES LAW to PROFESSOR BROWN.

United States Treasury Cattle Commission, Ithaca,
DEAR SIR, July 24, 1883.

IN view of the resolution recently passed in Parliament that no live cattle should be imported from countries in which foot-and-mouth disease exists, I take the liberty, as Chairman of the Treasury Cattle Commission, of drawing your attention to the fact that we can find no evidence of the existence of the disease in question in the United States. I make this statement, not as a simple assumption, based on a general belief or on the fact that no public complaint is made of the malady, but corroborated as it is by a most extended investigation conducted along the whole line of our cattle traffic from the Western Plains to the Eastern Seaboard, and by continued observation, up to the present, of the great eastern cattle marts at the terminus of our cattle traffic, and of the city dairies, which are continually replenished from these terminal marts. Permit me to call your attention to the evidence contained in our printed report accompanying this of the nature and extent of our investigation, made along the lines of cattle traffic two years ago, as showing how impossible it would have been for a disease so contagious as aphthous fever, and one marked by such prominent and unmistakable symptoms, to have existed along the line of our cattle traffic without detection. Had it been present, it could not have failed to show itself along a channel of transportation which it takes six days and upward to traverse, much less could it have escaped becoming localised and detected in the city dairies, the distillery, and other feeding stables, and in the herds of dairying districts along the line of travel.

Our Commission is in frequent receipt of information from all parts of the United States concerning diseases of stock supposed to be contagious, yet, apart from the cases to be referred to below, we have not had a single complaint of foot-and-mouth disease.

Dr. Thayer and I hold State appointments besides, which bring contagious diseases under our notice, yet neither of us has heard of this disease apart from the cases noted below.

I have lately made a number of personal observations in the great markets of New York and Jersey City, the terminus of our inland cattle traffic, but I have not been able to find a single case of this affection. So with regard to the city dairies at these places and at Baltimore.

Now the unwonted manifestations of this disease could not be passed over in silence by the American stockowner. In 1871, when it was imported into Montreal in two English shorthorns, when it entered the United States at Buffalo and Ogdensburg, and spread with great rapidity over Northern New York and New England, it produced a veritable panic. That invasion occurred in autumn, and was extinguished during the prolonged stabulation of the herds in the long northern winter that followed. But the great body of our farmers, even in the then infected States, have never seen the disease, and among these the consternation resulting from a renewed invasion would be as great to-day as it was in 1871.

Beside the invasion of 1871, I have only found the aphthous fever in this country on two occasions: the first was two years ago, when the S.S. "France" landed at New York a herd of Channel Island cattle direct from England, and in the acute stages of foot-and-mouth disease. They were secluded by the State authorities and the disease stamped out; but the steamer, after a supposed disinfection, was loaded with American cattle, which on their arrival in England were found to be suffering from the same plague. The second instance occurred in March last, when the S.S. "Nessmore" landed at Baltimore a herd of Channel Island cattle suffering from the aphthous fever. These were secluded, and the disease passed no further. The steamer, however, after a liberal dressing with quicklime and carbolic acid, was loaded with American cattle, and these on arrival in England were found to be suffering from foot-and-mouth disease, and became the occasion of questions in Parliament as to the arrival of diseased animals from America.

It is well known that on other occasions American beeves have been infected by the old and contaminated head-ropes brought from the English ports and used for the cattle on the return voyage to England.

I write to you thus freely as to a scientific man, above the bias of scribblers who would dismiss this letter as being merely the product of a party advocate. I trust you have followed my record closely enough to see and acknowledge that I have never sought to deny nor cover up the existence of contagious disease among American cattle. For 15 years I have been publicly proclaiming the existence of the cattle lung plague on a part of our eastern seaboard, and the report I send you bears witness that when State agents and governors have erroneously proclaimed their respective States free from this pestilence I have promptly and publicly denounced the error, confronted its authors with the exposure of cases of the disease in the so-called purified States, and called for an intelligent and thorough system of extinction. You will bear me witness that I have never complained of the compulsory slaughter of American cattle at English ports; my complaint has uniformly been that this great country should continue to give occasion for this handicapping of her immense western cattle industry, and to endanger this growing industry for all time by allowing the maintenance of the lung plague among what is comparatively but a mere handful of stock in the east.

This public denunciation of the lung plague will be extended to the foot-and-mouth disease the moment I find that that too has become domiciled on our territory. And in both cases the denunciation will be made in the interests of America and the American cattle industry. I would as soon think of closing the wound made by the fangs of a rabid dog without a preliminary cauterization as to deny or ignore either of these plagues when planted on American soil.

I have been delegated by the Commissioner of Agriculture at Washington to attend the forthcoming International Veterinary Congress at Brussels, and if my duties here will allow me to cross the Atlantic, I hope soon to have the pleasure of conferring with you in person.

Very respectfully,
Professor G. Brown. (Signed) JAMES LAW.

No. 60.

LETTER from the BRITISH CONSUL-GENERAL at New York to EARL GRANVILLE.

Commercial, No. 14.

British Consulate General, New York,
July 31, 1883.

MY LORD,

I HAVE the honour to report to your Lordship that, with the exception of Staten Island in this harbour, where contagious pleuro-pneumonia is reported still to exist among cattle, this consular district is generally free from such disease.

CORRESPONDENCE.

Many horses in the car stables in Brooklyn, and in Newark, New Jersey, have recently become affected with glanders. The diseased animals have been ordered to be shot.

I have, &c.
(Signed) WM. LANE BOOKER.

Her Majesty's Principal Secretary of State
for Foreign Affairs.

No. 61.

LETTER from the Hon. L. S. SACKVILLE WEST to EARL GRANVILLE.

Commercial, No. 202.

My Lord, Washington, August 3, 1883.

I HAVE the honour to enclose to your Lordship herewith printed copies of a Treasury circular respecting the importation of neat cattle into the United States, dated 30th of July.

I am informed that the regulations contained in this circular are substantially the same as those which existed before the passing of the new Tariff Bill, which, as it annulled all previous legislations on this subject, rendered their reinforcement necessary.

I have, &c.
(Signed) L. S. SACKVILLE WEST.

The Earl Granville, K.G.,
&c. &c. &c.

Enclosure in No. 61.

IMPORTATION OF NEAT CATTLE.

Department No. 104.

Treasury Department, Washington, D.C.
July 30, 1883.

To Collectors of Customs and others:

Sections 2493 and 2495 of the Revised Statutes, re-enacted in the Act approved March 3, 1883, as sections 2494 and 2495 respectively (page 6, T. I., new,) provide as follows:

§ 2494. "The importation of neat cattle and the hides of neat cattle from any foreign country into the United States is prohibited: Provided that the operation of this section shall be suspended as to any foreign country or countries, or any parts of such country or countries, whenever the Secretary of the Treasury shall officially determine, and give public notice thereof, that such importation will not tend to the introduction or spread of contagious or infectious diseases among the cattle of the United States; and the Secretary of the Treasury is hereby authorised and empowered, and it shall be his duty, to make all necessary orders and regulations to carry this law into effect, or to suspend the same as therein provided, and to send copies thereof to the proper officers in the United States, and to such officers or agents of the United States in foreign countries as he shall judge necessary."

§ 2495. "Any person convicted of a wilful violation of any of the provisions of the preceding section shall be fined not exceeding five hundred dollars, or imprisoned not exceeding one year, or both, in the discretion of the court."

An Act of March 3, 1883, page 613, Statutes of Second Session of 47th Congress, makes the following appropriation:

"To enable the Secretary of the Treasury to co-operate with State and municipal authorities and corporations and persons engaged in the transportation of neat cattle by land or water in establishing regulations for the safe conveyance of such cattle from the interior to the seaboard, and the shipment thereof, so that such cattle may not be exposed to the disease known as pleuro-pneumonia or lung plague, and to prevent the spread of said disease, and to establish quarantine stations, and provide proper shelter for neat cattle imported, at such ports as he may deem necessary, fifty thousand dollars."

Although sections 2494 and 2495 of the Revised Statutes as incorporated in the Act of March 3, 1883, are not materially changed, they have the force of new law, and the Secretary of the Treasury, by virtue thereof, hereby gives public notice that he has officially determined that the importation of neat cattle, subject to the conditions herein-after prescribed, will not tend to the introduction or spread of contagious or infectious diseases among the cattle of the United States. The operations of the sections of law prohibiting the importation of neat cattle and the hides of neat cattle into the United States are therefore suspended, but upon the condition that importers and owners of neat cattle shall submit to and abide by such orders and regulations as the Secretary of the Treasury has prescribed, or may from time to time prescribe, to carry the above laws into effect. All existing orders of the Department under the sections which have been revised will remain in force under the present provisions, except as herein modified.

All neat cattle arriving in the United States from any part of the world, except North and South America, will be subjected to a quarantine of 90 days, counting from the date of shipment. As the Dominion of Canada maintains quarantine for all imported cattle, no quarantine for cattle imported from Canada is provided.

For general information, it is deemed proper to state that permanent arrangements have been completed for quarantine accommodations of imported neat cattle as follows: At Deering, for Portland, Maine, for about 215 head; at Waltham, for Boston, Mass., for about 300 head; at Garfield, New Jersey, for New York, for about 450 head; and at Baltimore, Md., for about 350 head, full-grown animals, and that these arrangements will be extended as may be deemed necessary.

As each importation is kept isolated from all others, full numbers cannot always be accommodated, while larger numbers than the above estimates of small animals may be received.

It is obviously impossible to provide at each port for all the cattle that may be imported into the whole country, and all will see the necessity of using the accommodations, where not only shelter is provided at large expense, but veterinary inspectors or custodians are employed at annual salaries.

Experience already shows that importers have preferences as to the place of quarantine, so that the station at one port is full while that at another is nearly empty.

Importers of cattle, therefore, in order to secure accommodations at the port where the cattle are imported, should give notice to the collector of the expected importation, so as to secure quarantine accommodations, which will be provided in the order in which notice thereof is given. If, owing to lack of accommodations, cattle cannot be quarantined at the port where they arrive, they will be transferred, at the expense of the importer, to some other quarantine station where sufficient accommodations do exist, preference being given to stations where there is no danger of infection. Where there are more cattle for quarantine than the regular Government stations can accommodate, special arrangements for quarantine outside the stations may be made by the Collector of the port where they arrive upon consultation with the Cattle Commission or the superintendent in charge. The order by which importers have been allowed to quarantine cattle at such points as they might select, where cattle could be transported by water, is rescinded, and all imported cattle will be quarantined at the Government stations, except as above provided.

Consular officers abroad to whom this circular may be sent are requested to bring its contents to the notice of shippers of cattle, so that they may be fully informed of the regulations of this Department upon the subject before making shipments.

(Signed)   H. F. FRENCH,
Acting Secretary.

No. 62.

TELEGRAM from the INSPECTOR OF THE PRIVY COUNCIL at Liverpool to PROFESSOR BROWN.

August 9, 1883.

"BULGARIAN," from Boston, landed last night, Woodside Wharf, 482 cattle, one carcase, four overboard. Found two cases Splenic Fever, and three cases this morning. Sent by post last night box containing specimens. Arranged last night for manure in wharf to go to sea, whether from diseased animals or not, and arranged with shipping company this morning for sending manure on ship to sea, and notified sanitary officer who saw carcases last night.

No. 63.

During the months of August, September, October, and November, 1883, 28 cargoes of animals in which Texan Fever (splenic fever) was found to exist were landed at the port of Liverpool, and a tabular statement is here inserted, instead of printing the telegrams and letters received from the Inspector merely announcing in each instance the fact of the landing of animals affected with Texan Fever.

Tabular Statement.

Vessel.	From.	Landed Alive.	Landed Dead.	Thrown Overboard.	Diseased.
"Bulgarian"	Boston	482	1	4	156
"Missouri"	Boston	948	—	5	248
"Victoria"	Boston	619	—	1	307
"Mentmore"	Baltimore	475	—	25	297
"Istrian"	Boston	552	—	—	256
"Norseman"	Boston	860	1	2	211
"Bavarian"	Boston	476	—	8	60
"Palestine"	Boston	502	—	—	58
"Iberian"	Boston	540	1	9	74
"Humaco"	Baltimore	156	—	4	27
"Kansas"	Boston	976	—	—	132
"Murciano"	Baltimore	269	2	91	41
"Nessmore"	Baltimore	506	—	—	61
"Belgravia"	New York	434	—	16	53
"Iowa"	Boston	809	2	3	33
"Illyrian"	Boston	545	—	—	103
"Virginian"	New York	710	5	30	57
"Oranmore"	Baltimore	498	—	2	10
"Bulgarian"	Boston	478	—	10	25
"Missouri"	Boston	939	—	14	27
"Norseman"	Boston	886	2	13	22
"Istrian"	Boston	543	1	2	1
"Venetian"	New York	737	—	7	25
"Victoria"	Boston	846	1	15	28
"Palestine"	Boston	417	—	3	28
"Iberian"	Boston	532	—	10	13
"Kansas"	Boston	975	2	—	7
"Istrian"	Boston	398	1	2	4
		17,108	19	276	2,364

CORRESPONDENCE.

No. 64.
LETTER from the Hon. L. S. SACKVILLE WEST to EARL GRANVILLE.

Commercial, No. 208.

My Lord,   Washington, August 15, 1883.

WITH reference to my Despatch, No. 204 Commercial, of the 5th instant, I now have the honour to transmit an official copy of the Report of the United States Treasury Cattle Commission relative to the foot-and-mouth disease, which I have received from the Treasury Department.

I have, &c.
(Signed)   L. S. SACKVILLE WEST.

The Right Hon. the Earl Granville, K.G.,
&c.   &c.   &c.

Enclosure 1 in No. 64.

REPORT of UNITED STATES TREASURY CATTLE COMMISSION relative to the FOOT-AND-MOUTH DISEASE.

Department No. 106.

Treasury Department, Washington, D.C.,
August 4, 1883.

To COLLECTORS OF CUSTOMS AND OTHERS.

A RESOLUTION having been adopted by the British House of Commons opposing the importation into Great Britain of cattle from any country in which the foot-and-mouth disease prevails, and charges having been made in Parliament that such disease prevails in this country, an investigation has been made by the United States Treasury Cattle Commissioners, who find that there **is no evidence** that American herds are now suffering from the disease. **The report of the Commissioners is hereto appended.**

Should you at any time learn of the existence of such disease in this country, you will please inform this Department of the particulars without delay.

(Signed)   H. F. FRENCH,
Acting Secretary.

Enclosure 2 in No. 64.

United States Treasury Cattle Commission,
Sir,   Boston, Mass., July 21, 1883.

CHARGES having been recently made in the British Parliament that cattle were being shipped from our ports infected with the foot-and-mouth disease, and a majority of the House of Commons having voted for a resolution opposing the importation into Great Britain of cattle from any country in which said disease exists, we feel it our duty to state the facts of the case so far as this country is concerned.

After a most extended and almost exhaustive inquiry, your Commission have been able to find no trace of foot-and-mouth disease apart from herds just landed from Great Britain, and which herds have been in every case segregated until the infection has entirely disappeared. The nature and scope of our inquiry may be deduced from out Report for 1881. Beginning with the great rendezvous of cattle at Kansas City, Council Bluffs, and Omaha, we have made careful investigations along all the lines of cattle traffic as far as the eastern seaboard. In this investigation we have included all the great stockyards where cattle are detained for feeding, watering, sale, &c.; all the great feeding-stables connected with distilleries and starch, glucose, and other factories; all the city dairies where stockyards exist and where the herds are replenished from such stockyards, and to a large extent the great dairying districts, into which cows are drawn from the above-named stockyards and lines of travel. Up to the present date we have made observations in the stockyards at the seaboard—the terminal end of our cattle traffic, and that to which all infection must gravitate; but, apart from the imported cases above referred to, we have been unable to find a single case of the foot-and-mouth disease complained of.

The significance of the entire absence of this disease along the whole line of our cattle traffic and in the herds into which this traffic leads can only be appreciated when considered in its relation to the nature of the disease and the unmistakable symptoms by which it is manifested. The following points are especially to be noted:—

1st. The foot-and-mouth disease is perhaps the most contagious malady known. It rarely enters a herd without striking down all the members of that herd simultaneously, or nearly so.

2nd. The susceptibility to the disease is all but universal on the part of worm-blooded animals, but all cloven-footed animals are especially, and about equally, predisposed to it. It cannot be overlooked nor covered up, therefore, as can a disease which confines its ravages to a single genus, but sheep, goats, and swine coming within the range of the infection contract and manifest the disease as readily and in as marked a way as do cattle.

3rd. The period of latency on incubation is remarkably short, the eruption of the malady often taking place in 36 hours, and rarely being delayed, even in cold weather, beyond six days after exposure to infection. There is, therefore, no opportunity for concealment nor for the disposal of infected but still apparently sound animals, while a journey of four or six days from the west, with the attendant privations and febrile excitement, would infallibly determine the full eruption of the disease before the stock arrived at the eastern seaboard, and this although the infection had only been received after the shipment on the cars.

4th. The manifestation of the disease is not only so universal in the herd affected, but so prominent and unmistakable that it could not possibly be overlooked. No one could ignore for a moment

o 11711.

the swollen digits, the lameness, and the blisters or ulcers between the hoofs; the heat, tenderness, swelling, and blisters or raw sores on the udder and teats, and the abundant frothing and slobbering at the mouth; the frequent loud smacking noise made with the tongue and palate, and the large round blisters or red angry sores on the mucous membrane of the mouth. These cannot escape the attention of the owners and attendants, and especially when a whole herd of 10, 50, or 100 are suffering simultaneously. Much less can they escape the instructed eye of the professional veterinarian.

In this connexion it may be well to state that the invasion of foot-and-mouth disease that swept from Canada over Northern New York and New England in 1871 created something closely approaching a panic. The agricultural papers were full of the subject, State boards of agriculture convened and discussed the subject, a convention of delegates from different States met at Albany, N.Y., and it was the engrossing theme for every local farmers' club along the line of infection. This invasion, imported into Montreal with two English cows, fortunately occurred in autumn, and the long seclusion of the herds during the ensuing winter virtually stamped it out, the infection not having extended beyond herds in enclosed pasturages or buildings. Most of our farmers are as ignorant of the disease to-day as they were in 1871, and any new invasion could not fail to produce a similar excitement and consternation.

It should be added that our connexion with the States, as well as the United States, brings us constant complaints of diseases supposed to be contagious, but we have not found any evidence of the actual existence of the foot-and-mouth disease at any point among our home herds.

We cannot pass unnoticed the two latest importations of the disease from England. Two years ago the steamship "France," of the National Line, landed in New York a herd of Channel Island cattle suffering from foot-and-mouth disease. These were quarantined by the State authorities, and the infection stamped out. The "France," however, after an attempted disinfection, shipped a cargo of American beeves for the return voyage, and these, on arrival in England, were condemned as being infected with foot-and-mouth disease. This was undoubtedly contracted on board ship. The second case is that of the steamship "Nessmore," which, in March 1883, landed in Baltimore a herd of Channel Island cattle suffering from foot-and-mouth disease. These again were secluded, as soon as detected, by the Pennsylvania authorities, and no evil consequences to our home herds can be traced. But the steamship "Nessmore," after an attempted disinfection by the agents, shipped a cargo of American fat cattle, and these, on arrival in England, were found to be suffering from foot-and-mouth disease. This infection, unquestionably contracted on board ship, appears to have been the main, if not the sole, occasion of the recent questions and resolution in the British Parliament. That the infection was not derived from American herds, but from English, is beyond all dispute, alike in this case and in that of the "France," two years ago. The same is true of our extensive invasion in 1871, which was derived from two imported short-horn cows, and which was thoroughly extinguished without having gained any permanent foothold.

We do not deny that other cargoes of American cattle may have been found suffering from the disease in question on arrival in England, but this is amply accounted for by the occasional use for these cattle of head-ropes and other appliances that have been previously used for European cattle. But on this point we insist with the greatest confidence that there is no evidence whatever that our American herds are now suffering from foot-and-mouth disease, and that there is as strong evidence of its non-existence as can well be produced on the negative side of a question.

(Signed)   JAMES LAW,
E. F. THAYER,
United States Treasury Cattle Commissioners.

Hon. C. J. Folger,
    Secretary of the Treasury.

No. 65.

LETTER from the CLERK OF THE COUNCIL to the FOREIGN OFFICE.

(No. 80437.)

Agricultural Department, Privy Council Office,
44, Parliament Street, Westminster, S.W.,
August 16, 1883.

SIR,

I AM directed by the Lords of the Council to request that you will have the goodness to move Lord Granville that the immediate attention of the American Government may be called to the fact that the following vessels arriving at the port of Liverpool have brought animals which, on examination after landing, were found to be affected with Texan fever, namely, August 8th, the "Bulgarian" from Boston—August 14th, the "Missouri" from Boston—August 14th, the "Victoria" from Boston—and August 15th, the "Mentmore" from Baltimore.

I am, &c.
(Signed)   C. L. PEEL.

The Under Secretary of State,
    &c.   &c.

NOTE.—Letters to the above effect were sent to the Foreign Office whenever Texan Fever was discovered in the various cargoes that were subsequently landed in this country.

No. 66.

LETTER from the INSPECTOR OF THE PRIVY COUNCIL at London (Deptford) to PROFESSOR BROWN.

Park Lodge, Lee Green,
August 16, 1883.

SIR,

I BEG to report that on the 14th instant the S.S. "Persian Monarch" arrived at Deptford with 721 cattle from New York. On examination, two of the animals were found to be unwell, and were slaughtered in consequence.

From the post-mortem appearances, I have reason to believe they were the subjects of the disease known as splenic fever, in which I am confirmed by the opinion of Mr. Duguid, who had previously seen the disease at Liverpool.

The "Ludgate Hill" steamer also arrived on the 15th from New York with 574 cattle, two of which were similarly affected, and presented like appearances when slaughtered. Three others of the first-mentioned cargo have since been attacked with the disease, and slaughtered in consequence.

I have caused especial care to be taken with regard to disinfecting the manure, in which, I believe, the great risk of danger lies.

The cargoes are in course of slaughter, but unfortunately the trade is bad, so that this is not being carried out so quickly as could be desired.

I may add that the "Persian Monarch" lost 48 cattle on the voyage, and the "Ludgate Hill" 20.

I am, &c.
(Signed) S. G. HOLMANS.

No. 67.

LETTER from the FOREIGN OFFICE to the CLERK OF THE COUNCIL.

SIR,

Foreign Office, August 18, 1883.

I AM directed by Earl Granville to acknowledge the receipt of your letters of the 16th and 17th instant relative to animals affected with Texan Fever which have been landed in this country. I am to request that you will inform the Lords of the Council that copies of these letters will be sent to-day to Her Majesty's Minister at Washington with instructions to call the immediate attention of the United States Government to the matter.

I am, &c.
(Signed) EDMOND FITZMAURICE.

The Clerk of the Council,
 Veterinary Department.

No. 68.

LETTER from the BRITISH CONSUL-GENERAL at New York to EARL GRANVILLE.

Commercial, No. 15.

British Consulate General, New York,
August 24, 1883.

MY LORD,

I HAVE the honour to report to your Lordship that contagious pleuro-pneumonia has made its appearance among cattle in the southern part of the State of Connecticut. The disease is at present confined to two herds, and is said to have been brought there by a cow purchased in the State of New Jersey. The New York State Cattle Commissioners have directed both herds to be quarantined, and it is hoped thereby that the spread of the disease will be prevented.

There are also, it is publicly reported, cases of this disease in Brooklyn and in other parts of Long Island, in regard to which similar measures of quarantine have been adopted.

I have, &c.
(Signed) WM. LANE BOOKER.

Her Majesty's Principal Secretary of State
for Foreign Affairs.

No. 69.

MEMORANDUM from the INSPECTOR OF THE PRIVY COUNCIL at Bristol to PROFESSOR BROWN.

September 15, 1883.

DETECTED two cases of Splenic Fever (texan fever), one in each of the cargoes ex "Rhodora" from New York, landed on the 12th September, and ex "Cornwall" from New York, landed on the 14th September.

Every precaution taken with respect to manure, litter, &c.

No. 70.

LETTER from the BRITISH CONSUL at Philadelphia to EARL GRANVILLE.

Commercial, No. 9.   British Consulate, Philadelphia,
MY LORD,   September 17, 1883.

I HAVE to report that the disease pleuro-pneumonia has appeared amongst the cattle in Delaware, Chester, and York Counties, in the State of Pennsylvania.

So far, about 350 head of cattle in these counties have been affected, a dozen of which have been killed after a report of their condition from Doctor Bridge, the Official Veterinary Surgeon of the State Board of Agriculture.

Doctor Bridge states that about one fourth of the animals affected would die or become so diseased that it would be necessary to kill them; in Chester County 47 out of a herd of 50 head have the disease, and in other cases the per-centage is as large.

Doctor Bridge, who is directed as soon as the disease appears to make a careful and thorough examination of all the circumstances, says he has traced the disease in every case to a herd of cattle brought from Baltimore by one, John Noble, and sold in West Chester. Doctor Bridge thinks he has the disease well in hand, and that there is no fear of its spreading beyond the present centre of contagion. Except the three counties mentioned, there is no trace of the disease reported in this State.

I have, &c.
(Signed) ROBT. CHAS. CLIPPERTON.

The Right Hon. the Earl Granville, K.G.,
&c. &c. &c.

No. 71.

LETTER from the INSPECTOR of the PRIVY COUNCIL at London (Deptford) to PROFESSOR BROWN.

Foreign Cattle Market, Deptford,
September 18, 1883.

SIR,
I BEG to report the arrival here yesterday of 639 cattle ex S.S. "Assyrian Monarch" from New York, the whole of which were in an apparently healthy condition (and remain so), with one exception, which was in a dying condition when landed, and died very shortly afterwards.

The post-mortem examination of this animal has revealed a condition precisely similar to those ex S.S. "Persian Monarch" and "Ludgate Hill" on the 14th and 15th ultimo, which I reported at the time as being the subjects of splenic fever.

I may state that the "Assyrian Monarch" is reported to have lost only one other animal on the voyage.

I am, &c.
(Signed) S. G. HOLMANS.

CORRESPONDENCE.

No. 72.

LETTER from the BRITISH CONSUL-GENERAL at New York to EARL GRANVILLE.

Commercial, No. 16.

Her Britannic Majesty's Consulate-General,
New York, September 24, 1883.

MY LORD,

WITH reference to my Despatch, Commercial No. 15, of the 24th ultimo, I have the honour to state that, notwithstanding the precautionary measures adopted by the State authorities, two further cases of pleuro-pneumonia among cattle are reported on different farms at Salem, Connecticut.

Rigid quarantine of the infected district will continue to be enforced.

I have, &c.
(Signed) WM. LANE BOOKER.

Her Majesty's Principal Secretary of State
for Foreign Affairs.

No. 73.

LETTER from the ACTING BRITISH CONSUL at Portland, Maine, to EARL GRANVILLE.

Commercial, No. 15.

British Consulate, Portland (Maine),
October 1, 1883.

MY LORD,

I HAVE the honour to report to your Lordship that, according to information received from the local sanitary authorities, there has been no case of contagious or infectious disease amongst cattle or other animals in this State during the month of September last past, with the exception of one case of contagious farcy of a horse.

I have, &c.
(Signed) GEO. E. BIRD.

The Right Hon. the Earl Granville, K.G.,
&c. &c. &c.

No. 74.

LETTER from the BRITISH CONSUL at Baltimore to EARL GRANVILLE.

Commercial, No. 19.

MY LORD,　　　　　　　　　　Baltimore, October 1, 1883.

WITH reference to my Despatch, Commercial No. 18, of the 1st ultimo, I have the honour to report that the State Cattle Inspector informs me that no cases of cattle disease in this district have been developed in the month of September.

A charge was made in the newspapers that pleuro-pneumonia had been introduced into the State of Pennsylvania from some cattle purchased in the Baltimore market in July. The inspector positively denies that such was the case, and has proceeded to Pennsylvania for the purpose of tracing where the cattle came from that were charged with having introduced the disease into that State.

I have, &c.
(Signed)　　DENIS DONOHOE.

The Right Hon. the Earl Granville, K.G.,
　　&c.　　　&c.　　　&c.

No. 75.

LETTER from the BRITISH CONSUL at Philadelphia to EARL GRANVILLE.

Commercial, No. 10.　　British Consulate, Philadelphia,
MY LORD,　　　　　　　　　　October 9, 1883.

I BEG to report that pleuro-pneumonia is still prevalent in Chester County, Pennsylvania, the herds therein affected being those reported to your Lordship in my Despatch No. 9 of 7th ultimo, and two additional herds; the contagion in the latter being directly traced to animals which had been in contact with the diseased animals brought from Baltimore.

A notice has been issued from the United States Department of Agriculture at Washington to the effect that a convention of representatives of all classes interested in the animal industries of the United States will be held at Chicago, Thursday and Friday, November 15th and 16th next, for conference concerning contagious diseases among domestic animals.

I have, &c.
(Signed)　　ROBT. CHAS. CLIPPERTON.

The Right Hon. the Earl Granville, K.G.,
　　&c.　　　&c.　　　&c.

CORRESPONDENCE.

No. 76.

LETTER from the Hon. L. S. SACKVILLE WEST to EARL GRANVILLE.

Commercial, No. 238.

MY LORD,　　　　　　　　Washington, October 11, 1883.

I HAVE the honour to inform your Lordship that I have regularly reported to the United States Government the arrival of animals in England affected with Texan Fever, as notified by the several communications from the Agricultural Department of the Privy Council.

I have, &c.
(Signed)　　L. S. SACKVILLE WEST.

The Right Hon. the Earl Granville, K.G.,
&c.　　&c.　　&c.

No. 77.

LETTER from the FOREIGN OFFICE to the CLERK OF THE COUNCIL.

SIR,　　　　　　　　Foreign Office, October 17, 1883.

WITH reference to your letter of the 14th of September last, I am directed by Earl Granville to forward, for the consideration of the Committee of Council on Agriculture, the accompanying note from the United States Chargé d'Affaires respecting the regulations in force in the United States for preventing the spread of foot-and-mouth disease.

I am, &c.
(Signed)　　T. V. LISTER.

The Clerk of the Council,
　　Agricultural Department.

Enclosure 1 in No. 77.

　　　　　　　　Legation of the United States, London,
MY LORD,　　　　　　　　October 12, 1883.

REFERRING to Mr. Lowell's note of the 6th of September, and to your Lordship's reply of the 12th of September last, in relation to the existence of foot-and-mouth disease among the cattle of the United States, I have the honour to acquaint your Lordship that a despatch has been received to-day at this Legation from Mr. Frelinghuysen, in which he encloses a copy of a letter to the Department of State from the Acting Secretary of the Treasury, referring to a statement alleged to have been made recently in the House of Commons by Mr. Dodson, Chancellor of the Duchy of Lancaster, to the effect that the American quarantine system in reference to cattle diseases gives no security against the conveyance of disease by men attached to quarantine stations and by articles taken out of quarantine yards, and that the system takes into consideration only the animals themselves.

The Acting Secretary of the Treasury calls attention to the report of the Treasury Cattle Commission of the 21st of July last in regard to the foot-and-mouth disease among the cattle of the United States, which, while it admits that this disease did exist in herds of cattle imported from Great Britain, emphatically denies its present existence among American cattle.

A copy of this report was enclosed in Mr. Lowell's note to your Lordship of the 8th of September last.

I have the honour to forward herewith a copy of this letter from the Acting Secretary of the Treasury, dated the 20th of August last (Enclosure 2); of the letter from the same officer, dated the 1st of August last (Enclosure 3); and of the two circulars* accompanying the former communication; and I beg leave, in compliance with Mr. Frelinghuysen's instructions, to invite the special attention of Her Majesty's Government to the stringent regulations governing the quarantine of cattle which are established by those documents.

I have, &c.
(Signed) W. J. HOPPIN.

The Right Hon. the Earl Granville, K.G.,
&c. &c. &c.

Enclosure 2 in No. 77.

Treasury Department,
August 20, 1883.

SIR,

I HAVE the honour to enclose herewith a newspaper slip, containing a telegraphic despatch from London, England, in which it is alleged that Mr. Dodson, Chancellor of the Duchy of Lancaster, stated, on the 17th instant, in the House of Commons, that it was an undoubted fact that the foot-and-mouth disease in cattle had been carried from England to America, and that the American quarantine system in relation to cattle diseases gave no security against the conveyance of disease by men attached to quarantine stations, and by articles taken out of the quarantine yards, and that the system took into consideration only the animals themselves. I deem it due to American interests to state that if the honourable gentleman named made the remarks attributed to him, it must have been done without a knowledge of all the facts

---

* These Circulars are printed at pages 36 and 48.

of the case, and that in some respects such remarks are calculated to mislead the public mind on the subject.

Attention is called to the enclosed report of the Treasury Cattle Commission, dated the 21st ultimo, in regard to the foot-and-mouth disease among the cattle of the United States. While it is admitted that the disease did exist in herds of cattle imported from Great Britain, the Commission gives an emphatic denial to the present existence of the disease among the cattle of the United States. This statement is considered important, because it might be inferred from the remarks of Mr. Dodson, as quoted, that the disease which had thus been imported from Great Britain had not been eradicated. Ample quarantine stations exist in the districts of Boston, Mass., and Portland, Me., and as no contagious or infectious diseases among the cattle of those States exist, the possibility of these diseases being communicated to our cattle by cattle arriving at those ports (which are the only ports on the New England frontier where cattle are allowed to be quarantined) is quite remote. I call special attention to the stringent regulations governing the quarantine of cattle, herewith enclosed, which go far beyond the scope contemplated in the remarks attributed to Mr. Dodson.

I think if these regulations are properly carried out, as I assume they will be, they will prove sufficient to guard against the introduction of contagious diseases by the importation of foreign cattle at the ports where quarantine is established.

I have the honour to request that a copy of this letter and of its enclosures be sent to the British Minister at this capital for the information of his Government.

Very respectfully,
(Signed) H. F. FRENCH,
Acting Secretary.

Hon. F. T. Frelinghuysen,
Secretary of State.

Enclosure 3 in No. 77.

Treasury Department,
August 1, 1883.

SIR,

I HAVE to acknowledge the receipt of your letter dated the 25th ultimo, enclosing a copy of a despatch from Mr. Lowell, American Minister at London, in which he expressed the opinion that the legislation which recently passed the House of Commons indicates that the British Government will interdict the importation of cattle from all countries in which the laws for the extinction of disease are not comprehensive or severe enough or not rigidly enough enforced to satisfy the demands of the Privy Council.

The action of the House of Commons as well as the charge made in Parliament that the cattle were being shipped from our ports infected with the foot-and-mouth disease have already attracted the attention of this Department, and measures have been taken to ascertain whether that disease prevails among the cattle in this country.

A report, dated the 21st ultimo, upon the subject signed by Professor James Law and Dr. E. F. Thayer, United States Treasury Cattle Commissioners, in which they state with the greatest confidence that there is no evidence whatever that our American herds are now suffering from the foot-and-mouth disease, is enclosed herewith.*

It is suggested that measures be taken to bring the substance of the report to the attention of the British Government, through the Minister of the United States at London.

Very respectfully,
(Signed) H. F. French,
Acting Secretary.

Hon. F. T. Frelinghuysen,
Secretary of State.

No. 78.

LETTER from BRITISH CONSUL at Baltimore to EARL GRANVILLE.

Commercial, No. 20.

MY LORD, Baltimore, November 5, 1883.

WITH reference to my Despatch, Commercial No. 19, of the 1st ultimo, I have the honour to report that Dr. Ward, F.R.C.V.S., the State Cattle Inspector, informs me that there are a few cases of pleuro-pneumonia amongst the dairy cattle-farms about this city.

With reference to the last paragraph of my report of the 1st ultimo, Dr. Ward says, that after careful investigation he finds that the infected cows that were stated to have been purchased in Baltimore in July, taken to Pennsylvania, and caused the outbreak of pleuro-pneumonia in that State, were sent to this market from Pennsylvania, were sold here and purchased by a man living in another part of the State of Pennsylvania, and taken to his farm, where, in a short time, the disease was developed and spread amongst the other cattle on the farm.

I have the honour to enclose a draft of a Bill that will be brought before the Legislature of Maryland at its next sitting, in December, for the purpose of giving proper power to deal with outbreaks of cattle disease in the State.

This Draft Bill has been drawn up by Dr. Ward, but, at present, it is impossible for me to say whether it can be passed or not. It is a difficult thing to get a Bill giving such summary jurisdiction to a State officer to pass a State Legislature.

I have, &c.
(Signed) DENIS DONOHOE.

The Right Hon. the Earl Granville, K.G.,
&c.   &c.   &c.

---

* This Report is printed at page 48.

Enclosure in No. 78.

AN ACT to PREVENT the SPREAD of INFECTIOUS or CONTAGIOUS DISEASES among the LIVE STOCK of this STATE.

Section 1. Be it enacted by the General Assembly of Maryland, that it shall be the duty of the Governor of the State to take measures to promptly suppress any contagious or infectious disease which may make its appearance among the live stock of this State, and to prevent it from spreading.

Section 2. And be it enacted, that for such purpose the Governor shall appoint one Chief Veterinary Inspector, who shall be a graduate in good standing of some recognised school of veterinary medicine, at a salary of 2,000 dollars per annum and his travelling expenses, who shall hold his office at the pleasure of the Governor, whose duty it shall be to visit the stables of the city and counties wherever he has reason to believe contagious or infectious diseases may exist, and he may visit any such stable at any such hour of the day between sunrise and sunset, and shall have power, with the consent of the Governor, to order all animals which have been exposed to such contagion or infection to be secluded in such manner as the nature thereof may in his judgment render necessary to prevent the spreading of such disease; to order that any premises, farm or farms, stables or railway cars where such disease exists or has existed be put in quarantine, so that no domestic animal shall be removed from or brought to the premises or places so quarantined until the same shall have been properly disinfected; to prescribe such regulations as he may judge necessary or expedient to prevent infection or contagion being communicated in any way from the places so quarantined; to call upon all sheriffs and deputy sheriffs, constables, policemen, or any officers of the State, the city of Baltimore, or of any county, for information and assistance to carry out and enforce the provisions of such orders and regulations; to prescribe regulations for the destruction of animals affected with infectious and contagious diseases, and for the proper destruction of their hides and carcasses, and of all objects which might carry infection or contagion; provided that no animal shall be destroyed unless first examined by such veterinary inspector or one of his assistants; to prescribe regulations for the disinfection of all premises, buildings, and railway cars, and of all objects from which or by which infection or contagion may take place or be conveyed; to alter and modify from time to time, as he may deem expedient, the terms of all such orders and regulations, and to cancel or withdraw the same at any time; to order all or any animals coming into the State to be detained at any place or places for the purpose of inspection and examination; provided that animals coming from a neighbouring State that have been quarantined and discharged shall not be subject to the provisions of this Act; and it shall be the duty of all sheriffs and deputy sheriffs, constables, policemen, or other officers of the State, city of Baltimore, or counties, to obey and observe all orders and instructions which they may receive from the said veterinary inspector in the enforcement of the provisions of this Act.

Section 3. And be it enacted, that any person who shall transgress the terms or requirements of any order or regulation issued and prescribed by the said veterinary inspector, with the consent of the Governor under the authority of this Act, or shall refuse to said veterinary inspector or his assistants access to his or their premises, farms, or stables, or shall conceal the fact that contagious or infectious disease exists on his premises, shall be deemed guilty of a misdemeanor.

Section 4. And be it enacted, that any person who shall sell or otherwise dispose of an animal which he knows or has reason to believe is affected by any contagious or infectious disease, or has been exposed to the same, or shall permit the same to pass over or upon any public highway, street, lane, or alley of this State, shall, on conviction thereof, be fined not less than 50 nor more than 100 dollars for each animal.

Section 5. And be it enacted, that all the necessary expenses incurred under the direction or by the authority of the Governor in carrying out the provisions of this Act, including the salary and travelling expenses of said veterinary inspector, shall be paid by the treasurer out of any moneys not otherwise appropriated, and upon the warrant of the Comptroller on being certified as correct by the Governor.

Section 6. And be it enacted, that in the event of any building or buildings, sheds, or stables being reported to the Governor by said inspector as being incapable of proper disinfection, it shall be his duty to have such premises appraised, in a similar manner as prescribed in the succeeding section for appraisement of diseased animals, and destroyed.

Section 7. And be it enacted, that in the event of its being deemed necessary by the said veterinary inspector to prevent the spread of contagion or infection, to cause any animal or animals diseased to be slaughtered, the value of such animal or animals shall be fairly appraised by two appraisers, one of which to be appointed by the owner of said animal or animals, the other by said veterinary inspector, or in case the said owner shall neglect or refuse to name such appraiser, then by two appraisers to be appointed by said veterinary inspector, who, in case of disagreement, shall call in a third, which said appraisement shall be returned to the Comptroller by said veterinary inspector, and the Comptroller shall forthwith issue his warrant to the Treasurer for the three fourths of the amount of the appraisement of such animals as shall have been slaughtered in favour of the said owner or owners.

Section 8. And be it enacted, that the sum of 20,000 dollars for the year 1884 and 20,000 dollars for the year 1885, or so much thereof as may be necessary, be and the same is hereby appropriated to carry out the provisions of the last two preceding sections.

Section 9. And be it enacted, that in the event of the outbreak of an epidemic of contagious and infectious diseases among the live stock of this State, it shall be the duty of the Governor to appoint such assistants to said inspector as may be necessary to promptly suppress such epidemic and to fix their pay.

Section 10. And be it enacted, that all Acts or parts of Acts inconsistent herewith be and the same are hereby repealed.

No. 79.

LETTER from the BRITISH CONSUL at Baltimore to EARL GRANVILLE.

Commercial, No. 22.

MY LORD,　　　　　　　　　　　　　Baltimore, December 1, 1883.

WITH reference to my Despatch, Commercial No. 20, of the 5th ultimo, I have the honour to report that Dr. Ward, the State Cattle Inspector, informs me that one case of pleuro-pneumonia and one of Texas Fever (splenic fever) has occurred in the neighbourhood of Baltimore since my last report; that he considers the disease decreasing, and that in both these cases the cattle died.

The Texas Fever, the doctor has discovered, was introduced by a drove of 150 Texas cattle driven through Carroll and Harford counties, Maryland, in September last. It has appeared in other places along the route taken by these cattle, and many have died; but it does not seem to affect the Texas cattle, but remains latent in the system, and is readily communicated to northern cattle.

I notice that at a meeting of "stock-men" held in Chicago in November to take action towards stamping out contagious diseases amongst live-stock, that the meeting was presided over by Senator Williams, of Kentucky, and attended by about 200 delegates, and that the following resolution was passed:

"Whereas the existence of contagious pleuro-pneumonia among live-stock in certain portions of a few States on the Atlantic seaboard, introduced from time to time by the importation of livestock from foreign countries, constantly threatens the spread of the contagion to the Southern and Western States and territories, the disease is of such a character that State legislation can only give partial relief; prompt and appropriate legislation on the part of Congress to eradicate the disease in the affected districts is imperatively demanded, as, should the great ranges of the West become infected with the disease, it would be impossible to stamp out the plague except by the total destruction of herds, at a cost of hundreds of millions of dollars: Therefore, resolved, that we urge upon the proper authorities the imperative necessity of a thorough inspection of all live-stock and meat product shipped from foreign countries."

The convention also endorsed the action of the Secretary of the Treasury in enforcing a quarantine against all imported cattle, and decided to petition Congress to confer authority on

CORRESPONDENCE.

the Treasury Department by which such quarantine can be extended so as to cover sheep, swine, and goats.

From the above it is evident that the western stock-men do not consider that the action of the State Legislatures will be sufficient to prevent the spread of cattle diseases.

I have, &c.
(Signed)   DENIS DONOHOE.

The Right Hon. the Earl Granville, K.G.,
&c.   &c.   &c.

No. 80.

LETTER from the BRITISH CONSUL at Philadelphia to EARL GRANVILLE.

Commercial, No. 11.

MY LORD,   Philadelphia, December 12, 1883.

I BEG to report that no further outbreak of pleuro-pneumonia has occurred in this consular district since the cases reported in my Despatch No. 9 of this series, dated September 17th last.

The same herds are still undergoing quarantine.

I beg further to state that this district is entirely free from the contagious disease known as the foot-and-mouth disease in cattle. The only attacks which have occurred in the United States have, in each instance, as I am assured by Dr. Gadsden, a member of the Royal Veterinary College, London, been traced to importations of cattle from England.

I have, &c.
(Signed)   ROBT. CHAS. CLIPPERTON,
Her Majesty's Consul.

The Right Hon. the Earl Granville, K.G.,
&c.   &c.   &c.

No. 81.

LETTER from the BRITISH CONSUL at Baltimore to EARL GRANVILLE.

Commercial, No. 1.

MY LORD,   Baltimore, January 2, 1884.

WITH reference to my Despatch, Commercial No. 22, of the 1st ultimo, I have the honour to report that Dr. Ward, the State Cattle Inspector, informs me that no new cases of pleuro-pneumonia have occurred during the past month; he also states that any old cases are now in a satisfactory condition.

The Bill which is to be presented to the Legislature of Maryland next month, and of which I had the honour to enclose a copy in my Despatch, Commercial No. 20, of the 5th November, has been slightly modified, particularly as to the clause appropriating a stated salary to the inspector, and allowing a specified sum for the purpose of preventing the spread of cattle diseases; and Dr. Ward says that if it does pass it must place Maryland as first in the States that have legislated in a satisfactory manner on this subject.

        I have, &c.
      (Signed) DENIS DONOHOE.
The Right Hon. the Earl Granville, K.G.,
  &c.   &c.   &c.

No. 82.

LETTER from the HON. L. S. SACKVILLE WEST to EARL GRANVILLE.

Commercial, No. 6.

MY LORD,   Washington, January 11, 1884.

WITH reference to the correspondence which has passed respecting the exportation of diseased cattle, I have the honour to enclose to your Lordship herewith copies of a Bill which has been brought into the Senate for the establishment of a Bureau of Animal Industry, and which has been referred to the Committee on Agriculture.

        I have, &c.
      (Signed) L. S. SACKVILLE WEST.
The Right Hon. the Earl Granville, K.G.,
  &c.   &c.   &c.

Enclosure in No. 82.

In the SENATE of the UNITED STATES, December 4, 1883.

Mr. Willams asked and, by unanimous consent, obtained leave to bring in the following Bill, which was read twice and referred to the Committee on Agriculture.

A BILL for the establishment of a BUREAU of ANIMAL INDUSTRY to prevent the exportation of diseased cattle and the spread of infectious or contagious diseases among domestic animals.

Be it enacted by the Senate and House of Representatives of the United States of America in Congress assembled, that no railroad company within the United States whose road forms any part of a line of road from one State or territory to another, or from a State into the district of Columbia, or the owners or masters of any steam or sailing or other vessel or boat, shall receive for transportation, or transport, from one State or territory to another, or from any State into the district of Columbia, any live cattle affected with any contagious or infectious disease, and especially the disease known as pleuro-pneumonia; nor shall any person, company, or corporation deliver for such transportation to any railroad company, or master or owner of any boat or

o 11711.

vessel, any live cattle knowing them to be affected with any contagious or infectious disease; nor shall any person, company, or corporation drive on foot or transport in private conveyance from one State or territory to another, or from any State into the district of Columbia, any live cattle knowing them to be affected with any contagious or infectious disease, and especially the disease known as pleuro-pneumonia.

Sec. 2. That any person or persons operating any such railroad, or master or owner of any boat or vessel, or owner or custodian of or person having control over such live cattle, who shall knowingly violate the provisions of section 1 of this Act, shall be guilty of a misdemeanor, and, upon conviction, shall be punished by a fine of not less than 100 nor more than 5,000 dollars, or by imprisonment for not more than one year, or by both such fine and imprisonment.

Sec. 3. That the Commissioner of Agriculture shall organise in his department a Bureau of Animal Industry, and shall appoint a chief who shall be a competent veterinary surgeon, approved by the National Board of Health, and whose duty it shall be to investigate and report upon the number, value, and condition of the domestic animals of the United States, their protection and use, and also inquire into and report the causes of contagious and communicable diseases among them, and the means for the preservation and cure of the same, and to collect such information on these subjects as shall be valuable to the agricultural and commercial interests of the country. The Commissioner of Agriculture is hereby authorised to call to his aid in investigating said diseases in animals, and in providing means for the prevention and cure thereof, the National Board of Health, whose duty it shall be to render such aid and to employ such means as they deem necessary to obtain all information in regard to said diseases, their prevention and control; he is also authorised to employ two commissioners, one of whom shall be a practical stock-raiser, and one an experienced business man, familiar with questions pertaining to commercial transactions in live stock, whose duty it shall be to advise with regard to the best methods of treating, transporting, and caring for animals, and of providing against the spread of said diseases. The compensation of said commissioners shall be at the rate of not more than 10 dollars per diem, with all necessary travelling expenses while engaged in the performance of their duty under this Act. The salary of the Chief of Bureau shall be 3,000 dollars per annum; and the Commissioner of Agriculture shall appoint a clerk for said Bureau, with a salary of 1,800 dollars per annum; and any services rendered by the National Board of Health under the provisions of this Act shall be paid for as provided in the Act creating and organising such board.

Sec. 4. That in order to promote the exportation of live stock from the United States the Commissioner of Agriculture, through said Chief of Bureau, shall make special investigation as to the existence of pleuro-pneumonia, or any contagious or communicable disease, along the dividing line between the United States and foreign countries, and along the lines of transportation from all parts of the United States to ports from which live stock are exported, and make report of the results of such investigation to the Secretary of the Treasury, who shall establish such regulations concerning the exportation and transportation of live stock as the results of said investigation may require.

Sec. 5. That to prevent the exportation from any port of the United States to any port in a foreign country of live cattle affected with any infectious or contagious disease, and especially pleuro-pneumonia, the Secretary of the Treasury be and he is hereby authorised to take such steps and adopt such measures not inconsistent with the provisions of this Act as he may deem necessary.

Sec. 6. That it shall be the duty of the Commissioner of Agriculture, through said Chief of Bureau, in connexion with the National Board of Health, to prepare such rules and regulations as they may deem necessary for the speedy and effectual suppression and extirpation of said diseases, and to certify such rules and regulations to the executive authority of each State and territory, and invite said authorities to co-operate in the execution and enforcement of this Act.

Sec. 7. That the sum of 50,000 dollars, to be immediately available, or so much thereof as may be necessary, is hereby appropriated, out of any moneys in the Treasury not otherwise appropriated, to carry into effect the provisions of this Act.

Sec. 8. That whenever any infectious or contagious disease affecting domestic animals, and especially the disease known as pleuro-pneumonia, shall be brought into or shall break out in the district of Columbia, it shall be the duty of the Commissioners of said district to take measures to suppress the same promptly and to prevent the same from spreading; and for this purpose the said Commissioners are hereby empowered to order and require that any premises, farm or farms, where such disease exists or has existed be put in quarantine; to order all or any animals coming into the district to be detained at any place or places for the purpose of inspection and examination; to prescribe regulations for, and to require the destruction of, animals affected with infectious or contagious disease, and for the proper disposition of their hides and carcasses; to prescribe regulations for disinfection and such other regulations as they may deem necessary to prevent infection or contagion being communicated; and shall report to the Commissioner of Agriculture whatever they may do in pursuance of the provisions of this section.

Sec. 9. That it shall be the duty of the several United States district attorneys to prosecute all violations of this Act which shall be brought to their notice or knowledge by any person making the complaint; and the same shall be heard before any district or circuit court of the United States holden within the district in which the violation of this Act has been committed, or the person or corporation resides or carries on or has his or its place of business.

Sec. 10. That this Act shall take effect and be in force from and after its passage.

No. 83.

LETTER from the Hon. L. S. SACKVILLE WEST to EARL GRANVILLE.

No. 10.

My Lord,   Washington, January 14, 1884.

I HAVE the honour to transmit to your Lordship herewith copy of a resolution submitted to the Senate on the subject of the restrictions on the importation of alleged healthful meats from the United States.

I have, &c.
(Signed)   L. S. SACKVILLE WEST.

The Right Hon. the Earl Granville, K.G.
&c.   &c.   &c.

Enclosure in No. 83.

In the SENATE of the UNITED STATES.

January 9, 1884.—Ordered to be printed.

Mr. Anthony submitted the following Resolution:—

Resolved, That the Committee on Foreign Relations be instructed to inquire into the expediency of such legislation as shall enable the Executive to protect our interests against those Governments which have prohibited or restrained the importation of healthful meats from the United States.

No. 84.

LETTER from the BRITISH CONSUL at BALTIMORE to EARL GRANVILLE.

Commercial, No. 4.

My Lord,   Baltimore, February 1, 1884.

WITH reference to my Despatch, Commercial No. 1, of the 2nd instant, I have the honour to report that Dr. Ward, the State Cattle Inspector, informs me that there are no new cases of pleuro-pneumonia, and only two old cases, and the animals affected have been slaughtered.

As regards the Cattle Bill, I understand it will be introduced in the Maryland Legislature as soon as it is seen how the Bill before Congress on the same subject is disposed of.

I notice that the Sub-Committee on Agriculture of Congress has recommended an appropriation of 250,000 dollars, and that the States be required to contribute a sum equal to that apportioned amongst them by the general Government. This Bill was prepared by the " Cattle-breeders Convention " for the extirpation of diseases among domestic animals.

I have, &c.
(Signed) DENIS DONOHOE.
The Right Hon. the Earl Granville, K.G.,
&c. &c. &c.

No. 85.

LETTER from the HON. L. S. SACKVILLE WEST to EARL GRANVILLE.

Commercial, No. 17.

MY LORD, Washington, February 1, 1884.

WITH reference to my Despatch No. 12, of the 16th ultimo, I have the honour to enclose to your Lordship herewith the communication made to the President by the Secretary of State, to be transmitted to the House of Representatives, on the subject of the importation of American pork into France and Germany.

This communication deprecates retaliatory legislation, and recommends the appointment of a Commission of Scientists for the purpose of examining the question of the alleged prevalence of hog cholera in the United States. Your Lordship will perceive that the Secretary of State alludes to the reports of the British consular officers in the United States on this subject.

I have, &c.
(Signed) L. S. SACKVILLE WEST.
The Right Hon. the Earl Granville, K.G.,
&c. &c. &c.

Enclosure in No. 85.

EXTRACT from the NEW YORK TIMES of 31st January 1884.

AMERICAN PORK IN EUROPE—STATE DEPARTMENT EFFORTS TO PREVENT RESTRICTIONS.

Secretary Frelinghuysen lays the record before Congress; proof urged in place of retaliation.

Washington, Jan. 30.—Secretary Frelinghuysen has addressed to the President the following communication, to be transmitted to the House of Representatives, in response to the resolutions therein quoted :

TO THE PRESIDENT:

There have been referred to the undersigned for appropriate action thereon the two following resolutions of the House of Representatives.

I. *Resolved,* That the President be and he is hereby requested to furnish for the information of this House, if not incompatible with the public service, all communications, documents, and papers in his possession relating to the exclusion of and restriction upon the importation of American hog products into Germany and France.

II. Whereas Germany and certain other foreign Governments have interdicted the importation of the swine products of this country for the pretended reason that such products are not proper and wholesome for food; and

Whereas an invitation from this Government to said foreign Governments to send agents here to test said products has been declined, thus indicating that the pretended reasons given for such interdiction are not real reasons; and

Whereas it is the duty of this Government to act promptly and with energy to resent the injustice done by said charges, and to protect these great produces from said imputation; therefore

Resolved, That the President of the United States is hereby requested to transmit to this House, if in his opinion it be not incompatible with the public interest, copies of any and all correspondence had by the State Department with all foreign Governments on this subject, together with any and all information that he may have bearing upon this question.

Regarding these two resolutions jointly as embodying the wish of the popular branch of Congress to be possessed of whatever may throw light upon the measures adopted by foreign Governments to the detriment of an important branch of the export trade of the United States, and also of all that may tend towards a just and effective remedy for such detrimental measures, the undersigned has endeavoured to cover the whole ground embraced by both resolutions, by collecting and submitting to the President herewith copies of all pertinent matter found of record in the Department of State, to the end that it, or so much of it as the President may deem proper, may be communicated to the House of Representatives in response to its requests, and in so doing the undersigned avails himself of the occasion to submit to the President, as briefly as possible, such considerations, drawn from a general review of the action of this Government hitherto in the premises, as seem to him appropriate to the understanding of the general subject in its international bearing.

The action of the leading Governments of Europe took shape between 1879 and 1881, and was partially simultaneous in several countries. On the ground of the alleged frequent discovery of trichinæ in hogs' meat coming from Cincinnati into Italy, the Sanitary Department of that Government issued an order on the 20th of February 1879, prohibiting all pork imports of whatever character from the United States, a prohibition which was soon afterward,—May 6, 1879,—made general against all foreign pork. About September 1879, the Hungarian Council-General of Public Health caused a like prohibition in Hungary. Dr. Ludwig von Grosse, at the International Medical Congress of Amsterdam in September 1879, announced that the prevalence of trichinæ in pork products from America had led to consultation between the Austrian and Hungarian Governments, with a view to making the prohibition adopted in Hungary universal throughout the Austro-Hungarian Empire, which, however, was not accomplished until more than a year afterward. By an imperial decree of January 25, 1880, Germany prohibited the importation of chopped pork and sausages (but not of hams or bacon) from America. The French Government, as the result of the alleged discovery of trichinæ in some pork from America, issued a decree on the 18th of February 1881, upon the advice of the Consultative Committee of Public Health, forbidding the importation of salt pork coming from the United States. This action on the part of France was followed by several other States of Europe, and Turkey and Greece excluded the pork products of the United States, professedly in pursuance of the French example. The consideration of the same measure in Austria-Hungary, pending since 1879, was closed by the promulgation, March 10, 1881, of a decree prohibiting the importation of swine meat, lard, and sausages of every kind from the United States. Efforts were made for professed sanitary reasons to effect like prohibitory enactments in Belgium and Switzerland during the same time, but those Governments, holding rightly that no danger from trichinæ attended the consumption of properly cooked food products, abstained from the interdiction sought. Meanwhile, in England, popular excitement arose in the early part of 1880, caused by the publication of reports by several British consular officers in the United States alleging the prevalence of hog cholera in the West to an alarming extent, and imports of live swine and swine products to the British Islands were checked for a time, but no prohibitory legislation ensued. Apparently confined at first to scientific and hygienic considerations, the movement soon took, in the great European countries, an interested commercial aspect. The Governments of France, Germany, and Austria seem to have become subjected to pressure from adverse quarters. On the one hand, there became manifest a general tendency among men of science and practical economists to condemn the prohibition as unwise and needless; on the other, the local hog raisers and packers raised objection to the admission of a foreign product which, from its nature and manner of packing, they alleged could not be subjected, before entering into public consumption, to the same methods of investigation which legislation had prescribed for native swine products. Thus, the question debated in the press and legislatures of France and Germany, looked to determining whether the importation of pork products from the United States was, or was not, in fact, a source of danger to the public health. It now seemed no less the duty of the Government of the United States to investigate the question. A great industry, giving a prosperous export trade, had been declared pernicious to health and its products debarred from use abroad. The same considerations of public health which operated to bring about total prohibition abroad made it necessary that the alleged perniciousness should be no less searchingly investigated at home.

As a preliminary step, the Department of State, in March 1881, prosecuted an examination of the various phases of the pork industry in the Western States, from the raising of the hogs until their varied products are ready for marketable shipment. This investigation, made by Mr. Michael Scanlon, Chief of the Bureau of Statistics of the Department of State, covered all the possible causes which might operate to render the product dangerous to health. It embraced the diseases of swine, hog cholera receiving especial attention. The alleged presence of trichinæ among the swine of this country was rigidly inquired into. The results of that investigation appeared to the Department of State conclusive as to the healthfulness of a staple product, consumed without evil consequences by millions of our citizens. Not only were the asserted ravages of hog cholera disproved, but it was shown that unusual precautions had been universally taken to insure that the healthiest animals should be slaughtered for packing. It was shown, moreover, that the existence of trichinæ in the hog, although detected by proper tests in sundry cases, was not as widespread as among the swine of other countries; and that a much greater immunity from trichinosis existed throughout the great pork-consuming communities of the West than in the rural districts of Central Europe, where none but native pork products entered into consumption. The facts thus elicited warranted and constrained the Department of State to represent to the foreign Governments that the prejudicial judgment against the swine export of this country was ex parte and unfounded. How diligently the agents of this department abroad have endeavoured to overcome this adverse pre-judgment is shown in the correspondence communicated herewith. The result has hitherto not been of such a character as this Government felt it had good right to expect.

In France the discussion has passed through several phases. The French Government showed an earnest desire to meet the problem in a just sense. Ministers, legislators, and the most eminent men of science there united in declaring their conviction that the use of American pork, in any of its exported forms, whether as fresh meat or prepared for keeping, was absolutely innocuous to health. Not a single case of trichinosis traceable to American pork had been observed in France for many years. It was demonstrated that cooking destroyed the communicable forms of the parasite in the rare cases where it was detected. Science asserted that even the low temperature of 58° Fahrenheit sufficed to kill the trichinæ. But the difficulty seems to have lain in applying to imported pork the same examination which sanitary regulations provided for the native product. Various schemes of microscopic inspection on entry were devised, for the most part admittedly partial and fallacious, and all, according to the best judgment of this Government, needless and serving only to impede a traffic which had been shown to be harmless. At length, in November last, the Government repealed the prohibition. The immediate consequence was the renewed animation of the question in the French Chambers and a very decisive vote against the removal of the prohibition. The Government of the Republic has, therefore, with evident reluctance, been compelled to rescind its recent action, and, after a sufficient interval, to admit of shipments which had been made on the faith of the revocation of November. The interdiction is restored from the 20th instant. The correspondence herewith submitted will enable Congress to judge impartially the course of the matter in France.

In Austria, Hungary, and Italy the prohibition has been maintained. With Germany the representations of this Government took a different, and to some extent an unusual, direction. When, in February last, notwithstanding the proofs adduced to show that the restriction of pork imports into the Empire was not warranted by any state of facts known to prevail in the United States, but was rather at variance with the ascertained facts here, it was announced that the Imperial Government was about to submit to the Reichstag measures of total exclusion. Reasoning that the emergency justified any and every mode of appeal to the sense of justice and equality of the German Government against a measure believed to be no less injurious to the interests of the German people than to our export trade, the President directed that the Imperial Government should be informed of his intention to appoint an impartial and competent commission to investigate the asserted danger of American pork products to health, with a view to ascertaining and promulgating the exact facts in relation thereto, and that it should be invited to send one or more experts hither to make such investigation, either separately or jointly, with a United States commission. The invitation was declined, the reason, chiefly, being that in a matter concerning domestic sanitary legislation the German Government could not enter into any arrangement which might imply an obligation on its part to accept and be bound by a state of facts existing outside of its jurisdiction. The President has since appointed the commission then contemplated. It is composed of a representative of the New York Chamber of Commerce, Professor Charles F. Chandler; a representative of the Chicago Board of Trade, Mr. E. W. Blatchford; two members nominated by the Commissioner of Agriculture, Mr. F. D. Curtis, of Charlton, N.Y., and Professor D. E. Salmon; the whole under the chairmanship of the Commissioner of Agriculture. In point of scientific competence and elevated impartiality, the formation of the commission peculiarly fits it for the execution of its responsible task. To it should belong in great measure the shaping of the policy of this

Government toward the pork question in its domestic or foreign aspects.

In view, therefore, of the prominent part which the results reached by the Pork Commission must necessarily play in the further treatment of the question by the Executive or by Congress, the undersigned feels it incumbent upon him to advise that the President recommend Congress to abstain from any immediate legislative action until the report of the commission, soon to be presented, shall be before it. In advance of such report, and, indeed, without any knowledge of its probable import or intimation of the suggestions it may offer, the undersigned deems it his duty to lay before the President certain considerations, prompted by the language of the resolutions, to which he now responds.

The preamble to the second resolution above quoted indicates that Congress may feel impelled to take measures to resent the injustice which may be shown to have been done by the groundless charge that the same products of this country are not proper and wholesome for food. The President will see by the instruction of the undersigned to Mr. Sagent, of February 16, 1883, that there has been and is no disposition on the part of the Executive Department of this Government to prevent or to remonstrate, or in any way to interfere in the right of the German Empire to exclude the use or products which would be deleterious to the people. The question to be carefully, frankly, and honestly met is, whether the prepared meat products exported from this country are injurious to public health. We believe they are not, and have so represented. On the contrary, all the proofs which laborious and searching investigations have hitherto laid before us contain the belief that such products are promotive of the public health in those countries to which they are imported. Diligent inquiry has been made, as the correspondence shows, to trace out the cause of the sickness imputed to the use of imported meats, and such investigations show, we think, that it is in no case attributable to the pork exported from this country. Should it appear that the meat products of this country are, as we believe them to be, not deleterious but promotive of health, it is believed that those friendly nations which have put forth decrees inhibiting the importation of our meats would annul those decrees. The undersigned is aware that doubtless in those countries there are producers of meats who would be glad of the continuance of such inhibition, because they would profit by avoiding the competition which our exports create, but he has no belief that they can or would have any controlling influence on the Governments of those countries. If, however, in the face of clear proof, elicited both at home and abroad, that our meat products are free from disease or communicable germs of disease, proof which might be established to demonstration by actual inspection, as well as supported by a knowledge of the precautions which surround the raising and packing industries here, any nations with which we are on terms of intimacy and amity should, by legislation, discriminate against the trade of this country rather than protect the health of their people, it would then be the province of the Executive to call the attention of such nations to the provisions of treaties, with the confident expectations that those treaties would be respected.

The undersigned would suggest to the President that, as his message recommended that in certain cases, such as when a foreign nation, by onerous storage charges, exorbitant penalties, differential duties in favour of a competing flag, or by the misuse of some other incident of commerce, discriminated against the United States, there might, by legislation analogous to sections 2,502 and 4,228 of the Revised Statutes, be vested in the President power to adopt measures compensating for, and countervailing such misuse of, the incidents of commerce. It may be inferred that the suggestion extends to measures relating to the substance of commerce and affecting our commercial relations with other nations. It is submitted to the President that such measures are of an importance much greater than the administration of the incidents alluded to, and it would therefore seem to be proper that they receive the direct consideration and determination of Congress rather than that the subject should be disposed of by a reference to the Executive. It seems, however, very plain that our policy, in any event, should be to prove that our meat products are wholesome. This, the absence of trichinosis in this country, and particularly in our army and navy, where our meats are constantly used, goes far to demonstrate. Measures, however, might be taken to ascertain to an absolute certainty, by such means as a commission of scientists would devise, that our meats are or can be rendered innocuous.

With these observations the undersigned commits to the President the subjoined correspondence. Taken in connexion with the former correspondence, communicated to the House of Representatives on the 26th of May 1882, in answer to a resolution thereof (House ex doc. No. 209, 47th Congress, 1st session), it is believed that it presents a connected view of the efforts of this Government to impress upon other countries the conviction it holds, that the pork products of this country are not the means of disseminating disease and death they are represented to be, and to maintain the discussion of the international questions involved on the plane of disproving by fact and reason the sanitary argument put forth to justify the exclusion of those products from use as food in foreign lands.

Respectfully submitted,
FREDERICK T. FRELINGHUYSEN.
Department of State, Washington,
January 28, 1884.

No. 86.

LETTER from the FOREIGN OFFICE to the CLERK OF THE COUNCIL.

SIR, Foreign Office, February 20, 1884.

I AM directed by Earl Granville to transmit to you herewith, to be laid before the Lords of Her Majesty's Privy Council, for such action as their Lordships may see fit to take in the matter, copies of a note from the United States Minister at this Court and of a telegram from Her Majesty's Consul at Portland relative to the arrival at that port on the 2nd instant of the British steamer "Ontario" with cattle which were subsequently attacked with the foot-and-mouth disease; and the return of the same vessel to Liverpool with cattle and sheep on board.

I am, &c.
(Signed) T. V. LISTER.

The Clerk of the Council,
    Agricultural Department.

Enclosure 1 in No. 86.

Legation of the United States, London,
MY LORD, February 19, 1884.

I HAVE the honour to acquaint your Lordship that I have just received the following telegram from the Secretary of State :—

"Cattle entered at Portland, Maine, February 2nd, from S.S. 'Ontario,' developed hoof-and-mouth disease a day or two after landing. 'Ontario' cleared for Liverpool, February 9th, with cattle and sheep. Our Treasury officers say disease must have originated on steamship. Inform Foreign Office."

I have, &c.
The Earl Granville, (Signed) J. R. LOWELL.
  &c. &c.

Enclosure 2 in No. 86.

TELEGRAM from Mr. CONSUL ANNESLEY, Portland, Maine, to EARL GRANVILLE. February 19. Arrived 8.55 p.m.

"BRITISH steamer 'Ontario' arrived Portland 2nd instant from Liverpool. Cattle landed attacked with foot-and-mouth disease. 'Ontario' cleared for Liverpool on 9th with cattle and sheep. Submitted adoption precautionary measures on arrival 'Ontario' Liverpool."

CORRESPONDENCE.

No. 87.

TELEGRAM from the INSPECTOR OF THE PRIVY COUNCIL at Liverpool to PROFESSOR BROWN.

February 22, 1884.

"ONTARIO" landed 274 cattle, 630 sheep. About half of cattle affected with foot-and-mouth disease. Sheep will not be landed till too dark to examine them.

No. 88.

LETTER from the CLERK OF THE COUNCIL to the FOREIGN OFFICE.

(No. 83,893.)

Agricultural Department, Privy Council Office,
44, Parliament Street, Westminster, S.W.,
February 23, 1884.

SIR,

I AM directed by the Lords of the Council to request that you will have the goodness to move Earl Granville to cause the American Government to be informed that the S.S. "Ontario," arriving at the port of Liverpool from Portland on the 22nd instant, brought animals, 138 of which, on examination on landing, were found to be affected with foot-and-mouth disease.

I am, &c.
(Signed) C. L. PEEL.

The Under Secretary of State,
&c. &c. &c.

No. 89.

COPIES of TWO ORDERS OF COUNCIL passed in consequence of Foot-and-Mouth Disease on board the "Ontario."

(3110.)

At the Council Chamber, Whitehall, the 23rd day of February 1884.

By Her Majesty's most Honourable Privy Council.

THE Lords and others of Her Majesty's most Honourable Privy Council, by virtue and in exercise of the powers in them vested under The Contagious Diseases (Animals) Act, 1878, and of every other power enabling them in this behalf, do order, and it is hereby ordered, as follows :—

1. Notwithstanding anything in Article 92 (Time for Slaughter) of The Animals Order or in Article 6 (Slaughter) of The Foreign Animals Order of 1881, the slaughter of the animals landed on the 22nd day of February 1884 at the foreign animals wharf in the port of Liverpool from the vessel "Ontario," from Portland,

in the United States of America, shall be commenced forthwith, and the slaughter of those animals shall be completed as soon as practicable.

2. If the slaughter of the animals is not commenced as directed by the Privy Council under this Order, or completed in accordance with the provisions of this Order, the person failing to cause such slaughter to be so commenced or completed shall be deemed guilty of an offence against The Contagious Diseases (Animals) Act, 1878.

(Signed)   C. L. PEEL.

(3111.)

At the Council Chamber, Whitehall, the 25th day of February 1884.

By Her Majesty's most Honourable Privy Council.

PRESENT:

Lord President.
Mr. Dodson.

THE Lords and others of Her Majesty's most Honourable Privy Council, by virtue and in exercise of the powers in them vested under The Contagious Diseases (Animals) Act, 1878, and of every other power enabling them in this behalf, do order, and it is hereby ordered, as follows:

1. Animals shipped at the Port of Portland, in the State of Maine, in the United States of America, between the 27th day of February and the 12th day of March 1884, both days inclusive, shall not be landed in England or Wales or Scotland.

2. In this Order words have the same meaning as in The Contagious Diseases (Animals) Act, 1878.

(Signed)   C. L. PEEL.

No. 90.

LETTER from the INSPECTOR OF THE PRIVY COUNCIL at Liverpool to PROFESSOR BROWN.

SIR,   Birkenhead, February 24, 1884.

REFERRING to your instructions to isolate the cargo per "Ontario," I beg to inform you that I took the following steps to carry out such instructions:

The wicket-gates across the "run" leading from the stage to the lairs were fastened up so as not to allow anyone to cross it during the time the animals were being landed, and no one was allowed to enter the wharf. As soon as the vessel was berthed alongside the stage, I went on board, and having found some cattle with foot-and-mouth disease, I immediately had the fumigating box started, and every one of the cattle-men landed, and the drovers and others engaged in receiving the animals were made to go along the run into the wharf and undergo thorough fumigation under my own supervision. The slaughter of the diseased animals was commenced forthwith, and the hides and sheep skins were disinfected with a solution of carbolic acid. The heads, tongues, feet, and tripes were immersed for half an hour in a saturated solution of common salt.

Having made the necessary arrangements, the cattle salesmen gave instructions that their men were not to go into Woodside Wharf among the healthy animals, and I have reason to believe that this has been properly carried out. No one has been allowed, except on urgent business, to enter the wharf or lairs. The above precautions have been continuously carried out up to the present time, no one being allowed to leave the wharf without undergoing fumigation, washing the hands and disinfecting the boots, and they will be carried out until the wharf has been cleansed and disinfected.

All the head ropes will be destroyed by fire, either under my own or the wharfinger's supervision. The manifolds are being cut into pieces and covered with quicklime; they will not be moved out of the wharf until thoroughly destroyed.

All the butchers are required, before leaving the wharf, to wash their poleaxes, knives, &c., in hot water.

The cargo was confined to the eastern half of the lairage, leaving the western half intact.

I am, &c.
(Signed) JOHN W. T. MOORE.

No. 91.

LETTER from the CLERK OF THE COUNCIL to the FOREIGN OFFICE.

(No. 83,870A.)

Agricultural Department, Privy Council Office,
44, Parliament Street, Westminster, S.W.,
February 25, 1884.

SIR,

I AM directed by the Lords of the Council to state that in consequence of the S.S. "Ontario" having arrived at the port of Liverpool from Portland, United States of America, on the 22nd instant, with animals affected with foot-and-mouth disease, their Lordships have passed an Order of Council prohibiting from the 27th instant until the 12th proximo (both days inclusive) the landing in this country of animals shipped at Portland, and I am to request that you will have the goodness to move Earl Granville to direct a telegram to be immediately sent to the American Government to inform them of this Order, in order that the shipment of animals from Portland to this country may be stopped.

I am, &c.
(Signed)   C. L. PEEL.

The Under Secretary of State,
&c.   &c.   &c.

No. 92.

REPORT from the ASSISTANT INSPECTOR OF THE PRIVY COUNCIL to PROFESSOR BROWN.

SIR,   March 3, 1884.

I HAVE the honour to report that on Saturday, February 23rd, I went to Liverpool, accompanied by Mr. Barrett from Deptford, and on the following morning I met Mr. Moore at Birkenhead, and went with him to the foreign animals wharf at Wallasey, where the cargo of animals affected with foot-and-mouth disease ex "Ontario," from Portland, was landed on the previous Friday afternoon.

This cargo was perfectly isolated, there being no other animals at the time of their arrival in the wharf; and no person was allowed into the wharf while these animals were being slaughtered, except on business connected with the wharf.

At the time of my visit on Sunday morning the slaughter of these animals was being carried out quickly, and I only saw a few of the cattle then alive showing symptoms of the disease, the whole of the 274 cattle brought by the vessel were slaughtered by 11 a.m. on Monday, and the whole of the 638 sheep by midnight.

When Mr. Moore discovered the existence of foot-and-mouth disease in this cargo he gave orders that the landing stage and run leading to the lairs should be thoroughly washed, scrubbed, and limewashed, and this had been very satisfactorily carried out.

As soon as the whole of the cargo had been disposed of, a staff of men were started to wash and scrub the whole of the floors, woodwork, and walls of the lairs as high up as the animals could have come in contact, and then a good coating of freshly-made limewash was applied, not only to the woodwork and walls, but also to the floors, water-troughs, and all other fittings.

The fumigation of the sheds was afterwards carried out by burning a large quantity of sulphur, about 300 lbs., in three rows of small fires on the floor of the buildings; after these fires had been sometime lighted the fumes could be seen escaping from the louvre along the centre of the roof, and the atmosphere of the place was so dense that you could not see from one end of the building to the other, and could not breathe it if you attempted to enter. This dense atmosphere was entirely caused by the sulphur, no other fuel being used, the sulphur being ignited by means of hot irons, and simply allowed to burn itself out.

The manure was thoroughly mixed with quicklime, and the non-edible portions of the offal was cut up and laid in layers with quicklime, and not allowed to be sent away with the manure as is usually the case when no disease exists in the wharf.

The tongues, feet, &c. were steeped for a short time in salt and water before removal from the wharf.

The hides were disinfected by being sprinkled with carbolic acid and water.

So long as any of the animals remained alive every person leaving the wharf was required to disinfect himself and his clothes in the following manner:—Basins with soap and water were provided for washing the hands and a vessel with carbolic acid and water to disinfect the boots, and each person was afterwards enclosed (except his head) in a tightly fitted box in which sulphur was kept burning.

As soon as the whole of the meat was removed from the slaughter-houses, the walls, floors, and fittings of these were thoroughly washed and scrubbed with hot water. The whole of this cleansing and disinfecting was completed on Thursday, and on Friday the "Toronto," from Portland, landed a healthy cargo of animals, which were placed in the portion of the Wallasey lairage not occupied by the diseased cargo ex the "Ontario." During the whole of this time neither Mr. Moore nor myself went into any of the other wharves or landing places for foreign animals. Mr. Barrett took sole charge of them.

I went on board the "Ontario" in the Alexandra Dock and saw the washing and cleansing of the vessel being carried out; the feeding troughs, breast boards for the cattle, and the sheep-pen fittings were being burned as fuel for the donkey engine used on board for discharging cargo.

The manure from the vessel was put into suitable barges to be sent out to sea, and the vessel has been taken out of her regular turn, and will probably not leave Liverpool till the beginning of next month.

I called on the Managing Directors of the Dominion Line, to which the "Ontario" belongs, and they informed me that on the outward voyage to Portland the vessel carried 28 Hereford cattle shipped by Mr. Britten on the morning of January 17th. In endeavouring to discover the route by which these cattle were brought to Liverpool, I ascertained that 24 of these cattle were despatched from Leominster on January 16th, and were received and untrucked at the Canada dock cattle station of the London and North-Western Railway, and walked from thence to the ship on the following morning. This place where the cattle were untrucked is much used for other cattle, specially Irish cattle, and a market was held in it for several weeks while Stanley Market was closed.

o 11711.

With regard to the landing and embarkation of cattle at Portland, I was informed that a vessel carrying cattle takes up her usual berth and lands her cattle; then, when cargo has been taken in, cattle for embarkation would travel over the same ground as those previously landed.

         I have, &c.
   (Signed) W. DUGUID.

No. 93.

LETTER from the FOREIGN OFFICE to the CLERK OF THE COUNCIL.

SIR,   Foreign Office, March 5, 1884.

I AM directed by the Secretary of State for Foreign Affairs to transmit to you, to be laid before the Committee of Council on Agriculture for such observations as their Lordships may be pleased to offer, a note in original from the United States Minister at this Court stating that the cattle which arrived at Portland, Maine, by the ship "Ontario" shortly afterwards developed foot-and-mouth disease.

       I am, &c.
   (Signed) EDMOND FITZMAURICE.
The Clerk of the Council,
 Agricultural Department.

Enclosure in No. 93.

LEGATION of the UNITED STATES.

MY LORD,   London, March 4, 1884.

REFERRING to my note of the 19th ultimo, I have the honour to acquaint your Lordship that I have received a telegram from Mr. Frelinghuysen informing me that the cattle which arrived at Portland, Maine, by the ship "Ontario," from Liverpool, shortly afterwards developed foot-and-mouth disease. The "Ontario" cleared on the 9th of February for Liverpool, and I am instructed to impress upon Her Majesty's Government the fact that if disease has appeared among the cattle which she took back to this country it must have originated from the ship being infected by the diseased English cattle which she had previously brought to the United States.

       I have, &c.
   (Signed) J. R. LOWELL.
The Right Hon. the Earl Granville, K.G.,
  &c. &c. &c.

APPENDIX.

CONTENTS.

	Page
Proceedings of the Chicago Convention	84
American Neat Cattle into Great Britain	151
Summary of Report on Pleuro-Pneumonia	154
Compilation of Laws of Different States	158

PROCEEDINGS of a NATIONAL CONVENTION of CATTLE BREEDERS and OTHERS called in Chicago, Illinois, November 15 and 16, 1883, by the HON. GEO. B. LORING, Commissioner of Agriculture, to consider the subject of CONTAGIOUS DISEASES of DOMESTIC ANIMALS.

In September last the Commissioner of Agriculture of the United States issued the following circular call:

"UNITED STATES DEPARTMENT OF AGRICULTURE,
"*Washington, D. C., September* 21, 1883.

"A convention of representatives of all classes interested in the animal industries of the United States will be held in Chicago, Thursday and Friday, November 15 and 16, 1883, for conference concerning contagious diseases among our domestic animals.

"In addition to addresses and reports, the following topics are proposed for discussion.

"1. The extent to which contagious diseases exist among domestic animals in this country.

"2. The modes by which they are introduced or disseminated.

"3. Methods by which they may be eradicated or infected districts be isolated.

"4. The efficiency of existing legislation relative to such diseases.

"It is desired that this Convention may be national and thoroughly representative in its character. The time and place have been selected for the convenience of the large number of those directly interested in the questions to be discussed, who are expected to be in attendance at the Annual Fat Stock Show under the auspices of the Illinois State Board of Agriculture, and meetings of a number of important live stock associations to be held during the continuance of this show.

"Agricultural, live stock, and dairy associations are invited to send representatives, and all persons interested in breeding, rearing, transporting, importing or exporting any class of farm animals will be welcomed to the Convention.

"GEO. B. LORING,
"*Commissioner of Agriculture.*"

Pursuant to the place and date mentioned, the several delegates met and were called to order by Prof. G. E. Morrow, of the Illinois State University, at Champaign, Ill. He said:

GENTLEMEN: You are all aware that we meet as a National Convention of those interested in the animal industries of the country, at the call of the Commissioner of Agriculture, Dr. Loring, at whose request I have the honour to call you to order. I hold in my hand a letter from Dr. Loring explaining his enforced absence from this meeting, and I know that each and everyone present shares with me the deep regret I feel because of his absence. I know how thoroughly sincere Dr. Loring's words of regret are, and no one feels it more than we do. It was manifestly fitting that this call should proceed from a national source, thus removing it from any possible suspicion that it was from any one class or any one section. I can assure you that it is the earnest wish of Dr. Loring that this Convention shall be thoroughly representative, and I am glad to see before me quite a number of familiar faces, and whose names will be a sufficient guarantee of the successful outcome of our deliberations. In order, therefore, that we may be able to effect an organisation, I suggest that the roll of States be called and that the list of delegates be reported at once. With the understanding that it is Dr. Loring's desire that every gentleman interested directly in any branch of the animal industry shall be free to a voice in the proceedings of the meeting, the call of States will now be made.

Mr. J. H. SANDERS, of Illinois. I suggest, Mr. Chairman, that gentlemen present, without waiting for a formal call of States, hand in their list on slips of paper or any other convenient form, and then we can proceed to a temporary organisation.

Professor MCMURTRIE, of Illinois. I don't like to interpose a suggestion thus early in the proceedings, but I think it would be a good idea for the States to be called, and some member of the delegation could then hand in his list for entry and classification.

The Chairman then called the roll of States and Territories, and the following list of 175 delegates, representing 20 States and Territories, was reported and enrolled:—

Alabama—J. D. McFarland.

Arizona—J. G. Gosper.

Colorado—W. J. Wilson, H. T. Metcalf, G. W. Rusk, Carey Culver, —— Culver, —— Maxwell.

District of Columbia—Dr. D. E. Salmon.

Illinois—G. W. Curtis, J. K. Shaver, J. M. Thompson, D. N. Foster, J. M. Chambers, J. H. Sanders, D. W. Smith, J. R. Scott, A. B. Hostetter, J. H. Pickrell, C. M. Culbertson, Prof. G. E. Morrow.

Iowa—L. S. Coffin, W. R. Matthew, James Morgan, D. Moninger, H. C. Wheeler, Fitch B. Stacy, Hon. J. B. Grinnell, Hon. John Scott, Thomas B. Wales, R. D. Kellogg, W. R. Nugent, M. L. Dwin, J. Clark, D. Bonnett, George Chase, H. B. Griffin, Joseph Sproat, C. R. Smith, B. H. Taylor, W. T. Smith, E. F. Brockway, J. R. Shaffer, J. J. Snouffer, L. C. Baldwin, R. C. Webb, J. D. Brown.

Kentucky—Hon. J. S. Williams, James Chorn, B. A. Tracy, C. Thompson, C. Estell, B. F. Vanmeter, J. C. Hamilton, George Hamilton, C. R. Esten, W. W. Estell, W. W. Hamilton, A. W. Hamilton, D. A. Gay, W. Yarr, A. C. Bean, W. Garner, C. Scott, R. Owen, G. Hill, T. C. Anderson, C. Howell, W. Points, J. Kendall.

Minnesota—George E. Case.

Maryland—Edward B. Emory.

Massachusetts—Prof. L. S. Thayer.

Michigan—I. H. Butterfield, jr., William Ball, E. R. Phillips, —— Sweet, A. J. Murray, Prof. E. A. A. Grange, C. F. Moore, R. A. Remick, Edwin Phelps, R. B. Caruss.

Missouri—S. E. Ward.

New York—T. G. Yeomans, Prof. James Law, Col. F. D. Curtis, E. A. Powell, Joseph Harris, G. S. Miller, W. C. Brayton, Prof. J. P. Roberts, —— Wing.

Nebraska—Prof. S. R. Thompson, O. M. Donse, Watson Pickrell, Hon. William Dailey, P. Winslow.

New Jersey—John Crane.

Ohio—W. N. Cowden, L. B. Harris, W. I. Chamberlain, James W. Fleming, J. C. Levering, W. S. Foster, J. H. Brigham, L. N. Bonham, Leo Weltz, Frank Fleming, John Gould, M. J. Lawrence, Calvin Dodge, S. H. Todd, D. W. Todd, William Allwood, —— Lemnust, W. R. Parsons, Z. E. Shook, O. E. Niles, Prof. —— Niles, Prof. I. V. Newton,

I. S. Robinson, W. S. Delatast, M. P. Steddon, Prof. T. B. Cotton, J. Corwin, R. C. Skinner.

Pennsylvania—Edgar Huidekoper, J. C. Thornton, Julius LeMoyne, James L. Henderson, W. B. McKerrnan, Prof. John W. Gadsden, James B. Wilson, Samuel P. Fergus, W. M. Dinsmore, J. H. Clark, P. G. Walker, J. G. Paxton, J. M. Thompson.

Tennessee—W. P. Johnson, J. E. Wilcox, M.S. Cockrill, John Overton.

Texas—George B. Loving.

Wisconsin—Prof. —— Henry Hon. Hiram Smith.

Wyoming—Hon. J. M. Carey, Hon. Thomas Sturgis, Hon. W. C. Irvine, Hon. E. Teschemacher, Hon. A. H. Swan, J. H. Pratt, John Clay, May Goldschmidt, John Hunton, S. H. Hardin, W. H. Parker, R. A. Torrey, G. Holden, —— Stevens, George Morgan, Prof. James D. Hopkins.

West Virginia—J. M. Kirk, L. P. Sisson, T. R. Carskaden, T. H. Buchanan, I. B. Carskaden, C. P. Waugh, O. A. Lewis, O. M. Kirk, Obed Bath, Aaron Baker.

Mr. STURGIS, of Wyoming. Gentlemen of the Convention, in the absence of Dr. Loring I propose to you as your temporary chairman, Professor Morrow. I move that he be made temporary chairman.

The motion was agreed to.

Professor MORROW, of Illinois. I thank you heartily for this honour, for I count it an honor to preside, even temporarily, over so important a meeting. There are many things I should be glad to say, but I shall try to set an example by not occupying the time of the Convention in saying fancy things.

Mr. GOSPER, of Arizona. I move the appointment of Mr. Sturgis of Wyoming as temporary secretary.

Mr. STURGIS. I appreciate the gentleman's consideration, but I shall be unable to act, as I have duties in connexion with my own delegation.

The Hon. L. S. COFFIN, of Iowa, was thereupon nominated and elected temporary secretary.

The CHAIRMAN. Now, to expedite matters, though I leave it entirely in the hands of the Convention, I will suggest that a committee on permanent organisation be appointed, to consist of one member from each State and Territory represented.

A DELEGATE. I move that the plan suggested be adopted.

The motion was agreed to, and upon call the following named gentlemen were selected to represent their respective States upon the committee :—

Alabama, J. D. McFarland; Colorado, W. J. Wilson; District of Columbia, Dr. D. E. Salmon; Illinois, John R. Scott; Iowa, W. T. Smith; Kentucky, James Chorn; Maryland, Edward B. Emory; Massachusetts, Prof. L. S. Thayer; Michigan, I. H. Butterfield, jr.; Missouri, Col. S. E. Ward; Nebraska, Prof. S. R. Thompson; New York, Prof. James Law; Ohio, W. N. Cowden; Pennsylvania, J. C. Thornton; Tennessee, J. E. Wilcox; West Virginia, T. R. Carskaden; Wisconsin, Hon. Hiram Smith; Wyoming, Hon. J. M. Carey.

The CHAIRMAN. I will suggest that this committee retire and present a report as soon as possible. I would call the attention of the Convention to the fact that we have with us this morning two gentlemen from Canada. I think it would be well to have their names enrolled, but under a strict construction of the call the Chair would not be at liberty to do so.

A DELEGATE. I move that the provinces of Canada be called.

The motion was agreed to, and upon call Hon. M. H. Cockran

responded from the province of Quebec, and Prof. Simon Beatty from the province of Ontario.

The CHAIRMAN. I will take the liberty of nominating the Hon. W. T. Smith, of Iowa, as the chairman of the committee on permanent organization, at least until the committee takes further action.

Hon. J. S. WILLIAMS, of Kentucky. I wish to make one suggestion. It strikes me as almost impossible to get a large attendance in the day-time of the stock-men of the country. The fat-stock show is to be held here, beginning to-day and extending up to next Tuesday or Wednesday. There are engaged and interested in this exhibition three hundred or four hundred men—the very men we wish to meet—and but a small number of them can be here in the day-time. I want to ask if it will not be better, all things considered, to hold our meetings in the evening. Now, for instance, I see around me several who want to go to the sale of cattle this afternoon, and then there are other of these sales to-morrow and next day, and so on extending up to as late as next Wednesday, and the fat-stock show is going on all the time. Will it not be best for us to have our meetings in the evening? We certainly could get a much larger attendance.

Mr. THOMPSON, of Kentucky. I hope an organization will be made first, and then this matter can be considered.

Mr. WILLIAMS. I merely mentioned it now because it may be the intention to have a report made immediately.

The CHAIRMAN. The Chair will say that he fully appreciates the force of the remarks made by the gentleman from Kentucky (Mr. Williams), but this evening other important meetings are to be held. The American Hereford Association have a meeting, as do also two agricultural associations in the interest of the horse, not quite so directly connected with the specific object of this Convention perhaps, but there are some who would like to be present at some one of these meetings. Without wishing at all to dictate the action of the Convention I will suggest, with Mr. Thompson, that it will be well for us first to get our work somewhat in hand and started.

Mr. J. H. SANDERS, of Illinois. If you will indulge me a word in relation to this matter, I will say that there are two other organisations now meeting here, the sheep breeders and swine breeders. I presume after to-night the rush of these public meetings will be over, for this room at least, and I beg that this Convention will not attempt to rush its proceedings. I hope that it will proceed calmly and deliberately, and take time to thoroughly digest every step that shall be taken with care and due consideration. I do think it is impracticable at night to get a large proportion of these representative men at a meeting. They are all interested in some special meeting to be held to-night. These meetings were called a year ago, most of them, and it is impossible to make changes. I really think we should take ample time to digest every step that is taken.

The CHAIRMAN. Gentlemen, if you will pardon me, and I know you will, I have at my right a gentleman who is interested in agriculture in the State and nation, and I have taken the liberty in advance of inviting Governor Hamilton, of the State of Illinois, in which we meet to-day, to say a few words to you. [Applause.]

Governor HAMILTON. Mr. Chairman and gentlemen of the Convention: When I accepted the very kind and very urgent invitation of Professor Morrow and others to meet with you this morning for a short time, it was with the distinct understanding that I was not expected to deliver an address. I am very happy, however, to have the privilege of meeting, for a necessarily short time, inasmuch as my official duties call me this evening back to the capital, such a fine representative body of men—as fine in appearance and in general cast as a representative body of men can be in any direction or interest—as fully up to the standard of development and of good appearance in the line of animals called men as is the gathering over here in the Exposition Building in the line of animals called fat stock. [Applause.] I am most sincerely sorry, gentlemen, with all of you no doubt, that Dr. Loring is not present, for I have anticipated for some time the pleasure of listening to that distinguished gentleman.

I fully appreciate the importance of this conference, and of the objects of this Convention, as I understand them, to consider the subject of contagious diseases among animals, their cause, their ravages, and means of prevention and cure. We, in this State, are especially interested in this matter. Since it has been my privilege to preside as chief executive of the State of Illinois we have had considerable trouble in that direction among our stock raisers. During the session of the last legislature, last winter and spring, it became apparent that something must be done by the State government, and by legislative action, to prevent so far as possible the spread of the deadly disease known to stockmen as glanders among horses, which had made its appearance in some parts of the State. It happened that at that time we had upon the statute-books of Illinois an Act providing for the prevention and suppression of pleuro-pneumonia among cattle, under which Act a State veterinarian was provided, and also a fund to be used by him in connexion with his work. That fund, I am happy to say, however, it was unnecessary to use, at least any great portion of it, as the disease, pleuro-pneumonia, did not make its appearance. That Act was amended last winter so as to include measures for meeting the ravages of the disease called "glanders," which, as I said before, began to break out, as the Irishman said, "in spots here and there," but in a great many spots, and I have found out that the probabilities are that if it had not been for prompt legislative action we should have suffered to a very much greater extent than we have. The State veterinary surgeon, under my direction, has been very busy during the summer and fall in performing his duties under that Act. He has discovered a great many cases, and I doubt not has stopped, to a large extent, the ravages of the disease. The Act provides that after a visit and examination by the State veterinarian, the animal, if affected, may be condemned, or sequestered, or quarantined, as he may direct, and with these facilities, in connexion with certain local facilities and veterinary surgeons, if it is found that the animal is afflicted he may condemn it and have it destroyed, the State paying the amount of the assessment. The law has worked to the very great advantage of the State, and apparently with little friction. If other contagious diseases could be similarly dealt with, either through the action of State government, or even of the National Government, by appropriations for carrying out the provisions of law, it would be of very great value to the animal industry of the States and of the United States.

There is an affliction among swine which still exists to some extent, not only in this but other Western States. In this State it has not been very destructive, but if some measures could be agreed upon, or discovered by somebody, to stop the ravages of that disease, it would certainly save thousands, if not millions, of dollars to the stock raisers of the West. It seems to me there ought to be no difficulty since the experience we have had in this matter. About six years ago, while I was a member of the senate of this State, a gentleman proposed by way of a bill a very large reward to any one who should discover an unfailing remedy for hog cholera. It was simply proposed and mentioned in the newspapers. It was not passed into law, and no further action was taken upon it, and now I receive on an average five letters a week, asking for the particulars of that reward, and if there is still any way to get the money. I am sure that in this Convention, composed as it is of gentlemen of scientific attainment, and stockmen, and those skilled in veterinary surgery and other matters connected with stock raising, some practical action will be taken which I trust will result in the enactment of some wholesome law, under the operation of which our interests will be protected. I have been intensely interested in this matter, not only as chief executive, but in the operations of farming in this State. I have not come here for the purpose of delivering an address, for I have prepared none, and, as I have said before, none was expected from me; but I welcome you most heartily to the State of Illinois, in which your Convention, called for so important a purpose, meets to-day, and I bespeak for you abundant success in your efforts to secure for your interests all proper legislation. Thanking you for your attention, I bid you good day. [Applause.]

The CHAIRMAN. I would suggest that we now appoint a committee on order of business. I simply suggest this and leave it entirely in the hands of the Convention.

Mr. SMITH, of Iowa. I move that the Chair appoint a committee of five on order of business.

Mr. STURGIS, of Wyoming. I would like to ask the gentleman whether, in his motion for a committee on order of business, he contemplates the appointment of a committee to discuss the subjects that may come before the Convention, or is it simply to define the order of the questions to be discussed, or is there some other business which requires to have a routine arrangement.

The CHAIRMAN. The thought of the Chair was this : That at any such meeting there are many questions which come up, and there are many gentlemen who have important suggestions to make, and if all these could be reported to this committee, it would be competent for them to report what, in their judgment, should come before the Convention, but of course subject to the action of the Convention.

Mr. C. E. SMITH, of Iowa. I had in view that this committee, being small and not unwieldy, could report the order of procedure of the Convention, recommend time, and so forth.

The motion was agreed to; and the chairman appointed on the committee, Messrs. C. E. Smith, of Iowa; Pickrell, of Illinois; Murray, of Detroit, Michigan; Chamberlain, of Ohio; and Van Meter, of Kentucky.

Mr. GRINNELL, of Iowa. Mr. Chairman, I would make this suggestion, that as we have come together as stock raisers from all parts of the country, that we hear from gentlemen who have these afflictions that we have come here to seek remedy for, whether it is glanders or hog cholera, or anything of the kind, not an agreeable matter, it is true, but, sir, I am not advised as an agriculturist in regard to the prevalence of this disease that we have come here to combat. If any man has any trouble, not in his own immediate family [laughter], but in his neighbourhood, I think it is a good time to speak out and talk about it. We come here to learn and to sympathize if necessary. There is here a gentleman from the plains, and I refer to him because he happens to come from the State of Iowa,—a Mr. Swan. I suppose that his herd numbers about 49,000, and I should like to know if there is any Texas fever among them; and if there are other gentlemen who can give us information on this subject, I should like to hear from them.

The CHAIRMAN. One moment. The Chair desires to say that he is informed that Mr. John Dunn, the British Vice-consul, is present at the request of the British Government to attend this Convention. I think perhaps it will be the desire of the Convention to tender him its courtesy and grant him the privilege of a seat with us.

Mr. SANDERS, of Illinois. The Chair can do that without a formal motion.

The CHAIRMAN. Unless there be objection, the gentleman will be invited to a seat with us. The Chair will state that Dr. Salmon, the veterinarian of the Department of Agriculture, and who has been directed by Commissioner Loring to prepare a paper representing the information now in possession of the Department upon this subject, is present. I think it will be proper to have that paper early in the proceedings of the Convention. I await the pleasure of the Convention.

Mr. YEOMANS, of New York. I would suggest that if there are other gentlemen who have been invited to address this meeting that there is now an opportunity, until this committee are ready to report the subjects that are to be discussed and the order in which they be discussed.

The CHAIRMAN. Doubtless the members of the Convention have read at different times the call for this meeting. We meet as a body composed of all those interested in the cattle and other animal industries of the country. The Commissioner has left it free for the Convention to do what in its wisdom seems to be best; but he suggested in the original call certain topics as especially desirable, in his opinion, to be discussed.

The topics as set forth in the original call were then read.

Mr. KELLOGG, of Iowa. I was much pleased with the suggestion made by the Hon. Mr. Grinnell, and hoped to have heard a response reporting any disease of stock existing in any locality. Before he took his seat he called upon my friend Mr. Swan. There being no response from any gentleman present, the thought occurred to me whether this Convention was not, in a measure, crying fire when there is no blaze. I apprehend, sir, that it is possible that a call for such a Convention as this going out broadcast over the country and across the waters may effect a greater injury than any benefit we may derive from it. I question no man's motive, but I call upon gentlemen present to say if it is not true that any disease whatever among our stock is the exception and not the rule, and I suggest whether it will not be wisdom on our part to be cautious and not create an undue alarm that there are contagious diseases ravaging our country from one end to the other. If we are to establish that fact what will be the result in the sale of our meats? I presume that there may have been some action taken by foreign Governments inimical to the meat growers of this country, in the interest of their own product. That is all right. Nations look out for themselves as well as individuals; but now the cry of "hog cholera" has worn itself out, and it is about as hard to find as the milk sickness. You can find hundreds of people to-day who will guarantee to cure your hogs for ten cents each, and will guarantee to give you a dollar a pound for each one that is lost. It is a fact within the scope of my own observation that that disease prevails to a much more limited extent since farmers have come to get along better in the world, and have arranged their yards more in accordance with hygienic laws, and introduced purer water, and provided better in other ways for their stock. [Applause.] Farmers have come to know that a little common sense relieves them of most of this trouble, and in our western world, from here west, I know of no such thing as contagion among stock, unless it be glanders among horses, and generally when horses get that it is because they have breathed so long that they cannot breathe any longer. [Laughter.] I throw these remarks out as a suggestion. We should not magnify this matter of stock disease to our own detriment.

Mr. PARSONS, of Ohio. It has been my privilege to travel largely this past year among the cattle-raising districts of our country. My observation has been in my personal interest, and I have not found a herd where pleuro-pneumonia existed. I have travelled through the New England States, through New York and Pennsylvania. I learned that there was something like disease in Maryland, and that there had been a sprinkling of it in Pennsylvania; but westward in every direction there is not a shadow nor a semblance of it; there is one fact, however, among weaklings in calves; when the first cold weather struck some herds there was cold upon the lungs and some of those weaklings died, and some of those who have become frightened at this have scattered the news over the country that this was pleuro-pneumonia. It is just the same as a man taking a severe cold and having pneumonia, if neglected. But so far as any contagious disease of this or any other character is concerned, I have not known of a single case in all my travels.

Professor PRENTICE, of Illinois. I would like to say a few words on this subject. I have been eleven years connected with the State University of Illinois, and I can indorse what the gentleman has just said about bronchial pneumonia among calves, and I am certain that men who are not experienced would pronounce that to be contagious pleuro-pneumonia; but such is not the case.

Mr. KELLOGG. I would like to ask the gentleman before he takes his seat, if he has ever known of a case of contagious pleuro-pneumonia in this country?

Professor PRENTICE. Never, sir. I have seen plenty of it in England.

Mr. CLARK, of Iowa. Mr. Chairman, as a stock raiser since 1840, in Iowa, and as a citizen and farmer of that State, having mingled among the stockmen and stock farmers, buying, selling, and raising, I have yet to learn of a man of experience in raising and breeding stock in our State who has yet known the time himself when it was dangerous to go to any other herd in the State of Iowa to purchase stock for his purposes because there was contagious diseases among them. I have handled several thousand head of stock myself. I have wintered them, brought them from the different places west of Iowa, and from Illinois, to my farm, placed them together, cared for them from a year to two years, fattened them and brought them back to this market, and no animal has had a disease which was communicated to it by any other animal. Yet I have been in England and have seen cattle from my State, and some from my own neighbourhood, placed at a disadvantage of from $5 to $10 a hundred because of the sanitary regulations which barred out our stock from being shipped through Great Britain, and all because of the fears that have been built up that our stock was diseased. I am glad to know that there is a gentleman representing that country on this floor, and in his hearing I assert, as a stock raiser of Iowa, that the time has never been in Iowa when it was dangerous to bring stock from Illinois, Wisconsin, Michigan, Wyoming, or Utah for fear it would communicate disease. [Applause.]

Mr. COFFIN, of Iowa. I heartily agree with every word that has been said in regard to any contagious disease prevailing at present in these Western States. There is no question about it so far as the cattle disease, pleuro-pneumonia, is concerned; but for fear that this Convention shall be turned aside from the great point that I am so anxious it should meet, I feel called upon to reply to some of the remarks which have been just made. We rejoice and we feel like being grateful, and are grateful, that we have none of this contagious disease in the West; but we must acknowledge and own that we are not without danger. [Applause.] So long as contagious disease exists anywhere in this nation just so long are we in danger, and the object of this Convention is to plan some way and some method to eradicate every vestige of disease from our land. [Renewed applause.] My friend, Hon. Justice Clark, admits that we are discriminated against. Every shipper of a steer from here to England has to suffer a loss of from $10 to $20 from the very fact that there does exist somewhere in this nation a contagious disease, and we are meeting to devise some plan, some method, to remove the cause of that discrimination. [Applause.] Every man in this Convention who is intelligent enough to know anything knows that there exists along our eastern coast this pleuro-pneumonia. We cannot shut our eyes to that; and our steers going from the West have to pass through the Atlantic States. Our English cousins know this fact, and no steer can go from the West through Baltimore, New York, or Philadelphia without being more or less in danger of contagion. [Applause.] Then again, we are receiving now very largely breeding stock from the other country. Those cattle have to come through those ports, and I say it is a miracle of good luck that we never have had this disease brought into the West by that means. Now, shall we shut our eyes to the danger that is before us? We don't attempt to tell the world that we have this disease here in the West, and if we did we should tell a falsehood. What we are doing is the planning of measures to prevent and rid ourselves of a danger that we cannot shut our eyes to. [Applause.]

Mr. CLARK, of Iowa. I agree with Mr. Coffin that this Convention should do everything in its power in this direction What I desired to show was that we have none of this disease in the Western States. I am ready to join any gentleman present in making any arrangement to bring to the attention of Congress the dangers that surround us in order, if possible, that we may prevent this disease from being brought here and continue to be clear of it.

Dr. GADSDEN. I will not take up your time but a moment. What I desire to say is that England does not want any information from this Convention as to where contagious diseases exist in this country. I can assure you that they know where it is as well as we do. Every month they publish in a journal the exact location of all herds that are affected. They know full well that the West has never yet seen this disease. I make this suggestion in order to show that you need not trouble yourselves about England's information on this subject. Where they get it or who informs them I don't know. I was in England last year and I saw there copies of letters and reports from the Agricultural and Treasury Departments—all the information apparently that is in their possession. They know it all, gentlemen, and officially, too.

Mr. Smith, from the committee on permanent organisation, presented the following report, which was unanimously agreed to:

President—Hon. John S. Williams, of Kentucky.

Vice-Presidents—Prof. George E. Morrow, of Illinois; Hon. Alfred Batters, of Colorado; Edward A. Powell, of New York; Hon. M. H. Cochrane, of Dominion of Canada.

Secretary—Hon. Thomas Sturgis, of Wyoming.

Assistant Secretary—Edward B. Emory, of Maryland.

The newly-elected president of the Convention was thereupon conducted to the chair, and Professor Morrow said:

GENTLEMEN OF THE CONVENTION: I have the honour to introduce to you a gentleman who is widely known as one largely interested in agriculture and the subjects you are to discuss, and also for his public service in their behalf. [Applause.]

The PRESIDENT: Gentlemen of the Convention, I feel profoundly grateful to you for this very unexpected honour. I am here rather by accident than otherwise, but glad of an opportunity of meeting representative men from every section of our country, who are gathered together at this time to consider one of the most vital interests of the whole people of our land. I cannot, in accepting the honour and responsibilities of presiding over your deliberations, refrain from expressing my profound regret that the distinguished gentleman whom we all expected to preside over this Convention, the Commissioner of Agriculture, Dr. Loring, is detained at home by sickness. I know that he would have been able to instruct us upon the subjects that we have met to consider. I came here merely to learn, and not to instruct; for while there is not a more zealous man in this broad land in the advocacy of measures for your benefit, I am not in possession of information to instruct you. I have zeal but not knowledge. I have struggled in the Congress of the United States for years to procure some remedial legislation from the National Government that might reach the root of the evil. Perhaps I do not understand the full scope and objects of this meeting; but if I do understand them it is to attempt to procure measures for the interdiction of foreign and exotic diseases, especially of the cattle of the country. We do know that certain highly contagious diseases have been imported here from foreign countries, and have been planted in certain sections of our country; and yet these diseases are restricted within such narrow limits, that it is entirely possible and practicable for the National Government to stamp them out wherever they are found, and to take measures for the prevention of their further introduction. I have endeavoured for years to impress this idea upon Congress. I have laboured much upon that subject; and I have found one great difficulty to be that a majority of your Representatives had not sufficient information upon this subject and could not be induced to talk as they should have done. If you want anything done now you must express your determination. Also provide funds to send your delegation to Washington to pay its way; not to buy its way, but to pay its way, for they have got to stay there and lobby the bill through. Every other interest has its lobby there, and it is useless to talk about doing anything without money. The bankers, the iron men, the manufacturers, everybody has a lobby there except the farmers and stock-raisers, and if you expect to get any legislation in your interest you must adopt the necessary means to accomplish it. [Great laughter.] We represent the greatest interest of all. The cattle interest alone amounts to $750,000,000 annually—more than the tobacco; more than the wheat; more than everything else, and nearly as much as all others combined, but far more than any one interest; for those things which you produce, your corn and your grass, go into your stock. Animal productions amount to more than all the other products of the country combined. Well, now, this disease not only endangers your herds at home, for we know that they are contagious and incurable, but while they are yet confined to limited districts we feel certain they have not influenced the cattle trade from west to east; but, when it turns the other way, with the growth of the dairy, the production of milk and butter, how then will it be when shipment of improved bulls must be made West. The misfortune of the thing now is that these diseases are located at the very ports of entry from which you export your cattle, and they cast suspicion over everything you send to foreign countries. You want not only the disease exterminated, but you want that suspicion removed. [Applause.] In my judgment there is no power to do that except the almighty arm of the National Government, which is able to appropriate the necessary means. [Applause.] Foreign countries know us as one people only; they do not understand our dual form of government; that we are a great nation composed of independent commonwealths; they regard us only as the American Government, the Government of the United States; and Illinois and Kentucky and Pennsylvania and New York and Maryland and Virginia, do what they may, can never remove the suspicion of the people in the foreign markets of the world that our meats come to them in an unhealthy and unsound condition, and that the American Government takes upon itself the responsibility of giving clean bills of health. What do we lose by this? What might be our exports to foreign countries? Think of it. We are exporting $15,000,000 annually, and about as much of dead meat of the product of cattle, to say nothing about our hogs, and the suspicion that is cast upon your live stock has excluded your hogs and your pork from Germany and France, and means such restriction upon your live cattle going to England as to amount almost to a prohibition. Suppose we can remove this. Suppose we can satisfy the foreign countries that all our live animals are free from infection. What might be the extent of our exports? I can assure you that in time they would amount to more, much more, than all of our other exports combined. If we had a free market; if you men could send your 1,200 and 1,400 pound bullocks to England, and instruct your continental grazers to put them on their pastures and feed them turnips and rich succulent grasses, they would soon get over the heat and fever and bruises and sores of that long line of transportation from the extreme West, 1,500 miles by rail and 3,000 miles by sea; they could take them and finish them up and bring them back into the market, and they would bring as high a price as British beef. [Applause.] But as it is they have to be slaughtered in the pens immediately, and if there is a glut in the market at the time your beef is sold at a sacrifice, for they cannot be transported back, nor is there any ice there to preserve the meat, and you lose sometimes from $35 to $40 per head. Remove this taint and instead of shipping from $15,000,000 to $20,000,000 annually of live cattle you would ship from $250,000,000 to $300,000,000. Think of the advantage, you men of the West, if you could ship your 1,300 or 1,400 pound bullocks abroad and have them placed in the shambles there as fresh and as juicy and pure as the finest they could raise abroad. Instead of getting 3 cents a pound you would get 6 cents for cattle in this market; and if the market was free, instead of 4 cents for your hogs you would get 7 or 8 cents. This is indeed a mighty question; it is the greatest question of all that can be presented to the farmers of this country—the question of exterminating this disease and removing this suspicion [applause], and we never can prosper until that thing is done. [Renewed applause.] I shall not attempt to make you a speech. I am here merely to hear and to see how much help you are going to give me this winter in procuring the adoption of measures for the suppression of these plagues. I cannot do it alone. You have in your hands the means to influence your members of Congress—your Senators, and Representatives in the House—and let me assure you that you have got to bring that influence to bear upon them, you have got to knock loud and often, before they will listen to your appeals. [Applause.]

May I ask what is your order of business?

Mr. GOSPER, of Arizona Territory. I simply rise to request the Chairman to ask his secretary to rise and make a bow to the audience, so that we may be able to recognise him hereafter. [Great laughter.]

Mr. STURGIS, of Wyoming. I don't think that any remarks are necessary from me, Mr. Chairman.

A DELEGATE. Mr. President, I understand that the Committee on order of business is ready to report. Will the chairman of that committee rise and state the facts?

Mr. C. E. SMITH, of Iowa. We have hastily prepared a report, in order to give the Convention something to work upon, and the secretary will read the report.

Mr. COFFIN, of Iowa. I am very anxious to hear something from Mr. Sturgis, because he is one of the prime movers in this movement.

Mr. STURGIS, of Wyoming. Gentlemen, I am less unwilling to say a few words upon this occasion from the fact that a remark which was made here this morning seemed to me to furnish a text for your deliberations to-day which cannot be improved upon. It was said by one of the gentlemen, I think from Iowa, that this disease had never entered his State, and that he was able to buy cattle from the West without any fear of disease. Why is it that he says he is able to buy of my friend Mr. Swan without this fear? It is not because disease has not threatened Wyoming. We in that Territory take the very deepest interest in this question, and it arises from the fact that while with you, perhaps, this cattle interest is one of many industries in your States, with us it is the basis upon which the entire prosperity of our Territory rests. With us it is the one thing upon which rests, not only the taxation of the Territory, but the success of the stores, the manufacturing institutions, the banks, and everything. With us it is the one thing, and you cannot picture in brighter colours than we can imagine for ourselves the effect should one of these terrible bovine scourges invade our Territory. We have been alive to this for a long time past. It is no new measure; for we have taken all the means for local protection that our commonwealth can adopt. Over two years ago a very elaborate bill, combining not only the features of the Illinois law, but also all the best terms of printed legislation on the subject, was passed by our legislature, and under the provisions of that bill we have been locally protected for the past two years. I will not give you in detail the provisions of that Bill. I will simply say that it provides and makes obligatory on the owner of stock that every bull, every cow, every heifer that he brings into our Territory shall have from our Territorial veterinarian a clean bill of health before he leaves the first station at which he arrives within the Territory. This you understand is made obligatory. Our veterinarian has the right not only to detain, to quarantine, but destroy, and the fund for these purposes is received from a special tax. We have come here as a delegation appointed at a special meeting of our association, and as a member of that delegation I desire to impress upon you the necessity of shutting the stable door before the horse is stolen. As I say, we have provided at our own doors such measures as we can to prevent the introduction of this disease into our Territory. Now, we want to prevent the possibility of that disease ever coming to our doors, and to kill it where it now exists. [Applause.] It certainly would be foolish indeed for us to rest in fancied security and be misled into the belief that because we have not had previously much disease that we shall never have it. There can be no misleading about it, for in a publication of the Commissioner of Agriculture, a copy of which lies before me on the table, it is shown that this disease, especially the scourge of pleuro-pneumonia, exists in at least five of the Atlantic States, and in those States, in a mild form, in not less than 200 separate localities. That is not a thing that can be overlooked; it is not a thing that we can say exists there and will never exist anywhere else. We do believe that at present it is so isolated, and that it is in such localities that, with a moderate expenditure of money by the General Government, directed by careful, scientific, and professional men, it will be possible to eradicate this disease, and if we neglect it we just as earnestly believe that in a few years we shall be in the condition of the British Islands. The Wyoming delegation, gentlemen, is ready to enter upon the necessary work with time, and labour, and money. We are in favour of that sort of surgery that cuts off the leg in order to save the life. [Applause.]

The PRESIDENT. I understand that the committee on order of business is now ready to report. The secretary of the committee will read the report.

Mr. Chamberlain, from the committee, then presented the following report:—

"The committee on order of business beg leave to report that, in order that this Convention may at once proceed to its intended work, we recommend—

"First. That we at once listen to papers and addresses from Professor Law and J. H. Sanders, of the Treasury Commission, Dr. D. E. Salmon, of the Agricultural Department and Dr. Jas. D. Hopkins, of Wyoming, stating the present condition of investigation by their commissions and by the Department, and such recommendations as they may see fit to make to this Convention for its action, looking towards effecting necessary legislation.

"Second. That the Convention adjourn for dinner at 1 p.m., and hold other meetings at 3.30 and 9 p.m. to-day, and at 8 a.m. to-morrow, or until the objects of the Convention have been attained.

"The committee request that persons who have papers or addresses of a practical nature that they are ready to present should state the fact to the committee that it may arrange programme for future meetings to-day and to-morrow.

"The committee will meet this morning in this room at the reporter's table to listen to suggestions and receive names of parties that are likely to present papers of real value to the Convention.

"Respectfully submitted.
"CAREY R. SMITH, *Chairman*.
"W. I. CHAMBERLAIN, *Secretary*."

A DELEGATE. I move that the report be adopted by sections.
The motion was agreed to.
The first section was thereupon read and adopted.
Upon consideration of the second section the following discussion took place:—

Mr. LAWRENCE, of Ohio. It seems to me that half-past 3 is pretty late for our afternoon session.

Mr. CHAMBERLAIN. of Ohio. The reason for the action of the committee was that it was thought that a large part of the audience would wish to be present in other places between the time of adjournment and the hour named.

The PRESIDENT. I think it will be impossible for many to come even at that hour. These sales will be in progress, and I know there are many who wish to attend them. The sale is not only to-day but to-morrow and next day. I merely throw out this suggestion. It strikes me that we might have a morning session at which the committees could report and the routine business be discussed, but by all means let us have a night session. We are considering a very important matter, and we should have a meeting at night when these gentlemen can all be present. We can devote hours to it then, and sit until 1 o'clock if we choose. All these men are interested in this exhibition and in buying and selling high-bred stock. It is very important to have them with us. Their influence is worth a great deal to us, and I hope some one will move that we have a night session instead.

Mr. W. T. SMITH, of Iowa. I move that when this Convention adjourns it be to meet at 7 o'clock this evening.

Mr. CAREY E. SMITH, of Iowa. I would like to say in defence of the action of the committee, that we cannot hold any meeting at any hour that will not affect some one of the many meetings and attractions here. We also recognised the fact that there are gentlemen here who have come thousands of miles for the express purpose of moving in this work. We cannot put this off from time to time to accommodate this State and that State, therefore we tried to harmonise and hold the evening sessions rather late in order that some of these meetings could get through and their members could attend our meeting.

The second section was then adopted, and, upon motion, the remaining section was adopted.

Mr. GRINNELL, of Iowa. Mr. Chairman, I presume there are at least 50 persons present whom I should be glad to hear from; they are all able men, and some of them scientific gentlemen in the professions. I move, sir, in order that each may have a chance, that gentlemen occupying the time of the Convention be limited to one half an hour, and we can do as they do in Congress, give them "leave to print" [laughter] until they have been heard all around.

The PRESIDENT. I would say to the gentleman that some of the gentlemen who are here have been specially been called upon to address us, and that the time mentioned would neither be long enough nor fair to them.

Mr. GRINNELL. Well, sir, we can ask them to go on when the time has expired.

The PRESIDENT. In accordance with the recommendation of the committee on order of business, Professor Law's paper is first in order, and I have the pleasure of introducing that gentleman, who will now address you. [Applause.]

Professor Law, of Cornell University, then addressed the Convention. He said:

"Mr. PRESIDENT AND GENTLEMEN: No more important question can to-day engage the attention of the citizen or statesman than that of the contagious diseases of animals and the means of suppressing and extinguishing them. This subject has been too long neglected and is liable to continued neglect, for the reason that those who suffer pecuniarily from these affections have a deep personal interest in keeping the extent and even the very fact of their losses a profound secret. The city milkman who loses from the bovine lung plague in a single half year a number of cows equal to the entire herd that he holds at any one time would drive his customers to other dairies and invoke financial ruin if he published the fact of his heavy losses. The horse dealer would find his stock a drug in the market if he were injudicious enough to report that glandered animals had occupied his stalls. The flockmaster would throw away his chances of a remunerative sale if he let it be known that his sheep suffered from scab, lung-worms, or foot-rot. The swine-breeder might give up all hope of profit if he allowed

o 11711.

that his herds were infested with trichinæ or contaminated with swine-plague.

"Yet we well know that these are only examples of the animal contagia now existing among us and that threaten the whole of the live-stock industries of this great country.

"Texas Fever—Gulf-Coast Fever.

"Our entire southern coast is contaminated with a poison deadly to all bovine animals that have not been inured to it from the earliest dawnings of life, and Dr. Salmon has shown that this poison is steadily advancing northward, and for aught we yet know may one day cast its withering spell over our countless Northern herds as well. This poison is inherent in the soil, and in a suitable field may live and propagate in the earth independently of animal hosts. It is therefore in one sense even more redoubtable than those animal contagia which have little or no viability or power of self-propagation out of the living animal body. Happily for us, as yet this redoubtable poison cannot survive the winter frosts of our Northern States. Its yearly invasions of our northern pastures in summer and autumn are as yet effectually repelled by the winter's cold, and the disease has to make a fresh start the next year from its perennial home in the sunny south. Whether it can by a slow and gradual advance through the intermediate climates of the Middle States become finally acclimated and fitted for survival in the extreme north is a question that must be settled by carefully conducted experiment, unless, indeed, we elect to pursue our time-honoured policy of letting the experiment be wrought out in the natural way, and of ascertaining, mayhap when too late, that our northern herds are yearly scourged by the plague, and that our northern pastures have become permanently saturated with the deadly germs. The prevalence of this poison on the whole coast of the Gulf of Mexico and on the islands in the Gulf suggests that it is an indigenous germ generated in some way in that particular soil, and hence we must learn much more than we as yet know of its life-history before we can decide whether it will ever be possible for us to stamp it out. At present we can prevent its yearly summer invasions of the north and its slower but more permanent advances in the Middle States; we can even habituate young animals to its influence so that they may not fall victims to its ravages; but we cannot promise by any known measures to purify the already contaminated Southern States and guarantee them wholesome to cattle brought from without.

"Tuberculosis.

"Take another prevalent plague—tuberculosis. There can no longer be a shadow of doubt that this is a contagious disease, and I feel that I can no longer rationally doubt that it is caused by the infinitesimal germ, *Bacillus tuberculosis*, recently discovered by Koch. The fact that this scourge is common to man and a large class of domestic and wild animals places it on a height of sanitary importance that forbids us to ignore it or to contemplate it with feelings other than those of dread and apprehension. The vital statistics of New York City show that 29 per cent. of the mortality in its adult male population is from tuberculosis, and our examination of the herds that supply that city with milk reveals the astounding fact that in certain herds tuberculosis affects 20, 30, and, in some cases, even 50 per cent. Nor is this the worst showing that can be adduced. I have seen single herds of 50 and 60 head in the healthy country districts of New York, in which 90 per cent. were the victims of tuberculosis.

"Experiment has shown that this disease is propagated not only by direct inoculation, but by the consumption of the tuberculous flesh and milk, and by the inhalation into the lungs of the virulent particles diffused in the atmosphere in water spray. Nor does this complete the list of its channels of infection. I have recently witnessed in the biological laboratories of Europe the artificial cultivation of the tubercle bacillus on the freshly-cut surfaces of fruits and on sterilized bread, as well as on gelatinous preparations, and have seen the brute sufferers from tuberculosis that have been inoculated from these cultivations. In the face of these evidences that we and our animal possessions are liable to contract this fatal malady by the various channels of simple skin abrasions, ingestion with our food, animal and vegetable, and inhalation with our breath, no one will accuse me of underrating the magnitude of the danger, nor of seeking to undervalue any available measure for its restriction. One stands in wonder that in this conclusion of the 19th century the subject should still be comparatively unnoticed and untouched by Governments and by their local and national boards of health.

"But, great as is the need of sanitation in this field, and strongly as it appeals to the moral sense, as well as to the instincts of self-preservation of the individual and the community, the fact remains that the subject is too gigantic, the cost of restrictive measures too great, and the results promised us are too partial to warrant the expectation that the Government is prepared as yet to effectually grapple with the evil. The infected animals are scattered all over this great continent. They are found at least as abundantly in the herds of the countries adjoining us, and are liable to cross our frontier at any moment. The infection prevails not in one genus of animals only, but among all domesticated animals, especially the ruminants and omnivora. Thus, in men and domestic animals, we would have to inspect and control not less than 190,000,000 individuals scattered over an area of 3,000,000 square miles. But, in addition to all this, wild animals that successfully evade the domination and control of man, suffer equally with the tame. The poison can survive and multiply not only in a living animal medium, but also in dead vegetable matter; and, finally man himself furnishes so many victims that after we had done everything possible for the extinction of the poison in beast and vegetable, the sacredness of human life would still set a limit to our suppressive measures, and the virus would continue to be perpetuated everywhere in man, and at frequent intervals to be conveyed anew to the brute. Many millions might be spent on this affection to the great advantage of the community, with the effect of securing what might approximate to a temporary extinction of the active disease in the lower animals, yet, owing to the persisting consumptions among men, there would be no actual diminution of the infected area, and no one part of the country could be said to have been saved from the blighting presence of this disease. Critics would inveigh against the prophylactic measures with far more effect than they now do against the Jennérian vaccination, and, if unsupported by familiar contemporaneous instances in which contagious diseases had been completely extinguished, the sanitarians would find it hard to obtain a continued supply of the sinews of war and to maintain the humanitarian conflict. A failure after such a crusade had been inaugurated would mean a staggering blow to all sanitary legislation, and a serious retarding of the immeasurable boon which through this means may be secured for suffering humanity.

Great and ubiquitous as is the evil of animal tuberculosis, I would advise that for the present no veterinary sanitary legislation for its suppression be sought from the national Congress, but that the subject be for a time left in the hands of municipal health officers, physicians, and hygienists; in other words, let the individual and the local community adopt such protective measures as come within their power, or as the exigencies of their particular case may demand. All such isolated action is confessedly very imperfect and comparatively ineffectual, yet it will be of vast benefit, and will prove a stepping-stone to that national control which I trust many now present may live to see, and which should aim at the entire extinction of this bane of civilisation.

"Swine Plague.

"Turn to another of our great prevailing animal plagues. The so-called hog cholera or swine plague has become domiciled in all our great pork-raising districts. A few years ago the annual losses were estimated at $20,000,000, a sum which implies at once a decimation of over 50,000,000 swine, and a general prevalence of the disease wherever swine are bred on a large scale. The great area involved in these ravages, and the numbers of contaminated herds and infected premises, would make any effort to stamp out this disease a herculean task. Again, though there is a presumption that this disease once extirpated would be rooted out for good, still we are not yet certain that it does not arise indigenously on our own land, and that after all our labour and outlay we would not still be continually confronted by new centres of infection developed by unwholesome conditions among badly managed herds. It is more than questionable whether Congress would appropriate the means necessary to stamp out this plague and to thoroughly seclude and disinfect all infected premises, and no one can doubt that it would be next to impossible to secure a continuance of such appropriation if the disease persisted in cropping out anew at frequent intervals and at short distances after millions had been expended for its extinction.

"Other Contagious Diseases of Animals.

"I dare not try your patience by introducing the question of the other contagious diseases of animals, such as glanders, the various forms of anthrax, milk-sickness, diphtheria, actinomycosis, strangles, influenza, mange, and all the numerous and dangerous forms of animal parasitism; suffice it to say that no one of these presents to us the same favourable conditions for a perfect suppression as does the lung plague of cattle, and for none can we promise the same speedy and absolutely permanent extinction.

"Lung Plague and Texas Fever as affecting our Foreign Trade.

"In this connexion it is only just to state that Texas fever assumes a special importance in connexion with its occasional exportation to Great Britain in beef cattle. It may therefore be made the occasion of the maintenance of the present slaughtering clause, even after we shall have completely stamped out the lung plague. In this, as in the case of the lung plague, it is well at once to face the truth. The Texas fever has an average incubation or latency of one month, and even in cases communicated by inoculation this extends to 10 days. It stands, therefore, side by side with lung plague in the impossibility of checking its exportation by the simple expedient of a professional examination at the port of embarkation. It has been the rule for shippers from Boston and New York to have their cattle examined prior to shipment; but this has not prevented the exportation of 26 infected cargoes in the course of the present autumn. It is folly to expect anything like absolute protection from a professional examination without detention, in the case of such a disease, and to advocate such a measure is merely to invite discomfiture and discredit. No veterinarian who would be true to himself and his country would advocate such an examination as an effectual safeguard.

"The only protection of our northern herds and export cattle against the contagion of the Gulf-coast fever must be sought in the absolute prohibition of the movement northward of the cattle from infected districts excepting in the depth of winter. This we must one day secure, and if it is possible to obtain from the present Congress a measure which will accomplish this it will be a matter for profound thankfulness. But we need not close our eyes to the fact that the apprehension of such a law on the part of our Southern Representatives, has been a main cause of the defeat of every important measure for the stamping out of our animal contagia. While therefore strongly in favour of a law that will circumscribe the Southern or Gulf-coast fever, I am convinced that it will be highly injudicious to incorporate any such provision in a bill providing for the extinction of the lung plague. To do so is but to invite and insure defeat. Happily the Gulf-coast cattle fever may be ignored for a year or two without fear of its becoming permanent in any of the Northern localities into which it is yearly introduced. Again, any measures which we can at present adopt look not to its definite extinction but only to its limitation to its present area. It is, therefore, as preposterous as injurious to continue to combine these two subjects in any future Congressional bills.

"Special Urgency of the Lung Plague Question.

"The lung plague question is a more urgent one in every sense. This disease is an exotic, and if extinguished once would only reappear in case of a new importation from an already infected country. Its area of prevalence in the United States is so limited that it could be easily, with perfect certainty and (relatively to our other contagia) quickly and cheaply, extirpated. Unlike Texas fever, anthrax, and tuberculosis, it is not propagated in the soil, &c., nor is it capable of indefinite preservation and accidental increase out of the animal body, and therefore it may be easily extinguished. It is unlike the Texas fever in that it is comparatively unaffected by climate or season, and in that it tends to persist in any locality into which it has once been introduced and where susceptible cattle are found. Every day of its existence on our Eastern seaboard threatens our Western herds even to the coast of the Pacific. The infection of the West, the fountain of our cattle trade, means the infection not only of our roaming Western herds, but of all the channels of trade into which these gravitate, of all our stock-yards, of all our Middle and Eastern States and of our exports. Our present yearly losses from this plague are about $3,000,000; our losses in case of the extension we are supposing could not be less than $50,000,000, representing at 5 per cent. a capital of $1,000,000,000. Worse than all, such a tax once imposed can never be wiped out, as no land has ever succeeded in stamping out this disease among roaming herds on unfenced grazing grounds. It is this that is to be feared more than anything else, and if we leave the seed of this scourge to propagate itself on our Eastern seaboard this is what will happen to us sooner or later. On every ground, therefore, whether of commercial economy or of financial foresight, of the attainability of the necessary legislation, or of the assurance of the complete and permanent extinction of the malady to be dealt with, it may be safely claimed that lung plague demands the first measure of veterinary sanitary legislation. To neglect it is to woo a ruinous and irretrievable loss which must for ever after bear an invariable relation to our growing herds, and with their increase would ere long reach $100,000,000 in place of $50,000,000 per annum. The restriction of any one of our other animal plagues may be postponed without the overshadowing dangers that threaten from the neglect of this, and no one of these plagues gives the same assurance of a complete and early extinction of the poison under the application of proper methods. To handicap any bill for the extinction of this disease with provisions for any other affection, I cannot but consider as ruinous to the cause, not of anti-lung plague legislation only, but of all veterinary sanitary legislation and work.

"It is undoubtedly our duty as sanitarians and citizens to do all in our power to secure by legislation and every other available means the suppression of one and all of the animal plagues of which I have been speaking; but as it is impracticable to secure all this at once, as the demand for the whole would infallably lose us the whole, and as the lung plague is at once the most urgent and the simplest plague to deal with, and that on which we can go to work with the most perfect confidence of a complete success, this should be provided for in a separate bill, which should furnish ample power and means, and should take precedence of all others.

"THE LUNG PLAGUE OF AMERICA THE LUNG PLAGUE OF THE WHOLE WORLD.

"But we are reminded that we have in our midst stockmen who deny the existence of the genuine European lung plague in America, and who quote anonymous veterinarians in support of their assertion. I am in no wise disconcerted by this. In company with other sanitarians I had to meet the same assertions a quarter of a century ago, and the tactics now adopted are the same as were followed then. Then, as now, the agitation was ascribed to the cupidity of the agitators. Then, as now, the cattle dealers declared a lung plague a myth and quoted the late Professor Dick to the effect that it was only an inflammation of the lungs caused by impure air. The same professor denied the inoculability of hydrophobia, described rinderpest, as a mere impaction of the manifolds, and wrote an article to prove the non-contagiousness of epidemic diseases in general. We all know that personal interest and the love of notoriety will prompt certain men to promulgate dogmas that outrage the intelligence and common sense of the age. There are still, I believe, at Cambridge some learned men who assert that the earth is flat and that the sun revolves around it once in twenty-four hours.

"A loss of $500,000,000 from lung plague alone has taught England that she is not dealing with a myth but with a terrible and exacting reality, and a long and most intimate acquaintance with this lung plague has enabled England to pronounce without hesitation on the existence of the same disease in cattle exported from our shores.

"To come back to our own case; our self-appointed judges should have gone to the East and given some attention to the facts of the case before rendering their decision and visiting us with wholesale condemnation. They should have stood with us in the yards of the Blissville distillery in 1879 when the veterinarians who had been hired by Messrs. Gaff, Fleischmann and Co., and who had denounced our work in the public newspapers, and published a certificate that there was not a single case of lung plague in the distillery stables, were invited to select from the cattle we had condemned any that they considered sound, and were furnished in every case, on dissection, with ocular demonstration in the lung extensively and characteristically diseased. They should have stood with us in the field of John E. White, of Sagg, Suffolk County, New York, where nine cattle infected by a bull calf from Brooklyn stood ready to be shot; they should have seen the darkening faces of some scores of the inhabitants, and heard the denunciations and warnings that we would be held personally responsible for what they considered a grave error and a high-handed outrage on property in the slaughter of sound animals. They should have seen the urging necessary to get the executioner to do his duty, and they should have seen the restoration of universal confidence and support when the chests were opened and the masses of loathsome and characteristic disease exposed. They should have accompanied us in the rest of our inspections the same day and heard the men who had been the foremost to denounce us offering to pay out of their own pockets the value of the animals condemned in case they should not be found after death precisely as we had pronounced them. They should have attended us in the whole of our work in the east end of Long Island, and seen that wherever a farmer had taken in a calf out of the infected herd brought from Brooklyn by Billard, there the malady had broken out and decimated the herd. They should have visited with us the fine Jersey herd of Mr. Watrous, Perth Amboy, N.J., where an infected cow brought from a sale in New York City introduced the disease, which proved simply ruinous. They should have visited with us the extensive and valuable Jersey herd of Mr. James A. Hoyt, of Patterson, Putnam County, New York, when the introduction of the disease in four cows from New Jersey and Maryland led to the disease of his entire herd and to the loss of upwards of $20,000. They should have witnessed the invasion consequent on the introduction from the Union Stock Yards, New York, of infected animals into the stock farm of Mr. Baldwin, general live stock agent of the Erie Railway, and into the West Chester herd of Mr. Roach, of ship-building fame. They should have investigated the devastations caused in the herd of the Children's Hospital at Willow Brook, Staten Island, through an infected purchase, and of the herd of the Bloomingdale Lunatic Asylum through an infected cow coming to bull. They should have witnessed the thousands of similar cases in New York, New Jersey, Pennsylvania, Delaware, Maryland, and Virginia, and then they would have been in a position to decide justly whether we were dealing with a terribly contagious and fatal disease of the lungs.

"I mention these cases of recent infection, not as desiring to publish that any of the stocks specifically named are to-day tainted with this disease, for in every such instance the malady has been stamped out, and the herd can now be certified sound. I adduce them mainly as undeniable outbreaks occurring in the herds of men so well known that no one interested in the subject can have any difficulty in attesting their truth for himself. Let the objectors try to disprove these. There are plenty more such, not only in the past but to-day. The recent cases in Chester County, Pennsylvania, which have been sufficiently identified, a single diseased lung in particular cases having weighed 50 pounds in place of 3 pounds.

APPENDIX.

"Our Existing Lung Plague Imported.

"But some will even deny that the disease now prevalent on our Eastern seaboard is the genuine lung plague of Europe. Well, it was unknown in America until 1848, when Peter Dunn, of Brooklyn, bought an English cow from the ship Washington. This cow died in a few weeks of this lung affection, and the disease quickly spread to Dunn's other cows and to those of his neighbours, including the stables of the Skillman Street distillery, where it continued until 1862, and was recognised by Dr. Thayer and the other members of the Massachusetts commission. William Meakim, of Bushwick, had his herd infected in 1849 by a yoke of oxen employed in drawing grain from the Brooklyn distilleries, and lost 40 head in three months, and from 6 to 10 head yearly for 20 years thereafter, when he gave up the business. This brings it down to 1869. Since that date I have been frequently consulted about the disease, not in New York only, but also in the adjoining States on the south, and occasionally in Connecticut.

"Why has the Plague not Extended West?

"From New York the plague has extended 200 miles in a southward direction, and to-day holds its ground and continues to extend as opportunity offers. It has followed this direction simply because the traffic in live stock has been active from New York to the large cities in the South, and because in and around those large cities it has found that constant interchange of animals and intermingling of herds which insures its perpetuation by presenting an endless succession of fresh and susceptible subjects. The same extension would have taken place over all the large manufacturing cities of New England, but for the careful guardianship of the cattle commission of Connecticut, who, through all the years since the disease was imported, have been called upon at frequent intervals to stamp out circumscribed fires of infection lit up by importations from New York. The plague has not extended westward mainly because there has been so little cattle traffic in that direction. It would have been financial folly at any early time to send common cattle West from the great Eastern cities, and thanks to the Alleghanies, there is no large city within 200 miles of New York in that direction that would draw upon the market of the latter for dairy cows, or that was calculated to keep up the disease by the constant intermingling of herds.

"The dangers from thorough-bred cattle sent West were incomparably greater, but various conditions served to reduce the risks of infection by this channel. First. Thorough-breds were usually better guarded against danger of contamination, not being sold in the common stockyards. Second. Their owners are usually responsible and honourable men, who would be little likely to sell at the current high market rates animals they knew to be infected. Third. Thorough-breds are always sold with pedigree, and the buyer is fully acquainted with the position and standing of the seller, so that in case of a sale of infected animals the breeder would have been constantly subject to an action for damages. Fourth. Until recently thorough-bred cattle were comparatively seldom sent West to our unfenced pasturages, so that if some did carry infection into new herds, the latter were still on well-fenced farms, and were kept rigidly apart from other stock to secure the purity of the breed, and thus the infection had a good chance to attack all the herd and to die out for lack of fresh susceptible subjects.

"Such an immunity of a country in close proximity to an infected one is not at all unprecedented. Europe furnishes an exact parallel. For centuries the lung plague has prevailed in central Europe, where it is kept up by the active cattle traffic and the constant importations from the infected East. But Spain and Portugal, on the south, and Scandinavia, on the north, being out of the line of direct traffic, keep clear to the present day—a few invasions of the northern nations having been easily repelled by prompt isolation and slaughter, while the less enterprising Southern Peninsula has not even once been called upon to suppress an outbreak.

"Our Dangers Increasing.

"But our dangers of to-day are far greater than they have been in the past. Tens and hundreds of thorough-bred cattle are being constantly shipped to the West, and the great demand is for the unfenced ranges of the plains and beyond them. There the disease once introduced would find all those favourable conditions which have perpetuated it for centuries in the steppes of Eastern Europe and Asia, in spite of the best efforts of scientists, aided by the ungrudging support of the Government. These conditions are identical with those of Australia, where the disease has defied every effort to extirpate it, though they were carried out almost regardless of expense and of the numbers of animals that might have to be slaughtered. In New Zealand and South Africa the experience has been the same; the plague once planted on unfenced ranges, pastured in common by large herds, the property of different owners, has perpetuated itself in spite of every effort of man to suppress it.

"Nor is our danger alone from thorough-bred cattle. The great investments in cattle from the plains and the consequent enhanced prices have established a trade in common stock for the supply of the Western ranches, and young stock are extensively shipped from the middle and Eastern States to meet the demand. In years past the losses on the ventures in young calves have served to check the trade, but I regret to say it still continues to a considerable extent, and every such shipment is pregnant with danger.

"If there were any hope of the extinction of the lung plague after it had reached our unfenced pasturages we might find some excuse for those who would have us close our eyes to the danger; but when it threatens us with the infliction of a tax of $50,000,000 to $200,000,000 a year, a tax which must increase in ratio with the increase of our herds, and which no statesmanship and no financial ability can ever hope to arrest or abolish, we cannot but consider him as an enemy of his country and of humanity who would counsel or encourage apathy or inaction. Who would cry 'peace! peace!' while a remorseless enemy is at our doors, and his emissaries and battalions are even in our midst, ready to seize our strongholds? Who would claim health when the cancer was eating into the tissues and slowly extending towards the vitals? Who would claim security when the deadly cobra had been roused and had coiled himself for his fatal spring?

"If I speak strongly it is because I see the full measure of our danger; it is because I have traced the history of this disease in all historic time, and can speak from the unvarying experience of successive centuries and of different hemispheres; it is because I have been honoured with a great trust in this matter, and because I would be recreant to that trust, to the country, to my profession, and to myself, if I failed to give warning where danger threatens, and reassurance where our course is safe.

APPENDIX.

"Measures for Suppression and Extinction.

"In devising means for suppressing any plague we must give paramount attention to two considerations: First. Can we render the animal system *insusceptible* or *non-receptive of the poison?* and second, *can we destroy every vestige of the poison?* If we can perfectly accomplish either of these objects there will be an end of the plague at such a place. No plague can be propagated in the absence of susceptible subjects. No plague can survive if we destroy all its germs. The lung-plague virus is perfectly harmless to a community of horses, sheep, or swine. So it is to a great extent to cattle that have already passed through the disease and fully recovered. Just as a man does not readily contract small-pox a second time, so an ox does not usually suffer a second time from lung plague. I would not trouble you with this part of the subject but that some advocate the restriction of this plague by producing this comparative insusceptibility in the animals exposed.

"Methods of Seeking Insusceptibility.

"This insusceptibility to lung plague may be attained more or less perfectly by various methods.

"1st. *Keeping insusceptible breeds.*—Some breeds appear to be somewhat less receptive of lung plague than others. In some this has been acquired by a prolonged exposure of their ancestors to the plague, until the more susceptible strains of blood have died out, leaving only those that have a greater power of resistance to the contagion.

"This is merely 'a survival of the fittest.' In other cases cattle that are defective in muscular development, in loose connective tissue, and in the lymphatic apparatus, show a somewhat diminished susceptibility, as compared with those of an opposite habit of body. But in neither of these cases is the susceptibility ever completely eradicated from the race or family. Either of these conditions will to a slight extent reduce the losses, but neither separately nor together can they arrest the propagation of the poison nor prevent the progress of the disease. They are, therefore, only to be adopted as restrictive measures on open unfenced pasture ranges, covered with cattle, where the permanence of the disease is already assured and where no hope of its extinction can be held out. In other circumstances we can do incomparably better.

"2nd. *Passage of the young through the disease.*—In badly infected districts shrewd dairymen have profitably resorted to the expedient of exposing calves to the infection, realising that the pecuniary loss through the death of the individual animal at this age was small, while the survivors could afterward be exposed to infection with impunity.

"3rd. *Inoculation with fresh virus from the diseased lung.*—A more economical method is the inoculation of the susceptible cattle in the tail so as to exhaust their susceptibility. This, when properly managed, does not cause a loss of over 1 or 2 per cent., and the survivors acquire as perfect an immunity from lung plague as vaccinated people do from small-pox. This inoculation is extensively practised in Belgium and France, is obligatory in Holland, and is almost universal in Australia, Tasmania, New Zealand, South Africa, and certain parts of Great Britain and America. It has greatly diminished the losses in these countries, but in no one of them has it put an end to the plague. In the city of Edinburgh, where it is supplemented by the slaughter of the sick, and where it was loudly claimed that it had extinguished the disease, I found on my recent visit that the abattoir was furnishing frequent examples of lungs from city dairy cows with the characteristics lesions of lung plague. In Holland, where the compulsory inoculation is also supplemented by slaughter of the sick, the fat cattle from the great feeding stables frequently furnish, when killed, the unmistakable lung lesions of this disease, nor is this at all surprising. The inoculated poison propagated in the tissues of the tail not only protects the individual system but also secures the multiplication of the germs and their preservation in the stables, so that when an animal freshly introduced and inoculated fails to take, and to be protected, it has every opportunity of contracting the disease in the ordinary way in the lungs. The same result obtains where inoculation is practised on a large scale on cattle in open pasturages. Mr. Watson states as the result of his experience in Australia and New Zealand that on the occasions on which large herds of thousands or tens of thousands had been inoculated, a certain number of animals always failed to be brought in, and among these uninoculated animals there was in every case a very heavy per-centage of loss after they had mingled with the inoculated. Mr. Corbet gives the same testimony concerning his experience in Natal. 'The disease,' he says, 'is always lurking about ' and introduced to a greater or less extent each time of inoculation.'

"This is the great objection to inoculation as usually practised. It is a means of multiplying the disease germs, and while it protects the inoculated animal it furnishes material for the infection of every susceptible animal that may be brought in contact with it or with the premises where it has been. Inoculation is admissible as a means of self-protection by the individual owner in cases were the Government or local authorities take no efficient steps for the stamping out of the disease; but it is bad policy when our object is the complete extinction of the malady and when we are adopting other measures well calculated to secure this end. One suggestion more on this subject is, that from herds in which inoculation is permitted no animal should be allowed to pass out except to immediate slaughter. The premises become infected and the inmates may carry the infection on the surface of their bodies as well as in the lungs.

"4th. *Inoculation with weakened virus.*—The application of the method of Pasteur of inoculation with attenuated virus is advocated by some, but it is liable to all the objections urged against the simple inoculation. The attenuated virus is weakened, not sterilised; the germs continue to propagate their kind, and as their virulence has been lessened by culture under certain conditions, it can be enhanced by culture under conditions of an opposite kind. All such measures, which owe their efficacy to the propagation in the animal system of the diseased germ we seek to destroy, are to be deprecated and discarded whenever more radical measures of extinction can be adopted.

"5th. *Inoculation with sterilised virus.*—Two years ago I was led by my study of the manifestations of the lung plague in the system to suspect that the immunity, after a first attack, was acquired not by the contact of the living germ with the lung tissue, but of its chemical products or excretions. I accordingly took measures to kill the germ without altering the chemical condition of the virulent fluid, and inoculated the sterilised liquid on the susceptible animal. In 10 animals into which this liquid was injected there occurred no local swelling such as results from the inoculation with the living germ, and no one of these animals had local swellings when afterward inoculated with fresh virus containing living germs, nor had any lung plague when exposed for six months in infected herds and premises. In every case in which I tested the animals thus protected, by inoculating them with fresh living germs, I took the precaution of inoculating at the same time an unprotected subject, and in every such animal the disease appeared in a characteristic form; and when the inoculation had been made on the soft, loose tissues of the flank in a fatal one. I have since learned by experiments on animals that had already stood some time in infected buildings, that this inoculation with sterilised lymph is not protective of animals that have already taken the germs into their lungs. To be effective it must be practised on cattle before they have been exposed to the contagion; and its efficiency will be enhanced by a repetition after an interval of a week or more.

"This method, it will be observed, obviates the main objections to inoculation. By it there is no germ introduced into the animal system, nor any laid up in the buildings where inoculated beasts are kept. The method therefore may be safely applied to one of a score or a hundred susceptible cattle without endangering the rest, and the building where a thousand cattle have been operated on in this way may be at once filled with as many more fresh and susceptible animals without disinfection, and yet without any danger of evil consequences.

"The method is therefore immeasurably superior to any other that has been hitherto proposed, and in special cases may be resorted to with excellent results.

"The objections to its exclusive use are those that apply to all measures that come short of a speedy extinction of the disease: 1st. The keeping of diseased animals for the production of the virus is not without its dangers. 2nd. The application of the method over a wide district is necessarily slow. 3rd. The application to infected districts, extending over six different States, would entail a vast amount of machinery, and the perfection of the work would suffer in various ways; operators would fail for lack of care or ability; cattle would escape notice and afterwards fall victims to the disease; and the incessant additions of susceptible animals by birth and otherwise would present a serious difficulty. 4th. To operate on animals most satisfactorily it must be done before they enter the infected herds, and this would necessitate places of detention for such store animals outside the infected districts, and a considerable additional delay and outlay in cattle traffic. 5th. The expense for all this machinery would be largely prohibitory of the practice. 6th. Finally, we cannot expect of this any more than of any other inoculation, that it will prove absolutely protective in every case. We meet with second attacks of small-pox, measles, and even of lung plague. We cannot therefore hope that we shall be able to absolutely protect such exceptional animals as have a great inherent susceptibility to the lung plague. These exceptional cases forbid that we should adopt this as an exclusive method when we can resort to one that is absolutely certain in its results. This method may be of the greatest value for the protection of individual herds where there is no governmental measure for stamping out, and it may be conjoined with the ordinary method of extinction by slaughter without that danger of propagating the disease which always attaches to ordinary inoculation; but with all the many advantages which I can see in this, my own system, I am convinced that the Government can do incomparably better if it will.

"6th. *Preventive medication.*—In my experience of this disease in Great Britain, over 20 years ago, I found that a long course of certain tonics, and notably of the preparations of iron, fortified the system so that few animals fell victims to the contagion. But in this as in the other methods named the result is imperfect, and the protected animals soon reacquire the susceptibility after the tonic has been withdrawn.

"Destruction of the Poison.

"1st. *By disinfection of the air breathed.*—In many instances of infected herds I have found that a thorough fumigation with sulphur fumes for half an hour at a time, twice, or better, three times a day, has at once put a stop to the further extension of the infection. The cattle already infected would still suffer, but for the others the poison was destroyed before or soon after it entered the air-passages, and before it could make its way into the tissues, and no disease resulted. Like the other methods named this has its drawbacks. It requires suitable buildings and careful manipulation to secure a sufficient effect without danger to the animals, and as it requires such frequent application, it must be left in the hands of attendants who cannot always be relied on to carry it out safely and effectively.

"2nd. *By isolation, slaughter, and disinfection.*—Wherever the movement and intermingling of cattle can be prevented or sufficiently controlled, the method of stamping out by isolation, slaughter, and disinfection has ever been attended by the most perfect success. It has been ineffective in countries like Australia, where endless herds of cattle roam over the fenceless plains, but wherever lands are inclosed and where movement can be arrested or controlled, as in Norway, Sweden, Denmark, Oldenburg, Switzerland, and Massachusetts, it has resulted in the complete eradication of the malady. In New York in 1879 the same measures rooted out the disease from four of the eight infected counties, and restricted it to eight herds, which were temporarily preserved for lack of funds in two more counties, while in Kings county and the adjacent part of Queens, where local authorities had successfully opposed our work, the malady remained widely prevalent. While advocating the full efficacy of this method, it is needless to go into minor particulars further than to say that no additions from the public markets should be allowed to herds in infected districts, and that all additions to such herds, apart from natural increase, should be by special license from healthy districts, or from close markets which receive cattle only from such healthy districts; that every death in a herd in such proclaimed infected district should be promptly reported, and the carcass examined by a veterinary inspector; that no cattle should be moved from such herds in infected districts except to immediate slaughter, where examination of the carcass can be made by a veterinary inspector; or such movement should only be allowed after the herd and district have been certified by the inspector to have been sound and without dangerous additions for six months; that all infected animals, or far better, every infected herd, should be promptly slaughtered, and that a thorough disinfection should be made of all premises where infected animals have been.

"I have always held that the only sound and just method of dealing with this disease must be directed and sustained by the National Government. I quote from my monograph on the lung plague, published in 1879:

"'The plague threatens to reach our southern and western ranges, whence it will be as impossible to eradicate it as from the Russian steppes, Australia, and South Africa, and from which continuous accessions of infection will be thrown upon our Middle and Eastern States, and shall we hesitate to call upon the National Government to interfere? This is a question of incomparably more moment to the Western and Middle States than to Delaware, Maryland, or Virginia. To throw the burden of the extinction of this disease on these States is as impolitic as it is unjust. If ever there was a question which, in its future bearing, affected the United States, as a whole, it is this.

"'It would be highly appropriate that the agriculturists of the different States, Western and Southern as well as Eastern, should petition Congress to take this matter up and adopt such measures as would for ever rid our country of this most insidious of all animal plagues. At all hazards the work ought to be done, and that speedily. If State rights stand in the way, let the money at least be supplied, as it rightfully ought, from the national exchequer, and applied by the different States through their own officials under the supervision of some responsible Department—say the Agricultural Department, a live stock disease commission, the National Board of Health, or even the Treasury Department. It is folly and worse to quarrel about the means until the plague shall have passed beyond control. Action is wanted, of a prompt and decisive nature, by the General Government or with its assistance, and those who are most deeply interested in the subject should press this upon the Government until such action shall have been secured.'

"I would only add that, in my opinion, the Federal Government should provide and pay its own inspectors to act as experts in all the infected States, while the sheriffs or other State officials should conduct them into the herds to be examined, and, on behalf of the State, see to the appraisement and slaughter of all herds pronounced to be infected, to the safe disposal of the carcasses, and to the thorough disinfection of the premises. The sheriffs or other State officials should further deliver the certificates of such appraisements to the federal inspector, who should forward the same to the federal authority at Washington, and he should communicate with the owner of the herd, and on receipt of a signed receipt for the amount, should pay him the amount of indemnity for the animals slaughtered."

Mr. CHORN, of Kentucky. With the permission of Mr. Smith, the chairman of the committee on order of business, I wish to offer a resolution that we adjourn until 5 o'clock this evening, if that is in order, so that we can have those people here with us who are all vitally interested in these discussions.

The PRESIDENT *pro tempore* (Professor MORROW). I would suggest that you put your motion in the form of a reconsideration of the vote which has already fixed the time for meeting.

Mr. CHORN. Then I move that we reconsider that vote.

The motion to reconsider was agreed to.

MR. CHORN. Now, I renew my motion to adjourn until 5 o'clock.

Mr. CAREY, of Wyoming. There appears to be conflicting interests here. I am aware that many of the men who have come here are in attendance upon these stock sales, but we do hope that we shall devote all the time that we can until we attain the object of this meeting. Now, of course, there are a number of scientific articles that are to be read before this Convention, and we are anxious to hear them; but the final outcome of this meeting is what we are really anxious about. That means the appointment of a committee to go to Washington and lobby through Congress such measures as we deem necessary in our interest. I think that Senator Williams struck the key-note when he said that there must be a committee appointed who are willing to work, who are willing to pay their expenses, who are willing to give this matter sufficient time to have measures adopted that will accomplish something. Now we want a meeting this afternoon. If 3.30 is to early, why not say 4 o'clock? We can have a meeting before this evening, and these gentlemen can read their articles. Now, as I understand, there is a meeting this evening that will interfere; to-morrow there is a sale, and if we have to adjourn this meeting and let the stock sales take place, instead of going on, we will not be able to finish our work for a week.

I therefore move an amendment that when we adjourn we adjourn until 4 o'clock.

Mr. CHORN, of Kentucky. There are many of the very best breeders in this meeting who are directly and vitally interested in these stock sales. They cannot get here at 4 o'clock, but they can get here at 5 o'clock. We will be here at that hour and will give this important meeting our heartiest support, and we do beg for 5 o'clock.

Mr. CAREY, of Wyoming. Say 4.30, then. [Laughter.]

The amendment was not agreed to, and the motion of Mr. Chorn was carried.

The PREIDENT *pro tempore*. I beg to suggest the importance of the appointment of a committee on resolutions. I happen to know that there are likely to be a few resolutions which will conflict, some of them at least, with our purposes and views, and such a committee could consider these and report to this body.

Professor ROBERTS, of New York. I move that the Chair appoint a committee of three on resolutions.

A DELEGATE. I move to amend by inserting five.

The amendment was accepted, and the motion as amended was agreed to.

The PRESIDENT *pro tempore*. The Chair will name Professor Roberts as the chairman of that committee, and will reserve the appointment of the others until we meet again.

Professor ROBERTS. The Chair will please excuse me. I have more business than I can well attend to now. It will be inconvenient for me to serve. For one member of that committee I will suggest Professor Law.

The PRESIDENT *pro tempore*. The Chair will reserve, if you please, the appointment of the committee until later.

A DELEGATE. I move we now adjourn.

The motion was agreed to, and at 1 o'clock and 3 minutes the Convention adjourned.

The Convention met pursuant to adjournment, Senator Williams, the president, in the chair.

The PRESIDENT. Just before adjournment provision was made for the appointment of a committee on resolutions, with the intention of having referred to it all resolutions that may be offered by gentlemen, and to be by that committee reported to the Convention with its recommendations. That committee will consist of Messrs. Sanders, of Illinois; Chorn, of Kentucky; W. T. Smith, of Iowa; Bonham, of Ohio; and Redfield, of New York. I will announce now that Dr. Salmon, of the Department of Agriculture, has been commissioned by Dr. Loring to read a paper at this Convention, and if there is nothing further requiring the immediate action of the meeting, I would suggest that we now listen to Dr. Salmon.

Dr. SALMON then presented the following paper:—

"PREVENTION OF CONTAGIOUS DISEASES OF ANIMALS IN AMERICA.

" Among the many questions connected with the contagious diseases of animals those most suitable for discussion at this Convention are the ones which are nearest related to the subject of prevention. There are still too many people who cling to old ideas of the origin and nature of contagious diseases. Our popular writers still teach that they are the result of the 'absorption of foul matter from impure air, and that good ' ventilation and pure air are specific preventatives.' Good ventilation and pure air are excellent things, but if they are specific preventives how can we explain the cases of glanders which occur among horses that seldom see the inside of a stable; the cases of hog cholera in the open fields, and of chicken cholera among fowls which are never housed?

"Other writers, and their name is legion, tell us that the origin of hog cholera, for instance, is easily explained by the conditions under which hogs are raised, particularly in the West. Large numbers are kept together. They have the reprehensible habit of crowding each other to an uncomfortable degree in their sleeping places; they have so little regard for hygienic rules as to lie two or three deep. As a necessary consequence the under hog breathes terribly impure air; he even inspires so much dust that this alone would cause inflammation of the lungs. Couple this with his injudicious and irregular diet, and the origin of hog cholera is so clear that our friends are abundantly satisfied; they rather object to additional evidence for fear of unsettling beliefs now held with the most implicit confidence. We are even told that foot-and-mouth disease is as indigenous to England as the fogs and mists; that it always exists and always will, because it is provoked by the climate and the manner of keeping the cattle.

"But these remarkable conclusions are not so much the result of a long period of observations on the diseases themselves—they are rather the outcome of meditations as to what ought to be. 'Our enormous and 'well-appointed army,' said the French about 1870, 'will have no 'trouble in marching victoriously into Berlin;' but since the investigation of the size and equipment of that army was made in the office and not in the field, it resulted in a slight change of programme, which brought the German army to Paris and made the Frenchmen prisoners of war. And if we accept too hastily the conclusions to which I have referred—conclusions based upon an insufficient knowledge of these diseases, we also may invite disaster. The inflammation of the lungs seen in hog cholera is not a simple inflammation, due to mechanical irritation by inert particles of dust; the ulcers of the intestines are not the simple results of indigestion; the discharge and ulceration of glanders cannot be produced by lack of ventilation alone, nor the fever and eruption of foot-and-mouth disease by damp, and cold, and mud. These are contagious diseases, and an animal exposed to the virus contracts the disease, no matter what its conditions of life, just as your child contracts measles or scarlet fever when exposed to them, though it dwells in a palace, with the most perfect diet and surroundings. Hog cholera has been introduced into the South within the last 30 years, and now it is an annual scourge; but there is the same old breed of hogs, and they are allowed to roam at their own sweet will, just as has been the custom from time immemorial. If sleeping too many in a bed produces hog cholera to-day why did it not have the same effect 30 or 40 years ago?

"And so with chicken cholera. By making an insignificant wound with a lancet dipped in virus, or even by giving the virus with the food, I can destroy the greater part of the fowls upon any farm, and I care not what are the conditions of life or the quality of the food.

"Is pleuro-pneumonia produced by cold, bad feed, or filthy and unventilated stables? If so, why is it not found around some of your Western cities—Cincinnati, Saint Louis, Chicago? Surely the cow that kicked the lamp, that spilled the oil, that fired the straw, that burned the stable, &c., was not the last instance of improper stabling in or about this great city. And yet in many parts of Europe they talk about pleuro-pneumonia originating from improper conditions of life pretty much as our learned friends tell us that glanders, and hog cholera and chicken cholera and the rest of the list, originate in this country.

"Then there is rinderpest and sheep-pox and foot-and-mouth disease abroad, decimating the flocks and herds year after year and causing incalculable losses. Why do not these diseases appear as regularly among the animals upon our own grazing lands? Is it because there is something unfavourable to these diseases in our climate, or is it because the contagia—the germs—of those plagues have never yet been disseminated over our territory? There is not a particle of doubt in my mind that rinderpest, sheep-pox, and epizootic aptha would sweep America as they have swept Europe were they once fairly introduced among our animals.

"The truth seems to be, with most if not all of the contagious fevers, that every case is produced directly or indirectly from germs which were developed by a case which preceded it, just as every crop of corn is produced by seed from a preceding crop. I care not how well you prepare your ground, how favourable you make the conditions of life, you cannot get a crop of corn without seed; so a contagious fever is the result of the development of a living organism in the animal body, and you can no more get a crop of that organism without seed than you can the crop of corn.

"Just here I am usually met with an argument, apparently looked upon as invulnerable, for ever demonstrating the spontaneous production of animal plagues. These diseases, it is said, could not always have been contracted from pre-existing cases for the very reason that some time in the remote past there were no pre-existing animals—there must have been a first case of disease. No doubt of it; but this is one of those philosophical considerations which is not as practical as it appears upon its face. So, too, there must have been a first grain of corn, a first pig, a first sheep, a first calf; but let the young farmer of to-day put his land in the most favourable condition possible and sit upon the fence expecting the origin *de novo* of his corn, his pigs, his sheep, and his cattle—you know that he might sit there until his hair was white and his eyes dim with age without seeing such a phenomenon; no, not if his farm took in a continent and his field of vision embraced it all. And if the contagious organisms were as large as cattle, sheep, or pigs, or even as grains of corn, so that their goings and comings might be traced as we can trace these things, there would be no more question of the origin of glanders and hog cholera from the conditions of life than there is of cattle from the grass of your fields or corn from your fertile soil. Contagious fevers, then, are caused by specific germs, and so long as animals are exposed to these a considerable proportion will sicken and die in spite of hygienic surroundings, in spite of good and proper food, unless they are granted an immunity by methods analogous to vaccination.

"During the last decade we have had some of the most brilliant investigations and some of the most important discoveries that are to be found in the whole history of medicine; that greatest of all mysteries which enveloped contagious diseases in impenetrable darkness during the long ages of the past has at last, so far as concerns a number of these, been entirely solved. The cause of these diseases has been traced to microscopic organisms; to living things, capable of wonderfully rapid growth and multiplication, which can be seen and cultivated and studied. And by such studies we have learned that these organisms—germs if you please—may be made to change their nature and produce a mild instead of a fatal attack, from which the animal recovers and is enabled in the future to resist this virus even in its most malignant form. We have here a method, mysterious as the disease, which the omniscient Creator has provided that may be successful when all others have failed or where no others are applicable. It gives us hope that in the near

o 11711.

future we shall have efficient means for practically controlling the greater part of these destructive plagues.

"But to-day, gentlemen, as we review these diseases one by one, and consider the means which we have at hand for their suppression, we cannot doubt that they are yet, as they have been in the past, the most important and the most difficult problems which have engaged the attention of mankind, and that they will tax our intelligence and our ingenuity to the utmost before all the difficulties connected with them are overcome. With a single disease the new method of vaccination introduced by the illustrious Pasteur has proved successful in practice, and this success has been due to a character of stability in the virus which exists with but one other non-recurrent disease so far as our investigations have gone. Before this method can be applied to other diseases, and particularly to those with which we are most interested, there are new problems to be solved not less intricate and just as hard to grasp as were those so lately conquered. The direction has been pointed out to us, but the way is not open.

"Chicken Cholera

is one of the most widely distributed diseases, and certainly causes enormous aggregate losses. It is now as well understood as any of our contagious diseases, and it is one of the few in which the germs have been discovered and carefully studied. These germs under ordinary conditions must be taken into the stomach with the food or drink to produce their effects, and consequently by a proper use of disinfectants the disease may be almost entirely prevented. Fowls may also be made insusceptible to cholera by vaccination with a feeble virus, or by inoculation with a diluted virus. A few investigations to determine the best method of putting up the virus, and there is no doubt but that it could be sent to every part of the country in such a form that any one could use it.

"Black-Quarter

is another disease which is very destructive in localities of nearly every State in the Union. This has been recently investigated with much success in France, and we are told that it may be certainly prevented by both inoculation and vaccination.

"Hog Cholera.

"With hog cholera our investigations, owing to the difficulty of the subject, have not reached such satisfactory results. The germ has been isolated, cultivated, and studied, but not sufficiently to make us master of the conditions upon which the virulence depends. As I have cultivated it, it is one of the most unstable of viruses. The germ is easily cultivated, but its effects are far from uniform; a second, or third, or even fourth cultivation may produce fatal results, but it gradually loses its virulence until large quantities have no effect. During this diminution of virulence we get a vaccine which produces a mild attack and grants immunity, but it has been impossible to make this vaccine multiply itself without becoming too weak to be effectual, and it has been equally impossible to preserve it at the required strength a sufficient length of time to make its use practical over a very large section of the country. I do not say that this obstacle will not be overcome in the future; on the other hand, I am sanguine that it will be. We are just completing our arrangements at Washington to give this and our other contagious diseases a thorough investigation, and I can only say that, in spite of the assertion of Pasteur, until we learn more in regard to the virus vaccination cannot be used safely, nor is it sure to confer the desired immunity.

" Separation and disinfection are then the measures which must be depended upon for the present. These are already largely practised in many parts of the country, and have been the means of saving millions of dollars' worth of hogs since the first investigations of the Department of Agriculture demonstrated beyond question the contagiousness of the disease. There are still undoubtedly heavy losses which cannot be prevented in this way, and for such losses there appears to be but one practical remedy, and that is vaccination. Either we must fold our hands and allow the loss to go on as at present unchecked, or we must study the germs and master this secret of nature, which will make vaccination a possibility.

"Southern or Texas Cattle Fever.

" When we commenced the investigation of this disease a few years ago there was but little known of the district from which cattle would disseminate the infection; there was a vague and somewhat uncertain idea that the whole Gulf coast might be a dangerous district, but it was universally acknowledged that wherever there was frost and snow there the contagion of Texas fever could not survive, and cattle coming from such districts could be safely introduced upon our northern ranges.

" To-day we know that the infected district extends hundreds of miles from the Gulf coast, that in the East we may reach it by crossing the Rappahannock River in Virginia, that it is a long way this side of the line of frost and snow, and that, worse than all, it is advancing, slowly it is true, but steadily, surely advancing towards the best and most heavily stocked grazing lands in the country.

" In making this statement it is my desire to avoid the character of the mere alarmist. There is no occasion for immediate apprehension except in a few States, but there is occasion for immediate action. The advance of this disease can only be checked by laws regulating the movements of cattle, and with our present knowledge it is absurd to think of doing it in any other way. If the States along the border line of the infected district would adopt a law doing away with fences and consequently compel the owners of stock to prevent its running at large, and at the same time prohibit the driving of cattle from the infected to the uninfected district the advance of the disease would probably be arrested. As it is, an enormous territory has become infected, which comprises a considerable part of Virginia, two thirds of North Carolina, the whole of South Carolina, Georgia, Florida, Alabama, Mississippi, Louisiana, the greater part of Texas and Arkansas, and a large section in Tennessee. It will be instructive for every one interested in the American cattle industry to take a map of the United States and compare the part infected with this disease with that which is still free from it. Such a proceeding is well calculated to inspire an appreciation of the importance of giving this subject early and careful attention.

" Glanders.

" This disease, which causes at times such heavy losses with horses, and which produces a most horrible, loathsome, and fatal disorder in people, is now very inadequately dealt with in this country. Some States have no laws whatever in regard to it, and in most of the others they are imperfect, ineffectual, or not enforced. I have in mind now a case in a State where there is even a commission for suppressing this class of diseases. Some here will no doubt recognise it in the brief allusion which follows. Two horses were pronounced glandered by one or more veterinarians and quarantined by the State commission. As another practitioner considered the cases doubtful the highest talent in the American profession was consulted and inoculation experiments were made. A half dozen veterinarians unhesitatingly pronounced the disease to be glanders; the inoculation experiments proved this beyond question. In spite of this, however, the horses, instead of being slaughtered, were placed on pasture, the lesions of the disease were hidden by long and continued treatment, and then the owner goes to the legislature and obtains damages from the State for false quarantine. As a fitting climax to this absurd legal miscarriage these same horses were recently exhibited at the State fair, whether to show how easy it is to evade the laws in that State or whether to advertise the smartness of the owners it is difficult to say.

"Certainly with such a disease as this we should have effectual laws in every State, and when an animal is pronounced glandered by the State veterinarian it should be destroyed at once. No matter if the symptons are mild—no matter if there is a remote chance of covering them up or even of curing the animal; that animal is a centre of infection from which new cases will arise. It is a source of danger to human beings; it is a nuisance which ought not to be tole ated under any circumstances.

"Pleuro-Pneumonia.

"It is but a few months ago that the United States Department of Agriculture was charged with estimating the direct annual losses in this country from pleuro-pneumonia alone at $66,000,000. We were also charged with having published the statement that this disease had crossed the Missouri River and was affecting the great herds which roam the Western plains. That story, unfortunately, crossed the ocean. It went to the foreign markets of American beef; it was copied in the journals there as coming from the American Department of Agriculture, and you can judge for yourselves whether or not it had a tendency to remove any of the restrictions and obstacles which have been placed in the way of our exporters. Although the assertion was promptly contradicted abroad, it has not, so far as I am aware, received any public notice at home, and I only refer to the matter here for the purpose of stating that no one could have been more surprised at its publication than we were at the Department, for neither this statement nor anything resembling it has ever found its way into any of the Department publications.

"The time has come for speaking plainly in regard to the extent and losses from pleuro-pneumonia. I have never believed nor do I believe to-day that anything is gained in the long run by attempting to cover up the existence of a contagious disease by whitewashing reports or by any other form of deception. And, on the other hand, I must admit that I see no virtue in exaggeration, nothing but harm in the reports of enormous losses from pleuro-pneumonia and of its existence hither and yon in 30 different States which it has never entered. So far from the direct losses from this disease reaching up into the millions, it would undoubtedly be an exaggeration to say that they amount to $100,000 a year. So far from its having reached the Western plains, there has never been a case found west of the Alleghany mountains having the remotest resemblance to this plague, notwithstanding a pretty thorough ransacking of that great territory. And east of the Alleghanies, if you except a single farm in Connecticut, a half dozen farms in Pennsylvania, and perhaps a dozen in New Jersey, it may be truthfully said that there are no evidences of this disease at present beyond the immediate vicinity of a few large cities: New York, Brooklyn, Newark, Baltimore, and possibly Washington.

"Just what the situation is in these cities nothing but a thorough inspection will ever reveal. Brooklyn and Baltimore have a very bad reputation, but there have certainly been exaggerations in regard to the condition of the former. Taking the matter at the worst, I think it is evident that it would not be a herculean task to free ourselves from all suspicion of this foreign intruder. With energy and perseverance, a force of men who are able to identify this disease when they see it, and a very reasonable expenditure of money, we may be assured that the plague could be exterminated. But what are to be the details of this undertaking? Where is the money to come from? How is it to be used? Who should direct the work? How are they to get the necessary powers? These are questions which might be profitably discussed in this Convention, and if a practical scheme can be perfected, I doubt not it will be productive of much good.

"If I have left many points untouched and treated others in a superficial manner it is because I am unwilling to take more of your time than is absolutely necessary. I am anxious above all things that those most directly interested, those who put their money and their time in the live stock industry shall speak on these questions. I have no individual opinions or theories to inflict upon you, but the position with which I have been honoured has given me means of securing information which few others possess, and it is my earnest desire to give such evidence as may be needed to prevent the acceptance on the one hand of the extreme views of those who tell us that there are no dangerous diseases in the country, and on the other hand of those who insist that pleuro-pneumonia is ravaging an enormous territory, that other diseases are increasing from month to month by a sort of geometrical progression, and that our whole country is one great hot-bed of disease.

"I wish also to assure you that the United States Department of Agriculture fully appreciates the importance and is greatly interested in this subject of contagious animal diseases, and that it is willing, anxious, determined to do everything in its power to assist the stock owners of America in protecting their animals from these dreadful plagues."

The PRESIDENT *pro tempore* (Professor MORROW). I would ask if the committee on order of business has any further report to make, to add to that submitted at the morning session.

Mr. C. R. SMITH, of Iowa. We recommended this morning, in addition to the paper just read, that it be followed by a paper by Mr. Sanders, and we now recommend to follow the latter paper 10-minute practical speeches on this subject of pleuro-pneumonia by L. S. Coffin, Prof. J. D. Hopkins, Veterinarian, of Wyoming, J. M. Carey, and Mr. Crane, of New Jersey, to be followed by five-minute volunteer speeches on the subject. We have nothing further to recommend except that a thorough discussion and settlement of the subject of pleuro-pneumonia be had, and that no other subject be taken up until we have disposed of this one.

A DELEGATE. I move that we proceed in accordance with the recommendations of the committee.

The motion was agreed to.

Mr. SANDERS, of Illinois. Mr. Chairman, I do not know upon what authority or grounds anyone felt authorised to say that I had prepared a paper to be read at this Convention. I have never told anyone that I was going to read a paper here; no one ever asked me to do so, and I certainly have not prepared such a paper; and furthermore, I am in no kind of condition to make an extemporaneous talk to-night. I shall not attempt to inflict you with an address or lecture. There are one or two points that I merely wish to hint upon, which may serve as pointers to some extent for the discussions which may follow, and as my connexion with the Treasury Cattle Commission has caused me to pay a great deal of attention especially to pleuro-pneumonia and the quarantine regulations during the past two years, I shall be happy to answer any questions on the subject. I wish to say that I am exceedingly pleased with the manner in which Dr. Salmon has presented the question of pleuro-pneumonia. It is precisely in accordance with my own observation and my own views. There is no doubt that there has been a wonderful amount of idle talk upon the subject. There have been alarmists all over the country, and as secretary of the Treasury Cattle Commission, the member to whom the communications come (excepting those sent to Professor Law by his own personal acquaintances), I am in constant receipt of letters. In this general correspondence you would be surprised to see the number of letters complaining of this disease, There has scarcely been a week—scarcely two days—since the Commission was appointed, that letters have not been received at my office from Wyoming, Texas, Illinois, and so on, stating that pleuro-pneumonia had broken out somewhere. We have had these alarms sent in from every quarter. Of course, I have felt it my duty to institute certain inquiries in relation to these reports, and in every case it has proven to be a false alarm. The disease was not pleuro-pneumonia. This accounts largely for the false alarm on the subject. The Treasury Cattle Commission has been engaged in ascertaining for the Treasury Department where the disease actually exists in this country. We found no evidence that it existed, or ever had, west of the Alleghany mountains, and we so reported, and we found no evidence of the disease aside from the points mentioned by Professor Law in his address to-day and by Dr. Salmon. We have found that true, genuine contagious disease does exist in this country along the Atlantic seaboard in a few localities, as was presented so ably by Professor Law to-day. The reason for the fortunate circumstance that there is none of this disease in the West, is because the tide has been toward the centres around which the disease exists, and not away from them. Around New York the great tide is toward the butcher shops, and these dairymen about the great cities, who have been in the business a long time, know pleuro-pneumonia very well indeed, and just as soon as they find pleuro-pneumonia, their cattle go immediately to the butcher shops. This has very largely prevented the spread of the disease throughout the country. We found it existing in a number of these places. There is no question about its existence in New York, Brooklyn, New Jersey, some places at present in Pennsylvania, about Baltimore, and possibly about Washington. It has not spread to any alarming extent. The most forcible case is one that occurred in Pennsylvania this summer, and I wish Dr. Salmon had referred more to it. I allude to this simply to show that we have a precise knowledge as to where it exists, and also that there is a reason why the cattle men of the West, who are certainly free from this disease now, should feel some degree of this alarm. A gentleman bought some cattle in Baltimore in July last. A few of them were brought to Baltimore from Virginia, and put in the stock-yard at Baltimore, and a few others were brought from in and about the yards in Baltimore and were taken to Pennsylvania. They were sold in Chester, Delaware, and some other counties, and everywhere those animals went in about 40 days pleuro-pneumonia appeared, and Dr. Salmon has told me he never saw the disease manifest a more distinct type; never saw a case where he was more satisfied with the diagnosis. Supposing someone in the West had bought those cattle in Baltimore, and brought them here, to our Chicago stock-yards, to be sent to Wyoming, Colorado, Kansas, and other States, what would have been the result? In Pennsylvania they are practically protected, as the State authority quarantines, and I presume there is not a particle of danger of its spreading.

Now, if I have not stated the case fairly, it is because my recollection is at fault, and Dr. Gadsden, who knows more about it, will correct me. I hear gentlemen make their astounding statements, and congratulate themselves that the West is entirely free from contagious disease, that the whole country is entirely free in fact, and that they are able to take cattle from one part to another part of the country. It may be well enough perhaps to say that the British authorities are just as well informed of the precise condition of cattle disease in this country as any of our own people. Their consuls in every State are specially charged with keeping close watch upon this subject; and every despatch that goes into the Associated Press and every rumour that gets afloat is reported, and the facts, when they are ascertained to be facts, are also reported. The rumours are reported as well as the facts. Now, to say that we are free from disease in the West, for the simple purpose of affecting the British markets is perfectly useless. They know just as much about our Texas fever as we do. I was much surprised to hear the talk about the absolute freedom from contagious disease in Iowa. I have seen hundreds and hundreds of animals lying dead in that State which have died from Texas fever, and anyone who has lived in Iowa as long as I have will bear me out in that statement of affairs there at one time. We cannot misrepresent the matter to them in any way, gentlemen, and if you attempt to do so when you do tell them the exact facts, they will get no credit over there. In England, last summer, in a long conversation with Professor Brown, who is the chief veterinary adviser of the Privy Council, and upon whose advice they act, said to me: "We "are entirely satisfied that your whole country west of the Alleghanies "is perfectly free from pleuro-pneumonia. We have no doubt of the "ability of your cattle commission to arrange some plan by which cattle "can be brought from the West, through northern lines of travel, and "exported to Great Britain without any special danger of pleuro- "pneumonia, but our legislation is such that we must regard your whole "country as a nation. We don't know here anything about your "States, or lines, or regulations; we only know from our own reports "and from yours that what we call and know as pleuro-pneumonia "exists with you as a nation, and under the Act of Parliament the "Privy Council is absolutely powerless to remove these restrictions in "favour of the West, although we are sure it can be done with safety." I mention this to emphasize the point made by one speaker here to-day that this was a national affair, and that the proper power to take up and handle it was that of the general Government. We have been taking very strong measures during the past year to perfect a system of quarantine in order to prevent the further importation of animal plagues, and the condition of things in Great Britain has amply justified all the precaution we have taken. We have imported five times as many cattle as in any previous year in the history of the country, and there has never been a time when there has been so much foot-and-mouth disease as now. It is a most infectious disease. I am not a veterinary surgeon, but I know enough about it to know that it is a most dangerous thing, one to be dreaded; not because it is necessarily fatal and results in the decimation of the herd, but because it results in the loss of at least one year to the owner.

One more word. I know, Mr. Chairman, that there are many who have claimed that this was only a scare gotten up by veterinary surgeons in order to establish a business, and there are many who have that idea to-day. If they will go out one half as much as I have and make examinations for themselves they will get over that notion sure. I said to Mr. Brown this year, "Is it not possible that you are mistaken " as to the number of cases we have in the United States?" Said he, " I don't know, but I do know that we received five cases in the first " six months of last year." "Then," said I, "Is it not possible you are " mistaken in your diagnosis? Is it not acute pneumonia, or disease " engendered by bad ventilation on shipboard?" Said he, "We have " had too long and too costly an experience in Great Britain not to " know pleuro-pneumonia when we see it. It is what we call con- " tagious pleuro-pneumonia, and what we are going to continue to call " contagious pleuro-pneumonia." Now we can make up our minds that Parliament will not change any law that it has enacted in favour of any section of this country. There is no question that we have this disease in isolated places along the coast, and we must with the aid of the general Government, by some process or other, take some steps to wipe it out. But *how* to do it is the difficulty. I remember when I first became connected with this matter, that I thought I could draw up a Bill that would do the job. I tried my hand several times, but there are difficulties in the way—so many questions of State rights, and sovereignty and jurisdiction, and so many interests to consult that the man who is lawyer enough, and practical cattle man enough, and practical railroad man enough, and practical butcher enough, and practical veterinarian enough to draft a Bill that will provide the elaborate machinery that, without clashing with State laws, will stamp out this disease is a bigger man, and a better lawyer, and a better cattle man and a better newspaper man than I am. [Laughter.]

Mr. LAWRENCE, of Ohio. I would like to ask if you have had a case of genuine foot-and-mouth disease?

Mr. SANDERS. That is a question for a veterinarian to answer, but I will say that we have never had excepting those that have resulted from recent importations, and such as has been directly communicated by them.

Mr. LAWRENCE. It is entirely from imported cattle?

Mr. SANDERS. Yes; we had a cargo arrive in Baltimore last March afflicted with foot-and-mouth disease in the ship "Nessmore." Those cattle were placed in quarantine at once and the disease was stamped out and its spread prevented. But, without proper disinfection this infected ship was loaded with fat cattle at the port of Baltimore and sent back to England. Of course, when the ship landed those cattle were found to be suffering from this disease contracted from the infected ship. Another cargo arrived about the same time from Boston under similar circumstances, and the British people at once set up the hue and cry that we were sending them foot-and-mouth disease from this country; and in July last Mr. Chaplin called attention to this circumstance and introduced a motion, the intent and import of which was to absolutely prohibit the landing of live cattle from this country, because of the alleged prevalence of foot-and-mouth disease in America.

very thorough investigation by the Treasury Cattle Commission and other veterinarians enabled them to positively contradict that statement. This brought about a very decided change of feeling over there. I was met over there this summer by a strange remark from the American minister when I called upon him to officially assure him that we had no foot-and-mouth disease in this country. It was a day or two after Mr. Chaplin's motion had passed. When I told him that with the evidence in our possession I felt prepared to state positively that there was no such thing in this country, Mr. Lowell said: "We have told the " British people so many lies about the condition of cattle in our " country that they will not believe us now that we tell the truth." I will not take up more of your time.

Mr. LAWRENCE, of Ohio. In your opinion, the present precautionary measures are sufficient to protect us against the probability of contagious disease hereafter?

Mr. SANDERS. Not by any means. We have no authority to quarantine sheep, hogs, or goats. The Cattle Commission addressed a letter to the Secretary of the Treasury last September on that very subject, and urged him to direct the collector of each port to cause strict examination of all swine, sheep, &c. And while we have had no authority, our veterinary inspectors have been required to keep watch of the matter, and if they discovered anything in the direction of disease in these animals they have been instructed at once to notify the owners and invoke their assistance in preventing the spread of the affliction. I think this is of very great importance.

Mr. W. T. SMITH, of Iowa. Since arriving in the city I have learned from a gentleman certain facts. He said he had been out at the stock yards talking with a man who had one or two calves from the dairy district from New York to sell. He seemed pretty well posted about a man named Sanders who he said had spent a good deal of money without any return, and had tried very hard to break up this calf trade.

Mr. SANDERS. There is no doubt that this calf trade during the past three years has been the very greatest source of danger to us in the West in bringing the disease from the Eastern States by means of these calves. Many of them have been brought from Ohio and Michigan, which was all right, but as the demand became greater so that calves were brought from further east, the danger increased. Fortunately, or unfortunately, as you have a mind to call it, the men who have bought these calves all over the West have found it a losing business, and in many cases 40 per cent. of calves brought from the East, and sold to the people of the West, have died in less than six months. Thanks to the general warning by the agricultural press and others, the people have become very chary of these calves. There is a great danger always from these calves, because it is extremely difficult to tell where they come from.

Mr. BARTLETT, of Illinois. I have made a specialty of handling calves from the East for the last four years, and I have handled a large number of them. I want to say a few words in behalf of the dairy calves. There has been a great deal said in the last two years about the danger we were running in receiving those calves here. I know they are small and weak, and do not seem to have any frames, but I do insist that while for the last 12 years every year we have received in the neighbourhood of from 150,000 to 200,000 of these calves shipped from the East to the West, there has not been a case of contagious or infectious disease among one of them. Of course there is a certain rate of mortality among them. The calves are young and tender; but

I believe that the highest per-centage of loss in any year would not exceed 8 or 10 per cent. Two years ago Governor Cullom issued a proclamation at the request of some of the short-horn breeders scheduling certain counties, and I wrote Governor Cullom that that action was satisfactory to the dairy calf interest for the reason that it defined the region and gave additional assurance to the Western men. I told him that I considered myself fully posted in that business, and I defied any man to show to the contrary. There are conditions regarding the raising of these young calves which all do not understand. It is not profitable to raise calves in certain districts, consequently, in order to ship profitably, they have to be brought and gathered together within a short radius, where they are loaded on cars, and you cannot ship properly unless you get up a car-load, and unless your freights are right. It is not true that the demand is decreasing. I have had an order within the past year for 6,000 head. I can sell 1,000 head to-morrow. I am willing to sell when I can get them for $16 to $18 per head, and I have recently been offered $20 but I can't get them. There has been a vast amount of misrepresentation in this calf trade. The public has become some what excited over it and become frightened because they are told they will have pleuro-pneumonia; whereas the harmless creatures are simply doing the best they can to live. [Laughter.] I have seen them come back to the stock yards here as fine stock as you could ask for. I sold 100 head that went into a county in this State three years ago; every one of them lived except three, and two of them were killed in shipment, and the other got into a hay rick. [Laughter.] There has been quite enough of nonsense about this matter. What is the use of talking about the calf trade decreasing when the fact is that we can't get the calves fast enough. I am shipping calves to-day back to Ohio and Virginia. I have just received calves from Chautauqua County, New York, and they were loaded yesterday to go back to West Virginia.

Mr. THOMPSON, of Kentucky. Suppose that to be all true; what assurance have we that infected calves will not be shipped West after all. When prices increase, as they will with this great demand, the disposition to ship will be the greater, and calves will be bought and sold in New York and Pennsylvania, where they have not been sold before. What assurance have we that the danger will not be great in the future, even admitting that it has not been in the past?

Mr. BARTLETT. That might be if your cattle were thoroughbred cattle. That is where this contagious poison is. You never found it tin the cattle of commerce.

Mr. W. T. SMITH, of Iowa. I am sorry to learn that the business is profitable. If it was unprofitable the danger would be less; as long as it is profitable the danger is greater. Now, while I am willing to accept this gentleman's statement as true, I am certainly unwilling to believe he is the only gentleman who is shipping calves in this country. Others are in it, and perhaps they too get calves from every infected county, and here, I think, is where we are labouring under very great danger, shipping from the dairy districts in the East to this section. I think, as far as we are concerned, farmers, stockmen, and ranchmen, that we shall do very well to ascertain the history of the calves we buy from the time they were dropped, and where they were dropped and who brings them to us.

Professor LAW, of New York. Mr. Chairman, I wish to correct one or two impressions that have doubtless been conveyed. In the first place, Mr. Sanders was asked whether foot-and-mouth disease was ever found among our native cattle. Why, yes. If the question had been asked whether we are ever infected without infection from importations I should say no; a thousand times no. In 1870 it spread from Canada over Northern New York and over the greater part of New England. Dr. Thayer, my colleague on the Commission, met me in Albany to consider matters connected with this disease. With regard to the statement that Mr. Bartlett made that we had certain diseases among thoroughbred cattle only, it is utterly pretentious and thoroughly fallacious. Take the poor cattle on the steppes of Eastern Europe and Asia, and we find that we have there the home of the cattle plagues of Europe and Asia. They have the Russian plague there, and it is utter nonsense to talk of its being confined to thoroughbred cattle. Come to our own country and go south to Texas; there we find our worst indigenous cattle disease. And so we have here shown that the worst cattle of both continents are the subjects of contagious disease. So much for contagious disease belonging to thoroughbred cattle. There has been a reference made to the shipment of calves from Chatauqua County to the West. I happen to live in New York, and in Central New York, and I know a good deal about the state of affairs there. Now, then, a few weeks ago I had a letter from a gentleman in Cayuga County asking if he would be permitted to send two car-loads of calves to his ranch in Nebraska. In my reply I was sorry to have to say " Yes." I know that he was not likely to convey any infectious disease from there to Nebraska, and most certainly he was not likely to convey lung plague. But those calves have been received, to my knowledge, not only from Cayuga, but very largely from Chatauqua and other places as far east as Saint Lawrence. One more thing: I would like to say to Mr. Bartlett, in reference to this calf trade, that letters can be produced, I think, from sellers in the Chicago market requesting dealers in the Philadelphia market to send calves to Chicago for sale only.

The PRESIDENT *pro tempore*. The chairman of the committee on order of business has a further report to make.

Mr. C. R. SMITH, of Iowa. We have with us Prof. Jas. D. Hopkins, and also Professor Gadsden, both of whom have brief papers on this subject. We recommend that these papers be presented now.

The recommendation was adopted, and Prof. Jas. D. Hopkins, Territorial veterinarian of Wyoming, addressed the Convention as follows:—

Prof. HOPKINS. While I was inspector of cattle in New York, I had the good fortune to detect foot-and-mouth disease in a herd that was brought to the port of New York from London on the steamship "France." This herd was quarantined, and at the expiration of six months they were turned over to their owners.

Prof. Hopkins then read the following paper:—

"The extent to which contagious diseases exist among domestic animals in this country has been fully investigated, and exhaustive reports, accompanied by maps showing the infected localities, have been made by the veterinary division of the Agricultural Department, at Washington, D.C. These reports have been printed by the Commissioner of Agriculture and copies placed in the hands of our legislators, and widely distributed among the people, so that all persons interested in the cattle industry have had abundant opportunities of informing themselves concerning the different diseases our domestic animals may contract by coming in contact with those suffering with a contagious disease, or in journeys through infected roads, pastures, railway cars, or stock yards.

"It is not my intention to take up the time of this Convention by going into a detailed description of the various diseases which afflict the domestic animals of the different States, such as anthrax, Texas fever, hog cholera, glanders, and farcy, chicken cholera, or the different diseases of sheep.

"The original intention in calling this Convention was to consider the ways and means necessary to secure such legislation as will at an early day remove the restriction placed by the British Government upon our live stock export trade, and also to protect our great western country from an invasion of contagious pleuro-pneumonia among the cattle by stamping it out from where it now exists in the States of New York, New Jersey, Pennsylvania, Maryland, and Virginia.

"Pleuro-pneumonia is a highly contagious, febrile disease, peculiar to the ox tribe, having an incubative stage of 10 days to three and one-half months, at the end of which local complications arise in the form of extensive inflammatory exudations within the substance of the lung and pleuro, finally resulting in consolidation of some portion of the lungs and adhesion of the pleural surfaces. In some cases there is extensive and rapid destruction of lung tissue with death from suffocation, but most commonly the disease is of a lingering character, symptoms of great prostration manifesting themselves, with blood poisoning from absorption of the degraded pulmonary exudates and death from marasmus.

"Contagious pleuro-pneumonia never arises from any condition of keeping or feeding. The disease is *always* introduced into healthful herds through the addition of an animal from an infected locality. Stock yards and railroad cars in an infected district become centres of contagion, and cattle passing through them are exposed to infection. I saw a cow at the Union Stock Yards, New York, suffering with contagious pleuro-pneumonia. This cow was killed by the State authorities. I made the autopsy, and the remainder of the lot, 37 head, were sold to dairymen, thus spreading the contagion, for before leaving New York I was called on to visit three herds, whose owners had bought one each of this infected lot.

"Mr. Baldwin, of Paterson, N. J., bought a cow in December, 1881, at the Union Stock Yards, New York, and took her to his farm, where she sickened and died, spreading contagious pleuro-pneumonia to his herd of 34 milch cows, and my last official act in that State was to superintend the destruction and burial of this herd in April, 1882.

"How do stock yards become infected? Numberless instances are on record where pleuro-pneumonia is known to have broken out in herds whose owners have at once taken them to the yards and placed them on sale, rather than suffer the loss experience taught him was sure to follow.

"Again, the pernicious system of cow dealers who peddle cows, exchanging with dairies and returning them to stock yards, often leaving cows on trial at dairies known to be infected, and the cow is afterwards returned to the yards. These men are unscrupulous, and by their peculiar system of trade contagious pleuro-pneumonia is perpetuated and spread among all herds whose owners will trade with them.

"It is well known that many people find it profitable to keep cows on the suburbs of cities, where the large open commons furnish free pasturage and the distilleries and starch factories cheap food. These people let their cows run together on the commons, the infected and healthy. They rarely let a fat cow die of this disease, as at the first symptom of illness she is sent to the butcher.

These small herds and their stables are hotbeds of contagion in New York and Brooklyn. Pleuro-pneumonia is the most dangerous of all the cattle plagues, on account of the length of time between exposure to the contagion and the development of the disease, during which time the animal presents no abnormal symptom and might be transported to the extreme limits of the country.

"In 1882 the Treasury Cattle Commission, after a thorough investigation, made an exhaustive report of the history and spread of contagious pleuro-pneumonia among cattle in this country to the Secretary of the Treasury at Washington, D.C., and pointed out the dread consequences of allowing the disease to spread through the country, and advised the most energetic measures for its eradication. This report was the basis for several bills that were introduced before Congress at its last session. Most unfortunately nothing was done, and our export trade continues to suffer, and the whole country is threatened with an invasion of this terrible pestilence.

"Inoculation has been resorted to by the people of Europe, Great Britain, and Australia, which, while it limits the mortality, the disease continues to prevail. No country has ever got rid of contagious pleuro-pneumonia by inoculation, and to this country, where *so small* a territory is infected in comparison with the vast domain and interests involved, inoculation means perpetuation and spread of the disease. There is only one remedy applicable to this country — *the disease must be stamped out*. If this disease were wide-spread as in England, Europe, or Australia, we would be obliged to resort to inoculation. The work of stamping out pleuro-pneumonia from the States where it now exists is an immense undertaking even under the most favourable laws, and requires on the part of those entrusted with the work an extensive knowledge of the rights of individuals, and can be accomplished with very little interference with commerce. It has been demonstrated in Massachusetts, New York, and Connecticut, also in different parts of Europe, that the stamping out of this disease is the *only* effectual remedy. Eminent statesmen who have given this subject close attention cannot agree as to the constitutionality of any law of Congress giving authority to enter a State and prescribe rules and regulations governing the cattle traffic necessary to the slaughter of infected stock; in other words, 'The sovereignty of States must be respected.'

"If Congress *cannot* enact laws to stamp out contagion, then perhaps Congress *can* enact laws to keep it where it is. Therefore I would propose for your consideration that this Convention shall petition Congress to enact such laws that the Secretary of the Treasury shall appoint a commission of three or five, with authority to prohibit cattle leaving county or counties in any State where contagious pleuro-pneumonia among the cattle exists, except under special license. To prescribe the route all 'through cattle' must take in passing the infected district. To investigate all outbreaks of disease among cattle that may become epizootic, and have charge of the quarantine stations for imported cattle. To advise with State authorities as to the best methods of controlling contagious pleuro-pneumonia. To make it a misdemeanour for any one to violate the proclamation of the commission.

"If such a commission were appointed, the country would, in a measure, be relieved of its dread of the fatal contagion. But we can never breathe entirely free while we know that we harbour such an insiduous enemy to our live stock industry.

"To make this commission successful, their work must be continuous. Hence an abundant appropriation that will last until the next meeting of the Congress is a necessity.

"The moral effect of Federal prohibition on the movement of cattle *from* the infected States, would speedily result in the enactment of the necessary State laws and the stamping out of the contagion.

"It is a lamentable fact that with the exception of Illinois and

Wyoming Territory the different States pay no attention to the welfare of their live-stock industry. A few of the States have enacted laws against the introduction of pleuro-pneumonia, but they remain a dead letter on the statute book, for there is no provision made for their enforcement, and in the event of an outbreak of disease among the domestic animals they have no expert at hand to prevent the spread, and also much unnecessary loss among the people. Numerous instances have occurred during the past two years, where the injudicious handling of Southern cattle and Western hogs has spread Texas fever and hog cholera among the Northern and Eastern stock. Again, many animals perish annually, from anthrax, all over the country. Glanders and farcy among horses is a source of heavy loss. These and other diseases indigenous to our country should be a matter for the careful consideration of legislatures of every State and Territory. Therefore, I propose for your consideration that the legislature of every State and Territory shall be petitioned to enact such laws, giving the governor power to appoint a veterinary surgeon, whose duty shall be to investigate all outbreaks of disease among domestic animals, and upon the introduction of any contagious disease the governor shall have authority to quarantine any premises, farms, county, or counties where such disease may exist, and to prescribe such regulations as he may judge necessary to prevent contagion being communicated in any way from the places so quarantined; to call on all sheriffs and deputy sheriffs and police to enforce such rules and regulations; to prescribe regulations and order the destruction of all animals affected with contagious disease, and for the proper disposition of their hides and carcases, and thorough disinfection of all objects which might convey contagion; that the owners of all animals so condemned shall be indemnified at least two thirds sound value; that all persons transgressing any order of the governor shall be guilty of a misdemeanour; that a sufficient amount shall be appropriated to enable the governor to enforce the law.

" In the stamping out of a contagious disease I am in favour of a liberal indemnity being paid to owners of all condemned animals as the most economical and successful plan, because it secures the owner's hearty co-operation, and in large cities the Government must outbid the dealer and butcher. Then, again, by inducing the people to promptly report all sick cattle, it saves the most expensive professional supervision, and makes the work popular.

" Existing legislation, either State or Federal, does not control the movement of cattle. For instance, we have United States quarantine stations in which all cattle from Europe must undergo 90 days' detention on their arrival, while from the hot-beds of contagion around New York and Booklyn, Philadelphia, or Baltimore, cattle can be transported without let or hindrance to any part of the United States except Illinois and Wyoming Territory.

" Heretofore the tide of cattle traffic has been *from* the West, and to this fact we are indebted that contagious pleuro-pneumonia has not spread over the whole country, but at present the great demand for young stock for the Western ranches makes it an object for the trader to bring cattle from long distances, and unless prohibitive measures are adopted, we will soon see the cheap calves from the infected States brought West to develop pleuro-pneumonia.

" Our only safety lies in Congress enacting such laws as will place the prevention of the spread of this pestilence in competent hands, and to insure a continued prosperity it is a matter of necessity that each State shall have a veterinary department ready at all times to cope with any contagion that may be imported, and prevent the consternation and loss to the people consequent on the outbreak of disease among domestic animals.

" How this shall be done is a matter for the consideration of this Convention."

Dr. GADSDEN, of Pennsylvania. I would like to say one word in reply to an assertion that some gentleman made, that at the present time England was full of pleuro-pneumonia. Here is an official report —official because it comes from the Privy Council. It says:—

" During the five weeks ending September 29, 1883, there were reported in Great Britain 34 outbreaks of pleuro-pneumonia and 90 cattle attacked. In the corresponding period of 1882, there were 39 outbreaks, and 104 cattle attacked were reported."

This I am satisfied is true; and to let such an assertion go uncontradicted is not right.

Mr. CRANE, of New Jersey. I have lived in the midst of pleuro-pneumonia for 20 years. New Jersey was inoculated from that cow that was sold in Brooklyn to which Professor Law referred this morning, and it was introduced by selling calves from New York State. A friend of mine bought something like 100 of them, sold some to his neighbours, and took the rest to a pasture field in Morris County about 25 miles west. There the disease broke out, and all those calves that were distributed among these neighbours of his carried the disease with them. That was about 25 years ago, and there were efforts made to stamp it out, and I think it was pretty thorough, although we were troubled with it several years. About eight or nine years ago it was introduced into Newark, Jersey City, and Elizabeth, by cattle bought in Baltimore by these cow dealers. They could go there and buy cattle for from $10 to $15. Some of them showed signs of the disease. Those that had no signs were distributed among farmers, and the consequence was the disease was sown broadcast in four or five counties. This came to my knowledge and I felt it my duty to take action immediately. I went to the State board of health and stated what was going on, and from there we went to the legislature, and got it to enact laws, similar to those in Massachusetts, to stamp it out. The bill met with a good deal of opposition, especially among those who were afraid to make any appropriation for the purpose through fear their constituents would find fault. We had to labour three years before we got a law, and all this time it was being spread. Some had tried vaccination, but the relief seemed to be only temporary. About the time that Professor Law was attempting to find the disease in New York State the legislature made an appropriation of some $25,000, I think, and gave certain powers to Governor McClellan. He appointed General Sterling from my county, who pursued this thing pretty thoroughly, until the next meeting of the legislature. He had put a pretty effective stop to it by this vaccination and other means, until the State was comparatively quite free from it, and if we had only continued in that way for a year or two longer I think we would have stamped it out entirely. But of course there must be a change, and the matter is now in the hands of the State board of health, and Dr. Hunt is at the head of it; and at the last meeting he reported that there was but a single case, which, I think, came from Staten Island, New York. I have laboured hard, with other gentlemen, before the legislature, to create a popular opinion against this state of things. We believe that our State should have more effectual laws of some kind, and that the board of health or some other organisation should have power to stamp this disease out entirely and effectually. I believe that there is not nearly so much now as there was seven or eight years ago.

A DELEGATE. I move that we now adjourn until 9 o'clock p.m. The motion was agreed to; and at 6 o'clock and 47 minutes p.m., the Convention adjourned.

The Convention met at 9 o'clock, the president in the chair.

The PRESIDENT. I understand that in accordance with the report of the committee on order of business, adopted before we adjourned, the first business in order is the reading of a paper by Dr. Gadsden, of Pennsylvania.

Dr. GADSDEN. Before reading my paper, Mr. Chairman and gentlemen, I would like to read a very short paper about New Jersey. A gentleman speaking of New Jersey said there was no disease, or none to speak of there. I allude particularly to pleuro-pneumonia. Two inspectors under the State board of health called at my house on Saturday last and from them I gathered this information:

"There are five herds of cattle in quarantine with contagious pleuro-pneumonia. The animals number about 1,200 head. The number that have died in each herd is as follows: 22, 8, 10, 9, 5, in all 54. All the remainder are inoculated with virus from one of the first attacked. None of them have since died, but they have shown symptoms of contagious pleuro-pneumonia in a mild form, but every animal (cattle) brought into these herds of inoculated cattle (if not previously inoculated) have taken contagious pleuro-pneumonia and died or have been killed. They assert and say it can be proved that those cattle took this disease from a lot of 13 that was purchased in March last from a car-load of cattle at Flemington, N. J. They had just arrived from Bradford County, Pennsylvania. The disease was noticed in April last. Ten were put on one farm, three on another (this original 13), both belonging to one party. Contagious pleuro-pneumonia broke out on both farms about the same time, eight out of the 10 died, one of the three died, another was killed for virus to inoculate the rest, which are doing well. If this report is strictly true it goes a long way to show that inoculated cattle can spread this disease to other cattle coming in contact with them. This is very important, and goes to prove inoculation will not save our herds unless it is possible to inoculate them all, which, of course, is quite out of the question."

Mr. CRANE, of New Jersey. I would state that my authority was from Dr. Hunt.

Dr. GADSDEN. I know Dr. Miller and Dr. Rogers, and I believe every word of that is strictly true.

Mr. CRANE. I would state that I have been over New Jersey since June, and——

Dr. GADSDEN. I would here state that this herd was unknown to Dr. Hunt and Dr. Rogers last July. It was kept from the State authorities. Rather than to report it they thought proper to inoculate.

Professor LAW, of New York. Please tell us where Bradford County, Pennsylvania, is.

Dr. GADSDEN. Two hundred miles from Philadelphia, north-west.

Professor LAW. In the oil regions?

Dr. GADSDEN. I don't know; I haven't been there.

Professor LAW. West of the Alleghanies?

Dr. GADSDEN. It is close to them.

Professor LAW. I merely put the inquiry to show that the source is not to be relied upon.

Dr. GADSDEN. But the man who sold the 13 head says he is sure they came from Bradford County.

Dr. Gadsden then read the following paper :—

"CONTAGIOUS DISEASES IN CATTLE, HOW THEY ARE IMPORTED, AND WHAT THEY COST.

"There are three contagious diseases peculiarly affecting the bovine race, viz., rinderpest or cattle plague, contagious pleuro-pneumonia or lung plague, and sore foot and mouth disease; and the rapidity with which they spread, and the ease with which contagion is communicated, require the adoption of the most stringent measures to eradicate them where they now exist and prevent their further introduction.

"None of these plagues are indigenous to this country, but in every instance where they have appeared here the disease can be traced to infected animals that have been imported from Europe.

"Fortunately the first named has never made its appearance in this country, although several European nations have suffered terribly by its ravages, and some are still suffering from it.

"So far as is known it is incurable, and the only remedy is to guard carefully against its introduction by the enforcement of a strict embargo against all countries where it appears, and should it ever obtain lodgment here, adopt the most heroic measures to stamp it out at once. To give some idea of the rapid spread of rinderpest, and the immense loss caused by it, statistics gathered from official sources show that in 1865 and 1866 the loss from it in Great Britain was 12,000,000*l.* or $60,000,000, while in European Russia during the last four years over 1,000,000 cattle have perished with it.

"Contagious pleuro-pneumonia or lung plague has made its appearance at different times in this country, and efforts have been made by individual States to stamp it out. In this they have been successful for a time, and at comparatively small cost, but unfortunetely only to be again infected from neighbouring States that had taken no measures for the prevention of the spread of contagion.

"This disease has been known and dreaded in England for many years, and Dr. Fleming asserts that for the six years ending with 1860 more than 1,000,000 cattle perished from it, involving a loss of 12,000,000*l.*

"Some persons have denied the identity of the disease that has appeared here, with the scourge of the same name that caused such great loss in England, but having been an inspector in that country for a considerable time, and examined many diseased animals, and made numerous post-mortem examinations, and having had unusual facilities in this country to inspect both living and dead animals affected with the disease, I have no hesitation in pronouncing it *exactly the same disease* as is known as *pleuro-pneumonia* in England, and of its *contagious* character there can be no doubt.

"There have been occasional outbreaks of sore-foot and mouth disease in this country, always traceable to animals brought from Europe, but by the establishment of proper quarantine regulations it has been stamped out without extending to any great extent.

"Although this disease readily yields to treatment, it has been productive of great losses in other countries, not only among cattle but also has been communicated to swine and sheep.

"In 1871 there were 519,523 animals attacked with it in Great Britain; in 1872 the loss from it in England and Scotland was estimated at 13,000,000*l.*, and in 1875 at over 8,000,000*l.* In August of the present year 30,985 animals were attacked with it, and in September only six counties in all England were exempt from its ravages.

o 11711.

APPENDIX.

"Great Britain has adopted the most stringent laws, which are rigidly enforced, to prevent the introduction and spread of contagious diseases among her animals, going so far as to exclude the importation of live animals from countries that have any disease.

"This is not to be wondered at, when it is known that from 1839 to 1870 the loss in animals affected with contagious diseases amounted to the enormous sum of 100,000,000*l.* or $500,000,000.

"It is a matter of vital importance to this country to promptly take the necessary steps to prevent the importation and spread of these diseases, not only to protect our own food supply, but to prevent the total extinction of our trade in beef with foreign countries.

"When we take into consideration the losses sustained by England from these diseases and know that we have five times as many cattle in this country as they have, some idea may be had of the loss we should suffer if these diseases obtained a lodgment here.

"If they were once communicated to the vast herds on our western plains, the extirpation of the disease would be next to impossible and the loss which would ensue would be almost incalculable.

"The question then arises how are we to prevent so dire a calamity befalling us, for these diseases being purely *contagious*, certainly are *preventable*.

"The legislation to effect this object must be *national* in character, and its execution be under the control of the National Government, for if placed in the charge of local authorities, it must prove futile for two reasons: First, on account of favouritism that will naturally be shown to the owners of animals by local officers; and secondly, on account of the failure of certain localities to enact and enforce laws.

"There should be restrictions placed on the importation of all animals, animal products, and goods that have been in contact with animals from countries where disease is known to exist, and no animal should be permitted to enter the country until after having been placed in quarantine for a sufficient time to positively determine that it was perfectly free from disease, either in an incipient or active stage."

The Treasury Cattle Commission, to be sure, are taking certain preventive measures in the quarantine of cattle, but it is not thorough, and therefore it does not protect our country. For instance, we have a port at Philadelphia, but we have no quarantine station there, and these animals can come in there and be sent to all quarters of this vast country and these gentlemen know nothing about it.

"Secondly. Arrangements should be made for the reception of reports from all sections of the country at short intervals, and upon the appearance or suspicion of disease an inspection should be made by some person competent to detect it; all diseased animals, and those that have been in contact with them, placed in quarantine, and those, without doubt, affected with rinderpest or pleuro-pneumonia destroyed as speedily as possible and properly buried. The stables and other out-buildings that have been occupied by these animals should be thoroughly disinfected, and the quarantine maintained for at least three months after the disappearance of the last vestige of the disease.

"In the meantime careful inspection should be made from time to time of all animals in the neighbourhood.

"Animals that are killed should be paid for at a fair valuation, and thus the farmer will have no motive to conceal the appearance of disease for the purpose of saving his stock.

"When I speak of quarantine I mean a *complete isolation* of the animals from all others at some place remote from public roads, where they can by no possibility come in contact with any other animals.

"By adopting regulations of this character, and having them rigidly enforced by competent officials, under the supervision of some Department of the National Government that shall have the authority to destroy diseased animals and an appropriation to pay for them, such contagious diseases as at present exist can be eradicated from this country and their introduction in the future prevented.

"In this way, and in this way alone, can we prevent our vast Western herds from being infected and swept away, and restore to our Eastern seaports and Western cattle markets the trade of which they are now deprived by the English embargo, while the expense to the National Treasury will be trifling in comparison to the results attained."

There has been a further outbreak in Pennsylvania lately. I wish Thomas J. Edge was present, for he could give you not only the particulars of this but every other case they have had. The origin of this case rests with the sale in Baltimore of 16 calves. They were sold it July, and in six weeks the disease broke out. A local farrier, who is also a blacksmith, I believe, made an examination and said he would soon rectify that. Well, he did rectify it, and three of them died. Then the owner wrote to Mr. Edge. They soon found that they were affected. the State has paid $1,200 already for dead animals, and it is expected That it will cost $3,000 before they are through with it, and all on account of this man bringing 16 animals in there last July.

Professor LAW. I beg one word on the subject of Philadelphia. We did not establish a quarantine station there because we were told that Philadelphia steamships would not carry cattle, except under circumstances which were not at all likely to happen, and, therefore, a quarantine station would not be necessary. There is in force an order that all cattle should go to ports where a quarantine station has been established. Now I learn that they have been coming to Philadelphia, but we are not responsible for it. Moreover, we are not an executive body, but purely advisory. We can advise the Secretary of the Treasury, and there our power ends. We can do nothing else.

The PRESIDENT. Is it the duty of the revenue officer to remand those cattle back to the ship so they can land only at those points where there are quarantine regulations?

Professor LAW. The duty is to have them sent to the next port where there is a quarantine station.

The PRESIDENT. I understand the next paper is one by Mr. Coffin, of Iowa.

A DELEGATE. Mr. President, we have been listening to a good many papers, and it seems to me that we had better begin to think about taking some action now.

Mr. COFFIN. I have but a very crude paper, which I prepared on my way here. It is simply suggestive of some action, and perhaps the points have been covered by the papers already read. I hardly think it would be profitable to take up the time of the Convention with it.

The PRESIDENT. I presume the Convention would be glad to hear from Mr. Coffin. I was simply reporting to you the action of the Convention. According to the report of the committee Mr. Coffin was to have the floor following the reading of the paper of Dr. Gadsden.

There were several calls for Mr. Coffin, who came forward and presented the following paper:—

"The vastness of the interests here to be discussed is so beyond all grasp, it is useless to attempt to represent it in figures. Sufficient is it to say that no other one interest touches so many of the citizens of this nation. Now, when we look at the almost entire absence of all authoritative regulation by either the State or national power to protect this interest from danger, as well as the very poverty of the encouragement given for its better development, and of more general scientific and practical knowledge of its propagation and care and feeding, we may well stand filled with wonder and amazement at this lack of attention. Why this is so it is hard at this time to explain. I look upon the fact of this Convention as a most encouraging and auspicious move. Gathered here are representative men from all the stock-raising States and Territories of this nation. The eyes of the law-making powers of the country will be upon us. What this Convention may utter will, to a large extent, be taken as authority of what is actually needed. Hence, then, I feel very anxious that the deliberations here should be of the most calm, and at the same time far-reaching and exhaustive. As already said, the interest here represented is vastly important. At this present time the money value of the live stock of this nation runs up into figures too great to be well held in the human comprehension, and yet, great as it is, in the very near future it is to be increased to a wonderful degree. When one recognises the fact as to the great numbers of live stock that are now annually brought to our shores, and the value of each individual one, and at the same time keep in mind that each one of these imported animals is brought here for breeding purposes, and then takes into the account the millions already here which are used also for increasing the number, as well as the individual value of each added one, it does seem that the duty of a wise and thoughtful law-maker should be plain.

"What, then, are the demands now pressing, and what this Convention should with no uncertain sound announce as demanding the immediate attention of the national and State legislatures?

"(1.) Immediate steps to secure whatever other precautions that may be necessary to make it absolutely certain that no contagious disease of any kind be ever imported and lodged upon our shores.

"(2.) Such laws enacted and powers granted that can effectually and for ever stamp out at once whatever there is of contagious diseases among our live stock at the present time. I mean everything the words I use on this last item can bear.

"(3.) Under this head, the wants I design to mention may lead to a wide range of thought and discussion.

"We, as a nation, in comparison to what is done by many other governments to foster and encourage live-stock interest, are doing scarcely anything.

"Bear with me for a little while I present this matter as it lies in my own mind. As a nation we are growing rapidly rich. We are soon to to be, if our resources are wisely managed, one of the wealthiest peoples of the globe. Our revenues are to be enormous; our national debt is soon to be paid off; already is it a perplexing question with our statesmen what to do with our revenue. Is it not time that Congress should show its appreciation of that interest that lies at the very bottom of all our wonderful prosperity by turning some of this overflowing income that is well nigh bursting our Treasury and corrupting our officials into channels that will establish valuable experimental stations in every State, presided over by experienced and careful men, who will be able in a short time to give valuable information to all the agricultural interests of this land. As it is now we are, in almost every State, left entirely without protection and information.

"Let the lung plague break out in almost any of our Western States and we have no law, we have no State officer who has any power to act; we have no expert who can be called upon to decide on the character of the disease. We are all at sea. We have no standard or any fountain, no head centre of information to which we can look for real, certain, scientific truth on any of these matters. I do not wish to be understood that I am in favour of any objectionable centralisation of power, but I do want a plan by which a man or men whose business it would be to become experts in all these matters, no matter if to arrive at this expertness they shall have learned a great deal of the common, practical, level-headed farmer, as well as by scientific experimentation. But we want these stations and these men to scatter a more general and exact knowledge on agricultural matters; we want a man on whom the people can call, and whose duty and business it will be to go to any part of the State and examine any cases where dangerous diseases may actually or be supposed to exist.

"Is it not time that we moved in this direction of securing to the agricultural interests of the whole nation local experimental stations to foster, encourage, and protect all its interests?

"Is not a convention of such men as we have here a proper one to strike boldly out for these things in such a form and manner as its wisdom may dictate? We must remember that public sentiment, that gives birth to and maintains laws that are needed for and in the advancement of a great people's interests, is a matter of growth, and can we afford to neglect the cultivation of that kind of public sentiment that must be before we can reach the end so greatly desired and needed?"

A DELEGATE. I should be pleased to ask Professor Law what effect, in his judgment, the milk or flesh from an animal affected with pleuro-pneumonia would have upon the system of man?

Professor LAW. I am sorry to say that it will convey no actual disease to man. I have almost wished it were different, because if it was harmful to man it would be stamped out soon enough. Of course in the advanced stages of the disease the milk, what there is of it, is at least vastly impure, and the system is certainly saturated with obnoxious products; but we cannot trace any definite disease to man from this, other than perhaps a little ill-health. It never produces pleuro-pneumonia in man, or anything akin to it.

[Following this answer there occurred a running coloquy between Professor Law and a delegate, a large portion of which could not be heard at the reporter's table.]

Mr. SCOTT, of Iowa. Mr. Chairman, this Convention is composed of representative men—supposed to be representative men—who are interested in this question, and which was supposed by the Department of Agriculture to be of importance enough to call us together in a national Convention, and the time specified for its consideration was two days. One of those days, if my time be estimated properly and noted, has very nearly expired, and as yet it seems to me we are frittering away the little that is left of this first day in the discussion of some of the details in regard to questions that anyone could have settled for themselves by going to some of our libraries or consulting some of the publications that have been sent out gratuitously during the past year. Here for the last 10 minutes we have been listening to questions that any of those engaged could have had asked and answered either before or after we met. [Applause.] It seems to me, sir, that if we could rise to the dignity that belongs to a national Convention representing more than 50,000,000 of population and more than $60,000,000,000 of wealth, and more than $15,000,000,000 of annual productions—if we would rise to the dignity which belongs to men who represent interests of such great magnitude, we should address ourselves to the presentation of our views as a Convention, and the only practical manner, sir, that I can conceive of by which that can be done is by the usual method of a deliberative body—the expression of views through formal resolutions. [Applause.]

There are some things that are conceded. We have had the matter discussed to day, and it is conceded that in a comparatively small portion of this vast country there does exist infectious cattle disease. It is also conceded (probably an important fact to us) that it does occupy but a very small portion of our vast domain. It is further conceded also (and these things might, all of them, be embodied in a formal " whereas " this fact and " whereas " that fact, and " whereas " also this further fact) that it is only because the movement of the live stock of the country has been from the west to the east that we have been saved from a fearful disaster. Figures do not fairly convey to the human mind the terrible importance of this subject to us. No, neither figures nor language will convey it to us; at least I have not sufficient command over the language to represent to this Convention what our vast animal production means to this country, nor what it means should this disease get among our herds and scatter them like leaves before the autumn blast. [Applause.] Now, sir, you suggested in your remarks this morning, the time and the means which must be adopted to cause our Government to realise to some extent the precise facts in regard to this matter, and the necessity of prompt action. I am sure we all realise the necessity of using these means and of bringing them to bear upon the Government, and I make these remarks, Mr. President, with the view of calling forth from the committee on resolutions, or from any other source, some sort of action which shall bring us face to face with our duty in this matter before the day is entirely gone. [Applause.] I would ask if the committee on resolutions, or order of business, or any authority of the officers of this Convention, is prepared to present to this Convention any formal resolution through which this body can express tself only as a deliberative body can. [Applause.]

The PRESIDENT. There were several committees appointed, but I am not informed that either is ready to report at this time.

Mr. SCOTT. I trust we shall have something placed before this Convention at once that means action and business. [Applause.]

The PRESIDENT. Will the gentlemen make a motion to that effect?

A DELEGATE: We know that a large amount of money has been expended and a great deal of effort undertaken, and yet contagious lung plague still exists in this country. Now I think that the reason for that may be explained by the fact that the institutions of this country differ from those of other countries in which such organisations exist. Here in this country we have gone into some States and seen the plague extirpated from them, while in other States the disease has been quite prevalent, and little or no attempt made to stamp it out there. The question arises what practical method shall we adopt to eradicate this disease, and that question can be answered only in one way—there must be combined action on the part of the Federal Government and the State Government. This has already been alluded to by Professor Law, but in any attempt which shall be made to eradicate this disease the Federal Government must make a sufficient appropriation to carry on the work, and then the different States must adopt a uniform legislation, so that all States which are infected will take a united and harmonious action. Then we shall not have the spectacle of one State being free of the disease while another is still suffering from it. We can incorporate these principles in any resolution that may be brought before us. We must follow the principle of action by the Federal Government; and we must adopt, to a certain extent, the principle of the Government supervising the State action, but we cannot relegate the entire duty to the Federal Government; it must to a certain extent be carried out by the different States. I think that by recognising these two principles that we may ultimately see this country entirely free from the lung plague, and I think that in any resolution which is to be adopted by the Convention it will be well to limit our action to one disease. That is enough to grapple with at one time; and when we have seen the country rid of lung plague it will then be time for subsequent efforts to remove those other diseases which also inflict considerable loss upon us.

Professor MORROW. I heartily appreciate the force of the remarks made by my friend, Mr. Scott, of Iowa. I have also felt that the time had come when we should endeavour to get formal action before the Convention. As a means of securing this I would move that the committee on resolutions be requested to report to this Convention at the earliest practical moment a plan for our consideration and action.

The PRESIDENT. If any gentleman has a plan or resolution to offer let it be referred to this committee, in order that it may consider all suggestions together.

A DELEGATE. I suggest that the names of that committee be read.

The secretary read the list of names.

The DELEGATE from Wyoming. I am a very young man to even attempt to make a speech in a convention of this kind; but I do want to say that I hardly think the vast interests here are properly represented upon that committee. The delegation of which I am a part has come here from a long distance. That delegation represents on this floor from 12 to 20 millions of dollars invested on the plains, and I beg that we may have a representation upon that committee, and that the name of our president, Judge James Carey, be added to that committee. I think that his advice will be of great help.

The name of Mr. Carey was accordingly added to the committee.

Mr. POST, of Illinois. I would suggest that inasmuch as there may be those present who have prepared resolutions, or formulated some action for the Convention, that the roll be called for the purpose of allowing every one present to offer any such suggestion, and they be referred to the committee without debate. I make this suggestion in order that we may get some idea of the plan of operation that members have in mind. That will suggest other resolutions, and we shall know something of what we have before the Convention.

Mr. SCOTT, of Iowa. There seems to be some absent members of that committee. It appears to me that the number, 5, on so important a committee as this is to be is wholly inadequate to the proper representation of the feelings of our whole extent of country. By reason of this fact I move that the number be increased to 10, and the additional members be selected from those States not already represented upon the committee.

A DELEGATE. Will the gentleman not accept an amendment to make the committee consist of one member from each State represented here?

The amendment was accepted, and the motion, as amended, was adopted.

Mr. SCOTT. I rise to name Mr. Dailey, of Nebraska, as a member of that committee.

Mr. DAILEY, of Nebraska. I should like to present the name from my own State—Mr. S. R. Thompson.

The roll of States was called by the secretary, the nominations received and ratified, as follows:—

Wyoming, James Carey; Colorado, George W. Rusk; Pennsylvania,

Julius Le Moyne; Michigan, I. H. Butterfield, jr.; Arizona, J. J. Gosper; Wisconsin, Hiram Smith; Minnesota, George E. Case; West Virginia, J. M. Kirk; Nebraska, Prof. S. R. Thompson; Tennessee, Col. John Overton; Maryland, Edward B. Emory; District of Columbia, Dr. D. E. Salmon; Massachusetts, Dr. E. F. Thayer; Kansas, Governor Dick; Iowa, Hon. John Scott.

The committee thereupon retired, and, on motion, the Convention adjourned at 10 o'clock until 8 a.m. to-morrow.

November 16.

The Convention awaited the report of the committee on resolutions until 9 o'clock and 40 minutes, when it was called to order by the president.

Mr. CHORN, from the committee, said: With your permission, sir, the committee on resolutions is ready to report, and the secretary will read our report.

(The report was read. It appears hereafter in sections and in its amended form.—REPORTER.)

Mr. SANDERS, of Illinois. I move the adoption of the report.

Professor HOPKINS, of Wyoming. I notice that the first portion of the preamble refers to the matter as "disease among domestic animals." I would suggest that the disease be distinctly named. I believe that it will be better if we confine our influence to the one disease of contagious pleuro-pneumonia.

Mr. THOMPSON, of Nebraska. Mr. President, this matter was very fully discussed by the committee. This Convention was called, as we understand, to consider what measures are necessary to stamp out all classes of disease among domestic animals. The gentlemen who are interested in swine are particularly interested in this question, and we thought our action due to them, while the next portion of the preamble is fully directed toward this one disease of pleuro-pneumonia.

Mr. GRINNELL. I move the adoption of the first portion, and the amendments can come up in order.

A DELEGATE. I rise to make a motion that each speaker upon the report and amendments be confined to ten minutes.

(Suggestions of five minutes were heard from all parts of the room.)

The amendment was accepted, and the motion, as amended was agreed to.

Professor LAW. I now call for the reading of the first "whereas."

The secretary read as follows:—

"Whereas the existence of disease among animals in the United States has seriously affected the exportation of live stock, and the suspicion that attaches in foreign countries to all neat cattle and swine of the United States on account of the existence of disease in certain localities, has greatly lessened the sale of American meats in foreign markets."

This portion of the preamble was then adopted.

The secretary then read the second portion of the preamble as recommended by the committee, as follows:—

"And whereas the existence of pleuro-pneumonia in certain of the Atlantic States, introduced from time to time by the importation of livestock from European countries, constantly threatens the spread of the contagion to the Southern and Western States and Territories; that the disease is of such a character that State legislation can only give partial relief; that prompt and appropriate legislation on the part of Congress to eradicate the disease is imperatively demanded; that should the great ranges of the West become infected with the disease it would be impossible to stamp out the plague except by the total destruction of the herds, and at a cost of hundreds of millions of dollars."

Professor ROBERTS, of New York. If I quote it properly, that portion reads, "In certain Atlantic States" the disease prevails. I want to suggest that it be amended to read in "certain portions of the Atlantic States." As it is now, it is too sweeping. It conveys the impression that the disease exists all through certain Atlantic States, when the truth is, it is confined to small portions of a few of those States. I move that the words "small portions" be inserted.

Professor HOPKINS, of Wyoming. I think it would be better to name the States where the disease exists, as the locality is well-known all over the world. Why should we brand the whole Atlantic coast with the stigma of the disease when everybody knows that it is only certain States that have it? Why not name the States?

Mr. EMORY, of Maryland. I do not think it would be possible to name the States, because the disease is one that fluctuates from time to time. Maryland has been very much affected with pleuro-pneumonia. I don't think there is now one case in the State. We had an outbreak in Washington County a few weeks ago, but the animals were slaughtered and I don't think there is a single case in the State at the present time. I think that a few cases of Texas fever is now quarantined there, but to state that this disease exists there would not be fair. Of course we are liable to the disease there from time to time. It is brought from other States into the Baltimore stock-yards. It is liable to be carried through the State by the purchases of feeders from Virginia. The last case of pleuro-pneumonia was from West Virginia. I have been told by our State veterinarian that we have none there now, and to state that it exists there or in Pennsylvania might lead to trouble.

Dr. GADSDEN. With all respect to this committee on resolutions, I do hope that you will stick to this one fatal disease known as pleuro-pneumonia. If you go into swine-fever, chicken cholera, and all those other diseases, and everything else that is contagious in this country, I am afraid you will never succeed in getting one dollar from the national Treasury. The expense would be so great as to frighten those gentlemen at Washington. If you are going to render the country a service in your efforts to secure needed legislation, I do hope that you will confine your efforts to one thing at a time. Let that be pleuro-pneumonia, and I trust you will succeed in stamping out this dreaded pest from this country.

Professor LAW. With regard to the remarks of the gentleman from Maryland (Mr. Emory) I wish to say a word. Now I do not know where this disease exists in Maryland, but I am as confident that it does exist there as I am of my own existence. I don't blame our friends for standing by their State. They don't regret the existence of this plague any more than I do; but I am as confident that it is in Maryland as I am that I am in this room.

Mr. EMORY. We have a regular inspection in Maryland. We have a State veterinarian who visits the stock-yards every Monday morning and makes a thorough inspection.

Professor LAW. We had an inspection in New York in 1879, and the officer in charge of it had quite a number of inspectors employed in visiting the dairies constantly. They insisted that I would find no pleuro-pneumonia in the State of New York. Dr. Hopkins and Professor Salmon can tell what they found; we found it everywhere from Water Street on the south to Yonkers on the north. These inspections, unless they are thorough, and made for all the herds, and made continually, will miss of finding the disease. Now it is asserted that there is an inspection of the stock-yards, but I am as confident that it exists in Baltimore as it is possible to be, and a thorough inspection will show it.

Professor MORROW. I think the remarks to which we are listening illustrate the certainty that if we attempt to specify States we shall get into an interminable debate. There is a natural sensitiveness that States that have it shall not be named, and I therefore move that the second portion of the preamble be amended to read "a small portion of " the State of New York."

Professor ROBERTS, of New York. Oh, no ; a "very small portion of " a few of the Atlantic States."

Mr. CHORN, of Kentucky. The committee are willing to accept that amendment.

Professor HOPKINS. It has been published all over the world in what State or States it exists, and why should we place the stigma upon all the Atlantic States.

The PRESIDENT. The amendment is made to read " in small portions " of a few of the Atlantic States."

Professor HOPKINS. There are 2,000 miles of seaboard, and they should not be made to suffer the stigma when it has been published all over the world by the Treasury Cattle Commission and by the Department of Agriculture that that disease exists in New York, New Jersey, Pennsylvania, Maryland, and Virginia, and why should we say a "few " of the Atlantic States." Let us give it where it is known ; where the English Government know it exists ; where we have had inspectors who have found the disease. In 1879 the English Government sent Professor McEachran to the United States, and his report of finding this disease here was the basis whereby the restrictions upon our live-stock were placed. When they know, and when everybody knows, that the stock-yards in Baltimore and other cities are infected, let us give the name of the States, let the people know that we know where the disease exists, and that we are determined to do all in our power to stamp it out.

Mr. EMORY. In reference to what I said about the non-infection of the stock-yards in Baltimore, I believe, after conversation with Professor Ward before coming here, that the State is free from disease, and at the same time it may be thoroughly impregnated with the disease at any time. It would not, however, be proper to brand us to-day as an infected State. I would not state that the stock-yards were never infected. I have reason to believe that the disease is carried there from time to time, but we have a most rigid examination there now, and I believe we are entirely clear.

Professor LAW. How many animals are received at the stock-yards daily ?

Mr. EMORY. Several thousand.

Professor LAW. And he examines several thousand a day ; a pretty good day's work.

Mr. EMORY. Of course he does not examine every individual animal ; he visits the yards and looks over the stock. The Live-Stock Association of Maryland have taken hold of this question, and they propose to memorialize the legislature this winter to get proper legislation.

A DELEGATE. I move an amendment to the amendment ; that we insert the names of the States that have this disease.

Mr. W. T. SMITH, of Iowa. If we enter into these matters of detail we shall not get through in a month. We have attempted to deal in general terms, and have recommended the appointment of a committee whose duty it shall be to state the facts to Congress. I don't think it wise for this Convention to attempt to go into all the details. Leave that to the committee that we have provided for. I simply wish to offer the substance of what Mr. Roberts suggested, that for the words "in certain of the Atlantic States" this portion of the preamble be amended to read "in certain portions of the States on the Atlantic " seaboard."

The amendment was agreed to, the previous amendment being understood to have been withdrawn. The second portion of the preamble as amended was then adopted.

The PRESIDENT. The secretary will read the first resolution.

The secretary read as follows:—

"*Resolved,*—That we urge upon the proper authorities the importance of a thorough inspection of all live stock and meat products shipped to foreign countries."

A DELEGATE. I move its adoption.

Professor LAW. I think in this we are greatly increasing our expenditure without any corresponding benefit. The inspection of our live stock going to foreign countries cannot prevent the exportation of pleuro-pneumonia, nor yet Texas fever, the two great diseases that the English fear. Why should we ask for this examination? All exporters employ veterinarians and have an examination made on their own ground. The ship companies that insure the cattle have an examination on their account. The shipment of cattle suspected of the disease is never thought of, but the disease may remain latent in the system of an animal for at least three months. No inspector can detect that. The Texas fever may remain in the system from 30 to 60 days. No inspector can detect that. I propose that this resolution be eliminated as a matter of undue expense at the present time, and as likely to call upon Congress for too much money, and as likely to divert the money into other channels that will not have a correspondingly good effect. I move that this resolution be omitted from the report.

Mr. SANDERS, of Illinois. I am loth to differ with my associate and friend Professor Law upon anything, especially upon matters of this kind, for I acknowledge his very great learning upon every question of this nature; but I do hope that this resolution will be adopted exactly as reported by this committee. Among the very many things discussed by myself and Professor Brown was this question. He said to me explicitly that there was no one movement that this Government could undertake that would go farther toward securing the admission of our cattle there, and removing all restrictions, than an inspection under the sanction of Government. So far as I heard an expression among the American consuls in every city in Germany I visited, and from members of the German Government and people, it was unanimously to the effect that the very moment our Government adopts any sort of inspection they would remove their restriction upon American pork. I admit freely that inspection will not detect certain diseases, but an inspection as against foot-and-mouth disease and pleuro-pneumonia is not the only thing that we have to think of; they are not the only things that foreigners are afraid of.

Professor LAW. Mr. Sanders said yesterday that Professor Brown said that as long as there was pleuro-pneumonia here, just so long would the Government retain those restrictions. Professor Brown said to me that he fully appreciated the situation, and that as a scientific man he acknowledged the justice of our claims; but, said he, "What " we find when the cattle arrive here is that they have foot-and-mouth " disease." Examination cannot prevent foot-and-mouth disease, for it is contracted on board ship, and they will show it all the same whether there is an inspection here or not.

Dr. DETMERS, of Illinois. I simply have to say that thorough inspection of all the meat products is an impossibility in our country, as every one will see who is acquainted with the immense quantity of meat product furnished alone by Chicago. For instance, Armour and Company kill 7,000 hogs every day. How many men would it take to inspect that meat? It would be a great expense to our Government,

140 APPENDIX.

and no Congress man would be willing to vote for such an outlay. It cannot be done.

Mr. SCOTT, of Iowa. I favour the motion as made to strike this out, for the reason that this resolution departs from the objects of this Convention. We have not met here for the purpose of protecting European countries; we have met here for the purpose of inaugurating a movement that shall stamp out the disease in our own country. [Great applause.] If we undertake to do this, that, and the other thing for the purpose of pandering to the interest of exporters, and of those who are carrying on the trade, we shall depart from the objects which have called us here—which, as I understand, is to bring about such measures as shall stamp out this disease. Let us confine ourselves, then, to the business that has brought us together. [Applause.]

Professor HOPKINS of Wyoming. If it is the object of making an inspection of cattle going to European countries, to give them a clean bill of health, I will say that it is impossible for any veterinarian to detect disease by an inspection of cattle going on board. He must know where the cattle come from, and know their history for at least three months. It is impossible to do this thing. I have examined cattle and know all about it, and if at present in an examination I could discover no sympton of contagious disease, I would not give a clean bill of health to cattle going on board ship bound for Europe. I have examined thousands going to Europe.

Mr. GRINNELL, of Iowa. I hope, sir, that we will sustain the committee. I believe that resolution is drawn properly. It covers the ground, and in reply to my friend Governor Scott, who says this is not the purpose of this Convention, I want to say that I was sent here to do the very thing that this proposes to do. There is a cloud upon us, and I propose to remove it as far as possible. What are my friends here for from the West, from these ranges where they rear cattle that shall be good beef, above suspicion, to be sent abroad to bring the best prices. If we cannot do all that we profess to do, let us show the world that we are equal to this emergency; let us show to all Europe that there are men here from 20 States, who have come together to ask the national Congress to do all that we could do, to the end that we may send our product abroad with a clean bill of health. I hope, sir, you will pass this resolution as it stands, to show our good intent at least. I think my friend is not exactly right, because we are here, not only to stamp out what we have, but to rectify our reputation. We want to raise our reputation where it has fallen into straits. [Applause.]

Professor LAW. I wish to say this, that if we are to give a certificate of our cattle shipped from New York and Baltimore, on the basis of examination we will simply add one other instance to the other instances already quoted in which we tell them lies.

Dr. GADSDEN, of Pennsylvania. I have the honour of knowing Professor Brown as well as any man in this room. He is the advisor of the privy council where his advice has great influence, and he assured me last year that as long as we have one case of contagious disease these restrictions will ever be against us. That is the law of their land. They have placed this upon us because of the demand of their people, and you must remove the cause before they will remove the restriction. I went there for the purpose of getting Pennsylvania cattle released from the embargo. They told me that I need not trouble myself, as the law said as long as the disease existed in this country the restriction should be made. Unless we can get rid of this thing, the first thing we know we will have restrictions against receiving our cattle at all. It only wants proper working on the part of members over in Parliament, and if you do get it you will never get it wiped out.

Mr. SANDERS, of Illinois. I do not wish these veterinarians to understand that I make the assertion that Professor Brown told me that if we had an inspection the English Government would remove these restrictions. What he said was that it would be one of the best things we could do, and that we could not do any one thing that would be a greater step in the right direction, but you must stamp out your disease and inspect and keep up your inspection. Now, because we cannot do everything, I don't think any one should say that we ought not to do what we can do. Professor Brown urged me to recommend in my report this very thing, not as *the* one thing, but *one* of the things we could do.

Professor THOMPSON, of Nebraska. As a member of the committee I desire to say to the Convention that one object in recommending this resolution was to show our good intention. We may not be able to induce Congress to appropriate money necessary to appoint inspectors, but let us show to foreigners that we are willing to do the best we can. It was for the good effect, more than anything else, that we recommended this.

There were loud cries for the question, and, upon a division, the motion of Professor Law to strike out the resolution was agreed to— 27 to 25.

The secretary then read the second resolution, as follows:

"*Resolved*,—That this Convention heartily indorse the action of the Secretary of the Treasury in enforcing quarantine against all infected cattle, for the purpose of preventing the further importation of foreign contagious diseases, and we recommend that the regulations be enforced with rigid impartiality against all importers. And further that Congress should be asked to confer authority upon the Treasury Department to quarantine sheep, swine, and goats."

Mr. CAREY, of Wyoming. I move the adoption of the resolution.

Professor LAW. I object to this on similar grounds to those which actuated me in my motion with reference to the resolution before this. It is going to draw away considerable money for an object that can very well be left. Sheep and swine are not likely to convey disease to us, but at the same time the Treasury has the power to have all sheep and swine examined. So far as foot-and-mouth disease is concerned we know that it does show on arrival. They take the disease in from 24 hours to one week or thereabout. They pass through it on the ship, and in very many cases they are reasonably well over it when they arrive. At the same time the disease leaves such sores that any man who is worthy of his name can detect and will detect it on arrival. I don't know of an instance where a true veterinarian, I don't know of a person who is practising with a degree who has passed a lot of cattle, sheep, or swine afflicted with disease. At present we have the measures to prevent the importation of this disease. They will not take up pleuro-pneumonia or any of those long-continued diseases. We are not at all likely to import sheep-pox because they haven't it there, and because when they do get it they know precisely where it is. This is going to draw away a deal of money and afford no adequate compensation.

Mr. SANDERS, of Illinois. One word in reference to the reason why that resolution should pass. I drafted that resolution and I insist it should be adopted. There will be no necessity for Congress to compel the Secretary to quarantine all sheep and swine for 60 to 90 days. The object is simply to confer the authority to quarantine, and he can make such regulations in regard to the length or conditions as Professor Law may advise. There is this difficulty as the matter now stands: When we examine sheep and swine and find them infected with foot-and-mouth disease, or any other disease, the question is, what are you going to do with them? You have no authority in the world to say a thing about it. The owner may say, "They are not diseased and I am "going to take them home." And there is no law to prevent him. We can issue a circular to collectors of the port asking them to examine imported sheep, swine, and goats; but suppose we find disease, what are we going to do about it?

Professor LAW. Send it back.

Mr. SANDERS. There is no authority to send it back. All we can say is, "You ought not to take these infected hogs or sheep home." They can say, "We do not believe they are infected," and they can take them home and we cannot help it.

A DELEGATE. I move to strike out all reference to sheep, swine, and goats.

The motion was not agreed to.

The question then recurred upon the adoption of the resolution as reported by the committee, and it was agreed to without a division.

The secretary then read the third resolution, as follows:—

"*Resolved*, That we recommend that, for the purpose of reaching definite and conclusive action, a committee of five be appointed by the Chairman of the Convention, whose duty it shall be to present a memorial to Congress setting forth explicitly the loss and damage we have sustained in our business, not only by reason of the fact that contagious diseases do exist to a limited extent in this country, but also of the much greater loss and damage we sustain by reason of the embarrassing restriction, and, in some cases, prohibitory regulations which have been adopted by foreign Governments against American live stock and their meat products. We further recommend that said committee be instructed to confer with the Secretary of the Treasury, the Commissioner of Agriculture, and such other officials and persons as to them shall be deemed proper, and shall thereafter suggest to Congress such points of legislation as they may deem the best calculated to protect our interests and remove foreign prejudice against our meat productions. We further recommend that all live-stock organisations in the United States be invited to co-operate with us by advice, suggestions, and cash subscriptions, to be used in defraying the necessary expenses of said committee; and further, that the said invitation be extended to transportation and stock-yard companies, beef and pork packers and exporters, and all others having an interest in common with us in this matter."

Mr. GRINNELL, of Iowa. I move that where the word "five" occurs that the word "nine" be inserted. In the first place a committee of nine people from different sections may better combine and bring together the thoughts of the whole nation than five can; consequently, when we come to act upon Congress we want as many strings as possible. We want all sections, all interests, all parties represented in asking this action of the American Congress. Any gentleman who has been there knows how hard it is to procure legislation. A member of Congress has to do everything, as the president knows, except take in washing [great laughter], and we want a strong committee to induce these people to listen to us and heed our appeal; not a committee to go there simply to sit around and spend their time, but one that will go there and work in season and out of season, composed of those who will go to the houses of these members and meet them in committee and push this matter. My notion is, that if this Convention gives each of these

Congressmen notice that it is his political death for him to refuse to help us, and that he will lose the votes of his district if he fails to help in the matter, that you will get what you want. [Laughter and applause.] Let them understand that if they don't take care of you you will take care of them [laughter], and if they fail to aid you give them to understand that at the next election they will have need of the services of a political undertaker. [Great laughter.]

Professor HOPKINS, of Wyoming. I would rather it would be 19, and it would be still better if it were 1,900, and let them take Congress by storm.

The amendment of Mr. Grinnell was adopted.

The PRESIDENT. The Chair is not well enough informed to appoint this committee; and the best way to have it done is for the delegations to suggest one or two men from those States who are likely to be willing to act for us in this matter. I don't know the delegates well enough myself; I want to choose the very best men we have. I want the help of every one of you when I get there this winter. We want no drones there.

The resolution as amended was then agreed to.

Mr. STURGIS, of Wyoming. I wanted to make a motion to amend before the resolution was adopted. It would have been to this effect: That this committee shall consist of one member from each State and Territory represented here instead of the nine members provided for. Each State could name its member upon the roll call, and in my judgment we should then have an effective and representative committee.

A DELEGATE. I move a reconsideration of the last vote by which we adopted the resolution, with a view to amending the resolution as suggested by the secretary.

The motion to reconsider was agreed to.

The DELEGATE. I now move that the word "nine" be stricken out and that there be inserted "one member from each State and Territory represented."

The amendment was agreed to; and the resolution as amended was then adopted.

The secretary proceeded to call the roll of States.

Mr. COFFIN, of Iowa. Would it not be well to give time for each delegation to confer before they nominate their member of this committee?

Mr. SANDERS. I suggest, Mr. Chairman, that we all proceed to that without further formality. It is not essential that this committee should be announced at this meeting. The delegations can take their time to consult in order to select their best and strongest man.

The PRESIDENT. I think it is best to have the committee announced before we adjourn *sine die*.

A DELEGATE. I suggest that it will be well for us to dispose of this report of the committee before we take up any other business.

The PRESIDENT. The secretary will read the remainder of the report.

The secretary read as follows:—

"*Resolved*, That the thanks of this Convention are due to the Hon. George B. Loring, Commissioner of Agriculture, for the hearty and efficient manner in which he has co-operated with the live-stock breeders of the United States, and the efficient aid he has given us; and that the President of this Convention be requested to invite him to act as *ex officio* chairman of the committee which shall be appointed in accordance with the foregoing resolution."

The resolution was unanimously agreed to.

The full text of the preamble and resolutions adopted is as follows:—

"Whereas the existence of disease among domestic animals in the United States has seriously affected the exportation of live stock, and that the suspicion that attaches in foreign countries to all neat cattle and swine of the United States on account of the existence of diseases in certain localities has greatly lessened the sale of American meats in foreign markets; and

"Whereas the existence of pleuro-pneumonia in certain portions of the States on the Atlantic seaboard introduced from time to time by the importation of live stock from European countries, constantly threatens the spread of the contagion to the Southern and Western States and Territories, and the disease is of such a character that State legislation can only give partial relief; and since prompt and appropriate legislation on the part of Congress to eradicate the disease in the infected districts is imperatively demanded; and since, should the great ranges of the West become infected with the disease, it would be impossible to stamp out the plague except by the total destruction of the herds, and at a cost of hundreds of millions of dollars: Therefore,

Resolved, That this Convention heartily indorse the action of the Secretary of the Treasury in enforcing quarantine against all imported cattle for the purpose of preventing the further importation of foreign contagious diseases, and we recommend that the regulations be enforced with rigid impartiality against all importers. And, further, that Congress should be asked to confer authority upon the Treasury Department to quarantine infected sheep, swine, and goats.

"*Resolved*, That we recommend that, for the purpose of reaching definite and conclusive action, a committee to consist of one member from each State and Territory represented, be appointed by the chairman of this Convention, whose duty it shall be to present a memorial to Congress, setting forth explicitly the loss and damage we have sustained in our business, not only by reason of the fact that contagious diseases do exist to a limited extent in this country, but also of the much greater loss and damage we sustain by reason of the embarrassing restriction, and in some cases prohibitory regulations, which have been adopted by foreign Governments against American live-stock and dead-meat products. We further recommend that said committee be instructed to confer with the Secretary of the Treasury, the Commissioner of Agriculture, and such other officials and persons as to them shall be deemed proper, and shall thereafter suggest to Congress such points of legislation as they may deem the best calculated to protect our interests and remove foreign prejudice against our meat productions. We further recommend that all live-stock organisations in the United States be invited to co-operate with us by advice, suggestions, and cash subscriptions to be made in defraying the necessary expenses of said committee; and, further, that the said invitatton be extended to transportation and stock-yard companies, beef and pork packers, and exporters, and all others having an interest in common with us in this matter.

"*Resolved*, That the thanks of this Convention are due to Hon. George B. Loring for the hearty and efficient manner in which he has co-operated with the live-stock breeders of the United States, and the efficient aid he has given us, and that the president of this Convention be requested to invite him to act as *ex officio* chairman of the committee which shall be appointed in accordance with the foregoing resolutions."

Mr. W. T. SMITH, of Iowa. Before we adjourn, sir, representing the State of Iowa, which has more cattle than any State in this country except Texas, and more cattle than half a dozen Territories, I rise to say that our delegation has agreed upon the name of the Hon. J. B. Grinnell, ex-member of Congress, to represent Iowa upon this committee. [Applause.]

Mr. GOSPER, of Arizona. I rise pleasantly to ask the president of the Wyoming Cattle Association how many cattle they have in the Territory as compared with Iowa. There seems to be a disposition, perhaps, not exactly to ignore the fact that the great plains are alive with cattle, but there seems to be an ignorance on the part of some in relation to this matter. The Western men are more alive to this matter because they have so much more at stake.

Mr. W. T. SMITH, of Iowa. Well, I have owned cattle in Wyoming and Iowa. I may say to my friend from Arizona (Mr. Gosper) that Iowa contains, according to the last census, more than Nebraska, Wyoming, California, Utah, Colorada, Nevada——

Mr. GOSPER. Hold on; that is enough. [Great laughter.]

Mr. GRINNELL, of Iowa. I would like to say that it cost me $100 to get that information in advance. I shall not ask to have a contribution to remunerate me for the information, but the gentleman states a fact. [Laughter.]

Mr. CAREY, of Wyoming. I would like to ask the gentleman what census he refers to?

Mr. W. T. SMITH, of Iowa. To 1880.

Mr. CAREY, of Wyoming. I would like to inform the gentleman that he could not go to-day where the cattle roam in Wyoming, and buy them for $100,000,000, and he must remember that what has been done there has been done almost entirely since General Crook took possession there in 1876. [Applause.]

A DELEGATE. I move a recess for 15 minutes, for the purpose of enabling the delegates to confer upon nominations for this committee.

The motion was agreed to.

Upon re-assembling the secretary proceeded to call the roll of States, Territories, and the following nominations for membership upon the committee were ratified by the Convention:—

Wyoming.—Hon. J. M. Carey, Cheyenne.
Ohio.—Hon. Columbus Delano, Mount Vernon.
Colorado.—Hon. William J. Wilson, Denver.
New York.—Col. N. M. Curtis, Ogdensburg, N. Y.
Illinois.—Hon. D. W. Smith, Bates.
Pennsylvania.—Julius Le Moyne, Washington.
Iowa.—Hon. J. B. Grinnell, Grinnell.
Kentucky.—T. C. Anderson, Mount Sterling.
Texas.—Hon. George B. Loving.
Arizona.—J. J. Gosper.
Wisconsin.—Hon. Hiram Smith, Sheboygan.
West Virginia.—J. M. Kirk, Wheeling.
Nebraska.—Prof. S. R. Thompson, Lincoln.
Tennessee.—Col. John Overton, Nashville.
New Jersey.—Dr. E. M. Hunt, Trenton.
Maryland.—Hon. John M. Robinson, Centreville.
District of Columbia.—Dr. D. E. Salmon, Washington.
Massachusetts.—Levi Stockbridge, Amherst.
Michigan.—Hon. William Ball, Hamburg.

MR. STURGIS, of Wyoming, I wish to offer a resolution in connexion with this committee that has been appointed. It is that a secretary be appointed from a central point in the West who shall correspond with the members of the committee selected to go to Washington, shall ascertain what numbers will actually go, shall communicate with each of

o 11711.

those members who are to be their associates, and by appointing a fixed day for their meeting in Washington, thus insure unanimity of action. He shall provide the chairman with proper credentials and obtain proxies if originals cannot go. I move the adoption of the resolution.

The motion was agreed to.

Mr. STURGIS. I now nominate, with the consent of the Chair, the Hon. J. B. Grinnell as said secretary.

Professor MORROW, of Illinois. We all know Mr. Grinnell, and are all glad to have him upon this committee; but I am reminded that Mr. Grinnell is getting to be somewhat of an old man, and as the labour attaching to this office will be considerable I would suggest, without any consultation with him, the Hon. D. W. Smith, of Illinois. Of course if Mr. Grinnell will serve we should be glad to have him.

Mr. GOSPER, of Arizona. I understand that the secretary has such an assurance.

Mr. STURGIS, of Wyoming. I, of course, consulted some one before I took the liberty of proposing his name, and I was assured that he would throw himself into it, and do it with pleasure.

The nomination was agreed to unanimously.

Mr. CHORN, of Kentucky. I have a resolution which has been handed to the committee on resolutions, which I send to the secretary to be read.

The secretary read the resolution. It appears hereafter.

Mr. THOMPSON, of Nebraska. I will say that the resolution was handed me as a member of the committee on resolutions. The design is to call the attention of the States to this important subject, and to call their attention to their specific duty, and it contemplates that this shall be done through the committee of this body appointed to confer with Congress on a similar subject.

The PRESIDENT. Won't you amend that to read " several States or the executive authorities of the same ?"

Mr. THOMPSON, of Nebraska. I move that those words be inserted.

The motion was agreed to, and the resolution, as amended, was adopted. It is as follows:—

" Whereas it is the duty of State legislatures to take measures to protect the owners of domestic animals from loss arising from the importation and spread of contagious diseases.

" *Be it resolved*, That the committee of this Convention memorialize the legislatures of the several States, or the executive authorities of the same, urging upon them the importance of establishing a veterinary or health department for the prevention and spread of all such contagious diseases.

Mr. W. T. SMITH, of Iowa. We have had some very valuable articles read here upon the subject which was the cause of our convening. Of course the all-important object is to prevent the spread of this great disease among us. It seems to me that anything we do to educate our people as to what the disease is, its great danger, and how to prevent it, how it may be carried, &c., is an important branch of our business. I don't know what arrangments have been or are being made for the publication of these articles, but it seems to me it is an important part of our proceedings, and I have brought the subject before the Convention for the purpose of ascertaining if there have been any arrangements made by which they are to be published for the benefit of the public. If not we should make some arrangement before we adjourn. I don't know whether the live-stock journals have been represented here and have taken the proceedings with a view to their publication or not. If so, that will probably be sufficient.

PROCEEDINGS OF CHICAGO CONVENTION.

The PRESIDENT. Dr. Loring has had here during our sessions his stenographer, who has taken a full report of the proceedings, and I understand it is his intention to publish them from his Department.

Dr. SALMON. As the representative of the Department of Agriculture here to-day, I wish to say that Dr. Loring has expressed his intention of publishing the full proceedings of this Convention, together with the papers that have been read.

It was agreed that the committee on legislation should meet at 7 p.m.

Mr. CAREY, of Wyoming. Mr. President, I am not as sanguine about legislation as some others of the committee. I fear there are many members of it who think that all they will have to do will be to go to Washington and ask Congressmen to legislate for us. I know how very difficult it is to get a bill through both branches of Congress even when very favourable circumstances surround it. I think that Commissioner Loring did a very wise thing indeed when he called a Stock Convention to meet at this time and place. Now almost every other industry has a permanent organisation to consider that which affects their every interest. I therefore make this motion: That the president and secretary, or either of them, shall be authorised to call a convention of men representing the stock interests, to meet in this city next year at a suitable time during the progress of the Fat-Stock show, in order that we may hear and receive the report of the delegation we are sending to Washington, so that we gentlemen who have this matter so much at heart may know what is being done and what more is necessary to be done. The stock-growers of Wyoming issued a circular to the agricultural societies throughout the United States requesting them to send delegations to meet in this city and hold a convention during the time of this Fat-Stock show. The reason for our intense interest in this matter is not far to seek. We have men in that country who are importing from Europe; men who are producing the meat for this very market. We all know very well that if any contagious disease is introduced on the plains our business is surely ruined, and all the capital invested in that country will as surely pass out of existence. As an illustration of our watchfulness and of our dangers, and as showing the importance of this subject to us, one of our stock-growers went to Kentucky and bought, I think, 40 head. He unfortunately stopped those bulls in Saint Louis. They were met on the road by our authorised inspector, and the result was that those bulls were placed in quarantine, and I think 14 of them died. With regard to what my friend from Iowa (Mr. W. T. Smith) has said, I will state that, while we all acknowledge the importance and position of the cattle interest of Iowa, while we have no doubt that it is much larger than in any Territory, yet there is one fact in relation to the industry of Wyoming that must not be lost sight of, and in which it exceeds any State or Territory in the Union. The stock-raisers of our Territory went to the two States of Missouri and Iowa during the spring months of the present year to expend one million and a-half of dollars in young cattle. Now for this we want absolute protection, so far as it is possible, from any contact with disease by shipping your cattle out there. We want the risk entirely removed, and we ask these more Eastern States who have Congressmen to come to us in our need. We have no Congressman, only a delegate. Our hundred millions of dollars has really no power or influence, we may say, in the city of Washington. The men who have votes there are the men who can trade votes, and are those who can influence legislation. A Congressman who has a pet measure can go to another who has a pet measure, and they can trade and log-roll and secure the legislation. The Territories are put off always to the last, and they only get the crumbs that fall from the table in the distribution of the money. [Applause.] Our business for 100 days preceding the 1st of November enabled us to place upon the Chicago market a thousand beeves each day. Let us remember that this mighty development has come almost entirely from the business which has grown up there since General Crook took possession of the country occupied by roving, worthless bands of Indians, and remembering it let us believe that those States where we are expending our money can well afford to take hold of this matter and furnish us, so far as possible, with protection from those diseases which already exist in the East. [Applause.] Now I desire to say further in behalf of our young Territory—the youngest of all of them—while we have built up this great industry, which is tributary almost entirely to this great State, we have not been negligent in enacting the necessary legislation. Be it said to the credit of Mr. Sturgis, who occupies a position here, and to Mr. Swan and Mr. Irving, that they have laboured until they effected the passage of what we believe to be the best law ever passed on this subject. We have a salaried officer, an officer who has been very useful, and who has accomplished great good. We pay him, not a very large salary, but as much as is paid to any officers sent there by the United States. But the stock-men had to make this compromise; they agreed to come forward as men and furnish the requisite money for the indemnity fund. In other words, all animals destroyed on account of disease are paid for by a direct tax on the stock interests. They go before the legislature, which meets early in January, and advocate appropriations all of which shall be levied on this business.

Mr. Sturgis has vouched for the association, of which he has so long been secretary, that that association would pay the expenses of its delegatse. We ask no contribution. We only ask that every member of this committee be present in Washington, in season and out of season, if necessary; to go there this winter and to stay there urging this matter upon Congress until the dog days, if need be, in order to accomplish what is of so vast importance to these Western States and Territories. [Applause.] We have taken hold of this matter in advance. We have not had a case of pleuro-pneumonia in Wyoming so far as we know. Our men there who have bought cattle as far east as New York, especially those men who, like Mr. Swan, make large importations from Great Britain, want protection from this disease. You will find that the sentiment is unanimous among our stock-raisers, and we believe that this is the sentiment of those men who stand at the head of the stock-growing interests of the United States. Now we believe we do not ask anything unreasonable when we request this committee to do all in its power to get for us what almost every other interest in the United States gets—a certain amount of protection at the hands of Congress. The Territory asks for protection, and we shall ask Congress for it, and we trust we shall get it, if we knock until they answer us. [Applause.]

After a remark of a delegate to which Mr. Carey replied, and which was more or less personal in its nature, a delegate said:

A DELEGATE. I produce cattle in Iowa for the purpose of making fine beef, and fine men, and making men feel happy. Now, if we have any disease that passes through Iowa, going west to the plains, we cannot be secure in these results. I believe that one case across the Missouri River will wipe out $500,000,000. I believe that no atmospheric influences, no locality, no geographical position, nor heat, nor cold, nor degree of latitude will exterminate pleuro-pneumonia, as I have heard some gentleman say.

The motion of Mr. Carey was then agreed to.

MR. CLAY, of Illinois. I would like to move a vote of thanks to our chairman, who has so ably conducted the business of this meeting. It has been, I know, a gratification that the State of Kentucky, which I, as a stockman, look upon as one of our great stock-producing States, should send us our chairman. The labours of General Williams in behalf of our cattle interest are well known to us all, and I only hope that he will live long after this country has become clear of pleuro-pneumonia, and every other disease to which the animal kingdom is subject. There are very few who have had more experience in the stock business than I. This is a great question and this Convention has handled it well. I hope the interest you have all manifested here will not die out, and that every stockman in this country will assist you in your efforts to the best of his ability.

The motion was unanimously agreed to.

A DELEGATE. The thought suggested itself to me after the motion made by my friend from Wyoming (Mr. Carey) with reference to the calling of another convention, that it might be a wise thing to set on foot a movement for the purpose of organising a permanent national stock association. We meet now of course simply at the call of Commissioner Loring, and next year may be called together by our president and secretary, but will it be a permanent organisation?

A DELEGATE. I move that the committee on legislation be requested carefully to consider the question of a permanent organisation and that it, jointly with the president and secretary in due time, call a convention of delegates to complete a permanent organisation, about one year from this time.

A DELEGATE. While that may accomplish the object, it occurs to me that if we divide the duties of that committee the one great duty for which they were appointed may be neglected. It appears to me that it would be better if in the call to be made by the present president and secretary they announce the object, as they do in any call for similar organisations.

A DELEGATE. I move that a vote of thanks be tendered to the secretary for the able manner in which he has discharged his duties.

The motion was unanimously agreed to.

A motion of thanks to the press was also adopted.

Mr. W. T. SMITH, of Iowa. In your opening address, your honour took occasion to show the necessity for having money to pay the way of those who are to seek this legislation. It seems to me that one of the most important things for us to consider is how we can furnish this means of subsistence, and for carrying out legislation. I suggest that this should be considered.

The PRESIDENT. I should suppose that each State would pay the expenses of its own delegate.

Mr. SMITH. I don't propose to make any motion of that kind, but let us have an understanding about it. Let it be understood that each State and Territory is to defray its own expenses. There is to some extent a little injustice in that perhaps, but I presume it would not be proper or necessary that we pass a resolution of that kind, but let us understand it.

Mr. THOMPSON, of Nebraska. I trust that every member of this Convention who is here now, or who has been here will consider himself a committee of one to write to every member of Congress he knows, and urge upon him the importance of this matter. It will have a great effect in securing the help we need. I have seen the effect of these personal appeals, and I know that they are valuable.

The PRESIDENT. The Secretary will read a letter which has been placed in his hands, and which explains itself.

150 APPENDIX.

The Secretary read the following letter:—

"Chicago, Illinois, November 15, 1883.

"GENTLEMEN: I am instructed by the board of management of the World's Industrial and Cotton Centennial Exposition to invite your association to hold its next annual meeting at New Orleans, Louisiana, upon the occasion of the opening of the World's Exposition on the first Monday of December, 1884. Efforts are being made to secure the attendance of stock breeders from all parts of the world, and, whilst this exposition will be international in its character, it will specially exhibit the products of the soil, mines, and forests of the South, and of Mexico and Central America. The people of the section primarily interested in the inventions and labour-saving machinery of this age of progress are no less deeply interested in improving their breeds of horses, cattle, hogs, sheep, and poultry, and questions relating thereto. The holding of your convention at the opening of this World's Exposition would enlarge the scope of your labours, and in benefitting the section of country referred to would no doubt promote the objects you have in view.

"I am, very respectfully,
"C. A. BURKE,
"Director-General.

"President and Members National Stock Convention,
"Chicago, Illinois."

A DELEGATE. I move that a vote of thanks be tendered for this invitation.

The motion was agreed to.

Mr. CHORN, of Kentucky. I now move that we adjourn *sine die*.

The PRESIDENT (after putting the motion). The motion is agreed to, and this Convention stands adjourned without day. [Applause.]

MESSAGE from the PRESIDENT of the UNITED STATES, transmitting, in compliance with a resolution of the HOUSE of REPRESENTATIVES, a REPORT from the SECRETARY of STATE, touching the EXISTING RESTRICTIONS on the IMPORTATION of AMERICAN NEAT CATTLE into GREAT BRITAIN.

April 25, 1882.—Referred to the Committee on Agriculture and ordered to be printed.

TO THE HOUSE OF REPRESENTATIVES:

I TRANSMIT herewith a report of the Secretary of State, presented in compliance with the request of the House of Representatives in a resolution of the 10th instant, asking for information touching the existing restrictions on the importation of American neat cattle into Great Britain.

CHESTER A. ARTHUR.

Executive Mansion, Washington,
April 25, 1882.

TO THE PRESIDENT:

THE Secretary of State has had the honour to receive from the House of Representatives a resolution in the following terms:—

"Congress of the United States,
"In the House of Representatives,
"April 10, 1882.

"WHEREAS the English Government, with a view of guarding against the introduction and spread of pleuro-pneumonia among the cattle in England and Ireland, has established quarantine rules and prescribed and enforced regulations requiring that cattle imported into England from the United States shall be slaughtered at the port of entry, which said rules and regulations in their operation have tended to greatly injure our export trade in neat cattle; and

"Whereas careful investigation has disclosed the fact that no cattle infected with pleuro-pneumonia, or that are liable to said infection, are imported into England or Ireland from the United States; and

"Whereas it is deemed that it would be mutually advantageous to the people of the United States and England to encourage the commerce between the two nations of the character mentioned, and to that end there should be such modifications of the rules and regulations before mentioned as are consistent with the interests of both nations: Therefore

"*Be it resolved*, That the Secretary of State be, and he is hereby, required to inform this House touching the present condition of the export trade of the United States with England in neat cattle, and to report also what hindrances thereto exist, and what steps, if any, have been taken by our Government to modify or remove them; and, further, if any additional legislation is needful to adequately encourage said export trade and protect its interests.

"Attest:

' EDWD. McPHERSON,
Clerk."

In compliance with the foregoing resolution, the Secretary of State has the honour to lay before the President the following report:—

The resolution calls for information on three points:

1st. The present condition of the export trade of the United States with England in neat cattle;

2nd. The hindrances which exist to such trade, and the steps, if any, which have been taken toward their removal or modification; and

3rd. The legislation, if any be needful, which would encourage such export trade and protect its interests.

Upon the first of these points the Secretary of State has the honour to suggest that later and fuller information can be furnished by the Treasury Department than by the Department of State. The statistics collected by the agents of the Treasury Department are understood to show the export trade in cattle from all our ports to all foreign countries, while the information which this Department could give would be based only on the importation returns at the ports where consular officers of the United States are stationed.

On the second point, the Secretary of State may observe that for some years past the Department of State has been in consultation with the Treasury Department touching the conditions which are set by British legislation upon the importation of living cattle from foreign countries, and the especial effect of those conditions upon the cattle trade between the United States and Great Britain and Canada. In the course of correspondence with the British Government, either through our legation in London or the British legation in this country, the Department of State has communicated the views of the Treasury Department in the premises, and has received and communicated to that Department in reply the views of Her Majesty's Government. This correspondence has shown that the hindrances imposed are in accordance with the provisions of the British statute, while their removal, it has been intimated, was a question of the institution of a complete and effective system of domestic legislation to check and extirpate cattle diseases in the United States, joined to an adequate and trustworthy inspection of imported cattle, from the breeding grounds to the sea, with certification of their freedom from disease or contagious influences.

In like manner, the free exchange of cattle between Canada and the United States, and transit of herds from the West to the seaboard across Canadian territory, have been impeded by colonial legislation and regulation analogous to those of the mother country; and these, too, have had the attentive consideration of the Treasury Department.

While the Secretary of State would take pleasure in laying before the President for transmission to the House of Representatives the full correspondence of the State Department with the British Government on the general subject for some years past (although the resolution does not specifically call for the production of that correspondence), yet he deems it better to suggest that the Treasury Department be intrusted with the preparation of this much of the reply to the wish of the House of Representatives. The Treasury Department not only possesses in copy most, if not all, of the diplomatic correspondence on the subject, but it also has its own correspondence in relation thereto. The Secretary of State would, however, if deemed desirable, willingly co-operate with the Treasury Department in responding to the resolution by furnishing copies of the diplomatic correspondence here on file, as showing the efforts made to induce the British Government to relax the rigidity of the rule by which the slaughter of cattle on landing is made compulsory.

As to the third point, the Secretary of State begs leave to say that he feels it to be the especial province of the Secretary of the Treasury or the Commissioner of Agriculture to recommend the form of legislation necessary to establish an adequate scheme of cattle inspection, at the farms, in transit, and before shipment, which would admit of ascertaining and authoritatively certifying the absence of contagious disease and infectious influences among exported animals.

In conclusion, the Secretary of State has the honour to annex a copy of the British statute controlling the importation of cattle into the United Kingdom (Contagious Diseases (Animals) Act, 1878), as especially necessary to an understanding of the requirements of British legislation, and as suggesting the legislation by which those requirements may best be met, so as to insure the entry of American neat cattle into Great Britain in a living state.

Respectfully submitted.

FRED'K. T. FRELINGHUYSEN.

Department of State, Washington,
    April 24, 1882.

A Summary of the Report of the Cattle Commission on the Lung-Plague of Cattle, or Contagious Pleuro-Pneumonia, which was directed to be held by a Resolution of the Senate of the United States on February 10th, 1882.

Summary.

1st. Reasons for extension of the report so as to embrace history, nature, and extinction of lung-plague, as well as its present limits, and the question of imports and exports :—Introduction.

2nd. The designation lung-plague preferable to pleuro-pneumonia.

3rd. The whole history of lung-plague furnishes no ground for the conclusion that it arises otherwise than by contagion.

4th. The early history of this disease shows its great extensions to have been coincident with extensive wars in Central Europe, when cattle were drawn from all sources, infected and uninfected, for the supply of the armies in the field and constantly moving.

5th. During the intervals of such wars the lung-plague continued to prevail in the unfenced mountains and forests of Central Europe, where the few wandering herds had ample opportunity for mutual infection.

6th. Into the mountains and forests of Scandinavia, and the Spanish Peninsula, out of the region of the general wars, lung-plague did not penetrate.

7th. In recent times the increasing demand for cattle to feed on the refuse of distilleries, sugar factories, &c., in Western Europe, has led to great extensions of the disease.

8th. The British Isles, infected by imports from Holland, and infection kept up by the Free Trade Act, that admitted continental cattle free of duty.

9th. Ireland, which is not an importing country, has since kept up lung-plague by a most mischievous activity and method in her internal cattle traffic.

10th. The outbreaks in Sweden, Denmark, Norway, and Schleswig always traced to imported cattle and invariably stamped out.

11th. South Africa, Australia, Tasmania, and New Zealand infected by imported cattle, and infection rendered permanent by the impossibility of secluding the infected herds on the open, unfenced pastures, and by reason of the common employment of bullock waggons.

12th. Massachusetts, infected by imported cattle, found it possible to stamp out the disease, because she lay at the terminus of the American cattle traffic, in place of at its source or on its channel.

13th New York, New Jersey, Pennsylvania, Maryland, and Virginia, infected by imported cattle, have had the infection perpetuated by the mischievous nature of the city cow-trade, and the habit of pasturing on open commons and unfenced lots around the large and growing cities.

14th. Lung-plague failed to extend west and north because of the absence of such large cities and open pasturages, and because of the opposing current of the cattle traffic.

15th. The great profits on town dairies enable the owners to bear, without ruin, the losses caused by the plague.

16th. The risk of losing a lucrative milk-route makes the city dairyman unwilling to acknowledge the existence of disease in his herd, and this greatly injures the extinction of the plague.

17th. The practice of dealers in furnishing cows to city stables, receiving others from them, makes their sale stables hot-beds of infection.

18th. An unbroken chain of cases can be traced from the cow imported into Brooklyn in 1848 to the present day.

19th. Prior to that importation lung-plague was unknown on the American continent.

20th. The most inclement countries have failed to produce lung-plague.

21st. The most torrid regions have failed to produce lung-plague, though they aggravate it when once introduced.

22nd. Temperate climates apart from imported infection have failed to produce lung-plague.

23rd. Privations of travel have failed to produce lung-plague.

24th. Impure air has failed to produce lung-plague.

25th. Feeding distillery swill has failed to produce lung-plague.

26th. Feeding the refuse of glucose and starch factories has failed to produce lung-plague.

27th. No other conclusion is open to us than that lung-plague is caused in Western Europe and America by contagion only, and, if so, we have a perfect guarantee that it can be completely stamped out and permanently excluded.

28th. The infection of the herds on our unfenced Western and Southern pasturages would render it as impossible for us to stamp out the disease as it has been for the people of South Africa and Australia.

29th. The danger of such an infection is being constantly increased with the increase of the infected area in the East, with the increase of cattle imports, with the increase of thoroughbred herds, with the movement of thoroughbreds West and South for the improvement of native cattle, with the increased shipment of Eastern calves to be matured in the West, and with the improved railroad facilities.

30th. The virus of lung-plague retains its virulence for over a month in a hermetically sealed glass tube, for months in a close building, and for a variable time, according to exposure to air, in manure, fodder, clothes, &c.; so that the way is open for its propagation through different unsuspected channels.

Lung-plague is peculiar to the bovine genus; and other genera of animals, man included, can only assist in the dissemination of the disease by carrying the virus on the surface.

31st. The mortality from lung-plague varies much, but may reach 100 per cent. in hot climates and seasons. Hence the necessity for excluding it from the warmer portions of the continent.

32nd. The incubation of lung-plague, extending from a fortnight to three and half months, is one of the most dangerous features of this disease, and allows ample time for sending infected but still apparently healthy animals to the utmost confines of our territory. This long period of latency condemns the practice of passing animals as sound on a professional examination, and also the proposed method of sweeping over the country and killing all infected herds; for by reason of the many cases that must necessarily exist of infected animals not at the time showing symptoms of the disease, the process would have to be begun again as soon as it had been once performed.

33rd. This long incubation demands, as an essential concomitant of slaughter and disinfection, the entire prohibition or the most rigid control of all movements of cattle in an infected district.

34th. When an animal survives an attack of lung-plague there is usually left an encysted mass of dead (infecting) lung inclosed within the living. So that convalescent animals may be held as for a time capable of conveying the disease to others. These encysted masses often remain for over a year, and the bearers have often proved the centres of new outbreaks.

35th. Thoroughbred cattle, on account of their high value, are the most likely to be preserved, and if afterwards sent West, they become extremely dangerous because of these encysted masses. The large indemnity expected for a thoroughbred should therefore be no excuse for his preservation when infected.

36th. Inoculation for lung-plague is calculated to largely reduce the losses, but at the expense of a permanent preservation and general dissemination of the virus.

37th. Inoculation has never yet permanently rid any country of lung-plague.

38th. This, together with its expense and the impossibility of making it universal, condemns the measure as a palliation for America, so long as we can avail of the incomparably better method of extinction.

39th. A thorough investigation of the great centres for cattle feeding and cattle traffic has demonstrated that at the close of 1881 there was no lung-plague west of the Alleghanies; but that the disease was still confined to an area extending from Putnam county, New York, to Fairfax county, Virginia.

40th. We see no reason to conclude that the disease is disappearing under the present management; on the contrary, the absence of regular inspections in the infected districts leaves it to make its way unknown and unheeded, as it did prior to 1878.

41st. In the present status of the lung-plague and cattle trade it is impossible to guarantee the health of even Western cattle exported from New York, Philadelphia, or Baltimore.

42nd. It would be possible at present to guarantee the health of Western cattle exported from Boston or Portland, but if this led to the shipment to these ports of cattle from New York City, Philadelphia, or Baltimore, this guarantee would be at once invalidated.

43rd. As a prerequisite, therefore, to the furnishing of certificates of health with cattle shipped from Boston and Portland, the Federal Government must interdict the movement of cattle out of any infected State.

44th. This interdiction, supplemented by a control of the through traffic from the West, and the establishing of bonded markets at such places as Buffalo, Albany, and Pittsburgh, would not only protect our exports but secure us against any extension of the plague through the shipment of thoroughbreds or commoner cattle westward or southward.

45th. By providing bonded markets at the ports of New York, Philadelphia, and Baltimore, and by admitting to these cattle from sound States only, under proper regulations as to transit, we could further give certificates of health with Western cattle shipped from these points, and furnish the districts with the means of obtaining store cattle without danger of infection.

46th. The cleansing and disinfection of cars and ships (and their contents) conveying cattle to or from the bonded yards is an essential condition of any guarantee.

47th. The present method of quarantining imported cattle is objectionable, and should be exchanged for one requiring that the detention be for all alike, in premises at the port, provided for the purpose and kept under the control of the Federal Government.

48th. For export fat cattle we recognise the necessity for strong separate stalls on board ship, properly cleated to give firm foothold, and above all, that ample provision be made for ventilation by the use of a revolving fan, or by extraction by the heat of the furnace. This we recommend, not because impure air or other cause of injury on shipboard would be at all likely to produce lung-plague, but because the vitiated air is highly calculated to develop an inflammation of the lungs, which might arouse suspicion of lung-plague.

49th. To carry out the above objects, we recommend an ample appropriation by Congress, and the appointment of some Federal official or officials to control the work.

50th. For the extinction of the lung-plague in infected districts we consider it necessary that the authority, Federal or State, intrusted with the work should be clothed with the following power:

(*a*.) To abolish or regulate markets for store cattle in the infected districts.

(*b*.) To require the slaughter at the fat markets in infected districts of all cattle entering these markets. Fat cattle for slaughter elsewhere can be obtained at the bonded market.

(*c*.) To prohibit all movement of cattle in infected districts, except under special license.

(*d*.) To inspect all cattle in suspected districts.

(*e*.) To slaughter all infected cattle, and in exceptional cases those that have been exposed to infection.

(*f*.) To have the condemned animals appraised and the owners liberally indemnified.

(*g*.) To prohibit all exposure of cattle on highways, or on unfenced or insecurely fenced places in infected districts, or of suspected cattle on a lot adjoining one occupied by healthy cattle or bordering on a highway.

(*h*.) To prohibit all pasturage of more than one herd on one pasture in infected districts, unless under special license.

(*i*.) To disinfect all premises, fodder, and other articles that have been presumably exposed to infection.

(*j*.) To institute and enforce such minor rules as shall be demanded by the peculiar conditions of particular districts.

(*k*.) To provide and enforce suitable penalties for infringement of orders.

51st. In order to carry out these suggestions we recommend a liberal appropriation by Congress, to be disbursed by some designated Federal officer.

52nd. In case the work be delegated to the different States, we advise that a liberal appropriation be made from the Federal exchequer, sufficient to cover the greater part of the outlay; and that this be paid over to the executive of the infected State on the approval of the plan and execution of the work in the particular States by a veterinary sanitary organisation designated for the purpose by the Federal Government.

COMPILATION of the LAWS of DIFFERENT STATES in reference to DISEASES of FARM STOCK. From the Report of the United States Treasury Cattle Commission, 1882.

In the belief that a compilation of the laws of the different States bearing upon this subject might aid the Commission in the execution of their work, and furnish much valuable information to the Department and to Congress, in any effort that might be made to legislate thereon, and also to show how little has been done by the States themselves by way of precautionary and protective measures, a compilation which is believed to contain the substance of all the laws of the States and Territories relating to contagious diseases of cattle has been prepared by the Commission, and is herewith submitted.

	PAGE		PAGE
Connecticut	158	Minnesota	171
Illinois	158	Nebraska	172
Indiana	160	New Hampshire	173
Kansas	161	New Jersey	173
Maine	162	New York	175
Maryland	164	Pennsylvania	177
Massachusetts	166	Rhode Island	178
Michigan	171	Vermont	179

CONNECTICUT.

(House Bill No. 74.)

CHAPTER LXXIII.—AN ACT conferring upon the STATE BOARD of AGRICULTURE the POWER to KILL DISEASED ANIMALS.

Be it enacted by the Senate and House of Representatives in General Assembly convened:

SECTION 1. The State Board of Agriculture, or in case said board have or shall appoint commissioners on diseases of domestic animals, under the provisions of section 7 of the Act to which this is an addition, then said commissioners may, when in their judgment the public good shall require it, cause to be killed and to be disposed of afterwards as, in their judgment, may be expedient, any animal or animals which, in their judgment, are infected with or have been exposed to and are liable to communicate to other animals any contagious disease.

ILLINOIS.

AN ACT to SUPPRESS and PREVENT the SPREAD of PLEURO-PNEUMONIA among CATTLE.

SECTION 1. Be it enacted by the people of the State of Illinois, represented in the General Assembly, that the Governor of this State is hereby authorised and instructed to appoint a competent veterinary surgeon, who shall be known as State veterinarian or inspector, and whose duty it shall be to investigate any and all cases of contagious or infectious disease among domestic animals of the bovine species in this State, which may be brought to his notice by a competent veterinary surgeon or practising physician in the locality where such infectious or contagious disease may exist, and it shall be his duty to make visits of inspection to any locality where he may have reason to suspect that contagious or infectious disease may exist.

SEC. 2. In all cases of pleuro-pneumonia among cattle in this State, the State veterinarian shall have authority to order the quarantine of infected premises, and in case such disease shall become epidemic in any locality in this State, the State veterinarian shall immediately notify the Governor of the State, who shall thereupon issue his proclamation forbidding any animals of the kind among which said epidemic exists from being transported from said locality without a certificate from the State veterinarian showing such animals to be healthy. In case of epidemic, as aforesaid, the State veterinarian shall order the quarantine of infected premises, and shall order the slaughter of diseased animals thereon; and in cases of pleuro-pneumonia among cattle, he shall, as herein-after provided, order the slaughter of all cattle upon the premises which have been exposed to contagion; but before doing so he shall call in consultation with him two (2) reputable veterinarians or practising physicians residing within ten (10) miles of the infected premises, and shall not order the slaughter of any animals not actually diseased without a written order signed by one (1) or both of said veterinarians or practising physicians.

SEC. 3. Whenever it becomes necessary, as herein provided, to order the slaughter of animals, the State veterinarian shall notify the nearest justice of the peace, who shall thereupon summons three (3) disinterested freeholders of the neighbourhood as appraisers of the value of such animals; said appraisers, before entering upon the discharge of their duty, shall be sworn to make a true and faithful appraisement, without prejudice or favour. They shall, after making their appraisement, return a certified copy of their valuation to the justice of the peace by whom they were summoned, who shall, after entering the same upon his record, and making an endorsement thereon, showing the same to have been properly recorded, return it, together with the order of the State veterinarian, to the person or persons owning live stock ordered slaughtered.

SEC. 4. Whenever the Governor of the State shall have good reason to believe that such disease has become epidemic in certain localities in other States, or that there are conditions which render such domestic animals liable to convey disease, he shall thereupon, by proclamation, schedule such localities, and prohibit the importation of any live stock of the kind diseased into this State, unless accompanied by a certificate of health, properly signed by a duly authorised veterinary inspector. Any corporation or individual who shall transport, receive, or convey such prohibited stock shall be deemed guilty of a misdemeanour, and upon conviction thereof, shall be fined not less than one thousand dollars ($1,000) nor more than ten thousand dollars ($10,000) for each and every offence, and shall become liable for any and all damage or loss that may be sustained by any party or parties by reason of the importation or transportation of such prohibited stock.

SEC. 5. If any person or persons who shall have upon his premises any case of pleuro-pneumonia among cattle, and shall fail to immediately report the same to the State veterinarian, or if any person or persons shall wilfully and maliciously obstruct or resist the State veterinarian in the discharge of his duty, as herein-before set forth, he shall be deemed guilty of a misdemeanour, and upon conviction of either charge shall be fined not less than fifty ($50) nor more than five hundred dollars ($500) for each and every such offence, and upon conviction a second time shall, in addition to the above-named fine, be liable to not less than thirty (30) days nor more than six (6) months' imprisonment.

Sec. 6. The State veterinarian shall annually make a report to the Governor of all matters connected with his work, and the Governor shall transmit to the Department of Agriculture such parts of said report as may be of general interest to breeders of live stock, to be published with the proceedings of the State Board of Agriculture.

Sec. 7. All claims against the State arising from the slaughter of animals, as herein provided for, shall, together with the order of the State veterinarian and the award of the appraisers in each case, be submitted to the Governor, and he shall, after having examined each case, if satisfied of the justness of the same, indorse thereon his order to the State auditor, who shall thereupon issue his warrant on the State treasurer for the same so ordered paid by the Governor.

Sec. 8. The State veterinarian shall be entitled to receive for his service the sum of eight dollars ($8) per day for every day actually employed under the provisions of this Act, together with his necessary travelling expenses. He shall make an itemised account to the Governor, properly signed and sworn to, of the number of days he has served, and of the expenses which he has paid, and the Governor shall, if satisfied that the same is right and proper, indorse thereon his order on the State auditor for the amount. The appraisers, heretofore, provided for, shall be entitled to receive the sum of one dollar ($1) each for their services, to be paid out of the treasury of their respective counties, upon certificate of the justice of the peace summoning them. The justice of the peace shall be entitled to receive the ordinary fee for issuing summons, to be paid out of the town fund in counties under township organisation, and out of the county fund in counties not under township organisation. The physicians called in consultation shall be entitled to receive for their services the sum of two dollars ($2) per day, and mileage at the rate of ten (10) cents per mile one way; such compensation and mileage to be paid out of the veterinarian contingent fund. The State veterinarian shall have at his disposition the sum of two thousand dollars ($2,000), to be expended in disinfecting infected premises, and other incidental expenses connected with his work, for which he shall, before entering upon the discharge of his duties, give bond, with good and sufficient securities, in the sum of five thousand dollars ($5,000), and shall make a sworn statement to the Governor of the amounts he disburses. Any part of said two thousand dollars ($2,000) not used shall lapse into the State treasury.

Sec. 9. For the purpose of carrying out the provisions of this Act, the sum of eight thousand dollars ($8,000), or so much thereof as is necessary, is hereby appropriated out of the State treasury, to be paid as hereby provided out of any sums not otherwise appropriated.

INDIANA.

No law except the criminal code. Provides that a party who has cattle in a car not diseased, may claim damages if another party brings in cattle diseased, *knowing them to be so.*

KANSAS.

(Laws, 1881.)

CHAPTER 161.—CATTLE, PROTECTION OF, FROM CONTAGIOUS DISEASES.

An Act for the PROTECTION OF CATTLE against CONTAGIOUS DISEASES.

Be it enacted by the Legislature of the State of Kansas:

SECTION 1. That no person or persons shall drive or cause to be driven into or through any county in this State any cattle diseased with a disease known as Texas, splenic, or Spanish fever. Any person violating any provision of this Act shall on conviction be adjudged guilty of a misdemeanour, and shall be fined not less than one hundred and not more than one thousand dollars, and be imprisoned in the county jail not less than thirty days, and not more than one year.

SEC. 2. That upon the arrest of any person or persons charged with the violation of any of the provisions of this Act, all cattle found in his or their possession shall, during the arrest and trial of the offenders, be stopped and taken charge of by the officer or person executing the warrant of arrest, to abide the judgment of the court before whom the offender or offenders shall be tried.

SEC. 3. That upon a complaint made to any sheriff within the State, by any citizen thereof, that there are, within the county where said sheriff resides, wild or undomesticated cattle infected or diseased with what is commonly known as Texas, splenic, or Spanish fever, said sheriff shall forthwith take charge of said cattle and corral the same, or otherwise prevent their running at large, until said complaint shall be investigated as herein-after provided.

SEC. 4. It shall be the duty of such sheriff, upon taking charge of any cattle as provided in sections two and three of this Act, to immediately give notice thereof to any justice of the peace in his county; whereupon said justice shall immediately summon three resident citizens of the county to forthwith appear before him for the purpose of inspecting such cattle; and when the persons so summoned, or other persons summoned in their stead, shall appear, it shall be the duty of the justice to administer to them an oath, in writing, that they will faithfully discharge their duties as inspectors of the cattle aforesaid, and without delay make report to him of their finding in the premises.

SEC. 5. Upon taking the oath, as provided in section four of this Act, said inspectors shall immediately proceed to examine cattle so in the custody of the sheriff, and if upon such examination they shall find the condition of the same to be such as to endanger the health of other cattle in the vicinity by reason of probable contagion, they shall immediately report their findings to the justice aforesaid in writing, and thereupon the justice shall forthwith issue to the sheriff his order in writing, commanding him to keep such cattle in his custody and under his control until the first day of November next ensuing; and he may employ such assistance as may be required to properly care for such cattle, keeping a correct and itemised account of all such services and the cost thereof, as well as of all feed necessary to be used, and present a report thereof to the commissioners of the county at their next regular session, and if found by them to be correct and reasonable, they shall allow the same, and draw warrants upon the county treasurer therefor; and the sheriff shall be allowed for his services such compensation as the commissioners shall deem reasonable, taking as a basis for their estimate the fees allowed by law for similar services; and the inspectors shall be allowed in like manner for their services not to exceed **two**

o 11711.

162 APPENDIX.

dollars per day, for time actually spent in making the inspection, and ten cents per mile for every mile necessarily travelled in the discharge of their duties.

SEC. 6. That, in the trial of any person or persons charged with the violation of any of the provisions of this Act, proof that the cattle, of which such person or persons are charged with driving, are wild and of undomesticated habits, shall be taken as *primâ facie* evidence that said cattle are diseased with the disease known as Texas, splenic, or Spanish fever.

SEC. 7. Any person or persons who shall drive or cause to be driven into or through any county in this State any of the cattle mentioned in section one of this Act, in violation of this Act, shall be liable to the party injured for all damages that may arise from the communication of disease from the cattle so driven, to be recovered in civil action; and the party so injured shall have a lien upon the cattle so driven.

SEC. 8. Justices of the peace, within their respective counties, shall have criminal jurisdiction in all cases arising under the provisions of this Act.

SEC. 9. It shall be the duty of the prosecuting attorney of the proper county to prosecute on behalf of the State all criminal cases arising under this Act.

SEC. 10. Whenever any cattle are taken by the sheriff, or other officer, under the provisions of this Act, and shall remain in his possession, he shall, on the first day of November thereafter, deliver the same to their owner or owners, or his or their agent or agents: Provided, That before he shall deliver the same, all costs and expenses which have accrued by reason of the taking and detaining of such cattle as herein-before provided are paid into the county treasury; and in case such costs and expenses are not so paid within ten days after said first day of November, the sheriff shall advertise in the same manner as is by law provided in cases of sales of personal property that he will sell such cattle, or such portion thereof as may be necessary to pay such costs and expenses; and at the time and place so advertised he shall proceed to sell as many of said cattle as shall be necessary to pay such costs and expenses, and out of the proceeds of such sale he shall pay such amount into the county treasury, retaining the costs of sale.

SEC. 11. Nothing in this Act shall be construed to conflict with the provisions of section one, chapter one hundred and seventy-six, Laws of 1879, or Acts amendatory thereof.

SEC. 12. Article nine of chapter one hundred and five of the General Statutes of 1868, and all amendments thereto, entitled "An Act for the "protection of stock from disease," is hereby repealed.

SEC. 13. This Act to take effect and be in force from and after its publication in the official State paper.

Approved March 4, 1881.

MAINE.

Contagious Diseases among Cattle.

(Revised Statutes.—Chapter 14.)

SECTION 37. The municipal officers of towns, in case of the existence of the disease called lung murrain or pleuro-pneumonia, or any other contagious disease, shall cause the cattle in their towns infected, or which have been exposed to infection, to be secured or collected in some suitable place or places therein, and kept isolated; and when taken from the possession of their owners, one-fifth of the expense thereof is to be paid by the town, and four-fifths at the expense of the State, such isolation to continue so long as the existence of such disease or other circumstances render it necessary; or they may direct the owners thereof to isolate such cattle upon their own premises, and any damage or loss sustained thereby shall be paid as aforesaid.

SEC. 38. The municipal officers shall, within twenty-four hours after they have notice of the existence of such disease, or have reason to believe that it exists, cause the suspected animals to be examined by a veterinary surgeon or physician, by them selected, and if they are adjudged diseased, they may order them to be forthwith killed and buried at the expense of such town.

SEC. 39. When so killed they shall cause them to be appraised by three competent and disinterested men, under oath, at the value thereof at the time of appraisal, and the amount thereof shall be paid as provided in section thirty-seven.

SEC. 40. They may prohibit the departure of cattle from any inclosure, and exclude cattle therefrom.

SEC. 41. They may make regulations in writing to regulate or prohibit the passage from, to, or through their towns, or from place to place therein, of any neat cattle, and may arrest and detain, at the cost of the owners thereof, all cattle found passing in violation of such regulations, and may take all other necessary measures for the enforcement of such prohibition, and for preventing the spread of any such disease among the cattle in their towns and the immediate vicinity thereof.

SEC. 42. Such regulations shall be recorded in the records of their towns, and shall be published in such towns in such manner as such regulations provide.

SEC. 43. Any person who sells or disposes of any animal infected or known to have been exposed to infection within one year after such exposure, without the knowledge or consent of the municipal officers, shall be punished by fine not exceeding five hundred dollars, or by imprisonment not exceeding one year.

SEC. 44. Any person disobeying the orders of said municipal officers, made in conformity with the fortieth section, or driving or transporting any neat cattle contrary to the regulations made, so recorded and published, shall be punished as provided in section forty-three.

SEC. 45. Whoever knows or has reason to suspect the existence of any fatal contagious disease among the cattle in his possession or under his care shall forthwith give notice thereof to the municipal officers, and for failure to do so shall be punished as provided in section forty-three.

SEC. 46. Any town whose officers shall neglect or refuse to carry into effect the provisions of section thirty-seven, thirty-eight, thirty-nine, forty, forty-one, forty-two, and forty-three shall forfeit a sum not exceeding five hundred dollars for each day's neglect.

SEC. 47. All appraisals made under the provisions of section thirty-nine shall be in writing, and signed by the appraisers, and shall be certified by the municipal officers to the Governor and council, and to the treasurers of their towns.

SEC. 48. The municipal officers of towns may, when they deem it necessary to carry into effect the purposes of this chapter, take and hold possession, for a term not exceeding one year, of any land within their towns without buildings other than barns thereon, for inclosing and isolating any cattle, and they shall cause the damages sustained by the owners in consequence thereof to be appraised by the assessors thereof; and they shall further cause a description of such land, setting forth the boundaries thereof, and the area as nearly as may be estimated, together

164   APPENDIX.

with said appraisal, to be entered in the records of the town. The amount of said appraisal shall be paid as provided in the thirty-seventh section in such sums and at such times as they may order. If such owner is dissatisfied with the appraisal, he may, in an action of the case, recover from the town a fair compensation for the damages sustained by him; but no costs shall be taxed unless the damages recovered in such action, exclusive of interest, exceed the appraisal of the assessors, and the State shall reimburse any town four-fifths of any sum so recovered.

SEC. 49. Whenever such disease exists in any town, the municipal officers shall forthwith give notice thereof to the Governor and secretary of the Board of Agriculture, but if commissioners have been appointed as herein-after provided, such notice shall be given to them.

SEC. 50. The Governor may, when he deems it expedient, appoint commissioners who shall have full power to make all necessary regulations, and to issue summary orders relative thereto, for the treatment and extirpation of any contagious disease among cattle, and may direct the municipal officers to enforce and carry them into effect; and any such officer or other person refusing or neglecting to enforce, carry out, and comply with any regulations of the commissioners shall be punished by a fine as provided in section forty-three.

SEC. 51. When said commissioners shall make and publish any regulations they shall supersede the regulations made by the municipal officers, during the time those made by the commissioners are in force.

SEC. 52. All losses and damages and reasonable expenses sustained in consequence of execution of the orders of said commissioners shall be appraised as provided in the thirty-ninth section, and paid as provided in the thirty-seventh section.

SEC. 53. The commissioners shall keep record of their doings, and make report thereof to the next annual session of the legislature, on or before the tenth day of January, unless sooner required by the Governor; and such record or an abstract thereof shall be printed in the annual volume of transactions of the State Board of Agriculture.

SEC. 54. The Governor, with the advice and consent of the council, may terminate the commission, when, in his judgment, the public safety may permit.

MARYLAND.

(Chapter 439, Acts of the General Assembly of Maryland, 1880.)

AN ACT to PREVENT the SPREAD of INFECTIOUS or CONTAGIOUS PLEURO-PNEUMONIA among the CATTLE of this STATE.

SECTION 1. Be it enacted by the General Assembly of Maryland, that whenever it shall be brought to the notice of the Governor of this State that the disease known as contagious or infectious pleuro-pneumonia exists among the cattle in any of the counties of this State, or in the city of Baltimore, it shall be his duty to take measures to promptly suppress the disease and prevent it from spreading.

SEC. 2. And be it enacted, that for such purpose the Governor shall have power to issue his proclamation stating that infectious or contagious disease exists, in any county or counties of the State, or in the city of Baltimore, and warning all persons to seclude all animals in their possession that are affected with such disease or have been exposed to the infection or contagion thereof, and ordering all persons to take such precautions against the spreading of such disease as the nature thereof may, in his judgment, render necessary or expedient; to order that any premises, farm or farms, or stables where such disease exists or has existed, be put in quarantine, so that no domestic animal be removed from or brought to the premises or places so quarantined, and to prescribe such regulations as he may judge necessary or expedient to prevent infection or contagion being communicated in any way from the places so quarantined; to call upon all sheriffs and deputy sheriffs to carry out and enforce the provisions of such proclamations, orders, and regulations; and it shall be the duty of all sheriffs and deputy sheriffs to obey and observe all orders and instructions which they may receive from the Governor in the premises; to employ such and so many medical and veterinary practitioners and such other persons as he may from time to time deem necessary to assist him in performing his duty as set forth in the first section of this Act, and to fix their compensation; to order all or any animals coming into the State to be detained at any place or places for the purpose of inspection and examination; provided, that animals coming from a neighbouring State that have passed a veterinary examination in said State, and have been quarantined and discharged, shall not be subject to the provisions of this Act; to prescribe regulations for the destruction of animals affected with infectious or contagious disease, or of those in direct contact with such and liable to spread the disease, and for the proper disposition of their hides and carcases, and of all objects which might convey infection or contagion; provided, that no animal shall be destroyed unless first examined by a medical or veterinary practitioner in the employ of the Governor as aforesaid; to prescribe regulations for the disinfection of all premises, buildings, and railway cars, and of all objects from or by which infection or contagion may take place or be conveyed; to alter and modify, from time to time, as he may deem expedient, the terms of all such proclamations, orders, and regulations, and to cancel or withdraw the same at any time.

Sec. 3. And be it enacted, that any person who shall transgress the terms or requirements of any proclamation, order, or regulation issued or prescribed by the Governor under the authority of this Act, shall be deemed guilty of a misdemeanour.

Sec. 4. And be it enacted, that any person who shall sell or otherwise dispose of an animal which he knows, or has reason to believe, is affected by the disease, or has been exposed to the same, shall forfeit to the State not less than fifty nor more than one hundred dollars.

Sec. 5. And be it enacted, that all the necessary expenses incurred under direction or by authority of the Governor, in carrying out the provisions of this Act, shall be paid by the treasurer out of any moneys not otherwise appropriated, and upon the warrant of the comptroller on being certified as correct by the Governor.

Sec. 6. And be it enacted, that in the event of its being deemed necessary by the Governor, or any agent duly appointed by him under the provisions of this Act, to prevent the spread of contagion or infection to cause any animal not actually diseased to be slaughtered, the value of such animal or animals shall be fairly appraised, and a record kept and a report made thereof to the General Assembly at its session next ensuing, with a view to the reimbursement of the owners of such animals so killed, should provision therefor be made by law, it being provided that the carcasses of animals so killed and found entirely free from disease shall, if practicable, be sold, and the proceeds of such sale shall be paid over to the respective owners of the cattle, and the amounts so received and paid over noted against the appraised value thereof.

Sec. 7. And be it enacted that this Act shall take effect from the date of its passage.

Approved April 10, 1880.

MASSACHUSETTS.

(Supplement to the General Statutes, 1860, Chapter 192.)

AN ACT TO PROVIDE FOR THE EXTIRPATION OF THE DISEASE CALLED PLEURO-PNEUMONIA AMONG CATTLE.

SECTION 1. The Governor is hereby authorised to appoint three commissioners, who shall visit without delay the several places in this Commonwealth where the disease among cattle called pleuro-pneumonia may be known or suspected to exist, and shall have full power to cause all cattle belonging to the herds in which the disease has appeared or may appear, or which have belonged to such herds since the disease may be known to have existed therein, to be forthwith killed and buried, and the premises where such cattle have been kept cleansed and purified, and to make such order in relation to the further use and occupation of such premises as may seem to them to be necessary to prevent the extension of the disease.

SEC. 6. This Act shall take effect from its passage, and continue in force for the term of one year thereafter, and no longer. (April 4, 1860.)

CHAPTER 220, 1860.—AN ACT concerning CONTAGIOUS DISEASES among CATTLE.

SECTION 1. The selectmen of towns, and the mayor and aldermen of cities, in case of the existence in this Commonwealth of the disease called pleuro-pneumonia, or any other contagious disease among cattle, shall cause the cattle in their respective towns and cities which are infected or which have been exposed to infection to be secured or collected in some suitable place or places within such city or town, and kept isolated; and, when taken from the possession of their owners, to be maintained, one-fifth of the expense thereof to be paid by the town or city wherein the animal is kept, and four-fifths at the expense of the Commonwealth; such isolation to continue so long as the existence of such disease, or other circumstances, renders the same necessary.

SEC. 2. Said selectmen and mayor and aldermen, when any such animal is adjudged by a veterinary surgeon or physician, by them selected, to be infected with pleuro-pneumonia, or any other contagious disease, may, in their discretion, order such diseased animal to be forthwith killed and buried at the expense of such town or city.

SEC. 3. Said selectmen and mayor and aldermen shall cause all cattle which they shall so order to be killed to be appraised by three competent and disinterested men, under oath, at the value thereof at the time of the appraisal, and the amount of the appraisal shall be paid as provided in the first section.

SEC. 4. Said selectmen and mayor and aldermen within their respective towns and cities are hereby authorised to prohibit the departure of cattle from any inclosure, or to exclude cattle therefrom.

SEC. 5. Said selectmen and mayor and aldermen may make regulations in writing to regulate or prohibit the passage from, to, or through their respective cities or towns, or from place to place within the same, of any neat cattle, and may arrest and detain, at the cost of the owners thereof, all cattle found passing in violation of said regulations, and may take all other necessary measures for the enforcement of such prohibition, and also for preventing the spread of any such disease among the cattle in their respective towns and cities, and the immediate vicinity thereof.

SEC. 7. Said selectmen and mayor and aldermen are authorised to cause all cattle infected with such disease, or which have been exposed thereto, to be forthwith branded upon the rump with the letter P, so as to distinguish the animal from other cattle; and no cattle so branded shall be sold or disposed of except with the knowledge and consent of such selectmen and mayor and aldermen. Any person, without such knowledge and consent, selling or disposing of an animal so branded, or selling or disposing of an animal known to be affected with such disease, or known to have been exposed thereto within one year previous to such sale or disposal, shall be punished by a fine not exceeding five hundred dollars, or by imprisonment not exceeding one year.

Sec. 8. Any person disobeying the orders of the selectmen or mayor and aldermen, made in conformity with the fourth section, or driving or transporting any neat cattle contrary to the regulations made, recorded, and published as aforesaid, shall be punished by a fine not exceeding five hundred dollars, or by imprisonment not exceeding one year.

Sec. 9. Whoever knows or has reason to suspect the existence of any such disease among the cattle in his possession or under his care, shall forthwith give notice to the selectmen of the town or mayor and aldermen of the city where such cattle may be kept, and for failure so to do shall be punished by a fine not exceeding five hundred dollars, or by imprisonment not exceeding one year.

Sec. 10. Any town or city whose officers shall neglect or refuse to carry into effect the provisions of sections one, two, three, four, five, six, and seven shall forfeit a sum not exceeding five hundred dollars for each day's neglect.

Sec. 11. All appraisals made under the provisions of this Act shall be in writing and signed by the appraisers, and the same shall be certified to the Governor and council and to the treasurer of the several cities and towns wherein the cattle appraised were kept by the selectmen, and mayors and aldermen, respectively.

Sec. 12. The selectmen of towns, and mayor and aldermen of cities, are hereby authorised, when in their judgment it shall be necessary to carry into effect the purposes of this Act, to take and hold possession, for a term not exceeding one year, within their respective towns and cities, of any land, without buildings other than barns thereon, upon which it may be necessary to inclose and isolate any cattle, and they shall cause the damages sustained by the owner in consequence of such taking and holding to be appraised by the assessors of the town or city wherein the lands so taken are situated; and they shall further cause a description of such land, setting forth the boundaries thereof, and the area as nearly as may be estimated, together with said appraisal by the assessors, to be entered on the records of the town or city. The amount of said appraisal shall be paid as provided in the first section, in such sums and at such times as the selectmen or mayor and aldermen, respectively, may order. If the owner of any land so taken shall be dissatisfied with the appraisal of said assessors, he may by action of contract recover of the town or city wherein the lands lie a fair compensation for the damages sustained by him; but no costs shall be taxed, unless the damages recovered in such action, exclusive of interest, exceed the appraisal of the assessors, and the Commonwealth shall reimburse any town or city four-fifths of any sum recovered of such town or city in any such action.

Chapter 221, 1860.—An Act in addition to an Act concerning Contagious Diseases among Cattle.

Section 1. In addition to the commissioners appointed under the provisions of chapter one hundred and ninety-two of the Acts of the year one thousand eight hundred and sixty, the Governor, by and with the advice and consent of the council, is hereby authorised to appoint two additional persons to constitute, with those now in office, a board of commissioners upon the subject of pleuro-pneumonia, or any other contagious disease now existing among the cattle of the Commonwealth.

SEC. 2. When said commissioners shall make and publish any regulations concerning the extirpation, cure, or treatment of cattle infected with, or which have been exposed to, the disease of pleuro-pneumonia, or other contagious disease, such regulations shall supersede the regulations made by selectmen of towns and mayors and aldermen of cities upon the same subject-matter; and the operations of the regulations made by such selectmen and mayors and aldermen shall be suspended during the time those made by the commissioners as aforesaid shall be in force. And said selectmen and mayors and aldermen shall carry out and enforce all orders and directions of said commissioners to them directed, as they shall from time to time issue,

SEC. 3. In addition to the power and authority conferred on the selectmen of towns and mayors and aldermen of cities by the Act to which this is in addition, and which are herein conferred upon said commissioners, the same commissioners shall have power to provide for the establishment of a hospital or quarantine in some suitable place or places, with proper accommodations of buildings, land, &c., wherein may be detained any cattle by them selected, so that said cattle so infected or exposed may be there treated by such scientific practitioners of the healing art as may be appointed to treat the same. And for this purpose said commissioners may take any lands and buildings in the manner provided in the twelfth section of the Act to which this is in addition.

SEC. 4. The Governor, by and with the advice and consent of the council, is hereby authorised to appoint three competent persons to be a board of examiners to examine into the disease called pleuro-pneumonia, who shall attend at the hospital or quarantine established by the commissioners mentioned in the foregoing section, and there treat and experiment upon such number of cattle, both sound and infected, as will enable them to study the symptons and laws of the disease, and ascertain, so far as they can, the best mode of treating cattle in view of the prevention and cure of the disease, and who shall keep a full record of their proceedings and make report thereon to the Governor and council, when their investigations shall have been concluded: Provided, that the expense of said board of examiners shall not exceed ten thousand dollars.

SEC. 5. The selectmen of the several towns, and mayors and aldermen of the several cities, shall, within twenty-four hours after they shall have notice that any cattle in their respective towns and cities are infected with, or have been exposed to any such disease, give notice in writing to said commissioners of the same.

SEC. 6. The commissioners are authorised to make all necessary regulations for the treatment, cure, and extirpation of said disease, and may direct the selectmen of towns and mayors and aldermen of cities to enforce and carry into effect all such regulations as may from time to time be made for that end; and any such officer refusing or neglecting to enforce and carry out any regulation of the commissioners shall be punished by fine not exceeding five hundred dollars for every such offence.

SEC. 7. The commissioners may, when in their judgment the public good shall require it, cause to be killed and buried any cattle which are infected with, or which have been exposed to, said disease; and said commissioners shall cause said cattle to be appraised in the same manner provided in the Act to which this is in addition, and the appraised value of such cattle shall be paid, one-fifth by the towns in which said cattle were kept, and the remainder by the Commonwealth.

SEC. 8. Whoever shall drive or transport any cattle from any portion of the Commonwealth east of Connecticut River to any part west of said river before the first day of April next without consent of the commissioners shall be punished by fine not exceeding five hundred dollars, or by imprisonment in the county jail not exceeding one year.

SEC. 9. Whoever shall drive or transport any cattle from any portion of the Commonwealth into any other State before the first day of April next, without the consent of the commissioners, he shall be punished by fine not exceeding five hundred dollars, or by imprisonment in the county jail not exceeding one year.

SEC. 10. If any person fails to comply with any regulation made or with any order given by the commissioners, he shall be punished by fine not exceeding five hundred dollars, or by imprisonment not exceeding one year.

SEC. 11. Prosecutions under the two preceding sections may be prosecuted in any county in this Commonwealth.

SEC. 12. All appraisals made under this Act shall be in writing, and signed by the appraisers and certified by the commissioners, and shall be by them transmitted to the Governor and council and to the treasurers of the several cities and towns wherein the cattle appraised were kept.

SEC. 13. The provisions of chapter one hundred and ninety-two of the Acts of the year one thousand eight hundred and sixty, except so far as they authorise the appointment of commissioners, are hereby repealed; but this repeal shall not affect the validity of any proceedings heretofore lawfully had under the provisions of said chapter.

SEC. 14. The commissioners and examiners shall keep a full record of their doings, and make report of the same to the next legislature on or before the tenth day of January next, unless sooner required by the Governor; and the said record, or an abstract of the same, shall be printed in the annual volume of transactions of the State Board of Agriculture.

SEC. 15. The Governor, with the advice and consent of the council, shall have the power to terminate the commission and board of examiners whenever in his judgment the public safety may permit.

SEC. 16. This Act shall take effect from its passage.
(June 12, 1860.)

CHAPTER 41, 1861.—RESOLUTION providing for INDEMNIFICATION for CATTLE KILLED by ORDER of COMMISSIONERS.

Resolved,—That the commissioners appointed under this Act, approved April fourth, in the year eighteen hundred and sixty, and entitled "An Act to provide for the extirpation of the disease called "pleuro-pneumonia among cattle," be, and they hereby are, required to certify to the Governor and council the names of all persons whose cattle were killed by their authority for the reason that they appeared to be afflicted with the disease called pleuro-pneumonia, and not paid for, together with the number, description, and fair value of such cattle, at the time they were killed. Upon the receipt of such certificate, the Governor, with the advice and consent of the council, may draw his warrants in favour of such persons, and for such sums as shall appear to them to be justly due. The money so appropriated shall be taken from the appropriation for carrying into effect the provisions of the laws concerning contagious diseases among cattle. (March 28, 1861.)

CHAPTER 28, 1862.—AN ACT concerning CATTLE COMMISSIONERS.

SECTION 1. The Governor, with the advice and consent of the council, shall have power to appoint a board of cattle commissioners of not more than three members, whenever in his judgment the public safety may require, and may terminate their commissions whenever in his judgment the public safety may permit: Provided, that the compensation of said commissioners shall not exceed four dollars per day, for actual service, in addition to their travelling expenses necessarily incurred.

SEC. 2. The powers and duties of the commissioners shall be such as are set forth in Chapter 221 of the Acts of the year 1860.

SEC. 3. All commissions and appointments made under Chapters 192 and 221 of the Acts of the year 1860 are hereby abolished.

SEC. 4. This Act shall take effect upon its passage.
(February 18, 1862.)

CHAPTER 138.—AN ACT in addition to an ACT concerning CONTAGIOUS DISEASES among CATTLE.

SECTION 1. The Commissioners on contagious diseases among cattle are hereby authorised to examine under oath, in the several cities and towns of this Commonwealth, all persons possessing, or believing to possess, knowledge of any material facts concerning the existence or dissemination, or danger of dissemination of diseases among cattle; and for this purpose shall have and exercise all the powers vested in justices of the peace to take depositions, and to compel the attendance of the testifying witnesses, by the 131st chapter of the general statutes, and any other laws concerning the taking of depositions. All costs and expenses incurred in procuring the attendance of such witnesses shall be allowed and paid to the said commissioners from the treasury of the Commonwealth, upon the same being certified to the Governor and council, and approved by him. And the Governor is hereby authorised to draw his warrant therefor upon the treasury, the same to be paid out of any appropriation lawfully applicable to that purpose.

SEC. 2. Whenever cattle exposed to contagious diseases are killed by order of the commissioners, and upon a *post-mortem* examination shall be found to have been entirely free from disease, it shall be the duty of the commissioners to cause the same to be sold under their direction, first giving to the purchaser notice of the fact, and if the said purchaser or any other person shall sell said slaughtered cattle or any part thereof, they shall in like manner give notice to the parties to whom the same is sold; and the proceeds of the sales made by order of the commissioners shall be applied in payment of the appraised value of said cattle.

SEC. 3. Cattle commissions, now or hereafter appointed, shall keep a full record of their doings, and report the same to the legislature on or before the tenth day of January of each year, unless sooner required by the Governor; and an abstract of the same shall be printed in the annual report of the State Board of Agriculture.

SEC. 4. Whoever violates any of the provisions of this Act shall forfeit and pay a fine not exceeding one hundred dollars and costs of prosecution.

SEC. 5. This Act shall take effect upon its passage.
(April 25, 1862.)

MICHIGAN.

CHAPTER 46.—AN ACT to PREVENT the INTRODUCTION of CONTAGIOUS DISEASES in CATTLE. (Approved April 5, 1869.—Laws of 1869, p. 319.)

[1742.] SECTION 1. The people of the State of Michigan enact that when the Governor of the State of Michigan shall be satisfied of the necessity of the same, he shall have power to appoint three commissioners, to hold their office for two years, and make report annually to the secretary of the State Board of Agriculture. Such commissioners shall have power to use means to prevent the spread of dangerous diseases among animals, and protect the people of the State from the dangers arising from the consumption of diseased meat. Said commissioners shall have power to administer oaths and appoint assistants for such time as they may deem proper, and to place animals in quarantine, and to do generally whatever may be necessary to prevent the spread of contagious diseases among animals.

[1743.] SEC. 2. No animals shall be permitted to enter or pass through the State which shall be deemed by either of the commissioners capable of diffusing or communicating contagious diseases.

[1744.] SEC. 3. No cattle brought from Texas or the Indian territories shall be permitted to pass through this State, or any part of the same, from the first day of March to the first day of November, in each year.

SEC. 4. This Act shall take immediate effect.

MINNESOTA.

CHAPTER 101.—OFFENCES against the PUBLIC HEALTH.

SECTION 14.—*Importation of Texas or Indian cattle prohibited.*—That it shall not be lawful for any one to bring into the State or have in possession any Texas, Cherokee, Indian, or any diseased cattle, except as herein-after provided. (1869, c. 42, sec. 1.)

SEC. 15. *Exception as to cattle on hand.—Such cattle not to run at large.*—This Act shall not apply to any Texas, Cherokee, or Indian cattle, or other diseased cattle now on hand within this State; but persons having such shall be compelled to keep them within the bounds of their own premises, or separate from other cattle; and any damage that may accrue from allowing such cattle to run at large, and thereby spreading disease among other cattle, shall be recovered from the owner or owners thereof, who shall be liable to all the pains and penalties, as provided in section 4 of this Act. (*Id.*, sec. 2.)

SEC. 16. *Such cattle may be driven through State, when.*—Nothing contained in this Act shall be so construed as to prevent the transportation of such cattle through this State on railroads, or to prohibit the driving through any portion of this State such Texas or southern cattle as have been wintered, at least one winter, north of the northern boundary of the State of Missouri. (*Id.*, sec. 3.)

SEC. 17. *Penalty—disposition thereof—liability for damages.*—Any person who shall violate the provisions of this Act shall, for every such violation, forfeit and pay into the school-fund of the county where the offence is committed, a sum not exceeding one thousand dollars, or to be fined and imprisoned in the county jail, at the discretion of the court, though such time of imprisonment shall not exceed six months; and such person or persons shall pay all damages that may accrue to any person by reason of such violation of this Act. (*Id.*, sec. 4.)

NEBRASKA.

CHAPTER 3.—ANIMALS.—AN ACT to PROVIDE for the PROTECTION of STOCK from CONTAGIOUS DISEASES. (Passed, and took effect, June 20, 1867. Laws 1876, page 74.)

Be it enacted by the Legislature of the State of Nebraska:

[1.] SECTION 1. That every person shall so restrain his diseased or distempered cattle, or such as are under his care, that they may not go at large; and no person or persons shall drive any diseased or distempered cattle affected with any contagious or infectious disease, into or through this State from one point thereof to another. Any person or persons offending against this section shall, on conviction thereof before any justice of the peace, forfeit not less than five nor more than twenty-five dollars for every head of such cattle, and be liable for all costs and damages.

[2.] SEC. 2. Any justice of the peace, upon proof before him that any cattle are going at large or are driven in or through his county in violation of the preceding section, shall order a constable or sheriff to impound them, and the owner thereof shall be held liable for all costs and damages.

[3.] SEC. 3. The sheriff or constable who may execute the order of any justice of the peace as aforesaid, to impound any such cattle, shall have twenty-five cents per head for the first fifty, and five cents for each additional head, to be paid by the defendant upon conviction thereof, but in case the defendant be discharged then such costs to be paid by the complainant; and if any officer to whom any order under this law is directed should fail to execute (the same,) he shall forfeit, in case of a failure, a sum not less than one hundred dollars.

[4.] SEC. 4. It shall not be lawful for any person to use, let, sell, or permit to run at large any horse, mule, or ass diseased with the glanders. Any person violating the provisions of this section shall pay a fine not less than five, or more than fifty dollars, and shall be liable for all damages.

[5]. SEC. 5. All fines and forfeitures incurred under the provisions of this Act shall be recovered by action before any justice of the peace, and all such fines shall be paid into the school-fund, in and for the county having jurisdiction of the case.

[6.] SEC. 6. In all cases of conviction under the provisions of this Act, the justice shall enter judgment for the fine and costs against the defendant, and may commit him until the judgment is satisfied, or issue execution on the judgment for the use of the common schools of the county.

[7.] SEC. 7. All Acts and parts of Acts inconsistent with the provisions of this Act are hereby repealed.

[8.] SEC. 8. This Act shall take effect and be in force from and after its passage.

Approved June 20, 1867.

AN ACT to PREVENT the INTRODUCTION and SPREAD of HOG CHOLERA and kindred DISEASES in the STATE of NEBRASKA.

Be it enacted by the Legislature of the State of Nebraska:

SECTION 1. That from and after the 1st day of June, A.D. 1877, it shall be unlawful for any railroad company operating its road in this State to bring or cause to be brought into this State from an adjoining State any empty car used for transporting hogs or sheep, or any empty combination car used for carrying grain and stock, that has any filth of any kind whatever in the same; but the railroad company shall, before it allows said car or cars to pass into this State, cause the same to be thoroughly cleansed. Any person or persons or corporation violating any of the above provisions, and on conviction thereof, shall be fined in any sum not to exceed one hundred dollars.

Approved February 17, A.D. 1877.

NEW HAMPSHIRE.

(From GENERAL LAWS of the STATE of NEW HAMPSHIRE, chapter 116, entitled "DISEASES OF DOMESTIC ANIMALS.")

SECTION 1. Whenever any dangerous or troublesome disease prevails among cattle, horses, or other domestic animals, the Governor, with the advice of the council, may appoint a board of commissioners of not more than five persons, and may terminate its existence when the public safety may permit, or the Governor may direct that the Board of Agriculture may perform the duties and possess the powers herein specified.

The compensation of such board shall be limited to actual expenses, to be allowed by the Governor and council.

SECT. 2. Said board shall have the power to make regulations prohibiting the introduction or transportation of any domestic animals, by railroad or otherwise, and such other regulations as they may deem necessary to arrest or exclude any such infectious or troublesome disease, and modify or annul the same as circumstances may require.

Such regulations shall be in force until the existence and powers of the board shall be terminated by the Governor.

SECT. 3. Any person or corporation that shall violate any of the regulations of said board, shall be punished for such offence by fine not exceeding one hundred dollars.

SECT. 4. Any person or corporation that shall bring into the State, between the twentieth day of May and the twentieth day of October, any Texas or Cherokee cattle that have been kept north of the Ohio or Missouri river during the winter immediately preceding, shall be punished for such offence by a fine not exceeding twenty-five dollars for each and every animal so brought into this State.

The term Texas or Cherokee cattle shall be construed to mean the native cattle of Texas and Louisiana, and the classes of cattle known under these names.

SECT. 5. Selectmen shall enforce the provisions of this chapter within their respective towns at the expense of such towns.

NEW JERSEY.

CHAPTER CCXX.—A SUPPLEMENT to an ACT entitled "AN ACT to ESTABLISH a STATE BOARD of HEALTH," approved March ninth, one thousand eight hundred and seventy-seven.

1. Be it enacted by the Senate and General Assembly of the State of New Jersey, that in addition to the powers conferred by the Act to which this is a supplement, said board shall have full power and authority to examine and determine whether pleuro-pneumonia, rinderpest, or any other contagious or infectious disease exist among animals in any county in this State; and that the sum of five hundred dollars is hereby appropriated to defray the actual necessary expenses of said board while making such examinations.

2. And be it enacted, that in event of any contagious or infectious disease as aforesaid breaking out or being suspected to exist in any locality in this State, it shall be the duty of all persons owning or having any interest whatever in said cattle, immediately to notify the said board of health, or any one of them, of the existence of such disease, and thereupon it shall be the duty of said board of health, or any member thereof, to immediately proceed to the place or places where said disease is reported to exist, and to quarantine said animal or animals, and take such precautionary measures as shall be deemed necessary; to prescribe such remedies as in their judgment will be conducive to the recovery of such animal or animals, and to enforce such regulations as may be adopted by said board of health.

3. And be it enacted, that the board of health aforesaid, and all such assistants as they may appoint, whenever in their judgment or discretion it shall appear in any case that the disease is not likely to yield to any remedial treatment, or whenever it shall seem that the cost or worth of any such remedial treatment shall be greater than the value of the animal or animals so afflicted, or whenever in any case such disease shall threaten its spread to other animals, to cause the same to be immediately slaughtered, and their remains to be buried not less than four feet under ground, and all places in which said animals shall have been kept to be cleansed and disinfected.

4. And be it enacted, that in all cases where animals inflicted with, or which shall have been exposed, shall have been slaughtered or killed by the order of the said board of health, or their assistants, it shall be the duty of said board to appoint three competent and disinterested freeholders to appraise the value of the animals so killed or slaughtered, at the time they were so killed; who shall be affirmed or sworn, before proceeding to act, to make a just and true valuation of said animals so killed, at the time of their slaughter, two-thirds of which said valuation or appraisement shall be paid to the owner or owners by the State.

5. And be it enacted, that any person or persons refusing or neglecting to notify said board of health, or any of them, of the existence of pleuro-pneumonia, rinderpest, or any other contagious or infectious diseases among cattle, shall be deemed and adjudged guilty of a misdemeanor, and upon conviction shall be punished by a fine of not more than two hundred dollars, or by imprisonment not exceeding one year, or both, at the discretion of the court.

6. And be it enacted, that all bills for money expended under this Act shall be audited by the comptroller of this State and then submitted to the Governor for his approval. After being thus audited and approved by the Governor, shall be paid by the State treasurer upon warrant of the comptroller.

7. And be it enacted, that said board shall keep a full record of their proceedings, and shall publish the same in the annual report of the State Board of Agriculture, yearly and every year during the existence of the law.

8. And be it enacted, that if any person or persons shall knowingly either buy or sell or cause to be bought or sold, any animal or animals affected with pleuro-pneumonia, rinderpest, or any other contagious or infectious disease, all such person or persons shall be deemed and adjudged guilty of a misdemeanor, and upon conviction thereof shall be punished by a fine not exceeding two hundred dollars or imprisonment not exceeding one year, or both, at the discretion of the court.

9. And be it enacted, that in case an emergency shall arise and a larger sum shall be deemed necessary than the amount appropriated by

the preceding sections of this Act, said State Board of Health shall present the facts in evidence to the president of the State Agricultural Society, and the president and executive committee of the State Board of Agriculture, who shall authorise such additional expenditure as in their judgment they may deem the exigency of the occasion to demand: Provided, that in no case shall the amount of money thus authorised to be expended exceed the sum of five thousand dollars in any one year.

10. And be it enacted, that all Acts and parts of Acts inconsistent with this Act be and the same are hereby repealed, and that this Act take effect immediately.

Approved March 12, 1880.

NEW YORK.

(Laws of New York—by Authority.)

(Every law, unless a different time shall be prescribed therein, shall commence and take effect throughout the State on and not before the 20th day after the day of its final passage as certified by the Secretary of State.—Section 12, title 4, chapter 7, part 1, Revised Statutes.)

CHAPTER 134.—An ACT in relation to INFECTIOUS and CONTAGIOUS DISEASES of ANIMALS. (Passed April 15, 1878; three-fifths being present.)

The people of the State of New York, represented in Senate and Assembly, do enact as follows:

SECTION 1. Whenever any infectious or contagious disease affecting domestic animals shall be brought into or shall break out in this State it shall be the duty of the Governor to take measures to suppress the same promptly and to prevent the same from spreading.

SEC. 2. For such purpose the Governor shall have power:

To issue his proclamation stating that infectious or contagious disease exists in any county or counties in the State, and warning all persons to seclude all animals in their possession that are affected with such disease, or have been exposed to the infection or contagion thereof, and ordering all such persons to take such precautions against the spreading of such disease as the nature thereof may in his judgment render necessary or expedient.

To order that any premises, farm, or farms where such disease exists or has existed be put in quarantine, so that no domestic animal be removed from or brought to the premises or places so quarantined, and to prescribe such regulations as he may judge necessary or expedient to prevent contagion being communicated in any way from the places so quarantined.

To call upon all sheriffs and deputy sheriffs to carry out and enforce the provisions of such proclamations, orders, and regulations, and it shall be the duty of all sheriffs and deputy sheriffs to obey and observe all orders and instructions which they may receive from the Governor in the premises.

To employ such and so many medical and veterinary practitioners and such other persons as he may from time to time deem necessary to assist him in performing his duty as set forth in the first section of this Act and to fix their compensation.

To order all or any animals coming into this State to be detained at any place or places for the purpose of inspection and examination.

To prescribe regulations for the destruction of animals affected with infectious or contagious disease, and for the proper disposition of their hides and carcases and of all objects which might convey infection or contagion; provided that no animal shall be destroyed unless first examined by a medical or veterinary practitioner in the employ of the Governor aforesaid.

To prescribe regulations for the disinfection of all premises, buildings, and railway cars, and of all objects from which or by which infection or contagion may take place or be conveyed.

To alter and modify from time to time, as he may deem expedient, the terms of all such proclamations, orders, and regulations, and to cancel or withdraw the same at any time.

SEC. 3. Any person transgressing the terms of any proclamation, order, or regulation issued or prescribed by the Governor under authority of this Act, shall be guilty of a misdemeanour.

SEC. 4. All expenses incurred by the Governor in carrying out the provisions of this Act, and in performing the duty hereby devolved upon him, shall be audited by the comptroller as extraordinary expenses of the executive department, and shall be paid out of any moneys in the treasury not otherwise appropriated.

CHAPTER 306.—AN ACT in relation to INFECTIOUS and CONTAGIOUS DISEASES of ANIMALS. (Passed May 17, 1879, by a two-thirds vote.)

The people of the State of New York, represented in Senate and Assembly, do enact as follows:

SECTION 1. Whenever in his judgment for the more speedy and economical suppression, or for preventing the spread of any infectious or contagious disease of domestic animals, the public welfare shall be promoted thereby, the Governor shall have, in addition to the powers conferred upon him by chapter one hundred and thirty-four of the laws of eighteen hundred and seventy-eight, the power to cause to be slaughtered and to be disposed of afterwards as in his judgment may be expedient, any animal or animals which by contact or cohabitation with diseased animals, or by other exposure to infections or contagion may be considered or suspected to be liable to contract or to communicate the disease sought to be suppressed, or to be prevented from spreading.

SEC. 2. Whenever any animal shall be slaughtered under any order of the Governor for the purpose of suppressing or of preventing the spread of any infectious or contagious disease, the compensation to be made by the State to the owner shall be computed upon the basis of allowing for any diseased animal the actual value, if any, at the time of slaughter: for any animal that has been kept in the same stable, pen, field, pasture, or yard with a deceased animal, two-thirds of the sound value; and in the case of any other animal so slaughtered, the full value at the time of slaughter, without regard to the depreciation due to exposure, or suspicion of exposure, to infection or contagion: Provided, however, that if the carcass of any animal so slaughtered shall be sold for more than the amount which the owner would be entitled to receive as compensation aforesaid, the excess shall be paid to such owner: And provided further, that no compensation shall be made under the provisions of this section or otherwise to any person who shall wilfully have concealed the existence of disease among his animals or upon his premises, or who shall in any way by act or by wilful neglect have contributed to the spread of the disease sought to be suppressed, or prevented from spreading.

SEC. 4. This Act shall take effect immediately.

PENNSYLVANIA.

AN ACT to PREVENT the EXTENSION of DISEASE among CATTLE.

SECTION 1. Be it enacted, &c., that it shall not be lawful for any person who may own any cattle or sheep affected by the disease known as pleuro-pneumonia, or other contagious or infectious disease, to sell or otherwise dispose of any cattle, either alive or slaughtered, from the premises where such disease is known to exist, nor for a period of two months after such disease shall have disappeared from said premises.

SEC. 2. That no cattle or sheep shall be allowed to run at large in any township or borough where any contagious disease prevails; and the constables of such townships are hereby authorised and required to take up and confine any cattle to found running at large until called for and until all costs are paid. And in townships where there are no constables, it shall be the duty of the township clerk to perform this service; and the said officer shall be entitled to receive one dollar for each head of cattle so taken up. And any officer who shall refuse to perform the duties of this Act shall be liable to a fine of ten dollars.

SEC. 3. Any person offending against the provisions of the first section of this Act shall be guilty of a misdemeanor, and upon conviction be sentenced to pay a fine not exceeding five hundred dollars or undergo an imprisonment not exceeding six months.

Approved the 12th day of April, A.D. 1866.

AN ACT to PREVENT the SPREAD of CONTAGIOUS or INFECTIOUS PLEURO-PNEUMONIA among CATTLE in this STATE.

SECTION 1. Be it enacted, &c., that whenever it shall be brought to the notice of the Governor of this State that the disease known as contagious or infectious pleuro-pneumonia exists among the cattle in any of the counties in this State, it shall be his duty to take measures promptly to suppress the disease and prevent it from spreading.

SEC. 2. That for such purpose the Governor shall have power, and he is hereby authorised, to issue his proclamation stating that the said infectious or contagious disease exists in any county or counties of the State, and warning all persons to seclude all animals in their possession that are affected with such disease, or have been exposed to the infection or contagion thereof, and ordering all persons to take such precautions against the spreading of such disease as the nature thereof may in his judgment render necessary or expedient; to order that any premises, farm, or farms where such disease exists or has existed be put in quarantine, so that no domestic animal be removed from said places so quarantined, and to prescribe such regulations as he may judge necessary or expedient to prevent infection or contagion being communicated in any way from the places so quarantined; to call upon all sheriffs and deputy sheriffs to carry out and enforce the provisions of such proclamations, orders, and regulations; and it shall be the duty of all the sheriffs and deputy sheriffs to obey and observe all orders and instructions which they may receive from the Governor in the premises; to employ such and so many medical and veterinary practitioners, and such other persons as he may from time to time

o 11711.

deem necessary to assist him in performing his duty as set forth in the first section of this Act, and to fix their compensation; to order all or any animals coming into the State to be detained at any place or places for the purpose of inspection and examination; to prescribe regulations for the destruction of animals affected with the said infectious or contagious disease, and for the proper disposition of their hides and carcasses, and of all objects which might convey infection or contagion: Provided, that no animal shall be destroyed unless first examined by a medical or veterinary practitioner in the employ of the Governor as aforesaid; to prescribe regulations for the disinfection of all premises, buildings, and railway cars, and of objects from or by which infection or contagion may take place or be conveyed; to alter or modify, from time to time, as he may deem expedient, the terms of all such proclamations, orders, and regulations, and to cancel or withdraw the same at any time.

SEC. 3. That all the necessary expenses incurred, under direction or by authority of the Governor in carrying out the provisions of this Act, shall be paid by the treasurer upon the warrant of the auditor-general, on being certified as correct by the Governor: Provided, that animals coming from a neighbouring State that have passed a veterinary examination in said State and have been quarantined and discharged, shall not be subject to the provisions of this Act.

Approved the 1st day of May, A.D. 1879.

RHODE ISLAND.

PUBLIC STATUTES (revised 1881).

CHAPTER 84.—Of CONTAGIOUS DISEASE among CATTLE.

SECTION 1. Every person bringing into the State neat cattle or other animals which he knows to be infected with any infectious or contagious disease, or who shall expose such cattle or other animals known to him to be so infected, to other cattle and animals not infected with such disease, shall be fined not less than one hundred dollars nor more than five hundred dollars.

SEC. 2. The town councils of the several towns may pass such ordinances as they may think proper, to prevent the spread of infectious or contagious diseases among cattle and other animals within their respective towns, and may prescribe penalties for the violation thereof, not exceeding twenty dollars for any one offence.

SEC. 3. The State Board of Health may prohibit the introduction of any cattle or other domestic animals into that State. Every person who shall bring, transport, or introduce any cattle or other domestic animals into the State, after said board or any one of them shall have published for five successive days in such newspapers published in this State as the said board may direct, an order forbidding such introduction, shall be fined not exceeding three hundred dollars for every such offence; and every officer or agent of any company or other person who shall violate such order shall be subject to the fine aforesaid. In case of the introduction into the State of cattle or other domestic animals, contrary to the order of said board, the introduction of each animal shall be deemed a separate and distinct offence.

SEC. 4. Said board shall endeavour to obtain full information in relation to any contagious disease which may prevail among cattle or other domestic animals near the border of the State, and shall publish and circulate such information in their discretion; and should any such disease break out or should there be reasonable suspicion of its existence among cattle or other domestic animals in any town in the State, they shall examine the cases, and publish the result of their examination, for the benefit of the public.

SEC. 5. Said board may appoint suitable and discreet persons, on or near the several highways, turnpike roads, railroads, and thoroughfares in the State, who shall inquire into all violations of this chapter, and report the same to said board.

SEC. 6. Every person who shall sell, or offer to sell, any milk from any such cattle or other domestic animals, shall be fined not exceeding one thousand dollars, or to be imprisoned not exceeding two years, either or both, in the discretion of the court.

SEC. 7. Said board may make all necessary regulations for the prevention, treatment, cure, and extirpation of such disease; and the value of all cattle or other domestic animals killed on the written order of said board shall be appraised by three disinterested persons to be appointed by said board, such appraisal to be made immediately before the cattle or other domestic animals are killed, and the amount of such appraisal shall be paid by the State to the owner of such cattle or other domestic animals; and every person who shall fail to comply with any regulation so made shall be fined not exceeding three hundred dollars, or be imprisoned not exceeding one year.

SEC. 8. Whenever said board shall make and publish any regulations concerning the extirpation, cure, or treatment of cattle, or other domestic animals infected with or which have been exposed to any contagious disease, such regulations shall supersede the regulations made by the authorities of the several towns and cities upon the same subject; and the operation of such regulations made by said authorities shall be suspended during the time those made by said board shall be in force.

SEC. 10. All prosecutions for offences against the provisions of this chapter shall be commenced within thirty days after the same shall have been committed, and not afterwards.

In force on and after February 1, 1882.

VERMONT.

(REVISED LAWS, 1880.)

SECTION 4013. A person who drives or brings neat cattle into a town in this State from another State, or is accessory thereto, knowing that any of them have the disease or have been exposed to the disease known as pleuro-pneumonia, shall forfeit to the town not more than $500, or be imprisoned not more than twelve months and not less than one month, in the discretion of the court.

SEC. 4014. A town, at a meeting held for that purpose, may establish regulations, appoint officers or agents, and raise and appropriate money to prevent and arrest the spread or circumscribe the effect of the cattle disease known as pleuro-pneumonia as such town deems expedient.

SEC. 4015. The selectmen may perform all acts and make all rules and regulations for and in behalf of the town necessary to carry into effect the powers conferred on the town by this chapter, until the town otherwise orders at a meeting holden for that purpose.

SEC. 4016. Every person bringing into this State any neat cattle or other domestic animals which he knows to be infected with any infectious or contagious disease, or who shall expose such cattle or other animals known to him to be so infected to other cattle and animals not infected with such disease, shall be fined not less than $100 nor more than $500.

SEC. 4017. The selectmen of the several towns and the board of aldermen of the several cities of this State may make and enforce such regulations as they may think proper to prevent the spread of infectious or contagious diseases among cattle and other domestic animals within their respective towns and cities, and shall inquire into all such cases coming to their knowledge, and shall immediately report the same to the Governor. Any person who shall knowingly violate or refuse to obey any such regulation made by such town or city authorities shall be liable to a fine of $100.

SEC. 4018. The Governor may appoint a board of cattle commissioners, to consist of three members, whenever in his judgment the public safety may require, and may terminate their commissions whenever in his judgment the public safety may permit. The compensation of such commissioners shall not exceed three —— each per day for actual service, in addition to their travelling and other expenses necessarily incurred.

SEC. 4019. Such commissioners may prohibit the introduction of any cattle or other domestic animals believed to be infected with any contagious disease, or having been exposed thereto, into this State, but may not prohibit the transportation of the same in cars through the State, and every person who shall bring, transport, or introduce any cattle or other domestic animals into this State after said commissioners have issued an order forbidding the same, and such order shall have been published for three successive days in such newspapers published in this State as the commissioners may direct, shall pay to the treasurer of the State a fine of not more than $300 for every offence, and every officer or agent of any company, or other person who shall violate such order, shall be subject to the fine aforesaid. In case of the introduction into this State at the same time of a number of cattle or other domestic animals contrary to the orders of such commissioners, the introduction of each animal shall be deemed a separate and distinct offence.

SEC. 4020. Such commissioners shall endeavour to obtain full information in relation to any contagious disease which may prevail among cattle or other domestic animals near the borders of the State, and shall publish and circulate such information at their discretion; and should any such disease break out, or should their be reasonable suspicion of its existence among cattle or other domestic animals in any town in this State, they shall examine the cases and publish the result of their examination for the benefit of the public; such commissioners are also hereby authorised to examine under oath, in the several towns and cities in this State, all persons possessing or believed to possess knowledge of any material facts concerning the existence or dissemination or danger of dissemination of diseases among cattle or other domestic animals, and for this purpose shall have all the power now conferred by law upon justices of the peace to compel the attendance and testifying of such witnesses; and all costs and expenses incurred in procuring the attendance of such witnesses shall be allowed and paid to the commissioners from the treasury of the treasury of the State, upon the same being certified to the Governor and approved by him; and the auditor of accounts is hereby authorised to draw his order on the treasurer for such sum as shall be so certified and approved.

SEC. 4021. When any contagious disease exists in the State among cattle or other domestic animals, said board may quarantine all inflicted animals, or such as they suppose have been exposed to contagion; may prohibit any animal from passing on or over any of the highways near the place of quarantine; may enter upon any premises where there are animals supposed to be infected with any disease, and make all investigations and regulations necessary for the prevention, treatment, cure, and extirpation of such disease, and any person who shall knowingly violate or refuse to obey any regulation or order of such commissioners, shall be liable to a fine of one hundred dollars for each violation or refusal.

SEC. 4022. If any person during the existence of said board shall sell or offer to sell any cattle or other domestic animals, or any part or parts thereof, known to him to be infected with any contagious disease, or with any disease dangerous to the public health, he shall be fined not more than one thousand dollars, ro be imprisoned not exceeding two years, or both, at the discretion of the court.

SEC. 4023. The value of all cattle or other domestic animals killed by the written order of the commissioners shall be appraised by three disinterested persons, to be appointed by the commissioners, such appraisal to be made just before the cattle or other domestic animals are killed; and the amount of such appraisal shall be paid by the State to the owners of such animals; and every person who shall fail to comply with any regulation by them so made shall be fined not more than three hundred dollars, or be imprisoned not more than one year.

SEC. 4024. Whenever the commissioners shall make and publish any regulations concerning the extirpation, cure, or treatment of cattle or other domestic animals infected with or which have been exposed to any contagious disease, such regulations shall supersede the regulations made by the selectmen of the several towns, or the board of aldermen of the several cities upon the same subject; and the operation of such regulations made by said authorities shall be suspended during the time those made by the commissioners as aforesaid shall be in force.

SEC. 4025. The commissioners shall keep a record of their doings, and report the same to the Governor in the month of September next after their appointment, unless sooner required by the Governor.

SEC. 4026. All orders, appointments, and notices from the commissioners shall bear the signatures of a majority of said commissioners.

SEC. 4026. Any prosecution for a violation of any of the provisions of this Act shall be commenced within thirty days from the commission thereof.

LONDON: Printed by EYRE and SPOTTISWOODE,
Printers to the Queen's most Excellent Majesty.
For Her Majesty's Stationery Office.

FOREIGN OFFICE.

MISCELLANEOUS SERIES, 1886.

No. 2.

REPORTS ON SUBJECTS OF GENERAL AND COMMERCIAL INTEREST.

UNITED STATES.

REPORT FROM MR. VICTOR DRUMMOND

ON THE

EXTRACTION OF SUGAR FROM SORGHUM AND MAIZE.

REFERENCE TO PREVIOUS REPORT [C. 2472] Commercial No. 10, 1880.

Printed under the Superintendence of Her Majesty's Stationery Office,
By HARRISON AND SONS,
Printers in Ordinary to Her Majesty.
AND SOLD BY
Messrs. Hansard and Son, 13, Great Queen Street, W.C., and 32, Abingdon Street, Westminster;
Messrs. Eyre and Spottiswoode, East Harding Street, Fleet Street;
Messrs. Adam and Charles Black, Edinburgh;
Messrs. Alex. Thom and Co. (Limited), and Messrs. Hodges, Figgis, and Co., Dublin.

Price Twopence.

UNITED STATES.

Mr Drummond to the Earl of Rosebery.

My Lord,   *Munich, July* 5, 1886.

WHEN serving as Her Majesty's Secretary of Legation a Washington five years ago, there were two matters in which I took special interest, and upon which I reported at the time: one was ensilage, the other was the extraction of sugar from sorghum and maize. I believe I was the first person who brought to public notice in England by my reports these profitable aids to agriculture. The first I considered would be of advantage to our agriculturists at home, the second to our colonists. The former already holds an important position in England, and the second will, I feel sure, from the fresh statements I am enabled to bring to public attention, meet with that consideration which I consider due to those two gentlemen, Professor Collier and Mr. Stewart, who have now for some years devoted their time and intelligence towards bringing this new industry to success. In the future, I confidently believe that their labour will result in a profitable industry for our colonies and cheaper sugar for ourselves, and to this subject we should begin to pay particular attention, as it is possible if we do not do so that we shall find the United States sending us the sugar our own colonists should have produced. I consider it a duty to preface my statements by apologising for writing on a subject which no longer concerns me, having left the United States so long ago; but the fact is, I have never dropped the matter, having been in correspondence with Messrs. Collier and Stewart ever since I first reported upon the results they obtained in their production of sugar from the plants mentioned. They have apparently met with great success, and as they have been good enough to inform me of the progress they have made, I consider myself justified in continuing my remarks thereupon, which I now do in the following statement:— Every possible information was given in my reports of the 11th November, 1878, and of the 6th December, 1879,* and I hope that persons interested will refer back to them. Of course, it is well known that maize and sorghum contain sugar, but until lately no recognised process has been able to extract it profitably. *[Mr. Drummond's reports on sorghum sugar, 1878–1879.]*

Mr. A. C. Stewart, of Murrysville, Pennsylvania, was the first person to obtain the sugar in larger quantities than formerly, by what has been called the Stewart process. His experiments succeeded so well, that when I was at Washington in 1878 they attracted the attention of the then Director of Agriculture, my friend General W. Le Duc, who thereupon instructed Professor Collier, chemist of the Agricultural Department, to make experiments with Mr. Stewart's system. These were successfully carried out, and proved the use of Mr. Stewart's process, for the professor says in his first report: "In no case either with corn or sorghum did I fail to obtain satisfactory results in the way of crystallisation." I must add, however, that in later experiments the professor produced tons of sugar from these *[Mr. Stewart's first experiments. Mr. Stewart's method. Successful experiments carried out by Agricultural Department, Washington, 1878.]*

---

* Commercial No. 1 (1879), Commercial No. 10 (1880).

Other methods used successfully.

Mr. Stewart's new and important discoveries.

Maize more important than cane or sorghum for sugar production.

Mr. Stewart's reports upon mode of treatment of controlling the vital energies of corn or sorghum plants.

Sugar extracted from the tropical cane in its immature state.

Professor Collier's results obtained in production of sugar from sorghum.

Mr. Collier's reasons for believing that sorghum and not maize is

plants by other methods. I now come to the present state of progress made by both Professor Collier and Mr. Stewart. The latter wrote to me in January, 1884, that he had only just completed his final results of research, and that he had been rewarded with a discovery which placed maize far ahead of any other plant that can be grown in temperate climates for the production of sugar. He said, "This consists in the fact that the vital energies of the plant can be so controlled that it may be made to produce regularly not only a full crop of the ripened grain, but also, in addition, an increase in the saccharine secretion in the piece of the stem, equal to at least 30 per cent. above what it has heretofore been found to contain in its best normal condition. This is said to be brought about by simple means during the period of growth, the natural life of the plant being much prolonged by the operation, and a process of development in the stem inaugurated, which does not go on if the plant is left to itself." Mr. Stewart goes on to say, "When it is considered that the corn stalk thus reaches a development of saccharine richness, which ranks it fully with sugar-cane, that it is attained within a shorter season than is necessary to ripen sorghum generally, and that a full crop of grain (ripe) is secured at a mere trifling expense from the same plant, you can judge how far these results place us in advance of anything that could be done in 1880." The cost of the sugar all told it appears is 2 c. per lb. (say $1\frac{1}{4}d.$), and even less, for lower grades. In a printed report which I received last year from Mr. Stewart, and which I annex herewith, he enters more fully into the mode of treatment, and his statements are of such a nature as to warrant, it appears to me, the attentive interest of our agricultural scientists, for Mr. Stewart says "that he can control the vital energies of growing corn or sorghum, so as to prevent the exhaustion and death of the plant, naturally following the ripening of the grain;" and in the practical results obtained, it will be observed that he claims 55 per cent. of juice can be extracted, a grain of one-third above what is commonly obtained from sugar-cane; and in a letter to me he says that by the use of means both chemical and mechanical, which has taken years to develop, the new process now extracts nine-tenths of sugar.

Mr. Stewart also appears to be able to extract easily sugar of the best quality from the tropical cane in its immature state—a condition, he says, which it was thought to be suitable only for the production of an inferior syrup. Mr. Stewart is, I believe, taking steps for securing patents in Europe and the European colonies, and for the organisation of an English company to control them.

His process was to have been exhibited at the Inventions' Exhibition, but I was sorry to hear from him that in this he had been disappointed. I shall now pass from Mr. Stewart's results in the production of sugar from maize (which he believes is beyond the reach of rivalry from either sorghum or beet), and concern myself with the results obtained in the production of sugar from sorghum, the labour of Professor Collier, lately of the Agricultural Department at Washington, and who, owing to the means at his disposal when there, must have carried out even more experiments than Mr. Stewart here. I am on my own ground, for I constantly visited this courteous scientist in regard to the matter, and watched the progress he made to actual results with the interest of an enthusiast. Specimens of the sugar obtained at that time I forwarded to Mr. Giffen at the Board of Trade.

Mr. Collier differs from Mr. Stewart, inasmuch as he believes that sorghum is the sugar plant of the future, and not maize. This he explained some time ago before the New York Chambers of Commerce, and which, as far as I know, has not as yet been contradicted. He bases his argument in favour of sorghum on the fact that it can be planted much closer than maize, which would therefore give a larger quantity of sorghum stalks, together with seed. Again, maize is cured or dried on the stalk, and it would be difficult to dry it in any other way, whereas sorghum can be topped and dried upon the field. Also, maize juices, though often rich in sugar, are not so regular in their sugar contents in a general way as those of sorghum. In showing this result, I enclose herewith two tables I have taken from the report published by the Agricultural Department at Washington in 1881, together with some explanatory remarks thereupon by Mr. Collier, who is of opinion that the sorghum industry is to become one of the greatest and most profitable of industries; and what an advantage to consumers if, as he states, sugar can be made for 2 c. a pound, and ½ c. for the lowest grades. Mr. Collier is not in the least antagonistic to sugar being extracted from corn as an industry, and does not doubt of its success; on the contrary, he advocates it being carried out; he only maintains that sorghum as a sugar plant is far superior. Both Mr. Collier and Mr. Stewart are of opinion that sorghum and maize are the coming rivals of beet, and that later it will be driven out of the field in the race between these plants. *the sugar plant of the future.* *Messrs. Collier and Stewart believe sorghum and maize are the coming rivals of beet.*

The following statement made by Professor Collier at a meeting of the National Grange, held at Washington in 1884, may be read with advantage:— *Mr. Collier's statement at agricultural meeting at Washington, 1884.*

"In 1880 the States reporting approximately 1,000,000 gallons of sorghum syrup or more were as follows:—

	Gallons.
West Virginia	817,168
North Carolina	964,662
Georgia	981,152
Mississippi	1,062,140
Arkansas	1,118,364
Alabama	1,163,451
Ohio	1,229,852
Kansas	1,429,476
Indiana	1,741,853
Iowa	2,064,020
Illinois	2,265,993
Kentucky	2,962,965
Tennessee	3,776,212
Missouri	4,129,593

"As will be seen from the above, this industry is already widely distributed over the county, and has already reached large proportions. Already the acreage in sorghum, as shown by the last census, is sufficient to yield, if only the crop had been worked at the proper time for sugar, at the least 12 per cent. of all the sugar we import. From the recent results attained by the pioneers in this new sorghum sugar industry, I think there is no good reason to doubt, and indicate that within a very few years we may render ourselves as a people wholly independent of other nations for our sugar supply.

"Indeed, I think that it is possible to produce sugar from sorghum with greater profit than from sugar-cane in Cuba, even under the most favourable conditions. It may appear somewhat hazardous to venture any prediction, but I think that within a decade we shall produce our own sugar, and by 1900 shall export sorghum sugar to Europe. That such results to me appear possible and even probable will be seen to follow from these few well-established facts:—

"1. About 38 per cent. of all the cultivated land in the United States, including the grass lands, is at present devoted to the cultivation of

Indian corn, thus showing that the conditions of soil and climate in our country combine to make the production of maize profitable.

"2. The demands made upon the soil, and the conditions of climate necessary to the full development of sorghum, are practically identical with those made by and necessary to maize.

"3. The methods of cultivation of the two crops are identical, so that in every township of the country these methods are practically understood.

"4. The greater part of the maize consumed in this country is used for the purpose of feeding and fattening swine, and numerous analyses of several different varieties of sorghum seed have shown that the proximate chemical composition of sorghum seed is identical with that of maize, the sorghum seed differing no more from maize in composition than does one variety of maize from another.

"5. Numerous feeding experiments have established the fact that for feeding and fattening purposes sorghum seed is the equivalent of maize, and may be substituted for it.

"6. As much sorghum seed may be produced from an acre as of maize on the same land; and wherever maize may be grown successfully in this country, one variety or another of sorghum may be as successfully grown.

"7. Fully 99 per cent. of the sorghum grown in the world during the past 100 years has been grown solely for the seed and the forage obtained in the leaves, and abundant testimony is given that, for the seed alone, the crop may be profitably grown, while many of those using the stalks for syrup and sugar declare that the seed enables them to produce the stalks free of cost. Indeed, it is probably true that during the past 1,000 years more of the human family have mainly subsisted upon the seed of sorghum than upon wheat and corn together.

"8. It is only after the seed of any variety of sorghum is quite mature that the maximum of sugar in the stalks is attained, so that there is nothing to prevent the securing of both the maximum of seed and the maximum of sugar from the crop of sorghum.

"9. Many thousands of analyses of over 50 varieties of sorghum have conclusively established the fact that at maturity the stalk of sorghum contains an amount of sugar equal to that found in the best sugar-cane grown in Louisiana; and already as has been shown, by processes and appliances identical with those employed upon the sugar plantations of Cuba and Louisiana, several hundred tons of sorghum sugar have been put upon the market in competition with sugar from the tropical sugar-cane.

"10. The testimony of numerous manufacturers of syrups from sorghum shows that the syrup may be manufactured at an expense, varying in different localities and with different manufacturers, from 12 to 25 c. per gallon, from cane delivered free at the mill, even when working with small mills instead of the improved appliances of the large plantations.

"11. A yield of six to eight pounds of sugar from the gallon of syrup, made at the proper time, may be fairly expected, and thus the sugar would cost, according to the expense of manufacture above given, from $1\frac{1}{2}$ c. to 4 c. per pound, without any allowance for the molasses.

"12. Excellent sugar has been made from sorghum, and where an accurate account of all expenses was kept, including cultivation of crop, but no account made of the seed, the expense of production of the sugar did not exceed $4\frac{1}{2}$ c. per pound.

"In view of the results already attained, I have no doubt that sugar may even now be produced at an expense of not over 2 c. per pound, and I believe that within a decade it will be produced in this country from sorghum at an expense of not over 1 c. per pound."

I would particularly request attention to facts Nos. 6 to 13. Again, with respect to this great economical question, Mr. Collier, in his address before the Chambers of Commerce of the State of New York, states as follows with reference to his experiments from 1877 to 1880.

Mr. Collier's statement before Chambers of Commerce, New York.

In my preliminary experiments with sorghum and maize stalks, I demonstrated the fact that sugar could readily be obtained from both, and in quantity so great that the continuance of the investigation was rendered advisable. I succeeded in obtaining from syrup prepared from inferior sorghum, 34·6 per cent. of its weight of sugar polarising 94°; and from syrup from maize stalks, 32 per cent. of its weight in sugar polarising 90°. The molasses from the sorghum sugar was 65·4 per cent. of the weight of the syrup, and polarised 43°; that from the maize sugar was 68 per cent., and polarised 36°. In all, fifteen experiments were made from sorghum and maize stalks in 1878. In 1879 I planted four varieties of sorghum, and the crop was cultivated as maize, and when the crop had nearly reached its maximum in height, although not yet in blossom, daily examinations of stalks from each variety were made, and it was found that in the case of each of the four varieties the juice expressed contained at the first a small quantity (1 per cent. or less) of crystallisable sugar, and a comparatively large quantity (3 or 4 per cent.) of uncrystallisable sugar. It was found that, as the crop went on to maturity, the crystallisable sugar rapidly increased until it reached its maximum, and that this maximum was equal to the content of sugar in the juices of sugar-canes. It was also found that this maximum, when attained, was maintained for many weeks. It was also found that the uncrystallisable sugar slowly decreased as the sorghum matured, until it was no more in quantity than in the juice of sugar-cane, and also that this minimum of uncrystallisable sugar was contemporaneous with the maximum of crystallised sugar.

Sugar from sorghum and maize stalks.

Again, and most important of all, it was found in every case that this maximum of true sugar was never attained until the plant had perfectly matured its seed.

These results were abundantly confirmed in 1880, when 38 varieties were thus examined and 2,718 analyses made; in 1881, when 35 varieties were examined and 1,178 analyses made. In 1879 there were made 136 analyses of the four varieties. These results, therefore, which I submit, are obtained from a mass of testimony (4,032 analyses), as great as establishes the truth of any conclusion in science with which I am familiar, and it is only right that I quote here the unanimous opinion of this committee of the National Academy of Sciences, who, upon page 25 of their report, declare that the methods by which these results were ascertained "are among the best known to science;" and upon 26th page, where they say: "The care with which the methods for the determination of cane-sugar have been tested, and the probable error determined, enlists our confidence. The accuracy and constancy of the results have been ascertained as far as, in the present state of our knowledge, such end can well be attained. The reserve with which the chemist has refrained from accepting the results as conclusive, until, by repetition and variations in the methods, he had exhausted the means at his command to prove them to be erroneous, is in the true spirit of scientific research."

Sorghum jucies.

The average results obtained in 1880 are given in the following table; the successive stages, from 1 to 19, being reckoned from about a week before the seed head had made its appearance at the top of the p ant to many weeks after the complete maturity of the seed. Stage 5 was when the plant was in blossom, stage 7 was when the seed was in the milk, stage 9 was when the seed was in a doughy condition, and stage 11 was when the seed was dry, hard, and fully ripe :—

UNITED STATES.

GENERAL Average of the Composition of Sorghum Juices, at different Stages of Development, of 38 Varieties.

Stage of Development.	Length of Stalk, in feet.	Diameter of Stalk at Butt, in inches.	Unstripped Weight of Stalk, in pounds.	Stripped Weight of Stalk, in pounds.	Per cent. of Juice Expressed.	Specific Gravity of Juice.	Per cent. Sucrose in Juice.	Per cent. Glucose in Juice.	Per cent. Solids, not Sugars, in Juice.	Per cent. Available Sugar in Juice.	Number of Juices Analysed.
1	7·5	·9	1·93	1·34	59·06	1·031	1·76	4·29	1·75	−4·28	58
2	8·5	·9	1·93	1·46	59·60	1·036	2·96	4·45	1·86	−3·35	69
3	8·8	·9	1·78	1·39	59·67	1·037	3·51	4·50	1·78	−2·77	57
4	9·1	·8	1·83	1·44	61·61	1·041	4·34	4·34	1·91	−1·91	70
5	9·3	·9	1·96	1·55	63·05	1·045	5·13	4·15	1·92	−·84	75
6	9·7	·9	2·02	1·60	62·79	1·050	6·50	3·99	2·45	+·06	62
7	9·7	·9	2·11	1·55	63·85	1·052	7·38	3·86	2·19	1·33	70
8	9·3	1·0	2·10	1·63	65·68	1·055	7·69	3·83	2·37	1·49	111
9	8·8	·9	1·87	1·40	64·88	1·058	8·95	3·19	2·42	3·34	266
10	8·9	·9	1·81	1·38	64·83	1·061	9·98	2·60	2·50	4·88	217
11	9·1	·9	1·94	1·48	65·02	1·063	10·66	2·35	2·72	5·59	166
12	9·0	·9	1·81	1·87	63·39	1·065	11·18	2·07	2·83	6·28	170
13	9·1	·9	1·86	1·34	62·99	1·066	11·40	2·03	2·82	6·55	183
14	8·9	·9	1·82	1·32	61·72	1·067	11·76	1·88	2·96	6·92	191
15	8·9	·9	1·81	1·32	60·45	1·067	11·69	1·81	3·15	6·73	217
16	8·7	·9	1·73	1·22	61·20	1·070	12·40	1·64	3·32	7·44	339
17	7·7	·9	1·69	1·25	60·17	1·078	13·72	1·56	4·07	8·09	197
18	8·5	·9	1·44	1·15	62·09	1·069	11·92	1·85	3·42	6·65	191
19	8·5	1·0	1·81	1·53	56·04	1·080	12·08	3·09	3·62	5·37	30

By reference to the table it will be seen that the length and weight of the stalks at the first stage was equal to the length and weight at any subsequent stage, thus showing that, though the maximum weight of the crop had been attained at the first stage, there was less than 2 per cent. of sugar in the juice, while the average percentage of sugar in the juice at the 17th stage was 13·72.

It is also to be observed that the average amount of juice expressed during the earlier stages was appreciably less than at later stages, a result which few would predict.

In the column headed available sucrose is given the difference between the sucrose in the juice and the sum of the glucose and solids not sugars, since it is estimated that these two constitutents of the juice will hold in solution their own weight of sugar, so that only so much sugar can actually be obtained as sugar as is present in excess of the sum of glucose and solids not sugar.

It is also noticeable that during the first five stages, although there is an average of nearly 4 per cent. of sugar in the juice, none of it is available, and in fact the amount of available sugar is a minus quantity. The importance of this will be referred to at another place. It will be seen that the average available sugar for the last eight stages equals 6·76 per cent. of the juice, and also that it was not until after the eleventh stage (at which time the seed is ripe, hard, and dry) that the maximum of sugar in the plant is reached.

It is also to be remembered that the above table represents the average results of 38 varieties of sorghum, and of a large number of analyses at each separate stage—in all, 2,739 analyses—so that the above results may be regarded confidently as near approximations to the truth.

It will be observed how regularly the specific gravity of the juice increases with the increase in the percentage of sucrose.

In the following table the average results obtained from the examination of six well-known varieties of sorghum will fairly represent all the others.

The column headed "Days to ripen" represents the number of days required by each variety, from the day of planting to the thorough maturity of the seed, as at this time the maximum amount of sugar in the plant is attained; the other columns represent the average results of analyses of each variety after ripening of the seed. The stripped stalks was the amount actually obtained from that portion of an acre planted with each variety, and calculated to an acre. It will be seen that generally those varieties requiring longer time for maturity yielded a crop of cane proportionately heavier, so that it is desirable to plant, in any given locality, such varieties as may mature in succession, in order to have the longest possible season during which to manufacture the crop, and the largest possible crop of cane which can be grown.

	Days to Ripen.	Per cent. Sucrose in Juice.	Per cent. Glucose in Juice.	Per cent. Solids in Juice.	Per cent. Juice Expressed.	Pounds Stripped Stalks, per acre.
Early amber	80	13·21	1·54	3·28	59·02	28,000
White mammoth	102	13·51	1·18	3·45	62·31	29,340
Links hybrid	101	14·24	·93	3·43	63·53	34,450
Orange	117	13·18	1·58	3·39	61·67	49,000
Liberian	152	14·24	1·67	4·18	60·15	40,000
Honduras	163	12·93	2·11	3·92	64·68	47,250

UNITED STATES.

The average amount of available sugar per acre, indicated by the above results, is given in the following table, and is also estimated on the supposition of 90 per cent. of juice being present in the cane, although, as will be seen, the mill upon an average expressed only about 62 per cent.

	Early Amber.	White Mammoth.	Links Hybrid.	Orange.	Liberian.	Honduras.
Per cent. available sugar in juice	8·39	8·88	9·88	8·21	8·39	6·95
Pounds available sugar, per acre, obtained	1,387	1,623	2,128	2,481	2,019	2,124
Pounds available sugar, per acre, at 90 per cent. juice	2,114	2,345	3,063	3,621	3,020	2,956

It will be seen from the above that the average amount of available sugar present in the juice, actually expressed, from a crop actually grown, equalled 1,960 pounds per acre, while the amount of available sugar actually present in the crop, on the supposition of 90 per cent. of juice, was an average of 2,853 pounds per acre.

Now, surely these are astonishing results, but I believe them to be thoroughly reliable, for they have been fully confirmed not only in the United States, but also in France and Italy, where investigations have been made.

The Italian Government has had similar investigations instituted at the several agricultural experiment stations in Italy; and from the report of the Italian Minister of Agriculture it appears that, in 1883, the average results obtained at Modena, in Northern Italy, from sorghum cane, cut fully 15 days after the seed was quite ripe, were as follows:— *Investigations in Italy.*

Juice expressed from cane	60·53 per cent.
Specific gravity of juice	1·089
Sucrose in juice	17·66 per cent.
Glucose in juice	1·63 ,,

At Reggio, in Southern Italy, cane worked eight days after it had been cut, the average results were:—

Specific gravity of juice	1·072
Sucrose in juice	16·49 per cent.
Glucose in juice	2·20 ,,

The Italian Minister of Agriculture, in his conclusions as to the result of these investigations, says that "these results agree with those obtained in the United States, only the quantity of sucrose and the density of the juice were always somewhat greater in our experiments than was found in America." In the great majority of cases, it is reported, Italian canes which were cut after the seeds were ripe and analysed on the following day, showed a richness in available sugar which is fully equal to the best tropical canes.

In the report of the director of the Agricultural Experiment Station at Vaucluse, near Avignon, France, for 1883, he gives the following analysis of juice from sorghum:— *Investigations in France.*

Juice expressed by mill	60 to 65 per cent.
Sucrose in sugar	16·3 ,,
Glucose in juice	1·7 ,,

(M)

Sugar from sorghum equal to that in the sugar-cane.

He concludes as follows:—"Les résultats obtenus par Monsieur Peter Collier, chimiste du Gouvernement, concordent avec ceux que nous avons donnés plus haut sur la teneur en jus et en sucre."

The presence then in the stalks of fully-matured sorghum, of an amount of sugar practically equal to that found in the sugar-cane of Louisiana, is no longer a matter for doubt, as the following will further verify:—

Sugar in Sorghum.

Analysis of juices from sorghum stalks.

At Attawa-Kansas, from a juice which averaged on three analyses as follows:—

Sucrose	10·23 per cent.
Glucose	2·90 ,,
Other solids	2·80 ,,
Coefficients	64°·2

and which contained, therefore, 184 lbs. of sugar to the ton of cane, of which 118 lbs. were available, they actually obtained 95 lbs. of sugar and 16 gallons of molasses per ton of cane, the sugar being "washed and dried."

Mr. Collier informs me that he grew six varieties of sorghum, and the crop averaged 19 tons of stripped and topped stalks to the acre. The average analysis of the juices during a working period of 100 days was as follows:—

Sucrose	13·56 per cent.
Glucose	1·50 ,,
Other solids	3·61 ,,
Coefficients	72°·6

This shows 244 lbs. of sugar per ton of cane, of which 177 lbs. is available for sugar.

Comparisons of Sugar Canes and Sorghum.

72 juices of four varieties of sugar canes grown upon the Magnolia plantation of Governor Warmouth, 45 miles below New Orleans, gave upon the average the results below. 58 juices of several varieties of sorghum grown in Washington in 1884, and analysed by the same men and methods, gave the average results as below.

		Sugar Canes.	Sorghum.
Sucrose	Per cent ..	13·05	14·76
Glucose	,,	·67	1·27
Other solids	,,	2·82	3·65
Coefficient of purity		78°·9	75°·0
Sugar in ton of cane	Lbs.	235	266
Available sugar in ton of cane	,,	185	199

On the Belair plantation of John Dymond, of 1,200 acres of sugar cane, 25 miles below New Orleans, Louisiana, the following results were obtained as the average of 68 juices, and of the syrups made from these juices. The juices were from 40 varieties of sugar-cane.

			Juices.	Syrups.
Sucrose	.. ..	Per cent...	10·63	35·32
Glucose	.. ..	,,	1·36	6·11
Other solids	.. ..	,,	2·46	10·74
Coefficients	.. ..		73°·56	67°·70

It will be seen that there was a loss of nearly 6° in the coefficient of purity, and, therefore, of so much of the available sugar through their method of defecation.

By contrast, I give Mr. Collier's average results from the analysis of 92 juices from 14 varieties of sorghum, and of the 92 syrups made from these juices.

			Juices.	Syrups.
Sucrose	.. ..	Per cent...	13·55	54·47
Glucose	.. ..	,,	1·15	3·70
Other solids	.. ..	,,	2·79	7·73
Coefficients	.. ..		77°·48	82°·66

It will be seen that Mr. Collier's juices were purer and richer in sugar than the sugar-cane juices, and also that, as Mr. Collier points out, he increased by his defecation the coefficients over 5°, and consequently, by so much, increased the available sugar.

The above clearly demonstrates that sorghum juices will yield their sugar as readily as sugar-cane juices, and in Mr. Collier's 92 experiments there was not the least trouble in securing perfect crystallisation of the syrups. *Sorghum juices yield their sugar as readily as sugar-cane juices.*

An analysis of the foregoing results shows that while in the average results upon the Belair plantation there was a "gain" of at least 35 per cent. in the glucose, and a "gain" of at least 31 per cent. in the other solids, not sugars, by their methods of defecation, in Mr. Collier's work there was on the other hand a "loss" of at least 20 per cent. in the glucose, and a "loss" of at least 31 per cent. in the other solids, not sugars, which accounts for their "loss" in coefficient of purity, and Mr. Collier's "gain" in the coefficient of purity by his methods employed. *Mr. Collier's improved method of defecation.*

I will here add certain results secured last season, sustaining the conclusions of the above statements, furnished me by Mr. Collier. *Results obtained last year confirming statements made.*

Mr. Clinton Bozarth, of Cedar Falls, Iowa, grew and worked 85 acres of sorghum. His entire expenses, including 2 dol. 50 c. per acre rent of land, were 1,289 dol., say 258*l.*, and he sold his products for 5,020 dol., say 1,004*l.* Mr. Bozarth says that he can produce sugar at a cost of 2 c. per pound, and molasses at 5 c. per gallon. His net profits amounted to 43 dol. 76 c. per acre, or say 8*l.* 15s.

Mr. J. W. Shurmaker, of Dervilt, Nebraska, also gives detailed estimates, and shows a net profit per acre of 40 dol., or 8*l.*

Mr. J. T. Porter, Redwing, Minnesota, said that his syrups yield 50 per cent. of their weight in sugar, and that the molasses paid all expenses for cultivation and manufacture, leaving the sugar and seed as net profit, which amounted to over 30 dol. per acre, without counting the seed.

The following are a few noticeable points respecting sorghum cane:— *Sorghum cane and its usefulness.*

(M)

Yield of seed.		The average yield of seed is equal to that of corn, say 26 bushels an acre. This seed is food for man or beast, or for the manufacture of starch, alcohol, or glucose.
Yield of cane.		The yield of the sorghum cane on good corn land varies from 10 to 35 tons per acre.
Yield of sugar and molasses.		100 lbs. of sugar is a reasonable average per ton of cane, if worked when mature. Complete maturity from planting time varies from 90 to 180 days; but 132 lbs. of sugar from a ton of cane is entirely within practical limits, with 12 gallons of molasses.
Prices.		Average price of sorghum sugar in 1883, 6½ c. to 7⅛ c. per lb. (3d. to 3½d.) Molasses average 35 c. per gallon, or say 1s. 4½d. Syrup average, 45 c. per gallon, say 1s. 9d.
Bagasse: its importance.		By usual methods fully one-third of all the sugar found in the cane is left in the bagasse, as it comes from the mill. Now this bagasse is a very important factor. It not only contains a large amount of sugar, but other valuable constituents, and it is, as it comes from the mill, in a mechanical condition admirably adapted for the silo and for eating, as all animals greedily devour it. As ensilage it is excellent fodder.
Bagasse excellent as ensilage.		

The following table gives the average composition of 22 samples of bagasse and the leaves of sorghum; of 26 samples of ordinary ensilage of corn, and two samples of corn stalks, cut while in the silk:—

	Bagasse.	Ensilage.	Corn Stalks.
	Per cent.	Per cent.	Per cent.
Crude fibre	8·80	5·99	4·24
Ash	1·74	1·33	1·16
Albuminoids	2·15	1·37	1·19
Carbhydrates	25·93	10·08	10·48
Fats	··	·79	·57
Water	61·38	80·44	82·36
	100·00	100·00	100·00
Nutritive ratio	1.12	1·7·9	1·9·3

The value of 2,000 lbs. of each of the above, at the value assigned to the several food constituents, viz., 3·4 cents per lb. for albuminoids, 2·93 cents per lb. for fats, and ·72 cents per lb. for carbhydrates, would give the following results:—

	Bagasse.	Ensilage.	Corn Stalks.
	Dol. c.	Dol. c.	Dol. c.
Albuminoids	1 46	0 93	0 81
Fats	0 62	0 46	0 33
Carbhydrates	3 58	1 45	1 51
	5 66	2 84	2 65

From the above averages it appears that the actual money value of bagasse for food is almost exactly double that of ordinary ensilage.

Mr. Collier's new method for removing the sugar from the bagasse. In the United States it is calculated fully one-third of the sugar is lost by the inability of our best mills to press out the juice, but in 1880 Mr. Collier made a series of experiments to find a means to save this sugar, and he was successful in finding that there was no difficulty in removing the sugar entirely from the bagasse, and that a juice as rich in sugar could be obtained as was that expressed from the mill. Six per cent. of the weight of the bagasse was obtained as sugar. The bagasse was, after the experiments, submitted to the ordinary process for the preparation of paper pulp, and a sample was made and submitted to one of the largest paper manufacturers, who pronounced it to be of excellent quality, and worth 4½ c., or 1¾d. per lb. This industry may be added, then, to the production of sugar from sorghum cane, thus utilising a waste product and increasing the profits from the crop.

Bagasse, paper from.

To the above remarks I think I have given enough data as a foundation for the interesting study of what I consider to be a very important agricultural development in America—one which I will now leave to those who desire to pay attention to what may be a new opening to the wealth of agriculturists in our colonies. I have carried out a personal duty by finishing the work I commenced when in the United States, for the same reason that made me bring ensilage to notice, that it might be of advantage to my countrymen. It has been an outside work of pleasure, and I beg herewith to express my thanks both to Mr. Stewart and Mr. Collier for having made me cognisant of the advancement they have made towards securing for their own country results beneficial to those employed in farming.

Mr. Drummond trusts his remarks may be studied, and be useful to British colonists.

Thanks to Messrs. Collier and Stewart.

Any persons who may require further information can of course apply to Mr. Stewart, of Murrysville, Westmoreland county, Pennsylvania, or to Professor Collier, Agricultural Department, Washington, whose statements, I feel convinced, can be fully endorsed by the United States Minister in London, who, I have reason to believe, is friendly to the work the above-named gentlemen have given their time to perfect.

Persons interested should apply to Messrs. Collier and Stewart.

I have, &c.,
(Signed)   VICTOR DRUMMOND.

CORN CANE.

ABSTRACT of a Report on a Method of Perfecting the Development of Sugar in Indian Corn.

(To be submitted to the Committee of the National Academy of Science of the United States on Maize and Sorghum Sugar.)

In an article entitled "Maize and Sorghum as Sugar Plants," contained in the Report of the Department of Agriculture of the United States for the year 1877, afterwards reprinted in book form, I gave to the public the results of some researches of mine, which seemed to indicate that a new source of sugar supply had been found. The nature of the facts as made known, and the full confirmation of them by the public tests made at Washington as they progressed, awoke an interest in the matter as one of great public utility, which was not at all confined to citizens of our own country. As evidence of this, an official report on the subject to the English Government, embracing a reprint of the whole of the article above referred to, was prepared under the direction of Sir Edward Thornton, then British Minister at Washington, by the Hon. Victor Drummond, Secretary of Legation, and published at London in 1879.

But these investigations had not at that time been completed. In fact, so far as they related to Indian corn, they had progressed far enough merely to indicate a line of treatment for that plant which gave promise of final practical success.

The facts, as at first developed, were given to our Commissioner of Agriculture, General W. G. Le Duc, in the year 1878, at his special request (Rep. Dept. of Agriculture, 1877, p. 234), and on the express condition that the Government, as represented by his department, would test my claims in a thoroughly scientific manner, and publish the results, good or bad, to the world. This was done.

The work consumed much time, and partial reports were made during the next three years.

The investigation of the sugar millets (sorghum) having progressed the farthest, they first received attention, and the final results of the tests, as regarding them, were given to the public in a condensed form in the well-known report of the department's work on sorghum sugar in 1882, which was referred to a committee of the National Academy of Science for Investigation, and received its emphatic approval.

The suddenly-revived interest in sorghum following this work, and the substantial results already realised, diverted public attention from Indian corn. This was to be desired; for the reason that the original experiments necessary to determine the exact relative value of that plant for sugar production were not yet finished. Towards the completion of this work I have given much of my time during the past two years.

The outcome has far surpassed my expectations, or indeed any expectations which might reasonably have been based upon any previously known traits of this plant itself, or from analogies furnished by any allied plants. This consists mainly in the discovery which I have made and fully verified the past summer, that the vital energies of the growing corn can be so controlled as to prevent the exhaustion and death of the plant naturally following the ripening of the grain. As a consequence of this, the plant, instead of dying, takes a new lease of life and develops new powers. By a very simple mode of treatment, hereafter to be described, the same individual plant which has already given us its full yield of ripened grain, is now made to live on, secreting sugar, until the cells of the stalk have no more capacity to contain it in the liquid condition.

We have thus a combination never before presented—a cereal and a sugar cane, of the highest type of each, united together in the same individual

The sugar crop is made to follow the grain crop almost without abour or care, and a careful estimate, made with a knowledge of all the details, shows that the entire cost of this sugar, in an unrefined but well crystallised and merchantable condition, will not exceed $\frac{1}{2}$ c. a pound.

The removal of the ear at the proper period secures a full yield of ripe corn in at least as good condition as if the treatment necessary to charge the stalk with sugar had been omitted.

I find a difficulty in expressing this fact so as to convey its full meaning. If the feat could be performed of transforming a dead corn stalk into a living sugar-cane, it would be scarcely less remarkable than the change so produced. It would not only enlarge our ideas as to the limits of human control in the organic world, but, as a practical result, it would inevitably revolutionise sugar manufacture Yet, in effect, we have this transformation literally reproduced, with the difference only that the natural death of the plant invariably following the ripening of the grain is not permitted to ensue.

A man passing along the rows of ripening corn, at the proper time by a mere touch of his hand turns the vital current from the ear to the stem, and the work is done. Thenceforward, the whole economy of the plant is changed. The stalk, instead of dying, continues green, and within its cells the mysterious energy which before busied itself solely in perfecting the grain now works for the elaboration of the juice. What went before to form starch and gluten in the seed now goes to the storing up of sugar in the stalk. The change is not completed for a period of from three to six weeks, during which, if not interfered with, the plant attains its full saccharine development.

Up to the time when this new development is made to begin, the plant, as to its nature, requirements, and treatment under cultivation, is simply Indian corn, as we have always known it. When the change is completed, a glance at its condition, as revealed by the analyses given below, will show that to all intents and purposes it is then a sugar cane. I suggest that the term corn cane be used to designate it when in this new condition.

I have found that under similar conditions the law controlling the saccharine development affects all varieties of maize alike — common field corn as strongly as the so-called "sweet" varieties. Any of the large-stemmed sorts of either kind may be chosen with the utmost confidence in the results being such as above stated. Field corn, however, either white or yellow, is to be taken as the standard.

The history and nature of the changes going on in the living plant have been revealed and traced out in a series of analyses covering them at all points, during the past season, as will appear in the forthcoming report. They are very well expressed in the diagram given below.

		Sugar per ct.	
			— Oct. 10
		—17	
Sugar		—15	
		—13	— Sept. 10
	Grain ripe	—11	
	Ear in milk	—9	
		—7	— Aug. 10
		—5	
Grain	Ear forming	—3	
		—1	
	First silk	—0	
			— July 10
Early growth			— June 10
	Seed planted		— May 10

Explanation.—The light vertical line represents the period of growth of Indian corn, in the latitude of Pittsburgh, Pa., from planting time (about May 10th) to the flowering period. The broken line indicates the period from flowering to natural maturity and the ripening of the grain. With this period sugar formation begins. The heavy line shows the added period of true saccharine development. The per cent. of cane sugar in the juice at each stage is given in the column on the right.

The practical results are:—

1. The production of a full crop of ripened grain.
2. The production of a dense saccharine juice, equal in richness to

that of the sugar-cane, and yielding a sugar equal to that in all respects.

3. This sugar being the result of a natural process of development artificially extended after the ripening of the ear, costs nothing but the expense of manufacturing it.

4. The yield of sugar is greater than from any of the hard-stemmed canes. This comes from the peculiar texture of corn cane, which admits of the use of a new machine, but little, if any, more expensive than the ordinary sugar mill, by which 85 per cent. of juice can be extracted—a gain of one-third above what is commonly obtained from sugar-cane.

5. An entirely new chemical process for the purification of the juice has been put into operation, which secures the most perfect crystallisation and easy drainage of the sugar at an exceedingly low cost.

6. Stock feeding will be made a speciality in connection with this business. A proper use of the residual products of the sugar manufacture will be a source of immense advantage and of profit to the country. Those products are not only in the highest degree nutritious, but in the best condition possible for to animals. There will be no waste, and it will be within the power of our stock-growers to obtain at a low price, and in a compact, commercial form, food products so combined as to be adapted to any requirements. The magnitude of this business as an auxiliary to sugar production cannot but greatly exceed in all points cattle feeding as practised under the beet-sugar system in Europe; especially when we consider that maize not only excels the beet greatly in sugar, producing capacity, but also in its producing at the same time with the sugar, what the other furnishes no equivalent for whatever—its wonderful grain.

Not long ago the editors of the "Journal des Fabricants de Sucre," of Paris, the most influential newspaper in Europe, devoted to the interests of the beet-sugar industry, put into the hands of M. H. Pellet, a distinguished chemist, and member of the French Academy, for analysis, some of the unrefined sorghum sugar produced by the new process in the United States.

Commenting upon M. Pellet's report of the analysis, and the practical results known to have been realised in this country, the editors close a review of the whole subject with the following significant language (translated):—

"The facts which we have related deserve to attract the attention of the agriculturists of our southern districts, where sorghum may perhaps be cultivated under favourable conditions. The manufacturers of beet-sugar cannot longer be indifferent to results like these, which seem to us to announce as near at hand the rivalry of American sorghum."

It is now safe to say that, in all the great maize-growing regions of the globe, the great superiority of corn cane will put it beyond the reach of rivalry from either the beet or sorghum. The latter, however, has qualities which will make it a valuable auxiliary.

Amid many difficulties, I have now brought this work to a close. The full report of it will be given to the public with as little delay as possible. This brief outline is for the benefit of those who desire to know something of its general character and results. I refrain here from giving fuller details of the mode of treatment, to prevent the mistakes which would be made by those attempting to put it into practice without full and exact information of all the conditions upon which success depends.

One thing is now clearly established, which in a practical point of view embraces every other. Sugar can be produced from this new source at a mere fraction of its former cost. A system built up on such a basis cannot but be widespread and lasting In our modern life, no limit can be set to the demand for sugar cheaply produced. It is not over-production that is now paralysing the sugar industries of the world: it is the necessarily high cost of the raw sugar itself as obtained from the ordinary natural sources.

Nor can it be fabricated in any merely artificial way. The late Professor Joseph Henry uttered but the conviction of every investigator in this field when he said that he recognised in the vital influence in nature something "transcending the sagacity of the chemist, and producing groups of atoms of a complex form exceeding his highest skill; operating with the ordinary physical and chemical forces, but knowing no subjection to the laws by which they are governed. . . . The chemist has not yet been found who can make an atom of sugar from the elements of which it is composed."

The construction of the sugar atom is a function of life. It is nature's prerogative, and she holds it in her own hands. This power lies dormant in every stalk of growing corn. This discovery is that man can redress or develop it at his will. Nature presents to us an alternative. We take our choice. And thus the problem is solved.

F. L. STEWART.

Murrysville, Westmoreland, Co. Pa., U.S.A.,
March 30, 1885.

Comparative Value, during the Working Period, of Sorghum and Corn Stalks.

From the following table it is possible to judge quite accurately as to the comparative values of the different canes for the production of sugar. These values are applicable more especially to the latitude of "Washington," and it will be seen later that certain canes which do not stand high in the list, when grown in this section, are very likely to prove valuable where the growing season is longer.

Again, those which mature quickest, and also have a long working period, are the ones especially recommended for culture in more northern latitudes.

In this table the canes are arranged in the order of their comparative value, as shown from the large number of analyses recorded. It must not be inferred, however, that it is possible to state positively that this order may not be somewhat modified by future experience; it certainly would be somewhat changed were any one characteristic of the juice used as the basis of comparison to the exclusion of all others. It has been attempted to give due weight to all the factors which tend to show the good or bad qualities of the canes.

Among the points which have the most direct bearing on the determination as to the value of any cane for any locality are the following :—

1st. Other things being equal, that cane is best adapted to any locality which most quickly reaches the working stage, and longest continues workable. It will be noticed that, judged by this rule, the first eight varieties are superior to those that follow. It appears also that these varieties matured in from 77 to 89 days, and continued workable from 87 to 107 days, or, on an average, over three months. It is very important to have sufficient time in which to work up the crop.

2nd. The average purity of the juice is another very important consideration. This is shown by the column headed "Average exponent;" by this term is meant the percentage of pure crystallisable sugar in the total solids of the juice. As has already been stated in the discussion of the table of specific gravities, the exponent should not fall below 70 for the best results.

3rd. The average available sugar in the juice has very much to do with its value. The figures in this column were calculated by multiplying the figures in the column showing "average per cent. sucrose in juice" by the corresponding figures for "average exponent."

4th. The pounds of juice per acre has much to do with the amount of sugar that can be obtained.

As will be seen, the various canes do not differ very materially in the percentage of juice they can furnish; hence, the pounds of juice per acre depends more directly upon the number and weight of canes which can be raised. By reference to the tables for each variety, it will be seen that several of the varieties standing low in this list (Honduras, Honey Top, &c.) furnish canes much heavier then those standing near the first of the list; hence, if an equal number of such heavy canes could be grown on an acre, the amount of juice must be correspondingly greater.

If, then, the quality of the juice from heavy canes is as good as that from the light, and the season for working is greater, the heavy canes would be preferable, because they would furnish the larger amount of sugar per acre. Unfortunately, this is not the case in this latitude. The first two columns in this table show that the heavier canes do not attain their full growth and maturity in time to be worked up into sugar.

It is fully believed that these heavy canes are well adapted to the more southern parts of the United States, and that in those regions they will reach full maturity in time to leave an ample working period. In fact, several examinations of canes sent from South Carolina a year ago confirm these statements.

If it be supposed, for the sake of comparison, that an equal number of canes of each variety can be grown on an acre of land, the results given in the last three columns will show what amounts of stripped stalks, juice, and available sugar can be obtained on an acre from each variety of corn and sorghum. The number of stalks per acre has been placed at 24,000, which is believed to be a fair estimate.

In comparing these figures with those in the three columns just preceding them, which represent actual results of analyses, it will be seen that the figures do not differ greatly.

6th. After all, the real test of value for any cane is the amount of crystallisable sugar that can be actually separated from the juice obtained from the stalks grown on an acre. This amount will depend very greatly on the quantity and quality of the canes, and upon the promptness and care with which they are worked up after cutting. The figures here given in explanation of the various points which have been discussed have been derived from very carefully conducted work, and they are offered as fair statements of what can and should be attained by careful workers.

Among the essential points worthy of repetition are the following:—

1st. Select a cane that matures quickly; and has as long a working period as possible.

2nd. Do not work the cane too early; the seed should be well matured and quite hard, and the juice should have a specific gravity of 1·066, or higher.

3rd. After cutting the canes, work them up without great delay. It is best to draw directly from the field to the mill as may be needed.

UNITED STATES.

Table No. 96.—TABLE showing the comparative during the Working Period, of all Varieties of Sorghum and Corn Stalks here examined.

#	Name.	Source of Seed.	Number of Days to Maturity.	Number of Days for Working.	Number of Analyses.	Average per cent. Sucrose in Juice.	Average per cent. Glucose in Juice.	Average per cent. other Solids in Juice.	Average Exponent.	Average per cent. Available Sugar.	Average per cent. Juice.	Actually obtained. Stripped Stalks, per Acre. Lbs.	Actually obtained. Juice, per Acre. Lbs.	Actually obtained. Available Sugar, per Acre. Lbs.	Computed at 24,000 Stalks per Acre. Stripped Stalks, per Acre. Lbs.	Computed at 24,000 Stalks per Acre. Juice, per Acre. Lbs.	Computed at 24,000 Stalks per Acre. Available Sugar, per Acre. Lbs.
	VARIETIES OF SORGHUM.																
1	Early amber	D. Smith	77	99	80	12·42	1·55	2·98	73·15	9·11	60·02	27,073	16,249	1,480	25,520	15,317	1,395
2	"	Plant Seed Company	80	99	70	12·00	1·51	3·18	71·72	8·67	61·33	29,808	18,281	1,585	24,480	15,023	1,302
3	Early golden	A. B. Swain	80	104	76	11·47	1·76	3·09	70·24	8·12	60·03	24,611	14,774	1 200	24,480	14,695	1,352
4	Golden syrup	W. H. Lytle	87	82	67	12·48	1·42	2·99	73·65	9·24	61·36	15,822	9,708	897	24,480	14,023	1,388
5	White Liberian	D. Smith	88	101	39	13·43	1·31	3·17	74·98	10·08	63·82	32,165	20,528	2,069	31,920	20,371	2,053
6	Early amber	S. E. Evans	89	96	24	13·21	1·54	3·28	73·23	9·69	59·02	27,962	16,503	1,599	23,760	14,023	1,359
7	Black top	D. W. Aiken	87	87	35	12·69	1·21	3·07	74·75	9·51	61·35	21,907	13,440	1,278	22,800	13,977	1,329
8	African	W. E. Parks	87	107	83	11·50	1·46	3·14	70·38	8·13	62·92	21,716	13,664	1,111	27,840	17,517	1,424
9	White mammoth	Amos Carpenter	102	83	32	12·69	1·18	3·45	74·50	10·13	62·31	29,341	18,282	1,851	31,680	19,740	1,999
10	Oomseeana	Blymyer and Co.	115	77	54	13·51	1·49	3·07	74·38	8·81	62·31	19,522	12,523	1,103	27,840	17,859	1,573
11	Regular sorgho	"	101	93	71	12·16	1·49	3·43	72·43	8·70	60·77	26,611	16,172	1,407	30,720	18,669	1,624
12	Hybrid	E. Link	101	84	30	11·80	·93	3·03	76·08	10·84	63·53	34,477	21,903	2,374	42,240	26,835	2,909
13	Sugar cane	J. W. Barger	108	77	28	14·24	1·49	3·13	74·18	10·27	62·32	21,117	13,150	1,350	21,600	13,461	1,382
14	Oomseeana	D. W. Aiken	104	88	35	13·82	1·12	3·31	74·21	9·57	62·04	22,825	14,160	1,355	28,080	17,420	1,667
15	Neeazana	W. H. Lytle	136	58	38	12·84	1·93	3·18	72·13	9·48	61·58	23,467	14,451	1,360	26,400	16,257	1,441
16	Goose neck	P. P. Ramsey	111	72	44	13·16	1·46	2·99	73·29	7·58	62·12	27,362	16,997	1,288	30,480	18,934	1,435
17	Early orange	— Hedges	117	79	53	12·26	1·58	3·39	72·45	9·56	61·67	48,758	30,069	2,875	21,903	21,903	2,094
18	Neeazana	Blymyer and Co.	129	65	46	13·18	1·95	3·11	72·77	9·78	60·52	20,156	12,198	1,193	25,200	15,241	1,491
19	New variety	E. Link	108	84	31	13·45	1·19	3·35	73·93	9·50	65·22	30,731	20,042	1,904	28,320	18,470	1,755
20	Chinese	D. Smith	137	57	36	12·84	1·81	3·68	70·66	9·22	60·43	30,956	18,707	1,725	32,720	19,773	1,823
21	Wolf tail	E. Link	118	56	21	13·18	1·23	2·98	71·87	8·65	62·09	31,493	19,554	1,691	30,960	19,223	1,663
22	Gray top	H. C. Sealey	135	59	33	11·72	1·47	3·54	72·19	9·42	63·00	29,887	18,809	1,772	28,800	18,144	1,709
23	Liberian	Blymyer and Co.	131	38	22	13·03	2·05	3·22	71·23	9·39	62·02	45,580	28,269	2,654	45,120	27,983	2,628
24	"	W. H. Lytle	134	48	36	13·18	2·09	3·37	70·31	9·08	62·56	44,913	28,088	2,550	44,400	27,777	2,522
25	Oomseeana	W. I. Mayes and Co.	127	67	36	12·92	1·74	3·40	72·50	9·88	61·89	35,414	21,918	2,165	42,480	26,291	2,588
26	Sumac	W. Pope	152	31	14	13·62	1·67	4·18	70·82	10·09	60·15	39,919	24,011	2,423	39,360	23,675	2,389
27	Mastodon	D. W. Aiken	128	60	23	14·24	1·68	3·03	70·82	7·95	64·27	20,413	13,119	1,043	47,760	30,695	2,440
28	Imphee	"	155	37	9	14·21	1·76	3·61	72·56	10·31	61·67	37,031	22,837	2,354	37,920	23,385	2,411
29	New variety	J. W. H. Salle	172	7	5	13·99	2·02	3·73	70·88	9·92	58·57	26,090	15,287	1,516	25,920	15,181	1,506

UNITED STATES.

Table No. 96.—TABLE showing the Comparative Value, during the Working Period, of all Varieties of Sorghum and Corn Stalks here examined—(continued).

	Name.	Source of Seed.	Number of Days to Maturity.	Number of Days for Working.	Number of Analyses.	Average per cent. Sucrose in Juice.	Average per cent. Glucose in Juice.	Average per cent. other Solids in Juice.	Average Exponent.	Average per cent. Available Sugar.	Average per cent. Juice.	Actually obtained. Stripped Stalks, per Acre.	Actually obtained. Juice, per Acre.	Actually obtained. Available Sugar, per Acre.	Computed at 24,000 Stalks per Acre. Stripped Stalks, per Acre.	Computed at 24,000 Stalks per Acre. Juice, per Acre.	Computed at 24,000 Stalks per Acre. Available Sugar, per Acre.
												Lbs.	Lbs.	Lbs.	Lbs.	Lbs.	Lbs.
30	Sumac	J. H. Wighton	168	20	6	14·40	1·80	3·40	73·53	10·58	60·84	39,815	24,223	2,563	36,960	22,486	2,388
31	Honduras*	Arsenal	148	29	27	10·32	2·26	3·09	65·76	6·81	57·09	25,335	14,464	985	29,760	16,990	1,157
32	Honey cane†	J. H. Clark	133	43	21	10·80	2·56	2·51	67·76	7·37	65·08	50,017	30,301	2,233	53,760	34,987	2,579
33	Sprangle top*	W. Pope	153	38	20	11·21	2·61	2·94	66·79	7·51	65·91	46,634	30,736	2,308	44,880	29,580	2,221
34	Honduras	E. Link	157	10	4	12·83	1·80	2·95	67·98	10·06	65·06	45,695	29,729	2,991	50,740	33,011	3,321
35	Honey top, or Texas cane*	Brussels, Mo.	163	20	7	12·98	2·11	3·92	66·27	8·86	64·68	47,246	30,559	2,708	51,220	33,129	2,939
36	Honduras*	L. Brande	164	22	7	11·67	2·03	3·22	69·00	8·06	66·59	46,421	27,912	2,250	51,840	34,510	2,782
37	Sugar cane*	C. E. Miller	99	8	6	8·84	2·37	2·32	65·39	5·79	64·60	13,839	8,940	518	17,280	11,163	649
38	Hybrid	J. C. Moore	...	...	...	...	...	...	...	...	...	...	...	...	...	...	...
	VARIETIES OF CORN.																
39	Rice or Egyptian	Root and Hollingsworth	...	...	4	11·77	·59	3·90	72·32	7·51	42·41	18,497	7,845	589	10,320	4,377	329
40	Doura corn		...	...	3	12·75	1·97	3·87	68·59	8·75	43·56	39,900	17,380	1,521	22,080	9,618	842
41	Stowell's evergreen	W. R. Shelmire	...	...	5	10·92	1·05	3·26	71·70	7·83	55·30	8,835	4,886	383	14,640	7,975	624
42	Egyptian sugar		...	...	5	10·38	1·55	2·82	70·37	7·30	58·14	23,287	8,188	598	23,280	13,540	983
43	Lindsay's horse tooth	A. H. Lindsay	...	...	7	11·55	·94	3·53	72·10	8·33	57·58	24,753	14,253	1,187	41,040	23,631	1,968
44	White flat dent, 8-rowed	Washington Market	...	...	6	10·80	·88	2·96	73·77	7·97	59·68	22,256	13,282	1,059	36,720	21,914	1,747
45	Improved prolific	James M. Thorburn & Co.	...	...	5	10·47	·80	3·72	69·85	7·31	57·51	21,562	12,400	906	35,560	20,451	1,495
46	White dent	Thomas L. Jones	...	...	6	11·08	1·15	3·04	72·56	8·04	55·99	21,929	12,270	986	36,240	20,291	1,631
47	Sanford corn	F. B. Hatheway	...	...	5	9·33	1·12	3·51	66·85	6·24	47·63	6,187	2,947	184	10,320	4,915	307
48	Mammoth dent	M. J. Varney	...	...	7	10·86	·85	3·81	69·96	7·64	53·54	15,642	8,375	640	25,920	13,878	1,060
49	Early Minn. dent	M. J. Varney	...	...	3	10·92	1·08	4·75	65·20	7·12	36·15	4,278	1,546	110	6,960	2,516	179

* The juices of these five canes did not reach the exponent 70.
† The juice of this cane in some cases reached an exponent above 70.

FOREIGN OFFICE.

MISCELLANEOUS SERIES, 1886.

No. 11.

REPORTS ON SUBJECTS OF GENERAL AND COMMERCIAL INTEREST.

UNITED STATES.

FURTHER REPORT FROM H.M. LEGATION AT WASHINGTON

ON THE

EXTRACTION OF SUGAR FROM SORGHUM AND MAIZE.

REFERENCE TO PREVIOUS REPORT, Foreign Office Miscellaneous Series No. 2, 1886.

Printed under the Superintendence of Her Majesty's Stationery Office,

By HARRISON AND SONS,
Printers in Ordinary to Her Majesty.

AND SOLD BY

Messrs. HANSARD and SON, 13, Great Queen Street, W.C., and 32, Abingdon Street, Westminster;
Messrs. EYRE and SPOTTISWOODE, East Harding Street, Fleet Street;
Messrs. ADAM and CHARLES BLACK, Edinburgh;
Messrs. ALEX. THOM and Co. (Limited), and Messrs. HODGES, FIGGIS, and Co., Dublin.

Price One Penny.

New Series of Reports.

The following Reports from Her Majesty's Representatives abroad, on subjects of general and commercial interest, have been issued, and may be obtained from the sources indicated on the title-page:—

No.		Price.
1.	*Russia.*—Notes on a Visit to the City of Kieff	1d.
2.	*United States.*—Report on the Extraction of Sugar from Sorghum and Maize	2d.
3.	*Turkey.*—Report on Proposed Improvements in Bourgas Harbour..	1d.
4.	*Germany.*—Report on the Gotha Exhibition of European Manufactures in China	1d.
5.	*France.*—Report on the Publication of Official Statistics and the Establishment of Commercial Museums in France	2d.
6.	*Germany.*—Report on the Exhibition of European Manufactures in China	1d.
7.	*Japan.*—Report on the Import Trade of Great Britain with Japan	1d.
8.	*Spain.*—Report on Openings for British Enterprise in Catalonia	1d.
9.	*Germany.*—Report on the First German Wine Exhibition at Frankfort-on-Main	1d.
10.	*Africa* (*East Coast*).—Report on the Trade of the Somali Coast	4d.

(1)

WASHINGTON.

The Colonial Office to the Foreign Office.

Sir, *Downing Street, August* 21, 1886.

WITH reference to your letter of the 29th of July, enclosing a copy* of a report by Mr. Victor Drummond on the production of sugar from sorghum and maize, I am directed by Mr. Secretary Stanhope to transmit to you, for the information of the Earl of Iddesleigh, a copy of a letter from the Director of Kew Gardens, remarking on the report.

Mr. Stanhope would suggest that, as recommended in the last paragraph of this letter, information should be obtained as to the exact position of the sorghum and maize sugar industry in the United States at the present time.

I have, &c.
(Signed) E. WINGFIELD.

Royal Gardens, Kew, to Colonial Office.

Sir, *Royal Gardens, Kew, August* 10, 1886.

I am directed by Mr. Thiselton Dyer to acknowledge the receipt of your reference, dated the 6th August, forwarding copy of a report by Mr. Victor Drummond to Lord Rosebery on the extraction of sugar from sorghum and maize.

2. In reply, I am to state that the subject of the production of sugar from sorghum and maize has been followed at Kew with interest for some years, and the literature accumulated is of a very complete character.

3. Mr. Thiselton Dyer has been fully sensible of the importance of this subject, and believes that it is only necessary to glance at the range of distribution of the chief sugar-producing plants to show what the probable effects will be if sorghum ever takes the place of the cane or beet as the source of commercial sugars.

4. The sugar-cane proper (*Saccharum officinarum*), at present the chief sugar-producing plant of the world, is confined for the most part to tropical regions, and its range of remunerative cultivation extends only a short distance beyond them. The beet, which comes next to the sugar-cane as a source of commercial sugar, thrives best in cold temperate regions. The sorghum (of which *Sorghum vulgare*, grown in North Africa and elsewhere, may be accepted as a type), on the other hand, has a very extensive geographical range, extending from tropical and sub-tropical regions a considerable distance into the cold temperate zone—that is, an area equal to more than one-third of the habitable globe. Maize has a range almost identical with that of sorghum.

5. The extraction of syrups and a low class of sugar from sorghum is an invention of no recent date. In China soft sugar has been known for many centuries as the production of *Sorghum saccharatum*, and in Japan sorghum sugar has been long known as a commercial product,

* Miscellaneous Series of Foreign Office Reports, No. 2, 1886.

and yearly produced to the extent of 64,000,000 lbs. But it was not until the last few years—and not, indeed, until the subject was systematically taken up by the Department of Agriculture at Washington—that sorghum was used in the United States for any other purpose than the preparation of syrup, which latter was produced in 1880 to the extent of nearly 25,000,000 gallons. This syrup (or, as it is sometimes called, molasses) was an article of purely local consumption in the States, and did not enter into external commerce.

6. Whether good crystallisable (or hard) sugar can be produced largely in the United States from sorghum or maize to such an extent, and at such prices, as to compete successfully with cane sugar, remains to be seen. It is only right to point out that, at present, the facts cited by Mr. Victor Drummond are the result, for the most part, of laboratory experiments only. These results necessarily require to be tested and worked over large areas; and until this is done, and the article placed in the market on a commercial scale, it is obviously unadvisable to express a strong opinion either way.

7. Mr. Drummond's statements and conclusions are certainly of a very plausible and interesting character; but, without impugning their general accuracy, it may be permissible to point out that there are many statements in the report of a purely scientific character which are at variance with well-known facts in vegetable physiology. Explanation may be forthcoming; but, in the absence of such explanation, it is difficult to understand how it is possible with such a plant as sorghum "to produce regularly not only a full crop of the ripened grain, but also, in addition, an increase in the saccharine secretion of the stem." Again, in another portion of the report, Mr. Stewart claims "that he can control the vital energies of the growing corn (maize) or sorghum, so as to prevent the exhaustion and death of the plant naturally following the ripening of the grain." These statements appear to be self-contradictory, and opposed to the natural laws governing the habits of these plants; and although it is promised that the means whereby they are effected will be explained in the report, the subject is apparently overlooked. The following statement is quite incomprehensible as a scientific deduction from facts, and certainly requires further elucidation than is afforded in this report, viz.: "It is only after the seed of any variety of sorghum is quite mature that the maximum of sugar in the stalks is attained; so that there is nothing to prevent the securing of both the maximum of seed and the maximum of sugar from the (same) crop of sorghum."

8. Apart from these points, which I am to observe Mr. Thiselton Dyer deems it both necessary and desirable to pass under review, the information so ably and graphically summarised by Mr. Drummond is of the deepest possible interest to British tropical colonies, for, should sorghum or maize sugar be ultimately producible at a cheap rate, it must entirely take the place of cane and beet sugar, and hence the industrial interests connected with these latter would be completely revolutionised.

9. It is not stated in the report whether the extraction of sugar from sorghum and maize has already assumed commercial importance in the United States. The latest information to hand at Kew is dated 1883, and at that time several factories were about to engage in the extraction of crystallised sugar from sorghum and maize, and in this enterprise they were encouraged by special bounties offered by State Legislatures. It might be of advantage if information were obtained through the Foreign Office giving the exact position of the sorghum and maize sugar industry in the States at the present time. Such

information would prove of great interest to our colonial possessions, and would go far to support or correct the impression which must be produced by the publication of Mr. Drummond's present report.

    I have, &c.
    (Signed) D. MORRIS, Assistant-Director.

The Earl of Iddesleigh to Sir L. West.

Sir,   *Foreign Office, August* 28, 1886.

I enclose for your information a copy* of a report by Mr. V. Drummond on the extraction of sugar from sorghum and maize, and a copy of a letter to the Colonial Office from Mr. Thiselton Dyer making certain observations on the report. I should be glad to have a statement explanatory of the points adverted to by Mr. Thiselton Dyer.

    I have, &c.
    (Signed) IDDESLEIGH.

Sir L. West to the Earl of Iddesleigh.

My Lord,   *Washington, October* 5, 1886.

With reference to your Lordship's despatch of the 28th August last, I have the honour to enclose herewith a very complete report on the sorghum industry in this country, which has been carefully compiled by Mr. C. Hardinge.

    I have, &c.
    (Signed) L. S. SACKVILLE WEST.

Report on the Sorghum Industry of the United States.

In reply to Mr. Thiselton Dyer's comments on Mr. Drummond's report respecting the extraction of sugar from sorghum and maize, and in explanation of certain statements made therein and questioned by Mr. Thiselton Dyer, Mr. Norman Colman, Commissioner of the Department of Agriculture at Washington, states that Mr. Drummond's information has been gained from limited sources, and the facts upon which he has based his conclusions are apparently those derived from the laboratory experiments and opinions of Dr. Peter Collier, formerly Chemist of the Department of Agriculture, and do not take into consideration the results of practical experience in the country, and experiments conducted by the Department in the field during the past few years, under the direction of Dr. H. Wiley, at present in charge of this subject.

A considerable time has already elapsed since Professor Collier retired from his position as Chemist of the Department of Agriculture, the Commissioner having no further need of his services; and Mr. Stewart is not considered to be an authority on whose statements reliance should be placed in connection with the question of the sorghum sugar industry.

With regard to the following statement in Mr. Drummond's report, which Mr. Thiselton Dyer declares to be "quite incomprehensible as a scientific deduction from facts," and to require further elucidation—viz., "It is only after the seed of any variety of sorghum is quite mature that

* Miscellaneous Series of Foreign Office Reports, No. 2, 1886.

the maximum of sugar in the stalks is attained, so that there is nothing to prevent the securing of both the maximum of seed and the maximum of sugar from the (same) crop of sorghum"—Mr. Norman Colman asserts that it has been definitely settled, both by experiment and practice, that a full crop of seed is not only not incompatible with a large yield of sugar, but that full maturity is necessary to obtain the largest yield. On the other hand, Mr. Norman Colman characterises Mr. Stewart's claims in regard to controlling the vital energies of the growing plant as "certainly extravagant and hardly worthy of consideration."

As to the extent to which this industry has been developed, the extraction of marketable sugar from sorghum and maize has not yet assumed actual commercial importance, the entire production of the past 10 years in the United States not having exceeded, in the opinion of the Statistician of the Department of Agriculture, 5,000,000 lbs.

There were in 1884 several factories engaged in the extraction of crystallised sugar from sorghum and maize, and the following is a résumé of the results obtained by them, as reported to the Commissioner of Agriculture at Washington:—

The sugar factory at Hutchinson, Kansas, was one of the best equipped in the country, and in 1883 the services of Professor Swanson, of the Wisconsin University, well known for his ability in connection with this question, were secured as superintendent. The result of the season's work was 200,000 lbs. of sugar, which was heralded in Kansas as the solution of the sorghum sugar question. The facts, however, were that the cost of production was far in excess of the receipts, and the company became bankrupt. In 1884 another effort was made, with the result of 250,000 lbs. of sugar, but again at a heavy loss in cost of production. The report of the Hutchinson Sugar Works for 1884 is as follows:—

1. Acres of cane worked (100 for syrup only, 700 for syrup and sugar)	800
2. Tons of cane worked	6,100
3. Amount of seed (estimated)	10,000 bushels.
4. Amount of sugar made	250,000 lbs.
5. Amount of syrup made	50,000 gallons.
6. Average yield of sugar per ton of cane worked for sugar	47 lbs.
7. Average yield of syrup per ton of cane	7 gallons.
8. Average yield of sugar per acre	357 lbs.
9. Average yield of syrup per acre	53 gallons.
10. Value of plant	50,000 dol.
11. Number of hands employed during season (10 hours per diem)	22
12. Wages paid	1 dol. 50 c.
13. Fuel used (coal) per ton	5 dol.
14. Commenced milling	Aug. 22.
15. Closed milling	Oct. 30.
16. Cost of raising and delivering cane at factory, per ton	1 dol. 50 c.
17. Amount of juice expressed	40 per cent.
18. Working capital required	20,000 dol.

And Professor Swanson, in a letter to the Commissioner of Agriculture, dated the 12th December, 1884, makes the following statement:—"Under the present low prices the sorghum sugar industry is barely able to hold its own, but if, under favourable legislation, prices can be advanced from $\frac{1}{2}$ c. to 1 c. per lb., or if State or national aid to a like amount can be obtained for a limited time, till the best machinery can be procured and the methods of manufacture perfected, under these conditions we may safely hope to see the sorghum sugar industry established on a sound basis, and adding very materially to the wealth and prosperity of the country."

The works of the Sterling Sugar Company are at Sterling, Kansas, and in 1883 a new company was formed, with Professor Scovell as superintendent. In spite of every possible reduction in the cost of production, the season of 1884 resulted in heavy losses for the company, chiefly due to the extremely low price of sugar; and it was decided not to run the factory again unless a great improvement showed itself in the market. The following is Professor Scovell's report of the operations of the sugar works at Sterling:—

1. Acres of cane manufactured	1,000
2. Tons of cane manufactured	7,100
3. Price paid for cane delivered, per ton	2 dol.
4. Cost of production of cane, not estimating seed, per ton	1 dol. 57 c.
5. Seed not yet gathered, but will yield 15 to 30 bushels per acre.	
6. Amount of sugar made	169,000 lbs.
7. Amount of syrup made	75,000 gallons.
8. Value of manufacturing plant	80,000 dol.
9. Number of hands employed	50 to 60
10. Wages paid, per hour	15 c.
11. Cost of making sorghum cane into sugar and syrup, per ton	1 dol. 10 c.
12. Amount of juice expressed	50 to 60 per cent.
13. Percentage of feed furnished by bagasse	66⅔ ,,
14. Date of commencement of milling	Sept. 1.
15. Date of close	Oct. 31.
16. Working capital required	20,000 dol.

The works of the Franklin Sugar Company at Ottawa, Kansas—which had been thoroughly overhauled, and made into a well-equipped sugar factory, under the management of Mr. Parkinson—showed the following results for the season of 1884:—

1. Acres of cane manufactured	600
2. Tons of cane manufactured	6,100
3. Price paid for cane, per ton	2 dol.
4. Amount of seed	1,600 bushels.
5. Yield of sugar per ton of cane	30 lbs.
6. Yield of syrup per ton of cane	5 gallons.
7. Value of plant	60,000 dol.
8. Number of hands employed (12 hours per diem)	75
9. Wages of hands, per hour	14 c.
10. Fuel used (coal) per ton	3 dol. 35 c.
11. Commenced milling	Sept. 1.
12. Closed milling	Nov. 6.
13. Amount of juice expressed	40 per cent.
14. Working capital required	20,000 dol.

Thus, in the State of Kansas—which, from the nature of the soil and the temperature of the climate, has been shown to be specially adapted for the profitable prosecution of the sugar industry—a summary of the operations of the three largest sugar factories gives the following results:—

1. Number of factories operating for sugar	3
2. Capital invested in plant	190,000 dol.
3. Working capital	60,000 ,,
4. Number of hands employed	152
5. Average daily wages of hands, nearly	1 dol. 50 c.
6. Amount of sugar made	602,000 lbs.

(M)

7.	Amount of syrup made	..	..	..	..	155,500 gallons.
8.	Acres of cane worked..	..	..	..	..	2,490
9.	Tons of cane worked ..	..	..	..	..	19,300
10.	Value of cane worked	..	..	..	..	38,600 dol.

The sugars were sold at 5 c. to 6¾ c. per lb. wholesale, and the syrups at 15 c. to 30 c. per gallon wholesale.

The Champaign Sugar Company, whose works are at Champaign, Illinois, made in 1884 100,000 lbs. of sugar; but having sustained very severe losses, and sunk all the money invested, they concluded that they would not attempt to make any more sugar.

Mr. William Fraser, of Esofea, Vernon county, Wisconsin, being a careful operator, and with only a small centrifugal for sugar making, succeeded in producing 1,000 lbs. of sugar during the season of 1884, and made his factory pay a fair profit by making 5,000 gallons of syrup, which were sold to the home market at 40 c. per gallon.

Mr. Joseph Porter, of Red Wing, Minnesota, with a model factory for ingenuity of machinery, made 2,500 lbs. of sugar and 6,000 gallons of syrup, and, by selling his syrup at 35 c. to 50 c. per gallon, succeeded in making his mill a paying investment.

Mr. John Stuart, of Traer, Iowa, succeeded in producing from seven acres seven tons of cane per acre, from which, by a process of artificial evaporation, he produced 4,900 lbs. of sugar.

Messrs. Drummond of Wanensburg, Missouri, and Messrs. Belcher and Swartz of Edwardsville, Illinois, make now only syrup, having but small hopes that the manufacture of sugar of sorghum can be made a profitable business.

The Rio Grande Company, at Rio Grande, New Jersey, exported 385,000 lbs. of sugar, but no record has been obtained. This is also said to be a company whose business is a losing one.

Of all the above-mentioned factories, where in 1884 the extraction of sugar from sorghum was carried on, there exist at the present date only two where this industry is being prosecuted—one being that of the Rio Grande Company, and the second that of the Franklin Sugar Company, whose works have been removed from Ottawa to Fort Scott, where experiments are still being made under the superintendence of Dr. Wiley.

The amount of sugar made from sorghum during the season of 1884 may thus be safely based upon the following report:—

Name of Company.	Lbs.
Hutchinson Sugar Company, Kans.	250,000
Kansas ,, ,, Sterling	175,000
Franklin ,, ,, Ottawa	183,000
Champaign ,, ,, Illinois	100,000
Mr. Fraser, Esofea, Wisconsin	1,000
Mr. Porter, Redwing, Minn.	2,500
Mr. Stuart, Traer, Iowa	4,900
Rio Grande (exported)	385,000

making, roughly speaking, rather more than 1,000,000 lbs. in all.

By comparing this quantity of sugar derived from sorghum, with the annual consumption of cane sugar in the United States, viz., 1,170,000 tons (this being the quantity consumed in 1885), the fact is patent to all that this industry has not yet assumed "actual commercial importance;" and Mr. Thiselton Dyer's conclusion "that the production of good crystallisable sugar from sorghum to such an extent, and at such prices as to compete successfully with cane sugar remains to be seen," is essentially correct, although in the opinion of the Commissioner of Agriculture great hopes are to be entertained for the future of the industry.

From a study of the foregoing data of the operations in the field during the season of 1884, the only conclusion to be drawn is that the manufacture of sugar from sorghum has not proved hitherto successful. Great results were predicted, but the expectations of the least enthusiastic advocates of sorghum have not been realised, leaving the future of this industry still a matter of doubt. In the opinion of Dr. Wiley this state of things is due to many causes, of which the following are the most evident :—

1. The difficulties inherent in the plant have been constantly undervalued. By taking the mean of several seasons as a basis of computation, it can now be said that the juices of sorghum, as they come from the mill, do not contain over 10 per cent. of sucrose, while the percentage of other solids in solution is at least four, thus rendering the working of such a juice one of extreme difficulty.

2. The chemistry of the process is at present hardly known, and great development is necessary in this direction.

3. The area of land, where the climate and soil are best adapted for the cultivation of sorghum, is not nearly so extensive as was at first imagined, and investigation should be made in order to discover in which localities the necessary conditions are most favourable.

4. Commercial depression and the consequent low prices have affected this industry, and caused failure and losses in cases where all other conditions were favourable.

5. Lastly, the mechanical treatment of the juice is very imperfect, the machinery used in the mills being quite inefficient for the purposes intended.

With a view to the correction of the last-mentioned defect, it was decided by the Commissioner of Agriculture to apply the appropriation made by Congress to conducting experiments for the application of the process of diffusion on a practical scale. These experiments, although at first intended to take place in the season of 1884, had, owing to the difficulty of obtaining suitable machinery, to be postponed till the following year.

Dr. Wiley was entrusted with the direction of the experiments, and having obtained the best machinery possible, and erected the battery and necessary buildings in connection with the works of the Franklin Sugar Company at Ottawa, Kansas, the first trial of the process of diffusion was made on the 8th October, 1885. The cutters were at work from 8 a.m. until 5 a.m. of the following day. The weight of the diffused juice from 65 cells, capable of holding 1,400 lbs. each, was 96,140 lbs. The exhausted chips on analysis showed 0·10 per cent. of glucose, while the waste waters of diffusion showed 0·10 per cent. of sucrose and 0·10 per cent. of glucose, thus making the loss of sugars 0·10 per cent. of sucrose and 0·20 per cent. of glucose, or a total loss of 0·30 per cent. This, in Dr. Wiley's opinion, was a very satisfactory result, and makes it appear that diffusion can be successfully practised with sorghum cane, when the weight of the juice obtained is made about the same as that of the cane diffused. The mean specific gravity of the 32 charges, of 700 litres, each drawn from the first series of 32 cells, was 1·0394, at 25° or at 15° 1·0411, corresponding to 10·24 per cent. total solids. The average specific gravity of the juice of 32 charges, of 600 litres, each drawn from the second series of cells, was 1·0405 at 25° or 1·0424, corresponding to 10·55 per cent. total solids. Owing to the

(M)

great variation in the composition of the cane, no estimate of the degree of extraction could be made from the analysis of the cane juices.

The following analyses were made of the diffusion juices during the day:—

Articles.	First time 10·30 a.m.	Second time 3 p.m.
Total solids	10·84	9·70
Glucose	2·32	2·00
Sucrose	6·19	5·90
Solids not sugar	2·33	1·80

The weight of coal used during the diffusion amounted to 1½ tons, but half of this quantity might have been saved if the chips could have been promptly removed from the cells, so as to render it possible to make a diffusion every 10 minutes, in which case the whole experiment might have been completed in less than 12 hours.

The necessary force required and the expense incurred was:—

	Dol.	c.
One fireman (day) and one (night) at 1 dol. 50 c.	3	00
Four men on cane carrier (day) and four (night) at 1 dol. 25 c.	10	00
Four men at battery (day) and four (night) at 1 dol. 25 c.	10	00
One team to remove chips (day) and one (night) at 2 dol. 50 c.	5	00
One valve-man (day) and one (night) at 2 dol. 25 c.	4	50
One and a half tons of coal at 3 dol. 25 c.	4	88
Oil and lights	1	00
One boy (to sweep, &c.)	0	75
Total cost of diffusing 49 tons of cane	38	13

With some changes in the construction of the battery, and especially an enlargement of the cells, this rate of expense could be very much reduced, and the cost of diffusing a ton of cane would not exceed 30 c. It was estimated that about 15 horse-power was used in driving the machinery and heating the cells.

A careful estimate of the number of tons of the juice which was worked showed that 15 had been carbonated.

This yielded 4,320 lbs. of "masse cuite," containing 76·9 per cent. solid matter, or 11 per cent. on weight of cane worked.

The following analysis shows the composition of this "masse cuite":—

	Per cent.
Sucrose	53·48
Glucose	13·55
Water	23·10
Ash	4·74
Not sugar	5·13

The "masse cuite" was allowed to stand one week, and yielded 1,420 lbs., or about 30 per cent. of washed and dried sugar, or 95 lbs. per ton of cane worked.

Allowing 12 lbs. per gallon for the "masse cuite," the number of gallons per ton of cane was 24.

The sugar was of fine quality—the molasses of much better quality than that obtained in the usual way—and the whole product was in every way satisfactory.

Experiments were also made in carbonatation by the process so successfully used with beet juices. The process is simple, and consists in adding to the expressed juice a large excess of lime, and afterwards precipitating the greater part of it with carbonic acid. The whole is then sent to the filter press, where the precipitated carbonate of lime and impurities are separated from the juice. Owing to a large percentage of glucose in sorghum juice, the process is not conducted in the same manner as with beet juices.

On experimenting with the diffusion juices mentioned above, it was found that about $1\frac{1}{4}$ per cent. of lime was sufficient to produce perfect defecation; and in one day about 40,000 lbs. of juice were carbonated, with most satisfactory results. The juice came from the filter-press perfectly limped, and of a delicate amber colour. After passing through a sulphur box, this juice was sent to the evaporators, and reduced to a "masse cuite," which in colour, purity, and taste was greatly superior to the best product obtained by the usual method.

The carbonatation of sorghum juice, however, demands the greatest care. If too little lime is added, the precipitate does not settle readily, and filtration is slow and imperfect. The carbonatation must be continued until all but 0·2 per cent. of the lime has been removed. If more than this remains, the juice will darken and become bitter on boiling. If less than this quantity is left, the impurities appear to be redissolved, and a green scum forms on the top of the still liquor instead of sinking with the precipitate. With the help of proper test reagents, a little experience will enable the operator to carry the carbonatation to a successful completion.

It was found, also, that the temperature during carbonatation should not be allowed to exceed 40° C. Directly the carbonatation is completed, the juice is raised as rapidly as possible to the boiling-point, and sent at once to the filter-press. If allowed to stand, the liquor will quickly darken. Foaming is prevented by the addition of a little lard to the sugar, and by jets of steam from a perforated pipe near the top of the pan.

In all, 100,000 lbs. of juice were carbonated, and Dr. Wiley asserts that this process of defecation offers every evidence of being the one which should be brought into general use. In large sugar factories the saving in scums alone would pay for the carbonatation plant.

The mean coefficient of purity of the juices worked by the Franklin Sugar Company is 61·3, and Dr. Wiley stated his belief that by proper culture, fertilising, and selection, sorghum cane could be produced in which the juices would have a coefficient of purity of 75 to 80. The importance of securing such a cane is even greater than that of extracting all the sugar and properly defecating the juice.

The general results of the experiments of 1885 showed that:—

1. By the process of diffusion 98 per cent. of the sugar in the cane was extracted, and the yield was fully double that obtained in the ordinary way.

2. The difficulties to be overcome in the application of diffusion are purely mechanical, and by enlarging the diffusion cells to a capacity of 130 cubic feet, and by making a few changes in the apparatus, it would be possible to work 120 tons per diem.

3. The process of carbonatation for the purification of the juice is the only method which will give a limpid juice with a minimum of waste and a maximum of purity.

4. By a proper combination of diffusion and carbonatation, 95 per cent. of the sugar in the cane can be placed on the market, either as dry sugar or molasses.

At the termination of the foregoing experiments, Dr. Wiley received instructions from the Commissioner of Agriculture to proceed to Europe, for the purpose of inspecting and purchasing such forms of machinery as might appear most useful, also to gain such information as might secure the greatest success in this work; and much useful information, chiefly of a mechanical nature, was obtained by Dr. Wiley during the course of his visits to several of the most important sugar factories in France, Germany, and Spain.

During the present season of 1886 further experiments are being carried on at Fort Scott, under the direction of the Department of Agriculture; and it is reported that the results have not proved to be as satisfactory as was anticipated.

The foregoing account has been derived from information supplied by the Department of Agriculture, and shows the present phase of the sorghum sugar industry, as requested by Mr. Thiselton Dyer.

FOREIGN OFFICE.

1888.

MISCELLANEOUS SERIES.

No. 83.

REPORTS ON SUBJECTS OF GENERAL AND COMMERCIAL INTEREST.

UNITED STATES.

REPORT ON THE
MANUFACTURE OF SUGAR FROM SORGHUM IN KANSAS.

Presented to both Houses of Parliament by Command of Her Majesty,
FEBRUARY, 1888.

LONDON:
PRINTED FOR HER MAJESTY'S STATIONERY OFFICE,
BY HARRISON AND SONS, ST. MARTIN'S LANE,
PRINTERS IN ORDINARY TO HER MAJESTY.

And to be purchased, either directly or through any Bookseller, from
EYRE AND SPOTTISWOODE, EAST HARDING STREET, FLEET STREET, E.C., and
32, ABINGDON STREET, WESTMINSTER, S.W.; or
ADAM AND CHARLES BLACK, 6, NORTH BRIDGE, EDINBURGH; or
HODGES, FIGGIS, & Co., 104, GRAFTON STREET, DUBLIN.

1888.

[C.—5253—19.]   *Price One Penny.*

New Series of Reports.

The following Reports from Her Majesty's Representatives abroad, on subjects of general and commercial interest, have been issued, and may be obtained from the sources indicated on the title-page:—

No.		Price.
38.	*China.*—Report on the Manufactures of Native Cloth in the Consular District of Pakhoi	1d.
39.	*Netherlands.*—Report on the Cultivation of Cinchona in Java	1d.
40.	*Germany.*—Report on the Recent Currency Discussions in Germany	3d.
41.	*Austria-Hungary.*—Report on the History of the Austro-Hungarian Lloyd Steam Navigation Company	2d.
42.	*Italy.*—Report on the System and Working of Co-operative People's Banks in Italy	3d.
43.	*United States.*—Report on National and People's Banks in the United States of America	1d.
44.	*Italy.*—Further Notes on the Industries of the District of Biella (Province of Novara)	2d.
45.	*Brazil.*—Report on the General State of the Province of Rio de Janeiro	1d.
46.	*Japan.*—Report on the Ashiwo Copper Mines	4d.
47.	*Italy.*—Report on the Yield of Cocoons in Italy in 1886	1d.
48.	*Spain.*—Report on the Native Manufactures of the Philippine Islands	1d.
49.	*Japan.*—Reports on the Native Cotton Manufactures of Japan	2d.
50.	*Japan.*—Report on various Japanese Native Manufactures	1d.
51.	*Mexico.*—Report by Mr. Baker on the Condition of Agricultural Labourers in the State of Vera Cruz	1d.
52.	*Haïti.*—Report on the Trade and Finances of the Republic of Haïti	1d.
53.	*Portugal.*—Report on the Portuguese Mining Laws in South Africa	1d.
54.	*Italy.*—Report on the First National Congress of Italian Savings Banks held at Florence in November, 1886.	1d.
55.	*Russia.*—Notes on a Visit to the City of Kharkoff	1d.
56.	*Japan.*—Report on the Japanese Regulations controlling the Establishment of Exchanges	1d
57.	*Italy.*—Report on the Milan Millers' and Bakers' International Exhibition, 1887	1d.
58.	*Brazil.*—Report on the Province of Minas Geraes	2d.
59.	*Spain.*—Report on the Mining Industry of the District of Santiago de Cuba	1d.
60.	*Chile.*—Report on Native Woollen Manufactures in Chile	1d.
61.	*Chile.*—Further Report on the Condition of British Trade in Chile	5s. 8d.
62.	*Russia.*—Report on Pauperism, Benevolent Institutions, and Industrial Establishments in Russia	1d.
63.	*Tunis.*—Report on the Forests of Tunis	4d.
64.	*Mexico.*—Report on the Cotton Factories at Vera Cruz	1d.
65.	*Mexico.*—Report on the Commerce of Vera Cruz and the Future of that Port	1d.
66.	*Mexico.*—Report on the Mines and Minerals of the State of Vera Cruz	1d.
67.	*Sweden.*—Further Report on the Lulea-Ofoteu Railway	1d.
68.	*Russia.*—Report on the Russian Fiscal Policy	1d.
69.	*Spain.*—Report from Cadiz on the Vintage in Andalusia	1d.
70.	*Austria-Hungary.*—Report on Austrian Liquor Legislation	1d.
71.	*Russia.*—Report on the Commercial Importance of the Trans-Caspian Railway	4d.
72.	*France.*—Report on Frauds in the Brandy Trade	1d.
73.	*Switzerland*—Report on the Swiss Forest Laws	1d.
74.	*Germany.*—Report on the Working Men's Colony at Dornahof	1d.
75.	*Norway.*—Report on Bricklaying in Frosty Weather	1d.
76.	*Belgium.*—Report on the Commercial Institute of Antwerp	1d.
77.	*Germany.*—Reports on the German Grain Duties	1d.
78.	*United States.*—Report on Liquor Traffic Legislation in the United States	3d.
79.	*Switzerland.*—Report on the North-East Railway at Switzerland	1d.
80.	*United States.*—Report on the Oyster Fisheries of Maryland	1d.
81.	*Austria-Hungary.*—Report on the Timber Trade of Trieste	1d.
82.	*Russia.*—Report on Russian Agriculture, 1886–1887	2d.

No. 83.

UNITED STATES.

CHICAGO.

Consul Hayes Sadler to the Marquis of Salisbury.

My Lord,   Chicago, *January* 21, 1888.

I HAVE the honour to transmit herewith a Report on the Manufacture of Sugar from Sorghum in the State of Kansas, an industry which appears likely to become of much agricultural and manufacturing interest in that State.

                            I have, &c.
            (Signed)   J. HAYES SADLER.

Report on the Manufacture of Sugar from Sorghum in the State of Kansas.

In consequence of the presence of large amounts of cane sugar in sorghum-juice having been conclusively proved by the United States Department of Agriculture, practical experiments were instituted about seven years ago in the States of Illinois, Wisconsin, and Kansas, the results of which created much attention and interest. Aided by Government appropriations, continued experiments were made in the latter State, and these have led to a success in 1887, which, it is confidently believed, places sorghum sugar-making among the profitable industries of the country.

The first sorghum factory was built in Illinois in 1881, and in the following year three factories were in operation in Kansas, but, owing to the prices of sugar and syrup falling at that time to a low figure, the industry proved unprofitable, and the factories were closed. It was found that on account of the spongy and loose texture of the cane, it was impossible, with the heaviest and most modern crushers, to extract more than 40 per cent. of juice by the processes adopted, which were similar to those used in the South; and that, while the average amount of juice in the cane was about 90 per cent., half was lost in the first operation, and 10 per cent. of that obtained was lost in the subsequent treating. *[Early experiments.]*

The question, therefore, of obtaining a larger per-centage of juice was considered all-important, and efforts were made to try the process of diffusion, which had been successfully applied in the production of sugar from beet. As this would demand a considerable outlay, the aid of Congress was solicited, and an appropriation vote was obtained. Encouraged by this assistance, a battery was established in 1884 by the Franklin Sugar Company, at Ottawa, in the State of Kansas, where it was proved—though the appliances were yet imperfect—that by diffusion all the sugar could be extracted from the cane, or fully double that by the system of crushers; but the financial results were disastrous, and the company failed. In his report on these trials, Dr. Wiley stated that the difficulties in the application of diffusion were wholly mechanical, *[Diffusion tried.]*

(342)

though changes were necessary in the apparatus, with a view to the better working of the system. The result having been considered satisfactory, another appropriation was voted by Congress in 1885, and the Parkinson Sugar Company was established at Fort Scott, in Kansas, under an agreement whereby the United States Department of Agriculture should supply the machinery, and the company provide the cane and erect the buildings. The success of the method, consisting of diffusion and carbonation, was further assured; still the experiment failed to prove its commercial practicability. Great difficulty was experienced in inventing a machine to cut the cane, and to elevate and clean the chips, none being found successful; the acids of the cane also, together with the heat necessary for complete diffusion, caused another difficulty, the inversion of the cane sugar, and a large per-centage was thus changed into glucose, while the process of carbonatation, though securing a maximum yield of sugar, failed to make a marketable molasses from the blackening of the syrup on concentration caused by the small amount of lime remaining in the filtered juice. Dr. Wiley in his general review of the work in 1885, reported the absolute failure of the experiments to demonstrate the commercial practicability of manufacturing sorghum sugar, caused by the above difficulties. In 1886, 60,000 dols. (12,000*l*.) of the appropriation was expended in experiments. At the close of that year Professor Swenson reported that much had been accomplished, and the continued experiments and suggestions then made appear to have led to the means of overcoming the difficulties, and to the success which has resulted from the season's working in 1887.

Success in 1887.

All attempts to manufacture sugar from sorghum in Kansas having proved financially disastrous, early last year the State Legislature passed an Act to encourage the industry, and a bounty of 2 c. (1*d*.) per lb. for 5 years was granted on all sugar manufactured from beet, sorghum, or any other plant; and an inspector was appointed for the purpose of determining the per-centage, quantity and quality of the sugar produced, as well as to ascertain whether sugar-making in Kansas was a failure or a success. At the close of the year the inspector, Professor Cowgill, made his report, in which he shows that 842 packages, containing 234,607 lbs. of sugar, were inspected, and branded as provided by law, and that the packages so inspected, contained from 92 to 98 per cent. of crystallized sugar respectively; he also states that success has been at last attained, and that the result of the management at the Fort Scott works—the only factory in operation in the State—had been so far favourable as to place sorghum sugar-making on the basis of profitable business.

The season's work.

The season's work at the Parkinson Factory in 1887, as reported by the manager, shows the value of the product at 34,476·50 dol. (6,895*l*. 6*s*.), and the cost at 21,746·93 dol. (4,349*l*. 7*s*. 9*d*.), or a profit of 12,729·57 dol. (2,545*l*. 18*s*. 3*d*.); but, as the bounty is added in this calculation to the value of the product, the net profit should only amount to 1,607*l*. 9*s*. 8*d*. The total product of the season, and the total cost are thus stated:—

PRODUCT.

		Dollars.	Dollars.
Sugar, 235,826 lbs. at 5¾ c.		13,559·98	
„ State bounty at 2 c.		4,716·52	
			17,276·50
Syrups, 51,000 gallons (estimated) at 20 c.			10,200·00
Seed (estimated)			7,000·00
Value of total product			34,476·50

Cost.

	Dollars.	Dollars.
Cane, 3·84 tons. at 2 dol.	7,680	
Seed, 967 tons, al 2 dol...	1,934	
		9,614·00
Labour bill, August 15 to October 15, including labour for departmental experiments		5,737·16
Coal, including all experiments		1,395·77
Salaries, &c.		3,500·00
Insurance, sundries, &c...		1,500·00
Total cost		21,746·93

The working season is about 70 days, and the plant at Fort Scott is capable of working 135 tons of chips per day of 22 hours, equal to 170 tons of field cane. The crop contracted for was much less than the capacity of the works, so as to limit danger from loss, and the factory was only operated for three whole days of 22 hours, the remaining part of the season, owing to shortness of cane being worked at short time; only 3,840 tons of cane were bought, produced on about 450 acres of land. As 897 tons of this were used in experiments, and in the production of molasses, only 2,943 tons were worked in the production of sugar, and from this must be deducted 333 tons of leaves and blades. The actual cost per ton of cane, apart from the cost of experiments, taking an average day when in full operation, is calculated at 1 dol. (4s.) for labour and fuel, and 1 dol. (4s.) for expenses of management and control. The number of men employed was 38, at from 3 dol. (12s.) per day to 12½ c. (6d.) per hour. The working expenses might have been relatively less, but for the short supply of cane. To the above costs of 2 dol. (8s.), half for labour and fuel, and half for management, must be added the cost of the cane, reckoned at 2 dol. (8s.) per ton, and it is asserted that on this basis, taking the yield of cane and the product, a profitable business has been developed.

Cost of working.

The processes of making sugar from sorghum at the Parkinson Factory are as follows:—

The process.

1. The topped cane is delivered at the factory by the farmers who grow it.

2. The cane is cut by a machine into pieces about one and a quarter inches long. This is accomplished in the ensilage or feed-cutter, which is provided with three knives, fastened to three spokes of an iron wheel making 250 revolutions per minute, and carrying the knives with a shearing motion past a dead knife. The leaves, and nearly the entire sheaths, are thus freed from the pieces of cane, and the whole are then carried up by an elevator to the second floor.

3. The leaves and sheaths are separated from the cut cane by fanning-mills. The elevator empties into a hopper below, with a series of four or five fans arranged one below the other. The leaves are thus blown away, and finally taken from the building by an exhaust-fan; this separation of the leaves and refuse containing the greater part of colouring and deleterious matter being essential. The pieces of cane are then delivered by a screw-carrier to an elevator, which discharges into the final cutting-machine on the third floor.

4. The cleaned cane is cut into fine bits called chips. This machine consists of an eight-inch cast-iron cylinder, with knives like those of a planing machine, and revolves at the rate of 1,200 per minute; the knives, which are inserted in slots, and held in place with set screws, are carried past an iron dead knife, and the pieces are cut into fine chips,

which are then taken by an elevator and conveyed to the cells of the diffusion battery.

5. The chips are placed in iron tanks, and the sugar diffused soaked out with hot water. The diffusion battery consists of twelve iron tanks, arranged in a line, each with a capacity of 75 cubic feet, and holding nearly a ton of chips. These cells are supported near the middle by brackets, which rest on iron joists, and each is provided with a heater, through which the liquid is passed in the operation of the battery. They are also connected with pipes and valves, so that the liquid can be passed to the cells and from cell to cell at pleasure. The bottom of each cell consists of a door, closed on an annular rubber hose, placed in a groove, and filled with water under a greater pressure than the liquids in the cells are subject to, through which exhausted chips are passed into a truck below. The upper part is jug-shaped and secured with a lid held with a screw on rubber-packing. The cells are connected with a water-pipe, a juice-pipe, a compressed air-pipe, and the heaters by suitable valves, and the heaters are connected with a steam-pipe. These cells are filled with chips and water, turned on in the first till full, when by the process of diffusion the sugar is displaced. The condition under which sugar exists in the cane is one of solution in water, and the walls of the cells in which the sweetish liquid is contained, are porous. In a few minutes there is as much sugar in the liquid outside of the cane cells, as in the juice in these cane cells, *i.e.*, the water and the juice have divided the sugar between them. The liquid, always kept as nearly as possible at the boiling-point, is then passed into another cell full of fresh chips, and by the same process gains in strength, till, after being pressed forward and diffused successively through six cells of fresh chips, it is $\frac{31}{32}$ strength, and is then called juice, and drawn off; from this time forward one cell is emptied for every one filled. The difficulty experienced on account of the inversion of the sugar in the diffusion battery, is now successfully met; at the suggestion of Professor Swenson, a portion of freshly precipitated carbonate of lime is placed with the chips in each cell, which takes up any acid which may exist producing inversion, and remains inactive should none exist.

6. The juice obtained by diffusion, has its acids nearly or quite neutralised with milk of lime, and is heated and skimmed. The juice drawn off is taken from the measuring tanks into large deep vessels, called defecating tanks or pans, and provided with copper steam coils, for the purpose of heating the juice. Sufficient milk of lime is added to neutralise acids, the test being made with litmus paper. The juice, after being boiled, and as much scum removed as can be taken quickly, is then sent by a pump to the top of the building, when it is boiled and thoroughly reskimmed, all skimmings being returned to the different cells.

7. The defecated or clarified juice is boiled to a semi-syrup in vacuum pans. This is done by double-effect evaporation in two large closed pans provided with copper steam-pipes. The juice has now reached a condition in which it will keep, and is taken to the " strike-pan."

8. The semi-syrup is boiled " to grain " in a high vacuum in the " strike-pan."

This is a large air-tight iron vessel, where the semi-syrup is boiled in vacuo to the crystallizing density, air and vapour having been almost exhausted; this operation is delicate and requires much attention. The mixture is then called "melada" or "massuite," and is either drawn off into iron sugar-wagons and set in the hot room, or emptied direct into the mixer where it is brought to a uniform consistency.

2. The mixture of sugar and molasses from the strike-pan is passed through a mixing-machine into centrifugal machines which throw out the

molasses and retain the sugar. The molasses is now driven through the meshes of the wire cloth in the centrifugal machine, and the sugar, when sufficiently dried is taken out, and is ready for market, unless the further process of refining is required.

From the actual yield at Fort Scott last year and from the experience gained, it is thought safe to assume that an average of 100 lbs. of sugar and 12 gallons of molasses can be extracted from one ton of sorghum, and the conclusion come to is that an industry of vast importance has been developed. The diffusion battery is reported to work admirably; the difficulties in cutting, cleaning, and elevating the cane have been overcome, and the loss from inversion remedied, though improvements may yet be made to simplify the machinery and reduce the labour of operating. One great question is to determine the point at which the cane has arrived at such a degree of maturity as to have made its sugar; this must be done by chemical analysis, the manufacturer having no other means of testing the condition required. After being cut, the cane should not be exposed to the atmospheric influences of the earlier part of the season for any considerable time, whereby the sugar might be turned into glucose, great loss being sustained from damaged or injured cane. It should be worked the same day as cut in hot weather, or, if cut in the afternoon before 24 hours have passed, while in cooler weather, later in the season, the same despatch is not necessary. It must be passed rapidly through the different processes till it arrives at a keeping condition, that is, till the juice is reduced to semi-syrup. Analysis is also frequently requisite to observe whether during the work inversion is taking place, when the cause should be at once removed. Little has as yet been done to develop methods of separating the grape sugar, but grape sugar is a valuable content of sorghum, and about 63 lbs. are contained in a ton of cane.

Experience gained.

As the sweet sap is produced by the natural growth of the plant, and is easily lost through inversion in over-ripe or injured canes, as well as after cutting in warm weather, the farmer's part in the process of sugar-making is the first, and a most important one. It is thought a great deal may be done by experiments to improve the canes, on the same principle as beet for sugar-making purposes has been improved, by careful nursing, producing different hybrids, and preserving seed only from such cane as has been shown by analysis to contain the greatest amount of sugar. It is also thought that the length of the season for working sorghum may be extended by the development of earlier varieties, and by cultivation.

The farmer's part.

Experiments have been repeatedly made in keeping cane in sheds and in silo, so as to reduce the great cost of sugar operations by keeping the works open beyond the crop season, and from analysis of the "Orange" and "Link's Hybrid" varieties, it is thought that cane can be so kept with little depreciation of its contents of sugar for a greater part of the winter. The distance at which farmers can profitably grow the cane on account of quick delivery at the factory is not greater than three miles, unless railway communication is at hand.

The seed of sorghum is about equal value with corn for feeding purposes.

Taking seven and a half tons of clean cane as an average yield—and good cultivation can increase the yield to 10 and even 12 tons—an acre of land cultivated in sorghum, will produce 750 lbs. of sugar, 1,000 lbs. of molasses, 900 lbs. of seed, 1,500 lbs. of fodder, and 1,500 lbs. of exhausted chips, (dried); and the total value of the sugar, molasses and seed is about 59 dol. 50 c. (11*l*. 18*s*.). For the corresponding gross yield

Conclusion.

of 10 tons of sorghum at 2 dol. (8s.) per ton, the farmer will make 20 dol. (4l.) per acre for his crop, or more than double the yield of a crop of wheat or corn; while as a gross product of agriculture and manufacture it is said that six times as much per acre will be realised from this industy as is usually realised from cereals in the State of Kansas.

N.B.—For the convenience of this report, the exchange is calculated at five dollars per £ sterling.

LONDON:
Printed for Her Majesty's Stationery Office,
By HARRISON AND SONS,
Printers in Ordinary to Her Majesty.
(1125 2 | 88—H & S 342)

BOARD OF AGRICULTURE.

EXTRACTS

RELATING TO

PLEURO-PNEUMONIA

IN THE

UNITED STATES OF AMERICA

FROM THE

FIRST REPORT OF THE SECRETARY

OF

AGRICULTURE, WASHINGTON.

Presented to both Houses of Parliament by Command of Her Majesty.

LONDON:
PRINTED FOR HER MAJESTY'S STATIONERY OFFICE,
BY EYRE AND SPOTTISWOODE,
PRINTERS TO THE QUEEN'S MOST EXCELLENT MAJESTY.

And to be purchased, either directly or through any Bookseller, from
EYRE AND SPOTTISWOODE, EAST HARDING STREET, FLEET STREET, E.C., and
32, ABINGDON STREET, WESTMINSTER, S.W; or
ADAM AND CHARLES BLACK, 6, NORTH BRIDGE, EDINBURGH; or
HODGES, FIGGIS, & Co., 104, GRAFTON STREET, DUBLIN.

1890.

[C.—6146.]   *Price 1d.*

CONTENTS.

	Page.
EXTRACT from the REPORT OF THE SECRETARY OF AGRICULTURE, dated 26th October 1889	3
EXTRACTS from the REPORT OF THE CHIEF OF THE BUREAU OF ANIMAL INDUSTRY	5

Extract from the Report of the Secretary of Agriculture, dated 26th October 1889.

BUREAU OF ANIMAL INDUSTRY.

The work of the Bureau in the control and eradication of contagious pleuro-pneumonia has been vigorous, and I am happy to state successfully prosecuted. Thanks to these vigorous measures, the contagion has not spread to any new districts, and the infected territory has been so steadily reduced in extent that it is now entirely confined to the following mentioned States. In New York the disease has been eradicated from Orange and New York Counties, and to-day is only found in Kings and Queens Counties, and is there much less prevalent than it was a year ago. The reports from New Jersey indicate that the disease has been practically stamped out, and there is every reason to believe that a few months of supervision will remove the last trace of the contagion. Only two small outbreaks have been reported from Pennsylvania within the past year. The first was effectually stamped out and measures promptly taken on receipt of the report of the second by the State veterinarian, and the slaughter of two affected animals seems to have removed all apprehension of further danger. But three affected herds have been found in Maryland the past six months, and there seems to be no likelihood of further trouble there. My intention is to maintain a sufficient force of inspectors in each of these States to establish a strict supervision of cattle for three or four months after the last appearance of the disease, thus insuring against any subsequent development of it. It is gratifying to recall that the effectual measures taken by this Department have almost entirely prevented the periodical rumours and subsequent panics among those engaged in the cattle trade which a few years ago were so frequent and so disastrous to the cattle industry.

The number of cattle purchased for slaughter from July 1, 1888, to June 30, 1889, in order to secure the eradication of the plague, has been: in New York, 1,460 diseased, 3,011 exposed; in New Jersey, 255 diseased and 880 exposed; in Pennsylvania, 15 diseased, 68 exposed; and in Maryland, 217 diseased, 624 exposed.

The number purchased per month gradually decreased until it became much less than during corresponding periods of the preceding year. The total number of cattle found affected during the last-mentioned period with pleuro-pneumonia on *post-mortem* examination was: in New York, 1,561; in New

E 63470.   Wt. 7139.

Jersey, 302; in Pennsylvania, 29; in Maryland, 242; a total of 2,134. Reports received since June 30, 1889, indicate, as I have said, that the vigorous measures adopted have proved very effectual, and justify the most sanguine hopes in regard to the present control and proximate complete eradication of the disease.

* * * * * * *

Extracts from the Report of the Chief of the Bureau of Animal Industry.

PLEURO-PNEUMONIA.

The measures for the eradication of the contagious pleuro-pneumonia of cattle, as given in detail in former reports, have been continued during the year without interruption or modification. The progress of the work has been notable, though not as rapid as would be possible if the Department had sufficient authority to properly enforce its regulations. It has often been found difficult to secure the prosecution and conviction of parties who have violated the State laws under which the regulations are made. Some parties, who have flagrantly and persistently violated the regulations and even assaulted the officers of the Department, have had their cases dismissed by justices of the peace or by the grand juries before which the matter was brought, with the intimation that proscutions for such offences would not be countenanced by them.

The great obstacle to the speedy conclusion of this work is, therefore, not in any inherent difficulties in the work itself, but in the impossibility of securing under the present statutes a strict enforcement of the necessary rules. The infected area is, however, constantly decreasing, and the number of herds in which the disease is found is becoming smaller with each quarter. This improvement will be made plain in the tables which follow.

It is gratifying to be able to state that no outbreaks of pleuro-pneumonia have been discovered during the year in the section of the country west of the Alleghany Mountains. It is also fortunate that no extensions of the contagion have occurred in the Eastern States since the report for 1888 was submitted. The absence of such outbreaks has so increased the confidence of cattle-owners and shippers that our domestic traffic in cattle outside of the infected districts is no longer influenced to any appreciable extent by the presence of this contagion in the country.

Work in New York.

One year ago pleuro-pneumonia existed in the counties of Orange, New York, Kings, and Queens. No cases have been discovered in Orange and New York Counties since June, so that the disease has been confined for the last five months to Kings and Queens Counties. These two counties have long been the oldest and worst infected sections of the country. Many of the dairymen are unfavourably disposed towards the work of eradication and are unwilling to submit to the regulations. Cattle in many instances have been pastured upon the commons and moved from stable to stable without permit. Exposure in this way accounts for many of the new cases of disease which have been recently developed.

Many stables in the infected districts are without ventilation. They are so constructed that it is impossible to keep them in a proper sanitary condition. There are accumulations of filth under the floors, and the wood-work is rotten and porous. Such buildings cannot be satisfactorily disinfected, nor can they be held without stock a sufficient length of time after the diseased herds are removed to insure safety. The result is that in some cases the plague has appeared several times on the same premises.

To prevent these re-infections is one of the most difficult problems which is to be solved. In Maryland there was for a time the same difficulty, and it was removed in the worst cases by the State Live-Stock Sanitary Board condemning and destroying such buildings as could not be properly disinfected. The compensation in such cases was made from the State appropriation. This Department has up to the present declined to expend any part of the appropriation for the purchase and destruction of buildings, but in certain cases in the badly infected districts of Long Island such action may become necessary for the success of the work.

From December 1, 1888, the date to which the figures were given in the previous report, to November 30, 1889, there were inspected in New York 15,861 herds, containing 149,396 head of cattle. Of this number 137,688 were re-examined by the non-professional assistants, and 33,135 were tagged with numbers and registered upon the books of the Bureau.

There were 156 new herds found affected with pleuro-pneumonia during the year, and these herds contained 3,014 animals, 249 of which were pronounced diseased when the inspections were made. There were purchased for slaughter during the same time 1,053 affected cattle, at a cost of $28,210.05, an average of $26.79; also, 2,819 exposed cattle, at a cost of $59,908.93, an average of $21.25. The smaller cost of the exposed cattle as compared with the affected ones is due to the fact that the amount which the owner realised for the carcasses was deducted from the appraised value, the Department paying the balance.

It has been found necessary to disinfect 339 stables, stockyards, or other premises during the year, and also to make *post-mortem* examinations upon the carcasses of 15,375 bovine animals, of which 1,012 were found diseased with pleuro-pneumonia.

The total expenses in New York from December 1, 1888, to November 30, 1889, have been $187,814.99, of which $88,118.98 was paid for cattle purchased for slaughter as either diseased or exposed. The remainder constitutes the expense for disinfection, inspection, tagging, registering, supervising the movement of cattle, *post-mortem* examinations, and all the various expenses incident to a work of this character.

WORK IN NEW JERSEY.

In this State the operations have been almost entirely confined to Hudson County, with the exception of a large diseased herd found in the distillery stables at East Millstone, and three affected herds in Essex County which were infected by cattle taken by dealers from Hudson County in violation of the quarantine regulations.

The State Board of Health has for more than six months been desirous of removing the quarantine restrictions from Hudson County, but has consented to maintain them up to the present time upon the urgent representations of this Department that such action was necessary to the success of the work. It is doubtful if proper regulations can be continued in New Jersey under the present system of co-operation until the contagion is completed eradicated. The importance of success here is exceptionally great because of the traffic in cattle between the infected district in New Jersey and the neighbouring counties in New York. If the disease should again become prevalent in the former State it would be difficult if not impossible to prevent the re-infection of Westchester and New York Counties in the latter State. There would also be great danger of the infection of cattle destined for shipment to Europe from the port of New York, many of which go through the New Jersey stock-yards To properly protect this enormous trade between the States and with foreign countries greater powers are required than are now possessed by this Department.

From December 1, 1888, to November 30, 1889, there were inspected in New Jersey 8,455 herds, containing 76,001 head of cattle. Of this number 39,287 were re-examined by the non-professional assistants, 11,672 were tagged with numbers and registered upon the books of the Bureau.

There were 48 new herds found infected with pleuro-pneumonia during the year, and these herds contained 964 animals, 81 of which were pronounced diseased when the inspections were made. There were purchased for slaughter during the same time 116 affected cattle at a cost of $2,659, an average of $22.92 per head, also 704 exposed cattle at a cost of $16,592, an average of $23.57.

It has been found necessary to disinfect 208 stables, stock-yards, and other premises, and also to make *post-mortem* examinations upon the carcasses of 14,242 bovine animals, of which 189 were found diseased with pleuro-pneumonia.

The total expenses in New Jersey from December 1, 1888, to November 30, 1889, have been $69,345.42 of which $19,251 was paid for cattle purchased for slaughter, because they were either diseased or had been exposed.

THE WORK IN PENNSYLVANIA.

As indicated in the last report, quarantine restrictions at Philadelphia were removed on December 15, 1888, and at that time the greater part of the force of the Bureau stationed there was withdrawn. It was deemed advisable, however, to retain at that city two veterinary inspectors and two assistant inspectors for the purpose of maintaining a supervision of the Philadelphia stock-yards, and to watch the slaughter-houses and rendering works for a few months, in order that any re-appearance of disease might be promptly detected. The wisdom of this course was made apparent on December 31, when our inspectors discovered at the Philadelphia stock-yards a herd of cattle having contagious pleuro-pneumonia. These cattle had been shipped to Philadelphia from the Somerset Distillery stables at East Millstone, New Jersey. On being slaughtered, seventeen cases of contagious pleuro-pneumonia were found on *post-mortem* examination. All cattle that had come in contact with this herd were promptly quarantined and slaughtered, and the stock-yards were thoroughly disinfected. The railroad cars in which these cattle had been transported were traced to Altoona, Pa., where they were disinfected by officers of the Bureau.

Under date of September 11, the secretary of the State Board of Agriculture informed this Bureau that a herd had been discovered by the State officers in Chester County, Pa., having contagious pleuro-pneumonia, that the State veterinarian had killed two animals, and on *post-mortem* examination had pronounced them to be affected with contagious pleuro-pneumonia in an acute form. An officer of the Bureau was detailed to visit that locality, but failed to find any evidence of lung plague among animals there inspected. For the reason, however, that the premises on which the disease had been reported to exist was a public cattle or drove yard from which cattle were transported to Wilmington, Del., the stock-yards at Philadelphia, and into other channels of interstate commerce, it was thought necessary, in order to protect the cattle industry of the country from any possible danger, that these premises, and also all cattle that had been in contact with the herd reported to have been diseased, should be strictly quarantined. This was done; and in addition the stock-yards at Chester, where the disease was said to be, were thoroughly disinfected. The quarantine was maintained for ninety days, and at the end of that time no evidence of lung plague having developed, all restrictions were removed.

With these exceptions no contagious pleuro-pneumonia has been found in Pennsylvania during the year, and it is thought that the contagion no longer exists there.

From December 1, 1888, to November 30, 1889, there were inspected in Pennsylvania 1,311 herds, containing 24,003 head of cattle. Of this number 1,285 were re-examined by the non-professional assistants, and 1,513 were tagged with numbers and registered upon the books of the Bureau.

There were no herds in the State found by our inspectors to be affected with pleuro-pneumonia. There were purchased for slaughter eleven exposed cattle at a cost of $190, an average of $17.27 per head.

It was considered advisable to disinfect six stables, stock-yards, and other premises; 13,412 *post-mortem* examinations were made upon the carcasses of bovine animals, of which 17 were found diseased with pleuro-pneumonia.

The total expenses in Pennsylvania from December 1, 1888, to November 30, 1889, have been $8,856.25, of which $190 was paid for exposed cattle purchased for slaughter.

WORK IN MARYLAND.

The progress of the work in Maryland has been extremely satisfactory. With the active sympathy of the Governor and Attorney-General, and the earnest co-operation of the Live-Stock Sanitary Board, the quarantine regulations have been enforced and the contagion has been eradicated. Only five herds affected with pleuro-pneumonia have been discovered in the last ten months, and at this writing (December 20) three months have elapsed since a case of the disease has occurred.

We have here one of the most striking illustrations that the history of the world has furnished of the possibility of exterminating this plague from the worst infected of cities, and from the dairies of the adjoining country districts, within a reasonable time, by the application of proper sanitary measures. In the Old World it has always required many years under the regulations generally adopted to free a long infected district from the disease, while in some cities, as for example Paris, the work has gone on for years without appreciably diminishing the number of cases of disease which annually develop.

From December 1, 1888, to November 30, 1889, there were inspected in Maryland 10,904 herds, containing 79,606 head of cattle. Of this number 4,866 were re-examined by the non-professional assistants, and 10,534 were tagged with numbers and registered upon the books of the Bureau.

There were 18 new herds found infected with pleuro-pneumonia during the year, and these herds contained 295 animals, 21 of which were pronounced diseased when the inspections were made. There were purchased for slaughter during the same time 72 affected cattle at a cost of $2,254.27, an average of $31.31 per head; also 311 exposed cattle at a cost of $7,341.83, an average of $23.61 per head.

It has been found necessary to disinfect 35 stables, stockyards, and other premises during the year, and also to make *post-mortem* examinations upon the carcasses of 11,496 bovine animals, of which 76 were found diseased with pleuro pneumonia.

The total expenses in Maryland from December 1, 1888, to November 30, 1889, have been $57,488.96, of which $9,596.10 was paid for cattle purchased for slaughter as either diseased or exposed.

The Work as a Whole.

Including all the districts in which pleuro-pneumonia has existed, there were inspected from December 1, 1888, to November 30, 1889, a total of 36,531 herds of cattle, containing 329,006 animals. Of this number, 183,126 were re-examined by the non-professional assistants in addition to the veterinary inspections, and 56,854 were tagged with numbers and registered upon the books of the Bureau.

There were 222 new herds found affected with pleuro-pneumonia during the year, and these herds contained 4,273 animals, 351 of which were pronounced diseased when the inspections were made. There were purchased for slaughter during the same time 1,241 affected cattle at a cost of $33,123.32, an average of $26.69 per head; also, 3,845 exposed cattle at a cost of $84,032.76, an average of $21.86 per head.

It has been found necessary to disinfect 588 stables, stockyards, or other premises, and also to make *post-mortem* examinations upon the carcasses of 54,520 bovine animals, of which 1,294 were found diseased with pleuro-pneumonia.

The total expenses of the pleuro-pneumonia work from December 1, 1888, to November 30, 1889, have been $323,505.62, of which $117,156.08 was paid for cattle purchased for slaughter as either diseased or exposed. The remainder constitutes the expense for inspection, disinfection, tagging, registering, and supervising the movement of cattle, of *post-mortem* examinations, and of all the various expenses necessary to insure the prompt discovery of this plague when it appears in any herd, and to prevent the further extension of the infection.

The following table gives a résumé of the pleuro-pneumonia work from December 1, 1888, to November 30, 1889, as given in detail above:—

	New York.	New Jersey.	Pennsylvania.	Maryland.	Total.
Herds inspected	15,861	8,455	1,311	10,904	36,531
Cattle inspected	149,396	76,001	24,003	79,606	329,006
Cattle re-examined	137,688	39,287	1,285	4,866	183,126
Diseased cattle found by inspection.	249	81	—	21	351
Post-mortem examinations	15,375	14,242	13,412	11,491	54,520
Diseased carcasses found	1,012	189	17	76	1,294
Cattle tagged	33,135	11,672	1,513	10,534	56,854
New herds found affected	156	48	—	18	222
Animals in affected herds	3,014	964	—	295	4,273
Diseased cattle purchased	1,053	116	—	72	1,241
Exposed cattle purchased	2,819	704	11	311	3,845
Premises disinfected	339	208	6	35	588

A résumé of the expenditures in the pleuro-pneumonia work from December 1, 1888, to November 30, 1889, is made in the table which follows.

	New York.	New Jersey.	Pennsylvania.	Maryland.	Total.
	$	$	$	$	$
Salaries	81,863.02	36,600.58	7,630.53	37,712.99	163,807.12
Travelling expenses	11,746.78	10,629.92	614.83	8,903.87	31,895.40
Miscellaneous expenses	6,086.21	2,863.92	420.89	1,276.00	10,647.02
Affected cattle	28,210.05	2,659.00	—	2,254.27	33,123.32
Exposed cattle	59,908.93	16,592.00	190.00	7,341.83	84,032.76
Average paid for affected cattle	26.79	22.92	—	31.31	26.69
Average paid for exposed cattle	21.25	23.57	17.27	23.61	21.86

Comparison with the previous Year.

The progress accomplished by this work can only be estimated by comparing the number of new herds found affected during the year and the total number of cases of pleuro-pneumonia found on *post-mortem* examination with similar data gathered from the reports of the preceding year. As the carcasses of all animals which die or are slaughtered from the quarantine districts are examined, we have in the returns of the *post-mortem* examinations the total number of cases of pleuro-pneumonia which have developed.

The following table shows the number of new herds found affected, the number of *post-mortem* examinations that were made, and the number of carcasses found affected with pleuro-pneumonia at the *post-mortem* examinations for the years from December 1, 1887, to November 30, 1888, and from December 1, 1888, to November 30, 1889 :—

States.	No. of New Herds affected.		No. of Post-mortem Examinations.		No. of Carcasses affected with Pleuro-pneumonia.	
	1888.	1889.	1888.	1889.	1888.	1889.
New York	347	156	15,826	15,375	2,374	1,012
New Jersey	216	48	6,892	14,242	536	189
Pennsylvania	23	—	13,157	13,412	72	17
Maryland	96	18	6,165	11,491	596	76
Total	682	222	42,040	54,520	3,578	1,294

The above table shows that there were less than half as many new herds found affected in New York during the last year as in the preceding year. There were also less than half as many diseased carcasses found on *post-mortem* examination in 1889 as in 1888, although the number of carcasses examined was nearly the same. In New Jersey there were only about one-fourth as many affected herds and about one-third as many affected animals, although a greatly increased number of carcasses was examined. In Pennsylvania and Maryland the reduction as shown by the table is even more marked, and is still greater than the figures indicate, as the malady has entirely disappeared from those States during the last quarter of the year.

* * * * * * *

Notwithstanding the fact that the number of cattle in this country per thousand of population has been slowly decreasing during the past four years, the large proportion of these animals that are being marketed still keeps the market overstocked, and makes it extremely important that every effort should be made to maintain the export trade at least to its present extent, and, if possible, to increase it. The only danger to the trade in live cattle which has been suggested during the year is the occasional discovery of an animal which the English veterinary authorities supposed to be affected with contagious pleuro-pneumonia. It is impossible to understand how any of the beef cattle going abroad can be infected with this disease. After the most careful and extended investigations in the United States, this Bureau has been unable to discover any pleuro-pneumonia in any section from which steers are shipped. The only districts in which this disease does exist are two counties on Long Island and one county in New Jersey. The Long Island district is isolated, and no cattle from it go into the stock-yards through which the export cattle pass. The infected district in New Jersey is very nearly free from the disease, and while it is not isolated like the Long Island district, no steers are raised for beef in this section, and the stock-yards are believed to be thoroughly protected.

For the reasons given above, we are led irresistibly to the conclusion that the disease found in the lungs of American steers when slaughtered on the English wharves is a sporadic inflammation, which probably in most cases arises from exposure during the voyage. It is well known that generally no special characters are found by which contagious pleuro-pneumonia can be distinguished with certainty from the sporadic form of inflammation of the lungs and pleura. In making a diagnosis the veterinarian is always assisted by the history of contagion in the herds in which the disease is found, and, in the absence of such a history, if a single case of inflammation of the lungs and pleura is discovered, it is difficult or impossible to make a positive diagnosis. With American steers slaughtered in England it is impossible, under existing conditions, to have any history of the animals, and as but a single steer is usually found affected in a whole cargo, there is nothing to indicate that the malady discovered is of a contagious nature.

It is plain that the diagnosis of the English veterinarians in the cases of supposed pleuro-pneumonia among our steers must be more or less uncertain and open to doubt, without reflecting in the least upon the professional ability and competency of the inspectors making the examination. As this trade has grown to such an extent, and is of such great importance to the cattle industry of this country, it would seem very proper that we should take some means to determine whether the animals pronounced affected with contagious pleuro-pneumonia are really suffering from this disease. This fact could probably be determined by stationing one or more agents of the Department in

England to examine the lungs of animals pronounced diseased, and to determine as accurately as possible the exact conditions of their organs. The animals going abroad might also be numbered at the time of their shipment from the American ports, according to some system by which any individual animal might be traced back to the herd from which it came. In this way it would be possible to determine whether such an animal had been in any way exposed to the contagion of pleuro-pneumonia. With such precautions it would seem possible to settle this long contested question as to whether the disease found by English inspectors in American steers is or is not contagious pleuro-pneumonia.

*   *   *   *   *   *   *

LONDON: Printed by EYRE and SPOTTISWOODE,
Printers to the Queen's most Excellent Majesty.
For Her Majesty's Stationery Office.

FOREIGN OFFICE.

1892.

MISCELLANEOUS SERIES.

N°. 245.

REPORTS ON SUBJECTS OF GENERAL AND COMMERCIAL INTEREST.

UNITED STATES.

REPORT (WITH PLATES) ON THE

PRUNE INDUSTRY OF CALIFORNIA.

Issued during the Recess and Presented to both Houses of Parliament by Command of Her Majesty.

LONDON:
PRINTED FOR HER MAJESTY'S STATIONERY OFFICE,
BY HARRISON AND SONS, ST. MARTIN'S LANE,
PRINTERS IN ORDINARY TO HER MAJESTY.

And to be purchased, either directly or through any Bookseller, from
EYRE & SPOTTISWOODE, EAST HARDING STREET, FLEET STREET, E.C., and
32, ABINGDON STREET, WESTMINSTER, S.W.; or
JOHN MENZIES & Co., 12, HANOVER STREET, EDINBURGH, and
90, WEST NILE STREET, GLASGOW; or
HODGES, FIGGIS, & Co., 104, GRAFTON STREET, DUBLIN.

1892.

[C. 6813—5.]   *Price Elevenpence Halfpenny.*

New Series of Reports.

The following Reports from Her Majesty's Representatives abroad, on subjects of general and commercial interest, have been issued, and may be obtained from the sources indicated on the title-page:—

No.		Price.
210.	*Borneo.*—Notes on a Visit to Sarawak, and its Trade	1d.
211.	*Italy.*—Report on the Condition of Labour in Italy	6d.
212.	*Germany.*—Report on the Present State of the Labour Question in Germany	2d.
213.	*France.*—Report on the Present State of the Labour Question in France	1½d.
214.	*Belgium.*—Report of the Present State of the Labour Question in Belgium	3d.
215.	*Norway.*—Report on the Fisheries of Norway, 1890	½d.
216.	*Argentine Republic.*—Report on Emigration to Argentine Republic, and Demand for Labour, 1891	3d.
217.	*Russia.*—Report on the Condition of Labour in Russia	1½d.
218.	*Argentine Republic.*—Report on the Salt Industry of the Argentine Republic	½d.
219.	*Austria-Hungary.*—Report on the Timber Trade of Bosnia and the Herzegovina	1½d.
220.	*Netherlands.*—Report on the Evidence taken at Rotterdam and Amsterdam by the Dutch Labour Commission	1½d.
221.	*Netherlands.*—Report on Legislation for Protection of Women and Young Children Employed in Factories, &c.	1d.
222.	*Tunis.*—Report on Projected Extension of the Tunisian Railway System	1d.
223.	*Bulgaria.*—Translation of New Law on Mines	½d.
224.	*Netherlands.*—Report on the Effects of the Law of 1889 for the Protection of Women and Children Engaged in Factory and other Work	2d.
225.	*Egypt.*—Report on the Aloe Fibre Industries of Somali Land	½d.
226.	*Roumania.*—Report on Roumanian Trade, Agriculture, and Danube Navigation from 1881 to 1890	1d.
227.	*Denmark.*—Statistics of the Town of Copenhagen	½d.
228.	*Austria-Hungary.*—Report on Vine Culture in Bosnia and the Herzegovina	½d.
229.	*Belgium.*—Report on the History and Progress of Telephone Enterprise in Belgium	1d.
230.	*Denmark.*—Further Report on the Progress of the Works of the Free Port of Copenhagen	½d.
231.	*Japan.*—Report on the Native Industries of Japan	2d.
232.	*Morocco.*—Report on the Present Condition of British Trade in Morocco	2d.
233.	*Belgium.*—Report on the Creation and Constitution of a Higher Council of Labour	1d.
234.	*Bavaria.*—Summary of Reports of Bavarian Inspectors of Factories for 1891	½d.
235.	*United States.*—Report on the Earnings of Labour and Cost of Living in the Consular District of Chicago	3d.
236.	*Mexico.*—Report on the Henequen Hemp Industry at Yucatan	1d.
237.	*Germany.*—Report on the Progress of the Trade, &c., of Hamburg for the Years 1841-90	1½d.
238.	*Austria-Hungary.*—Report on the Condition of Labour in Hungary	3d.
239.	*Russia.*—Report on the Iron Industry of the Province of Ekaterinoslav for 1891	½d.
240.	*Denmark.*—Report on the New Danish Maritime Code, more particularly in its bearing on Questions of General Average	1½d.
241.	*France.*—Report on the Shipping and Harbour Improvements at Rouen (with plans)	7d.
242.	*Russia.*—Further Report on Provisions of Industrial Population on Old Age	½d.
243.	*Switzerland.*—New Swiss Regulations respecting Commercial Travellers	½d.
244.	*Switzerland.*—Report on the Condition of Labour in Switzerland	6d.

No. 245.

UNITED STATES.

SAN FRANCISCO.

Consul Donohoe to the Marquis of Salisbury.

My Lord,   *San Francisco, May* 23, 1892.

I HAVE the honour to enclose herewith a Report on the History and Method of Prune Culture in the State of California, which has been prepared by Mr. Vice-Consul Moore of this Consulate. This Report gives very full particulars as to the cultivation of this fruit and will prove of great value to anyone intending to pursue this industry in California. The cultivation of the prune has reached large proportions of late years, and is becoming one of the leading fruit products of the State.

I have, &c.
(Signed)   DENIS DONOHOE.

Report on the Prune Industry of California.

ABSTRACT of Contents.

	PAGE
Origin and growth of industry	2
Habitat of the prune	3
Cultivation, soil and stock	4
Planting and systems of orchard	5
Different varieties; propagation	6
Necessity of careful cultivation	8
Irrigation; pruning	9
Pests affecting prunes, and remedies; yield; picking and curing	11
Grading	12
Finishing	14
Packing; production and markets	15

UNITED STATES.

The following Report on the above subject is compiled from the Annual Report of the State Board of Horticulture of the State of California:—

Introduction into California.

It is to France that California is indebted for this healthful and profitable fruit. Louis Pellier, a French sailor, who had visited many parts of the world, arrived in San Francisco in 1849, and went to work in the mines in Trinity County. He did not succeed well there, and finally removed to San José early in the fifties. Here he established a nursery. He soon after induced his brother Pierre, whom he had left in France, to join him in California, and the two brothers worked the nursery together until the spring of 1856, when Pierre returned to France in order to marry a girl to whom he was engaged. Combining business with pleasure, he secured a large number of cuttings of prunes, grapes and other fruits, which he brought back with him on his return. His bride and his brother Jean accompanied him, and, together with the box of precious cuttings, they made the voyage successfully, crossing the Isthmus of Panama and arriving in San Francisco in December, 1856.

The prune cuttings were procured in the Ville Neuve d'Agen, from whence the common Californian prune derives it name of Petit Prune d'Agen. They were carefully packed in a box about sixteen inches square by four feet in length, which was lined with cloth, and every precaution was taken to insure the safe arrival of what has since proved the germ of one of the most important industries of California. Upon its arrival the shipment was at once transmitted to Louis Pellier at San José, and a number of plum roots were grafted to the newly arrived prunes. This started the first prune nursery on the Pacific Coast.

The importance of Pellier's experiment was not at first appreciated. A German nurseryman named B. Kamp, procured some grafts from Pellier, and also worked for the introduction of the prune. He was one of the first to put out prune trees in orchard row. But comparatively little attention was paid to prune growing, as a speciality, for a quarter of a century after its introduction into the State. The superiority of California as a fruit-growing State, however, at last forced itself upon public attention, and, among other fruits, the prune was given a trial, and it soon proved its great capacity as a profitable crop, and to-day it ranks among the leading industries of the Golden State.

Growth of the industry.

Probably the oldest orchard of any size in the State is the Bradley orchard, on Steven's Creek Road, about two miles out of San José. This was set out in 1870. The success of this led others to go into prune growing, and the O'Banion and Kent orchard, near Saratoga, was planted in 1878-9, and the Dr. Handy orchard of 100 acres, at Saratoga, followed in 1880-81; in 1881 the Buxton orchard, also at Saratoga, was planted, and prune growing and curing on a large scale became a fixed fact.

From that time the growth of the industry has been phenomenal. The prune industry has been practically the growth of the past decade, for within that period the planting of orchards, their cultivation, and the proper care of their product, have grown into a system. In the prune centre of Santa Clara county, which ten years since produced not a pound of this fruit, it is now exported by the carload. Above Los Gatos, Mr. Morrell was then one of the heaviest producers, and his output was from five to six tons per annum; he now packs from five to six carloads each season from the same orchard.

Santa Clara county was from the beginning the centre of the prune industry, and there was demonstrated the fact that prune growing would pay, that no extraordinary care was required in cultivation or mysterious skill in preparation. As soon as these facts were known other counties took up the pursuit, until now the prune is found in all except the highest mountain counties in the State. In 1870 there were but 19,059 prune trees in the State, while the Assessors' reports for 1886, which are probably 25 per cent. too low, give the number in the various countries that year at 1,077,841 trees.

The Assessor's reports for 1891 show a very large increase in the past five years in those counties which have made returns.

A large portion of these trees, perhaps one-half, are not yet in full bearing. It is estimated that when the trees now growing into Santa Clara county alone shall have matured the annual product will be over 40,000,000 pounds of dried fruit.

The prune is a very hardy tree, and will thrive in a wide range of climate and soil and at various elevations. Wherever the greengage plum will grow, the prune can be grown. It will stand severe winter weather, and will grow where the thermometer touches zero. Its favourite habitat, however, is a temperate climate and a warm, generous soil. It can be grown in the Eastern states, but the short seasons there, the numerous pests, and the unfavourable conditions for drying which exist, prevent the East from ever entering the field as a competitor to California in the prune industry. Even in California, while the tree will grow in nearly all the counties, there are but few favoured localities in which it appears at its best. In some sections of this State where the prune makes a thrifty growth and yields heavily, there is a lack of saccharine matter in the fruit that deprives it of its best qualities, and when dried a very inferior product is the result. In other localities large juicy fruit will be grown, which decreases heavily in drying. The prime requisites in the prune are solid, firm flesh, that will not ferment at the pit in drying, a rich fruity flavour and bouquet, and a keeping quality that will stand the test of months or years without serious loss from shrinkage, and those sections which possess the peculiarities of soil and climate which ensure these in their greatest perfection are the true prune sections. The drying quality of the prune varies very greatly owing to the varieties

Habitat of the prune.

of soil in which it is grown. In some localities it will shrink in drying from four to one, while in others two-and-a-half pounds of green fruit will make one pound of dried. The fruit will also vary in different places in thickness and toughness of skin.

The prune is a gross feeder, and wants for its best development a rich and heavy soil with sufficient moisture to feed it. The foothills of Santa Clara county have long been regarded as especially favourable to the prune, but, as experiments in its growth have been made, other sections have been found that furnish all the required conditions, and while Santa Clara county is still, and probably always will be, the centre and most important section of this industry, it is not now the only prune county of the State. The most extensive single prune orchard in the State is now in the Salinas Valley, in San Luis Obispo county, in the eastern slope of the coast range, near the town of Templeton. In this orchard the are nearly 300 acres of prunes in one body, containing 324,000 trees. Some very excellent prunes are produced in Los Angeles, Orange, San Bernardino, San Diego, Ventura, Alameda, Monterey, Napa, Sonoma, and in the counties of the San Joaquin and Sacramento Valleys, while especially good results have been reported from Tehama, Shasta, Humboldt, Sutter, and Yuba counties. It is not improbable that in time the different localities of the State will discover certain lines in which each excels, and the production of specialities in that line will result in the fruit from each being known for its own peculiarities.

Methods of cultivation.

Soil and stock.

The soil required for prunes depends largely upon the stock used, or rather, perhaps, the stock should be selected to suit the soil. A light, deep, sandy loam, not too moist and well-drained, is adapted to peach stock, which does well on the sedimentary deposits of the higher valleys. Such soils are warm and light, and experience has proved that peach stock will do better here than on the heavy, clayey lands of the bottoms.

In the heavier soils, plum stock does better than peach, and the Myrobalan or wild plum stock is the favourite. It is hardy, forms a good union with its graft, and does not sucker as other plum stock will.

The almond stock is a favourite with many growers who have a rocky subsoil, as it does well in such land, even better than the peach.

The preparation of the soil depends largely upon its peculiarities. If heavy, it should be deeply ploughed and subsoiled. If there is a hardpan subsoil, this should also be broken, which can be done with any good subsoil plough; in any event, the ground should be ploughed deep and well stirred up for ventilation. It is well, when practicable, to begin the preparation of the land for an orchard some time before the planting of it. It should be thoroughly and deeply-ploughed early in the autumn, leaving the surface rough and exposed to the air during the winter. This facilitates the access of air to the lower layers and gives vitality to the soil. Following in the furrow with a subsoil plough is desirable, especially in the conversion of old grain lands into orchards, as it breaks up the old hardpan which has probably formed through years of shallow culture. The preparation may continue through the following summer, and, where practicable, hoed crops can be grown, or the land can be left to summer-fallow, care being taken to keep it thoroughly pulverized and free from weeds. If it is desirable to fertilize the land, manure can be applied in the winter, before the trees are planted. If this is not done then, the work should be left until the trees are planted, and the manure should be evenly spread over the surface during the winter, to be ploughed under in the spring. Care should be taken to spread it evenly and not mass it around the young trees, unless it is to be applied as a mulch to prevent evaporation after spring cultivation.

If it is desired to plant the land immediately after breaking up, the work should be commenced as early in the fall (autumn) as it is possible to do, deep ploughing, and the ground should be stirred to a depth of 10 inches, or 12 inches or more, if practicable, and should afterwards be thoroughly harrowed. If it is still early, cross plough deeply and follow with a subsoil plow, working to a depth of 14 inches or more. Harrow again thoroughly and the land is ready for the trees.

Planting the orchard. In laying off the orchard it is desirable to have it symmetrical and to economise the land. A little thought and care displayed at the commencement will save much annoyance in after years, and it is no greater task to have the orchard neat in appearance and symmetrical in outline than to have it in a haphazard condition. There are three objects to be considered in laying out the orchard: symmetry of appearance, economy of space, and facility for future care. Of course, the first thing is to get the trees in straight rows, at equal distances apart, and everyone thinks he can accomplish this. But there are various methods of disposing of the straight row, and these methods all have their advocates and each one its advantages. The principal forms are the square, the quincunx, and the hexagonal or septuple. The methods most common in use are the square and the quincunx systems. The most generally adopted is the square system, as the orchard can be changed to quincunx after being planted, even after a number of years' growth, by the addition of a tree planted in the centre of each square.

The square system of planting. The square system is the most approved. The orchard is laid off in lines crossing each other, with equal intervals of space, and a tree planted at each crossing of the lines. By this method, at 20 feet apart, 108 trees are planted to the acre.

In the proper planting of trees a little care is an absolute necessity, as it is in all branches of orchard work. Rules that would apply to one locality and under one set of conditions will fail in another. Some of the most successful orchardists advise the removal of the top dirt carefully, then digging a hole of liberal depth and placing the surface soil in the bottom;

(1355)

upon this the tree roots are to be set, and the hole filled up with top dirt. Where there is a subsoil of cold, heavy clay, this plan is admirable, but in warmer, sandy soils it is unnecessary. One of the most experienced prune growers in Santa Clara County advises the throwing out of a dead furrow after the land has been prepared, in which the trees are to be set at proper distances, and the soil thrown back on them with a plough, and afterwards pressed closely around the roots.

The more careful method is the best, as it gives the young tree better root hold, and affords a larger area from which to derive its nourishment during its early period of growth.

The distances at which trees are planted in orchard row varies from 18 to 24 feet, 20 feet being the favourite, and under most conditions probably the best distance. On very strong soil the greater distance would be better, as where more closely planted the limbs of the full grown trees are liable to become intertwined, and to render cultivation and gathering inconvenient. At a distance of 20 feet apart, planted by the square plan, there would be 108 trees to the acre, and by the hexagonal plan 126. After planting the young trees should be cut back to 18 inches from the ground, and they should be protected during the first season from the heat of the sun by a shade on the south side. Three or four buds should be allowed to grow at the top, and the terminal buds of the lower branches, should be pinched back after they have grown out a little, so that the buds will put out leaves and shade the stalk the first year.

Varieties. The principal varieties are the California (the Petite Prune d'Agen), the Bulgarian, the Fellenberg, the German, the Hungarian, and the Hungarian Date Prune, the Robe de Sergent, the Silver, and the Tragedy. Of these the first named is by far the most popular, and forms the true shipping prune of California.

Propagation of the prune. The first prunes were grafted on plum stock, but this has grown into disfavour on account of the tendency of plums to throw out suckers; and other stocks, the peach, the apricot, and lastly the Myrobalan plum, have come into use.

There is an intimate relation between soil and stock. For light, sandy soil the peach stock is yet in great favour, and many growers prefer it over all others. Upon heavier soils it does not do so well as does the Myrobalan. For some time apricot stock was the favourite, but it has now fallen into total disuse. Experience has taught fruit growers a severe lesson. The prune makes a very poor union with the apricot, and when the tree gets to be large enough to catch the wind it invariably breaks off at the joint of the two stocks. In one instance a fruit grower lost 1,000 trees in an orchard.

Those who have prunes grafted on apricot root can prevent their loss in the following manner:—As the peach makes a good union with both the prune and the apricot, it can be used as an aid; the soil must be removed from the tree so as to get

THE PRUNE INDUSTRY.

THE CALIFORNIA PRUNE.
(P. d'Agen.)

at the union of it. The peach cion must be cut in such a way as to be inserted above and below the union. It will form an arch with the trunk of the tree. On small trees two such grafts will suffice, but on large trees at least four should be placed. These grafts will eventually thicken and form a complete trunk for the tree.

The Myrobalan, or cherry plum (Prunus Myrobalana) has of late come into great favour as a stock for the prune. It is claimed by some growers that the fruit on Myrobalan stock is smaller than on peach stock, but that its flesh is more solid and dries heavier. The influence of the root on the cured fruit is, however, still a mooted question.

The Myrobalan stock comes from France. It is a wild plum of great thriftiness, and is used very extensively in that country for budding stock of the prune. It grows readily from seed and cuttings, and is easily propagated. The seeds are generally sent to this coast in the middle of October, and then they are at once sprouted. There has been considerable discussion during the last few years as to what is the true Myrobalan, and it must be acknowledged that some of the refined distinctions which have been mooted do not seem to be well placed. Seedlings grown from the seed of the Myrobalan vary, as do other fruit seedlings, both in fruit and in foliage and habit of trees; and perhaps this fact has given rise to the distinction between "true" and "false" Myrobalan, so-called. Practice has proceeded without much reference to the discussion, and whether grown here from seed of trees imported long ago, or from cuttings of the same, or whether seedling stocks are imported directly from France, as large quantities are, the Myrobalan of French origin is now the accepted plum stock for California. It has largely displaced the St. Julien and the Myrabelle, as well as the peach. Though described by some authorities as a dwarfing stock, it is found to be sufficiently free growing in California to suit all purposes, and to form a good foundation for full standard trees. Its leaves are smaller and its shoots finer than the cherry plum tree, grown for its fruit in this State.

Whether Myrobalan shall be grown from seed or from cuttings is an open question in California practice. Large quantities have been grown from cuttings, as in the French practice, according to Baltet. Other propagators hold, with W. H. Pepper, of Petaluma, that plum cuttings form a mass of fibrous roots at the lower end of the cutting, and when transplanted fail to send out strong supporting roots. As for the durability of trees grown from cuttings, there can easily be found old, thrifty orchards planted with such trees, though it must be acknowledged a better root system would be expected from a seedling, and there are instances in which trees from cuttings are held to be diseased in the root, while seedling roots are healthy. Possibly longer experience may yield a demonstration of the question.

Experience has shown that the Myrobalan stock thrives in this State both in low, moist, valley lands, in comparatively dry lands, and in stiff upland soils. Thus it has come to be accepted as an all-round stock for the prune.

It is urged against peach stock for damp, heavy soils, that it does not do well; that the sap sours and the fruit will not set well, while the root is subject to root knot, borers, and other pests that do not affect the Myrobalan stock on the heavier soils.

The prune is propagated by both budding and grafting. It is customary to bud the young stock first, as, if the bud does not take, it affords an opportunity to graft later in the season, thus giving the nurseryman two chances. The budding season extends from the middle of July to the end of August. The young trees are stripped of their leaves and twigs about 6 inches above the ground, at which place the bud is inserted. The grafting season is in January and February, at which time grafts are inserted in all the plants in which the buds have not taken. The grafting is done as near the surface of the soil as convenient, usually about 2 or 3 inches from the ground. The whole process of budding and grafting is described at length in the present report, under the marginal note, " Propagation of the prune," and can be dismissed here without further notice.

Cultivation.

In the prune orchard, as in all others, careful cultivation pays. A double object is attained by keeping the surface well pulverised. First, the weeds, which draw heavily upon the vitality of the soil, which should be devoted to tree and fruit growth, are destroyed, and the fertilising qualities which they would extract from the land are left for the benefit of the growing fruit. Secondly, it prevents the rapid evaporation of moisture of the soil, the loose surface acting as a mulch, and on dry lands especially, renders the need of irrigation less frequent. Further advantages are found in the neat appearance of the orchard, making it pleasing to the eye, and, further, rendering its penetration easy both to teams and men. A neglected orchard, overrun with weeds, takes money out of the pocket of the owner.

It is customary to plough deeply in the early spring, usually as soon as the weeds are fairly started. The seeds of these are given a fair chance to germinate, in order that the plough may turn under and destroy as many as possible, rendering subsequent cultivation much easier. Near the tree rows, shallow ploughing must be the rule, taking care to avoid injuring the roots as much as possible. After ploughing, the land should be thoroughly harrowed and left in as good condition as it can be made. After the spring ploughing, a cultivator, or weed cutter, should be run through the orchard from two to four times in the season as may be needed, to keep the weeds down and the surface loose. Particular pains should be taken in the last cultivation to leave the ground beneath the trees as fine and smooth as it can be made Many growers work it fine with a rake, breaking carefully all lumps, smoothing down all hillocks or inequalities, and leaving a perfectly level and smooth surface, upon which the ripened fruit fruit can fall without injury. In foothill land it is usual after the harvest to plough a furrow on the low side of the row, which is left during the winter to catch the rainfall and prevent its escape to the lower lands. By this means the land gets the benefit of the entire winter precipitation, which is husbanded for summer use.

The matter of irrigation is another thing that must be left to the individual orchardist, for it depends wholly upon the character of the soil upon which the orchard is growing. Some lands producing excellent prunes are so damp that drainage has to be resorted to in order to prevent the surplus water from drowning out the trees, while upon others, notably in the southern part of the State, where intense evaporation and dry land are the rule, irrigation must be frequent and thorough, and careful cultivation must follow each period of irrigation. In portions of the Santa Clara Valley, it is believed that at least 20 inches of rain are necessary to insure good crops, and winter irrigation is resorted to, the land being thoroughly soaked while the trees are in their dormant state, and no water is applied in the summer. Upon this question there is as great diversity of opinion as there is in regard to soil, and each grower must use his own best judgment, taking into consideration the characteristics of the land upon which his orchard is situated. In sections where irrigation is practised for all orchard crops, the prune is treated the same as is the peach, the apricot, or the almond.

Irrigation.

The training of the young tree requires thought, care, and judgment. In the first three years of its life it is to assume the form which it is to retain during its whole existence. Here, again, the individual judgment must be exercised, and conditions of soil, climate and requirements must be considered. Two schools, in regard to pruning, have sprung up, each advocating a system diametrically opposed to the other, and each backing its opinions with plausible arguments—the one favouring high pruning, the other low; one heavy pruning, the other light. It is argued in favour of the high-cut tree that it is much easier to cultivate the orchard when a horse can be driven under the limbs, than when it is necessary to work under them with a hoe, as when they are trained low. The advocates of high pruning, in answer to the objections that high-pruned trees in hot climates are liable to sun-burn, state that they may be planted closer together and thus afford shade for each other. In favour of low pruning it is urged that the limbs bending beneath their weight of fruit will find support on the ground, that the trunks are protected from the sun, and that the fruit is easier to gather.

Pruning.

Mr. W. H. Aiken, of Wrights, gives the following rules for training the young tree:—

"Cut back the trees after planting to 18 inches from the ground, and shade on south side by some convenient shade. Three or four buds should be allowed to grow at the top, and the terminal buds of those below pinched back after they have grown out a little, so that the buds will put out leaves and shade the stalk the first year. The second year remove them and cut back the limbs to a foot in length; the third, two feet, &c., the object in view being to shape a handsome tree with strength and bearing span, which can be attained only by low training and intelligent pruning.

"After about six years of age, when in full bearing, the tree does not need cutting back as much as it does thinning out of cross limbs, if any, and pruning out unfruitful wood. The sprays or small twigs in body of the French prune tree should be cut back to one or two fruit buds, so that the fruit may be large. Some, however, advise the removal of all such sprays, as the fruit on them is small at the best.

It is important in pruning to select buds on the upper side of the limbs, as they will have a greater weight-bearing power than buds forming branches from under side of boughs. Summer pruning is not advisable. A full season's growth properly pruned back in the winter, and trained low so that the branches take a natural upward and oblique direction, will shape a tree that will be strong and broad enough to live long and be fruitful.

"My idea of pruning the prune tree is to make a handsome tree with plenty of limbs, and prune it back so that it will give the limbs great strength and bearing space. In that way you can raise a large amount of good plums or prunes. The tree should not be thinned out much unless the limbs cross, because when they begin to bear the tree opens very nicely. I have eight year old French prune trees, and though they did not average it, many of them had 800 pounds of prunes on this year, without much affecting the form or shape of the tree. They were so pruned and so strong, and with such a broad bearing space, that they bore that amount of prunes and very easily, although it has been a dry year, and they were not quite as large as they would have been if there had been a little more moisture. I think the great mistake in raising the prune is leaving too few limbs, say one limb up in the air, and the other one in another direction, like two arms. On such a tree you can raise very little fruit, and it would be of very little profit. I am of the opinion, too, that this pruning should go on each year, and give a fine form and strength and bearing space, and when the tree bears and gets to be over six years old, and is in good bearing, you do not need so much pruning back. Indeed, I think when the tree is eight, or nine or ten years old, it does not need much, if any, pruning back; of course, take out the old limbs to keep it in good form or shape."

Low training and little pruning after the fourth year have grown in favour of late, and are the systems which have the largest support among prune growers. The work of pruning should be commenced as soon as the sap stops flowing, which will depend upon the season, but as soon as the green leaves are gone, and no danger is to be apprehended from "bleeding," pruning may be advantageously begun.

Plum Aphis ("Aphis prunifolia").—These plant lice appear on the under side of the young leaves in spring, and increase very rapidly, so as to cover the new growth in a few weeks. In the last few years this pest has been on the increase. Plant lice, as a general rule, are hard to destroy, owing to their oily excrement. So far whale-oil soap has proved the best remedy. If a tree is badly infested the lice produce such quantities of honeydew as to make the leaves and fruit very sticky to handle. *Pests affecting the prune, and their remedies.*

Peach Moth ("Anarsia lineatella").—This insect attacks the young shoots of the tree, bores into the pith, and causes the shoot to wither. Last year it proved very destructive, and caused many a fruit grower to become alarmed. The lime, salt, and sulphur remedy applied in winter checks it to a great extent.

Tree Cricket ("Oecanthus latipennis").—The limbs of the prune are bored into by this insect, and the eggs are found in the pith. When these crickets are numerous the young limbs become seriously damaged. The best remedy is to cut off all infested limbs and burn them.

The Black Scale ("Lecanium olea"), Apricot Scale ("Lecanium armeniacum"), Frosted Scale ("Lecanium pruniosum"), and Pernicious Scale (Aspidiotus perniciosus") are those scale insects which trouble the prune tree most. Some orchards have not produced good crops on account of having been so badly infested with these pests, the quantity of scale preventing the fruit from growing large and being marketable. The different scale remedies given elsewhere have been well tested and proved to be efficient, provided diligence and pains are taken by the fruit grower when he prepares them.

Root Borer ("Ægeria existosa").—Trees grown on peach stock imported from the East must be carefully examined, and if found infested with the pest must be destroyed. These insects will ruin a tree in a very short time.

The prune is a prolific bearer, and can be relied upon for annual crops. Unlike many fruits, it does not take an occasional season's rest, but will yield its average returns every season. If properly cultivated some fruit may be gathered the third year, and the fourth year will field a fairly profitable crop; the fifth year will give from 50 to 60 lbs. to the tree, which the sixth year should double. From this time on the tree can be considered as in full bearing, and will give from 150 to 300 lbs. of green fruit annually. The average yield for Santa Clara county is about 300 lbs. per tree. In some instances 600 to 800 lbs. to the tree are reported, and one six-year old tree in Visalia is credited with 1,102 lbs. of green fruit in one season. *Yield.*

The prune is picked from the tree when fully ripe, which is *Picking and curing.*

UNITED STATES.

Process of gathering.

indicated when it passes from light reddish to purple, and by the withering condition of the fruit. It is very important that the fruit be thoroughly ripe, or else when dried it will be devoid of that rich flavour so essential in a marketable fruit. In most sections the prune upon ripening has a tendency to drop to the ground, which fruit is gathered and processed with the rest of the crop. The picking of the fruit, simple as the process appears, is one of the most particular things in prune cultivation. Many of the leading growers go over their orchards eight or ten times, gathering the ripest fruit each time. People are kept continually at work in the season gathering the ripe fruit. Starting at one end of the orchard they will work it over, and by the time they have got through the part first gathered is ready for the second picking, and this is repeated until the entire crop is harvested. The object is to get the fruit in its prime condition—rich, full, meaty, and thoroughly ripe. If it dries on the tree a little and begins to shrivel it is none the worse. The fruit is usually allowed to drop on the ground, from whence it is gathered, and no greater assistance is given it in falling than the gentlest tap on the trunk of the tree; a severe shaking even is not allowed. At the last picking the fruit that remains on the tree is gathered with that which has fallen. By this method the fruit is assured of positive ripeness, is solid, and is charged with saccharine matter so desirable in the cured article. The prune will generally drop from the tree when fully ripe, and will not rot even if left on the ground under the trees for several days. As the fruit shows indications of ripening the ground under the trees is generally cleared of all rubbish and worthless fruit, so that when the mature fruit does fall it can be gathered by itself, free from rubbish. Sometimes a sheet is placed upon the ground under the tree, and the ripe fruit is shaken into it, after which the sheet is picked up by the corner, and the fruit turned into boxes and loaded on a wagon, to be taken to the drying ground.

Grading and curing.

Prunes are generally graded before drying, and various home-made contrivances are employed. Some use inclined planes of adjustable slats, the grader being thus available for other fruit than prunes; the large fruit rolls along into receptacles at the bottom, while the small fruit falls through into other receptacles. Other grading devices are made with wire screens, or riddles of different sizes of mesh. Some of them work on the principle of a fanning mill—three or four riddles placed one above the other, each with a slight incline, and a spout on the side, where each grade drops into a box. Some have a long riddle, say 12 feet long, with three different sizes of wire screen on it. This riddle is hung upon four ropes, with an incline; the prunes are thrown in at the higher end, and by shaking it they roll down and fall through the holes into boxes underneath. The first piece of screen should be small, to let only stems and dirt through, and no prunes. This long, hanging screen is also used to grade prunes after drying.

The object to be attained by grading before drying is equality in drying. The smaller fruit dries more rapidly than the larger, and by grading it into two or three sizes, as it comes from the tree, greater uniformity in evaporation is secured, and a more even quality of finished fruit is the result. The grader also removes all twigs, leaves, or other foreign substances which may have become mixed with the fruit in picking.

The next process to which the fruit is subjected is known as dipping. This is one of the most important processes in the whole preparation of the prune for market, and much of the success of the pack will depend upon the person having it in charge. The ripeness of the fruit, the toughness of the skin, and other peculiarities of the fruit have to be considered in the preparation of the lye into which it is dipped, so that no certain rule can be laid down. The object to be attained is to remove the bloom, which fills up the pores, and at the same time crack the skin of the fruit so that evaporation may take place more rapidly. In its natural state the skin of the prune is almost impervious, and unless dipped the fruit would consume weeks if not months in drying. The usual strength of the dip is about 1 lb. of concentrated lye to each 10 gallons of water. The proper strength, however, must be left to the judgment of the operator, and the lye must be sufficiently strong to crack the skin of the prune. The lye must be kept boiling hot during the operation, and not allowed to cool by the immersion of the fruit. The length of time required for immersion also varies according to the toughness of the skin, the soil upon which the fruit is grown, and the age of the orchard, fruit from old orchards and heavy land being tougher than that from young orchards and freer soils. The average time required is about 30 seconds, but the fruit must be withdrawn as soon as the skin shows minute cracks on its surface. If left too long the sugar will ooze through the cracks in drying, rendering the fruit sticky and disagreeable to handle, and causing it to lose much of its best qualities; if it is removed too soon it will not dry well. After their removal from the lye bath, the scalded prunes are next plunged into clean, fresh water, which rinses off all the lye that may have adhered to them in the first operation. This water must be changed frequently to prevent its becoming too heavily impregnated with lye. For dipping the fruit is put into wire baskets, or galvanised pails with perforated sides and bottoms. In the Buxton orchard, at Campbell, in Santa Clara County, a very ingenious device is used, which does the work automatically. The prunes are taken direct from the orchard, and unloaded into a bin. Elevators raise them to the grader, which removes all twigs, leaves, and rubbish, and assorts the fruit into two sizes. These two sizes each fall into an endless apron, provided with carrying slats, and are carried through the lye baths, which are kept at a boiling pitch by steam pipes, a separate bath being provided for each sized fruit. The apron continues from the lye bath into the rinsing bath, which is kept fresh by a continuous stream of pure water which flows through it, and from the rinsing bath the fruit is delivered to the trays.

Drying is done wholly by the sun. A number of experiments with driers have been made, but the machines were found wholly inadequate to handle the crops, and sunshine was found so much superior that they have fallen into almost complete disuse, and are now used to so limited an extent as to require no consideration in connection with the prune industry. After the fruit comes from its second, or fresh-water bath, it is spread evenly on trays of a convenient size, usually about two by three feet, made of thin timber and easy to handle, and these trays are placed on the drying ground, a space which has been carefully selected with a view to its full exposure to the sun. The drying season extends from the middle of August until the beginning of November. The length of time required for the complete dessication of the fruit depends upon the weather, its heat, and the humidity of the atmosphere.

In hot, dry conditions, the fruit requires a shorter exposure than where it is cool and moist. The drying period will vary under these circumstances from a week to a month, and the time at which to remove the fruit from the drying grounds must be left to the judgment of the operator. It should, however, be sufficiently well dried to warrant its keeping under all conditions, but not so dry as to rattle. When sufficiently dried the fruit is taken to the processing house, where it is put into bins to "sweat." This operation requires from two to three weeks, during which period the fruit must be carefully shovelled over several times and thoroughly intermixed. At the end of the sweating season it assumes a black, glossy appearance, and resumes somewhat of its original plumpness.

Finishing.

The next process is that of "finishing." This comprises a second bath, to which the now dried fruit is subjected. This bath is simply boiling water, to which is added such ingredients as the judgment or the whim of the individual grower may fancy will improve the appearance or quality of his fruit. The objects to be obtained in the second dipping are to destroy whatever insect germs may have become attached in drying, and to soften the skin. The fruit should be left in the bath until partially cooked and these ends are accomplished. Some growers add sufficient salt to the dip to make it a fairly strong brine, and this has the advantage of increasing the heat of the water several degrees beyond that to which fresh water can be heated, and making its effect surer. Others add a small quantity of glycerine, glucose, fruit juices, and some few logwood or indigo. This is done for the purpose of improving the appearance of the fruit and adding to its gloss and colour. Many of the most experienced packers decry the addition of any of the last-named articles, claiming that they are ineffective and do not add either to the quality or appearance of the fruit. In about three hours the fruit will be sufficiently dry for packing.

Before passing the finishing process the fruit is once more run through the grader and assorted into standard sizes for the market. There are usually six sizes: first, those ranging from 40 to 50 to the pound; second, 50 to 60 to the pound; third, 60 to 70 to the pound; fourth, 70 to 80 to the pound; fifth, 80 to 90 to the pound; and sixth, all below 90.

Packing. The final operation in the handling of the prune is packing, and here again great judgment is required in putting up a thoroughly good article, that will present an attractive appearance and force its way on the market. Great care must be exercised that no fruit be packed until all surplus moisture between the fruit has entirely disappeared, for if packed while damp the fruit will mould in the packages; at the same time all fruit that is overdried must be thrown out. The skilful packer can tell by the sense of touch just what fruit is fit for packing, and that which is not, as he runs his fingers over the piles before him. Much of the fruit is packed in boxes of 10 lbs., 25 lbs., and 50 lbs. each, but of late there is a growing demand for fruit in sacks, and large quantities are now shipped to the Eastern States in 100 lb. sacks, where it is either boxed by the eastern dealer or sold direct from the sacks to the consumer.

Production and markets. The principal markets for California prunes are Chicago and New York, by far the greater portion being shipped to Chicago. Some smaller shipments are also sent to Philadelphia and Pittsburg. From these central points the product finds its way to the retailers, and thence to the consumers of the country. Although but a comparatively new aspirant for public favour, the California prune has forced its way in advance of the imported article, and brings from 2 c. to 2½ c. (1d. to 1¼d.) per lb. more than the French prune sold in competition with it. The proportion of pit and skin to meat in the California fruit is much less than in that of the French article, while the proportion of saccharine matter is much greater.

These features give our domestic fruit its great advantage over the imported article. This popularity should be no surprise, as the California French prune is a different article from the imported French prune. Our prunes, as every consumer knows, are more like dates, and when cooked are of a most delicious flavour. Besides this, dealers have found out that the California prune keeps better and longer without sugaring than the imported goods.

The prune crop of 1889 was variously estimated at from 15,000,000 lbs. to 18,000,000 lbs., and it was sold at fair prices, ranging from 5 c. to 9 c. (2½d. to 4½d.) per lb., the average in the market being 2 c. (1d.) higher than the imported. The crop of 1890 was expected to fall short, owing to excessive rain upon the bloom, and the excessive moisture in the soil, which caused much of the fruit to drop after having attained a fair size At the end of the season it was apparent that the output was but very little, if at all, less than the preceding year. Prices for green fruit delivered at the driers' ranged from 21 dol. to 30 dol. (4l. 6s. 9d. to 6l. 4s.) per ton.

The amount of prunes now consumed in the United States is enormous, but the consumption is capable of great enlargement as the superior quality of the Pacific Coast product becomes better known. It will be years before the demand on this side of the Atlantic can be supplied, and when that shall have occurred there will be the market of Europe and the rest of the world to supply. The immense area devoted to prune culture this season (1891) testifies to the profound confidence felt in the future of the industry by the people of California, and that confidence certainly appears well founded.

The following table gives the foreign import and California production for the six years from 1885 to 1891, inclusive:—

Year.	Foreign Imports, by years, ending June 30th. Quantity.	Value in currency.	California Production, by years, ending December 31st. Quantity.	Value in sterling.
	Pounds.	Dollars.	Pounds.	£ s. d.
1885	57,631,820	2,147,505	..	443,699 7 4
1886	64,995,545	2,026,595	2,000,000	418,717 19 4
1887	92,032,625	2,999,648	1,825,000	619,761 19 6
1888	70,626,027	2,197,150	2,100,000	453,956 12 1
1889	46,154,825	1,423,304	15,200,000	294,071 1 5
1890	58,093,410	1,789,176	12,200,000	369,663 19 2
1891	34,281,322	2,054,486	27,000,000	424,480 11 5

The importation of prunes into the United States for the year 1890, to December 31st, was 61,905,782 lbs. valued at 2,819,420 dol. (582,524l. 15s. 8d.), an increase over the importations of 1889 of 18,188,429 lbs., and an increased value of 584,029 dol. (120,667l. 2s. 11d.) The product of the State of California for the same period is given for 1889 at 15,200,000 lbs., and 1890 at 12,200,000 lbs, or 28,517,353 lbs. less than were imported in 1890. It would appear that while the United States imports from three to four times the quantity of prunes produced by California, there is still a large field for our domestic fruit, and that with our continually increasing population, the danger of over supply is still very remote, and prune growing in California may be relied upon as a profitable industry for years, if not for generations, yet to come.

I enclose five illustrations showing the prune d'Agen; a six-year-old orchard; a six-year-old prune tree in bearing; a prune orchard in full bearing and drying-grounds; and prune drying-grounds of 10,000 trays.

The rate of exchange in this report is calculated at 4 dol. 84 c. to the pound sterling.

(75 7 | 92—H & S 1355)

FOREIGN OFFICE.

1894.

MISCELLANEOUS SERIES.

N°. 326.

REPORTS ON SUBJECTS OF GENERAL AND COMMERCIAL INTEREST.

UNITED STATES.

REPORT ON

TEA RAISING IN SOUTH CAROLINA.

Presented to both Houses of Parliament by Command of Her Majesty,
MARCH, 1894.

LONDON:
PRINTED FOR HER MAJESTY'S STATIONERY OFFICE,
BY HARRISON AND SONS, ST. MARTIN'S LANE,
PRINTERS IN ORDINARY TO HER MAJESTY.

And to be purchased, either directly or through any Bookseller, from
EYRE & SPOTTISWOODE, EAST HARDING STREET, FLEET STREET, E.C., and
32, ABINGDON STREET, WESTMINSTER, S.W.; or
JOHN MENZIES & Co., 12, HANOVER STREET, EDINBURGH, and
90, WEST NILE STREET, GLASGOW; or
HODGES, FIGGIS, & Co., Limited, 104, GRAFTON STREET, DUBLIN.

1894.

[C. 7294—2.] *Price One Halfpenny.*

New Series of Reports.

The following Reports from Her Majesty's Representatives abroad, on subjects of general and commercial interest, have been issued, and may be obtained from the sources indicated on the title-page:—

No.		Price.
282.	*Norway.*—Notes on the Condition of Peasant Proprietors in Norway	½d.
283.	*Germany.*—Report on Labour Time and Labour Wages in Germany	2½d.
284.	*Mexico.*—Translation of Circulars relating to Mexican Mining Laws	½d.
285.	*Spain.*—Report on the Marble Quarries of Macael in the Sierra de los Filabres	½d.
286.	*Denmark.*—Report on the Stamping and Control of Meat Supply	7½d.
287.	*Greece.*—Report on the New Greek Customs Law and Tariff	3d.
288.	*Turkey.*—Report on the Jaffa-Jerusalem Railway (with plans)	7d.
289.	*United States.*—Report on the Working of the Sugar Bounty Clause of the McKinley Act, with Statistics respecting the Consumption, &c., of Sugar in the United States for the year ended June 30, 1892	1½d.
290.	*Sweden and Norway.*—Further Report on the Telephone Systems of Sweden and Norway	4d.
291.	*Austria-Hungary.*—Notes on Landed Estates in Hungary	½d.
292.	*United States.*—Report on the Inauguration and Condition of the World's Columbian Exposition	1d.
293.	*Russia.*—Report on the Cultivation of the Vine at Berdiansk	½d.
294.	*Russia.*—Report on the Salt Industry in Astrakhan	1d.
295.	*France.*—Report on Poultry Yards and Dairy Farms in France	1d.
296.	*Tunis.*—Further Report on the Railway System of Tunis	½d.
297.	*Italy.*—Report on the Sulphur Industry of Sicily	1½d.
298.	*Argentine Republic.*—Report on Immigration and Emigration in 1892-93	3d.
299.	*Japan.*—Report on the National Debt of Japan	1d.
300.	*Turkey.*—Report on Irrigation and Orange Growing at Jaffa	1d.
301.	*Spain.*—Report on the Textile Industries at Catalonia	1d.
302.	*Mexico.*—Report on the Effect of Depreciation of Silver on Mexico	2d.
303.	*Greece.*—Report on the Mineral Resources of the Island of Milo (with Plan)	5½d.
304.	*Portugal.*—Report on the Port Wine Trade of Oporto	1d.
305.	*China.*—Report on the Effect of the Fall in Value of Silver on Prices of Commodities in China	2d.
306.	*Portugal.*—Report on the Railway Route from Beira to Mashonaland	½d.
307.	*Russia.*—Report on the Manganese Ore Industry of Sharopan	3d.
308.	*France.*—Report on Sugar Cultivation in the Society Islands	½d.
309.	*Mexico.*—Report on the Railways of Mexico	4d
310.	*Chile.*—Report on Chile as a Field for Emigration	1d.
311.	*Germany.*—Report on the Regulations respecting the Manufacture of Lucifer Matches in Germany and Prussia	½d.
312.	*Germany.*—Report on Life Insurance in Germany	½d.
313.	*Austria-Hungary.*—Report on the Plum Trade of Bosnia for the Year 1893	½d.
314.	*United States.*—Report on the Close of the World's Columbian Exposition at Chicago	2½d.
315.	*Japan.*—Report on Japanese Currency	1d.
316.	*Germany.*—Précis of Memoranda laid before the Reichstag respecting the German South-West African and East African Protectorates	1½d.
317.	*Corea.*—Report on the Cultivation of Cotton in Corea	½d.
318.	*Corea.*—Report on the Commercial Condition of the Ports of Fusan and Wönsan	1d.
319.	*France.*—Report on the Cultivation of Vanilla in Tahiti	½d.
320.	*Austria-Hungary.*—Report on the Sugar Industry in Bosnia	½d.
321.	*United States.*—Report on the Coal Mines of West Virginia	1½d.
322.	*Columbia.*—Report on the Cultivation of Cacao, Bananas, and India-rubber in Districts surrounding the Sierra Nevada of Santa Marta	1½d.
323.	*Argentine Republic.*—Report on Baron Hirsch's Jewish Colonisation Scheme	4d.
324.	*United States.*—Further Report on Liquor Traffic Legislation in the United States since 1889	4½d.
325.	*Germany.*—Report on the Question of Employers' Liability in Germany	2½d.

No. 326.

UNITED STATES.

CHARLESTON.

Consul Rawson-Walker to the Earl of Rosebery.

My Lord, Charleston, February 24, 1894.

I HAVE the honour to transmit, herewith enclosed, to your Lordship a Report on the Experimental Tea Farm at Summerville, a suburb some 20 miles distant from this town, which, owing to the climatic conditions of this part of the State of South Carolina, gives promise that great success will attend the afore said cultivation of the plant in question.

I have, &c.
(Signed) E. H. RAWSON-WALKER.

Report on Tea Raising in South Carolina.

The cultivation of tea at Dr. Shepard's Experimental Tea Gardens at Summerville, some 20 miles from Charleston, South Carolina, having been carried on very successfully of late by Dr. Shepard, a gentleman of property and scientific tastes, I have considered it might be interesting to give a few extracts from a report that gentleman has made to the Hon. J. M. Rusk, Assistant-Secretary of Agriculture, Washington.

From this report it would appear that the first tea plant in this section of the United States was planted by the French botanist, Michaux, in 1804, at Middleton Barony, on the Ashley River, distant some 15 miles from Charleston. With it was planted out the first representative of its cousin, the Camelia Japonica. Dr. Shepard states that he saw the former tree a few years ago, and that it had grown into a small tree, about 15 feet in height, while of the latter there were many specimens fully twice as tall.

The publications of the United States Patent Office and the United States Department of Agriculture record the results of many subsequent attempts to inaugurate an American tea

(1699)

industry. It would appear that repeated failure has not checked the ardour of those engaged in these experiments, who constantly enjoy the realisation that their climate is especially favourable for the cultivation of the Camelia Japonica, Azalea Indica (subtropical plants), and have read that the flora of the tea-producing countries of the East finds, to a certain extent, its counterpart here. The little patches, and, in some instances, large gardens, which have resulted from these attempts, have produced tea of fine flavour, although very generally devoid of that strength of infusion which appears to constitute a most desirable quality for many tea-drinkers. It may be presumed, however, that this failure in pungency was largely due to defective curing, and especially to inadequate rolling of the leaf, in consequence of which the cup qualities were not fully developed. So far as is generally known it remained for the National Department of Agriculture to begin, about 10 years ago, the first serious attempt to produce American commercial tea on a scale sufficiently large to arrive at a decisive result. The retirement from office of Commissioner William G. le Duc, to whose great interest in this subject the inception of the experiment was due; the death of Mr. John Jackson, under whose experienced management the gardens were established; the great distance of the station from its source of management, and the opinion of the United States Commissioner, George B. Loring, that the climatic conditions were not favourable for it (Report for 1883), combined to cause the total abandonment by the Government of the gardens which it had established at great expense on a plantation called Newington, about a mile distant from Pinehurst Farm, which also constituted a part of the same large estate.

The present experiment owes its undertaking to the belief that the previous trials to produce tea in the United States were arrested before reaching definite conclusions—that more careful cultivation and preparation, which might be the result of a lengthened local observation, and the subsequent production of a higher class of teas might reverse the generally entertained opinion that, as an industry, the cultivation of tea in this country must always prove a failure; and that, if successful, this new field for agricultural enterprise would furnish a wide and comparatively easy out-door employment for many who are unequal to those rougher operations, whose accomplishment under a summer's sun can be borne but by few in this climate.

It needed only the announcement of the revival of tea experiments in this country to excite the liveliest interest and assistance for the undertaking. The United States Department of Agriculture, under the direction of the Secretary, the Hon. J. M. Rusk, and Assistant-Secretary, Edwin Willets, has manifested a deep concern in the project, and has generously borne a considerable part of the expenditure for procuring consignments of tea seed from Asia. The Department of State has kindly issued orders to its Consuls at the tea ports to obtain these samples, and the foreign representatives of the United States Government have spared no effort to secure the best quality of seed.

CHARLESTON.

Quality of Tea produced at Pinehurst Tea Farm.

During the past summer of 1893 some of the Pinehurst plants were sufficiently advanced to warrant picking the leaf. The great majority of them had been raised from seed in 1889 and planted out that autumn; a limited number were a few months older. They belong to the Assam hybrid variety, *i.e.*, the cross between the Assamese and Chinese sorts, and come from stock that had been thoroughly acclimated by probably 30 years' growth in this country. The plants had been systematically "topped" with garden shears, and afterwards carefully pruned with a knife during the winter of 1891–92, and throughout their growth had been carefully cultivated and generously manured—they covered small areas on various soils, viz., under-drained pond and high swamp, the slope of a clay hill, and a flat, sandy pineland. So free had been the artificial enrichment of all these plants that no material difference in the quality or quantity of yield were observed. It was designed to test by these first experiments whether commercial tea could be raised at all.

Below are given the results from picking and curing such leaf as appeared to be suitable for manufacture, and might be spared without impairing the subsequent luxuriant development of the plants.

Report on Sample of Tea produced at Pinehurst Tea Farm, by the United States Secretary of Agriculture, dated November, 1892.

I wish to say that we are much pleased with the samples. A sample was sent to a travelling agent of a large tea firm in Detroit for his judgment, advising him as to where the tea was produced. He took the tea to his store, and without giving them any information with regard to the same, it was tested by two of the leading members of the firm, each making a separate test—they pronounced it very excellent English breakfast tea, and as I recollect claimed that it was better than any breakfast tea they had in the store or at least equally good, and when the information was given them as to the place of production, they were very much surprised and wished to know if any considerable amount could be purchased.

Opinion of Mr. Gilbert Gill, of Martin, Gilbert and Co., celebrated Tea Merchants of Baltimore, Maryland, United States, as published in the "Sun" of that City and other papers.

The first marketable tea ever produced in the United States was brought to Baltimore by Mr. Charles M. Shepard, of Summerville, South Carolina, who grew and cured the plant on his farm.

The American tea was tested by Mr. Gilbert Gill who pronounced it equal to the best high grade English breakfast tea and superior to many grades that come from India and China—the samples are all of one quality and character, black, crisp and well scented, it makes a strong beverage, this quality is said by Mr. Gill to be due solely to its treatment in fermentation and curing; other methods of curing the American product will produce tea similar to the several brands that come from India and China.

Opinion of Mr. Charles Kerr Reid, Tea Expert and Merchant, of Philadelphia.

Picking of June 14, season 1892. Report on samples from four grades into which the tea was sifted. No. 1. Rather handsome, rather small even blackish leaf with Pekoe flower, strictly extra fine tea, strong, full, and with South Carolina Pekoe flavour, value 32 c. to 35 c. wholesale.

No. 2. Blackish even leaf with a few Pekoe tips—fine to extra fine tea, strong, brisk South Carolina Souchong Pekoe flavour, value 25 c. to 30 c. wholesale.

No. 3. Rather bold, evenish curled black leaf, middling tea (or preferred), strong, brisk, fresh burnt, South Carolina Souchong flavour, value 22 c. to 25 c. wholesale.

No. 4. Bold, black, uneven curly leaf middling tea, rather strong, fresh burnt, South Carolina Souchong flavour, value 20 c. to 21 c. wholesale.

Yield of Tea.

Colonel Money, an expert on tea planting, gives the following estimate of the probable yield per acre on flat land, good soil in a good tea climate (which Summerville, near Charleston, South Carolina, is considered to be), this is with hybrid plants, if really high cultivation and liberal manuring is carried out:—

Year.	Yield of Tea per Acre.
	Lbs.
First	..
Second	..
Third	40
Fourth	160
Fifth	320
Sixth	400
Seventh	480
Eighth	560
Ninth	600
Tenth	640

The Pinehurst plants had been set out at a greater distance than is the practice in the East, with the object of substituting cultivators and ploughs drawn by mules for hand labour and the spade. After making due allowance for this difference and for average vacancies (where plants have died), and thus estimating the production by the same number of plants, we find the average of the Pinehurst gardens for the past season to have reached about 37½ lbs. of cured tea per acre of the earlier "flushes," as the successive crops of young and tender leaves are called, purposely very little was picked of the midsummer ones, we were careful to confine the pickings to the smallest leaf, and in the autumn we had at least one abundant flush that was permitted to remain on the bushes—in other words the standard production as laid down by the same authority might readily have been attained. Indeed, in view of subsequent events, it would have been better to have picked the late (October) flush, as probably thereby we might have prevented the florescence of the plants, with all its attendant drain on the resources, and subsequent entailed cost of picking off the incipient seed, in order to prevent the yet further exhaustion of the bushes by its full development through the next season. But we will assume that the Indian grower exercises as much care with his own gardens, and we will rest our case on the actual figures submitted. The results at Pinehurst are all the more gratifying as they were obtained on plants exhibiting great difference in form and luxuriance of growth and flushing—the seed from which they sprang had been brought from India long before the inauguration of the recent successful attempt to raise the grades of those teas by a judicious selection of seed and most careful cultivation. From the gardens now being established at Pinehurst, and in consequence of the great care bestowed on their composition, it is hoped to obtain much finer teas in the future.

LONDON:
Printed for Her Majesty's Stationery Office,
By HARRISON AND SONS,
Printers in Ordinary to Her Majesty.
(75 3 | 94—H & S 1699)

FOREIGN OFFICE.

1895.

MISCELLANEOUS SERIES.

N⁰. 360.

REPORTS ON SUBJECTS OF GENERAL AND COMMERCIAL INTEREST.

UNITED STATES.

REPORT ON THE

AGRICULTURAL CONDITION OF THE UNITED STATES AND THE PROBABLE COMPETITION WITH BRITISH AGRICULTURE IN THE FUTURE.

Presented to both Houses of Parliament by Command of Her Majesty,
MAY, 1895.

LONDON:
PRINTED FOR HER MAJESTY'S STATIONERY OFFICE,
BY HARRISON AND SONS, ST. MARTIN'S LANE,
PRINTERS IN ORDINARY TO HER MAJESTY.

And to be purchased, either directly or through any Bookseller, from
EYRE & SPOTTISWOODE, East Harding Street, Fleet Street, E.C., and
32, Abingdon Street, Westminster, S.W.; or
JOHN MENZIES & Co., 12, Hanover Street, Edinburgh, and
90, West Nile Street, Glasgow; or
HODGES, FIGGIS, & Co., Limited, 104, Grafton Street, Dublin.

1895.

[C. 7582—21.] *Price Twopence.*

New Series of Reports.

The following Reports from Her Majesty's Representatives abroad, on subjects of general and commercial interest, have been issued, and may be obtained from the sources indicated on the title-page:—

No.		Price.
320.	*Austria-Hungary.*—Report on the Sugar Industry in Bosnia	½d.
321.	*United States.*—Report on the Coal Mines of West Virginia	1½d.
322.	*Colombia.*—Report on the Cultivation of Cacao, Bananas, and India-rubber in Districts surrounding the Sierra Nevada of Santa Marta	1½d.
323.	*Argentine Republic.*—Report on Baron Hirsch's Jewish Colonisation Scheme	4d.
324.	*United States.*—Further Report on Liquor Traffic Legislation in the United States since 1889	4½d.
325.	*Germany.*—Report on the Question of Employers' Liability in Germany	2½d.
326.	*United States.*—Report on Tea Raising in South Carolina	½d.
327.	*Switzerland.*—Summary of Laws in force in Switzerland with regard to the Treatment of Inebriates	1½d.
328.	*Germany.*—Report on the Provision of the Treaty of Commerce between Russia and Germany	2½d.
329.	*Germany.*—Report on the Treaty of Commerce between Russia and Germany	2d.
330.	*China.*—Summary of First Decennial Report on the Chinese Imperial Maritime Customs	2½d.
331.	*Colombia.*—Report on the Mineral Products of the Republic of Colombia, with Summary of Mining Laws	2½d.
332.	*Switzerland.*—Report on Life Insurance in Switzerland	1½d.
333.	*Switzerland.*—Report on the Secondary Schools of the Canton of Zurich	1d.
334.	*Würtemberg.*—Summary of Reports of Würtemberg Factory Inspectors for 1893	½d.
335.	*Würtemberg.*—Report on the Railway, Telegraph, and Postal Services of Würtemberg	1d.
336.	*Bavaria.*—Summary of Reports of Bavarian Factory Inspectors for 1893	1d.
337.	*Italy.*—Report for the Year 1893 on the Position of the Labour Question in Italy	2½d.
338.	*Russia.*—Report on the Russo-German Commercial Treaty and its Probable Effect on Trade with Russia	2½d.
339.	*Russia.*—Report on the Iron Industry of European Russia	2½d.
340.	*Germany.*—Commercial Relations of Germany with Foreign Countries	2½d.
341.	*Tunis.*—Report on the New Port of Bizerta	6d.
342.	*France.*—Report on Canal Traffic in France	5½d.
343.	*Persia.*—Report on the Proposed Establishment of a Sugar Industry in Persia under Belgian Auspices	1½d.
344.	*Portugal.*—Further Report on the Railway from Beira to Mashonaland	½d.
345.	*Germany.*—Report on the Inland Waterways of Germany (with Plans)	10d.
346.	*Germany.*—Report on the German Colonies in Africa and the South Pacific	6½d.
347.	*Russia.*—Report on the Position of Landed Proprietors in Poland	1½d.
348.	*Russia.*—Report on the Coal, Iron, Salt, and Quicksilver Industries in the Consular District of Taganrog	1d.
349.	*Norway.*—Translation of New Law relating to the Sale of Spirits	1d.
350.	*Servia.*—Report on the Mines of Servia	2d.
351.	*Denmark.*—Further Report on the Free Port of Copenhagen	11½d.
352.	*Italy.*—Report on the Volterra Alabaster Industry	7½d.
353.	*Italy.*—Report for the Years 1892-93 on the Yield of Cocoons in Italy, and on the Condition of the Italian Silk Trade to May, 1894	1d.
354.	*Austria-Hungary.*—Report on the Mining Industry in Bosnia and Herzegovina	1d.
355.	*Russia.*—Report on the Peasantry and Peasant Holdings in Poland	2½d.
356.	*Russia.*—Report on the Agricultural Position of Russia	1d.
357.	*Siam.*—Report on the Teak Trade in Siam	4d.
358.	*Paraguay.*—Report on the "New Australia" Colony in Paraguay	1½d.
359.	*Bavaria and Würtemberg.*—Abstract of the Reports for the Year 1894 of the Bavarian and Würtemberg Factory Inspectors	½d.

No. 360.

UNITED STATES.

WASHINGTON.

Sir J. Pauncefote to the Earl of Kimberley.

My Lord,   *Washington, March* 29, 1895.

I HAVE the honour to forward herewith a Report, compiled by Mr. Gough, at the desire of the Royal Commission on Agriculture, on the Agricultural Position of the United States and the probable competition with which British Agriculturists must in the future reckon.

            I have, &c.
        (Signed)   JULIAN PAUNCEFOTE.

Report on the Agricultural Position of the United States and the probable competition with which British Agriculturists must in the future reckon.

ABSTRACT of Contents.

	Page
Existence of depression	2
Dependence of farmers on Liverpool market	4
Causes of depression	7
Over-production	7
Appreciation of gold	11
Depreciation of silver	11
Options and futures	14
Prospects of improvement	14
Government aid to agriculture	15
Dairy business and oleomargarine	16

NOTE.—The report of the Senate Committee on Depression, No. 787, and that of the House Committee on the same subject, No. 1999, contains evidence from all parts of the country reported in full.

(1940)

UNITED STATES.

Existence of agricultural depression.

Owing to the vast extent of the United States territory, any general statement that its agricultural interests are depressed must be considered as subject to numerous exceptions. Individuals here and there are still prosperous, but a series of inquiries recently held by the Government and by the Legislature prove that prosperity is in abeyance, and that generally the financial condition of the farmers is bad, the cost of production almost equalling the value of the produce raised.

The date given by most authorities as that when prices began to fall is 1873; but it is within the last 3 years that the depression has been felt to an alarming extent.

Absolute destitution has been prevented from reaching even the most unfortunate, but this arises partly from the open-hearted charity everywhere characteristic of the people of this country, partly from the climatic advantages of the Southern States, and partly from the extreme cheapness of the absolute necessaries of life.

Decline in price of cereals.

A few figures only need be quoted in proof of the losses sustained by farmers.

The following tables were recently prepared by the Department of Agriculture.

TABLE showing the Farm Prices of Cereals per Bushel in the United States for each Year from 1868–92.

Year.	Indian Corn.	Wheat.	Rye.	Oats.	Barley.
	Cents.	Cents.	Cents.	Cents.	Cents.
1868	63·0	142·9	127·7	56·0	130·3
1869	75·3	94·1	97·1	47·6	81·6
1870	54·9	104·2	81·5	43·3	84·5
1871	48·2	125·8	79·0	40·1	80·6
1872	39·8	124·0	76·3	33·6	73·8
1873	48·0	115·0	76·2	37·4	91·5
1874	64·7	94·1	85·8	52·0	92·1
1875	42·0	100·0	76·9	36·5	81·1
1876	37·0	103·7	66·9	35·1	66·4
1877	35·8	108·2	59·2	29·2	63·9
1878	31·8	77·7	52·6	24·6	58·0
1879	37·5	110·8	65·6	33·1	58·9
1880	39·6	95·1	75·6	36·0	66·6
1881	63·6	119·3	93·3	46·4	82·3
1882	48·4	88·2	61·5	37·5	62·8
1883	42·0	91·0	58·0	33·0	58·7
1884	35·7	64·5	51·9	28·0	48·7
1885	32·8	77·1	57·9	28·5	56·3
1886	36·6	68·7	53·8	29·8	53·6
1887	44·4	68·1	54·5	30·4	51·9
1888	34·1	92·6	58·8	27·8	59·0
1889	28·3	69·8	45·7	22·9	42·7
1890	50·6	83·8	62·9	42·4	64·8
1891	40·6	83·9	77·4	81·5	54·0
1892	39·4	62·4	54·8	31·7	47·2

WASHINGTON.

This shows an average decline during the whole period of wheat 35 per cent., maize 32 per cent., rye 32 per cent., oats 30 per cent., barley 40 per cent. The general average decline in price being 35 per cent.

During the same period oxen and other cattle declined in value 35 per cent., and milch cows 40 per cent.; sheep and pigs remain as they were.

The yield of wheat per acre has been well maintained, but the value of the returns has been much lessened, as shown in the following table.

Calendar Year.	Average Yield per Acre in Bushels.	Average Value of Yield per Acre.
		Dol. c.
1869	13·5	12 76
1870	12·4	12 94
1871	11·5	14 56
1872	11·9	14 87
1873	12·7	14 59
1874	12·3	11 66
1875	11·0	11 16
1876	10·5	10 86
1877	13·9	15 2
1878	13·1	10 16
1879	13·8	15 27
1880	13·1	12 48
1881	10·1	12 3
1882	13·6	12 2
1883	11·6	10 56
1884	13·0	8 38
1885	10·4	8 5
1886	12·4	8 4
1887	12·1	8 25
1888	11·1	10 30
1889	12·9	8 98
1890	11·1	9 28
1891	15·3	12 86
1892	13·4	8 35

The other cereals have gone down proportionately.

Recently the Commissioners of Labour for the State of Michigan found that among 5,000 farm labourers in that State the average decrease in wages during 1892 had been 13 per cent. *Labourers' wages.*

The cotton growers of Alabama propose to cut down this year's production 50 per cent. if they can obtain the adhesion of three-fourths of the cotton growers of the South. *Cotton.*

Mr. Consul Monaghan recently sent to the State Department a table showing the prices of cotton each year since 1814, when it sold for 2s. 5½d. per lb., and down to 1894, when the price, on November 12, was by far the lowest ever known, namely, 2·93 pence. In the northern American cotton belt, by aid of artificial fertilizers, the cotton cost to grow 7 cents per 1 lb.; in Texas, with no fertilizers, 5·2 cents. The prices obtained for these in Liverpool were 3d. (about 6 cents). Deduct 10 per cent. for waste, 0·6 for handling,

(1940)

1·25 for freight from Texas, inland expenses 0·25, and the Texan planter receives 3·90 for cotton that cost him 5·20, and 3·90 goes to the northern cotton belt planter, whose product cost him 7 cents.

A recent report of a Committee on Agriculture states that "cotton cannot, except under the most favourable circumstances, be raised profitably at less than 8 cents a lb., nor without loss under 7. cents," and that the price of cotton has continued to fall until January 1895, when it reached the lowest point ever known.

Tobacco. In South Carolina tobacco is being increasingly grown in lieu of cotton, and the change proves remunerative.

Dependence of United States farmers on admission of their surplus cattle duty free in the United Kingdom. During the 9 months ending September 30, 1894, the farmers and stock-raisers of the United States sold in the United Kingdom 305,910 live beef cattle, valued at 5,300,000*l.* During the same period of 1893 they sold 182,611 such cattle, valued at 3,300,000*l.* Canada is practically the only competitor with the United States for the English live cattle trade, and in both cases the cattle are killed on arrival.

363,535 live beef cattle were exported and marked after inspection during the year 1893, an increase of 25 per cent. over 1892.

During the first 6 months of 1894 the United States sent to the United Kingdom 112,000,000 lbs. of dressed beef, valued at nearly 2,000,000*l.*, and the Secretary of Agriculture deems such meat exportation more advantageous to farmers here than the export of live cattle.

Government inspection of cattle. The Secretary of Agriculture, on November 20 last, stated as follows:—

"European Governments are constantly declaring live animals from the United States diseased. These declarations are sometimes made for fear of infection of their own herds, and at other times, it is believed, for economic reasons. If all American beef going abroad is shipped in carcases, and it is all stamped 'inspected' as wholesome and edible by authority of the Government of the United States, it certainly cannot be shut out afterwards on account of alleged Texas fever, pleuro-pneumonia, tuberculosis, or any other disease. But if certain European nations continue to demand legally authorised microscopic inspection of American pork, and require also veterinary inspection for beef with Government certification to each, then why ought not the Government of the United States to demand that all imports from foreign countries for human consumption—either edibles or beverages—must likewise be certified by the authorities of those foreign Governments as wholesome and unadulterated before they are permitted to be sold in the United States?"

In February, when the French Government prohibited the importation into France of United States cattle, the Secretary of Agriculture added:—

"The condition of our cattle, and the extent and character of our inspection system, made the allegation that such restrictions were required for sanitary reasons the merest pretence. We have better opportunities now than ever for knowing the condition of our cattle, for we are inspecting more than ever before—12,000,000 head last year. Moreover, that Germany and France have confidence in the efficiency of our inspection was shown by the enormous increase in our exports of inspected pork to these countries. These have increased in the past 6 months more than 30 per cent. over the exports of the corresponding period a year ago, and this inspection was microscopic.

"The meat-producers of the United States send only the very best grades of live cattle and dressed and cured meats to the European markets. American dealers expect to hold those markets against all comers by offering the very best, most wholesome, and desirable meats which careful feeding, skilled slaughtering, and scientific preserving can produce.

"It is claimed by the United States international dealers in meats that all the hue and cry against the edibleness of American meats, and all the charges against the sanitary conditions of American live cattle sent abroad, are inspired by the land-owning Protectionists of Germany and France. They desire, it is said, to make cattle and meat higher in the German and French markets, by making cattle and beef scarcer The scarcity is brought about by excluding, for alleged sanitary reasons, the American cattle and meat products. It is not claimed, however, by Protectionists in Germany, as it is by Protectionists in the United States, that making scarcer will make them cheaper.

"The herds of cattle and swine, in fact all the domestic animals of the United States, are in splendid condition. There has not been a case of pleuro-pneumonia in any of the United States or territories during the last 3 years. There is no contagious, infectious, or communicable disease now prevalent among the domestic animals in any State or territory of the American Union. There has not been, and there will not be, shipped to any European port any animal, or the product of any animal, which has not been inspected and declared healthy, wholesome, and edible. The United States will continue to furnish all meatless Europe with the best and cheapest pork and beef in the world."

Speaking on the same subject, on February 25, Mr. N. Morris, of Chicago, said:—

"We shipped 3,600,000*l*. worth of cattle and products to France alone last year, and this great trade is absolutely destroyed by the order of the French Government. I knew this was coming some months ago, and with the exception of two or three boat loads not any cattle or product has been sent to France in the last ten days. [*Exclusion of cattle from France.*]

"The effect of the German and Belgium embargo has been to reduce the price of cattle of the classes shipped to these countries by 10 dol. a head, and this French edict will even more injuriously affect the stock yards. This has been the effect on prices, notwithstanding the fact that the supply of cattle has been cut down to two-thirds on account of feed.

"The effect on the product is even greater than on the live cattle trade, especially so far as France is concerned.

"We were shipping 7,000 cattle a week, and as many or more in addition in the form of the product. France has been taking a great deal of lean cattle for soups, and this branch of the trade will be very injuriously affected by the new edict, while as to dressed beef and pork and products the result will be even more far reaching."

New law for inspection of cattle.

The new law of March 2, 1895, amends the Cattle Inspection Act, and provides that the Secretary of Agriculture shall cause to be made a careful inspection of all live cattle, the meat of which is intended for exportation to any foreign country, with a view to ascertaining whether such cattle are free from disease and their meat sound and wholesome, and may appoint inspectors, who shall be authorised to give an official certificate, clearly stating the condition in which the cattle and meat are found. No clearance shall be given to any vessel having on board any fresh or prepared beef for exportation to any foreign country until the shipper shall obtain from an inspector a certificate that the cattle are free from disease, and that their meat is sound and wholesome.

The cattle thus inspected are required to be stamped or labelled, and a heavy penalty is fixed for counterfeiting the labels. The Secretary of Agriculture is also authorised to require the destruction of all cattle found by inspection to be diseased, and a penalty is fixed for violation of the department regulations by packers and owners of slaughter-houses.

In the same month the Secretary of Agriculture issued an admirable series of regulations for the safe and humane transport of cattle to other countries; the following is a summary of these regulations:—

"Cattle or sheep must not be carried on any part of the vessel where they will interfere with the proper management of the vessel, or with the efficient working of the necessary lifeboats, or with the requisite ventilation of the vessel. Cattle must have 6 feet vertical space on all decks, free of obstructions.

"No cattle or sheep shall be allowed on the poop deck or within 20 feet of the breakwater on the spar deck between October 1 and April 1. If cattle are carried on the bridge deck, proper runways shall be provided for loading and unloading.

"When it is desired to carry cattle upon the third deck a special permit must be obtained from the inspector of the port.

"Suitable arrangements shall be made to provide at all times sufficient light for the proper tending of all animals.

"No cattle shall be loaded upon hatches or decks above cattle, nor upon third deck hatches when cattle are carried upon such decks, nor shall any merchandise, freight, or food for cattle be loaded upon said hatches, but said hatches shall at all times be kept clear.

"All vessels shall carry hogsheads of not less than 400 gallons total capacity for each 100 head of cattle, and these shall be filled with fresh water before sailing and refilled as emptied.

"Cattle or sheep suffering from broken limbs or other serious injuries during the voyage shall be slaughtered by the captain of the vessel.

"The employment of all cattle attendants shall be under the control of owners or agents of steamships, and men so employed shall be reliable, and signed as part of the ship's crew, and shall be furnished with well-lighted and well-ventilated quarters. Not less than one-half of the cattle attendants must be experienced men who have made previous trips with cattle. There shall be one experienced man in charge of each 150 sheep during the winter months, and one to each 200 sheep during the summer months.

"No vessel shall be allowed to take on board any cattle or sheep unless the same have been at the port of embarkation at least 24 hours before the vessel sails, except in special cases and by direction of the inspector, nor until the loading of the other cargo has been completed."

Bacon. In 1893 263,824,000 lbs. of bacon, worth 5,370,000*l*., were exported by the United States to England.

In 1894 the quantity increased, but the price obtained was slightly lower.

The price obtained by Danish bacon in England is considerably higher than the price of United States bacon.

The following table, compiled by Mr. Ford, Chief of the Bureau of Statistics, gives the quantities and values of bacon, hams, pork, &c., shipped into the United Kingdom from the United States during the year ending June 30, 1894:—

Product.	Quantity.	Value.
	Lbs.	£
Bacon	334,985,389	6,273,368
Hams	73,894,248	1,646,157
Pork, fresh and pickled	14,272,957	231,863
Lard	150,655,158	2,705,797

Live cattle. In further illustration of the same subject, Mr. Ford shows that during the 7 months ending January 31, 1894, the United Kingdom took 2,967,673*l*. worth of live cattle from the United States, while all other countries took during the same period only 12,771*l*. worth.

Value of exports to United Kingdom. In the year ending December 31, 1893, the United Kingdom paid to American producers for bread-stuffs, provisions, cotton, and tobacco more than 65,000,000*l*. That is to say, the British market bought more than one-half of all the farm exports of the United States during that year. Including 2,000,000*l*. worth of mineral oil, the United Kingdom took 56·31 per cent. of all that was exported from the United States, nearly all entering duty free.

The export of wheat to Germany, which was 6,302,102 tons in 1892, fell to 3,149,282 tons in 1893, and to 3,054,669 tons in 1894.

Causes of the depression. It is not easy to state the causes of the depression or the proposed remedies without entering upon controversial ground. Neither political parties nor private persons are in general agreement upon this subject, and the different views must, consequently, be briefly stated without comment. The principal crops of the United States are cereals, and, cereals being annual productions, their market values are affected more or less by large or small yields from year to year. This is true, not only as to local prices but to market values of the surplus generally. Effects produced from this cause are much less now than in years before facilities for distribution had reached their present state of development. When 30 to 40 days were required for the passage of a ship with a cargo of 10,000 bushels of wheat across the Atlantic Ocean, before telegraph wires and cables were used to convey information concerning crops, before the Suez Canal was opened for traffic, and before steamships were built that can carry 100,000 bushels of grain from New York to Liverpool in 10 days, a very heavy crop or a very light crop of any particular kind of grain in the United States materially affected market prices here for the surplus. Now, however, with present conveniences for handling, storing, and shipping grain, with low rates of transportation over long distances, it is the world's production, and not that of any one country, that affects the market values of grain that go into the channels of commerce.

If farm products were the only articles which have fallen in price, we should probably find some special reasons for it, reasons not however broad enough to cover the whole field of commerce. Depression has been so general, affecting so wide a range of prices, that where articles are found whose market values have been well maintained, they appear to be exceptions, which may be explained by circumstances and conditions that are exceptional rather than general. At all events it may be stated that depression is found to exist among many articles of manufacture as well as among the products of agriculture.

While on the general average all prices have declined about 10 per cent. since 1883, the average for the farm has been three times as great as that. And while the immediate causes for this decline are general in their nature, they have borne with greater weight on agriculture than on any other department of industry.

The depression in agriculture cannot properly be attributed to one cause only; many things have operated, each in its own peculiar way, to aid in the general decline.

Over-production. Whilst enumerating the supposed causes of agricultural depression in the United States it should be remembered that these are generally the same as those given for agricultural depression in Europe.

Although it is so often repeated that wheat prices being fixed at Liverpool, they are beyond the control of the United States farmer, yet it is the enormous surplus from this country which keeps those prices down. Of the 243,000,000 bushels of wheat annually required to supply the demand outside the United States, about one-third on the average is furnished by the United States.

The wheat required by Great Britain and Belgium compose

the quantity which is known as the world's demand, to supply which the farmers of all wheat exporting countries are in continual competition.

The annual average export of wheat from the United States has been about 80,000,000 bushels during the last 7 years, the export from India being about half that amount.

Those who deny that over-production is the cause of low prices point out that the United States wheat crop of 1891 was larger by 25 per cent. than it had ever been before, and that nevertheless better prices were obtained than in the preceding year, when the crop was lighter, but a similar rise would naturally occur whenever the demand exceeded the world's supply, not merely the supply of the United States.

An enormous extension in the productive capacity of the United States has taken place within the last 25 years owing to the extension of railways. The capital of the railways in 1892 (as stated in a recent report to the Senate) was nearly 2,000,000,000*l.* sterling, which is said to be double their value, and the loss of capital suffered by the public has contributed to swell the general depression of business. *Railways.*

The development of the food-producing industry has been too rapid and has more than kept pace with the increasing population of the United States and of the world.

Improvement in transportation reduces the cost of produce, but, as the railways are more in number than the country can make profitable, many of the companies have become insolvent. Mr. Newlands stated in the House of Representatives, on February 6, that one quarter of the mileage of the country is in the hands of receivers.

Thrifty and saving persons have seen much of what they saved disappear, and are disinclined to adventure the remainder, so that business generally has been bad for some years. At the end of 1892, and again in the spring of 1894, there was serious financial depression amounting almost to a crisis.

Apart from the railways, over-production has been caused by the cheapness of borrowed money. It would have been natural, when distant parts of the country were first farmed, for the farming adventurer to pay from 10 to 15 per cent. interest for the occasional temporary advances of which he might be in urgent need. This deterrent to borrowing may even now be seen in operation in Brazil, where farmers have been comparatively little interfered with from outside. *Cheapness of borrowed money.*

Not only does such a charge deter from borrowing, but it makes it indispensable for the farmer to keep up the prices of his produce.

This barrier to low prices was broken through by numerous money lending companies from the Eastern States and elsewhere, who competed with one another and lowered the rate of interest almost to half the above-mentioned figures. The average interest paid on the 217,000,000*l.* of existing farm mortgages is stated by the "Census Bulletin" of January 24, 1895, to be 7·07 per cent.

UNITED STATES.

The result of their interference with the natural value of capital in newly occupied districts was that fresh territory was constantly occupied by farmers whose capital was borrowed. Railways were simultaneously constructed, sometimes even in advance of the cultivated land, and the future profits of both farmers and railways were calculated on the basis of existing prices of produce.

Indebtedness of farmers. From 1880 to 1890 an immense indebtedness was incurred by the farmers of the United States, largely however a renewal of old obligations incurred many years earlier.

Of the farmers, 34 per cent. hire their land, 66 per cent. own it, and thus experience the full force of the depression, not only in their produce but in the value of their land.

Area of crops. The farming area has been greatly enlarged since the war. The following table shows the acreage devoted to particular crops in certain years:—

Year.	Area.		
	Wheat.	Indian Corn.	Oats.
	Acres.	Acres.	Acres.
1870	18,992,591	38,646,977	8,792,395
1880	37,986,717	62,317,842	16,187,917
1892	38,554,430	70,626,658	27,062,825

Thus the wheat area was doubled between the years 1870 and 1880, while the increase from 1880 was only 567,713 acres.

Milling industry. Concurrently with increased area of wheat land, the milling industry has been developed. Men of great resources—and the same men—are frequently found engaged in buying and selling grain, and in manufacturing and exporting flour. They have facilities for collecting and storing grain scattered along all the railway lines in the grain States, and at the milling and trading centres. They are in constant touch with the speculative markets at one end of the line and with their agents out among the farmers at the other end. The local buyer does not purchase on his own account; he is the agent of men or companies at headquarters. There is an enormous concentration of wealth and business talent at the grain marts dealing with products of the farm. Minneapolis dealers bought 70,000,000 bushels of wheat in the year 1892, and the 21 flouring mills there turned out 9,750,000 barrels of flour in the same time.

Speaking generally, farm lands in all the grain-growing and stock-raising States are in as good a condition for tillage now as they ever were.

Production and area of wheat. The following table shows the production and area of wheat for the years 1869 to 1892 inclusive.

WASHINGTON.

TABLE showing Production and Area of Wheat for the Years 1869-92.

Calendar Year.	Total Production.	Total Area of Crop.	Average Yield per Acre.
	Bushels.	Acres.	Bushels.
1869	260,146,900	19,181,004	13·5
1870	235,884,700	18,992,591	12·4
1871	230,722,400	19,943,893	11·5
1872	249,997,100	20,858,359	11·9
1873	281,254,700	22,171,676	12·7
1874	308,102,700	24,967,027	12·3
1875	292,136,000	26,381,512	11·0
1876	289,956,500	27,627,021	10·5
1877	364,194,146	26,277,546	13·9
1878	420,122,400	32,108,560	13·1
1879	448,756,630	32,545,950	13·8
1880	498,549,868	37,986,717	13·1
1881	383,280,090	37,709,020	10·1
1882	504,185,470	37,067,194	13·6
1883	421,086,160	36,455,545	11·6
1884	512,765,000	39,475,885	13·0
1885	357,112,000	34,189,246	10·4
1886	457,218,000	36,806,184	12·4
1887	456,329,000	37,641,783	12·1
1888	415,868,000	37,336,138	11·1
1889	490,560,000	38,123,859	12·9
1890	399,262,000	36,087,154	11·1
1891	611,780,000	39,916,897	15·3
1892	515,949,000	38,554,430	13·4

Taking all cereals as one, the increase of production has been about 120 per cent. since 1869, while the enlargement of the area on which grain is grown is somewhat less.

The production of potatoes increased nearly 100 per cent.

From 1868 to 1892 the number of horses increased from 5,756,940 to 16,206,802, mules from 855,685 to 2,331,128, milch cows from 8,691,568 to 16,424,087, oxen and other cattle from 11,942,484 to 35,954,196, sheep from 38,991,912 to 47,273,553, swine from 24,317,258 to 46,094,807. *Increase of animals.*

It is clear that the area of farming lands has been greatly extended, that their fertility has been well maintained, and that their returns have been increased, in the aggregate, more than 100 per cent. within 25 years.

The range and ranch cattle business began about the year 1868, and in 17 years it had grown to fabulous proportions. With the building of railways in Texas, Kansas, and the far west and north-west, began a movement of cattle from Texas northward and eastward. Young cattle were driven and afterwards carried on railroads to the grazing lands of Wyoming and Montana, and fatted animals were carried to St. Louis and Chicago. Improved breeding animals were taken from the eastern herds to cross with the natives from Texas and the Indian Territory. By the year 1884 it was estimated that about 7,500,000 head of cattle were on the ranges east *Ranch business.*

of the Rocky Mountains and north of New Mexico and Texas, and their value was put at 187,500,000 dol.

The influence of this abnormal development of the cattle industry was felt on every farm in the country where cattle were raised and fed for slaughter. With the use of land without taxes, the use of grass without cost, young cattle at low figures, and tranportation at favourable rates, ranchmen were able to flood the markets and defy competition.

Marketing cattle. While the cattle business was growing on the ranges, facilities for handling the animals marketed developed in equal proportions. Packing houses are among the great institutions of the country.

One great packing establishment in Chicago killed 1,750,000 pigs, 850,000 cattle, and 600,000 sheep during the year 1892.

The value of the sales made by one company during that year was 18,000,000*l.* and of another 15,000,000*l.*

In the course of 1894 there were received at the Kansas City stockyards and sold 2,549,742 pigs, 1,695,000 cattle, 586,000 sheep and 44,378 horses and mules, a large increase in each sort over 1893.

Prices of cattle have been depressed more than any other class of live stock, and the principal firm of packers is said to have lost money on each head of cattle handled in 1894. However, in March and April, 1895, the price of beef rose considerably, and on May 1 Mexican cattle for grazing, after being long excluded, were readmitted.

Recent falling-off in exports. It should be stated that during the past 8 months there has been a considerable falling off, both in quantities and average prices, of agricultural exports, as compared with the same 8 months of the year preceding. The internal commerce of the country has, as stated elsewhere in this report, been showing a gradual and gratifying improvement; but while the total number of farm animals, *i.e.*, horses, mules, milch cows, oxen and other cattle, sheep and swine on January 1, 1894, was 161,783,453, on January 1, 1895, a falling off of 6,228,402, or 3·85 per cent., was reported. Oxen and other cattle have fallen from 36,608,168 to 34,366,216, or 6·13 per cent., not only has their value per capita declined a little, but the aggregate value has decreased from 107,358,000*l.* to 96,600,000*l.*

Appreciation of gold. Some attribute the depression in the prices earned by agricultural products to the appreciation of gold, which causes a constant increase in the value of money as compared with the value of things. This is alleged to arise from the locking up since 1873 of vast masses of gold, principally by France and Germany, and from the inability of the gold mines of the world to fill up the void thus caused.

The United States Government cannot by any direct action of theirs remedy this ill, as their store of gold is insufficient, even if released, to materially lower the value of gold universally.

Depreciation of silver. The cause to which agricultural depression is most usually attributed is the depreciation of silver, and constant agitation is in progress in favour of re-commencing its coinage at 16 to 1, irrespective of the action of any other nation with whom commercial relations are being carried on. Some of these thorough-going advocates of free silver coinage are singularly ill-equipped with consistent or perspicuous ideas of the subject, but they gain apparent strength owing to their occasional identification with the bi-metallist party, which is numerously represented in Congress, and owing to the almost universal desire for the restoration of silver bullion to at least an approximate equality with its coinage value.

Should the thorough-going advocates of free silver coinage gain their point the Government would, probably, discontinue holding gold and silver at par, and the United States would at once become a purely silver using country. The farmer would then receive for 10 bushels of wheat 10 dol. (at 10 dol. to the 1*l*.), in lieu of the present 5 dol. (at 5 dol. to the 1*l*.). He would pay both capital and interest on previously made mortgages with ease, and if he chose to sell his 10 bushels for a little less than 10 dol. (at 10 dol. to the 1*l*.) he would undersell Indian and Argentine wheat at Liverpool, but in doing so would still farther depress the earnings of the British wheat grower. The same thing would occur in regard to other agricultural exports, so that farmers in the United Kingdom would suffer more than ever. *Probable effects of change of standard.*

An ounce of silver buys the same quantity of wheat or cotton now as it did in 1873, and it is supposed would continue to do so, even after a change such as described above.

It is alleged that some of the eastern States, in which much of the capital of the country is situated, are specially adverse to any experiments being made in matters of currency.

Mr. Joseph Choate stated in an address to the Supreme Court, on March 13, that if income tax be enforced on persons with incomes of 800*l*. a year, the States of New York, New Jersey, Massachusetts, and Pennsylvania would pay nineteen-twentieths of the total amount raised.

A Committee of the House of Representatives appointed to inquire into the causes of the prevailing agricultural depression has recently prepared a report, in which it says:—

"It is unnecessary for the Committee to enter into or dwell upon the fact that agriculture is depressed in every branch of this most important industry; that the values of land and farm products, unless under exceptionally rare conditions, have depreciated steadily as the purchasing power of the dollar has increased. But while the value of property owned by the American farmers has decreased in 30 years from nearly one-half of the total wealth in 1860 to less than one-fourth in 1890, of which 30 per cent. is now under mortgage, taxes have steadily increased, and debts now require four times the labour to be paid off than was then required. The purchasing capacity of the dollar to secure the farmers' land and produce has increased fourfold, while the power to pay his taxes and debts have remained at a standstill. In 1873 wheat sold from 1 dol. 55 c. to 2 dol. 25 c. a bushel (according to Spofford's Almanac), in New York; in 1894 it sold at 50 c. *Suggestions of a committee.*

"To secure relief we suggest:—

"1. That silver should be remonetized at the ratio of 16 to 1.

"2. That so long as the present unjust and unequal system of protection continues agriculture should receive its just proportion, and as this cannot be secured by a protective tariff a bounty on exported agricultural staples should be allowed, similar to that on fish in 1813.

"3. That gambling in futures should be prevented by law.

"4. That a national pure food law should be enacted."

It would be beyond the scope of the present summary to cite statements of the consequences which it is apprehended would ensue to other than agricultural interests by a change of the law.

Congressional opinions. It will suffice to quote a declaration made in the House of Representatives on February 14, by Mr. McDearmon, in favour of silver coinage at 16 to 1, and a declaration made in that House, by Mr. Springer, on March 3, with the object of showing how injudicious a change would be.

Mr. McDearmon said:—"From the day that silver was stricken from the list of coins authorised by law to be turned out by our mints it began to decline. The principal use to which that metal had been put was thereby destroyed and prohibited by law. It was made a commodity, and its use restricted and curtailed; hence, in obedience to the universal laws of trade and commerce, it naturally declined, as would any other commodity. When the Indian mints were closed to silver coinage the work of demonetisation was completed. Over 4,000,000,000*l.* of the standard money, the money of ultimate redemption, was destroyed. The measure of all the wealth of the world was diminished one-half. Thereafter, all wealth has been measured alone by the gold coin in existence. The result has clearly demonstrated the truth of the doctrine laid down by all writers on political economy and finance that the decrease of the volume of money lowers and the increase raises prices.

"A gradual but steady and constant shrinking and decline in almost every commodity, including silver, began simultaneously with the demonetisation of silver, and has continued ever since, not only in this country but in every nation of the civilised world.

"If I am correct in my premises, the remedy is apparent. Undo by law the wrong which was done by law. Increase the measure of values by re-establishing the double standard. Restore to silver its principal use, that of being converted into money at the ratio of 16 to 1, and it will, by the inexorable laws of trade and commerce, enhance in value and be equal with gold."

Mr. Springer's speech was as follows:—"Those who favour the remonetisation of silver at 16 to 1 assert, in effect, that Congress could by law make 1 oz. of silver, which is now worth only 60 c., worth 129 c. A proposition which is so improbable needs only to be stated to be refuted. But if silver will not be enhanced in value to this extent, the effect would be to place this country on a silver basis. Mr. Sibley has said in effect that if we will remonetise silver at 16 to 1, wheat would be worth 1 dol. per bushel and cotton 10 c. per lb. That is double the price they are bringing here. That would be so if we go to a silver basis. Mexico is upon a silver basis. If you will go to Mexico, were there is free and unlimited coinage at the ratio of $16\frac{1}{2}$ to 1, you will find cotton worth 10 c. per lb. and wheat 1 dol. per bushel; and they will be worth that in this country when we go to a silver basis, and not until then. If gentlemen who are advocating silver prices will ship their products to Mexico they can be gratified. The price of wheat in this country is fixed by the price in Liverpool, on a gold standard; and the price of cotton is fixed in Liverpool, on a gold standard. And if we were to put all the silver in the world into circulation in the United States it would not raise the price of wheat in Liverpool one iota; and we sell on the Liverpool price. Not only does the Liverpool price fix the price of all articles which are exported, but the same articles when consumed in this country are sold here on the basis of the Liverpool prices."

One of the minor causes which have tended to lower the price of wheat is alleged to be the practice of speculating in options and futures. *Speculating in options and futures.*

This can be done in three ways:—1. Where a farmer or other person, having grain of his own, sells it for a price then agreed upon, with the understanding that it is to be delivered within or at a certain time in the future; 2. Where a dealer, having no grain of his own, contracts a sale of grain to be delivered in future, expecting to purchase the grain in the market in time for delivery according to the terms of the contract, at a price agreed upon at the time of sale; 3. Where two persons enter into a contract by which it is stipulated that one of them will deliver to the other, at a future time mentioned, a certain quantity of grain at a price named at the time of making the contract, reserving the option to deliver the wheat or not, on condition that if any loss would come to the other by reason of failure or refusal to make delivery, he will make good the loss.

The wheat sales reported as having been made in New York city in the 2 years, 1892–93, amounted to 2,203,456,000 bushels or at least 30 bushels for every 1 bushel that was actually sold or that was on hand to be sold, an amount equal to more than twice as much as all the wheat grown in the country during those 2 years, not more than one-thirtieth part of which could have been in New York for sale there. When prices are regulated by a market which appears to be very full they will tend downward.

Such extravagant estimates of the supply of wheat may certainly have done harm, and a bill was brought into Congress (though not passed) to prohibit the worst sides of this practice.

A feeling exists that the prevailing depression will shortly diminish and that business generally is about to revive, and this confidence in the approaching return of prosperity tends to the fulfilment of the expectation. *Prospects of diminution of the depression.*

A good-natured optimism is characteristic of the people

(1940)

generally, and no positive proof can be given of the early cessation of agricultural prostration.

In 1894 there was an advance in the price of pigs and in the price of maize. The production of rice is increasing in the Southern States, and may profit by the war in the East.

Those States produced an enormous crop of cotton in 1894, though the prices were quite unremunerative, but it is expected that some of the great Pennsylvania cotton factories will move down to the South and thus save the expense of transportation.

Wheat is expected, by the Secretary of Agriculture, to remain at a relatively low price for all time, and to cease to be the staple product of the United States.

Much is expected of the next Congress, which meets in December, in the way of legislation to relieve the distressed condition of the country.

Mr. Funk stated, on February 20, in the Agricultural Committee of the House of Representatives, that the farmers of Illinois have never been so well off as they are to-day.

Federal and State support of agriculture. Farmers, as a class, in the United States are much better informed than formerly, not only concerning their particular vocation but also concerning the business of the classes that purchase, carry, and exchange farm products.

The productive age of men begins at 20, which is 5 years earlier than in some parts of Europe, and this is one reason for the industrial energy displayed by the United States.

Agricultural colleges and experiment stations have been serviceable in teaching the art of farming from a scientific standpoint. It is common in some parts of the country to find graduates of these colleges busily engaged in the practical work of agriculture.

The educational influences of the county fair have been greatly lessened by the modern tendency to horse racing and other species of gambling. But the fair has been superseded by farmers' institutes and other forms of meeting, where men of learning mingle with plain farmers, and together they discuss practical matters pertaining to the daily work of the farm. In Wisconsin a State officer has charge of institute work. In Kansas and some other States teachers in the agricultural colleges fix dates for holding institutes in different portions of their respective States as often as they can do so without neglecting their duties at the college, and the places for meeting are so arranged as to reach all parts of the State in the course of a few years. In some States, State agricultural societies manage the institute work.

In some of the States departments of agriculture have been created as State offices, and this has been found to be an efficient means of collecting and disseminating information of special benefit to all persons interested in the business of farming.

Through the operation of these and other instrumentalities before-mentioned, the intellectual horizon of farmers has been greatly widened within the last 25 years.

The Secretary of Agriculture carefully studies and enumerates the demand for American agricultural products in all parts of the world. He considers that "it matters little to the farmer what the price of wheat may be if he may buy his goods in the same markets where he is compelled to sell. In selling, the farmer competes with all the world.

"To give him an equal chance he ought also to be allowed to buy where all the world competes."

On the other hand, Governor McKinley, speaking on February 13, said: "We not only want to keep our home market, but we want a foreign market for our surplus products of manufacture and agriculture. We do not want it, however, at the loss of our home market."

Out of the total exports of the United States for the fiscal year 1894, amounting in value to 174,000,000*l.*, farm products represent 126,000,000*l.* and other articles 48,000,000*l.*; that is respectively 72 per cent. and 28 per cent. of the total.

The whole question of the assistance rendered by Government to agriculture is fully described in Mr. Goschen's report from this Embassy of February 28, 1894, printed in a Parliamentary Paper, No. 3 Commercial of 1894.

Dairy business. The dairy business in the United States has grown immensely within the last few years, and it has done so in proportion to the growth of cities.

Boston, for instance, with 750,000 inhabitants consumes annually 82,000,000 quarts of milk. This earns for the farmers, on an average, nearly 1,000,000*l.*

The number of milch cows on January 1, 1893, was 16,424,087. There were 63,313 more in January, 1894, and a further increase of 17,129 up till January, 1895.

The export of butter has fallen off. It amounts to 9,000,000 lbs. as compared to 90,000,000 lbs. of oleomargarine exported. Denmark sells 24 times as much butter to the United Kingdom as is sold by the United States.

Oleomargarine. Mr. Whittaker, at a meeting of the National Dairy Congress on February 27, stated that whilst large quantities of oleomargarine were in fact exported to South America, none was sold there as such. Also that a great deal of oleo oil is exported to Holland and Denmark for adulterating purposes.

The correctness of Mr. Whittaker's last statement may be questioned, but the following statement recently issued by the New York Mercantile Exchange proves that misleading practices are occasionally adopted to the injury of the pure butter trade.

"In July, 1891, the oleomargarine men prevailed upon Internal Revenue Commissioner Mason to rule that the 'case' in which the tins of oleomargarine were packed was the 'package' referred to in the law. As soon as this interpretation was given the oleomargarine exporters ceased to brand the tins oleomargarine and branded them butter and the outer case oleomargarine, and from that time until the spring of 1894 90 per cent. of all the oleomargarine cleared for foreign markets was so marked. All sorts of frauds were used, such as 'Western Dairy,' 'Suffolk Creamery,' 'Garden City Creamery,' 'Empire Creamery.'

(1940)

"In the spring of 1894 a committee was appointed by the New York Mercantile Exchange to look into the matter and found that outside of the clearance of oleomargarine there was no regard paid to the law, and all of the exports were branded butter. The committee waited upon Commissioner Miller, called his attention to these abuses, gave him proofs that the statements of the committee were correct, and he ruled that the case was not the package referred to in the law, but the tins were, and that the oleomargarine exporters and manufacturers must cease branding their goods butter or any name that inferred butter in any language of the islands or countries for which goods were intended, such as 'beurre' for goods intended for the French West Indies Islands, and 'mantiquila' for goods for the Spanish Islands and South American countries, but he did not rule that they must brand it oleomargarine, nor has he so ruled up to this time, and large quantities of oleomargarine are being shipped marked with favourite terms by which butter is known, such as 'Fancy Goshen,' 'Extra Elgin Creamery,' 'I.X.L. Dairy,' and other marks that signify butter and nothing but butter, and these goods are leaving New York so marked this week.

"In some cases the tins are entirely blank, with no mark whatever upon them, while the case is branded oleomargarine, and butter labels are sent by express or mail to ports of destination and there put upon the goods.

"The importations of butter into Brazil are 6,000,000 dol. (1,200,000*l*.) annually, and into Rio Janeiro, 2,500,000 dol. (500,000*l*.), and since the introduction of oleomargarine the prejudice against our butter has become so great that our exports to Brazilian ports for the past year will be less than ever before, barely reaching 100,000 dol. (20,000*l*.). South American countries are now sending their butter orders to Denmark, that Government guaranteeing the quality and purity of its goods, and a purchase in a Danish market means to the buyer a delivery of what he pays for."*

Butter, both real and artificial, enjoys the protection of a duty of 4 c. (2*d*.) per 1 lb.

There has been a doubt as to whether the laws of certain States restricting the sale of oleomargarine were constitutional, but the question having recently come before the Supreme Court Mr. Justice Harlan decided in favour of those statutes.

In Iowa, within the last few months, a specially stringent law has been passed, as the former laws on the subject were evaded. Oleomargarine must be sold in its natural white colour, and in fact is hardly sold at all.

In Massachusetts, a new law, called the "colouration law," prohibits the manufacture and the sale of any imitation of yellow butter, and there are other laws in force in that State equally intended to save butter from unfair competition.

A bill intended to carry out the same object was introduced into Congress in its last session but did not become law.

* Quoted from "Star," March 5, 1895.

No one knows how cheaply crops can be grown. When prices of produce go down the immediate result is loss to the grower, but presently extra industry, economy, and good management reduce the cost of growing crops, and the farmer may regain his margin of profit. If bad crops and bad prices come together, then the farmer must lose, but the prevailing depression in the United States is not caused by bad crops, but solely by bad prices. Wheat and cotton are now selling at prices unremunerative to most farmers, but the crops have been raised at far less cost than heretofore. *Depression met by cheaper production.*

There is an evident tendency in many places to possess and to cultivate large tracts of land under one ownership. In such cases machinery can be used within the closest limits of economy, and labour can be applied to the best advantage. The production of large quantities of wheat or corn by one management, and the raising of a great many animals by one person or firm for sale serve to secure for their owners many advantages among dealers and carriers.

A system exists, called "bonanza" farming, carried on by persons who work large tracts of land. *Bonanza farming.*

These great farms are common in Wyoming, Montana, North and South Dakota, and the Pacific States.

The Official Northern Pacific Railroad Guide gives a description of one of them in the following paragraphs:—

"Messrs. George W. Cass and Benjamin P. Cheney, both heavy capitalists and directors in the railroad company, having faith in the fertility of the land, determined to test its capacity for wheat production. They first bought, near the site of the present town of Casselton, 7,680 acres of land from the railroad company, and then secured the intervening Government sections with Indian scrip, thus obtaining compact farming grounds of enormous area. Mr. Oliver Dalrymple, an experienced wheat farmer, was engaged to manage the property, and in June, 1875, he turned his first furrow, ploughing 1,280 acres, and harvested his first crop in 1876. The acreage was increased in each succeeding year, until, in 1882, there were not less than 27,000 acres under cultivation. This immense farm does not lie in one body. One part of it, known as the Grandin farm, is situated in Traill county, 30 miles north of Casselton. The entire area embraced by the three tracts is 75,000 acres. Farming operations conducted on so gigantic a scale seem almost incredible to persons who are only familiar with the methods of the older and more settled States. In managing the affairs of a 'bonanza farm' the most rigorous system is employed, and the cost of cultivation averages about 1 dol. (4s.) per acre less than smaller estates. The plan adopted by Mr. Dalrymple and all the other 'bonanza' men is to divide the land into tracts of 6,000 acres each, and these are subdivided into farms of 2,000 acres each. Over each 6,000 acres a superintendent is placed, with a bookkeeper, headquarters' building, and a storehouse for supplies. Each subdivision of 2,000 acres is under the charge of a foreman, and is provided with its own set of buildings, comprising boarding-houses for the hands, stables, a granary, a machinery hall, and a blacksmith's shop, all connected with the superintendent's office by telephone. Supplies of every description are issued, only upon requisition, to the several divisions. Tools and machinery are bought by the carload from manufacturers; farm animals are procured at St. Louis and other principal markets; stores of every description for feeding the army of labourers are purchased at wholesale; and the result of the thorough system and intelligent economy in every department is found in the fact that wheat is raised and delivered at the railroad at a cost varying little from 35 c. (1s. 5d.) per bushel. The net profit on a bushel of wheat is seldom less than 10 c. (5d.), and the average yield per acre may safely be put at 15 bushels, although it often exceeds that quantity.

"On this great farm, or rather combination of farms, the 20,000 acre tract at Casselton, 400 men are employed in harvesting and 500 to 600 in threshing. 250 pairs of horses or mules are used, 200 gang ploughs, 115 self-binding reapers, and 20 steam threshers. About August 1 the harvester is heard throughout the length and breadth of the land, and those who have witnessed the operation of securing the golden grain will never forget the scene. The sight of the immense wheat fields, stretching away farther than the eye can reach, in one unbroken sea with golden waves, is in itself a grand one. One writer describes the long procession of reaping machines as moving like batteries of artillery, formed 'en echelon' against the thick-set ranks of grain. Each machine is drawn by three mules or horses, and with each gang there is a superintendent who rides along on horseback and directs the operations of the drivers. There are also mounted repairers who carry with them the tools for repairing any break or disarrangement of the machinery. When a machine fails to work, one of the repairers is instantly beside it, and, dismounting, remedies the defect in a trice, unless it proves to be serious. Thus the reaping goes on with the utmost order and the best effect. Travelling in line together these 115 reaping machines would cut a swath one-fifth of a mile in width, and lay low 20 miles of grain in a swath of that great size in the course of a single day."

This method of farming has brought the cost of producing wheat down to about 35 c. (1s. 5d.) per bushel on an average yield in two States, North Dakota and South Dakota. The crop in 1889, which was below an average crop year there, yielded nearly 43,000,000 bushels (42,929,583 are the census estimates first published and subject to correction) of wheat, nearly 10 per cent. of the total wheat crop of the whole country, and of this amount at least 30,000,000 bushels were surplus thrown on the market, an amount equal to more than one-fifth of the average annual exportation of wheat, including wheat flour.

When it is considered that the market price of the surplus wheat is fixed in Liverpool, England, and that the export price to a large extent controls the price for what is sold in the home markets, it is readily seen that so large a quantity of 35 c. wheat thrown on the market must have a depressing effect on the general average of profits in wheat farming.

In California there are "bonanza" wheat farms of 50,000 acres, 100,000 acres, and one considerably larger.

The President of the Agricultural Society of California (Mr. Boggs) thus describes the methods of raising wheat on the large farms of California.

"For instance, we do all our summer ploughing (more properly speaking, spring ploughing) with gang ploughs. As large farming is done with these gangs, which consist generally of 8 ploughs attached together, or 8 ploughs in 1 frame, 1 man with a team of 6 or 8 horses can plough 6 acres per day. In seeding the ground we use the common broadcast seeder followed by an 8-horse harrow. Under this system we can seed 20 acres per day in good order.

"In harvesting our crops we use the combined harvesters, which cut from 28 to 30 acres per day. A harvester with an 18-foot cut of sickle will, in an average grain field, cut and thrash from 350 to 400 sacks, or 800 to 900 bushels per day, at a cost, counting wear and tear of machinery, feed of animals, wages and board of men, not to exceed 1 dol. per acre."

Under the old methods of farming in California, the cost of producing an acre of wheat was from 5 dol. (1*l*.) to 6 dol. (1*l*. 4*s*.), while now it is done for half that amount, and the cost of producing a bushel of wheat has been reduced accordingly to about 22 c. on an average crop.

The wheat harvest extends, usually, over a period of 60 to 90 days. It is rare that rain falls on the wheat fields between May and September. During so long a harvest one machine can cut over an immense area, and a modern California harvester is a ponderous machine. It is drawn by a team consisting (according to size and capacity of the machine) of 16 to 30 horses, and cuts, threshes, and sacks the grain at the rate about an acre to the horse each day. The horses are worked 8 abreast, the first 2 or 3 tiers, with 4 or 2 in the lead. A 26 horse team has 3 tiers of 8 horses each, with 2 horses in front, and a 28-horse team has 4 horses leading. One man drives the team, one looks after the machine, while a third sews the sacks as they are filled. Thus 3 men dispose of 25 to 30 acres—often much more—of wheat in 1 day. Men with 2 or 4 horse wagons follow the machines at proper intervals of distance and gather up the sacks and haul them to the owner's warehouses, on the railroad. These large farms extend many miles along the roads.

In 1889 California produced over 40,000,000 bushels of wheat, of which at least 30,000,000 bushels were exported. This amount, added to the produce of Dakota gives a total of 60,000,000 bushels of surplus wheat, that is more than two-fifths of the average annual export of the United States.

The produce of wool by the United States is about 300,000 lbs. annually, which is about 70 per cent. of the consumption.

Protection and bounties.

The remaining 30 per cent. is chiefly imported from Australia and South America.

The home producers of wool are not protected by a duty on imports, wool being required as raw material by the manufacturers who are strictly protected. On February 26, 1895, Senator Mitchell proposed that a bounty of 5 c. per lb. should be granted to wool grown in the United States, but the Senate refused this proposal.

Protective duties not effective.

The other agricultural products are nominally protected, but as they could not be delivered from elsewhere as cheaply as they can be made at home, the United States farmer cannot be said to enjoy protection but rather the contrary, as the cost of such manufactured goods as he has to buy is increased by their being protected, thus diminishing the purchasing power of his produce. Owing to the geographical situation of Canada some agricultural products have been imported thence even under the McKinley Tariff, and more would doubtless arrive if allowed to enter free, but prices would not be materially affected owing to their being fixed not here but in Europe.

Sugar bounties.

Sugar is in a special position owing to repeated legislation for its encouragement.

From 1890 it received a bounty under the McKinley Act. In the spring of 1894 this bounty was regarded by the Government as abolished under the Wilson Tariff Act, and on January 8, 1895, the following decision was given against payment of this bounty by the Court of Appeals:—

"The Court of Appeals yesterday, in an opinion written by Mr. Justice Shepard, affirmed the judgment of the court below (Judge McComas) in the case of the Miles Planting and Manufacturing Company, of Louisiana, against the Secretary of the Treasury and Commissioner of Internal Revenue. The case was one in which the company, manufacturers, and planters of sugar, sought by mandamus to compel the Secretary and Commissioner to carry out the regulations provided for by the McKinley Tariff Act, granting a bounty to producers of sugar. Judge McComas, in the court below, refused to grant the mandamus, holding that the recent Tariff Act had repealed the McKinley Act. That decision the Court of Appeals yesterday affirmed.

"The Court held that the three questions at issue were whether the case is one in which a mandamus could be ordered, whether the repealing clause of the law now in force had the effect to at once repeal the sugar bounty clauses of the McKinley Act, taking away all claims thereunder, and whether the bounty law was constitutional.

"As to the first question, the Court holds that the matter has already been sufficiently passed upon in the cases of Seymour against State of South Carolina, and International Construction Company against Lamont, the latter case having already been affirmed by the United States Supreme Court. Respecting the second question, the Court says that the repealing clause of the recent Tariff Act is not only a direct repeal of that part of the

McKinley Act which granted a sugar bounty, but is also an express prohibition of any further payment of such bounty.

"Referring to the question as to the constitutionality of the bounty, the Court says that no amount of incidental public good or benefit will render valid taxation, or the appropriation of revenues to be derived therefrom, for a private purpose. If Congress be conceded the power to grant subsidies from the public revenues to all objects it may deem to be for the general welfare, then, says the Court, it follows that this discretion, like all admitted powers of taxation, is absolute. Such a doctrine would destroy the idea that this is a Government of 'delegated, limited, and enumerated powers,' render superfluous all the special delegations of power contained in the constitution, and open the way for a flood of socialistic legislation, the specious plea for all of which has ever been 'the general welfare.'

"Such a doctrine, says the Court, it cannot subscribe to, and it is still less able to subscribe to a doctrine that legislation may be enacted by Congress 'in pursuance of a national policy analogous to that adopted by Germany and France,' or any other Government on the face of the earth.

"In conclusion, the Court says that if there has been a practice by Congress, uniform and generally acquiesced in, our opinion is so clearly against the validity of this Act (the McKinley bounty clause) that we could not be controlled by it in the performance of our duty. No time, no acquiescence, no estoppel runs against the people under the protection of our written Constitution. It follows that the judgment below must be in all things affirmed, and it is so ordered, with cost to the appellees.

"In a concurring opinion, Mr. Chief Justice Alvey says that while he fully concurs in the affirmance of the judgment below he does so on the distinct grounds that the Sugar Bounty Act was expressly repealed by the Tariff Act of 1894. Even were that not so, he says, the case, as presented to the court, showed no sufficient foundation for a writ of mandamus. He explains that he did not deem it necessary, for any purpose of the case, to discuss and decide the constitutional question of the power of Congress to provide for the payment of bounties in such case as that provided for by the Tariff Act of 1890, the Chief Justice explaining that he prefers to express no opinion upon that subject."

The above decision is quoted as incidentally illustrating the different views held on the subject of bounties.

Subsequently to the above decision, and during the last days of the session, Congress again granted the full bounty (up to August 28, 1894, when the new tariff went into effect) to those who had not yet received it, and also eight-tenths of a cent. per pound bounty on all sugars above 80 per cent. polariscope test produced up to June 30, 1895.

This grant of a bounty may be regarded as a gift of 1,047,600*l*. to sugar growers in compensation for the unexpected removal of the bounty in 1894, when they had made their calculations on the basis of such a grant being continued.

(1940)

The sugar growers are also protected by large duties on import (except from Hawaii), and have been assisted by a sum of 102,000*l.* voted for experiments in the manufacture of sugar in different parts of the country from 1885 to the present date. Of this amount 44,000*l.* was expended in machinery and materials by the Secretary of Agriculture.

Condition of sugar industry.

On February 26 Senator Gorman described the state of the sugar industry as follows. He said:—

"That it was his firm conviction, after the most careful and patient investigation for the last two or three months, that the sugar provision of the last tariff law (in view of the evolution that had taken place in the manufacture of sugar throughout the world), had placed the American sugar industry in the most unfortunate position. He believed that, with the bounties paid by other governments, it was impossible either for the beet industry or the cane sugar industry to live in this country 5 years. He did not believe that sugar could be refined in this country 5 years longer, except the higher grades, such as cut loaf, if the Germans continued to produce sugar as they had done in the last year. He regretted that the great sugar industry should be destroyed in this country. There was no parallel to the success which the Germans had had under their system, by which they not only manufactured all the sugar for their own consumption, but exported sugar to England and America; and in this year, 1894–95, they had produced 1,000,000 tons more than in the previous year. The price of the German sugar to-day was, delivered in Baltimore or New York, within a fraction of the cost of production in the United States."

Sugar mills.

The Secretary of Agriculture has recently circulated information as to the cheap price at which sugar mills can now be obtained. A mill with a capacity of $16\frac{1}{2}$ tons of beets per hour costs, with equipment, 36,730*l.* at Havre in France.

Cuban sugar.

The Spanish colonies in the West Indies supply the United States with about 75 per cent. of the sugar imported into the country, and they escape a duty of one-eighth of a cent. per 1 lb. which has to be paid by sugar from bounty paying countries, in addition to the 40 per cent. duty payable on all (except Hawaiian) imported sugars.

Protectionist remedy for depression.

The remedy of the Protectionist party for the agricultural depression was summed up before a committee of the House of Representatives by Mr. Baker on 16 February, 1895, in the following words.

"The true remedy lies in the employment of so many people in the other industries as to use the agricultural products of our people among ourselves. Then we shall secure prosperity for both agriculture and manufactures, labour will be permanently employed and well paid, every industry will be promoted, our currency will be regulated without reference to the money centres of Europe, our people will be contented and happy, and the American nation self-sustaining and honoured as never before among the nations."

Recapitulation.

In recapitulation of the statements of the above report it is submitted that they tend to show that:—

WASHINGTON.

(1.) Agriculture in the United States is now and has been for some years gravely depressed.

In exceptional cases the depression of prices has been successfully met by the cheapening of cost of production.

A widespread feeling exists that business generally, including agriculture, is about to revive.

(2.) The depression is attributed to the fall of prices consequent on the appreciation of gold and to overproduction, and, even more generally, to the depreciation of silver. The depression began 20 years ago and has been progressive; the main cause of the fall of prices being the progressive competition in the world's market, owing to decreased cost of production and transportation, together with the great development of internal competition due to the improvement of industrial machinery.

(3.) The area under wheat has been increasing, but less rapidly in recent years, and the system of cultivation tends to be changed.

(4.) The popular remedy for the depression advocated in meetings and writings is national free coinage of silver independently of the action of other nations. Decrease of transportation charges, prohibition of speculation in the case of wheat, and prohibition of imitation in the case of butter are also asked for, while almost all parties advocate an international bimetallic standard if possible.

(5.) The Government is actively supporting and assisting agriculture in numerous indirect ways, such as inspection of meat products, with guarantee of their purity, information as to the requirements of foreign markets, advice on best modes of cultivation, bounty and protection for sugar, and in general by every means which suggest themselves to a highly trained and sympathizing corps of experts held at the disposal of the Secretary for Agriculture since the year 1889.

(6.) Protective duties exist, but as agricultural profits depend on the sale abroad of surplus produce, these duties do not serve their purpose. In the case of wheat especially there can be no protection against the competition of India and the Argentine Republic in the English market.

(7.) The British agriculturist must probably in the future reckon with the same competition as heretofore in wheat, meat, and dairy produce. If anything, the competition would appear likely to become more severe as either the cost of production will continue to decrease in the same way as hitherto, or, should the United States change their currency basis from gold to silver, the cost of produce will be reduced when paid for in gold.

LONDON:
Printed for Her Majesty's Stationery Office,
By HARRISON AND SONS,
Printers in Ordinary to Her Majesty.
(75 5 | 95—H & S 1940)

FOREIGN OFFICE.

1896.

MISCELLANEOUS SERIES.

Nº. 403.

REPORTS ON SUBJECTS OF GENERAL AND COMMERCIAL INTEREST.

UNITED STATES.

REPORT ON THE

UNITED STATES CATTLE-RAISING INDUSTRY IN 1896, AND THE EXPORT OF CATTLE AND BEEF TO GREAT BRITAIN.

Presented to both Houses of Parliament by Command of Her Majesty,
AUGUST, 1896.

LONDON:
PRINTED FOR HER MAJESTY'S STATIONERY OFFICE,
BY HARRISON AND SONS, ST. MARTIN'S LANE,
PRINTERS IN ORDINARY TO HER MAJESTY.

And to be purchased, either directly or through any Bookseller, from
EYRE & SPOTTISWOODE, EAST HARDING STREET, FLEET STREET, E.C., and
32, ABINGDON STREET, WESTMINSTER, S.W.; or
JOHN MENZIES & Co., 12, HANOVER STREET, EDINBURGH, and
90, WEST NILE STREET, GLASGOW; or
HODGES, FIGGIS, & Co., Limited, 104, GRAFTON STREET, DUBLIN.

1896.

[C. 8278—2.]   *Price Three Halfpence.*

New Series of Reports.

The following Reports from Her Majesty's Representatives abroad, on subjects of general and commercial interest, have been issued, and may be obtained from the sources indicated on the title-page:—

No.		Price.
366.	*France.*—Report for the Year 1894 on the Fluvial Traffic of Rouen and the Waterways of the Seine Basin..	11½d.
367.	*Brazil.*—Report on a Tour in the German and Italian Colonies in the Valley of the River Cahy	3½d.
368.	*Greece.*—Report on the Emery Districts of Naxos	10d.
369	*Argentine Republic.*—Report on the Agricultural and Pastoral Condition and Prospects of the Argentine Republic	1½d.
370.	*Colombia.*—Report on the Agricultural Products of Tolima	1d.
371.	*Russia.*—Report on Measures Adopted for Improving the Commercial Prosperity of Archangel	½d.
372.	*Russia.*—Report on the Associations of Working Men known as "Artels"	1½d.
373.	*Africa (Central).*—Report on the Botanical Aspects of British Central Africa	1½d.
374.	*Colombia.*—Report on the Commercial Importance of the Port of Barranquilla	2d.
375.	*Greece.*—Report on the Deposits of Magnesite Ore and the Manufacture of Magnesite Fire-Bricks in Euboea	2d.
376.	*Denmark.*—Special Report on the Agricultural Condition of Denmark..	1d.
377.	*Denmark.*—Report on the Port of Frederikshavn..	4½d.
378.	*Italy.*—Report on the Pumice Stone Industry of the Lipari Islands	½d.
379.	*France.*—Report on the Principal Fibres obtainable in the Society Islands	½d.
380.	*Servia.*—Report on Apiculture in Servia	½d.
381.	*Belgium.*—Report on the Ivory Trade of Antwerp	½d.
382.	*Germany.*—Report for the year 1893-94 on the German Colonies in Africa and the South Pacific	5d.
383.	*France.*—Report on the Bordeaux International Exhibition of 1895	1d.
384.	*Brazil.*—Report on the Causes which have brought about a Diminution in the Receipts at the Custom-house at Rio de Janeiro	½d.
385.	*Mexico.*—Report on the Cultivation of Cacao, Vanilla, Indiarubber, Indigo, and Bananas in Mexico	2½d.
386.	*France.*—Report on the International Congress on Technical, Industrial, and Commercial Education, held at Bordeaux in September, 1895	1d.
387.	*Portugal.*—Report on the East Coast Route to Mashonaland	1d.
388.	*Austria-Hungary.*—Report on the Iron Industry in Styria and the Betler Ironworks in Hungary	5d.
389.	*Belgium.*—Report on the Output of Coal, Iron, and Steel in Belgium in 1894-95	½d.
390.	*Japan.*—Report on the Railways of Japan (with Plans)	13½d.
391.	*Egypt.*—Report on the Commercial Relations of Great Britain and Egypt	2½d.
392.	*Germany.*—Report on the Wine Trade of Germany, 1893-95	1d.
393.	*Mexico.*—Report on the Cultivation of Coffee in Mexico..	1d.
394.	*Switzerland.*—Report on the Various Institutions and Agricultural Development of Switzerland	1½d.
395.	*Germany.*—Report on the Reduction of Railway Tariff for Coal from the Silesian Mines	½d.
396.	*Austria-Hungary.*—Report on the Treatment of Habitual Drunkards in Austria and the "Curatel" Procedure	½d.
397.	*Brazil.*—Report on the Productions, Commerce, and Finances of the States of Amazonas and Pará	2½d.
398.	*Portugal.*—Report on the Port and Railway of Lorenzo Marques	2d.
399.	*Germany.*—Report on the Society for Insurance against Want of Employment in Winter and the General Labour Registry at Cologne..	1½d.
400.	*Switzerland.*—Report on the Extent of State Encouragement to Commercial Education	½d.
401.	*Mexico.*—Further Report on the Various Vegetable Products of Mexico	2d.
402.	*Germany.*—Report for the Year 1894-95 on the German Colonies in Africa and the South Pacific	6d.

No. 403.

UNITED STATES.

WASHINGTON.

Sir J. Pauncefote to the Marquis of Salisbury.

My Lord, Washington, July 24, 1896.

I HAVE the honour to transmit herewith a Report, prepared by Mr. O'Beirne, Third Secretary of this Embassy, on the United States Cattle Raising industry in 1896 and the Export of Cattle and Beef to Great Britain.

I have much pleasure in expressing my appreciation of the ability with which this useful Report has been drawn up, and of the care and industry bestowed upon it.

I have, &c.
(Signed) JULIAN PAUNCEFOTE.

Report on the United States Cattle Raising Industry in 1896, and the Export of Cattle and Beef to Great Britain.

ABSTRACT of Contents.

	PAGE
Growth of ranching business	2
Profits of the business	2
Its decline—and present extent	2
Corresponding change in results of cattle industry	3
Decrease in numbers of cattle	3
Concentration of cattle industry in the West	5
Decrease in Western States	6
Decrease due to reduction of profits	6
Present profits of breeders	7
" of feeders	9
Industry conducted partly at a loss	11
Conclusion as to tendency of numbers	11
Growth of demand	11
Estimated annual slaughter	12
Relation between present stock and demand now met	13
Present year's heavy supplies	13
Special reason for	13
Annual supply now available	14
Prices in American market	15
Present low prices	15
Connected with depression of trade	15
Growth of exports	15
Present year's export to England	17
Special reasons for increase	17
Export of chilled beef	18
Tables	19—21

(2241)

The extent of the influence on English prices of the import of American cattle and beef, may be estimated from the fact that the United States in 1894 provided some three-fourths of the total imports of live cattle, and nearly six-sevenths of the import of fresh beef into Great Britain. While the imports both of States cattle and beef for the 5 months, January—May last, have been so large as to make it probable that the current year's import will show an increase over all previous years, the American agricultural returns, on the other hand, show so remarkable a diminution in the total stock of cattle during the past 4 years, that the question necessarily suggests itself how far it is probable that the exportation will keep pace, in the near future, with the growing English demand for fresh beef. The following report is intended to supply a short statement of the facts connected with the present position of cattle raising in the States, and the present situation in the American cattle markets, which have seemed material to this question.

Growth of the ranching business. In order to appreciate the actual condition of the cattle raising industry in the United States, it is necessary to glance at the history of the development of the "ranching" business, and its marked decline in the past few years. Prior to the year 1870, a herd of cattle on a Texas ranch was worth, roughly speaking, the price of its hides and bristles. With the extension of the railway system the cattle became available for the chief meat markets of the country, and the owner of the herd found his property suddenly trebled in value. The ranching business sprang at once into first-rate importance; large capitals were attracted into the new enterprise; and from Texas the business spread quickly over the Western and North-Western States, until the herds, multiplying with great rapidity, had gradually occupied the most suitable ranges of prairie country from the Mississippi to the Rocky Mountains.

Profits of the business. Under the ranching system the cost of raising cattle is reduced to a minimum. In the earlier days the business, when ranchmen enjoyed not only the free use of the public domain, but also a complete immunity from taxation, the expense of maintaining a herd was in fact the expense of maintaining the staff of mounted cowboys necessary to control it, and the cost of keeping a bullock on the ranches was then estimated at from 75 c. to 1 dol. (4s.) per year. Nowadays the ranch-owners do not altogether escape from taxation, and their expenses have increased in other minor respects; but the profit on a steer raised on the ranch, to be afterwards fattened in the corn-growing States, is still extremely large, and it is yet larger in the rare cases where the ranch is rich enough to produce cattle ready for the butcher. On the other hand there have always been heavy chances of losses of cattle from exposure and scarcity of food in winter, and from drought in summer; the herds are liable to be plundered by cattle thieves, and in the wilder regions by grey wolves; and other risks peculiar to a far western ranch have contributed to make the business, even in its best days, a highly speculative one.

Its decline. By the year 1885, which forms the high-water mark of the industry, the number of cattle on the western ranches had reached a total of 16,000,000 head, or nearly one-third of the entire number then in the States. Since then the ranching business has steadily declined in importance. The risk of losses of cattle from scarcity of food, which from the first had been considerable, became more serious as time went on. Vast as was the area at the disposal of the cattlemen, it was found that with the increasing number of herds, the ranches were very liable to become so far overstocked as not to permit of the complete renewal of the nutritive grasses; and in these conditions a dry summer producing a small crop of grass, followed by a hard winter, might easily result in such a shortness of feed as to amount to a disaster. But the principal cause of the decline of ranching has, of course been the progress of settlement. As settlement has slowly advanced from the south and east, the extension of irrigation and the gradual breaking up of the land for agriculture, the introduction of wire-fencing, the operation of "herd laws" requiring herd owners to keep their cattle off unfenced crops, and the competition of sheep farmers for range, have all combined to push the ranchman steadily back into the remoter districts. In the more settled regions the ranch has necessarily given way to less primitive, and much less economical, systems of cattle raising—in small herds, and fenced pastures, with artificial shelter, and on corn and every variety of food stuffs. At the present day, of the chief cattle States lying west of the Mississippi, Kansas and Nebraska have passed entirely out of the "free range" stage, and Colorado may be classed in the same category; a limited extent of range survives in Texas, partly on the borders of New Mexico; while the ranching business is still in vigour in the more northerly States of Wyoming, Montana, and North Dakota. In Missouri and Iowa it has never existed—at least, of recent times. The total number of cattle in the two chief ranching States, Montana and Wyoming, is under 2,000,000. *Its present extent.*

Under conditions thus altered, the cattle-raising industry has shown a remarkable change in its results. Between 1870 and 1885 the total number of cattle in the United States, exclusive of dairy cows, had risen with the development of ranching, from 15,000,000 to 35,000,000; between 1885 and 1892, though the decline of ranching had now commenced, the number of cattle continued slowly to advance, till it reached the total of 37,500,000 in 1892. Since that year the returns show a rapid decline. In the four years from January, 1892, to January, 1896, it is estimated to have fallen from 37,500,000 to 32,000,000, being an average decrease of over 1⅓ million per year. In each of the two last years of this period it has decreased by about 2,000,000 head, or over 5 per cent. *Corresponding change in results of cattle industry. Decrease of numbers of cattle.*

The following are the official returns of the Department of Agriculture from which these figures are taken:—

UNITED STATES.

Table showing Number of Cattle in the United States on January 1.

	1870.	1885.	1892.	1893.	1894.	1895.	1896.
Milch cows	10,095,000	13,904,000	16,416,000	16,424,000	15,487,000	16,504,000	16,137,000
Oxen and other cattle	15,338,000	35,513,000	37,651,000	35,954,000	36,608,000	34,364,000	32,085,000

NOTE.—(1). The returns must be taken as only approximately correct. They are arrived at by actual count only in census years; in other years estimates are obtained from the various districts of the increase or decrease since preceding year.

(2). The number of "oxen and other cattle" shown for 1885 is the result of a special investigation made at the time by Mr. Nimmo, chief of the Bureau of Statistics; it is considerably larger than that given in the ordinary departmental returns.

(3). The total returned as "milch cows" consists chiefly of cows reserved exclusively for the dairy, which generally belong to breeds unsuitable for the beef market, and the numbers of which have consequently little influence on the total number of beef cattle. Thus the largest cattle-producing States, such as Texas, are returned as having, relatively, the smallest number of milch cows. The heading also includes a large (but not ascertainable) proportion of cows used for breeding meat cattle, the rest being shown under "oxen and other cattle."

It is important to take note of the extent of the decrease shown in a limited number of Western States, in which the cattle industry of the whole country is largely concentrated. As will be seen from the detailed figures given in the Appendix, the following 10 States—Texas, Illinois, Iowa, Indiana, Missouri, Kansas, Nebraska, Montana, Wyoming, and Colorado, all with the exception of Illinois and Indiana lying west of the Mississipi—provide some $17\frac{1}{2}$ millions oxen and other cattle, or considerably more than half the total number returned for the 48 States and Territories. Or, if we leave out of consideration the Pacific Coast States, which may be regarded as far as the cattle industry is concerned, as forming a region apart—the 10 States named above supply over $\frac{17}{30}$ of the oxen and other cattle in the whole country east of the Rocky Mountains.

The concentration of cattle industry in the West.

This remarkable concentration of the industry in a small number of Western States has become possible through the agency of the great slaughtering and packing houses which have grown up in Chicago, Kansas, and other western cities, and have given the "dressed meat" trade its present enormous importance. The bulk of the western cattle are brought from the fatteners by these firms, and butchered and dressed on an immense scale, and at a great saving of expense. The dressed beef is distributed through the country in refrigerator railway cars, and sold to the consumer in local meat stores, which have largely superseded the old-fashioned butcher's shop. The result has been that the cattle raising industry of all but the most southerly of the Eastern States has been seriously affected by the competition of the western stock-growers, who, though their own expenses have been on the increase, still retain a great advantage in that respect over their eastern competitors.

The following table, showing the receipts of cattle in recent years of the chief packing centres, illustrates the growth of the dressed beef trade, and the increasing extent to which the West has become the beef supplier of the country. Allowance must, of course, be made for the cattle slaughtered for local consumption in the cities in question. It will be noted that Kansas, Omaha, and St. Louis have gained at the expense of Chicago:—

(2241)

UNITED STATES.

COMPARATIVE Yearly Receipts of Cattle at Kansas City, Omaha, Chicago, and St. Louis, from 1884-95.

Year.	Kansas City.	Chicago.	Omaha.	St. Louis.
1884	535,526	1,817,697	88,603	390,569
1885	506,627	1,905,518	116,963	311,702
1886	490,971	1,963,900	148,515	307,244
1887	669,224	2,382,008	239,337	387,709
1888	1,056,086	2,611,543	355,923	453,918
1889	1,220,343	3,023,281	473,094	396,095
1890	1,472,229	3,484,280	615,337	510,755
1891	1,270,917	3,290,359	602,002	630,356
1892	1,479,078	3,571,796	755,059	653,337
1893	1,660,807	3,133,406	852,456	756,485
1894	1,699,193	2,974,363	821,512	663 657
1895	1,613,454	2,588,558	586,103	733,526

Decrease of numbers in the Western States.

In the 10 States enumerated above, which have thus come to represent to so large an extent the cattle industry east of the Rocky Mountains, the estimated decrease of "oxen and other cattle" since 1892 has been from 21,250,000 to 17,400,000, or nearly 4,000,000. In the great breeding State of Texas the decrease is from 7,000,000 to 5,500,000. Indiana has lost about one-fifth, Illinois over one-sixth. The only one of these States showing a slight increase is Montana, where ranching is in full vigour; while the corn-growing and "feeding" States, such as Missouri, Kansas, and Nebraska, all show some decrease.

Decrease due to reduction of profits.

On a review of the past few years' history of the cattle industry, it is difficult to avoid the conclusion that what has been mainly responsible for the decrease in numbers of cattle is the reduction in the profits of cattle raising. In the 5 years preceding 1885 prices were high, and the ranching business, with its tempting profits, had a wide extension, and we have seen that the total number of cattle increased from 35,000,000 to 49,000,000. During the five following years, prices of all classes of cattle fell by as much as 35 per cent., partly from causes affecting the price of commodities in general, but chiefly as the result of the excessive supplies of cattle thrown on the market with the rapid development of ranching. At the same time the ranching area was rapidly diminishing, and ranching was being replaced by more expensive and less profitable methods of cattle raising. A corresponding change followed in the results shown by the industry, although not until some years later. The number of cattle continued to increase, although slowly, up to 1892; but since then low prices and small profits have had their effect in a rapid and continuous diminution of the stock.

Present profits.

The question of the future tendency of the numbers of cattle, therefore, seems to turn to a large extent upon the question whether the inducements offered to cattle-raising under existing conditions, and at present prices are sufficiently strong to check the falling-off in results shown by the industry in the past years. It is of course correct to say that the States can produce an indefinitely larger stock of cattle than they now possess. But the question is not so much of the capacity of the country to produce, as of the conditions that must intervene before the capacity will be exercised; and while inducements to cattle-raising are no higher than they have been in recent years, there is no reason to expect any decided change in the course of cattle production. Some idea may be gained of the actual position of breeders and fatteners from the following estimates obtained partly from private inquiry, but chiefly from published statements.

With regard, first, to the cost of raising a steer up to the time when he is sold to the feeder as a 2-year old, rising three, weighing some 900 lbs., to be finally fattened for the butcher. *Profits of breeders.*

In these estimates no charge is made for the cost of keeping the cow, which is supposed to be covered by the sale of the portion of her milk not consumed by the calf. In many districts, however, there is no sale for the milk, so that the column of expenses should be increased by the keep of the cow. The land is assumed to be good land, bought at 30 dol. per acre, or rented at 2 dol. 50 c. per year.

Cost of Raising 1-Year Old Steer in Iowa. (Privately furnished Estimate.)

	Cost.	
	Dol.	c.
Interest on cow (cost 40 dol.)	2	80
,, bull	2	0
Summer—		
Meal, corn, and oat chop	1	50
Pasture	1	0
Winter, 5 months, 150 days—		
Oilcake, 150 lbs., at 1 c.	1	50
Meal, 300 lbs., at ½ c.	1	50
Rough feed, hay, &c., with attendance	4	0
(Estimated weight of 12 months steer, 700 lbs.)		
Total	14	30

Cost of Raising 2-Year Old Steer in Illinois. (Estimate published in Live Stock Report.)

	Cost.
	Dol. c.
Interest on cow	(Not charged)
,, bull	2 50
Pasture and small feed (summer)	1 80
Wintering (6 months, at 1 dol. 50 c. per month)	9 0
Labour, insurance, tax	1 28
	14 58
Pasture, 6 months, at 1 dol.	6 0
Wintering, peck of corn per day (45 bushels, at 20 c.)	9 0
Labour, insurance	3 2
Total	32 60

In these two calculations the amount of grain allowed for feed is extremely large; the land is dear, and with 2-year old feeders selling at 3 dol. 50 c. per 100 lbs., the result would be a loss to the breeder. The author of the second estimate, indeed, concludes that "breeders of thoroughbred stock are being driven out of the business."

The case is different in localities where pastureland is cheap, and it is practicable to raise stock with little grain feed. From a large number of inquiries kindly made for the purposes of this report by the Acting British Vice-Consul at Kansas City, Mr. Evans, it results that the average price of pastureland in the States of Kansas and Nebraska is only from 8 to 12 dol. per acre, although the "tame grassland" (blue grass, clover, and timothy), is valued at 30 to 50 dol. The cost of raising an 8 months' old calf being roughly estimated at 10 dol., the cost thereafter of each summer's pasture (on the cheaper sort of land), is put at 2 dol. 50 c., that of rough feed in winter at 2 dol. 50 c., little or no grain being given; and the total cost of the 2-3-year old steer is thus estimated at from 20 to 25 dol. No allowance, however, is here made for cost of attendance, taxes, &c., nor for keep of cow (though there is generally no sale for the milk), so that the whole cost would really stand somewhat higher. Still there remains a large margin of profit; and the profits are, of course, far larger in the case of animals raised on the ranches of Wyoming, Montana, or North Dakota.

The question of the comparative costliness of pasture in summer and hay in winter in the various districts is of course closely connected with that of the thickness of the population. The fact is well illustrated by a remark made by Mr. Allen, Manager of the Standard Cattle Company, of Nebraska, in a paper printed in the report of the Senate Committee on Agricultural Depression, 1895. Mr. Allen says:—"At present the great advantage . . . . of the country west of the Missouri lies in the low cost of hay, but as

WASHINGTON.

our agriculture changes to meet the demands of an increasing population, the area of hay-land in this district, which is now very great, will become less, and the advantage of this low-priced food will be lost."

It is difficult to obtain any exact estimate of the returns yielded by capital invested in the ranches. But it is very generally admitted that the profit on steers raised on the ranches, which are usually sold as 3-year olds to feeders, are extremely large. We have seen, however, that the ranching area has been greatly reduced in recent years; and there are causes at work which tend to restrict it further (vide supra.)

With regard next to the position of the "Feeder" who buys the steer as a 2–3-year old and fattens him for the butcher. *Profits of feeders.*

ESTIMATED Cost of Fattening 150 Steers in Minnesota. (Live Stock Report.)

	Cost.	
	Dol.	c.
Cost of 150 steers, September 1, 1895, average 1,200 lbs., at 3¼ c.	5,850	0
First 90 days, 35 lbs. corn per day per steer, at 20 c. per bushel	1,937	0
Next 60 days, 28 lbs. corn per day per steer, at 20 c. per bushel	900	0
Last period, 3 lbs. oil-meal per day per steer, at 17 dol. per ton	229	0
Pasture, 2 months, at 50 c. per steer per month	150	0
Use of feeding lot, barns and yards for 90 days	90	0
Services of man and teams, 150 days, at 1 dol. 50 c. per day	225	0
Interest at 7 per cent. on average cost of steers for 5 months	164	85
Insurance at 3 per cent. per annum for 5 months on average cost	98	91
60 days hay and straw, 12 lbs. per steer per day, at 2 dol. 40 c. per ton	129	0
Interest on 200 pigs, 7 dol. 50 c. each (average for period), 7 per cent., 90 days	26	25
Insurance on 200 pigs, 7 dol. 50 c. each (average for period), 3 per cent., 90 days	11	25
Interest on 200 pigs, 7 dol. 50 c. each (average for period), 7 per cent., 60 days	18	73
Insurance on 200 pigs, 7 dol. 50 c. each (average for period), 3 per cent., 60 days	5	25
Total	9,835	24
	Dol.	c.
Gain on 200 pigs, first 90 days, 3½ c., at farm, 1 lb. per day each .. 630 0		
Gain on 250 pigs, last 60 days, 3½ c., at farm, 1 lb. per day each .. 315 0		
	945	0
Cost of cattle, when fat, at farm	8,890	24

Gain on cattle 70 lbs. per head per month, 52,500 lbs.; total cost to make 52,500 lbs., 3,240 dol., or 6⅙ c. per lb. of gain. Weight of each animal at farm 1,550 lbs.; shrinkage in shipment to Chicago 70 lbs.; freight, yardage, commission and feed, 5 dol. 9 c., making cost of each steer in Chicago 64 dol. 35 c., or 4 dol. 35 c. per 100 lbs.

The feeder probably lost money on this transaction as this price was only obtainable for steers of quite exceptional quality at the time to which the calculation refers.

ESTIMATED Cost of Fattening 16 Steers in Illinois. (Live Stock Report.)

	Cost.	
	Dol.	c.
16 cattle, averaging 1,000 lbs., at 4 c. per lb.	640	0
Interest, 6 months, at 7 per cent., on 640 dol.	22	40
24 hogs, averaging 100 lbs., at 3½ c. per lb.	84	0
Interest, 6 months, at 7 per cent., on 84 dol.	2	94
1,280 bushels of corn, at 24 c. (80 bushels per steer)	307	20
Interest, 6 months, at 7 per cent., on 307 dol. 20 c.	10	75
180 days' shock fodder, twice a day, 10 c per shock	36	0
Labour of feeding	20	0
Salt	2	25

On the assumption that the average feeder gains 50 lbs. per month in weight, the author of the estimate supposes the 16 steers to have gained 4,800 in 6 months. The outlay, after deducting estimated gain on hogs, is 250 dol. 34 c., or 5 dol. 21 c. per 100 lbs. On this calculation the report observes, "Summing up the original cost of the cattle and hogs and the expense of feeding throughout 6 months a total of 1,125 dol. 54 c. is found. The cattle . . . have therefore got to bring 4 dol. 25 c. and the hogs 3 dol. 75 c. per 100 lbs. on the farm to let the feeder out even. This is equivalent to practically 4 dol. 55 c. for the cattle, and 4 dol. 10 c. for the hogs on the Chicago market. When freight, shrinkage, &c. are taken into consideration, it would be difficult indeed to find cattle or hogs good enough to bring anywhere near those figures." It must be said, however, that the original cost of the steers was very high.

The following is an estimate of the cost of finishing the two-year old steer estimated to have been raised for 32 dol. 60 c. (vide supra).

	Cost.	
	Dol.	c.
Cost of raising 2-year old	32	60
Pasture, 6 months, at 1 dol. 25 c. per month	7	50
Corn, 4 months in pasture (peck per day, 30 bushels, at 20 c.)	6	0
Corn, 2 months full feed ($\frac{1}{2}$ bushel per day, 30 bushels, at 20 c.)	6	0
Interest, insurance, tax, labour	5	45
(Estimated weight of 3-year steer, 1,400 lbs.)		
Total	57	55

The cost of raising and finishing this steer, weighing perhaps 1,500 lbs., was therefore 57 dol. 55 c., or 3 dol. 83 c. per 100 lbs. on the farm. And the writer points out that for every steer raised there will be a heifer of much less value.

In these calculations the cost of corn has been taken as low as 20 c. per bushel; it has frequently been much higher in recent years. But it seems that the corn can be grown at an outlay of 15 c. and therefore farmers who feed corn they have grown themselves are in a better position than the estimates would show.

The calculations we have quoted above can of course only apply strictly in all respects to the localities to which they happen to refer, and need to be considerably modified in minor particulars, before they can fully correspond to the special local conditions prevailing in the various cattle growing districts. But subject to this limitation they may be taken as fairly representing the position of the cattle raisers and feeders through a great part of the Western States.

The conclusion to be drawn from them is that there is a large profit in raising stock cattle on the ranches, and a considerable profit in regions where pasture land and meadow are abundant and cheap, but that there are important parts of the cattle-growing region where, owing chiefly to greater thickness of population, pasture and hay are relatively dear, and here there is little profit in the business. The business of fattening cattle for the butcher yields a profit under specially favourable conditions, and notably where the fattener grows his own feed; but a large proportion of the feeding is, at present prices, necessarily carried on at a loss. *Cattle industry conducted partly at a loss.*

There is nothing in these results which can be regarded as affording any great stimulus to the industry as a whole. Looking at the past few years' course of production, the probability seems to be that the numbers of cattle will undergo a further diminution; at any rate, it may be reasonably supposed that while present conditions continue unchanged, they will not show any material increase. *Conclusion as to tendency of numbers.*

While the total supply of cattle, therefore, shows some signs of a further diminution, and may at the best be regarded as stationary; the demand for American beef on the other hand, is of course growing with great rapidity. The population of the States at the *Growth of demand.*

rate of increase shown in the period 1880–90 will, in five years, be some 8½ millions, and in ten years some 18 millions, larger than it is now. There will be a simultaneous growth of the demand for American beef with the growth of wealth and population in England; although against this latter consideration must be set the increasing ratio of the importation from Canada and Argentina, and, for the present, the prohibition of the importation of American cattle into Germany and France.

Relation between present stock and demand now met.

It may be thought, however, that the stock of the cattle in the United States is so vast that although it is stationary or decreasing, while the demand to which it ministers is certainly increasing, there can be no present prospect of any sensible scarcity of the supply. Some light may be thrown upon this point by a rough comparison between the total stock of cattle, as it now stands, and the extent of the demand which it actually meets.

Estimated annual slaughter.

There are no reliable statistics as to the consumption of beef in the United States; but the consumption per head of population may be taken as certainly not less than that of the United Kingdom—setting off the negro population of the south against the classes of the British population which from poverty do not eat much butcher's meat; and considering also the smaller consumption of mutton in America. The total yearly consumption of beef by the States is therefore larger in the proportion of 70 to 38 than that of the United Kingdom, which according to the most recent estimates is over 2,555,500,000 lbs.* Or, taking the average dressed weight of mature cattle to be 600 lbs., the States' consumption represents a slaughter of over 7½ millions head per year. If, to this number we add 300,000 head annually exported alive, the export of fresh beef representing some 300,000 head, and of salt and canned beef representing 200,000 head, we arrive at a total of over 8,300,000 cattle which the States are annually called upon to provide for slaughter.

To meet this there are 32,000,000 "oxen and other cattle." But from this number it is necessary to make a large deduction on account of cows used for breeding meat cattle, which are returned in great part under "other cattle," the head "milch cows" referring, as has been noted, primarily to dairy cattle. If we look, for instance, at three of the cattle States where dairy farming is least developed, we have the following returns:—

* Cf. Professor Long, "Nineteenth Century," of January last. The estimated weight of cattle is somewhat lower than that usually taken, to allow for the earlier age at which they are now matured.

	Number.	
	Milch Cows.	Oxen and Other Cattle.
Texas	784,000	5,518,000
Montana	42,000	1,153,000
Wyoming	18,000	751,000
Total	844,000	7,422,000

Here it is evident that we must set apart at least a fourth of the "oxen and other cattle" as breeding cows; and similarly for the whole country, without attempting a more exact estimate, which the returns are not sufficiently definite to warrant, we may conclude that the number of head actually destined for the meat market falls far below the 32,000,000 returned as "oxen and other cattle." Now, on the assumption that the average age of killing is no higher than 3 years, it is conceivable that a third of this residuum might under certain circumstances be annually available for slaughter. But when we allow for the vast area over which the American cattle industry is distributed, for losses from drought and fever in the south, from extreme cold in the north, and from a multitude of other causes, it is evident that the total of beef cattle in the country at a given time does not represent —at the most liberal estimate—more than one-fourth of that number annually available for the butcher.

A rough calculation, based on the estimated British consumption would therefore seem to indicate that the stock of cattle has already so far diminished as not to be equal to furnishing the number of head at present annually slaughtered except at the cost of a further depletion of the herds. The obvious objection to such a conclusion is that all the chief cattle markets of the country have been so heavily supplied during the past winter as to force prices down to a figure approaching the lowest reached in past years; and that the exports for the first 5 months of the current year have been so large that it seems probable that the year's export will be considerably above the average. If the present supplies were only obtainable by the marketing of an excessive proportion of heifers, it is hardly to be supposed that there should not have resulted before now a sensible tightening of the market. *Present year's heavy supplies.*

This objection, however, loses much of its weight on a closer examination. It was to be anticipated that the present year should be marked by an abundance of supply of finished beeves; because the scarcity of corn feed in 1895, consequent upon the failure of the corn crop of 1894, had the result that a large number of cattle which in the ordinary course should have been fattened in 1895, were instead held over until the following year. How great a number of the mature cattle due for 1895 were thus reserved until 1896, may be judged from the falling-off in the *Special reason for.*

receipts for 1895 of the four chief western markets (vide Table above). The increase of receipts at these markets for first 5 months of the current year over the receipts for the same months of 1895 has, however, been quite inconsiderable, as appears from this table :—

RECEIPTS of Cattle at Western Markets, January–May.

	Number.	
	1895.	1896.
Chicago	922,379	1,025,968
Kansas City	539,347	530,259
South Omaha	184,005	182,728
East St. Louis	278,084	252,006
Total	1,923,815	1,990,961
Increase, 1896..	..	67,146

Decrease of receipts in past 2 years.

At this rate, the receipts at the western markets for the whole of the current year will show only a small increase on those of 1895; and when allowance is made for the special circumstances which threw a number of the 1895 cattle into the year 1896, it will be seen that this result is equivalent to a continuous and substantial falling-off of the receipts in the past 2 years.

The supposition that the existing abundance of supply of finished beeves is to a certain extent a temporary feature of the trade, the result of the scarcity of corn in 1895, receives some confirmation from the fact that while supplies of mature cattle have been heavy and prices low, "stockers and feeders" on the other hand have been comparatively scarce and dear. The Live Stock Report of May 1 (Messrs. Clay, Robinson and Co., of Chicago) notes as a curious fact that "feeders should be selling for as much per hundredweight as good fat beeves. This week 3 dol. 85 c. and 3 dol. 90 c. have been paid for two or three lots, while 3 dol. 75 c. has been paid in quite a number of cases."

Annual supplies now available.

It appears, then, that while the markets are at present heavily supplied, there has been a considerable falling-off of the receipts during the past 2 years, taken as a whole; and there is, therefore, nothing in the present state of the trade which can be regarded as altogether inconsistent with the conclusion yielded by the calculation stated above, that the supply of cattle which is at present annually furnished for slaughter is obtainable only at the cost of depleting the herds. The data upon which that calculation was based are, however, perhaps not sufficiently well ascertained to justify us in placing complete confidence in all its results. Without, therefore, accepting the more precise conclusions to which a comparison between the total stock of cattle, and the number of head annually slaughtered, would seem to lead, we shall confine ourselves to noting the general fact which it brings out, that the number of cattle which the United States with their present stock of cattle can furnish annually for slaughter, large as it is, is yet far below the number which the same stock could supply if distributed over a lesser area, and one subjected to less rigorous climatic conditions.

Prices in American market. The future course of prices in the American markets must be determined by the operation of the two factors which have been discussed above—a stationary or possibly diminishing supply, and a steadily increasing demand. There are, however, some facts of the past 2 years' history of prices which may be noticed as possibly throwing some further light on the question of the tendency of the market. We have seen that the receipts for the current year at the western markets have been far less than the receipts for the same period in 1894, and only slightly heavier than the receipts for 1895. The falling-off of the receipts in 1895 had a most marked effect in raising prices; and it might, therefore, have been expected that prices in the present year should have been only slightly lower than last year. **Present low prices.** Yet they have, as a fact, fallen, and are indeed now little better than in 1894, as will be seen from this table.

Description.	March 27, 1896. From—	March 27, 1896. To—	March 29, 1895. From—	March 29, 1895. To—	March 30 1894. From—	March 30 1894. To—
	Dol. c.	Dol. c.	Dol. c.	Dol. c.	Dol. c.	Dol. c.
Extra prime steers	4 20	4 40	6 30	6 50	4 50	4 75
Export and shipping steers, 1,450 to 1,600 lbs. average	3 90	4 10	5 75	6 10	4 30	4 50
Export and shipping steers, lacking quality	3 60	3 80	5 50	5 70	3 90	4 20
Good dressed beef and shipping steers, 1,150 to 1,400	3 70	4 0	5 15	6 20	3 50	4 20
Fair to medium grades	3 40	3 70	4 50	5 50	3 15	3 65
Good to choice cows and heifers	3 0	3 90	4 10	4 85	3 0	3 25
Fair to medium grades	2 25	2 75	3 0	3 50	2 40	2 75
Canners	1 50	2 0	1 80	2 60	1 50	2 20
Export and butcher bulls	2 65	3 25	3 50	4 75	2 50	3 0
Stock, feeding, and bologna bull	2 25	2 65	2 40	3 25	1 90	2 25
Good stockers and feeders	3 10	3 60	3 75	4 75	3 0	3 60
Common stockers and feeders	2 75	3 0	2 90	3 75	2 50	3 0
Calves, 300 lbs. upward	2 50	3 0	2 25	3 0	2 0	3 0
Calves, 100 to 180 lbs.	3 25	5 40	3 0	5 25	3 50	5 50

Connected with depression of trade. The fact must be explained by a great falling-off of the American consumption and this is attributed to general depression of trade, which has especially weakened the demand in such great eastern markets as New York and Boston. If that explanation is the true one, it would seem that one of the chief causes of present depression in the American cattle market is essentially temporary in character and that a more prosperous state of general trade may be looked forward to as likely to have a very marked effect on prices of cattle.

Growth of exports. The export of cattle and beef to Great Britain grew to its present volume in the period 1885-92 when the rapid development of the ranching industry had given the country an enormous accession to its normal supply of cattle, the western markets were flooded with cheaply raised stock, and American prices were correspondingly

(2241)

depressed. The export of live cattle to British ports, which in the 5 years preceding 1885 had averaged some 100,000 head, more than trebled itself between that year and 1892, when it reached a total of 378,000 (vide infra). Similarly, the export of fresh beef rose from 111,000,000 lbs. in 1885 to 219,000,000 lbs. in 1892.

Live cattle. Conditions of the export trade.

The cattle exported alive to Great Britain are for the most part 3 and 4-year olds, selected from the highest class of beeves raised in the cattle States west of the Mississippi and marketed in Chicago. They are there bought by the exporting firms, the great bulk of the purchases being made by a limited number of the great slaughtering and packing houses among which may be mentioned Messrs. Armour, Swift and Co., and Nelson, Morris and Co. The cattle are shipped almost entirely to London, Liverpool, or Glasgow, where their meat sells slightly below the corresponding class of English beef from the force of a lingering prejudice against the foreign article. The total of the exporters' expenses between the Chicago and the English market varies from 20 to 25 dol. (4l. to 5l.) per head, according to the rates of ocean freight. The items of expense are approximately as below:—

	Per Head.
	Dol. c.
Railroad freight from Chicago to New York..	7 0
Feed on ocean	3 0
Ocean freight (about)	9 0
Insurance	0 85
Attendance	1 0
Yardage, commission, &c., on English side	3 0
Incidental	1 0
Total	24 85

It is calculated, making due allowance for loss of weight on the voyage, that a difference of some 6 to 7 c. per 1 lb. between the Chicago and English prices (live weight, and estimated dressed weight respectively) is just sufficient to enable the exporter to recover his outlay with a fair profit, supposing the shipment to be of heavy cattle; and the prices in the two markets tend in the long run to adjust themselves in this relation. A difference in price of more than 7 c. has an immediate effect in stimulating purchases for export at Chicago; a very slight advance of prices at Chicago, or decline at Liverpool, bringing the difference in price below 6 c., is sufficient to make exportation a losing business. The exporter having generally been forced to engage ocean freight some months in advance has then to choose between sacrificing his freight or shipping at a certain loss. Thus the business has admittedly been one of great uncertainty and risk.

The following table shows the export to Great Britain of live cattle and of fresh beef during the past 10 years:—

Year.	Cattle.	Fresh Beef.
	Head.	1,000 lbs.
1886	114,193	97,149
1887	96,960	81,917
1888	124,562	93,466
1889	193,167	137,286
1890	300,589	171,032
1891	345,797	192,456
1892	378,167	219,103
1893	280,996	205,911
1894	345,734	193,331
1895	305,068	190,736

The export of live cattle which, as has been seen, rose rapidly in the years preceding 1892, has since averaged a figure somewhat below that then reached, and has been subject to extreme variations. The great decrease shown in 1895 is to be accounted for by the scarcity of corn in that year, which as has been noticed above caused a considerable reduction of the receipts at the western markets, and a large rise of prices at Chicago.

Present year's export to England. The export to Great Britain for the first 5 months of the current year was 175,000 head, as compared with 112,000 for the same period last year. If this rate per month be sustained, the year's export will be over 400,000 or larger even than in 1892. The London and Liverpool markets have been so heavily supplied that the prices of American beeves have there fallen as low as 9 to $9\frac{1}{2}$ c. per 1 lb. (estimated dressed weight); while export steers were being quoted at Chicago at 3·75 to 4 c. per 1 lb. live weight. At these rates shipments must have been at a loss.

Special reasons for increase. The increase of the export in the present year, like the decrease of last year may be explained in part by last year's shortness of feed, which threw a portion of the 1895 cattle into the present year, and contributed to bring about a temporary congestion of the Chicago and other western markets; the heavy cattle, of the class suitable for exportation being those which have most suffered in price.

We have seen, further, that the receipts for the first 5 months of this year, though slightly heavier than last year, were considerably lower than in 1894; and the fact that, with far smaller supplies, the prices have sunk almost as low as 1894 led to the inference that the American demand had temporarily weakened owing to general depression of trade. Any decrease of the home consumption, of course, increases the surplus available for exportation; and since the home consumption is extremely large relatively to the export, the effect of any decrease of the former in increasing the volume of export is disproportionately large.

To the extent to which these two special circumstances, the scarcity of corn in 1895 and the trade depression in the present year have contributed to depress the Chicago market, the increase of exports to England during the past 5 months must be considered as a temporary feature of the trade. The course of the exports

(2241)

Chilled beef export.

in future years must be governed mainly by the abundance or the scarcity of supplies at Chicago and other western markets; and the volume of those supplies, and its relation to the demand, will be determined by the conditions which we have already discussed.

The course of development of the chilled beef export trade has been very similar to that of live cattle. Taking 600 lbs. as the average weight of cattle slaughtered for the dressed beef trade, last year's export of fresh beef to Great Britain represented a number of cattle nearly equal to that exported alive, the latter being, however, heavier cattle. The past 5 months' export of chilled beef was 108,759,600 lbs., as compared with 81,841,065 lbs. for the same period last year. At this rate the year's export will be some 60,000,000 lbs. greater than in 1892. It seems still a matter of doubt which of the two branches of the trade offers the largest profits. The Secretary of Agriculture in his report for 1895 says: "It appears to work out more profitably to transport the live cattle. They are carried on parts of the ship that would otherwise be unoccupied. They do not require such special fittings and appliances as to debar the vessel from carrying other cargo when cattle are not available." The ocean freight on the 4 quarters of a steer varies from 5 to 6 dol.

The following table shows the London prices of American chilled beef in 1895 compared with those of Deptford killed American, and of English and Scotch beef:—

WASHINGTON.

Average Wholesale Prices of Dressed Meats at the London Central Meat Market, 1894-95. (Compiled from the Board of Agriculture Returns and from the Meat Trades Journal.)

Per 100 Lbs.

Beef.	First Quarter, 1895. From—	First Quarter, 1895. To—	Second Quarter, 1895. From—	Second Quarter, 1895. To—	Third Quarter, 1895. From—	Third Quarter, 1895. To—	Average for 1894. From—	Average for 1894. To—
	Dol. c.	Dol. c.	Dol. c.	Dol. c.	Dol. c.	Dol. c.	Dol. c.	Dol. c.
Scotch—								
Short sides	12 12½	12 87½	13 12½	14 12½	12 12½	14 62½	12 62½	13 62½
Long sides	11 25	11 75	12 12½	12 62½	12 12½	13 62½	11 37½	11 75
English prime	11 25	11 75	11 75	12 37½	11 0	12 87½	11 12½	12 37½
Cows and bulls	7 75	9 25	7 25	9 75	6 0	10 0	.. ..	.. ..
American—								
Deptford killed	10 50	11 0	11 0	11 50	9 0	11 50	9 25	11 0
Birkenhead killed	10 50	11 0	10 75	11 50	9 75	11 50	9 25	11 0
Refrigerated hind quarters	10 50	11 50	11 75	12 87½	10 50	13 50	9 12½	10 62½
Refrigerated fore quarters	8 0	8 75	6 25	7 75	4 50	7 50	5 25	8 0

UNITED STATES.

Estimated Number of Animals on Farms and Ranches, Total Value of each kind, &c.

States and Territories.	Milch Cows. Number.	Average Price. Dol. c.	Value. Dollars.	Oxen and other Cattle. Number.	Average Price. Dol. c.	Value. Dollars.
Maine	175,879	26 50	4,660,794	152,664	24 74	3,776,920
New Hampshire	106,122	26 50	2,812,233	113,846	23 48	2,673,550
Vermont	239,335	24 33	5,823,021	165,688	22 26	3,687,798
Massachusetts	176,476	32 72	5,774,295	96,799	25 78	2,495,797
Rhode Island	24,524	32 0	784,768	11,950	28 73	343,269
Connecticut	136,246	29 14	3,970,208	100,111	29 3	2,905,812
New York	1,552,217	26 18	40,637,041	775,798	26 67	20,693,631
New Jersey	189,035	35 0	6,616,225	63,845	28 75	1,835,731
Pennsylvania	929,091	25 25	23,459,548	835,222	22 17	18,514,790
Delaware	31,020	25 75	798,765	27,941	23 33	651,941
Maryland	147,541	26 21	3,867,050	121,044	21 79	2,637,328
Virginia	280,252	22 25	6,235,607	419,523	17 24	7,233,456
North Carolina	269,379	17 60	4,741,070	390,446	11 59	4,526,990
South Carolina	155,009	20 31	3,148,233	204,126	12 88	2,629,043
Georgia	354,583	18 0	6,382,494	569,200	9 86	5,613,450
Florida	56,600	15 0	849,000	553,727	9 2	4,994,120
Alabama	311,774	15 0	4,676,610	445,007	9 0	4,006,179
Mississippi	312,265	14 75	4,605,909	419,946	7 97	3,346,971
Louisiana	179,354	17 10	3,066,953	298,688	10 1	2,989,123
Texas	868,811	14 25	12,380,557	7,024,496	8 85	62,177,330
Arkansas	342,286	13 75	4,706,433	725,794	8 75	6,353,236
Tennessee	373,736	16 50	6,166,644	469,556	10 48	4,921,187
West Virginia	183,555	22 71	4,168,534	292,269	18 67	5,455,723
Kentucky	320,264	21 75	6,965,742	467,060	16 97	7,923,866
Ohio	783,403	25 0	19,585,075	871,662	22 44	19,559,404
Michigan	459,475	24 24	11,137,674	508,938	20 67	10,521,389
Indiana	657,048	23 25	15,276,366	1,085,236	19 28	20,925,520
Illinois	1,104,861	22 23	24,561,060	1,747,731	18 88	32,992,610
Wisconsin	701,774	20 54	14,414,488	836,975	16 43	13,749,322
Minnesota	577,254	19 25	11,112,140	641,946	15 87	10,187,680
Iowa	1,304,184	18 77	24,479,534	2,707,049	18 76	50,792,352
Missouri	869,726	17 50	15,220,205	1,928,269	16 50	31,821,846
Kansas	773,489	18 40	14,232,198	1,978,520	16 78	33,207,282
Nebraska	530,338	18 75	9,943,838	1,614,676	16 59	26,780,200
California	290,521	26 95	7,829,541	602,904	17 39	10,481,668
Oregon	106,122	25 0	2,653,050	797,051	16 42	13,090,374
Nevada	14,903	27 50	409,833	317,498	14 77	4,689,446
Colorado	60,416	26 0	1,570,816	1,037,814	16 49	17,112,302
Arizona	17,797	25 0	444,925	761,254	15 0	11,418,810
North Dakota	65,000	21 19	1,377,350	272,000	17 17	4,669,587
South Dakota	133,000	19 0	2,527,000	410,000	16 25	6,662,500
Idaho	32,709	27 0	883,143	515,338	15 25	7,858,905
Montana	35,705	28 75	1,026,519	1,025,967	16 30	16,725,323
New Mexico	18,775	20 0	375,500	1,288,182	11 1	14,179,659
Utah	54,497	22 21	1,210,378	402,731	14 10	5,679,512
Washington	96,605	35 0	3,381,175	447,690	20 88	9,345,532
Wyoming	13,395	32 0	428,640	1,107,062	14 37	15,910,696
Total	16,416,351	21 40	351,378,132	37,651,239	15 16	570,749,155

WASHINGTON.

Estimated Number of Milch Cows and of Oxen and other Cattle on Farms and Ranches, average Price per Head, and Total Value of each kind, January, 1896.

States and Territories.	Milch Cows. Number.	Milch Cows. Average Price.	Milch Cows. Value.	Oxen and other Cattle. Number.	Oxen and other Cattle. Average Price.	Oxen and other Cattle. Value.
		Dol. c.	Dollars.		Dol. c.	Dollars.
Maine	192,077	28 14	5,405,047	117,802	24 46	2,880,939
New Hampshire	127,694	29 50	3,766,973	84,723	24 40	2,067,306
Vermont	258,471	24 82	6,415,250	143,643	21 20	3,044,576
Massachusetts	174,572	34 63	6,045,428	80,476	26 36	2,121,662
Rhode Island	24,763	38 33	949,166	11,596	23 81	276,120
Connecticut	136,206	29 90	4,072,559	69,390	25 15	1,745,494
New York	1,445,232	24 30	35,119,138	597,428	23 12	13,813,491
New Jersey	200,347	34 38	6,887,930	47,487	26 35	1,251,502
Pennsylvania	947,766	24 22	22,954,893	610,776	20 70	12,642,879
Delaware	34,174	29 0	991,046	25,482	19 99	509,258
Maryland	150,477	24 50	3,686,687	116,045	19 31	2,241,000
Virginia	265,635	18 14	4,818,619	386,675	15 88	6,138,896
North Carolina	272,046	14 40	3,917,462	363,585	10 12	3,680,393
South Carolina	129,388	16 88	2,184,069	158,450	10 11	1,601,346
Georgia	312,711	16 95	5,300,451	540,916	9 11	4,926,936
Florida	114,332	13 32	1,522,902	361,054	7 97	2,878,718
Alabama	308,439	10 91	3,365,069	523,329	6 70	3,507,352
Mississippi	293,870	13 81	4,058,345	485,695	7 49	3,636,691
Louisiana	166,889	14 10	2,353,135	312,122	8 34	2,603,311
Texas	783,936	17 89	14,024,615	5,518,644	12 60	69,520,010
Arkansas	295,827	12 87	3,807,293	516,695	8 49	4,388,084
Tennessee	330,690	15 53	5,135,616	519,124	10 58	5,493,215
West Virginia	175,029	20 54	3,595,096	296,613	15 35	4,553,985
Kentucky	303,682	20 38	6,189,039	506,997	17 33	8,786,669
Ohio	759,597	24 25	18,420,227	686,285	21 41	14,693,645
Michigan	468,523	25 16	11,788,039	398,656	17 61	7,018,495
Indiana	637,404	24 70	15,743,879	798,414	20 60	16,447,970
Illinois	1,018,443	27 46	27,966,445	1,430,976	20 42	29,214,530
Wisconsin	802,902	22 21	17,832,453	673,250	17 37	11,693,824
Minnesota	600,515	21 44	12,875,042	694,321	15 3	10,434,540
Iowa	1,202,560	25 78	31,001,997	2,336,973	21 46	50,159,389
Missouri	723,309	24 0	17,359,416	1,686,990	19 30	32,565,492
Kansas	622,892	22 12	13,778,371	1,766,245	19 20	33,903,604
Nebraska	534,197	21 92	11,709,598	1,062,469	17 86	18,980,269
South Dakota	292,874	20 41	5,977,558	399,814	16 50	6,597,768
North Dakota	156,571	21 63	3,386,631	255,502	19 81	5,061,518
Montana	42,086	27 90	1,174,499	1,153,557	17 24	19,882,720
Wyoming	18,332	24 50	449,134	751,849	16 48	12,389,717
Colorado	79,975	25 0	1,999,375	926,560	17 17	15,910,331
New Mexico	18,383	23 0	422,809	793,506	10 15	8,056,069
Arizona	15,622	25 0	390,550	636,512	10 14	6,457,164
Utah	57,271	15 20	870,519	369,374	11 51	4,253,114
Nevada	18,196	24 50	445,802	259,078	12 7	3,126,940
Idaho	28,034	20 25	567,689	395,852	14 10	5,583,492
Washington	117,381	22 8	2,591,772	381,550	15 21	5,803,002
Oregon	113,732	18 43	2,096,081	788,452	12 64	9,962,640
California	335,646	23 75	7,971,593	888,832	15 82	14,057,319
Oklahoma	28,888	19 75	570,538	155,645	15 20	2,365,031
Total, 1896	16,137,586	22 55	363,955,545	32,085,409	15 86	508,928,416
,, 1895	16,504,629	21 97	362,601,729	34,364,216	14 6	482,999,129
Decrease	367,043	0 58*	1,353,816*	2,278,807	1 80*	25,929,287*
Decrease (per cent.)	2·2	2·6*	0·4*	6·6	12·8*	5·4*

* Increase.

LONDON:
Printed for Her Majesty's Stationery Office,
By HARRISON AND SONS,
Printers in Ordinary to Her Majesty.
(75 10 | 96—H & S 2241)

FOREIGN OFFICE.
1897.
MISCELLANEOUS SERIES.

No. 423.

REPORTS ON SUBJECTS OF GENERAL AND COMMERCIAL INTEREST.

UNITED STATES.

REPORT ON THE
PROSPECTS OF FARMERS IN THE STATE OF CALIFORNIA.

Presented to both Houses of Parliament by Command of Her Majesty,
MAY, 1897.

LONDON:
PRINTED FOR HER MAJESTY'S STATIONERY OFFICE,
BY HARRISON AND SONS, ST. MARTIN'S LANE,
PRINTERS IN ORDINARY TO HER MAJESTY.

And to be purchased, either directly or through any Bookseller, from
EYRE & SPOTTISWOODE, EAST HARDING STREET, FLEET STREET, E.C., and
32, ABINGDON STREET, WESTMINSTER, S.W.; or
JOHN MENZIES & Co., 12, HANOVER STREET, EDINBURGH, and
90, WEST NILE STREET, GLASGOW; or
HODGES, FIGGIS, & Co., Limited, 104, GRAFTON STREET, DUBLIN.

1897.

[C. 8278—22.] *Price One Penny.*

New Series of Reports.

The following Reports from Her Majesty's Representatives abroad, on subjects of general and commercial interest, have been issued, and may be obtained from the sources indicated on the title-page:—

No.		Price.
383.	*France.*—Report on the Bordeaux International Exhibition of 1895	1d.
384.	*Brazil.*—Report on the Causes which have brought about a Diminution in the Receipts at the Custom-house at Rio de Janeiro	½d.
385.	*Mexico.*—Report on the Cultivation of Cacao, Vanilla, Indiarubber, Indigo, and Bananas in Mexico	2½d.
386.	*France.*—Report on the International Congress on Technical, Industrial, and Commercial Education, held at Bordeaux, in September, 1895	1d.
387.	*Portugal.*—Report on the East Coast Route to Mashonaland	1d
388.	*Austria-Hungary.*—Report on the Iron Industry in Styria and the Betler Ironworks in Hungary	5d.
389.	*Belgium.*—Report on the Output of Coal, Iron, and Steel in Belgium in 1894–95	½d.
390.	*Japan.*—Report on the Railways of Japan (with Plans)	13½d.
391.	*Egypt.*—Report on the Commercial Relations of Great Britain and Egypt	2½d.
392.	*Germany.*—Report on the Wine Trade of Germany, 1893–95	1d.
393.	*Mexico.*—Report on the Cultivation of Coffee in Mexico	1d.
394.	*Switzerland*—Report on the various Institutions and Agricultural Development of Switzerland	1½d.
395.	*Germany.*—Report on the Reduction of the Railway Tariff for Coal from the Silesian Mines	½d.
396.	*Austria-Hungary.*—Report on the Treatment of Habitual Drunkards in Austria and the "Curatel" Procedure	½d.
397.	*Brazil.*—Report on the Productions, Commerce and Finances of the States of Amazonas and Pará	2½d.
398.	*Portugal*—Report on the Port and Railway of Lorenzo Marques	2d.
399.	*Germany.*—Report on the Society for Insurance against Want of Employment in Winter and the General Labour Registry at Cologne	1½d.
400.	*Switzerland.*—Report on the Extent of State Encouragement to Commercial Education	½d.
401.	*Mexico.*—Further Report on the Various Vegetable Products of Mexico	2d.
402.	*Germany.*—Report for the Year 1894–95 on the German Colonies in Africa and the South Pacific	6d.
403.	*United States.*—Report on the United States Cattle-Raising Industry in 1896, and the Export of Cattle and Beef to Great Britain	1½d.
404.	*United States.*—Report on the Distress Caused to British Emigrants to California by Fraudulent Land Syndicates and Emigration Agencies	1½d.
405.	*Chile.*—Report on the Maintenance of British Trade at Iquique and Northern Chile	½d.
406.	*Netherlands.*—Report on the Balata Industry of Dutch Guiana	1d.
407.	*Persia.*—Report on the Cultivation of Olives in the Districts of Ghilan	½d.
408.	*Portugal.*—Reports on the Fruits and Fruit Trade of Madeira	1½d.
409.	*Russia.*—Report on the Nijni Novgorod Exhibition, 1896	1½d.
410.	*Belgium.*—Report on the Herstal Arms Factory	½d.
411.	*Roumania.*—Report on the Petroleum Industry in Roumania	2d.
412.	*Belgium.*—Report on the Metallurgical Industries of the Province of Liége during 1895	1d.
413.	*Germany.*—Report on the Finances of the German African Colonies for 1897–98	1d.
414.	*Germany.*—Report on Molasses and Peat Fodder	1d.
415.	*China.*—Report on the Revenue and Expenditure of the Chinese Empire	3d.
416.	*Russia.*—Report on the Drink Question in Russia	½d.
417.	*Italy.*—Report on the Economic and Financial Situation in Italy	4d.
418.	*Germany.*—Report on the Operation of the Insurance Laws for 1895	1d.
419.	*Netherlands.*—Report on the German Competition with British manufactures in the Netherlands	½d.
420.	*Germany.*—Report on the Wine Trade of Germany, 1895–96	1d.
421.	*Mexico.*—Report on the Tampico Branch of the Mexican Central Railway	1d.
422.	*Netherlands.*—Report on the Gold Industry of Dutch Guiana	5½d.

No. 423.

UNITED STATES.

SAN FRANCISCO.

Consul-General Warburton to the Marquess of Salisbury.

(Received at Foreign Office, May 6, 1897.)

My Lord,

I HAVE the honour to inclose a Report on various matters bearing on the Prospects of Farmers in the State of California, viz., the fall in the value of land and horses, the prospects of fruit growers and the beet sugar industry.

I have, &c.
(Signed)   J. W. WARBURTON.

Report on Various Matters Bearing on the Prospects of Farmers in the State of California.

Table of Contents.

	Page
Fall in the value of land	1
Prospects of fruit growers	3
Diseases of the vine	6
Pests of citrus fruits	7
Beet sugar industry	8
Fall in the value of horses	10

Fall in the Value of Land in California.

Land in California has fallen greatly in value during the last few years, probably as much as from 25 to 50 per cent., according to quality. Indeed, any but the best lands are now almost unsaleable. There has, however, it is said, been of late a slight general recovery owing partly to the result of the Presidential election, and in the case of wheat lands to the great rise in the price of wheat. The farmers of California, unfortunately, did not benefit much if at all by the rise as their crops had been sold before it came.

(2383)

There was sold by auction last summer an estate, known as the Martin Murphy Estate, near Mountain View, in the Santa Clara Valley. The estate is said to be one of the finest, and is situated in one of the most beautiful and fertile districts in California. It was sold in three portions, and in small lots, averaging about 10 acres. The sale of the first portion took place in June, and realised prices ranging from 240 dol. down to 120 dol. per acre. It is admitted that the land was sold cheap, and that those who bought got bargains.

The second portion was sold in August, and the prices realised ranged from 165 dol. down to 119 dol. per acre. The third portion was sold in October, and realised from 110 dol. down to 78 dol. per acre. This portion is described as seed and garden land. After the sale four remaining parcels were sold at from 150 dol. down to 135 dol. per acre.

According to the newspapers the auctioneer expressed the opinion that, considering everything, fair prices had been realised.

Last February an estate known as the Oak Lawn Farm, described as "the finest in San Joaquin County," and consisting of 850 acres, situated about 6 miles from the city of Stockton, was sold at public auction. It is stated that the owner had spent 250,000 dol. on it, and that there were numerous fine buildings thereon. There were only two bids, the first of 40,000 dol., the second of 73,525 dol. This bid was made by the Stockton Savings and Loan Society who had a mortgage of that amount on the property, and to whom it was knocked down. The price was, therefore, about 86 dol. 50 c. per acre, without taking the buildings into account.

Early in March the Tobre Vista Ranch, near the town of Sonoma, was sold for 42,000 dol. It consists of 810 acres of land, heavily wooded on the hillsides with a vineyard, a great olive orchard, and an orchard of general character, and a residence which is said to have cost 30,000 dol. 15 years ago. There are also wine cellars, barns, and other outhouses. The property is said to have cost the late owner 150,000 dol., and one of the newspapers observed that "on the basis of" the purchase price (which was believed to be 65,000 dol.) "it will be income-producing as well as a princely country seat for its new proprietor." The estate is an ornamental residential one, "with ideal location and climate," not a farming one, but the low price paid serves to indicate the extent of the fall in the value of land.

Considering the great fall in the price of land, and the fact that land can now be bought at a fair value, and if the view which now appears to be generally taken that the Constitutional Amendment of 1894 does not affect the right of aliens in the matter of "the acquisition, possession, enjoyment, transmission," &c., of real estate, the opportunities for settlers to buy land are at the present time unquestionably good; but intending purchasers must exercise due caution, and make careful enquiries through respectable solicitors and estate agents before purchasing.

SAN FRANCISCO.

Prospects of Fruit Growers in California.

The State Board of Equalisation, in a report recently issued, gave the numbers of all the fruit trees in the State for the years 1895–96, with the exception of apple trees. In reply to my enquiry as to the cause of this omission, the Secretary to the Board informed me that the returns of apple trees were not sufficiently accurate to be included in the official report, none having been received from six counties. For the rest of the State the figures were approximately 895,575 in bearing, and 541,730 not in bearing in 1896.

The returns are based upon the sworn statements of fruit-growers, and as they are taxed on the number of their trees they would not be likely to return more than they possessed. The returns, moreover, appear to be not quite complete. For, at least, three counties there are no returns at all.

It may, therefore, be not unfairly assumed that the number of fruit trees is under rather than over-estimated.

The official returns then show that there were in the spring of the two years 1895–96 respectively the following number of fruit trees of all kinds, excepting apples, in this State, viz.:—

Year.	In Bearing.	Not in Bearing.	Total.
1895	12,179,224	12,566,459	24,745,683
1896	14,032,284	13,625,485	27,657,769

The figures show an increase in bearing trees in 1896 over 1895 of 1,853,060, and in all trees of 2,912,086; and as the nursery stock is not included in the returns, and fresh trees come into bearing every year and the younger bearing trees come gradually into maturity and yearly increase their produce, and as, moreover, new orchards are being continually planted, it is not unreasonable to assume that the output of fruit will be doubled within a very few years.

It may be interesting here to give the numbers of the different kinds of fruit trees for 1896 as shown by the returns referred to :—

| | Number. ||
	In Bearing.	Not in Bearing.
Apricot	1,630,887	1,289,934
Cherry	634,953	181,704
Fig	181,500	106,996
Olive	267,704	820,259
Peach	3,120,743	2,641,917
Pear	1,248,426	738,997
Prune (French)	3,537,255	3,568,013
,, (other kinds)	474,049	406,338
Lemon	230,453	963,572
Orange	1,464,332	1,969,940
Almond	1,001,926	643,930
Walnut	240,056	293,885
Total	14,032,284	13,625,485

For some years there has been more fruit produced in the State than there was a profitable market for, and at times large quantities have been allowed to go to waste in the orchards because it was not worth while to pick it, and the serious question arises, what will become of the fruit when the crop is doubled? An outlet for a part of the produce has been found in Chicago and New York, but this is limited. It may, perhaps, be increased and markets opened up in other parts of the United States. It may also be possible to send fruit profitably to London at some future time, but so far the experiment has not proved a success. As, however, carriage is very expensive overland, and the fruit season here is not earlier than that of the South of France, and not much more so than the English season, the English market is likely to be very limited.

The amount of fruit sent to New York in 1896 is stated to have been 1,133 carloads (a carload is 10 tons), an increase of 149 loads over 1895, but a decrease of 30 from 1894. The amount sent to Chicago is said to have been about the same as in 1895.

In September a report was published of the results of the shipment of fresh fruits to London last summer, from which I quote the following extracts:—"The shipment of California fruits to London this year began with the middle of July, when a consignment of 4,000 boxes of pears and plums from Sacramento were transported over the sea in the American Line steamship 'St. Louis.' English buyers had been rendered cautious by their experiences in other years, and the prices obtained in the London market were unsatisfactory to the sellers. The complaint was made that some of the boxes were damaged, and both pears and plums were too small to command good prices.

"The average selling price of Bartlett's* was from 1 dol. 32 c.

---

* The "Bartlett" pear is the same as what we call "William" at home. It is the best pear I have met with here.—J. W. W.

to 1 dol. 92 c. per box of 50 lbs., and plums were sold for 1 dol. 80 c. per crate. Making allowance for freight, insurance, and cost of handling, the prices realised were lower than those then prevalent in New York. At a sale in London on the last day of July pears brought 1 dol. 38 c. to 1 dol. 80 c., while plums brought 2 dol. 28 c., an advance upon the price at the previous sale.

"Two weeks later a consignment of 10,600 half-cases from California, consisting of peaches, pears, and plums, arrived in London. They were of superior size and quality, and in fine condition. Nevertheless the selling price was very low. Peaches ranged from 84 c. to 1 dol. 56 c., plums from 72 c. to 1 dol. 92 c., William pears from 72 to 84 c. and Hardy's were disposed of at 1 dol. 44 c. Large lots were taken by German and Russian buyers. It was said the prices were depressed on account of the abundance of French and English fruits in London.

"On August 28, 5,000 half-cases arrived in London from California. The prices were low, though the fruit was in good condition. Peaches, 72 c. to 1 dol. 24 c.; pears, 48 to 84 c.; plums, 48 c. to 2 dol. 4 c. for a very superior quality. There were again great quantities of French and English fruits in the London market.

"In the first week of the present month of September a consignment of 5,000 half-cases from California were put up at auction in London. The prices realised were better than at the previous week's sale, owing to the scarcity of fruit in the market. Peaches brought 1 dol. 8 c. to 1 dol. 32 c.; pears, 90 c. to 1 dol. 32 c.; plums, 1 dol. 74 c. All fruits were excellent, except a lot of pears, which were small and hard, and brought only 78 c. The prices obtained at several sales since the first consignment was delivered have certainly been discouraging to the California fruit-raisers, as also to the exporters."

As regards local sales of fruit, the growers are said to be very much at the mercy of the middleman and speculators. To remedy this grievance the question of establishing a free public market in this city for the sale of fruit and other perishable products has for some time past been under discussion, and attempts have been made to procure a site for the market. But so far conflicting interests have proved too strong for the realisation of the project.

The report of the State Board of Horticulture says, with reference to local sales, that "the successful methods of marketing citrus fruits in the southern part of the State are entirely due to co-operative associations or exchanges."

Mexican competition in the near future is greatly feared. The Mexicans are said to be giving their serious attention to fruit-growing, and to have agents in all the markets of the eastern United States, who are studying the best system of packing, &c. The soil and climate of Mexico are well suited to the production of many fruits, especially oranges and lemons. Land and labour also are cheap, and there are considerable railway facilities northwards.

(2383)

Canada also is likely to prove a competitor for some kinds of fruit. A newspaper on November 6 published a telegram from Ottawa which stated that "the yield of peaches and grapes has been above the average, while the yield of apples is extraordinary, thousands of barrels being despatched to Montreal daily for shipment to England. From one little station, Winona, on the Grand Trunk Railway, near Hamilton, 2,000,000 lbs. of grapes have been shipped within the last six weeks."

At present, therefore, the prospects of the Californian fruit-growers would seem to be somewhat gloomy, and their remedy to lie in the direction of extending the canned and dried fruit industry, with the exception perhaps of raisins, and in sending these goods to Europe and other parts of the United States, and in establishing co-operation and combination for the purpose.

In order to aid the dried fruit industry, arrangements have been made with the Southern Pacific Railway to ship such goods for Europe from the principal points in this State at the following rates, which came into effect on September 17:—

From—	To—	Rate per 100 lbs. in United States Gold Coin.	
		In Boxes.	In Sacks.
		Dol. c.	Dol. c.
San Francisco	London	1 10	1 30
Oakland	Liverpool	1 10	1 30
San José	Glasgow	1 15	1 35
Stockton	Bordeaux	1 25	1 45
Sacramento	Havre	1 25	1 45
Marysville	Hamburg	1 15	1 35
Los Angeles	Bremen	1 15	1 35
Main line intermediate points in California	Antwerp	1 10	1 30
	Amsterdam	1 15	1 35
	Rotterdam	1 15	1 35
	Copenhagen	1 25	1 45
	Stockholm	1 25	1 45

NOTE.—These rates are for carload lots of not less than 24,000 lbs., and only apply over the Sunset route to New Orleans, whence the Morgan line of steamers will convey the consignments to New York. There close connection will be made for the port of destination.

As regards viticulture, it is probable that wine and brandy making will prove more profitable to grape-growers than making raisins, for the present at any rate, and great efforts are being made to improve the quality of wines.

Phylloxera and other Diseases of the Vine.

Instructor Hayne, of the College of Agriculture at the State

University, went last summer on a tour of inspection of the vineyards in the Upper Napa Valley. The object of this tour was partly to determine if the so-called "Riparia disease" was the same as the "Anaheim disease," and partly to examine the condition of the selected resistant vines which the University imported for distribution last spring, and of which samples were sent to various localities for trial before the general distribution, which is to take place this spring.

Concerning the mysterious disease which was stated to attack only the riparia, Mr. Hayne has said, "that whatever the trouble was it was of a surety not the Anaheim disease. Were it the Anaheim disease I should feel very much discouraged, for no one knows what this is. It is a contagious disease that since 1887 has swept out of existence over 30,000 acres of fine vines south of Tehachapi, but the cause of which is unknown and so far has been found incurable.

"From hasty examination it is impossible to say definitely what the trouble is at St. Helena. It is probably due to a complication of troubles, mainly bad varieties, and those in no way suited to the soil; but nothing definite can be said till fuller investigation has been made."

Pests, &c., of Citrus Fruits.

Some alarm has recently been felt by orange growers in the southern counties at the possible introduction from Mexico of an orange worm which is said to be prevalent in that country. This pest is the larva of a small fly of the *Dyptera* order called *Trypeta Ludens*. It burrows into the pulp of the orange, causing the fruit to decay. According to Dr. L. O. Howard, United States entomologist, it was found infesting Mexican oranges imported into New Orleans as long ago as 1884, but he knows of no case where the worm has been found in the native oranges of the State.

There is said to be great danger of introducing this fly in cars that have been used in transporting Mexican oranges to eastern markets, and an effort is being made to stop the introduction of oranges from the State of Morelos, where the fly is found.

A newspaper recently reported that another pest had lately been discovered which was making great havoc among oranges and lemons shipped to the east from Southern California. It was alleged to be a species of fungus, but whether an entirely new variety or not had not been decided. It further stated that the so-called fungus was engaging the attention of the professors at the Agricultural College of the State University.

Some papers say that the markings noticed on citrus fruits are not caused by a fungus but are due to the effects of the gas used in the fumigation of the trees; that they are only found on fruit grown in orchards where the trees have been fumigated, that they have long been known, and that the percentage of fruit marked is very small, and that it causes no injury to the fruit, occurring only where there was some abrasion of the skin.

UNITED STATES.

Beet Sugar Industry.

Several of the local newspapers recently published articles on the position of the beet-sugar industry of this State.

One, in an article on "California's possibilities with sugar beets," says, while persons largely interested in sugar producing have "expressed the highest opinions of the prospects and possibilities" of the State in the matter, the farmers "who have turned their attention to raising the sugar beet are finding it very hard to make both ends meet."

In referring to the struggles of the first beet-sugar factory in the United States, established several years ago at Alvaredo in Alameda County, and of the beet-growing farmers, it says, "in time, however, these difficulties were overcome, and the McKinley tariff with its sugar bounty clause going into effect, the business of the factory was established on a firm basis. The repeal of the McKinley law has again embarrassed the sugar factories, and as the price paid to the farmers is dependent upon the price obtained for the sugar, the farmers also have suffered."

The article then gives a list of other factories which "under the fostering influence of the sugar bounty under the McKinley tariff" have been established in various parts of the State, or "are being considered." It goes on to show that the conditions of California are peculiarly favourable to the production of the sugar-beet, but adds that "the prices of land and labour prevent the industry being profitably established in competition with foreign sugar." It estimates the number of acres in the State suitable for the production of sugar at 1,250,000, and the possible production at 4,631,250,000 lbs. The amount and value of sugar imported into the United States during the year ended June 30, 1895, are stated to have been respectively 3,574,510,454 lbs. and 76,462,836 dol. The article concludes, "Under favourable legislation" (*i.e.*, protection and bounties) "California could have produced this sugar, and nearly 80,000,000 dol., instead of being sent abroad, would be distributed among the farmers of this State."

Another paper, in a leader on "the sugar-beet issue," says: "The farmers of Pajaro, Salinas, and San Juan Valleys are in trouble. Under Harrison's Administration they began the culture of the sugar-beet with flattering prospects, having a home market for their products and cash in hand. The outlook for great and growing prosperity was of the best. With the election of a Democratic President and a Congress composed of . . . . radical free traders . . . . the sugar bounty was repealed, and every beet grower in the United States was put on short pay." The article proceeds to say that the United States, with a soil that will raise all the sugar it needs, pays foreign countries 130,000,000 dol. per annum for the sugar it uses.

The object of these articles is, of course, to advocate protection and the restoration of the sugar bounty, but there is no reason, so far as I am able to ascertain, to doubt the correctness of the statements as to the condition of the beet-growing farmers.

A third paper published a long report of an investigation made by an agent of the paper into the condition and prospects of the beet-growing farmers on the Chino Ranch, who supply the Chino Sugar Factory. This report shows the condition of those farmers to be most unsatisfactory. So far I have not seen any contradiction of the statements contained in the report.

Notwithstanding, however, the complaints about the position of the beet sugar factories, and whatever may be the condition of the farmers, it is generally believed that the farmers are making good profits, and this opinion would seem to be borne out by the fact that a new factory is being built, and is near completion, on the Los Alamitos Ranch about 20 miles from Los Angeles, not far from Chino, and that there is now a scheme on foot for erecting in Salinas Valley, Monterey County, what it is said will be the largest sugar factory in the world. It is stated that when completed it will crush daily over 3,000 tons of beets, and produce 1,000,000 lbs. of sugar. One of the principal local papers recently said that "although the time is not definitely fixed, it is not far removed when active operations will be begun in the erection of the great factory."

The existing factories in the State and their capacity are given as follows:—Watsonville, 1,000 tons of beets; Chino, 750 tons; and Alvaredo, 500 tons, a total of 2,250 tons or 750 tons less than that of the new factory will be.

The report above referred to states that beets grown on the Chino Ranch vary in the percentage of sugar from 9 to 19, both these figures, however, being so rare "as to simply indicate the possibilities, and not the probabilities of the outcome of the crop," and that 12 per cent. is the average. A very well informed paper says that the "run of the factory at Alvaredo was recorded by weeks, showing that the average percentage of sucrose ranged from 11·9 to 15·4 per cent." This would give a general average of 13·6 per cent. Also it states that the production of beets ranged from 15 to 26 tons per acre, the average being 19·5.

Professor Hilgard, of the Agricultural Department of the University of California, in answer to my enquiries, writes as follows:—"The highest sugar percentage obtained by our analysis was 22 per cent. from beets grown on the Chino Ranch. Higher percentages are claimed, but we cannot vouch for them. The figure you note, 19 per cent., is of quite frequent occurrence, having been found by us in beets from Isleton, Sacramento County, Santa Maria, San Luis Obispo County, and at the Chino Ranch. At Alvaredo some years ago it was stated that a 'run' of some 15 hours was made on beets ranging from 19 per cent. to 21 per cent. The average there is, I believe, about 13 per cent. At Chino the price is set for a 15 per cent. beet as a standard, above which a premium is paid, below which a reduction is made. Two years ago the average of sugar in the juice of our beet crop (about 8 acres) on the Chino Ranch, for which we received pay from the factory, was 15·6 per cent.

"I think there can be no question that sugar beets carefully grown on the right kind of land in California yield a higher average percentage than is attained elsewhere, to which it must be added that the high grade beets as regards sugar percentage, almost always have a correspondingly high 'purity co-efficient,' ranging between 85 and 92."

A letter written by a gentleman who was investigating the beet-sugar industry in 1894, which was published in the "Transactions of the California State Agricultural Society during the year 1895," says:—"Germany leads all other countries, and their average is about 12 tons of beet to the acre, carrying 14 per cent. saccharine matter on an average 80 per cent. fine, while California's average is 12 tons to the acre carrying 15 per cent. saccharine matter, 80 per cent. fine."

It is stated that the average percentage of saccharine matter in German beets is 14 and in French 11. It would therefore seem that the actual average results in California are considerably higher than those obtained in Europe, and that on the best lands, and with careful cultivation, still higher average results may not unreasonably be expected.

On the Chino Ranch there are stated to be 10,000 acres suitable for beet cultivation. The greater part of this quantity is now appropriated.

Fall in the Value of Horses.

It was recently stated in one of the local newspapers that statistics issued by the Federal Department of Agriculture, showed that the horses of the United States had decreased during the past year 4·8 per cent. in number and 13·3 per cent. in value. To use the words of a local newspaper, they have become in some of the Western States a "drug in the market."

One newspaper says, "While electricity and bicycles have been increasing in popular favour for several years past, great bands of horses have been roaming over the bunch-grass hills of Eastern Washington. Rapidly increasing in number their value has diminished in like proportion, until many owners do not now consider it worth while to feed them through the winter. A few days ago an Eastern Washington stockman arrived here (Tacoma) with two carloads of horses which he hoped to market on Puget Sound. He found the market glutted, both here and in Seatle, and finally sold his horses to get money to pay the freight bill. They brought 3 dol. to 15 dol. each, the receipts just about covering the expense of bringing them across the mountains. Stockmen say there are about 100,000 horses in Eastern Washington ranges, and they are destroying feed that would support three times that number of cattle and sheep. The latter animals are being housed and fed during the stormy weather, while the horses are left on the ranges to starve, unless they can paw through the snow to the surface. Cattlemen desire that the larger portion of the horses perish during the winter, that the bunch-grass ranges may be preserved for sheep and beef cattle.

They say that in that event the horses left will be worth as much as the unnumbered thousands now roaming at large."

Another newspaper, writing on the same subject, stated that there was in the summer of last year a herd of about 125,000 horses roaming about the prairies of Montana, North Dakota, Washington, and North Idaho. No buyers could be found for these horses, which included coach horses and Clydesdales, and descendants of very high-priced stallions.

With a view of getting rid of, and at the same time making use of, them, a plant was erected at Portland, Oregon, for the purpose of slaughtering them and canning the meat for export to France. The plant was operated for less than a year and failed.

"The question as to what shall be done with Oregon horses," says a newspaper, "is being effectively settled on Eastern Oregon ranges, where animals are perishing by hundreds and even thousands this winter. Roaming over the ranges of the mountain slopes are numberless bands of horses that are dying through starvation and exposure. The winter is unusually severe in the mountains, and even cattle which are taken care of have suffered some. The ranges are barren, and it passes the memory of the settler when the conditions were such as they now are. Whole herds of horses are seen along the stage road. The famished beasts have gnawed each other's tails and manes off; they are so weak that they can scarcely more than walk. Frequently half-a-dozen horses will be found frozen in a snow-bank, where they have stumbled and stuck fast, and are unable to get out."

There were several sales in this city in November and December of yearlings, mostly thoroughbred, and raised at well-known ranches in the States.

At the first, on November 12, 35 thoroughbred colts and fillies sold for 5,765 dol., an average of 165 dol. The highest price realised was 610 dol.

At the second sale, on November 17, 19 thoroughbred yearlings and horses in training, from another establishment, sold for 4,850 dol., an average of 255 dol.

At the third sale, November 24, 14 thoroughbreds from one establishment brought 1,660 dol., an average of 119 dol., the highest price being 425 dol. Nine from another stable realised 1,392 dol. 50 c., an average of about 155 dol. The top price was 400 dol.

The fourth sale took place on December 15 and 16, when 48 yearlings from one stable were sold for 11,310 dol., an average of 235 dol. per head, the highest prices being 750 dol., 600 dol., 500 dol., 410 dol., 400 dol., 375 dol. (two), and 350 dol. At this sale four others from another stable sold for 830 dol.; one of these realised 500 dol.

Another sale was held on December 17. I did not succeed in getting particulars of the prices realised, but they were stated to have been unsatisfactory, even as compared with the previous sales.

Good young horses can be bought in the country for a few pounds; good trained saddle and carriage horses here from 15*l.* to 30*l.* Fine carriage horses, thoroughly broken in, range from 50*l.* to 200*l.* a pair, but the latter price is very uncommon, and would be for something exceptionally fine and well matched.

LONDON:
Printed for Her Majesty's Stationery Office,
By HARRISON AND SONS,
Printers in Ordinary to Her Majesty.
75 5 | 97—H & S 2383)

FOREIGN OFFICE.
1897.
MISCELLANEOUS SERIES.

No. 425.

REPORTS ON SUBJECTS OF GENERAL AND COMMERCIAL INTEREST.

HAWAIIAN ISLANDS.

REPORT ON
COFFEE CULTURE IN THE HAWAIIAN ISLANDS.

Presented to both Houses of Parliament by Command of Her Majesty,
MAY, 1897.

LONDON:
PRINTED FOR HER MAJESTY'S STATIONERY OFFICE,
BY HARRISON AND SONS, ST. MARTIN'S LANE,
PRINTERS IN ORDINARY TO HER MAJESTY.

And to be purchased, either directly or through any Bookseller, from
EYRE & SPOTTISWOODE, EAST HARDING STREET, FLEET STREET, E.C., and
32, ABINGDON STREET, WESTMINSTER, S.W.; or
JOHN MENZIES & Co., 12, HANOVER STREET, EDINBURGH, and
90, WEST NILE STREET, GLASGOW; or
HODGES, FIGGIS, & Co., Limited, 104, GRAFTON STREET, DUBLIN.

1897.

[C. 8278—24.] *Price Three Halfpence.*

New Series of Reports.

The following Reports from Her Majesty's Representatives abroad on subjects of general and commercial interest, have been issued, and may be obtained from the sources indicated on the title-page :—

No.		Price.
384.	*Brazil.*—Report on the Causes which have brought about a Diminution in the Receipts at the Custom-house at Rio de Janeiro..	½d.
385.	*Mexico.*—Report on the Cultivation of Cacao, Vanilla, Indiarubber, Indigo, and Bananas in Mexico	2½d.
386.	*France.*—Report on the International Congress on Technical, Industrial, and Commercial Education, held at Bordeaux, in September, 1895	1d.
387.	*Portugal.*—Report on the East Coast Route to Mashonaland	1d.
388.	*Austria-Hungary.*—Report on the Iron Industry in Styria and the Betler Ironworks in Hungary	5d.
389.	*Belgium.*—Report on the Output of Coal, Iron, and Steel in Belgium in 1894–95	½d.
390.	*Japan.*—Report on the Railways of Japan (with Plans)	13½d.
391.	*Egypt.*—Report on the Commercial Relations of Great Britain and Egypt	2½d.
392.	*Germany.*—Report on the Wine Trade of Germany, 1893–95	1d.
393.	*Mexico.*—Report on the Cultivation of Coffee in Mexico..	1d.
394.	*Switzerland.*—Report on the Various Institutions and Agricultural Development of Switzerland	1½d.
395.	*Germany.*—Report on the Reduction of the Railway Tariff for Coal from the Silesian Mines	½d.
396.	*Austria-Hungary.*—Report on the Treatment of Habitual Drunkards in Austria and the "Curatel" Procedure	½d.
397.	*Brazil.*—Report on the Productions, Commerce, and Finances of the States of Amazonas and Pará	2½d.
398.	*Portugal.*—Report on the Port and Railway of Lorenzo Marques	2d.
399.	*Germany.*—Report on the Society for Insurance against Want of Employment in Winter and the General Labour Registry at Cologne..	1½d.
400.	*Switzerland.*—Report on the Extent of State Encouragement to Commercial Education	½d.
401.	*Mexico.*—Further Report on the Various Vegetable Products of Mexico..	2d.
402.	*Germany.*—Report for the Year 1894–95 on the German Colonies in Africa and the South Pacific	6d.
403.	*United States.*—Report on the United States Cattle-Raising Industry in 1896, and the Export of Cattle and Beef to Great Britain	1½d.
404.	*United States.*—Report on the Distress Caused to British Emigrants to California by Fraudulent Land Syndicates and Emigration Agencies..	1½d.
405.	*Chile.*—Report on the Maintenance of British Trade at Iquique and Northern Chile	½d.
406.	*Netherlands.*—Report on the Balata Industry of Dutch Guiana	1d.
407.	*Persia.*—Report on the Cultivation of Olives in the Districts of Ghilan..	½d.
408.	*Portugal.*—Report on the Fruits and Fruit Trade of Madeira	1½d.
409.	*Russia.*—Report on the Nijni-Novgorod Exhibition, 1896	1½d.
410.	*Belgium.*—Report on the Herstal Arms Factory	½d.
411.	*Roumania.*—Report on the Petroleum Industry in Roumania	2d.
412.	*Belgium.*—Report on the Metallurgical Industries of the Province of Liége during 1895	1d.
413.	*Germany.*—Report on the Finances of the German African Colonies for 1897–98	1d.
414.	*Germany.*—Report on Molasses and Peat Fodder..	1d.
415.	*China.*—Report on the Revenue and Expenditure of the Chinese Empire	3d.
416.	*Russia.*—Report on the Drink Question in Russia	½d.
417.	*Italy.*—Report on the Economic and Financial Situation in Italy	4d.
418.	*Germany.*—Report on the Operation of the Insurance Laws for 1895	1d.
419.	*Netherlands.*—Report on the German Competition with British manufactures in the Netherlands..	½d.
420.	*Germany.*—Report on the Wine Trade of Germany, 1895–96	1d.
421.	*Mexico.*—Report on the Tampico Branch of the Mexican Central Railway	1d.
422.	*Netherlands.*—Report on the Gold Industry of Dutch Guiana	½d.
423.	*United States.*—Report on the Prospects of Farmers in the State of California	1d.
424.	*Italy.*—Report on the Straw Hat Industry of Tuscany	1d.

No. 425.

HAWAIIAN ISLANDS.

HONOLULU.

Consul-General Hawes to the Marquess of Salisbury.

(Received at Foreign Office, May 11, 1897.)

My Lord,

I HAVE the honour to forward a Report which I have drawn up on the Possibilities of Coffee Culture in these Islands, to which I have added an appendix on the method of cultivation, taken from a pamphlet recently published under the auspices of this Government.

In submitting this Report to your Lordship, I have the honour to state that very valuable information has been afforded to me by Mr. Charles D. Miller, a coffee planter of great experience both in Ceylon and in these Islands.

I am also indebted to Mr. A. Cockburn for assistance, and I take this opportunity of acknowledging the courteous treatment shown to me by the planters whilst I was visiting the various coffee districts of Hawaii.

I have, &c.
(Signed)   A. G. S. HAWES.

Report on the Coffee Culture of the Hawaiian Islands.

TABLE of Contents.

	PAGE
Introductory remarks	2
Necessary conditions	2
Areas available for coffee	3
Soil	3
Fertilising	3
Lay and aspect	3
Rainfall	4
Wind	4
Temperature	5
Labour	5
Wages	5
Facilities of transport	6
District of Kona recommended	6
Concluding remarks	7
Appendix by the Commissioner of Agriculture	8

(2387)

Introductory Remarks.

Coffee its future as an article of export.

Coffee culture is attracting much attention in these islands at present, and promises to develop an important produce for export. Though yet in its infancy and in a somewhat experimental stage, coffee planting has nevertheless made great strides in the past 5 years, and there is every reason to believe that ultimately the industry will be placed on a sound and profitable footing. Before that end has been attained, however, it is not improbable that several failures and disappointments will take place from various causes.

This is nothing more than might be expected from a new industry, in many cases under the supervision of men who were entirely unfamiliar with the plant or its proper mode of culture and with all their experience to gain.

The situation at the present time is very similar to that of Ceylon in the early days, when plantations were started in all sorts of unsuitable places without any regard to soil or elevation; the result being that many estates were abandoned and large sums of money were lost before coffee planting in that island could be called a success or a profitable investment.

That the Hawaiian Islands are eminently adapted to the successful cultivation of the plant there can be no doubt, for the appearance of the numerous patches of wild coffee trees throughout the islands, and particularly in the district of Kona, in Hawaii, clearly demonstrate this fact; but whether they will produce trees yielding crops year after year, which will prove remunerative to the planter, with the high price of labour as compared with other countries, is quite another matter, and is one on which, thus far, no authentic data are obtainable.

Necessary conditions.

Before embarking on the coffee industry, whether in Hawaii or elsewhere, certain conditions must exist, four of which are imperative, otherwise failure will inevitably follow. The four absolutely necessary conditions are:—First, a suitable and available labour supply; second, a moderate rainfall well distributed throughout the year, though at the same time divided into distinct wet and dry seasons, with ample sunshine; third, an absence from severe or continuous winds; fourth, a temperature characterised by neither extremes of heat nor cold, with an average of 60° to 80° Fahr. in the shade.

Amongst the conditions which are also important in the proper development of the plant, may be mentioned a good friable soil, which should not be ferruginous, or consist to any great extent of clay in its composition, and free from slab rock as a sub-stratum. A favourable "lay" of land, neither too steep nor entirely level, in order to ensure good drainage. A suitable "aspect," that is, situated in such a direction as will permit the sun's rays to thoroughly penetrate every portion of the estate during the greater part of the day, and not obscured half the time by neighbouring high mountains or tall belts of forest. Lastly, good and readily accessible transport facilities.

Throughout this group of islands there are vast areas of land at elevations of from 500 to 2,400 feet well suited for coffee. In the Island of Hawaii it is estimated that there are over 200,000 acres of land on which the coffee plant will grow to more or less advantage; at the present time probably less than one-tenth of this land is under cultivation. *Areas available for coffee.*

The soil of the Hawaiian Islands being of volcanic origin is extremely rich and fertile, but there is a great variety of soils throughout the districts, or rather soils in the various stages of decomposition in the formation. *Soil.*

In the Islands of Maui, Kuai, and Oahu, and in the districts of Kau, Hamakua, and Hilo, in the Island of Hawaii, the soil is a deep friable loam with subsoil drainage; in the districts of Puna and Kona, in Hawaii, it is more or less rocky; in some places the land is actually covered with stones, not a vestige of soil to be seen, and certainly most uninviting to the eyes of a planter; yet native coffee is to be found growing, flourishing, and producing heavy crops under such peculiar conditions. The line, however, should be drawn sharply at all such formations as the latter, especially when situated at lower altitudes, for although coffee trees planted in such localities appear to thrive equally as well as those of formations with an abundance of soil, and even to bear a good crop, after the fifth or sixth year they invariably show signs of exhaustion, turn yellow, and drop their foliage. This may be attributed to the fact that the soil in such localities is confined in pockets, so to speak, exceedingly rich and forcing in its character, which acts as a stimulant to the young plant for a time. When the tree has assumed larger proportions and expands its roots in search of plant food amongst the rocks, exposed to the heat of the sun through the crevices, deriving temporary nourishment from what scanty soil may be left, it soon becomes impoverished, and eventually dies for lack of further sustenance.

To maintain the virgin generosity of the soil nitrogen must be introduced. In plantations where the trees are seven feet by eight feet apart, and the plough or cultivator can be used, this is best done by sowing lupin beans around each coffee plant about two feet from its stem. The lupin will flower in about four months; it should then, in wet or showery weather, be ploughed under. In addition to the nourishment thus given, the ploughing itself stimulates the growth of the coffee plant, if carefully performed, having the same effect on the roots that pruning has on the branches; when ploughing cannot be done the hoe may be used. *Fertilising.*

A careful application of water-slaked lime should also be made to eliminate the potash and phosphoric acid from the soil.

The lands facing the west and gradually ascending from the shore by gentle slopes to the mountains insure good drainage, at the same time preventing wash, which obviates the necessity for draining or terracing, both costly works, but necessary where lands are steep. *Lay and aspect.*

During bright sunshine the general lay of the land is situated

(2387)

in such a direction that it receives the full benefit of the sun's rays from 8 a.m. till sunset.

Rainfall.

Under this heading it may be broadly stated that although coffee apparently seems to thrive and grow luxuriantly in districts here in which the rainfall is excessive, from 150 to 200 inches per annum, unless this is compensated for by an unusual amount of heat such as is to be found in countries lying nearer the equator, it will very likely be found that such districts will never produce large crops, from the fact that a great percentage of the blossoms will not set, and many of the berries will fail to reach maturity for the want of sufficient sunshine.

In the temperate climate of Hawaii, at elevations ranging say from 1,000 to 2,000 feet above sea level, a rainfall of 100 inches per annum is sufficient for all purposes.

From careful records kept during the last five years in the district of Kona on the leeward side of the island, the average yearly rainfall for the elevation of 900 and 1,800 feet may be placed at 75 and 90 inches respectively; from another source it was found that at a low level on the same side of the island the rainfall from July 1, 1894, to June 30, 1895, was only 51 to 21 inches, whilst at Olaa, on the windward side of the island, at an elevation of 2,000 feet, where coffee is being tried, the rainfall during the same period was 176 to 82 inches.

Dry months from October to March.

The seasons are fairly regular; the dry months, though not absolutely without occasional showers, may be looked for from October to March, after which the showers are more frequent, increasing until the wet season proper sets in, about the latter part of May or beginning of June, when the rains are more or less continuous until the month of September. Such conditions are most favourable to the coffee planter, as they ensure the proper setting of the blossom, facilitate pruning operations, and replenish his water supply at a time when it is in most demand for the pulping and washing of coffee.

One curious feature in connection with the rainy season in the district of Kona, in Hawaii, is the fact that a wet morning is a very rare occurrence, the rains generally setting in towards the afternoon, between the hours of 1 and 2. This is quite an important feature, as it enables the drying of parchment to proceed in the morning during the wet season.

Wind.

Wind in any form is admitted by all authorities to be the worst enemy to which the coffee tree can be subjected; on exposed situations the trees become stunted, and in some cases have the appearance of having been attacked by frost; when such conditions exist they may partially be remedied by leaving portions of the forest standing to give shelter from the wind, or, on lands devoid of forest, suitable trees for the purpose should be planted. After all, such precautions are only half measures, for in the most carefully laid-out situations it will be found that the wind has a way of circling over the tree tops from all points of the compass, and whirling around in the coffee fields with great fury, causing irreparable damage. It is far wiser to be satisfied with inferior soil in a sheltered location, than to plant coffee in the richest of forest soil, when, after the land has been cleared, it becomes exposed to the full force of the prevailing winds, for the former can be remedied by the application of manure, while the latter can only be partially alleviated.

The records of maximum and minimum temperatures covering the same period as that for rainfall returns, and kept in the same district, show a fairly uniform average, rarely exceeding 85° Fahr. in the shade, only for a few nights in the months of December and January falling as low as 50° at an elevation of 1,800 feet. The average temperature of Kona may therefore be considered as favourable to the successful growth of the coffee plant. *Temperature.*

In the matter of sunshine there is ample, even at the higher altitudes in the rainy seasons; although clouds may set in towards the afternoon, the mornings are generally fine.

With regard to labour for coffee culture there appears to be a diversity of opinion. The best authorities here are opposed to the contract system, which has been in practice in the past on the various sugar plantations, and is still greatly in vogue. Doubtless the contract plan was the only one at first open to the planter that secured him means for controlling and retaining his labourers on his plantation, but it was open to many serious abuses, and has caused from time to time endless trouble and disputes. *Labour.*

At present the feeling is strongly in favour of the monthly free labourer, and the Japanese as a class, when properly handled, are found to be steady, good workmen. The Chinese also make excellent field hands, but they are very scarce for such purposes. The native Hawaiian cannot be recommended, being by some considered totally unfit as a labourer on a coffee plantation, as he is most unreliable, and from his nature seems to abhor any employment which demands constant and regular attendance. Other, again, have great hopes that he will become useful in the coffee fields, and that the more intelligent may ultimately, like the Japanese, be even trusted with pruning and planting. In some cases, such as for employment on cattle ranches, and in contract work in building stone walls for instance, he is an excellent workman.

The question of labour for picking when the various plantations have come to full maturity, is one that will require serious attention, not only to ensure careful picking, but also to be certain of having a cheap supply of labour sufficient for the demand.

Some form of co-operation or planting on shares might be successfully carried out to the mutual advantage of the labourer and the employer; but before any such schemes could be put in operation, it will be necessary to have absolute data as to the actual return from coffee trees under cultivation, which up to the present time are not forthcoming.

At present, the wages paid to contract labourers are 12 dol. *Wages.*

50 c. per month, and to free labourers at the rate of 15 dol. per month. The latter, when compared with the ruling rates in other countries, is unquestionably high, but there are other points which must be taken into consideration when making comparisons between the price of labour in Hawaii and in other parts of the world.

In Ceylon, as an example, costly works were required in connection with coffee planting, which will be unnecessary in Hawaii, such as roading, draining, manuring, &c., the latter, on some estates, requiring the maintenance of elaborate cattle-sheds stocked with hundreds of stall-fed cattle for the purpose of supplying manure alone. Then the yield per acre will play an important factor in the final result of total expenditure and returns.

In regard to the works above mentioned, roading is much less costly in this country from the nature and easy lay of the lands, as also from the fact of fewer roads being necessary; draining, so far as Kona is concerned, will never be required, except under very extraordinary circumstances; manuring will doubtless be found beneficial when the proper time arrives, but on virgin land with rich volcanic soil, it may to any great extent be dispensed with for many years. As to the productiveness of the coffee tree in Hawaii, experience shows that the yield will be greatly in excess of that of Ceylon, where a return of 6 cwt., or 672 lbs. per acre, as an average, was considered a very good crop. In Kona, for cultivated coffee, properly managed, a yield of 1 lb. per tree, or 1,000 lbs. per acre in the fourth year may reasonably be expected. In subsequent years, with thorough pruning and a little judicious fertilizing, it is possible that from $1\frac{1}{2}$ to 2 lbs. per tree may be harvested.

Facilities of transport. In the past the want of good roads throughout Hawaii, especially in the district of Kona, has been a great drawback to the development of the coffee industry. At the present time, however, the Government is vigorously pushing ahead with this work, and it will only be a matter of a very short time, when the greater part of the island will be traversed with fine carriage roads laid out in easy gradients.

There are numerous harbours along the western coast with excellent landing, which is effected throughout the year, with the exception of the month of December, in smooth water. These landings are in many cases connected with the coffee fields by good cart roads. Regular communication is maintained with Honolulu by tolerably fast and commodious steamers.

District of Kona recommended. The district of Kona, being situated to windward or on the leeward side of Hawaii, is blessed with perpetual calms. At intervals of many years' duration a storm known as a "Kona" wind sweeps over the face of the country, and is more or less boisterous while it lasts, but the damage sustained from such is felt more at the beach and lower elevations, the higher lands not being affected.

With its wonderfully rich soil, absence from wind, medium

rainfall, with regular wet and dry seasons, there is no reason why a coffee plantation laid out on a carefully selected site, and under the supervision of a practical and experienced planter, should not turn out a profitable investment.

In regard to the product, Kona has already established for itself a name in the foreign markets, for the bean is undoubtedly of a superior quality, although until very lately no proper pains have been taken in its preparation. One very favourable feature is the large percentage of pea berry produced, in many cases ranging from 12 to 15 per cent. High authorities state that the cup quality of coffee grown on soil interspersed with the lava rock in its state of disintegration combines the excellent properties of Mocha coffee.

The soil of the Kona uplands answers this requirement, and undoubtedly to a great extent accounts for the fine quality of the bean, but it should not be overlooked that climate, more particularly as regards rainfall and temperature, is an important factor in the good results produced in this district. When picking operations are properly conducted and the careful preparation of the bean is more appreciated, the coffee of Kona will hold its own in the foreign market and eventually create a demand.

In conclusion, I venture to say a few words in regard to Hawaii as a prospective field for young Englishmen with capital at their command desirous of trying their fortunes abroad. *Concluding remarks.*

At the present time it may be a risk for young men of means to come to these islands, for the success of coffee planting is, as it were, hanging in the balance, not that it will not eventually prove a profitable investment, but that in the next two years results will probably fall so far short of expectation, especially in unsuited districts, that the consequence will be a general reaction from the eager rush displayed everywhere just now in setting out acres broadcast, and Hawaii as a coffee country will experience a temporary check. The question of elevation and the most suitable district will by that time be decided, and after a while coffee planting will again be prosecuted more vigorously than ever but under very different circumstances. That will be the proper time for men desirous of investing to come in, for lands will be cheap, there will be all the errors and experience of the past seven years to profit by, and an industry will be built up that will become permanent, not only with profit to the investor, but to the country at large.

The following appendix is extracted from a pamphlet recently published under the auspices of the Hawaiian Government for the purpose of giving information to those intending to invest in the industries of these islands. It has been compiled by the Commissioner of Agriculture, whose authority on the subject may be relied on as being correct. It gives in a clear, practical, and concise manner information that is being continually applied for by British colonists and others, and on that account may prove a valuable and useful addition to this report.

In the estimates which form the concluding portion of the extract, the price fixed per lb. for the sale of coffee is probably too high, and it would be safer perhaps to calculate on a basis of 15 c. per lb.

It may be added that fairly good coffee land can often be leased from private individuals at from 2 to 4 dol. per acre per annum for terms varying from 20 to 25 years. This method of obtaining land does not necessitate the holder becoming a denizen of the country.

Cultivation of the Coffee Tree in the Hawaiian Islands.

In order to obtain the best results the coffee tree requires to be properly planted, and during its lifetime needs frequent and intelligent cultivation.

The various operations incidental to the opening and carrying on of a coffee plantation will be taken up in their proper order and described in as plain language as possible, and as briefly as is consistent with a clear explanation of the subject.

The very first thing the planter should do after obtaining possession of his land is to plant a nursery, so that he may have, as soon as possible, an abundant supply of strong healthy plants. Many planters have planted their fields with wild stumps, these are young coffee plants that are found under wild growths of coffee trees. The young trees are cut off about 6 inches above the ground, they are then taken up and the lateral roots trimmed close to the tap root. The thready end of the tap root is cut off and the stump is ready to plant. In some cases the young plants are taken up from under the wild trees, and planted just as they are. This method can be dismissed at once as the worst possible method of planting the coffee tree. The very best plants are strong healthy nursery plants, that is, plants that have been grown from the best seed in a properly prepared nursery. The next best plants to use are nursery stumps. These are nursery trees that have grown too large to safely transplant. By cutting them down and trimming the roots they can be safely transplanted to the field, where they will grow into good healthy trees. Stumps soon after planting send up several shoots, these, with the exception of the strongest one, are taken off. This latter shoot is to grow and make the coffee trees.

Making the nursery. The size of the nursery will depend on how large the plantation is to be. For a 75-acre plantation, 1 acre of ground will more than supply all the plants required. It is always desirable to have a greater number of plants than is needed to just plant the acreage the plantation is to be, for after the fields are planted some of the plants may get injured from dry weather and require replacing with plants from the nursery. Any surplus left, after the trees in the fields are well established, can be sold to some later planter, who will find it to his advantage to purchase good nursery plants for his first planting and thereby save one year of time. It is advisable for all planters to buy plants for their first planting, but for the second year's planting they should have a nursery of their own from which they can select the strongest and most forward plants.

The land for the nursery should be selected as close as possible to where the plantation is to be. It should be on a slight slope to ensure drainage, and free from rocks and stones. The soil should be ploughed or dug over to the depth of 1 foot and made as fine as possible. Beds should be thrown up 6 inches high and 3 feet wide. The surface of the beds should be made quite smooth and level; the seed should be planted 6 inches apart and $\frac{3}{4}$ inch deep. A good way to ensure even and regular planting is to make a frame 3 feet wide each way. Pegs, $\frac{3}{4}$ inch long and $\frac{5}{8}$ inch diameter, should be fastened to one side of the frame, placing them exactly 6 inches apart. The frame, thus prepared, is placed, pegs down, on the bed A slight pressure will sink the pegs into the soil. The frame is now lifted and you have the holes for the seeds all of one depth and equi-distant from each other. The seeds can now be dropped one in each hole. The seeds should be placed flat side down, and covered by brushing over the surface of the bed. If the weather is at all dry it is a good plan to mulch the surface of the bed with dry grass or fern leaves. The soil should be kept moist, and if there is not sufficient rain the beds must be kept watered. In six or seven weeks the seeds should sprout and show above ground. The mulching should now be moved from over the plants and arranged in the rows. It has been the practice of some planters to plant the seed much closer than 6 inches apart, but it will be found that plants 6 inches apart can be more easily and safely transplanted than from close planted beds. It will be advisable in taking up plants from the beds, to take only every other one, this will give the remaining plants more room to develop and grow more stocky than would be the case if all the plants were taken up from each bed as they were required.

The next thing for the planter to do is to get his land cleared. *Clearing the land.* This can be done more satisfactorily and cheaply by contract than can be done by days' work. Gangs of Chinese and Japanese undertake the clearing of land, and will make a contract to clear the land as per specification. In the Olaa district land costs from 20 to 50 dol. per acre to clear, according to the kind of clearing done. The land is forest land, and some planters have the trees cut down and everything burned, making the land quite clear, while others just have the vines and ferns cut and the trees felled, leaving everything on the land to rot. This method, while costing much less than burning up everything, makes it work expensive to lay out and plant the land. The planter must decide for himself which of the two methods he will pursue. However, it can be said in the case of those who only cut and fell, in a few years everything, trees, vines and ferns rot down and greatly increase the fertility of the soil. The next thing is to lay out the land for the digging of the holes where it is intended to set out the young trees. There is a wide diversity of opinion as to the proper distance apart to plant coffee trees. From 10 feet by 12, down to 5 feet by 6, and all intermediate distances are practised. It is a significant fact that planters who formerly planted their trees at the wider distances are now setting out trees as close as 6 feet by 5. Trees planted 6 by 6 will probably yield better results per acre than trees planted at a wider or closer distance. Having fixed upon the distance apart the trees are to be planted, the planter proceeds to mark with pegs the places where he wants the holes dug. This is usually done with a line or rope that has pieces of red rag fastened in the strands at the distance apart at which it is intended to dig the holes. The line is drawn tightly across one end of the clearing and a peg driven into the soil at every place that is marked on the line. The men, holding the two ends of the line, are each provided with a stick the exact length that the rows are to be apart. After one row is pegged, the line is advanced one length of the stick and the operation repeated until the whole clearing is pegged. After the first line is pegged a line should be laid at exactly right angles to the first line, so that the rows will be straight both ways. The pegging being completed, the holes should be dug not less than 18 inches wide and 18 inches deep. The top soil should be carefully placed on one side of the hole and the subsoil on the other, the holes should remain open as long as possible and should only be filled in a week or so before planting the trees. The bottoms of the holes should be explored with a light crowbar, and if any rocks or stones are found they should be removed. In filling the holes the top soil (that has been placed on one side) should be placed in the bottom of the hole and other top soil should be taken from between the rows until the hole is full, the subsoil can now be disposed of by scattering it between the rows. The holes after filling should have the marking pegs replaced in the centre of the filling, this will serve as a guide for planting the trees.

Planting

There is no operation in all the work of establishing a coffee plantation that requires such careful supervision as that of planting out the young trees. If the work is carelessly done and the slender tap root is doubled up, or if it is shortened too much, the tree will never thrive. It may grow fairly well for a time, perhaps until the time for the first crop, then the foliage will turn yellow and the tree show every sign of decay. The effort to produce a crop is too much for the tree, and the sooner it is pulled up and replaced by a properly planted tree the better.

The closest supervision is necessary in order that the planter may be certain that the tap roots are placed perfectly straight in the ground, and the lateral roots placed in a natural position. In order to effect this with the least amount of trouble, transplanters have been used. A transplanter that has been used with success is made as follows: two pieces of sheet-iron (galvanised) are bent into two half circles, which, when placed together, form a cylinder 3 inches in diameter and 7 inches long. A piece of hoop iron is bent to a ring, that will fit over the cylinder, and riveted. The mode of using is as follows: the two halves of the cylinder are pressed into the ground, one on each side of the young coffee tree. They are pressed down until the upper ends are level with the surface of the soil. The hoop iron ring is then pressed over the heads of the two halves of the cylinder, binding them firmly together. The cylinder can now be lifted from the ground, bringing with it the young tree with all its roots in the position in which they grew. In this condition the young trees are carried to the field and, the holes being opened, the cylinder, holding the tree, is placed in the ground and the soil packed firmly around it. The hoop iron ring is then removed and the two halves of the cylinder withdrawn. The soil is again compacted around the roots and the tree is planted. There is another transplanter, invented in America, that would probably be better and more economical in working than the one described above. This transplanter consists of a cylinder of thin sheet steel. These are made in America of various sizes to suit different kinds of trees. For a coffee tree a good size would be 7 inches long and five inches in diameter. The cylinder has an opening, five-eighths of an inch wide, running the whole length of the cylinder, and exactly opposite this opening a handle is riveted. This handle is of half inch round iron, 18 inches long, with a cross bar on top. The rod is bent outward in the form of a bow, so that in working the branches of the young tree may not be injured. The mode of working the transplanter is as follows: the cylinder is placed on the ground with the tree in the centre of the cylinder. This can be done by allowing the stem of the young tree to pass through the slot in the cylinder. Then, by means of the cross handle, the cylinder is turned and pressed into the soil until the upper end is level with the surface of the ground. Then, by lifting on the stem of the tree and the handle of the transplanter at the same time, the tree is taken from the ground with its roots undisturbed. Should the end of the tap root project below the end of the cylinder, the thready end should be pinched off with the thumb nail. By placing the lower end of the cylinder on the bottom of a box and inserting a wedge-shaped piece of wood in the slot, the cylinder is sprung open and can be withdrawn, leaving the young tree, with a cylinder of earth around its roots, standing on the bottom of the box. This operation can be repeated until the box is full of the young trees, when it is carried to the field and the trees placed one at each hole. By using a duplicate transplanter a cylinder of earth is removed from the spot where the tree is to be placed, and the tree with its cylinder of earth is placed in the round hole, which it exactly fits, the earth being slightly compacted around the roots. The tree is thus planted with the absolute certainty that the roots are in their natural position.

Weeding.

The old adage, "a stitch in time saves nine," will bear its fullest application in the care and weeding of a coffee estate. From the time the land is first cleared, weeding should commence, and it is astonishing how little it will cost if care is taken that no weed be allowed to run to seed. The bulk of Hawaiian coffee lands is situated in the forests where the land is covered with a dense undergrowth of ferns and vines and there are no pernicious weeds to bother. But soon after clearing, the seeds of weeds are dropped by the birds and are carried in on the feet and clothing of the labourers and visitors. We have no weeds that run to seed in less than 30 days, and if the fields are gone over, once a month, and any weed that can be found pulled up and buried, the work of weeding will be reduced to a minimum. But if the weeds, that are bound to spring up, are allowed to run to seed, the work of weeding will be greatly increased and will require the labour of a large gang to keep the fields in order. If taken in time, the labour of one man will keep from 15 to 25 acres quite clean. During the first year after setting out the fields, all that is required is to keep the fields clear of weeds and the replacing, with a healthy tree from the nursery, any tree that from any cause looks sickly and does not come along well.

It will be found that in parts of the field some trees, while looking healthy, do not grow as fast as the average of the trees; this is often due to the soil not being of as good a quality. Knolls and side hills are not generally so rich as the hollows and valleys, and the coffee trees planted in the poorest parts of the field should be fertilized until they are as vigorous as the trees in the best parts.

Handling.

During the second year the young trees will have begun to make a good growth, and will require handling. In order to make clear the description of the operations of handling and pruning, it may be well to describe here the component parts of the coffee tree.

The underground portion consists of a tap root and numerous lateral or side roots. The parts above ground consist of:—

(1.) The stem or trunk.

(2.) The primaries or first branches; these grow from the trunk in pairs at intervals of from two to four inches; the two primaries, making a pair, grow one opposite to the other, the pair above radiating out at a different angle, and so on to the top of the tree.

(3.) The secondaries; these are the branches that grow in pairs from the primaries.

(4.) The tertiaries; these are the third branches that grow in pairs from the secondaries in the same manner as the secondaries grow on the primaries.

(5.) The leaves that grow on all the branches.

During the whole of the second year the field should be gone over at least every two months, and all the secondaries that make their appearance should be rubbed off; this can be done by a touch of the fingers if the secondaries are not more than two or three inches long. If allowed to grow longer, the knife must be used, or there is danger of tearing out the eye or bud, which we depend upon for growing new secondaries at the proper time. During the second year the secondaries will make their appearance only on the lower sets of primaries, the upper sets as they grow being too young to grow secondaries. At the beginning of the third year all the secondaries should be allowed to grow till they attain a length of six inches; then the trees should be carefully gone over, and all but five of the secondaries on each primary cut off with a sharp pruning knife. No pairs should be left, and only the strongest and most vigorous should be retained. They should be disposed on alternate sides of the primary, and none left in a space of six inches from the stem of the tree. The object of this is to allow the light to penetrate to the centre of the tree, for the coffee tree bears fruit in greater profusion on branches that are exposed to the light, than on those that are shaded.

During this third year the tree will blossom and bear the first or maiden crop. In some cases the tree will blossom in the second year, but it is a wise plan to rub all the blossoms off, as it only weakens the tree to bear a crop at such an early age. It is of the utmost importance that in the first crop, as well as in all future crops, the tree should not be overburdened with a superabundance of growing wood. If left to itself, the lower primaries will grow a mass of secondaries, so much so that no blossom will set on them, and the first crop will come only on the upper primaries, and be only a third or fourth of the crop that would be produced if the trees were properly handled. By handling, as described above, the tree is relieved of all superfluous wood, and only such secondaries are left as are needed to bear the fourth year's crop, and the maiden crop will grow on the primaries. It may be well to mention here that coffee only grows on wood of the second year's growth, and does not grow on the same wood twice.

During the third year, the secondaries will come on the upper primaries. When they are well set they should be reduced in number, and in no case should more than five be left to grow. In some cases four or even three will be sufficient. Whatever the number that may be left, it must be understood that these are the branches that will bear the crop for the fourth year. During the third year new secondaries will grow from the places where the former secondaries grew. Sometimes two will grow from one bud, they should all be removed, the trees being gone over two months, but at the last handling before blossoming time, which varies greatly with the elevation above sea-level, enough of these new secondaries should be left to make wood for the fifth year's crop. From this time on the coffee planter should be able to point out the wood on which the present and next year's crop will be borne, and it is this wood, and this only, that should be allowed to grow. All other shoots, suckers, &c., should be rubbed off each time the tree is handled, provision being made each year for the wood for the crop two years hence.

During the third year the trees will require topping. As to the height at which a coffee tree should be topped, there is a great diversity of opinion. Some planters advocate topping as low as four and a half feet, others at six or seven feet; as a matter of fact the coffee tree will bear fruit if topped as low as one and a half feet, or if not topped at all. The only valid reason for topping as low as four and a half feet is for the convenience of picking the crop. Five and a half or six feet is a good height to top a coffee tree on the rich lands of the Hawaiian Islands. In fact, the planters should not be guided by the number of feet, but by the number of primaries he desires the tree to carry. 18 to 20 pairs is a reasonable number for a coffee tree to carry in this country, and it will be found that by not counting those primaries that grow on the stem within 15 inches from the ground, 18 or 20 pairs of primaries will come on the stem within six feet from the ground. Before topping the tree, it should be allowed to grow somewhat higher than it is intended to top, so that the wood may be hardened and not decay as it sometimes does if topped when the wood is too young. Topping is performed by cutting off the top of the tree at a point an inch above a pair of primaries. Both primaries should also be cut off an inch from the stem. This will leave the top in the form of a cross; a knot will form at this point from which the tree will constantly send up shoots striving to make a new top. These should be torn off every time the tree is handled.

We have now arrived at the time when the tree is bearing the first or maiden crop. Through careful handling the tree has been divested of all superfluous shoots, branches, &c., and the crop is maturing on the primaries. If the trees are situated on good rich soil, and the trees are well grown, there should be at least 13 pairs of primaries bearing crop. At an average of 50 berries to each primary, there will be a yield of over $1\frac{1}{4}$ lbs. of clean coffee to the tree. This yield for the first crop has been much exceeded in this country, but it can only be assured by careful cultivation and handling, as described in this paper.

We will now take a look at the condition of our three years' old trees. They have all been topped, and are carrying from 36 to 40 primaries, of which all except the upper six or eight are carrying four or five secondaries that are well advanced, and which will bear the crop for the fourth year. There will also be four or five secondaries that are one or two months old, which are intended to bear the fifth year's crop. All other growth should be removed as before up to the time of blossoming for the fourth year's crop. This may be estimated as follows:—There should be at least 24 primaries that have on each of them, say, four bearing secondaries. At 30 berries to each secondary, the yield would be close to 3 lbs. of clean coffee to each tree. This again has been exceeded in this country for four year old trees, but it must be borne in mind that, in order to obtain these results, proper cultivation, handling, and pruning must be done. Without proper care such results would be impossible; the coffee tree cannot grow an abundance of wood and coffee at the same time. As soon as the crop of the fourth year is gathered, the work of pruning must commence without delay. This consists of cutting off with a sharp knife the secondaries that have borne the crop. They must not be cut so close as to injure the eye or bud. About three-sixteenths of an inch from the stem of the primary will be quite safe, and the secondaries for the fifth year's crop will soon make their appearance. Care should be taken to leave the stem of the tree clear of shoots and foliage for a space of six inches from the stem; the tree will want all the light it can get. The coffee tree can be said to be in full bearing when all the primaries are carrying bearing secondaries. During the life of the coffee tree the planter must keep a close watch on his trees, and restrict their wood-bearing propensities to the wood that is to bear his crops; nothing else should be allowed to grow. If the work is commenced rightly, and carried on systematically, it will not be difficult, and no crops will be lost. But on the other hand, if the work is neglected, the trees will become matted, and all the lower primaries die off. These, if once lost, will not grow again. The tree under these conditions will only bear a tithe of the crop it would bear with proper attention, and furthermore it is a most difficult matter to bring a neglected tree into proper shape, and it can only be done at a loss of one and perhaps two years' time. There are many minor details connected with the care of the coffee tree which would occupy too much space to describe here, and which the coffee planter can easily learn as he carries on the work of coffee planting.

HAWAIIAN ISLANDS.

ESTIMATE of Cost of Establishing and Maintaining a Coffee Plantation of 75 Acres, from the First to the Seventh Year.

	Amount.	Total.
	Dollars.	Dollars.
FIRST YEAR.		
Purchase of 100 acres of Government land at 10 dol. per acre	1,000	
Manager's house and water tank	600	
Labourers' quarters and water tank	350	
Clearing 50 acres of land, at 20 dol. per acre	1,000	
Fencing	300	
Purchase of 65,000 one-year-old coffee plants, at 5 dol. per thousand	325	
Lining, holing, and planting 50 acres	600	
Manager's salary	1,200	
Labour of six Japanese, one year, at 15 dol. per month	1,080	
Purchase of tools and starting nursery	500	
		6,955
SECOND YEAR.		
Manager's salary	1,200	
Labour, six Japanese	1,080	
Extra labour, lining, holing, and planting 25 acres	300	
Sundries	500	
		3,080
		10,035
THIRD YEAR.		
Manager's salary	1,200	
Labour, nine Japanese	1,620	
Pulping shed and drying house	500	
Pulper, with engine and boiler	500	
Extra help for picking, pulping, and drying 20,000 lbs. of coffee from 50 acres (at 4 c. per lb.)	800	
Hulling, polishing, and grading 20,000 lbs. of coffee, at 1 c.	200	
Sundries: bags, freights, &c.	250	
		5,070
Credit.		15,105
By sale of 20,000 lbs. of coffee, at 18 c.	..	3,600
FOURTH YEAR.		11,505
Manager's salary	1,200	
Labour, nine Japanese	1,620	
Extra labour, picking, pulping, and drying 50,000 lbs. of coffee from 50 acres (at 4 c. per lb.)	2,000	
10,000 lbs. from 25 acres (three-year-old trees)	400	
Hulling, polishing, and grading 60,000 lbs., at 1 c.	600	
Sundries: bags, freights, &c.	400	
		6,220
Credit.		17,725
By sale of 60,000 lbs. of coffee, at 18 c.	..	10,800
		6,925

HONOLULU.

ESTIMATE of Cost of Establishing and Maintaining a Coffee Plantation of 75 Acres, from the First to the Seventh Year—continued.

	Amount.	Total.
	Dollars.	Dollars.
Brought forward	..	6,925
FIFTH YEAR.		
Manager's salary	1,200	
Labour, nine Japanese	1,620	
Picking, pulping, and drying 60,000 lbs. coffee from 50 acres, and 25,000 lbs. from 25 acres, at 4 c.	3,400	
Hulling, polishing, and grading 85,000 lbs. (at 1 c. per lb.)	850	
Sundries: bags, freight, &c.	500	
		7,570
Credit.		14,495
By sale of 85,000 lbs. coffee, at 18 c.	..	15,300
Balance on hand	..	805
SIXTH YEAR.		
Manager's salary	1,200	
Labour, nine Japanese	1,620	
Picking, pulping, and drying 75,000 lbs. of coffee from 50 acres, and 25,000 lbs. from 25 acres, 100,000 lbs. at 4 c.	4,000	
Hulling, polishing, and grading 100,000 lbs., at 1 c.	1,000	
Sundries: bags, freight, &c.	1,000	
		8,820
Credit.		
By sale of 100,000 lbs. of coffee, at 18 c.	..	18,000
Balance on hand	..	9,985
SEVENTH YEAR.		
Manager's salary	1,200	
Labour, 12 Japanese	2,160	
Picking, pulping, and drying 125,000 lbs. of coffee, at 4 c.	5,000	
Hulling, polishing, and grading 125,000 lbs., at 1 c.	1,250	
Sundries: bags, freight, &c.	1,200	
		10,810
Credit.		
By sale of 125,000 lbs. of coffee, at 18 c.	..	22,500
Balance to credit of plantation at end of seventh year	..	21,675

The yields, as given in the above estimate, are far below what may be attained by thorough cultivation and fertilising. The coffee tree responds readily to good treatment, but will disappoint its owner if neglected.

LONDON
Printed for Her Majesty's Stationery Office,
By HARRISON AND SONS,
Printers in Ordinary to Her Majesty.
(75 5 | 97—H & S 2387)

No. 480 Miscellaneous Series.

DIPLOMATIC AND CONSULAR REPORTS.

UNITED STATES.

NOTES ON THE

AGRICULTURE OF THE STATE OF MAINE, U.S.A.

Presented to both Houses of Parliament by Command of Her Majesty,
SEPTEMBER, 1898.

LONDON:
PRINTED FOR HER MAJESTY'S STATIONERY OFFICE,
BY HARRISON AND SONS, ST. MARTIN'S LANE,
PRINTERS IN ORDINARY TO HER MAJESTY.

And to be purchased, either directly or through any Bookseller, from
EYRE & SPOTTISWOODE, EAST HARDING STREET, FLEET STREET, E.C., and
32, ABINGDON STREET, WESTMINSTER, S.W.; or
JOHN MENZIES & Co., 12, HANOVER STREET, EDINBURGH, and
90, WEST NILE STREET, GLASGOW; or
HODGES, FIGGIS, & Co., Limited, 104, GRAFTON STREET, DUBLIN.

1898.

[C. 9045—8.] *Price One Penny.*

CONTENTS.

	PAGE
Preliminary remarks	3
Farms	4
Hay making and potatoes	5
Good roads	5
Ice harvesting	5
Dairy cream	6
Cheese factories	6
Cattle inspection	7
Regulations for the sale of milk in Portland	7
Wool growers	7
Agricultural societies	8
State College	9
Experiment Station	9

No. 480. **Miscellaneous Series.**

Notes on the Agriculture of the State of Maine, U.S.A.,
By Mr. Vice-Consul Keating.

(Received at Foreign Office, September 10, 1898.)

It is not intended in this report to cover all matters of agricultural interest throughout the State of Maine, but to draw attention, as briefly as possible, to a few subjects of interest.

From the inquiries I have made of many competent authorities I gather that the condition of the Maine farmer has been steadily improving in every way during the last 40 years, and the neat, progressive, and thriving farms now existing throughout the State, stand as proofs of this statement. It seems to be the general opinion that a great deal of this progress and prosperity is due to the Maine Liquor Law. I am told that a little over 40 years ago a farmhouse shingled or clap-boarded was rarely to be seen, and that the average farmer of that period who was able to give his front door a coat of red paint was considered fairly well off. The farm labourer at that date before commencing his daily work required an allowance of Medford or Jamaica rum, and his refreshment during the day is stated to have consisted of alcoholic liquor instead of oatmeal water.

It is universally admitted that the Maine Liquor Law is certainly not enforced in the cities, but I think it may safely be said that throughout the rural districts the law has had a wonderfully good effect, and whenever the mass of the inhabitants desire its enforcement, the law is on the statutes to support them. While, however, it is allowed that temperance may be credited with much of the improvement that has taken place during the last 40 years, it must also be remembered that the covering of the State with railroads, the opening up of new markets, and the work performed by the Experiment Station and agricultural societies has also had much to do with the present condition of the Maine farmer.

As connected with agricultural products, I may allude in passing to the efforts which are being made by the State Board of Trade, assisted by the Boston Board of Trade, to obtain reciprocity with Canada. Resolutions favouring the project have been adopted and forwarded to Washington.

The financial depression which has prevailed in the country for some years past first manifested itself in the West, and there

Preliminary remarks.

naturally the first indications of returning prosperity made their appearance. Of course, public opinion is divided as to the chief causes that are responsible for the agreeable change, which made its appearance during the latter part of the year 1897, some claiming that the favourable crop outlook, with the prospect of good prices for farm products, had much to do with it, and that it would have come about without the aid of the Dingley Tariff. Others contend that the Dingley Tariff undoubtedly proved an important factor in the evolution of prosperity, and that the passage of the Bill has brought certainty to some of the most important business conditions for the next three years to come. The agriculturist and the manufacturer can unquestionably count upon a virtual monopoly of the home market, which is perhaps his best market. That is to say, he is sure of a demand for his products and for his manufactures, and unless the country is unfortunately embroiled with some foreign Power, there seems to be no reason why the wave of prosperity should not continue. I think that the monied interests of the country are agreed, that what the country needs more than anything else is an opportunity to work without distractions.

Farms. Value, &c. A depreciation in the market value of farms is generally claimed, but it does not appear that the productive capacity of the farms has diminished. The low price of the farm products which has prevailed in recent years has not only produced a depression in farm values, but also unfavourably affected every branch of trade and industry in the State.

The total area of Maine is 19,000,000 acres; occupied by farms (cultivated lands), 3,500,000 acres; occupied by farms (enclosed woodlands), 9,000,000 acres; occupied by lakes (1 square mile of lake to each 13·3 of area) and streams (5,151 of which are to be found on the map of Maine), 3,000,000 acres.

In other words Maine has an area of 19,132,800 acres (or in round numbers 30,000 square miles), 7,000,000 of said acres are enclosed as farms, one-half of which, or 3,500,000 acres, are under cultivation. Of these farms there are 65,000, representing a cash value of 38,511,523*l.*, a capital which annually produces farm products valued at 4,200,000*l*. Over 62,000 of the 65,000 farms are cultivated by their owners. The farms in extent range from 1 to 150 acres, the average being 50 acres.

The varied soils, natural vegetable products, abundant and pure water, and the most favourable climatic conditions of Maine, favour the highest agricultural development. The State presents a great variety of soils adapted to all kinds of crops, clay, clayey loam, sandy loam, mountain interval, river bottom, salt marsh and fresh meadows. As a consequence there are many agricultural specialities grown in Maine.

Near the cities and especially about the city of Portland, where exceptional market facilities exist, many market gardens thrive whose owners consider 10 acres sufficient, keeping their limited farms under high cultivation, and forcing the early fruits and table delicacies for the Boston markets.

MAINE.

Hay making and potatoes.

A directly opposite system of extensive culture is met with on the great hay farms of the Kennebec Valley and the potato fields of Aroostook.

The rainy season affected the crops of hay very much, and up to August 1 a large part of the hay crop was still uncut in the fields. The crop at this period was very good, and considered to be one of the largest ever known. The haymakers come from Canada in large numbers every year, and after the season is closed return to Canada.

The potato crop suffered greatly from rust, and in Aroostook county the farmers lost half their potato crop as a consequence. The shipment from this county usually commences about August 20, but last year no potatoes were shipped out of the county until the latter part of September. The total number of bushels of potatoes forwarded from Aroostook county for 1896 was 2,371,847 bushels; in 1895, 1,586,267 bushels; and in 1894, 1,496,928 bushels. There were forwarded to points out of New England 337 car loads, New York city taking 190. It took about 4,743 cars to move the 1896 crop. Added to this an immense quantity is consumed in the manufacture of starch in the numerous starch mills of the State, from which was shipped in 1896, 13,520,112 lbs.

Good roads.

Perhaps one of the most difficult tasks on the hands of the Maine State Board of Agriculture is the problem how they can secure good roads for the farmer, and enable him to carry his products safely and readily to the various markets. The system of highway labour now on the statute books permits people to work out their taxes in repairing the roads. There is no doubt, if one may judge by the freely expressed criticism of all classes, and by the condition of the roads, that this system is far from being a success. The matter of good roads is unquestionably important for the Maine farmer, and particularly so when the cost entailed in getting his products to the nearest railroad station is considered. At the present rates it costs him about a $\frac{1}{2}d.$ a ton per mile on the railroads, and more than a $\frac{1}{2}d.$ a cwt. per mile by team.

Ice harvesting.

As a contrast to the farming industry, and while the ground which borders the Kennebec River is buried under drifting snows, thousands of men are employed in harvesting ice. As near as can be ascertained the beginning of the ice business was about the year 1826, and the ice was shipped in a small brig named the "Orion," of Gardner, Maine, the cargo being taken to Baltimore and sold for 140*l*. The business has constantly grown until it is now estimated that the annual value of exports amounts to 400,000*l*. It is not unusual for upwards of 2,300 men to be employed harvesting ice, and they are assisted by over 1,200 horses. The wages of the men employed average 6*s*. to 8*s*. per diem. The companies pay 5*s*. a day for each horse hired. The men are lodged in the companies' boarding houses, where they are required to board, and for which they are charged from 14*s*. to 16*s*. per week.

(274)

MAINE.

Dairy cream. The dairy interests of Maine are in a prosperous condition. Prices for cream have ruled higher during the past year than for nearly any other commodity sold from the farms, and the output is slightly increased. Several new creameries have started into successful operation during the past year, and one factory established for condensing milk. There are 4,784 farms furnishing milk or cream to the associated creameries, and it takes 25,515 cows to contribute their product to the 33 creameries, the farms receiving in payment 184,270*l*. The Babcock method of testing cream is becoming better understood, and gives great satisfaction, the novice being enabled at a glance to ascertain whether or not the separation of the fat is complete. A modification of the Babcock method of milk testing is being discussed at the Experiment Station, and a number of comparative tests made. A State law requires all the glassware to be tested, and all the users of the test to be certified by the superintendent of the dairy schools. This requirement has undoubtedly resulted in increased confidence by the average creamery patron.

Cheese factories. There are several cheese factories in the State, and from reports of three of them, it is ascertained that the milk furnished comes from 800 cows.

The farms receive 3,280*l*. for the product. Altogether there are 5,500 farmers patronising the associated creameries and cheese factories, and they have about 30,000 cows furnishing milk or cream. So far as can be ascertained, the farmers receive in payment about 206,000*l*. From the State assessor's return it would seem that there are, in the State, 143,000 cows. This would leave about 113,000 whose milk is worked up in some other way than by the associated creameries. From the agricultural statistics I learn that a little more than one-fifth of the cows of the State contribute their products to the associated creameries, and that the product from a little less than four-fifths is worked up in the homes of the farmers. The farmers annually receive about 50,000*l*. from the sale of sweet cream direct, and the annual income of the farm averages about 7*l*. 4*s*. for each cow. Some, however, receive as high as 12*l*. From reports made at the Dairy Meeting, this average is considered far from satisfactory, and the reason given by experts is that the Maine farmers' goods are lacking in quality. They admit that the colour, grade and texture is satisfactory, but that the flavour is not. I notice, however, that at the Dairy Meeting, Professor G. M. Gowell takes exception to the opinion of the experts, and states in his report the trouble is, "That the butter we get from the creameries in Maine is uneven, and sometimes a creamery sends butter for a number of months, and it runs well, the quality is even and we are satisfied. But all at once it drops down. This is true with all the creameries in Maine, a great deal more than in Vermont. The difficulty is that we have so few cows, and they are distributed over our State so sparsely, that instead of collecting cream every day, it is done every other day, or every third or fourth day, and sometimes only once a week. When that stock gets into the hands of the creamer's man, it is in poor condition to make high-priced butter, because the ripening of that cream is going on in the farmers' cream tanks under varying conditions. The 100 or 200 patrons furnish 100 or 200 different qualities of cream to work from, and however expert the butter maker may be, he cannot make the finest quality of butter out of it."

From the Cattle Commissioner's report for the year 1896, the following information is derived. The Commissioners made over 300 inspections, which were secured all over the State, containing cattle to the number of 328,543, and 110,719 horses, either boarding or owned upon 65,400 farms in Maine. In 1895, 43 head of horses were condemned and destroyed, at an appraisal of 385*l*. 8*s*., and 79 head of cattle were also condemned and destroyed at an appraisal of 492*l*., the total amount of appraisals for that year being 877*l*. In 1896, 43 head of horses were condemned and destroyed at an appraisal of 394*l*., 200 head of cattle were also condemned and destroyed at an appraisal of 1,413*l*.

Inspection of cattle.

In May, 1897, the Portland Board of Health adopted certain rules and regulations for the sale of milk within the city of Portland, and which were afterwards approved by the Justices of the Supreme Judicial Court. In brief, the regulations enacted that all milk offered for sale in this city shall come only from tuberculin tested cows, or from cows certified to after a physical examination, and provided also that these cows shall be examined in the month of June each year by a veterinary approved by the Board of Health, and the regulations provided for a fine of not more than 10*l*. for each violation of the rules. Immediately following the issue of these regulations the farmers protested, and a lively discussion arose between the farmers, veterinary surgeons, and the Board of Health. It looked as if Portland would have a milk famine. The Board of Health thereupon postponed the enforcement of their regulations. At a meeting of the Maine Veterinary Medical Association, the secretary touched upon the matter of tuberculosis and moved the adoption of the following resolutions:—

Regulations for the sale of milk in Portland.

" Resolved that we believe in the efficiency of the tuberculin test, as a sure method of diagnosing tuberculosis.

" That the physical examination as a means of diagnosing tuberculosis is false and misleading, and entirely untrustworthy, and is so conceded by all noted scientists.

" That we absolutely refuse to make any physical examinations as a means of diagnosing tuberculosis, and believe it to be a means of spreading the disease by giving the public a source of security which does not exist."

As a matter of fact, the rules and regulations adopted by the Portland Board of Health are now dormant, and no special effort is at present being made to secure healthy milk. I am, however, informed that the matter will very shortly be taken up again, and it is anticipated that the health regulations of May, 1897, will be enforced.

It is generally claimed by the Maine wool growers that a large quantity of shoddy is used in the manufacture of so-called woollen

Wool growers.

goods, and that this fact tends to lower the price of wool in the markets, and as a consequence lessens the income of the sheep raisers. The attention of the Maine legislators has been drawn to this state of affairs, and it is hoped that by a concerted action in all the States of the Union interested, some law will be passed to remedy the complaint. As a matter of fact, a Bill has been already reported to the State legislature, and referred to the committee on manufactures. The object of this Bill is to adopt a law which will compel retailers to tag each piece of cloth, so that the purchaser may know exactly what percentage of shoddy is in the cloth.

Agricultural societies.

It is generally conceded that the agricultural societies have accomplished a great deal for the benefit of the farmer and stock raiser, more than 15,000*l*. being annually distributed at the numerous agricultural fairs.

The following is an abstract of the amounts awarded, and also a table showing how, and from what sources the finances are derived for the payment of these awards:—

Analysis of Awards.

	Amount.
	£
Amount of premiums paid—	
Trotting-bred stallions	105
,, brood mares	62
Draught-stock stallions	31
,, brood mares	32
Family horses	29
Gentlemen's drivers	66
Matched carriage horses	29
Colts	182
To horses for draught	144
Thoroughbred bulls and bull calves	153
,, cows, heifers, and heifer calves	217
Grade bulls and bull calves	58
,, cows, heifers and heifer calves	24
Herds	103
Working oxen and steers	175
Matched oxen and steers	91
Trained steers	31
Beef cattle	56
Town teams	159
Oxen and steers for draught	240
Sheep	160
Swine	73
Poultry	162
Grain and root crops	309
Fruit and flowers	394
Bread and dairy products	123
Honey, sugar, and syrup	35
Agricultural implements	14
Household manufactures and needlework	384
For objects not named above	407
Total amount of premiums and gratuities paid	4,048

MAINE.

FINANCES.

	Amount.	Total.
	£	£
Amount received from the State	1,683	
Receipts for membership	689	
,, from loans	1,246	
,, ,, entry fees for trotting purses	2,531	
,, ,, all other sources	30,093	
		36,242
Amount expended in improvements	2,234	
,, ,, trotting purses	6,173	
Expenses during the fair	5,353	
		13,760
Value of property belonging to Society		29,671
Amount of liabilities		9,842

Out of the amount received from the United States appropiation for the year ending June 30, 1897, the following details show that the sum of 3,000l. was expended by the Experiment Station at Orono:—

	Amount.
	£
Salaries	1,803
Labour	267
Publications	104
Postage and stationery	62
Freight and express	41
Heat, light, and water	111
Chemical supplies	51
Seeds, plants, and sundry supplies	118
Fertilisers	13
Feeding stuffs	90
Library	42
Tools, implements, and machinery	7
Furniture and fixtures	46
Scientific apparatus	60
Live-stock	7
Travelling expenses	50
Contingent expenses	128
Total	3,000

Maine State College. Apparently the course of agriculture at the State College is not successful in educating the sons of farmers, or at least in fitting them for the vocation of a farmer. I glean from the statistics of the Maine Board of Agriculture for 1896, that out of 468 living graduates of the State College, only 37 are engaged in agricultural pursuits (a little less than 8 per cent.). This seems remarkable, when it is considered how much such a college is capable of doing for the education of the up-to-date farmer.

Experiment Station. The work of the Maine Experiment Station during the past year has been on practically the same lines as heretofore, which includes investigations on the food and nutrition of man and domestic animals, box and field experiments with fertilisers, horticultural experiments, botanical and entymological investigations, and work in veterinary science and practice. Feeding experiments were made with cows, and digestion experiments with sheep, box experiments on the availability of phosphoric acid were continued. In horticulture, studies in plant breeding have constituted the most important branch of inquiry. Greenhouse experiments have been made with tomatoes, fruits, vegetables and ornamental plants. Co-operative experiments in horticulture have also been conducted, especially in Aroostook county. The question of the food and nutrition of man has been examined, including special studies on bread made from different kinds of flour, and investigations with the bomb calorimeter. Under State laws the station has the inspection of fertilisers, cream, glassware, food stuffs and seeds (the laws relating to feeding stuffs and seeds came into effect last autumn). In order to get a better understanding of the disease of tuberculosis, an affected herd of 10 animals was kept isolated from all other animals (a small barn 38 by 40 feet being erected for their accommodation). The points stated were: (1) the progress of the disease in affected animals; (2) the conditions under which tuberculin will cause a rise in temperature in tuberculous cows; (3) the effect of good hygienic conditions on the progress and outcome of the disease. The report of progress was made by a Dr. Russell, veterinary at the State College, and I would be pleased to forward this report to anyone requesting me to do so. Also a sketch of a model barn which was erected at this college. There are other interesting matters dealt with at the Experiment Station, which I am sure would be of interest to farmers, but as space will not permit me to give the details in this report, I will merely refer to them, and should the full particulars be of interest to anyone, I shall, of course, have much pleasure in forwarding the same. Under this heading I would mention: analysis of feeders and feeding stuffs, growth of sunflowers and English horse beans for a silage crop, tests of separators, feeding experiments with milch cows, gluten meal compared with cottonseed meal as food for milch cows, effects of tuberculin on tuberculous cows, orchard notes, notes on winter gardening, notes on plants and insects, &c.

(75 9 | 98—H & S 274)

No. 481 Miscellaneous Series.

DIPLOMATIC AND CONSULAR REPORTS.

UNITED STATES.

REPORT ON THE

CATTLE INDUSTRY OF THE UNITED STATES, JUNE, 1896, TO JUNE, 1898.

REFERENCE TO PREVIOUS REPORT, Miscellaneous Series No. 403.

Presented to both Houses of Parliament by Command of Her Majesty,
SEPTEMBER, 1898.

LONDON:
PRINTED FOR HER MAJESTY'S STATIONERY OFFICE,
BY HARRISON AND SONS, ST. MARTIN'S LANE,
PRINTERS IN ORDINARY TO HER MAJESTY.

And to be purchased, either directly or through any Bookseller, from
EYRE & SPOTTISWOODE, EAST HARDING STREET, FLEET STREET, E.C., and
32, ABINGDON STREET, WESTMINSTER, S.W.; or
JOHN MENZIES & Co., 12, HANOVER STREET, EDINBURGH, and
90, WEST NILE STREET, GLASGOW; or
HODGES, FIGGIS, & Co., Limited, 104, GRAFTON STREET, DUBLIN.

1898.

[C. 9045—9.] *Price Twopence.*

CONTENTS.

	PAGE
Present numbers of cattle	3
Recent decrease	3
Average price in 1897	5
Course of rise in price	6
Course of receipts at markets	7
Improvement in demand	8
Scarcity of young stock	9
Increase of imports	10
Increased movement of cattle from South-west	10
Exhaustion of South-western ranges	11
Texas fever	12
Conditions in North-western range country	14
Effects of increased price	15
Conditions at close of period reviewed	16
Shortage in Texas	16
Tendency of United States markets	18
Increase of exports to Great Britain	19
Business partly at a loss	21
Conclusions as to prospects of British farmers	22

No. 481.   **Miscellaneous Series.**

Reference to previous Report, Miscellaneous Series No. 403.

Report on the Cattle Industry of the United States, June, 1896, to June, 1898, by Mr. Hugh O'Beirne, Second Secretary at Her Majesty's Embassy at Washington.

(Received at Foreign Office, September 10, 1898.)

Present numbers of cattle.

The total number of cattle in the United States at the opening of the year 1898 is returned by the United States Department of Agriculture at:—

	Head.
Milch cows	15,840,886
Oxen and other cattle	29,264,197

Recent decrease.

These figures represent a decrease of 100,841 milch cows and 1,244,211 "oxen and other cattle" in the course of the previous 12 months. How the country's present stock of cattle compares with that which it has held at different periods during the past 10 years may be seen from the following table, showing the numbers of milch cows, oxen and other cattle on January 1, 1885, and the same date of the years 1892 to 1898 inclusive. It will be noticed that since the commencement of 1892, in which year the number of cattle of the United States was the highest ever attained in the history of the industry, there has been a decrease in "oxen and other cattle" of some 8,387,000 head, or about 22 per cent. The decrease has been continuous since the year 1894, averaging about 1,800,000 head annually; but during the last two years under consideration, the rate of diminution has been much less rapid than in the previous two-year period, the loss amounting roughly to 4,523,000 head between January, 1894, and January, 1896, as against 2,821,000 head from January, 1896, to January, 1898.

(275)

UNITED STATES.

NUMBER of Cattle in the United States on January 1 of Years Named.

Year.	In Round Numbers.	
	Milch Cows.	Oxen and other Cattle.
1885..	13,904,000	35,513,000
1892..	16,416,000	37,651,000
1893..	16,424,000	35,954,000
1894..	15,487,000	36,608,000
1895..	16,504,000	34,364,000
1896.	16,137,000	32,085,000
1897..	15,942,000	30,508,000
1898..	15,841,000	29,264,000

NOTE (1).—The number of "oxen and other cattle" shown for 1885 is the result of a special investigation made at the time by Mr. Nimmo, Chief of the United States Bureau of Statistics; it is considerably larger than that given in the ordinary departmental returns.

(2). The total returned as "milch cows" consists chiefly of dairy cows, not belonging to beef breeds. Thus, the largest cattle-producing States, such as Texas, are returned as having, relatively, the smallest number of milch cows. The heading also includes a large (but not ascertainable) proportion of cows used for breeding beef cattle, the rest being shown under "oxen and other cattle."

The annual returns of cattle numbers issued by the Agricultural Department are not, it must be noted, intended to be taken as absolutely correct. The figures are arrived at by actual count only in census years; in other years estimates are obtained from the various districts of the increase or decrease since the preceding year; and at this distance of time from the last census it is evident that the numbers returned may vary considerably from the actual figures. Nevertheless, there is no reason to doubt that the annual estimates of decrease or increase are sufficiently accurate to give a correct idea of the tendency of the numbers from year to year.

Decrease in Mid Western States. Turning to the detailed returns printed in the appendix, giving the figures relating to the several States, it will be found that the great corn-growing and cattle-feeding region of the Middle West, comprising the seven States (named in the order of their cattle numbers) Iowa, Kansas, Missouri, Illinois, Nebraska, Indiana and Ohio, has suffered a decrease during the two years, January, 1896, to January, 1898, of only about 100,000 head out of a total of some 9,500,000 head—their loss thus falling much below the proportion shown for the whole country. These seven States play so important a part in the cattle industry of the United States as a whole that it will be convenient to give figures relating to them in a separate form. The following table shows the number of cattle in each State on January 1, 1892, 1896, and 1898 respectively:—

UNITED STATES.

NUMBER of Cattle in the Seven great Corn Growing and Cattle Feeding States of the Middle West, on January 1 of Years Named.

	Number.		
	1892.	1896.	1898.
Iowa	2,707,049	2,336,973	2,207,739
Kansas	1,978,520	1,766,245	2,035,774
Missouri	1,928,269	1,686,990	1,537,523
Illinois	1,747,731	1,430,976	1,304,192
Nebraska	1,614,676	1,062,469	1,213,764
Indiana	1,085,236	798,414	675,698
Ohio	871,662	686,285	606,127
Total	11,933,143	9,768,352	9,580,817

It will be seen from this table that while six of the States named all show some decrease, the number of cattle in Kansas has actually increased since 1896 by over 200,000 head, thus reducing the loss for the Mid Western region as a whole to the comparatively small figure shown in the table. Like the Mid Western districts the ranching region of the North-west (including Montana, Wyoming, and the Dakotas) has suffered a very small loss since 1896 out of a total of over 2,000,000 head. On the other hand, the South-western region (Texas, Arizona, and New Mexico) shows the very heavy loss of nearly 900,000 head out of a total of under 7,000,000; this being the region, as we shall find, from which the North-west and Central West have recently obtained the largest part of the young cattle which they needed to replenish their stock. The States of the Pacific slope have suffered rather largely in proportion to their cattle numbers, and all the more important cattle-producing Eastern States show some decrease.

Decrease in South-western region.

From a careful review of daily quotations on the Chicago Market, the "Chicago Live-Stock Report" finds the average price* for corn-fed "native" steers (or steers the product of the Mid Western States, as distinguished from Texas cattle and North-western Range cattle) during the year 1897 to have been 18s. 9d. per 100 lbs. (live weight), or about 1s. 10½d. per 100 lbs. higher than the average price in 1896. The improvement has been sustained during the first six months of the current year, prices having remained with no very great variations, at or about the level of the average of the year 1897. A comparison between the prices of the 18 months, January, 1897, to June, 1898, and those of the previous three years, is furnished by the following table. The prices quoted are for "natives," the values of Texans and "Westerns"† ranging somewhat lower:—

Average price in 1897.

---

* The exchange is taken at 1*l*. = 4 dol. 80 c. throughout this report.
† The term "Westerns" is generally used of North-western range cattle.

UNITED STATES.

AVERAGE Price of Fed "Native" Steers at Chicago in the Years 1894–97, per 100 lbs. (live weight).

Year.	Average Price.
	s. d.
1894	17 8½
1895	18 9
1896	16 10½
1897	18 9
1898 (January to June) .. (about)	18 9

It will be observed that the prices in 1897 and the first half of 1898 have been on an average equal to the prices of 1895, in which year the values of fed cattle were temporarily raised by a scarcity of corn which resulted in a considerable falling-off of the numbers sent to market. There is some improvement on both the other years named, and the increase in value as compared with 1896 amounts, as has been said, to 1s. 10½d. per 100 lbs., or about 11 per cent.

Course of rise in price. The improvement commenced in the late autumn of 1896, during the first nine months of which year values had been exceedingly depressed; and continued, as is shown by the subjoined table, throughout the winter and spring of 1897. The highest point was touched in September, 1897, after which there was a temporary falling-off. During the spring of the present year, however, prices again recovered the level of the earlier part of 1897, that is to say, averaging approximately 18s. 9d. per 100 lbs. for all classes of native steers; and they have remained at that level down to the close of the period under review, export and shipping steers being quoted on June 20 last at 17s. 4½d. to 21s. 3d.

UNITED STATES.

AVERAGE Price (per 100 lbs., live weight) of Fed "Native" Steers for each Month of the Year 1897.

Year.	Steers Weighing 1,350 to 1,500 lbs.	Steers Weighing 1,200 to 1,350 lbs.	Steers Weighing 1,050 to 1,200 lbs.
	s. d.	s. d.	s. d.
January	19 2	17 8½	16 8
February	18 6½	17 3½	16 5½
March	19 4½	17 11	17 3½
April	19 7	18 4	17 11
May	19 9½	18 9	18 1½
June	19 7	18 6½	17 11
July	19 4½	18 4	17 8½
August	20 5	19 9½	18 9
September	20 10	19 9½	18 11½
October	20 5	19 4½	18 11½
November	19 4½	18 6½	17 8½
December	18 6½	17 6	16 10½

Cf.—Export and shipping steers (1,350 to 1,600 lbs.) on June 30, 1898, quoted at 17s. 4½d. to 21s. 3d.

It is somewhat surprising to find that this considerable improvement in the prices of fed cattle cannot be regarded as resulting (immediately, at any rate) from the decrease, above recorded, in the total numbers of the American herd; inasmuch as the supply of finished cattle arriving at the markets during the last 18 months of the period under review shows no signs of any falling-off as compared with the previous year. It is true that the diminishing volume of the herd has, as we shall find presently, been attended by a marked scarcity of young stock; and the high prices obtaining for that class of cattle have necessarily had the effect of strengthening the market in fed cattle. But whilst the supplies of cattle of the latter class continue to arrive in undiminished numbers, it is evident that the diminished bulk of the herd can scarcely be held mainly responsible for the fact that they have risen in price. *Causes of rise in price.*

The following are the returns of the total receipts of cattle at the four principal Western markets, Chicago, Kansas City, Omaha, and East St. Louis, for the years 1893-97:— *Course of receipts at Western markets.*

Year.	Receipts.
1893	6,403,154
1894	6,148,725
1895	5,528,629
1896	5,693,888
1897	5,971,077
1898 (first 4 months)	1,732,950
1897 (")	1,682,684

It will be seen that the total receipts of cattle at these four markets have been on the increase since 1895, in which year, as has been already noted, they fell off largely, owing to a scarcity of corn. The total receipts during the year 1897 were larger by nearly 300,000 head than during the previous year, 1896, and the receipts for the first four months of the present year are about 50,000 head larger than those for the same period of 1897. As these figures include the arrivals of feeding stock and other classes, the net receipts of finished cattle can only be roughly computed. But it is estimated that there has been an increase in the arrivals of feeding stock in 1897 as compared with 1896, which is about sufficient to account for the growth of the total receipts; and we shall not be far wrong in concluding that the average receipts of finished cattle during the 18 months, January, 1897, to June, 1898, have been about equal to, or slightly larger than, the average for 1896.

It is true that the receipts of fed cattle at these four points do not supply us with any conclusive test of the course of the aggregate receipts, during the years named, at all the United States markets; because there is a constant tendency for the great Western centres of the cattle trade to absorb a larger share of the business formerly done at other points. There are, however, indications enough, apart from these figures, that the market as a whole has been liberally supplied with fed cattle during the 18 months ending with last June. In the latter part of the summer of 1897 (about which time prices touched the highest point of the year) there were some complaints of a deficiency of fed steers of good quality. But with this exception the market reports for the period generally indicate decidedly heavy arrivals; and it seems clear, though no exact figures can be obtained on the point, that the average of the receipts was at least equal to that of 1896.

Improvement in demand. The supply of fed cattle not having fallen off, the recent rise in the price must certainly be considered as the result, chiefly, of a marked improvement which has taken place in the demand. One of the chief causes contributing to bring about the extremely low prices of 1896 was unquestionably a great falling-off in the American consumption of beef, the result of a depression of trade extending over a prolonged period, which had materially lessened the purchasing powers of the mass of consumers.* With the recent improvement in the general conditions of business there has, of course, been a recovery in the country's powers of consumption, especially noticeable in the case of the great industrial centres of the East, New York, Boston, Philadelphia, &c.; and Chicago and the other Western markets have felt the effect of the stronger demand on the part of buyers for Eastern shipment. The demand at Chicago for export to Great Britain is also reported to have shown an appreciable improvement

* *Vide* F.O. Report on "United States Cattle-Raising Industry in 1896," Miscellaneous Series No. 403.

throughout the year 1897, as compared with 1896; although it appears from the British agricultural returns that there was only a very moderate advance in prices on the British markets.

This improvement in the demand accounts to a great extent for the rise in the American price of fed cattle. But it must also be noticed that the decreasing volume of the herd has been attended, during the two years under review, by a marked scarcity of young stock cattle which, though not so considerable as to curtail the receipts of fed steers at the markets, caused a strong advance in values of feeding stock and thus contributed to raise prices of all other classes. *Scarcity of young stock.*

A great deal of light was thrown on this subject by an inquiry undertaken last summer at all the best informed sources, by the "Live-Stock Report" of Chicago, into the question of how the numbers of cattle then on feed in the Mid-Western States compared with the numbers the previous year. The results of this investigation may be thus summarised:—

Illinois, Iowa, and Missouri show a decrease of the number of cattle on feed as compared with the same period of the previous year, which was generally estimated at from 10 to 15 per cent. Feeding stocks had been scarce and high, and while all available supplies had been called into requisition, there still remained abundant pasture and feed "crying out for cattle." In Iowa, a prominent stockman gave it as his experience that young stock had not been so scarce for the past 25 years; while every available animal, from yearlings upward, had been put on feed, there were yet, in this gentleman's opinion, not nearly enough cattle to meet the requirements of farmers. The case was similar in Indiana, where large tracts of grazing land were reported to be wholly denuded of stock. All these States had drawn largely for their supply of young cattle on the great resources of the South-western States (notably Texas, Arizona, and New Mexico), and upon the herds of the North-western range States, and Iowa is mentioned as importing considerable numbers of Canadians. From two of the greatest corn-growing and cattle-raising States, indeed, Kansas and Nebraska, there were not the usual complaints of the scarcity of young cattle; but this was only because they succeeded in fully renewing their stock by importation from the South and West, having some advantage in that respect from their geographical position. Generally speaking, the upshot of the reports from the cattle districts of the Middle West was that the stock of "natives" had of late been so heavily drawn upon for the market as to produce a distinct scarcity of that class of cattle, and to render these districts dependent, in an unusually large degree, for the renewal of their stock on importations from Canada and Mexico, and on the resources of other parts of the United States where the stock of cattle had been less heavily exploited.

The scarcity of young stock thus led immediately to two noticeable results. It stimulated the importation of foreign cattle, and it produced a greatly increased movement of young cattle to the Middle West from other portions of the United States.

Increase of imports.

The imports of cattle into the United States have grown as the numbers of cattle in the country have diminished; increasing, as will be seen from the following figures, from 2,168 head in the year ending June 30, 1892, to 217,628 in the year ending June 30, 1896, and 328,977 in the year ending June 30, 1897. It is interesting to note that they now represent some three-fourths of the total number of live cattle exported.

TOTAL Imports of Cattle into the United States.

Year ending June 30—	Number.
1892	2,168
1893	3,293
1894	1,592
1895	149,781
1896	217,826
1897	328,977
1898—	
Canada 116,477	
Mexico 172,171	
Other countries.. .. 2,907	
	291,555

The imports are practically wholly from Mexico and Canada, which in the year ending June 30, 1898, supplied 172,171 and 116,477 head respectively. The Mexican cattle are stunted and poor in quality, and the numbers available for export from the northern provinces are said to be running low. The Canadians are imported chiefly into the more northerly of the Mid Western States, such as Ohio, Illinois, and Iowa. But recently they have been taken in considerable numbers by Kansas and Missouri, as also by the ranching States of the North-west. It is estimated that nearly 20,000 steers (an altogether unprecedented quantity) were imported last winter from Ontario into Illinois, Iowa, Nebraska, and Missouri. The ranchmen of the North-western States are said to find it more profitable to procure Canadian stock from the North-west Territory of Canada, even from points remote from the railway, than to buy young cattle in the United States. The duty on imported cattle under the Dingley Tariff is estimated to represent about 25 per cent. ad valorem on the average class of cattle imported.

Increased movement of cattle from the South-west.

It is, however, mainly from the South-western region (Texas, Arizona, and New Mexico) that the Mid Western States have replenished their stock of young cattle, and the stock-growing industry of this region has been very noticeably affected by the rapid growth of the demand made on its resources. Writing on this subject last winter, a correspondent of the "Live-stock Report" described the changing conditions of the business by saying that whereas a short time ago men went South to the Panhandle (the North-western region of Texas) to buy steers, buyers now go South from the Panhandle for the same purpose. That is

UNITED STATES.

to say, as the more northerly districts of the South-west have successively felt the effect of the demand for young stock, the line below which cattle are plentiful and cheap has been shifted constantly to the South. The Southern States, as the writer explains, have always been looked upon by Northern stockmen as able to furnish unlimited quantities of cheap cattle at short notice, and not long ago there were thousands of such cattle for sale in the South, for which there was practically no demand. But the position, he goes on to say, has become completely altered with the reduction of the herds both in the Northern and Southern districts, and the young cattle of South Texas, Arizona, and New Mexico are now eagerly sought after by purchasers from all sections of the central cattle districts, from the North-west and even from the Pacific slope.

In addition to a large number of young cattle which are sent directly from Texas to the corn-growing States of the Middle West, there is also a smaller but still very considerable number of young Texans annually sent to the North-western ranching States, whence they eventually find their way to the Middle West either as feeders or as finished cattle, so that of the annual supplies of cattle which the Mid Western region draws from the North-west a considerable portion originates from Texas. Thus during the nine months February 15 to November 15, 1897, there were sent from the portions of Texas not infected with Texas fever* 100,000 head of young cattle to Kansas, and 27,000 to Nebraska, while over 15,000 head went to each of the ranching States, Montana and Wyoming. The bulk of these cattle are forwarded by rail, but considerable numbers are driven to the feeding grounds along trails formed by the constant passage of the herds northward, the number thus driven to Montana (a distance of over 1,000 miles) and Kansas forming an important part of the totals sent to those States. Finally, in addition to her shipments of young cattle, Texas also provides a large complement of finished cattle for the central markets. These are fattened chiefly on cotton-seed, and a large proportion, owing to quarantine regulations against Texas fever, are shipped for immediate slaughter.

The deficiencies of the Mid Western cattle districts being thus made good in the last resort, mainly from the resources of the South-west, it was to be expected that any strain on the country's general cattle resources should make its effects felt specially in the numbers of the South-western herds, and it is not surprising to find that these should have suffered the very heavy losses shown in the returns. But there is an additional circumstance which has contributed largely to bring about the same result—the rapid exhaustion of the carrying capacity of the Texas range. It should be explained that Texas, Arizona, and New Mexico in the South-west, with Montana, Wyoming, and the Dakotas in the North-west, now form the two principal regions in the United States containing large areas of "range country." In the earliest days of ranching, prior to the advent of the railway, the ranges of Texas

Exhaustion of South-western range.

* See p. 12.

are described as thickly covered with grasses averaging from 1 to 3 feet in height, and often reaching the back of a well-grown steer, and they were then estimated to be easily capable of supporting some 300 head of cattle per acre. The cattlemen in those days had no legal title to the tracts of country which they controlled, which were generally the property of the State, and this condition of things continued down to the extension of the railway system to Central Texas in 1882, although by that time the range had been to a great extent parcelled out into railway lands and private properties, the owners, however, having for the most part not yet appeared to take up their claims. With the construction of the railway and the appearance of the owners upon the ground, cattlemen realised that the days of free grass were numbered, and it became their object to make the utmost possible profit out of the land while they still remained in possession.

There followed a period of speculation in cattle and reckless overstocking of the ranges; the grasses were eaten and trampled down, until, 10 years ago, the carrying capacity of the range had fallen, it is estimated, to one head of cattle per five acres. The area of range has since then, of course, considerably decreased with the progress of settlement, and the ranchmen now generally own, or pay a substantial rent for, a portion at least of their ranch, though they still rent a part at a nominal rate from the railroads; nevertheless, the process of overstocking has continued and it is now the exception to find a tract capable of supporting one head of cattle per five acres. The average is probably not over one per 10 acres. The general opinion among farmers seems to be that the wasting of the range has already gone so far as to be beyond remedy, but there are some good judges who hold that a great deal might yet be effected by resting portions of the range in rotation, and by encouraging the growth of the most nutritive grasses.

Improvement in South-western cattle. The increased use of Southern cattle to take the place of "natives" has been facilitated by recent improvements effected in the Southern herds by successful intermixture of high-class stock. Texas now owns several herds of beef cattle which compare favourably with any in the United States. The wild appearance which formerly characterised the Southern cattle has been considerably softened as the herds have been "graded up" and the practice of polling has been generally adopted with a view partly to that end; though it is also considered to make the cattle more profitable feeders, and has great practical advantages in the case of cattle forwarded to market by rail.

Texas fever. A circumstance, however, which has greatly impeded the Southern industry in the past, and must apparently continue to have this effect, is the prevalence throughout a large portion of the Southern States of the destructive disease known as Texas fever. The nature of this disease is still a matter of discussion; but it may be now regarded as settled that it is caused and propagated by the ticks which generally infest the hides of the Southern cattle. These parasites do not necessarily affect the health of the

UNITED STATES.

Southern herds which are inured to their presence, but on being transferred to Northern cattle they cause an immediate outbreak of the fever. The disease is recognised to be in the highest degree infectious; it is almost necessarily contracted by Northern cattle having access to places where fever-infected animals have recently passed or stood; and there is even a perfectly well authenticated case of its breaking out among herds grazing along the course of a railroad by which infected cattle were forwarded North—the supposition in this instance being that the fever ticks dropping from the railway trucks, laid their eggs in the pastures adjoining the line.

To guard against the infection of the Northern herds, the Federal Authorities have adopted the most rigorous measures of quarantine. A line is drawn, subject to modification by the Secretary of Agriculture from year to year, across the entire breadth of the United States from a point on the coast of Central California on the West to Chesapeake Bay on the East. The region South of this line is declared infected with Texas fever and the shipment of cattle from the Southern to the Northern side (unless for immediate slaughter) is only allowed during the three winter months—November 15 to February 15, when the cold is supposed to remove the danger of infection. Some of the States, not satisfied with the efficacy of the Federal regulations, enforce specially severe quarantine measures of their own against the Southern districts.

The quarantine line as at present drawn includes within

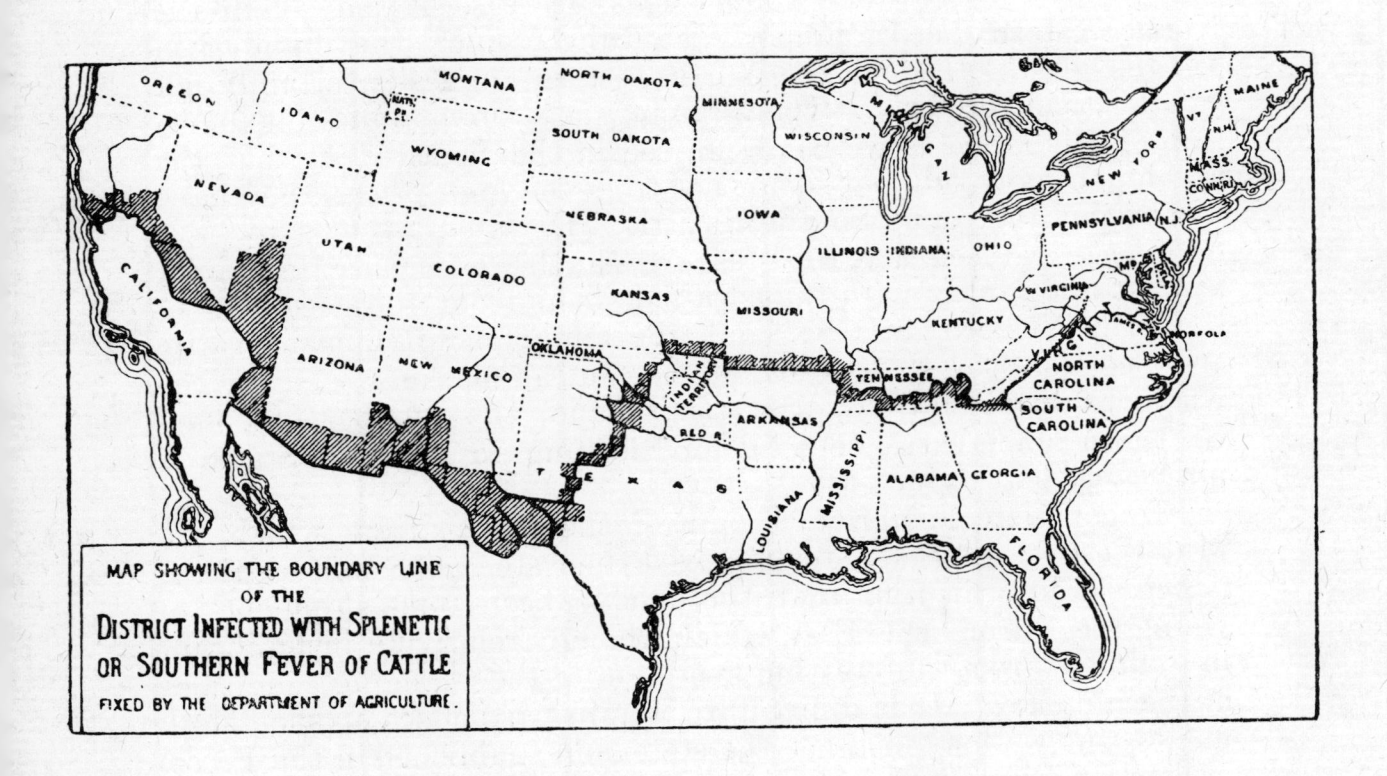

MAP SHOWING THE BOUNDARY LINE OF THE DISTRICT INFECTED WITH SPLENETIC OR SOUTHERN FEVER OF CATTLE FIXED BY THE DEPARTMENT OF AGRICULTURE.

the infected area the southern fringe of Arizona and New Mexico and the entire area of the South-eastern States, Mississippi,

Alabama, Georgia, Louisiana, &c. The great cattle-breeding section in the North-west of Texas known as the "Panhandle" lies north of the line; but it is estimated that some 70 per cent. of the Texas cattle belong to districts within the infected area. The Texas cattle-men are, therefore, for the most part obliged to ship all their young cattle Northwards during the three winter months, which are in certain respects unfavourable for the introduction of Southern cattle to the Northern feed lots; while in regard to their shipments of fed cattle they have the choice between crowding these on the markets during the short season when the quarantine is removed, and consigning them at a considerable sacrifice of price to the quarantine division of the market for immediate slaughter. It is apparent that these restrictions must operate to the great prejudice of the industry; and numerous efforts have been made to devise a practical method for disinfecting the Southern cattle, though it is still too early to judge with what success.

Conditions in North-western range country

The North-western ranching region sends a much lesser number of young cattle (exact statistics are not available) to the Central West for feeding purposes, than do the South-western States; and of these shipments a considerable proportion, as we have already noticed, is composed of cattle originating from Texas. On the other hand, the number of fed North-westerns arriving at the central markets is larger than that of Texans. The total number of cattle in the three chief North-western ranching States, Montana, Wyoming and North Dakota, is now about 2,000,000 head, showing a decrease of some 400,000 head since 1892 and only about 100,000 since 1896. This decrease is mainly in the North-western herds, properly so called, since the number of Texans passing through the North-western ranges is certainly not smaller than formerly. There are no such complaints of exhaustion of the range as we have noticed in the South-west; but the ranchmen have suffered somewhat from the high prices they have had to pay for young Southern cattle. Of late it seems to have become recognised that the grass-fed North-western cattle cannot compete profitably with the corn-fed steers from the feed lots of the Mid-Western States; and the numbers of finished cattle arriving from the North-west at the central markets tend on the whole to diminish.* On the other hand, the number of young Northern ranch cattle sent for final feeding to the corn States is noticeably on the increase.

To complete this brief account of the sources from which the Mid-Western districts have renewed their stock of young cattle, it is necessary to mention that there have been some shipments of young stock from the East, which, though relatively insignificant in number, are an interesting symptom of the changing conditions of the industry. It is difficult to obtain particulars of such shipments, but we may instance the statement (published in the Press) of a buyer connected with certain Southern cattle companies who mentions that he had consigned some 20,000 head of young

* Although the number arriving this year is larger than last year.

Georgia and Florida cattle to the Indian Territory last spring; adding that such a transaction had been unknown for years. This case is probably typical of a good many others.

It need scarcely be said that the advance in prices of 10 per cent. has had a considerable effect on the rate of profits derived from the cattle industry. *Effects of increased price.*

In 1896 a comparison between the prices then ruling and the estimated cost of production, led to the conclusion* that as regards breeders, while there was a large profit in raising cattle on the range, and a considerable profit in regions where pasture land and meadow were abundant and cheap, there were important parts of the cattle-growing region where, owing chiefly to greater density of population and the consequent dearness of pasture and hay, there was little profit in the business. As regards feeders, it was concluded that the business of fattening cattle for the butcher yielded a profit only under especially favourable conditions, and notably when the feeder grew his own corn; but a large proportion of the feeding was necessarily conducted at a loss. It was then evident that the recent reductions in the profits of cattle-raising had been largely responsible for the decrease in the numbers of the herd; and the prevailing low prices gave ground for anticipating a continuance of the decline in numbers, which has in fact taken place.

Conditions have greatly altered since then. Speaking of the change in the situation of herd-owners in the South-western districts, which have no doubt profited as much as any others by the advance in values, a Western paper records the fact that many Arizona herds of 2,000 and 3,000 head of cattle which were vainly offered for sale in the summer of 1896 at 2*l.* and 2*l.* 8*s.* per head, have recently sold for 4*l.* 4*s.* and 4*l.* 8*s.*; and gives a typical instance of a cattle company, which having since 1892 levied annual assessments on its stock, has now resumed the payment of dividends. It is also a very significant fact that "cattle paper" is now reported to be once more good in the South. Cattle paper, or obligations issued by cattlemen on the security of their herds, has for some time been looked upon with general suspicion and disfavour in consequence of the heavy losses of recent years. Its recovery is the best evidence of the present prosperity.

In regard to the position of breeders generally, a collection of communications from its correspondents, published at the end of last December, by the "Breeders' Gazette," gives a very favourable account of the business during the year then closing. Stock raisers from all parts of the country are unanimous in reporting a great growth in the demand, at remunerative prices, for young cattle belonging to recognised beef breeds. The year has been one of such prosperity as had not been seen for five or six years; and there was a general revival of activity in the business—breeders, according to one writer, "who had become partially discouraged, having started in with renewed vigour, recorded their cattle," and now enjoying "a good demand for all they desire to sell." The *Prosperity of breeders.*

* *Vide* F.O. Report No. 403 Miscellaneous Series.

tone of these communications is throughout in marked contrast with the complaints heard in 1896 that breeders of thoroughbred stock were being driven out of the business; and it is evident that one important factor in the recent decrease of United States cattle—the discouragement of breeders—has for the present been removed.

Position of feeders. The position of feeders has certainly not been quite so satisfactory, as the great demand for young cattle kept the prices of stores at a level very little below those of finished cattle. Indeed, the prices of good stores at different times rose considerably above the average price for fed cattle (18s. 9d. per 100 lbs., live weight), and it is reported that many farmers sold their cattle back to market last winter at less than these had cost them as stores. Reviewing the cost of the business during the year 1897, the "Live Stock Report" estimates that "cattle feeders have, as a rule, realised decidedly more satisfactory returns from their labour and investment (than in the previous year, which, however, had been a ruinous one); money has been more easily obtained, and with good crops in 1896 and fair yields in 1897 their position is by no means unfortunate." On the whole it may be gathered that while feeders have not been by any means as well off as breeders, business has not been so unremunerative as to have any marked tendency towards discouraging the industry.

Conditions at close of period reviewed. The state of the country's supply of cattle at the close of last year was summed up by the "Breeders' Gazette" in the words: "a shortage of general stocks with abundance in the feed lots"; and this description will apply roughly to the position of the industry at the close of the period under review, although the scarcity of young cattle was not so much felt about that time as had been the case during the spring.

Shortage in stock cattle. The demand of graziers and feeders for store cattle has been checked occasionally by circumstances affecting the business for the time being—such as the outbreak of war, drought, threatening the corn crop, extreme heat in the feeding districts, and other such causes. But the supply of stock cattle has on the whole been felt to be short in relation to requirements. The strength of the competition for them was particularly noticeable during the spring, when thousands of calves were reported to have been contracted for before their birth, and six-months calves of good form and breeding changed hands freely at 4l. to 5l. Since then, prices of young stock have remained very high as compared with those of finished cattle; and good yearlings were largely quoted at Chicago on June 30, 1898, the last day of the period under review, at 19s. 2d. to 19s. 9½d. per 100 lbs.

Shortage in Texas. In Texas, trade in young cattle was somewhat interfered with on the outbreak of the Spanish War by the scarcity of money. But this obstacle disappeared with the early American successes, and the demand was soon reported as having again become too heavy for the supply available. The Texas "Stockman and Farmer" describes buyers as "scouring the scrub" to furnish themselves with the stock they need, in good time.

The condition of the supply in Texas and the South-west generally is of especial importance from the fact that it is from this region, as we have noticed, that the North-western range country and the Mid-Western feeding States principally depend for the renewal of their stock. The following is a summary estimate, given in a report to the Missouri Agricultural Department, of the numbers of cattle in Texas last December as compared with the preceding winter:—

> *Panhandle.*—" About as many cows and young steers, but not nearly so many aged steers."
> *West Texas.*—" Very few aged steers."
> *South Texas.*—" About as many cattle, but not so many aged steers."
> *Central and North Texas.*—" Not so many cattle, and cattle not in as good shape."

This report has been cited as furnishing the most moderate account that has recently appeared of the visible shortage in the Texas herds. The Texas " Stockman and Farmer " gives one a far stronger idea of its extent; and this is rather what we should have expected from the very large falling-off shown in the returns, some 700,000 head during the last two years.

It is worth noticing that the special reduction shown in the numbers of aged steers forms part of the process which has been general throughout the country during the past few years. It has of late become general in America, following the example of Great Britain, to mature stock cattle at a far earlier age than was formerly the case, and with the establishment of this practice a great part of the whole stock of cattle of three years and over has been killed off, and not replaced. The result must, of course, have been, for the time being, to increase the numbers of cattle marketed, and this process has no doubt had some bearing on the course of receipts during the past few years. Probably, however, it had ceased to have much influence by the time we come down to the period under review.

Conditions in North-western region. In the North-western range country the summer has been remarkable for a good crop of grass, and a much larger number of cattle have been brought into condition for the block than was the case last year. The result has been greatly to increase the numbers of fed " Westerns " in the markets, but to reduce the supply of feeders available for the corn-feeding States. An unprecedented number of range cattle were purchased as stores last summer and autumn, and there is no doubt that they would be readily taken this year also were they available for the same purpose.

Effects of war. The first effects of the Spanish War on the cattle market were felt in the increased demand for the lower class of butcher stock, suitable for canning purposes. Later very large contracts were given out for fresh (chilled) beef for the use of troops in camp in the United States and within reach of sea ports in Cuba and Porto Rico; and shipments of fresh beef continue to home camps and to the Philippines. Complaints of the tightness of money heard at the outbreak of hostilities ceased in the earlier stages of the war, and its effects may, therefore, be said to have been on the whole distinctly beneficial to the trade.

Tendency of United States market. The foregoing brief account of the recent course of the cattle industry may serve to throw some light on the question of the general tendency of the United States market. It is clear in the first place that what scarcity of stock cattle there has been, during the two years under review, must be regarded, for the present, as a permanent element in the situation. The conditions described were not the result of any circumstance specially affecting the cattle supply for the time being, but the outcome of a process which dates, as the returns will show, at least as far back as the year 1892. It is true that what has been one of the chief factors of this process, the discouragement, that is, of stock growing through falling profits, has now, with the advance in the value of young stock, entirely lost its force. There has been a great accession of activity in the breeding business which will henceforth undoubtedly operate to check the decline in cattle numbers, and may be expected eventually to reverse it. But it must be remembered that that country's general stock of cattle cannot be materially increased from one year's end to another as is practicable, for instance, in the case of hogs. That must be a matter of more than one year or even two or three years; and in the meantime we have to deal with a stock of cattle which has lately been felt to be distinctly short in relation to the requirements of buyers.

It is, however, somewhat difficult to estimate the value of this limitation in the stock of young cattle as a factor influencing the fed cattle market. It has not, as we have seen, prevented the receipts of fed cattle from being fully sustained, if not increased, during the two years under review. Its chief visible effect has been to make it difficult for graziers and feeders to obtain the quantity of feeding stock they needed. The resulting competition for stock cattle has brought about an advance in the values of that class, which has had the result of considerably strengthening the prices of all others, including fed steers. In this way the deficiency of stock cattle has indirectly helped to raise the price of fed cattle, but it has not up to the present immediately affected the market by checking the receipts.

The strongest reason for supposing that its effects tend to become more decidedly felt is certainly to be found in the state of the supply in Texas, taken in connection with the increasing difficulty of importation from Mexico. The great resources of Texas and the South-west generally have hitherto sufficed to make good a large proportion of the deficiency in other portions of the country. But the increasing demands made on the stock of South-western cattle, together with the exhaustion of the range, have told heavily on the cattle numbers throughout this region. The strength of the herds has everywhere been greatly reduced; young stock cattle which not long ago were forthcoming in unlimited numbers, are now short of the requirements of purchasers, and eagerly sought after, and it is becoming increasingly difficult and costly for Northern cattlemen to obtain the supplies of Southern cattle which they need.

As regards the question of importation, the returns show how important a part Canadians and Mexicans have lately come to play in keeping up the country's supply. Speaking of the increasing difficulty of obtaining such cattle, the writer of a very able review which appeared in the "Breeders' Gazette" last April observes that importations must be checked by the Dingley increase of duties, and goes on to say that "Northern Mexico is nearly depleted of cattle, poor as these are in quality," and adds that in any case Mexico will have a better market in Cuba next year. The demand of Cuba for cattle, once a normal condition of things is restored in the island, is likely to prove an element of considerable importance, as it will no doubt be supplied largely from the Southern districts of the United States, of which the cattle are proof against the Cuban climate.

Considered in themselves these conditions would point to the likelihood of less liberal supplies for some time to come. But on the other hand, the history of the past few years makes it difficult to believe in any decided change in the course of receipts. The total numbers of cattle, as we have seen, have steadily fallen off; the difficulty and costliness of obtaining young stock have very sensibly increased, and yet the receipts of fed cattle at the markets have been regularly sustained and even increased. This experience makes one cautious of attaching too much value to the scarcity in the visible supply of stock, although this is now noticeable in the regions that have hitherto made good the deficiencies of other parts of the country. What can be safely concluded in regard to the question of supply is probably resumed by saying that there has been for some two years past a noticeable shortage of stock cattle as compared with the demand of feeders and the average of previous years; this must be regarded, at any rate so far as the next two or three years are concerned, as a permanent factor in the situation, and its effect on the price of beef cattle tends to become more decided than it has been up to the present.

As regards the demand, it is generally agreed that the recovery which has taken place during the two years under review does not represent the whole of the improvement which there is ground for expecting. With signs of a continued growth of business activity it is reasonable to anticipate a further development of the country's consumption of beef; and the prospects of a stronger demand in the cattle market are on the whole distinctly encouraging.

Increase of exports.

The following table (taken from the British agricultural returns) gives the numbers of live cattle exported from the United States to Great Britain in the years 1894 to 1897 inclusive:—

(275)

Year.	Number of Head.
1894	381,932
1895	276,533
1896	393,119
1897	416,290

The export for 1895 was specially affected by the scarcity of corn, to which reference has been made, and may be left out of the comparison as the result of exceptional conditions; but taking the figures for 1894, 1896, and 1897, we have an increase over the three-year period averaging some 11,000 head per year.

The exports of fresh (chilled) beef and of canned beef to the United Kingdom, for the years ending June 30, 1894 to 1898 inclusive, were, according to the United States returns, as follows:—

Year ending June 30—	Fresh Beef.	Canned Beef.
	Lbs.	Lbs.
1894	193,331,292	42,544,532
1895	190,736,136	40,310,196
1896	224,507,040	40,092,098
1897	290,007,772	34,714,439
1898	274,700,000*	(Not available)

* Approximately.

It will be noticed that the latest returns of fresh beef shipments show a certain falling-off as compared with the previous year but the export on the whole has been strongly increasing.

Particulars of export trade.
The export of chilled beef during the year ending June, 1897 (the latest period for which details are obtainable), was practically wholly to the United Kingdom. Of the live cattle exported, all but about one-thirtieth were shipped to the United Kingdom, the balance going to Belgium, Holland, Germany (633 head), and the West Indies and South America. The total export of canned beef was 54,000,000 lbs. so that the United Kingdom took about three-fifths of the whole. Germany and France bought the largest part of the remainder.

The cattle exported generally belong to the best class of "natives" raised in the corn-growing States. In 1897 some two-thirds of the whole number exported were marketed in Chicago. They are usual ly heavy steers, weighing some 1,350 to 1,500 lbs., as the freight is the same on light as on heavy animals; and they are admittedly of excellent quality. In the course of the last two years there have also been some shipments of Texans from New Orleans to England—about 2,000 head in 1897. In the case of Northern cattle shipped from Northern ports there is, of course, practically no question of infection from Texas fever; but New

Orleans lies in the heart of the fever district, and the probability is that a part of the cattle shipped from that port would be infected. There is nothing to prevent such cattle from being exported at times of the year when they are prohibited from being sent to the Northern States (except for immediate slaughter), and there have in fact been some shipments to England in the summer months. There is, however, a Government inspection before exportation; and since the animals are slaughtered on landing there is no serious danger of infection to English herds unless English cattle (not about to be slaughtered) should have access to places where Southern cattle have passed or stood.

It has been a very noticeable feature of the export business that the price of American cattle and beef on the British markets during the year 1897 did not show an improvement as compared with the previous year corresponding to that shown by prices of cattle in the United States markets. The average value of fed steers in Chicago for the year 1897 is estimated, as we have seen, at about 1s. 10½d. per 100 lbs. (live weight) above the average for 1896. The prices of American imported fresh beef in the English market for these two years compare thus, according to the British returns:— *Price of American cattle on English market.*

Year.	Per Cwt.
	£ s. d.
1896	1 17 10
1897	1 18 5

giving an addition per cwt. of only 7d. This estimate (the only one available) of the average of recent prices of American imported beef is based on the "declared values," which are perhaps not altogether reliable; but it is clear from the general course of quotations that the advance in prices of American beef on the English market was at any rate considerably less than the advance in Chicago. The improvement in price of British cattle was also less marked than that in the United States markets; the estimated average price in the London Metropolitan Market being 1s. 2d. per cwt. (estimated dressed weight) higher in 1897 than in 1896. (*Vide* British returns.)

The difference between the English and the American prices seems thus to have been scarcely large enough to afford a fair profit on exportation; and the year 1897 is described by the "Live Stock Report" as a busy, but not a very profitable one for exporters. The cost of placing a steer bought in Chicago on the English market is estimated roundly at 5l., with some variation from changes in ocean freights,* and it is reckoned that in the case of heavy weight cattle such as are exported, a difference of from 3d. *Export trade partly at a loss.*

---

* For particulars of cost of exportation, *vide* F.O. Report No. 403 Miscellaneous Series before referred to.

to $3\frac{1}{2}d.$ per lb. between the prices in the two markets* is about sufficient, allowing for shrinkage in transit, to yield a reasonable profit to the exporter. Of the cattle shipped to England in 1897, about two-thirds were bought in Chicago, at prices ranging from $2d.$ to $2\frac{7}{10}d.$ per lb., largely from $2\frac{3}{10}d.$ to $2\frac{1}{2}d.$ per lb. The price of American cattle on the Deptford market ranged from $4\frac{1}{2}d.$ to $6\frac{1}{4}d.$; but the top price seldom reached the latter figure, being more generally about $5d.$ to $5\frac{3}{4}d.$, so that the margin appears frequently to have fallen below the $3d.$ necessary, according to our estimate, to furnish a profit. We give for convenience of reference the prices of export steers in Chicago and Deptford for each week of June, the last month under review:—

Week ending—	Chicago. Live Weight.	Deptford. Estimated Dressed Weight.
June 9	$2\frac{1}{4}$ to $2\frac{1}{2}$	5 to $5\frac{1}{2}$
,, 16	$2\frac{1}{4}$ $2\frac{1}{2}$	5 $5\frac{1}{2}$
,, 23	$2\frac{1}{4}$ $2\frac{1}{2}$	5 $5\frac{1}{4}$
,, 30	$2\frac{3}{10}$ $2\frac{6}{10}$	$5\frac{3}{8}$ 6

It will be seen that the lowest priced cattle in three weeks out of the four did not bring the difference of price in England requisite for a profit, and the highest priced steers barely fetched the necessary price, except in the last week.

It may be inferred that exporters, to keep their hold on the English trade, have done some considerable part of their business at a sacrifice. A well-known firm, in answer to an inquiry, kindly gave this explanation of the matter:—"There is no doubt whatever of exporters having for a long time operated with more or less loss, but where they have vessel space contracted ahead it must either be filled or sacrificed. Lower freight and ocean rates . . . . to some extent offset lower markets, but until the British market makes a considerable improvement . . . . American exporters will continue to operate at little or no profit." It may be observed, besides, that the great firms which now control the export trade also do an immense packing and dressed meat business in the United States, and can afford to conduct one branch of their trade for a time without return.

Conclusions as to prospects of British farmers.

In the long run, however, the export will of course continue only at such a difference between the two prices as is sufficient to give a fair profit on the trade; and when the question of the relative prices in the two countries is taken into account, the

* The Chicago quotations are on the live weight of the cattle; the English quotations on the estimated dressed weight; so that the difference between the prices is really considerably less than would appear from these figures.

prospect for British farmers is by no means so disheartening as has been inferred from the increase of the American exportation. The export of cattle and beef to Great Britain has increased; but the price at which they can be profitably brought to the English consumer has not been lowered, and there is no prospect of its being so. The past few years, as we have seen in the course of this report, have brought about a restriction in the American supply which tends for the present to strengthen American prices, and there has been a recovery in the demand, which still continues. The former of these conditions is to be reckoned with for some time to come as the principal factor influencing the American market, though the increasing activity in the breeding business may be expected gradually to correct it. Looking somewhat further ahead, the fact principally to be noticed is that the cost of production of American cattle tends on the whole to increase, as compared with that of British. With the decline of ranching and the substitution of dearer methods of cattle-raising, the average cost of making beef in the United States has for some years been on the increase; and this process is now very noticeable in the South-western region, which is of peculiar importance as the source from which the country has in recent times drawn enormous supplies of cheap cattle. In parts of the West, where ranching has long since disappeared, the cost of cattle-raising also tends to increase slowly as population becomes thicker, and pasture and hay become less abundant and dearer.

There is, therefore, no reason to anticipate that as time goes on the American stock grower will find himself in a better position to undersell producers in the older country. On the contrary, the terms on which the two compete tend in the long run to become less unfavourable to the British farmer.

UNITED STATES.

Annex A.—NUMBER of Oxen and other Cattle on Farms and Ranches, January 1, 1896, and January 1, 1898.

States and Territories.	1896.	1898.
Maine	117,802	107,294
New Hampshire	84,723	76,327
Vermont	143,643	135,139
Massachusetts	80,476	74,134
Rhode Island	11,596	10,676
Connecticut	69,390	65,282
New York	597,428	554,375
New Jersey	47,487	42,406
Pennsylvania	610,776	550,981
Delaware	25,482	23,953
Maryland	116,045	109,175
Virginia	386,675	356,360
North Carolina	363,585	321,228
South Carolina	158,450	152,160
Georgia	540,916	503,593
Florida	361,054	350,295
Alabama	523,329	442,736
Mississippi	485,695	370,876
Louisiana	312,122	220,108
Texas	5,518,644	4,823,295
Arkansas	516,695	305,522
Tennessee	519,124	379,168
West Virginia	296,613	253,604
Kentucky	506,997	392,162
Ohio	686,285	606,127
Michigan	398,656	348,505
Indiana	798,414	675,698
Illinois	1,430,976	1,304,192
Wisconsin	673,250	607,541
Minnesota	694,321	593,922
Iowa	2,336,973	2,207,739
Missouri	1,686,990	1,537,523
Kansas	1,766,245	2,035,774
Nebraska	1,062,469	1,213,764
South Dakota	399,814	432,079
North Dakota	255,502	245,282
Montana	1,153,557	1,082,498
Wyoming	751,849	688,092
Colorado	926,560	935,826
New Mexico	793,506	731,216
Arizona	636,512	509,082
Utah	369,374	322,464
Nevada	259,078	241,201
Idaho	395,852	349,142
Washington	381,550	294,862
Oregon	788,452	667,030
California	888,832	810,615
Oklahoma	155,645	212,814
Total	32,085,409	29,264,197

UNITED STATES.

Annex B.—NUMBER of Milch Cows on Farms and Ranches, January 1, 1896, and January 1, 1898.

States and Territories.	1896.	1898.
Maine	192,077	195,919
New Hampshire	127,694	132,840
Vermont	258,471	266,276
Massachusetts	174,572	174,554
Rhode Island	24,763	25,258
Connecticut	136,206	138,930
New York	1,445,232	1,402,164
New Jersey	200,347	208,421
Pennsylvania	947,766	928,905
Delaware	34,174	35,554
Maryland	150,477	151,982
Virginia	265,635	252,512
North Carolina	272,046	258,607
South Carolina	129,388	130,682
Georgia	312,711	303,392
Florida	114,332	117,785
Alabama	308,439	296,194
Mississippi	293,870	267,657
Louisiana	166,889	138,184
Texas	783,936	722,476
Arkansas	295,827	223,645
Tennessee	330,690	279,863
West Virginia	175,029	167,240
Kentucky	303,682	264,051
Ohio	759,597	729,441
Michigan	468,523	454,561
Indiana	637,404	605,916
Illinois	1,018,443	1,003,218
Wisconsin	802,902	814,384
Minnesota	600,515	633,993
Iowa	1,202,560	1,214,345
Missouri	723,309	666,530
Kansas	622,892	654,286
Nebraska	534,197	571,591
South Dakota	292,874	341,579
North Dakota	156,571	167,719
Montana	42,086	42,713
Wyoming	18,332	17,960
Colorado	79,975	85,669
New Mexico	18,383	19,126
Arizona	15,622	18,222
Utah	57,271	55,564
Nevada	18,196	18,105
Idaho	28,034	29,167
Washington	117,381	120,297
Oregon	113,732	115,427
California	335,646	342,392
Oklahoma	28,888	35,590
Total	16,137,586	15,840,886

LONDON:
Printed for Her Majesty's Stationery Office,
By HARRISON AND SONS,
Printers in Ordinary to Her Majesty.
(75 10 | 98—H & S 1986)